Tribal Names of the Americas

Tribal Names
of the Americas

*Spelling Variants and Alternative
Forms, Cross-Referenced*

PATRICIA ROBERTS CLARK

McFarland & Company, Inc., Publishers
Jefferson, North Carolina, and London

LIBRARY OF CONGRESS CATALOGUING-IN-PUBLICATION DATA

Clark, Patricia Roberts, 1948–
Tribal names of the Americas : spelling variants and
alternative forms, cross-referenced / Patricia Roberts Clark.
p.   cm.
Includes bibliographical references.

ISBN 978-0-7864-3833-4
softcover : 50# alkaline paper ∞

1. Names, Indian—Dictionaries.   2. Names, Ethnological—America—
Dictionaries.   3. Names, Geographical—America—Dictionaries.
4. Names, Personal—America—Dictionaries.   I. Title.
E54.5.C55   2009   929.4'4—dc22   2009022057

British Library cataloguing data are available

Front cover: Sundancer ©2009 Shutterstock; map background ©2009 Clipart.com
Back cover: Arrowhead ©2009 Shutterstock

Manufactured in the United States of America

*McFarland & Company, Inc., Publishers
Box 611, Jefferson, North Carolina 28640
www.mcfarlandpub.com*

Contents

To my parents,
Billie J. and Mary Scala Roberts

Preface

I have been a reference librarian for twenty-five years and have enjoyed my interaction with books, people, and computers. I work at Texas Tech University's Southwest Collection/Special Collections Library as Reference Archivist (what's in a name?) and am still referencing away.

The most fun I ever had occurred while I was working in the History/Genealogy Department of the Los Angeles Public Library's Central Library. While I was there, I was the unofficial expert of the Indians of North, Central and South America section of books, and what a collection it was! Books had been collected for years and I got to read most of them. These included hundreds of older out-of-print books that had been written at the time of establishment of archaeology in the United States at the end of the nineteenth century when the West's history began to be documented. The range was from then to modern times and I was able to expand my knowledge greatly.

Among the thousands of books at my disposal were complete sets of the annual reports and Bulletins of the Bureau of American Ethnology. I started my learning with them and read studies of many indigenous groups written by well-known, well-respected archaeologists and linguists. Somewhere, very early on in my reading, I began to see the following patterns:

- There were few cross references in books written before 1950.
- There were in those writings footnotes that gave vital information, but it was not included in the few cross references that did exist.

- Variant spellings of Native tribal names abounded, depending on the hearing, educational levels, and nationalities of the writers.
- Governments mandated standardized names for tribes, and the resulting names had little or nothing to do with tribal self-designations or the names that their neighbors called them. My own beloved Library of Congress subject headings chose and codified the standardization of many "recognized" tribes and ignored the rest.
- There was little or no effort to pull the variations together into an organized cross-reference.

Although I was annoyed by this state of affairs, I tended to rely on my "institutional memory" to recognize variations. But as I grew older, and the number of books I read skyrocketed, my memory started to fail me. This was brought home to me by a junior high student who brought in her textbook with the spelling of a California tribe on which she had to do a report. This desperate young lady was sent to me by her frustrated branch librarian who could not find anything on what the textbook had dubbed "a well-known tribe." Two hours and over twenty books on California tribes later I found the variant spelling documented by the state-chosen textbook. I had read all those books but could not remember that the name was for the Chumash, definitely a well-known California tribe. No longer trusting my memory, I wrote the information down on an index card. This book was born, but it took me more than twenty years and 200 boxes of index cards before I completed it.

Because anthropologists, linguists, and archaeologists have been discussing for years what a "tribe" is and what a "name" is, I chose to make my own simple definitions for this book. A "tribe" became a group of people, any size, who lived together and called each other by the same designation. A "name" was a designation whether self-chosen or given by outside peoples. To keep these outside names intelligible, I omitted the linguistic representations of the pronunciations of different languages. I tried to represent the different designations of individual tribes where they were clearly stated by my sources and I left the linguistic contortions to those who will not be confused by them.

I used the format of letter-by-letter alphabetization because of my experiences with the computer-educated young adults who came into the public libraries where I worked. Complicated print indexes with classified systems seem to frustrate and defeat them. I chose to try to create a manner that simplified the search and made it quick. Many short words may or may not be prefixes, and since so many languages are being collected in these pages, I am employing strict letter-by-letter alphabet. By my more sophisticated users, I hope thereby to be excused for the resulting simplicity. I hope the book will be of use to all who seek information about variant tribal designations.

I employ abbreviations for ease of use. Following this Preface is a How to Use This Book section that explains how to read the entries and how to interpret the abbreviations. Users will please note that there are no linguistic abbreviations being used.

In my readings I found many, many entries based on saints' names with varying ways to abbreviate the "saint" designation. I chose to congregate them all under "saint" and alphabetize them by the name of the saint. Thus, the user will find Felipe, S.; Felipe, Saint; Felipe, San; Felipe, Sant; Felipe, St.; and Fellipe, S., all in a row, not divided by pages of intervening text. Again, this is to simplify the search, not to confuse.

I did not read every book ever written about indigenous peoples, so I do not claim to have compiled a thorough book on the subject. I did, however, read the sources I quote as thoroughly as I could. If I have omitted any names, it is because I did not come across them in my reading, not for any other reason. I encourage communication from any and all who wish to have information included and the sources they suggest I use next time.

I wish to send my appreciation to the following people who have helped me along my path. First, I thank my parents: Maria Adrianna Scala Roberts, who has put up with over 200 boxes of index cards through two moves and encouraged my slaving over the computer to enter all the information; and my father, Billie Jean Roberts, gone now but not forgotten, who always encouraged my scholarship. Second, I thank my bosses at Los Angeles Public Library, Frank Louck and Jane Nowak, who always respected my subject specialty. Third, I thank my supervisor at the Southwest Collection/Special Collections Library at Texas Tech University, Dr. Tai Kreidler, who has insisted that I not give up. *Grazie a tutti*.

How to Use This Book

1. Use the Header

Tribal name [Designation] **Approximate Location** *Parent Group* (Source)

An entry may contain some or all of the above elements. They are distinguished typographically and appear in the order above. Their meanings are as follows:

A. "Tribal name" denotes the name of the group.
B. "Designation" indicates a name for something other than a band or a tribe; for example, it might be a language or a clan.
C. "Approximate Location" is the original physical location of the tribe given in the source material.
D. "Parent Group" is a larger group with which this group is affiliated.
E. "Source" is the original material in which this group was found by this author. To find the complete entry, the user is directed first to the abbreviations and then to the bibliography.

2. Use the Abbreviations

Main entries: For example, the entry "Apwaruge [Lang] [*Atsugewi*] (CA-8)" is interpreted to be "Apwaruge is a language of the Astsugewi group. This information was taken from *The Handbook of North American Indians, volume 8*."

"See" entries: For example, "Aleche (H) *see* Eyeish (BE)" means that to find information on the Aleche as cited in (H) or Hodge, the reader must look under the Eyeish in (BE), the publication by Swanton.

"See also" entries: For example, "Acoma (Hdbk10) *see also* Arahomo (Hdbk10)" means that although Acoma has a separate identity and is treated as such in the source, *The Handbook of North American Indians, volume 10*, the editors of the source want the researcher to find more information under "Arahomo."

3. Use the Saint Section

In the S section beginning where the word "saint" would appear, the user will find all "saint" entries regardless of the abbreviations used. This includes S., Saint, San, Sant, Santa, Sante, Sn., St., Ste., and Sto. To find information in this section, the user will look for the saint name first. For example, when searching for "Saint Felipe," one will look for "Felipe" first, and will then look between "Felipe, S." and "Felipe, San." This not only allows the user to find all Felipes together without skipping around through pages of material, but it allows him to choose which entry is the appropriate one.

Abbreviations

AI	Gibson. *American Indians*
AIQ	*American Indian Quarterly*
AIR	*American Indian Report*
AK	Alaska
AL	Alabama
AlGeo	*Alaska Geographic*
Almanac	Champagne (ed.) *Native North American Almanac*
Alta	Barker. *Archaeology of Alta California*
AN	*Akwesasne Notes*
Andrews	Andrews. *Curtis' Western Indians*
ANM	*Akwesasne Notes Magazine*
Anthro	University of California. *Anthropological Records, v. 1–28.*
AR	Arkansas
Arch	*Archaeology Magazine*
Arg	Argentina
Athena	*Athena Review*
AtInd	Waldman. *Atlas of the North American Indian*
Axel	Axelrod. *Chronicle of the Indian Wars*
AZ	Arizona
AzH	*Arizona Highways*
BaC	Baja California
Bah	Bahamas
BC	British Columbia
BE	Swanton. *The Indian Tribes of North America: Bulletin of American Ethnology, # 145*
Beals	Beals. *California Indians I*
Bel	Belize
Bklst	*Booklist*
Black	Burton. *Black, Red and Deadly*
BO	Bolivia
Br	Brazil
BrH	British Honduras
Brinton	Brinton. *The American Race*
Bull	Smithsonian Institution. Bureau of American Ethnology. *Bulletin*
Bush	Bush. *Photograph and the American Indian*
[CA]	California
(CA)	Kroeber. *Handbook of the Indians of California*
CAd	*Cherokee Advocate*
CA-8	Heizer. *California: v. 8: Handbook of North American Indians*
CAH	*California History*
Calif	*California Indians I*
CAm	Central America
Can	Canada
Can'd	Canadian Association in Support of the Native Peoples. *Bulletin*
Cardozo	Cardozo. *Native Nations*
CH	Chile
Chapman	Chapman. *Ten'a Texts and Tales*
Char	Fay. Charters, *Constitutions, and By-laws of the Indian Tribes of North America, v. 1–14*
Chron	*Chronicles of Oklahoma*
Circl	Smithsonian Institution. Bureau of American Ethnology. *Circular of Information Regarding Indian Popular Names*
Circle	Gattuso. *Circle of Nations*
Clan	Gens or part of a family
CO	Colorado
Coe	Coe. *Atlas of Ancient America*
Col	Colombia
Coll	Maine Historical Society. *Collections*
Contri	Department of the Interior. *Contributions*
CR	Costa Rica
Crow	McGinnis. *Crow People*
Crying	Anderson. *Crying for a Vision*

5

CT	Connecticut
Cu	Cuba
CUC	University of California, Berkeley, *Contributions*
DC	Washington, D.C.
DE	Delaware
DO NOT SEE	The two groups are not identical nor are they to be confused with one another.
Docu	Prucha. *Documents of United States Indian Policy,* 2nd ed.
DR	Domincan Republic
DTQ	*Dog Town Territorial*
Eagle	*Eagle*
Early	Fleming. *Indians of North America in Early Photos*
Earth	Eargle. *Earth Is Our Mother,* 2nd ed.
EC	Ecuador
EP	El Palacio
ES	El Salvador
Et	*Ethnohistory*
Ex	*Expedition*
Family	Social group within a tribe
Fausz	Fausz. "Fighting 'Fire' with Firearms," in Nichols
FL	Florida
Fleming	Fleming. *Grand Endeavors of American Indian Photography*
Forg	Hines. *Forgotten Tribes*
FrG	French Guiana
GA	Georgia
Gens	Clan or part of a family
GL	Great Lakes
GPQ	*Great Plains Quarterly*
Gr	Greenland
Great	Tanner. *Atlas of Great Lakes Indian History*
Gu	Guam
Gua	Guatemala
Guy	Guyana
H	Hodge. *Handbook of American Indians North of Mexico,* 2 v., reprint
HA	Haiti
Haines	Haines. *American Indian (Uhnish-in-na-ba)*
HawkH	*Hawkeye Heritage*
Hdbk	Sturtevant. *Handbook of North American Indians, v. 1–*
Hdbk4	Washburn. *History of Indian-White Relations: v. 4: Handbook of North American Indians,* ed. Sturtevan
Hdbk5	Damas. *Arctic: v. 5: Handbook of North American Indians,* ed. Sturtevant
Hdbk6	Jelm. *Subarctic: v. 6: Handbook of North American Indians,* ed. Sturtevant
Hdbk7	Suttles. *Northwest Coast: v. 7: Handbook of North American Indians,* ed. Sturtevant
Hdbk9	Ortiz. *Southwest: v. 9: Handbook of North American Indians,* ed. Sturtevant
Hdbk10	Ortiz. *Southwest: v. 10: Handbook of North American Indians,* ed. Sturtevant
Hdbk11	D'Azevedo. *Great Basin: v. 11: Handbook of North American Indians,* ed. Sturtevant
Hdbk12	Walker. *Plateau: v. 12: Handbook of North American Indians,* ed. Sturtevant
Hdbk15	Trigger. *Northeast: v. 15: Handbook of North American Indians,* ed. Sturtevant
Hdbk17	Goddard. *Languages: v. 17: Handbook of North American Indians,* ed. Sturtevant
HdCan	Hodge. *Handbook of Indians of Canada, facsimile edition*
He	Heizer. *Languages, Territories and Names of California Indian Tribes*
Heye	*Contributions from the Heye Museum, # 1–9*
HeyeLeaf	*Leaflets: Heye Museum*
HH	*Heritage and History*
HI	Hawaii
His/T	McKenney. *History of the Tribes of North America,* 3 v.
Hon	Honduras
Hook	Hook. *Geronimo: Last Renegade of the Apache*
IA	Iowa
ICT	*Indian Country Today*
ID	Idaho
IL	Illinois
IN	Indiana
IndL	Denver. *Indian Leaflet Series*
IndN	Denver. *Indian Notes*

IndT	*Indian Trader*		NJ	New Jersey
IT	Indian Territory		NM	New Mexico
J/Anthro	*Journal of California Anthropology*		NMM	*New Mexico Magazine*
JA	Jamaica		NPeos	*Native Peoples*
JCB	*Journal of California Anthropology and Great Basin Anthropology*		NS	Nova Scotia
			NT	*Navajo Times*
			NV	Nevada
JCS	*Journal of Cherokee Studies*		NVAP	Nevada State Museum. *Anthropological Papers*
John	*Southern Quarterly*, v. 95, no. 2 (Oct. 1991), pp. 139-176		NVHQ	*Nevada Historical Society Quarterly*
JSW	*Journal of the Southwest*			
JW	*Journal of the West*		NY	New York
KS	Kansas		O	Olson. *Indians of Central and South America*
KY	Kentucky			
LA	Louisiana		O'Brien	O'Brien. *American Indian Tribal Governments*
Lab	Labrador			
Lang	Language		OH	Ohio
LAT	*Los Angeles Times*		OK	Oklahoma
LC	*Library of Congress Subject Headings,* 14th ed.		Ont	Ontario
			OR	Oregon
LT	Lakota Times		Oregon	Webber. *Indians Along the Oregon Trail*
Luchetti	Luchetti. *Women of the West*			
M Mag	*Montana Magazine*		OW	*Old West*
MA	Massachusetts		PA	Pennsylvania
Man	Manitoba		PacN	Pacific Northwest
MD	Maryland		Palm	*Palm Springs Life*
ME	Maine		Pan	Panama
MI	Michigan		PAnthro	*Plains Anthropologist*
MM	*Malki Matters*		Par	Paraguay
MN	Minnesota		Partial	Lippard. *Partial Recall*
MO	Missouri		PC	Cross-reference to punctuation differences in spellings
Moiety	A kinship group			
MS	Mississippi		PE	Peru
MT	Montana		People	Trimble. *The People*
MX	Mexico		Phratry	Group of clans
NA	North America		Plateau	*Plateau*
NAmI	Curtis. *North American Indian, v. 1–20*		PR	Puerto Rico
			Prehis	Indiana Historical Society. *Prehistory Research Series, v. 1–*
NatNat	Curtis. *Native Nations*			
NatPeos	Champagne. *Native America*		Pub	American Ethnological Society. *Publications*
NAW	Women's Studies Program. *Native American Women*			
			Q	Quebec
NB	Nebraska		QCH	*Queen City Heritage*
NC	North Carolina		QSAIA	*Quarterly of the Southwestern Association of Indian Affairs*
ND	North Dakota			
NDH	*North Dakota History*		R	*Reader (Los Angeles)*
NE	Nevada		Rachlis	Rachlis. *Indians of the Plains*
NEng	New England		Raven	Healy. "Flags of the Native Peoples of the United States," *RAVEN*
NewB	New Brunswick			
News	*News from Native California*			
NH	New Hampshire		Red	Burrows. *Indian Names, bicentennial ed.*
NI	Nicaragua			

RedI	*Red Ink*
Report	*Report on the Americas*
RI	Rhode Island
Ruby	Ruby. *Indians of the Pacific Northwest*
Rus	Russia
SA	South America
SanD	Santo Domingo
Sas	Saskatchewan
SC	South Carolina
Scherer	Scherer. *Indians*
SD	South Dakota
SDQ	*South Dakota Quarterly*
see	Refers reader to what the bibliographic source considers the authentic name of a group
see also	Refers reader to a tribal group that has a separate identity from what the source quoted says it does. Some sources clump related tribes into one term but the tribe did not consider itself part of that group.
Self-designation	An individual group's name for itself
Sept	Clan
Shasta	Renfro. *The Shasta Indians of California and Their Neighbors*
Sherrow	Sherrow. *Political Leaders and Peacemakers*
SHQ	*Southwestern Historical Quarterly*
Sib	Siberia
Social group	Not a formal society but a group within a tribe
Society	Social group within a tribe
SoML	*Southwest Museum Leaflets*
Spi	Walker. *Spiritual Leaders*
SR	*Southwest Review*
Stockel	Stockel. *Women of the Apache Nation*
Subclan	Division of a clan
Subgens	Division of a gens
T/Linds	*Indians (Time/Life)*
TDF	Tierra del Fuego
TH	*Texas Highways*
TL	*Talking Leaf*
TN	Tennessee

Totem	Bancroft-Hunt. *People of the Totem*
Trans	American Ethnological Society. *Transactions*
TT	*Tundra Times*
TW	*True West*
2000	Laboratory of Anthropology. *I Am Here*
TX	Texas
UAz	University of Arizona. *University of Arizona Anthropological Papers*
UNMPubs	University of New Mexico. *Publications in Anthropology # 1–14*
Ur	Uruguay
UT	Utah
UW	University of Washington. *Publications in Anthropology*
VA	Virginia
VanI	Vancouver
VC	*Ventura County Historical Society Quarterly*
VE	Venezuela
VI	Virginia
VT	Vermont
W	Waldman. *Who was Who in Native American History*
WA	Washington
WaldAt	Waldman. *Atlas of the North American Indian*
Was	*Wassaja*
Way	*Way We Lived*
Weibel	Weibel-Orlando. *Indian Country, L.A.*
WHQ	*Western Historical Quarterly*
WI	Wisconsin
WInd	West Indies
Wis	Wall. *Wisdom's Daughter*
Wr	Wright. *A Guide to the Indian Tribes of Oklahoma*
WTHA	*West Texas Historical Association*
WV	West Virginia
WW	*Wild West*
WY	Wyoming
Ye	Yenne. *Encyclopedia of North American Indian Tribes*

The Tribal Names

-A-

Aacus *see* Acoma
Aainen [Self-designation] *see* Atsina
Aaingang *see* Kaingangue
A-a-ko-za *see* Iyakoza
Aakoza *see* Iyakoza
Aaltu *see* Ala
A-ampkua amim *see* Umpqua
Aampkuqamim *see* Umpqua
Aa'ninena *see* Atsina
Aaninena *see* Atsina
Aanu'hawa *see* Hanahawunena
Aanuhawa *see* Hananawunena
Aanunhawa *see* Hananawunena
aapanahkiiha *Delaware* (Hdbk15)
Aarapahoes *see* Arapaho
A-ar-ka *see* Hopi
A-ar-ke *see* Hopi
Aarke *see* Hopi
Aas *see* Eyeish
Aatam *see* Pima
A-a-tam [Self-designation] *see* Pima
A-a'tam A'kimult *see* Pima
Aatam Akimult *see* Pima
Aatsosni [Clan] *Navajo* (H)
A-auh-wauh *see* Ahahweh
Aauhwauh *see* Ahahweh
Aaya *see* Eyeish
Aays *see* Eyeish
Ababco [MD] *Choptank* (H)
Ababeve *see* Ababco
Abacoes *see* Abihka
A'bahoko *see* Navajo
Abahoko *see* Navajo
Abajoses *see* Navajo
Abalache *see* Apalachee
Abalachi *see* Apalachee
Abanakee *see* Abnaki
Abanaki *see* Abnaki
Abanaqui *see* Abnaki
Abanaquois *see* Abnaki
Abane *see* Baniva
Abani [VE] *Achagua* (O)
Abapco's Indians *see* Ababco
Abarginny *see* Aberginian
Abasopalme [MX] *Concho* (BE)
Abasusiniguara [MX] *Coahuiltecan* (Hdbk10)
Abbato-Tena (Contri, v.1, pp.32–33)
Abbato-Tena *see* Abbatotine
Abbatotena *see* Abbatotine
Abbatotenah *see* Abbatotine
Abbatotine [Can] *Nahane* (H)
Abbatotinneh *see* Abbatotine
Abbatotinney *see* Abbatotine
Abbetika *see* Abitibi
Abbetiki *see* Abitibi
Abbitibbe *see* Abitibi

Abbitibi *see* Cree
Abbo *see* Abo
Ab-boin-ee Sioux *see* Dakota
Abboinee Sioux *see* Dakota
Ab-boing-ug *see* Dakota
Ab-boin-ug *see* Dakota
Abboinug *see* Dakota
Abbwoi-nug *see* Dakota
Abbwoinug *see* Dakota
Abcha *see* Abihka
Abeca *see* Abihka
Abecaes *see* Abihka
Abecka *see* Abihka
Abeica *see* Abihka
Abeika *see* Abihka
Abeka *see* Abihka
abémadenaïak *see* Huron of Lorette
Abenaka *see* Abnaki
Abenake *see* Abnaki
Abenaki *see* Abnaki
Abenakias *see* Abnaki
Abenakiss *see* Abnaki
Abenakkis *see* Abnaki
Abenaque *see* Abnaki
Abenaqui *see* Abnaki
Abenaquioict *see* Abnaki
Abenaquiois *see* Abnaki
Abenaquioue *see* Abnaki
Abenati *see* Abnaki
Abeneaguis *see* Abnaki
Abenequa *see* Abnaki
Abenkai *see* Abnaki
Abenquois *see* Abnaki
Abergeny *see* Aberginian
Aberginian [MA] (H)
Aberieney *see* Aberginian
Abernaqui *see* Abnaki
Abica *see* Abihka
Abicetava *see* Bribri
Abigira *see* Awishiri
Abi'hka *see* Abihka
Abihka [AL] *Muskogee* (BE)
Abihka-in-the-West [OK] *Abhika* (BE)
Abihki *see* Abihka
Abihkutchi [2 tribes in AL] *Muskogee* (BE)
Abihkutci [OK] *Okfuskee* (BE)
Abijira *see* Awishiri
Abika *see* Abihka
Abikaw *see* Abihka
Abimiouec *see* Illinois
Abinaqui *see* Abnaki
Abinohkie *see* Abnaki
Abio *see* Abo
Abipon *see* Abipone
Abipone [Lang] [Arg, Par] *Guaycuna* (LC)
Abiquiu *Pueblo Indians* (H)
Abira *see* Awishiri
Abitibi [Can] *Algonkin* (LC)
Abitibiwinni *see* Abitibi

Abittibbe *see* Abitibi
Abittibi *see* Abitibi
Abixira *see* Awishiri
Abnaki [Can, ME, NH, VT] (LC)
Abnaki Confederacy (Who)
Abnaqui *see* Abnaki
Abnaquies *see* Abnaki
Abnaquiois *see* Abnaki
Abnaquois *see* Abnaki
Abnaquotii *see* Abnaki
Abnasque *see* Abnaki
Abnekais *see* Abnaki
Abneki *see* Abnaki
Abo [Lang] *Piro* (H)
Abo [NM] *Tompiro* (H)
Ab-oin *see* Dakota
Aboin *see* Dakota
Aboinug *see* Dakota
Abolachi *see* Apalachee
Abonakies *see* Abnaki
Abonnekee *see* Abnaki
Aborginny *see* Aberginian
Abra [CAm] *Guetar* (BE)
Absahrokee *see* Crow
Absaraka *see* Crow
Absarako *see* Crow
Ab-sar-o-ka *see* Crow
Absaroka *see* Crow
Absaroke *see* Crow
Absaroki *see* Crow
Absentee Shawnee (BE)
Absoroka *see* Crow
Abubae [CR] (O)
Abucios *see* Acoma
Abuscal *see* Abascal
Abwoinug *see* Dakota
Acacafui [NM] *Tigua* (H)
Acacagua [NM] *Pueblo Indians* (H)
Acachme *see* Juañeno
Acadians *see* Micmac
Acagchemem [CA] *Saddleback Valley* (JCB, v.11, no.2, p.9)
Acaguayo *Akawaio* (O)
Acahuayo *Akawaio* (O)
acakudakwa tibiwaga'yu *see* Atsakudoka tuviwarai
Acana *see* Kechipauen
Acancuara [MX] *Coahuiltecan* (Hdbk10)
Acani *see* Ocana
Acansa *see* Quapaw
Acansea *see* Quapaw
Acansia *see* Quapaw
Acapato *see* Atsina
A c'araho [MN] *Crow* (BE)
Acarred Arms *see* Cheyenne
Acasaquastlan [Hon] *Nahuatl* (BE)
Acateco [Gu] *Mayan* (O)
Acateco [Lang] [CAm] *Western Mayan* (O)

Acatoyan [MX] *Coahuiltecan* (Hdbk10)

Acawai [Br, Guy, VE] *Cariban* (LC)

Acawaoi *see* Acawai

Acawoio *see* Acawai

Acaxee [MX] (LC)

Accahanock *see* Accohanoc

Accance *see* Quapaw

Accancea *see* Quapaw

Accawai *see* Acawai

Accawmack *see* Accomac

Accawmacke *see* Accomac

Accerri [CAm] *Guetar* (BE)

Acco *see* Acoma

Accocesaw *see* Arkokisa

Accocick *see* Conoy

Accockesaw *see* Arkokisa

Accohanoc [VA] *Powhatan* (BE)

Accohanock *see* Accohanoc

Accokesaus *see* Arkokisa

Accokesaw *see* Arkokisa

Accokicke *see* Conoy

Accomac [VA] *Powhatan* (LC)

Accomack *see* Accomac

Accomentas *see* Accominta

Accominta [ME] *Pennacook Confederacy* (H)

Accominticus *see* Accominta

Accomintycus *see* Accominta

Accomynticus *see* Accominta

Acconeechy *see* Occoneechee

Accotronack *see* Accohanoc

Accowmack *see* Accomac

Acewaio *see* Acawai

Acha *see* Picuris

Achagua [Col, VE] *Maipurean* (LC)

Achague *see* Outchougai

Achalaque *see* Cherokee

A-cha-o-tin-ne *see* Etchareottine

Achaotinne *see* Slave Indians

Achaotinne *see* Etchareottine

Achaque *see* Outchougai

Achastas *see* Rumsen

Achastli *see* Rumsen

Achastlian *see* Rumsen

Achastlien *see* Rumsen

Achastlier *see* Rumsen

Achastlies *see* Rumsen

Ache *see* Guayaqui

Achedoma *see* Alchedoma

Achee *see* Yuchi

Acheha [Phratry] *Timucua* (H)

Achena *see* Atsina

Acheotenne *see* Etchareottine

Acheotenne *see* Slave Indians

Ache-pa-ba-cha *see* Achepabecha

Achepabacha *see* Achepabecha

Achepabecha *Crow* (H)

Aches *see* Pawnee

A-che-to-e-ten-ni *see* Etchareottine

Achetoetenni *see* Etchareottine

Acheto-e-Tinne *see* Etchareottine

Achetoetinne *see* Slave Indians

Achetoetinne *see* Etchareottine

Acheto-tena *see* Etchareottine

Achetotena *see* Etchareottine

Achetotinna *see* Titshotina

Ache-to-tin'neh *see* Etchareottine

Acheto-tinneh *see* Titshotina

Achetotinneh *see* Etchareottine

Achi [Gu] *Eastern Mayas* (O)

Achiganes *see* Sooke

Achilia *see* Hitchiti

Achiligouan [Can] (H)

Achiligouiane *see* Achiligouan

Achiote [PE] *Witoto* (O)

Achiout (His/T)

Achipaye *see* Chipaya

Achipoes *see* Chippewa

Achipoué *see* Chippewa

Achire [MX] *Guasave* (BE)

Achirigouan *see* Achiligouan

Achiritouan *see* Achiligouan

Achistas *see* Tumsen

Achjuch-Aliat *see* Imaklimiut

Achjuch-Aliat *see* Inguklimiut

Achjuchaliat *see* Imaklimiut

Achjuchaliat *see* Inguklimiut

Achkingkesacky *see* Hackensack

Achkinkehacky *see* Hackensack

Achkinkes hacky *see* Hackensack

Achkinkeshacky *see* Hackensack

Achkugmjuten *see* Aglemiut

Achkugmjuten *see* Kaniagmiut

Ach-min-de-cou-may *see* Kalispel

Achmindecoumay *see* Kalispel

Achomawan *see* Achomawi

Achomawe *see* Achomawi

A-cho-ma-wi *see* Achomawi

Acho-ma-wi *see* Achomawi

Achomawi [CA] (LC)

Achomawi [Lang] *Shastan* (LC)

Achonechy *see* Occaneechi

Achote *see* Nonuya

Achote *see* Achiote

Achoto-e-tenni *see* Etchareottine

Achotoetenni *see* Etchareottine

Achquegenonck *see* Aquackanonk

Achquickenough *see* Aquackanonk

Achquickenunck *see* Aquackanonk

Achquickenunk *see* Aquackanonk

Achquikanuncque *see* Aquackanonk

Achsisagheck *see* Missisauga

Achsissaghecs *see* Missisauga

Achual *see* Achuale

Achuale [Lang] [EC, PE] (LC)

Achuara *see* Achuale

Achuare *see* Achuale

Achumawi *see* Achomawi

Achupaya *see* Chipaya

Acihi *see* Ashihi

Acihicine *see* Ashihi

Acinay *see* Caddo

Acipoya *see* Chipaya

acipwe-wake *see* Ojibwa

A-ci-wi *see* Zuni

Aciwi *see* Zuni

Acjachemen *see* Juaneño

Acjachemen *see* Juañeno

Ackinckesaky *see* Hackensack

Ackkinkas-hacky *see* Hackensack

Ackkinkashacky *see* Hackensack

Ackquekenon *see* Aquackanonk

Acmaat *see* Acoma

A-co *see* Acoma

Aco *see* Acoma

Acogiya *see* Acoma

Acohamock *see* Accomac

Acohanock *see* Accohanoc

Aco-ke-sa *see* Arkokisa

Acokesa *see* Arkokisa

Acolapissa [LA] *Choctaw* (BE)

Acolhua (LC) *see also* Tezcucan (LC)

Acolhua [MX] (BE)

Acoli [NM] *Pueblo Indians* (H)

Acolocu *see* Chilili [Tigua]

Acolta *see* Lekwiltok

Acoma (Hdbk10) *see also* Arahomo (Hdbk10)

Acoma (LC) *see also* Yaquina (BE)

Acoma [NM] (LC)

Acomack *see* Accomac

Acomak *see* Accomac

Acoman *see* Acoma

Acomayo [PE] (BE)

Acome *see* Acoma

Acomense *see* Acoma

Acomese *see* Acoma

Acomo *see* Acoma

Acona *see* Acoma

Aconagua *see* Halona

Aconcagua [CH] (BE)

Aconeche *see* Occoneechee

Aconechos *see* Occoneechee

Aconeechy *see* Occoneechee

Aconia *see* Acoma

Aconichi *see* Occoneechee

Acoonedy *see* Occoneechee

Acopalca [PE] (BE)

Acossesaw *see* Arkokisa

Acosta *see* Koasati

Acoste *see* Koasati

Acquackanonk *see* Aquackanonk

Acquera [FL] *Utina* (H)

Acquia *see* Acoma

Acquicanunk *see* Aquackanonk

Acquiggenonck *see* Aquackanonk

Acquikanong *see* Aquackanonk
Ac-quin-a-nack-su-ack *see* Acquintanacsuak
Acquinanacksuack *see* Acquintanacsuak
Acquinoshionee *see* Iroquois
Acquinta *see* Pocomoke
Acquintanacsuah *see* Acquintanacsuak
Acquintanacksuak *see* Acquintanacsuak
Acquintanacksuck *see* Patuxent
Acquintanacsuak [MD] *Conoy* (BE)
Acquintanacsuck *see* Acquintanacsuak
Acquintunachsuah *see* Acquintanacsuak
Acquinuskionee *see* Iroquois
Acquiora *see* Bagiopa
Acquitanase *see* Acquintanacsuak
Acu *see* Acoma
Acuan-Shavante *see* Akwe-Shavante
Acua-Shavante *see* Akwe-Shavante
Acubadaos [TX] (H)
Acubados *see* Arbadaos
Acuca *see* Acoma
Acucan *see* Acoma
Acuco *see* Acoma
Acucu *see* Acoma
Acuen-Xavante *see* Akwe-Shavante
Acuera (H) *see also* Acquera (H)
Acuera [FL] *Timucua* (BE)
Acuique *see* Pecos
A-cu-lah *see* Pecos
aculah *see* Pecos
Aculah *see* Pecos
Acuria *see* Akurio
Acus *see* Acoma
Acuti-Tapuya [Col] *Wakuenai* (O)
Acux *see* Acoma
Acuye *see* Pecos
Adae *see* Adai
Adage *see* Adai
Adahi *see* Adai
Ada-i *see* Adai
Adai [LA] (BE)
Adaic *see* Adai
Adaice *see* Adai
Adaies *see* Adai
Adaihe *see* Adai
Adaisses *see* Adai
Adaizan [Lang] *see* Caddoan
Adaizan Indians *see* Adai
Adaize *see* Adai
A da ka'da ho *see* Arikara
Adakadaho *see* Arikara
A'dal-k'ato'igo *see* Nez Perce
Adalkatoigo *see* Nez Perce

Adams Lake [BC] *Shuswap* (H)
Adam's Lake Indians (H) *see also* South Andrian (H)
Adamstown Indians *see* Upper Mattapony
Adawadeny *see* Potawatomi
Adawe *see* Ottawa
Aday *see* Adai
Adayes *see* Adai
Addaise *see* Adai
Addaize *see* Adai
Addee *see* Adai
Addick *see* Ahdik
Addies *see* Adai
Ad-dik *see* Ahdik
Addik *see* Ahdik
Ad-dik-kun-maig *see* Udekumaig
Addikkunmaig *see* Udekumaig
Addle-Heads *see* Menominee
Adee *see* Adai
Adena Culture (LC)
Adene *see* Athapascan
Adero *see* Ardeco
Adeyche *see* Adai
Adgecantchook *see* Arosaguntacook
Adiais *see* Adai
Adi'kamag *see* Udekumaig
Adikamag *see* Udekumaig
Adirondac *see* Adirondack
Adirondack [Can] *Algonquian* (H)
Adirondak *see* Adirondack
Adirondax *see* Adirondack
Adirontak *see* Adirondack
Adisonka *see* Adirondack
Ad-je-jawk *see* Ojeejok
Adjejawk *see* Ojeejok
Admitial [MX] *Coahuiltecan* (Hdbk10)
Adnondeck *see* Adirondack
Adose *see* Adai
Adshusheer [Lang] *Catawba* (H)
Adshusheer [NC] (H)
Adusta *see* Edisto
Adwanuqdji *see* Atsugewi
Adye *see* Adai
Adyi Kaporur-ri *see* Asurini I
Adzaneni [VE] *Wakuenai* (O)
Adzumawi *see* Achomawi
Aenay *see* Hainai
Aents [Self-designation] *see* Aguaruna
Aents [Self-designation] *see* Jivaro
Aequeya *see* Acuera
Aes *see* Eyeish
Aesetooue *see* Uzutiuhi
Aesopus *see* Esopus
Affagoula *see* Ofo
Affats-tena *see* Abbatotine
Afotige *see* Apinage
Afulakin *see* Wasco

Agace *see* Maca
Agace *see* Payagua
Agaideka (Hdbk11) *see also* Tukudeka (Hdbk11)
Agaideka [Hdbk11] *see also* Lemhi in Idaho (Hdbk11)
Agaideka *Northern Shoshone* (Hdbk11)
agaidika-a *see* Aga'ipaninakokado
agaidika'a *see* Koa'aga'itoka
agaidikadi *see* Aga'idokado
Aga'idokado *Northern Paiute* (Hdbk11)
Agai Duka *see* Agaideka
A-gai-du-ka *see* Agaihtikara
Agaiduka *see* Agaideka
A-gai-du-ka *see* Aga'idokado
Agaiduka *see* Aga'idokado
Agaiduka *see* Agaihtikara
Aga'ih-tika'ra *see* Agaihtikara
Agaihtikara [NE] *Paviotso* (H)
agaipani-n-adi *see* Aga'ipaninadokado
agaipaninadi *see* Aga'ipaninadokado
Agaipaninadokado *see* Aga'ipaninadokado
Aga'ipaninadokado *Northern Paiute* (Hdbk11)
A-gai-ti-kut-teh *see* Agaihtikara
A-gai-ti-kut-teh *see* Aga'idokado
Agaitikutteh *see* Aga'idokado
Agaitikutteh *see* Agaihtikara
Agai'tukeda *see* Aga'idokado
Agaitukede *see* Aga'idokado
A-gai-va-nu-na *see* Aga'ipaninadokado
Agaivanuna (Hdbk11) *see also* Aga'ipaninadokado (Hdbk11)
Agaivanuna [NE] *Paviotso* (H)
Agalec-qua-maya *see* Halyikwamai
Agalecquamaya *see* Halyikwamai
Agamenticus *see* Accominta
Aganushioni *see* Iroquois
Agata *see* Aguata
Agaucateco *see* Aguatec
A-ga Uo-no *see* Agawano
Agavotoqueng [Br] (O)
Agawam [MA] (BE)
A-ga-wa-no *see* Agawano
Agawano [NM] *Pueblo Indians* (H)
Agaz *see* Payagua
Agerones *see* Kainai
Aggey [NM] *Pueblo Indians* (H)
Ag-gi-tik-kah *see* Tazaaigadika
Aggitikkah *see* Tazaaigadika
Aghsiesagichrone *see* Missisauga
Agin *see* Pecos
Agiu *see* Pecos
Aglahmute *see* Aglemiut
Aglaxtana *see* Aglemiut

Aglegmguten *see* Aglemiut
Agleg'mut *see* Aglemiut
Aglemiut (Hdbk5) *see also* Aglurmiut (Hdbk5)
Aglemiut [AK] *Eskimos* (LC)
Aglemut *see* Aglemiut
Aglurmiut [AK] *Eskimos* (Hdbk5)
Aglurmiut [Lang] [AK] *Yupik* (Hdbk15)
Agnechronon *see* Mohawak
Agnée *see* Mohawk
Agneehronon *see* Mohawk
Agnengeronon *see* Mohawk
Agneronon *see* Mohawk
Agnez *see* Mohawk
Agnic *see* Mohawk
Agnié *see* Mohawk
Agniehronnon *see* Mohawk
Agniehroron *see* Mohawk
Agnierhonon *see* Mohawk
Agnieronnon *see* Mohawk
Agnieronon *see* Mohawk
Agnierrhonon *see* Mohawk
Agniers *see* Mohawk
Agniez *see* Mohawk
Agnizez *see* Mohawk
Ago *see* Acoma
Agolegma *see* Aglurmiut
Agolegmiut *see* Aglemiut
Agolegmiut *see* Aglurmiut
Agolegmiuty *see* Aglurmiut
Agolegmute *see* Aglemiut
Agolegmuten *see* Aglurmiut
Agolegmyut *see* Aglurmiut
Agolemuten *see* Aglemiut
Agomiut [Can] *Eskimos* (H)
Agoneaseah *see* Iroquois
Agones *see* Iowa
Agonnonsionni *see* Iroquois
Agonnousioni *see* Iroquois
Agonnsionni *see* Iroquois
Agoolmute *see* Aglemiut
Agotsagane *see* Mahican
Agotsagene *see* Mahican
Agouais *see* Iowa
Agoual *see* Iowa
Agoues *see* Iowa
Agouisiri *see* Awishiri
Agozhagauta *see* Mahican
Agto *Greenland Eskimos* (BE)
Agua *see* Carijona
Agua Blanca [Col] *Tunebo* (O)
Aguacadiba [JA, WInd] (BE)
Aguacaleyquen *see* Utina
Agua Caliente [CA] (H)
Agua Caliente [Lang] [*Luiseño-Kawia*] (H)
Aguacateca *see* Aguacatec
Aguacateca *see* Aguatec
Aguacatec I [MX] *Mayan* (BE)
Aguacatec II [Gu] *Zoque* (BE)
Aguacateco *see* Aguatec
Aguacero *Coahuiltecan* (Hdbk10)

Aguachacha [AZ, CA] *Yuman* (H)
Aguacoata *Coahuiltecan* (Hdbk10)
Agua Dulce [CA] *Shoshonean* (BE)
Agua Dulce [FL] *Timucua* (BE)
Aguahun *see* Aguaruna
Aguajun *see* Aguaruna
Agualo *see* Betoi
Agualohe *Coahuiltecan* (Hdbk10)
Aguana [MX] *Coahuiltecan* (Hdbk10)
Aguano [PE] (BE)
Aguanoxgi *see* Abnaki
Aguanu *see* Aguano
Agua Nueva [NM] *Piro* (H)
Aguapalam *Coahuiltecan* (Hdbk10)
Aguaque [MX] *Coahuiltecan* (Hdbk10)
Aguarnauguara [MX] *Coahuiltecan* (Hdbk10)
Aguaruna [EC, PE] *Jivaran* (LC)
Aguasajuchim *see* Ahwaste
Aguasajuchium *see* Uchium
Agua Salada *Navajo* (H)
Aguas Calientes [MX] (LC)
Aguastaya [TX] *Coahuiltecan* (BE)
Aguasto *see* Ahwaste
Agua Supai *see* Havasupai
Aguata [MX] *Coahuiltecan* (Hdbk10)
Aguateca [Gu, MX] *Mamean* (O)
Aguatinejo *Coahuiltecan* (Hdbk10)
Aguauono *see* Agawano
agudutsyam *see* Kawaiisu
Aguegnonke *see* Aquackanonk
Aguene *see* Doguene
Agueynaba [PR] (BE)
Aguial *see* Aigual
Aguica [MX] *Coahuiltecan* (Hdbk10)
Aguico *see* Hawikuh
Aguicobi *see* Hawikuh
Aguierhonon *see* Mohawk
Aguijampo *see* Aquijampo
Aguimaniguara *see* Saguimaniguara
Aguiniguara [MX] (Hdbk10)
Aguiocobi *see* Hawikuh
Aguiquegua (Hdbk10)
Aguirtiguera [MX] *Coahuiltecan* (Hdbk10)
Aguivira *see* Quivira
Aguljmjuten *see* Aglemiut
Agulmiut *see* Chnagmiut
Agulmut *see* Kuskwogmiut
Agulmuten *see* Aglemiut
Aguscal *see* Abascal
Aguskemai *see* Eskimos
Agustin culture, San (Col) (LC)
Agustin de la Isleta, San *see* Isleta
Agustin del Isleta, San *see* Isleta

A-gutch-a-ninne *see* Hidatsa
Agutchaninne *see* Hidatsa
A-gutch-a-ninne wug *see* Hidatsa
Agutchaninnewug *see* Hidatsa
Aguti *see* Marinawa
Aguti *see* Sharanahua
Agutit *see* Kinipetu
Agutit *see* Caribou Eskimos
agutushyam *see* Kawaiisu
A-gu-yu *see* Pecos
Aguyu *see* Pecos
A-ha-chae *see* Osage
Ahachae *see* Osage
Ahachik *see* Ahacik
Ahacik *Crow* (H)
Ah-ah *see* Ahalakalgi
Ahah *see* Ahalakalgi
Ahaharopironopa *Crow* (H)
Ahaharropirnopa *see* Ahaharopirnopa
Ahah-ar-ro-pir-no-pah *see* Ahaharopirnopa
Ahahawa *see* Amahami
Ahahaway *see* Amahami
Ahahnelin *see* Atsina
Ah-ah-pi-ta-pe *see* Ahahpitape
Ahahpitape [MN] *Piegan* (BE)
Ah-ah-wai *see* Ahahweh
Ahahwai *see* Ahahweh
Ah-ah-wauk *see* Ahahweh
Ahahwauk *see* Ahahweh
Ah-ah-weh *see* Ahahwah
Ahahweh [Phratry] *Chippewa* (H)
Ahaknanelet *see* Aivillirmiut
A-hak-nan-helet *see* Aivillirmiut
Ahaknanhelet *see* Aivillirmiut
Ahaknanhelik *see* Aivillirmiut
Ahalakalgi [Clan] *Creek* (H)
Ah-alakat *see* Chemehuevi
Ahalakat *see* Chemehuevi
Aha'lpam *see* Santiam
Ahalpam *see* Santiam
Ahandshiyuk *see* Ahantchuyuk
Ahandshuyuk *see* Ahantchuyuk
Ahantchuyuk [OR] (BE)
Ahantcuyuk amim *see* Ahantchuyuk
Aharaibu *see* Guaharibo
Ahatchwoop *Choptank* (Hdbk15)
Ah-auh-wauh *see* Ahahweh
Ahauhwauh *see* Ahahweh
Ah-auh-wauh-ug *see* Ahahweh
Ahauhwauhug *see* Ahahweh
Ahawhwauk *see* Ahahweh
Ahayadal *see* Southern Arapaho
Ahbahto dinne *see* Abbatotine
Ahbahtodinne *see* Abbatotine
Ah-co *see* Acoma
Ahco *see* Acoma
Ahdik [Clan] *Chippewa* (H)
A-he-alt *see* Ahealt
Ahealt [AK] *Koluschan* (H)

Ahearmiut *see* Ahiarmiut
Ahehoen *see* Ahehouen
Ahehoenes *see* Ahehouen
Ahehouen [TX] (H)
Ahei'pudin *see* Lower Chinook
Aheipudin *see* Lower Chinook
Ahekouen *see* Ahehouen
Ah-e-o-war *see* Amahami
Ah-e-o-war *see* Iowa
Aheowar *see* Amahami
Aheowar *see* Iowa
Ahepat Okla *see* Oypatukla
Ahgytecittech *see* Agaihtikara
Ahgy-tecitteh *see* Agaihtikara
Ahgyweit *see* Agaihtikara
Ah-ha-chick *see* Ahacick
Ahhachick *see* Ahacick
Ahhitape *see* Siksika
Ah-hi'-ta-pe *see* Siksika
Ahhousaht *see* Ahousaht
Ahiahichi *see* Eyeish
Ahialt *see* Ahealt
Ahiarmiut [AK] *Qairnirmiut*
  (Hdbk5)
Ahiarmiut *Caribou Eskimos*
  (Hdbk5)
Ahihinin *see* Pawnee
Ah-i-hi-nin *see* Pawnee
Ahihinon *see* Pawnee
Ahijados *see* Eyeish
Ahijados *see* Tawehash
Ahijaos *see* Eyeish
Ahijaos *see* Tawehash
Ahijitos *see* Eyeish
Ahijitos *see* Tawehash
Ahinai *see* Hainai
Ah-in-aub-ag *see* Chippewa
Ahjados *see* Eyeish
Ahk *Sitka* (Contri, v.1, p.38)
Ah-kaik-sum-ik *see* Ahkaiksumik
Ahkaiksumiks [MN] *Kainah*
  (BE)
Ah-kai-nah *see* Kainah
Ahkainah *see* Kainah
Ah-kai-po-kaks *see* Ahkaipokaks
Ahkaipokaks [Can] *Kainah* (BE)
Ah-kai-yi-ko-ka-kin-iks *see*
  Ahkaiyikokakiniks
Ahkaiyikokakiniks [MN] *Piegan*
  (BE)
Ah-knaw-ah-mish *see* Hahuamis
Ahknawahmish *see* Hahuamis
Ah-know-ah-mish *see* Hahuamis
Ahknowahmish *see* Hahuamis
Ah-ko *see* Acoma
Ahko *see* Acoma
Ahkonapi *see* Akonapi
Ahkootskie *see* Auk
Ahk-o-tash-iks *see* Ahkotashiks
Ahkotashiks [Can, MN] *Kainah*
  (BE)
Ah-kuh-ne-nak *see* Akuninak
Ahkuhnenak *see* Akuninak

Ah-kwo-nis-tsists *see* Ahkwon-
  istsists
Ahkwonistsists [Can, MN]
  Kainah (BE)
Ah-le-la *see* Shipaulovi
Ahlela *see* Shipaulovi
Ahlelq *see* Shipaulovi
Ah-lunk-soo *see* Ahlunksoo
Ahlunksoo [Clan] *Abnaki* (H)
Ah-mah-oo *see* Komogue [Gens]
Ahmahoo *see* Komogue [Gens]
Ah mau dah ka *see* Anadarko
Ahmaudahka *see* Anadarko
Ah-meek *see* Ahmik
Ahmeek *see* Ahmik
Ahmeekkwun-eninnewug (H)
Ah-mik *see* Ahmik
Ahmik [Clan] *Chippewa* (H)
Ah-mo-kai *see* Hopi
Ahmokai *see* Hopi
Ahnahanamete (H) *see also* Ama-
  hami (BE)
Ahnahanamete *Hidatsa* (H)
Ahnahaway *see* Amahami
Ah-nah-ha-nah-me-te *see* Ahna-
  hanamete
Ahnahhanamete *see* Ahna-
  hanamete
Ah-nan-dah-ka *see* Anadarko
Ahnandahka *see* Anadarko
Ahnaudahka *see* Anadarko
Ahnaudaka *see* Anadarko
Ahnenin *see* Atsina
Ahni-ninn *see* Atsina
Ahnininn *see* Atsina
Ahola *see* Tonto Apache
Ahola *see* White Mountain
  Apache
Ahomama [MX] *Lagunero* (BE)
Ahome [MX] *Guasave* (BE)
Ahondihronnons *see*
  Aondironon
Ahonekenke *see* Southern
  Tehuelche
Ahonicanka *see* Southern
  Tehuelche
Ahoniken *see* Southern
  Tehuelche
Ahonnekenke *see* Southern
  Tehuelche
Ahorio *see* Moro
Ahosett *see* Ahousaht
Ahotireitsu [CA] *Shasta* (BE)
Ahouandate *see* Huron
Ahouenrochrhonons *see* Wenro
Ahousaht [VanI] *Nootka* (BE)
Ahouset *see* Ahousaht
Ahowartz *see* Ahousaht
Ahowsaht *see* Ahousaht
Ah-owz-arts *see* Ahousaht
Ahowzarts *see* Ahousaht
Ah-pai-tup-ik *see* Ahahpitape
Ahpaitupik *see* Ahahpitape

Ahpakosea [Clan] *Miami* (H)
Ah-pa-kose-e-a *see* Ahpakosea
Ah-pe-ki *see* Apikaiyiks
Ahpeki *see* Apikaiyiks
Ah-pe-ki-e *see* Apikaiyiks
Ahpekie *see* Apikaiyiks
Ahpenope *see* Arikara
Ah-pen-ope-say *see* Arikara
Ahrenda *see* Arendahronon
Ahrendaronon *see* Arendahronon
Ahrowah (PC) *see also* Arukhwa I
  (H)
Ah-ro-wha *see* Arukwa I
Ahrowha [Clan] *Oto* (H)
Ah-se-pon-na *see* Ahseponna
Ahseponna [Clan] *Miami* (H)
Ah-shee-wai *see* Zuni
Ahsheewai *see* Zuni
Ah-shin-na-de-ah *see* Ashinadea
Ahshinnadeah *see* Ashinadea
Ah-shi-wi *see* Zuni
Ahshiwi *see* Zuni
Ah-shu-ah-har-pen *see* Salish
Ahshuahharpen *see* Salish
Ah-Supai *see* Havasupai
Ahsupai *see* Havasupai
Aht *see* Nootka
Ahtawwah *see* Ottawa
Ah-tena *see* Ahtena
Ahtena [AK] *Athapascan* (LC)
Ahtinne *see* Ahtena
Ahtinue *see* Ahtena
Ahtna-khotana *see* Ahtena
Ahtnakhotana *see* Ahtena
ahtu-tsuhka'is *see* Flathead
ahtutsuhkais *see* Flathead
a-hu-a-cha *see* Apache
ahuacha *see* Apache
Ahuachapan [ES] *Pokomam* (BE)
Ahuaches *see* Pawnee
Ahuadje *see* Tonto Apache
Ahuadje *see* White Mountain
  Apache
Ahuata *see* Aguata
Ahuatcha *see* Mescalero Apache
Ahucan *see* Yaochane
Ahuishiri *see* Awishiri
Ahwahacknanhelett *see* Aivillir-
  miut
Ahwahawa *see* Amahami
Ahwahaway *see* Amahami
Ah-wah-ha-way *see* Amahami
Ahwahhaway *see* Amahami
Ahwahnachee *see* Awani
Ahwahnechee *see* Awani
Ah-wah-sis-sa *see* Awausee
Ahwahsissa (PC) *see also* Awausee
  (H)
Ahwahsissa [Clan] *Chippewa* (H)
Ahwakilu *see* Chimakum
A-hwa-ki-lu [Self-designation]
  see Chimakum
Ahwandate *see* Huron

Ahwa-paia-kwanwa *see* Tonto Apache
Ahwapaiakwanwa *see* Tonto Apache
Ah-wash-te *see* Ahwaste
Ahwashte *see* Ahwaste
Ah-wa-sis-se *see* Awausee
Ahwasisse *see* Awausee
Ahwaste [CA] *Costanoan* (H)
Ah-weh-soo *see* Ahwehsoo
Ahwehsoo [Clan] *Abnaki* (H)
Ahweksoo [Clan] *Abnaki* (H)
Ah-wha-mish *see* Hahuamis
Ahwhamish *see* Hahuamis
Ahwishiri *see* Awishira
Ahya'to *see* Arapaho
Ahyches *see* Eyeish
Ai *see* Pilaga
A'i [Lang] *see* Cofan
Ai [Lang] *see* Cofan
Ai-aha *see* Chiricahua Apache
Aiaha *see* Chiricahua Apache
Aiahan *see* Chiricahua Apache
Aiaichi *see* Eyeish
Aiamiqta *see* Aia'miqta
Aia'miqta [WI] *Menominee* (BE)
Aiano *see* Kanohatino
Aiaouais *see* Iowa
Aiaouez *see* Iowa
Aiapai [CA] (H)
Aiapi *see* Oyampi
Ai-a'-ta *see* Apache
Ai-a-ta *see* Apache
Aiata *see* Apache
Aiauoua *see* Iowa
Aiauway *see* Iowa
Aiavvis *see* Iowa
Aiaye *see* Guaja
Aibali *see* Betoi
Aibamo *see* Alabama
Aibine (Hdbk10) *see also* Eudeve (LC)
Aibine [MX] *Xixime* (BE)
Aibino [MX] *Pueblo Indians* (Bull44)
Aibino [NM] (Bull44)
A-ic *see* Eyeish
Aic *see* Eyeish
Aiches *see* Eyeish
Ai-dik-a-da-hu *see* Arikara
Aidikadahu *see* Arikara
Aieways *see* Iowa
Aigngutdesu [Br] (O)
Aigspalo *see* Klamath
Aigspaluma *see* Klamath
Aigspaluma *see* Modoc
Aigual *Coahuiltecan* (Hdbk10)
Aiha *see* Chiricahua Apache
Aijados *see* Eyeish
Aijados *see* Tawehash
Aijaos *see* Eyeish
Aijaos *see* Tawehash
Aijas *see* Eyeish

Aijoues *see* Iowa
Aika *see* Kammatwa
Aikana [Br] (O)
A'ikoka *see* Acoma
Aikoka *see* Acoma
Aikspalu *see* Klamath
Aimara *see* Aymara
Aimaro *see* Aymara
Aimbore *see* Botocudo
Aimore *see* Botocudo
Aimoro *see* Aymara
Ainai *see* Hainai
Ainawimomowi *see* Hamaru-amomowi
Aingshi [Clan] *Zuni* (H)
Ainjshi-kwe *see* Aingshi
Ainones *see* Iowa
Ainoves *see* Iowa
Ain'shi-kwe *see* Aingshi
Ainshikwe *see* Aingshi
Ainsle Creek [BC] *Ntlakyapamuk* (H)
A-i-nun *see* Crow
Ainun *see* Crow
Aioaez *see* Iowa
Aioma *see* Acoma
Aiomo *see* Acoma
Aiouez *see* Iowa
Aiounouea *see* Iowa
Aiowais *see* Iowa
Aipatse [Br] (O)
Aipi *see* Oyampi
Ais (H) *see also* Eyeish (BE)
Ais [FL] *Muskhogean* (BE)
Aisa *see* Ais
Aise *see* Eyeish
A-ish *see* Eyeish
Aish *see* Eyeish
Ai-sik-stuk-ik *see* Aisikstukiks
Aisikstukiks [MN] *Siksika* (BE)
Aisnous *see* Iowa
Aispalu *see* Klamath
Aiticha (H) *see also* Iticha (H)
Aiticha [CA] *Kings River Yokuts* (BE)
Ai-tiz-zart *see* Ehatisaht
Aitizzart *see* Ehatisaht
Aitzart *see* Ehatisaht
Aiviktok [*Inuit (Quebec)*] (Hdbk5)
Aivilik Eskimos *see* Iglulik
Aivilingmiut [AK] *Iglulik* (LC)
Aivilirmiut *see* Aivillirmiut
Aivillirmiut [Can] *Central Eskimos* (BE)
Aivino [MX] *Pueblo Indians* (Bull44)
aivirtuuq *see* Aiviktok
Aivitumiut [Can] *Labrador Eskimos* (BE)
Aiwahokwu *see* Aiyaho
aiwa'nat (Hdbk5) *see also* Saint Lawrence Islanders (Hdbk5)

aiwa'nat *see* Chaplinski
aiwanat (PC) *see also* Chaplinski (Hdbk5)
aiwanat (PC) *see also* Saint Lawrence Islanders (Hdbk5)
Aiwanat [Sib] *Yuit* (BE)
Aiwateri [Br, VE] (O)
Aix *see* Eyeish
Aixai *see* Eyeish
Aixaj *see* Eyeish
Aixaos *see* Eyeish
Aixaos *see* Tawehash
Ai-yah-kin-nee *see* Hopi
Aiyahkinnee *see* Hopi
Aiyaho [Clan] *Zuni* (H)
Aiyaho-kwe *see* Aiyaho
Aiyahokwi *see* Aiyano
Ai-yan *see* Hankutchin
Aiyan *see* Hankutchin
Ai-ya-na *see* Hankutchin
Aiyana *see* Hankutchin
Aiyuwe *see* Iowa
Ai'yuwe *see* Iowa
Aizes *see* Eyeish
Ajaga *see* Achagua
Ajana *see* Oyana
Ajana *see* Urukuyana
Ajaouez *see* Iowa
Ajijagua *see* Ayagua
Ajouas *see* Iowa
Ajouelle *see* Avoyel
Ajoues *see* Iowa
Ajouez *see* Iowa
Ajuipiaijaigo [MX] *Coahuiltecan* (Hdbk10)
A-juma *see* Pit River Nation
Ajuma *see* Pit River Nation
Ajuma wi *see* Ajumawi
Ajumawi [CA] (CA)
Ajumawi [Lang] *Achomawi* (CA-8)
Ajuru *see* Wayoro
Ajuyap *see* Ujuiap
A'ka'a inihak'acin'a *see* Kanse
A'ka'a iniyak'acin'a *see* Kanse
Akainihakacina *see* Kanse
Akaitchi [OR] (H)
Akaitikka *see* Lemhi
akaitikka *see* Tukudeka
Akakashi *see* Mandan
Akama *see* Quapaw
Akamnik [BC] *Upper Kutenai* (H)
Akamsca *see* Quapaw
Akamsea *see* Quapaw
Akamsian *see* Quapaw
Akanaquint [UT] *Yampa* (H)
Akanca *see* Quapaw
A Kancea *see* Quapaw
Akancea *see* Quapaw
Akanekunik [BC] *Upper Kutenai* (H)
Akansa *see* Quapaw
Akansaes *see* Quapaw

Akansas *see* Quapaw
Akansca *see* Quapaw
Akansea *see* Quapaw
Akansis *see* Quapaw
Akanssa *see* Quapaw
Akanza *see* Quapaw
Akasquy [TX] (H)
Akauwenchaka *see* Akawantca'ka
Akavais *see* Acawai
Akawai *see* Acawai
Akawaio (LC) *see also* Akawai
  (LC)
Akawaio [Br, VE] (O)
Akawantca'ka [NC] *Tuscarora*
  (BE)
Akawenchaka *see* Akawantca'ka
Akawentc'aka *see* Akawantca'ka
Akawoio *Abanaki* (BE)
Ak'-ba-su'pai *see* Havasupai
Akbasupai *see* Havasupai
akbinnaxxu-we' *see* Kalispel
Ak Chin *see* Papago
Ak-e-ji *see* Santa Clara [NM]
akeji *see* Santa Clara [NM]
A'kemorl-Oohtam *see* Pima
Akemorl oohtam *see* Pima
Akenatzie *see* Occaneechee
Akenatzy *see* Occaneechee
Akensa *see* Quapaw
Akenuq'la'lam *see* Okinagan
Akhrakouaehronon *see* Conestoga
Akhrakoueahronon *see* Susquehanna
Akhrakuaronon *see* Conestoga
akimel o'odham *see* Gila River Pima
akimel o'odham *see* Pima
A'kimmash *see* Clackamas
Akimmash *see* Clackamas
Akinsaw *see* Quapaw
Akiskenukinik [BC] *Upper Kutenai* (H)
Akiskinookanik *see* Akiskenukinik
Akiyenik [BC, ID] *Upper Kutenai* (H)
Akkolear *see* Akuliarmiut
Ak-kon *see* Auk
Akkon *see* Auk
Ak-min-e-shu-me *see* Kalispel
Akmineshume *see* Kalispel
Ako *see* Abo
Ako *see* Acoma
A'ko [Self-designation] *see* Acoma
Akochakanen *see* Mahican
Akoeria *see* Akurio
akokavi *see* Acoma
Akoki *see* Acoma
Akokisa [TX] (BE)
Akoklako *see* Lower Kutenai
Akol [Clan] *Pima* (H)

Ako-ma *see* Acoma
Akoma *see* Acoma
akomage *see* Acoma
Akome *see* Acoma
Akonapi [IN, OH] (H)
Akonichi *see* Occoneechee
Akononsionni *see* Iroquois
Akonye [AZ] *Apache* (H)
Akoroa *see* Koroa
A-ko-t'as'-ka-ro'ren *see* Tuscarora
A-ko-tas-ka-ro-ren *see* Tuscarora
Akotaskaroren *see* Tuscarora
A-ko-tca-ka'nen *see* Delaware
Akotcakanen *see* Delaware
Akotcakanha *see* Delaware
A-ko-tca-nha *see* Delaware
Akotsakannha *see* Abnaki
A-kots-ha-ka-nem *see* Delaware
Akotshakanem *see* Delaware
Akowini *see* Akonapi
Akroa (O) *see also* Karoa (BE)
Akroa [Br] (O)
Aksanas [CH] (O)
Aktayatsalgi [Clan] *Creek* (H)
a-ku *see* Acoma
aku *see* Acoma
Akuawa-Asurini *see* Asurini
Akuchaklacta *see* Lower Kutenai
Akudliarmiut *see* Akuliarmiut
Akudnirmiut [Can] *Central Eskimos* (BE)
Akuen *see* Akwe
Akuen *see* Xavante
Akuesu-pai *see* Havasupai
Akuesupai *see* Havasupai
Akuliak-Eskimos *see* Akuliarmiut
Akuliarmiut [Can] *Central Eskimos* (BE)
Akuliyo *see* Akurio
Akulliakatagmiut [Can] *Central Eskimos* (BE)
akulmiut (Hdbk5)
akuma *see* Acoma
Akunigmiut *Kotzebue Sound Eskimos* (Hdbk5)
Akuninak *Sauk and Fox* (H)
Akuri *see* Akurio
Akurijo *see* Akurio
Akurio [Br, Su] *Tiriyo* (LC)
Akuriyo *see* Akurio
A-ku-tca-ka-nha *see* Delaware
Akutcakanha *see* Delaware
Akutskoe *see* Auk
akutusyam *see* Kawaiisu
Akwa [Lang] *Ge* (BE)
Akwaala *see* Akwa'ala
Akwa'ala [BaC, MX] *Yuman* (LC)
A-kwa-amish *see* Hahuamish
Akwaamish *see* Hahuamish
akwa'hnki *see* Delaware
akwahnki *see* Delaware
Akwawa-Asurini *see* Asurini II

Akwe (BE)
Akwech *Wichita* (H)
Akwen *see* Akwe
Akwesh *Wichita* (BE)
Akwe-Shavante [Br] (LC)
Akwe-Shavante [Lang] (LC)
Akwe-Xavante *see* Akwe-Shavante
Akwe-Xavante *see* Xavante
Akwilget *see* Hwotsotenne
Akwinoshioni *see* Iroquois
Akwits [OK] *Wichita* (BE)
Ala [Phratry] *Hopi* (H)
Alabama [AL] (LC)
Ala Bamer *see* Alabama
Alabamer *see* Alabama
Alabamu *see* Alabama
Alacaloof *see* Alacaluf
Alacalouf *see* Alacaluf
Alacaluf [CH] (LC)
Alacaluf [Lang] (LC)
Alacalufan *see* Alacaluf
Alachua [FL] *Seminole* (Ye)
Alacrane [MX] *Apache* (H)
Alaculoof *see* Alacaluf
Alaculuf *see* Alacaluf
Aladndesu [Br] *Southern Nambicuara* (O)
Ala'dshush *see* Chinook
Aladshush *see* Chinook
Alagonkin *see* Algonkin
Alaguilac [Gu] (BE)
Alaho *see* Kansa
A-laho *see* Osage
Alaho *see* Osage
Alaho-ateuna [Phratry] *Zuni* (H)
Alakaluf *see* Alacaluf
Alakatdesu [Br] *Southern Nambicuara* (O)
Alakea *see* Palaquesson
Alakema'yuk *see* Luckiamute
alakiwon *see* Aliklik
Alakwisa [CA] (Pub, v.16, no.8, p.472)
Alalengya *see* Ala-Lengya
Ala-Lengya [Phratry] *Hopi* (H)
Ala-Leñiya *see* Ala-Lengya
Alalenya *see* Ala-Lengya
Alama [EC, PE] *Quechua* (O)
Alamama [MX] *Lagunero* (BE)
Alameda *Tigua* (H)
Alameda la Isleta *see* Isleta
Alamillo [Lang] *Tigua* (H)
Alamillo *Piro* (H)
alammi *see* Modoc
alammig *see* Modoc
Alammimakt ish *see* Klamath
alammimakt ish *see* Modoc
A-lan-sar *see* Atsina
Alansar *see* Atsina
Alaoqui [MX] *Coahuiltecan* (Hdbk10)
Alapaguem *see* Saulapaguem

Alasapas [TX] *Coahuiltecan* (BE)
Alaskan Yupik [Lang] [AK]
  (Hdbk5)
Alatska *see* Clatskanie
A'latske *see* Clatskanie
A'latskne-i *see* Clatskanie
A'latskne-i *see* Tlatskanai
Alatsknei *see* Tlatskanai
Alawahku [Clan] *Pueblo Indians*
  (H)
Ala wiñwu *see* Ala
Albama *see* Alabama
Albenaqui *see* Abnaki
Albenaquioue *see* Abnaki
Albikas *see* Abihka
Albivi (H)
Alcalerpaguet *Coahuiltecan*
  (Hdbk10)
Alcea *see* Alsea
Alcea (H) *see also* Halchidhoma
  (CA)
Alcea (H) *see also* Maricopa (LC)
Alchedoma [AZ, CA] *Yuman* (H)
Alchedome *see* Alchedoma
Alchedum *see* Alchedoma
Alchedum *see* Halchidhoma
Alcheduma *see* Alchedoma
Alchidoma *see* Alchedoma
Alchones *see* Olhon
Alcojolado *see* Paraujano
Alcuco *see* Acoma
Aldeano [EC, PE] (O)
Aldefonso, San *see* San Ildefonso
Alebamah *see* Alabama
Alebamon *see* Alabama
Alebdoma *see* Halchidhoma
Aleche *see* Eyeish
Aleguapiame [MX] *Coahuiltecan*
  (Hdbk10)
Al-e-is *see* Cascades
Aleouteans *see* Aleuts
Alesar *see* Atsina
Aleuten *see* Aleuts
Aleutians *see* Aleuts
Aleuts [AK] (LC)
Alexander Archipelago *Tlingit*
  (Ye)
Alexandria Indians *see* Tautin
Aleya *see* Alsea
Aleyut *see* Aleuts
Algic [Lang] (LC)
Algic Indians *see* Oibwa
Algic Languages *see* Algonquian
Algique *see* Algic
Algodomes *see* Alchedoma
Algodonne *see* Alchedoma
Algokin *see* Algonkin
Algomeequin *see* Algonkin
Algomequin *see* Algonkin
Algommequin *see* Algonkin
Algommequin de l'Isle *see* Kich-
  esipirini
Algomquin *see* Algonkin

Algongin *see* Algonkin
Algongoncain *see* Algonkin
Algongoquois *see* Algonkin
Algonic *see* Algonkin
Algonkian *see* Algonquian
Algonkian-Mosan [Lang] (BE)
Algonkin [Can] (LC)
Algonkin of the Islands *see* Kich-
  esipirini
Algonmequin *see* Algonkin
Algonovin *see* Algonkin
Algonquen *see* Algonkin
Algonquian [Lang] (LC)
Algonquian of Portage de Prairie
  [Can] *Chippewa* (H)
Algonquian-Ritwan [Lang] (Coe)
Algonquin *see* Algonkin
Algonquins à tetes de Boule *see*
  Tetes de Boule
Algonquins of Rainy Lake *see*
  Kojejewininewug
Algonquins Superieurs *see* Ot-
  tawa
Algoomenquini *see* Algonkin
Algoquin *see* Algonkin
Algouinquin *see* Algonkin
Algoumekin *see* Algonkin
Algoumequin *see* Algonkin
Algoumequini *see* Algonkin
Algumenquini *see* Algonkin
Aliaska Penninsula *see* Aglemiut
Aliata *see* Ietan
Aliatan *see* Ietan
Aliatan *see* Shoshone
Aliatans of la Playes *see* Ietan
Aliatans of the West *see* Ietan
Aliatin *see* Northern Shoshone
Aliatons *see* Ietan
Aliatons of the West *see* Ietan
Alibam *see* Alabama
Alibama *see* Alabama
Alibamies *see* Alabama
Alibamo *see* Alabama
Alibamon *see* Alabama
Alibamous *see* Alabama
Alibamu *see* Alabama
Alibanis *see* Alabama
Alibanon *see* Alabama
Alich *see* Eyeish
Aliche *see* Eyeish
Alickas *see* Eyeish
Aligatalingmiut *see* Aligattaling-
  miun
Aligattalinmiun [AK] *Qairmir-
  miut* (Hdbk5)
Alijae *see* Tilijaes
Alikacaluf *see* Alacaluf
Alikalif *see* Alacaluf
Alikaluf *see* Alacaluf
Alikhoolip *see* Alacaluf
Alikoolif *see* Alacaluf
Alikuluf *see* Alacaluf
Al-i-kwa *see* Yurok

Alikwa *see* Yurok
Alile *see* Paraujano
Alimamu *see* Alabama
Alimibegoueci *see* Alimibegouek
Alimibegouek [Ont] *Cree* (H)
Alimouek *see* Illinois
Alimouk *see* Illinois
Alinconguin *see* Algonkin
Aliniouek *see* Illinois
Alinoueck *see* Illinois
Alipoti [NM] *Pueblo Indians* (H)
Alis [FL] (Ye)
Alish *see* Eyeish
Alishes *see* Eyeish
Alitan *see* Ietan
Aliton *see* Ietan
Aliut *see* Aleuts
Alkali Lake [BC] *Shushwap* (H)
Alkansa *see* Quapaw
Alkonkin *see* Algonkin
Alkunwea *Laalaksentaio* (H)
Al-la-ka-we-ah *see* Allakaweah
Allakaweah [MT] (H)
Allayume *see* Aleuts
Alle [NM] *Pueblo Indians* (H)
Allebome *see* Comanche
Allegan *see* Cherokee
Allegany *see* Alleghany
Allegewe *see* Cherokee
Allegewi *see* Cherokee
Allegewy *see* Cherokee
Alleghan *see* Cherokee
Alleghany (H) *see also* Cherokee
  (LC)
Alleghany [DE] *Shawnee* (H)
Allegheny *see* Alleghany
Allegwi *see* Cherokee
Allenemipigon *see* Chippewa of
  Lake Nipegon
Allentiac [Lang] *Paezan* (LC)
Allequas *see* Yurok
Allh [VanI] *Salish* (H)
Allianies *see* Miami
Alliatan *see* Ietan
Alliatans of the West *see* Ietan
Allibama *see* Alabama
Allibami *see* Alabama
Allibamon *see* Alabama
Allibamous *see* Alabama
Allico *see* Hawikuh
Alligany (H) Alleghany (H)
Alligewi *see* Cherokee
Allihewi *see* Cherokee
Alliklik [CA] (LC)
alliklikini *see* Alliklik
Allinoueck *see* Illinois
Allu [Clan] *Pecos* (H)
Almaguero *see* Quecha
Almotipu [ID] *Nez Perce* (BE)
Almotu [WA] *Paloos* (BE)
Alnanbai *see* Abnaki
Alobja *see* Pitalac
Alokolup *see* Alacaluf

Alomas *see* Acoma
Alona *see* Halona
Alonagua *see* Halona
Alooculoof *see* Alacaluf
Alookooloop *see* Alacaluf
Aloqui *see* Hopi
Alpowe'ma [ID] *Nez Perce* (BE)
Alquequin *see* Algonkin
Alse *see* Alsea
Alsea [OR] (LC)
Alseya *see* Alsea
Al-si *see* Alsea
Alsi [Self-designation] *see* Alsea
Alsigantegwi *see* Arosaguntacook
Alsiia *see* Alsea
Alsi-me tunne *see* Alsea
Alsimetunne *see* Alsea
Alsiya *see* Alsea
Al-tah-mo *see* Altahmo
Altahmo [CA] *Costanoan* (H)
Altajumi *see* Altahmo
Altajumo *see* Altahmo
Altamaha (BE) *see also* Tama (BE)
Altamaha [GA] *Yamassee* (BE)
Altamuskeet *see* Machapunga
Al-ta-tin *see* Sekani
Altatin *see* Sekani
Al-ta-tin of Bear Lake *see* Saschutkenne
Altatin of Bear Lake *see* Saschutkenne
Altatmo *see* Altahmo
Altau [Self-designation] *see* Altinun
Altekas *see* Texas
Altenkin *see* Algonkin
Altignenonghac *see* Attigneenongnahac
Altihamaguez *see* Attikamegue
Altikamek *see* Attikamegue
Altikameque *see* Attikamegue
Altinun [CA] *Yokuts* (H)
Alu [Clan] *Pecos* (H)
Alucaluf *see* Alacaluf
Alucuyana *see* Oyana
A lu'hl *see* Awluhl
Aluhl *see* Awluhl
Alukoeluf *see* Alacaluf
Alukulup *see* Alacaluf
Alukuyana *see* Oyana
Aluplishlish *see* Ataplili'ish
Alutiiq (Hdbk5) *see also* Aleuts (LC)
Alutiiq [AK] (AlGeo, v.23, no.2, 1996)
Alvayelilit *see* Eskimos
A'lvaye'litit *see* Eskimos
Alwasa-Ontilka *see* Coast Yuki
Amacaba *see* Mohave
Amacabo *see* Mohave
Amacabos *see* Mohave
Amacacore *see* Iquito
Amacahuri [Clan] *Timucua* (H)

Amacano [FL] (BE)
Amacapiras *see* Macapiras
Amacaua *see* Mohave
Amacava *see* Mohave
Amachave *see* Mohave
Amacuaguaramara [MX] (Hdbk10)
Amacuyero [MX] *Coahuiltecan* (Hdbk10)
Amador [Lang] [CA] *Miwok* (Pub, v.6, no.3, p.353)
Amage *see* Amuesha
Amaguaco *see* Amahuaca
Amaguagua *see* Mohave
Amagues *see* Amuesha
Amahami [ND] *Siouan* (BE)
Amahim *see* Anaham
Amahiyukpa [AZ] *Wikedjasapa* (BE)
Amahuaca [Lang] [Br, PE] *Panoan* (LC)
Amahuaka *see* Amahuaca
Amahuaya *see* Mohave
Amajaba *see* Mohave
Amajava *see* Mohave
Amaje *see* Amuesha
Amajo *see* Amuesha
Amajuaca *see* Amahuaca
Amakaraongky *see* Aquackanong
A-mak-ava *see* Mohave
amakava *see* Mohave
Amakhaba *see* Mohave
Amalecite *see* Malecite
Amalicite *see* Malecite
Amalingan *see* Malecite
Amaliste *see* Malecite
Amamanage *see* Amanaye
Amamati *see* Yamamadi
Amanage *see* Amanaye
Amanaje *see* Amanaye
Amanajo *see* Amanaye
Amanajoz *see* Amanaye
Amanakoa *see* Amonokoa
Amananiu *see* Amanaye
Amanasu [MX] *Coahuiltecan* (Hdbk10)
Amanaye [Br] (LC)
Amancoa [MX] *Coahuiltecan* (Hdbk10)
Amandaicoes *see* Anadarko
Amapoala [MX] *Coahuiltecan* (Hdbk10)
Amaque *see* Hopi
Amaquei [HA, WInd] *Bainoa* (BE)
Amaqui *see* Hopi
Amaracaire *see* Amarakaeri
Amarakaeri [PE] *Mashco* (O)
Amarakaire *see* Amarakaeri
Amaraquisp [MX] *Coahuiltecan* (Hdbk10)
Amarascoggin *see* Arosaguntacook

Amarascogin *see* Arosaguntacook
Amarescoggin *see* Arosaguntacook
Amariba [Br] *Wapisiana* (O)
Amaripa *see* Amariba
Amariscoggin *see* Arosaguntacook
Amarizama [Col, VE] *Achagua* (O)
Amarizan *Acahgua* (BE)
Amarizina [Lang] *Maipurean* (O)
Amaroscoggen *see* Arosaguntacook
Amasaconticook *see* Amaseconti
Amasacontoog *see* Amaseconti
Amasaguanteg *see* Amaseconti
Amasagunticook *see* Arosaguntacook
Amasconly *see* Amaseconti
Amascontie *see* Amaseconti
Amasconty *see* Amaseconti
Amasecontee *see* Amaseconti
Amaseconti [ME] *Abnaki* (BE)
Amashi *see* Hidatsa
Amasi *see* Amahami
Amassacanty *see* Amaseconti
Amassaconty *see* Amaseconti
Amatam [MX] *Coahuiltecan* (Hdbk10)
A-ma-te-wat-se *see* Amahami
Amatewatse *see* Amahami
Amatiha [ND] *Hidatsa* (BE)
A ma tiha mi *see* Amahami
A-mac-ha-ve *see* Mohave
Amatihami *see* Amahami
Amatisenge [PE] *Campo* (O)
Amatsenge *see* Amatisenge
Amawaca *see* Amahuaca
Amawaka *see* Amahuace
Amaxa [NM] *Pueblo Indians* (H)
Amayes *see* Jemez
Amaza [NM] *Pueblo Indians* (H)
Amazonia *see* Amazon River Region or Valley
Amazon River Region (LC)
Amazon River Valley (LC)
Ambahtawoot *see* Abbatotine
Ambah-tawut-dinni *see* Abbatotine
Ambahtawutdinni *see* Abbatotine
Ambataut tine *see* Abbatotine
Ambatauttine *see* Abbatotine
Ambatawwoot *see* Abbatotine
Ambawtamoot *see* Abbatotine
Ambawtawhootdinneh *see* Abbatotine
Ambawtawhoot Tinneh *see* Abbatotine
Ambawtawhoottinneh *see* Abbatotine
Ambawtawoot *see* Abbatotnine
Ambawtowhoot *see* Abbatotine
Ambure *see* Botocudo

Amdowapuskiyapi *Sisseton* (H)
Amdustez *see* Conestoga
Ame *see* Zuni
Amediche (H) *see also* Nabedache (BE)
Amediche [TX] (H)
Amedichez *see* Amediche
Amedichez *see* Nabedache
Amege *see* Jemez
Ameguara [MX] *Coahuiltecan* (Hdbk10)
Amehouest *see* Amikwa
Ameias *see* Jemez
Ameie *see* Jemez
Amejes *see* Jemez
Ameleste *see* Malecite
Amelick *see* Malecite
Amelinga *see* Malecite
Ameliste *see* Malecite
Amelistis *see* Malecite
Amena-Diapa [Lang] *Catuquina* (O)
Amena-Diapa Indians *see* Catuquina
Ameneci *see* Malecite
Amentis *see* Munsee
Ameralik *Greenland Eskimos* (BE)
Amerascogen *see* Arosaguntacook
Amereangan *see* Arosaguntacook
Amerescogin *see* Arosaguntacook
American Valley [Lang] [CA] *Maidu* (CA-8)
Ameries *see* Jemez
Ameriscoggin *see* Arosaguntacook
Amerrisscoggin *see* Arosaguntacook
A-me-she *see* Hidatsa
Ameshe *see* Hidatsa
Ameuhaque *see* Amahuaca
Ameyao [JA, WInd] (BE)
Amgutsuish *see* Umpqua
Ami *see* Zuni
Amicawaes *see* Amikwa
Amicoa (H)
Amicois *see* Amikwa
Amicouës *see* Amikwa
Amicour *see* Amikwa
Amicoures *see* Amikwa
Amic-ways *see* Amikwa
Amicways *see* Amikwa
Amiemhuaca [PE] *Campa* (O)
Amies *see* Jemez
Amiguara [Lang] [MX] *Quinigua* (Hdbk10)
Amihouis *see* Amikwa
Amik *see* Ahmik
Amikois *see* Amikwa
Amikones *see* Amikwa
Amikouai *see* Amikwa
Amikouas *see* Amikwa
Amikouek *see* Amikwa
Amikoues *see* Amikwa

Amikouest *see* Amikwa
Á Mikouest *see* Amikwa
Amikouet *see* Amikwa
Amikouis *see* Amikwa
Amikouy *see* Amikwa
A-miks-eks *see* Inuksiks
Amikseks *see* Inuksiks
Amikwa [Can] *Algonquian* (LC)
Amilcou (H)
Amilicite *see* Malecite
Amimenipaty [DE] *Unalachtigo* (BE)
Amios *see* Jemez
Amircankanne *see* Arosaguntacook
Amireaneau *see* Arosaguntacook
Amires *see* Jemez
Amirgankaniois *see* Narraganset
Amiscogging *see* Pequawket
Amishgo *see* Amuzgo
Amitaga *see* Amituaga
Amito [MX] *Coahuiltecan* (Hdbk10)
Amitons *see* Yankton
Amitormiut [Can] *Eskimos* (H)
Amitsi *see* Atsugewi
Ami'tsi *see* Atsugewi
Amitturmiut [AK] *Iglulingmiut* (Hdbk5)
Amituaga [MX] *Cerralvo* (Hdbk10)
Amiyaya [MX] (Hdbk10)
Amkepatine *see* Hunkpatina
Am-khark-hit-ton *see* Ankakehittan
Amkharkhitton *see* Ankakehittan
Amkora *see* Arikara
Ammarascoggin *see* Arosaguntacook
Ammarescoggin *see* Arosaguntacook
Ammascoggen *see* Arosaguntacook
Ammassalik Eskimos *see* Ammassalimmiut
ammassalimmiut *East Greenlanders* (Hdbk5)
Ammisk-watchee-thinyoowuc *see* Paskwawininiwug
Ammuchaba *see* Mohave
Amniape [Br] (O)
Amo (BE) *see also* Mosetenos (LC)
Amo (O) *see also* Chimane (LC)
Amo [NM] *Pueblo Indians* (H)
Amoama [MX] *Coahuiltecan* (Hdbk10)
A-moc-ha-ve *see* Mohave
Amochave *see* Mohave
A'moekwikwe *see* Hopi
Amoekwikwe *see* Hopi
Amoguama [MX] *Coahuiltecan* (Hdbk10)

Amohah *see* Mohave
Amohak *see* Mohawk
Amoishe *see* Amuesha
Amojave *see* Mohave
Amokebit *see* Mocobi
A-mo-kini *see* Hopi
Amokini *see* Hopi
A-mo-kwi *see* Hopi
Amokwi *see* Hopi
Amolelish *see* Molala
Amonces [CA] *Yokuts* (H)
Amonokoa *Illinois* (H)
Amonoscoggan *see* Arosaguntacook
Amonoscoggin *see* Arosaguntacook
Amoroa (O)
Amorua [Col] (O)
Amoscongen *see* Arosaguntacook
Amosequonty *see* Amaseconti
Amo-shium-qua *see* Amushungkwa
Amoshiumqua *see* Amushungkwa
Amoskeag [NH] *Pennacook* (H)
Amoxunqua *see* Amushungkwa
Amoxunque *see* Amushungkwa
Amo-zium-qua *see* Amushungkwa
Amoziumqua *see* Amushungkwa
Ampalamuyu [OR] *Luckiamute* (BE)
Ampapa *see* Hunkpapa
Ampape *see* Hunkpapa
Ampishtna [OR] *Calapooya* (BE)
Ampkoknimaklaks *see* Umpqua
Ampkua *see* Umpqua
Ampxankni *see* Wasco
Amresscoggin *see* Arosaguntacook
Amu [Clan] *Pecos* (H)
Amu-chaba *see* Mohave
Amuchaba *see* Mohave
Amucho *see* Amuzgo
Amueixa *see* Amuesha
Amueixa [Lang] *see* Lorenzan
Amuesa *see* Amuesha
Amuesa [Lang] *see* Lorenzan
Amuese *see* Amuesha
Amuesha [PE] (LC)
Amueshua *see* Amuesha
Amuetamo *see* Amuesha
Amuexa *see* Amuesha
A'muhak *see* Mohawk
Amuhak *see* Mohawk
A'-mu-kwi-kwe *see* Hopi
Amukwikwe *see* Hopi
Amusaya [Clan] *Timucua* (H)
Amusgo *see* Amuzgo
Amushungkwa [NM] *Jemez* (H)
Amusteack *Choptank* (Hdbk15)
amutcakaiem [Clan] [CA] *Serrano* (Pub, v.26, 1929)

Amuzgo [MX] *Miztecan* (LC)
Ana (BE) *see also* Cree (LC)
Ana, Sta *see* Santa Ana [NM]
Ana [Clan] *Zuni* (H)
Anaashashi *see* Santa Clara [NM]
Anaashashi *see* Tewa
Anabaidaitcho *see* Nabedache
Anacaioury *see* Yao
Anacamegishca (His/T)
Anacan *Coahuiltecan* (Hdbk10)
Anacana *see* Aracanaes
Anacasiguais *see* Anachiquaies
Anachiquaies [MX] *Tamaulipec*
    (BE)
Anacostan *see* Nacotchtank
Anacostank *see* Conoy
Anacostin *see* Conoy
Ana-da-ca *see* Anadarko
Anadaca *see* Anadarko
Anadacao *see* Anadarko
Anadaghcoes *see* Anadarko
Anadahcoe *see* Anadarko
Anadahha *see* Anadarko
An-a-dah-has *see* Anadarko
An-a-dah-kas *see* Anadarko
Anadahkoes *see* Anadarko
Anadahkos *see* Anadarko
Anadaka *see* Anadarko
An-a-dak-ha *see* Anadarko
Anadakha *see* Anadarko
Anadakka *see* Anadarko
Anadako *see* Anadarko
Anadaku *see* Anadarko
Anadarco *see* Anadarko
Anadarko (H) *see also* Nadarko
    (BE)
Anadarko [TX] *Caddoan Confederacy* (H)
Anadarko [TX] *Hasinai Confederacy* (BE)
Anadoghes *see* Anadarko
Anadorko *see* Anadarko
Anagado *see* Anegado
Anagansetts *see* Narragansett
Anagonge *see* Abnaki
Anaguanoxgi *see* Abnaki
Anaguas *see* Mohawk
Anaham [BC] *Tsilkotin* (H)
An-ah-dah-koes *see* Anadarko
Anahdahkoes *see* Anadarko
An-ah-dah-kos *see* Anadarko
Anahdahkos *see* Anadarko
Anahdaka *see* Anadarko
Anahem *see* Anaham
Anahim *see* Anaham
Anahon *see* Osage
Anainiyakacina *see* Kanse
Anais *see* Haisai
Anajot *see* Oneida
Anake *see* Auake
Anakew *see* Ana
Anakwancki *see* Delaware
Ana-kwan'ka *see* Delaware

Anakwanki *see* Delaware
Ana-kwe *see* Ana
Analac *see* Analoa
Analco [NM] *Tewa* (H)
Analoa [AR] (H)
Anamari *see* Yamamadi
Anambe [Br] (BE)
Aname *see* Aranama
Anana *see* Guanano
Ananare *see* Avavares
Anancock *see* Accomac
Anancock *see* Onancock
Anandaga *see* Onondaga
Anandarkoes *see* Anadarko
Anani *see* Biloxi
Ananis *see* Biloxi
Anano *see* Guanano
Anantooeah *see* Seneca
Anapaho *see* Arapaho
Anapati [PE] *Campa* (O)
Anapia *see* Carijonia
Anaqua *see* Nahukwa
Anarkat *Greenland Eskimos* (BE)
Anasaguntacook *see* Arosaguntacook
Anasaguntacook *see* Arsigantenok
Anasaguntakook *see* Arosaguntacook
Anasagunticook *see* Arosaguntacook
Ana Santa [NM] (BE)
Anasazi (LC)
Anasazi *Pueblo Indians* (LC)
Anasazi Culture (LC) *see also*
    Pueblo Indians (LC)
Anasgua [MX] *Coahuiltecan*
    (Hdbk10)
Anasuguntakook *see* Arosaguntacook
Ana Sushi *see* Santa Clara [NM]
Anasushi *see* Santa Clara [NM]
Anauqua *see* Nafuqua
Anauya [Lang] *Maupurean* (O)
Anavare *see* Avavares
Anawmanient *see* Onawmanient
Anaxi *see* Biloxi
Anaxis *see* Biloxi
Anaya [JA, WInd] (BE)
Anayents *see* Oneida
Anayints *see* Oneida
Anayot haga *see* Oneida
Ancalagresses (H)
Ancash [PE] (O)
Ancash-Huanuco [Lang] *Quechua*
    (O)
Ancashiguy *Coahuiltecan*
    (Hdbk10)
Ancavistis *Faraon Apache* (H)
Ancerma *see* Anserma
Anchipawah *see* Chippewa
Anckutere *see* Angotera
Ancoalla (BE)

Ancocus [NJ] *Delaware* (Hdbk15)
Ancutena *see* Angotera
Ancutera *see* Angotera
Ancutere *see* Angotera
Andacaminos [TX] *Coahuiltecan*
    (BE)
Andacui *see* Andaqui
Andagueda [Pan] *Embera* (O)
Andaico *see* Anadarko
Andaki *see* Andaqui
Anda-koen *see* Eskimos
Andakoen *see* Eskimos
Andaqui [Col, PE] (LC)
Andarco *see* Anadarko
Andaslaka *see* Conestoga
Andastaehronon *see* Conestoga
Andastaeronnon *see* Conestoga
Andastaes *see* Conestoga
Andastagueus *see* Conestoga
Andastaguez *see* Conestoga
Andastaka *see* Conestoga
Andaste *see* Susquehanna
Andastes *see* Conestoga
Andastfs *see* Conestoga
Andastiguez *see* Conestoga
Andastiquez *see* Conestoga
Andastoe *see* Conestoga
Andasto'e'r *see* Conestoga
Andastoerhonon *see* Conestoga
Andasto'e'ronnon *see* Conestoga
Andastoeronnon *see* Conestoga
Andastoerrhonon *see* Conestoga
Andastogne *see* Conestoga
Andastogue *see* Conestoga
Andastoguehronnon *see* Conestoga
Andastogueronnon *see* Conestoga
Andastohe *see* Conestoga
Andastonez *see* Conestoga
Andastoui *see* Conestoga
Andastracronnon *see* Conestoga
Andata honato *see* Ottawa
Andatahouat *see* Ottawa
Andatahouats *see* Eskimos
Andatohat *see* Ottawa
Andaye *see* Adai
And-dai-coes *see* Anadarko
Ande *see* Campa
Andean *see* Andes Region
Anderson Lake [BC] *Upper Lillooet* (H)
Anderson's River Esquimaux *see*
    Kitegareut
Andes Region (LC)
Andira *see* Maue
Ando *see* Shimigae
Andoa *see* Shimigae
Andoke [Lang] [Col] *Paezan* (LC)
Andoouanchronon *see*
    Ataronchronon
Andoque *see* Andoke
Andoquero [Lang] [Col] *Witoto*
    (O)

Andosagues *see* Conestoga
Andostaguez *see* Conestoga
Andostoue *see* Conestoga
Andowanchronon *see* Ataronchronon
Andrejanouschen Aleuten *see* Atka
Androscoggin *see* Arosaguntacook
Andshankualth [OR] *Yamel* (BE)
Andshimmampak [OR] *Yamel* (BE)
Anduico *see* Anadarko
Anega *see* Henya
Anegado [TX] *Coahuiltecan* (H)
Anenepit *see* Kopagmiut
A-ne-po *see* Anepo
Anepo [MN, Can] *Kainah* (BE)
Angaite [Lang] [Par] *Mascoian* (H)
Angaite [Par] (BE)
Angakok (H)
Angalla *see* Oglala
Angam *see* A-ngam
A-ngam [Lang] *Papago* (Hdbk10)
Angé *see* Mohawk
Angechag'emut *see* Ekogmut
Angechag'emut *see* Ankachagmiut
Angeles (H) *see also* Pecos (BE)
An-ghem-ak-ti-koo *see* Accominta
Anghemaktikoo *see* Accominta
Anghethade *see* Gunghethaidagai
Anghichia *see* Piankashaw
Angit Haade *see* Gunghethaidagai
Anglemiut [AK] *Eskimos* (H)
Angmagsalingmiut *Greenland Eskimos* (BE)
Angmagsalink Indians *see* Angmagsalingmiut
Angmagssalik [Lang] *see* Kalatdlisut
Angotera [EC] *Secoya* (O)
Angotero [PE] *Western Tukanoan* (O)
Angutera *see* Angotera
Angwassag [MI] *Chippewa* (H)
Ang-wush-a *see* Angwusi
Angwusi [Clan] *Hopi* (H)
Anhawa *see* Amahami
Aniaka-haka *see* Mohawk
Anibiminanisibiwininiwak [Ont, MN] *Chippewa* (BE)
Anichapanama *Coahuiltecan* (Hdbk10)
Anié *see* Mohawk
Aniers *see* Mohawk
Aniez *see* Mohawk
Anigatagewi *see* Ani-Gatagewi
Ani-gatagewi [Clan] *Cherokee* (His/T, p.398)

Anigilah (PC)
Ani-Gila'h [Clan] *Cherokee* (His/T)
Ani-Gili *see* Congaree
Anigili *see* Congaree
Ani-Gu'sa *see* Muskogee
Ani-Gu'sa *see* Creek
Anigusa *see* Creek
Anigusa *see* Muskogee
Anikawi *see* Ani-Kawi
Ani-Kawi [Clan] *Cherokee* (H)
Ani-Kawita *see* Lower Creek
Anikawita *see* Lower Creek
Ani-Kitu'hwagi *see* Cherokee
Anikituhwagi *see* Cherokee
Anikoessa *see* Creek
Ani-Ku'sa *see* Upper Creek
Ani-Kusa *see* Upper Creek
Anikusa *see* Upper Creek
anilt'anii *see* Navajo
Animay *see* Ione
Ani-Na'tsi *see* Natchez
Aninatsi *see* Natchez
A'ninin *see* Gros Ventre
Ani-Nun'dawe'gi *see* Seneca
Aninundawegi *see* Seneca
A'nipahu *see* Arapaho
Anipahu *see* Arapaho
Aniporspi *see* Nez Perce
Aniraniguara [MX] (Hdbk10)
Ani-Saha'n (His/T)
Anisahan *see* Ani-Saha'n
A-ni-sa-ha-ni *see* Asahani
Anisahani *see* Asahani
Ani-Saha'ni [Clan] *Cherokee* (His/T)
Ani-Sawanu'gi *see* Shawnee
Anisawanugi *see* Shawnee
Ani-Se'nika *see* Seneca
Anishinabe *see* Chippewa
Anishinabeg *see* Chippewa
An-ish-in-aub-ag *see* Chippewa
Anishinaubag *see* Chippewa
Ani-Skala-li *see* Tuscarora
Aniskalali *see* Tuscarora
Ani-Suwa'la *see* Cheraw
Anisuwala *see* Cheraw
Ani-Suwa'li *see* Cheraw
Anisuwali *see* Cheraw
Ani'ta'gua *see* Catawba
Anitagua *see* Catawba
Ani-Tsa-ta *see* Choctaw
Anitsata *see* Choctaw
Ani'Tsi'ksu *see* Chickasaw
Anitsiksu *see* Chickasaw
Anitsiskwa *see* Ani-Tsiskwa
Ani-Tsiskwa [Clan] *Cherokee* (His/T, p.398)
Ani-Wa'di (His/T, p.398)
Aniwadi *see* Ani-Wa'di
Ani-Wasa'si *see* Osage
Aniwasasi *see* Osage
Aniwaya *see* Ani'wa'ya

Ani'wa'ya [Clan] *Cherokee* (H)
Ani-yun-wiga *see* Cherokee
Ani-Yun-wiga *see* Cherokee
Aniyunwiga *see* Cherokee
Ani-Yun-wiya *see* Cherokee
Aniyunwiya *see* Cherokee
Ani-yun-wiya [Self-designation] *see* Cherokee
Ani-Yu'tsi *see* Yuchi
Aniyutsi *see* Yuchi
Anjoues *see* Iowa
Ankachagmiut [AK] *Chnagmiut Eskimos* (H)
Ankakehittan [AK] *Koluschan* (H)
Ankappa-nukkicicimi *see* Cedar
An-Kutchin *see* Hankutchin
Ankutchin *see* Hankutchin
Ankwa *see* Umpqua
Anligmuts *see* Kaviagmiut
Anlygmuten *see* Kaviagmiut
Anmesoukkanti *see* Amaseconti
Anmessukkantti *see* Amaseconti
Anmissekanti *see* Amaseconti
Anmoughcawgen *see* Arosaguntacook
Ann, Saint *see* Santa Ana [NM]
Anna *see* Anxau
Anna, S. *see* Santa Ana [NM]
Anna, Santa *see* Santa Ana [NM]
Annacostin *see* Conoy
Annadahkoes *see* Anadarko
Annadahoes *see* Anadarko
Anna-darcoes *see* Anadarko
Annadarcoes *see* Anadarko
Annah *see* Cree
Annahawa *see* Amahami
Annaho *see* Osage
Annamessex *see* Pocomoke
Annamessick (Hdbk15) *see also* Pocomoke (Hdbk15)
Annamessick [MD] *Nanticoke* (BE)
An-namu *see* Anu
Annamu *see* Anu
Annapolis [NS] *Kespoogwit Micmac* (BE)
Annas [TX] *Coahuiltecan* (BE)
Annawon [MA] *Wampanoag* (BE)
Annay *see* Hainai
Anndggho *see* Anadarko
Annegouts *see* Oneida
Anniegue *see* Mohawk
Anniehronnon *see* Mohawk
Anniene *see* Mohawk
anñieneeronnon *see* Mohawk
Anniener'onon *see* Mohawk
Anniengehronnon *see* Mohawk
Annienge'ronnon *see* Mohawk
Annienhronnon *see* Mohawk
Annieronnon *see* Mohawk
Annieronon *see* Mohawk
Annierronnon *see* Mohawk
Annies *see* Mohawk

Anniez see Mohawk
Anninici [HA, WInd] *Bainoa* (BE)
Annirkakan see Arosaguntacook
Annocchy see Biloxi
An-no-dar-coes see Anadarko
Annodarcoes see Anadarko
Annogonge see Abnaki
Annu [Self-designation] see Paraujano
Anoeg see Eno [NC]
A-nog-i-na jin see Anoginajin
Anoginajin *Wakpaatonwedan* (H)
Anogongaar see Abnaki
Anoixi [AR] *Caddoan* (H)
Anonotha [Self-designation] see Nonuya
Ano's-anyotskano see Arapaho
Anosanyotskano see Arapaho
Anoyints see Oneida
Anpan [Clan] *Quapaw* (H)
Anpanenikashika [Clan] *Quapaw* (H)
Anq'a'ke hit tan see Ankakehit-tan
Anquimamiomo [MX] *Coahuiltecan* (Hdbk10)
Anserma [Col] (LC)
Anseus see Kansa
An-shi-i-que see Aingshi
Anshiique see Aingshi
Anskowinis [SD] *Cheyenne* (BE)
Anskowinis [SD] *Cheyenne* (BE)
Antaniri [PE] *Campa* (O)
Antarianunts [UT] *Southern Paiute* (Hdbk11)
Antastoez see Conestoga
Antastogue see Conestoga
Antastouais see Conestoga
Antastouez see Conestoga
Ante see Campa
Antelope-eaters see Kwahari
Antelope Skinners see Kwahari
Anthontan see Teton
Anthoutanta see Oto
Anti see Arawak
Anti see Campa
Antiguos *Coahuiltecan* (Hdbk10)
Antoinede Senecu, S. see Senecu
Antoniano [CA] (LC)
Antoniano [Lang] [CA] *Salinan* (He)
Antoniño [CA] *Salinan* (Pub, v.10, no.4, p.104)
Antonio, S. see Senecu
Antonio, San [CA] (BE)
Antonio, San [Lang] [CA] *Sallinan* (Pub, v.14, no.1)
Antonio, San [Pueblo] [NM] *Tigua* (H)
Antonio de la Isleta, San see Isleta
Antonio de la Ysleta, San see Isleta

Antonio de Padua, Sant see Puaray
Antonio de Senaca, S. see Senecu
Antonio de Sencen, S. see Senecu
Antonio de Seneci, S. see Senecu
Antonio de Senecu, S. see Senecu
Antonio de Senecu Sant see Senecu
Antonio of Sinolu, San see Senecu del Sur
Antonio Seneca, San see Senecu del Sur
Antontu'tua [PE] *Taushiro* (O)
Antony, St. see Senecu
Antouaronons see Neutral Nation
Antouhonoron see Seneca
Antouhonoron see Oneida
Antouoronon see Seneca
antovorino see Seneca
Anu [Clan] *Hopi* (H)
Anue'nes see Anuenes
Anuenes [Clan] *Nanaimo* (H)
Anumania (O) see also Aueti (O)
Anumania [Br] (O)
Anun see Paraujano
Anunze see Nambicuara
Anuu see Paraujano
A-nu wunwu see Anu
Anuwunwu see Anu
Anuxa see Ocaina
Anvik-Shageluk [AK] *Ingalik* (BE)
Anwuci winwu see Angwusi
An-wu-si wun-wu see Angwusi
Anwusi wunwu see Angwusi
Anxau *Coahuiltecan* (Hdbk10)
Anyganset see Narraganset
Anyukwinu [NM] *Jemez* (H)
Anzerma see Anserma
Aoais see Iowa
Aoaqui see Auake
Aoat see Awata
Aocola [MX] *Coahuiltecan* (Hdbk10)
Aoechisacronon see Missisauga
Aoechisaeronon see Mississauga
Aoeni-Kunk see Southern Tehuelche
Aoge see Apinage
Ao-gitana-i see Aogitunai
Aogitunai [BC] *Masset* (H)
Aoiatenon see Wea
Aokeawai [Clan] *Skittagetan* (H)
Aome see Tohome
Aona see Ona
Aonarktormiut see Hauniqtuur-miut
Aonays see Iowa
Aondironon [Can, NY] *Neutral Nation* (BE)
Aonik see Ona
Aonik see Southern Tehuelche

Aoniken see Southern Tehuelche
Aonikenk see Southern Tehuelche
Aonikenke see Southern Tehuelche
Aoniko-tshonk see Southern Tehuelche
Aonukun'k see Southern Tehuelche
Ao-qe'awa-i see Aokeawai
Aoqeawai see Aokeawai
Aorta Band see Heviq-ni'pahis
Aostlanlnagai [Clan] [Can] *Skittagetan* (H)
Aouas see Iowa
Aouasanik see Ouasourini
Aouayeille see Avoyel
Aouciatenon see Wea
Ao ya ku lnaga i see Aoyakulnagai
Aoyakulnagai [Clan] *Skittagetan* (H)
'apaai see Papago
apac see Navajo
Apacachodegodegi (BE) see also Mbaya (LC)
Apacachodegodegi *Caduveo* (BE)
Apacachodeguo *Caduveo* (O)
Apacatchudeho *Caduveo* (O)
Apacatsche-e-tuo (BE) see also Apacachodegodegi (BE)
Apaca-tsche-e-tuo (BE) see also Apacachodegogedi (BE)
Apacatscheetuo see Apacachodegodegi
Apacatscheetuo see Apaca-tsche-e-tuo
Apaca-tsche-e-tuo *Caduveo* (O)
Apacci see Apache
Apacha see Apache
Apachas see Apache
Apache [AZ, NM, TX, MX] (LC)
Apachean [Lang] (Hdbk10)
Apache Arivapah see Arivaipa
Apache Band of Pharaoh see Faraon
Apache de Nabajo see Navajo
Apache Indians of Nabaju see Navajo
Apache Mimbrenos see Mimbreno Apache
Apache Mohave see Yavapai
Apache-Mojaoes see Yavapai
Apache-Mojaves see Yavapai
Apache Peaks *San Carlos Apache* (BE)
Apacherian see Apache
Apachesa see Apache
Apaches Broncos see Chiricahua Apache
Apaches Carlanes see Carlane
Apaches Chiricaguis see Chiricahua Apache

Apaches Colorados *Vaqueros* (Hdbk10)

Apaches Conejeros (Hdbk10)

Apaches Conexeros *see* Apaches Conejeros

Apaches de Chilmo (Hdbk10)

Apaches de Chiricahui *see* Chiricahua Apache

Apaches de Gila (Hdbk10)

Apaches de Jicarilla *see* Jicarilla Apache

Apaches del Acho (Hdbk10)

Apaches de la Xicarilla *see* Jicarilla Apache

Apaches del Cuartelejo *see* Apaches de Quartelejo

Apaches del Mechon (Hdbk10)

Apaches del Natafe *see* Natage

Apaches del Natage *see* Natage

Apaches de los Chipaynes *see* Chilpaines

Apaches del Perrillo [NM] (H)

Apaches del Quartelejo [KS] *Jicarilla Apache* (H)

Apaches de Nabajoa *see* Navajo

Apaches de Nabaju *see* Apache

Apaches de Nabaju *see* Navajo

Apaches de Nauajo *see* Navajo

Apaches de Navaio *see* Navajo

Apaches de Navajo *see* Navajo

Apaches de Navajo *see* Navajo

Apaches de Navajox *see* Navajo

Apaches de Nementina *see* Apaches de Trementina

Apaches de Peryllo *see* Apaches del Perrillo

Apaches de Quinia (Hdbk10)

Apaches de Siete Rios (Hdbk10)

Apaches de Trementina (Hdbk10)

Apaches de Xicarilla *see* Jicarilla Apache

Apaches de Xila *see* Gila Apache

Apaches de Xila *see* Apaches de Gila

Apaches Faraones *see* Faraon

Apaches Farones *see* Faraon

Apaches gileños *see* Gila Apache

Apaches jileños *see* Gila Apache

Apaches Lipanes *see* Lipan Apache

Apaches Llaneros *see* Mescalero Apache

Apaches Mansos [AZ] (H)

Apaches Mescaleros *see* Mescalero Apache

Apaches Mescalorez *see* Mescalero Apache

Apaches Nabajai *see* Navajo

Apaches of Arkansas River *see* Kiowa Apache

Apaches of Seven Rivers *see* Mescalero Apache

Apaches of the Plains *see* Kiowa Apache

Apaches orientaux *see* Querecho

Apaches Pharaones *see* Faraon

Apaches Taraones *see* Faraon

Apaches Vasqueras *see* Querecho

Apaches Vasqueros *see* Querecho

Apaches Xicarillas *see* Jicarilla Apache

Apache Tonto *see* Tonto Apache

Apache Tontoes *see* Tonto Apache

Apache Yuma *see* Tulkepaia

apachide *see* Apache

Apachies *see* Apache

apachin *see* Apache

Apachis *see* Apache

Apacho *see* Apache

Apachos Mescaleros *see* Mescalero Apache

Apachu *see* Apache

Apaci *see* Apache

Apades *see* Apache

apaeci *see* Jicarilla Apache

Apaehe *see* Apache

Apafan *see* Nestucca

Apahlahche *see* Apalachee

apaho-pa'is *see* Nez Perce

A-pa-huache *see* Apache

Apahuache *see* Apache

Apaichi *see* Apyachi

apaksisttohkihkini-tsitapi-koana *see* Flathead

Apalaccium *see* Apalachee

Apalacha *see* Apalachee

Apalache *see* Apalachee

Apalachean *see* Apalachee

Apalachecolo *see* Apalachicola

Apalachee [AL, FL] *Muskhogean* (LC)

Apalachen *see* Apalachee

A'palachi *see* Apalachee

Apalachi *see* Apalachee

Apalachia *see* Apalachee

Apalachian *see* Apalachee

Apalachias *see* Apalachee

Apalachicola [GA] (LC)

Apalachicolo *see* Apalachicola

Apalachicoloes *see* Apalachicola

Apalachicoly *see* Apalachicola

Apalachicoulys *see* Apalachicola

Apalachin *see* Apalachee

Apalachino *see* Apalachee

Apalachita *see* Apalachee

Apalachite *see* Apalachee

Apalachoocla *see* Apalachicola

Apalachucla *see* Apalachicola

Apalai (LC) *see also* Aparai (LC)

Apalai [Br, Su] *Carib* (LC)

Apalakire *see* Apalakiri

Apalakiri [Br] (LC)

Apalans *see* Apalachee

Apalaquiri *see* Apalakiri

Apalatchee *see* Apalachee

Apalatchia *see* Apalachee

Apalatchukla *see* Apalachicola

Apalatchy *see* Apalachee

Apalatchy-Cola *see* Apalachicola

Apalatci *see* Apalachee

Apalay *see* Apalai

Apalchen *see* Apalachee

Apalehen *see* Apalachee

Apallachian *see* Apalachee

Apalousa *see* Opelousa

Apalusa *see* Opelusa

Apamatecoh *see* Appomattoc

Apamatica *see* Appomatoc

Apamatick *see* Appomattoc

Apamatuck *see* Appomattoc

Apamatuk *see* Appomattoc

Apamona *Coahuiltecan* (Hdbk10)

A-pa-nax-ke *see* Abnaki

Apanaxke *see* Abnaki

Apa n de *see* Lipan Apache

Apande *see* Lipan Apache

Apani *see* Pawnee

Apaniekra [Br] (O)

A-pan-to-pse *see* Arikara

Apantopse *see* Arikara

Apanyecra *see* Apaniekra

Apanyekra *see* Apaniekra

Apaomateke *see* Appomattoc

A-pa-o-pa *see* Nez Perce

Apaopa *see* Nez Perce

A'pap *see* Apap

Apap *Pima* (H)

Apapocuva [Br] (LC)

Apapokuva *see* Apapocuva

Apapokuva *see* Avachiripa

Apapovoteng *see* Avachiripa

Apaqssos *see* Apaq'ssos

Apaq'ssos [Clan] *Menominee* (H)

Aparai [Lang] [UAz, v.28]

Aparai Indians *see* Apalai

Aparano *see* Mosetenos

Apatch *see* Apache

Apatche *see* Apache

a'patche-ahua *see* Apache

Apatcheahua *see* Apache

Apatches *see* Apache

Apa-tche tai'nin *see* Apache

Apatchetainin *see* Apache

Apatchim *see* Apache

A'patchu *see* Navajo

Apatchu *see* Navajo

A-pa-tci'm *see* Apache

Apats *see* Apache

Apatschee *see* Apache

Apatsh *see* Apache

Apa-tsil-tli-zhi'hi *see* Apatsiltlizhihi

Apatsiltlizhihi [NM] *Jicarilla Apache* (BE)

A'patsjoe *see* Navajo

Apatsjoe *see* Navajo

Apayi *see* Apaysi

Apaysi *Coahuiltecan* (Hdbk10)

Apayxam (H) *see also* Ebahamo (H)

Apayxam *Coahuiltecan* (BE)
Apedes *see* Apache
Apeica *see* Arara
Apeiran'di [Br] *Kawahib* (O)
Apelash *see* Apalachee
Apeloussa *see* Opelousa
Apelusa *see* Opelousa
Apena [NM] [Pueblo Indians] (H)
Apennapem *Coahuiltecan* (Hdbk10)
Apeolatei *see* Apalachee
Apes *see* Hapes
A-pe-tup-i *see* Ahahpitape
Apetupi *see* Ahahpitape
Apewan tanka *see* Apewantanka
Apewantanka *Brule* (H)
aphache *see* Apache
Apiaca [Br] (LC)
Apiachi *see* Apyachi
Apiaka *see* Apiaca
Apiche *see* Apache
Apiches *see* Eyeish
Apichi (H) *see also* Apache (LC)
Apichi [Clan] *Timucua* (H)
Apieaca *see* Arara
apihavatum [Clan] *Serrano* (Pub, v.26, 1929)
A-pi-kai-yiks *see* Apikaiyiks
Ap-i-kai-yiks *see* Apikaiyiks
Apikaiyiks [Can, MN] *Kainah* (BE)
Apilache *see* Apalachee
Apilash *see* Apalachee
Apinage [Br] (LC)
Apinaje *see* Apinage
Apinaye *see* Apinage
Api'nefu *see* Chepenafa
Apinefu *see* Chepenafa
Apingui [Lang] (UAz, v.28)
Apingui Indians *see* Arara
Apinulboines *see* Assiniboin
Apis *see* Hapes
Apiscas *see* Abihka
Apistekaihe [Can] *Cree* (BE)
Apistonga [AL] (H)
Apitala [MX] *Coahuiltecan* (Hdbk10)
Ap-la-che *see* Aplache
Aplache [CA] (H)
Apoche *see* Apache
Apohola [Clan] *Timucua* (H)
Apolacka *see* Apalachee
Apolashe *see* Apalachee
Apomatock *see* Appomattoc
Aponitre *Pueblo Indians* (H)
Apopokuva *see* Apapocuva
Apopokuva *see* Avachiripa
Apopovoteng *see* Avachiripa
Aporige [CA] *Atsugewi* (H)
Apostata [MX] *Tamaulipec* (BE)
Apoya [Clan] *Zuni* (H)
Apoya-kwe *see* Apoya

Appache *see* Apache
Appachee *see* Apache
Appalache *see* Apalachee
Appalachian *see* Apalachee
Appalachicola *see* Apalachicola
Appalachite *see* Apalachee
Appalacho *see* Apalachee
Appallatcy *see* Apalachee
Appallatta *see* Apalachee
Appalousa *see* Opelousa
Appamatox *see* Appomattoc
Appamatricx *see* Appomattoc
Appamattoc *see* Appomattoc
Appamattuck *see* Appomattoc
Appamatuck *see* Appomattoc
Appeche *see* Apache
Appelatha *see* Apalachee
Appellachee *see* Apalachee
Appelousa *see* Opelousa
Applegate Creek *see* Hupa
Applegate River Indians *see* Dakubetede
Appomatock *see* Appomattoc
Appomattake *see* Appomattoc
Appomattoc (H) *see also* Matchotic (H)
Appomattoc [VA] *Powhatan* (BE)
Appomatuck *see* Appomattoc
Appomatux *see* Appomattoc
Appomotack *see* Appomattoc
Ap-sah-ro-kee *see* Crow
Apsahrokee *see* Crow
Apsaroke *see* Crow
Apsarraka *see* Crow
Apsaruka *see* Crow
Apsharooke *see* Crow
Ap-sha-roo-kee *see* Crow
Apuasto *see* Ahwaste
A'puki *see* Apuki
Apuki [Clan] *Pima* (H)
A-pu-pe *see* Nez Perce
Apupe *see* Nez Perce
Apurina *see* Ipurina
Aputere *see* Mbya
Aputere *see* Caingua
Ap-ut-o-si-kai-nah *see* Aputosikainah
Aputosikainah [Can, MN] *Kainah* (BE)
Apwaruge [Lang] *Atsugewi* (CA-8)
Apwarukei *see* Apwaruge
A-pwa-tci *see* Apache
Apwatci *see* Apache
Apyachi [CA] [CA-8]
Apytere *see* Mbya
Aqathine'na [WY] *Arapaho* (BE)
A-q'iu *see* Pecos
Aqiu *see* Pecos
Aqk'a'mnik *see* Akamnik
Aqk'amnik *see* Akamnik
Aqka'mot [WI] *Menominee* (BE)
Aqk'anequ'nik *see* Akanekunik
Aqk'anequnik *see* Akanekunik

Aqkiskanukenik *see* Akiskenukinik
Aqki'sk-enu-kinik *see* Akiskenukinek
Aqkoqtla'tlqo *see* Lower Kutenai
Aqkoqtl'atlqo [Lang] *Kitunahan* (H)
A-qo *see* Acoma
Aqo *see* Acoma
Aqokulo *see* Chimakum
Aquaauchuque *see* Atquanochuke
Aquachonongue *see* Atquachanonk
Aquackanonk [NJ] *Unami* (BE)
Aqua Dulce *see* Agua Dulce
Aquahpa *see* Quapaw
Aquahpah *see* Quapaw
Aquamachuke *see* Atquanochuke
Aquamachuque *see* Atquanochuke
A-qua-mish *see* Hahuamis
Aquamish *see* Hahuamis
Aquanachuke *see* Atquanochuke
Aquaninoncke *see* Aquackanonk
Aquannaque *see* Abnaki
Aquannaque *see* Algonkin
Aquanoschioni *see* Iroquois
Aquanuschioni *see* Iroquois
Aquanuschionig *see* Iroquois
A-qua-pa *see* Quapaw
Aquapa *see* Quapaw
Aquaquanuncke *see* Aquackanonk
Aquas-saw-tee *see* Koasati
Aquatsagane *see* Mahican
Aquatzagane *see* Mahican
Aqueckenonge *see* Aquackanonk
Aqueckkonunque *see* Aquackanonk
Aquelegua *see* Gualegua
Aqueloa pissa *see* Acolapissa
Aquelon Pissa *see* Acolapissa
Aquelou pissa *see* Acolapissa
Aqueyquinunke *see* Aquackanonk
Aqui *see* Haqui
Aqui *see* Pecos
Aquia *see* Acoma
Aquicabo *Pueblo Indians* (H)
Aquicato *see* Aquicabo
Aquickanucke *see* Aquackanonk
Aquickanunke *see* Aquackanonk
Aquico *see* Hawikuh
Aquieeronon *see* Mohawk
Aquiers *see* Mohawk
Aquijampo [MX] *Coahuiltecan* (Hdbk10)
Aquima *see* Kiakima
Aquiman *see* Kiakima
Aquinoshioni *see* Iroquois
Aquinsa [NM] *Zuni* (H)
Aquintankee *see* Pocomoke
Aquinteca *see* Pocomoke

Aquinushionee *see* Iroquois
Aquira-Otam *see* Pima
Aquitadotdacam *Coahuiltecan* (Hdbk10)
Aquiu *see* Pecos
Aquoechononque *see* Aquack-anonk
Aquohanock *see* Accohanoc
Aquqenu'kqo *see* Lower Kutenai
Aquqtla'tlqo *see* Lower Kutenai
A-qu-sta *see* Tolowa
Aqusta *see* Tolowa
Ara (H) *see also* Karok (LC)
Ara [MX] (BE)
Ara-ara *see* Karok
Araara *see* Karok
Arabasca [Lang] *see* Athapascan
Arabaskaw *see* Athabasca
Arabela [PE] (LC)
Arabo [HA, WInd] *Caizcimu* (BE)
Aracaju [Br] (O)
Aracanaes [MX] *Tamaulipec* (BE)
Aracari *see* Arikara
Aracate *Coahuiltecan* (Hdbk10)
A-rach-bo-cu *see* Mandan
Arachbocu *see* Mandan
Aracuay *Coahuiltecan* (Hdbk10)
Aracuna *see* Arecuna
Aragaritka (H)
Aragaritka (H) *see also* Neutral Nation (LC)
Arahasomi [Clan] *Timucua* (H)
Arahatteak *see* Arrohattoc
Arahoma (Hdbk10)
Arahuac *see* Arawak
Arahuna *see* Araona
Araibayba *see* Pauserna
Araivapa *see* Arivaipa
A ra ka da ho *see* Arikara
Arakadaho *see* Arikara
Ara-k'c *see* Eskimos
Arake *see* Eskimos
Arakwayu *see* Apalai
Aramacoutou *see* Aramagoto
Aramagoto [Br, Su] *Tiriyo* (BE)
Aramagotou *see* Aramagoto
Aramakoto *see* Aramagoto
Aramana [Ha, WInd] *Caizcimu* (BE)
Aramayana *see* Aramagoto
Aramgoto *see* Aramagoto
Aramichaux *see* Aramisho
Aramicho *see* Aramisho
Aramihitcho *see* Aramisho
Aramisa *see* Aramisho
Aramisho [Br, Su] *Tiriyo* (O)
Aramiso *see* Aramisho
Aramogoto *see* Aramagoto
Aranama [TX] *Coahuiltecan* (BE)
Araname *see* Aranama
Aranau *Botocudo* (BE)
Araona [BO, Br] (LC)

Araona [Lang] *Tacana* (LC)
Araote *Warrau* (BE)
Arapaco *see* Arapaso
Arapaha *see* Arapaho
Arapahay *see* Arapaho
Arapaho [WY, Can] (LC)
Arapahoe *see* Arapaho
Arapahoo *see* Arapaho
Arapakata *see* Arapaho
Arapaso [Col] *Tucano* (BE)
Arapha *see* Arapaho
Araphoco *see* Arapaho
Arapium *see* Maue
Arapiyu *see* Maue
Arapohaes *see* Arapaho
Arapoho *see* Arapaho
Arapohose *see* Arapaho
Arara (LC) *see also* Koaia (O)
Arara (O)
Arara [Br] (LC)
Ararandeuara *see* Amanaye
Ararandewa *see* Amanaye
Arara-Tapuya [Clan] *Karutana* (O)
Ararawa *see* Arawete
Arasa [Lang] (LC)
Arasaeri [PE] (O)
Arasairi *see* Arasa
Arathapescoas *see* Athabaska
Arathapescoas [Lang] *see* Athapascan
Araua [Lang] (O)
Arauak *see* Arawak
Arauan *Botocudo* (BE)
Arauc *see* Arhuaco
Araucanian [Arg, CH] (LC)
Araucano *see* Araucanian
Arauco *see* Arhuaco
Araukan *see* Araucanian
Aravaco *see* Arawak
Aravaipa *see* Arivaipa
Aravapa *see* Arivaipa
Aravapai *see* Arivaipa
Aravapa Piñals *see* Arivaipa
Arawa [Lang] [Br] (O)
Arawac *see* Arawak
Arawak [WInd] (LC)
Arawakan [Lang] [WInd] (LC)
Arawete (O) *see also* Arawine (O)
Arawete [Br] (LC)
Arawine [Br] (O)
Arawna *see* Araona
Araza *see* Arasa
Araza *see* Arasaeri
Arazaire *see* Arasa
Arazaire *see* Arasaeri
Arbadaos [TX] (H)
Arbadoes *see* Arbadaos
Arbapaoes *see* Arapaho
Arcahamo *see* Tacame
Arcahomo *Coahuiltecan* (Hdbk10)
Arcanca *see* Quapaw
Arcansa *see* Quapaw

Archaic Age (AI, pp.22–25)
Archaree *see* Arikara
Archirigouan *see* Achiligouan
Archouguet *see* Outchougai
Arc Indians *see* Quapaw
Arc Plattes *see* Lower Kutenai
Arcs-a-plats *see* Lower Kutenai
Arcs-Brises *see* Tinazipeshicha
Arcs-Plats *see* Lower Kutenai
Arcs-plattes *see* Lower Kutenai
Arctic Highlanders *see* Ita
Arctic Highlanders *see* Polar Eskimos
Ardeco [AR] (H)
Ardnainiq *Central Eskimos* (H)
Are (BE) *see also* Heta (LC)
Are [Br] (BE)
Arecibo [PR] (BE)
Arecuna (LC) *see also* Arekena (LC)
Arecuna [Br, Col, VE] [*Parukoto-Pemon*] (LC)
Arekaina *see* Arekena
Arekena [Br, Col, VE] (LC)
Arekuna *see* Arecuna
Arenda *see* Arendahronon
Arendachronon *see* Arendahronon
Arendacronon *see* Arendahronon
Arendaenhronon *see* Arendahronon
Arendaenronnon *see* Arendahronon
Arendae'ronnon *see* Arendahronon
Arendaeronon *see* Arendahronon
Arendageronnon *see* Arendahronon
Arendah *see* Arendahronon
Arendahronon *Huron* (H)
Arendarhononon *see* Arendahronon
Arendaronnon *see* Arendahronon
Arendaronon *see* Arendahronon
Arendarrhonon *see* Arendahronon
Arendoronnon *see* Arendahronon
Areneños *see* Papago
Arepaha *see* Arapaho
Arepina *see* Maue
Arequena *see* Arekena
Arequipa (O)
Aresaguntacook *see* Arosaguntacook
Are Sheta *see* Heta
Aresheta *see* Heta
A-re-tear-o-pan-ga *see* Atsina
Aretearopanga *see* Atsina
Aretin [Coahuiltecan] (Hdbk10)
Aretines [MX] *Tamaulipec* (BE)
Aretino [MX] *Tamaulipec* (BE)
Aretpeguem *Coahuiltecan* (Hdbk10)

Arhosett see Ahousaht
Arhouaques-Kaggaba see Kagaba
Arhua [TX] (H)
Arhuac see Arhuaco
Arhuaca [Lang] see Ica
Arhuaco (LC) see also Ica (LC)
Arhuaco [Col] (LC)
Arhuak see Arhuaco
Ariana see Omagua
Aribaipa see Arivaipa
Aribapais see Arivaipa
Aribay see Caribay
Aricapu see Arikapu
Aricara see Arikara
Aricaree see Arikara
Aricari see Arikara
Aricarie see Arikara
Ariccaree see Arikara
Aricharay see Arikara
Arichard see Arikara
Arichimamoica (Hdbk10)
Arickara see Arikara
A-rick-a-ra-one see Arikara
Arickaraone see Arikara
Arickaraw see Arikara
Arickaree see Arikara
Aricuni see Arecuna
Aricuni see Arekena
Aridgevoak see Norridgewock
Aridgevoak see Kennebec
Aridgewoak see Norridgewock
Aridgewoak see Kennebec
Aridian [AZ] (H)
Arikapu [Br] (O)
A-ri-ka-ra see Arikara
Arikara [ND] (LC)
Arik-are see Arikara
Arikare see Arikara
Arikaree see Arikara
Arikari see Arikara
Ariken [Br] [Tupi-Guarani] (O)
Arikera see Arikara
Arikiena see Arekena
Arikkara see Arikara
Arikpaktsa see Aripaktsa
Arimigoto see Arimihoto
Arimihoto [Br, Su] Tiriyo (O)
Arimikoto see Arimihoto
Arimiyana see Arimihoto
Arino see Tapanyuna
Aripa [BaC, MX] Waicuri (BE)
Aripahoes see Arapaho
Aripaktsa [Br] (O)
Aripaktsa [Lang] see Rikbaktsa
Ariquepa see Arequipa
Ariquipay see Arequipa
Arisaguntacook see Arosagunta-
cook
Ariscapana (Hdbk10)
Aristeti [MX] Coahuiltecan
(Hdbk10)
Ariti [Self-designation] see Pa-
ressi

Arivaipa [AZ] San Carlos Apache
(BE)
Arivapa see Arivaipa
Arivapa Apaches see Arivaipa
Arivapais see Arivaipa
Arivaypa Apaches see Arivaipa
Arizonian Pimas see Pima
Arkandada see Oglala
Arkansa (H) see also Quapaw (LC)
Arkansa (H) see also Santsukhdhin
(H)
Arkansa Osage (Ye)
Arkansas Indians see Quapaw
Arkansaw see Quapaw
Arkansaw see Santsukhdhin
Arkansaw Osages see Santsukhd-
hin
Arkansea see Quapaw
Arkanses see Quapaw
Arkanza see Quapaw
Arkensa see Quapaw
Arkensas see Quapaw
Arkensaw see Quapaw
Arkensea see Quapaw
Arkokisa [TX] (H)
Armacoutou see Aramagato
Armagoto see Aramagoto
Armeomeck see Armewamex
Ar-me-shay see Hidatsa
Armeshay see Hidatsa
Armewamex Delaware (Hdbk15)
Armewamus see Armewamex
Armos see Auk
Aroaqui see Arawak
Aroaqui see Taruma
Arockamecook see Rocameca
Aroeck see Arseek
Arogisti see Conoy
Aroostook [ME] Micmac (BE)
Arosagantakuk see Arosagunta-
cook
Arosaguntacook [ME] Eastern Ab-
naki (LC)
Arosaguntakuk see Arosagunta-
cook
Arosario see Malayo
Aroua see Arua
Arouage see Arawak
Arouen see Arua
Arouseguntecook see Arosagun-
tacook
Arra-Arra see Karok
Arrahatecoh see Arrohattoc
Ar-rah-pa-hoo see Arapaho
Arrahpahoo see Arapaho
Arransoak see Norridgewock
Arransoak see Kenebec
Arrapaha see Arapaho
Arrapaho see Arapaho
Arrapaoes see Arapaho
Arrapapa see Chantapeta's Band
Arrapha see Arapaho
Arrapho see Arapaho

Arrapoho see Arapaho
Arrasaguntacook see Arosagunta-
cook
Arrasaguntacook see Arsigan-
tenok
Arrawac see Arawak
Arreaguntecook see Arosagunta-
cook
Arreguntenock see Arosagunta-
cook
Arrekara see Arikara
Arrenamuse see Aranama
Arrepaha see Arapaho
Arreraguntecook see Arosagunta-
cook
Arreruguntenock see Arosagunta-
cook
Arresagontacook see Arosagunta-
cook
Arresaguntacook see Arosagunta-
cook
Arreseguntecook see Arosagunta-
cook
Arreseguntoocook see Arosagun-
tacook
Arresuguntoocook see Arosagun-
tacook
Arricara see Arikara
Arricaree see Arikara
Arrickara see Arikara
Arrickaraw see Arikara
Arrickaree see Arikara
Arriekari see Arikara
Arrikora see Arikara
Arripaho see Arapaho
Arrivapi see Arivaipa
Arrockaumecook see Rocameca
Arrohateck see Arrohattoc
Arrohattoc [VA] Powhatan (BE)
Arrohattock see Arrohattoc
Arrow Creek People see Kas-
naikotkaiya
Arrowhatock see Arrohattoc
Arrowhatoes see Arrohattoc
Arrowmen see Moiseyu
Arruague see Arawak
Arsahattock see Arrohattoc
Arseek [MD] (H)
Arseguntecoke see Arosagunta-
cook
Arsek see Arseek
Arsenipoitis see Assiniboin
Arsenipoits see Assiniboin
Arsigantegwiak see Arsigantenok
Arsigantenok Western Abnaki
(Hdbk15)
Arsikanteg see Arosaguntacook
Arspahas see Arapaho
Arssateck see Arrohattoc
Arsuk Greenland Eskimos (BE)
Artez-kutchi see Ahtena
Artez-kutshi see Ahtena
Artez-Kuttchin see Ahtena

Artieda *see* Guaymi
Artieda *see* Northern Guaymi
Arts-milsh *see* Atsmitl
Artsmilsh *see* Lower Chehalis
Aru *see* Jaqi
Arua [Br] (O)
Aruac *see* Arawak
Aruaco *see* Arhuaco
Aruak *see* Arhuaco
Aruaki *see* Arawak
Aruashi [Br] (O)
Arucui *see* Urarina
Arucuye *see* Urarina
Arucuyi *see* Urarina
Arukhwa I [Clan] *Oto* (H)
Arukhwa II [Clan] *Iowa* (H)
Arundac *see* Adirondack
Arundax *see* Adirondack
Arupati (O) *see also* Kamaiura
   (LC)
Arupati [Br] (O)
A-ru-qwa *see* Arukhwa I
A-ru-qwa *see* Arukhwa II
Aruqwa *see* Arukhwa I and II
Aruseguntekook *see* Arosagunta-
   cook
Arutani *see* Auake
Arveqtormiut [Can] *Central Eski-
   mos* (BE)
Arvertormiut *see* Arviqtuurmiut
Arviligjuarmiut *see* Arvili-
   gyuarmiut
Arviligyuarmiut [Can] *Central Es-
   kimos* (BE)
arvilimmiut [Can] [*Inuit
   (Quebec)*] (Hdbk5)
Arviqtuurmiut [AK] *Eskimos*
   (Hdbk5)
Arwacahwa *see* Amahami
Arwachaon *see* Amahami
A-sa *see* Asa
Asa [Clan] *Hopi* (H)
A-sa-ha-ni *see* Asahani
Asahani [Clan] *Cherokee* (H)
Asahaptin *see* Nez Perce
As-a-ka-shi *see* Mandan
asa-ke-w *see* Sauk
asakew *see* Sauk
asá-ki-wa *see* Sauk
asakiwa *see* Sauk
asa-ki-waki *see* Sauk
asakiwaki *see* Sauk
Asan *Coahuiltecan* (BE)
Asani *see* Yscani
Asan'ka *see* Kutenai
Asanka *see* Kutenai
A-sa-nyu-mu *see* Asa
Asanyumu *see* Asa
Asau *see* Anxau
Asaukee *see* Sauk
Asay *see* Hopi
Ascahcutoner *Plains Indians* (H)
Ascani *see* Yscani

Ascani *see* Caddo
Aschatliens *see* Esselen
Aschochimi *see* Wappo
Asco *see* Doosedoowe
Aseny *see* Caddo
A'sepuna *see* Ahseponna
Asepuna *see* Ahseponna
Asequimoa [MX] *Coahuiltecan*
   (Hdbk10)
Ashaninca [PE] *Campa* (O)
Ashbochia *Crow* (H)
Ashbochiah *see* Ashbochia
Ash-bot-chee-ah *see* Ashbochia
Ashbotcheeah *see* Ashbochi
Ash-colored Indians *see* Gray-
   ones
Ashcroft [BC] *Shuswap* (H)
Asheninca [Self-designation] *see*
   Pajonalino
Ashepoo [SC] *Cusabo* (BE)
A-she-we *see* Zuni
Ashewe *see* Zuni
A-shi-ap-ka-wi *see* Biktasatetuse
Ashiapkawi *see* Biktasatetuse
Ashihi [Clan] *Navajo* (H)
Ashinadea *Crow* (H)
Ashinanca [PE] *Campa* (O)
Ashinance *see* Ashinanca
Ashiri *see* Awishiri
A-shi-ui *see* Zuni
Ashiui *see* Zuni
Ashiwi *see* Zuni
A'shiwi [Self-designation] *see*
   Zuni
Ash-kane-na *see* Ashkanena
Ashkanena *Crow* (H)
Ashkimeq *see* Eskimos
Ashley River Indians *see* Etiwaw
Ashluslay [Arg, BO, Par] (LC)
Ashluslay [Lang] *see* Chulupi
Ashnola [Br] *Okinagan* (H)
Ashnola [WA] *Similkameen* (BE)
Ashnuhumsh *see* Snohomish
Ashochemie *see* Wappo
Ash-o-chi-mi *see* Wappo
Ashochimi *see* Wappo
Asht-ia-la-qua *see* Astialakwa
Ash-tyal-a-qua *see* Astialakwa
Asht-ya-laqua *see* Astialakwa
Ashtyalaqua *see* Astialakwa
A-shu-e-ka-pa *see* Salish
Ashuekapa *see* Salish
Asiagmiut [Can] *Central Eskimos*
   (BE)
Asiagmut *see* Asiagmiut
Asiatic Eskimo (Hdbk5) *see also*
   Siberian Yupik (Hdbk5)
Asiatic Eskimos (Hdbk5)
Asidahech *see* Asidahetsh
Asidahetsh [OK] *Wichita* (BE)
Asihi *see* Ashihi
Asihidine *see* Ashihi
A-Simaes *see* Caddo

Asimaes *see* Caddo
A-Simais *see* Caddo
Asimais *see* Caddo
Asinaes *see* Caddo
Asinais *see* Caddo
Asinay *see* Caddo
Asinbols *see* Assiniboin
Asiniboels *see* Assiniboin
Asi-ni-bwan *see* Assiniboin
Asinibwan *see* Assiniboin
Asinibwanak *see* Assiniboin
A-si-ni-poi-tuk *see* Assiniboin
Asinipoituk *see* Assiniboin
Asinipovales *see* Assiniboin
Asinskau-winiuuk [Can]
   Paskwawininiwug (BE)
Asistagueronon *see* Mascouten
Asistagueronon *see* Potawatomi
Asistaguerouon *see* Mascouten
Asivoriches *see* Seuvarits
A-Skala-li *see* Tuscarora
Askalali *see* Tuscarora
Askikouaneronon *see* Nipissing
askime *see* Eskimos
askime-w *see* Eskimos
askime-winini *see* Eskimos
askipo'k *see* Eskimos
Askwalli *see* Nisqualli
As-ne-boines *see* Assiniboin
Asnecoines *see* Assiniboin
Asomoche [DE, NJ] *Unalachtigo*
   (BE)
asona *see* Pojoaque
Asoni *see* Caddo
Asonsaht *see* Ahousaht
Asoomaches *see* Asomoches
Asopus *see* Esopus
Asotin *Nez Perce* (Who)
Asoutheague *see* Assateague
Asperousa *see* Opelousa
Asphalashe *see* Apalachee
Assabaoch [Ont] (H)
Assaca *see* Masacuajulam
Assagunticook *see* Arosagunta-
   cook
Assagunticook *see* Arsigantenok
Assanpink *see* Assunpink
Assar *Coahuiltecan* (Hdbk10)
Assateague *Delaware* (LC)
Assatege *see* Assateague
Assategue *see* Assateague
Asseenaboine *see* Assiniboin
Asseeneepoytuck *see* Assiniboin
Assegun [Can, MI] (H)
Assegun [Can, MI] (H)
Assegunaig *see* Sauk
Asseinpink *see* Assunpink
Assekale *see* Hathawekela
Assekelaes *see* Hathawekela
Asselibois *see* Assiniboin
Assenepoil *see* Assiniboin
Asseni *see* Caddo
Asseniboines *see* Assiniboin

Asseniboualak *see* Assiniboin
Assenipoel *see* Assiniboin
Assenipoil *see* Assiniboin
Assenipoual *see* Assiniboin
Assenipoualac *see* Assiniboin
Assenipoualak *see* Assiniboin
Assenipouel *see* Assiniboin
Assenipoulac *see* Assiniboin
Assenipoulaes *see* Assiniboin
Assenipoulak *see* Assiniboin
Assenipouval *see* Assiniboin
Assenipoval *see* Assiniboin
Assenjigun *see* Osage
Assenniboin *see* Assiniboin
Assenpoel *see* Assiniboin
Assestagueronon *see* Mascouten
Assestagueronon *see* Potawatomi
Asseteague *see* Assateague
Assetegue *see* Assateague
As-sich-oots *see* Panguitch
Assichoots *see* Panguitch
Assigunaick *see* Assegun
Assigunaig *see* Assegun
Assigunaigs *see* Osage
Assikanna *see* Seneca
Assilibouel *see* Assiniboin
assimeu *see* Eskimos
assime-w *see* Eskimos
Assimpouel *see* Assiniboin
Assinaboes *see* Assiniboin
Assinaboil *see* Assiniboin
Assinabwoines *see* Assiniboin
Assinais *see* Caddo
Assinapi (H)
Assinay *see* Hasinai Confederation
Assinay *see* Caddo
Assine *see* Caddo
Assineboes *see* Assiniboin
Assineboin *see* Assiniboin
Assinebwannuk *see* Assiniboin
Assinepoel *see* Assiniboin
Assinepoin *see* Assiniboin
Assinepotuc *see* Assiniboin
Assinepoualaos *see* Assiniboin
Assiniboel *see* Assiniboin
Assiniboelle *see* Assiniboin
Assiniboel of the South *see* Assiniboin of the Plains
Assiniboels of the North *see* Northern Assiniboin
Assiniboels of the North *see* Tschantoga
Assiniboesi *see* Assiniboin
Assiniboil *see* Assiniboin
Assiniboile *see* Assiniboin
Assiniboin *see* Assiniboin
Assiniboin [Can, MN, ND] (LC)
Assiniboin des Plaines *see* Assiniboin of the Plains
Assiniboine *see* Assiniboin
Assiniboine *see* Assiniboin
Assiniboin of the Plains [Can] *Assiniboin* (H)

Assiniboins des Forets *see* Tschantoga
Assiniboins of the Forest *see* Tschantoga
Assiniboins of the North *see* Tschantoga
Assiniboins of the Rocky Mountains *see* Tschantoga
Assinibois *see* Assiniboin
Assiniboleses *see* Assiniboin
Assiniboualas *see* Assiniboin
Assinibouane *see* Assiniboin
Assinibouel *see* Assiniboin
Assinibouel of the Meadow *see* Assiniboin of the Plains
Assinibouet *see* Assiniboin
Assinib'wan *see* Assiniboin
Assinibwan *see* Assiniboin
Assinipi *see* Assinapi
Assinipoal *see* Assiniboin
Assinipoel *see* Assiniboin
Assinipoil *see* Assiniboin
Assinipoile *see* Assiniboin
Assinipoileu *see* Assiniboin
Assiniponiel *see* Assiniboin
Assinipotuc *see* Assiniboin
Assinipoual *see* Assiniboin
Assinipoualac *see* Assiniboin
Assinipoualak *see* Assiniboin
Assinipouar *see* Assiniboin
Assinipoulac *see* Assiniboin
Assinipour *see* Assiniboin
Assinipoval *see* Assiniboin
Assini-poytuk *see* Assiniboin
Assinipoytuk *see* Assiniboin
Assinipwanak *see* Assiniboin
Assinnaboin *see* Assiniboin
Assinnaboines *see* Assiniboin
Assinnee-Poetuc *see* Assiniboin
Assinni *see* Caddo
Assinnibain *see* Assiniboin
Assinniboan *see* Assiniboin
Assinniboine *see* Assiniboin
Assinopoil *see* Assiniboin
Assinpouele *see* Assiniboin
Assinpoul *see* Assiniboin
Assinpoulac *see* Assiniboin
Assisagh *see* Missisauga
Assisagigroone *see* Missisauga
Assista *see* Mascouten
Assista Ectaeronnon *see* Mascouten
Assistaeronon *see* Potawatomi
Assistagueronon *see* Mascouten
Assistagueronon *see* Potawatomi
Assistaqueronon *see* Mascouten
Assistaqueronon *see* Potawatomi
Assitaronon *see* Mascouten
Assitigue *see* Assateague
Assiwikale (H) *see also* Hathawekela (BE)
Assiwikale *Shawnee* (H)
Assoni *see* Caddo

Assony *see* Caddo
Assotoue *see* Uzutiuhi
Assunpink [NJ] *Unami* (BE)
Assurini *see* Asurini I
Assurinikin *see* Asurini I
Assuti [ID] *Nez Perce* (H)
Asswekalaes *see* Shawnee
Asswekale *see* Hathawekela
Asswikale *see* Hathawekela
Asswikales *see* Shawnee
Asswikalus *see* Hathawekela
Assynais *see* Caddo
Astakiwi [CA] *Achomawi* (BE)
Astari'wa *see* Astariwawi
Astariwawi [Lang] *Achomawi* (CA-8)
Astialakwa *Jemez* (H)
Asto [PE] (LC)
Astouregamigoukh [Can] (H)
Asumpcion *see* Sandia
Asuncion *see* Sia
Asuncion *see* Zuni
Asuncion *see* Sandia
Asuncion de Tepave *see* Tepahue
Asuncion Tepahue *see* Tepahue
Asurini I [Br (Xingu River)] (LC)
Asurini II [Br (Tocantins River)] (LC)
As-wun-wu *see* Asa
Aswunwu *see* Asa
A-ta-a *see* Ataakwe
Ataa *see* Ataakwe
Ataakwe [Clan] *Zuni* (H)
Atacal *see* Ataxal
Atacama *see* Atacameno
Atacamenian [Lang] *see* Cunza
Atacameno [BO, CH] (LC)
Atac-Apa *see* Attacapa
Atacapa *see* Attacapa
Atacapaz *see* Attacapa
Atac-assa *see* Attacapa
Atach *see* Tachi
A-tache *see* Tachi
Atache *see* Tachi
Atachiopa [AZ] *Wikedjasapa* (BE)
Ataconchronon *see* Ataronchronon
A-tagui *see* Lipan Apache
Atagui *see* Lipan Apache
Atagwa *see* Catawba
Ata'gwe *see* Catawba
Atahontaenrat *see* Tohontaenrat
Atai-kutchin *Loucheux* (IndN, v.2, no.3, July 1925, pp.172–77)
Atajal *Coahuiltecan* (BE)
Atakapa *see* Attacapa
Atakapan *see* Attacapa
Atakhtans *see* Ahtena
Ata'kini *see* Sichomovi
Atakwa *see* Catawba
Atalala *see* Vilela
Atalan (H)

A'tali (H) *see also* Alali (W)
Atali (PC) *see also* Alali (W)
Atali (W) *see also* A'tali (H)
Atali [Lang] *Mountain Cherokee* (W)
A'tali [Lang] *Upper or Mountain Cherokee* (H)
Atanaguaypacam *Coahuiltecan* (Hdbk10)
Atanum [WA] *Klikitat* (BE)
Atanumlema *see* Atanum-lema
Atanum-lema [WA] *Yakima* (BE)
Ataouabouscatouek *see* Bouscoutton
At'aplili'ish *see* Ataplili'ish
Ataplili'ish (JCB, v.4, no.2, pp.222) *see also* Alliklik (LC)
Ataplili'ish [Lang] [CA] (JCB, v.4, no.2, pp.222)
Ataronch *see* Ataronchronon
Ataronchronon *Huron* (H)
Atasi [AL] *Muskogee* (BE)
A-t'as'ka'lo'len *see* Tuscarora
A-tas-ka-lo-len *see* Tuscarora
Ataskalolen *see* Tuscarora
Atastagonies [TX] *Coahuiltecan* (BE)
Atawawa *see* Ottawa
Ataxal *Coahuiltecan* (Hdbk10)
Atayo *see* Adai
Atayos (H) *see also* Toho (BE)
Atayos *Coahuiltecan* (Hdbk10)
Atcansas *see* Quapaw
Atchaer *see* Atka
Atchashti ame'nmei *see* Chastacosta
Atchasti amim *see* Chastacosta
Atchatchakangouen [IL, IN] *Miami* (H)
Atchaterakangouen [WI] (H)
Atchialgi [Clan] *Creek* (H)
Atchihwa *see* Maricopa
Atchiligouan *see* Achiligouan
Atchixe'lish *see* Chehalis
Atchougek (H) SE Outchougia (H)
Atchoughe *see* Outchougia
Atchougue *see* Outchougia
Atchouguet *see* Outchougia
Atchuara *see* Achuale
Atcik-hata [Lang] [GA] (BE)
Ateacari [MX] *Cora* (H)
Ateakari *see* Ateacari
Ateanaca *see* Ateacari
A-teet-sa *see* Tangeratsa
Ateetsa *see* Tangeratsa
Atena *see* Ahtena
Atena *see* Shuswap
Atepira *see* Atepua
Atepua [NM] *Pueblo Indians* (H)
Ateyala-keokva *see* Astialakwa
Atfalati [OR] *Kalapooian* (BE)
Athabascan [Lang] *see* Athapascan

Athabaska (BE) *see also* Cree (LC)
Athabaska [Can] *Chipewyan* (BE)
Athabaska Lake Cree *see* Ayabaskawininiwug
Athabaskawithiniwuk *Sakawithiniwuk* (H)
Athapacca *see* Athapascan
Athapache *see* Athapascan
Athapasca Indians *see* Athabasca
Athapascan (LC) *see also* Kutchin (LC)
Athapascan [Lang] (LC)
Athapascow *see* Athabasca
Athapaskan [Lang] *see* Athapascan
Athapasque *see* Athapascan
Athapuscow *see* Athabasca
Athapuskow *see* Cree
Athistaeronnon *see* Mascouten
Athistaeronnon *see* Potawatomi
Athlameth *see* Klamath
Athlashimih *see* Carrier Indians
Athlets *see* Paviotso
Athnaer *see* Ahtena
Atiaonrek *see* Neutral Nation
Atica [NM] *Pueblo Indians* (H)
Aticum *see* Atikum
Atiec [HA, WInd] *Bainoa* (BE)
Atigagnongueha *see* Attigneenongnahac
Atignaouantan *see* Attignawantan
Atignenongach *see* Attigneenongnahac
Atignenonghac *see* Attigneenongnahac
Atignouatitan *see* Attignawanta
Atigyahointin *see* Attignawantan
Atik *see* Ahdik
Atikamegue *see* Attikamegue
Atikum [Br] (O)
Atilama *see* Alabama
Atimaco *see* Timucua [FL]
Atimuca *see* Timucua [FL]
Atimuqua *see* Timucua [FL]
Atingueennonnihak *see* Attigneenongnahac
Atingyahointan *see* Attignawantan
Atingyahoulan *see* Attignawantan
Atinionguin *see* Neagwaih
Atinniaoenten *see* Attignawantan
Atinniawentan *see* Attignawantan
Atinouaentan *see* Attignawantan
Atintans *see* Teton
Atintons *see* Teton
Atiouandaronk *see* Neutral Nation
Atiouendaronk *see* Neutral Nation
Atiouendaronk *see* Neutral Nation
Atiragenratka *Neutral Nation* (H)
Atiraguenrek *see* Atiragenratka

Atiraguenrek *see* Neutral Nation
Atirhagenrat *see* Neutral Nation
Atirhagenrenret *see* Neutral Nation
Ati-rhagenret *see* Neutral Nation
Atirhagenret *see* Neutral Nation
Atirhaguenreck *see* Neutral Nation
Atiri (O) *see also* Nomatsiguenga (LC)
Atiri [PE] *Campa* (O)
Atiwandaronk *see* Neutral Nation
Atka [AK] *Aleuts* (BE)
Atkan *see* Atka
Atkan (Hdbk5) *see also* Atha (BE)
Atkan *Western Aleut* (Hdkb5)
Atkha *see* Atka
Atlachaco *see* Acoma
Atlantic Bribri [Pan] *Bribri* (O)
Atlashimih *see* Takulli
Atna *see* Shuswap
Atna *see* Ahtena
Atnachtjaner *see* Ahtena
Atnäer *see* Ahtena
Atnah *see* Ahtena
Atnahs *see* Shuswap
At-naks *see* Shuswap
Atnaks *see* Shuswap
Atnalis *see* Tautin
Atnan *see* Ahtena
Atnans *see* Shuswap
Atnatana *see* Ahtena
Atnatena *see* Ahtena
Atnaxthynne *see* Ahtena
Atnuk *Bering Strait Eskimos* (Hdbk5)
A-to-co *see* Atoko
Atoco *see* Atoko
Atoko [Clan] *Hopi* (H)
Atoko winwu *see* Atoko
A-to-ko wunwu *see* Atoka
Atoko wunwu *see* Atoko
Atokume *see* Apache
Atokuwe *see* Apache
Atonaxo *see* Masacali
Atonthratarhonon (H) *see also* Totontaratonhronon (H)
Atonthratarhonon *see* Atonthrataronon
Atonthrataronon [Lang] (H)
Atontrataronnon *see* Atonthrataronon
Atontrataronnon *see* Totontaratonhronon
Atontratas *see* Atonthrataronon
Atontratas *see* Totontaratonhronon
Atontratoronons *see* Atonthrataronon
Atontratoronons *see* Totontaratonhronon
a-too-ha-pe *see* Salish

atoohape *see* Salish
Atorad *see* Atorai
Atorai [Br] *Wapishana* (O)
Atorya *see* Atorai
Atotchasi *see* Uzutiuhi
Atowa *see* Ottawa
Atowateany *see* Potawatomi
Atoyo *see* Adai
Atoyos *see* Toho
At-pasha-shliha *see* Hitchiti
Atpashashliha *see* Hitchiti
Atquanachuck *see* Atquanochuke
Atquanachuke *see* Atquanochuke
Atquanahuckes *see* Atquanochuke
Atquanochuke [NJ] (H)
Atquinachunk *see* Atquanochuke
Atra'kwae'ronnon *see* Susquehanna
Atra'kwae'ronnon *see* Conestoga
Atrakwer *see* Conestoga
Atrato *see* Embera
Atripuy [NM] *Jumano* (H)
Atroahi [Br] *Waimiri* (O)
Atroahy *see* Atroahi
Atroai *see* Atroahi
Atroari *see* Atroahi
Atroari *see* Waimiri
Atroari *see* Yawaperi
Atruahi *see* Waimiri
Atruahi *see* Atroahi
Atruahi *see* Yawaperi
Atrutons *see* Teton
Atsahuaca [Lang] (O)
Atsakudoka tuviwarai *Northern Paiute* (Hdbk11)
Atsawaca *see* Atsahuaca
Atsayongky *see* Mahican
Atsayonock *Delaware* (Hdbk15)
At-se-na *see* Atsina
Atsena *see* Atsina
Atsharoke *see* Crow
A-tsho-to-ti-na (H) Etchareottine (H)
Atshototina *see* Etchareottine
Atsina [Can, MN] (LC)
Atsiri *see* Campa
Atsiri [Self-designation] *see* Pajonalino
Atsista *see* Mascouten
Atsistaehronon *see* Mascouten
Atsistaehronon *see* Potawatomi
Atsistagherronnon *see* Mascouten
Atsistaghronnon *see* Mascouten
Atsistaheroron *see* Mascouten
Atsistaheroron *see* Mascouten
Atsistaheroron *see* Potawatomi
Atsistarhonon *see* Mascouten
Atsistarhonon *see* Potawatomi
Atskaaiwawixpu [ID] *Nez Perce* (BE)
Atsmitl [WA] *Chinookan* (H)
At-soo-ka-e *see* Atsugewi

Atsookae *see* Atsugewi
Atsuge (CA) *see also* Pit River Nation (CA)
Atsuge [Lang] [CA] (CA-8)
Atsugei *see* Atsugewi
Atsuge'wi *see* Atsugewi
Atsugewi [CA] (LC)
Atsugewi [Lang] [CA] (CA-8)
Attacapa [LA, TX] (LC)
Attacapaca *see* Attacapa
Attacapan [Lang] [LA, TX] (H)
Attacappa *see* Attacapa
Attakapa *see* Attacapa
Attakapo *see* Attacapa
Attamasco *see* Timucua [FL]
Attamuskeet *see* Machapunga
Attaquapa *see* Attacapa
Attaraya *see* Atorai
Attawa *see* Ottawa
Attawawa *see* Ottawa
At-ta-wits *see* Kadohadocho
Attawits *see* Kadohadocho
Attayes *see* Tyigh
Attegheny *see* Alleghany
Attekamek *see* Attikamegue
Attencapa *see* Attacapa
Attenkin *see* Algonkin
Attenmiut [AK] *Malemiut* (H)
At'tenmut *see* Attenmiut
Attenmut *see* Attenmiut
Attenonderonk *see* Neutral Nation
At-te-shu-pe-sha-loh-pan-ga *see* Les Noire Indians
Atteshupeshlohpanga *see* Les Noire Indians
Attibamegue *see* Attikamegue
Attibuni [HA, WInd] *Bainoa* (BE)
Atticameoet *see* Attikamegue
Atticameouec *see* Attikamegue
Atticamique *see* Attikamegue
Atticamoet *see* Attikamegue
Atticmospicayes *see* Thlingchadinne
Attignaoouentan *see* Attignawantan
Attignaouantan *see* Attignawantan
Attignaouentan *see* Attignawantan
Attignawantan [Ont] *Huron Confederacy* (H)
Attigneenongnahac [Ont] *Huron Confederacy* (H)
Attignenonghac *see* Attigneenongnahac
Attignouaatitan *see* Attignawantan
Attigouantan *see* Attignawantan
Attigouantine *see* Attignawantan
Attigouautan *see* Attignawantan
Attiguenongha *see* Attigneenonghac

Attihouandaron *see* Neutral Nation
Attikameg *see* Attikamegue
Attikamegouek *see* Attikamegue
Attikamegue [Can, Q] *Montagnais* (H)
Attikameguekhi *see* Attikamegue
Attikamek *see* Attikamegue
Attikameque *see* Attikamegue
Attikamigue *see* Attikamegue
Attik Iriniouetch *see* Attikiriniouetch
Attikiriniouetch [Can, Q] *Montagnais* (H)
Attikouetz *see* Attikamegue
Attikou Iriniouetz *see* Attikiriniouetch
Attikouiriniouetz *see* Attikiriniouetch
Attimopiquay *see* Thlingchadinne
Attimospiquaies *see* Thlingchadinne
Attimospiquais *see* Thlingchadinne
Attingueennonniahak *see* Attingneenongnahac
Attingueenongnahac *see* Attigneenonghac
Attigueenongnahac *see* Attigneenongnahac
Attinguenongnahahak *see* Attigneenongnahac
Attinguenongnahac *see* Attigneenongnahac
Attinniaoenten *see* Attignawantan
Attinoindaron *see* Neutral Nation
Attinquenongnahac *see* Attigneenongnahac
Attionandaron *see* Neutral Nation
Attionidaron *see* Neutral Nation
Attiouandaronk *see* Neutral Nation
Attiouendarankhronon *see* Neutral Nation
Attiquenongnah *see* Attigneenongnahac
Attiquenongnahai *see* Attigneenongnahac
Attistae *see* Mascouten
Attistae *see* Potawatomi
Attistaehronon *see* Mascouten
Attistaehronon *see* Potawatomi
Attistaeronon *see* Mascouten
Attistaeronon *see* Potawatomi
Attiuoindaron *see* Neutral Nation
Attiwandaronk *see* Neutral Nation
Attiwendaronk *see* Neutral Nation

Attiwondaronk *see* Neutral Nation

Attochingochronon *see* Ojeejok

Attorraidi *see* Atorai

Attuan *Western Aleut* (Hdbk5)

Attuckapa *see* Attacapa

Atuami [CA] *Achomawi* (BE)

A-tu-a-mih *see* Atuami

Atuamih *see* Atuami

aturaviatum [Clan] *Serrano*(Pub, v.26, 1929)

Atures *see* Piaroa

Atuyama [NM] *Pueblo Indians* (H)

Atwagannen *see* Ontwaganha

Atwa'msini *see* Atwamsini

Atwamsini [Lang] *Achomawi* (CA-8)

Atzigues *see* Tiwa

Atzinca *see* Ocuiltec

Atzinca [Lang] *see* Ocuiltec

Atzinca [MX] *Matlatzinca* (BE)

Atziqui *see* Tiwa

Atziri *see* Campa

Auaicu [Br] (O)

Auake [Br, VE] (O)

Auaque *see* Auake

Aubecuh *see* Abihka

Aubinaukee *see* Abnaki

Aubocoes *see* Abihka

Aub-sa-ro-ke *see* Crow

Aubsaroke *see* Crow

Auburn [Lang] *Nisenan* (CA-8)

Auca [CH] *see* Araucanian

Auca [EC] *see* Huao

Auca [Self-designation] *see* Waorani

Auca [Self-designation] *see* Waorani

Aucan *see* Araucanian

Aucanian *see* Araucanian

Aucano *see* Araucanian

Aucas [Br] *Araucanian* (O)

Auches *see* Eyeish

Aud-je-jauk (H) SES Ojeejok (H)

Audusta *see* Edisto

Aueti [Br] (O)

Aueto *see* Aueti

Augallalla *see* Oglala

Augustin, St. [Can] [*Montagnais-Naskapi*] (BE)

Augustin de la Isleta, San *see* Isleta

Augustin del Isleta, San *see* Isleta

Augutge *see* Gavioes

Auhishiri *see* Awishiri

Auishiri *see* Awishiri

Auiti *see* Aueti

Aujuiap *see* Ujuiap

Auk [AK] *Tlingit* (BE)

Auka *see* Araucanian

a'ukckni [OR] *Klamath* (BE)

Auke *see* Auk

Auke-Qean *see* Auk

Au Kotchin *see* Hankutchin

Aukotchin *see* Hankutchin

Aukpaluk [Can] [*Inuit (Quebec)*] (Hdbk5)

Auksiwash *see* Klamath

A-uksni *see* Klamath

Auksni [Self-designation] *see* Klamath

Au-kwu-cta *see* Tolowa

Aukwucta *see* Tolowa

Aulpapa *see* Hunkpapa

Aumane *see* Jumano

Aumesoukkantti *see* Amaseconti

Aunghim *see* Tanotenne

Auniers *see* Mohawk

Aunies *see* Mohawk

Auolasus *see* Southern Paiute

Auolasus *see* Paiute

aupaluk *see* Aukpaluk

Auquitsaukon *see* Delaware

Aura *see* Waura

Aurananean *see* Aranama

Auricara *see* Arikara

Aurickaree *see* Arikara

Auroguac *see* Arhuaco

A-ushkni *see* Klamath

Aushkni *see* Klamath

Ausinabwaun *see* Assiniboin

Ausotunnoog *see* Stockbridge

Autawa *see* Ottawa

Authontanta *see* Oto

Autire *see* Kikalsik

Autl *see* Aueti

Autouack *see* Ottawa

Autrechaha *see* Osage

Auve [PE] *Iquito* (O)

Aux Ares *see* Ozark

Auxira *see* Awishiri

A-uya *see* Kickapoo

Auya *see* Kickapoo

Auyapaguim *Coahuiltecan* (Hdbk10)

Auyapem *Coahuiltecan* (Hdbk10)

A-uyax *see* Kickapoo

Auyax *see* Kickapoo

Ava [Br] (O)

Ava-Chiriguano *see* Chiriguano

Avachiriguano *see* Chiriguano

Ava-Chiripa *see* Avachiripa

Avachiripa [Par] (LC)

Ava-Guarani *see* Chiriguano

Ava-Guarani *see* Chiripa

Avaguarani *see* Chiriguano

Avaguarani *see* Chiripa

Ava-Katu-Ete *see* Avachiripa

Avakatuete *see* Avachiripa

Ava-Kue-Chiripa *see* Chiripa

Avakuechiripa *see* Chiripa

Ava-mbiha *see* Mbya

Avambiha *see* Mbya

Avanersuarmiut *see* Polar Eskimos

Avani *see* Baniva

Avani *Baniva* (LC)

Avaraes *see* Avavares

Avares *see* Avavares

Ava-Supies *see* Havasupai

Avasupies *see* Havasupai

Avauwais *see* Iowa

Avavares [TX] (H)

Avesupai *see* Havasupai

Avijira *see* Awishiri

Avipa Apache *see* Arivaipa

Avirxiri *see* Awishiri

Avitumiut [Can] *Labrador Eskimos* (BE)

Avixira *see* Awishiri

Avogal *see* Avoyel

Avovelle *see* Avoyel

Avoy *see* Iowa

Avoyall *see* Avoyel

Avoyel [LA] (BE)

Avoyella *see* Avoyel

Avoyelle *see* Avoyel

Avvagmiut [Can] *Mackenzie Eskimos* (BE)

A-vwa-tsu *see* Apache

Avwatsu *see* Apache

awaaca *see* Apache

Awachawi *see* Amahami

awaci *see* Jicarilla Apache

Awaete *see* Asurini I

A-wa-ha-wa *see* Amahami

Awahawa *see* Amahami

A-waha-way *see* Amahami

Awahaway *see* Amahami

Awahe *see* Pawnee

Awahi *see* Pawnee

Awahu *see* Pawnee

Awahun *see* Aquaruna

Awaika *see* Auaicu

Awaike *see* Auaicu

A'wa-ilala *see* Awaitlala

Awaitlala [BC] *Kwakiutl* (BE)

Awaitlala [Lang] *Kwakiutl* (H)

Awalache *see* Awani

Awallache *see* Awani

awamish *see* Skihwamish

A-wa-ni *see* Awani

Awani [CA] *Miwok* (H)

Awano *see* Aguano

A-wa-oo *see* Tlaaluis

Awaoo *see* Tlaaluis

Awasatciu *see* Ouasourini

Awash [Clan] *Tonkawa* (H)

Awasko ammim *see* Wasco

Awaso *see* Ahwehsoo

A-was-shetan-qua *see* Cheyenne

a-was-she-tan-qua *see* Cheyenne

Awasshetanqua *see* Cheyenne

Awassissin *see* Awausee

Awaswas [Lang] [CA] *Northern Costanoan* (CA-8)

A-wa-ta *see* Awata

Awata [Clan] *Hopi* (H)

Awata winwu *see* Awata
A-wata wun-wu *see* Awata
Awata wunwu *see* Awata
Awatch *see* Apache
Awatche *see* Apache
Awate *see* Asurini I
Awatixa *Gros Ventre* (Ye)
A-waus-e *see* Awausee
Awausee [Phratry] *Chippewa* (H)
A-waus-e-wug *see* Awausee
Awausewug *see* Awausee
A-waus-is-ee *see* Awausee
Awausisee *see* Awausee
Awaxawi *Gros Ventre* (Ye)
"Away-from-here Shawnee" *see* Absentee Shawnee
A-we *see* Akwe
A-we *see* Akwe-Xavante
A-we *see* Xavante
Awe *see* Akwe
Awe *see* Akwe-Xavante
Awe *see* Xavante
Aweatsiwaenhronon *see* Winnebago
Aweatsiwaenrrhonon *see* Nipissing
Awechisaehronon *see* Missisauga
Aweikoma *see* Shokleng
Awenatchela *see* Wenatchi
Awena'techela *see* Wenatchi
Aweti *see* Aueti
Awi-adshi *see* Klickitat
Awighsaghroene *see* Awighsaghroone
Awighsaghroone [Can] (H)
Awikenox *see* Oowekeeno
Awikyenoq *see* Oowekeeno
Awirimomowi *Guahibo* (O)
A-wish-in-aub-ay *see* Chippewa
Awishinaubay *see* Chippewa
Awishira *see* Awishiri
Awishiri [PE] (O)
Awk *see* Auk
Awl-heart *see* Skitswish
Awluhl [Clan] *Taos* (H)
Awo *see* Pawnee
Awokanak *see* Etchaottine
Awokanak *see* Etchareottine
Awo-pa-pa *see* Maricopa
Awopapa *see* Maricopa
Aw-o-tum *see* Pima
Awotum *see* Pima
Awp *see* Apache
A'wp-pa-pa *see* Maricopa
Awppapa *see* Maricopa
Axauti *Pueblo Indians* (H)
Axehinen *see* Pawnee
Axion (Hdbk15) *see also* Atsayonck (Hdbk15)
Axion [NJ] *Unami* (BE)
Axipaya *Coahuiltecan* (Hdbk10)
Axol [NM] *Tewa* (H)
Axoytre *see* Axol

Axshihhaye-runu *see* Chippewa
Axtaos *see* Eyeish
Axtaos *see* Tawehash
Axua *see* Comeya
axwa *see* Apache
axwaatca *see* Apache
Axwe'lapc *see* Kwalhioqua
Ayabasca *see* Athapascan
Ayabaskan Indians *see* Athabasca
Ayabaskawininiwug [Can] *Sakawininiwug* (BE)
Ayabaskawiyiniwag *see* Sakawithiniwuk
Ayache *see* Eyeish
Ayacucho [PE] (O)
Ayacucho-Cuzco [Lang] *Quechua* (O)
Ayagua *Coahuiltecan* (Hdbk10)
Ayahanisino [Clan] *Timucua* (H)
Ayahkini *see* Hopi
Ayahkini *see* Walpi
Ayahwa *see* Iowa
Ayaman [VE] (LC)
Ayamare *see* Aymara
Ayan *see* Hankutchin
Ayanai *see* Hainai
Ayancuara (Hdbk10)
Ayane *Baniva* (LC)
Ayankeld *see* Yoncalla
Ayanna *see* Oyana
Ayano *see* Kanohatino
Ayano *see* Baniva
Ayapi *see* Oyanpik
Ayas *see* Eyeish
a-yascime-w *see* Eskimos
ayascimew *see* Eskimos
a-yaskime-w *see* Eskimos
ayaskimew *see* Eskimos
a-yaskyime-w *see* Eskimos
ayaskyimew *see* Eskimos
ayassime-w *see* Eskimos
Ayatchinini *see* Siksika
Ayatchiyinim *see* Siksika
Ayatchiyiniw *see* Siksika
A-ya-to *see* Arapaho
Ayato *see* Arapaho
Ayauais *see* Iowa
Ayauvai *see* Iowa
Ayauwais *see* Iowa
Ayauwas *see* Iowa
Ayauwaus *see* Iowa
Ayauway *see* Iowa
Ayavois *see* Iowa
Ayawai *see* Iowa
Ayaways *see* Iowa
Ayays *see* Eyeish
Aybamo *see* Alabama
Aycalme [MX] *Concho* (BE)
A-y-chart *see* Hachaath
Aychart *see* Hachaath
Ayche *see* Eyeish
Aychis *see* Eyeish
Aycubaverrenay *Achagua* (O)

Ayeche *see* Eyeish
Ayenguara [MX] (Hdbk10)
Ayeni *see* Hainai
Ayenni *see* Hainai
Ayennis *see* Yojuane
Ayeouais *see* Iowa
Ayeraguara [MX] (Hdbk10)
Ayerapaguana [MX] *Coahuiltecan* (Hdbk10)
Ayes *see* Eyeish
Aygual *see* Aigual
Ayhuttisaht *see* Ehatisaht
Ayiches *see* Eyeish
Ayish *see* Eyeish
Ayisiyiniwok *see* Cree
Ayjados *see* Tawehash
Ayjaos *see* Eyeish
Ayjaos *see* Tawehash
ayluymiut *see* Aglurmiut
Aymamon [PR] (BE)
Aymara [Lang] [Arg, BO, CH, PE] *Jaqi* (LC)
Aymore *see* Aymara
Aynais *see* Hainai
Aynay *see* Hainai
Aynics *see* Hainai
Ayoa *see* Iowa
Ayoes *see* Iowa
Ayoman *see* Ayaman
Ayomano *see* Ayaman
Ayonai *see* Hainai
Ayoois *see* Iowa
Ayook *see* Mixe
Ayoouais *see* Iowa
Ayooues *see* Iowa
Ayore *see* Moro
Ayorei *see* Moro
Ayoreiodo *see* Moro
Ayoreo *see* Moro
Ayoreode *see* Moro
Ayoua *see* Iowa
Ayouahs *see* Iowa
Ayoues *see* Iowa
Ayouez *see* Iowa
Ayouwa *see* Iowa
Ayouwais *see* Iowa
Ayouways *see* Iowa
Ayovai *see* Iowa
Ayovois *see* Iowa
Ayowa *see* Iowa
Ayoway *see* Iowa
Ayoweo *see* Moro
Ayqueroa [HA, WInd] *Guaccaiarima* (BE)
Ayqui *Pueblo Indians* (H)
Ays *see* Ais
Ays *see* Eyeish
Ayses *see* Eyeish
Aytch-arts *see* Hachaath
Aytharts *see* Hachaath
Ayticha [Lang] *Kings River* (CA-8)
Ayuguama *see* Cuatache

Ayuhba *see* Iowa
Ayuhuwahak *see* Iowa
Ayuhwa *see* Iowa
Ayukba *see* Iowa
Ayundiguiguira [MX] (Hdbk10)
Ayunini *see* Ayyuini
Ayutan *see* Ietan
Ayuwa *see* Iowa
Ayyuini (Early)
Ayzes *see* Eyeish
Azadyze *see* Adai
Azana *see* Atsina
Aziagmiut *Kaviagmiut* (H)
Aziag-mut (Contri, v.1, p.16) *see
also* Asiagmiut (H)
Aziag-mut *see* Aziagmut
Aziagmut *see* Unaligmiut
Aztec *see* Aztecs
Azteca *see* Aztecs
Aztecan *see* Aztecs
Aztec Confederacy [MX] (BE)
Aztecoidan [Lang] [MX] [*Uto-
Aztecan*] (BE)
Azteco-Tanoan [Lang] [MX]
(LC)
Aztecs [MX] *Nahuatl* (LC)
Azzuei [HA, WInd] *Bainoa* (BE)

-B-

Baachinena *see* Northern Ara-
paho
Ba'achinena *see* Nakasinena
Baachinena *see* Nakasinena
Ba-akush *see* Dakota
Baakush *see* Dakota
Baakuune'nan *see* Nakosinena
Baantctiine'na *see* Nakasinena
Baanticiine'nan [WY] *Arapaho*
(BE)
Baasanwuune'nan *see* Arapaho
Babane *Coahuiltecan* (Hdbk10)
ba'bawi-o'odham *see* Papago
Babawi oodham *see* Papago
Babayoula *see* Bayogoula
Babco *see* Ababco
Babin *see* Nataotin
Babina *see*
Babina *see* Nataotin
Babine (H) *see also* Hwotsotenne
(BE)
Babine (H) *see also* Nataotin (BE)
Babine [BC, Can] *Carrier* (LC)
Babini *see* Babine
Babini *see* Nataotin
Babol *see* Bobol
Babor *see* Pabor
Babor *see* Bobol
Baburi *Coahuiltecan* (Hdbk10)
Bacabi *Hopi* (Hdbk9)

Bacairi *see* Bakairi
Bacaja *see* Xikrin
Bacaranan *see* Bacora
Bachilmi [MX] *Concho* (BE)
Bachipkwasi [Clan] *Hopi* (H)
Bachom's Country *see* Tankiteke
Baciroa [MX] *Teracahitian* (BE)
Backbook *see* Backhook
Back Hook *see* Backhook
Backhook [Lang] *Eastern Siouan*
(H)
Backhook [SC] (H)
Backward Clans *see* Tutoimana
Bacobi *see* Bacabi
Bacora *Coahuiltecan* (Hdbk10)
Bacoram *see* Bacora
Bacoregue *see* Vacoregue
Bacorehui *see* Vacoregue
Bad *see* Oyateschicha
Bad Arms *Brule* (H)
Bad Bows (H) Tinazipeshicha (H)
Bad Coup *see* Eskepkabuk
Bad Faces *see* Waquithi
Bad Faces *see* Iteshica
Bad-hearts *see* Kiowa Apache
Bad Honors *see* Esekepkabuk
Badies *see* Bidai
Bad Leggings *see* Esachkabuk
Bad Leggins *see* Esachkabuk
Bad Looking Ones *see*
Glaglahecha
Bad-people *see* Etchaottine
Bad Pipes [WY] *Northern Arapaho*
(BE)
Bad River Band *Lake Superior
Chippewa* (Char, v.2, pt.1, p.6)
Badwis'ha *see* Badwisha
Badwisha (Pub, v.4, no.3, p.122)
see also Balwisha [CA] (BE)
Badwisha [CA] *Mariposa* (H)
Badwunun *see* Palwunun
Baenan [Br] (O)
Baenna *see* Baenan
Baffin Island Eskimos (Hdbk5)
Baffinland Eskimos [AK] *Central
Eskimos* (Hdbk5)
Bagaces [CR] *Aztecoidan* (BE)
Bagiopa *Shoshonean* (H)
Bagname *Coahuiltecan* (Hdbk10)
Bagoache [Ont] *Chippewa* (H)
Bagopa *see* Bagiopa
Bagowits *see* Navajo
Bagowitz *see* Navajo
Baguacat [NM] *Pueblo Indians*
(H)
Baguaja *see* Bahuajjas
Baguajairi *see* Bahuajjas
Baguajairi *see* Ese Ejja
Baguame *see* Bagname
Baguanimabo [HA, WInd]
Caizcimu (BE)
Bagueja *see* Ese Ejja
Bahacecha [AZ] (H)

Bahakosin *see* Cheyenne
Bahamo *see* Ebahamo
Bahka-bo'm-foka *Patwin* (Pub,
v.29, no.4)
Bahkanapul *see* Tubatulabal
Bahkanapul *see* Pahkanapils
Bahohata (H) *see also* Ba-ho-ha-ta
(H)
Ba-ho-ha-ta [Clan] *Hidatsa* (H)
Bahohata *Hidatsa* (H)
Bahuajja (O) *see also* Ese Ejja
(LC)
Bahuajja [PE] (O)
Bahwetego-weninnewug *see*
Atsina
Bahwetig *see* Atsina
Baimena [MX] *Zoe* (BE)
Bainoa [HA, WInd] (BE)
Baiohaigua [HA, WInd] *Cahibo*
(BE)
Baiougoula *see* Bayogoula
Bairira [Col] (O)
Baisimete *see* Bersiamite
Baiyu *see* Bai-yu
Bai-yu [Maidu] (Contri, v.3,
p.282)
Bajino Diegueño (CA-8)
Bajiopas *see* Bagiopa
Bakab *see* Pakab
Bakabi *see* Bacabi
Bakairi [Br] *Xingu* (LC)
Bakavi *see* Bacabi
Bakhkanapul [Self-designation]
see Tubatulabal
Bakihon *Upper Yanktonai* (H)
Bakiri *see* Bakairi
Balamiha [Self-designation] *see*
Aguateca
Baldam *Mosquito* (BE)
Bald Head *see* Peshla
Bald Heads *see* Comanche
Bald Hill [Lang] *Wintu* (CA-8)
Bald Hills Indians *see* Chilula
Bald Mountain *Northern Tonto
Apache* (BE)
Bale [Self-designation] *see* Bare
ba-lew *see* Northern Paiute
balew *see* Northern Paiute
Ballokai [CA] *Pomo* (H)
Bal-lo Kai Pomo *see* Ballokai
Baloh *see* Paviotso
Baluusha *see* Balwisha [CA]
Baluxa *see* Biloxi
Balwisha (H) *see also* Badwisha
(H)
Balwisha [CA] (Contri, v.16, no.2,
p.38)
Balwisha [NV] *Northern Paiute*
(BE)
Bambana [MX] [*Mosquito-Sumo*]
(BE)
Bamoa [MX] *Cahita* (BE)
Banabeouiks *see* Winnebago

Banac see Bannock
Ban-ack see Bannock
Banai'ti see Bannock
Bana'kwut see Bannock
Banakwut see Bannock
Banani see Bannock
Ban-at-tee see Shoshone
Ban-at-tees see Bannock
Banava-Jafi [Br] (O)
Banax see Bannock
Band of the Lights see Chagu
Band That Don't Cook *Yanktonai*
(H)
Band that eats no buffalo see
Pteyuteshni
Band That Eats No Geese *Yank-
tonai* (H)
Band That Wishes the Life *Yank-
tonai* (H)
Bangeklachi see Bankalachi
Bani [Cu] (BE)
Baniatho see Cherokee
Baniba see Baniva
Banimamam see Bibiamar
Baniua do Icana see Baniva
Baniva [Br, Col, VE] *Arahuaco*
(LC)
Baniva do Icana see Baniva
Baniwa (O) see also Wakuenai (O)
Baniwa [Br, VE] (O)
Bankalachi [CA] *Shoshonean* (H)
Bannach Snakes see Bannock
Bannack see Bannock
Banneck see Bannock
Ban-ni-ta see Bannock
Bannita see Bannock
Bannock [ID, WY] *Shoshonean*
(LC)
Bannock [Lang] [*Mono-Paviotso*]
(H)
Bannock [*Ute-Chemehuevi*] (H)
Bannock Creek Shoshone
(Bull120)
Banumints see Serrano
Baopapa [MX] *Concho* (BE)
Baouichtigouin see Chippewa
Bapua Bara [Col] *Barasana* (O)
Ba-qa-o see Makah
Baqao see Makah
Baquero see Querecho
Baquioba see Bagiopa
Baquiva see Bagiopa
Baquiziziguara [MX] *Coahuiltecan*
(Hdbk10)
Bara [Br, Col] *Barasana* (O)
Baracoa [Cu] (BE)
Baraconos see Paraconosko
Barafiri [Br] *Yanoama* (O)
Barajagua [Cu] (BE)
Barajiri see Barafiri
Bara Maku see Macu
Barama River Carib [Lang] *Galibi*
(Uaz, v.28)

Baranawa see Barrawana
Barasana [Br, Col] (LC)
Barasana del Norte [Lang] (LC)
Barasana del Sur [Lang] [Col]
(LC)
Barasano see Barasana
Ba-ra-shup-gi-o see Dakota
Barashupgio see Dakota
Barauana see Barawana
Barawana [Br] (O)
Barbacoa [Lang] [Col, Cu] (BE)
Barbado see Umotina
Barbara, Santa [Lang] [CA] *Chu-
mashan* (H)
Barbara Indians, Santa (LC) see
also Chumash (CA)
Barbara Indians, Santa [CA] *Mis-
sion* (LC)
Barbara Islands, Santa [Lang]
[CA] *Shoshonean* (Pub, v.4,
no.3, pp.152–53)
Barbareno [CA] *Chumash* (CA)
Barbarole see Brule
Barbarole see Chakute
Barbera, Santa see Chumash
Barbipian see Ervipiame
Barbudo see Umotina
Barbudo see Mayoruna
Bare [Col, VE] *Arawak* (O)
Bar-har-cha see Pahatsi
Barharcha see Phatsi
Bari [Col, VE] (O)
Barira see Bari
Bark Tribe see Ecore
Barrados see Jumano
Barrancas [Pueblo] *Piro* (H)
Barre see Bare
Barren Ground [Can]
[*Montagnais-Naskapi*] (BE)
Barren Ground [Can] *Sakaw-
ininiwug Cree* (BE)
Barria *Achagua* (O)
Barricade Falls people see Kaka'-
pa'kato Wini'niwuk
Barriere [Can] *Algonkin* (BE)
Barro Negra [Col] *Tunebo* (O)
Barrosos *Coahuiltecan* (Hdbk10)
Bartholomew, St. see Cochiti
Bartolome, San see Puaray
Bartolome de Jongopavi, San see
Shongopovi
Bartolomede Jougopavi, San see
Shongopovi
Bartolome de Xongopabi, San see
Shongopovi
Bartolome de Xonogopavi , San
see Shongopovi
Basanwune'nan see Basawunena
Ba'sawune'na see Basawunena
Basawunena [WY] *Arapaho* (BE)
Bascoram see Bacora
Basdece-sni see Basdecheshni
Basdecheshni *Sisseton* (H)

Basdetce-cni see Basdecheshni
Base'lelotsed [WA] *Skagit* (BE)
Base-tlo-tinneh see Tatsanottine
Bashabas see Abnaki
Bashalabsh see Basha'labsh
Basha'labsh [WA] *Nisqually* (Ore-
gon)
Basiroa [MX] *Nevome* (H)
Baska'dsadsiuk [WA] *Skagit* (BE)
Baskaiya (Pub, v.20, no.6,
pp.102–103)
Baske'kwiuk [WA] *Skagit* (BE)
Basketmaker see Basket-Makers
Basket-Makers *Pueblo Indians*
(LC)
Basket People see Colville
Baslo'halok [WA] *Skagit* (BE)
Basosuma [AZ] *Sobaipuri* (H)
Basses Rivieres see Lower Creek
Bastard see Nakotcho-kutchin
Bastard Beaver Indians see
Etcheridiegottine
Bastard Loucheux (BE) see also
Kutchin (LC)
Bastard Loucheux [Can] (H)
Bas-Tchinouks see Lower Chi-
nook
Bastchinouks see Lower Chinook
Batajagua [MX] *Coahuiltecan*
(Hdbk10)
Batang see Patung
Batang-a see Patang
Batanga see Patang
Batard-Loucheux see Bastard
Loucheux
Batard Loucheuz see Bastard
Loucheux
Batawat [CA] *Wiyot* (BE)
Ba-tci'p-kwa-si see Bachipkwasi
Batcipkwasi see Bachipkwasi
Batemdaikai see Kato
Batem-da-kai-ee see Kato
Ba-tem-da-kaii see Kato
Batemdakaii see Kato
Baticola see Mbya
Baticola see Kaiwa
Batin-da-kia see Kato
Bat Indians see Cashinawa
Batki see Patki
Batkinyamu see Patki
Baton Rouge see Mikasuki
Battle-le-mule-emauch see
Methow
Batucari [MX] *Cahita* (H)
Batuco see Euduve
Batueari see Batucari
Baure [Lang] [BO] *Maipurean*
(LC)
Bauruco [HA, WInd] *Bainoa*
(BE)
Bawichtigouek see Chippewa
Bawichtigouin see Chippewa
Bawihka [Hon, NI] *Sumo* (BE)

Baxumomowi *Guahibo* (O)
Bayagola *see* Bayogoula
Bayagouba *see* Bayogoula
Bayagoula *see* Bayogoula
Bayaguaniguara *see* Bazaniguara
Bayamo [Cu, PR] (BE)
Bayano (O) *see also* San Blas (O)
Bayano [MX] *Cuna* (BE)
Baya-Ogoula *see* Bayogoula
Bayaquitiri [Cu] (BE)
Bay du Noc [MI, WI] *Chippewa* (H)
Bay Indians *see* Winnebago
Bay Indians *see* Oklahannali
Bay-ma-pomas *see* Sinkyone
Baymas *see* Guayma
Bay Miwok (He) *see also* Saclan (LC)
Bay Miwok [Lang] [CA] (He)
Baymunana *Sumo* (BE)
Bayogola *see* Bayogoula
Bayogoula [LA] (BE)
Bayonne Ogoula *see* Bayogoula
Bayoodzin *see* Southern Paiute
Bayouc Agoula *see* Bayogoula
Bayouc Ogoula *see* Bayogoula
Bay River *see* Bear River
Bayugla *see* Bayogoula
Bayuk-okla *see* Bayogoula
Baziniguara [MX] (Hdbk10)
Beadeye *see* Bidai
Bean People *see* Papago
Beansmen *see* Papago
Bear Clan (BE) *see also* Kishkakon (BE)
Bear Gens (BE) *see also* Kishkakon (BE)
Bear Gens (Bull85)
Bear Indians *see* Clatchotin
Bear Indians *see* Matonumanke
Bear Lake [Can] *Subarctic* (Ye)
Bear Lake Indians (H) *see also* Saschutkenne (H)
Bear Nation *see* Attignawantan
Bear People *see* Attignawantan
Bear River [CA] (BE)
Bear River [Lang] *Athabascan* (He)
Bear River [NC] (LC)
Bear's Paw Mountain *see* Shiptetza
Beathook *see* Beothuk
Beatty band *Northern Paiute* (Hdbk11)
Beauquiecho *Caduveo* (O)
Beaux Hommes *see* Quapaw
Beaux Hommes *see* Siksika
Beaver (H) *see also* Etcheridiegottine (BE)
Beaver (H) *see also* Intermediate Dene (H)
Beaver (H) *see also* Pakhtha (H)
Beaver (H) *see also* Tsattine (LC)

Beaver [UT] *Southern Paiute* (Hdbk11)
Beaver Clan [BC] *Haisla* (Anthro, v.2, no.6)
Beaver Hill Cree *see* Paskawaw-ininiwug
Beaver Hunters *see* Tsattine
Beaver Indians *see* Tsattine
Beaver Indians *see* Amikwa
Beaver Islands [MI] *Chippewa* (H)
Beaver-men *see* Tamakwapi
Beaver People *see* Ahmeekkwun-eninnewug
Beaver People *see* Shapeinihkashina
Becaes *see* Abihka
Becancour [Lang] *Eastern Algonquian* (Hdbk15)
Bedah-marek *see* Bidamarek
Beddies *see* Bidai
Bedees *see* Bidai
Bedies *see* Bidai
Be-don-ko-he (Hdbk10)
Bedonkohe *see* Be-don-ko-he
Bedzaqetcha *see* Chippewa
Bedzietcho *see* Chippewa
Beehai *see* Jicarilla Apache
Be Esa Ntsai *see* Maricopa
Beesantsai *see* Maricopa
Be-ga-kol-kizjin *see* Mogollon
Begakolkizjin *see* Mogollon
Begging people *see* Hitoune'nan
Behathook *see* Beothuk
Beicas *see* Abihka
Beico do Pau [Br] *Cayapo* (O)
Be-ku (Contri, v.3, p.393)
Beku *see* Be-ku
Belantse-etea *see* Hidatsa
Belautse-etea *see* Hidatsa
Belbellah *see* Bellabella
Belen *Pueblo Indians* (H)
Belenista *Caduveo* (O)
Belhoola *see* Bella Coola
Beliche *see* Huilliche
Bella-Bella *see* Bellabella
Bellabella [BC] *Kwakiutl* (LC)
Bellabella [Lang] *Heiltsuk* (H)
Bellacoola *see* Bella Coola
Bella Coola [BC] *Coast Salish* (LC)
Bellaghchoolas *see* Bella Coola
Bellahoola *see* Bella Coola
Bell-houla *see* Bella Coola
Bellichoola *see* Bella Coola
Belochy *see* Biloxi
Belocse *see* Biloxi
Beloxi *see* Biloxi
Beluxi *see* Biloxi
Beluxy *see* Biloxi
Bemontire *see* Xikrin
Benaki *see* Western Abnaki
Benaqui *see* Abnaki
Ben-Diapa [Lang] *Catuquina* (O)

Beneme *see* Serrano
Benyeme *see* Serrano
Beothick *see* Beothuk
Beothics *see* Beothuk
Beothik *see* Beothuk
Beoths *see* Beothuk
Beothuc *see* Beothuk
Beothuck *see* Beothuk
Beothue *see* Beothuk
Beothugs *see* Beothuk
Beothuk [New] (LC)
Beothunkan [Lang] [Can] (BE)
Bering Strait Eskimos (Hdbk5)
Bernabe Jongopavi, S. *see* Shongopovi
Bernardo de Jongopabi, San *see* Shongopovi
Berry-eaters [Clan] [MN] (BE)
Bersami *see* Bersiamite
Bersiamit *see* Bersiamite
Bersiamite [Can] *Algonquian* (H)
Bersiamitt *see* Bersiamite
Bersimis [Can] [*Montagnais-Naskapi*] (BE)
Bertiamiste *see* Bersiamite
Bertiamite *see* Bersiamite
Bertolomeo, San *see* Cochiti
Berttipame *see* Ervipiame
Be-sde-ke *see* Fox
Besdeke *see* Fox
Beshde'ke *see* Fox
Bes-he-kwe-guelts *see* Miseek-wigweelis
Beshekweguelts *see* Miseekwig-weelis
Be-sheu *see* Besheu
Besheu [Clan] *Chippewa* (H)
Be'shiltcha *see* Kiowa
Beshiltcha *see* Kiowa
Bessebes *see* Abnaki
Bes-tchonhi-Gottine *see* Bistchonigottine
Bestchonhigottine *see* Bistchonigottine
Bethsiamit *see* Bersiamite
Bethuck *see* Beothuk
Bethuk *see* Beothuk
Betidee *see* Arapaho
Betoi [Col] *Tukanoan* (O)
Betoi [Lang] [Col] *Paezan* (O)
Betoi Jirarru *see* Betoi
Be-ton-auk-an-ub-yig *see* Betonukeengainubejig
Betonaukanubyig *see* Betonu-keengainugejig
Be-ton-uk-eeng-ain-ub-e-jig *see* Betonukeengainubejig
Betonukeengainubejig [WI] *Chippewa* (BE)
Betoya *see* Betoi
Betoye *see* Betoi
Betsiamit *see* Bersiamite
Betsiamite *see* Bersiamite

Betumki *see* Mitomkai
Beuteubo *Caduveo* (O)
Bevan-acs *see* Dakota
Bewanacs (H) SE Dakota (LC)
Be'xai *see* Jicarilla Apache
Bexai *see* Jicarilla Apache
Beyuma [BO] *Araona* (O)
Bibiamar *Coahuiltecan* (Hdbk10)
Bibit *Coahuiltecan* (Hdbk10)
Bica'ni *see* Bithani
Bicani *see* Dsihlthani
Biccaree *see* Arikara
Bicowetha (H) *see also* Piqua (BE)
Bi-co-we-tha *see* Bicowetha
Bicowetha [MO] *Shawnee* (H)
Bidai [TX] (BE)
Bidais *see* Bidai
Bidaises *see* Bidai
Bidamarek [CA] *Pomo* (H)
Biday *see* Bidai
Bidayes *see* Bidai
Biddaquimamar *see* Vid-
  daquimamar
Bidias *see* Bidai
Bidwell Bar [Lang] [CA] *Konkow*
  (CA-8)
Bierai *see* Laguna
Bieride *see* Laguna
Bierni'n *see* Keres
biernin *see* Keres
Big Ankle Band *see* Iyakoza
Big Bayou *see* Boguechito
Big Bead *see* Araphano
Big bellied *see* Gros Ventres
Bigbellies *see* Gros Ventres
Big-bellys *see* Gros Ventres
Big Devils *Assiniboin* (H)
Big Eagle's band *see* Ohanhanska
Big Feet *see* Maangreet
Big Grizzard People *see*
  Mamakitce-wiinuuk
Big Heads *see* Maskegon
Big-Heads *see* Tetes de Boule
Bighorn People *see* Abbatotine
Bighorn People *see* Esbataottine
big island people *see* Qikiqta-
  grungmiut
Big Jim's Band *see* Kispokotha
Big-legged Horses *see* Iyakoza
Big-Lips *see* Nataotin
Big Meadows [Lang] *Maidu* (CA-
  8)
Big Pauch *see* Gros Ventres
Big Paunch *see* Gros Ventres
Big Plume's Band *see* Bloods
  Atsina
Big River [Can] [*Montagnais-
  Naskapi*] (BE)
Big River People *see*
  Nekwichoujik-kutchin
Big Rock [MI] *Chippewa* (H)
Big Siconese *Delaware* (Hdbk15)
Big Stone Lake Band *see* Inkpa

Big Thicket *see* Bidai
Big Tohome [AL] *Tohome* (BE)
Big Topknots *see* Miawkinaiykis
Big Track *see* Santsukhdghin
Bik-ta-sa-te-tu-se *see* Biktasate-
  tuse
Biktasatetuse *Crow* (H)
Bik-ta-she *see* Northern
  Shoshone
Bik-ta-she *see* Shoshone
Bilexe *see* Biloxi
Bilhoola *see* Bella Coola
Billechoola *see* Bella Coola
Billikula *see* Bella Coola
Billoxi *see* Biloxi
Billoxie *see* Biloxi
Bilocchi *see* Biloxi
Bilocchy *see* Biloxi
Bilochi *see* Biloxi
Bilochy *see* Biloxi
Biloci *see* Biloxi
Biloui *see* Biloxi
Biloxi [Lang] *Siouan* (H)
Biloxi [MS] (LC)
Biloxy *see* Biloxi
Bilqula *see* Bella Coola
Bilusi *see* Biloxi
Bi'lxula *see* Bella Coola
Bilxula *see* Bella Coola
bini-edine *see* Western Apache
Bi-ni-e-dine *see* Western Apache
Bin-i-ette She-deck-a *see* San
  Carlos Apache
Biniette Shedecka *see* San Carlos
  Apache
Binii edinende *see* Western
  Apache
Bintuca *see* Ica
Bintuk [Lang] *see* Ica
Bintuka *see* Arhuaco
Bintuka [Lang] *see* Ica
Bintukwa *see* Arhuaco
Bintuncua [Col] *Arhuaco* (O)
Binuxsh *see* Biloxi
Binuxshi *see* Biloxi
Birch Bay Indians *see* Semiah-
  moo
Birch Creek Kutchin *see*
  Tennuth-kutchin
Birch Indians *see* Tennuth-
  kutchin
Birch-rind *see* Tatsanottine
Birch-Rindmen *see* Tatsanottine
Birch River Indians *see* Tennuth-
  kutchin
Birnik Culture [AK] (Hdbk5)
Biroros *see* Piro *Pueblo*
Bisanigua *see* Guayabero
Biscatronge *see* Coaque
Biskatronge *see* Coaque
Bissarhar *Apache* (H)
Bisserain *see* Nipissing
Bisserein *see* Nipissing

Bisserinien *see* Nipissing
Bissirinien *see* Nipissing
Bistchonigottine [Can] *Etchaot-
  tine* (H)
Bita'ni *see* Bithani
Bitani *see* Dsihlthani
Bithani [Clan] *Navajo* (H)
Bitomkhai *see* Mitomkai
Bitoupa *see* Ibitoupa
Bituncua [Col] *Arhuaco* (O)
Black-arms *see* Cheyenne
Black Bears *see* Yakima
Blackbird [MI] *Chippewa* (H)
Black Blood *see* Siksahpuniks
Blackblood *see* Siksahpuniks
Black Carib (LC) *see also* Garifuna
  (O)
Black Carib [Lang] [WInd] (LC)
Black-dog *see* Ohanhanska
Black Dog's band *see* Ohanhan-
  ska
Black Doors *see* Sikokitsimiks
Blackduck Culture (LC)
Black Eagle *see* Hangatanga
Black Elks *see* Siksinokaks
Black Fat Roasters *see* Sikopoksi-
  maiks
Black-feet Scioux *see* Sihasapa
Blackfeet (H) *see also* Siksika (LC)
Blackfeet (LC) *see also* Sihasapa
  (LC)
Blackfeet Tetons *see* Sihasapa
Blackfoot (H) *see also* Sihasapa
  (LC)
Blackfoot (LC) *see also* Siksika
  (LC)
Black-footed ones *see* Sihas-
  apakhcha
Blackfoot Lodges *see* Ashkanena
Blackfoot Sioux (Oregon)
Black Hawk's band (Hdbk11) *see
  also* Moanunts (Hdbk11)
Black Hawk's Band *Sauk* (His/T,
  v.2, p.137)
Blackhead [NE] *Kitkehahki* (H)
Black Hook Indians *see* Back-
  hook
Black Indians *see* Inkesabe
Black Lodges (BE) *see also*
  Mine'sepere (BE)
Black Lodges [SD] *Cheyenne* (BE)
Black Minqua *see* Honniasont
Blackmouths *see* Sukhutit
Black Muscogee [MX] *Muscogee*
  (H)
Black Patched Moccasins *see*
  Sikutsipumaiks
Black Pawnee *see* Wichita
Black Pawnee *see* Arikara
Black River [KS, OK] *Chippewa*
  (BE)
Black River Kutchin *see* Tranjik-
  kutchin

Black-Tailed Deer *Hidatsa* (H)

Blacktailed Deers [Society] *Hidatsa* (H)

Black Tiger [SD] *Dakota* (BE)

Black Tomahawk *see* Tacanhpisapa

Black Water *see* Opelousa

Blanchard's Fork [OH] *Ottawa* (H)

Blas, San [Pan] *Cuna* (BE)

Blewmouths [GA] (H)

Bloodies *see* Kainah

Blood Indians *see* Kainah

Blood Indians *see* Blackfeet

Blood People *see* Kainah

Bloods [Can] *Sarsi* (BE)

Bloods [MN] *Atsina* (BE)

Bloody Piegans *see* Ahahpitape

Blount Indians (LC) *see also* Apalachicola (LC)

Blount Indians [AL, FL] *Seminole* (H)

Blue Bead *see* Arapaho

Blue Earth band *see* Mankato

Blue Earth Indians *see* Nez Perce

Blue Ground People *see* Dalsokaiya

Blue-lipped *see* Blewmouths

Blue Mud Indians *see* Nez Perce

Blue Muds *see* Nez Perce

Bluff Indians *see* Prairie Band of Potawatomi

Blu-kci *see* Biloxi

Blukci *see* Biloxi

B'luksi *see* Biloxi

Blunt *see* Blount Indians

Blunt *see* Apalachicola

Bluski *see* Biloxi

Blut Indianer *see* Kainah

Boa [NI] *Sumo* (BE)

Bobol [MX] *Coahuiltecan* (Hdbk10)

Bobor *see* Pabor

Boboram *see* Bobol

Bocalo [Lang] [MX] (Hdbk10)

Boca Negra [Br] *Kawahib* (O)

Boca Preta [Br] *Kawahib* (O)

Bocas Prietas *Coahuiltecan* (Hdbk10)

Bocootawwanauke *see* Bocootowwonauke

Bocootawwonauke [VA] *Algoquian* (LC)

Bocootowwonough *see* Bocootawwonauke

Bocootowwonock *see* Bocootawwonauke

Bo'dalk'inago *see* Comanche

Bodalkinago *see* Comanche

Bodega (H) *see also* Olamentka (H)

Bodega [CA] *Miwok* (BE)

Bodega [Lang] [CA] (CA-8)

Boder'wiumi *see* Paleuyami

Boeothick *see* Beothuk

Boeothuck *see* Beothuk

Boethick *see* Beothuk

Bogoache [WI] *Chippewa* (BE)

Boguechito [MS] *Choctaw* (H)

Bogue Chitto *see* Boguechito

Bohnapobatin [CA] (H)

Bohogue *Shoshone* (Anthro, v.8, no.3, p.264)

Boiguera [MX] *Coahuiltecan* (Hdbk10)

Boijero *see* Boiguera

Boin-acs *see* Dakota

Boine *see* Dakota

Boinug *see* Dakota

Bois brule *see* Brule

Boise *Shoshone* (Ye)

Boise Forte *see* Sugwaundugahwininewug

Bois Fort Chippewa *see* Sugwaundugahwininewug

Bois Forts *see* Sugwaundugahwininewug

Boka *see* Bo-ka

Bo-ka *Maidu* (Contri, v.3, p.282)

Bokeai *see* Hopi

Bokeya [CA] *Central Pomo* (Pub, v.40, no.2)

Boklai *see* Hopi

Bokninuwad *see* Bokninwad

Bokninwad [CA] [*Tule-Kaweah*] (CA)

Bokninwad [Lang] [CA] (CA-8)

Bokninwal *see* Bokninwad

Bolamomowi *see* Awirimomowi

Bolamomowi *see* Guahibo

Bolbon *see* Bolbone

Bolbone [CA] *Cholovone* (H)

Boli *see* Buli

Bolinas [CA] (H)

Bolixe *see* Biloxi

Bolixie *see* Biloxi

Bollanos *see* Bolinas

Boluxa *see* Biloxi

Boluxe *see* Biloxi

Boluxie *see* Biloxi

Bonack *see* Bannock

Bonair [Lang] *Waiwai* (UAz, v.28)

Bonaparte [BC] *Shuswap* (BE)

Bonarch *see* Bannock

Bonarch Diggers *see* Bannock

Bonarch Diggers *see* Shoshone

Bonark *see* Bannock

Bonasila [AK] *Ingalik* (BE)

Bone Indians *see* Osage

Bone Indians *see* Assegun

Bone People *see* Tanintauei

Bongee *see* Sarsi

Bonnack *see* Bannock

Bonnak *see* Bannock

Bonnax *see* Bannock

Bonner's Ferry [ID] *Kutenai* (BE)

Bonnet *see* Ekupabeka

Bonoch *see* Bannock

Bons Irocois *see* Huron

Booadasha *Crow* (H)

Boonack *see* Bannock

Boothians *see* Netchilirmiut

Boothroyd [BC] *Ntlakyapamuk* (H)

Boothroyds [BC] *Upper Thompson* (H)

Boquiguera [MX] (Hdbk10)

Bora [Col] *Witoto* (LC)

Bora-Muinane *see* Muinane

Boran [Lang] *Col* (O)

Born in the middle *see* Chegnakeokisela

Boro (LC)

Bororo [Lang] [BO, Br] (LC)

Bororo Oriental [Br] *Eastern Bororo* (O)

Borrado (BE) *see also* Jumano (LC)

Borrado [MX, TX] *Coahuiltecan* (BE)

Boruca [CR] (LC)

Boruca [Lang] [CR] *Chibchan* (LC)

Borun *see* Botocudo

Boshgisha *see* Poskesa

Bo'tcaced *see* Sinkiuse-Columbia

Botcaced *see* Sinkiuse-Columbia

Botecudos *see* Botocudo

Bot-k'in-ago *see* Atsina

Botkinago *see* Atsina

Botocudo *Aweikoma* (O)

Botocudo [Br] (LC)

Botshenin *see* Occoneechee

Botshenin *see* Patshenin

Bounding-Wind *see* Kiyuksa *Mdewakanton*

Bouscoutton [NY] *Cree* (H)

Bouscouttous *see* Bouscoutton

Bove *see* Ildefonso

Bow Indians *see* Quapaw

Bow People *see* K'andankaiya

Bowpith *see* Sans Arcs

Bow String Society *see* Himatanohis

Bowwetegoweninnewug *see* Atsina

Bowwetig *see* Atsina

Boxelder Indians [UT] *Shoshone* (H)

Boya Band [CA] *Pomo* (Earth)

Boyaca [Cu] (BE)

Braba *see* Taos

Bracamo *see* Ebahamo

Brada *see* Taos

Brandywine *see* Wesorts

Brandywine Indians *Delaware* (Hdbk15)

Bread Nation *see* Pascagoula

Breakers of the custom see
    Kiyuska *Oglala*
Breech-cloths [Clan] [MN] *Atsina*
    (BE)
Breed Nation see Pascagoula
Bribri [CR, Pan] *Chibcha* (LC)
Bridgeport [CA] (Pub, v.11, no.5)
Bridge River Indians [BC] *Upper*
    Lillooet (H)
British Band *Sauk* (H)
Broad Belt Indians see Cinta
    Larga
Broad Grass [Can] *Sarsi* (BE)
Broken Arrows [SD] (BE)
Broken-Moccasin see Bannock
Broken Tooth *Chippewa* (H)
Broncos see Chiricahua Apache
Brotherton [NJ, NY] (LC)
Brothertown see Brotherton
Broule see Brule
Brucellares see Brule
Brule [SD] *Teton* (LC)
Brule Dakotas see Brule
Brulees see Brule
Brules of the Platte [SD] *Brule*
    (H)
Brulie see Brule
Brunca see Boruca
Bruneau [ID] *Wihinasht* (H)
Brunka see Borunca
Brushwood Indians see Etchaot-
    tine
Brushwood Indians see
    Etchareottine
Bu see Timbira
Bua see Pira-Tapuyo
Bubol see Wowol
Bucinka [Col] *Arhuaco* (O)
Bucintaua see Bucinka
buckberry eaters see wiyitaka'a
Buckskin Creek Band *Fraser River*
    Shuswap (Hdbk15)
Buda [BO] *Araona* (O)
Bue see Witoto
Buekete see Guaymi
Buekete see Northern Guaymi
Buen. de Mossaquavi, S. see Mis-
    hongnovi
Buenaventura see Mishongnovi
Buenaventura, San [Lang] [CA]
    Chumashan (H)
Buenaventura, Sant see Picuris
Buena Ventura de Cochita, San
    see Cochiti
Buenaventura di Cochiti, San see
    Cochiti
Buenaventura Indians, S. see Co-
    chiti
Buena Vista [CA] *Miwok* (LAT,
    Sec.E, N 14, 1994, E1, E4)
Buena Vista [CA] *Yokuts* (LC)
Buena Vista [Lang] *Foothill* (CA-
    8)

Buffalo (H) *see also* Chedunga (H)
Buffalo (H) *see also* Tesinde (H)
Buffalo [NY] *Seneca* (H)
Buffalo Bull see Chedunga
Buffalo-bull warriors see Maho-
    hivas
Buffalo Dung see Kahmitaiks
Buffalo Eater Band see Kotsoteka
Buffalo-Eaters see Kutsshundika
Buffalo-Hip see Tanin'ta'bin
Buffalo-humps see Tendons
Buffalo Hunters see Querecho
Buffalo Indians see
    Cheikikarachada
Buffalo Indians see Kotsoteka
Buffalo Indians see Lamtama
Buffalo Province see Zuni
Bugre see Shokleng
Buhagana see Macuna
Buhayana [Col] (O)
Buhk'herk see Hopi
Buiaz [HA] *Bainoa* (BE)
Buigana see Macuna
Buigana see Buhayana
Buketa see Guaymi
Bukin see Hopi
Bukina see Uru
Bulbone see Bolbone
Buldam see Bul-dam
Bul-dam *Pomo* (Contr, v.3, p.155)
Buli [Clan] *Hopi* (H)
Bu-li-nya-mu see Buli
Bulinyamu see Buli
Bu-li-so see Buliso
Buliso [Clan] *Hopi* (H)
Bu-li win-wu see Buli
Buli winwu see Buli
Bull Dog [SD] *Teton* (H)
Bullheads see Tetes de Boule
Bulls see Okos
Bulls *Hidatsa* (H)
Buluxi see Biloxi
Buma see Suma
Bungee see Chippewa
Bungi see Chippewa
Buntigwa (O) *see also* Ika (O)
Buntigwa [Col] (O)
Burica [CR, Pan] *Chibcha* (BE)
Burned see Brule
Burney Valley see Wamari'i
Burnt-face see Iteghu
Burnt Hip see Brule
Burnt Thighs see Brule
Burnt Woods (H) *see also* Brule
    (LC)
Burnt Woods [MI, WI] *Chippewa*
    (H)
Burrard Saw Mills Indians [BC]
    Squamish (H)
Burubora see Purubora
Burucaca [CR] *Chibcha* (BE)
Burururau [CR, Pan] *Terraba* (O)
Busada [Br] see Sakbwatsuk

Busha'labsh [WA] *Nisqualli* (BE)
Bush People see Saka-winouuk
Bus-in-as-see see Businausee
Businassee see Businausee
Bus-in-aus-e see Businausee
Businausee [Phratry] *Chippewa* (H)
Bus-in-aus-e-wug see Businausee
Businausewug see Businausee
Businka see Ika
Busintana see Ika
Buskipani see Capanahua
Busquipani see Capahahua
Bussenmeus see Bersiamite
Butchers see Oosabotsee
buxide see Hopi
buxiek see Hopi
Bwan see Dakota
Bwan-acs see Dakota
Bwoinug see Dakota
Bwoirnug see Dakota
Byssirinien see Nipissing

-C-

Ca see Sa
Ca see Sha
Ca see Shana
Caa see Dakota
Caagua see Cayuse
Caan see Dakota
Caanqti see Dakota
Caaygua see Mbya
Cabadilapo see Kato
Cabahiba see Parintintin
Cabaies see Kabaye
Cabaiva see Kawahib
Ca-ba-na-po see Khabenapo
Cabanapo see Khabenapo
Cabanatith see Toba-Maskoy
Cabassaguntiquoke see Cabbasa-
    gunti
Cabazon [CA] *Mission Indians*
    (Palm, v.39, no.2)
Cabbasaqunti [Can, Q] (H)
Cabbassaguntiac see Cabbasa-
    gunti
Cabbisseconteag see Cabbasa-
    gunti
Cabecar [CR] *Talamanca* (BE)
Cabecare see Cabecar
Cabeca Seca see Zoro
Cabecaseca see Zoro
Cabellos realzados see Chippewa
Caberre see Puinave
Cabesa see Cabezas
Cabessa see Cabezas
Cabezas [MX] (BE)
Cabia (H) *see also* Kabaye (H)
Cabia (Hdbk10) *see also* Cauya
    (Hdbk10)

Cabia *Coahuiltecan* (BE)
Cabicujapa [MX] *Coahuiltecan*
(Hdbk10)
Cabinoios *see* Cahinnio
Cabishi *see* Kabixi
Cabishinana *see* Kabixiana
Cabishi-Pareci *see* Kozarene
Cabixi *see* Kabixi
Cabixiana *see* Kabixiana
Cabiyari [Col] (LC)
Cabiyeri *see* Cabiyari
Cabras *see* Kiabaha
Cabri *see* Zuni
Cabyamaraguam *Coahuiltecan*
(Hdbk10)
Cac *see* Ke
Caca *see* Cacan
Cacachia *see* Kaskaskia
Cacafes *Coahuiltecan* (BE)
Cacahouanous *see* Shawnee
Cacaje *see* Jacao
Cacalote [MX] *Tamaulipec* (BE)
Cacalotes *Coahuiltecan* (Hdbk10)
Cacalotito [MX] *Concho* (BE)
Cacamacao *see* Cacamegua
Cacamara *Coahuiltecan* (Hdbk10)
Cacamegua [MX] *Coahuiltecan*
(Hdbk10)
Cacan [Lang] (LC)
Cacana *see* Cacan
Cacani *see* Cheyenne
Cacaopera (LC) *see also* Matagalpa
(LC)
Cacaopera [ES, Hon] (BE)
Cacapam *Coahuiltecan* (Hdbk10)
Cacaste *see* Cacaxte
Cacataibo [Lang] *see* Cashibo
Cacaxte [MX] *Coahuiltecan*
(Hdbk10)
Cacchi *see* Kekchi
Cacchouma *see* Chakchiuma
Cacchuma *see* Chakchiuma
Cachae *see* Ione
Cachapostate *see* Cachopostales
Cache Creek [Lang] *Patwin* (CA)
Cachee's band *see* Central Chir-
icahua Apache
Cache River People *see* Tranjik-
kutchin
Cache Valley Shoshone (Bull120)
Cachibo *see* Cashibo
Cachichi *see* San Felipe [Keres]
Cachies *see* Kichai
Cachinaua *see* Cashinawa
Cachiquel *see* Cakchikel
Cachise Apache *see* Central
Chiricahua Apache
Cachise Indians *see* Central
Chiricahua Apache
Cachnawayes *see* Conoy
Cachomashiri *see* Caquinte
Cachopostal *see* Cachopostales
Cachopostales [TX] (BE)

Cachopostate *see* Cachopostales
Cachsaputal *see* Cachopostales
Cachuena [Lang] *Carib* (UAz,
v.28)
Cacibo *see* Cashibo
Caclasco *see* Wasco
Cacopa *see* Cocopa
Cacore *see* Shakori
Cactan-qwut-me' tunne *see*
Umpqua
Cacua [Macu] (LC)
Caculipalina *see* Caculpaluniame
Caculpaluniame [MX] (Hdbk10)
Cacupa *see* Cocopa
Cadadoquis *see* Kadohadacho
Cadapouces *see* Catawba
Cadaquis *see* Kadohadacho
Cadaudacho *see* Kadohadacho
Cadaux *see* Kadohadacho
Caddo (H) *see also* Kadohadacho
(BE)
Caddo [LA, TX] (LC)
Caddoan [Lang] (BE)
Caddoan Indians *see* Caddo
Caddo Confederacy (H)
Caddo-dacho *see* Kadohadacho
Caddodacho *see* Kadohadacho
Caddoe *see* Kadohadacho
Caddokies *see* Kadohadacho
Caddons *see* Kadohadacho
Caddoques *see* Kadohadacho
Caddoquies *see* Kadohadacho
Caddoquis *see* Kadohadacho
Caddow *see* Kadohadacho
Cadeaux *see* Kadohadacho
Cadecha [FL] *Timucua* (H)
Cadica *see* Cadecha
Cadiguegodi *see* Caduveo
Cadiheo *see* Caduveo
Cadima *see* Cadimas
Cadimas [MX] *Tamaulipec* (BE)
Cadinias *see* Cadimas
Cadioeo (LC)
Cadioeo (LC) *see also* Caduveo
(LC)
Cadique *see* Cadioeo
Cadloes *see* Kadohadacho
Cado *see* Kadohadacho
Cado *see* Peticado
Cadodaccho *see* Kadohadacho
Cadodache *see* Kadohadacho
Cadodacho *see* Kadohadacho
Cadodaguios *see* Kadohadacho
Cadodakis *see* Kadohadacho
Cadodaquinons *see* Kadohadacho
Cadodaquio *see* Kadohadacho
Cadodaquiou *see* Kadohadacho
Cadodaquioux *see* Kadohadacho
Cadodaquis *see* Kadohadacho
Cadoes *see* Kadohadacho
Cadogdacho *see* Kadohadacho
Ca-do-ha-da-cho *see* Kadohada-
cho

Cadohadacho *see* Kadohadacho
Cadojodacho *see* Kadohadacho
Cadoque *see* Coaque
Cadouch *see* Comanche
Cadoux *see* Kadohadacho
Cadrons *see* Kadohadacho
Caduveo [BO, Br] (LC)
Caecena *see* Cayuishana
Caenoestoery *see* Iroquois
Caensa *see* Taensa
Caeujes *see* Cayuga
Caeuquias *see* Cahokia
Cafuenchi *see* Cajuenche
Ca Gaba *see* Kagaba
Cagaba *see* Kagaba
Cagabegux *see* Cayabegux
Cagabo *see* Kagaba
Cagan *see* Shakian
Cagatsky *see* Aleuts
Caghnawaga *see* Caughnawaga
Cagnaguet [BaC] *Laimon* (H)
Cagnajuet *see* Cagnaguet
Cagnawaga *see* Caughnawaga
Cagu *see* Chagu
Caguaumama [Lang] *Quinigua*
(Hdbk10)
Caguayoguam [MX] (Hdbk10)
Cagubiguama [MX] *Coahuiltecan*
(Hdbk10)
Caguchuarca [MX] *Coahuiltecan*
(Hdbk10)
Caguchuasca [MX] *Coahuiltecan*
(Hdbk10)
Caguiamiguara [MX] (Hdbk10)
Caguilipan [MX] *Coahuiltecan*
(Hdbk10)
Caguilla *see* Kawia *Luiseño*
Caguinachi *see* Coguinachi
Caguiniguara [MX] *Coahuiltecan*
(Hdbk10)
Caguiraniguara [MX] *Coahuilte-
can* (Hdbk10)
Caguisniguara [MX] (Hdbk10)
Cagulla *see* Kawia *Luiseño*
Ca'ha *see* Dakota
Caha *see* Dakota
Cahahaguillas *see* Cahuilla
Cahainihoua *see* Cahinnio
Cahainohoua *see* Cahinnio
Cahakies *see* Cahokia
Ca'han *see* Dakota
Cahan *see* Dakota
Cahata *see* Kiowa Apache
Cahau *see* Cahokia
Cahaymi [HA] *Guaccaiarima*
(BE)
Cahaynohaoua *see* Cahinnio
Cahenhisenhonon *see* Toryohne
Cahiagua *see* Kiowa
Cahi'a iye'skabin [MN] *Assiniboin*
(BE)
Cahibo [HA] (BE)
Cahieca *see* Cheyenne

Cahigua see Kiowa
Ca-hiks-i-ca-hiks see Pawnee
Cahiksi-cahiks see Pawnee
Cahinnio [AR, TX] Caddo (BE)
Cahinoa see Cahinnio
Cahirmois see Cahinnio
Cahita [MX] (LC)
Cahitan [Lang] Taracahitian (BE)
Cahivo see Cashibo
Cahlahtel [CA] (H)
Cahnilla see Kawia Luiseño
Cahnillo see Kawia Luiseño
Cahnowa see Conoy
Cahoco [BO] Araona (O)
Cahoki see Cahokia
Cahokia Illinois (H)
Cahokian see Cahokia
Cahokies see Cahokia
Cahoque see Coaque
Cahoqui see Cahokia
Cahoquias see Cahokia
Cahroc see Karok
Cahroes see Karok
Cahto see Kato
Cahuahiva see Kawahib
Ca-hual-chitz see Paiute
Cahualchitz see Paiute
Cahuanas see Kahwan
Cahuapana [PE] (O)
Cahuapanan [Lang] see Jeberoan
Cahuarano [PE] (O)
Cahuga see Cayuga
Cahuilla (H) see also Kawia
   Luiseño (H)
Cahuilla [CA] (LC)
Cahuillan Linguistic Family
   [Lang] (Pub, v.4, no.3, p.131)
Cahuillo see Kawia Luiseño
Cah-wa see Kawia Yokuts
Cahwa see Kawia Yokuts
Cah-wee-o see Kawia Luiseño
Cahweeo see Kawia Luiseño
Cahwia see Kawia Yokuts
Cah-wi-ah see Kawia Yokuts
Cahwiah see Kawia Yokuts
Cah-willa see Cahuilla
Cahwilla see Cahuilla
Caiabi see Kayabi
Caiapa see Cayapo
Caiapo see Cayapo
Caiasban (H)
Cai-a-wa see Kiowa
Caiawa see Kiowa
Caicaches [TX] (H)
Caicana see Cataican
Caicoa [HA, WInd] Caizcimu
   (BE)
Caigua see Kiowa
Caigua see Caingua
Caiguara see Kiowa
Caihua see Kiowa
Caijougas see Cayuga
Caijouge see Cayuga

Cailloux see Cayuse
Caiman see Caimanes
Caiman see San Blas Cuna
Caimanes Cuna (BE)
Caimbe see Kaimbe
Cainamero see Gallinomero
Caingang see Kaingangue
Caingangue see Kaingangue
Cainge see Cayuga
Caingua [Arg, Br, Par] (LC)
Caiouga see Cayuga
Caiougo see Cayuga
Caiougue see Cayuga
Caipotorades see Moro
Caishana see Cayuishana
Caita see Cahita
Caitsdammo [LA] (H)
Caiua see Caingua
Caiushana see Cayuishana
Caiwa see Kiowa
Caiyonga see Cayuga
Cai-yu-cla see Siuslaw
Caizcimu [HA, WInd] (BE)
Cajages see Cayuga
Cajamarca [PE] (O)
Cajanibi [MX] Coahuiltecan
   (Hdbk10)
Cajapanama [MX] Coahuiltecan
   (Hdbk10)
Cajaquepa [MX] Coahuiltecan
   (Hdbk10)
Cajoeger see Cayuga
Cajouga see Cayuga
Cajouge see Cayuga
Cajougoes see Cayuga
Cajouse see Cayuse
Cajuala see Paiute
Cajuala Sevinta see Shivwits
Cajuales see Paiute
Cajubama [MX] Coahuiltecan
   (Hdbk10)
Cajubama [MX] Coahuiltecan
   (Hdbk10)
Cajubicena see Cayuishana
Cajuenche (BE) see also Kohuana
   (BE)
Cajuenche (BE) see also Kohuana
   (BE)
Cajuenche (Hdbk10) see also Kah-
   wan (Hdbk10)
Cajuenche (Hdbk10) see also Kah-
   wan (Hdbk10)
Cajuenche [AZ] Yuman (H)
Cajuenche [CA, AZ] (H)
Cajuenes see Kahwan
Cajuga see Cayuga
Cajuge see Cayuga
Cajugu see Cayuga
Cajuka see Cayuga
Cajyouga see Cayuga
Cajyuga see Cayuga
Cakainikova see Cahinnio
Cakchi see Kekchi

Cakchikel [Gu] (LC)
Cakchiquel see Cakchikel
Cake see Kake
cakge-nkni see Molala
Cakinonpa see Kakinonba
Cakkiptaco see Cattachiptico
Cakwaleñya winwu see Shak-
   walengya
Ca-kwa-len-ya wuñ-wu see
   Shakwalengya
Calabaw see Catawba
Ca-la-bi see Cheli
Calabi see Cheli
Calahpoewah see Calapooya
Calajomanes see Gallinomero
Cal-a-mex see Tillamook
Calamex see Tillamook
Ca-la-mox see Tillamook
Calamox see Tillamook
Calanay see Calany
Calancheño Coahuiltecan
   (Hdbk10)
Calanio see Calany
Calany [FL] Timucua (H)
Calapalo see Apalakiri
Calapelin see Kalispel
Calapooa see Calapooya
Calapooah see Calapooya
Calapooga see Calapooya
Calapooia see Calapooya
Calapoolia see Calapooya
Calapoosa see Calapooya
Calapooya [OR] (BE)
Calapooyan [Lang] see Kalapuya
Calapuaya see Calapooya
Calapuya see Calapooya
Calasthocle (H) see also Killax-
   thokle (H)
Ca-last-ho-cle see Killaxthokle
Ca-last-ho-cle see Quinault
Calasthocle [WA] Quinault (BE)
Calasthorte see Calathocle
Calatouches (Hdbk12) see also
   Paloos (LC)
Calatouches [WA] (Hdbk12)
Calbo see Calvo
Calcefar [NJ] Unami (BE)
Calchaqui [Arg] [Diaguitá] (LC)
Calcharnies see Kulchana
Calciati Pueblo Indians (H)
Caldono [Col] Paez (O)
Cale see Olagale
Calespelin see Kalispel
Calespell see Kalispel
Calespin see Kalispel
Calexpaquet see Alcalerpaquet
Calibi see Galibi
Caliente see Kawaiisu
Caliente Trumoyo see Kawaiisu
Caliente Tumoyo see Kawaiisu
California [Lang] (BE)
Californian [Lang] (BE)
Calima culture [Col] (LC)

Calina *see* Culina
Calina [Self-designation] *see*
   Carib
Calinya *see* Carib
Calinya [Black Carib] *see* Black
   Carib
Calipoa *see* Calapooya
Calipoa *see* Catawba
Calipocate [MX] *Coahuiltecan*
   (Hdbk10)
Calipooia *see* Calapooya
Calipooya *see* Calapooya
Calipoya *see* Calapooya
Calipuyowe *see* Calapooya
Calispell *see* Kalispel
Calkobins *see* Tautin
Callaga *Abipone* (LC)
Callageheah *see* Cherokee
Cal-lah-po-e-ouah *see*
   Calapooya
Callahpoeouah *see* Calapooya
Cal-lah-po-e-wah *see* Calapooya
Callahpoewah *see* Calapooya
Callahuaya [Lang] [BO] (LC)
Cal-la-mak *see* Tillamook
Callamak *see* Tillamook
Cal la mox *see* Tillamook
Callamox *see* Tillamook
Callamucks *see* Tillamook
Callapipa *see* Calapooya
Callapooia *see* Calapooya
Callapooiale *see* Calapooya
Callapooka *see* Calapooya
Callapooto *see* Calapooya
Callapooya *see* Calapooya
Callapooyah *see* Calapooya
Calla puya *see* Calapooya
Callapuya *see* Calapooya
Callapuye *see* Calapooya
Callawalla *see* Callahuaya
Callawpohyeaa *see* Calapooya
Callemax *see* Tillamook
Callemex *see* Tillamook
Callimix *see* Tillamook
Calling River Band *see*
   Katepoisipi-winuuk
Calliseca *see* Sipibo
Call-law-poh-yea-a *see*
   Calapooya
Callo *see* Calousa [CA]
Callo *see* Calusa [FL]
Calloosa *see* Calousa [CA]
Calloosa *see* Calusa [FL]
Caloait *see* Skilloot
Calooit *see* Skilloot
Caloort *see* Skilloot
Caloosa *see* Calousa [CA]
Caloosa *see* Calusa [FL]
Calopissa *see* Acolapissa
Calos *see* Calousa [CA]
Calos *see* Calusa [FL]
Calouche [FL] (H)
Calousa [CA] *River Patwin* (BE)

Calt-sop *see* Clatsop
Caluca *see* Okelousa
Calusa (His/T, v.2, p.345) *see also*
   Calousa [CA] (BE)
Calusa [FL] (LC)
Calusa [FL] (LC)
Calvo *Apache* (Hdbk10)
Cama [BO] *Araona* (O)
Camacaluira [MX] *Coahuiltecan*
   (Hdbk10)
Camacan *see* Kamakan
Camachi [CR] (O)
Camacuro [MX] *Coahuiltecan*
   (Hdbk10)
Camaguey [Cu] (BE)
Camahan *Coahuiltecan* (Hdbk10)
Camai *Coahuiltecan* (BE)
Camaie [HA] *Bainoa* (BE)
Camaiguara [MX] *Coahuiltecan*
   (Hdbk10)
Camaleones *Coahuiltecan*
   (Hdbk10)
Camaleones [MX] *Tamaulipec*
   (BE)
Camalucano [MX] *Coahuiltecan*
   (Hdbk10)
Camancee *see* Comanche
Camanche *see* Comanche
Camaniguara [MX] *Coahuiltecan*
   (Hdbk10)
Camaracoto (O) *see also* Puricoto
   (LC)
Camaracoto [VE] (LC)
Camarakoto *see* Caramacoto
Camarakoto *see* Karamacoto
Camaroua *see* Tamaroa
Camarsche *see* Comanche
Camasari *see* Camahan
Camas Eaters *see* Saituka
Camas People *see* Kalispel
Camasuqua *Pamaque* (Hdbk10)
Camatonaja [MX] *Coahuiltecan*
   (Hdbk10)
Camaya [BO] *Araona* (O)
Camayopalo [MX] *Coahuiltecan*
   (Hdbk10)
Camayula *see* Kamaiura
Camayura *see* Kamaiura
Camba (Hdbk15) *see also* Ken-
   nebec (Hdbk15)
Camba (LC) *see also* Chiriguano
   (LC)
Camba [BO] (O)
Cambas *see* Norridgewock
Cambeba *see* Omagua
Cambela *see* Omagua
Came *see* Zuni
Camejeya [Self-designation] *see*
   Yucuna
Camel-el-poma *see* Usal
Cam-el-lel-Poma *see* Usal
Camellel Poma *see* Usal
Cami *see* Zuni

Cami-isubaba [MX] *Coahuiltecan*
   (Hdbk10)
Camiltpaw [WA] *Wenatchi* (BE)
Camilya *see* Coneya
Camilya *see* Kamia
Camiopajamara (Hdbk10)
Camisnimat [MX] *Coahuiltecan*
   (Hdbk10)
Camoavi [BO] *Araona* (O)
Camole [TX] (H)
Camone *see* Camole
Camowev *see* Chemehuevi
Campa [PE] (LC)
Campa Caquinte *see* Caquinte
Campacua *see* Tampacua
Campa del Alto Perene [PE]
   Campa (O)
Campa del Pichis [PE] *Campa* (O)
Campa Nomatsiguenga *see* No-
   matsiguenga
Campa Pajonalino *see* Pajonalino
Campa Ucayalino *see* Ucayalino
Campaz *see* Colorado [SA]
Campe [Br] (O)
Campeba *see* Omegua
Campiti *see* Campa
Campoa *see* Pampopas
Campo Nambicuara *see* South-
   ern Nambicuara
Camp Verde Apache (Char, v.4)
Camsa [Col] (LC)
Camuchininbara [MX] (Hdbk10)
Camyula *see* Kamaiura
Cana (H) *see also* Sana (BE)
Cana (Hdbk10) *see also* Canua
   (Hdbk10)
Cana (Hdbk9) *see also*
   Kechipauan (Hdbk9)
Cana [PE] *Aymara* (O)
Canaba *see* Kennebec
Canabaco [HA, SanD] *Hubabo*
   (BE)
Canabas *see* Norridgewock
Canabecuma [MX] *Coahuiltecan*
   (Hdbk10)
Canabi *see* Kechipauan
Canacabala [MX] *Coahuiltecan*
   (Hdbk10)
Canagesse *see* Conoy
Canaghkonje *see* Iroquois
Canaghkouse *see* Iroquois
Canaghquieson (Great, pp.57–67)
Canaguiague [MX] (Hdbk10)
Canaguiapem *see* Quiniacapem
Canai *see* Conoy
Canaine [MX] *Coahuiltecan*
   (Hdbk10)
Canais *see* Conoy
Canaitoca [MX] *Coahuiltecan*
   (Hdbk10)
Canamari [Br] *see* Kanamari
Canamarigui [MX] *Coahuiltecan*
   (Hdbk10)

Canamary [BO] *Araona* (O)
Canamau [MX] *Coahuiltecan* (Hdbk10)
Canameo [MX] *Coahuiltecan* (Hdbk10)
Cananarito [MX] *Coahuiltecan* (Hdbk10)
Canaoneuksa *see* Mohawk
Canapanama *see* Cajapanama
Canapeo [MX] *Coahuiltecan* (Hdbk10)
Canapouce *see* Catawba
Canapu *see* Canapes
Canaranaguio [MX] *Coahuiltecan* (Hdbk15)
Canaresse *see* Canarsee
Canari [EC] (LC)
Canarian [Lang] [EC] (LC)
Canarian Indians *see* Canari
Cañaris-Cajamarca (O)
Canarise *see* Canarsee
Canarisse *see* Canarsee
Canarse *see* Canarsee
Canarsee [NJ] *Unami* (BE)
Canarsee [NY] *Metoac* (H)
Canarsii *see* Canarsee
Canastoga *see* Conestoga
Canastoge *see* Conestoga
Canastogue *see* Conestoga
Canatino *see* Kanohatino
Canaumano *see* Gallinomero
Canavest *see* Conoy
Canawaroghare *see* Oneida
Canaway *see* Conoy
Canawese *see* Conoy
Canawest *see* Conoy
Canayna *see* Canaynes
Canaynes [MX] *Tamaulipec* (BE)
Canbroiniguera [MX] *Coahuiltecan* (Hdbk10)
Canceas *see* Quapaw
Cancer *see* Lipan Apache
Cancere *see* Lipan Apache
Cances *see* Lipan Apache
Cancey *see* Apache
Cancey *see* Kiowa Apache
Cancey *see* Lipan Apache
Canceze *see* Kansa
Cancezs *see* Kansa
Canchez *see* Kansa
Canchi [PE] *Aymara* (O)
Canchy *see* Lipan Apache
Canchy *see* Cancy
Cancon *see* Konkow
Cancy (H) *see also* Lipan Apache (LC)
Cancy *Apache* (Hdbk10)
Candadacho *see* Kadohadacho
Candaungack *see* Cantauncack
Candia *see* Sandia
Candoshi [PE] (LC)
Candoxi *see* Candoshi
Cane *see* Ocana

Canechi *see* Canichana
Canecis *see* Lipan Apache
Canecy *see* Cancy
Canee *see* Lipan Apache
Caneeci *see* Lipan Apache
Cañegacola *see* Cañogacola
Canela (O) *see also* Canella (LC)
Canela *Eastern Timbira* (O)
Canella [Br] (LC)
Canelo [EC] (LC)
Canelos Quichua *see* Canelo
Canel Pomo [CA] *Northern Pomo* (Pub, v.40, no.2)
Canendeshe *see* Naogeh
Canesi *see* Canichana
Canestoga *see* Conestoga
Canestogo *see* Conestoga
Canga-Peba *see* Omagua
Canggaree *see* Congaree
Can-han *see* Dakota
Canhan *see* Dakota
Canhaway *see* Conoy
Caniba [Lang] *Algonquian* (Bull3)
Caniba Indians *see* Kennebec
Canibas *see* Norridgewock
Canice *see* Takulli
Canichana [BO] (LC)
Canicon *see* Tanico
Caniengo *see* Mohawk
Canimairo *see* Gallinomero
Canimare *see* Gallinomero
Canim Lake [BC] *Lake Shuswap* (Hdbk12)
Caniouis *see* Kannehouan
Canips *see* Kansa
Canisi *see* Canichana
Canistage *see* Conestoga
Canistoge *see* Conestoga
Can-kaga-otina *see* Chank-aghaotina
Cankagaotina *see* Chank-aghaotina
Cankia *see* Caholia
Cannabas *see* Norridgewock
Cannaha *see* Kannehouan
Cannahios *see* Kannehouan
Cannarse *see* Canarsee
Cannassoone *see* Iroquois
Cannecis *see* Lipan Apache
Cannecy *see* Lipan Apache
Cannehovanes *see* Kannehouan
Cannensis *see* Lipan Apache
Cannessi *see* Lipan Apache
Cannetquot [NY] *Patchoag* (H)
Canney *see* Cancy
Cannibal *see* Potiguara
Cannibalier *see* Potiguara
Cannibas *see* Norridgewock
Cannissoone *see* Iroquois
Canniungaes *see* Mohawk
Cannohatinno *see* Kanohatino
Cannohatino *see* Kanohatino

Cannokantimo *see* Kanohatino
Cannon-gageh-ronnon *see* Abnaki
Cannossoene *see* Iroquois
Cano *see* Canua
Canoatinno *see* Kanohatino
Canoatino *see* Kanohatino
Canocan (H)
Canoe Creek [BC] *Shuswap* (H)
Canoe Creek Band [BC] *Fraser River Shuswap* (Hdbk12)
Canoe Indians *see* Mahican
Canoe Indians *see* Alacaluf
Canoe Indians *see* Yaghan
Canoeiro [Br] (LC)
Canoe Lake [BC] *Upper Thompson* (H)
Canoemen *see* Malecite
Canoera *see* Ava
Cañogacola [FL] (H)
Canohatino *see* Kanohatino
Canohattino *see* Kanohatino
Canoise *see* Conoy
Canon *see* Canua
Canonchahonronon *see* Osswehgadagaah
Canon Division [Can] *Shuswap* (BE)
Cañon Indians *see* Lower Thompson
Canorise *see* Canarsee
Canossoone *see* Iroquois
Canostoga *see* Conestoga
Canouhanan *see* Kanohatino
Canowaroghere *see* Oneida
Canowes *see* Conoy
Canoy *see* Conoy
Canoyeas *see* Conoy
Canoyias *see* Conoy
Cans *see* Kansa
Cansa *see* Kansa
Canses *see* Kansa
Cansez *see* Kansa
Cantajes *see* Kiowa Apache
Cantanual *see* Simaomo
Cantauhaona *see* Simaomo
Cantauncack [VA] *Algonquian* (Hdbk15)
Cantaunkack *see* Cantauncack
Cantcy *see* Cancy
Cantensapue (H)
Cantey *see* Lipan Apache
Cantona *see* Simaoma
Cantonaes *see* Simaomo
Canton Indians *see* Iroquois Confederacy
Cantonment Cheyenne (Who)
Cantujuana *see* Simaomo
Cantuna (H) *see also* Simaomo (BE)
Cantuna *Coahuiltecan* (BE)
Canua *Coahuiltecan* (Hdbk10)
Canum Mentulae *see* Cuntce'bi

Canungas *see* Mohawk
Canyon Creek *San Carlos Apache*
(BE)
Canyon Division [BC] *Shuswap*
(Hdbk12)
Canzas *see* Kansa
Canze *see* Cancy
Canzes *see* Kansa
Canzez *see* Kansa
Caodacho *see* Kadohadacho
Caokia *see* Cahokia
Caoque *see* Coaque
Caoquias *see* Cahokia
Caos *see* Cahokia
Caouaouce *see* Cahokia
Caouquias *see* Cahokia
Capa (H) *see also* Quapaw (LC)
Capa [BO] *Araona* (O)
Capabagua *see* Capanahua
Capache *Coahuiltecan* (Hdbk10)
Capachequi [FL] (BE)
Capae [MX] *Coahuiltecan*
(Hdbk10)
Capagui [MX] *Coahuiltecan*
(Hdbk10)
Capaha *see* Quapaw
Capaheni [BO] *Araona* (O)
Capanagua *see* Capanahua
Capanahua [Br, PE] (LC)
Capanary [BO] *Araona* (O)
Capanawa *see* Capanahua
Capangu *see* Capanahua
Capapacho *see* Cashibo
Caparaz (BE) *see also* Capachequi
(BE)
Caparaz [FL] (BE)
Capate *see* Capote
Capatuu [MX] *Coahuiltecan*
(Hdbk10)
Capawec *see* Martha's Vineyard
Capechene [BO] *Araona* (O)
Cape Dorset Inuktitut *see* Kin-
ngarmiut
Cape Espenberg *Bering Strait Es-*
kimos (Hdbk5)
Cape Farewell *West Greenlandic*
(Hdbk5)
Cape Fear [Lang] *Catawba* (H)
Cape Fear [NC] (BE)
Cape Flattery *see* Makah
Cape Florida *see* Calusa
Cape Florida Indians *see* Calusa
Cape Fox *see* Sanyakoan
Cape Indians *see* Nauset
Cape Nome *Bering Strait Eskimos*
(Hdbk5)
Cape People *see* Makah
Cape St. James Tribe *see*
Gunghet-hadagai
Cape Suble Indians [NS] *Micmac*
(H)
Capina *see* Capinans
Capinans [MS] (BE)

Capiri [PE] *Campa* (O)
Capitanesse *see* Biloxi
Ca-po *see* Santa Clara [NM]
Capo *see* Santa Clara [NM]
Ca-po-cia band *see* Kapozha
Capocia band *see* Kapozha
Capohn *Acawai* (LC)
Capong *Acawai* (LC)
Capoo *see* Santa Clara [NM]
Capoque *see* Coaque
Caposepock [VA] *Algonquian*
(Hdbk15)
Caposho *see* Masacali
Ca-po-ta *see* Capote
Capota *see* Capote
Capote [CO, NM] *Ute* (LC)
Cappa *see* Quapaw
Capt. Sutter's Indians *see* Nishi-
nam
Capu [BO] *Araona* (O)
Capuchies *see* Capote
Capuibo [BO] *Pacanuara* (O)
Capujaquin [MX] *Coahuiltecan*
(Hdbk10)
Caquetio [VE] (LC)
Caquima *see* Kiakima
Caquinte [PE] *Campa* (LC)
Cara [EC] (LC)
Carabayo *see* Karabayo
Carabere *see* Pauserna
Carabisi *see* Carib
Caraca [Lang] *Tamanec* (UAz,
v.28)
Caracati *see* Krikati
Caracontauon *see* Coiracoentanon
Caracotanon *see* Coiracoentanon
Caraguists *see* Karigouistes
Caraib *see* Carib
Caraja [Br] (LC)
Caramanes *see* Karankawa
Caramanta [Col] *Choco* (O)
Caramapana [MX] (Hdbk10)
Caramaperiguan [MX] (Hdbk10)
Caramariguanes [MX] *Tamaulipec*
(BE)
Caramiguaies [MX] *Tamaulipec*
(BE)
Caramiguay *see* Caramiguaies
Caramunigua [MX] (Hdbk10)
Caraña [MX] *Coahuiltecan*
(Hdbk10)
Carana-Cuna *see* Yecuana
Caranca *see* Caranga
Carancaguacas *see* Karankawa
Carancaguazes *see* Karankawa
Carancahua *see* Karankawa
Carancahuases *see* Karankawa
Carancahuazes *see* Karankawa
Carancahueses *see* Karankawa
Carancanay *see* Karankawa
Carancouas *see* Karankawa
Caranga [BO] *Aymara* (O)
Caranhouas *see* Karankawa

Caranine *see* Coree
Carankahua *see* Karankawa
Carankawaes *see* Karankawa
Carankonas *see* Karankawa
Carankouas *see* Karankawa
Carankoways *see* Karankawa
Carantouani *see* Conestoga
Carantouannais *see* Conestoga
Carapana [Lang] *Col Tucano* (LC)
Cara Preta *see* Mudurucu
Carare [Lang] *Opone* (O)
Caravare *see* Kuruaya
Caraya *see* Caraja
Carbama *see* Caurame
Carcarchia *see* Kaskaskia
Carcarilica *see* Kaskaskia
Cardeche *see* Cadecha
Caree *see* Kahra
Careluta *see* Moro
Careneri (O) *see also* Arasa (LC)
Careneri [PE] *Mashco* (O)
Carfaray (H)
Cargua *see* Kiowa
Cariaya [Lang] (O)
Carib [Hon, WInd] (LC)
Cariban [Lang] (LC)
Cariban Indians *see* Carib
Caribayes [MX] *Tamaulipec* (BE)
Caribe [Self-designation] *see*
Carib
Caribice *see* Carib
Caribisi [Lang] *Western Cariban*
(UAz, v.28)
Cariboo Eaters *see* Etheneldeli
Cariboo Eaters *see* Eastern Dene
Caribou [*Western Canada (Inuit-*
Inupiaq)] (Hdbk5)
Caribou-Eaters *see* Etheneldeli
Caribou Eskimos [AK] *Central*
Eskimos (Hdbk5)
Caribou gens *see* Oueschek-
gagamiouilimy
Caribou Indians *see* Tutchone
Carihona *see* Carijona
Carijo *see* Fulnio
Carijona [Col] (LC)
Carijona [Lang] *Cariban* (UAz,
v.28)
Carina *see* Carib
Cariniaco [Lang] *Western Cariban*
(UAz, v.28)
Carinya *see* Kariña
Caripuna *see* Karipuna
Cariri *see* Kariri
Cariri-Sapuya *see* Sapuya
Carises [CA] (H)
Cariso *see* Carrizo [NM]
Caritiana *see* Karitiana
Carjuenche *see* Cajuenche
Carlana (Hdbk10) *see also* Sierra
Blanca (Hdbk10)
Carlana [CO] *Plains Apache*
(Hdbk10)

Carlene [NM] *Jicarilla Apache* (H)
Carlin *see* Calusa [FL]
Carlos *see* Calusa [FL]
Carlos, San [AZ] *Apache* (BE)
Carmelo Eslenes *see* Esselen
Carmeneh *see* Siksika
Carnijo *see* Fulnio
Carolina [Lang] *Eastern Algonquian* (Hdbk15)
Caromanie [Gens] *Winnebago* (H)
Carp River *see* Ommunise
Carquin *see* Karkin
Carrechias *see* Cahokia
Carree *see* Kahra
Carriba *see* Kennebec
Carribas *see* Norridgewok
Carrien *see* Takulli
Carrier-Indians (H) *see also* Takulli (H)
Carrier Indians [BC] *Subarctic* (LC)
Carriso *see* Carrizo [MX]
Carrizalleño *see* Carrizo [NM]
Carrizo [MX] *Tamaulipec* (BE)
Carrizo [NM] *Cibecue* (BE)
Carrua *see* Charrua
Carruco *see* Chorruco
Carson Lake *see* Toedokado
Car-soos *see* Kassovo
Cartaka *see* Castake
Caruama *see* Caurame
Carutana [Lang] *Maipurean* (O)
Carutana Indians *see* Karitana
Carvilla *see* Kawia *Luiseño*
Cas *see* Kaskaskia
Casaga *Coahuiltecan* (Hdbk10)
Casapullas *see* Cusabo
Casarba [SD] *Dakota* (BE)
Casas Chiquitas *Coahuiltecan* (BE)
Casastales *Coahuiltecan* (BE)
Cascachias *see* Kaskaskia
Cascacia *see* Kaskkaskia
Cascade (BE) *see also* Watlala (BE)
Cascade (Oregon) *see also* Watlala (BE)
Cascade [OR] *North Basin* (Ye)
Cascade Phase (AI, p.20)
Cascades (Hdbk12)
Cascades Indians (Forg) *see also* Watlala (BE)
Cascakia *see* Kaskaskia
Cascakiaki *see* Kaskaskia
Cascaquia *see* Kaskaskia
Cascarba *Dakota* (H)
Cascashia *see* Kaskaskia
Cascaskia *see* Kaskaskia
Cascasquia *see* Kaskaskia
Casharari *see* Kaxarari
Cashchevatebka *see* Kotsoteka
Cashchokelka Comanche *see* Kotsoteka

Cashhook *see* Clowwewalla
Cashibo [PE] (LC)
Cashinahua *see* Cashinawa
Cashinawa [Br, PE] (LC)
Cashiniti *see* Kashiniti
Cashiniti *see* Paressi
Cashook *see* Clowwewalla
Casibo *see* Cashibo
Casimariguan *see* Simariguan
Casino *see* Havasupai
Casjoukia *see* Cahokia
Caskaguia *see* Kaskaskia
Caskakia *see* Kaskaskia
Caskaquia *see* Kaskaskia
Caskarorin *see* Tuscarora
Caskaroun *see* Tuscarora
Caskaskia *see* Kaskaskia
Caskinampo *see* Kakinonba
Casnino *see* Havasupai
Caso *see* Kotsava
Casor *see* Coosa
Casquasquia *see* Kaskaskia
Casqui (BE) *see also* Kaskinampo (BE)
Casqui *Quapaw* (H)
Casquiar *see* Kaskaskia
Casquias *see* Kaskaskia
Casquin *see* Kaskinampo
Cas-sans *see* Kassovo
Cassans *see* Kassovo
Cassapecock [VA] *Powhatan* (H)
Cassia *see* Kichai
Cass Lake Band *see* Gamiskwakokawininiwak
Cas-soes *see* Kassovo
Cassoes *see* Kassovo
Casson *see* Kassovo
Cassoos *see* Kassovo
Cassotis (H)
Castabana *see* Castahana
Castahama *see* Castahana
Castahana (H)
Cas-ta-ha-na *see* Castahana
Cas-take *see* Castake
Castake [CA] (H)
Castanoe *see* Cree
Castapana *see* Castahana
Castcheteghka-Comanches *see* Kotsoteka
Castixes *see* San Felipe [Keres]
Castor *see* Amikwa
Castors *see* Tsattine
Castors des Prairies *see* Sarsi
Ca-ta *see* Choctaw
Cata *see* Choctaw
Cataara [MX] *Coahuiltecan* (Hdbk10)
Cataba *see* Catawba
Cataban *see* Catawba
Catabaw *see* Catawba
Catada *see* Dhatada
Catago *see* Castake
Cataha *see* Kiowa Apache

Catahoula [LA] (H)
Cataican *Coahuiltecan* (Hdbk10)
Catajuno *see* Kutuhano
Ca'taka *see* Kiowa Apache
Cataka *see* Kiowa Apache
Catamarca-la Rioje *see* Quechua
Catamareno *see* Cacan
Catanamepaque *see* Cotonam
Catanoneaux *see* Kutenai
Cataoulou *see* Catahoula
Catapa *Chibcha* (BE)
Catapaw *see* Catawba
Catapolitani [Lang] *Maipurean* (O)
Catareaguemara [MX] *Coahuiltecan* (Hdbk10)
Cataruberi *Achagua* (O)
Catathoy *see* Kamakan
Catauba *see* Catawba
Cataubo *see* Catawba
Cataupa *see* Catawba
Catawahay *see* Kutenai
Catawba [Lang] *Siouan* (H)
Catawba [Lang] [Siouan] (H)
Catawba [SC] (LC)
Catawbau *see* Catawba
Catawbaw *see* Catawba
Catawian *see* Katawian
Catawishi *see* Catuquina
Catawishi *see* Katawixi
Cataxtle *see* Cacaxte
Catcho *see* Kadohadacho
Catelamet *see* Cathlamet
Cat Fish Indians *see* Manumaig
Ca-tha *see* Comanche
Catha *see* Comanche
Cath Camette *see* Cathlamet
Cathelamett *see* Cathlamet
Cathlacomatup [OR] *Mulnomah* (BE)
Cathlacommatup *see* Cathlacomatup
Cathlacumup [OR] *Multnomah* (LC)
Cathlahaw *see* Thlakalama
Cath-lah-com-ma-tup *see* Cathlacomatup
Cathlahcommatup *see* Cathlacomatup
Cathlahcumup *see* Cathlacumup
Cath-lah-nah-quiah *see* Cathlanaquiah
Cathlahnahquiah *see* Cathlanaquiah
Cath-lah-poh-tle *see* Cathlapotle
Cathlahpohtle *see* Cathlapotle
Cath-lak-a-heckit *see* Cathlakaheckit
Cathlakaheckit (Hdbk12) *see also* Cascades (Hdbk15)
Cathlakaheckit [OR] *Watlala* (BE)

Cathlakahikit *see* Cathlakaheckit
Cathlakamap *see* Cathlacumup
Cath-la-ma *see* Cathlamet
Cathlama *see* Cathlamet
Cathlamah *see* Cathlamet
Cathlamak *see* Cathlamet
Cathlamat *see* Cathlamet
Cathlamet [Lang] [WA] *Chinookan* (Oregon)
Cathlamet [WA] (BE)
Cathlaminimim *see* Kathlaminimin
Cathlamut *see* Cathlamet
Cathlamux *see* Cathlamet
Cathlanahquiah *see* Cathlanaquiah
Cathlanamenamen *see* Kathlaminimin
Cathlanaminim *see* Kathlaminimin
Cathlanam nimin *see* Kathlaminimin
Cathlanaquiah [OR] *Multnomah* (BE)
Cathlapootle *see* Cathlapotle
Cathlapooya *see* Calapooya
Cathlapotle [WA] (BE)
Cathlapoutle *see* Cathlapotle
Cathlapoutte *see* Cathlapotle
Cathlapouyea *see* Calapooya
Cathlas *see* Wasco
Cathlascan *see* Wasco
Cathlascon [Lang] *Chinookan* (Bull15)
Cathlascon Indians *see* Wasco
Cathlasko *see* Wasco
Cathlasko *see* Wasco
Cathlassis *see* Wasco
Cathlathla *see* Cathlathlala
Cath-lath-la-la *see* Cathlathlala
Cathlathlala [OR] *Watlala* (BE)
Cathlathlaly *see* Cathlathlala
Cathlatsco *see* Wasco
Cathlawah *see* Cathlamet
Cathlayackty *see* Cathlakaheckit
Cathlayackty *see* Cascades
Cath-le-yach-e-yach *see* Cascades
Cathleyacheyach *see* Cascades
Cath-le-yach-e-yachs *see* Shahala
Cathleyacheyachs *see* Shahala
Cathlumet *see* Cathlamet
Catiene *see* Shathiane
Cat Indians *see* Erie
Catio [Col, Pan] (LC)
Catiokia *see* Cahokia
Catiokiah *see* Cahokia
Catkil *see* Catskill
Catlahma *see* Cathlamet
Catlipoh *see* Cathlapotle
Catlipok *see* Cathlapotle
Catlo'ltq *see* Comox
Catloltq *see* Comox

Catloltx *see* Comox
Catlo'ltx [Self-designation] *see* Comox
Cat Nation *see* Erie
Cato [MA] *Massachuset* (BE)
Catomae *see* Guahibo
Catomao *see* Catomavo
Catomavo [MX] *Coahuiltecan* (Hdbk10)
Catoquina [Br] (LC)
Catoquino *see* Catoquina
Catouinayo [LA] (H)
Catriti *see* San Felipe [Keres]
Cat-sa-nim *see* Yakima
Catsanim *see* Yakima
Catskil *see* Catskill
Catskill [NY] *Munsee* (BE)
Cattaba *see* Catawba
Cattabaw *see* Catawba
Cattachipico *see* Cattachiptico
Cattachiptico [VA] *Algonquian* (Hdbk15)
cattail eaters *see* Toedökado
Cattako *see* Kiowa Apache
Cat-tan-a-haw *see* Kutenai
Cattanahaw *see* Kutenai
Cattanahowe *see* Kutenai
Cattawba *see* Catawba
Cattleputle *see* Cathlapotle
Cattoway *see* Catawba
Cattskill *see* Catskill
Catujan *see* Catujano
Catujan *see* Katuhano
Catujano (Hdbk10) *see also* Katuhano (Hdbk10)
Catujano [MX] *Coahuiltecan* (Hdbk10)
Catujuan *see* Catujano
Catujuan *see* Katuhano
Catukina *see* Catoquina
Catukinaru *see* Catoquina
Catukino *see* Catoquina
Catuquina *see* Catoquina
Catuquinaru *see* Catoquina
Catuquino *see* Catoquina
Catuxanes *see* Kutuhano
Catuxano *see* Kutuhano
Cauaripan *see* Cauripan
Caucan [CH] (O)
Caugh *see* Kansa
Caughnawaga [Q] (LC)
Caughnowaga *see* Caughnawaga
Cauhuahipe *see* Kawahib
Cau-i *see* Chaui
Caui *see* Chaui
Cauila *see* Coahuileño
Cauishana *see* Cayuishana
Cauixana *see* Cayuishana
Caujana *see* Cayuishana
Caujucko *see* Cayuga
Cauldrons *see* Colville
Caumuche *see* Comanche
Caunbitant *see* Corbitant

Cauneeyenkees *see* Mohawk
Caunoa [HA, WInd] *Bainoa* (BE)
Caunouche *see* Comanche
Caurame *Coahuiltecan* (Hdbk10)
Cauripan *Coahuiltecan* (Hdbk10)
Cautawba *see* Catawba
Cautonee *see* Kutenai
Cautonies *see* Kutenai
Cauxana *see* Cayuishana
Cauya *Coahuiltecan* (Hdbk10)
Cauyari (O) *see also* Cabiyari (LC)
Cauyari [Lang] *Maipurean* (O)
Cauyary *see* Cabiyari
Cauyary *see* Cauyari
Cauyguama *Coahuiltecan* (Hdbk10)
Cauzes *see* Kansa
Cava [TX] *Tonkawan* (BE)
Cavaianes *see* Kouyani
Cavecara [CR] *Cabecar* (O)
Cavesi *see* Cabezas
Cavessa *see* Cabezas
Caveza *see* CAbezas
Cavina *see* Araona
Cavinena [Lang] *see* Cavineno
Cavineno [BO] (LC)
Cavio *see* Kawia *Luiseño*
Caviseras [MX] *Lagunero* (BE)
Cavua *see* Caduveo
Caw *see* Kansa
Caw-a-chim *see* Cowichan
Cawachim *see* Cowichan
Cawahib *see* Parintintin
Cawahib *see* Kawahib
Cawahiwa *see* Kawahib
Cawala *see* Shawala
Cawala *see* Shawnee
Cawalitz *see* Cowlitz
Cawana *see* Shawnee
Cawasumseuck [NEng] (H)
Cawaupugos *see* Cumumbah
Cawa'xamux *see* Nicola
Cawaxamux *see* Nicola
Caw-Caw *see* Konkow
Cawcaw *see* Konkow
Caweo *see* Kawia *Luiseño*
Cawesitt *see* Coweset
Cawina (BE) *see also* Kohuana (BE)
Cawina [AZ, CA] (H)
Ca-witchan *see* Cowichan
Cawitchan *see* Cowichan
Caw-mainsh *see* Comanche
Cawmainsh *see* Comanche
Cawnacome *see* Coneconam
Cawnee *see* Koni
Cawra *see* Kahra
Caw-ree *see* Kahra
Cawree *see* Kahra
Caxibo [Lang] *see* Cashibo
Caxinaua *see* Cashinawa
Caxuiana [Br] (O)
Caya (H) *see also* Shaya (H)

Caya [AR] (H)

Cayabi see Kayabi

Cayacacamegua see Cacamegua

Cayaga see Cayuga

Cayaguaga see Cayaguaguin

Cayaguaguin [MX] Coahuiltecan (Hdbk10)

Cayaguam see Caguayoguam

Cayaguayo [Cu] (BE)

Cayague [MX] Coahuiltecan (Hdbk10)

Cayahasomi [Clan] [FL] Timucua (H)

Cayaki see Cherokee

Cayamo see Cayapo

Cayanapuro [MX] Coahuiltecan (Hdbk10)

Cayani see Cheyenne

Cayanoguanaja [MX] Coahuiltecan (Hdbk10)

Cayanwa see Kiowa

Cayapa [EC] (LC)

Cayapo [Br] (LC)

Cayase see Caya

Cayauga see Cayuga

Cayauge see Cayuga

Cayaughkia see Cahokia

Cay-au-wa see Kiowa

Cay-au-wah see Kiowa

Cayauwah see Kiowa

Cayawah see Kiawaw

Cayawash see Kiawaw

Cayaywa see Kiowa

Caycua see Kiowa

Caycuge see Cayuga

Cayeuge see Cayuga

Cayeugo see Cayuga

Caygua see Kiowa

Cayhuga see Cayuga

Cayingahaugas see Mohawk

Caymus see Wappo

Caynga see Cayuga

Cayoga see Cayuga

Cayohua see Kiowa

Cayonge see Cayuga

Cayoogo see Cayuga

Cayoose see Cayuse

Cayoosh Creek Band [BC] Upper Lilliooet (Hdbk12)

Cayoque see Coaque

Cayoquit see Kyuquot

Cayote see Coyotero Apache

Cayouga see Cayuga

Cayouge see Cayuga

Cayougue see Cayuga

Cayouse see Cayuse

Cayoush see Cayoosh Creek

Cayoux see Cayuse

Cayowge see Cayuga

Caypa see Santa Clara [NM]

caysi see Washo

Cayua see Caingua

Cayuaga see Cayuga

Cayubaba see Cayuvava

Cayubicena see Cayuishana

Cayuga (H) see also Kiowa (LC)

Cayuga [NY, Ont] Iroquois Confederacy (LC)

Cayuge see Cayuga

Cayugo see Cayuga

Cayuishana [Br] (O)

Cayuker see Cayuga

Cayunga see Cayuga

Cayupine [MX] Coahuiltecan (Hdbk10)

Cayuquet see Kyuquot

Cayus see Cayuse

Cayuse [OR, WA] (LC)

Cayuvava [BO] (LC)

Cazaby Pah-Utes see Katsava

Cazancanay see Karankawa

Cazazhita (BE) see also Wannawegha (H)

Cazazhita Teton (BE)

Cazcan [Lang] [MX] Nahuatlan (LC)

Cazulpaniale [CA] Coahuiltecan (Hdbk10)

Cebola see Zuni

Cebolla see Zuni

Cebollians see Zuni

Ceboynas see Lucayan

Cecigha [Lang] Siouan (Contri, v.6)

Cecilville [CA] (BE)

Cecocawanee see Secacawoni

Cecocawonee see Secacawoni

Cecomocomoco see Secowocomoco

Cecoughtan see Kecoughtan

Cedar [UT] Southern Paiute (Hdbk11)

Ce-ecl-tunne see Sheethltunne

Ceecltunne see Sheethltunne

Ceetshongos see Brule

Cegiha [Lang] Siouan (BE)

Cegiha [Self-designation] (H) see also Omaha (LC)

Cegiha [Self-designation] (H) see also Ponca (LC)

Cegnake-okisela see Chegnakeokisela

Ce-go-ni-na see Shungikikarachada

Cegonina see Shungikikarachada

Ce-ha-na-ka see Chegnakeokisela

Cehanake see Chegnakeokisela

Ceh-huha-ton see Chekhuhaton

Cehhuhaton see Chekhuhhaton

Cehmeque-sabinta see Shivwits

Ceichasaw see Chickasaw

Cekacawone see Secacawoni

Cekakawwon see Secacawoni

Ce'kiwere see Chiwere

Cekiwere see Chiwere

Celdal see Tzeltal

Celeste see Siletz

Celetze see Siletz

Celilo [OR] Great Basin (Ye)

Cemanlo see Comanche

Cems see Quems

Ceneca see Seneca

Cenecu see Senecu

Cenepisa see Acoplapissa

Cenesean see Caddo

Cenesian see Caddo

Ce-ngoqedi'na see Shunkukedi

Cengoqedina see Shunkukedi

Ceni see Caddo

Ceniocane see Heniocane

Cenis see Hasinai Confederation

Cenizo Coahuiltecan (Hdbk10)

Cenizos see Senisos

Ceno see Sioni

Cenokipe see Sinoquipe

Cenola see Zuni

Censoc see Sinicu

Censoc see Cenizo

Censoo see Sinicu

Central-Alaskan-Yupik Eskimos (Hdbk15)

Central Aleut [Lang] (Hdbk5)

Central Algonquian [Lang] Can (Hdbk5)

Central Chiricahua Apache [AZ, MX] (Hdbk10)

Central Chumashan [Lang] (H)

Central Eskimos [Can] (BE)

Central Foothill [Lang] [CA] Yokuts (Anthro, v.10, no.1–2)

Central Miwok [CA] (BE)

Central Nomlaki [Lang] [CA] Wintun (He)

Central Numic [Lang] [Uto-Aztecan] (Hdbk10)

Central Pomo [CA] Pomo (BE)

Central Pomo [Lang] Pomo (Pub, v.6, no.1, pp.159–182)

Central Siberian Yupik [Lang] (Hdbk5)

Central Sierra see Tuolumne

Central Sierra Miwok [Lang] Eastern Miwok (CA-8)

Central Wappo [CA] Wappo (BE)

Central Wappo [Lang] Yuki (Pub, v.6, no.1, p.266)

Central West Greenlandic Greenland Eskimos (Hdbk5)

Central Wintun Wintu (Pub, v.29, no.4)

Central Yana [CA] Yana (BE)

Central Yana [Lang] [CA] Yana (CA-8)

Central Yuman [Lang] [CA] (He)

Ceny see Caddo

Ce-oliba see Cheokhba

Ceoliba see Cheokhba

Ceona see Sioni

Ce-pa-le-ve *see* Shipaulovi
Cepaleve *see* Shipaulovi
Ceqemen *see* Siccameen
Ce'qtamux *see* Ntlakyapamuk
Ce'qtamux *see* Thompson
Ceqtamux *see* Ntlakyapamuk
Ceqtamux *see* Thompson
Cerabo *see* Mayoruna
Cere *see* Seri
Ceri *see* Seri
Ceries Assonys *see* Caddo
Cetguanes *see* Yuma
Cetguanes *see* Kahwan
Ceuala *see* Zuni
Ceuola *see* Zuni
ceux du Feu *see* Mascouten
Cevola *see* Zuni
Cex-e-ni-nuth *see* Cexeninuth
Cexeninuth [BC] (H)
cexkekwenk *see* Buckskin Creek
Band
cexwepkemx *see* Empire Valley
Band
Chaa *see* Cheyenne
Chaadulam *see* Sulujam
Chaahl-lana [Clan] [Can] *Haida*
(H)
Chaas *see* Ais
Chabin [Clan] *Assiniboin* (H)
Chacahengua *see* Miami
Chacahuaztli [MX] *Pueblo Indians*
(BE)
Chacakengua *see* Atchatchakan-
gouen
Chacato *see* Chatot
Chacato *see* Choctaw
Chacchooma *see* Chakchiuma
Chacchuma *see* Chakchiuma
Chacci Cuma *see* Chakchiuma
Chaccicuma *see* Chakchiuma
Chacci Ouma *see* Chakchiuma
Chacciouma *see* Chakchiuma
Chaccoux *see* Chactoo
Chacehouma *see* Chakchiuma
Chachachouma *see* Chakchiuma
Chachakingoya *see* Miami
Chachakingua *see* Atchatchakan-
gouen
Chachamatses *see* Hahamatse
Chachambitmanchal [OR] *At-
falati* (H)
Chachanim [OR] *Atfalati* (H)
Chachapoya [Lang] *Quecha* (O)
Chachapoyas-Lamas [Lang]
Quecha (O)
Chachelis *see* Chehalis
Chachemewa *see* Chachimewa
Chachi (LC) *see also* Cayapa (LC)
Chachimahiyuk [OR] *Atfalati* (H)
Chachimewa [OR] *Atfalati* (H)
Chachiscos *see* Santo Domingo
Chachokwith [OR] *Atfalati* (H)
Chachouma *see* Chakchiuma

Chachua'mis *see* Hahuamis
Chachuma *see* Chakciuma
Chaci [EC] (Ex, v.33, no.1, 1991,
pp.53–62)
Chaci [EC] (Ex, v.33, no.1,
pp.53–62)
Chacif [OR] *Atfalati* (H)
Chackchicoma *see* Chakchiuma
Chacksihooma *see* Chakciuma
Chaclan *see* Saclan
Chaclanes *see* Saclan
Chacobo [BO] (LC)
Chacouma *see* Chakchiuma
Chacoume *see* Chakchiuma
Chacrow *see* Coos
Chacsihoma *see* Chakchiuma
Chacsihooma *see* Chakchiuma
Chacta *see* Choctaw
Chactah *see* Choctaw
Chactany *see* Choctaw
Chactaw *see* Choctaw
Chactchi-Ouma *see* Chakchiuma
Chactiouma *see* Chakchiuma
Chactoo [LA] (H)
Chactot *see* Chatot
Chacxouma *see* Chakchiuma
Chadadoquis *see* Kadohadacho
Chadeca *see* Cadecha
Chafalote [NM] *Apache* (H)
Chafan *see* Tsanchifin
Chaganons *see* Shawnee
Chageluk settlements *see* Jugel-
nute
Chagindueftei [OR] *Atfalati* (H)
Chagnet *see* Chugnut
Chagnutt *see* Chugnut
Chagoteo *Caduveo* (O)
Chagu *Yankton* (H)
Chaguan (Hdbk10) *see also*
Siaguan (BE)
Chaguan *Warrau* (O)
Chaguanaco *see* Chiriguano
Chaguane *see* Chiriguano
Chaguanguano *see* Akanaquint
Chaguanos *see* Shawnee
Chaguantapam *Coahuiltecan* (BE)
Chaguena [Lang] [CR] *Talaman-
can* (O)
Chagustapa *Coahuiltecan* (BE)
Chaguyenne *see* Cheyenne
Chahalis [WA] *Coast Salish* (LC)
Chahcowah (H) *see also* Charcowa
(H)
Chahcowah [OR] *Clowwewalla*
(Oregon)
Chahelim [OR] *Atfalati* (H)
Chahiksi-chahik [Self-
designation] *see* Pawnee
Chahiksichahiks *see* Pawnee
Chahis *see* Cree
Chah-ra-rat *see* Dakota
Chahrarat *see* Dakota
Chah-shm *see* Apache

chahshm *see* Apache
Cha'hta *see* Choctaw
Chah'ta *see* Choctaw
Chahta *see* Choctaw
Chahtulelpi [BC] *Salish* (H)
Chahuginde *see* Rancheria of El
Ligero
Chaic-cles-aht *see* Chaicclesaht
Chaicclesaht [VanI] *Nootka* (BE)
Chaienne *see* Cheyenne
Chaikikarachada [Clan] *Win-
nebago* (H)
Chailkitkaituh *see* Chail-kut-kai-
tuh
Chail-kut-kai-tuh (Contri, v.3,
p.73)
Chai-nim-ai-ni *see* Choinumni
Chainimaini *see* Choinumni
Chaizra [Clan] *Hopi* (H)
Chak [Phratry] *Tlingit* (H)
Chakaiha *see* Chickasaw
Chakankni [OR] *Molala* (BE)
Chakchiuma [MS] (BE)
Chake *see* Motilon
Chake *see* Yukpa
Chakeipi [OR] *Atfalati* (H)
Chakhtogmut *see* Shaktoligmiut
Chakobo *see* Chacobo
Chaktaw *see* Choctaw
Chakutpaliu [OR] *Atfalati* (H)
Chakwaina *Hopi* (H)
Chala [Can] (H)
Chalakee *see* Cherokee
Chalakki *see* Cherokee
Chalal [OR] *Atfalati* (H)
Chalam *see* Clallam
Chalaque *see* Cherokee
Chalaquies *see* Cherokee
Chalawai [OR] *Atfalati* (H)
Chalchuapa [MX] *Pokomam* (BE)
Chaliva (BE) *see also* Northern
Guaymi (O)
Chaliva *Guaymi* (BE)
Challenge [Lang] *Konkow* (CA-8)
Chalon [CA] *Costanoan* (H)
Chalon [Lang] *Northern
Costonoan* (CA-8)
Chalone *see* Chalon
Chalosas (H)
Chalta *see* Choctaw
Chalula *see* Chilula
Chama *see* Sipibo
Chama *Tacanan* *see* Ese Ejja
Chamacoco [BO, Par] (LC)
Chamak *see* Tsamak
Chamakoko [Lang] *see* Chama-
coco
Chamalquay *see* Chimalakwe
Chamampit [OR] *Atfalati* (H)
Chambira *see* Urarina
Chambirino *see* Urarina
Chamelcon [Hon] (BE)
Chamers *see* Santsukhdhin

Chami [Col] *Embera* (LC)
Chamicolo *see* Chamicuro
Chamicura *see* Chamicuro
Chamicuro [PE] (O)
Chamifu [OR] *Santiam* (BE)
Chamifu [OR] *Yamel* (BE)
Chamila *see* Chimila
Chamiwi [OR] *Yamel* (BE)
Chamkhai [CA] *Pomo* (H)
Chamna'pum *see* Chamnapum
Chamnapum [WA] *Wanapam* (BE)
Chamoappan *see* Shanwappom
Champikle [OR] *Yamel* (BE)
Chamula *see* Tzotzil
Chana (H) *see also* Sana (BE)
Chana [Lang] *Charna* (LC)
Chana [Self-designation] (O) *see also* Tereno (LC)
Chanabal [Gu, MX] (LC)
Chañabal [Lang] [CA] (Bull44)
Chanabale *see* Chanabal
Chana-Bohave [Br] *Tereno* (O)
Chanaguan *see* Siaguan
Chana-Mbegua [Br] *Tereno* (O)
Chana-Timbu [Br] *Tereno* (O)
Chanatya [Clan] *Keres* (H)
Chanatya-hano *see* Chanatya
Chanca [PE] (LC)
Chancay culture [PE] (LC)
Chances *see* Santsukhdhin
Chanchampenau *see* Chanchampeneau
Chanchampeneau [OR] *Santiam* (BE)
Chanchantu [OR] *Santiam* (BE)
Chanco *see* Aymara
Chanco [Lang] *see* Waunana
Chancre *see* Lipan Apache
Chandalar Kutchin *see* Natsitkutchin
Chandinahua (LC) *see also* Sharanahua (LC)
Chandinahua (O) *see also* Shahindawa (O)
Chandinahua *Jaminaua* (O)
Cha-ne *see* Chaui
Chane *see* Tereno
Chane *see* Chaui
Chane [Lang] [BO, Par] *Maipurean* (LC)
Chaneabal *see* Chanabal
Chaneers *see* Santsukhdhin
Chanes *see* Sana
Cha-net-kai *see* Shnalkeya
Chanetkai *see* Shnalkeya
Changa *see* Chanca
Chang Doa *see* Kang
Chango [CH] (O)
Changuaguane *see* Akanaquint
Changuena [CR, Pan] (BE)
Changuina *see* Changuena
Chan Han *see* Chiricahua Apache

Chanhan *see* Chiricahua Apache
Chaniers band *see* Santsukhdhin
Chaninawa *see* Chandinahua
Chanka *see* Chanca
Chankaghaotina *Wahpeton* (H)
Chankaokhan *Hunkpapa* (H)
Chankute *Sisseton* (H)
Chanona *Upper Yanktonai* (H)
Chanousanons *see* Shawnee
Chansdachikana *Sisseton* (H)
Chanshushka *see* Chansuushka
Chan-shu-shka *see* Chansuushka
Chansuushka *Dakota* (BE)
Chan-ta-ko-da *see* Hupa
Chantakoda *see* Hupa
Chan-ta-ko-ta *see* Cheindekhotding
Chantakota *see* Cheindekhotding
Chantapeta's Band *Sioux* (H)
Chantaquiro [Lang] *Arawakan* (LC)
Chantkaip [OR] *Santiam* (BE)
Chanundadies *see* Tionontati
Chanwappan *see* Shanwappom
Chanzes *see* Lipan Apache
Chaoenne *see* Cheyenne
Chaoenon *see* Shawnee
Chaoesnon *see* Shawnee
Chaonanons *see* Shawnee
Chaoni *see* Shawnee
Chaonists *see* Chowanoc
Chaouacha [LA, MS] (H)
Chaouannon *see* Shawnee
Chaouanon *see* Shawnee
Chaouanong *see* Shawnee
Chaouanonronon *see* Shawnee
Chaouanons *see* Shawnee
Chaouanoua *see* Shawnee
Chaouans *see* Shawnee
Chaouen *see* Shawnee
Chaouennon *see* Shawnee
Chaouenon *see* Shawnee
Chaounon *see* Shawnee
Chaouoinon *see* Shawnee
Chaovanon *see* Shawnee
Chaovenon *see* Shawnee
Chaowanon *see* Shawnee
Chapa *see* Shapra
Chapacura *see* Txapakura
Chapagera [Hon] (BE)
Chapagua [Hon] *Nahuatl* (BE)
Chapakura *see* Txapakura
Cha'palaachi *see* Cayapa
Chapalaachi *see* Cayapa
Chapamaco *Coahuiltecan* (BE)
Chapanaghtin [OR] *Atfalati* (H)
Chapanec *see* Chiapanec
Chapaqua [Hon] *Nahuatl* (O)
Cha'parahihu *see* Hupa
Chaparahihu *see* Hupa
Chaparro *see* Yukpa
Chaplinski (Hdbk5) *see also* Central Siberian Yupik (Hdbk5)

Chaplinski [Lang] *Siberian Eskimos* (Hdbk5)
Chaplintsy *see* Chaplinski
Chapokele [OR] *Atafalati* (H)
Chapopine *see* Chayopin
Chapopines *see* Tiopines
Chapoteños *Coahuiltecan* (Hdbk10)
Chappunish *see* Nez Perce
Chapra *see* Shapra
Chaptico *see* Conoy
Chapticoe *see* Choptank
Chapticon [MD] (H)
Chapulines *Coahuiltecan* (Hdbk10)
Chapungathpi [OR] *Atfalati* (H)
Chaquantie [LA] *Caddo Confederacy* (H)
Chaque *see* Yukpa
Chaque [Lang] *Motilon* (UAz, v.28)
Chaquesauma *see* Chakchiuma
Chaqueta *see* Choctaw
Chaquita *see* Choctaw
Cha-ra *see* Chaikikarachada
Chara *see* Chaikikarachada
Charabana *see* Echoaladi
Charac *see* Cheraw
Characuay *Coahuiltecan* (Hdbk10)
Charah *see* Cheraw
Charakee *see* Cherokee
Charakey *see* Cherokee
Charame *see* Xarame
Charankoua *see* Karankawa
Charanon *see* Shawnee
Charca [BO] *Aymara* (BE)
Charcawah *see* Charcowa
Char-cheine *see* Satchin
Charcheine *see* Satchin
Charcowa [OR] *Clowwewalla* (H)
Charcowah *see* Charcowa
Chargeurs *see* Takulli
Charibbs *see* Carib
Charikee *see* Cherokee
Charioquois *see* Huron
Charitica *see* Arapaho
Charokee *see* Cherokee
Charraw *see* Cheraw
Charrom *see* Xarame
Charrow *see* Cheraw
Charrua [Lang] [Ur, Arg, Br] (LC)
Charrua [Ur, Arg, Br] (LC)
Charrua-Minvan *see* Charrua
Charruan *see* Charrua
Charucco *see* Chorruco
Chascoso *see* Campa
Chaskpe [IL] (H)
Chasmu'na *see* Chasmuna
Chasmuna *Dakota* (BE)
Chaspa *see* Atsahuaca
Chasta (H) *see also* Shasta (CA)
Chasta [OR] *Umpqua* (H)

Chasta band of the Rogue Rivers
 see Chasta
Chastacosta (H) *see also* Shis-
 takoostee (H)
Chasta-Costa *see* Chastacosta
Chastacosta [OR] (BE)
Chasta-Scotan *see* Chasta-
 Skoton
Chasta Scoten *see* Chasta-Skoton
Chasta Scoton *see* Chasta-Skoton
Chasta-Skoton [OR] (H)
Chastay *see* Chasta
Chasunous *see* Shawnee
Chasutino [PE] (O)
Chata *see* Chala
Chataba *see* Catawba
Chatagithl [OR] *Atfatali* (H)
Chatagshish [OR] *Atfalati* (H)
Chataka *see* Choctaw
Chatakuin [OR] *Atfalati* (H)
Chatamnei [OR] *Atfalati* (H)
Chataw *see* Choctaw
Chatilkuei [OR] *Atfalati* (H)
Chatino [Lang] [MX] (Bull44)
Chatino [MX] *Zapotec* (LC)
Chat-Ka *see* Choctaw
Chatkaw *see* Choctaw
Chato [MX] *Matagalpa* (BE)
Chatot [FL] (BE)
Chats *see* Erie
Chats-hadai [AK] *Koeta* (H)
Chatsop *see* Clatsop
Chatta *see* Choctaw
Chattoes *see* Choctaw
Chattoo *see* Chactoo
Chauanon *see* Shawnee
Chaucha *see* Chaouacha
Chauchila *see* Chawchila
Chau-chil-la *see* Chowchilla
Chau-chil-la *see* Chawchila
Chauchilla *see* Chawchila
Chaudiere *see* Colville
Chauenese *see* Shawnee
Chauenous *see* Shawnee
Chaugane *see* Chaguan
Chaugueronon *see* Montagnais-
 Naskapi
Chau-i *see* Chaui
Chaui [NB] *Pawnee* (BE)
Chaulamas *see* Xarame
Chaumene *see* Jumano
Chaunis *see* Shawnee
Chaunundadies *see* Wyandot
Chaunys *see* Shawnee
Chaushila [CA] *Yokuts* (H)
Chavanon *see* Shawnee
Chavante *see* Akwe-Shavante
Chavante *see* Akwe
Chavante *see* Xavante
Chavante Acuan *see* Akwe-
 Shavante
Chavante-Akwe *see* Akwe-
 Shavante

Chavavares *see* Avavares
Chavin culture [PE] (LC)
Chavite [AR] *Southern Caddo* (H)
Chavouanon *see* Shawnee
Chawache *see* Chaouacha
Chawack *see* Cheewack
Chawagis-stustae *Stusta* (H)
Chawano *see* Chowanoc
Chawanock *see* Chowanoc
Chawanoes *see* Shawnee
Chawanoke *see* Chowanoc
Chawanon *see* Shawnee
Chawanook *see* Chowanoc
Chawari *see* Tsawarii
Chawas *see* Cheyenne
Chawasha [LA] (BE)
Chawayed [OR] *Atfalati* (H)
Chawchila [CA] (CA-8)
Cha-we *see* Chaui
Chawe *see* Chaui
Chawenon *see* Shawnee
Chaweta *see* Choctaw
Chawi *see* Pawnee
Chawi *see* Chayahuita
Chawon *see* Chowanoc
Chawonack *see* Chowanoc
Chawonest *see* Chowanoc
Chawonoack *see* Chowanoc
Chawonock *see* Chowanoc
Chawonok *see* Chowanoc
Chawoon *see* Chowanoc
Chawraw *see* Cheraw
Chawwonock *see* Chowanoc
Chawwonoke *see* Chowanoc
Chayabita *see* Chayahuita
Chayahuita [PE] (LC)
Chayahuite *see* Chayahuita
Chayankeld [OR] *Yoncalla* (BE)
Chayanne Indians *see* Oglala
Chayavita (O) *see also* Chayahuita
 (LC)
Chayavita [Lang] [PE] *Jeberoan*
 (O)
Chayawita *see* Chayahuita
Chayenne *see* Cheyenne
Chayhuita *see* Chayahuita
Chaykisaht *see* Chaicclessaht
Chayma [Lang] *Tamanaco* (UAz,
 v.28)
Chayopin [TX] *Tonkawa* (H)
Chayopines *see* Tiopines
Chea *see* Sia
Chealis *see* Chehalis
Cheaptin *see* Nez Perce
Chearhaw *see* Chiaha
Cheattee [OR] *Tutuni* (H)
Che-baah-ah-bish *see*
 Chobaabish
Chebaahahbish *see* Chobaabish
Chebaylis *see* Chehalis
Cheberbo *see* Jebero
Chebero-Munichi *see* Parana-
 pura

Cheboigan *see* Cheboygan
Chebois *see* Chippewa
Chebonte [CA] (H)
Cheboygan [MI] *Ottawa* (H)
Checaldish *see* Chehalis
Checalish *see* Chehalis
Checepiok *see* Chesapeake
Chechehet [Lang] *Pampas* (LC)
Chechili *see* Chehalis
Chechohomynaies *see* Chicka-
 hominy
Chechohomynies *see* Chicka-
 hominy
Chechotank *see* Kecoughtan
Checka Hamania *see* Chicia-
 hominy
Checkahomanies *see* Chicka-
 hominy
Checkesaw *see* Chickasaw
Checklesit *see* Chaicclesaht
Che-com *see* Shigom
Checom *see* Shigom
Chectaw *see* Choctaw
Chedaik *see* Shediac
Che-dong-ga *see* Chedunga
Chedongga *see* Chedunga
Chedtokhanye [Clan] *Arukhwa II*
 (H)
Chedtoyine [Clan] *Arukhwa II*
 (H)
Chedunga [Clan] *Kansa* (H)
Cheecer Ree *see* Brule
Chee-Chinook [Lang] *see* Chi-
 nookan jargon
Cheehalis *see* Chehalis
Cheelake *see* Cherokee
Cheelcat *see* Chilkat
Cheelhaat *see* Chilkat
Cheelkaat *see* Chilkat
Chee-luck-kit-le-quaw *see*
 Chilluckittequaw
Cheeluckkitlequaw *see*
 Chilluckittequaw
Cheenalies *see* Chehalis
Cheenook *see* Chinook
Cheerake *see* Cherokee
Cheerakee *see* Cherokee
Cheeraque *see* Cherokee
Cheerns [VanI] *Songish* (H)
Cheerokee *see* Cherokee
Cheesecake *see* Chiskiac
Cheesehahchamuk [MA]
 Wampanoag (BE)
Cheewack [BC] *Salish* (H)
Chee-zhoo *see* Tsishuutseped-
 hungpa
Cheezhoo *see* Tsishuutseped-
 hungpa
Chee-zhoo peace-makers *see*
 Tsishuwashtake
Cheezhoo peace-makers *see*
 Tsishuwashtake
Cheghita [Clan] *Iowa* (H)

Cheghita [Clan] *Missouri* (H)
Cheghita [Clan] *Oto* (H)
Chegnakeokisela *Hunkpapa* (H)
Chegua *see* Tigua
Cheguas *see* Tiwa
Chegwalis [Clan] *Abnaki* (H)
Chehales *see* Chehalis [Can]
Chehalis [Can] *Stalo* (BE)
Chehaw *see* Chiaha
Chehaylis *see* Chehalis
Cheh-chewe-hem *see* Chuchu-
    nayha
Chehchewehem *see* Chuchu-
    nayha
Chehelim *see* Chahelim
Chehelu [Clan] *Timucua* (H)
Cheh-he-ta *see* Cheghita
Chehheta *see* Cheghita
Chehokette *see* Chettrokettle
Chehuelchu *see* Tehuelche
Cheikikarachada [Gens] *Win-
    nebago* (H)
Chein *Pueblo Indians* (H)
Cheindekhotding (H)
Chekahomanies *see* Chicka-
    hominy
Chekalis *see* Chehalis
Chekasaw *see* Chickasaw
Chekasschee *see* Skaischiltnish
Chekhuhaton *Oglala* (H)
Chekilis *see* Chehalis
Che-kiss-chee *see* Skaischiltnish
Chekisschee *see* Skaischiltnish
Chekohomini *see* Cjickahominy
Chekwa [Clan] *Potawatomi* (H)
Chel-a-ke *see* Cherokee
Chelakee *see* Cherokee
Chelamela [OR] (BE)
Chelan [WA] *Middle Columbia
    River Salish* (Hdbk12)
Chelaque *see* Cherokee
Chelekee *see* Cherokee
Cheli [Clan] *Hano* (H)
Cheli [Clan] *Tewa* (H)
Chelibas (O) *see also* Changuena
    (BE)
Chelibas [CR] (O)
Chelkatskie *see* Chilkat
Chellicothee *see* Chillicothe
Chellokee *see* Cherokee
Cheloculgee *see* Cherokee
Chelokee *see* Cherokee
Chelouel *see* Natchez
Che-luc-it-te-quaw *see*
    Chilluckittequaw
Chelucittequaw *see* Chilluckitte-
    quaw
Che-luck-kit-ti-quar *see*
    Chilluckittequaw
Cheluckkittiquar *see* Chilluckit-
    tequaw
Chelukamanche *see* Luckiamute
Chelukimauke *see* Luckiamute

Che-ma-hua-va *see* Chemehuevi
Chemahuava *see* Chemehuevi
Chemahuevi *see* Chemehuevi
Chem-a-hue-vi *see* Chemehuevi
Chema-keem *see* Chimakum
Chemakeem *see* Chimakum
Chemakeum *see* Chimakum
Chemakum *see* Chimakum
Chem-a-kum *see* Chimakum
Chem-a-pho *see* Chemapho
Chemapho *Kalapuya* (H)
Che-ma-wa-wa *see* Chemehuevi
Chemawawa *see* Chemehuevi
Chemchuevi *see* Chemehuevi
Chemebat *see* Chemehuevi
Chemebat Quajala *see* Paiute
Chemebet *see* Chemehuevi
Chemegeraba *see* Chemehuevi
Chemeguaba *see* Chemehuevi
Chemeguabas Sevintas *see* Shiv-
    wits
Chemeguagua *see* Chemehuevi
Chemeguava *see* Chemehuevi
Chemegué *see* Southern Paiute
Chemegue *see* Chemehuevi
Chemegue Cajuala *see* Paiute
Chemegue Cuajala *see* Paiute
Chemegue-sevicta *see* Shivwits
Chemegue Sevinta *see* Shivwits
Chemeguet Cajuala *see* Paiute
Chemehnevi *see* Chemehuevi
Chem-e-hue-vi *see* Chemehuevi
Chemehuevi [CA] *Southern Paiute*
    (LC)
Chemehuevi [Lang] *Shoshonean*
    (H)
Chem-e-hue-vitz *see* Cheme-
    huevi
Chemehuevitz *see* Chemehuevi
Chemehuewa *see* Chemehuevi
Chemeketa [OR] *Kalapuya* (H)
Chemeonaha *see* Chemehuevi
Chemequaba *see* Chemehuevi
Chemeque *see* Chemehuevi
Chemeque-caprala *see* Paiute
Chemetunne *see* Yahshute
Chemicum *see* Chimakum
Chemiguabo *see* Chemehuevi
Chemiheavi *see* Chemehuevi
Chemihuahua *see* Chemehuevi
Chemihuara *see* Chemehuevi
Chemihuave *see* Chemehuevi
Chemihueva *see* Chemehuevi
Chemihuevi *see* Chemehuevi
Cheminare *see* Chemehuevi
Chemmesyan *see* Chimmesyan
Chemoco *Coahuiltecan* (LC)
Chemonchovanistes *see*
    Chomonchouaniste
Chemovi *see* Sichomovi
Chenachaath *Toquart* (H)
Chenakisses *see* Chiakanessou
Chenandoanes *see* Seneca

Chêniers *see* Santsukhdhin
Chenku *see* Chonque
Chenondadees *see* Tionontati
Chenondadees *see* Wyandot
Chenook *see* Chinook
Chenook *see* Choynok
Chenoux *see* Chinook
Chenoya *see* Atsugewi
Chenoyana *see* Atsugewi
Chen-po-sel *see* Chenposel
Chenposel [CO] *Patwin* (H)
Chenuke *see* Chinook
Chenundaddey *see* Wyandot
Chenundady *see* Tionontati
Chenundady *see* Wyandot
Chenundies *see* Tionontati
Cheokee *see* Cherokee
Cheokhba *Hunkpapa* (BE)
Chepalis *see* Copalis
Chepawa *see* Chippewa
Che-pa-wy-an *see* Chipewyan
Chepawyan *see* Chipewyan
Chepayan *see* Chipewyan
Chepecho *see* Pamunkey
Chepeco *see* Cattachiptico
Chepenafa [OR] (BE)
Chep-en-a-pho *see* Chepenafa
Chepenapho *see* Chepenafa
Chepeo *see* Sipibo
Chepewa *see* Chippewa
Chepeway *see* Chippewa
Chepewayan *see* Chipewyan
Chepewyan *see* Chipewyan
Chepeyan *see* Chipewyan
Chepo *see* Cuna
Chepo *see* San Blas
Cheponssea *see* Chepoussa
Chépontia *see* Chepoussa
Cheposhkeyine *Arukhwa II* (H)
Chepousca *see* Chepoussa
Chepouscia *see* Chepoussa
Chepoussa *Illinois* (H)
Chepoussea *see* Chepoussa
Chepowa *see* Chippewa
Cheppewe *see* Chippewa
Cheppewyan *see* Chipewyan
Cheppeyan *see* Chipewyan
Chequelcho *see* Tehuelche
Chequiack *see* Chiskiac
Cheraguee *see* Cherokee
Cherahe *see* Cherokee
Cherakee *see* Cherokee
Cheraki *see* Cherokee
Cheraquee *see* Cherokee
Cheraqui *see* Cherokee
Cheraw [Lang] *Eastern Siouan*
    (H)
Cheraw [NC] (LC)
Cherecaquis *see* Chiricahua
    Apache
Cherechos *see* Keres
Cherente *see* Sherente
Cherermon *see* Shawnee

Cheres *see* Keres
Chericahui *see* Chiricahua
  Apache
Cherickee *see* Cherokee
Cherikee *see* Cherokee
Cheroenhaka [Self-designation]
  see Nottoway
Che-ro-ho-ka *see* Nottoway
Cherohoka *see* Nottoway
Cherokee [Lang] *Konkow* (CA-8)
Cherokee [TN, GA, AL] (LC)
Cheroki *see* Cherokee
Cherookee *see* Cherokee
Cheroquee *see* Cherokee
Cherrackee *see* Cherokee
Cherrokee *see* Cherokee
Cherrykee *see* Cherokee
Chesapeach *see* Chesapeake
Chesapeake [VA] *Powhatan* (BE)
Chesapeiack *see* Chesapeake
Chesapeian *see* Chesapeake
Chescaik *see* Chiskiac
Chescheak *see* Chiskiac
Chesepian *see* Chesapeake
Chesepioock *see* Chesapeake
Chesepiuc *see* Chesapeake
Che-shap *see* Navajo
Cheshap *see* Navajo
Che-she-gwa *see* Kenabig
Cheshegwa *see* Kenabig
Cheskyake *see* Chiskiac
Chester Valley Indians *see* Shasta
Chestes *see* Shasta
Chesthltishtun [Gens] [CA]
  Tolowa (H)
Chetac Lake [MI] *Chippewa* (H)
Cheta-ut-tdinne *see* Etchareottine
Chetauttdinne *see* Etchareottine
Cheta-ut-tinee *see* Tsetautkenne
Chetauttinne *see* Tsetautkenne
Chetco (H) *see also* Cheattee (H)
Chetco [Or, CA] (LC)
Chetemacha *see* Chitimacha
Chethl' *see* Chak
Cheticnewash *see* Chititiknewas
Chetimacha *see* Chitimacha
Chetkoe *see* Chetco
Chetleschantunne [OR] *Tututni*
  (BE)
Chetl-e-shin *see* Chetleschan-
  tunne
Chetleshin *see* Chetleschantunne
Chetlesiyetunne *see* Chetleschan-
  tunne
Chetlessentan *see* Chetlessentun
Chetlessenten *see* Chetlessentun
Chet-less-en-tun *see*
  Chetleschantunne
Chetlessentun [OR] *Tututni* (H)
Chet-less-in-gen *see*
  Chetleschantunne
Chetlessingen *see* Chetleschan-
  tunne

Cheto Kette *see* Chettrokettle
Chetro Ketl *see* Chettrokettle
Chetro Ketle *see* Chettrokettle
Chettro-Kettle *see* Chettrokettle
Chettrokettle [NM] *Pueblo Indi-
  ans* (H)
Cheueux ou poils leue *see* Ot-
  tawa
Cheueux releues *see* Ottawa
Cheveriches *see* Seuvarits
Chevet *see* Shivwits
Cheveux leves *see* Missisauga
Cheveux relevez *see* Missisauga
Che-wae-rae *see* Oto
Chewaerae *see* Oto
Chewelah [ID] *Kalispel* (BE)
Chewenee (H) SE Choinumni
  (CA)
Cheyenne [Lang] *Arapaho* (Pub,
  v.12, no.3, p.73)
Cheyenne [SD] (LC)
Cheyenne River Sioux (LC)
Cheyinye [Clan] *Arukhwa II* (H)
Chez-ye-na *see* Tzecheschinne
Chia *see* Chua
Chia *see* Sia
Chiaas *see* Ais
Chiabel-na-poma *see* Kelispoma
Chiacantefous *see* Chiakanessou
Chiacasa *see* Chickasaw
Chiachi-Oumo *see* Chakchiume
Chiagmiut [Lang] *Eskimo* (Bull1)
Chiaguan *see* Siaguan
Chiaha [GA] (BE)
Chiahnesou *see* Chikanessou
Chiakanessou (H)
Chiamacoco *see* Chamacoco
Chian *see* Cheyenne
Chiaouenon *see* Shawnee
Chiapanec [MX] (LC)
Chiapanecan [Lang] (BE)
Chiapas *see* Chiapanec
Chiappawaw *see* Chippewa
Chias *see* Ais
Chi'a-tai'na *see* Chiataina
Chiataina [Clan] [NM] *Taos* (H)
Chibcha [Col] (LC) Chibchan
  [Lang] (LC)
Chibchan Indians *see* Chibcha
Chibois *see* Chippewa
Chicaca *see* Chickasaw
Chicacha *see* Chickasaw
Chicacho *see* Chickasaw
Chicahamanias *see* Chicka-
  hominy
Chicama *see* Halyikwamai
Chicana *see* Hoti
Chicaraguis *see* Chiricahua
  Apache
Chicasa *see* Chickasaw
Chicasan *see* Chickasaw
Chicasauns *see* Chickasaw
Chicasaw *see* Chickasaw

Chicasou *see* Chickasaw
Chicassa *see* Chickasaw
Chicawchaw *see* Chickasaw
Chicaza *see* Chickasaw
Chicconessick *see* Chiconessex
Chichaca *see* Chickasaw
Chichacha *see* Chickasaw
Chichasau *see* Chickasaw
Chichasaw *see* Chickasaw
Chichasha *see* Chickasaw
Chichava *see* Hoti
Chichedec *see* Chisedec
Chichedek *see* Chisedec
Chichequaa *see* Rancoca
Chichigoue *Algonquian* (H)
Chichigouek *see* Chichigoue
Chichilli *see* Chilili *Tigua*
Chichimec *see* Chichimecs
Chichimeca [Lang] [MX]
  (Bull44)
Chichimeca Indians *see*
  Chichimecs
Chichimeca-Jonaz [MX] (LC)
Chichimeco *see* Chichimecs
Chichimecs [MX] (LC)
Chichiti *see* Chilili *Tigua*
Chichominy *see* Chickahominy
Chichuich *see* Pecos
Chickahamanias *see* Chicka-
  hominy
Chickahamine *see* Chickahominy
Chickahomine *see* Chicka-
  hominy
Chickahomini *see* Chickahominy
Chickahominy [VA] *Powhatan
  Confederacy* (BE)
Chickahomone *see* Chicka-
  hominy
Chickahomonie *see* Chicka-
  hominy
Chickakone *see* Secacawoni
Chick-a-lees *see* Chehalis
Chickalees *see* Chehalis
Chickamauga *Cherokee* (H)
Chickanee *see* Wateree
Chickanossous *see* Chiakanessou
Chickasaw [MS] (LC)
Chickassa *see* Chickasaw
Chick-atat *see* Klikitat
Chickatat *see* Klikitat
Chickataubut [MA] *Massacuset*
  (BE)
Chickcahomaniacke *see*Chicka-
  hominy
Chickchi (LT, v.10, no.41, p.6)
Chickeeles *see* Chehalis
Chickelis *see* Chehalis
Chicken-hawk *see*
  Khuyeguzhinga
Chickesaw *see* Chickasaw
Chicketaw *see* Chickasaw
Chickiaes *see* Chiskiac
Chickisaw *see* Chickasaw

Chickitat *see* Klikitat

Chicksah *see* Chickasaw

Chickshau *see* Chickasaw

Chicktaghicks *see* Illinois

Chicktaw *see* Choctaw

Chico [CA] *Maidu* (Pub, v.33, no.2, 1932/34)

Chicoa *see* Chiricoa

Chicocoan *see* Secacawoni

Chicohominies *see* Chicka-hominy

Chicomuceltec [Lang] [MX] *Huastec* (BE)

Chicomuceltec [MX] *Mayoid* (BE)

Chicomucelteca [Lang] *see* Chicomuceltec

Chiconamians *see* Chickahominy

Chiconessex (H) *see also* Siconesse (BE)

Chiconessex *Accomac* (Hdbk15)

Chicora (H) *see also* Cusabo (BE)

Chicora [SC] (H)

Chicoria *see* Chicora

Chicorie *see* Chicora

Chicous [Br] (LC)

Chicoutimi [Can] [*Montagnais-Naskapi*] (BE)

Chictaghicks *see* Illinois

Chictaw *see* Choctaw

Chidikaagu *see* Chiricahua Apache

Chiduma *see* Alchedoma

Chidumas *see* Halchidhoma

Chi-e *see* Chie

Chi-e *see* Warm Springs Apache

Chie *Chiricahua Apache* (H)

Chien *see* Cheyenne

Chien-Flancs *see* Thlingchadinne

Chienne *see* Cheyenne

Chigasaw *see* Chickasaw

Chigilousa (H)

Chigilousa (H) *see also* Chiti-macha (LC)

Chiglit *see* Kopagmiut

Chiglit [Lang] *see* Mackenzie River Delta

Chiglit Inuvialuktun [Lang] *Western Canada* (Hdbk5)

Chigmiut [AK] *Chugatchigmut* (H)

Chigmut *see* Chigmiut

Chigoula *see* Chicora

Chigtaghcicks *see* Illinois

Chigua *see* Tigua

Chiguan *see* Siaguan

Chiguas *see* Tiwa

Chiguicagui *see* Chiricahua Apache

Chihales *see* Chehalis

Chihalis *see* Chehalis

Chiheeleesh *see* Chehalis

Chiheeles *see* Chehalis

Chihelish *see* Chehalis

Chihenne *see* Chi-hen-ne

Chi-hen-ne *Warm Springs Apache* (Hdbk10)

Chihochockies *see* Unalachtigo

Chihokokis *see* Unalachtigo

Chiholacki *see* Unalachtigo

Chihupa *Dakota* (H)

Chiihende *Mescalero Apache* (Hdbk10)

Chikacha *see* Chickasaw

Chikahominy *see* Chickahominy

Chikailish *see* Chehalis

Chikaka *see* Chickasaw

Chikalish *see* Chehalis

Chikasah *see* Chickasaw

Chikasaw *see* Chickasaw

Chik'asha *see* Chickasaw

Chikasha *see* Chickasaw

Chikataubut *see* Chickataubut

Chikauach [Can] *Songish* (BE)

Chikchi *see* Siberian Eskimos

Chikeelis *see* Chehalis

Chikelis *see* Chehalis

Chi-ke-lis *see* Chehalis

Chikena [Lang] *Carib* (UAz, v.28)

Chikilishes *see* Chehalis

Chikimini *see* Unalachtigo

Chikini *see* Unalachtigo

Chikiriaba *see* Xakriaba

Chikitaw *see* Chickasaw

Chikkasah *see* Chickasaw

Chikkasaw *see* Chickasaw

Chikkash *see* Chickasaw

Chikkatabak *see* Chickataubut

Chikkesh *see* Chickasaw

Chiklisilkh [WA] [*Chehalis (CS)*] (H)

Chikohoki [DE] *Unalachtigo* (BE)

Chikoilish *see* Chehalis

Chikonapi (H)

Chiksah *see* Chickasaw

Chiktachiks *see* Illinois

Chilaca [PE] *Aguano* (O)

Chilacoffee *see* Chillicothe

Chi-lah-cah-tha *see* Chillicothe

Chilahcahtha *see* Chillicothe

Chilahcahtha *Shawnee* (H)

Chilaka *see* Chilaca

Chi-la-ka-tha *see* Chillicothe

Chilakatha *see* Chillicothe

Chilanga [ES] *Lenca* (BE)

Chilano [LA, TX] (H)

Chilcah *see* Chilkat

Chilcahdilkloge [AZ] *San Carlos Apache* (H)

Chilcak *see* Chilkat

Chilcale *see* Chilkat

Chilcat *see* Chilkat

Chilcate *see* Chilkat

Chilchadilklogue *see* Chilchadilkloge

Chilcotin [BC] (LC)

Chilcotin Mouth Band [BC] *Canyon Shuswap* (Hdbk12)

Chilcow *see* Chiricahua Apache

Chileatin *see* Chilcotin

Chilecago *see* Chiricahua Apache

Chile Cowes *see* Chiricahua Apache

Chilecowes *see* Chiricahua Apache

Chileons *see* Tsiltaden

Chili *see* Chilili [Tigua]

Chilian *see* Tsiltaden

Chilicagua *see* Chiricahua Apache

Chilicague *see* Chiricahua Apache

Chilicoatens *see* Chilcotin

Chilicotens *see* Chilcotin

Chilicothe *see* Chillicothe

Chilicotin *see* Chilcotin

Chilikoffi *see* Chillicothe

Chilile *see* Chilili *Tigua*

Chilili [FL] *Utina* (H)

Chilili *Tigua* (H)

Chililo *see* Chilili *Utina*

Chilily *see* Chilili *Tigua*

Chilily *see* Chilili *Utina*

Chilion *see* Tsiltaden

Chilivik *see* Selawigmiut

Chilkaht *see* Chilkat

Chilkahtkwan *see* Chilkaht-kwan

Chilkaht-tena (H) *see also* Taku-tine (BE)

Chilkaht-tena *Nehaunee* (Contri, v.1, pp.33–34)

Chilkast *see* Chilkat

Chilkat [AK, BC] *Tlingit* (LC)

Chilkat-kwan *Tlingit* (Contri, v.1, p.37)

Chilkat-qwan *see* Chilkat-kwan

Chilkatskoe *see* Chilkat

Chilkhat *see* Chilkat

Chilkho'tenne *see* Chilcotin

Chilko-tin *see* Chilcotin

Chillacothe *see* Chillicothe

Chillates *see* Chehalis

Chillcoatens *see* Chilcotin

Chillicothe (H) *see also* Chilahc-ahtha (H)

Chillicothe [OH, TN] *Shawnee* (BE)

Chillili *see* Chilili *Tigua*

Chilliwack [BC] *Stalo* (LC)

Chilliwack [Lang] *Coastal Salis-han* (CA-8)

Chilliwhack *see* Chilliwack

Chillo Kittequaw *see* Chilluckit-tequaw

Chillokittequaw *see* Chilluckitte-quaw

Chillons *see* Tsiltaden

Chilluckit-te-quaw (Hdbk12) *see also* White Salmon Indians (Hdbk12)

Chilluckittequaw see White
  Salmon Indians
Chilluckittequaw [WA] (BE)
Chilluckkittaquaw see
  Chilluckittequaw
Chil-luck-kit-tequaw see
  Chilluckittequaw
Chilluckkittequaw see
  Chilluckittequaw
Chillukittequa see Chilluckitte-
  quaw
Chillukittequaw see Chilluckitte-
  quaw
Chillukkitequaw see Chilluckit-
  tequaw
Chil-luk-kit-te-quaw see
  Chilluckittequaw
Chillukkittequaw see Chilluckit-
  tequaw
Chillula see Chilula
Chil-lu-la see Chilula
Chillulah see Chilula
Chillulah see Chilula
Chillwayhook see Chilliwack
Chillwayuk see Chilliwack
Chillychandize [OR] Kalapuya (H)
Chilmos see Apaches de Chilmo
Chilocathe see Chillicothe
Chilocotin see Chilcotin
Chilon see Tsiltaden
Chilook see Skilloot
Chiloweyuk see Chilliwack
Chilowhist see Methow
Chilpaines (H) see also Tsihli-
  nainde (H)
Chilpaines Plains Apache
  (Hdbk10)
Chilpanines see Chilpaines
Chiltneyadnaye [AZ] Apache (H)
Chiltokin see Chilcotin
Chilts see Chehalis
Chiltz see Chehalis
Chilucan [FL] Timucua (BE)
Chilukki see Cherokee
Chilu'ktkwa see Chilluckitte-
  quaw
Chiluktkwa see Chilluckittequaw
Chilukweyuk see Chilliwack
Chilula [CA] (LC)
Chilula [OR] Umpqua (H)
Chil-way-uk see Chilliwack
Chilwayuk see Chilliwack
Chimacu see Urarina
Chimacum see Chimakum
Chim-a-kim see Chimakum
Chimakim see Chimakum
Chimaku see Urarina
Chimakuan [Lang] (BE)
Chima-kum see Chimakum
Chimakum [WA] (BE)
Chi-mal-a-kwe see Chimalakwe
Chimalakwe (Pub, v.5, no.4,
  p.296) see also Chimariko (LC)

Chimalakwe [CA] (H)
Chimalaquay see Chimalakwe
Chimalpa see Zoque
Chimane [BO] (LC)
Chimanisa see Chimane
Chimarikan [Lang] [CA] (H)
Chim-a-ri-ko see Chimariko
Chimariko [CA] (LC)
Chimawava see Chemehuevi
Chimbuiha [OR] Molala (BE)
Chimchinve see Chemehuevi
Chimedoc see Chumidok
Chimehueva see Chemehuevi
Chimehueve see Chemehuevi
Chimehwhuebe see Chemehuevi
Chimewawas of Arizona see
  Chemehuevi
Chimheva see Chemehuevi
Chimicum see Chimakum
Chim-i-dok see Chumteya
Chim-i-dok see Cumidok
Chimidok see Chumidok
Chimidok see Chumteya
Chimigae see Shimigae
Chi-mi-hua-hua see Chemehuevi
Chimihuahua see Chemehuevi
Chimila [Col] (O)
Chimile see Chimila
Chimmesyan [AK, BC] (LC)
Chim-nah-pan see Chimnapum
Chimnahpan see Chimnapum
Chim-nah-pum see Chimnapum
Chimnahpum see Chimnapum
Chim-nah-pun see Chimnapum
Chimnahpun see Chimnapum
Chimnapoo see Chimnapum
Chimna-pum see Chimnapum
Chimnapum [WA] Paloos (BE)
Chimnapun see Chimnapum
Chimohueois see Chemehuevi
Chimook see Chinook
Chimopovi see Shongopavi
Chimopovy see Shongopavi
Chimpsain see Tsimshian
Chimseyan see Tsimshian
Chimsyan see Chimmesyan
Chimteya see Chumteya
Chimu [Lang] [PE] Paezan (LC)
Chim-ue-hue-va see Cheme-
  huevi
Chimuehueva see Chemehuevi
Chim-woy-o see Chemehuevi
Chimwoyo see Chemehuevi
Chin see Takulli
China Hat [Lang] [Can] Heiltsuk
  (H)
Chin-a Ka-na Tze-shu-ma see
  Pueblo Caja del Rio
Chin-a-kum see Chimakum
Chinantec [MX] (LC)
Chinantecan [Lang] [MX] (LC)
Chinantee see Chinantec
Chinarihuan see Simariguan

Chinarra [MX] Concho (BE)
Chincal see Chinchal
Chinchal [OR] Yamel (BE)
Chine [FL] Chatot (BE)
Chine-a-kum see Chimakum
Chinga see Cayuga
Chingigmiut [AK] Eskimos (BE)
Chingoteague see Pocomoke
Chingwawateick see Conoy
Chingwoatyke see Conoy
Chin-hook see Chinook
Chinhook see Chinook
Chininoas see Cahinnio
Chinipa (H) see also Varohio (BE)
Chinipa [MX] (BE)
Chinkakum see Chimakum
Chinko Illinois (H)
Chinkoa see Chinko
Chinloes see Natliatin
Chinnahpum see Chimnapum
Chin-na-pum see Chimnapum
Chinnapum see Chimnapum
Chin Nation see Lillooet
Chin-nook see Chinook
Chinnook see Chinook
Chinock see Chinook
Chin ook see Chinook
Chinook (LC) see also Choynok
  (CA)
Chinook [WA] (LC)
Chinookan [Lang] [WA] (LC)
Chinookan Indians see Chinook
Chinookan jargon (LC)
Chinouk see Chinook
Chinoun see Hopi
Chin-poo see North Thompson
  Band
Chinpoo see North Thompson
  Band
Chintagottine [Can] Kawchottine
  (BE)
Chinuc see Chinook
Chinuk see Chinook
Chinunga [Clan] Hopi (H)
Chiouanon see Shawnee
Chipawa see Chippewa
Chipawawa see Chippewa
Chipaway see Chippewa
Chipaweigh see Chippewa
Chipaya [BO] (LC)
Chipaynes see Chipaines
Chipeo see Sipibo
Chipeouaian see Chipewyan
Chipewa see Chippewa
Chipewan see Chipewyan
Chipeway see Chipewyan
Chipeway see Chippewa
Chipewayan see Chipewyan
Chipewegh see Chippewa
Chipewigh see Chippewa
Chipewyan [Can] (LC)
Chipewyan People see
  Tcipoaian-winiuuk

Chipewyan Tinney *see* Chipewyan

Chipio *see* Sipibo

Chipiouan *see* Chipewyan

Chipiwa *see* Chippewa

Chipoes *see* Chippewa

Chipoussa *see* Chepoussa

Chippanchickchick [WA] (H)

Chippawa *see* Chippewa

Chippawee *see* Chippewa

Chippeouay *see* Chippewa

Chippewa [Ont, MN] (LC)

Chippewaes *see* Chippewa

Chippewais *see* Chippewa

Chippewa of Lake Nipegon [Ont] (H)

Chippewa of Red Lake *see* Miskwagamiwisagaigan

Chippewas of Lake Superior *see* Kitchigumiwininiwug

Chippewaus *see* Chippewa

Chippeway *see* Chippewa

Chippewayan *see* Chipewyan

Chippewayan *see* Chipewyan

Chippewayanawok *see* Chipewyan

Chippewayans proprement dits *see* Thilanottine

Chippeways of Leach Lake *see* Pillagers

Chippeways of Red Lake *see* Miskwagamiwisagaigan

Chippeways of the Burnt Woods *see* Burnt Woods

Chippeweigh *see* Chippewa

Chippeweyan *see* Chipewyan

Chip-pe-wi-yan *see* Chipewyan

Chippewiyan *see* Chipewyan

Chippewyan *see* Athapascan

Chippewyse *see* Chippewa

Chippoway *see* Chippewa

Chippowyen *see* Chipewyan

Chippuwa *see* Chippewa

Chipunish *see* Nez Perce

Chipunnish *see* Nez Perce

Chipwa *see* Chippewa

Chipwaes *see* Chippewa

Chipway *see* Chippewa

Chipwayan *see* Chipewyan

Chipwayanawok *see* Chipewyan

Chipweyan *see* Chipewyan

Chip-wyan *see* Chipewyan

Chipwyan *see* Chipewyan

Chiquacha *see* Chickasaw

Chiquende *see* Mimberno Apache

Chiquillam *see* Puelche

Chiquillanes [CH] (O)

Chiquimitaca *see* Baure

Chiquimitica *see* Baure

Chiquitano [BO] *Chiquito* (O)

Chiquitano [Lang] [BO] (LC)

Chiquito (BO) [(LC)

Chiquola *see* Chicora

Chirakue *see* Cherokee

Chiricagua *see* Chiricagui [Apache]

Chiricagui (H) *see also* Chiricahua Apache (LC)

Chiricahni *see* Chiricahua Apache

Chiricahua Apache [AZ, NM] (LC)

Chir-i-ca-huans *see* Chiricahua Apache

Chiricahuans *see* Chiricahua Apache

Chiricahues *see* Chiricahua Apache

Chi-ri-ca-hui *see* Chiricahua Apache

Chiricahui *see* Chiricahua Apache

Chiricaqui *see* Chiricahua Apache

Chiricau *see* Chiricoa

Chiricoa [VE, Col] *Guahibo* (O)

Chiricoy *see* Chiricoa

Chiricua *see* Chiricoa

Chiricuegi *see* Chiricahua Apache

Chirigua *see* Achagna

Chiriguano [BO] (LC)

Chirikahwa *see* Chiricahua Apache

Chiripá [Br] (LC)

Chiripinon *see* Assiniboin

Chiripo (O) *see also* Chirripo (O)

Chiripo [Lang] [CR] *Chibcan* (O)

Chiripuno *see* Arabela

Chiriquans *see* Chiricahua Apache

Chiriqui *see* Guaymi

Chirocahue *see* Chiricahua Apache

Chiroky *see* Cherokee

Chirripo (O) *see also* Chiripo (O)

Chirripo [CR] *Cabecar* (O)

Chiru [Pan] (BE)

Chirumas *see* Yuma

Chisapeack *see* Chesapeake

Chisapean *see* Chesapeake

Chi-sapi-ack *see* Chesapeake

Chisapiack *see* Chesapeake

Chisca *see* Yuchi

Chisedec [Can] [*Montagnais-Naskapi*] (BE)

Chisedech *see* Chisedec

Chiserhonon [Can] (H)

Chishamne'e [Arg, Par] *Ashluslay* (O)

Chi-she *see* Mescalero Apache

Chishe *see* Apache

Chishe *see* Mescalero Apache

Chishende *Chiricahua Apache* (Hdbk10)

Chish-hind *see* Chiricahua Apache

Chishhind *see* Chiricahua Apache

Chishi *see* Chiricahua Apache

Chishye *see* Apache

Chiska *see* Yuchi

Chiskact *see* Chiskiac

Chiskiac [VA] *Powhatan* (BE)

Chiskiack *see* Chiskiac

Chiskokaiya *Wailaki* (Pub, v.20, no.6, pp.106–107)

Chisnedinadinaye *Pinal Coyoteros* (H)

Chisos [MX] *Concho* (Hdbk10)

Chisro [Clan] *Hopi* (H)

Chit-ah-hut *see* Klikitat

Chitahhut *see* Klikitat

Chit-at-hut *see* Klikitat

Chitathut *see* Klikitat

Chit-che-ah *see* Chitsa

Chitcheah *see* Chitsa

Chit-hut *see* Chithut

Chithut [WA] (H)

Chitimacha [LA, MS] (LC)

Chitimachan [Lang] (H)

Chitimachan Indians *see* Chitimacha

Chititi *see* Chilili *Tigua*

Chititiknewas [CA] *Bankalachi* (H)

Chit-les-sen-ten *see* Chetleschantunne

Chitlessenten *see* Chetleschantunne

Chitl-kawt *see* Chilkat

Chito [Clan] *Choctaw* (H)

Chitodawa *see* Chitonahua

Chitola [Clan] *Zuni* (H)

Chitola-kwe *see* Chitola

Chitonahua *Jaminaua* (O)

Chit-o-won-e-augh-gaw *see* Seneca

Chitowoneaughgaw *see* Seneca

Chitsa (H) *see also* Tchitcheah (H)

Chit-sa *see* Chitsa

Chitsa [AK] *Kutchakutchin* (H)

Chitsah *see* Chitsa

Chit-saugh *see* Chitoa

Chitsaugh *see* Chitsa

Chitwout *see* Similkameen

Chiuga *see* Cayuga

Chiugachi *see* Chugatchigmiut

Chiu-taiina *see* Chiutaiina

Chiutaiina [Clan] [NM] *Taos* (H)

Chivari *see* Jivaro

Chivipane *see* Ervipiame

Chi-vo-la *see* Zuni

Chivola *see* Zuni

Chiwaro *see* Jivaro

Chiwaro [Lang] *see* Jivaro

Chiwere [Lang] *Siouan* (BE)

chiwetha *see* Isleta

Chixaxia *see* Chickasaw

Chiz-ches-che-nay *see* Tizsessi-
naye
Chizcheschenay *see* Tizsessinaye
Chizhu *Ponca* (H)
Chizhuwashtage [Clan] *Kansa* (H)
Chizo [MX] *Concho* (BE)
Chkungen [Can] *Songish* (BE)
Chlach-a-jek *see* Yakutat
Chlukoach-adi *see* Hlukahadi
Chnagmiut [AK] *Eskimos* (BE)
Choaenne *see* Cheyenne
Choam Cha-di-la Pomo [CA]
(Contri, v.3, p.155)
Choan *see* Chowanoc
Choanik *see* Tehuelche
Choanist *see* Chowanoc
Choanoke *see* Chowanoc
Choarana *see* Echoaladi
Cho-ba-abish *see* Chobaabish
Chobaabish [WA] *Salish* (H)
Cho-bah-ah-bish *see* Chobaabish
Chobahahbish *see* Chobaabish
Chocama *see* Waunana
Chocataus *see* Choctaw
Chocchuma *see* Chakciuma
Choccomaw *see* Chakchiuma
Chochenyo [Lang] *Northern
Costanoan* (CA-8)
Chochite *see* Cochiti
Chochiti *see* Cochiti
Choch-Katit *see* Siksika
Chochkatit *see* Siksika
Chocho [Lang] [MX] (Bull44)
Chocho [MX] (BE)
Chocho *Tlapanec see* Tlapanec
Chochocois *see* Shoshoko
Chochones *see* Shoshone
Chocktaw *see* Choctaw
Choco (LC) *see also* Popoloca
(LC)
Choco (LC) *see also* Shoco (LC)
Choco [Br] (LC)
Choco [Br] (LC) *see also* Shoco
(LC)
Choco [Pan, Col] (LC)
Choco [Pan, Col] (LC)
Choco [Pan, Col] (LC) *see also*
Popoloca (LC)
Cho-co-men-a *see* Chukaymina
Chocomena *see* Chukaymina
Cho-co-nish *see* Nez Perce
Choconish *see* Nez Perce
Chocorbo (O)
Chocorvo *see* Chocorbo
Chocreletan [OR] *Tututni* (H)
Choctaugh *see* Choctaw
Choctaw [MS, LA] (LC)
Chocto *see* Choctaw
Cho-e-nee *see* Choynok
Choenee *see* Choynok
Cho-e-nem-nee *see* Choinumni
Choenemnee *see* Choinumni
Cho-e-nim-na *see* Choinumni

Choenimna *see* Choinumni
Choe-nim-ne *see* Choinumni
Cho-e-nim-nee *see* Choinumni
Choenimnee *see* Choinumni
Cho-e-nook *see* Choynok
Choenook *see* Choynook
Cho-e-nuco *see* Choynok
Choenuco *see* Choynok
Choe-wem-nim-nee *see*
Choinumni
Choewemnimnee *see* Choinumni
Choguan *see* Siaguan
Chohomes *see* Tohome
Cho-ho-nut *see* Chunut
Chohonuts *see* Chunut
Chohoptin *see* Nez Perce
Choimimnee *see* Choinumni
Choinimni *see* Choinumni
Choinoc *see* Choynok
Choinok *see* Choynok
Choinook *see* Choynok
Choi-nook *see* Choynok
Choinuck *see* Choynok
Choi-nuck *see* Choynok
Choi-nuk *see* Choynok
Choinuk *see* Choynok
Choinumne *see* Choinumni
Choinumni [CA] *Yokuts* (CA)
Choinux *see* Choynok
Chois *see* Zoe
Choiz *see* Zoe
Chokatowela *Brule* (H)
Chokchoomah *see* Chakchiuma
Cho-ke-me-ne *see* Chukaymina
Chokemene *see* Chukaymina
Cho-ke-min-nah *see*
Chukaymina
Chokeminnah *see* Chukaymina
Cho-kem-nies *see* Chukaymina
Chokemnies *see* Chukaymina
Choke-tar-to-womb *see* Coka-
towela
Choketartowomb *see*Chokatowela
Chokiamauve *see* Chukaymina
Chokimauve *see* Chukaymina
Cho-ki-me-na *see* Chukaymina
Chokimena *see* Chukaymina
Cho-ki-min-ah *see* Chukaymina
Chokiminah *see* Chukaymina
Chokitapia *see* Siksika
Chokonen *see* Central Chiric-
ahua Apache
Chokonen *see* Chokonni
Cho-kon-nen *see* Chokonni
Chokonni (H) *see also* Pinalino
Apache (H)
Chokonni *Chiricahua Apache*
(Hdbk10)
Choktah *see* Choctaw
Choktau *see* Choctaw
Choktaw *see* Choctaw
Cho Kune *see* Chiricahua
Apache

Chokune *see* Chiricahua Apache
Chokuyen *see* Cho-ku-yen
Cho-ku-yen [CA] (Contri, v.3,
p.195)
Chol [Lang] *Western Mayan* (LC)
Chola *see* Chula
Chol Lacandon [MX] *Chol* (BE)
Cholo [Col] (H)
Cholo [Pan] *Choco* (BE)
Cholo [PE, BO, EC] (O)
Cholobone *see* Cholovone
Choloid [Lang] *Mayan* (BE)
Choloid Indians *see* Chol
Cholon [PE] (O)
Cholos Penonomenos [Pan] (O)
Cholovone [CA] *Mariposan* (H)
Cholti *see* Chol
Cholutec [Hon] *Mangue* (BE)
Choluteca *see* Cholutec
Choluteca [Lang] *see* Mangue
Chomaath [Sept] *Toquart* (H)
Choman *see* Jumano
Chomane *see* Jumano
Chomene *see* Jumano
Chomocouaniste *see* Chomon-
chouaniste
Chomonchouaniste [Q] (H)
Chon [Lang] [Arg] [*Panoan-
Tacanan*] (O)
Chonakera [Clan] *Winnebago* (H)
Chonanon *see* Shewanee
Chondal *see* Chontal
Choneca *see* Tehuelche
Chonek *see* Tzoneca
Chongaskabe *see* Congasketon
Chongas Kabi *see* Sisseton
Chongaskabion *see* Chongaske-
ton
Chongaskaby *see* Sisseton
Chongaskethon *see* Chongaske-
ton
Chongasketon *Sisseton* (H)
Chongonsceton *see* Chongasketon
Chongousceton *see* Chongaske-
ton
Chongue *see* Chonque
Chongyo [Clan] *Hopi* (H)
Chonik *see* Tehuelcha Chongas-
keton
Chono [CH] (LC)
Chonoan *see* Chono
Chonondedeys *see* Tionontati
Chonondedeys *see* Wyandot
Chonontouaronon *see* Seneca
Cho-nook *see* Choynok
Chonook *see* Choynok
Chonot *see* Chunut
Chonque [MS] *Choctaw* (H)
Chonsgaskaby *see* Chongasketon
Chonta [PE] *Campa* (O)
Chontader *see* Piro [Peru]
Chontal [Lang] [MX] *Western
Mayan* (LC)

Chontal [NI, ES, CR] (O)
Chontal [Oaxaca] [Lang] [MX]
  (LC)
Chontal [Tobasco] [MX] *Mayas*
  (LC)
Chontaquiro *see* Chuntaquiro
Chonuke *see* Chinook
Chonuntoowaunee *see* Seneca
Chonut *see* Chunut
Choochancey *see* Chukchansi
Choo-enu *see* Choynok
Chooenu *see* Choynok
Choogak *see* Chugachigmut
Chookchances *see* Chukchansi
Chook-chan-cie *see* Chukchansi
Chookchancie *see* Chukchansi
Chook-chancy *see* Chukchansi
Chookchancy *see* Chukchansi
Chook-cha-nee *see* Chukchansi
Chookchanee *see* Chukchansi
Chook-chau-ce *see* Chukchansi
Chookchauce *see* Chukchansi
Chook-chaw-ce *see* Chukchansi
Chookchawce *see* Chukchansi
Chook-chuncy *see* Chukchansi
Chookchuncy *see* Chukchansi
Choomedoc *see* Chumidok
Choomedoc *see* Chumteya
Choo-mi-ah *see* Huchnom
Choomiah *see* Huchnom
Choomuch *see* Chumuch
Choomwit *see* Chumwit
Choo-nemne *see* Choinumni
Choonemne *see* Choinumini
Choonke *see* Tehuelche
Choo-nut *see* Chunut
Choonut *see* Chunut
Chootchancer *see* Chukchansi
Chopannish *see* Nez Perce
Chopeminish *see* Nez Perce
Chopi [Clan] *Laguna* (H)
Chopi-hano *see* Tyupi
Chopihano *see* Tyupi
Chopi-hanock *see* Tyupi
Chopihanock *see* Tyupi
Choponiesh *see* Nez Perce
Choponish *see* Nez Perce
Choponsca *see* Chepoussa
Choppunish *see* Nez Perce
Choptank *Algonquian* (Hdbk15)
Choptank [MD] *Nanticoke* (LC)
Choptico *see* Chapticon
Chopticon *see* Chapticon
Chopunish *see* Nez Perce
Chopunmohee *see* Nez Perce
Cho pun-nish *see* Nez Perce
Chopunnish *see* Nez Perce
Choquichouman *see* Chakchi-
  uma
Chora *see* Cora
Choraki *see* Cherokee
Chorchake *see* Corchaug
Chori *see* Siriono

Choro *see* Chosro
Chorofa [Clan] *Timucua* (H)
Choropi [Arg] *Ashluslay* (O)
Chorote [Par] (O)
Chorotega [CR] (LC)
Chorotega-Mangue *see* Mangue
Chorotega-Mangue *see*
  Chorotega
Chorotegan [Lang] *Otomauguean*
  (BE)
Choroti [Arg] (LC)
Chorouacha *see* Chaouacha
Chorruco [TX] *Karankawa* (H)
Chorti [Gua, Hon, Arg, BO]
  Chorote (LC)
Chorti [Lang] *Western Mayan*
  (LC)
Choruico *see* Chorruco
Chorzh *see* Chosro
Chorzh-namu *see* Chosro
Chosh'ka-hano *see* Soshka
Cho-shon-ne *see* Shoshone
Choshonne *see* Shoshone
Chosro [Clan] *Hopi* (H)
Chota *see* Cora
Chouaca *see* Chaouacha
Chouacoet *see* Sokoki
Chouacta *see* Choctaw
Chouala *see* Cheraw
Chouanon *see* Shawnee
Chouanong *see* Shawnee
Chouanous *see* Shawnee
Chouchilla *see* Chawchilla
Chouchille *see* Chawchilla
Chou-chillies *see* Chawchilla
Chouchillies *see* Chawchilla
Chouchouma *see* Chakchiuma
Chouenon *see* Shawnee
Chouesnon *see* Shawnee
Chougaskabee *see* Chongasketon
Chougasketon *see* Chongasketon
Choula [MS] (BE)
Chouman *see* Jumano
Choumane *see* Jumano
Choumay *see* Jumano
Choumene *see* Jumano
Chouontouarouon *see* Seneca
Chouqui *see* Tehuelche
Chousa *see* Sutaio
Choushatta *see* Koasati
Chovala *see* Cheraw
Chowah *see* Chowanoc
Chowan (H) *see also* Chowanoc
  (BE)
Chowan [NC] (BE)
Chowane *see* Chowanoc
Chowanoake *see* Chowanoc
Chowanoc [NC] (BE)
Chowanock *see* Chowanoc
Chowanok *see* Chowanoc
Chowanooke *see* Chowanoc
Chow-chi-la *see* Chawchilla
Chow-chi-lier *see* Chawchilla

Chowchilla *see* Chawchilla
Chowchillier *see* Chawchilla
Chow-chill-ies *see* Chawchilla
Chowchillies *see* Chawchilla
Chowcille *see* Chawchilla
Chowcla *see* Chawchilla
Chowee *see* Chaui
Chow-e-nim-ne *see* Choinumni
Chownimne *see* Choinumni
Chowou *see* Chowanoc
Choya'ha *see* Yuchi
Choyapin *Coahuiltecan* (BE)
Choyapin [Lang] *Tonkawan* (BE)
Choynimni [Lang] *see*
  Choinumni
Choynok *Yokuts* (CA-8)
Choyopan [Clan] *Tonkawa* (H)
Chozetta [Lang] *Siouan* (Bull22)
Chratka-ari *see* Katkaayi
Chrelch-kon *see* Hehlkoan
Chrelejan *see* Sulujame
Chreokee *see* Cherokee
Christaneaux *see* Cree
Christanna Indians [VA] (H)
Christanna Indians [VA] (H)
Christenaux *see* Cree
Christeneaux *see* Cree
Chris-te-no *see* Cree
Christeno *see* Cree
Christenoes *see* Cree
Christenois *see* Cree
Christianaux *see* Cree
Christianeaux *see* Cree
Christian Indians *see* Munsee
Christian Indians *see* Christanna
  Indians
Christianux *see* Cree
Christinaux *see* Cree
Christineaux *see* Cree
Christinos *see* Cree
Christinou *see* Cree
Chua [Phratry] *Hopi* (H)
Chuala *see* Echoaladi
Chualpay *see* Colville
Chuanoes *see* Shawnee
Chuapas *Coahuiltecan* (BE)
Chubio [Clan] *Hopi* (H)
Chu-chacas *see* Keres
Chuchacas *see* Keres
Chu-cha-chas *see* Keres
Chuchachas *see* Keres
Chuchillones (CA-8)
Chuchtononeda [NY] *Mohawk*
  (H)
Chuchunayha [BC] *Okinagan* (H)
Chuchures [Pan] (BE)
Chuchuwayha *see* Chuchunayha
Chuckbuckmiut [Can] *Labrador*
  (BE)
Chuckchee [Lang] (BE)
Chuckehalin *see* Chukchansi
Chucknutt *see* Chugnut
Chucuna *see* San Blas *Cuna*

Chucunaque (O) *see also* San Blas Cuna (O)

Chucunaque *Cuna* (BE)

Chueskweskewa [Clan] *Chippewa* (H)

Chu-fan-ik-sa *see* Chufaniksa

Chufaniksa [Clan] *Choctaw* (H)

Chuga *see* Chugatchigmut

Chugach *see* Chugatchigmut

Chugachi *see* Chugatchigmut

Chugachigmiut *see* Chugatchigmut

Chugach'ig-mut *see* Chugatchigmut

Chugachik' *see* Chugatchigmut

Chugachimute *see* Chugatchigmut

Chugachugmiut *see* Chugatchigmut

Chugackimute *see* Chugatchigmut

Chugant *see* Chugnut

Chugatch *see* Chugatchigmut

Chugatchigmut [AK] *Eskimos* (BE)

Chughnot *see* Chugnut

Chugnues *see* Chugnut

Chugnut [NY] (H)

Chuh *see* Chuj

Chuh-hla *see* Chuhhla

Chuhhla [Clan] *Chickasaw* (H)

Chuijuger *see* Cayuga

Chuj [Lang] [Gu] *Western Mayan* (LC)

Chuje [Lang] (BE)

Chujean *see* Chuj

Chukai [Clan] *Hopi* (H)

Chu-kai-mi-na *see* Chukaymina

Chukaimina [CA] *Yokuts* (H)

Chukaimina [Lang] (BE) *see also* Chukaymina (CA-8)

Chukanedi [Clan] *Tlingit* (H)

Chukanende *see* Ch'uk'anende

Ch'uk'anende *Chiricahua Apache* (Hdbk10)

Chukansi *see* Chukchansi

Chukaw *see* Choctaw

Chukaymina [Lang] *Kings River* (CA-8)

Chukchagemiut [AK] *Chnagmiut* (H)

Chukchag'emut *see* Chukchagemiut

Chukchancy *see* Chukchansi

Chuk-chan-cy *see* Chukchansi

Chukchansey *see* Chukchansi

Chuk-chan-si *see* Chukchansi

Chukchansi [CA] *Yokuts* (CA)

Chuk-chi *see* Yuit

Chukchi-Namolly *see* Siberian Eskimos

Chukchuk *see* Chukchagemiut

Chu-ke-chan-se *see* Chukchansi

Chukechanse *see* Chukchansi

Chukesw *see* Chickasaw

Chukluk'mut *see* Yuit

Chuklu'k-mut *see* Yuit

Chukohukomute *see* Yuit

Chukotalgi [Clan] *Creek* (H)

Chula *see* Choula

Chu-la *see* Tsulalgi

Chula *see* Tsulalgi

Chulajam *see* Sulujame

Chulajame *see* Sulujame

Chulamni [CA] *Yokuts* (CA)

Chulpun *see* Khulpuni

Chuluaam *see* Sulujame

Chulufichi [Phratry] [FL] *Timucua* (H)

Chulukki *see* Cherokee

Chulupe *see* Ashluslay

Chulupi *see* Ashluslay

Chulupie *see* Ashluslay

Chu-mai-a *see* Yuki

Chumaia *see* Yuki

Chumakum *see* Chimakum

Chumano *see* Chimane

Chumash [CA] (H)

Chumashan [Lang] [CA] (H)

Chu-ma-wa *see* Chumawi

Chumawa *see* Chumawi

Chumawi [CA] *Shastan* (H)

Chumeto *see* Chumteya

Chu-mi-dok *see* Chumidok

Chumidok [CA] (H)

Chum-te-ya *see* Chumteya

Chumteya [CA] (H)

Chumu [BO] *Araona* (O)

Chumuch (H) *see also* Chumteya (H)

Chu-much *see* Chumuch

Chumuch [CA] (H)

Chumula *see* Chumulu

Chumulu [Pan] *Chibchan* (BE)

Chumwit (H) *see also* Chumteya (H)

Chum-wit *see* Chumwit

Chumwit [CA] (H)

Chuna-kon *see* Huna

Chuncho *see* Campa

Chuncho *see* Leco

Chuncho *see* Yuracare

Chunco *see* Guaycuru

Chunemme *see* Choinumni

Chunnapun *see* Chimnapum

Chun-nut *see* Chunut

Chunoiyana *see* Atsugewi

Chunotachi *see* Chunut

Chuntaquiro [Lang] (LC)

Chuntaquiro [PE] *Piro* (LC)

Chunupi *see* Ashluslay

Chunupi *see* Mataco

Chu-nut *see* Chunut

Chunut [CA] *Yokuts* (CA)

Chunute *see* Chunut

Chuoanous *see* Shawnee

Chupacho [PE] (LC)

Chu-ran *see* Churan

Churan [NM] *Isleta* (H)

Churchcates [SC] (H)

Churchers [NEng] (H)

Churehu [Clan] *Isleta* (H)

Churehu-t'ainin *see* Churehu

Churitana [PE] *Muniche* (O)

Chuructas [CA] *Wintu* (JCB, v.2, no.3, pp.24–25)

Churupa [BO] (O)

Churuptoy [CA] *Patwin* (H)

Churuya [Lang] *Guahiboan* (O)

Chushan *see* Yuma

Chusute *see* Chunut

Chu-su-te *see* Chunut

Chutes (H)

Chuts-ta-kon *see* Hutsnuwu

Chutznou *see* Hutsnuwu

Chuunake *see* San Blas

Chuwon *see* Chowanoc

Chuxoxi [Lang] [CA] *Buena Vista* (CA)

Chuyenmani *see* Choinumni

Chwachamaju *see* Khwakhamaiu

Chwachmaja *see* Khwakhamaiu

Chyan *see* Cheyenne

Chyanne *see* Cheyenne

Chyenne *see* Cheyenne

Chym-nah-po *see* Chimnapum

Chymnapom *see* Chimnapum

Chymnapum *see* Chimnapum

Chymseyan *see* Chimmesyan

Chymshean Nation *see* Tsimshian

Chynne *see* Cheyenne

Chyppewan *see* Chipewyan

Chyuga *see* Cayuga

Cia *see* Sia

Ciadsier *see* Saesse

ciae-hwip-ta *see* Isleta

Ciamacoco *see* Chamacoco

Cia'mectix *see* Seamysty

Ciamectix *see* Seamysty

Ciapynes *see* Chilpaines

Ciawani *see* Chaguan

Ciawani *see* Chiriguano

Ciawi *see* Kiowa

Cibaiigan *see* Cheboygan

Cibala *see* Zuni

Cibao *see* Cahibo

Ciba-riches *see* Seuvarits

Cibariches *see* Seuvarits

Cibecue *San Carlos Apache* (BE)

Cibola *see* Zuni

Cibolae *see* Zuni

Cibolal *see* Zuni

Cibolan Indians *see* Zuni

Cibolas (H)

Cibola-Zuñi *see* Zuni

Cibole *see* Zuni

Cibolian *see* Zuni

Cibolo *see* Zuni

Ciboney (Cu, WInd, HA) (LC)
Cibora *see* Zuni
Cicaca *see* Chickasaw
Cicaque *see* Jicaque
Cice *see* Sia
Ci-cho-mo-oi *see* Sichomovi
Cichomooi *see* Sichomovi
Cichomovi *see* Sichomovi
Ci-cin-xau *see* Salmon River
Cicinxau *see* Salmon River
Cicoua *see* Pecos
Cictaqwutmetunne *see* Umpqua
Ci-cta-qwyt-me'tunne *see*
 Umpqua
Cicui *see* Pecos
Cicuic *see* Pecos
Cicuica *see* Pecos
Cicuich *see* Pecos
Cicuick *see* Pecos
Cicuie *see* Pecos
Cicuio *see* Pecos
Cicuiq *see* Pecos
Cicuique *see* Pecos
Cicuje *see* Pecos
Cicuya *see* Pecos
Cicuyan Indians *see* Pecos
Cicuye *see* Pecos
Cicuyo *see* Pecos
Ci-da-hetc *see* Asidahech
Cidahetc *see* Asidahech
Cidika-go *see* Chiricahua Apache
Cieguaje [EC] *Secoya* (O)
Cien *see* Cheyenne
Cigom *see* Shigom
Ciguana [SanD, WInd, HA]
 Hubabo (BE)
Ciguayo *see* Hubabo
Ci-hene *see* Eastern Chiricahua
Cihene *see* Eastern Chiricahua
Ci-hu-pa *see* Chihupa
Cihupa *see* Shongopovi
Cihwahmu-ca *see* Navajo
Cijame *see* Sijame
Cikaga *see* Chickasaw
Cikcitcela *see* Shikshichela
Cikcitcena *see* Shikshichena
Cileños *see* Gila Apache
Cilla *see* Sia
Ciloba *see* Zuni
Cil-tar-den *see* Tsiltaden
Ciltarden *see* Tsiltaden
Cimarron *see* Urarina
Cimarron Utes *see* Moache
Cimataguo *Coahuiltecan* (BE)
cimbu'ihe *see* Molala
Ci-mo-pavi *see* Shongopovi
Cimopavi *see* Shongopovi
Ci-motk-pivi *see* Shongopovi
Cimotkpivi *see* Shangopovi
Cinal [CA] *Northern Pomo* (Pub,
 v.40, no.2)
Cinaloa *see* Sinaloa
Cinaloa *see* Yaqui

Cina-luta-oin *see* Shinalutaoin
Cinalutaoin *see* Shinalutaoin
Cinanctec *see* Chinantec
Cinecu *see* Senecu del Sur
Cinela *see* Conestoga
Cingacuchusca *see* Urarina
Cingpoil *see* Sanpoil
Cinique *see* Seneca
Cinnakee *see* Seneca
Cinnigo *see* Seneca
Cinnoko *see* Seneca
Cinola *see* Zuni
Cinoquipe *see* Sinoquipe
Cinquaoteck *see* Conoy
Cinta Larga [Br] (LC)
Cintu-aluka *see* Comanche
Ci-nyu-muh *see* Hopi
Cinyumuh *see* Hopi
Ci-o-ho-pa *see* Cheokhba
Ciohopa *see* Cheokhba
Ciona *see* Sioni
Cioua *see* Dakota
Cioux *see* Dakota
Cipaulire *see* Shipaulovi
Ci-pau-lovi *see* Shipaulovi
Cipaulovi *see* Shipaulovi
Cipias *see* Tsipiakwe
Cipiwiniuuk *see* Cipi-winiuuk
Cipi-winiuuk [Can] *Paskwaw-*
 ininiwug (BE)
Cipoliva *see* Shipaulovi
Ci-pow-lovi *see* Shipaulovi
Cipowlovi *see* Shipaulovi
Ciquique *see* Pecos
Cirabo *see* Mayoruna
Circee *see* Sarsi
Circuic *see* Pecos
Ciriana *see* Sanuma
Ciries *see* Sarsi
cisin *see* Chiricahua Apache
Cisquiouws *see* Karok
Cissapeack *see* Chesapeake
cisse-kwe *see* Western Apache
Cissitons *see* Sisseton
Ci-sta-qwut *see* Umpqua
Cistaqwut *see* Umpqua
Ci-sta-qwut-me tunne *see*
 Kuitsch
Cistaqwutmetunne *see* Kuitsch
Ci-sta-qwut ni-li t'cat' tunne *see*
 Nahankhuotane
Cistaqwutnilitcattunne *see* Na-
 hankhuotane
Ci-sta-qwut-qwut *see* Umpqua
Cistaqwutqwut *see* Umpqua
Citara [Pan] *Embera* (O)
Citchumwi *see* Sichomovi
Citcumave *see* Sichomovi
Ci-tcum-wi *see* Sichomovi
Cithinistinee *see* Cree
Citisans *Sioux* (H)
Citizen Potawatomi [KS, IT] (H)
Ciuola *see* Zuni

Civilized Farmers *see* Farmers
 Band
Civola *see* Zuni
Civoli *see* Zuni
Civona *see* Zuni
Ci-wa-nu wun-wu *see* Shiwanu
Ciwanu wunwu *see* Shiwanu
Ciwere *see* Chiwere
Ci-wi-na-kwin *see* Zuni
Ciwinakwin *see* Zuni
Ci-wo-na *see* Zuni
Ciwona *see* Zuni
Ciya *see* Sia
ciyahwipa *see* Isleta
ciyawihpa *see* Isleta
Ciyo-subula *see* Shiyosubula
Ciyo-tanka *see* Shiyotanka
Cizentetpi *Pueblo Indians* (H)
Ckac-tun *see* Shkashtun
ckatahka *see* Apache
Ckiyi *see* Skidi Pawnee
Ckwa-ri-nan *see* Toryohne
ckweylexw *see* Pavilion Band
Cla *see* Sia
Clackamas [OR] (LC)
Clackami *see* Clackamas
Clackamo *see* Clackamas
Clack-a-mu *see* Clackamas
Clackamur *see* Clackamas
Clackamus *see* Clackamas
Clackanur *see* Clackamas
Clackarner *see* Clackamas
Clackemur *see* Clackamas
Clackemus *see* Clackamas
Clackimis *see* Clackamas
Clacksstar *see* Tlatskanai
Clack-star *see* Tlatskanai
Clack-star *see* Clatskanie
Clackstar *see* Clatskanie
Clackstar *see* Tlatskanai
Clackster *see* Tlatskanai
Cladachut *see* Klikitat
Cladsap *see* Clatsop
Clahclallah *see* Clahclellah
Clahclellah (Hdbk12) *see also* Cas-
 cades (Hdbk12)
Clahclellah [OR] *Watlala* (BE)
Clahclellar *see* Clahclellah
Clah-in-na-ta *see* Claninnata
Clah-in-nata *see* Claninnata
Clahinnata *see* Claninnata
Clahnahquah *see* Clahnaquah
Clahnaquah [OR] *Multnomah*
 (BE)
Clahoose [Can] *Comox* (BE)
Claiakwat *see* Clayoquot
Clakamu *see* Clackamas
Clakema *see* Clackamas
Clakstar *see* Tlatskanai
Clalam *see* Clallam
Clallam [WA] (LC)
Clallem *see* Clallam
Clal-lu-i-is *see* Tlaaluis

Clalluiis *see* Tlaaluis
Clallum *see* Clallam
Clal-lums Indians *see* Clallam
Clalskanie *see* Clatskanie
Clamakum *see* Chimakum
Clamath *see* Klamath
Clamcoches *see* Karankawa
Clamcoet *see* Karankawa
Clamet *see* Klamath
Clammitte *see* Klamath
Clam-nah-min-na-mun *see*
  Kathlaminim
Clamnahminnamun *see* Kath-
  laminimin
Clamore *see* Santsukhdhin
Clamouth *see* Klamath
Clamut *see* Klamath
Clamuth *see* Klamath
Clan (H, pp.303–305)
Clanaminamum *see* Kathlamin-
  imin
Clan-in-na-ta's *see* Claninnata
Clanimata *see* Claninnata
Clannahminnamun *see* Kath-
  laminimin
Clan-nah-quah *see* Clahnaquah
Clannahquah *see* Clahnaquah
Clannahqueh *see* Clahnaquah
Clan-nah-queh's Tribe of Mult-
  nomah's *see* Clahnaquah
Clan-nar-min-a-mon *see* Kath-
  laminimin
Clannarminamon *see* Kathlamin-
  imin
Clannarminimun *see* Kathlamin-
  imin
Clannarminnamun *see* Kath-
  laminimin
Clanninnata [OR] *Multnomah*
  (BE)
Clao-qu-aht *see* Clayoquot
Claoquaht *see* Clayoquot
Clap-sott *see* Clatsop
Clapsott *see* Clatsop
Clara, S. *see* Santa Clara [NM]
Clara, Santa [CA] *Mission* (BE)
Clara, Santa [NM] *Pueblo* (BE)
Clara, Sta. *see* Santa Clara [NM]
Clarkame *see* Clackamas
Clarkamee *see* Clackamas
Clarkamo *see* Clackamas
Clarkamu *see* Clackamas
Clark Lake [AK] *Tanaina* (BE)
Clasap *see* Clatsop
Claskanio *see* Tlatskanai
Class-can-eye-ah *see* Tlatskanai
Classcaneyeah *see* Tlatskanai
Classet *see* Makah
Classical Aztec [Lang] (Hdbk10)
Classop *see* Clatsop

Clastop *see* Clatsop
Clatacamin *see* Tlatskanai
Clatchotin [AK] *Tanana* (BE)
Clatochin *see* Clatchotin
Clat-sa-canin *see* Tlatskanai
Clatsacanin *see* Tlatskanai
Clatsaconin *see* Tlatskania
Clatsap *see* Clatsop
Clatset *see* Makah
Clatskanie (BE) *see also* Tlatskanai
  (BE)
Clatskanie [OR] (BE)
Clat-sop *see* Clatsop
Clatsop [OR] (BE)
Clatstoni *see* Tlatskanai
Clatstop *see* Clatsop
Clatsup *see* Clatsop
Claucuad *see* Clayoquot
Claugh-e-wall-hah *see* Clowwe-
  walla
Claughewallhah *see* Clowwewalla
Claw-et-sus *see* Tlauitsis
Clawetsus *see* Tlauitsis
Claxtar *see* Tlatskanai
Clax-ter *see* Tlatskanai
Claxter *see* Tlatskanai
Clayhoosh *see* Clahoose
Clayoquat *see* Clayoquat
Clayoquot [BC, VanI] *Nootka*
  (LC)
Clayoquotoch *see* Clayoquot
Clear Lake Indians (H) *see also*
  Laguna (CA)
Clear Lake Indians [CA] (H)
Clear Lake Pomo [CA] (Pub,
  v.29, no.4)
Clear Lake Wappo [Lang] [CA]
  Yuki (Pub, v.6, no.1, pp.274–
  79)
Cle-Hure *see* Clahoose
Clehure *see* Clahoose
Cle-Huse *see* Clahoose
Clehuse *see* Clahoose
Cle-li-kit-te *see* Clelikitte
Clelikitte [BC] (H)
Clemaks *see* Tillamook
Clem-clem-a-lat *see* Clem-
  clemalats
Clemclemalats [VanI] *Cowichan*
  (BE)
Clem-clemalet *see* Clemclemalats
Clemclemalet *see* Clemclemalats
Clem-clem-a-lit *see* Clem-
  clemalats
Clemclemalit *see* Clemclemalats
Clermont's band *see* Santsukhd-
  hin
Clermo's band *see* Santsukhdhin
Clicitat *see* Klikitat
Click-a-hut *see* Klikitat
Clickahut *see* Klikitat
Clickatat *see* Klikitat
Clicketat *see* Klikitat

Clickitat *see* Klikitat
Clickquamish *see* Cloquallam
Cliff-dwellers (LC)
Clikatat *see* Klikitat
Climath *see* Klamath
Clin-ar-par *see* Tzlanapah
Clinarpar *see* Tzlanapah
Clingat *see* Tlingit
Clintinos *see* Cree
Clinton [BC] *Shuswap* (H)
Clinton Band (Hdbk12) *see also*
  Whispering Pines Band
  (Hdbk12)
Clinton Band [BC] *Fraser River
  Shuswap* (Hdbk12)
Clipalines *see* Shipaulovi
Clipper Gap [Lang] [CA] *Nisenan*
  (CA-8)
Clishhook *see* Clowwewalla
Clistenos *see* Cree
Clistinos *see* Cree
Clkwan-ti-ya tunne *see* Thlk-
  wantiyatunne
Clockstar *see* Tlatskanai
Clock-toot *see* Clocktoot
Clocktoot [BC] *Shuswap* (H)
Clo-kar-da-ki-ein *see*
  Klokadakaydn
Clokardakiein *see* Klakadakaydn
Cloquallam [WA] *Kwaiailk* (BE)
Cloquallum *see* Cloquallum
Closset *see* Makah
Clotsop *see* Clatsop
Clough-e-wal-hah *see* Clowwe-
  walla
Cloughewalhah *see* Clowwewalla
Clough-e-wal-lah *see* Clowwe-
  walla
Cloughewallah *see* Clowwewalla
Clover-Eaters *see* Poatsi-
  tuhtikuteh
Clover eaters *see* poz'idadikadi
Clowetoos *see* Tlauitsis
Clow et sus *see* Tlauitsis
Clowetsus *see* Tlauitsis
Clowewalla *see* Clowwewalla
Clow-we-wal-la *see* Clowwewalla
Clowwewalla [OR] (BE)
Clts'us-me tunne *see* Thltsusme-
  tunne
Club Indians *see* Yuma
Club Indians *see* Quechan
Cluetau *Coahuiltecan* (BE)
Clukema *see* Clackamas
Clulwarp *see* Shuswap
Clunsus *see* Ntlakyapamuk
Clunsus *see* Thompson Indians
Clymclymalat *see* Clemclemalats
Clyoquot *see* Clayoquot
Clyquot *see* Clayoquot
Cneis *see* Caddo
Cnistineaux *see* Cree
Cnongasgaba *see* Chngasketon

Coahuanes see Kahwan
Coahuia see Cahuilla
Coahuila see Kawia *Luiseño*
Coahuila see Cahuilla
Coahuileño [MX] (Hdbk10)
Coahuilla see Cahuilla
Coahuiltecan [Lang] [MX, TX]
 (LC)
Coahuilteco see Coahuiltecan
Coaiker see Cuaiquer
Coaiquer see Cuaiquer
Coajiro see Goajiro
Coama see Kahwan
Coamo [PR] (BE)
Coana see Kohuana
Coana see Kahwan
Co-a-ni-nis see Havasupai
Coaninis see Havasupai
Coano (Hdbk10) see also Kahwan
 (Hdbk10)
Coano [MX] *Cora* (BE)
Coanopa (H)
Coapite [TX] (BE)
Coapuliguan [MX] (Hdbk10)
Coaque [TX] (BE)
Coaqui see Coaque
Coaquina see Kwakina
Coarae see Quarai
Coaruama see Caurame
Coashatay see Koasati
Coashatta see Koasati
Coassatti see Koasati
Coast [Lang] [CA] *Central Pomo*
 (Pub, v.6, no.1, pp.162–166)
Coast [Lang] [CA] *Northern Pomo*
 (Pub, v.6, no.1, pp.131–135)
Coast [Lang] [CA] *Southern Mo-
 quelumnan* (Pub, v.6, no.1,
 pp.307–309)
Coast [Lang] [CA] *Southwestern
 Pomo* (Pub, v.6, no.1, pp.228–
 235)
Coastal Chumash (CA-8)
Coastal Diegueño see Ipai
Coastal Eksimos (Hdbk5)
Coast Cree see Maskegon
Coast Indians see Costanoan
Coastmen see Costanos
Coast Miwok [CA] *Miwok* (BE)
Coast Miwok [Lang] [CA] *West-
 ern Miwokan* (CA-8)
Coast of Dogs see
 Thlingchadinne
Coast Salish [BC, WA] (LC)
Coast Yuki [CA] *Yuki* (CA)
Coast Yuki [Lang] [CA] *Yuki*
 (Pub, v.6, no.1, pp.260–263)
Coast Yurok [Lang] [CA] *Yurok*
 (He)
Coatae see Cuatache
Coaxa *Coahuiltecan* (Hdbk10)
Coayo [TX] (H)
Cobajais see Kawaiisu

Cobaji see Kawaiisu
Co'bajnaaj see Thobazhnaazhi
Cobajnaaj see Thobazhnaazhi
Co'bajnaaji see Thobazhnaazhi
Cobajnaaji see Thobazhnaazhi
Cobane see Kohani
Cobarde *Ute* (H)
Cobari [Br] *Yanoama* (O)
Cobaria [Col] (LC)
Cobaro [PE] *Campa* (O)
Cobbeo see Cubeo
Cobb Indians see Hopahka
Cobbisseconteag see Cabbasa-
 gunti
Cobewa see Cubeo
Coca [MX] *Cazcan* (LC)
Cocama [PE] (LC)
Cocamaricopa see Maricopa
Cocamegua see Cacamegua
Cocamilla [PE] (LC)
Cocao see Coosa
Cocapa see Cocopa
Cochaboth see Maca
Cochali [TN, AL] (H)
Cochaly see Cochali
Cochatties see Koasati
Coche see Camsa
Cochee see Central Chiricahua
 Apache
Co-che-ta-cah see Kotsoteka
Cochetacah see Kotsoteka
Co-che-ta-ka see Kotsoteka
Cochetaker see Kotsoteka
Cocheteka see Kotsoteka
Cocheti see Cochiti
Cocheto see Cochiti
Cochieme see Cochimi
Cochile see Cochiti
Cochilis see Cochiti
Cochima see Cochimi
Cochime see Cochimi
Cochimi [BaC, MX] *Yuma* (BE)
Cochimies see Cochimi
Cochimy see Cochimi
Cochinean see Havasupai
Cochini see Cochimi
Cochis see Yuracare
Cochise Chiricahua see Central
 Chiricahua Apache
Cochit see Cochiti
Cochita see Cochiti
Cochite see Cochiti
Co-chi-te-mi see Cochiti
Cochitemi see Cochiti
Cochiteño see Cochiti
Cochiteumi see Cochiti
Cochiti [NM] *Keres* (LC)
Cochitino see Cochiti
Cochito see Cochiti
Cochitti see Cochiti
Cochity see Cochiti
Cochnewwasroonaw see Conoy
Cochnichno see Havasupai

Cochopa see Cocopa
Cocluti see Cochiti
Coco (BE) see also Coaque (BE)
Coco (H) see also Acoma (LC)
Coco [NI, Hon] *Sumo* (BE)
Coco [NI, Hon] *Sumo* (O)
Coco [TX] (BE)
Cocoaipara [MX] *Coahuiltecan*
 (Hdbk10)
Cocojupara [MX] *Coahuiltecan*
 (Hdbk10)
Cocomacaque [MX] [Pima Bajo]
 (BE)
Cocomarecopper see Maricopa
Cocomari see Maricopa
Cocomaricopa see Maricopa
Cocomaricopa see Kavelchadom
Cocomarisepa see Maricopa
Cocomeioje *Coahuiltecan* (BE)
Cocomiracopa see Maricopa
Co-con-cah-ra see Cocoueahra
Coconcahra see Cocoueahra
Coconino see Havasupai
Co-co-noon see Coconoon
Coconoon [CA] *Yokuts* (BE)
Coconuco (O) see also Gambiano
 (O)
Coconuco [Lang] [Col] (LC)
Co-co-pa see Cocopa
Co-co-pah see Cocopa
Cocopa [AZ, MX] (LC)
Cocopa [Lang] *Delta* (Hdbk10)
Cocopah [AZ] [Adopted officially
 in 1974] (Hdbk10, p.111)
Cocora [NI] (BE)
Co-cou-eah-ra see Cocoueahra
Cocoueahra [CA] (H)
Cocoye [NM] (H)
Cocoyome [MX] (BE)
Cocto see Coto
Codakai see Shodakhai
Coddoque see Kadohadacho
Codogdacho see Kadohadacho
Coen [CR] *Cabecar* (O)
Coeni see Caddo
Coenossoeny see Iroquois
Coeruna [Br] (O)
Coetzal see Gueiquesales
Coeur d'Alene [ID] (BE)
Coeur d'Alene (BE) see also
 Skitswish (LC)
Coeur d'Alienes (H) see also
 Coeur d'Alene (BE)
Coeur d'Alienes see Skitswish
Coeur d'Eiene see Skitswish
Coeur d'Eleine see Coeur d'A-
 lene
Coeur d'Eleine see Skitswish
Coeur d'Eliene see Coeur d'A-
 lene
Coeur d'Helene see Coeur d'A-
 lene
Coeur d'Helene see Skitswish

Coeurs d'Aleines *see* Coeur d'A-
  lene
Coeurs d'Aleines *see* Skitwish
Coeurs d'aliene *see* Coeur d'A-
  lene
Coeurs d'aliene *see* Skitwish
Coeurs-piontus *see* Skitwish
Coeurs-pointus *see* Coeur d'A-
  lene
Cofa [GA] (H)
Cofan [Col, EC] (LC)
Cofane *see* Cofan
Coffee [MN] *Atsina* (BE)
Cofitachequi *see* Kasihta
Cogapacori [PE] *Machiganga* (O)
Coghui *see* Kagaba
Cogninas *see* Havasupai
Coguana *see* Kohuana
Cogui (O) *see also* Kagaba (LC)
Cogui [Col] (O)
Coguifa *see* Kawia *Luiseño*
Coguinachi [MX] *Opata* (H)
Cohainihoua *see* Cahinnio
Cohainotoas *see* Cahinnio
Cohakia *see* Cahokia
Cohakies *see* Cahokia
Cohannies *see* Kohani
Cohas [NY] (H)
Cohass *see* Coosac
Cohassiac *see* Coosac
Cohes [CA] *Maidu* (H)
Cohias *see* Cohes
Cohila Apache *see* Chiricahua
  Apache
Cohonina *see* Yavapai
Cohonina culture [AZ] (LC)
Cohonino *see* Havasupai
Cohoss *see* Coosac
Cohpap *see* Maricopa
Cohuana *see* Kohuana
Cohuilla *see* Kawia *Luiseño*
Cohuilla *see* Cahuilla
Cohuilla *see* Cahuilla
Cohuille *see* Kawia *Luiseño*
Coiacohhanauke *see* Quiouco-
  hanock
Coiaheguxes *see* Coyabegux
Coiba [Pan] (BE)
Coiejue *see* Cayuga
Coiencahes *see* Karankawa
coika'a *see* Nez Perce
Coira *see* Koroa
Coirachietanon *see* Coiracoen-
  tanon
Coiracoentanon *Illinois* (H)
Coiracoitaga [NEng] (H)
Coitch *see* Panamint
Cojage *see* Cayuga
Cojate *see* Cuatache
Cojnino *see* Havasupai
Cojoge *see* Cayuga
Cojonina *see* Havasupai
Cojoye [MX, NM] (H)

Cojuenchi *see* Cajuenche
Cojuklesatuch *see* Uchucklesit
Cokah [Can] *Cree* (BE)
Co-kanen *see* Central Chiricahua
  Apache
Cokanen *see* Central Chiricahua
  Apache
Coka-towela *see* Chokatowela
Cokatowela *see* Chokatowela
Coke *see* Coaque
Cokesilah *see* Koksilah
Cokoa [CA] *Central Pomo* (Pub,
  v.40, no.2)
Cokomaricopa *see* Maricopa
Colan [PE] (O)
Colapessa *see* Acolapissa
Colapissa *see* Acolapissa
Colasthocle [WA] *Quinault* (BE)
Colcene (H) *see also* Quilene (H)
Colcene (Pams, v.6, pp.605–606)
  see also Kolsid (BE)
Colcene [WA] *Twana* (H)
Colcharney *see* Kulchana
Colchatta *see* Koasati
Colchin *see* Kolsid
Colching *see* Kulchena
Colchopa [BC] *Salish* (H)
Colcin *see* Colcene
Colcin *see* Kolsid
Cold Country Indians [NY] (H)
Colespelin *see* Kalispel
Colespell *see* Kalispel
Colfax [Lang] *Nisenan* (CA-8)
Coligua *see* Koroa
Colima *see* Koroa
Colimies *see* Cochimi
Colina (O) *see also* Culina (LC)
Colina [NM] *Apache* (H)
Colipasa *see* Acolapissa
Colla [BO, PE, Arg] (LC)
Collagua [PE] *Colla* (LC)
Collahuaya *see* Callahuaya
Collao *see* Colla
Collapissa *see* Acolapissa
Col-lap-poh-yea-ass *see*
  Calapooya
Collappohyeaass *see* Calapooya
Collotero *see* Coyotero Apache
Collville *see* Colville
Coloa *see* Koroa
Coloclan *see* Colotlan
Coloma *see* Koloma
Coloosa *see* Calousa [CA]
Coloosa *see* Calusa [FL]
Colorado [EC] (LC)
Colotlan [MX] (BE)
Colouse *see* Korusi
Colseed *see* Colcene
Colseed *see* Kolsid
Colteches *see* Kawaiisu
Coltshanie *see* Kulchana
Columbia Indians *see* Sinkiuse-
  Columbia

Columbia Lake Indians *see*
  Akiskenukinik
Columbia Lake Indians *see* Lakes
Columbian [Lang] *Interior Salish*
  (Hdbk12)
Columbians [PacN] (H)
Columbias *see* Sinkiuse
Colusa *see* Korusi
Colusi *see* Korusi
Colville [Lang] (WA, BC) *Salis-
  han*
Colville [WA, BC] (LC)
Colville River Eskimos [AK] *Inte-
  rior North Alaska Eskimos*
  (Hdbk5)
Comabo [Lang] *see* Cashibo
Co-mai-yah *see* Comeya
Co-mai-yah *see* Kamia
Comaiyah *see* Comeya
Comance *see* Comanche
Comancha *see* Comanche
Comanche [Lang] *Central Numic*
  (Hdbk10)
Comanche [Lang] [*Shoshone-
  Comanche*] (H)
Comanche [TX, NM] (LC)
Comanchee *see* Comanche
Comanchero *see* Comanche
Comancho *see* Comanche
Comande *see* Comanche
Comandus *see* Comanche
Comaniopa *see* Maricopa
Comanito [MX] (BE)
Comanshima *see* Comanche
Comantz *see* Comanche
Comaricopa *see* Maricopa
Comauch *see* Comanche
Combahee [SC] *Cusabo* (BE)
Combec *Accomac* (Hdbk15)
Comea-kin *see* Comiakin
Comecamotes [MX] *Tamaulipec*
  (BE)
Comechingon *see* Comechingone
Comechingone [Arg] (LC)
Comecrudo (H) *see also* Carrizo
  [MX] (BE)
Comecrudo *Coahuiltecan* (BE)
Comecrudo [MX] *Tamaulipec* (BE)
Comeda *see* Comeya
Comeda *see* Kamia
Comenha (NAW)
Comenopales *see* Cometunas
Comeperros *Bocas Prietas*
  (Hdbk10)
Come Pescado (H) *see also* Tim-
  paiavats (H)
Come Pescado (Hdbk10)
Come Pescado (Hdbk11) *see also*
  Timpanogots (Hdbk11)
Comepescados *Coahuiltecan*
  (Hdbk10)
Comesacapem *see* Gumme-
  sacapem

Cometunas *Coahuiltecan* (Hdbk10)
Comeya (LC) *see also* Kamia (LC)
Comeya [CA] (H)
Comi *see* Zuni
Comia *see* Barasana
Comiaken *see* Comiakin
Comiakin [VanI] *Cowichan* (BE)
Comina *see* Havasupai
Comino *see* Havasupai
Comité [MX] (Hdbk10)
Comiteco *see* Chanabal
Commagsheak *see* Comox
Commanche *see* Comanche
Common Dogs *see*
  Shungikcheka *Hunkpatina*
Como [TX] (H)
Comocaura [MX] (Hdbk10)
Comopori [MX] *Vacoregue* (H)
Comoripa [MX] *Pimo Bajo*
  (Bull44)
Comosellamos *Coahuiltecan*
  (Hdbk10)
Co-moux *see* Comox
Comoux *see* Comox
Comox [BC] (LC)
Comoya *see* Kamia
Co-mo-yah *see* Comeya
Comoyah *see* Comeya
Comoyatz *see* Comeya
Comoyatz *see* Kamia
Comoyee *see* Comeya
Co-mo-yei *see* Comeya
Como-yei *see* Kamia
Comoyei *see* Comeya
Comoyei *see* Kamia
Compori [MX] *Guasave* (BE)
Comupaui *see* Shongopavi
Comupavi *see* Shongopavi
Comuxes *see* Comox
Conahomana *see* Wappo
Conaliga [AL] [*UpperCreek*] (H)
Conarie *see see* Canarsee
Conarise *see* Canarsee
Conarsie *see* Canarsee
Conastagoe *see* Conestoga
Conastoga *see* Conestoga
Conastogy *see* Conestoga
Concee *see* Lipan Apache
Conception *see* Tome
Concha *see* Conshac
Conchac *see* Conshac
Conchaes *see* Conshac
Conchakus *see* Conshac
Conchaque *see* Apalachicola
Conchaque *see* Conshac
Conchaque *see* Koasati
Conchata *see* Koasati
Conchatez *see* Conshac
Conchatez *see* Koasati
Conchati *see* Koasati
Conchatta *see* Koasati
Conchayon *Taensa Confederacy*
  (H)

Conches *see* Conshac
Concho [MX] (BE)
Conchtta *see* Koasati
Concon *see* Konkow
Conconcully *Lower Okinagan* (Ye)
Con-Con's *see* Konkow
Con-Cous *see* Konkow
Concous *see* Konkow
Concow *see* Konkow
Con-Cow *see* Konkow
Concow *see* Konkow
Concuyapem *Coahuiltecan*
  (Hdbk10)
Coneconam [MA] *Wampanoag*
  (LC)
Conejeros [Coahuiltecan]
  (Hdbk10)
Conejo [CA] *Diegueño* (H)
Conejo [MX] *Concho* (BE)
Coneliskes *see* Cowlitz
Conerd Helene *see* Skitwish
Conestego *see* Conestoga
Conestoga (BE) *see also* Susque-
  hanna (LC)
Conestoga (Ye) *see also* Susque-
  hannock (Ye)
Conestoga [MD] (LC)
Coneston *see* Conestoga
Conestogue *see* Conestoga
Confederated River Tribes (AI)
Confederated Tribes of Warm
  Springs (HN, v.48, no.2,
  pp.22–25)
Confederate Indians *see* Iroquois
Confederate Nations *see* Iroquois
Confederates *see* Iroquois
Congare *see* Congaree
Congaree [Lang] [SC] *Siouan* (H)
Congaree [SC] (BE)
Congere *see* Congaree
Congeree *see* Congaree
Conge-wee-cha-cha *see* Con-
  gewichacha
Congeweechacha *see* Con-
  gewichacha
Congewichacha *Dakota* (BE)
Congree *see* Congaree
Conguaco (BE) *see also* Popoluca
  (LC)
Conguaco [Gu] (BE)
Congue [MX] (Hdbk10)
Conguse *see* Cayuse
Conibo [PE] (LC)
Conicari [MX] (BE)
Conicoricho [MX] (Hdbk10)
Conina *see* Havasupai
Conipigua *Coahuiltecan* (Hdbk10)
Conis *see* Yuracare
Conistoga *see* Conestoga
Conittekook *see* Connecticut
Conivo *see* Conibo
Conkasketonwan *see* Changaske-
  ton

Conkhandeenrhonon [Can] *Iro-
  quois* (H)
Connamox *see* Coree
Connastago *see* Conestoga
Connay *see* Conoy
Connectacut *see* Connecticut
Connecticut [CT] (H)
Connegticut *see* Connecticut
Connessi *see* Cancy
Conneuaghs *see* Tahltan
Conninggahaughgaugh *see* Mo-
  hawk
Connino *see* Havasupai
Con-no-harrie-go-harrie *see*
  Onoalagona
Connoharriegoharrie *see*
  Onoalagona
Connoy *see* Conoy
Connoye *see* Conoy
Con-nugh-harie-gugh-harie *see*
  Onoalagona
Connughhariegughharie *see*
  Onoalagona
Conoatino *see* Kanohatino
Conob *see* Kanjobal
Conoies *see* Conoy
Conois *see* Conoy
Conostaoga *see* Conestoga
Conoy [MD, WV] (LC)
Conoy-uch-such *see* Conoy
Conoyucksuchroona *see* Conoy
Conqeree *see* Congaree
Consejo Regional Indigine [Col]
  (O)
Conshac (H)
Conshac (H) *see also* Koasati
  (LC)
Conshach *see* Conshac
Conshaes *see* Koasati
Conshakis *see* Conshac
Conshatta *see* Koasati
Contamis *see* Kutenai
Contauba *see* Catawba
Contenay *see* Kutenai
Contonnes *see* Kutenai
Contotol *see* Contotor
Contotoli *see* Contotor
Contotor [MX] (Hdbk10)
Contznoo *see* Hutsnuwu
Convivo *see* Conibo
Cooc [MX] *Guatare* (BE)
Coochchotellica *see* Kotsoteka
Cooch-cho-teth-ca *see* Kotsoteka
Coochchotethca *see* Kotsoteka
Coocheetaka *see* Kotsoteka
Coo-er-ee *see* Kuyuidika
Cooeree *see* Kuyuidika
Coofer *see* Puaray
Coofert *see* Puaray
Cookchaney *see* Chukchansi
Cookkoo-oosee *see* Coos
Cookkoooose *see* Coos
Cookoose *see* Coos

Cook's Ferry [BC] *Ntlakyapamuk*
(H)
Cools-on-tick-ara *see* Kotsoteka
Coon *see* Mikaunikashinga
Cooniac [WA] *Skilloot* (Oregon)
Coopanes *see* Kopano
Coopspellar *see* Kalispel
Coos (H) *see also* Coosuc (BE)
Coos (LC) *see also* Hanis (BE)
Coos [OR] (LC)
Coosa [SC, AL] *Cusabo* (BE)
Coosada *see* Koasati
Coosadi *see* Koasati
Coosah *see* Coosa
Coosas *see* Coos
Coosauda *see* Koasati
Coosaudee *see* Koasati
Coo-sau-dee *see* Koasati
Coosaw *see* Coosa
Coosawda *see* Koasati
Coosawder *see* Koasati
Coosawdi *see* Koasati
Coos Bay *see* Coos
Co-ose *see* Coos
Coose *see* Coos
Coose Bay *see* Coos
Cooses *see* Coos
Coose Taylors *see* Coos
Cooshates *see* Koasati
Cooshatties *see* Koasati
Coosida *see* Koasati
Coospacam *Coahuiltecan*
(Hdbk10)
Coospellar *see* Kalispel
Coos-pel-lar Nation *see* Kalispel
Cooss *see* Coos
Coosuc [NH] (BE)
Coosuck *see* Coosuc
Cootajam *see* Cotoname
Cootenai *see* Kutenai
Cootenay *see* Kutenai
Cootounies *see* Kutenai
Cootstooks pa tah pee *see* Salish
Coowarsartdas *see* Koasati
Coowersortda *see* Koasati
Cooyoko *see* Shooyoko
Cooyuweeweit *see* Kuyuidika
Copa *see* Creek
Copalis [WA] (BE)
Copane *see* Cofan
Copanes *see* Kopano
Copatta *see* Quapaw
Cop-eh *see* Copeh
Copeh (Pub, v.6, no.1, p.285) *see
also* Wintu (LC)
Copeh [CA] *Patwin* (H)
Copehan [Lang] (LC) *see also*
Wintu (LC)
Copehan [Lang] [CA] (H)
Copehan Indians *see* Copeh
Co-pi-yar *see* Kewevikopaya
Copiyar *see* Kewevkapaya
Copper (H) *see also* Tsattine (LC)

Copper [Lang] *Western Canada*
(Hdbk5)
Copper Eskimos (H) *see also* Kid-
nelik (H)
Copper Eskimos [AL] *Central Es-
kimos* (Hdbk5)
Copper Indians *see* Tatsanottine
Copper Indians *see* Ahtena
Copper-Mine *see* Tatsanottine
Coppermine *Chiricahua Apache*
(Hdbk10)
Coppermine *Mimbreno Apache*
(Hook)
Copper Mine Apache *see* Cop-
permine
Copper People *see* Tatsanottine
Copper River Indians *see* Ahtena
Copuchiniguara [MX] (Hdbk12)
Co-qani *see* Thokhani
Coqani *see* Thokhani
Coque *see* Zoque
Coquell *see* Mishikhwutmetunne
Coquet-lane *see* Coquitlam
Coquetlum *see* Coquitlam
Coquiapan *see* Caguilipan
Coquilain *see* Coquitlam
Coquill *see* Mishikhwutmetunne
Coquilla *see* Mishikhwut-
metunne
Coquille *see* Mishikhwut-
metunne
Coquille *see* Nasumi
Coquilth *see* Kwahiutl
Coquins *see* Tututni
Coquite *see* Pecos
Coquitlam [BC] *Stalo* (BE)
Coquitlan *see* Coquitlam
Coquitlane *see* Coquitlam
Coquitlum *see* Coquitlam
Cora [BaC] *Waicuri* (BE)
Cora [Lang] *Corachol* (Hdbk10)
Cora [MX] (LC)
Corachol *Sonoran* (Hdbk10)
Coramine *see* Coree
Coran-cana *see* Karankawa
Coranine *see* Coree
Corankoua *see* Karankawa
Coras *see* Nevome
Coras *see* Cora
Corazo *see* Moro
Corazu *see* Moro
Corbeau *see* Crow
Corbeaux *see* Crow
Corbitant [MA] *Wampanoag* (BE)
Corbonamga [Lang] [CA] (Pub,
v.8, n.1, p.11)
Corchaug [NY] *Montauk* (BE)
Corchong *see* Corchaug
Corchoug *see* Corchaug
Cord People *see* Attigneenongna-
hac
Core *see* Coree
Corechos *see* Querecho

Coree [NC] (BE)
Coreguaje [Col] (O)
Corica *see* Yorica
Corinto [Col] *Paez* (O)
Corn Band [SD] *Sioux* (H)
Corn Creek Band of Paiutes *see*
Pahranagat
Corn Eaters *see* Arikara
Corneille *see* Amahami
Corn Indians *Southern Brule*
(TW, v.39, no.6, p.49)
Corn Peoples *see* Zuni
Cornplanter Indians [NY] *Seneca*
(H)
Coroa *see* Koroa
Coroa *see* Cayapo
Coroado *see* Kaingangue
Coroaso *see* Kaingangue
Corobici [CR] *Chibchan* (BE)
Corobisi *see* Corobici
Coroha *see* Koroa
Corois *see* Koroa
Coro Marikopa *see* Maricopa
Coronkawa *see* Karankawa
Coronks *see* Karankawa
Corotomen *see* Cuttatawomen
Corpus Christi de Isleta *see* Isleta
Corrhue [CR] *Cabecar* (O)
Corroas *see* Koroa
Corrois *see* Koroa
Corroys *see* Koroa
Coruano [CA] (H)
Corumbiara *see* Aikana
Corusies *see* Korusi
Corveset *see* Coweset
Cosah *see* Coosa
Cosapuya *see* Cusabo
Coschotghta *see* Kotsoteka
Cosemene *see* Cosume
Coshatta *see* Koasati
Coshattee *see* Koasati
Cosina *see* Goajiro
Cosnina *see* Havasupai
Cosnino *see* Havasupai
Coso *see* Kassovo
Coso *see* Panamint
Coss *see* Coos
Costano *see* Costanoan
Costanoan [CA] (LC)
Costanoes *see* Costanoan
Costanos (CA-8) *see also*
Costanoan (CA-8)
Costanos [CA] (H)
Cos-tche-tegh-ka *see* Kotsoteka
Costcheteghka Comanches *see*
Kotsoteka
Coste *see* Koasati
Costehe *see* Koasati
Costeño *see* Costanoan
Costonoan [Lang] *Utian* (CA-8)
Costrowers *see* Kassovo
Cosume [CA] (H)
Cosumne *see* Cosume

Cosumnies see Cosume
Cosuttheutun [OR] *Tututni* (H)
Coswas see Kassovo
Co-ta-plane-mis see Cotoplane-
mis
Cotaplanemis see Cotoplanemis
Cotappo see Catawba
Cotawpec see Catawba
Co'tcalsicaya see Thochalsithaya
Cotcalsicaya see Thochalsithaya
Cotchita see Cochiti
Cotchiti see Cochiti
Cotes-de-Chien see
Thlingchadinne
Cotipiniguara [MX] (Hdbk10)
Coto *Chibchan* (BE) *see also*
Boruca (LC)
Coto [CR] (BE)
Coto *Tucanoan* see Orejon
Cotoayagua [Lang] (Hdbk10)
Cotober see Catawba
Cotogeho *Caduveo* (O)
Cotogcuo *Caduveo* (O)
Cotogudeo *Caduveo* (O)
Cotomavo see Cotonam
Cotonam [TX] (BE)
Cotoname see Cotonam
Cotones see Kutenai
Co-to-planemis see Cotoplane-
mis
Cotoplanemis [CA] (H)
Cotoy [HA, WInd] *Cahibo* (BE)
Cotshimi see Cochimi
Co'tsoni see Thotsoni
Cotsoni see Thotsoni
Cottonois see Kutenai
Cottonwood Bannock see
Shohopanaiti
Cottonwoods see Dau-pom
Cottonwood-Salmon-Eaters see
Shohoaigadika
Cou-chan see Yuma
Couchan see Yuma
Couchate see Koasati
Cou-Cows see Konkow
Coucows see Yuma
Coueracouitenon see Coiracoen-
tanon
Couexi see Coosa
Coujouga see Cayuga
Coulapissa see Acolapissa
Coulonge see Dumoine
Couna *Pueblo Indians* (H)
Counarrha see Kutenai
Counica see Tunica
Coup de Fleches [TX] (H)
Coupe see Tsankupi
Coupes see Cuts
Coup-gorges see Dakota
Cour d'Aleine see Coeur d'Alene
Cour d'Aleine see Skitswish
Cour d'Alenes see Coeur d'Alene
Cour d'Alenes see Skitswish

Cour d'Aline see Coeur d'Alene
Cour d'Aline see Skitswish
Cour de Lion see Coeur d'Alene
Cour de Lion see Skitswish
Couroas see Koroa
Courois see Koroa
Courterrielle see Ottawa
Courtes Oreilles see Ottawa
Courtoreiller see Ottawa
Cousatee see Koasati
Coushatta (LC) *see also* Koasati
(LC)
Coushatta [TX] (LC)
Cousoudee see Koasati
Coussac see Koasati
Coussati see Koasati
Coussehate see Koasati
Coutah-wee-cha-cha see
Kutawichasha
Coutanies see Kutenai
Coutaria see Kutenai]
Couteaux see Ntlakyapamuk
Couteaux see Thompson Indians
Couteaux Jaunes see Tatsanottine
Couteaux Jeaunes see Tatsanot-
tine
Coutenay see Kutenai
Couthaougoula *Taensa Confeder-
acy* (H)
Coutnees see Kutenai
Coutonais see Kutenai
Coutonois see Kutenai
Coutouns see Kutenai
Covaji see Kawaiisu
Cove-chance see Chukchansi
Coville see Colville
Cow-ang-a-chem see Serrano
Cowangachem see Serrano
Cowassuck (H) *see also* Coosuc
(BE)
Cowasuck (H) *see also* Coosuc
(BE)
Cowasuck [Q, VT, NH] *Western
Abnaki* (Hdbk15)
Co-wa-ver see Kewevikopaya
Cowaver see Kewevkapaya
Cow Buffalo see Arukhwa I
Cow-cow see Konkow
Cowchilla see Chawchilla
Cow Creek see Nahankhuotane
Cow Creek (LC) *see also* Umpqua
(LC)
Cow Creek [OR] (Oregon)
Cowegan see Cowichan
Cowela see Cahuilla
Cowela see Kawia *Luiseño*
Cow-e-lis-ke see Cowlitz
Coweliske see Cowlitz
Cow-e-lis-kee see Cowlitz
Coweliskee see Cowlitz
Cowelits see Cowlitz
Cowelitz see Cowlitz
Cow-e-na-chino see Cowlitz

Cowenachino see Cowlitz
Cowes see Coos
Coweset [MA, RI] *Nipmuc* (BE)
Cowesett see Coweset
Coweta [AL] *Muskogee* (BE)
Cowe-wa-chin see Cowichan
Cowewachin see Cowichan
Cowhuilla see Kawia *Yokuts*
Cowiah see Kawia *Yokuts*
Cowichan [BC, VanI] (LC)
Cowichan Lake [VanI] *Nootka*
(H)
Cowichan of Fraser River see
Stalo
Cowichin see Cowichan
Cowila see Cahuilla
Cowilla see Cahuilla
Cowilla see Kawia *Luiseño*
Cow-iller see Kawia *Yokuts*
Cowiller see Cahuilla
Cowiller see Kawia *Yokuts*
Cowitchen see Cowichan
Cowitchin see Cowichan
Cowlitch see Cowlitz
Cowlits see Cowlitz
Cowlitsick see Cowlitz
Cowlitsk see Cowlitz
Cowlitsk see Cowlitz
Cowlitz (LC) *see also* Scowlits (BE)
Cowlitz [WA] (LC)
Cow-nan-ti-co see Cownantico
Cownantico [OR] *Skoton* (H)
Cowweset see Coweset
Cowweseuck see Coweset
Cowwesit see Coweset
Cowwilla see Kawia *Yokuts*
Coxane see Kohani
Coya see Colla
Coyabegux [TX] (H)
Coyahero see Coyotero Apache
Coyaima [Col] (LC)
Coyaima [Lang] *Motilon* (UAz,
v.28)
Coyamit [MX] *Concho* (BE)
Coyatero see Coyotero Apache
Co-ye-ta see Koyeti
Coyeta see Koyeti
Co-ye-te see Koyeti
Coyete see Koyeti
Coyetero see Coyotero Apache
Co-ye-tie see Koyeti
Coyetie see Koyeti
Co'yetlini see Thoyetlini
Coyetlini see Thoyetlini
Coyoleno see Coyotero Apache
Coyolxauhqui [MX] *Aztecs* (BE)
Coyoquipiguara *Coahuiltecan*
(Hdbk10)
Coyotaro see Coyotero Apache
Coyote see Coyotero Apache
Coyotens see Coyotero Apache
Coyote People see Stoam Ohimal
Coyotero Apache (Hook) *see also*
Western Apache (Hdbk10)

Coyotero Apache (SoQ, v.95, no.2, pp.138–176) *see also* Tonto Apache (LC)

Coyotero Apache [AZ] *Chiricahua Apache* (H)

Coyotes (H) *see also* Oto (LC)

Coyotes *Pima* (H)

Coyote Society *see* Himoiyoqis

Coyouge *see* Cayuga

Coyouger *see* Cayuga

Coyoukon *see* Koyukukhotana

Coystero *see* Coyotero Apache

Co-Yukon *see* Koyukukhotana

Coyukon *see* Koyukukhotana

Cozaby Pah-Utes *see* Kutsavi-dokado

Cozao *see* Coosa

Cozarini *see* Kozarene

Cqa'neza *see* Thkhaneza

Cqaneza *see* Thkhaneza

Cqa'neza'ni *see* Thkhaneza

Cqanezani *see* Thkhaneza

Cqa'paha *see* Thkhapaha

Cqapaha *see* Thkhapaha

Cqa'tcini *see* Thkhatshini

Cqatcini *see* Thkhatshini

Cqesxenemx *see* Canim Lake

Craho [Br] *Eastern Timbira* (LC)

Craho [Lang] *see* Canella

Cran *see* Tapuya

Crane People *see* Petkhaninikashina

Crao *see* Craho

Craw-fish Band *see* Chakchiuma

crawfish eaters *see* Beatty Band

Credit Indians [Ont] *Missisauga* (H)

Cree [Ont, MT] (LC)

Cree-Assiniboine *see* Niopwatuk

Creek [AL, GA] (LC)

Creek Confederacy [AL, GA] (BE)

Creek Nation *see* Creek Confederacy

Cree of Cross Lake *see* Sakittawawininiwug

Cree of the lowlands *see* Maskegon

Cree of the Woods *see* Sakawithiniwuk

Creston Band [BC] *Kutenai* (BE)

Crevas *see* Osage

Cri *see* Cree

Crichana [Br] *Carib* (LC)

Crichana [Lang] *Yauapery* (UAz, v.28)

Crie *see* Cree

Criq *see* Cree

Crique *see* Cree

Cris [Lang] *see* Cree

Crisca *see* Akwe-Shavante

Crishana *see* Crichana

Crishana *see* Yanoama

Crishana *see* Yawaperi

Cristeneaux *see* Cree

Cristinaux *see* Cree

Cristineaux *see* Cree

Cristinos *see* Cree

Crists *see* Cree

Criza *see* Akwe-Shavante

Croatan Indians (LC) *see also* Lumbee (LC)

Croatan Indians [NC, VA] (BE)

Croix Indians, St. *see* Passamaquoddy

Cross Sound Indians *see* Huna

Crosswick Indians [NJ, DE] (Hdbk15)

Crow (H) *see also* Kaka (H)

Crow [Lang] *Hidatsa* (H)

Crow [MT, WY] (LC)

Crow-Chief's band *see* Sarsi

Crow-Child's Band *see* Broad Grass

Crow Creek Sioux (Char, v.1)

Crown King Indians *see* Wikenichepa

Crow People (H) *see also* Tutchone (BE)

Crow People *Crow* (H)

Crow River Kutchin *see* Vuntakutchin

Crow-wing [MN] *Chippewa* (H)

Crow Wing River [MN, ND, SD] *Chippewa* (H)

Crucifero *see* Yavapai

Cruel *see* Dakota

Crus *see* Cree

Cruz, Santa [CA] *Coastanoan* (BE)

Cruz, Santa [MX] *Mayas* (BE)

Cruzado *see* Yavapai

Cruz Island, Santa [Lang] [CA] *Chumashan* (H)

Cu *see* Shu

Cuabajai *see* Serrano

Cuabajai *see* Kawaiisu

Cuabajai *see* Gitanemuk

Cuabajay *see* Serrano

Cuabajay *see* Kawaiisu

Cuachichil [Lang] [MX] (Hdbk10)

Cuacua *see* Mapoyo

Cuagila *see* Coahuileño

Cuagilla *see* Coahuileño

Cuaguijamiguara [MX] (Hdbk10)

Cuahcomeca [MX] (BE)

Cuaiker *see* Cuaiquer

Cuaiquer [EC, Col] (LC)

Cuajala *see* Southern Paiute

Cuambia *see* Moguex

Cuame *see* Sia

Cuampes *see* Cuampis

Cuampis *Faraon Apache* (H)

Cuanes *see* Cocopa

Cuapas *see* Quapaw

Cuaques *see* Zuaque

Cuaquinacaniguara [MX] (Hdbk10)

Cuarac *see* Quarai

Cuarai *see* Quarai

Cua-ray *see* Quarai

Cuaray *see* Quarai

Cuarra *see* Quarai

Cuarry *see* Quarai

Cuartelejo [KS] *Plains Apache* (Hdbk10)

Cuatache [MX] (Hdbk10)

Cuatahe *see* Cuatache

Cuatganes *see* Yuma

Cuatganes *see* Kahwan

Cuayker *see* Cuaiquer

Cubana [HA, WInd] *Cahibo* (BE)

Cubanacan [Cu] (BE)

Cubao [SanD, WInd] *Hubabo* (BE)

Cubeo [Br, Col] (LC)

Cubeo Maku *see* Cacua

Cubeo Maku *see* Kakwa

Cubeus *see* Cubeo

Cubsuvi *Coahuiltecan* (Hdbk10)

Cubulco Achi [Gu] *Achi* (LC)

Cucapa *see* Cocopa

Cucapacha *see* Cocopa

Cucassus *see* Cocopa

Cuchan *see* Yuma

Cuchana *see* Yuma

Cu-cha-no *see* Yuma

Cu-cha-no *see* Quechan

Cuchano *see* Quechan

Cuchano *see* Yuma

Cuchans *see* Quechan

Cuchantica *see* Kotsoteka

Cuchaus *see* Yuma

Cuchaus *see* Quechan

Cuchendado [TX] (H)

Cuchi *see* Yuracare

Cuchian *see* Cuchillones

Cuchian *see* Yuma

Cuchian *see* Quechan

Cuchili *see* Cochiti

Cuchillones [CA] *Costanoan* (H)

Cuchimies *see* Cochimi

Cuchin *see* Cochiti

Cuchinochi *Coahuiltecan* (Hdbk10)

Cuchinochil *see* Cuchinochi

Cuchinu *see* Cochimi

Cuchiti *see* Cochiti

Cuciba [Cu] (BE)

Cucompners *see* Cucoomphers

Cucoomphers [CA] (H)

Cucopa *see* Cocopa

Cucua *see* Kakwa

Cuculato [CA] *Yuma* (H)

Cuculute *see* Cuculato

Cu-cu-pah *see* Cocopa

Cucupah *see* Cocopa

Cucutades *see* Moro

Cucuyama *see* Sucuyama
Cucuye *see* Pecos
Cudeve *see* Eudeve
Cuechuntica *see* Kotsoteka
Cueganas *see* Yuma
Cueganas *see* Kahwan
Cuelcaje-ne *see* Llanero
Cuelcajen-ne *see* Guhlkande
Cuelcajenne *see* Llanero
Cueloce *see* Quelotetrey
Cuelotetry *see* Quelotetrey
Cuepane [MX] (Hdbk10)
Cuercomache [AZ] *Yavapai* (H)
Cuercos quemados [MX]
    Tamaulipec (BE)
Cueres *see* Keres
Cuerez *see* Keres
Cueros Crudos *Coahuiltecan*
    (Hdbk10)
Cueros Quemados *see* Cuercos
    quemados
Cuerro *see* Quarai
Cuesi [BO] *Araona* (O)
Cuesnina *see* Havasupai
Cueva (LC) *see also* Cuna (LC)
Cueva [Pan] (LC)
Cufan *see* Cofan
Cugadika'a *see* Nez Perce
Cuhana *see* Cocopa
Cuhanas *see* Kahwan
Cuhanes *see* Cocopa
Cuhtzuteca *see* Kotsoteka
Cuiba *see* Cuiva
Cuibo *see* Caiva
Cuicatec [Lang] [MX] *Mixtecan*
    (LC)
Cuicatecan [Lang] [MX] *Mixtecan*
    (BE)
Cuicateco *see* Cuicato
Cuichan *see* Yuma
Cuichan *see* Quechan
Cuichana *see* Yuma
Cuicuro *see* Kuikuru
Cuicuru *see* Kuikuru
Cuicutl *see* Kuikuru
Cuiminipaco [MX] (Hdbk10)
Cuimnapum *see* Chimnapum
Cuipoco *see* Piapoco
Cuismer *see* Havasupai
Cuisnur *see* Havasupai
Cuitlatec *see* Cuitlateco
Cuitlateco (LC) *see also* Teco (LC)
Cuitlateco [Lang] [MX] (LC)
Cuitoas [KS] (H)
Cuiukguo *see* Cajuga
Cuiva [VE, Col] *Guahibo* (LC)
Cuivira *see* Quivira
Cuivres *see* Tatsanottine
Cujanes *see* Kohani
Cujano *see* Kohani
Cujareno [PE] (O)
Cujisenayeri [Lang] *Maipurean*
    (O)

Cujubicena *see* Cayuishana
Culane *see* Shuhlanan
Culantro *see* Guaymi
Culantro *see* Northern Guaymi
Culcahende *see* Rancheria of
    Pasqual
Culdoah *see* Kauldawa
Culina (LC) *see also* Colina (O)
Culina [Br] (LC)
Culino *see* Culina
Culinonisna *see* Havasupai
Culisnur *see* Havasupai
Culs-coupe *see* Kishkakon
Cultalchulches *see* Cutalchich
Cumana (Hdbk10) *see also* Kah-
    wan (Hdbk10)
Cumana (LC) *see also* Kamia (LC)
Cumana [VE] (LC)
Cumanagoto (LC) *see also*
    Cumano (LC)
Cumanagoto [Lang] *Tamanaco*
    (UAz, v.28)
Cumanasho *see* Mascali
Cumanche *see* Comanche
Cumania *see* Comanche
Cum-ba-twas *see* Kumbatuash
Cumbatwas *see* Kumbatuash
Cumcloup *see* Kamloop
Cumeehe *see* Comanche
Cum-i-um-has *see* Cumumbah
Cumiumhas *see* Cumumbah
Cum-min-tahs *see* Cumumbah
Cummintahs *see* Cumumbah
Cummoaqui *see* Hopi
Cummooqui *see* Hopi
Cumpes *see* Cumumbah
Cumpquekis *see* Komkyutis
Cum-que-kis *see* Komkyutis
Cumumbah [UT] *Ute* (H)
Cum-um-pah *see* Cumumbah
Cumumpah *see* Cumumbah
Cuna [Pan] (LC)
Cuna-Cueva *see* Cuna
Cunacuna *see* Cuna
Cunacuna *see* Mainland Cuna
Cuñai *see* Cuñeil
Cuñai *see* Cuñeil
Cuñai *see* Kamia
Cuname *see* Sia
Cunan [Lang] *Chibchan* (O)
Cuncaae *see* Caacat
Cuñeil (H) *see also* Kamia (LC)
Cuñeil [CA] *Yuman* (H)
Cuneskapi *see* Naskapi
cunge *see* Pecos
Cunhate *see* Koasati
Cuni *see* Zuni
Cuniba *see* Conibo
Cunibo *see* Conibo
Cun-iktceka *see* Shungikcheka
Cuniktceka *see* Shungikcheka
Cun-i-um-hah *see* Cumumbah
Cuniumhah *see* Cumumbah

Cunivo *see* Conibo
Cunkaha-nap'in *see* Chungka-
    hanapin
Cunka-yute-cni *see*
    Shungkayuteshni
Cunkayutecni *see*
    Shungkayuteshni
Cunk i-ki-ka-ra-tca-da *see*
    Shungikikarachada
Cunkikikaratcada *see*
    Shungikikarachada
Cunk-tcank i -ki-ka-ra-tca-da *see*
    Shungikikarachada
Cunktcankikikaratcada *see*
    Shungikikarachada
Cunmikase *see* Shomakoosa
Cunopavi *see* Shongopavi
Cunquilipinoy *Piro* (H)
Cuntce'bi [MN] *Assiniboin* (BE)
Cunuana (O) *see also* Yecuana
    (LC)
Cunuana [Lang] *Maquiritare*
    (UAz, v.28)
Cunyeel *see* Cuñeil
Cunza [Lang] (LC)
Cuouex *see* Dakota
Cupacha *see* Cocopa
Cupan [Lang] *Shoshonean* (LC)
Cupan [Lang] *Tapic* (Hdbk10)
Cupdan *Coahuiltecan* (BE)
Cupeño [CA] (LC)
Cupeño [Lang] [CA] *Cupan*
    (Hdbk10)
Cupeño [Lang] [CA] [*Luiseño-
    Cahuilla*] (BE)
Cupisnique [PE] (LC)
Curabare *see* Kuruaya
Curancahuases *see* Karankawa
Curano [PE] *Campa* (O)
Curaye *see* Kuruaya
Curbo *see* Crow
Curibary *see* Kuruaya
Curibeo *see* Conibo
Curierai *see* Kuruaya
Curino *see* Culina
Curiuaia *see* Kuruaya
Curiuaye *see* Kuruaya
Curivare *see* Kuruaya
Curivere *see* Kuruata
Curois *see* Koroa
Curoton *see* Heta
Curricaro *see* Curriccarro
Curricarro [VE] (O)
Currierai *see* Kuruaya
Curripaco [VE, Br, Col] *Wakue-
    nai* (O)
Curripako *see* Curripaco
Curtaka *see* Castake
Curtoze-to-gah Comanches *see*
    Kotsoteka
Curtz-e Ticker Comanches *see*
    Kotsoteka
Curuahe *see* Kuruaya

Curuara *see* Kuruaya
Curuari *see* Kuruaya
Curuaya *see* Kuruaya
Curuaye *see* Kuruaya
Curubare *see* Kuruaya
Curueye *see* Kuruaya
Curupi [BO] *Araona* (O)
Curuton *see* Heta
Cusabo [SC] (BE)
Cuscarawaoc [MD, DE] *Nanticoke* (BE)
Cuscarawaoke *see* Cuscarawaoc
Cushans *see* Quechan
Cushatee *see* Koasati
Cush-eh-tah *see* Koasati
Cushehtah *see* Koasati
Cushhouk *see* Clowwewalla
Cushkarawaock *see* Cuscarawaoc
Cushna [CA] *Maidu* (H)
Cushooks [OR] *Clowwewalla* (Oregon)
Cuskoetehwaw-thesseetuck *see* Siksika
Cussadies *see* Koasati
Cusseta *see* Kasihta
Cusshetaes *see* Koasati
Custenau [Lang] *Maupurean* (O)
Custenau Indians *see* Kutenabu
Cutagamies *see* Fox
Cutahaco *see* Tutahaco
Cutalches *see* Cutalchich
Cutalchich [TX] (H)
Cutalchiches *see* Cutalchich
Cutans [NA] (H)
Cutasho *see* Kamakan
Cut bank *see* Micacuopsiba
Cut Beards *see* Pabaska
Cutcana *see* Yuma
Cutcanas *see* Kahwan
Cutchamekin *see* Kutshamakin
Cutchanas *see* Yuma
Cutchanas *see* Quechan
Cutchate *see* Koasati
Cuteanas *see* Yuma
Cuteanas *see* Kahwan
Cuteco [MX] *Varohio* (H)
Cutgana *see* Kohuana
Cutgana *see* Kahwan
Cutgana *see* Yuma
Cutgana *see* Kohuana
Cutganes *see* Yuma
Cutganes *see* Kahwan
Cutguanes *see* Yuma
Cutguanes *see* Kahwan
Cuthalchuches *see* Cutalchich
Cut heads *see* Pabaska
Cuthlamuh *see* Cathlamet
Cuthlamuk *see* Cathlamet
Cutinano *see* Aguano
Cutlashoot *see* Ootlashoot
Cut Offs *see* Kiyuksa *Oglala*
Cuts *Sihasapa* (H)
Cutsahnim *see* Yakima

Cut-sah-nim *see* Yakima
Cut-sa-nim *see* Yakima
Cutsanim *see* Yakima
Cutshamakin *see* Kutshamakin
Cutshamequin *see* Kutshamakin
Cutshamewquin *see* Kutshamakin
Cutshamoquen *see* Kutshamakin
Cuts-sah-nem *see* Yakima
Cutssahnem *see* Yakima
Cuts-sah-nim *see* Yakima
Cutssahnim *see* Yakima
Cuttako *see* Kiowa Apache
Cuttambo *see* Catawba
Cuttatawoman *see* Cuttatawomen
Cuttatawomans *see* Cuttatawomen
Cuttatawomen [VA] *Pawhatan* (BE)
Cuttawa *see* Catawba
Cut-throats *see* Dakota
Cutthroats *see* Dakota
Cutu [PE, EC] (O)
Cutugueo *Caduveo* (O)
Cut wrists *see* Cheyenne
cux *see* Nunivak Central Yupik
Cuyacapo *see* Gueyacapo
Cuyahuga *see* Cayuga
Cuyama [CA] *Chumash* (BE)
Cuyama [Lang] [CA] *Chumash* (He)
Cuyamunque [Lang] *Tewa* (H)
Cuyanes *see* Kohani
Cuyba *see* Cuiva
Cuybira *see* Quivira
Cuyentemari [PE] *Campa* (O)
Cuyuhasomi [Phratry] *Timucua* (H)
Cuyuhasomiaroqui [Clan] *Timucua* (H)
Cuyuhasomiele [Clan] *Timucua* (H)
Cuyuse *see* Cayuse
Cuyuteca [MX] (BE)
Cuza *see* Quarai
Cuzadan *see* Koasati
Cu-za-ya *see* Quarai
Cuzaya *see* Quarai
Cuzco *see* Quecha
Cwarennoc *see* Coree
cwexemx *see* Canoe Creek Band
Cybaho [HA, WInd] *Cahibo* (BE)
Cycuyo *see* Pecos
Cyininook *see* Cree
Cynago *see* Sinago
Cyneper *see* Seneca
Cyniker *see* Seneca
Cyotlero *see* Coyotero Apache
Cypowais plunderers *see* Pillagers
Cypoway *see* Chippewa
Cypress bulb eaters *see* Tovusidokado
Cyuse *see* Cayuse

-D-

Daahl [Clan] [NM] *Jemez* (H)
Daahl [Clan] [NM] *Pecos* (H)
Da'at'hl *see* Daahl *Jemez*
Daathl *see* Daahl *Jemez*
da-bahu *see* Navajo
dabahu *see* Navajo
Dabaigua [HA, WInd] *Bainoa* (BE)
Dabo-tena *see* Etagottine
Dacabimo *see* Navajo
Dacacmuri *Coahuiltecan* (Hdbk10)
Dachi *see* Tachi
Dachizh-o-zhi-n *see* Dachizhozhin
Dachizhozhin [NM] *Jicarilla Apache* (BE)
Dacorta *see* Dakota
Dacota *see* Dakota
Dacota errans *see* Gens du Large
Dacotah *see* Dakota
Dacotas of the St. Peter's *see* Santee
Da-da-ze ni-ka-cin-ga *see* Southern Paiute
Da-da-ze ni-ka-cin-ga *see* Pauite
Dadaze nikacinga *see* Paiute
Dagaeoga *see* Mohawk
Dadaze nikacinga *see* Southern Paiute
Da-ga-e-o-ga *see* Mohawk
Daganasel *see* Dagangasel
Dagangasel [*Kona-ketawi*] (H)
Dahaboon [HA, WInd] *Cahibo* (BE)
Daha-dinneh *see* Etagottine
Dahadinnes *see* Etagottine
Daha-dtinne *see* Etagottine
Da-ha-dumies *see* Etagottine
Dahadumies *see* Etagottine
Dahcinci [Lang] [CA] *Patwin* (CA)
Dahcota *see* Dakota
Dahcotah *see* Dakota
Dahibonici [HA, WInd] *Bainoa* (BE)
Dahkota *see* Dakota
Dah-ko-tah *see* Dakota
Dahmi *see* Santa Ana
Dahodinni *see* Etagottine
Daho-tena *see* Dahotena
Daho-tena *see* Etagottine
Dahotena (PC) *see also* Etagottine (BE)
Dahotena [CA] *Nehaunee* (Contri, v.1, p.33)
Daigano *see* Diegueño
Daiyuahl-lanas [Clan] *Haida* (H)
Dakanmanyin [*Han (Kansa)*] (H)
Dakats [Clan] *North Fork Mono* (Pub, v.11, no.5, p.293)

Dakaz *see* Tukkuthkutchin
dakca-mala *see* Modoc
dakca-wana *see* Modoc
Dakkadhe *see* Tukkuthkutchin
Dakla-weti *see* Daktlawedi
Daklaweti *see* Daklawedi
Dakota (LC) *see also* Lakota (Annual, v.15, no.2, pp.157–158)
Dakota (LC) *see also* Sioux (BE)
Dakota [SD] (LC)
Dakotah *see* Dakota
Dakotha *see* Dakota
Daktlawedi [AK] *Chilkat* (H)
Daktlawedi [AK] *Hutsnuwa* (H)
Daktlawedi [Clan] *Tlingit* (H)
Dak-tsaam-al-a *see* Klamath
Daktsaamala *see* Klamath
Dak-tsaew-an-a *see* Klamath
Daktsaewana *see* Klamath
Dakubetede [CA, OR] (BE)
Dala *see* Tala
Dalinche [CA] (H)
Dalinchi [CA] (CA)
Dalles (Hdbk12) *see also* Wasco (LC)
Dalles [CA] *Tennino* (H)
Dalls Indians *see* Dalles
Dallus *see* Mayoruna
Dalsokaiya (Pub, v.20, no.6, p.107)
Damiche *see* Odamich
Dancer Band *see* Genega's Band
Dancer Indians *see* Cahuilla
Dancers *see* Kawia *Luiseño*
Dane (H) *see also* Athapascan (LC)
Dane (H) *see also* Kaiyuhkhotana (BE)
Dane (H) *see also* Tsattine (LC)
Dane *Tinne* (H)
Dane Esclaves *see* Etchareottine
Da-nem-me *see* Tanima
Danemme *see* Tanima
Dani [Br] (O)
Danite *see* Athapascan
Danites Esclaves *see* Etchareottine
Danoha *see* Danoxa
Danokeya [CA] *Pomo* (Pub, v.40, no.2)
Danoxa [CA] *Eastern Pomo* (Pub, v.36, no.6)
Danzarine *see* Cahuilla
Danzarine *see* Kawia [Luiseño]
Daparabopos [MX] *Lagunero* (BE)
Dapishul *see* Da-pi-shul
Da-pi-shul [CA] *Pomo* (Contri, v.3, p.155)
Daq'lawe'di *see* Daktlawedi
Daquinatinno [TX] (H)
Daquio [TX] (H)
Darazhazh *see* Pawnee

Darcota *see* Dakota
Darcotah *see* Dakota
Dareotas *see* Dakota
Dariena *see* Embera
Dark Hands *see* Manos Prietas
Dark Rocks People *see* Aravaipa
Dark Tree *see* Ta'neeszahni
Da'sha-i *see* Kadohadocho
Dashai *see* Kadohadacho
Dashiton *see* Deshuhittan
Dasingahaga *see* Hangatanga
Da-sin-ja-ha-ga *see* Hangatanga
Dasoak [Clan] *Huron* (H)
Datcho (H) *see also* Kadohadacho (BE)
Datcho [TX] (H)
Da-thun-da *see* Tesinde
Dathunda *see* Tesinde
Datse-a *see* Comanche
Da'tse-a *see* Comanche
Datsea *see* Comanche
Da'tse-an *see* Comanche
Datsean *see* Comanche
Datuana [Col] *Yahuna* (LC)
Datumpa'ta *see* Kiowa
Daunom *see* Dau-nom
Dau-nom [CA] *Wintu* (BE)
Daupom *see* Dau-pom
Dau-pom [CA] *Wintu* (BE)
Dau-pum *see* Dau-pom
Daupum *see* Dau-pom
Daurai *see* Atorai
Dauri *see* Atorai
Davaxo *see* Navajo
Davis Inlet [Can] [*Montagnais-Naskapi*] (BE)
Dawaganha *see* Ontwaganha
Dawaganhaes *see* Ontwaganha
Dawamish *see* Dwamish
Dawhoot-dinneh *see* Etagottine
Dawnom *see* Dau-nom
Dawpom *see* Dau-pom
Dawta *see* Dakota
Daygótcheerah *see* Ojibwa
Dayton-Elmo *Kutenai* (BE)
De [Clan] *Pueblo Indians* (H)
Deadman's Creek (Hdbk12) *see also* Skeetchestn (Hdbk12)
Deadman's Creek (Hdbk12) *see also* Skemqinemx (Hdbk12)
Deadman's Creek [BC] *Kamloop Shuswap* (H)
Deadose [TX] (BE)
Deagheta [Clan] *Ponca* (H)
Deagothee Loochoo *see* Tukkuthkutchin
Deaguane *see* Doguene
Dearuwa *see* Pioroa
Decano *see* Desana
De Chentes *see* Des Chutes
De'citan *see* Deshuhittan
Decitan *see* Deshuhittan
De Corbeau *see* Crow

De'cuana *see* Dekuana
Decu'hit tan *see* Deshuhittan
Decuana *see* Dekuana
de Curbo *see* Crow
De-d'a tene *see* Mishikhwut-metunne
Dedatene *see* Mishikhwut-metunne
Deegothee *see* Tukkuthkutchin
Deep Creek [CA] *Gosiute*
Deep Creek [WA] *Spokan* (H)
Deer Eaters *see* Beatty band
Deer Head *see* Tapa [Omaha]
Deer-Horn Esquimaux *see* Nageuktormiut
Deerhorn Mountaineers *see* Etchaottine
Deer People *see* Tohontaenrat
Deer Purple *see* Pimtainin
Deer Skins *Northern Athapascan* (H)
Deeshcii'nii [Clan] [*Navajo* (People, p.123)
Deewano *see* Twana
Degathee Dinees *see* Tukkuthkutchin
Degothees *see* Tukkuthkutchin
Degothi-Kutchin *see* Tukkuthkutchin
Deguene *see* Doguene
Degutbee Dinees *see* Tukkuthkutchin
Deguthee Dennee *see* Takkuthkutchin
Deguthee Dine *see* Tukkuthkutchin
Deguthee Dinees *see* Takkuthkutchin
Dehkewi *see* Kutchin
Deis *see* Sandia
Deja *see* Piapoco
Dejabi [BO] *Araona* (O)
Dekuana [VE] *Yecuana* (O)
Dekuhana *see* Dekuana
Dekujana *see* Dekuana
Delamattanoes *see* Huron
Delamattenoes *see* Huron
Delamattenoes *see* Wyandot
de la Nation du Castor *see* Amikwa
Delawar *see* Delaware
Delawara *see* Delaware
Delaware [NJ] (LC)
De Lawarr *see* Delaware
Delaway *see* Delaware
Del-dje *see* Tonto Apache
Deldje *see* Tonto Apache
Deldzje *see* Tonto Apache
Delemattanoes *see* Huron
Delewar *see* Delaware
Deleware *see* Delaware
Deleway *see* Delaware
Deliette *see* Tamaroa

Dellamattanoes *see* Huron
Delta [Lang] *Yuman* (Hdbk10)
Delta-Californian [Lang] *Yuman* (Hdbk10)
Deluas *see* Delaware
Demingo, Santa *see* Santo Domingo
Dena'ina *see* Tanaina
Denaina *see* Tanaina
De-na-vi *see* Tanima
Denavi *see* Tanima
De-na-ways *see* Tanima
Denaways *see* Tanima
Dena'xtax *see* Tenaktak
Denaxtax *see* Tenaktak
Dendjye *see* Athapascan
Dendjye *see* Kuyedi
Dene (H) *see also* Athapascan (LC)
Dene (H) *see also* Kawchottine (LC)
Dene [Can] *Tinne* (Can'd, v.17, no.1, pp.24–26)
Dene Couteaux-Jaunes *see* Tatsanottine
Dene des Montagnes-Rocheuses *see* Nahane
Dene-Dindjie *see* Athapascan
Dene Esclaves *Tinne* (H)
Dene Etcha-Ottine *see* Etchaottine
Deneh-Dindschieh *see* Athapascan
Dene Peaux-de-Lievre *see* Kawchodinne
Dene Tchippewayan *see* Chipewyan
Deni *see* Dani
Denondadies *see* Tonontati
Denver Ute *see* Grand River Ute
Deonondade *see* Tionontati
Deonondade *see* Wyandot
Deonondadies *see* Tionontati
Depso [Pan, CR] *Terraba* (O)
De'sa *see* Kadohadacho
Desa *see* Desana
Desa *see* Ipeca
Desa *see* Kadohadacho
Desaguadero [MX, NI, CR] (BE)
Desana [Br, Col] (LC)
Desana Makú *see* Yohop
Desano *see* Desana
Deschitan *see* Deshuhittan
Des Chutes *see* Chutes
Deschutes *see* Chutes
Des Chutes *see* Wayam
Des Coupes *see* Cuts
Desert Cahuilla [CA] (BE)
Desert Culture *Paleo* (AI, pp.20–21)
Desert Diegueño *see* Southern Diegueño
Desert Pimans *see* Papago

Deshoot *see* Des Chutes
Deshtchin *see* Destchin
Deshuhittan [AK] *Tlingit* (H)
des Naiz percez *see* Amikwa
Desnedekenade [Can] *Dine Chipewyan* (BE)
Desnedeyarelott [Can] *Dene Esclaves* (H)
Desnedeyarelottine [Can] *Etchaottine* (BE)
Des-nedhe-kke-nada *see* Desnedekenade
Desnedhekkenada *see* Desnedekenade
Des-nedhe-yape-l'Ottine *see* Desnedeyarelottine
Desnedheyape l'Ottine *see* Desnedeyarelottine
Desonontage *see* Onondaga
Dessana *see* Desana
Destcaraguetaga [NEng] (H)
Destchetinaye [AZ] *Coyotero Apache* (H)
Destchin [AZ] *Apache* (H)
Destsini *see* Theshtshini
Desumana *see* Jumano
Detame *see* Dotame
De-tdoa *see* De
Detlk-oe'de *see* Tahlkoedi
Detsana *see* Desana
Detsanayuka [TX] *Comanche* (BE)
Detseka'yaa *see* Arapaho
Detsenei *see* Tariana
Detuana *see* Datuana
De-Ushene *see* Teuesh
Deushene *see* Teuesh
Devil's Lake Sioux *see* Pabaksa
Devil's-medicine-man Band (H) *see also* Wakan (H)
Devil's Medicine-man Band *Sihasapa* (H)
Dewagama *see* Ottawa
Dewagana *see* Ottawa
Dewaganas *see* Ontwaganha
Dewagunha *see* Ottawa
De-wa-ka-nha *see* Chippewa
Dewakanha *see* Chippewa
Dewamish *see* Dwamish
Dewoganna's *see* Chippewa
Dewogannas *see* Ontwaganha
Dhatada [Clan] *Omaha* (H)
Dhegiha [Lang] *Siouan* (LC)
Dhighida [Clan] *Chizhu* (H)
Dhighida [Clan] *Ponca* (H)
Dhihida *see* Deagheata
Dhiu *Piro* (H)
Diagano *see* Diegueño
Diaguitá [Arg, CH] (LC)
Diaguo [HA, WInd] *Bainoa* (BE)
Diahoi [Br] *Kawahib* (O)
Diarroi [Br] (H)
Diau *see* Trio

Dibe Lizhini *see* San Felipe
Didu [BaC, MX] *Waicuri* (BE)
Diegana *see* Diegueño
Diegano *see* Diegueño
Diegeeno *see* Diegueño
Diegene *see* Diegueño
Diegeno *see* Diegueño
Diegino *see* Diegueño
Diegmon *see* Diegueño
Diego, S. *see* Tesuque
Diego de la Congregacion, San *see* Jemez
Diego de los Jemez, San *see* Jemez
Diego de Tesuque, San *see* Tesuque
Diegueño [CA] (LC)
Diegueño [Lang] *Central Yuman* (LC)
Diegueño [Lang] [*Hokan-Yuman*] (H)
Dieguino *see* Diegueño
Dieguno *see* Diegueño
Dienondade *see* Tionontati
Dienondade *see* Wyandot
Dienteños *Bocas Prietas* (Hdbk10)
Dies, St. *see* Sandia
Digene *see* Diegueño
Digger (Ye) *see also* Maidu (LC)
Digger *Shoshone* (Ye)
Diggers (BE) *see also* Bannock (LC)
Diggers (BE) *see also* Southern Paiute (BE)
Diggers (H) *see also* Paiute (LC)
Diggers (H) *see also* Shoshoko (H)
Diggers (Hdbk11) *see also* Shoshone (LC)
Diggers [CA] (H)
Diggers [UT] *Paiute* (H)
Digger Ute *see* Ute
Digothi *see* Takkuthkutchin
Digothi-Kutchin *see* Tukkuthkutchin
Di-go-thi-tdinne *see* Kutchin
Digothitdinne *see* Kutchin
Digu [Br] (O)
Digut *see* Gavioes
Dihai-kutchin [AK] (BE)
Dihit *see* Ponca
Dildzehi *see* Thildzhe
Dillaway *see* Delaware
Dillewar *see* Delaware
Dilwishne *see* Wiyot
Dil-zha *see* Yavapai
Dilzha *see* Yavapai
Dilzhan *see* Tonto Apache
Dil-zhay *see* Mohave
Dil-zhay *see* Tonto Apache
Dil-zhay *see* Tulkepaia
Dilzhay *see* Mohave
Dilzhay *see* Tonto Apache
Dilzhay *see* Tulkepaia

Dil-zhay's *see* Yuma
Dilzhays *see* Yuma
Dilzhe'e *see* Yavapai
Dilzhehe *see* Yavapai
Dilzhi'i *see* Yavapai
Dimadeni [Br] *Dani* (O)
Dinais *see* Athapascan
Dindjie (H) *see also* Kutchin (LC)
Dindjie [Can] *Tinne* (H)
Dindjie Loucheux *see* Kutchin
Dindjitch *see* Athapascan
Dine *see* Athapascan
Dine [Self-designation] *see*
 Navajo
Dine Chipewyan [Can] *Tinne* (H)
Dine'e [Self-designation, plural]
 see Navajo
Dineh *see* Navajo
Dinetah *see* Navajo
Dinne *see* Athapascan
Dinne *see* Navajo
Dinnee *see* Athapascan
Dinneh *see* Athapascan
Dinni *see* Athapascan
Dinondadi *see* Tionontati
Dinondadies *see* Tionontati
Dinondodies *see* Tionontati
Diogene *see* Diegueño
Diokaya [Self-designation] *see*
 Ocaina
Dionnondadees *see* Tionontati
Dionondade *see* Tionontati
Dionondade *see* Wyandot
Dionondadies *see* Tionontati
Dionondadoes *see* Tionontati
Dionondadoes *see* Wyandot
Dionondages *see* Tionontati
Dionondes *see* Tionontati
Dionoudadie *see* Tionontati
Diore *see* Xikrin
Diria [NI] *Mangue* (BE)
Dirian [Lang] [SA] (Bull44)
Dis-cheine *see* Destchin
Discheine *see* Destchin
Discovery Island *see* Skingenes
Disguino *see* Diegueño
Diskaden *see* Tseskadin
Disko *Greenland Eskimos* (BE)
Ditche-ta-ut-tinne *Loucheux*
 (IndN, v.2, no.2, no.3, pp.172–
 177)
Ditiapode *see* Pira-tapuya
Ditsa-kana *see* Ditsakana
Ditsakana [TX] *Comanche* (BE)
DiuJuan *see* Yoyuane
Diurhet *see* Puelche
Dixie Valley *see* Atsugewi
Dixie Valley Indians *see* Ap-
 waruge
Dj'aaquig'it'ena'i *see* Djahui-
 gitinai
Djaaquigiteneai *see* Djahui-
 gitinai

Djaaqui'sk-uatl'adaga'i *see*
 Djahui-skwahladagai
Djaaquiskuatladagai *see* Djahui-
 skwahladagai
Djahai-gitinai [Clan] [BC] (H)
Djahai-hlgahet-kegawai [Clan]
 [BC] [*Hlaghet-gitinai*] (H)
Djahai-skwahladagai [Clan] [BC]
 Haida (H)
Dja'tie *see* Tchatchiun
Djatie *see* Tchatchiun
Dja'tien *see* Tchatchiun
Djatien *see* Tchatchiun
Djemez *see* Jemez
Djene *see* Navajo
Djimaliko [Self-designation] *see*
 Chimariko
Djiquaahl-lana [Clan] *Haida* (H)
Dji'wi *see* Santo Domingo
Djobokubi *see* Motilon
Djonontewake *see* Seneca
Djore *see* Xikrin
Djulalgi *see* Tsulalgi
Djushade *see* Djus-hade
Djus-hade [Clan] [BC] (H)
Djus xade *see* Djus-hade
Djusxade *see* Djus-hade
Dl'ia'len k-eowai *see* Hlielung-
 keawai
Dnaine *see* Athapascan
Doage *see* Nanticoke
Doags *see* Conoy
Doaquioydacam *Coahuiltecan*
 (Hdbk10)
Dobozubi *see* Bari
Dochkafuara *see* Tuyuca
Dock-sous *see* John Day Indians
Dockspus *see* John Day Indians
Docota *see* Dakota
Doeggs *see* Tauxenent
Doegs *see* Nanticoke
Doegs *see* Conoy
Doegs *see* Tauxenent
Does-to-e *see* Doestoe
Doestoe *Apache* (H)
Dog *Fox* (H)
Dog Coast *see* Thlingchadinne
Dog Creek (H) *see also* Canoe
 Creek Band (Hdbk12)
Dog Creek [BC] *Fraser River
 Shuswap* (H)
Dog-Drivers *see* Aglemiut
Dog-Eaters *see* Arapaho
Dog-feet *see* Manos de Perro
Dogi [VA] (H)
Dog Indians *see* Cheyenne
Dog Indians *see* Cheyenne
Dogitunai *see* Do-gitunai
Do-gitunai [Clan] [BC] (H)
Dog Nation *see* Cheyenne
Dogrib [Can] (Ye)
Dog-ribbed *see* Thlingchadinne
Dog Rib Indians (BE)

Dog-rib Indians (H) *see also*
 Thlingchadinne (LC)
Dog River (Oregon) *see also* Wat-
 lala (BE)
Dog River *Wasco* (BE)
Dog River Indians (Hdbk12) *see
 also* Hood River Indians
 (Hdbk12)
Dog River Wascos (Hdbk12) *see
 also* Hood River Indians
 (Hdbk12)
Dogs [Society] *Hidatsa* (H)
Dogs Naked *see* Emitahpahk-
 saiyiks
Dog Tribe *see* Cherokee
Do'gu'at *see* Wichita
Doguat *see* Wichita
Doguene [TX] (H)
Do-ha-kel'ya *see* Kekin [Kansa]
Dohakelya *see* Kekin [Kansa]
Doheme *see* Eudeve
Dohe'nks *see* Carrizo [MX]
Dohenks *see* Carrizo [MX]
Dohkapoara *see* Tuyuca
Do'hleli'p *see* Tulalip
Dohlelip *see* Tulalip
Dohme *see* Eudeve
Do'kana *see* Wichita
Dokana *see* Wichita
Doki's Band [Can] *Chippewa*
 (H)
Doleguas [Pan] *Guaymi* (BE)
Dolores *see* Sandia
Dom. de Cochiti, Sto. *see* Santo
 Domingo
Dominga, Santa *see* Santa
 Domingo
Domingo *see* Santo Domingo
Domingo, San *see* Santo
 Domingo
Domingo, Santa *see* Santo
 Domingo
Domingo, Santo (LC)
Domingo de Cochiti, Santo *see*
 Santo Domingo
Domingo de Cuevas, Santo *see*
 Santo Domingo
Domingo de Cuevas, Sto. *see*
 Santo Domingo
Dominic, Saint *see* Santo
 Domingo
Domongo. St. *see* Santo
 Domingo
Donondades *see* Tionontati
Donondades *see* Wyandot
Dononiiote *see* Oneida
Don't Laugh *see* Kutaiimiks
Doo-ese-doo-we *see* Doose-
 doowe
Dooesedoowe *see* Doosedoowe
Doo-goo-son *see* Tegotsugn
Doogooson *see* Tegotsugn
Doosedoowe [Clan] (H)

Do-qua-chabsh *see* Nukwat-samish
Doquachabsh *see* Nukwatsamish
Doraskean [Lang] [CAm] (LC)
Dorasque (BE) *see also* Doraskean (LC)
Dorasque [Pan] (BE)
Dospan *see* Tisepan
Dostlan-Inagai [BC] [*Stelenga-lana*] (H)
Do-ta ma *see* Dotame
Dotama *see* Dotame
Dotame (H)
Do-ta me *see* Dotame
Dotchtonne [TX] (H)
Dothliuk [WA] *Muckleshoot* (BE)
Dotuskustl [BC] [*Sagua-lana*] (H)
Douaganha *see* Chippewa
Douaganha *see* Ontwaganha
Douesdonqua *see* Doustioni
Douglas [BC] *Lower Lillooet* (H)
Douglas Bad [BC] *Douglas Tribe* (Hdbk10)
Douglas Indians *see* Lillooet River
Douglas Lake [WA] *Okinagan* (BE)
Douglas Tribe [BC] *Lower Lil-looet* (Hdbk12)
Doune [Can] *Tinne* (H)
Dounes Flancs-de-Chien *see* Thlingchadinne
Dounie [Can] *Tinne* (H)
Dounie' Espa-tpa-Ottine *see* Es-bataottine
Doustiany *see* Doustioni
Doustioni [LA] *Caddo Confeder-acy* (BE)
Douwaganha *see* Chippewa
Douwaganha *see* Ontwaganha
Dovaganhaes *see* Chippewa
Dovaganhaes *see* Ontwaganha
Dowaganah *see* Chippewa
Dowaganha *see* Chippewa
Dowaganha *see* Ontwaganha
Dowaganha *see* Ojibwa
Dowaganhaa *see* Ontwaganha
Dowaganhaes *see* Chippewa
Dowaganhaes *see* Ontwaganha
Dowaganhoes *see* Ontwaganha
Dowangaha *see* Shawnee
Downstream Halotesu [Br] *South-ern Nambicuara* (O)
Draguane *see* Doguene
Dreamer Indians *see* Tsattine
Drifting Goose Band *see* Putetemini
Drinkers of the Dew *see* Keres
Drio *see* Trio
Dscilcani *see* Dsihlthani
Dshipowe-haga *see* Chippewa
Dsihlnaothihlni [Clan] *Navajo* (H)

Dsihltlani [Clan] *Navajo* (H)
Dsilanoci'lni *see* Dsihlnaothihlni
Dsilnaocilcine *see* Dsihlnaoth-ihlni
Dsilnaocilni *see* Dsihlnaothihlni
Dsiltani *see* Dsihlthani
Dsiltla'ni *see* Dsihltlani
Dtakhtikianpandhatazhi [Sub-gens] *Nikapashna* (H)
'Dtchatatauttunne *see* Tse-tautkenne
'Dtcha-ta-uttinne *see* Etchaot-tine
'Dtchatauttinne *see* Etchaottine
'Dtcheta-ta-ut-tunne *see* Tse-tautkenne
Dtedhezedhatazhi [Subgens] *Washabe* (H)
Dtepaitazhi [Subgens] *Dhatada* (H)
Dtepaitazhi [Subgens] *Washabe* (H)
Dtesanhadtadhishan [Subgens] *Hanga* (H)
Dtesinde [Subgens] *Washabe* (H)
Dtesindeitazhi [Subgens] *Naka-pashna* (H)
Dtinne *see* Tinne
'Dtinne *see* Athapascan
ducay *see* Eskimos
Duck Lake [BC] *Okinagan* (H)
Duck Valley *Shoshone* (Char, v.11)
Duckwater Shoshone (Char, v.11)
Dudley Indians (LC)
Dudu [NI, Hon] *Sumo* (BE)
dudutcyatikadu *see* Beatty band
Dughdwabsh *see* Dwamish
Du Haade *see* Dostlan-Inagai
Duhaade *see* Dotlan-Inagai
Duhaimomowi *see* Baxumomowi
Du-hle-lip *see* Tulalip
Duhlelip *see* Tulalip
duhu tcyatikadu *see* Beatty band
Dukaiya *Ocaina* (O)
Du'kwakni *see* du'kweakni
dukweakni *see* du'kweakni
du'kweakni [OR] *Klamath* (BE)
Du-lay-lip *see* Tulalip
Dulaylip *see* Tulalip
Dulchanois *see* Doustioni
Dulchinois *see* Doustioni
Dulcioni *see* Doustioni
Dule (BE) *see also* Chato (BE)
Dule *Hon* (BE)
Dumna (H) *see also* Tumna (H)
Dumna [CA] *Yokuts* (CA)
Dumoine [Can] *Algonkin* (BE)
Dune *see* Athapascan
Dung-of-a-buffalo-bull *see* Tatankachesli
Dung-on-the-river-banks *see* Mine'sepere
Dunne-za *see* Tsattine

Dus-ga-o-weh *see* Tuscarora
Dusty Nose *see* Iowa
Dusty-ones [Clan] [MN] *Atsina* (BE)
Dutagami *see* Fox
dutna *see* Eskimos
Duuxuga [Self-designation] *see* Tucuna
Duwa'ha [WA] *Skagit* (BE)
Duwamish *see* Dwamish
Duwano *see* Twana
Duy [MX] *Chibchan* (BE)
duzcay *see* Eskimos
Dwahmish *see* Dwamish
Dwa-ka-nen *see* Chippewa
Dwakanen *see* Chippewa
Dwa-ka-nha *see* Chippewa
Dwakanha *see* Chippewa
D'Wamish *see* Dwamish
Dwa-mish *see* Dwamish
Dwamish [WA] (LC)
D'ya'mi *see* Dyami *Keres*
Dyami [Clan] [NM] *Keres* (H)
D'yami-hano *see* Dyami *Keres*
Dyami-hanuch *see* Dyami
Dya'ni *see* Dyani
Dyani [Clan] [NM] *Keres* (H)
Dyani-hano *see* Dyani
Dye *see* D'ye
D'ye [Clan] *Tewa* (H)
Dye-tdoa *see* D'ye
Dyi-wa *see* Santo Domingo
Dzase *see* Piapoco
Dza'wadeenoxu *see* Tsawatenok
Dzawadeenoxu *see* Tsawatenok
Dzawinai [VE] [*Wakuenai*] (O)
Dzaze *see* Piapoco
Dzitgais'ani *see* Faraon
Dzitgha a *see* Western Apache
Dzitgha'i *see* Western Apache
Dzitsiistas *see* Cheyenne
Dzi'tsiistas [Self-designation] *see* Cheyenne
Dzitsi'stas *see* Cheyenne
Dzitsistas *see* Cheyenne
Dzos haedrai *see* Djus-hade
Dzubukua (O) *see also* Motilon (LC)
Dzubukua [Br] (O)

-E-

E. Scihous *see* Santee Sioux
Eagle *see* Katshikotin
Eagle *see* Khuya
Eagle eyed Indians *see* Migichi-hiliniou
Eagle-Head *see* Tintaotonwe
Eagle Head's Band *see* Tintao-tonwe

Eagle Hills Assiniboin [Can] (H)
Eagle Nest Band *see* Oglala
Eagle People *see* Cheghita
Eagle people *see* Hangkaahutun
Eambosandata *see* Khemnichan
Eamuses *see* Yamassee
Eanbosandata *see* Khemnichan
Eano *see* Eno [NC]
E-an-to-ah *see* Jatonabine
Eantoah *see* Jatonabine
Earbob Indians *see* Kalispel
E-ar-ke *see* Hopi
Earke *see* Hopi
Early Finished Eating *see*
　Tsinksistsoyiks
Earring People *see* Kalispel
Earring People *see* Pfialola
Ear Rings *see* Kalispel
Earth *see* Manyika
Earth Eaters *see* Hokandika
Earth-lodge *see* Mandhinkagaghe
Eascab *see* Jatonabine
East Bay Costanoan *see*
　Chochenyo
East Central Sierra Miwok [Lang]
　[CA] *Eastern Miwokan* (CA-8)
Easterlings *see* Accomac
Eastern Abnaki [Lang] [ME]
　Penobscot (Hdbk15)
Eastern Aleut [Lang] (Hdk5)
Eastern Algonquian [Lang]
　(Hdbk15)
Eastern Apache (H) *see also*
　Querecho (H)
Eastern Apache (Hdbk9)
Eastern Archaic (AI, pp.24–25)
Eastern Bakairi [Br] (O)
Eastern Bororo [Br] (O)
Eastern Canada [*Inuit-Inupiaq*]
　(Hdbk5)
Eastern Carib [Lang] (UAz, v.28)
Eastern-Central [Lang] *Arapaho*
　(Pub, v.12, no.3, p.73)
Eastern Cherokee *see* Treaty Party
Eastern Chiricahua [NM]
　(Hdbk10)
Eastern Comanche *see* Penateka
Eastern Denes *Tinne* (H)
Eastern Dieguéño *see* Southern
　Dieguéño
Eastern Eskimos *see* Inuit-
　Inupiaq
Eastern Folks *see* Etheneldeli
Eastern Indians (H)
Eastern Keres [Lang] (H)
Eastern Mayan [Lang] (O)
Eastern Miwokan [Lang] *Utian*
　(CA-8)
Eastern Mono *see* Owens Valley
　Paiute
Eastern Niantic [RI, CT] (BE)
Eastern Pomo [CA] (Pub, v.36,
　no.6)

Eastern Pomo [Lang] [CA] (Pub,
　v.6, no.1, pp.182–204)
Eastern Province [Lang] (AI)
Eastern Riparian (AI)
Eastern Shawnee [OH] (H)
Eastern Shore Indians *see* Acco-
　mac
Eastern Shoshone [WY] (Hdbk11)
Eastern Shuswap [Lang] [BC] *In-
　terior Salish* (Hdbk12)
Eastern Siouan [Lang] (H)
Eastern Sioux (H)
Eastern Sioux (H) *see also* Santee
　(LC)
Eastern Suya [Br] (O)
Eastern Tarahumara [Lang]
　(Hdbk10)
Eastern Timbira [Br] (O)
Eastern Tucano [Br, Col] (O)
Eastern Tukano [Lang] [Br, Col]
　(O)
Eastern White Mountain Apache
　San Carlos Apache (BE)
Eastern Woodlands (Bull180,
　no.10, pp.77–82)
East Greenlanders *Greenland Es-
　kimos* (H)
East Greenlandic *Greenland Eski-
　mos* (Hdbk5)
Eastlanders *see* Abnaki
Eastmain [Can] [*Montagnais-
　Naskapi*] (BE)
Eastward Indians *see* Eastern In-
　dians
Ea-tau-bau *see* Catawba
Eataubau *see* Catawba
Eaters *see* Omisis
Eat-no-buffalo-cows *see*
　Pteyuteshni
Eat the Ham *Sans Arc* (H)
Eat-the-scrapings-of-hides *see*
　Takhuhayuta [Hunkpatina]
Ebahamo [TX] (H)
Ebahumo *see* Ebahamo
Ebicerings *see* Nipissing
Ebicerinys *see* Nipissing
Ebidoso [BO, Par] *Chamacoco*
　(O)
Ebikuita *see* Mescalero Apache
Ebitoso *see* Ebidoso
Ecclemach *see* Esselen
Ece'je *see* Ese Ejja
Echebool *see* Tlakluit
Echebool *see* Wishram
E-chee-lute *see* Tlakluit
E-chee-lute *see* Wishram
Echeelute *see* Tlakluit
Echeelute *see* Wishram
Echeetee *see* Hitchiti
Echele *see* Hitchiti
E-che-loot *see* Wishram
E-che-loot *see* Tlakluit
Echeloot *see* Tlakluit

Echeloot *see* Wishram
E-che-lute *see* Tlakluit
E-che-lute *see* Wishram
Echelute *see* Wishram
Echelute *see* Tlakluit
Echemin *see* Malecite
Eche-mo-hua-va *see* Cheme-
　huevi
Echemohuava *see* Chemehuevi
Echenoana *see* Echoaladi
Echeta *see* Hitchiti
Echete *see* Hitchiti
Echetee *see* Hitchiti
Echeti *see* Hitchiti
Echetii *see* Hitchiti
Echiguego [SA] *Caduveo* (O)
Echi-mo-hua-va *see* Chemehuevi
Echimohuava *see* Chemehuevi
E-chip-e-ta *see* Siksika
Echipeta *see* Siksika
Echiti *see* Hitchiti
Echito *see* Hitchiti
E-cho *see* Itchualgi
Echo *see* Itchualgi
Echoaladi [Br] *Tereno* (O)
Echoja *see* Ese Ejja
Echuntica *see* Kotsoteka
Eclemaches *see* Esselen
Ecorce [Can] *Nipissing* (H)
Ecoree *see* Ecorce
Ecquamish *see* Hahuamis
Ecrevisses rouges *see* Chakchi-
　uma
Ecselen *see* Esselen
Ecselenas *see* Esselen
Ecselenes *see* Esselen
Ecuary [BO] *Araona* (O)
Ecureuil [Q] *Montagnais* (H)
Ecusgina *Abipone* (LC)
Edawika *see* Kadohadacho
Edchautawoot *see* Etchareottine
Edchawtashoot dinneh *see*
　Etchareottine
Edchawtawhoot tinneh *see*
　Etchareottine
Edchawtawoot *see* Etchareottine
Ede-but-say *see* Kainah
Edebutsay *see* Kainah
Eden Valley Yuki (NamI, v.14)
Edisto [SC] *Cusabo* (BE)
Edistoes *see* Edisto
Edistow *see* Edisto
Ediu-Adig [Self-designation] *see*
　Caduveo
Edjeho [SA] *Caduveo* (O)
Edjieretrukenade [Can] *Athapas-
　can* (H)
E'd-ohwe *see* Kikatsuk
Edohwe *see* Kikatsik
Edshawtawoot *see* Etchareottine
Edu [BaC, MX] *Waicuri* (BE)
Eduria (O) *see also* Tabaino (O)
Eduria [Col] *Barasana* (O)

E-eh see Eeh
Eeh [CA] *Iruwaitsu* (H)
Eeksen [VanI] *Salish* (BE)
Eel River [IN, OH] *Miami* (H)
Eelrivers see Eel River
Eel River Wailaki [Lang] [CA]
  (He)
Eemitches see Imiche
Eeno see Eno [NC]
Eenthlit [Self-designation] see
  Langua
Eert-kai-lee see Kutchakutchin
Eertkailee see Kutchakutchin
Ees-tey-toch see Eesteytoch
Eesteytoch [BC] *Bella Coola* (H)
E'esxen see Eeksen
Ee-ta-sip-shov see Sans Arcs
Eetasipshov see Sans Arcs
Eexsen see Eeksen
Efaca [Clan] *Timucua* (H)
Egan's band see To-gwing'-a-ni
Egavik *Bering Strait Eskimos*
  (Hdbk5)
Egedesminde *Greenland Eskimos*
  (BE)
Egeish see Eyeish
Egue see Eudeve
Eh-aht-tis-aht see Ehatisaht
Ehahttisaht see Ehatisaht
Ehanktonwanna see Yanktonai
E-hank-to-wana see Yanktonai
Ehanktowana see Yanktonai
E-hart-sar see Ehartsar
Ehartsar *Crow* (H)
Ehateset see Ehatisaht
Ehatisaht [Can] *Nootka* (BE)
E'hatisath see Ehatisaht
Ehatt-is-aht see Ehatisaht
Ehattisaht see Ehatisaht
E-hawn-k-t-wawn see Yanktonai
Ehawnktwawn see Yanktonai
E-hawn-k't'wawn-nah see Yank-
  tonai
Ehawnktwawnnah see Yanktonai
Ehelute see Tlakluit
Ehelute see Wishram
Ehesepiooc see Chesapeake
Eh-ha-tza see Ehartsar
Ehhatza see Ehartsar
Ehhen see Eh-hen
Eh-hen [VE] (O)
Ehihalis see Chehalis
Ehonkeronon see Kichesipirini
Ehressaronon [Can] (H)
Ehriehronnon see Erie
Ehta-Gottine see Etagottine
Ehtagottine see Etagottine
Ehta-tcho-Gottine see
  Etatchogottine
Ehtatchogottine see Etatchogot-
  tine
Ehuskemay see Eskimos
E-in-a-ke see Einake

Einake [Society] *Ikunuhkatsi* (H)
Einontu'tua [PE] *Tanshiro* (O)
Eioestures see Eneeshur
Eiotaro see Coyotero Apache
Eirichtih-Aruchpahga see Ara-
  paho
Eithinyook see Cree
Eithinyoowuc [Self-designation]
  see Cree
Eivesteurs see Eneeshur
Eivillinmiut see Aivillirmiut
Eiwhue'lit see Eiwhuelit
Eiwhuelit (Hdbk5) see also Saint
  Lawrence Islanders (Hdbk5)
Eiwhuelit [AK] *Yuki* (BE)
Eiwillik see Ais
Ejueo [SA] *Caduveo* (H)
Ekaluktogmiut [Can] *Central Es-
  kimos* (BE)
e-ka-to-pi-staks see Ekatopistaks
Ekatopistaks *Piegan* (H)
Ekeantoton [Can] *Amikwa* (H)
Ekeenteeronnon see Huron
ekeenteeronnon see Huron of
  Loretta
Ekogmut (Contri, v.1, p.17)
Ekog'mut see Ekogmut
Ekogmut (H) see also Ikogmiut
  (BE)
Ekog'mut see Ikogmiut
E-koolth-aht see Ekoolthaht
Ekoolthaht [PacN, Can] *Nootka*
  (BE)
E-ko-to-pis-taxe see Ekatopistaks
Ekotopistaxe see Ekatopistaks
Ekpimi see Shasta
Ekriehronom see Erie
Eku'lath see Ekoolthaht
E-ku-pa-be-ka see Ekupabeka
Ekupabeka [Clan] *Hidatsa* (H)
Ekwa'ahle see Akwa'ala
e-kwe-ka-pi-ya see Cocopa
ekwekapiya see Cocopa
Elati [Lang] [SC, GA] *Lower
  Cherokee* (H)
Elaw see Catawba
Elder Brothers see Hathawekela
Elder Osage see Pahatsi
El'e-idlin-Gottine see Eleidlinot-
  tine
Eleidlingottine see Eleidlinottine
Ele-idlin-ottine see Eleidlinot-
  tine
Eleidlinottine [Can] *Etchaottine*
  (BE)
El Gusano see Seyupa
Elixguegue see Iliguigue
Elizabeth Islands [MA]
  Wampanoag (BE)

Elizu cathlans-coon-hidery see
  Naikun-kegawai
Elk see Huwanikikikarachada
Elk'ba-sumh see Bellabella
El-ke-ai see Sia
Elkeai see Sia
Elk-la'sum see Bellabella
Elk Mountain [Col] *Ute* (BE)
Elk Mountain Utes see Seuvarits
Elk Mountain Yutas see Seuvarits
Elk River Tribe see Eel River
Elks (H)
Eloot see Tlakluit
Eloot see Wishram
Eloquale see Olagale
Elosedabsh see Elo'sedabsh
Elo'sedabsh [WA] *Sahehwamish*
  (BE)
Elpom [CA] *Wintu* (BE)
El Pueblo de los Siete Arroyos see
  Tenabo
El Pueblo Quemado see Tzenatay
Elqi-mie see Tsimshian
El Santisimo Sacramento see
  Isleta
E-lute see Tlakluit
E-lute see Wishram
Elute see Tlakluit
Elute see Wishram
Em-alcom see Homalko
Emalcom see Homalko
Emamoueta (H)
emasi see Jemez
Emat see Emet
Embena see Embera
Embeno [Lang] see Catio
Embera [Col, Pan] *Northern
  Choco* (LC)
Emberak see Embera
Embogodegi see Caduveo
Emeaes see Jemez
Emeges see Jemez
Emejeita [Col] (O)
Emejes see Jemez
Emenes see Jemez
Emerenon see Emerillon
Emerillon [Lang] [Br] (LC)
Emerilon see Emerillon
Emerion see Emerillon
Emes see Jemez
Emet [TX] (BE)
Emexes see Jemez
Emidio, San [CA] *Chumushan* (H)
Emigdiano [Lang] [CA] *Chumash*
  (CA)
Emissourita see Missouri
E-mi-tah-pahk-sai-yiks see Emi-
  tahpahksaiyiks
Emitahpahksaiyiks [MN] *Siksika*
  (BE)
E-mi-taks see Emitaks
Emitaks [Society] *Ikunuhkahtsi*
  (H)

Emlh-wilh-laht see Ucluelet
Emmes see Jemez
Emoa see Macuna
Emoamasa [Col] *Macuna* (O)
Emok see Toba
Empera see Embera
Empera [Lang] see Catio
Empire Valley Band [BC] *Fraser River Shuswap* (Hdbk12)
Em-tim-bitch see Intimbich
Emtimbitch see Intimbich
Enacaga [SA] *Caduveo* (O)
E-nagh-magh see Tiwa
E-nagh-magh see Tigua
Enaghmagh see Tigua
Enaghmagh see Tiwa
Enagua see Piapoco
Enansa see Quapaw
Enanthayonni see Toryohne
Enapa see Panare
E'napa [Self-designation] see Panare
Enarhonon see Arendahronon
E-nat-za see Hidatsa
Enatza see Hidatsa
Enauene-Naue see Saluma
Enawene-Newe see Saluma
Encabellado (O) see also Secoya (O)
Encabellado (O) see also Siona (O)
Encabellado [EC] (O)
Encaquiagualcaca *Piro* (H)
Enclataw see Lekwiltok
Enclit see Lengua-Mascoi
Encogido [EC, PE] (O)
Endastes see Conestoga
Endimbich see Entimbich
E-ne-churs see Eneeshur
Enechurs see Eneeshur
E-nee-sher see Eneeshur
Eneesher see Eneeshur
Eneeshur (H) see also Tapanash (BE)
E-nee-shur see Eneeshur
Eneeshur [WA] (H)
Enenslet see Lengua-Mascoi
Enepiahe see Ervipiame
Enepiahoe see Ervipiame
Enesher see Eneeshur
E-ne-show see Eneeshur
Eneshow see Eneeshur
E-ne-shur see Eneeshur
Eneshur see Eneeshur
Eneshure see Eneeshur
Enesteurs see Enneshur
Enete see Yuracare
Engarico see Ingariko
Engerakmung see Botocudo
English Indians see Apalachicola
English Towns see Oklahannali
Engna see Henaggi
Enias [BC] *Upper Lillooet* (H)

E'Niepa [VE] *Mapoyo* (O)
Eni-Maca see Maca
Enimaca see Maca
Enimaga (LC) see also Maca (LC)
Enimaga [Par] *Matacoan* (O)
E-ni'tunne see Enitunne
Enitunne [OR] *Mishikwut-metunne* (H)
En-ke-map-o-tricks see Nkamaplix
Enkemapotricks see Nkamaplix
En-ke-mip (H) Nkamip (BE)
Enkemip see Nkamip
Enk-ka-sa-ba see Inkesabe
Enkkasaba see Inkesabe
En-na-k'e see Eskimos
Enna-k'e see Eskimos
Ennake see Eskimos
En-na-k'ie see Eskimos
Ennakie see Eskimos
Ennas see Cree
Enneyuttehage see Oneida
Eno [BO] *Araona* (O)
Eno [Lang] *Catawba* (H)
Eno [NC] (BE)
Enoe see Eno [NC]
Enoqua [LA] (H)
Enquisacoes see Arkokisa
Ensen see Esselen
Ensenes see Esselen
Enskiae'ronnon see Saulteaux
Enslet see Angaite
Enta-otin see Tautin
Entaotin see Tautin
Entari ronnin see Cherokee
Enthlit see Langua
Entiat [WA] *Middle Columbia River Salish* (Hdbk12)
Entiatook see Entiat
Entimbich (H) see also Intimbich (H)
Entimbich [CA] *Mono* (H)
Entimbich [Lang] [CA] *Kings River Foothill* (CA-8)
Entimbitch see Entimbich
Entkasaba see Inkesabe
Entouhonoron see Seneca
Entouhonorono see Seneca
Entouohonoron see Seneca
Entron [EC, PE] (O)
Entwohonoron see Seneca
E-nyae-va Pai see Yavapai
Enyaevapai see Yavapai
E-oh see Eeh
Eoh see Eeh
Eokoro see Arikara
Eoote-lash-Schute see Ottlashoot
Eototo [Clan] *Kokop* (H)
Eototo winwu see Eototo
E-o-to-to wun-wu see Eototo
Eototo Wunwu see Eototo
E-pa see Hualapai
Epena [Col] (O)

Epera see Embera
Epera [Lang] see Catio
Epesengles see Nipissing
Ephi see Agua Caliente
Epicerinyen see Nipissing
Epicerinyes see Nipissing
Epicerinys see Nipissing
Epiciriniens see Nipissing
Epiminguia *Quapaw* (H)
Epinette [Ont] *Chippewa* (H)
Episingle see Nipissing
Epissingue see Nipissing
Epitoupa see Ibitoupa
Epkhie see Agua Caliente
E-poh-si-miks see Ipoksimaiks
Epohsimiks see Ipoksimaiks
Equalett see Ekoothaht
Equi see Eudeve
Equijati [BO, PE] *Ese Ejja* (O)
Equiliquinao see Kinikinao
Equinipicha see Acolapissa
Equiniquinao see Kinikinao
Erabacha see Uzutiuhi
Erahidaunsu [Br] *Southern Nambicuara* (O)
Erarapi'o [MN] *Crow* (BE)
Erawika see Kadohadacho
Ercansaques see Kansa
Erchipeetay see Siksika
Erettchi-ottine see Etcheridiegot-tine
Erians see Erie
Erie [OH] (LC)
Erieckronois see Erie
Erieehronon see Erie
Eriehronon see Erie
Erielhonon see Erie
Erieronon see Erie
Eriez see Erie
Erigas see Erie
Erigbaagtsa see Aripaktsa
Erigbactsa see Aripaktsa
Erigoanna [TX] (H)
Erigpactsa see Aripaktsa
Erigpatsa see Aripaktsa
Erikbaktsa see Ribaktsa
Erikbaktsa see Aripaktsa
Erikpaktsa see Rikbaktsa
Erikpaktsa see Aripaktsa
Eriniouai see Illinois
Eriniwek see Illinois
E-ri-o see Erio
Erio [CA] *Pomo* (H)
Eriwonec [NJ] *Unalachtigo* (BE)
Erkileit see Kutchin
Erocoise see Iroquois
Eromaha see Omaha
Errieronon see Erie
Ersegontegog see Arsigantegok
Ersengontegog see Arosagunta-cook
Erusi [CA] *Pomo* (H)
E-rus-si see Erusi

Erussi *see* Erusi
Ervipiame [TX] (BE)
Esachkabuk *Crow* (H)
Esa-Esa *see* Esa Ejja
Esa-exa *see* Esa Ejja
E-sah-ate-ake-tar-par *see* Esa-
  hateaketarpar
Esahateaketarpar *Brule* (H)
E-sah-ka-buk *see* Esachkabuk
Esanties *see* Santee
Esau *see* Catawba
Esaurora *see* Tuscarora
Esaw *see* Catawba
Esba-t'a-ottine *see* Esbataottine
Esbataottine [BC] *Nahane* (BE)
Escaba [TX] *Coahuiltecan* (BE)
Escaba-Cascastes *see* Escaba
Escabel [MX] (Hdbk10)
Escalante Band *see* Kaiparowits
Escamacu (H) *see also* Uscamacu
  (H)
Escamacu [SC] *Cusabo* (BE)
Escanjaques *see* Kansa
Escansaques *see* Kansa
Escanxaques *see* Kansa
Escelen *see* Esselen
Escelenes *see* Esselen
Escequatas *see* Mescalero Apache
Escihous *see* Santee
Esclaves (H) *see also* Etchaottine
  (BE)
Esclaves (H) *see also* Etchareottine
  (H)
Esclaves (H) *see also*
  Thlingchadinne (LC)
Esclaves *Tinne* (H)
Escoria [Pan] (BE)
Escoumains [Q] *Montagnais* (BE)
Escoumins *see* Eskimos
Escurieux *see* Ecureuil
Ese-eja *see* Ese Ejja
Eseejja *see* Ese Ejja
Ese Ejja [Arg] (LC)
Ese Ejje *see* Ese Ejja
Eseexa *see* Ese Ejja
Ese-kep-ka-buk *see* Esekepkabuk
Esekepkabuk *Crow* (H)
esekwita-go *see* Mescalero
  Apache
Eselenes *see* Esselen
Esgemag *see* Eskimos
Esgemao *see* Eskimos
esgimow *see* Eskimos
Esha'ktlabsh [WA] *Puyallup* (BE)
Eshkibod *see* Eskimos
Esikwita *see* Kiowa Apache
Esikwita *see* Mescalero Apache
Eskaleutian *see* Eskimo-Aleut
Eskeemoes *see* Eskimos
Eskegawage [Can] *Kespoogwit*
  (BE)
Eskeimoes *see* Eskimos
Eskelen *see* Esselen

E-skel-lute *see* Tlakluit
Eskellute *see* Tlakluit
Eskeloot *see* Tlakluit
Eskeloot *see* Wishram
E-ske-lute *see* Wishram
Eskelute *see* Wishram
Eskemoes *see* Eskimos
esket *see* Alkali Lake Band
Eskewi [Lang] [CA] *Konkow* (CA-
  8)
Eskiaeronnon *see* Chippewa
Eskiaeronnon *see* Saulteaux
Eskima *see* Eskimos
Eskimantsik *see* Eskimos
Eskima'ntzik *see* Eskimos
Eskimauan [Lang] (BE)
Eskimauen *see* Eskimauan
Eskimauk *see* Eskimos
Eskimaux *see* Eskimos
Eskimeaux *see* Eskimos
Eskimesi *see* Eskimos
Eskimo-Aleut [Lang] (BE)
Eskimo of the East *see* Kopag-
  miut
Eskimos [AK, Can] (LC)
Es-kin *see* Eskin
Eskin [CA] *Maidu* (Contri, v.3,
  p.282)
e-skipot *see* Eskimos
eskipot *see* Eskimos
Es ko-pik *see* Naskapi
Eskopik *see* Naskapi
Eskoro *see* Arikara
Esk-sin-ai-tup-iks *see* Esksi-
  naitupiks
Esksinaitupiks [MN] *Piegan* (BE)
Eslen *see* Esselen
Eslenajan *see* Esselen
Eslenes *see* Esselen
Esmeralda [Lang] [EC] [*Macro-
  Chibchan*] (O)
Esnime [ID] *Nez Perce* (BE)
Esopes *see* Esopus
Esopus [NY] *Munsee* (LC)
Esopuz *see* Esopus
Es-pa-to-ti-na *see* Esbataottine
Espatotina *see* Esbataottine
Espa-tpa-Ottine *see* Esbataottine
Espatpaottine *see* Esbataootine
Espejos [MX] *Mescalero Apache*
  (H)
Espeminkia *Illinois* (H)
Espicheates *see* Spichehat
Espopolames [TX] *Coahuiltecan*
  (BE)
Espopulam *see* Espopolames
Esquansaques *see* Kansa
Esquiate *see* Hesquiat
Esquimalt [Clan] *Songish* (H)
Esquimantsic *see* Eskimos
Esquimau *see* Eskimos
Esquimaud *see* Eskimos
Esquimaude *see* Eskimos

Esquimaun *see* Eskimauan
Esquimaux *see* Eskimos
Esquimaux-caribous *see* Caribou
  Eskimos
Esquimawes *see* Eskimos
Esquimeaux *see* Eskimos
Esquimones *see* Eskimos
Esquimos *see* Eskimos
Es-ree-que-tee *see* Mescalero
  Apache
Esreequetee *see* Mescalero
  Apache
Es-sah-ah-ter *see* Santee
Essahahter *see* Santee
Essanape (H)
Essanape (H) *see also* Isanyati (H)
Es-san-a-pis *see* Essanape
Essanapis *see* Essanape
Essannape *see* Essanape
Essaqueta *see* Kiowa Apache
Essejja *see* Ese Ejja
Es-se-kwit-ta *see* Mescalero
  Apache
Essekwitta *see* Mescalero Apache
Esselen [CA] (H)
Esselene *see* Esselen
Esselenian [Lang] [CA] (H)
Esselenian Indians *see* Esselen
Essenape *see* Essanape
Esse-qua-ties *see* Mescalero
  Apache
Essequaties *see* Mescalero Apache
Essequeta *see* Mescalero Apache
Essequeta *see* Kiowa Apache
Essinaboin *see* Assiniboin
Esson *see* Santee
Estanxaques *see* Kansa
E-sta-pa *see* Histapenumanke
Estapa (PC) *see also* Histapenu-
  manke (H)
Estapa *Mandan* (H)
Esteban de Acoma. San *see*
  Acoma
Estechemain *see* Malecite
Estechemin *see* Malecite
Estechemine *see* Malecite
Estecuenopo [MX] *Coahuiltecan*
  (Hdbk10)
Estegueno [MX] *Coahuiltecan*
  (Hdbk10)
Estequenepo *see* Estecuenopo
Estero [CA] (H)
Estevan, St. *see* Acoma
Estevan Acoma, St. *see* Acoma
Estevan de Acoma, S. *see* Acoma
Estevan Queres, St. *see* Acoma
Estevau de Acama, S. *see* Acoma
Estguama [MX] *Coahuiltecan*
  (Hdbk10)
Estiaghes *see* Chippewa
Estiaghes *see* Saulteaux
Estiaghick *see* Chippewa
Estiaghick *see* Saulteaux

Estiajenepo [MX] *Coahuiltecan* (Hdbk10)

Estjage *see* Chippewa

Estok pakai peyap *see* Comecrudo

Estok pakawaile [Selfdesignation] *see* Pakawa

Estrella [CR] *Cabecar* (BE)

Estward Indians *see* Eastern Indians

Eta *see* Cree

Etaa [Clan] *Zuni* (H)

Etaa-kwe *see* Etaa

Etabosle *see* Maca

E-tach-e-cha *see* Iteshica

Etachecha *see* Iteshica

Eta-gottine *see* Etagottine

Etagottine [Can] *Nahane* (BE)

Etah *see* Ita

Etah *see* Polar Eskimos

E-tah-leh *see* Arapaho

Etahleh *see* Arapaho

Etak-bush *see* Etakmehu

Etakmehu [WA] *Salish* (H)

Etakmurs *see* Etakmehu

E-ta-ni-o *see* Atsina

Etanio *see* Atsina

E-tans-ke-pa-se-qua *see* Assiniboin

Etanskepasequa *see* Assiniboin

Eta-Ottine *see* Etagottine

Etaottine *see* Etagottine

Etarita [Clan] *Tionontati* (H)

Etatchogottine [Can, AK] *Kawchottine* (BE)

Etcha-Ottine *see* Etchaottine

Etchaottine (LC) *see also* Slave Indians (LC)

Etchaottine [Can] *Etchareottine* (BE)

Etchape-ottine *see* Etchareottine

Etchareottine (LC) *see also* Slave Indians (LC)

Etchareottine [MA] (H)

Etcheetee [Lang] *see* Hitchiti

Etchemin *see* Malecite

Etchemon *see* Malecite

Etcheridiegottine [Can, MA] *Etchaottine* (BE)

Etchian-Koet *see* Chitsa

Etchimin *see* Etechemin Indians

Etchipoes *see* Chippewa

Etchipoës *see* Ojibwa

Etchita *see* Hitchiti

Etchmin *see* Malecite

Etechemies *see* Malecite

Etechemin *see* Passamaquoddy

Etechemin [Lang] (BE)

Etechemin Indians *Malecite* (BE)

Etecheneus *see* Malecite

Ete-ches-ottine *see* Etechesottine

Etechesottine [Can] *Etchaottine* (BE)

Etechimes *see* Malecite

Etechiminii *see* Malecite

Etehua *see* Ashluslay

Etelena *see* Tereno

Etelene *see* Tereno

Etelenoe *see* Tereno

Etemankiak *see* Malecite

Eteminquois *see* Malecite

Etewaus *see* Etiwaw

Etharita *see* Etarita

Ethelena *see* Tereno

Ethelene *see* Tereno

Ethen-eldeli *see* Etheneldeli

Etheneldeli [Can] *Chipewyan* (BE)

Ethen-elteli *see* Etheneldeli

Ethenelteli *see* Etheneldeli

Ethinu *see* Cree

Ethinyer *see* Cree

Etichimene *see* Malecite

Etichita *see* Hitchiti

Etionnontatehronnon *see* Tionontati

Etionnontates *see* Tionontati

Étionnontatés *see* Wyandot

Etishoka *Hidatsa* (H)

E-tish-sho-ka *see* Etishoka

Etiwan *see* Etiwaw

Etiwaw [SC] *Cusabo* (BE)

Etnemitane *see* Umpqua

Etnemi-teneyu *see* Umpqua

Etnemiteneyu *see* Umpqua

Etocale *see* Ocale

Etocale *see* Olagale

Etschimin *see* Malecite

Etsh-tawut-dinne *see* Etchareottine

Etsitu'biwat *see* Ditsakana

Ets-kai-nah *see* Etskainah

Etskainah (PC) *see also* Eskainah (H)

Etskainah [Society] *Ikunuhkahtsi* (H)

Ettchaottine *see* Etchaottine

Ettcha-ottine *see* Etchaottine

Ettchaottine *see* Ettchaottine

Ettchaottine (LC) *see also* Slave Indians (LC)

Et-tcheri-die-Gottine *see* Etcheridiegottine

Ettcheridiegottine *see* Etcheridiegottine

Ettcheridieottine *see* Etcheridiegottine

Ettine-tinney *see* Etheneldeli

Etzamish *see* Songish

Euchas *see* Yuchi

Euchas *see* Yuma

Euchee *see* Yukichetunne

Euchee *see* Yuchi

Eucher *see* Yukichetunne

Euches *see* Yukichetunne

Euchitaw *see* Hitchiti

Euchre *see* Yukichetunne

Euchre Creek *see* Yukichetunne

Euclataw *see* Lekwiltok

Euclitus *see* Lekwiltok

Eudebe *see* Eudeve

Eudeva *see* Eudeve

Eudeve [Lang] [MX] *Opata* (LC)

Eufala [AL] *Muskogee* (BE)

Eugene Molala *see* Southern Molala

Euhchee *see* Yuchi

Euimes *see* Jemez

Eukas *see* Yuki

E-ukshikni *see* Klamath

Eukshikni [Self-designation] *see* Klamath

Eukshiknimaklaks *see* Klamath

Eukshikni maklaks *see* Modoc

E-ukskhik-ni maklaks *see* Klamath

E-uks-kni *see* Klamath

Eukskni *see* Klamath

Eu-o-tal-la *see* Umatilla

Eu-qua-chee *see* Yukichetunne

Euquachee (PC) *see also* Yukichetunne (BE)

Euquachee [OR] *Tututni* (H)

Eu-quah-chee *see* Yukichetunne

Euquahchee *see* Yukichetunne

Euquatop *see* Mescalero Apache

Euroc *see* Yurok

Eus-a-nich *see* Sanetch

Eusanich *see* Sanetch

E-ushkni *see* Klamath

Eusquemays *see* Eskimos

Eutah *see* Ute

Eutaw *see* Ute

Eutchee *see* Yuchi

Eu-tem-pe-che's *see* Intimbich

Eutempeche's *see* Yukichetunne

Euyron *see* Huron

Eves *see* Erie

Evi-sts-uni'pahis *see* Heviqsni'pahis

Ewahoos *see* Ewawoos

Ewarhoyana [Br] (O)

Ewarhoyana Kahgawa *see* Ewarhogana

Ewa-woos *see* Ewawoos

Ewawoos [BC] *Stalo* (BE)

Ewa'wus *see* Ewawoos

Ewawus *see* Ewawoos

Ewemala *see* Alabama

Ewinte *see* Uinta

Ewlbwiehaht *see* Ucluelet

Ewl-hwilh-aht *see* Ucluelet

Ewlhwilhaht *see* Ucluelet

Ewmitilly *see* Umatilla

E-wu-ha-wu-si *see* Northern Shoshone

E-wu-ha-wu-si *see* Shoshone

Ewuhawusi *see* Northern Shoshone

Ewuhawusi *see* Shoshone
e-wu-xa wu-si *see* Shoshone
ewuzawusi *see* Shoshone
Excanjaque *see* Kansa
Excausaquex *see* Kansa
Excelen *see* Esselen
Excellemaks *see* Esselen
Excomminqui *see* Eskimos
Excomminquois *see* Eskimos
Ex e ni nuth *see* Cexeninuth
Exeninuth *see* Cexeninuth
Exepiahohe *see* Ervipiame
Exmalquio (Hdbk10)
Exteban de Asoma, San *see*
  Acoma
Exvayum [CA] *Luiseño* (Pub, v.8,
  no.3, p.161)
E'yack-im-ah *see* Yakima
Eyackimah *see* Yakima
Eyak [AK, BC] (LC)
Eyakema River Indians *see*
  Sokulk
Eya Kimu [WA] (Hdbk12)
Eyakini dine *see* Hopi
Eyank-ton-wah *see* Yanktonai
Eyeish [TX] (BE)
Eyibogodegi [SA] *Caduveo* (O)
Eyish *see* Eyeish
Eythinyuwuk [Self-designation]
  see Cree

-F-

Faai *see* Fa-ai
Fa-ai [Bora] (O)
Facullies *see* Takulli
Fallatah *see* Atfalati
Fallatrah *see* Atfalati
Fall Indians *see* Atsina
Fall Indians *see* Clowwewalla
Fall Indians *see* Des Chutes
Fall Islands *see* Atsina
Fallon Reservation (Char, v.14)
Falls Indians *see* Des Chutes
Falsavins *see* Menominee
Faraon *Mescalero Apache* (BE)
Faraona *see* Faraon
Faraone *see* Faraon
Faraones *see* Faraon
Fardones *see* Faraon
Farmers Band [MN] *Mdewakan-
  ton* (BE)
Farreon *see* Faraon
Farute *Warrau* (O)
Fat Roasters *see* Ipokimaiks
Fat-Smokers *see* Waci'azi hyabin
Faux Tetes-Plates *see* Salish
Fa-wac-car *see* Tawakoni
Fawaccar *see* Tawakoni
Fawalomne *see* Tuolumne

Feather Falls [Lang] [CA] *Konkow*
  (CA-8)
Feather People *see* Pfia
Feimamar *see* Tumamar
Fejua *see* Tejua
Felepe, San *see* San Felipe [Keres]
Felip, S. *see* San Felipe [Keres]
Felipe, S. *see* San Felipe [Keres]
Felipe, San [NM] *Keres* (BE)
Felipe, Sant *see* San Felipe [Piro]
Felipe de Cueres, S. *see* San Fe-
  lipe [Keres]
Felipe de Cuerez, S. *see* San Fe-
  lipe [Keres]
Felipe de Jesus, San *see* San Fe-
  lipe [Keres]
Felipe de Keres, San *see* San Fe-
  lipe [Keres]
Felipe de Queres, San *see* San
  Felipe [Keres]
Felipo, San *see* San Felipe
  [Keres]
Felippe, San *see* San Felipe
  [Keres]
Felles avoins *see* Menominee
Fellipe, San *see* San Felipe
  [Keres]
Fernandeño [CA] (CA)
Fernandeño [Lang] [CA]
  Gabrielino (Hdbk10)
Fernie Band [MN] *Tobacco Plains*
  (BE)
Fetutlin [AK] *Han* (BE)
Feuille's band *see* Kiyuksa [Mde-
  wakanton]
Few That Lived *Yantonai* (H)
Fiaroa *see* Piaroa
Fiaroankomo *see* Piaroa
Fighting-alone *see* Bloods
  [Atsina]
Fig People *Coahuiltecan* (Hdbk10)
Filifaes *see* Tilijaes
Filijayas *see* Tilijaes
Filixaye *see* Tilijaes
Fire Heart's Band *see* Chan-
  tapeta's Band
Fire Indians *see* Mascouten
Fire Lodge [SD] *Lakota* (BE)
Fire Nation *see* Potawatomi
Fire Nation *see* Mascouten
firewood people *see* Chishende
First Christian Party [WI] *Oneida*
  (H)
fish catchers *see* Booadasha
Fish Clan *see* Huinikashika
Fish-Eaters (H) *see also* Assiniboin
  (LC)
Fish Eaters (H) *see also* Mameoya
  (BE)
Fish Eaters (H) *see also* Taza-
  aigadika (H)
Fish Eaters (H) *see also* Timpaia-
  vats (H)

Fish Eaters (Hdbk11) *see also*
  painkwithikka (Hbk11)
Fish eaters (Hdbk11) *see also* Tim-
  panogots (Hdbk11)
Fish Eaters *Western Shoshone*
  (Hdbk11)
Fish Gens *see* Huinikashika
Fish River *Bering Strait Eskimos*
  (Hdbk5)
Fish Ute *see* Moanunts
Fish Utes *see* Seuvarits
Fiskernaes *Greenland Eskimos*
  (BE)
Fitita *see* Witoto
Five Canton Nations *see* Iroquois
  Confederacy
Five Civilized Tribes [IT, OK]
  (LC)
Five Indian Cantons *see* Iroquois
  Confederacy
Five Lodges *see* Tizapan
Five Mohawk Nations *see* Iro-
  quois Confederacy
Five Nations *see* Iroquois Con-
  federacy
Five Nations [after 1717] *see* Six
  Nations
Five Nations of the Sciota Plains
  see Mingo
Flachbogen *see* Lower Kutenai
Flancs de chien *see*
  Thlingchadinne
Flandreau Indians [SD] *Santee*
  (BE)
Flat Bow *see* Lower Kutenai
Flatbows *see* Lower Kutenai
Flat bows *see* Kutenai
Flat Bows *see* Puhksinahmahyiks
Flathead (BE) *see also* Catawba
  (LC)
Flathead (BE) *see also* Chinook
  (LC)
Flat Head (BE) *see also* Choctaw
  (LC)
Flathead (BE) *see also* Choctaw
  (LC)
Flathead (BE) *see also* Waxhaw
  (BE)
Flathead (H) *see also* Nez Perce
  (LC)
Flat-head *see* Histapenumanke
Flathead (Hdbk12) *see also* Lower
  Chinook (H)
Flathead (Hdbk12) *see also* Spokan
  (LC)
Flathead (LC) *see also* Salish (LC)
Flathead (PC) *see also* Flat Head
  (PC)
Flathead (PC) *see also* Histapenu-
  manke (H)
Flathead [MT] (Hdbk12)
Flat head Indians *see* Flathead
Flathead Kootanie *see* Kalispel

Flat Heads *see* Spokan
Flat heads *see* Flathead
Flathead-Salish *see* Salish
Flathead-Spokan [Lang] [MT] (Hdbk12)
Flats *see* Choctaw
Flat-side Dogs *see* Thlingchdinne
Flattery Indians *see* Makah
Flechas de Palo *Plains Apache* (Hdbk10)
Flok-o *see* Lo-lon-kuk
Flores Creek *see* Thltsusmetunne
Flowpahhoultin [BC] *Salish* (H)
Follaties *see* Atfalati
Folleavoine *see* Menominee
Folle Avoines *see* Menominee
Folles Avoines *see* Menominee
Fols Avoin *see* Menominee
Fols Avoines *see* Menominee
Folsavoins *see* Menominee
Fols-avoise *see* Menominee
Folsom culture (LC)
Folsovoins *see* Menominee
Fond du Lac [MC, ND, SD] *Chippewa* (H)
Fon du Lac Loucheux *see* Tatlit-kutchin
Fonechas *see* Phonichi
Foolish Dogs [Society] *Hidatsa* (H)
Foot Assiniboines *see* Gens de Pied
Foothill [Lang] *Yokutsan* (CA-8)
Foot Indians *see* Ona [SA]
Foremost *see* Hanga
Forest Potawatomi [WI] (Ye)
Forked Horn [MN] (H)
Fork Indians [NJ] *Delaware* (Hdbk15)
Fork People *see* Nassauaketon
Forks-of-the-river Men [WY] *Northern Arapaho* (BE)
Fort Albany Band [Can] *Sakaw-ininiwug* (BE)
Fort George band *see* Tanotenne
Fort Hall Bannock *see* Pohogwe
Fort Hall Shoshone *see* Pohogwe
Fort Hope *see* Sakahl
Fort Indians *see* Kutchakutchin
Fort McDermitt Paiute (Char)
Fort Rupert Indians *see* Kwakiutl
Fort Simpson Indians *see* Tsimshian
Fort Steele Band [BC] *Kutenai* (BE)
Fort Thompson *Sioux* (Char, v.1)
Fossil Creek Band *Northern Tonto Apache* (BE)
Fou-ka-was *see* Tonkawa
Fountain [BC] *Shuswap* (H)
Fountain Band [BC] *Upper Lillooet* (Hdbk12)

Fountain Indians [BC] *Upper Lillooet* (H)
Four Creeks Tribes [CA] *Yokuts* (H)
Four Nations (H)
Four Peak Indians *see* Tonto Apache
Fox *Arikara* (H)
Fox [Society] *Hidatsa* (H)
Fox [WI] (LC)
Franceses *see* Pawnee
Francis, Saint [Lang] *Eastern Algonquian* (Hdbk15)
Francisco, San (BE) *see also* Ramaytush (CA-8)
Francisco, San [CA] *Costanoan* (BE)
Francisco, San [NM] (H)
Francisco de los Epañoles, Sant *see* Yugeuinegge
Francisco de Nambe, San *see* Nambe
Francisco de Sandia, San *see* Sandia
Francisco Pajague, San *see* Pojoaque
Francis Indians, San [NH] *Abnaki* (BE)
Francis Xavier, St. [MI, WI] *Chippewa* (H)
Fraser River [BC] *Upper Lillooet* (BE)
Fraser River [Can] *Shuswap* (BE)
Fraser River Division [BC] *Shuswap* (HDbk12)
Freckled Panis *see* Wichita
Frederikshaab *Greenland Eskimos* (BE)
French Gulch [Lang] *Wintu* (CA-8)
French Prairie Indians *see* Ahantchuyuk
Frentone *see* Mocobi
Frentones *see* Toba
Fresh meat necklace people *see* Talonapin
Fresh Water Indians *see* Agua Dulce
Frog Indians *see* Manta
Frozen Indians [MN] *Atsina* (BE)
Fuchs-Aleuten *see* Unalaska
Fuegians [TF, Arg, CH] (LC)
Fuegino [CH] (O)
Fulawin *see* Menominee
Fulnio [Lang] [Br] (LC)
Fulsowine *see* Menominee
Fus-hatchee [AL] *Muskogee* (BE)
Fushi [Clan] *Chickasaw* (H)
Fusualgi [Clan] *Creek* (H)
Fwah *see* Fwaha
Fwa-ha *see* Fwaha
Fwaha [Clan] *Pecos* (H)

-G-

Ga-a-penoxu *see* Koprino
Gaapenoxu *see* Koprino
Gabilan *Coahuiltecan* (BE)
Gabriel, San *see* Gabrielino
Gabriel, San *see* Yugeuinegge
Gabriel, Sant *see* Yugeuinegge
Gabriel del Yunque, San *see* Yugeuinegge
Gabriele, San *see* Yugeuinegge
Gabrieleño *see* Gabrielino
Gabrielino [CA] *Mission Indians* (LC)
Gabrielino [Lang] [*Serrano-Gabrielino*] (Hdbk10)
Gabrielino Mission Indians (R) *see also* Tongva (R)
Gacare *see* Jacao
Gacheos *see* Cayuga
Gachnawas-haga *see* Conoy
Gachoi *see* Cayuga
Gachoo *see* Cayuga
Gachpa *see* Cayuga
Gachwechnagechga [PA] *Unami* (BE)
Gadinchin [AZ] *Pinal Apache* (H)
Gae *see* Shimigae
Gagaba *see* Cogui
Gaga'nhit tan *see* Kaganhittan
Gaganhittan *see* Kaganhittan
G-ag-g-ilak-a *see* Gyagyilakya
Gaggilaka *see* Gyagyilakya
Gagihetnas-hadai [Subclan] [AK] *Haida* (H)
Gagnieguez *see* Mohawk
Gahe'wa *see* Kiowa
Gahewa *see* Kiowa
Gahkwas *see* Erie
Gahooskins *see* Yahuskin
Gah-tau-go ten-ni *see* Chintagottine
Gahtaugotenni *see* Chintagottine
Gah-tow-go tin-ni *see* Chintagottine
Gahtowgotinni *see* Chintagottine
Gaigwu *see* Kiowa
Ga-i-gwu [Self-designation] *see* Kiowa
Gaiqueri *see* Guayqueri
Gaitchim *see* Juaneño
Gaiuchker *see* Cayuga
Gai'wa *see* Kiowa
Gaiwa *see* Kiowa
Gajuka *see* Cayuga
Gajuqua *see* Cayuga
Gakao *see* Cayuga
Gakpomute [Clan] *Mahican* (H)
Gala'naqoa-ix *see* Cathlanaquiah
Galanaqoaix *see* Cathlanaquiah
Galasq'o *see* Wasco
Galcani *see* Kulchana

Galchedunes *see* Halchidhome
Gal-doe *see* Kauldaw
Galdoe *see* Kauldaw
Galeece Creek Indians *see* Taltushtuntude
Galera [Br] *Nambicuara* (O)
Galia'moix *see* Katlamoik
Galiano Island [VanI] *Penalakut* (H)
Galibi [Br, FrG] (LC)
Galibi [Lang] *Northern Carib* (UAz, v.28)
Galibi [Lang] *Western Carib* (UAz, v.28)
Galibi-Marorne (O)
Galibi-Marworne *see* Galibi-Marworno
Galibi-Morworno [Br, FrG] *Galibi* (O)
Galice Creek Indians *see* Taltushtuntude
Galisteo *Pueblo Indians* (BE)
Galleace Creek *see* Taltushtuntude
Gallinomero (H) *see also* Southern Pomo (BE)
Gal-li-no-me-ro *see* Gallinomero
Gallinomero [CA] *Pomo* (H)
Galtzanen *see* Kulchana
Galzanen *see* Kulchana
Galzani *see* Kulchana
Gamacan *see* Kamakan
Gamakan *see* Kamakan
Gambellites *see* Saint Lawrence Islanders
Gambia *see* Moguex
Gambiano (LC) *see also* Moguex (LC)
Gambiano [Col] (O)
Gamgamtelatl [Gens] *Kwakiutl* (H)
Gamiskwakoka-wininiwak *see* Gamikswakokawininiwak
Gamiskwakokawininiwak [MN] *Chippewa* (H)
Gamutwa *see* Kammatwa
Ganahadi [AK] *Chilkat* (H)
Ganahadi [BC] *Tlingit* (H)
Ganahadi [Social group] [Can] *Takee* (H)
Ganàwagohóno *see* Conoy
Ganaway *see* Conoy
Ganawense *see* Conoy
Ganawese *see* Conoy
Ganawoose *see* Conoy
Ganawses *see* Conoy
Ganaxa'di *see* Ganahadi
Ganaxte'di *see* Ganahadi
Gandastogue *see* Conestoga
Gandostogega *see* Conestoga
Ganeagaonhoh *see* Mohawk
Ganeagaono *see* Mohawk
Ga-ne-ag-o-no *see* Mohawk

Ga-ne-ga-ha-ga *see* Mohawk
Ganegahaga *see* Mohawk
Gangascoe *see* Gingaskin
Gangawese *see* Conoy
G-anhada *see* Kanhada
Ganhada *see* Kanhada
Gani-inge-haga *see* Mohawk
Ganiingehaga *see* Mohawk
Ganingehage *see* Mohawk
Gannaouen *see* Conoy
Gannentaha *see* Onondaga
Ganniagwari *see* Mohawk
Ganniataratich-rone *see* Nanticoke
Ganniegehaga *see* Mohawks
ganniegehronnon *see* Mohawk
Ganniegeronon *see* Mohawk
Ganniegez *see* Mohawk
Ganniegue *see* Mohawk
Ganniekez *see* Mohawk
Ganniessinga *see* Conoy
Ganningehage *see* Mohawk
Gano-a-lo-hale *see* Oneida
Ganochgeritawe *see* Seneca
Ganossetage *see* Conestoga
Ganstero *see* Yuma
Gantsi *see* Kiowa Apache
G'anyakoilnagai *see* Aoyakulnagai
Ganyakoilnagai *see* Aoyakulnagai
Gappa *see* Quapaw
Ga-qua-ga-o-no *see* Erie
Gaquagaono *see* Erie
Gaqui *see* Yaqui
Garabito [CR] *Cabecar* (O)
Garabito [MX] *Guetar* (BE)
Garennajenhaga *see* Huron
Garif *see* Black Carib
Garifuna (LC) *see also* Black Carib (LC)
Garifuna [Lang] [Bel, Gua, NI, Hon] *Cariban* (O)
Garii *see* Northern Yana
Garote *see* Yuma
Garotero *see* Yuma
Garretero *see* Yuma
Garroteros *see* Yuma
Garroteros *see* Quechan
Garrotes *see* Yuma
Garza *Coahuiltecan* (Hdbk10)
Gasakaskuatchimmekak [MN, ND, SD] *Chippewa* (H)
Gashowu (H) *see also* Kassovo (H)
Gashowu [CA] *Kings River Yokuts* (CA-8)
Gashwusha *see* Kassovo
Gaspar Gaspesian *see* Gaspesien
Gaspesians *see* Micmac
Gaspesien [Q] (H)
Gaspesies *see* Gaspesien
Gaspi *see* Walpi
Gataea *see* Kiowa Apache
Gatagetegauning [MI, WI] *Chippewa* (H)

Gatai *see* Central Yana
Gata'ka *see* Kiowa Apache
Gataka *see* Kiowa Apache
Ga ta ka *see* Kiowa-Apache
gatatala *see* Cascades
Gatlanakoa-iq *see* Cathlanaquiah
Ga'tlap'otlh *see* Cathlapotle
Gatlapotlh *see* Cathlapotle
Gatohua *see* Cherokee
Gatsalghi *see* Cheyenne
Gatschet *see* Illinois
Gattacka *see* Kiowa Apache
Gattochwa *see* Cherokee
Gatuya Pain [Self-designation] *see* Sioni
Ga-u-gweh *see* Cayuga
Gaugweh *see* Cayuga
Gaviano *see* Krikati
Gaviao *see* Gavioes
Gavioes [Br] *Eastern Timbira* (LC)
Gawababiganikak [MN, ND, SD] *Chippewa* (H)
Gawia (H) *see also* Kawia [Luiseño] (H)
Gawia [CA] (CA)
Gawia [Lang] [*Tule-Kaweah*] (CA-8)
Gawunena [WY] *Arapaho* (BE)
Gawya *see* Gawia
Gayhead *see* Gay Head
Gay Head [MA, CT] *Wampanoag* (LC)
Gayuga *see* Cayuga
Ge [Lang] [Br] (LC)
Geaji *see* Ge'Aji
Ge'Aji [Lang] *Papago* (Hdbk10)
Gecualme *see* Tecual
Gecuiches *see* Cahuilla
Gecuiches *see* Kawia [Luiseño]
Gediak *see* Shediac
Ge-e-way *see* Santo Domingo
Geeway *see* Santo Domingo
Ge-e-we *see* Santo Domingo
Geewe *see* Santo Domingo
Geghdageghroano *see* Illinois
Geghtigeghroones *see* Illinois
G'eg'o'te *see* Gyegyote
Gegote *see* Gyegyote
Geie *see* Geyer
Geier *see* Geies
Geies [TX] *Coahuiltecan* (BE)
G'eighe-t-nas-had-a-i *see* Gagihetnas-hadai
Geighetnashadai *see* Gagihetnas-hadai
Gelinos *see* Gila Apache
Gemes *see* Jemez
Gemex *see* Jemez
Gemez *see* Jemez
Ge-nega's Band *see* Genega's Band
Genega's Band [NV] *Paviotso* (H)

General Aztec [Lang] [*Southern Uto-Aztecan*] (Hdbk10)
General Central Yupik [Lang] *Alaskan Yupik* (Hdbk5)
Genicuiches *see* Serrano
Geniegueronon *see* Mohawk
Genigneihs *see* Serrano
Genigueches *see* Serrano
Genigueh *see* Serrano
Geniguieh *see* Serrano
Geniocane *see* Heniocane
Genizaro (H) *see also* Tome (H)
Genizaro [NM] (H)
Gens *see* Ouikaling
Gens de bois *see* Tutchone
Gens de Bois *see* Hankutchin
Gens de bouleau *see* Tennuth-kutchin
Gens de Bouleaux *see* Tennuth-kutchin
Gens de butte *see* Tenankutchin
Gens de Castor *see* Tsattine
Gens de Feu *see* Mascouten
Gens de Feuillees *see* Tschantoga
Gens de Feuilles *see* Itscheabine
Gens de Feuilles *see* Tschantoga
Gens-de-fine *see* Hankutchin
Gens de Fous *see* Hankutchin
Gens de Fous *see* Hankutchin
Gens de Foux *see* Hankutchin
Gens de la Barbue *see* Marameg
Gens de l'abri *see* Tatsakutchin
Gens de Lac *see* Mdewakanton
Gens de la Feuille *see* Itscheabine
Gens de la fourche du Mackenzie *see* Eleidlinottine
Gens de la Grande Riviere *see* Nakotcho-kutchin
Gens De Lai *see* Mdewakanton
Gens de la Loutre *see* Nikikouek
Gens de la Mer [Can] *Algonquian* (H)
Gens de la montagne *see* Etagot-tine
Gens de la montagne la Corne *see* Etechesottine
Gens de Large *see* Natsitkutchin
Gens de la riviere au Foin *see* Klodesseottine
Gens de la Sapiniere [Can] (H)
Gens de Milieu *see* Tangeratsa
Gens d'En-haut *see* Etagottine
Gens de Paise *Sioux* (H)
Gens de Panse *see* Allakaweah
Gens de Pied [Can] *Assiniboin* (H)
Gens de Pitie *see* Shoshoko
Gens-de-ralt *see* Tukkuthkutchin
Gens de rats *see* Takkuth-kutchin
Gens de rats *see* Tukkuthkutchin
Gens de Roche *see* Jatonabine
Gens de Roches *see* Jatonabine
Gens des Bois *see* Esbataottine

Gens des Bois *see* Hankutchin
Gens des Bois *see* Tschantoga
Gens des Butte *see* Tenankutchin
Gens des Chaudieres *see* Colville
Gens des chevres *see* Esbataottine
Gens des Corbeau *see* Crow
Gens de Serpent *see* Shoshone
Gens des Faux *see* Hankutchin
Gens des fees *see* Itscheabine
Gens des filles *see* Itscheabine
Gens des Foux *see* Tutchone
Gens de siffleur *see* Teachinkutchin
Gens des Lacs *Sioux* (H)
Gens des Montagnes *see* Chabin
Gens des Montagnes *see* Chipewyan
Gens des Montagnes-Rocheuses *see* Etagottine
Gens des Osayes *see* Tanintauei
Gens des Rats *see* Vuntakutchin
Gens des rosches *see* Jatonabine
Gens des Serpent *see* Shoshone
Gens des Soulier *see* Amahami
Gens des Tee *see* Itscheabine
Gens des Terres *see* Tetes de Boule
Gens des Vache *see* Arapaho
Gens de Tee *see* Tshantoga
Gens-de-wiz *see* Tutchone
Gens du Caribou *see* Attikirin-iouetch
Gens du Cuivre *see* Tatsanottine
Gens du Feu *see* Potawatomi
Gens du fond du Lac *see* Tatlit-kutchin
Gens du Fort-de-pierre *see* Etheneldeli
Gens du Fort Norman *see* Desnedeyarelottine
Gens du Lac *see* Mdewakanton
Gens du Lac *see* Minishinakato
Gens du lac la Truite *see* Etchaottine
Gens du Large (BE) *see also* Nat-sitkutchin (LC)
Gens du Large *Dakota* (H)
Gens du Nord *see* Northern Assiniboin
Gens du Nord *see* Tschantoga
Gens du Petun *see* Tionontati
Gens du Poil *see* Chintagottine
Gens du Rat *see* Vuntakutchin
Gens du Sable *see* Sable
Gens du Sang *see* Kainah
Gens du Sant *see* Miskouaha
gens du Sault *see* Saulteaux
Gens du Serpent *see* Northern Shoshone
Gens du Serpent *see* Shoshone
Gens du vache *see* Arapaho
Gens en l'air *see* Etagottine
Gens feu *see* Potawatomi

Gentlemen Indians *see* Waco
gents puants *see* Winnebago
Genuvskoe *see* Henya
George, Saint *Southern Paiute* (Hdbk11)
Geral (O) *see also* Nheengatu (O)
Geral [SA] (O)
Gerano, San [Col] *Yuki* (O)
Gergecensens [CA] *Thamien* (H)
Gerguensens *see* Gergecensens
Gerzuensens *see* Gergcensens
Get-an-max *see* Kitanmaiksh
G-e'xsem *see* Gyeksem
Gexsem *see* Gyeksem
Geyer *Coahuiltecan* (Hdbk10)
Gha-hi-taneo *see* Khahitan
Ghec-chi *see* Kekchi
Ghecham [Self-designation] *see* Luiseño
Ghuil-chan *see* Kulchana
Ghula'napo *see* Kuhlanapa
Ghuylliche *see* Huilliche
Giajepocotiyo *see* Goajopocayo
Giamina [Lang] [CA] (He)
Gi-aucth-in-in-e-wug *see* Hi-datsa
Giauctchininewug *see* Hidatsa
Gi-autch-in-ne-wug *see* Hidatsa
Giautchinnewug *see* Hidatsa
Gibari *see* Jivaro
Gibbaway *see* Chippewa
Gibola *see* Zuni
Gicarilla *see* Jicarilla Apache
Gicocoge *Coahuiltecan* (Hdbk10)
gicpahlo'As *Tsimshian* (Anthro, v.9, no.3, p.160)
Gidanemuik *see* Serrano
Gidanemuik *see* Gitanemuk
Gidanemuk *see* Gitanemuk
Gidu'tikad [CA] *Northern Paiute* (Pub, v.31, no.3)
Gigabu *see* Kickapoo
Gigabuhak *see* Kickapoo
G-i-g-ilgam *see* Gyigyilkam
Gigilgam *see* Gyigyilkam
gigilqAm [Clan] *Kwexa* (Anthro, v.9, no.3, p158)
Gigimai adia [Lang] *Papago* (Hdbk10)
Gigue *see* Santo Domingo
Gijames *see* Hihames
Gijames *see* Sijame
Gikapu *see* Kickapoo
Gi'kats *see* Shasta
Gikats [OR] *Shasta* (Shasta, p.15)
Gi'katsakitsu *see* Shasta
Gikatsakitsu *see* Shasta
Gikidanum *see* Serrano
Gikidanum *see* Gitanemuk
Gila Apache (Hdbk10) *see also* Eastern Chiricahua (Hdbk10)
Gila Apache [NM] (H)
Gila'lelam *see* Nisal

Gilalelam *see* Nisal
Giland *see* Coyotero Apache
Gilans *see* Gila Apache
Gila Pimas *see* Pima
Gila'q!ulawa *see* Kwalhioqua
Gilaqulawa *see* Kwalhioqua
Gila'wewalamt *see* Clowwewalla
Gilawewalamt *see* Clowwewalla
Gila'xicatck *see* Watlala
Gilay'wee-walamt *see* Clowwe-
   walla
Gileñas *see* Gila Apache
Gileñas *see* Gilenos
Gileños (H) *see also* Gila Apache
   (H)
Gileños (Hdbk10) *see also* Eastern
   Chiricahua (Hdbk10)
Gileños [AZ] *Upper Piman*
   (Hdbk10)
Gileños Apaches *see* Gila Apache
Gillamook *see* Tillamook
Gilserhyu [Phratry] *Carrier Indi-
   ans* (Bull133)
giltusa *see* giluts'a
giluts'a *Tsimshian* (Anthro, v.9,
   no.3, p.160)
Gilxicatck *see* Watlala
Gi'manoitx *see* Kitlope
Gimanoitx *see* Kitlope
Gimiel (H) *see also* Comeya (H)
Gimiel (H) *see also* Kamia (LC)
Gimiel [BaC] *Yuma* (H)
Ginabo *see* Sinabu
ginadoiks *Tsimshian* (Anthro, v.9,
   no.3, p.160)
Gina's *see* Kiowa Apache
ginaxangik *Tsimshian* (Anthro,
   v.9, no.3, p.160)
Ginebigonini *see* Northern
   Shoshone
Ginebigonini *see* Shoshone
Ginetwei Sawanogi *see* Absentee
   Shwanee
Gingascoe *see* Gingaskin
Gingaskin *Accomac* (Hdbk15)
Gingaskoyne *see* Gingaskin
Gingateege *see* Pocomoke
Gingo Teague *see* Pocomoke
Gingoteque *see* Pocomoke
Giopas *see* Ojipas
Giopino (Anthro, v.9, no.3,
   p.158)
Gioricane *see* Heniocane
Gi-oshk *see* Gyaushk
Gioshk *see* Gyaushk
Giowaka-a *see* Santa Clara [NM]
Giowatsa-a *see* Santa Clara
   [NM]
Gipane *see* Lipan Apache
Gi-pu-y *see* Santo Domingo
Gipuy *see* Santo Domingo
Giriguana *see* Chiriguano
Giriguano *see* Chiriguano

Girl's band *see* Itscheabine
Girtrhatin *see* Kithateh
Giry [BO] *Araona* (O)
Gitamtanyer [Phratry] *Carrier In-
   dians* (Bull133)
gitando *Tsimshian* (Anthro, v.9.
   no.3, p.160)
Gitanemok *see* Gitanemuk
Gitanemuk [CA] *Serrano* (Pub,
   v.4, no.3, pp.135–139)
Gitanemuk [Lang] *Serrano* (Pub,
   v.4, no.3, pp.135–139)
Gitanemum *see* Gitanemuk
Gitanemum *see* Serrano
Git-an-max *see* Kitanmaiksh
Gitanmax *see* Kitanmaiksh
Gita'qemas *see* Clackamas
Gita'q emas *see* Clackamas
Gitaqemas *see* Clackamas
Gitenmaks *see* Gitanemuk
Gitenmaks *see* Kitanmaiksh
Gitibo *see* Setebo
Gitin-gi'djats *see* Gitin-gidjats
Gitin-gidjats [Clan] *Haida* (H)
Gitksan (LC) *see also* Kitksan
   (LC)
Gitksan [BC] (H)
Gitksan [Lang] [BC] *Chim-
   meweyan* (H)
Gitksan [Lang] [BC] *Southern
   Coast Tsimshian* (Anthro, v.9,
   no.3, p.160)
gitlan *Tsimshian* (Anthro, v.9,
   no.3, p.160)
Gitla'tlpe'leks *see* Palux
Gitlatlpeleks *see* Palux
Gitla'we-walamt *see* Clowwe-
   walla
Gitlawewalamt *see* Clowwewalla
Gits'aji *see* Kichai
Gitsaji *see* Kichai
Gitsegyukla *see* Kitsegukla
gitsilasu *see* gits'ilasu
gits'ilasu *Tsimshian* (Anthro, v.9,
   no.3, p.160)
Gittci's *see* Kitzeesh
Gituns [Family group] [BC]
   Haida (H)
gitwilgyo'ts *Tsimshian* (Anthro,
   v.9, no.3, p.160)
Gitwinksilk *see* Kitgigenik
Gitwinlkul *see* Kitwancool
Gitwinsilk *see* Kitgigenik
gitzis *Tsimshian* (Anthro, v.9,
   no.3, p.160)
Givaro *see* Jivaro
gixsAm *Koskimo* (Anthro, v.9,
   no.3, p158)
Glagla-heca *see* Glaglahecha
Glaglahecha *Sihasapa* (H)
Glagla-hetca *see* Glaglahecha
Glakhmiut *see* Aglurmiut
Gleese Cleek *see* Taltushtuntude

Glen-Vowell Band [Lang] [BC]
   Kitksan (H)
Gleta *see* Isleta
Gnacsitare [MN] (H)
Gnacsitaries *see* Gnacsitare
Gnapaw *see* Quapaw
Go-about Band *see* Detsanayuke
Goagiro *see* Goajiro
Goahibo *see* Guahibo
Goahiva *see* Guahibo
Goahivo *see* Guahibo
Goajir *see* Goajiro
Goajiro [VE, Col] (LC)
Goajopocayo *Coahuiltecan*
   (Hdbk10)
goasek *see* Coosac
Goasi *see* Coosac
goasiak *see* Coosac
goasiak *see* Cowasuck
Goasila [Lang] *Kwakiutl* (BE)
Goch [Phratry] *Tlingit* (H)
Gocoyome [MX] *Toboso* (BE)
Godamyon *see* Kwatami
Godbout [Can] [*Montagnais-
   Naskapi*] (BE)
Godhavn *Greenland Eskimos* (BE)
Godthaab *Greenland Eskimos* (BE)
Gogouin *see* Cayuga
Gohlkahin *see* Golkahin
Gohun *see* Yavapai
Gohun *see* Tonto Apache
Go-hun *see* Tulkepaia
Gohun *see* Tulkepaia
Goianaz *see* Kaingangue
Goiogoen *see* Cayuga
goiögoinronnon *see* Cayuga
Goiogouen *see* Cayuga
Goiogouioronon *see* Cayuga
Gojogouen *see* Cayuga
Gokapatagan *see* Kickapoo
Go-ke-nim-non *see* Bokinwad
Gokenimnon *see* Bokinwad
Golden Lake [Ont] *Algonkin* (H)
Gol-doe *see* Kauldaw
Goldoe *see* Kauldaw
Go'lkahin *see* Golkahin
Golkahin [NM] *Jicarilla Apache*
   (BE)
Goltzane *see* Kulchana
Golzan *see* Kulchana
Golzanen *see* Kulchana
Gomez *see* Jemez
Gonaho [AK] *Tlingit* (BE)
Gonana *see* Nahane
Go'naxo qoan *see* Gunachonken
Gonaxoqoan *see* Gunachonken
Gonega *see* Genega's Band
Gonoois *see* Conoy
Gontiel [Clan] [AZ] *San Carlos
   Apache* (H)
Goodhope *Bering Strait Eskimos*
   (Hdbk5)
Good Iroquois *see* Huron

Good Knife *see* Tanetsukanu-
manke
Good-night *see* Beothuk
Goodnight *see* Beothuk
Goodroad's Band *see* Oy-
ateshicha
Goodrod's Band *see* Oyateshicha
Gooiogouen *see* Cayuga
Goolkizzen *Apache* (H)
Goose Creek Diggers *see* Tus-
sawehe
Goose Lake Modoc (Hdbk12)
G-o-p'enox *see* Koprino
Gopenox *see* Koprino
Gophers *see* Tashnahecha
Goricas *see* Yorica
Gorotire [Br] *Northern Cayapo*
(O)
Gorretas *see* Manso
Gorrita *see* Manso
Go-sha-ute *see* Gosiute
Goshaute *see* Gosiute
Goshee Utes *see* Gosiute
Goshen Utes *see* Gosiute
Goship *see* Gosiute
Goship Shoshones *see* Gosiute
Go-ship-Utes *see* Gosiute
Goshiss *see* Gosiute
Goshoot *see* Gosiute
Gosh-sho-o *see* Kossovo
Goshshoo *see* Kassovo
Goshute *see* Gosiute
Go-shutes *see* Gosiute
Gosh Yuta *see* Gosiute
Gosiute [UT, NV] *Western
Shoshone* (LC)
Go-si Utes *see* Gosiute
Gos-ta Utes *see* Gosiute
Gosta Utes *see* Gosiute
Gos ventres *see* Gros Ventres
Got [Phratry] *Haida* (H)
Gotane [MX] *Chibchan* (BE)
Gotc *see* Goch
Gotchti *see* Cochiti
Gotocogegodegi *Caduveo* (O)
Goulapissa *see* Acolapissa
Goxica *see* Yorica
Goyagouin *see* Cayuga
Goyana *see* Kaingangue
go'y'atikadu *see* Beatty Band
goyatikadu *see* Beatty Band
Goyode *see* Navajo
Goyogan *see* Cayuga
Goyogoan *see* Cayuga
Goyogoin *see* Cayuga
Goyogouan *see* Cayuga
Goyogouen *see* Cayuga
Goyogouin *see* Cayuga
Goyoguan *see* Cayuga
Goyoguen *see* Cayuga
Goyoguin *see* Cayuga
Goyoguoain *see* Cayuga
Go-yo-gwen *see* Cayuga

Goyogwen *see* Cayuga
Goyoteros *see* Yuma
Gpaughettes *see* Kishpachlaots
Grail *Sioux* (H)
Granada *see* Kawihuh
Grand Eaux *see* Pahatsi
Grand Eskimaux *see* Labrador
Eskimos
Grandes pagnes *see* Paskwaw-
ininiwug
Grand Gens *Loucheux* (IndN, v.2,
no.3, July 1925)
Grand Osage *see* Pahatsi
Grand Pan *see* Chaui
Grand Pani *see* Chaui
Grand Pans *see* Chaui
Grand Pawnee *see* Chaui
Grand Portage [MN, SD, ND]
Chippewa (H)
Grand Quivira *see* Tabira
Grand River [UT, CO] *Ute* (H)
Grand River Indians (BE) *see also*
Ute (LC)
Grand River Indians [Ont] *Iro-
quois* (H)
Grand River Utahs *see* Grand
River
Grand River Ute (Hdbk11) *see also*
White River (Hdbk11)
Grand River Ute (LC) *see also*
Yampa (LC)
Grands *see* Chaui
Grands Akansas *Quapaw* (H)
Grand Saux *Dakota* (H)
Grands Panis *see* Chaui
Grands Taensas *see* Taensa
Grand Tuc *see* Pahatsi
Grand Zo *see* Pahatsi
Grand Zue *see* Pahatsi
Granite Peak Band *see* Wikutepa
Gran Quivira *see* Quivira
Gran Quivra *see* Tabira
Grasshopper Indians *see* Ute
Grasshoppers *see* Masi'kota
Grass House People *see*
Shoshone
Grass People *see* Sakutenedi
Grass Sound Indians *see* Huna
Gray-ones [Clan] [MN] *Atsina*
(BE)
Gray Ponka [Subclan] *Ponca* (H)
Gray Squirrel Gens *see* Sinago
Grease Creek Indians *see* Tal-
tushtuntude
Greasy Faces [WY] *Northern Ara-
paho* (BE)
Great Basin (Hdbk11)
Great Basin [Lang] *Shoshonean*
(AI)
Great Belly Indians *see* Gros
Ventres
Great Kammas Indians *see*
Tukuarika

Great Kitkehahki [NE]
Kitkehahki (H)
Great Lakes (LC)
Great Osage (BE) *see also* Big
Osage (AtInd)
Great Osage *see* Pahatsi
Great Osage [MO] *Osage* (BE)
Great Ossage *see* Pahatsi
Great Ozage *see* Pahatsi
Great Pawnee *see* Chaui
Great Plains (LC)
Great Sand Bar people *see* Matc
Sua'mako Tusi'niniu
Greenland *Greenland Eskimos*
(BE)
Greenland Eskimos [Lang] [*Inuit-
Inupiaq*] (Hdbk5)
Green Paint Indians *see* Nez
Perce
Green River Band *see*
Akanaquint
Green River Indians *see*
Skopamish
Green River Snakes *Eastern
Shoshone* (Hdbk11)
Green River Utahs *see*
Akanaquint
Green River Ute *see* Akanaquint
Green Timber Band [BC] *Lake
Shuswap* (Hdbk12)
Green Wood Indians *see* Nez
Perce
Gregoio de Abo, S. *see* Abo
Gregoria de Abo, S. *see* Abo
Gregorio Abbo, San *see* Abo
Gregorio de Abo, S. *see* Abo
Gregory, St. *see* Abo
Grey Eagle Band [MN] *Dakota*
(BE)
Grey Eyes *see* Inshtasanda
Grey-Iron *see* Magayuteshni
Grigas *see* Gris
Grigra (BE) *see also* Gris (BE)
Grigra [MS] (BE)
Grimes [CA] (BE)
Grimes [Lang] [CA] *River Patwin*
(BE)
Grinaiches (H)
Gris (BE) *see also* Grigra (BE)
Gris [LA] (BE)
Gritone *see* Sinabu
Groote Siconese *see* Big Siconese
Grosse Ventres *see* Gros Ventres
Gross Vantres *see* Gros Ventres
Grossventers *see* Gros Ventres
Gross Ventres *see* Gros Ventres
Grosvantres *see* Gros Ventres
Grosventres *see* Hidatsa
Gros Ventres [ND, Can] (LC)
Gros Ventres des Plaines *see*
Atsina
Gros Ventres des Prairies *see*
Atsina

Gros Ventres of the Falls *see* Atsina

Gros Ventres of the Missouri *see* Gros Ventres

Gros Ventres of the Plains *see* Atsina

Gros Ventres of the Prairie *see* Atsina

Grosventres of the Prairie *see* Atsina

Gros-Vents *see* Gros Ventres

Groundhog Eaters *see* Yahandeka

Groundhog-eaters *see* Gidu'tikad

Grouse Men *see* Sipushkanu-manke

Grovan *see* Gros Ventres

G-tinkit *see* Tlingit

Gtinkit *see* Tlingit

Guabaqua [HA] *Guaccaiarima* (BE)

Guacacamegua *see* Cacamegua

Guacachina [MX] *Coahuiltecan* (Hdbk10)

Guacanahua *see* Ese Ejje

Guacata [FL] (BE)

Guacaya *see* Waccamaw

Guaccaiarima [HA] (BE)

Guachama [CA] *Serrano* (Pub, v.4, no.3, p.132)

Guachanahua *see* Ese Ejje

Guachichil *see* Guachichile

Guachichila *see* Guachichile

Guachichile [MX] (LC)

Guacurure *see* Pilaga

Guadalupe *see* Pojoaque

Guadalupe *see* Zuni

Guadepa *Coahuiltecan* (Hdbk10)

Guaes [KS] *Kansa* (H)

Guagaqua [HA] *Guaccaiarima* (BE)

Guage-johe (BE) *see also* Kwahari (BE)

Guagejohe *see* Guage-johe

Guage-johe [TX] *Comanche* (BE)

Gua-ge-jo-ho *see* Guage-johe

Guagenigronnon *see* Mohawk

Guagibo *see* Guahibo

Guagiva *see* Guahibo

Guaguatu (H)

Guaguatu (Hdbk11) *see also* Capote (LC)

Guagui [MX] *Coahuiltecan* (Hdbk10)

Guahabba [HA] *Bainoa* (BE)

Guaharibo [Br, VE] (LC)

Guaharivo *see* Guaharibo

Guahiba *see* Guahibo

Guahibo [Col, VE] (LC)

Guahiboan [Lang] [Col, VE] (O)

Guaiana *see* Guayana

Guaiana *see* Kaingangue

Guaiapy *see* Oyampi

Guaiaqui *see* Guayaki

Guaiba *see* Guahibo

Guaibo *see* Guahibo

Guaica *see* Waica

Guaicamaopa *see* Yacum

Guaicuro *see* Guaycura

Guaicuru *see* Guaycura

Guaigua *see* Guahibo

Guaika *see* Waica

Guaika *see* Yanoama

Guaikiare *see* Wokiare

Guaikuru *see* Guaycuru

Guailopo [MX] *Varohio* (H)

Guaimaro [Cu] (BE)

Guaimi *see* Guaymi

Guaino *see* Huayno

Guaipuinave *see* Puinave

Guaiquairo *see* Yabarana

Guaivo *see* Guahibo

Guaja [Br] (BE)

Guajajara [Br] (O)

Guajajara-Tenetehara [Br] *Tenetehara* (O)

Guajaribo *see* Yanoama

Guajibo *see* Guahibo

Guajima [BO] *Araona* (O)

Guajira *see* Goajiro

Guajiro (O) *see also* Goajiro (LC)

Guajiro [Lang] *Maipurean* (O)

Guajivo *see* Guahibo

Guajolote [MX] *Coahuiltecan* (Hdbk10)

Guak-s'n'a'mish *see* Squaxon

Gualaca [MX] *Chibchan* (BE)

Gualahuis *see* Hualahuis

Gualala (BE) *see also* Southwestern Pomo (BE)

Gua-la-la *see* Gualala

Gualala [CA] *Coast Pomo* (H)

Gualciones *see* Guaycones

Guale [GA] (LC)

Gualegua [MX] *Coahuiltecan* (Hdbk10)

Gualiba *see* Hualapai

Gualpi *see* Walpi

Gualta (H)

Guamaca *see* Damana

Guamaca [Lang] [Col] *Chibchan* (O)

Guamahaya [Cu] (BE)

Guamar [Lang] [MX] (Hdbk10)

Guambia *see* Moguex

Guambia-Coconuco *see* Guahibo

Guambiana [Lang] [Col] *Chibchan* (O)

Guambiano *see* Gambiano

Guamepeje [MX] *Coahuiltecan* (Hdbk10)

Guamichicorama [MX] *Concho* (BE)

Guamo *see* Guayqueri

Guamoa *see* Guamua

Guamoayagua [MX] *Coahuiltecan* (Hdbk10)

Guampe [MX] *Coahuiltecan* (Hdbk10)

Guampexte [MX] *Coahuiltecan* (Hdbk10)

Guamua (Hdbk10) *see also* Navajo (LC)

Guamua [AZ, CA] (H)

Guana (LC) *see also* Kaskiha (O)

Guana (O) *see also* Tereno (LC)

Guana [Arg, Par, Uru] (LC)

Guana [Lang] *Mascoian* (LC)

Guanabepe [AZ, CA] (H)

Guanacahibe [Cu] (BE)

Guanama [HA] *Caizcimu* (BE)

Guananesses *see* Conoy

Guanano [Br] (LC)

Guanano [Lang] [Br] *Eastern Tukanoan* (LC)

Guanapujamo [MX] *Coahuiltecan* (Hdbk10)

Guanavepe *see* Guanabepe

Guanbiano *see* Gambiano

Guandastogue *see* Conestoga

Guandostague *see* Conestoga

Guane [Col] (LC)

Guanexico [NI] *Ulua* (BE)

Guanica [PR] (BE)

Guaniguanico [Cu] (BE)

Guanipas [TX] *Coahuiltecan* (BE)

Guapa *see* Wappo

Guape *Coahuiltecan* (Hdbk10)

Guapishana *see* Wapisiana

Guapo *see* Wappo

Guapore Namiquara *see* Nambicuara

Guaputu *see* Guaguatu

Guaputu *see* Capote

Guaque [Lang] *Carijona* (UAz, v.28)

Guaracata *see* Iguaracata

Guarama *see* Caurame

Guarani [Lang] [BO, Par, Arg, Br] *Tupi* (LC)

Guaranne *see* Warrau

Guarano *see* Warrau

Guaranoca *see* Moro

Guaranu *see* Warrau

Guarao *see* Warrau

Guarao *see* Warao

Guaraon *see* Warrau

Guaraoun *see* Warrau

Guaraouno *see* Warrau

Guaraounoe *see* Warrau

Guararini *see* Warrau

Guarasteguara [Lang] [Br] *Tupi* (O)

Guarasteguara [MX] (Hdbk10)

Guarasu *see* Pauserena

Guarasug'we [Self-designation] *see* Pauserna

Guaratagaja *see* Guarategaja

Guarategaja [Br] (O)

Guarau *see* Warrau

Guarauana *see* Warrau
Guarauna [Lang] *Carib* (LC)
Guaraune *see* Warrau
Guarauno *see* Warrau
Guarauno *see* Warao
Guaraunun *see* Warrau
Guarayo (LC) *see also* Chiriguano (LC)
Guarayo [BO, Par] (LC)
Guarayo [Tacanan] *see* Ese Ejje
Guarayu *see* Guarayo
Guarayu-ta *see* Pauserna
Guarco [MX] *Guetar* (BE)
Guarehena *see* Arekena
Guarequena [VE] *Arahuac* (O)
Guarequena [VE] *Wakuenai* (O)
Guariba *Macu* (O)
Guarijio [Lang] *Tarahumaran* (Hdbk10)
Guarijio [MX] (Hdbk10)
Guarina *see* Palenque
Guarino [Col] (LC)
Guarionex [PR] (BE)
Guariqueche *Coahuiltecan* (Hdbk10)
Guariquena *see* Arekena
Guariquena *see* Warikyana
Guarizo [Lang] [BO] *Tacanan* (O)
Guarpe (LC)
Guarpe (LC) *see also* Allentiac (LC)
Guarpe (LC) *see also* Huarpe (LC)
Guarricco [HA] *Bainoa* (BE)
Guaru [Lang] *Maipurean* (O)
Guas *see* Guaes
Guasachis *see* Osage
Guasama *see* Cathlamet
Guasapar [MX] *Varahio* (BE)
Guasas [TX] (H)
Guasave [MX] *Cahita* (BE)
Guasco [TX] *Hasinai Confederacy* (BE)
Guasers *see* Guasas
Guasi'la *see* Goasila
Guastec *see* Huastec
Guasurango *see* Tapiete
Guatari *see* Watereee
Guatiadeo *Caduveo* (O)
Guatiguara [MX] (Hdbk10)
Guatijigua [ES] *Lencan* (BE)
Guatinicamame *Mazatec* (BE)
Guato [BO, Br] (LC)
Guatsenok *see* Quatsino
Gua'ts'enoq *see* Quatsino
Gua'ts'enox *see* Quatsino
Guatsenox *see* Quatsino
Guatuso [CR] *Chibchan* (LC)
Guauaenok *Kwakiutl* (BE)
Guauaenok [Lang] [BC] *Kwakiutl* (H)
Guau'aenoq *see* Guauaenok
Guau'aenox *see* Guauenok

Guaviare [Col] (O)
Guaxiquero [Hon] *Lenca* (BE)
Guayabero [Col] *Guahibo* (LC)
Guayagua *see* Cayague
Guayaki *see* Guayaqui
Guayaki-Ache *see* Guayaqui
Guayana [Br, Sur, FrG] (LC)
Guayapi *see* Oyanpi
Guayaqui [Par] (LC)
Guayaro *see* Itene
Guayba *see* Guahibo
Guaycari *see* Guayqueri
Guaycones [TX] *Coastal Coahuiltecan* (Hdbk10)
Guaycuru (LC) *see also* Tereno (LC)
Guaycuru [Lang] [Arg, Par] (LC)
Guaycuruan *see* Guaycuru
Guaygata [JA] (BE)
Guaykuru *see* Guaycuru
Guayma [MX] *Seri* (BE)
Guaymi (Hdbk10) *see also* Guayma (BE)
Guaymi [CR, Pan] *Chibchan* (LC)
Guaymie [Lang] *see* Guaymi
Guaynungomo *see* Mayongong
Guayotri *Tigua* (H)
Guayqueri [VE] [Tamanaco] (O)
Guayquiri *see* Guayqueri
Guayu *see* Goajiro
Guayva *see* Guahibo
Guaza *see* Kiowa
Guazapar [MX] *Tarahumara* (Hdk10)
Guazas *see* Guasas
Guazave [MX] *Vacoregue* (H)
Gubates *see* Tano
Guehegaia *see* Walapai
Gueimas *see* Guayma
Gueiquesal *see* Gueiquesales
Gueiquesal *see* Hueyhueyquetzal
Gueiquesales (H) *see also* Guisoles (BE)
Gueiquesales [TX] (H)
Gueiquizales *see* Guiequesales
Guelamoye [MX] *Coahuiltecan* (Hdbk10)
Guelasiguicme [MX] *Concho* (BE)
Guentuse *see* Maca
Guereches *see* Querecho
Guerecho *see* Querecho
Gueren (LC) *see also* Tapuya (LC)
Gueren [Br] (O)
Gueres *see* Keres
Guergaida *see* Guerjuatida
Guericochal *Coahuiltecan* (Hdbk10)
Gueripiamo *see* Ervipiame
Guerjuadan *see* Guerjuatida
Guerjuatida *Coahuiltecan* (BE)
Guerrero [MX] *Mazatec* (BE)
Guerriers *see* Dakota

Guerriers de la Roche *see* Assiniboin
Guerriers de pierre *see* Assiniboin
Guesal *see* Hueyhueyquetzal
Guesol *see* Hueyhueyquetzal
Guetala *see* Guetela
Guetar [CR] (LC)
Guetare *see* Guetar
Gueteadeguo *Caduveo* (O)
Guetela [Clan] [BC] *Kwakiutl* (H)
Guetiadegodi *Caduveo* (O)
Guetiadeo *see* Caduveo
Gueyacapo [MX] (Hdbk10)
Gueymura (H) *see also* Kamia (LC)
Gueymura [BaC] (H)
Gueyniotiteshesgue [Phratry] *Caughnawaga* (H)
Gueza [SC] (BE)
Guhlkainde [NM] *Mescalero Apache* (H)
Guhunes *see* Tonto Apache
Guiagua [HA] *Caizcimu* (BE)
Guianapaqueno *see* Quiniacapem
Guiaquita [MX] *Concho* (BE)
Guibisnuches *see* Weeminuche
Guical *see* Hueyhueyquetzal
Guicasal *see* Hueyhueyquetzal
Guichais *see* Kichai
Guichita *see* Wichita
Guichola *see* Huichol
Guichyana *see* Yuma
Guicopasico [MX] *Coahuiltecan* (Hdbk10)
Guicuru *see* Kuikuru
Guigouin *see* Cayuga
Guiguigoa *Coahuiltecan* (Hdbk10)
Guiguimuches *see* Weeminuche
Guiguipacam *Coahuiltecan* (Hdbk10)
Guiguitamcar [Lang] [CA] (Pub, v.8, no.1, p.11)
Gui'gyilk-am *see* Gyigyilkam
Guijacal *see* Hueyhueyquetzal
Guilford Indians *see* Wappinger
Guiliche *see* Huilliche
Guilistinons *see* Cree
Guilitoy [CA] *Patwin* (H)
Guillica *see* Guilitoy
Guiluco *see* Guilitoy
Guimen [CA] *Olamentke* (H)
Guinaima [MX] (Hdbk10)
Guinala [MX] *Coahuiltecan* (Hdbk10)
Guinau [Lang] *Maipurean* (O)
Guinau Indians *see* Winao
Guineas (LC)
Guipaolave *see* Shipaulovi
Guipaulavi *see* Shipaulovi
Guipui *see* Santo Domingo
Guiquitamcar *see* Guiguitamcar
Guiriguana *see* Chiriguano

Guisnai *see* Ashluslay
Guisnai *see* Mataco
Guisnay *see* Mataco
Guisoles (BE) *see also* Gueique-
  sales (H)
Guisoles [TX] *Coahuiltecan* (BE)
Guisolotes [MX] *Tamaulipec* (BE)
Guithla'kimas *see* Clackamas
Guithlakimas *see* Clackamas
Guithlameth *see* Cathlamet
Guithlamethl *see* Cathlamet
Guithlasko *see* Wasco
Guithlia-ishalxi *see* Ktlaeshatlkik
Guithlia-kishatchk *see* Upper
  Chinook
Guitoto *see* Witoto
Guitzeis *see* Kichai
Guiyu *see* Ditsakana
Gulgahen *Jicarilla Apache*
  (Hdbk10)
Gu'l ka-i-nda *see* Guhlkainde
Gulkainde *see* Guhlkainde
Gull Lake [MN, ND, SD]
  Chippewa (H)
Gull Lake [MN] *Kitchisibiwinini-
  wug* (H)
Gumbatkni *see* Kumbatuash
gumbotkne *see* gu'mbotkni
gu'mbotkni [OR] *Klamath* (BE)
Gummesacapem *Coahuiltecan*
  (Hdbk10)
Gunachokon *see* Gunachonken
Gunachonken [AK] *Tlingit* (H)
Gunana *see* Athapascan
Gunghet-gitinai *see* Gunghet-
  kegawai
Gunghet-haidagai [BC] *Haida*
  (H)
Gunghet-kegawai [Clan] *Haida*
  (H)
Guniam *see* Itene
Gunlock *Southern Paiute*
  (Hdbk11)
Gununa-kene *see* Pampa
Gununa-kene *see* Northern
  Tehuelche
Gununa-kene *see* Tehuelche
Guocotegodi *Caduveo* (O)
Guoyagui *see* Guayaqui
Gurequena *see* Arekena
Gusiquesal *see* Hueyhueyquetzal
Gus-shil-la *see* Goasila
Gusshilla *see* Goasila
Gutah *see* Ute
Gu'ta'k *see* Kiowa Apache
Gutak *see* Kiowa Apache
Gutgune'st nas'had'a'i *see*
  Gutgunest-nas-hadai
Gutgunets-nas-hadai *Haida* (H)
Guthlameth *see* Cathlamet
Guth-le-uk-qwan *see* Ugalak-
  miut
Gu'tskia'we *see* Cree

Gutskiawe *see* Cree
Guuylliche *see* Huilliche
Guyaki *see* Guayaqui
Guyana *see* Guayana
Guyana *see* Urukuyana
Guyandot *see* Wyandot
Guyandot *see* Conestoga
Guyandot *see* Huron
Guyapi *see* Oyampi
Guyas *see* Guaes
Guylpunes *see* Khulpuni
Guymen *see* Guimen
Gwaitu *see* Utu Utu Gwaiti
Gwaugueh *see* Cayupa
Gwe a'ndas *see* Gweudus
Gweandas *see* Gweudus
Gweudus *Haida* (H)
Gwe-u-gweh-o-no *see* Cayuga
Gweundu *see* Gweudus
Gwhunnughshonee *see* Iroquois
Gwich'in [AK] (NPeos, v.7, no.1,
  pp.22–29)
Gwich'in [Lang] *see*
  Kutchakutchin
Gyagyilakya [Gens] *Kwakiutl* (H)
Gyai-ko *see* Comanche
Gyandotte *see* Huron
Gyarzobi *see* Gyazru
Gyaushk [Gens] *Chippewa* (H)
Gya-zro *see* Gyazru
Gyazro *see* Gyazru
Gyazru [Clan] *Hopi* (H)
Gyazru winwu *see* Guazru
Gyegyote [Gens] *Tlatlasikoala* (H)
Gyekolekoa [Gens] *Kwakiutl* (H)
Gyeksem [Clan] [BC] *Hahuamis*
  (H)
Gyeksem [Clan] [BC] *Kwakiutl*
  (H)
Gyeksem [Clan] *Koskimo* (H)
Gyeksemsanatl [Clan] *Koskimo*
  (H)
Gye'qsem *see* Gyeksem
Gyeqsem *see* Gyeksem
Gyidesdzo *see* Kittizoo
Gyidnada'eks (H) SE Kinuhtoiah
  (H)
Gyidzaxtla'tl *see* Kitsalthlal
Gyidzi's *see* Kitzeesh
Gyigyekemae [Gens] *Kwakiutl*
  (H)
Gyi'gyelk-am *see* Gyigyilkam
Gyigyelkam *see* Gyigyilkam
Gyigyilkam [Clan] [BC] *Kwakiutl*
  (H)
Gyigyilkam [Clan] [VanI] *Ko-
  mogue* (H)
Gyigyilkam [Gens] [BC]
  Hahuamis (H)
Gyigyilkam [Gens] *Goasila* (H)
Gyigyilkam [Gens] *Guauaenok*
  (H)
Gyikshan *see* Kitksan

Gyilaktsaok [BC] *Tsimshian* (H)
Gyilots'a'r *see* Kilutsai
Gyimanoitq *see* Kitlope
Gyisg-a'hast *see* Gyisgahast
Gyisgahast [BC] *Niska* (H)
Gyisgahast [Clan] *Kitzegukla* (H)
Gyiskabenak [BC] *Niska* (H)
Gyispaqla'ots *see* Kishpachlaots
Gyispawaduweda [Clan]
  Tsimshian (H)
Gyispayo'ko *see* Kishpiyeoux
Gyispotuwe'da *see* Gyis-
  pawaduweda
Gyit'ama't *see* Kitamat
Gyitamat *see* Kitamat
Gyit'anma'kys *see* Kitanmaiksh
Gyitanmakys *see* Kitanmaiksh
Gyit'enda *see* Kitunto
Gyitenda *see* Kitunto
Gyitg-a'ata *see* Kitkahta
Gyitgaata *see* Kitkahta
Gyitgyigyenik [Phratry] *Niska* (H)
Gyitingits'ats *see* Gitin-gidjats
Gyit'ingyits'ats *see* Gitin-gidjats
Gyitingyitsats *see* Gitin-gidjats
Gyit'i'ns *see* Gituns
Gyitins *see* Gituns
Gyitkadok [Phratry] [BC] *Niska*
  (H)
Gyitksa'n *see* Kitksan
Gyitkshan *see* Kitksan
Gyitktsaktl [BC] *Kitzilas* (H)
Gyitla'n *see* Kitlani
Gyit'laqda'mike *see* Kitlakdamix
Gyitlaqdamike *see* Kitlakdamix
Gyitlo'p *see* Kitlope
Gyitqa'tla *see* Kitkala
Gyitsaek [Clan] [BC] *Niska* (H)
Gyits'ala'ser *see* Kitzilis
Gyitsalaser *see* Kitzilis
Gyitsigyu'ktla *see* Kitzegukla
Gyits'umra'lon *see* Kitzimgaylum
Gyitsumralon *see* Kitzimgaylum
Gyitwulgya'ts *see* Kitwilgioks
Gyitwulkesba *see* Kitwilksheba
Gyitwulnakeyl [BC] *Niska* (H)
Gyitwung-a *see* Kitwingach
Gyitwuntlko'l *see* Kitwinskole
Gyuungsh [Clan] [NM] *Pecos* (H)
Gyuunsh *see* Guungsh

-H-

Haai'alik-anae *see* Haailakyemae
Haaialikyauae *see* Haailakyemae
Haai'lak-emae *see* Haailakyemae
Haailakyemae [Clan] [BC]
  Matilpe (H)
Haailakyemae [Clan] [VanI] *Ko-
  moye* (H)

ha'aiyilikyawi [Clan] *Kwexa* (Anthro, v.9, no.3, p.158)
Haak'oh *see* Acoma
Haak'ohni *see* Acoma
Haami [Clan] *Keres* (H)
Haami-hano *see* Hami
haanalino *see* ha'anaLi'no
ha'anaLi'no [Clan] *Kwexa* (Anthro, v.9, no.3, p.158)
Haanatlenok [Gens] [VanI] *Komoyue* (H)
Haaninin *see* Atsina
Haaninin *see* Hitoune'nan
Ha'a'ninin [Self-designation] *see* Hitoune'nan
Haatsu [Clan] *Keres* (H)
Haatsu-hano *see* Hatsi
Haauneiri *see* Yamaica
Habachaca [Clan] [FL] *Timucua* (H)
Habacoa [HA] *Guaccaiarima* (BE)
Ha-ba-soo-pi-ya *see* Havasupai
Habasoopiya *see* Havasupai
Ha-ba-soo-py-a *see* Havasupai
Habasoopya *see* Havasupai
Habasto *see* Ahwaste
Habasopi *see* Havasupai
Habbamala *see* Alabama
Habe-napo *see* Khabenapo
Habenapo [CA] *Eastern Pomo* (Pub, v.36, no.6)
Ha-bi-na-pa *see* Khabenapo
Habinapa *see* Khabenapo
Hab-koo-kee-ah *see* Acoma
Habkookeeah *see* Acoma
Habutas *see* Tano
Habuwi [BO] *Araona* (O)
Haca'ath *see* Hachaath
Hacansacke *see* Hackensack
Haccinsack *see* Hackensack
Hachaaht [VanI] *Nootka* (BE)
Hachepiriinu *Arikara* (H)
Hachinghsack *see* Hackensack
Hachkinkeshaky *see* Hackensack
Hachos *see* Apaches del Acho
Hackensack [NJ] *Unami* (LC)
Hackinckesaky *see* Hackensack
Hackinghesaky *see* Hackensack
Hackinghsack *see* Hackensack
Hackinghsackin *see* Hackensack
Hackinghsakij *see* Hackensack
Hackingkesacky *see* Hackensack
Hackingkescaky *see* Hackensack
Hackingsack *see* Hackensack
Hackinkasacky *see* Hackensack
Hackinkesackingh *see* Hackensack
Hackinkesacky *see* Hackensack
Hackinkesaky *see* Hackensack
Hackinsack *see* Hackensack
Hackinsagh *see* Hackensack
Hackquickanon *see* Aquackanonk

Hackquinsack *see* Hackensack
Hacksensack [NJ] *Unami* (LC)
Haclli *see* Haglli
Ha-coom *see* Yacum
Hacoom *see* Yacum
hacpa *see* Pima
hacpa 'amay *see* Papago
Hacquickenunk *see* Aquackanonk
Hacquinsack *see* Hackensack
Hacu *see* Acoma
Hacuqua *see* Acoma
Ha-cu-quin *see* Acoma
Hacuquin *see* Acoma
Hacus *see* Acoma
Hadai *see* Adai
Ha-de-pi-ri-i-nu *see* Hachepiriinu
Hadepiriinu *see* Hachepiriinu
Hadinia'den [Clan] *Seneca* (H)
Hadinion'gwaiiu [Clan] *Seneca* (H)
Hadishwengaiiu *see* Hadi'sh-wen'gaiiu
Hadi'shwen'gaiiu [Clan] *Seneca* (H)
Hadi'twiwi *see* Atsugewi
Hadley Indians [MA] (H)
Hadovesaves *see* Dakota
Hadovessians *see* Dakota
Hadsapoke's Band [NV] *Paviotso* (H)
Hadtuitazhi [Clan] *Omaha* (H)
Haeeltruk *see* Bellabella
Haeeltsuk *see* Bellabella
Haeeltz *see* Bellabella
Haeeltzuk *see* Bellabella
Haeetsuk *see* Bellabella
Haelli *see* Haglli
Haeltzuk *see* Heiltsuk
Hae-mis *see* Jemez
Haemis *see* Jemez
Haesar (Hdbk10) *see also* Saesse (Hdbk10)
Haesar *Coahuiltecan* (BE)
Haghquagenonck *see* Aquackanonk
Hagilana *see* Hagi-lana
Hagi-lana [BC] *Haida* (H)
Haglli *Yuma* (H)
Hagueti *see* Cashibo
Haguna *see* Laguna
Haha *see* Assiniboin
Hahamatse (H) *see also* Walitsum (H)
H'ah'amatse *see* Hahamatse
Hahamatse [Sept] [BC] *Lekwiltok* (H)
Hahatona *see* Chippewa
Hahatonwan *see* Chippewa
Hahatonway *see* Chippewa
Ha-hat-tong *see* Chippewa
Hahattong *see* Chippewa

Ha-ha-tu-a *see* Chippewa
Hahatua *see* Chippewa
Ha-ha-twawn *see* Chippewa
Hahatwawn *see* Chippewa
Ha-ha-vasu-pai *see* Havasupai
Hahavasupai *see* Havasupai
Hahderuka *see* Crow
Hahekolatl [Gens] *Tlatlasikoala* (H)
Hahel-topa-ipa *see* San Carlos Apache
Hahel-topa-ipa *see* Tsiltaden
Hah-hah-ton-wah *see* Chippewa
Hahhahtonwah *see* Chippewa
Hah-koo-kee-ah *see* Acoma
Hahkookeeah *see* Acoma
Hahtz-nai koon *see* Atsina
H'ah'uamis *see* Hahuamis
Hahuamis [BC] *Kwakiutl* (BE)
Hahuamis [Lang] *Wakashan* (H)
Ha-hwad-ja *see* Pinalino Apache
Ha-hwadsha *see* Pinalino Apache
Hahwadsha *see* Pinalino Apache
Ha'i'aha *see* Chiricahua Apache
Ha'i'aha *see* Mescalero Apache
Haiaha *see* Chiricahua Apache
Haiaha *see* Mescalero Apache
Hai-ai-nima *see* Sanpoil
Hai-ai'nima *see* Sanpoil
Haiainima *see* Sanpoil
Hai-ankutchin *see* Hankutchin
Haiankutchin *see* Hankutchin
Hai'bata *see* Santa Clara [NM]
Haibata *see* Santa Clara [NM]
Haiba'yu *see* Santa Clara [NM]
Hai-da *see* Haida
Haida [BC, AK] *Skittagetan* (LC)
Haida [Lang] *Skedans* (Anthro, v.9, no.3, p.157)
Haidah *see* Chimmesyan
Haidah *see* Haida
Haidahs *see* Kaigami
Haideroka *see* Crow
Haiish *see* Eyeish
Hailtsa *see* Heiltsuk
Hailtsuk *see* Heiltsuk
Hailtzuk *see* Bellabella
Ha-ilt-zukh *see* Bellabella
Hailtzukh *see* Bellabella
Hai'luntchi *see* Cayuse
Hailuntchi *see* Cayuse
Ha-im *see* Haim
Haim [BC] *Salish* (H)
Haimaaksto [Tsentsenkaio] (H)
Hai-maaxsto *see* Haimaaksto
Haimaaxsto *see* Haimaaksto
Hain *see* Cayuse
Hainai (W) *see also* Ione (CA)
Hainai [TX] *Caddo* (BE)
Hai-ne-na-une *see* Tanima
Hainenaune *see* Tanima
haipaai *see* Santa Clara [NM]
Haiphaha *see* Santa Clara [NM]

Hair Shirts *see* Isisokasimiks
Hairy-Men's band *see*
   Hevhaita'nio
Hais *see* Eyeish
Haisai (BE)
Haiseas *see* Yscani
Ha-ish *see* Eyeish
Haish *see* Eyeish
Hai-shi-la *see* Kitamet
Haishila *see* Kitamat
Haishilla *see* Kitamat
Haisla [Can] *Bellabella* (LC)
Haisla [Lang] [Can] *Kwakiutl*
   (LC)
haisndayin [Self-designation] *see*
   Jicarilla Apache
Haita *Western Shoshone* (Hdbk11)
Haitch Point *see* Hatch Point
Haitlin *see* Tait
Haiwal [Clan] *Tonkawa* (H)
Ha ka *see* Kiowa Apache
Haka (PC) *see also* Kiowa Apache
   (LC)
Haka [Clan] *Acoma* (H)
Haka-hanoq *see* Hakan
Hakahanoq *see* Hakan
Haka-hanoqch *see* Hakan
Hakahanoqch *see* Hakan
Hakan [Clan] *Keres* (H)
Hakan-hano *see* Hakan
Ha-kan-ni *see* Hakan
Hakanyi [Clan] *Keres* (H)
Hakanyi-hano *see* Hakanyi
Hakanyi-hanuch *see* Hakanyi
Hakataya Culture [AZ] (Hdbk10)
Hakawhatapa *see* Haka-whatapa
Haka-whatapa [AZ] *Tolkepaya*
   (BE)
Hakayopa [AZ] *Wikedjasapa* (BE)
Hakehelapa [AZ] *Western Yavapai*
   (Pub, v.29, no.4)
Hakehelapa Wiltaikapaya [AZ]
   Tolkepaya (BE)
Hakesian *see* Haqui
Hakia tce-pai [AZ] *Walapai* (BE)
Hak-koo-kee-ah *see* Acoma
Hakkookeeah *see* Acoma
Hakoopin *see* Agua Caliente
Hakouchirmiou (H)
Ha-ku *see* Acoma
Haku *see* Acoma
haku-ka *see* Acoma
Hakukia *see* Acoma
Ha-ku Kue *see* Acoma
Hakukue *see* Acoma
Hakupakapa (BE) *see also* Tolke-
   paya (BE)
Hakupakapa [AZ] (BE)
Hakwiche *see* Cahuilla
Hakwiche *see* Kawia [Luiseño]
Halakwulup *see* Alacaluf
Hal-alt *see* Hellelt
Halalt *see* Hellelt

Halaut (H) *see also* Neskainlith (H)
Halaut (Hdbk12) *see also* Neskon-
   lith Band (Hdbk12)
Hala'ut *see* Neskonlith Band
Halaut [BC] *Shuswap* (H)
Halbama *see* Alabama
Halchadhoma *see* Halchidoma
Halchedoma *see* Halchidhoma
Halchedunes *see* Halchidhoma
Halchidhoma (CA) *see also*
   Chemehuevi (LC)
Halchidhoma [CA, AZ] (CA)
Halchidhoma [Lang] *Yuman* (CA)
Half breech cloth people *see*
   Chegnakeokisela
Half breech clout people *see*
   Chegnakeokisela
Half-breed Band [SD] *Cheyenne*
   (BE)
Half-breeds *see* Mixed Bloods
Half-Cheyenne band *see* Sutaio
Half Crees *see* Cahi'a iye'skabin
Halhaiktenok [Clan] *Bellabella*
   (H)
Halisanes *see* Ietan
Halitanes *see* Ietan
Haliti *see* Paressi
Halkome'lem *see* Stalo
Halkome'lem *see* Cowichan
Halkomelem *see* Stalo
Hallapoota *see* Olulato
Halliquamalla *see* Halyikwamai
Halliquamaya *see* Quigyuma
Halona (Hdbk9)
Halona (Hdbk9) *see also* Zuni
   (LC)
Ha-lo-nah *see* Zuni
Halonah *see* Zuni
halona-wa *see* Zuni
Halotesu [Br] *Southern Nam-
   bicuara* (O)
Halpadalgi [Clan] *Creek* (H)
Haltalt *see* Hellelt
Halthwypum *see* Klickitat
Haltso *see* Khaltso
Haltsodine *see* Khaltso
Ha-lum-mi *see* Lummi
Halummi *see* Lummi
Ha'lx'aix'tenox *see* Halhaiktenok
Halxaixtenox *see* Halhaiktenok
Halyikwamai [AZ] (BE)
Halyikwamai [Lang] *Delta Yuman*
   (Hdbk10)
Hamacore *see* Iquito
Ha-ma-kaba-mitc kwa-dig *see*
   Apache
Ha-ma-kaba-mitckwa-dig *see*
   Apache
Hamakabamitckwadig *see*
   Apache
Hamakha-v *see* Mohave
Hamakhava [Self-designation] *see*
   Mohave

Hamakhave *see* Mohave
Hamak-have *see* Mohave
Hamalakyauae (H) *see also* Gyigy-
   ilkam (H)
Hamalakyauae [Clan] *Nimkish* (H)
Hamano [Gens] *Quatsino* (H)
Hamapu [BO] *Araona* (O)
Hamaruamomowi *Guahibo* (O)
Hamawi (BE) *see also* Hammawi
   (CA)
Hama'wi *see* Humawhi
Hamawi (PC) *see also* Humawhi
   (H)
Hamawi [CA] *Achomawi* (BE)
Hamburg Indians *see* Kammatwa
Hamechuwa [CA] *Comeya* (H)
Ha-mef-kut-tel-li *see* Atuami
Hamefkuttelli *see* Atuami
Hamefuitellies *see* Atuami
Ha'meyisath *see* Hameyisath
Hameyisath [Sept] [Can] *Nootka*
   (H)
Ha-mi *see* Hami
Hami [Clan] [NM] *Pueblo Indi-
   ans* (H)
Hami-hano *see* Hami
Hamilton Creek [Can] *Salish* (H)
Haminal *see* Gitanemuk
Hamine-chan *see* Khemnichan
Hammawi (CA-8) *see also*
   Hamawi (BE)
Hammawi (CA-8) *see also* Hu-
   mawhi (H)
Hammawi [CA] *Achomawi* (Pub,
   v.23, no.5)
Hammawi [Lang] *Achomawi* (CA-
   8)
Ham-met-wel-le *see* Hometwoli
Hammetwelle *see* Hometwoli
Hammonasset [CT] *Wappinger*
   (LC)
Hamockhaves *see* Mohave
Hamokaba *see* Mohave
Hamokavi *see* Mohave
Ham-oke-avi *see* Mohave
Hamoke-avi *see* Mohave
Hamokeavi *see* Mohave
Hamokhave *see* Mohave
Hamtolops *see* Humptulips
Hamtsit [BC] *Bella Coola* (H)
Hamtsit [Clan] *Taliomh* (H)
Hamukahava *see* Mohave
Han [AK] (BE)
Han [Clan] *Kansa* (H)
Han [Lang] *Athapascan* (BE)
Han [TX] (H)
Hana [Clan] *Menominee* (H)
Hanag *see* Henaggi
Hanaga *see* Henya
Ha'nahawunena *see*
   Hanakawunena
Hanahawunena [WY] *Arapaho*
   (BE)

Hanakwiche *see* Serrano
Hanakwiche *see* Jenequich
Hanalelti *see* Ha'nale'lti
Ha'nale'lti [CA] *Washo* (BE)
Hanamana [Cu] (BE)
Haname *see* Cotonam
Hananaxawuune *see* Hana-
hawunena
Hananaxawuune'nan *see* Ara-
paho
Hanctons *see* Yankton
Hand Cutters *see* Dakota
Handsome Men *see* Quapaw
Hane *see* Jano
Hanega *see* Henya
Hanera *see* Barosana
Haneragmiut [Can] *Central Eski-
mos* (BE)
Hanetones *see* Yankton
Hanga [Subgens] *Omaha* (H)
Hangacenu *see* Hangashenu
Hanga jinga *see* Ibache
Hangajinga *see* Ibache
Hanga-qti *see* Dtesanhadtadhis-
han
Hangaqti *see* Dtesanhadtadhis-
han
Hangashenu *Omaha* (H)
Hanga tanga *see* Hangatanga
Hangatanga [Gens] *Kansa* (H)
Hanga utanandji *see* Hangatanga
Hangautanandji *see* Hangatanga
Hanging Ears *see* Kalispel
Hanginihkashina *Tsishu* (H)
Hangka [Clan] *Quapaw* (H)
Hangka *Osage* (H)
Hangkaahutun *Hangka* (H)
Hangkaenikashika [Gens] *Qua-
paw* (H)
Hangkautadhantsi *Hangka* (H)
Hangnikashinga [Subgens] *Han*
(H)
Hanichina *see* Isleta
Hanieas *see* Henya
Haningayormiut [Can] *Central
Eskimos* (BE)
Haninikashina *Haninihkashina*
(H)
Hanis [OR] (BE)
Hankpape *see* Hunkpapa
Han-kutchi *see* Hankutchin
Hankutchi *see* Hankutchin
Han kutchin *see* Hankutchin
Hankutchin [AK] *Kutchin* (H)
Han-kut'qin *see* Loucheux
Hankutqin *see* Loucheux
Han-kuttchin *see* Hankutchin
Hankuttchin *see* Hankutchin
Hannakalal *see* Hannakallal
Hannakallah *see* Hannakallal
Han-na-kal-lal *see* Hannakallal
Hannakallal [PacN] *Athapascan*
(H)

Hannanaxawune'nan *see* Hana-
hawunena
Hannesuk [CA] *Northern Valley
Yokuts* (BE)
Hannetons *see* Yankton
Hannikashinga [Subgens] *Han*
(H)
Hanningayurmuit [AK] *Eskimos*
(Hdbk5)
Hano (H) *see also* Jano (BE)
Hano *see* Tewa [after 1936]
Hano *Northern Tewa* (BE)
Hanoki *see* Hano
Hanom *see* Hano
Ha-no-me *see* Hano
Hanome *see* Hano
Hanomuh *see* Hano
Hano Oshatch *see* Oshach
Han-te-wa *see* Hantiwi
Hantiwi [CA] *Achomawi* (BE)
Hantiwi [CA] *Shasta* (H)
Hanyuveche *see* Serrano
Hapai [Clan] *Laguna* (H)
Hapai-hano *see* Hapanyi
Hapai-hanock *see* Hapanyi
hapanahkih *see* Delaware
hapanahkiyah *see* Delaware
Hapan-hano *see* Hapanyi
Ha-pan-ni *see* Hapanyi
Hapanni *see* Hapanyi
Hapanyi [Clan] *Keres* (H)
Hapanyi-hano *see* Hapanyi
Hapanyi-hanoq *see* Hapanyi
Hapanyi-hanuch *see* Hapanyi
hapasma *see* Papago
ha-pas-ma *see* Papago
Hapeka *see* Hopi
Ha-pe-ka *see* Hopi
Ha'pudtukede *see* Sawawaktodo
tuviwari
Hapes [TX, MX] *Coahuiltecan*
(LC)
Hapitu *see* Hopi
Hapsa-rokay *see* Crow
Hapsaroke *see* Crow
Hapudtukede *see* Sawawaktodo
tuviwari
Haqihana [WY] *Arapaho* (BE)
Haqua'mis *see* Hahuamis
Haquequenunck *see* Aquack-
anonk
Haqui [TX] (H)
Haquicqueenock *see* Aquack-
anonk
Hara'c hit tan *see* Kayashkidetan
Harahey *see* Pawnee
Harakmbet [Lang] [PE] (O)
Harame *see* Xarame
Harames [MX] *Coahuiltecan* (BE)
Har-dil-zhay *see* Yavapai
Har-dil-zhay *see* Mohave
Har-dil-zhay *see* Tonto Apache
Har-dil-zhay *see* Tulkepaia

Hardilzhay *see* Mohave
Hardilzhay *see* Tonto Apache
Hardilzhay *see* Tulkepaia
Hardilzhay *see* Yavapai
Hardwoods *see* Sugwaundugah-
wininewug
Hare *see* Eskimos
Harefoot Indians *see* Kawchot-
tine
Hare Indians *see* Peau de Lievre
Hare Indians *see* Kawchottine
Hareskins *see* Kawchottine
Harno *see* Hano
Haro *see* Hano
Harones *see* Huron
Harrison Mouth *see* Scowlits
Harrison River [BC] *Cowichan*
(H)
Hartley Bay *see* Kitqata
Hartley Bay *see* Kitkahta
Harvaktormiut *see* Harvaqtuur-
miut
Harvaqtormiut (Hdbk5) *see also*
Harvaqtuurmiut (Hdbk5)
Harvaqtormiut [Can] *Central Es-
kimos* (BE)
Harvaqtuurmiut [Lang] *Caribou
Eskimos* (Hdbk5)
Harwaneki *see* Southern
Tehuelche
Hashi *see* Cora
Hasinai (W) *see also* Ione (CA)
Hasinai [Self-designation] (H) *see
also* Caddo (LC)
Hasinai [TX] (LC)
Hasinai Confederacy (BE)
Hasinai Confederation *see* Hasi-
nai Confederacy
Hasinninga *see* Hassinunga
Haskanhatso *see* Khaskankhatso
Haskanhatsodine *see*
Khaskankhatso
haskwáhkihah *see* Fox
Hasli'zdine *see* Khashhlizhni
Hasli'zni *see* Khashhlizhni
Hasotino [ID] *Nez Perce* (BE)
Hassinienga *see* Hassinunga
Hassinuga *see* Hassinunga
Hassinunga [Lang] [VA] *Eastern
Siouan* (H)
Hassinunga [VA] *Manahoac* (BE)
Hass-lin-tung *see* Hupa
Hasslintung *see* Hupa
Hassnungaes *see* Hassinunga
Hastriryini *see* Taensa
Hatakfushi [Clan] *Chickasaw* (H)
Hatarask *see* Hatteras
Hatawa [CA] *Comeya* (H)
Hatca'ath *see* Hachaath
Hatchita *see* Hitchiti
Hatch Point [VanI] *Salish* (H)
Hatchswamp *see* Hatsawap
Hat Creek Indians *see* Atsugewi

Hat Creek Indians *see* Atsuge
Hate *see* Harakbet
Ha'tene *see* Coos
Hatene *see* Coos
Hathawekela (H) *see also* Assi-
    wikale (H)
Hathawekela [TN] *Absentee
    Shawnee* (BE)
Ha-tha-we-ke-lah *see*
    Hathawekela
Hathawekelah *see* Hathawekela
Ha-tha-we-ki-lah *see*
    Hathawekela
Hathawekilah *see* Hathawekela
Hati'hshi-ru'nu *see* Winnebago
Hatihshirunu *see* Winnebago
Hatilshe *see* Mohave
Hatilshe *see* Tulkepaia
Hatilshe *see* Yuma
Hatindia'ointen *see* Wyandot
Hatinieyerunu *see* Mohawk
Hatiron'taks *see* Adirondack
Hatishe' *see* Yuma
Hatiwanta-runh *see* Neutral Na-
    tion
Hatorask *see* Hateras
hat-pa *see* Pima
Hatpa *see* Pima
Hatsawap *Choptank* (Hdbk15)
Hatsi [Clan] [NM] *Laguna* (H)
Hatsi [Clan] [NM] *San Felipe* (H)
Hatsi-hano *see* Hatsi
hat-spa *see* Pima
hatspa *see* Pima
hats-pas *see* Pima
Hatswampt *see* Hatsawap
Hattack-falaih-hosh *see* Ok-
    lafalaya
Hattahappa *see* Attacapa
Hattakappa *see* Attacapa
Hattchenae *see* Unakhotana
Hatteras (LC) *see also* Lumbee
    (LC)
Hatteras [Lang] *Algonquian* (BE)
Hatteras [NC] (BE)
Ha'tunne *see* Coos
Hatunne *see* Coos
Hatweme [ID] *Nez Perce* (BE)
Hauaniker-Tsonik *see* Southern
    Tehuelche
Hauenayo [Clan] *Timucua* (H)
Haughgoghnuchshionee *see* Iro-
    quois
Hauheqtormiut [Can] *Central Es-
    kimos* (BE)
Hauico *see* Hawikuh
Haukoma [CA] *Pomo* (H)
Hauneqtormiut *see* Hauniqtuur-
    miut
Hauniqtuurmiut [AL] *Caribou
    Eskimos* (Hdbk5)
Hauscari *see* Cedar
Haush [Arg] (O)

Hautcu'k-tles'ath *see* Uchucklesit
Hautlatin *see* Huntlatin
Hauts-Tchinouks *see* Upper
    Chinook
Havana [Cu] (BE)
Havasopi *see* Havasupai
Havasua Pai *see* Havasupai
Ha-va-su-pai *see* Havasupai
Havasupai [AZ] (LC)
Havasupai [Lang] *Upland Yuman*
    (Hdbk10)
Hava-su-pay *see* Havasupai
Havasu-pay *see* Havasupai
Havasupay *see* Havasupai
Haveniken *see* Tehuelche
Haverstraw [NY] *Unami* (BE)
Haverstroo *see* Haverstraw
Havesu-pai *see* Havasupai
Havico *see* Hawikuh
Havilah *see* Wiwayuk
Havisua Pai *see* Havasupai
Hawalapai *see* Hualapai
Hawaneki *see* Southern Tehuelche
Ha-waw-wah-lah-too-waw *see*
    Jemez
Hawawwahlahtoowaw *see* Jemez
Hawesidoc *see* Ha-we-si-doc
Ha-we-si-doc [CA] *Achomawi*
    (BE)
Hawiche *see* Cahuilla
hawikku *see* Hawikuh
Hawikuh *Zuni* (Hdbk9)
Hawitche *see* Hewchi
Hawmanao [Gens] *Kwakiutll* (H)
Haw-on-chee *see* Hewchi
Haw-quo-e-hov-took *see* Chasta
Hawquoehovtook *see* Chasta
Haxaancine'nan [OK] *Arapaho*
    (BE)
Haxua'mis *see* Hahuamis
Haya-a *see* Chiricahua Apache
Ha-yah *see* Hayah
Hayah [Clan] [NM] *Pecos* (H)
Hayaha *see* Chiricahua Apache
Haychis *see* Eyeish
Hayfork [CA] *Wintu* (CA)
Hayfork [Lang] [CA] *Wintu* (CA-
    8)
Haynaggi *see* Henaggi
Hay-narg-ger *see* Henaggi
Haynargger *see* Henaggi
Haynargie *see* Henaggi
Hayno (LC)
Haynokes *see* Eno [NC]
Hazaname *see* Aranama
Hazoa [HA] *Caizcimu* (BE)
Hazue [HA] *Cahibo* (BE)
H'doum-dei-kih *see* Kadohada-
    cho
Heabenoma *see* Hoabonoma
Head of the Lake Band (BE)
Head of the Lake Band *see*
    Komaplix

Headwater People *see* Ihuruhana
Heard Swamp *see* Hatsawap
Hebahamo *see* Ebahamo
Hebohamo *see* Ebahamo
Hebonuma *see* Hoabonoma
Hechoaladi *see* Echoaladi
He'ckwiath *see* Hesquiat
Heckwiath *see* Hesquiat
Heda-haidagi [Clan] *Haida* (H)
Hedatse *see* Hidatsa
Hegue *see* Eudeve
He-ha-me-tawe *see* Hehametawe
Hehametawe [Subgens] *Kwakiutl*
    (H)
Hehighenimmo *see* Sanpoil
He-hih-e-nim-mo *see* Sanpoil
Hehl [AK] *Tlingit* (BE)
Hehlkoan [AK] *Tlingit* (H)
Hehonqueronon *see* Kich-
    esipirini
Hehue *see* Eudeve
Heiche *see* Eyeish
He'iltsuk *see* Heiltsuk
Heiltsuk (LC) *see also* Bellbella
    (LC)
Heiltsuk [Lang] [Can] *Kwakiutl*
    (LC)
Heiltsuk [Lang] [Can] *Wakashan*
    (BE)
He'iltsuq *see* Heltsuk
Heiltsuq *see* Heiltsuk
Hekhalanois [Gens] *Koskimo* (H)
Hekinxtana *see* Ikogmiut
Hekpa [Clan] *Hopi* (H)
Hekwach *see* Agua Caliente
Hel-alt *see* Hellelt
Helalt *see* Hellelt
Helikilika [Gens] *Kwakiutl* (H)
Hel-lalt *see* Hellelt
Hellalt *see* Hellelt
Hellelt [VanI] *Salish* (H)
Hellet [Can] *Cowichan* (BE)
Hellwits *see* Tlakluit
Hellwits *see* Wishram
Helowna *see* Okanagan Lake
Helto *see* Hel-to
Hel-to [CA] *Maidu* (Contri, v.3,
    p.282)
Helwit *see* Tlakluit
Helwit *see* Wishram
He-mai *see* Jemez
Hemai *see* Jemez
Hemeos *see* Jemez
Hemes *see* Jemez
Hemeshitse *see* Jemez
He-me-shu-tsa *see* Jemez
Hemeshutsa *see* Jemez
Hemez *see* Jemez
He-mi *see* Jemez
Hemi *see* Jemez
He-mi-ma *see* Jemez
Hemima *see* Jemez
He-mini-canj *see* Khemnichan

Heminicanj *see* Khemnichan
Hemishitz *see* Jemez
he-misi *see* Jemez
hemisi *see* Jemez
he-misi-ce *see* Jemez
he-misice *see* Jemez
hemisice *see* Jemez
Hemnica *see* Khemnichan
Hemnicanj *see* Khemnichan
He-mni-conj *see* Khemnichan
Hemp Gatherers *see* Skaru'ren
He-nag-gi *see* Henaggi
Henaggi [CA] *Tolowa* (H)
He-nakyalaso *see* Henakyalaso
Henakyalaso [Gens] *Kwakiutl* (H)
Henarhonon *see* Arendahronon
Henex *see* Jemez
Henicohio *Tigua* (H)
Heniocane [TX] *Coahuiltecan*
  (BE)
Henja-kon *see* Henya
henna *see* Northern Paiute
Henneega [Can] [*Sitka-kwan*]
  (Contri, v.1, p.38)
Hennega *see* Henya
Henne-ga-kon *see* Henya
Hennegakon *see* Henya
Henne'sh *see* Choctaw
Hen-ta-pah-tu *see* Hunkpatina
Hentapahtu *see* Hunkpatina
Hen-tee-pah-tee *see* Hunkpatina
Henteepahtee *see* Hunkpatina
Henuti [Clan] [NM] *Sia* (H)
Henya [AK] *Tlingit* (BE)
Henya qoan *see* Henya
Hepowwoo [CA] *Comeya* (H)
Hequi *see* Eudeve
Herechene *see* Horicon
Herechenes *see* Horicon
Hereckene *see* Horicon
Heri *see* Seri
Heries *see* Erie
Hernes *see* Jemez
Hesley *see* Makhelchel
Hesquiaht *see* Hesquiat
Hesquiat [Can] *Nootka* (BE)
Hessler *see* Makhelchel
He-stands-both-sides *see* Anogi-
  najin
Hesweiwewipu [ID] *Nez Perce*
  (BE)
Heta [Br] (LC)
Heth-to-ya (H) *see also* Hittoya
  (H)
Hethtoya *see* Heth-to-ya
Hethtoya *see* Hittoya
Heth-to-ya [CA] *Miwok* (Contri,
  v.3, p.349)
Heuchi *see* Hewchi
Hev'a tan i u *see* Hevhaita'nio
Hevataniu *see* Hevhaita'nio
Heve *see* Eudeve

Hevhaitan *see* Hevhaita'nio
Hev-hai-ta-ni-o *see* Hevhaita'nio
Hevhaitanio *see* Hevhaita'nio
Hevhaita'nio [SD] *Cheyenne* (BE)
Hevi-qsin *see* Heviqs-ni'pahis
Heviqsin *see* Heviqs-ni'pahis
Heviqs-ni'kpahis *see* Heviqs-
  ni'pahis
Heviqs'ni'pa *see* Heviqs-ni'pahis
Heviqsnipahis *see* Heviqs-
  ni'pahis
Heviqs-ni'pahis [SD] *Cheyenne*
  (BE)
He-wa *see* Jemez
Hewa *see* Jemez
He-wa-kto-kta *see* Hidatsa
Hewaktokta *see* Hidatsa
Hewaktokto *see* Hidatsa
He-war-tuk-tay *see* Hidatsa
Hewartuktay *see* Hidatsa
Hewa-ta-niuw *see* Hevhaita'nio
Hewchi [CA] *Northern Valley
  Yokuts* (CA-8)
Hewi *see* Huwi
Hewis'dawi *see* Hewisedawi
Hewisedawi [CA] *Achomawi*
  (Pub, v.23, no.5)
Hewisedawi [Lang] *Achomawi*
  (CA-8)
Heya *see* Chiricahua Apache
Heyata-otonjwe *see* Kheyatao-
  tonwe
Heyata tonwan *see* Kheyatao-
  tonwe
Heyata wicasa *see* Khey-
  atawichasha
Heye *see* Geyer
Heyquetzal *see* Hueyheuyquetzal
H'hana *see* Khana
Hi-a *see* Hia
Hia (Hdbk10) *see also* Guarihio
  (Hdbk10)
Hia *Arikara* (H)
Hiabu [TX] *Coahuiltecan* (BE)
Hiac'ed O'odham adia [Lang] *Pa-
  pago* (Hdbk10)
hiaki *see* Yaqui
hiakim *see* Yaqui
Hianacoto *see* Carijona
Hianacoto-Umaua *see* Carijona
Hianagouy [TX] (H)
Hiantatsi [TX] (H)
Hiaque *see* Yaqui
Hiaqui *see* Yaqui
Hi-ar *see* Chiricahua Apache
Hiar *see* Chiricahua Apache
Hiazus *see* Yazoo
Hibaro *see* Jivaro
Hicaque *see* Jicaque
Hichakhshepara [Gens] *Win-
  nebago* (H)
Hichapulvapa [AZ] *Wikedjasapa*
  (BE)

Hicheta *see* Hitchiti
Hich'hu *see* Hupa
Hichucio [MX] *Tehueco* (H)
Hickory *see* Jicarilla Apache
Hickory Indians [PA, DE] (H)
Hictoba *Dakota* (H)
Hidatsa [Can, ND] (LC)
Hidatsa [Lang] *Siouan* (H)
Hidatsa after 1920 *see* Gros Ven-
  tre
Hidatza *see* Hidatsa
Hide Strap Clan *see* Piqosha
Hidhatsa *see* Hidatsa
Hiem-ai *see* Jemez
Hiemide *see* Jemez
hiemma *see* Jemez
Hierbipiam *see* Ervipiame
Hierbipiames *see* Ervipiame
Hieroquodame *see* Terocodame
Hietan *see* Comanche
Hietanes *see* Ietan
Hietans *see* Ietan
Higaali *see* Jicarilla Apache
Higabu *see* Kickapoo
Higgahaldahu *see* Tillamook
Higgahaldshu *see* Tillamook
High Bar [BC] *Shuswap* (H)
High Bar Band [BC] *Fraser River
  Shuswap* (Hdbk12)
High-House People *see* Kinaani
Highland [Lang] *Pima* (Hdbk10)
Highland Brule *see* Khey-
  atawichasha
Highlander *see* Chipewyan
Highlanders *see* Nochpeem
Highland Eskimos *see* Polar Es-
  kimos
Highland Indians (H) *see also*
  Nochpeem (BE)
Highland Indians *Delaware*
  (Hdbk15)
Highland Mayan *see* Quichoid
Highland Munsee [Lang]
  (Hdbk15)
Highland Piman [Lang] (Hdbk15)
Highland Sicangu *see* Khey-
  atawichasha
High-minded people *see* Siksika
High Village *see* Meteahke
Higos [TX] (H)
Higuey [HA] *Caizcimu* (BE)
Hi-ha kanhanhan win *see* Hi-
  hakanhanhanwin
Hihakanhanhanwin *Brule* (H)
hihakim *see* Yaqui
Hihame (Hdbk10) *see also* Sijame
  (BE)
Hihames [MX] *Coahuiltecan* (BE)
Hihaneton *see* Yankton
Hihighenimmo *see* Sanpoil
Hi-high-e-nim-mo *see* Sanpoil
Hihighenimo *see* Sanpoil
Hihinkiava *see* Kawaiisu

Hiits Hanyi *see* Itrahani
Hijames *see* Hihames
Hijames *see* Sijame
Hikanagi *see* Mahican
Hika-pu *see* Kickapoo
Hikapu *see* Kickapoo
Hilabia *Creek* (Ye)
Hilchittee *see* Hitchiti
Hilend's Gila Indians *see* Coyotero Apache
Hiletsuck *see* Bellabella
Hiletsuck *see* Heiltsuk
Hiletsuk *see* Bellabella
Hiletsuk *see* Heiltsuk
Hilibi [AL] (BE)
Hilini *see* Illinois
Hiliniki *see* Illinois
Hilleamuck *see* Tillamook
Hillini-Lle'ni *see* Cree
Hill Maidu *Northwestern Maidu* (Pub, v.29. no.4)
Hill Nomlaki [Lang] [CA] (CA-8)
Hill Patwin [CA] (CA-8)
Hill Patwin [Lang] *Wintuan* (CA-8)
Hiluys [BC] (H)
Himatanohis [Society] *Cheyenne* (H)
Himeri [MX] *Pima* (BE)
Himoiyoqis *see* Hi'moiyoqis
Hi'moiyoqis [Society] *Cheyenne* (H)
Hinana'e'inan *see* Arapaho
Hinanae'inana *see* Arapaho
Hinanashiu [Gens] *Menominee* (H)
Hinana'shiuv [Clan] *Menominee* (H)
Hinasso *see* Wichita
Hine [MX] *Xixime* (BE)
Hingutdesu [Br] *Southern Nambicuara* (O)
Hinhan-cun-wapa *see* Hinhanshunwapa
Hinhanshunwapa *Brule* (H)
Hini *see* Hainai
Hinienima *see* Kawaiisu
Hiniima *see* Kawaiisu
Hinimiut [AK] *Netsilik* (Hdbk5)
Hinkaneton *see* Yankton
Hinsepu [ID] *Nez Perce* (BE)
hiokuo'k *see* Pecos
Hiorna *see* Yorica
Hios [MX] *Nevome* (H)
Hipa [Clan] *Mohave* (H)
Hirequodame *see* Terocodame
Hirocoi *see* Iroquois
Hiroon *see* Huron
Hiroquais *see* Iroquois
Hiroquois *see* Iroquois
Hisada [Gens] *Ponca* (H)
hisatok *see* Washo

Hiscas *see* Yscani
Hishkaryana *see* Hixkaryana
Hishquayaht *see* Hesquiat
Hisiometanio *see* Hisiometa'nio
Hisiometa'nio [SD] *Cheyenne* (BE)
Hiskaryana *see* Hixkaruyana
Hisotoko [CA] (H)
His-scarlet-people *see* Kapozha
Hissi o me tan i u *see* Hisiometa'nio
Hissiometaniu *see* Hisiometa'nio
Histapenumanke (H) *see also* Estapa (H)
Hista pe nu-man-ke *see* Histapenumanke
Histapenumanke *Mandan* (H)
Histoppa *see* Histapenumanke
His-tu-i'ta'ni-o *see* Atsina
Histuitanio *see* Atsina
Hitaniwo'iv *see* Arapaho
Hi-tan-ne-wo-i-e *see* Arapaho
Hitannewoie *see* Arapaho
Hitanwo'iv *see* Arapaho
Hitasi'na *see* Cheyenne
Hi-tca-qce-pa-ra *see* Hichakhshepara
Hitcaqcepara *see* ichakhshepara
Hitchatee *see* Hitchiti
Hitchetaw *see* Hitchiti
Hit-che-tee *see* Hitchiti
Hitchetee *see* Hitchiti
Hitchi *see* Kichai
Hitchies *see* Hitchiti
Hitchies *see* Kichai
Hitchiti [GA] (BE)
Hitchittee *see* Hitchiti
Hitch-ity *see* Hitchiti
Hitchity *see* Hitchiti
Hitnu *see* Guahibo
Hitote *see* Witoto
Hitoune'nan [Self-designation] *Arapaho* (Pub, v.12, no.3, p.74)
Hittoya [CA] *Miwok* (H)
Hitunena *see* Atsina
Hitu'nena *see* Atsina
Hitunenina *see* Atsina
hiuqua *see* Pecos
Hive *see* Oivimana
Hivi [Self-designation] *see* Guahibo
H'iwana *see* Apache
Hi'wana *see* Apache
Hiwana *see* Apache
Hiwi [Self-designation] *see* Chiricoa
Hiwi [Self-designation] *see* Guahibo
Hixkaryana [Br] *Parukoto* (LC)
Hiyaraba [Clan] *Timucua* (H)
Hizantinton *see* Santee
Hizo [MX] *Varohio* (H)
Hlahloalgi [Clan] *Creek* (H)

Hlgagilda-kegawai [Sub-family] *Haida* (H)
Hlgahet-gitinai [Clan] *Haida* (H)
Hlgahet-kegawai [Sub-clan] *Haida* (H)
Hlgaiu-lana [Clan] [BC] *Haida* (H)
Hlielung-keawai [Sub-clan] [BC] *Haida* (H)
Hlielungkun-lnagai [Sub-clan] *Haida* (H)
Hlielung-stustae [Sub-clan] [BC] *Haida* (H)
H'lilush *see* Tutuni
Hlilush *see* Tututni
Hlimul-naas-hadai *see* Hlimulnaas-hadai
Hlimulnaas-hadai [Sub-clan] *Haida* (H)
Hlingwainaes-hadai [Sub-family] *Haida* (H)
Hlkaonedis [Sub-clan] [AK] *Haida* (H)
Hlkoayedi [Clan] [AK] *Tlingit* (H)
Hlukahadi [Clan] [AK] [Chilkat] (H)
Hmi'sis *see* Omisis
Hoabonoma [AZ] (H)
Hoahonomo *see* Hoabonoma
Ho'aiath *see* Oiaht
Hoaiath *see* Oiaht
Hoak *Maidu* (Contri, v.3, p.282)
Ho-al-kut-whuh *see* Whilkut
Hoancut *see* Honkut
Hoan-kut *see* Honkut
Hoba *see* Jova
Hobaks *see* Ho'baks
Ho'baks [WA] *Swinomish* (BE)
Hobatinequasi [Clan] *Timucua* (H)
Hobonoma *see* Hoabonoma
Hoc-bo-a *see* Hosboa
Hoc-bo-a wun-wu *see* Hosboa
Hoccanum [CT] (H)
Hochangara *see* Winnebago
Hochelaga (BE)
Ho-chon-chab-ba *see* Hochonchabba
Hochonchabba [Clan] *Chickasaw* (H)
Hochonchapa *see* Hochonchabba
Hochungohrah *see* Winnebago
Hočipwe-ki *see* Oibwa
Hockanoanco *see* Hoccanum
Hockquackanonk *see* Aquackanonk
Hockquackonong *see* Aquackanonk
Hockquecanung *see* Aquackanonk
Hockquekanung *see* Aquackanonk

Hockquickanon *see* Aquackanonk
Hocktem *see* Hoitda
Hoctata *see* Oto
Ho-dash *see* Khotachi
Hodash *see* Khotachi
Ho-de-no-sau-nee *see* Iroquois
Hodenosaunee *see* Iroquois
Ho-de-san-no-ge-ta *see*
  Onondaga
Hodesannogeta *see* Onondaga
Hodesaunee *see* Houdenosaunee
  Confederacy
Hodidaion'ga [Clan] *Seneca* (H)
Hodidjionni'ga [Clan] *Seneca* (H)
Hodigen'gega [Clan] *Seneca* (H)
Ho-di-hi-dan-ne *see* Pawnee
Hodihidanne *see* Pawnee
Hodinesiiu *see* Hodi'ne'si'iu
Hodi'ne'si'iu [Clan] *Seneca* (H)
Hodinon'deoga [Clan] *Seneca* (H)
Ho-di-non'syon'ni *see* Iroquois
Hodinonsyonni *see* Iroquois
Hoeras [MX] *Lagunero* (BE)
Hoesh *see* Penateka
Hoganlani *see* Khoghanhlani
Hogapa'goni *see* Southern Paiute
Hogapa'goni *see* Paiute
Hogh-na-you-tau-agh-taugh-
  caugh *see* Oneida
Hogiopas *see* Cocopa
Hoglanders *see* Nochpeem
Hogloge *see* Yuchi
Hogologe *see* Yuchi
Hogologee [GA] *Yuchi* (H)
Hoh [WA] (BE)
Ho-ha *see* Assiniboin
Hoha *see* Assiniboin
Hohandika (Hdbk11) *see also*
  Hukunduka (Hdbk11)
Ho'handi'ka *see* Hukunduka
Hohandika [UT] *Shoshone* (H)
Hohe *Sihasapa* (H)
Hoheh *see* Hohe
Ho-he-i-o *see* Assiniboin
Hoheio *see* Assiniboin
Hoh-hay *see* Assiniboin
Hohhay *see* Assiniboin
Ho hill po *see* Hohilpo
Hohillpo *see* Hohilpo
Hohilpo (H) *see also* Salish (LC)
Ho-hil-po *see* Hohilpo
Hohilpo *Tushepaw* (H)
Hohio (H)
Hohodene [Lang] *Maipurean* (O)
Hohodene [VE] *Wakuenai* (O)
Hohoka-hano *see* Hooka
Hohokam (LC)
Hohota *Piro* (H)
Hohota *Tigua* (H)
Hohu *see* Hoko
Hoidarhonon [Can] (H)
Hoidxnous *see* Hutsnuwu
Hoilkut-hoi *see* Whilkut

Ho in de borto *see* Hunkpatina
Hoindeborto *see* Hunkpatina
Ho-is *see* Penateka
Hois *see* Penateka
Hoitda [CA] *Maidu* (H)
Ho iv i ma nah *see* Oivimana
Hoivimanah *see* Oivimana
Hojomes *see* Jocome
Hok [CA] (CA)
Hokamish *see* Skokomish
Hokan [Lang] (CA)
Hokandika *see* Hukunduka
Ho-kan-dik-ah *see* Hohandika
Ho-kan-dik-ah *see* Hukunduka
Hokandikah *see* Hohandika
Hokandikah *see* Hukunduka
Hokan Indians *see* Hok
Hokan-Siouan Phylum [Lang]
  (BE)
Hokan-ti-kara *see* Hohandika
Hokan-tikara *see* Hukunduka
Hokantikara *see* Hohandika
Hokantikara *see* Hukunduka
Ho-ka-rut-cha *see* Hokarutcha
Hokarutcha [Society] *Crow* (H)
Hoke *see* Ho'ke
Ho'ke [MN] *Assiniboin* (BE)
Hokedi [AK] *Tlingit* (H)
Hoko [Clan] *Hopi* (H)
Hoko winwu *see* Hoko
Ho-ko wun-wu *see* Hoko
Hoko wunwu *see* Hoko
Ho-kwaits *see* Hokwaits
Ho-kwaits *see* Las Vegas
Hokwaits (PC) *see also* Las Vegas
  (Hdbk11)
Hokwaits [CA] *Chemehuevi* (BE)
Holbama *see* Alabama
Holcuma *see* Holkoma
Hol-cu-ma *see* Holkoma
Hole *see* Hoh
Holechame [CA] (H)
Ho-len-mah *see* Holkoma
Holenmah *see* Holkoma
Hol-en-na *see* Holkoma
Holenna *see* Holkoma
Holilepa *see* Ololopa
Holil-le-pa *see* Ololopa
Ho-lil-li-pah *see* Ololopa
Holillipah *see* Ololopa
Holiwahali [AL] *Muskogee* (BE)
Holkoma [CA, NV] *Mono* (BE)
Hol-ko-mah *see* Holkoma
Holkomah *see* Holkoma
Hol-mie-uh *see* Holmiuk
Holmieuh *see* Holmiuk
Holmiuk [CA] (H)
Holoaloopi *see* Ololopa
Hol-o-kommah *see* Holkoma
Holokommah *see* Holkoma
Hololipi *see* Ololopa
Hol-o-lu-pai (H) *see also* Ololopa
  (H)

Hololupai *see* Ololopa
Hol-o-lu-pai [CA] *Maidu* (Con-
  tri, v.3, p.282)
Holonagu *see* Halona
Holstenborg *Greenland Eskimos*
  (BE)
Holy Cross-Georgetown [AK]
  Inglaik (BE)
Holy Easter *see* San Pascual [CA]
Holy Sabbath *see* Santo
  Domingo
Ho-ma *see* Hotachi
Homa *see* Houma
Homa *see* Hotachi
Ho-ma-ha *see* Omaha
Homaha *see* Omaha
Homalco *see* Homalko
Homaldo [CA] *Nomlaki* (CA-8)
Homalko [BC] *Salish* (BE)
Homalko [Lang] *Comox* (BE)
Homamish *see* Shomamish
Ho-man-han *see* Omaha
Homanhan *see* Omaha
Ho'ma yin'e *see* Homayine
Homayine [Subclan] *Iowa* (H)
Hometwoli [CA] *Buena Vista
  Yokuts* (CA)
Hometwoli [Lang] [CA] *Buena
  Vista* (CA-8)
Ho-mna *see* Homna
Homna *Brule* (H)
Honabanou *see* Ouabano
Honaga'ni *see* Khonagani
Honan *see* Honau
Honanduk *see* Adirondack
Honani [Clan] *Hopi* (H)
Ho-na-ni-nyu-mu *see* Honani
Honani wiwu *see* Honani
Ho-na-ni wun-wu *see* Honani
Ho-nan-ne-ho-ont *see* Seneca
Honannehoont *see* Seneca
Ho-nau *see* Honau
Ho-nau *see* Ke
Honau (PC) *see also* Ke (H)
Honau [Clan] *Hopi* (H)
Ho-nau-uh *see* Honau
Honauuh *see* Honau
Honau winwu *see* Honau
Honawuu *see* Honau
Honcopampa [PE] (Ex, v.33,
  no.3, 1991, pp.27–36)
Honcpatela band *see* Hunkpatina
Honctons *see* Yankton
Honcut *see* Honkut
Hone-cha-da *see* Chonakera
Honechada *see* Chonakera
Honeches *see* Waco
Honepapa *see* Hunkpapa
Honepatela Yanctonnais *see*
  Hunkpatina
Hone-ta-par-teen *see*
  Hunkpatina
Honetaparteen *see* Hunkpatina

Hone-ta-par-teen-waz *see* Hone-taparteenwaz
Honetaparteenwaz *Yankton* (H)
Honey-Eaters *see* Penointikara
Honey Eaters *see* Penateka
Honey Lake Paiute (NVAP, no.4, 1960)
Hongashan *see* Hangashenu
Hongashanno *see* Hangashenu
Hon-ga-sha-no *see* Hangashenu
Hong-Kutchin *see* Hankutchin
Hongkutchin *see* Hankutchin
Honigeters *see* Penateka
Ho-ni-i-tani-o *see* Pawnee
Ho-ni-i-ta-ni-o *see* Pawnee
Honiitanio *see* Pawnee
Honin nyumu *see* Honau
Honk pa pa *see* Hunkpapa
Honkpapa *see* Hunkpapa
Honkut [CA] *Maidu* (H)
Hon-namu *see* Honau
Honnamu *see* Honau
Honnat'haiion'ni [Clan] *Seneca* (H)
Honnehiouts *see* Oneida
Honniasont [Lang] *Iroquoian* (BE)
Honniasont [PA] (BE)
Honniasontkeronon [KY] (H)
Honnontage *see* Onondaga
Honnont-gondjen *see* Hodi-non'deoga
Honnontgondjen *see* Hodi-non'deoga
Honnonthauan *see* Seneca
Honontonchionni *see* Iroquois
Honorucco [HA] *Bainoa* (BE)
Honosonayo [Clan] [FL] *Timu-cua* (H)
Honoso Nays *see* Honosonayo
Honosuguaxtu-wane *see* Cayuga
Ho-now *see* Ho'nowa
Ho'nowa [SD] *Cheyenne* (BE)
Honow *see* Ho'nowa
Honowa (PC) *see also* Ho'nowa (BE)
Honowa *Cheyenne* (H)
Honqueron *see* Kichesipirini
Honqueronon *see* Kichesipirini
Hontc'i-ki-ka-ra-tca-da *see* Chonakera
Hontouagaha *see* Ontwaganha
Ho-n-u *see* Honau
Honu *see* Honau
Hon-wun-wu *see* Homai
Honwunwu *see* Honani
Hooch *see* Hoh
Hoochenoo *see* Hutsnuwu
Hoochinoo *see* Hutsnuwu
Hoochnom *see* Huchnom
Hoodchenoo *see* Hutsnuwu
Hood River Indians [WA, OR] (Hdbk12)

Hoodsinoo *see* Hutsnuwu
Hoodsna *see* Hutsnuwu
Hoods-Nahoos *see* Hutsnuwu
Hoodsnahoos *see* Hutsnuwu
Hooh *see* Hoh
Hooh-oh-ah-lat *see* Hoh
Hoohohahlat *see* Hoh
Hoo-ish *see* Penateka
Hooish *see* Penateka
Hook [SC] (H)
Ho-o-ka *see* Hooka
Hooka [Clan] *Keres* (H)
Hooka-hano *see* Hooka
Hookchenoo *see* Hutsnuwu
Hookluhmic *see* Lummi
Hookooeko *see* Marin-Bodega
Hooks [Lang] *Eastern Siouan* (H)
Hoo-ma *see* Hotachi
Hooma *see* Hotachi
Hooma [Clan] *Oto* (H)
Hoonah *Tlingit* (Ye)
Hoonah Kow *see* Huna
Hoonchenoo *see* Hutsnuwu
Hoone-ah *see* Huna
Hooneah *see* Huna
Hoone-ak *see* Huna
Hooneak *see* Huna
Hoo-ne-boo-ey (Hdbk11) *see also* Hunipuitoka (Hdbk11)
Hoonebooey (Hdbk11) *see also* Hunipuitoka (Hdbk11)
Hoonebooey [OR] *Shoshone* (H)
Hoo-ne-boo-ly *see* Hoonebooey
Hoo-ne-boo-ly *see* Hunipuitoka
Hoonebooly *see* Hoonebooey
Hoonebooly *see* Hunipuitaka
Hooniah *see* Huna
Hoonid *see* Huna
Hoonyah *see* Huna
Hoopa *see* Hupa
Hoo-pah *see* Hupa
Hoopah *see* Hupa
Hoosatunnuk *see* Stockbridge
Hooshkal [WA] *Chehalis* (H)
Hootsinoo *see* Hutsnuwu
Hootz-ah-tar-qwan *see* Hutsnuwu
Hootznahoo *Tlingit* (Ye)
Hoo-wal-ya-pia *see* Walapai
Hoowalyapia *see* Walapai
Hoo-wun-na *see* Huwanikikikarachada
Hoowunna *see* Huwanikikikarachada
Ho-pah *see* Hupa
Hopah *see* Hupa
Hopahka [MS] *Choctaw* (H)
Hope *see* Sakahl
Ho-pee *see* Hopi
Hopee *see* Hopi
Hopetcisa'th *see* Opitchesaht
Hopewell Culture (LC)
Hopi [AZ] (LC)

Hopi [Lang] *Shoshonean* (H)
Hopi [Lang] [*Uto-Aztecan*] (Hdbk10)
Hopii *see* Hopi
Ho-pil-po *see* Hohilpo
Hopisinom *see* Hopi
Hopite *see* Hopi
Hopi-Tewa *see* Tano
Hopitu *see* Hopi
Hopituh *see* Hopi
Ho-pi-tuh-ci-nu-muh *see* Hopi
Hopituhcinumuh *see* Hopi
Ho-pi-tuh-ci-nyu-muh *see* Hopi
Hopituhcinyumuh *see* Hopi
Ho-pi-tuh-lei-nyu-muh *see* Hopi
Hopituhleinyumuh *see* Hopi
Hopitu-shinumu [Self-designation] *see* Hopi
Hopokohacking [DE] *Unalachtigo* (BE)
Hopungieasaw *see* Piankashaw
Hopungiesas *see* Piankashaw
Hoquiam [WA] *Chehalis I* (H)
Ho-ra-ta-mu-make *see* Horatamumake
Horatamumake *Mandan* (H)
Horcaquisac *see* Arkokisa
Horconcito *see* Arkokisa
Horcoquisa *see* Arkokisa
Horcoquisaes *see* Arkokisa
Hores *see* Keres
Horicon [NY] (H)
Horikan *see* Horicon
Horio *see* Orio
Horn Mountain Indians *see* Etechesottine
Horruque *see* Surruque
Hosboa [Clan] *Hopi* (H)
Hosboa winwu *see* Hosboa
Hosh-que-aht *see* Hesquiat
Hoshqueaht *see* Hesquiat
Hoskies *see* Eskimos
Hos-ler *see* Hupa
Hosler *see* Hupa
Hostaqua *see* Yustaga
Hostaque *see* Yustaga
Ho-suk-hau-nu-ka-re-ri-hu *see* Hosukhaunukarerihu
Hosukhaunukarerihu *Arikara* (H)
Hotachi [Clan] *Missouri* (H)
Hotagastlas-hadai [Sub-clan] [AK] *Haida* (H)
Hota'mi massau *see* Hotamimsaw
Hotamimassau *see* Hoamimsaw
Hotam-imsaw *see* Hotamimsaw
Hotamimsaw [Society] *Cheyenne* (H)
Hotamita'nio [Society] *Cheyenne* (H)
Hotanka *see* Winnebago
Ho-tashin *see* Mescalero Apache

Hotashin see Mescalero Apache
Ho-ta-tci see Hotachi
Ho-tatci see Khotachi
Hotatci see Hotachi
Hotatci see Khotachi
Hotavila see Hotevilla
Hotavilla see Hotevilla
Hotcangara see Winnebago
Hotchon tchapa see Hochonch-
abba
Ho-te-day see Kikatsik
Hoteday see Kikatsik
Hotel'ena see Eskimos
Hote-shog-garah see Winnebago
Hoteshoggarah see Winnebago
Hotevila see Hotevilla
Hotevilla Hopi (Hdbk9)
Hothliwahali [GA] Upper Creek
(BE)
Hoti [VE] (O)
Hoti'nestakon see Sauk
Hotinnonchiendi see Iroquois
Hotinnonsionni see Iroquois
Hotinonsionni see Iroquois
Hotlimamish see Shotlemamish
Hotlugee see Hutalgalgi
Hotnas-hadai [AK] Haida (H)
Hoto see Oto
Hotoa-nutqiu see Mahohivas
Hotoanu'tqiu see Mahohivas
Hotoanutqui see Mahohivas
Ho-to-la-bixh see Humptulips
Hotolabixh see Humptulips
Ho-tor-lee see Hutalgalgi
Hotorlee see Hutalgalgi
Hottimamish see Shotlemamish
Hottunamish see Shotlemamish
Ho-tum-mi-hu-is see
Shungkayuteshni
Hotummihuis see
Shungkayuteshni
Houandate see Huron
Houaneiha [LA] (H)
Houaroux see Warrau
Houatoctota see Oto
Houattoehronon (H)
Houattoehronon (H) see also Sauk
(LC)
Houdenosaunee Confederacy (AI)
Houechas see Waco
Houeches see Waco
Hou-etchu see Hewchi
Houetchu see Hewchi
Houjets [LA] (H)
Houkpapa see Hunkpapa
Houlton Band see Malecite
Houma [Lang] Muskhogean (LC)
Houma [MS, LA] (LC)
Hounena see Crow
Houpin Guaymas see Upan-
guayma
Houron see Huron
Housatannuck see Stockbridge

Housatonic see Stockbridge
Housatonnoc see Stockbridge
Houssatonnoc see Stockbridge
Houssatunnuck see Stockbridge
Houtaqua see Yustaga
Houtchi see Yuchi
Houtouagaha see Ontwaganha
Hova see Jova
How-a-chez see Hewchi
How-ach-ee see Hewchi
Howachee see Hewchi
Howachez see Hewchi
Ho-wah see Iowa
Howah see Iowa
Howakeeas [NY] (H)
Howa'laa-pai see Hualapai
Howalaapai see Hualapai
Howalek [CA] Eastern Pomo
(Pub, v.36, no.6)
Howchee see Hewchi
How-chuck-les-aht see Uchuck-
lesit
Howchucklesaht see Uchucklesit
Howchucklus-aht see Uchuckle-
sit
Howchuk-lis-aht see Uchucklesit
Howchuklisaht see Uchucklesit
Howchuklisat see Uchucklesit
How-ech-e see Hewchi
Howeche see Hewchi
How-ech-ee see Hewchi
Howechee see Hewchi
How-ge-chu see Ogeechee
Howgechu see Ogeechee
How'ku'ma see Hauoma
Howkuma see Haukoma
How-mox-tox-sow-es see Man-
dan
Howmoxtoxsowes see Mandan
How-ru-ma see Haukoma
Howruma see Haukoma
Howschueselet see Uchucklesit
Hoxsuwitan see Wichita
Ho-ya see Hoyala
Hoya (PC) see also Hoyala (BE)
Hoya [Clan] Haida (H)
Hoyala [Can] Kwakiutl (BE)
Hoyero see Saidinde
Hoyima [CA] Northern Valley
Yokuts (CA-8)
Hoyma see Hoyima
Hrah-hrah-twaun see Chippewa
Hu [Clan] Quapaw (H)
Hua'amu'u see Navajo
Huaamuu see Navajo
Huabi see Huave
Huacacasa (Hdbk10) see also
Juanca (Hdbk10)
Huacacasa Coahuiltecan (BE)
Huachi [Lang] [SA] Txapakura
(O)
Huachipaire see Wachipaeri
Huachipairi see Wachipaeri

Huachipairy see Wachipaeri
Huaco see Waco
Huadjinaas-hadai [Sub-family]
[BC] Haida (H)
Huados [Clan] [BC] Haida (H)
Huaino see Hayno
Hualahuis [MX] Coahuiltecan
(Hdbk10)
Hua'la-pai see Hualapai
Hualapai (Hdbk10) see also Wala-
pai (BE)
Hualapai [AZ] (LC)
Hualapi see Hualapai
Hualga [Clan] Mohave (H)
Hualipai (Hdbk10) see also Wala-
pai (BE)
Huallaga see Cocamilla
Huallapai see Walapai
Huallop see Walapai
Hualopai see Walapai
Hualpai see Hualapai
Hualpais see Colville
Huamachuco [Lang] [SA] Quecha
(O)
Huambisa [EC, PE] (LC)
Huambisa [Lang] Jivaro (LC)
Huambise see Huambisa
Huambiza see Huambisa
Huanca [PE] (LC)
Huancavilca [EC, PE] (LC)
Huanchane see Waco
Huanes [TX] Coahuiltecan (BE)
Huanuco [Lang] Quecha (O)
Huanuco [PE] (O)
Huanyam see Pakaanova
Huanyam see Wanam
Huao [EC] (LC)
Huaorani see Huao
Huaorini see Waorani
Huaraijia see Guarijio
Huarani see Awishiri
Huaraque Coahuiltecan (Hdbk10)
Huaraya see Ese Ejja
Huarayo see Guarayo
Huarayo [Tacanan] see Ese Ejja
Huari [PE, BO, Br] (LC)
Huariapano [Self-designation] see
Panobo
Huarpe [Arg] (LC)
Huary [BO] Araona (O)
Huarymodo [BO] Araona (O)
Huascari (Hdbk11) see also Cedar
(Hdbk11)
Huascari [UT] (H)
Huash [Arg] (O)
Huash [Lang] Chon (O)
Huashasha see Osage
Huasioto see Oto
Huasipunguero [EC] (O)
Huastec [Lang] [MX] Mayan
(LC)
Huasteca see Huastec
Huatanis see Mandan

Huatocta *see* Oto

Huattoehronon *see* Houattoehronon

Huatuso *see* Guatuso

Huave [Lang] *Mizocuavean* (LC)

Huave [MX] (LC)

Huavean Family [Lang] *Mizocuavean* (BE)

Huaxtec *see* Huastec

Huayaalis [PacN] (Anthro, v.9,
no.3, p.158)

Huayan [Lang] *Txapakura* (O)

Huayaru *see* Ese Ejje

Huaynamota [MX] *Cora* (BE)

Hubabo [HA, SanD] (BE)

Hubales *see* Tano

Hubates *see* Tano

Hubites *see* Tano

Hubol *see* Wowol

Huch *see* Hoh

Huch'-nom *see* Huchnom

Huchnom [CA] (CA)

Huchnom [Lang] *Yukian* (CA)

Huchun *see* Uchium

Huc-klic *see* Nung

Hucklic *see* Nung

Huda [Clan] *Yuchi* (H)

Huda taha *see* Huda

Hudataha *see* Huda

Hudcoadama *see* Alchedoma

Hudcoadan *see* Alchedoma

Hud-Coadan *see* Halchidhoma

Hudcoadanes *see* Alchedoma

Hudecabin *see* Hu'deca'bin

Hu'deca'bin [MN] *Assiniboin*
(BE)

Hudsunu [Can] [*Sitka-kwan*]
(Contri, v.1, p.38)

Hue-la-muh *see* Stalo

Huelamuh *see* Cowichan

Huelamuh *see* Stalo

Hue-la-muh [Self-designation]
see Cowichan

Hue-lang-uh *see* Songish

Huelanguh *see* Songish

Hueplapiaguilam *see* Lugplapiagulam

Huequetzal *see* Gueiquesales

Huereo [JA] (BE)

Hueripane *see* Ervipiame

Huero [JA] (BE)

Huertas (H)

Hueshuo *see* Mataco

Huetar *see* Guetar

Hu-e-ya *see* Khuya

Hueya *see* Khuya

Hueyanguh *see* Clallam

Hue-yang-uh [Self-designation]
see Clallam

Hueyhueyquetzal [MX] (Hdbk10)

Hughchee *see* Yuchi

Hu-hlo *see* Hlahloalgi

Huhlo *see* Hlahloalgi

Huhuula *see* Hu-hu'ula

Hu-hu'ula [Lang] *Papago*
(Hdbk10)

Huhuwos [Lang] *Papago*
(Hdbk10)

Huhuygam *Coahuiltecan*
(Hdbk10)

Huichol [Lang] *Carachol*
(Hdbk10)

Huichol [MX] (LC)

Huichola *see* Huichol

Huiknu *see* Makaguane

Huikuayaken [BC] *Squawmish*
(H)

Huiliche *see* Huilliche

Huilli *see* Huilliche

Huilliche [CH] *Araucanian* (LC)

Huillicos *see* Huilliche

Huinihkacina *see*
Hanginihkashina

Huinihkashina [Gens] *Osage* (H)

Hu i'nikaci'ka *see* Huinikashika

Huinikacika *see* Huinikashika

Huinikashika [Gens] *Quapaw* (H)

Huisocal *see* Gueiquesales

Huita [MX] *Cahita* (H)

Huitata *see* Witoto

Huitcole *see* Huichol

Huite [Lang] *Taracahitian* (BE)

Huite [MX] (BE)

Huititnom *see* Huititno'm

Huititno'm [CA] *Round Valley
Yuki* (BE)

Huitnu [Self-designation] *see*
Makaguane

Huito *see* Witoto

Huitoto *see* Witoto

Huke Eaters *see* Hukunduka

Huki Eaters *see* Hukunduka

hukkuntikka *see* Hukunduka

Hukunduka (Bull120) *see also*
Promontory Point Shoshone
(Bull120)

Hukun duka *see* Hukunduka

Hukunduka [UT] *Northern
Shoshone* (Hdbk11)

Hukwats *see* Yuma

Hukwats *see* Mohave

Hulanapo *see* Kuhlanapo

Huldanggat [Clan] [BC] *Haida*
(H)

Hull-loo-el-lell *see* Hullooetell

Hullooellell *see* Hullooetell

Hullooetell [WA] *Skilloot* (BE)

Hul-loo-et-tell *see* Hullooetell

Hul-lu-et-tell *see* Hullooetell

Hulluettell *see* Hullooetell

Hulmeca *see* Olmecs

Hulpunes *see* Khulpuni

Huma *see* Jumano

Huma *see* Houma

Humacao [PR] (BE)

Humakam *see* Tepecano

Hu-ma-kam [Self-designation]
see Tepecano

Hum-a-lah *see* Skagit

Humalah *see* Skagit

Hum-a-luh *see* Skagit

Hum-a-luh *see* Stalo

Hum-a-luh *see* Cowichan

Humaluh *see* Cowichan

Humaluh *see* Skagit

Humaluh *see* Stalo

Humana *see* Jumano

Humana de Tompires *see* Jumano

Humana de Tompiros *see* Jumano

Humano *see* Jumano

Humasko *see* Creek

Humaskogi *see* Creek

Humaskogi *see* Muskogee

Hu-mat-kam *see* Tepecano

Humatkam *see* Tepecano

Hu-ma-whi *see* Humawhi

Humawhi [CA] *Shasta* (H)

Humboldt Bay Indians *see*
Wiyot

Humboldt Indians [NV] *Paviotso*
(H)

Humbra *see* Anserma

Hume [Lang] *Chinantec* (BE)

Hume [MX] *Xixime* (BE)

Hume [TX] *Coahuiltecan* (BE)

Humetwadi *see* Hometwoli

Humptulips [WA] *Chehalis I* (BE)

Hump-tu-lups *see* Humtulips

Humptulups *see* Humptulips

Humro *see* Huna

Humunas de Tompires *see* Jumano

Humurana *see* Omurano

Huna [AK] *Tlingit* (BE)

Huna cow *see* Huna

Huna-kon *see* Huna

Hunga *see* Hanga

Hung-ga ni-ka-shing-ga *see*
Hangatanga

Hungganikashingga *see*
Hangatanga

Hungotinga *see* Hangatanta

Hun-go-tin-ga *see* Hangatanga

Hunguh *see* Hanga

Huniedes *see* Oneida

hunipuitika'a *see* Hunipuitoka

Hunipuitoka (Hdbk11) *see also*
Hoonebooey (Hdbk11)

Hunipuitoka *Northern Pauite*
(Hdbk11)

Hunkappa *see* Hunkpapa

Hun-koo-chin *see* Hankutchin

Hunkoochin *see* Hankutchin

Hunkpapa [Lang] *Teton* (H)

Hunkpapa *Sioux* (LC)

Hunk-pate *see* Hunkpatina

Hunkpate *see* Hunkpatina

Hunkpa-te-dans *see* Hunkpapa
Hunkpatedans *see* Hunkpapa
Hunkpatee *see* Hunkpatina
Hunkpatidan *see* Hunkpatina
Hunkpatina (BE) *see also* Upper
  Yanktonai (BE)
Hunkpatina [SD] *Yanktonai* (H)
Hunkplatin *see* Hunkpatina
Hun-kutch-in *see* Hankutchin
Hun-Kutchin *see* Hankutchin
Hunkutchin *see* Hankutchin
Hunkuwanicha *Brule* (H)
Hunku-wanitca *see*
  Hunkuwanicha
Hunkuwanitca *see*
  Hunkuwanicha
Hunna *see* Huna
Huno *see* Puquina
Huno *see* Uru
Hun-sa-tung *see* Hupa
Hunsatung *see* Hupa
Hunskachantozhuha *Hunkpapa*
  (H)
Hunters *see* Etagottine
Huntlatin [AK] *Tanana* (BE)
Hunzpuzlugut *see* Unpuncliegut
Huokarawaoch *see* Cuscarawaoc
Hupa [CA] (LC)
Hupa [Lang] [CA] *Athabascan*
  (H)
Hupachisat (Anthro, v.9, no.3,
  p.157)
Hupda *see* Jupda
Hupdu *see* Jupda
Hupi *see* Hopi
Hupo *see* Hupa
Huramomowi *Guahibo* (O)
Hures *see* Ures
Hurini [Self-designation] *see*
  Asurini II
Huro *see* Uru
Huron (BE) *see also* Wyandot
  (BE)
Huron [Ont] (LC)
Hurones *see* Huron
Huronnes *see* Huron
Huron of Lorette (Hdbk15)
Hurons at Lemikariagi *see*
  Wyandot
Hurons of Missilimakinac *see*
  Wyandot
Hurons of the Tobacco Nation
  see Wyandot
Hurripacuxi *see* Tocobaga
Hurron *see* Huron
Hurry People *see* Hankutchin
Husada [Sub-gens] *Kansa* (H)
Husadta [Sub-gens] *Osage* (H)
Husadtawanu [Sub-gens] *Osage*
  (H)
Husadtawanun *see* Husadtawanu
Hushkoni [Clan] *Chickasaw* (H)
Huskchanoes *see* Conestoga

Huskemaw *see* Eskimos
Huskey *see* Eskimos
Huskhoskey *see* Kaskaskia
Huskie *see* Eskimos
Huskoni *see* Hushkoni
Husky *see* Eskimos
Hus'ky *see* Eskimos
Husoron [MX] *Varohio* (H)
Huspah [SC] *Yamasee* (H)
Huspoa *see* Hosboa
Hu-tab Pa-da-nin *see* Pawnee
Hutab Padanin *see* Pawnee
Hu-ta-ci *see* Lipan Apache
Hutaci *see* Lipan Apache
Hutalgalgi [Clan] *Creek* (H)
Huta-napo *see* Kuhlanapo
Hutanapo *see* Khulanapo
Hutanga *see* Kansa
Hutashi *see* Tsiltaden
Hutchistanet *see* Onondaga
Hute-pa *see* Papago
Hutepa *see* Papago
Hutsawap [MD] *Choptank* (H)
Hutsnuwu [AK] *Tlingit* (BE)
Huuka [Clan] *San Felipe* (H)
Huuka-hano *see* Hooka
Huumbo *see* Yumbo
Hu-umui *see* Omaha
Huumui *see* Omaha
Huwaka [Clan] *Acoma* (H)
Huwaka-hanoqeh *see* Huwaka
Hu-wan-i-ki-ka-ra-tca-da *see*
  Huwanikikikarachada
Huwanikikaratcada *see*
  Huwanikikikarachada
Huwanikikikarachada [Gens]
  Winnebago (H)
Huwi [Clan] *Hopi* (H)
Hu-wi win-wu *see* Huwi
Huwi winwu *see* Huwi
Huxal *see* Lipan Apache
Huyupurina *see* Ipurina
Huzaa *see* Osage
Huz-zau *see* Osage
Huzzau *see* Osage
Huz-zaw *see* Osage
Huzzaw *see* Osage
Hvattoehronon *see* Sauk
Hwahwatl [VanI] *Puntlatsh* (BE)
hwa'mu *see* Navajo
hwamu *see* Navajo
Hweroi *see* Santa Ana [NM]
Hwotso'tenne *see* Hwotsotenne
Hwotsotenne [Can] *Babine* (BE)
Hyaquez *see* Yaqui
Hyaquin *see* Yaqui
Hyaquis *see* Yaqui
Hyda *see* Haida
Hydah *see* Kaigani
Hydah *see* Chimmesyan
Hydah *see* Haida
Hyder *see* Haida
Hyem Tu-ay *see* Puretuay

Hyeroquodame *see* Terocodame
Hyo-qua-hoon *see* Pecos
Hyoquahoon *see* Pecos
Hyperina *see* Ipurina
Hyroquoise *see* Iroquois
Hyroquose *see* Iroquois
Hyroquoyse *see* Iroquois
Hyscani *see* Yscani
Hyshalla *see* Kitamat

-I-

Iacchi [HA] *Bainoa* (BE)
Iacovane *see* Yojuane
Iagohaiucho [HA] *Bainoa* (BE)
Iagua [Cu] (BE)
I-a-kar *see* Ietan
Iakar *see* Ietan
Iakema *see* Yakima
Iakim *see* Yaqui
I-akima *see* Yakima
Iakima *see* Yakima
Iakon *see* Yakonan
Iakon *see* Yaquina
Ialo'stimot *see* Ialostimot
Ialostimot [BC] *Bella Coola* (H)
Ialostimot [BC] *Talio* (H)
Ialostimot [Clan] *Taliomh* (H)
Iamamadi *see* Yamamadi
Iaminawa *see* Jaminaua
Iamoacos *see* Yamasee
Ia'na *see* Iana
Iana [Clan] *Taos* (H)
Ianaizi [Ha] *Guaccaiarima* (BE)
Iana-taiina *see* Iana
Iano *see* Hano
I-an-to-an *see* Jatonabine
Iantoan *see* Jatonabine
Iapies *see* Hapes
Iasica *see* Farmers Band
I-at *see* Mohave
Iat *see* Mohave
Iata *see* Ietan
Iatago *see* Ietan
Iata-go *see* Ute
Iatago *see* Ute
Iataina *see* Taos
Iatan *see* Ietan
I-a-tans *see* Ietan
I'at'apalliklik *see* Alliklik
Iate *see* Fulnio
Iaualapiti [Br] (O)
Iauaulapiti [Lang] *Arawakan* (O)
Iawai *see* Iowa
Iawalapiti *see* Iualapiti
Iawano [Br] (O)
Iawano [Lang] *Panoan* (O)
Iawas *see* Iowa
Iawavo *see* Iawano
Iaway *see* Iowa

Ibache [Clan] *Kansa* (H)
Ibaja *see* Guale
Ibatc-e *see* Ibache
Ibequi *see* Yaqui
Ibi *see* Yui
Ibirayara *see* Cayapo
Ibitoupa [MS] (BE)
Ibotsa *see* Ibo'tsa
Ibo'tsa [SA] *Ocaina* (O)
Ica (LC) *see also* Ika (BE)
Ica [Col] (LC)
Ica [Lang] *Chibchan* (LC)
Icabia *Coahuiltecan* (Hdbk10)
Icafui [FL] *Timucua* (BE)
Icaguate [EC] *Secoya* (O)
Icaiche [MX] *Mayas* (BE)
Icarilla Apache *see* Jicarilla
  Apache
Icasqui *see* Kaskinampo
Icaura *Coahuiltecan* (Hdbk10)
Icbewa *see* Chippewa
Icca *see* Incha
Iccarilla Apache *see* Jicarilla
  Apache
Iccuje-ne *see* Mimbreno Apache
Ice *see* Nukhe
Ichagoteguo [SA] *Caduveo* (O)
Icharilla Aapche *see* Jicarilla
  Apache
Ic-ha-she *see* Kanze [Kansa]
Ichashe *see* Kanze [Kansa]
Ichhasualgi [Clan] *Creek* (H)
Ichiti *see* Hitchiti
Ichualgi [Clan] *Creek* (H)
I-chu-ar-rum-pats *see*
  Ichuarumpat
I-chu-ar-rum-pats *see* Moapa
Ichuarumpat [NV] *Paiute* (H)
Icna'umbisa [MN] *Assiniboin*
  (BE)
Icosans (H)
icsluit *see* Wishram
Ictans *see* Ietan
Ictasanda *see* Inshtasanda
Ictunga *see* Ishtunga
Icuano *Coahuiltecan* (Hdbk10)
Icuara *see* Icaura
Idahi *see* Comanche
Ida-kara-wak-a-ha *see* Idakariuke
Idakarawakaha *see* Idakariuke
Ida-ka-riuke *see* Idakariuke
Idakariuke [CA] *Shasta* (H)
I'dats'e *see* Kanse
Idatse *see* Kanse
Id-do-a *see* Kikatsik
Iddoa *see* Kikatsik
Idemasa [Col] *Macua* (O)
I-do-ka-rai-uke *see* Idakariuke
Idokaraiuke *see* Idakariuke
idza'a-teaga-tekade *see*
  Makuhadokado
Iean, S. *see* San Juan [NM]
Iean, Saint *see* Etarita

Iebathu [Clan] [NM] *Isleta* (H)
Iebathu [Clan] [NM] *Tigua* (H)
Iebathu-t'ainin *see* Iebathu
Iechur [Clan] *Isleta* (H)
Iechur [Clan] *Tigua* (H)
Iechur-t'ainin *see* Iechur
Iefeu [Clan] *Isleta* (H)
Iefeu [Clan] *Tigua* (H)
Iefe'u-t'ainin *see* Iefeu
Iekidhe [Gens] *Omaha* (H)
Iekuana *see* Yecuna
Ielan *see* Ietan
Ienecu *see* Senecu del Sur
Ieshur [Clan] *Isleta* (H)
Ieshur [Clan] *Tigua* (H)
Ieshur-t'ainin *see* Ieshur
Ieskachincha *Oglala* (H)
Ieska cinjca *see* Ieskachincha
Ieskacinjca *see* Ieskachincha
Ie-ska-pi *see* Jatonabine
Ieskapi *see* Jatonabine
Ieska-tcintca *see* Ieskachincha
Ieskatcintca *see* Ieskachincha
Ietam *see* Ietan
Ietan (H)
Ietan (H) *see also* Ute (LC)
Ietanes *see* Ietan
Ieuontowanois *see* Seneca
Iewatse (H)
I-e-wat-se *see* Iewatse
ígabu *see* Kickapoo
Igalik [AK] *Subarctic Indians* (Ye)
Igdlorssuit *Greenland Eskimos*
  (BE)
Igdlumiut (H) *see also* Tahagmiut
  (H)
Igdlumiut *Inuit* (Hdbk5)
Igihua'-a *see* Apache
Iglaka tehila *see* Iglakatekhila
Iglakatehila *see* Iglakatekhila
Iglakatekhila *Oglala* (H)
Iglaka-teqila *see* Iglakatekhila
Iglakateqila *see* Iglakatekhila
Igloolik *see* Iglulik
Igloolikmiut *see* Iglulirmiut
Iglulipmiut *see* Iglulirmiut
Iglulik [AK] *Eskimos* (LC)
Iglulik *Central Eskimos* (Hdbk5)
Iglulik [Lang] *Eastern Canada*
  (Hdbk5)
Iglulingmiut (LC) *see also* Iglulir-
  miut (LC)
Iglulingmiut [Lang] *Iglulik*
  (Hdbk5)
Iglulirmiut [WA] *Central Eskimos*
  (LC)
Iglu-miut *see* Tahagmiut
Iglumiut *see* Tahagmiut
Iglurarsome [*Innuit (Quebec)*]
  (Hdbk5)
Ignaciano (LC) *see also* Moxo
  (LC)
Ignaciano [Lang] *Aawakan* (LC)

Ignacio *see* Ignaciano
Ignacio de Soniquipa, San *see*
  Sinoquipe
Ignacio Sinoquipe, San *see* Sino-
  quipe
Ignerhonon *see* Mohawk
Igneri *see* Island Carib
Ignierhonon *see* Mohawk
Ignituk *Bering Strait Eskimos*
  (Hdbk5)
Iguaces *see* Yguases
Iguaja *see* Guale
Iguana *see* Icuano
Iguanas *see* Iguanes
Iguanes [AZ] *Yuman* (H)
Iguaracata *Coahuiltecan* (Hdbk10)
Iguases *see* Yguases
Iguiguipacam *see* Guiguipacam
Iha-ca *see* Ihasa
Ihaca *see* Ihasa
Iha'gtawa Kataxka *see* Yankton
Ihagtawa Kataxka *see* Yankton
Iha-isdaye *see* Ihaisdaye
Ihaisdaye *Yankton* (H)
Ihank'tanwin *see* Yanktonai
Ihanktanwin *see* Yanktonai
Ihanktewans *see* Yanktonai
Ihanktonwan (H) *see also* Yankton
  (LC)
Ihanktonwan *Brule* (H)
Ihanktonwanna *see* Yankton
I-hank-ton-wan-na *see* Yankton
Ihanktonwanna Dakotas *see*
  Yankton
Ihanktonwe *see* Yankton
Ihan-k'tow-wan-nam *see* Yank-
  tonai
Ihanktowwannan *see* Yankton
Ihanktuwan Dacotah Oyate *see*
  Yankton
Ihank-t'wan *see* Yankton
Ihanktwan *see* Yankton
Ihank-t'wan-ahs *see* Yanktonai
Ihanktwanahs *see* Yankton
Iha-sa *see* Ihasa
Ihasa *see* Ihasha
Ihasha [SD] *Hunkpatina* (H)
Ihauk-to-wa-na *see* Yankton
Ihauk-t'wan *see* Yankton
Ihauk-t'wan-ah *see* Yankton
Ihldene *see* Navajo
I'hl-dene *see* Navajo
Ihon-a-Does *see* Juniata
Ihonadoes *see* Juniata
Ihoway *see* Iowa
Ih-po-se-ma *see* Ipoksimaiks
Ihposema *see* Ipoksimaiks
Ihuruana [Lang] *Maquiritare*
  (UAz, v.28)
Ihuruhana [VE] *Yecuana* (O)
Iicarrilla *see* Jicarilla Apache
Iiwilkamepa [AZ] *Wikedjasapa*
  (BE)

Ijca *see* Ica
Ijirang *Eskimos* (H)
Ijka *see* Ica
I-ka *see* Kammatwa
Ika (O) *see also* Arhuavo (LC)
Ika (PC) *see also* Kammatwa (BE)
Ika [BaC, MX] (BE)
I-ka-du *see* Kickapoo
I-ka-du *see* Osage
Ikadu *see* Kickapoo
Ikadu *see* Osage
Ikake *see* Jicaque
Ikanafaskalgi *see* Seminole
Ikan-faski *see* Seminole
Ikanfaski *see* Seminole
I-ka-nuck *see* Ikaruck
Ikanuck *see* Ikaruck
Ikanuiksalgi *see* Seminole
Ika-ruck *see* Ikaruck
Ikaruck [CA] *Shasta* (H)
Ike *see* Ica
Ikherkhamut [AK] *Ahtena* (BE)
Ikiruka'tsu [CA] *Shasta* (Shasta, p.14)
Ikito *see* Iquito
Ik-kil-lin *see* Kutchakutchin
Ikkillin *see* Kutchakutchin
Ikmun *Yankton* (H)
Ikogmiut (Hdbk5) *see also* Kuig-pagmiut (Hdbk5)
Ikogmiut (Hdbk5) *see also* Russian Mission (Hdbk5)
Ikogmiut [AK] *Eskimos* (BE)
Ikogmjut *see* Ikogmiut
Ikogmute *see* Ikogmiut
Ikoklag'mut *see* Ekogmut
Ikoleec [Self-designation] *see* Gavioes
Ikoro *see* Gavioes
Ikouera *see* Koroa
Iku *see* Ika
Ikunuhkahtsi [Society] (H)
Ikvogmute *see* Ikogmiut
Ilamatt *see* Klamath
Ilaoquatsh *see* Clayoquot
Ila'xluit *see* Wishram
Ila'xluit *see* Tlakluit
Ilaxluit *see* Tlakluit
Ilaxluit *see* Wishram
Il de Conso, San *see* San Ildefonso
Ildefonse, S. *see* San Ildefonso
Ildefonsia, S. *see* San Ildefonso
Ildefonso *see* San Ildefonso
Ildefonso, S. *see* San Ildefonso
Ildefonso, San [Lang] *Northern Tewa* (BE)
Ildefonso, San [Pueblo] [NM] (BE)
Ildefonzo, San *see* San Ildefonso
Ildephonso, San *see* San Ildefonso
Ildjunai-hadai [BC] *Haida* (H)

I'ldjunai xa'dai *see* Ildjunai-hadai
Ilefonso, San *see* San Ildefonso
Ilefonso, Sant *see* San Ildefonso
Ileños *see* Gileños
Ilesta *see* Isleta
Ilet *see* Isleta
Ilet Suck *see* Bellabella
Iletsuck *see* Bellabella
Ilga't *see* Chehalis [WA]
Ilgat *see* Chehalis [WA]
Ilghi'mi *see* Bella Coola
Ilgonquines *see* Nipissing
Iliamna [AK] *Tanaina* (BE)
Iliguigue [MX] *Coahuiltecan* (Hdbk10)
Ilihasitumapa (BE) *see also* Walka-mepa (BE)
Ilihasitumapa [AZ] (BE)
Ilimoüec *see* Illinois
Ilimouek *see* Illinois
Iline *see* Illinois
Ilinese *see* Illinois
Ilinesen *see* Illinois
Iliniouek *see* Illinois
Ilinois *see* Illinois
Ilinoués *see* Illinois
Ilinouets *see* Illinois
Ilinouetz *see* Illinois
ilinwe *see* Illinois
Ilionois *see* Illinois
Ilisees [LA, TX] (H)
Ilivilermiut *see* Ilivilirmiut
Ilivilirmiut [AK] *Eskimos* (Hdbk5)
Ilkodankaiya [CA] (Pub, v.20, no.6)
Ill Creek Bands *see* Chasta
Illenois *see* Illinois
Illenonecks *see* Illinois
Illicoueck *see* Illinois
illimiut sic] *see* Igdlumiut
Illimouec *see* Illinois
Illinese *see* Illinois
Illinesen *see* Illinois
Il-li-ni *see* Illinois
Illini *see* Illinois
Illiniens *see* Illinois
Illiniwek *see* Illinois
Illinoias *see* Illinois
Illinois [IL] (LC)
Illinois Confederacy (BE)
Illinois River Indians *see* Takelma
Illinoix *see* Illinois
Illinonecks *see* Illinois
Illinoneeks *see* Illinois
Illinoüec *see* Illilnois
Illinouecks *see* Illinois
Illinoüek *see* Illinois
Illmawees *see* Ilmawi
Illonese *see* Illinois
Illonois *see* Illinois
illuajuk *see* Iglurarsome
illuajummiut *see* Iglurarsome

illualummiut [Can] [*Inuit (Quebec)*] (Hdbk5)
Illuni *see* Illinois
Il-ma-wi *see* Ilmawi
Ilma'wi *see* Ilmawi
Ilmawi [CA] (BE)
Ilmawi [Lang] *Ilmawi* (CA-8)
Ilthkoyape *see* Colville
Iltte-Kai-Mamits *see* Ithkye-mamits
Ilttekaimamits *see* Ithkyemamits
Iluilermiut [Can] *Central Eskimos* (BE)
Ilyamna People *see* Knaiakhotana
Ima *see* Quapaw
I'ma *see* Quapaw
Imach-leet *see* Imaklimiut
Imaha [TX] *Kwapa* (BE)
Imahans *see* Quapaw
Imah-kli-mut *see* Imaklimiut
Imahklimut *see* Imaklimiut
Imakleet *see* Imaklimiut
Imaklig'amut (Contri, v.1, p.15)
Imaklimiut [AK, Rus] *Eskimos* (BE)
Imaklit *see* Imaklig'amut
Imaklitgmut *see* Imaklimiut
Imapari *see* Iñapari
Imbaya *see* Cara
Imiacolomo [MX] *Coahuiltecan* (Hdbk10)
Imiche (H) *see also* Wimilchi (H)
Imiche [CA] (H)
Imihita [SA] *Bora* (O)
Imikie [Col] *Yucuna* (O)
Imimule [MX] *Coahuiltecan* (Hdbk10)
Imipecte [MX] *Coahuiltecan* (Hdbk10)
Imiri, San *see* Emidio
Imirio, San *see* Emidio
I'mlach-no'm *see* Round Valley Yuki
Imlachnom *see* Yuki [CA]
Immokalee Seminole (Eagle, v.8, no.1, p.8)
Imnama [ID] *Nez Perce* (BE)
Imp-qua *see* Umpqua
I-na-cpe *see* Nez Perce
Inacpe *see* Nez Perce
I-na-ha-o-win *see* Inyanhaoin
Inahaowin *see* Inyanhaoin
Inaja [CA] *Mission* (PC)
Iñaken *see* Southern Tehuelche
Ina'khtek *see* Ina'qtek
Inakhtek *see* Ina'qtek
Inalugmiut *see* Imaklimiut
Inalugmiut *see* Inguklimiut
Inantoinu [ID] *Nez Perce* (BE)
Inapanam *Coahuiltecan* (Hdbk10)
Iñapari [Br, PE] *Mashco* (O)
Iñapari [Lang] *Maupurean* (O)
Inapaw *see* Quapaw

Inaqtek *see* Ina'qtek
Ina'qtek [Clan] *Menominee* (H)
In-as-petsum *see* Nespelim
Inaspetsum (PC) *see also* Nespelim (LC)
Inaspetsum [WA] *Nez Perce* (H)
Inatahin *see* Mescalero Apache
Incas (O) *see also* Quechua (LC)
Incas *Andeas Region* (LC)
Incaura *see* Icaura
Incha (H)
Inchulukhlaites *see* Inkalich
Income-can-etook *see* Income-canetook
Incomecanetook *Okinaga* (H)
Incuero *Coahuiltecan* (Hdbk10)
Inda *see* Comanche
Inde [Self-designation] *see* Apache
Indelchidnti [AZ] *San Carlos Apache* (H)
Indian Peak Tribe *see* Beaver
Indian River Indians *see* Assateague
Indians of Rice Lake *see* Missisauga
Indians of Rice Lake *see* Rice Lake [Chippewa]
Indians with many bundles *see* Bissarhar
Indian Valley [Lang] *Maidu* (CA-8)
Indiens Cuivres *see* Tatsanottine
Indiens du Sang *see* Kainah
Indiens-Loups *see* Skidi Pawnee
Indiens-Pierre *see* Assiniboin
Indiens-Serpents *see* Shoshone
Indilche-dentiene *see* Indelchidnti
Indilchedentiene *see* Indelchidnti
Inekatu *see* Nheengatu
Inewakhubeadhin [Subgens] *Omaha* (H)
Inez, Santa [Lang] [CA] *Chumashan* (H)
Inga [Col] (O)
Ingain *see* Kaingangue
Ingaleek *see* Ingalik
Ingalete *see* Ingalik
Ingal'igmut (Contri, v.1, p.15)
Ingalik (H) *see also* Kaiyuhkhotana (BE)
Ingalik [Self-designation] [AK] (LC)
Ing'aliki *see* Ingalik
Ingaliki *see* Ingalik
Ingalit *see* Ingalik
Ingaliuk *see* Ingali'igmut
Ingano [Col] (LC)
Ingarica *see* Ingariko
Ingarico *see* Ingariko
Ingariko [Br, Guy] (O)
Ingariko [Lang] *Carib* (O)

Ingdhe-zhide *see* Ingdhezhide
Ingdhezhide [Clan] *Omaha* (H)
Ingekasagmi *see* Ingalik
Ingeletes *see* Ingalik
Ing-gera-je-da *see* Ingdhezhide
Inggerajeda *see* Ingdhezhide
Ingkdhunkashinka [Subclan] *Osage* (H)
Inglutal'igemut *see* Inglutal-igemiut
Inglutalikgemiut [AK] *Malemiut* (H)
Inglutalkik *Bering Strait Eskimos* (Hdbk5)
In-gra-zhe-da *see* Ingdhezide
Ingrazheda *see* Ingdhezhide
Ing-uh-kli-mut *see* Inguklimiut
Inguhklimut *see* Inguklimiut
Inguklimiut [AK] *Eskimos* (BE)
Ing-we-pi-ran-di-vi-he-man *see* Keres
Ingwepirandiviheman *see* Keres
inhabitants of the narrow place *see* Amitormiut
inhuit [Self-designation] *see* Polar Eskimos
Ini *see* Hainai
Inic *see* Hainai
Inie *see* Hainai
Inie *see* Ione
I-nik-si-kah-ko-pwa-iks *see* Inuksikahkowpaiks
Iniliki *see* Unakhotana
Ini-maca *see* Maca
Inimaca *see* Maca
Ininauumbi *see* Ini'na u'umbi
Ini'na u'umbi [MN] *Assiniboin* (BE)
Ininwezi [Ont] *Algonquian* (IndN, v.5, no.2, Apr.1928, pp.173–178)
Ininyu-we-u *see* Cree
Ininyuweu *see* Cree
Injame *see* Sijame
Inka *see* Incas
Inkalich [AK] *Kaiyuhkhotana* (H)
Inkalichljuaten *see* Inkalich
In-kal-ik *see* Ingalik
Inkalik *see* Ingalik
Inkalil-Ingelnut *see* Jugelnute
Inkalilingelnut *see* Jugelnute
Inkalite *see* Ingalik
Inkaliten *see* Ingalik
Inkaliten *see* Kuskwogmiut
Inkaliten *see* Magemiut
Inkba *see* Inkesabe
Inkesabe [Gens] *Omaha* (H)
Inkilik *see* Ingalik
Inkiliken *see* Ingalik
Ink-ka-sa-ba *see* Inkesaba
Inkkasaba *see* Inkesaba
Inkpa [MN] *Wahpeton* (H)
Inkpatonwan *see* Inkpa

Inkuluchluatan *see* Inkalich
Inkuluchluaten *see* Unakhotana
Inkulukhlaites *see* Inkalich
Inkuluklaities *see* Inkalich
Inltane *see* Navajo
Innatcha *see* Natchez
Innies *see* Hainai
Inninyu-wuk *see* Cree
Innoit *see* Eskimos
Innok *see* Eskimos
Innondadese *see* Tionantati
Innu *see* Montagnais-Naskapi
In-nu *see* Eskimos
Innu *see* Eskimos
Innuees *see* Eskimos
Innuin *see* Eskimos
Innuit (BE) *see also* Inuit (BE)
Innuit *see* Eskimos
Innuit *see* Eskimauan
In'nuit *see* Eskimos
Ino [BO] *Araona* (O)
inoca [Self-designation] *see* Illinois
Inocoples [MX] *Tamaulipec* (BE)
Inocopolo *see* Inocoples
Inoschujochen *see* Inoschuochn
Inoschuochn [Clan] [AZ] *San Carlos Apache* (H)
Inparavi *see* Shipaulovi
Inpaton *see* Inkpa
Inquero *see* Incuero
Inquoi *see* Iroquois
In'shin *see* Konkow
Inshin *see* Konkow
Inside Fat *see* Kakapoya
In-spellum *see* Nespelim
Inspellum *see* Nespelim
Inshtasanda [Subgens] *Omaha* (H)
Inta *see* Ute
In-tem-peach-es *see* Intimbich
Intempeaches *see* Intimbich
Interior North Alaska Eskimos (Hdbk5)
Intermediate Denes *Tinne* (H)
Intermediate Foothill [Lang] *Yokutsan* (CA-8)
Intibucat [Hon] *Lenca* (BE)
Inti-etook *see* Intietook
Inti-etook *see* Entiat
Intietook *see* Entiat
Intietook *Okinaga* (H)
Intimbich [CA] *Mono* (H)
In-tim-peach *see* Intimbich
Intimpeach *see* Intimbich
Intimpich *see* Intimbich
Intogapid *see* Itogapuk
Intruder Peoples (AI)
Intruder Peoples (AI) *see also* Southwest Tribes (AI)
Intsi Dindjich *see* Ahtena
Intsi-Dindjitch *see* Koyukukhotana

Intujen-ne *see* Faraon
Inugleet *see* Inguklimiut
Inugsuk culture [Gr] (Hdbk5)
In-uhk-so-yi-stam-iks *see* In-uhksoyistamiks
Inuhksoyistamiks [MN] *Kainah* (BE)
Inuin (H) *see also* Eskimos (LC)
Inuissuitmiut *Eskimos* (H)
Inuit (BE) *see also* Eskimos (LC)
Inuit *Labrador* (Hdbk5)
Inuit [Lang] *Eskimos* (Bull1)
Inuit *Quebec* (Hdbk5)
Inuit [Self-designation after 1977] (Hdbk5)
Inuit-Inupiaq [AK] *Eskimos* (Hdbk5)
inuit kumpaimiut *see* Inuit [Quebec]
inuk *see* Eskimos
Inuksikahkopwaiks [MN] *Piegan* (BE)
I-nuks-iks *see* Inuksiks
Inuksiks *Piegan* (H)
Inuna-ina *see* Arapaho
Inuñaina [Self-desgination] *see* Arapaho
Inupiaq [Lang] [AK] [*Inuit-Inupiaq*] (Hdbk5)
Inupiat [AK] *Eskimos* (Hdbk5)
Inupik *see* Inuit-Inupiaq
inuvialuit (Hdbk5) *see also* Eskimos (LC)
Inuvialuit [Can] (NatPeos, pp.381–382)
inuvialuk *see* Eskimos
Inverted Society *see* Himatanohis
Invna-ina *see* Arapaho
Inyancheyaka-atonwan [MN] *Wahpeton* (H)
Inyangmani [MN] *Wahpeton* (H)
Inyan-ha-oin *see* Inyanhaoin
Inyanhaoin *Miniconjou* (H)
Inyan-tceyaka-atonwan *see* Inyancheyaka-atonwan
Inyantceyakaatonwan *see* Inyancheyaka-atonwan
Inyantonwan *see* Jatonabine
Inyantonwanbin *see* In'yanton'wanbin
In'yanton'wanbin [MN] *Assiniboin* (BE)
Inya-vape *see* Yavapai
Inyavape *see* Yavapai
Inyo [CA] (Pub, v.11, no.5)
Inyokapa *see* Hakupakapa
Inyopacan *Coahuiltecan* (Hdbk10)
Ioewaig *see* Iowa
Iofoka *see* Io'foka
Io'foka *Wintu* (Pub, v.29, no.4)
Iogopani *see* Shongopavi
Iogopapi *see* Shongopovi
Iojuan *see* Yoyuane

Iondes *see* Hainai
Ione [CA] (CA)
Ionees *see* Hainai
Ioni *see* Ione
I-on-i *see* Hainai
Ioni *see* Hainai
Ionias *see* Hainai
Ionie *see* Ione
Ionies *see* Hainai
Ionnondadese *see* Wyandot
Ionontady-Hagas *see* Tionontati
Ionontady Hagas *see* Wyandot
I-oo-guneintz *see* Kaibab
Iooguneintz *see* Kaibab
Iotan *see* Ietan
Iotteca *see* Juniata
Iowa [IA] (LC)
Iowa [Lang] *Chiwere* (H)
Iowaulkeno *see* Tawakoni
Ioway *see* Iowa
Ipai [CA] (CA-8)
Ipajuiguara [Lang] *Quinigua* (Hdbk10)
Ipajuiguara [MX] (Hdbk10)
Ipa-n'de *see* Lipan Apache
Ipa-nde *see* Lipan Apache
Ipandes *see* Lipan Apache
Ipandi *see* Lipan Apache
Ipapana [Lang] *Totonacan* (BE)
Ipapana [MX] (BE)
Ipataraguites *see* Jumano
Ipeca [Lang] *Maipurean* (O)
Ipeka *see* Ipeca
Ipewi *see* Kreen-Akrore
Ipitinere *see* Amahuaca
Ipoilq *see* Sanpoil
I-pok-si-maiks *see* Ipoksimaiks
Ipoksimaiks [MN] *Piegan* (BE)
Ipotewat [Br] *Kawahib* (O)
Ipuricoto *see* Purikoto
Ipurina [Br] (LC)
Ipurucoto *see* Purikoto
I-qer-qa-mut *see* Ikherkhamut
Iqerqamut *see* Ikherkhamut
Iquahsinawmish *see* Squaxon
Iqugmiut *see* Kuigpagmiut
Iqugmiut *see* Russian Mission
Iquita *see* Iquito
Iquito [Lang] *Zaparo* (LC)
iquymiut *see* Kaugpagmiut
iquymiut *see* Russian Mission
Iranche *see* Iranxe
Iranshe *see* Iranxe
Irantxe *see* Iranxe
Irantze *see* Iranxe
Iranxe [Br] (LC)
Irapa [Col, VE] (LC)
Ira-Tapuya [Col] *Wakuenai* (O)
Irecoies *see* Iroquois
Irequois *see* Iroquois
Irinions *see* Illinois
Iriquoi *see* Iroquois
Iriquois *see* Iroquois

Irkpeleit *see* Athapascan
Irkpeleit *see* Kutchin
Iroca *see* Iroka
Irocois *see* Iroquois
Iroequois *see* Iroquois
Irognas *see* Iroquois
Iroka [Col] *Yuko* (O)
Irokesen *see* Iroquois
Iron Cloud *see* Makhpiyamaza
Iron Cloud's Village *see* Makhpiyamaza
Ironeyes *see* Hainai
Ironeyes *see* Ione
Ironies *see* Hainai
Ironois *see* Iroquois
Iroondock *see* Adirondack
Iroquaes *see* Iroquois
Iroque *see* Iroquois
Iroquese *see* Iroquois
Iroqueze *see* Iroquois
Iroquiese *see* Iroquois
Iroquoi *see* Iroquois
Iroquoian Family [Lang] (H)
Iroquoian Indians *see* Iroquois
Iroquois [NY] (LC)
Iroquois Confederacy (H)
Iroquois d'enbas *see* Mohawk
Iroquoise Chippeways [Q] (H)
Iroquois Inferieurs *see* Mohawk
Iroquois League *see* Iroquois Confederacy
Iroquois Nation *see* Iroquois Confederacy
Iroquois Superieurs (H)
Iroquos *see* Iroquois
Irriquois *see* Iroquois
Irrironnon *see* Erie
Irrironon *see* Erie
Irritila [MX] *Lagunero* (BE)
Irrohatock *see* Arrohattoc
Irroquays *see* Iroquois
Irroquois *see* Iroquois
Iruai'tsu *see* Iruaitsu
Iruaitsu [CA] *Shasta* (BE)
I'ruwai *see* Iruaitsu
Iruwai *see* Iruaitsu
Iruwaitsu *see* Iruaitsu
Is *see* Ais
Isallanic race *see* Cherokee
Isalwakten [BC] *Salish* (H)
Isalwalken *see* Isalwakten
Isamis [BC] *Salish* (H)
Isammuck *see* Isamuck
Isamuck [BC] *Salish* (H)
Isanati *see* Santee
Isanisk *see* Sanetch
Isanti *see* Santee
Isantie Dakotas *see* Santee
Isanties *see* Santee
I-san-tis *see* Santee
Isantis *see* Santee
Isantiton *see* Santee
Isanyate *see* Santee

Isanyati (H) *see also* Santee (LC)
Isanyati *Brule* (H)
I-sa-po-a *see* Crow
Isapoa *see* Crow
Isashbahatse *see* Sarsi
Isatis *see* Santee
Isa-ttine *see* Tsattine
Isattine *see* Tsattine
Isaunties *see* Santee
I-sau-uh wun-wu *see* Ishauu
Isauuh wunwu *see* Ishauu
Isauu winwu *see* Ishauu
Isawisnemepu [ID] *Nez Perce*
   (BE)
Iscani *see* Caddo
Iscapana [MX] *Coahuiltecan*
   (Hdbk10)
Iscaycinca [PE] (LC)
Iscobaquebu [Self-designation]
   see Isconahua
Isconahua [Lang] *Panoan* (O)
Isconahua [PE] (O)
Isconis *see* Yscani
Iscuande *see* Cuaiquer
Isebene [BO] *Araona* (O)
Iselle *see* Isleta
Iseta *see* Isleta
Isfanalgi [Clan] *Creek* (H)
Is-fa-nul-ke *see* Isfanalgi
Isfanulke *see* Isfanalgi
Ish *see* Ishauu
I-sha-hue *see* Ishauu
Ishahue *see* Ishauu
Ishango *see* Brule
Ishauu [Clan] *Hopi* (H)
Ishawu *see* Ishauu
I'shawuu *see* Ishauu
Ishawuu *see* Ishauu
Ishfanalgi *see* Isfanalgi
Ishfanalgi *see* Ishauu
Ishir [Self-designation] *see*
   Chamacoco
Ishira *see* Chamacoco
Ishisagek Roanu *see* Missisauga
Ish-pan-ee *see* Ishpanee
Ishpanee [Phratry] *Chickasaw* (H)
Ishpani *see* Ishpanee
Ish-ta-sun-da *see* Inshtasanda
Ishtasunda *see* Inshtasanda
Ish-te-pit-e *see* Siksika
Ishtepite *see* Siksika
Ishti semoli *see* Seminole
Ishto [Clan] *San Felipe* (H)
Ish'to-hano *see* Ishtowa
Ishtohano *see* Ishtowa
Ishtowa [Clan] [NM] *San Felipe*
   (H)
Ishtowa [Clan] [NM] *Sia* (H)
Ishtowa-hano *see* Ishtowa
Ishtunga *Kansa* (H)
Isi [Clan] [NM] *San Felipe* (H)
I'si-hano *see* Isi
Isihano *see* Isi

Isiis *see* Isis
Isimpshean *see* Tsimshian
Isipopolames *see* Espopolames
Isir *see* Orio
Isira *see* Chamacoco
Isis (BE) *see also* Yscani (BE)
Isis *Wichita* (BE)
I-sis-o-kas-im-iks *see*
   Isisokasimiks
Isisokasimiks [MN] *Kainah* (BE)
I'sium-ita'niuw *see* Hi-
   siometa'nio
Isiumitaniuw *see* Hisiometa'nio
Iskayouse *see* Cayuse
Iskemay *see* Eskimos
Iskoman [Lang] [CA] (Pub, v.16,
   no.3, p.104)
is-ksi-na-tup-i *see* Esksinaitup-
   piks
isksinatupi *see* Esksinaitupiks
Iskulani [Clan] *Choctaw* (H)
Isla *see* Isleta
Island [CA] *Chumash* (CA)
Island Carib [Lang] [WInd] (LC)
Island Innuit *see* Okiogmiut
Isle aux Noix *see* Illinois
Isle-de-Peins *see* Sinkiuse
Isle-de-peiree *see* Sinkiuse
Isle de Pierre *see* Moses-
   Columbia
Isle-de-Pierre *see* Sinkiuse-
   Columbia
Islella *see* Isleta
Isle-River Indians *see* Eel River
Isleta [Lang] *Tiwa* (BE)
Isleta [NM] *Tigua* (LC)
Isletabuh *see* Isleta
Isleta del Paso *see* Isleta
Isleta del Sur *see* Isleta
Isletans *see* Isleta
Isleta of the South *see* Isleta
Isleteños *see* Isleta
Isletta *see* Isleta
Islinois *see* Illinois
Ismiquilpas [TX] (H)
Ismuracanes [CA] (H)
Isnihoyelps *see* Colville
Isoletta *see* Isleta
Isonkuali [Self-designation] *see*
   Okinagan
Isonnontoan *see* Seneca
Isonnontonan *see* Seneca
Isonontouanes *see* Seneca
I-sonsh-pu-she *see* Cheyenne
I-sonsh-pu-she *see* Cheyenne
Isonshpushe *see* Cheyenne
Isosena *see* Izoceno
Isowasson *see* Sweathen
Ispani *see* Ishpanee
Ispipewhumaugh [WA] (H)
Ispipichimack [WA] (Hdbk12)
Issa *see* Catawba
Issanti *see* Santee

Issappo *see* Crow
Issappo'ekuun *see* Crow
Issaqui *see* Santee
Issaquy *see* Santee
Issati *see* Assiniboin
Issati *see* Santee
Issatie *see* Santee
Issatrians *see* Santee
Issi [Clan] *Chickasaw* (H)
Issi-chupioha *see* Siksika
Issirriberrenai *Achagua* (O)
Issis *Wichita* (NAmI, 1978, v.19,
   pp.223–224)
Issi-Schupischa *see* Siksika
Issischupischa *see* Siksika
Is-sui *see* Issui
Issui [Society] *Piegan* (H)
Istam [Moiety] [CA] (Pub, v.16,
   no.6)
Istasunda *see* Inshtasanda
Istet [BC] *Bellabella* (Anthro, v.9,
   no.3, p.159)
Isti seminole *see* Seminole
Istiseminole *see* Seminole
Isti simanole *see* Seminole
Istisimanole *see* Seminole
Is-tsi-kai-nah *see* Istsikainah
Istsikainah [MN] *Kainah* (BE)
Isty-semole *see* Seminole
Istysemole *see* Seminole
Iswa [SC] *Catawba* (BE)
Ita (Hdbk5) *see also* Polar Eski-
   mos (Hdbk5)
Ita *Greenland Eskimos* (BE)
Ita anyadi *see* Itaanyadi
Itaanyadi [Clan] *Biloxi* (H)
Itacayuna *see* Xikrin
I-tach-ee *see* Iticha
Itachee *see* Iticha
Itaches *see* Iticha
Ita-Eskimos *see* Ita
Ita Eskimos *see* Polar Eskimos
I ta ha taki *see* Dakota
Itahataki *see* Dakota
Ita ha'tski *see* Dakota
Itahatski *see* Dakota
Itah-Ischipahji *see* Cheyenne
Itahischipahji *see* Cheyenne
Itahzipchois *see* Itazipcho
Ita-Iddi *see* Arapaho
Itaiddi *see* Arapaho
Itakule [PE] *Urarina* (O)
Italua lako *see* Apalachicola
Italualako *see* Apalachicola
Italwo lake *see* Apalachicola
Italwolake *see* Apalachicola
Itamalgi [Clan] *Creek* (H)
Ita'mi *see* Ita
Itami *see* Ita
Itaner *see* Ita
Itaner *see* Polar Eskimos
Itanese *see* Ita
It-ans-ke *see* Dakota

Itanske *see* Dakota
Itasi'na *see* Cheyenne
I-ta-su-pu-zi *see* Cheyenne
I-ta-su-pu-zi *see* Cheyenne
Itasupuzi *see* Cheyenne
Itasupuzu *see* Cheyenne
Itatin *see* Pauserna
Itaywiy [CA] *Comeya* (H)
Itazipcho *Sans Arcs* (H)
Itazipco *see* Itazipcho
Itazipcoes *see* Itazipcho
Itazipco-hca *see* Itazipcho
Itazipko *see* Itazipcho
Itaziptco-qtca *see* Itazipcho
Itchali *see* Kutchakutchin
Itcheabudah *see* Ditsakana
It-chet-a-bud-ah *see* Ditskana
Itchhasualgi [Clan] *Creek* (H)
Itchi-mehueve *see* Chemehuevi
Itchualgi [Clan] *Creek* (H)
Ite *see* Itene
Itean *see* Ietan
I-te-che *see* Iticha
Iteche *see* Iticha
I-techees *see* Iticha
Itechees *see* Iticha
Itechi *see* Taushiro
Ite'chi [Self-designation] *see*
   Taushiro
Ite-citca *see* iteshica
Itecitca *see* Iteshica
Ite-citca-etanhan *see*
   Iteshichaetanhan
Itecitcaetanhan *see* Iteshichaetan-
   han
Iteghu [SD] *Hunkpatina* (H)
Ite gu *see* Iteghu
Itegu *see* Iteghu
Iten *see* Itene
Itene [BO, Br, EC] (LC)
Iteneo *see* Itene
Itenez *see* Itene
Iteshica [SD] *Oglala* (H)
Iteshicha *see* Iteshica
Iteshichaetanhan [SD] *Oglala* (H)
Ite-sica *see* Iteshica
Itesica *see* Iteshicha
Ite-xu *see* Iteghu
Itexu *see* Iteghu
Ithale teni *see* Mishikhwut-
   metunne
Ithaleteni *see* Mishikhwut-
   metunne
Ithale tuni *see* Mishikhwut-
   metunne
Ithaletuni *see* Mishikhwut-
   metunne
Ithkyemamits [WA] (H)
It-i-cha *see* Iticha
Iticha [CA] *Yokuts* (H)
Iticha [Lang] [CA] *Marioposan*
   (H)
Itimpachis *see* Kaibab

Itivimiut [Can] [*Inuit (Quebec)*]
   (Hdbk5)
Itivimiut [Can] *Labrador Eskimos*
   (BE)
Itivimmiut [Lang] *Eastern Canada*
   (Hdbk5)
Itiwa Ateuna [Phratry] *Zuni* (H)
It-kagh-lie *see* Kutchakutchin
Itkaghlie *see* Kutchakutchin
It-ka-lya-ruin *see* Kutchakutchin
It-kal-ya-ruin *see* Tinne
Itkalyaruin *see* Kutchakutchin
It-kalyi *see* Tinne
I't-ka-lyi *see* Kutchakutchin
Itkalyi *see* Kutchakutchin
Itkalyi *see* Tinne
Itkepelit *see* Kutchakutchin
Itkilak [WA] *Klickitat* (Oregon)
Itkpe-leit *see* Kutchakutchin
Itkpeleit *see* Kutchakutchin
Itkpe'lit *see* Kutchakutchin
Itku'dlin *see* Kutchakutchin
Itlalyaruin *see* Tinne
Itoaten *see* Tautin
I-to-ches *see* Iticha
Itoches *see* Iticha
Itoebehe *see* Kawahib
Itogapuk [Br] *Kawahib* (O)
Itokah-tina *see* Itokakhtina
Itokahtina *see* Itokakhtina
Itokakhtina *Sisseton* (H)
Itokaq-tina *see* Itokakhtina
Itokaqtina *see* Itokakhtina
Itomapa (H)
Itonama [Lang] [Col] *Paezan* (LC)
Itoreauhip [Lang] *Txapakura* (O)
Itra [Clan] *Cochiti* (H)
Itrahani [Clan] [NM] *Cochiti* (H)
I'trahani hanuch *see* Itrahani
Itrahani hanuch *see* Itrahani
It-sa-a-ti-a-ga *see* Itsaatiaga
It-sa'-a-ti-a-ga *see*
   Makuhadokado
Itsaatiaga [NV] *Paviotso* (H)
Itsa'tawi *see* Itsatawi
Itsatawi [CA] (Pub, v.23, no.5)
Itsatawi [Lang] [CA] *Achomawi*
   (CA-8)
I-tsa-ti *see* Santee
Itsati *see* Santee
Itscheabine *Assiniboin* (H)
Itsisihisa *see* Siksika
I tsi si pi sa *see* Siksika
Itsisipisa *see* Siksika
Ittawan *see* Etiwaw
It-t'ha-gi *see* Sichomovi
Itthagi *see* Sichomovi
Ittibime [Can] [*Inuit (Quebec)*]
   (Hdbk5)
ittoqqortoormeermiit *East Green-
   landers* (Hdbk5)
Itucale *see* Itakule
Itucale *see* Urarina

Itukale *see* Itakule
I-tun-i-wo *see* Arapaho
Ituniwo *see* Arapaho
It-us-shi-na *see* Cheyenne
Itusshina *see* Cheynne
Itynai *see* Tinne
Itynai *see* Athapascan
Itza [Gua, BrH] *Mayas* (LC)
Itza [Lang] *Yucatec* (BE)
It-ze-su-pe-sha *see* Siksika
Itzesupesha *see* Siksika
Itzuco [MX] (BE)
Iualapiti (O)
Iuan Baptista, San *see* San Juan
   Bautista [NM]
I'uka tene *see* Yukichetunne
Iukatene *see* Yukichetunne
iu'la'lonkni [OR] *Klamath* (BE)
Iumana *see* Jumano
Iumane *see* Jumano
Iumano *see* Jumano
Iumbucanis *see* Yubuincariri
I-um O'otam *see* Kamia
I-um o-otam *see* Comeya
Ium Ootam *see* Comeya
Ium O'otam *see* Kamia
Iuruna *see* Yuruna
Iuta *see* Ute
Ivagmute *see* Magemiut
Ivapare *see* Heta
Ivap'i *see* Karok
Ivapi *see* Karok
Ivigtut *Greenland Eskimos* (BE)
I vists tsi nih pah *see* Heviqs-
   ni'pahis
Iviststsinihpah *see* Heviqs-
   ni'pahis
Iwalapiti *see* Iaualapiti
Iwatoinu [ID] *Nez Perce* (BE)
Iwayusota [SD] *Oglala* (H)
Iwi [Clan] *Caddo Confederacy* (H)
Iwi [Clan] *Kadohadacho* (H)
Iwo'rien *see* Kikhtog'amut
Ixcani *see* Yscani
Ixcatec *see* Ixcateco
Ixcateco [MX] *Otomanguan* (LC)
Ixignor *see* Awishiri
Ixil [Gua] *Mayas* (LC)
Ixil [Lang] *Eastern Mayan* (LC)
I-ya-aye *see* Iyaaye
Iya-aye *see* Iyaaye
Iyaaye *San Carlos Apache* (H)
Iyakhba *see* Iowa
Iyakhwa *see* Iowa
Iyak'oza *see* Iyakoza
Iyakoza *Brule* (H)
Iyama Ateuna [Phratry] *Zuni* (H)
Iyanough [MA] *Nauset* (BE)
Iyemi *see* Karutana
Iyemi *see* Yurapari-Tapuya
Iyich *see* Tyigh
Iyiniwok [Self-designation] *see*
   Cree

Iyuhba *see* Iowa
Iyutagjen-ne *see* Navajo
Izacanis *see* Yscani
Izalco [ES] (BE)
Izaneni [Lang] [SA] *Maipurean* (O)
Izatys *see* Santee
izicidi tibiwaga'yu *see* Tsoso odo tuviwarai
Izocenio *see* Izoceno
Izoceno [BO] [*Tupi-Guarani*] (O)
Izoceno-Chiriguano *see* Izoceno
Iztacans (H)
Iztepeque [ES] *Pokomam* (BE)

-J-

Jaakema *see* Yakima
Jaba *see* Jova
Jabesua *see* Havasupai
Jaboti *see* Jabuti
Jabuti [Br] (O)
Jabutifed [Br] *Kawahib* (O)
Jacaltec *see* Jacalteca
Jacalteca [Lang] [MX, Gua] *Western Mayan* (LC)
Jacalteco *see* Jacalteca
Jacao *Coahuiltecan* (Hdbk10)
Jacarilla Apache *see* Jicarilla Apache
Jackhuthath *see* Yakutat
Jack Indians [Can] (H)
Jack-quy-ome *see* Jackquyome
Jackquyome [BC] *Salish* (H)
Jacome *see* Jocome
Jacomi *see* Jocome
Jacon *see* Yakonan
Jacon *see* Yaquina
Jacoquin *Coahuiltecan* (Hdbk10)
Jacum *see* Yacum
Jae *see* Geyer
Jagavans [TX] (H)
Jaguallapai *see* Walapai
Jaguallapai *see* Hualapai
Jahui *see* Diahoi
Jahui *see* Kawahib
Jaimamar *see* Tumamar
Jakechdune *see* Alchedoma
Jak huthath *see* Yakutat
Jakis *see* Sauk
Jakobshavn *Greenland Eskimos* (BE)
Jakon *see* Yakonan
Jakon *see* Yaquina
Jakou *see* Yazoo
Jakutat *see* Yakutat
Jakutat-kon *see* Yakutat
Jalam *see* Xarame
Jalchedon *see* Alchedoma
Jalchedon *see* Halchidhoma

Jalchedum *see* Alchedoma
Jalchedun *see* Alchedoma
Jalchedun *see* Halchidhoma
Jalchedunes *see* Halchidhoma
Jallicuamai *see* Quigyuma
Jallicuamay *see* Quigyuma
Jallicumay *see* Halyikwamai
Jallicumay *see* Quigyuma
Jalliquamai *see* Quigyuma
Jalliquamai *see* Halyikwamai
Jalliquamay *see* Quigyuma
Jalliquamay *see* Halyikwamai
Jamaja *see* Mohave
Jamajab *see* Mohave
Jamajaba *see* Mohave
Jamajama *see* Mohave
Jamajiri *see* Yamamadi
Jamala *see* Mohave
Jamamadi *see* Yamamadi
Jamamandi *see* Yamamadi
Jamamiri *see* Yamamadi
Jamasees *see* Yamassee
Jambalo [Col] *Paez* (O)
Jameco [NY] (H)
James *see* Jemez
Jamez *see* Jemez
Jaminahua *see* Jaminaua
Jaminaua [Lang] [Br, PE, BO] *Panoan* (LC)
Jaminawa *see* Jaminaua
Jaminawa *see* Yaminawa
Jamkallie *see* Yoncalla
Jamo *see* Jano
Jamul [CA] (CA)
Jamunda *see* Uaboi
Janadoah *see* Oneida
Janambre [MX] (BE)
Janambre-Pison [Lang] [MX] (Hdbk10)
Janapas [MX] *Coahuiltecan* (Hdbk10)
Janata nikacinga *see* Yankton
Jancas *see* Tonkawa
Janena [Col] *Barasana* (O)
Janequeila *see* Serrano
Janero *see* Jano
Janitos *see* Oneida
Jano (BE) *see also* Tano (Hdbk9)
Jano [MX, NM] *Apache* (BE)
Janogualpa *see* Hano
Janondadies *see* Wyandot
Jantamais (H)
Jantonees *see* Yanktonai
Jantonnais *see* Yanktonai
Jantonnois *see* Yanktonai
Jantons *see* Yankton
Jantous *see* Yankton
Jaos *see* Taos
Japiam *see* Yapiam
Japiel *see* Japul
Japies *see* Hapes
Japreria [Lang] *Motilon* (UAz, v.28)

Japreria [VE] *Yukpa* (O)
Japui *see* Japul
Japul (H)
Jaqaru [Lang] [PE] *Jaqi* (O)
Jaqi [Lang] [PE, BO] (O)
Jaquiripamona [MX] *Coahiltecan* (Hdbk10)
Jarame *see* Xarame
Jarames *see* Harames
Jaraname *see* Aranama
Jarecouna *see* Arekena
Jarecoune *see* Arecuna
Jaricuna *see* Arecuna
Jaricuna *see* Taulipang
Jarosoma *see* Apache
Jarquin *see* Karkin
Jaru *see* Jora
Jarú *see* Pakaanova
Jaruara [Br] *Yamamadi* (O)
Jaruna *see* Yuruna
Jaruya *see* Witoto
Jason *see* Yazoo
Jatapaina *see* Pima
Jatche-then-juwue *see* Yatchee thinyoowuc
Jatonabine [Clan] *Assiniboin* (H)
Jaucar *see* Juanca
Jaue'nikacika *see* Zhawenick-ashika
Jauenikacika *see* Zhawenick-ashika
Jauja-Huanca [Lang] [SA] *Quechua* (O)
Java [Br] *Caraya* (O)
Javahe *see* Javae
Javaje *see* Javae
Java Supais *see* Havasupai
Javensa *see* Havasupai
Je *see* Ge
Jeaga [FL] (BE)
Jean, S. *see* San Juan [NM]
Jean des Chevaliers, Saint *see* San Juan [NM]
Jeapes *see* Hapes
Jebero [PE] (O)
Jeberoan [Lang] [PE] (O)
Jece *see* Ais
Jecorilla *see* Jicarilla Apache
Jecuche *see* Cahuilla
Jecuche *see* Kawia [Luiseño]
Jecueche *see* Cahuilla
Jecuiche *see* Cahuilla
Jecuiche *see* Kawia [Luiseño]
Jediuk *see* Shediac
Jehua *see* Tewa
Jemaco *see* Jameco
Jemas *see* Jemez
Jemes *see* Jemez
Jemex *see* Jemez
Jemez [NM] (LC)
Jemmes *see* Jemez
Jemos *see* Jemez
Jeneckaw *see* Seneca

Jenecu *see* Senecu del Sur
Jenegueches *see* Serrano
Jeneguechi *see* Serrano
Jenequich [CA] (H)
Jenequiches *see* Serrano
Jenies *see* Jemez
Jenigueche *see* Serrano
Jenigueich *see* Serrano
Jenigueih *see* Serrano
Jeniguieh *see* Serrano
Jennings Band [MN] *Kutenai* (BE)
Jennitos *see* Oneida
Jenondades *see* Tionontati
Jenondades *see* Wyandot
Jenondage *see* Onondaga
Jenondathese *see* Tionontati
Jenondathese *see* Wyandot
Jenontowano *see* Seneca
Jenundadees *see* Tionontati
Jenundadees *see* Wyandot
Jequiche *see* Kawia [Luiseño]
Jerez *see* Keres
Jermz *see* Jemez
Jerome, San *see* Taos
Jeruiwa [Col] *Yucuna* (O)
Jetam *see* Ietan
Jetans *see* Ietan
Jeures *see* Jemez
Jibaro *see* Jivaro
Jibewa *see* Chippewa
Jicaque [Hon] (LC)
Jicara *see* Jicarilla Apache
Jicaragrande *Coahuiltecan* (Hdbk10)
Jicarello *see* Jicarilla Apache
Jicarila Apache *see* Jicarilla Apache
Jicarilla Apache [CO, NM] (LC)
Jicarillero *see* Jicarilla Apache
Jicarillo *see* Jicarilla Apache
Jiccarrilla Apache *see* Jicarilla Apache
Jicho [BO] *Araona* (O)
Jickorie *see* Jicarilla Apache
Jicorilla *see* Jicarilla Apache
Jicorilla Apache *see* Jicarilla Apache
Jijame *see* Sijame
Jimenez *see* Jemez
Jiminiguara [MX] (Hdbk10)
Jimiopa [MX] *Coahuiltecan* (Hdbk10)
Jiniapa [MX] *Coahuiltecan* (Hdbk10)
Jiniguara [MX] (Hdbk10)
Jinipiguara *see* Jiniguara
Jinotega [Lang] [NI] [*Macro-Chibchan*] (O)
Jirajira [Lang] *Paezan* (O)
Jitipo *see* Setebo
Jivara *see* Jivaro
Jivaran [Lang] (LC)

Jivaro [Lang] [EC, PE] (LC)
Jivaroan *see* Jivaran
Jivira *see* Jivaro
Jldefonso, San *see* San Ildefonso
Joan, Saint *see* San Juan [NM]
Joan Batista, Sant *see* San Juan [NM]
Joanne, S. *see* San Juan [NM]
Joaquin, San [CA] (H)
Joaquin's Band, San [NV] *Paviotso* (H)
Joara *see* Cheraw
Jo-as-seh *see* Joasseh
Joasseh [Clan] *Iroquois* (H)
Joba *see* Jova
Jobal *see* Jova
Jocome [MX] (BE)
Jocomeos *see* Jocome
Jocomis *see* Jocome
John, S. *see* San Juan [NM]
John, Saint *see* San Juan [NM]
John-a-does *see* Juniata
Johnadoes *see* Juniata
John Day Indians (BE) *see also* Tukspush (BE)
John Day Indians [CA] *Tenino* (H)
John Days *see* John Day Indians
John Day's River *see* John Day Indians
John's, St. *see* Etarita
Johns, St. *see* San Juan [NM]
John's River, St. *see* Malecite
John's tribe , St. *see* Malecite
Jollillepa *see* Ololopa
Jonaz-Chichimeca *see* Chichimeca-Jonaz
Jongoapi *see* Shongopovi
Jongopabi *see* Shongopovi
Jongopai *see* Shongopovi
Jongopavi *see* Shongopovi
Jonies *see* Hainai
Jon-ion-cali *see* Shongopovi
Jonioncali *see* Shongopovi
Jonkta *see* Chankuti
Jonontadyhnago *see* Tionontati
Joqualan [MX] *Coahuiltecan* (Hdbk10)
Jora [BO] *Guarani* (O)
José, San (H) *see also* Pecos (BE)
Jose de la Laguna, San *see* Laguna
Josef de La Laguna, San *see* Laguna
Joshua Indians [OR] *Tututne* (BE)
Josimnin *see* Khosminin
Joso *see* Hopi
Jotans *see* Ietan
Jotars [TX] (H)
Jotoy [Arg, Par] *Ashluslay* (O)
Joukiousme *see* Jukiusme
Jouskiousme *see* Jukiusme

Jova [Lang] *Opata* (Bull44)
Jova [MX] (BE)
Jovahe *see* Caraja
Jowai *see* Iowa
Jowas *see* Iowa
Joways *see* Iowa
Joylraua *see* Opata
Joyl-ra-ua [Self-designation] *see* Opata
Joyvan (H) *see also* Yojuane (BE)
Joyvan [AR] (H)
Jsleta *see* Isleta
Juacanas *see* Tawakoni
Juacano *see* Tawakoni
Jualati *see* Atfalati
Juamaca (BE) *see also* Juanca (Hdbk10)
Juamaca *Coahuiltecan* (BE)
Juampa *see* Juanca
Juan, San [CA] (H)
Juan, San [Lang] [NM] *Northern Tewa* (BE)
Juan, San [NM] (BE)
Juana Kitaunlhu [Br] *Southern Nambicuara* (O)
Juan Baptista, San *see* San Juan Bautista [NM]
Juan Bautista, San [CA] *Costanoan* (BE)
Juan Bautista, San [NM] (H)
Juanca *Coahuiltecan* (Hdbk10)
Juan Capistrano, San (Pub, v.4, no.3, p.149) *see also* Juaneño (LC)
Juan de Cabalenos, San *see* San Juan [NM]
Juan de los Caballeros, San *see* San Juan [NM]
Juaneño [CA] *Mission Indians* (LC)
Juaneño [Lang] [*Luiseño-Cahuilla*] (Pub, v.4, no.3, pp.149–150)
Juaneño [Lang] [*Luiseño-Kawia*] (H)
Juaneros, San *see* San Juan [NM]
Juaners, San *see* Saint Lawrence [Eskimos]
Juan Paiute, San [AZ] (JCB, v.5, nos.1/2, Sum./Win.1983, pp.199–207)
Juan Quivira *see* Tabira
Juaquialan *see* Joqualan
Juchium *see* Uchium
Jueinzum *Coahuiltecan* (BE)
Jugelnute [AK] *Kaiyuhkhotana* (H)
Jugelnuten *see* Jugelnute
Jugelnuts *see* Jugelnute
Ju-i *see* Penateka
Jui *see* Penateka
Juichen [CA] *Costanoan* (H)
Juina Kitaunlhu *see* Nambicuara

Juke-yunke see Yugeuinegge
Jukeyunke see Yugeuinegge
Jukiusme [CA] Moquelumnan (H)
Jukumani [BO] (LC)
Juliam see Sulujame
Julianehaab Greenland Eskimos
  (BE)
Julime [MX] Concho (BE)
Julimeño [MX] (H)
Juma (H) see also Jumano (LC)
Juma (H) see also Yuma (LC)
Juma [Br] (O)
Juma [Lang] [Br] Panoan (O)
Jumana see Jumano
Jumana see Tawehash
Jumane see Jumano
Jumane see Tawehash
Jumano (H) see also Tawehash
  (BE)
Jumano [MX, TX] (LC)
Jume see Hume
Jumee see Hume
Jumez see Jemez
Jumpanguaymas see Upan-
  guayma
Jumpers see Chippewa
Jum-pys see Yavapai
Jumpys see Yavapai
Juna see Pamoa
Junachotana see Unakhotana
Junakachotana see Unakhotana
Juncata see Juanca
Juncatas Coahuiltecan (BE)
Junced Coahuiltecan (BE)
Juncks'es see Tunxis
Juneauta see Juniata
Junetre see Tajique
Juni see Zuni
Juniata [PA] (H)
Juniguis see Serrano
Junikuin [Self-designation] see
  Cashinawa
Junin [PE] (O)
Junnachotana see Unakhotana
Junnakachotana see
  Koyukukhotana
Junnaka-chotana see
  Koyukukhotana
Junnakachotana see Unakhotana
Juntunen Culture (BE)
Jupangueimas see Upanguayma
Juparivi see Shipaulovi
Jupda [SA] Macu (LC)
Jupde see Macu
Jupe see Disakana
Jupichiya [Self-designation] see
  Matapi
Jupurina see Ipurina
Jurame see Xarame
Juris, Juris see San Emidio
Juruhuna see Yuruna
Jurumi [Col] Yucuna (O)
Juruti see Yuruti

Juskwaugume see Nipissing
Jut joat see Ute
Jyuo-tyu-te Oj-ke see San Juan
  [NM]

-K-

Ka-ack see Kake
Kaack see Kake
Kaadg ett ee see Katchandi
Kaadgettee see Katchandi
Kaadi see Kadohadacho
Kaadnaas-hadai [Clan] [AK]
  Haida (H)
Kaady-ett-ee see Katchadi
Kaadyettee see Katchadi
Ka-ah see Kau [Clan]
Ka-ai see Konglo
Kaai see Konglo
Kaake [Can] Salish (BE)
Kaake [Lang] Comox (BE)
Kaana [Clan] [NM] Taos (H)
Kaana-taiina see Kaana
Ka anjou see Kansa
Kaanjou see Kansa
Ka anzou see Kansa
Kaanzou see Kansa
Ka'aor see Urubu
Kaapo see Tuerto
Kaapor see Urubu
Kaas-ka-qua-tee see Kaskakoedi
Kaba [Br] Cinta Larga (O)
Ka-bah-seh see Kabaseh
Kabahseh [Clan] Abnaki (H)
Kabalemomowi Guahibo (O)
Kabasa see Kabahseh
Kabaye (H) see also Cabia (BE)
Kabaye [TX] (H)
Ka-bi-na-pek see Khabenapo
Kabinapek see Khabenapo
Kabiriari see Cabiyari
Kabishiana see Kabixiana
Kabixi (O) see also Sarare (O)
Kabixi [Br] (O)
Kabixiana [Br] (O)
Kabiyar see Cabiyari
Kabiyeri see Cabiyari
Kabo [NI] Mosquito (BE)
Kacaskia see Kaskaskia
Kacchiquel see Cakchikel
ka-ce-kwe-su see Eskimos
kacekwesu see Eskimos
Kacha-Pomo [CA] River Pomo
  (Pub, v.36, no.6)
Kacharadi see Kaxarari
Kacharari see Kaxarari
Ka-che-kone-a-we-so-uk see
  Ketchigumiwisuwugi
Kachekoneawesouk see Ketchigu-
  miwisuwugi

Kachgiya [Clan] Knaiakhotana
  (H)
Ka-chi-e see Kechayi
Kachie see Kechayi
Kachina [Clan] Hano (H)
Kachina-towa see Kachina
Kachkachkia see Kaskaskia
Kachkaska see Kaskaskia
Ka-cho-'dtinne see Kawchottine
Kachodtinne see Kawchottine
Kacht'ya see San Felipe [Keres]
Kacia [CA] Southwestern Pomo
  (Pub, v.40, no.2)
ka-ciku-su see Eskimos
kacikusu see Eskimos
Kackapoes see Kickapoo
Kaclasko see Wasco
Kacouchakhi see Kakouchaki
Kadakaman [BaC] Laimon (H)
Kadapau see Catawba
Kadapaw see Catawba
K'adas ke'e'owai see Kadusgo-
  ketawai
Kadaskeeowai see Kadusgo-
  kegawai
Kaddepaw see Catawba
Kaddipeaw see Catawba
Kaddo see Kadohadacho
Ka-di see Kadohadacho
Kadi see Kadohadacho
Kadiagmuts see Kaniagmiut
Kad'iak see Koniag
Kadiak see Kaniagmiut
Kadiak see Koniag
Kad'iakfsy see Koniag
Kadiakfsy see Koniag
Kadiakia see Kaniagmiut
Kad'iakskii see Koniag
Kadiakskii see Koniag
Kadiaski see Kaniagmiut
Kadieo see Caduveo
Kadieueu see Caduveo
Kadiko see Tonkawa
Kadiu-Diapa [Lang] Catoquina
  (O)
Kadiweu see Caduveo
Kadjacken see Kaniagmiut
Kadjakians see Kangmaligmiut
Kado see Kadohadacho
Kadodakio see Kadohadacho
Kadodakious see Kadohadacho
Kadodaquious see Kadohadacho
Ka-dohada'cho see Kadohadacho
Kadohadacho [TX, AR] (BE)
Kadohadacho Confederacy (BE)
Kaduapuritana [Col] Wakueni
  (O)
Kadusgo-kegawai [Clan] [BC]
  Haida (H)
Kaduveo see Caduveo
Kaduwot-kedi see Hlukahadi
Kaekibi [NM] Hopi (H)
Kaenna see Kainah

Kaernermiout *see* Qairnirmiut
Kaeso *see* Carrizo [MX]
Kaetage *see* Kein
Ka-e-ta-je *see* Kein
Kaetaje *see* Kein
Kaeyah-Khatana *see* Kaiyuhkhotana
Kafoka *see* Ka-foka
Ka-foka *Eastern Pomo* (Pub, v.29, no.4)
Kagaba [Col] (LC)
Kagagi (H) *see also* Kakake (H)
Kagagi [Clan] *Chippewa* (H)
Kagahanin [Clan] *Caddo Confederacy* (H)
Ka'g'aih *see* Kagaih
Kagaih [Clan] *Caddo Confederacy* (H)
Kaga'kwisuwag *see* Kagakwisuwag
Kagakwisuwug [Clan] *Sauk and Fox* (H)
K'agan hit tan *see* Kaganhittan
Kaganhittan [AK] *Tlingit* (H)
Kagataya-Koungins *see* Aleuts
Kaggaba *see* Kagaba
Kagiats-kegawai [Clan] *Haida* (H)
Kagiciwuinuwuk Indians *see* Katepoisipi-wiinuuk
Ka gmalik *see* Kangmaligmiut
Kagmalik *see* Kangmaligmiut
Kagmalirmiut [AK] *Eskimos* (BE)
Kagmallirmiut [AK] *North Alaska Coast Eskimos* (Hdbk5)
Kagotan *see* Kagwantan
Kagouse *see* Cayuse
Kagwahib *see* Kawahib
Kagwahiv (O) SE Kawahib (O)
Ka'gwantan *see* Kagwantan
Kagwantan [AK] *Tlingit* (H)
K'agyalsk-e'owai *see* Kagials-kegawai
Kagyalskeowai *see* Kagials-kegawai
Kah *see* Kansa
Ka-ha-bi *see* Kahabi
Kahabi [Clan] *Hopi* (H)
Kahansuk [NJ, DE] *Unalachtigo* (BE)
Kah-cho tinne *see* Kawchottine
Kahcottine *see* Kawchottine
Ka'heaheawastsik *see* Cheyenne
Kahelamit *see* Cathlamet
Kahepaia *see* Cofan
Kahepain *see* Cofan
Ka-he-ta-ni-o *see* Khahitan
Kahetanio *see* Khahitan
Kahinoa *see* Cahinnio
Kahk-ah-mah-tsis *see* Hahamatse
kahkoestseataneo'o *see* Flathead
Kah-Kwah *see* Erie
Kahkwah *see* Erie

Kahkwas *see* Neutral Nation
Kahl [Clan] *Hopi* (H)
Kahlchanedi [AK] *Tlingit* (H)
Kahlguihlgahet-gitinai [BC] *Haida* (H)
Kahligua-gitinai [Sub-clan] [BC] *Haida* (H)
Kah-lis-pelm *see* Kalispelm
Kahlispelm *see* Kalispelm
Kahmetahwungaguma [MN, ND, SD] *Chippewa* (H)
Kahmi-atonwan *see* Kakhmiatonwan
Kah-milt-pah *see* Camiltpaw
Kahmiltpah *see* Camiltpaw
Kah-mi-taiks *see* Kahmitaiks
Kahmitaiks [MN] *Piegan* (BE)
Kahna *see* Kainah
Kahokia *see* Cahokia
Kahoquia *see* Cahokia
Ka'hosadi *see* Shasta
Kahosadi [OR] *Shasta* (BE)
Ka'hpagi *see* Quapaw
Kahpagi *see* Quapaw
Kah-po *see* Santa Clara [NM]
Kahpo *see* Santa Clara [NM]
Kah-po-sia *see* Kapozha
Kahposia *see* Kapozha
Kahpozhah *see* Kapozha
Kahpozhay *see* Kapozha
Kahquas *see* Erie
Kahra [MN] *Sisseton* (H)
Kahruk *see* Karok
Ka-hua-i-ko *see* Laguna
Kahuaiko *see* Laguna
Kahuene *see* Kohuana
Kahuilla *see* Cahuilla
Kahuilla *see* Kawia [Luiseño]
Kahvichpak *see* Ikogmiut
Kahvichpaks *see* Unakhotana
Kahwan [Lang] *Delta Yuman* (Hdbk10)
Kah-we-a *see* Kawia [Luiseño]
Kahwea *see* Kawia [Luiseño]
Kahweah *see* Kawia [Yokuts]
Kahweak *see* Cahuilla
Kahweak *see* Kawia [Luiseño]
Kah-we-as *see* Cahuilla
Kahwe'n *see* Kahwan
Kahweyah *see* Kawia [Luiseño]
Kah-wis-sah *see* Kawaiisu
Kahwissah *see* Kawaiisu
Kai [Clan] *Navajo* (H)
Kaiabi *see* Kayabi
Kaiaby *see* Kayabi
Kaiaganies *see* Kaigani
Kaiahl-lanas [Clan] [BC] *Haida* (H)
Kaialigamut *see* Kaialigmiut
Kaialigmiut (BE) *see also* Kayaligmiut (Hdbk5)
Kaialigmiut [AK] *Eskimos* (BE)
Kai-a-lig-mut *see* Kaialigmiut

Kaialigmut *see* Kaialigmiut
Kaialigmute *see* Kayaligmiut
Kaialigumute *see* Kayaligmiut
Kaialligmiute (Hdbk5) *see also* Kayaligmiut (Hdbk5)
Kaiapo *see* Cayapo
K-ai-atl la'nas *see* Kaiahl-lanas
Kaiatllanas *see* Kaiahl-lanas
Kaiawa *see* Kiowa
Kaibab [UT] *Southern Paiute* (BE)
Kai-bab-bit *see* Kaibab
Kaibabbit *see* Kaibab
Kaibabit *see* Kaibab
Kaibab-its *see* Kaibab
Kaich *see* Koso
Kaichichekaiya (Pub, v.20, no.6, p.107)
Kai-da-toi-ab-ie *see* Kaidatoiabie
Kaidatoiabie [NV] *Paviotso* (H)
Kaidine *see* Kai [Clan]
Kaidju-kegawai [BC] *Haida* (H)
Ka'i-e *see* Kau
Kaie *see* Kau
Kai-e-na *see* Kainah
Kaiena *see* Kainah
Kaigan *see* Kaigani
K!aiga'ni *see* Kaigani
Kaigani [AK] *Haida* (BE)
Kaigans *see* Kaigani
Kaiganskoi *see* Kaigani
Kaigwa *see* Kiowa
Kai-gwa *see* Kiowa
Ka-i-gwu *see* Kiowa
Ka'igwu *see* Kiowa
Kaigwu *Kiowa* (BE)
Ka-ih *see* Kein
Kaih *see* Kein
Kaihatin [Clan] *Apache* (H)
Kaiihl-lanas [BC] *Haida* (H)
Kaiipa *see* Santa Clara [NM]
Kai-it-ko-ki-ki-naks *see* Ahkaiyikokakiniks
Kaiitkokikinaks *see* Ahkaiyikokakiniks
Kaijous *see* Cayuse
Kaikichekaiya *Wailaki* (Pub, v.20, no.6, p.107)
Kaikoma *see* Sinkyone
Kaimbe [Br] (O)
Kaime (H) *see also* Kainah (LC)
Kai-me *see* Kaime
Kaime (O) *see also* Witoto (LC)
Kaime [CA] *Pomo* (H)
Kai-na *see* Kainah
Kaina *see* Kainah
Kainah (LC) *see also* Bloods (BE)
Kainah [Can] *Siksika* (LC)
Kai-nama *see* Gallinomero
Kainama *see* Gallinomero
Kai-na-meah *see* Gallinomero
Kainameah *see* Gallinomero
Kai-na-me-ro *see* Gallinomero

Kainamero *see* Gallinomero
Kai'nau *see* Kainah
Kainau *see* Kainah
Kaingang *see* Kaingangue
Kaingangue [Br] (LC)
Kaingua *see* Caingua
Kainhkhotana *see* Kaiyuhkhotana
Kainoe-koon *see* Kainah
Kai-no-meah *see* Gallinomero
Kainomeah *see* Gallinomero
Kainomero *see* Gallinomero
Kaiova [Br] (O)
Kai-o-wa *see* Kiowa
Kaiowa *see* Kiowa
Kaiowan *see* Kiowa
Kaiowe *see* Kiowa
Kai'p'a *see* Santa Clara [NM]
kaipa *see* Santa Clara [NM]
kaipaa *see* Santa Clara [NM]
kaipa-picicimi *see* Kaibab
Kaiparowits *Southern Paiute*
    (Hdbk11)
Kai Pomo *see* Kato
Kaiquariegahaga (BE)
Kaiquariegahaga *see* Contestoga
Kairaikome *see* Laguna
Kaispa *see* Dakota
Kaitana *see* Knaiakhotana
Kaitc *see* Panamint
K'a'itchin *see* Cowichan
Kait-ka *see* Calapooya
Kaitka *see* Calapooya
Kaitlen *see* Kwantlen
Kaitze *see* Katsey
Kaivanungavidukw (H) *see also*
    Kidutokado (Hdbk11)
Kai-va-nung-av-i-dukw *see*
    Kaivanungavikukw
Kaivanungavidukw [CA] *Paviotso*
    (H)
Kaivavwit *see* Kaibab
Kai-vav-wits *see* Kaibab
Kaiviat-am *see* Serrano
Kai-vwav-uai Nu-ints *see* Kaibab
Kaivwavuainuits *see* Kaibab
Kai-wa *see* Kiowa
Kaiwa (PC) *see also* Kiowa (LC)
Kaiwa [Br, Par] (O)
Kaiwaika *see* Laguna
Kai-wane *see* Kiowa
Kaiwane *see* Kiowa
Kaiwiem *Serrano* (Pub, v.26)
Kaiyau [CA] (H)
Kaiyekiyahang *Wailaki* (Pub,
    v.20, no.6, p.96)
Kaiyuhkatana *see* Kaiyuhkhotana
Kai-Yuh-Kho-Ta'Na *see*
    Kaiyuhkhotana
Kaiyuhkho-tana *see*
    Kaiyuhkhotana
Kaiyuhkhotana [AK] (BE)
Kaiyuhkhotenne *see* Kaiyuh-
    kho-tenne

Kaiyuh-kho-tenne *Loucheux* (H)
Kaiyuk-a-kho-tan'a *see*
    Kaiyuhkhotana
Kaiyukhotana *see* Kaiyuhkhotana
Kajabi *see* Kayabi
Ka-jech-adi *see* Kajechadi
Kajechadi [AK] *Tlingit* (H)
Kaji *see* Kichai
Kajingahaga *see* Mohawk
Kaj-Kai *see* San Juan [NM]
Kajkai *see* San Juan [NM]
Ka-ka *see* Kaka
Kaka (LC) *see also* Cacan (LC)
Kaka *Arikara* (H)
Kakachkiouek *see* Kaskaskia
Ka-kag-she *see* Kakagshe
Kakagshe [Clan] *Potawatomi* (H)
Ka-kaik *see* Kakake
Kakaik *see* Kakake
Ka-ka-i-thi *see* Salish
Kakaithi *see* Salish
Kakak *see* Kaka'k
Kaka'k [Clan] *Crow* (H)
Ka-kake *see* Kakake
Kakake [Clan] *Chippewa* (H)
Ka-ka-kwis-so-uk *see* Kagak-
    wisuwug
Kakakwissouk *see* Kagakwisuwug
Kakamatsis *see* Hahamatse
Ka-kan *see* Kakhan
Kakan *see* Cacan
Kakan *see* Kakhan
Kakana *see* Cacan
Kakanikone Tusininiwug *see*
    Kaka'nikone Tusi-niniwug
Kaka'nikone Tusi-niniwug [WI]
    Menominee (BE)
Kakapakato Wininiwuk *see*
    Kaka'pa'kato Wini'niwuk
Kaka'pa'kato Wini'niwuk [WI]
    Menimonee (BE)
Kakapoya (H) *see also* Inuks-
    sikahikipwaiks (BE)
Ka-ka-po-ya *see* Kakapoya
Kakapoya *Piegan* (H)
Kakaskigi *see* Kaskaskia
Kakasky *see* Kaskaskia
Kakawatilikya [Gens] *Tsawatenok*
    (H)
Kakchiquel *see* Cakchikel
Kake [AK] *Tlingit* (BE)
Kakega *see* Kakegha
Kakegha *Brule* (H)
Kakekt [VanI] *Salish* (BE)
Kak'exa *see* Kakegha
Kakexa *see* Kakegha
Kakhan [Clan] [NM] *Laguna* (H)
Kakhan-hanoch *see* Kakhan
Kakhmiatonwan *Sisseton* (H)
Kakhuana *see* Cajuenche
Kaki [Br] *Cinta Larga* (O)
Kakia *see* Caholia
Kakick [TN, AL] (H)

Kakigue *see* Kakick
Kakima *see* Kiakima
kaki-ma *see* Kiakima
Kakinonba [KY] (H)
kakkakkia *see* Kaskaskia
Kakmalikg *see* Kangmaligmiut
Ka-ko-is-tsi-a-ta-ni-o *see* Salish
Kakoistsiatanio *see* Salish
kakora *see* Pecos
Kakoshittan *see* Kakos-hit-tan
Kakouagoga *see* Neutral Nation
Kakouchac *see* Kakouchaki
Kakouchakhi *see* Kakouchaki
Kakouchaki (H) *see also* Piek-
    ouagami (H)
Kakouchaki [Q] *Montagnais* (H)
Kaksatis *see* Kiksadi
Kakso-hit-tan [AK] *Shunkukedi*
    (H)
Kaktsik [OR] (Shasta)
Kakus *see* Kake
Kakwa [Col, Br] *Macu* (O)
Kakwa [NA] *see* Erie
Kak-wits *see* Wailaki
Kakwits *see* Wailaki
kalaaleq [Self-designation] *see*
    Greenland Eskimos
kalaallit *see* Greenland Eskimos
kalaallit *see* West Greenlanders
Ka-la-ci-au-u *see* Kalashiauu
Kalaciauu *see* Kalashiauu
Kaladlit *see* Greenland Eskimos
Kalalik *see* Greenland Eskimos
Kalalit *see* Greenland Eskimos
Ka-la-muh *see* Shuswap
Kalamuh *see* Shuswap
Kalapalo (LC) *see also* Apalakiri
    (LC)
Kalapalo [Lang] [*Kakairi-
    Nahukwa*] (UAz, v.28)
Kalapooiah *see* Calapooya
Kalapooian [Lang] [OR] (BE)
Kalapooya *see* Calapooya
Kalapooyah *see* Calapooya
Kalapouya *see* Calapooya
Kalapuaya *see* Calapooya
Kalapuya (H) *see also* Calapooya
    (BE)
Kalapuyan *see* Kalapuya
Kalashiauu [Clan] *Hopi* (H)
Kalatdlisut [Lang] *Greenland Es-
    kimos* (LC)
Kalatekoe *see* Kilatika
Kala-Walset *see* Kalawatset
Kalawatset [PacN] (H)
Kalawatshet *see* Kalawatset
Kalespel *see* Kalispel
Kalespilium *see* Kalispel
Kalespilum *see* Kalispel
Kali [Clan] [AK] (H)
Kaliana [VE] (O)
Kalino [Self-designation] *see*
    Carib

Kalinya *see* Carib
Ka-lis-cha *see* San Felipe [Keres]
Kalischa *see* San Felipe [Keres]
Kalispel [ID] (LC)
Kalispel [Lang] *Interior Salish*
  (BE)
Kalispelim *see* Kalispel
Kalispeline *see* Kalipsel
Kalispell *see* Kalispel
Kalispelm *see* Kalispel
Kalispelum *see* Kalispel
Kalispelusses *see* Kalispel
Kalistcha *see* San Felipe [Keres]
Ka-lis-te-no *see* Cree
Kalisteno *see* Cree
Kaljuschen *see* Tlingit
Kalka'lak [WA] *Puyallup* (BE)
Kallapoea *see* Calapooya
Kallapooyah *see* Calapooya
Kallapuga *see* Calapooya
Kallawaya *see* Callahuaya
Kalmath *see* Klamath
Kalmish, St. *see* Sekamish
Kal-namu *see* Kahl
Kalnamu *see* Kahl
Kalokta [Clan] [NM] *Zuni* (H)
Ka'lokta-kwe *see* Kalokta
Kaloosas *see* Calousa [CA]
Kaloosas *see* Calusa [FL]
Kaloshes *see* Tlingit
Kaloshians *see* Tlingit
Ka-lox-la-tce *see* Kadohadacho
Kaloxlatce *see* Kadohadacho
Kaltsergheatunne [OR] *Tututni*
  (H)
Kal-ts'e-rxe-a tunne *see* Kalt-
  sergheatunne
Kaltserxeatunne *see* Kaltserghea-
  tunne
Kalusa *see* Calousa [CA]
Kalusa *see* Calusa [FL]
Kaluschian *see* Tlingit
Kalu-xnadshu *see* Kadohadacho
Kalu-xnad-shu *see* Kadohadacho
Kaluxnadshu *see* Kadohadacho
Kama *see* Cacua
Kama *see* Kakawa
Kamadeni [Br] *Dani* (O)
Kamaiura [Br] (LC)
Kamakan [Lang] [Br] (O)
Kam-a-lel Pomo *see* Usal
Kamalel Pomo *see* Usal
Kamaloo'la-pa *see* Kamloop
Ka-man-tci *see* Comanche
Kamantci *see* Comanche
Kamaracoto *see* Puricoto
Kamarakoto *see* Camaracoto
Kamaru [Br] *Kariri* (O)
Kamayura *see* Kamaiura
Kambeba *see* Omagua
Kambiwa [Br] (O)
Kamdot [CA] *Southeastern Pomo*
  (Pub, v.36, no.6)

Kameintza *see* Camsa [Lang]
Kamentxa *see* Camsa
Kamia (H) *see also* Comeya (H)
Kamia (H) *see also* Diegueño (LC)
Kamia (H) *see also* Kamiah (H)
Kamia [CA, MX] (LC)
Kamia [Lang] [CA] *Yuman* (He)
Kamia-ahwe *see* Diegueño
Kamia-akhwe *see* Comeya
Kamiah [ID] *Nez Perce* (H)
Kamiai *see* Kamia
Kamiaxpu [ID] *Nez Perce* (BE)
kam-idikadi *see* Kamodokado
kamidikadi *see* Kamodokado
Kamillary *see* Cabiyari
Kamilt-pah *see* Camiltpaw
Kamiltpah *see* Camiltpaw
Kamiskwa-wa'ku'ka-wininuwag
  see Gamiskwakokawininiwak
Kamiskwawa'ku'ka-winiwiwag *see*
  Gamiskwakokawininiwak
Kamiyahi *see* Diegueño
Kamiyahi *see* Kamia
Kamiyai *see* Diegueño
Kamiyai *see* Kamia
Kamloop [BC] *Shuswap* (BE)
Kamloops Division [BC] *Shuswap*
  (Hdbk12)
Kammack *see* Kammuck
Kammas Prairie Tribe *see*
  Tukuarika
Kammat'wa *see* Kammatwa
Kammatwa [CA] *Shasta* (BE)
Kammedeka *Northern Shoshone*
  (Hdbk11)
kammitikka *see* Kammedeka
Kammuck [BC] *Salish* (H)
Kam-ne *see* Kainah
Kamne *see* Kainah
Kamodokado *Northern Paiute*
  (Hdbk11)
Kampa *see* Campa
Kamsa *see* Camsa
Kamse *see* Kansa
Kamuduka (Bull120) *see also* Ban-
  nock Creek Shoshone (Bull120)
Kamuduka *see* Kamu duka [ID]
  Shoshone
Kamu duka [ID] *Shoshone* (An-
  thro, v.8, no.3)
Kamu-inu *see* Nez Perce
kamu'tukede *see* Tasiget tuvi-
  warai
Kamutukede *see* Tasiget tuvi-
  warai
Kamya *see* Kamia
Kan [Clan] [*San Juan (NM)*] (H)
Kanaa *see* Conoy
Kanaai *see* Conoy
Kanaatino *see* Kanohatino
Kanach-adi *see* Ganahadi
Kanach-tedi *see* Ganahadi
Kanagist *see* Koniag

Kanai *see* Conoy
Kanaizer *see* Tinne
Kanamanti [BR] (O)
Kanamara *see* Gallinomero
Kanamari [Br] (O)
Kanamari *Tamanawa* (O)
Ka'nani *see* Kanani
Kanani [Clan] *Navajo* (H)
Ka-nan-in *see* Arikara
Kananin *see* Arikara
Kanastoge *see* Conestoga
Kanatat *see* Klikitat
kanati-cimi *see* Kaibab
Kanawa (BE)
Kanawa (BE) *see also* Conoy (LC)
Kanawa (H) *see also* Cayuga (LC)
Kanawa (H) *see also* Mohawk
  (LC)
Kan-Ayko *see* Laguna
Kan-ayko *see* Sitsime
Kanayko *see* Laguna
Kanayko *see* Sitsime
Kancas *see* Kansa
Kances *see* Kansa
Kancho *see* Kawchottine
Ka-nc za-wa *see* Kanwasowaua
Kanczawa *see* Kanwasowaua
Kandankaiya *see* K'andankaiya
K'andankaiya [CA] (Pub, v.20,
  no.6)
Kandoshi *see* Candoshi
K'an-dzi *see* Lipan Apache
Kandzi *see* Lipan Apache
Ka'neahea-wastsik *see* Cheyenne
Kaneaheawastsik *see* Cheyenne
Ka'neaheawatsik *see* Cheyenne
Kanela *see* Canela [Eastern Tim-
  bira]
Kanela *see* Canella
Kanela *see* Canelo [EC]
Kaneskies *see* Knaiakhotana
Kang [Clan] *Tewa* (H)
Kangamiut *Greenland Eskimos*
  (BE)
Kangatsiak *Greenland Eskimos*
  (BE)
Kangerdlugsiatsiak *Greenland Es-
  kimos* (BE)
Kangguatl-lanas [Sub-clan] *Haida*
  (H)
Kanghiryuachiakmiut [Can] *Cen-
  tral Eskimos* (BE)
Kanghiryuarmiut [Can] *Central
  Eskimos* (BE)
Kanghishunpegnaka *Sihasapa* (H)
Kanghiyuha *Brule* (H)
Kangialis *see* Kangmaligmiut
Kangianirmiut *North Alaska Coast
  Eskimos* (Hdbk5)
Kangigmiut *Kotzebue Sound Eski-
  mos* (Hdbk5)
Kangikhlukhmut [AK] *Ahtena*
  (BE)

Kang-iq-xlu-q'mut *see* Kangikhlukhmut

Kangiqxluqmut *see* Kangikhlukhmut

Kangirlugyarmiut [AK] *Igluling-miut* (Hdbk5)

kangirsualujjuag *see* Kangiva

kangirsuk *see* Payne Inuit

Kangite *see* Ipurina

Kangiti *see* Ipurina

Kangitoka *see* Crow

Kangiugdlit *see* Kangmaligmiut

kangiva [Can] [*Inuit (Quebec)*] (Hdbk5)

kangivamiut [Can] [*Inuit (Quebec)*] (Hdbk5)

Kangivamiut [Can] *Sukinimiut Eskimos* (H)

Kan-gi-wi-ca-sa *see* Crow

Kangiwicasa *see* Crow

Kan-gi yu-ha *see* Kanghiyuha

Kangi-yuha *see* Kanghiyuha

Kangjulit *see* Chnagmiut

Kangmali-enyui *see* Kangmaligmiut

Kangmalienyui *see* Kangmaligmiut

Kangmaligmeut *see* Kangmaligmiut

Kangmaligmiut [AK] *Arctic Eskimos* (H)

Kangmalig-mut *see* Eskimos

Kangmalig-mut *see* Innuit

Kangmali'gmut *see* Kangmaligmniut

Kangmaligmut *see* Kangmaligmiut

Kangmaligmut *see* Innuit

Kang-ma'li-innuin *see* Kopagmiut

Kangmali-innuin *see* Kangmaligmiut

Kangmaliinnuin *see* Kangmaligmiut

Kangoot Mute *see* Kungugemiut

Kangootmute *see* Kungugemiut

Kangormiut [Can] *Central Eskimos* (H)

Kang-orr-Moeoot *see* Kangormiut

Kangorrmoeoot *see* Kangormiut

K'anguatl la'nai *see* Kangguatllanas

Kanguatllanai *see* Kangguatllanas

Kan-gukelua'luksoagmyut *see* Kangivamiut

Kangukelualuksoagmyut *see* Kangivamiut

Kangutu *see* Ipurina

Kanhada [Clan] *Chimmesyan* (H)

Kanhadda *see* Kanhada

Kanhatki *see* Kan-hatki

Kan-hatki [FL, AL] *Muskogee* (BE)

Kanhawa *see* Conoy

Kanhaway *see* Conoy

Ka'nhe'nko *see* Carrizo [MX]

Kanhenko *see* Carrizo [MX]

Kanhobal *see* Kanjobal

Kanhutyi [Clan] [MN] *Atsina* (BE)

Ka-ni (H) *see also* Koni (H)

Kani *see* Ka-ni

Ka-ni [CA] *Miwok* (H)

Kaniagi *see* Kaniagmiut

Kaniagi *see* Koniag

Kaniagist *see* Kaniagmiut

Kaniagmiut (Hdbk5) *see also* Koniag (Hdbk5)

Kaniagmiut [AK] *Eskimos* (LC)

Kaniagmut *see* Kaniagmiut

Kaniag-mut *see* Kaniagmiut

Kanianermiut [AK] *Eskimos* (BE)

Kaniapiskau [Can] [*Montagnais-Naskapi*] (BE)

Kaniba *see* Norridgewock

Kaniba *see* Kennebec

Kanibals *see* Norridgewock

Kanibat *see* Norridgewock

Kanibat *see* Kennebec

Kanibesinnoak *see* Norridgewock

Kanibesinnoak *see* Kennebec

Kanibessinnoak *see* Norridgewock

Kanichana *see* Canichana

Kanieke-haka *see* Mohawk

Kaniengehaga [Self-designation] *see* Mohawk

Kanienge-onon *see* Mohawk

Kaniengeonon *see* Mohawk

Kanikaligamut [AK] *Knaiakhotana* (H)

Kanikgmut *see* Kungugemiut

Kanimare *see* Gallinomero

Kanimarre *see* Gallinomero

Kanim Lake *see* Kenim Lake

Ka'nina *see* Havasupai

Kanina *see* Havasupai

Kaninahoic *see* Arapaho

Kaninahoich *see* Arapaho

Kaninahoish *see* Arapaho

Kaninavish *see* Arapaho

Kaninim Lake *see* Kenim Lake

Kaninis' Tribe *see* Kenim Lake

Ka-nip-sum *see* Kenipsim

Kanipsum *see* Kenipsim

Ka'ni-qa-li-ga-mut *see* Kanikaligamut

Kaniqaligamut *see* Kanikaligamut

Kanisiana *see* Canichana

Kanisky *see* Knaiakhotana

Kanit *see* Mandan

Kanithlualukshuamiut [Can] *Labrador Eskimos* (BE)

Kaniulit *see* Ekogmiut

Kaniulit *see* Chnagmiut

Kanjagi *see* Koniag

K'anjobal *see* Kanjobal

Kanjobal [Gua] *Western Mayan* (LC)

Kan'ka *see* Ponca

Kanka *see* Ponca

Kañ'kan *see* Ponca

Kankan *see* Ponca

Kankau *see* Konkow

Kankaways *see* Tonkawa

Kankete *see* Ipurina

Kankiti *see* Ipurina

Kankuna *see* Knaiakhotana

Kankunats kogtana *see* Knaiakhotana

Kank'utla'atlam *see* Okinagan

Kankutlaatlam *see* Okinagan

Kanlax [BC] *Upper Lillooet* (H)

Kanmali-enyuin *see* Kangmaligmiut

Kan-na *see* Kanna

Kanna [Clan] *Tuscarora* (H)

Kanneastoka-roneah *see* Conestoga

Kannehonan *see* Kannehouan

Kannehouan [TX] (H)

Kanoatina *see* Kanohatino

Kanoatinno *see* Kanohatino

Kanoatino *see* Kanohatino

Kanoe [Br] (O)

Kano Hatino *see* Kanohatino

Kanohatino [TX] (H)

Ka'noqtla'tlam *see* Kalispel

Kanoqtlatlam *see* Kalispel

Kanosh *Paiute* (Hdbk11)

Kanoutinoa *see* Kanohatino

Kanozawa [Clan] *Miami* (H)

Kanp-meut *see* Kangormiut

Kanpmeut *see* Kangormiut

Kanq-or-mi-ut *see* Kangormiut

Kanqormiut *see* Kangormiut

Kans *see* Kansa

Kansa [KS, OK] (LC)

Kansa [Lang] *Dhegiha* (H)

Kansae *see* Kansa

Kanse (H) *see also* Kansa (LC)

Kanse [Clan] *Osage* (H)

Kansez *see* Kansa

Kanshak *see* Creek

Kansies *see* Kansa

Kantcati *see* Kan-tcati

Kan-tcati [AL, FL] *Muskogee* (BE)

Kan-tdoa *see* Kang

Kantdoa *see* Kang

Kantha *see* Kansa

Kants *see* Kansa

Kantsi *see* Kiowa Apache

Kantsi *see* Lipan Apache

Kanuktlualuksoagmyut *see* Kangivamiut

Kanwasouwau *see* Kanozawa

Kanwasowaua [Clan] *Miami* (H)

Kanxi-cun-pegnaka *see* Kanghishunpegnaka

Kanxicunpegnaka *see* Kanghishunpegnaka

Kanxi-yuha *see* Kanghiyuha

Kanxiyuha *see* Kanghiyuha

Kanyag *see* Koniag

Kanykgmiut *see* Kangigmiut

Kanyuksa Istichati [FL] *Seminole* (H)

Kanzas *see* Kansa

Kanze (H) *see also* Kansa (LC)

Kanze [Clan] *Kansa* (H)

Kanze [Subgens] *Omaha* (H)

Kanzeis *see* Kansa

Kaockhia *see* Cahokia

Kaockia *see* Caholia

Kao-ke-owai *see* Aokeawai

Kaokeowai *see* Aokeawai

Kaokia *see* Cahokia

Kaokies *see* Cahokia

Kaons *see* Coos

Kaoquias *see* Cohokia

Kaouai *see* Salmon River

Kaouanoua *see* Kannehouan

Kaouechias *see* Cahokia

Kaoukia *see* Cahokia

Kaoulis *see* Cowlitz

Kapa *see* Quapaw

Kapaha *see* Quapaw

Kapaits [Phratry] [NM] *Laguna* (H)

Kapana *see* Yamamadi

Kapanahu *see* Capanahua

Kapanawa *see* Capanahua

K'a-pa'te *see* Apache

Kapate *see* Apache

K'a-pa-top *see* Kiowa Apache

K'a-patop *see* Kiowa Apache

K'a-patop *see* Apache

Kapatop *see* Apache

Kapatop *see* Kiowa Apache

Kap-ho *see* Santa Clara [NM]

Kapho *see* Santa Clara [NM]

Kapiekran *see* Ramkokamekra

Kapinamari *see* Yamamadi

Kapixana *see* Kanoe

Ka-po *see* Santa Clara [NM]

Ka-po *see* Tuerto

Kapo *see* Santa Clara [NM]

Kapo *see* Tuerto

Kapoga *see* Kapozha

Kapohn *Acawai* (O)

Kap'oja *see* Kapozha

Kapo'ja *see* Kapozha

Kapoja *see* Kapozha

Kapojay *see* Kapozha

Kapon [Self-designation] *see* Kapohn

Kapong *Acawai* (O)

Ka-Poo *see* Santa Clara [NM]

Kapoo *see* Santa Clara [NM]

Kaposia *see* Kapozha

Ka-po-sias *see* Kapozha

Kapota *see* Kapozha

Kapota *see* Capote

Kapoti *see* Capote

Ka-pou *see* Santa Clara [NM]

Kapou *see* Santa Clara [NM]

Ka-po-za *see* Kapozha

Kapoza *see* Kapozha

Kapozha [MN] *Mdewakanton* (H)

Kappa Akansea *see* Quapaw

Kappas *see* Quapaw

Kappaws *see* Quapaw

Kappawson-Arkansas *see* Quapaw

Ka-pu-lo *see* Kapulo

Kapulo [Clan] *Hano* (H)

Kapulo-towa *see* Kapulo

Kapung *see* Santa Clara [NM]

kapu-ta *see* Capote

Kap Yorker *see* Polar Eskimos

Kap York Eskimoer *see* Polar Eskimos

Kaqmi-atonwan *see* Kakhmia-tonwan

Karabayo [Col] (O)

Karadza *see* Caraja

Karaja *see* Caraja

Karajak *Greenland Eskimos* (BE)

Karakoenitanon *see* Coiracoentanon

Karakuka [Lang] [CA] (H)

Karaler *see* Eskimos

Karalit *see* Eskimos

Karamanta *see* Caramanta

Karamaracoto [*Parukoto-Pemon*] (O)

Karankawa [TX] (LC)

Karankawan [Lang] [TX] (H)

Karankaway *see* Karankawa

Karankoas *see* Karankawa

Karankoo-as *see* Karankawa

Karapana *see* Carapana

Karapana-Tapuya *see* Carapana

Kararaiho *see* Kararao

Kararao [Br] (O)

Ka-rasch-kidetan *see* Kayashkidetan

Karaschkidetan *see* Kayashkidetan

Karawaka [NI] *Panamaka* (BE)

Karawala [NI] *Panamaka* (BE)

Karaya *see* Caraja

Karekateye *see* Krenkateye

Kareneri *Mashco* (O)

Karese *see* Lipan Apache

Kareses *see* Kiowa Apache

Karezi (H)

Kar-gwan-ton *see* Kagwantan

Kargwanton *see* Kagwantan

Karhadage [Can] (H)

Karhagaghrooney [Q] (H)

Karhaski *see* Kaskaskia

Karib *see* Carib

Kariban *see* Cariban [Lang]

Karigouistes [Can] (H)

Karijona *see* Carijona

Kariko *Tonkawan* (BE)

Kariña [Lang] *Galibi* (UAz, v.28)

Kariña [Lang] *Western Carib* (UAz, v.28)

Kariña [VE, Br] (O)

Karinya (LC) *see also* Carib (LC)

Karinya *see* Kariña

Karipuna [Br] *Panoan* (O)

Karipuna [Br] *Tupi* (O)

Kariri [Br] (LC)

Kariri-Sapuya *see* Sapuya

Karitiana [Br] (LC)

Karkadia *see* Kaskaskia

Karkin [CA] (H)

Karkin [Lang] *Northern Costonoan* (CA-8)

Karkinonpois *see* Kakinonba

Karmowong *see* Kaumauangmiut

Karnijo *see* Fulnio

Karo *see* Gyazru

Karo *see* Arara

Karoa [MS] (LC)

Ka-rok *see* Karok

Karok [CA] (LC)

Karok [Lang] *Yana* (CA-8)

Karo-xnadshu *see* Kadohadacho

Karoxnadshu *see* Kadohadacho

Karquines *see* Karkin

Karrihaet [Can] (H)

Karro *see* Gyazru

Kar-sa *see* Kansa

Karsa *see* Kansa

Karsea *see* Kansa

Kartar [WA] *Sinkaietk* (BE)

Kartchottee [Family] *Tahltan* (H)

Karu [VE] *Wakunai* (O)

ka-ruk *see* Karok

Karuk *see* Karok

Karupaka *see* Wakuenai

Karutana [Br] *Baniva* (O)

Kar-wee-wee *see* Atsmitl

Karweewee *see* Atsmitl

Kasaha unun *see* Chickasaw

Kasahaunun *see* Chickasaw

Kasas *see* Kansa

Kaschke-kon *see* Kashkehoan

Kaschkekon *see* Kashkehoan

Kasgresquois *see* Kaskaskia

Kashahara [CA] *Wintun* (H)

Kashapaokla *see* Kushapokla

Kashap-ukla *see* Kushapokla

Kashapukla *see* Kushapokla

Kasharari *see* Kaxarari

Kash-a-woosh-ah *see* Kassovo

Kashawooshah *see* Kassovo

Kashawooshah *see* Nim

Kashaya [CA] *Pomo* (LC)

Kashinaua *see* Cashinawa

Kashinawa *see* Cashinawa

Kashiniti [Br] *Pareci* (O)
Kashkekoan [AL] *Tlingit* (H)
Kashuyana [Lang] [*East-West Guiana Carib*] (UAz, v.28)
Kasihta *Muskogee* (BE)
Kasispa [WA] *Palouse* (BE)
Kaska [BC] *Nahana* (LC)
Kaskaias *see* Kiowa Apache
Kaskaisas *see* Kaskaskia
Kaskaiska *see* Kaskaskia
Kaskakia *see* Kaskaskia
Kaskakies *see* Kaskaskia
Kaskakoedi *Tlingit* (H)
Kaskaroren *see* Tuscarora
Kaskascia *see* Kaskaskia
Kaskasia *see* Kaskaskia
Kaskaskey *see* Kaskaskia
Kaskaskia [IL] (LC)
Kaskaskian *see* Kaskaskia
Kaskaskies *see* Kaskaskia
Kaskasquia *see* Kaskaskia
Kaskaya *see* Kiowa Apache
Kaskia *see* Kiowa Apache
Kaskiha (O) *see also* Guana (LC)
Kaskiha [Par] (O)
Kaskinampo [TN] (BE)
Kaskkasies *see* Kaskaskia
Kaslanas *see* Kas-lanas
Kas-lanas [Family] *Haida* (H)
Kasnaikotkaiya [CA] (Pub, v.20, no.6)
Kasoongkta (H)
K'asq'ague'de *see* Kaskakoedi
Kasqaguede *see* Kaskakoedi
Kasq!akue'di *see* Kaskakoedi
Kasqakuedi *see* Kaskakoedi
Kasqui *see* Kaskaskia
Kasquias *see* Kaskaskia
Kasquinanipo *see* Kakinonba
Kasquuasquia *see* Kaskaskia
Kasseya *see* Kadohadacho
Kasseye-i *see* Kadohadacho
Kassiluda *see* Sandatoton
Kas-so-vo *see* Kassovo
Kassovo [CA] *Yokuts* (H)
Kassra-kuedi *see* Kaskakoedi
Kassrakuedi *see* Kaskakoedi
Kasta-kegawai *see* Daiyahl-lanas
Kastakegawai *see* Daiyahl-lanas
K'astak'e-rauai *see* Daiyuahl-lanas
Kastakerauai *see* Daiyahl-lahas
Kas-tel *see* Kastel Pomo
Kastel Pomo (H) *see also* Kato (LC)
Kastitchewanuk [NY] *Cree* (H)
Kasupa *see* Aikana
K'at'a *see* Kata
Kata *Kiowa* (BE)
Kataba *see* Catawba
Ka-ta-ge-ma-ne *see* Katagemane
Katagemane *Piegan* (H)
Kataghayekiki *see* Aleuts

Katagottine (BE) *see also* Chintagottine (BE)
Katagottine (H) *see also* Kawchottine (LC)
K'a-t'a-gottine *see* Kawchottine
Kat'a-got-tine *see* Kawchottine
Katagottine [AK] *Kawchodinne* (H)
Katagwadi [AK] *Tlingit* (H)
Katahba *see* Catawba
Katahka *see* Apache
Ka-ta-ka *see* Kiowa Apache
Kataka *see* Kiowa Apache
Katake *see* Kiowa Apache
Katalamet *see* Cathlamet
Kataubah *see* Catawba
Katawba *see* Catawba
Katawian [Br, Sur] (O)
Katawishi *see* Catoquina
Katawishi *see* Katawixi
Katawixi [Br] *Cataquina* (O)
Kataxka *see* Kiowa Apache
Katca [CA] *Northern Pomo* (Pub, v.40, no.2)
K atc'a'de *see* Katchadie
Katcade *see* Katchadi
Katce *see* Siksika
Katchadi [AK] *Tlingit* (H)
Katchadi *Kake* (H)
Katchan *see* Yuma
Katchekakuashiueu *see* Eskimos
K'a-tcho-gottine *see* Kawchogottine
Katchogottine (PC) *see also* Kawchogottine (BE)
Katchogottine [AK, Can] *Kawchodinne* (H)
Katco-Ottine *see* Kawchogottine
Kat-chu *see* Katsalgi
Katchu *see* Katsalgi
Ka-tci-na *see* Kachina
Katcina *see* Kachina
Ka-tci-na nyu-mu *see* Kachina
Katcina nyumu *see* Kachina
Katcina win-wu *see* Kachina
Ka-tci-na wun-wu *see* Kachina
Katcina wunwu *see* Kachina
Katditalhu [Br] *Southern Nambicuara* (O)
Kate *see* Kake
Katenuaka *see* Ka'te'nu'a'ka
Ka'te'nu'a'ka [NC] *Tuscarora* (BE)
Katepoisipi-wiinuuk [Can] *Paskwawininiwug* (BE)
Katezie *see* Katsey
Kathagi *see* Kansa
Kathlamet *see* Cathlamet
Kat-hlamet *see* Cathlamet
Kathlaminimim [OR] *Multnomah* (BE)
Kathlamit *see* Cathlamet

Kathlamut *see* Cathlamet
Kathlapootle *see* Cathlapotle
Kathlaram [BC] *Salish* (H)
Kathlarem *see* Kathlaram
Kathlemit *see* Cathlamet
Katihcha *see* San Felipe [Keres]
Katio *see* Catio
Ka-ti-ru *see* Katiru
Katiru [CA] *Shasta* (H)
katisca *see* San Felipe [Keres]
Ka-tish-tya *see* San Felipe [Keres]
Kat-ish-tya *see* San Felipe [Keres]
Katishtya *see* San Felipe [Keres]
Kat-ist-ya *see* San Felipe [Keres]
Katistya *see* San Felipe [Keres]
Ka-ti-tya *see* San Felipe [Keres]
Katitya *see* San Felipe [Keres]
Ka-ti-ya-ye-mix *see* Kutaiimiks
Katiyayemix *see* Kutaiimiks
Katkaayi [AK] *Tlingit* (H)
Katlagakya *see* Watlala
Katlagakya *see* Cascades
Katlagakya [Self-designation] *see* Shahala
Katlagulak [OR] *Chinookan* (H)
Katlamak *see* Cathlamet
Katlamat *see* Cathlamet
Katlaminim *see* Kathlaminimim
Katlammet *see* Cathlamet
Katlamoik [OR] *Chinookan* (H)
Katlaportl *see* Cathlapotle
Katlawewalla *see* Clowwewalla
Katluchtna [Clan] *Knaiahkhotana* (H)
K'at nas had'a'i *see* Kaadnaas-hadai
Katnashadai *see* Kaadnaas-hadai
Kato [CA] (LC)
Kato [CA] *Kuneste* (H)
Kato [Lang] [CA] *Wailaki* (He)
Ka-to pomo *see* Kato
Katowa *see* Cherokee
Katsalgi [Clan] *Creek* (H)
Katschadi *see* Katchadi
Katsey [Can] *Stalo* (BE)
katshekuashueu *see* Eskimos
Ka-tshik-otin *see* Katshikotin
Katshikotin [AK] *Han* (BE)
Katskil *see* Catskill
Katskill *see* Catskill
Kattahawkee *see* Kitkehahki
Kattanahaw *see* Kutenai
Kattarbe *see* Catawba
Kattaupa *see* Catawba
Katteka *see* Kiowa Apache
Kattera *see* Tutelo
Katuhano (Hdbk10)
Katukina *see* Catoquina
Katukina do Bia/Jutai *see* Catoquina
Katukino *see* Catoquina

Katuku *see* Chastacosta
Kau (W) *see also* Kansa (LC)
Kau [Clan] *Hopi* (H)
Ka-uay-ko *see* Laguna
Kauayko *see* Laguna
Kauia (H) *see also* Kawia [Yokuts] (BE)
Kauia *see* Kau-i-a
Kau-i-a *Yokuts* (Contri, v.3, p.370)
Kauitchin *see* Cowichan
Kaul-daw *see* Kauldaw
Kauldaw [BC] *Kitksan* (H)
Kau-lits *see* Cowlitz
Kaulits *see* Cowlitz
Kaumainsh *see* Comanche
Kaumanang *see* Kaumauangmiut
K'aumauangmiut *see* Kaumauangmiut
Kaumauangmiut *Labrador Eskimos* (H)
Kaus *see* Coos
Kausas *see* Kansa
Kautanohakau *see* Tuscarora
Kauvuya (H) *see also* Kawia [Luiseño] (H)
Kauvuya [Lang] *Southern California Shoshonean* (Pub, v.4, no.3, p.131)
Kauvuyas *see* Cahuilla
Kauwerak *Bering Strait Eskimos* (Hdbk5)
Kauwetseka *see* Akawantca'ka
Kauwetseka *see* Tuscarora
Kau win-wu *see* Kau
Ka'u wun-wu *see* Kau
Kau wunwu *see* Kau
Kau-yai-chit *see* Cahuilla
Kau-yai-chit *see* Kawia [Luiseño]
Kau-yai-chit *see* Las Vegas
Kauyaichits (PC) *see also* Cahuilla (LC)
Kauyaichits (PC) *see also* Kawia [Luiseño] (H)
Kauyaichits (PC) *see also* Las Vegas (Hdbk11)
Kauyaichits [CA] *Chemehuevi* (BE)
Kauzau *see* Kansa
Kavagan *see* Kouyam
Kavayo *see* Cahuilla
Kavayo *see* Kawia [Luiseño]
Kavea *see* Kuviagmiut
Kaveak *see* Kaviagmiut
Kavechia *see* Cahokia
Kavelchadom [Lang] [AZ] *Yuman* (Hdbk10)
Kaveltcadom *see* Kavelchadom
Kaverong Mutes *see* Kaviagmiut
Kaviacks *see* Kaviagmiut
Kaviagamute *see* Kaviagmiut
Kaviagmiut [AK] *Eskimos* (BE)
Kaviagmut *see* Kaviagmiut

Kaviagmute *see* Kaviamiut
Kaviagmyut *see* Kaviagmiut
Kaviaks *see* Kaviagmiut
Kaviatam *see* Serrano
Kaviawach (BE) *see also* Parusanuch (Hdbk11)
Kaviawach [UT] (BE)
Kaviazagamute *see* Kaviazagmiut
Kaviaza'gemut *see* Kaviazagmiut
Kaviazagmiut *Kaviagmiut* (H)
Kavixi *see* Kabixi
Kavvachia *see* Cahokia
Kavvchia *see* Cahokia
Kavvkia *see* Cahokia
Kavwaru-Maup *see* Cahuilla
Kavwaru-maup *see* Kawia [Luiseño]
Kaw *see* Kansa
Kawa *see* Kiowa
Kawaaisu [Lang] [*Ute-Chemehuevi*] (H)
Kawahib [Br] (O)
Kawahyb *see* Kawahib
Kawahykaka *see* Laguna
Kawaibatunya [Clan] *Hopi* (H)
Kawaihkaa *see* Laguna
Kawaiisu [CA] (LC)
Kawaik *see* Laguna
Ka-waik [Self-designation] *see* Laguna
Ka-waika *see* Laguna
Kawaika *see* Laguna
Kawaikama *see* Laguna
Kawaikame *see* Laguna
Kawaik-ka-me *see* Laguna
Kawaikkame *see* Laguna
Kawaiko *see* Sitsime
Kawaikome *see* Laguna
Kawapabikuni'kag *see* Gawababiganikak
Kawapa'tu *see* Apache
Kawapatu *see* Apache
Kawarakis *Pitahauerat* (BE)
Kawarakish *see* Kawarakis
K'a-was *see* Kawas
Kawas [Family] *Haida* (H)
Kawa-Tapuya [Col] *Wakuenai* (O)
Kawatskin *see* Cowichan
Kawchodinne *see* Kawchottine
Kawchogottine [Can] *Kawchottine* (BE)
Kawchottine [Can, AK] (LC)
Kaweach *see* Cahuilla
Kaweah *see* Cahuilla
Kaweisa *see* Kawaiisu
Kawelitsk *see* Cowlitz
Kawesqar [Lang] *see* Alacaluf
Kawia (BE) *see also* Cahuilla (LC)
Kawia (BE) *see also* Gawia (CA)
Kawia (H) *see also* Cahuilla (LC)
Kawia [CA] *Luiseño* (H)
Kawia [Lang] [CA] [*Luiseño (Kawia)*] (H)

Kawia *Yokuts* (BE)
Ka-wi-a-suh *see* Ta-hi-cha-pa-han-na
Ka-wi-a-suh *see* Kawaiisu
Kawiasuh *see* Ta-hi-cha-pa-han-na
Kawiasuh *see* Kawaiisu
Kawichen *see* Cowichan
Kawillary *see* Cabiyari
Ka-wi-na-han *see* Siksika
Kawinahan *see* Siksika
Kawirimomowi *Guahibo* (O)
Kawishm *see* Kawaiisu
Kawita *Creek Confederacy* (H)
Kawitchen *see* Cowichan
Kawitshin *see* Cowichan
Kawitskin *see* Cowichan
Kawiyeri *see* Cabiyari
Kawkawling [MI] *Chippewa* (H)
Kawki (O) *see also* Jaqaru (O)
Kawki [PE] (O)
Kawkia *see* Cahokia
Kaws *see* Kansa
Kaw-sa *see* Kansa
Kawsa *see* Kansa
Kaw-za *see* Kansa
Kawza *see* Kansa
Kaxanawa *see* Cashinawa
Kaxarari [Br] (O)
Ka-xi *see* Crow
Kaxi *see* Crow
Kaxinaw *see* Cashinawa
Kaxinawa *see* Cashinawa
Kaxiniti *see* Kashiniti
Kaxiniti *see* Pareci
Kaxuiana [Br] (O)
Kaxuyama *see* Kaxuiana
Kaxuyana *see* Kaxuiana
kaxwa'n *see* Kahwan
Kayabi [Br] (LC)
Kaya'ckidetan *see* Kayashkidetan
Kayackidetan *see* Kayashkidetan
Kayagua *see* Kiowa
Kayaligmiut [AK] *Eskimos* (Hdbk5)
Kayamaici [TX] (BE)
Kayapo *see* Cayapo
Kayapwa *see* Zaparo
Kayashkidetan [AK] *Tlingit* (H)
Kayaway *see* Kiowa
Kayjatin *see* Kaihatin
Kaykovskie *see* Kake
Kaynaguntl *Apache* (H)
Kayo-kath *see* Kyuquot
Kayokath *see* Kyuquot
Kayokuaht *see* Kyuquot
Kayomasho [Phratry] *Laguna* (H)
Kayouse *see* Cayuse
Kayouuik *see* Cayuse
Kayova *see* Caingua
Kayova *see* Kaiova
Kayowa *see* Kiowa
Kayowe *see* Kiowa

Kayowgaw *see* Cayuga
Kayowu *see* Kiowa
Kay-tzen-lin *see* Kaihatin
Kaytzenlin *see* Kaihatin
Kayua *see* Caingua
Kayugua *see* Kiowa
Kayugueonon *see* Cayuga
Kayul *see* Cayuse
Kayuse *see* Cayuse
Kayuse Creek *see* Cayoosh Creek
Ka'yuwa *see* Kiowa
Kayuwa *see* Kiowa
Kayuxes *see* Cayuse
K'ce-qwuc tunne *see* Siuslaw
Kchegagonggo [Gens] *Abnaki* (H)
K'che-sepi-ack *see* Chesapeake
Kchesepiack *see* Chesapeake
K'chick-aham-min-nough *see*
   Chickahominy
Kchikcahamminnough *see*
   Chickahominy
Kcop-tagui *see* Jicarilla Apache
K'cu-quic'tunne *see* Siuslaw
Kcuquictunne *see* Siuslaw
Kcuqwictunne *see* Siuslaw
Kdhun [Gens] *Osage* (H)
Ke (H) *see also* Kekin [Kansa] (H)
Ke [Clan] *Pueblo Indians* (H)
Kea [Clan] *Tewa* (H)
Kealedjii [AL] *Muskogee* (BE)
Keasas *see* Kiyuksa [Oglala]
Ke-at *see* Koso
Ke-at *see* Panamint
Keat *see* Koso
Keat *see* Panamint
Keawa *see* Kiowa
Keawah *see* Kawia [Yokuts]
Keawaw *see* Kiawaw
Keaway *see* Kiowa
Keawe *see* Keyauwee
Keawee *see* Kayauwee
Kea-wit-sis *see* Tlauitsis
Keawitsis *see* Tlauitsis
Ke-ax-as *see* Kiyuksa [Oglala]
Kebiks *see* Montagnais-Naskapi
Kecapo *see* Kickapoo
Kecchies *see* Kichai
Kecha *see* Kichai
Ke'cha *see* Kichai
Kechayi [CA] (BE)
Kechayi [Lang] *Northern Foothill*
   Yokuts (BE)
Kechayi [Lang] *Northern Valley*
   Yokuts (Anthro, v.11, no.3)
Kech-eel *see* Kechayi
Kecheel *see* Kechayi
Kechegummewininewug [MN]
   Chippewa (BE)
Kechekame Wenenewak *see*
   Kitchigumiwininiwug
Kechemeche [NJ] *Delaware* (H)
Kechepukwaiwah [MI, WI]
   Chippewa (H)

Ke-che-se-be-win-in-e-wug *see*
   Kitchisibiwininiwug
Kechesebewininewug (PC) *see also*
   Kitchisibiwininiwug (H)
Kechesebewininewug [MI]
   Chippewa (BE)
Ke-che-se-be-win-o-wing *see*
   Kitchisibiwininiwug
Kechesebewinowing *see* Kitchisi-
   biwininiwug
Kechi *see* Luiseño
Kechies *see* Kichai
Kechipauan *Zuni* (Hdbk9)
kechipa-wa *see* Kechipauan
Kechis *see* Kichai
Kechtawangh *see* Kitchawank
Kechua *see* Quechua
Kecopes *see* Kickapoo
Kecotan *see* Kecoughtan
Kecoughtan [VA] *Powhatan* (BE)
Kedada [Br] [*Pira-Tapuyo*] (O)
Kedalana *see* Keda-lana
Keda-lana [BC] [*Hagi-lana*] (H)
Kee *see* Arikara
Kee-ark-sar *see* Kiyuksa [Yank-
   tonai]
Keearksar *see* Kiyuksa [Yank-
   tonai]
Keeawawe *see* Keyauwee
Keeche (PC) *see also* Kitzeesh (H)
Keeche [CA] (LC)
Keeche-gumme-winine-wug *see*
   Kitchigumininiwug
Keechers *see* Kichai
Kee-ches *see* Kitzeesh
Keechi *see* Kichai
Keechies *see* Kichai
Kee-chis *see* Kitzeesh
Keechis *see* Kitzeesh
Kee-chum-a-kai-lo *see* Kitzim-
   gaylum
Keechumakailo *see* Kitzimgay-
   lum
Kee-chum akarlo *see* Kitzimgay-
   lum
Keechumakarlo *see* Kitzimgay-
   lum
Keechy *see* Kichai
Kee-hat-sa *see* Crow
Keehatsa *see* Crow
Keeheet-sa *see* Creek
Kee-kat-sa *see* Creek
Keekatsa *see* Creek
Keek heat la *see* Kitkala
Keekheatla *see* Kitkala
Keen-ath-toix *see* Kinuhtaoiah
Kee-nip-saim *see* Kenipsim
Keenipsaim *see* Kenipsim
Kee-nip-sim *see* Kenipsim
Keenipsim *see* Kenipsim
Keeowaw *see* Keyauwee
Keeowee *see* Keyauwee
Keequotancke *see* Kecoughtan

Kee-tah-hon-neet *see* Tongass
Keetahhonneet *see* Tongass
Keet-heat-la *see* Kitkala
Keetheatla *see* Kitkala
Keethratlah *see* Kitkala
Keetoowah Society (AI, pp.505–
   506)
Keetsas *see* Kichai
K-e'etse *see* Katsey
Keetse *see* Katsey
Kee-uke-sah *see* Kiyuksa [Yank-
   tonai]
Keeukesah *see* Kiyuksa [Yank-
   tonai]
Keew-ahomomy *see* Tuscarora
Ke-ga-boge *see* Kickapoo
Kegaboge *see* Kickapoo
Kegarnie *see* Kaigani
Ke-gi *see* Kegi
Kegi [Clan] *Tewa* (H)
Kegiizhi *see* Papago
Kegiktowrigemiut *Unaligmiut* (H)
Kegiktowrig'emut *see* Kegik-
   towrigemiut
Kehabou *see* Kickapoo
Keh-chen-wilt *see* Quaitso
Kehchenwilt *see* Quaitso
Kehk (H) *see also* Kake (BE)
Kehk [Can] [*Sitka-kwan*] (Contri,
   v.1, p.38)
Kehons *see* Kake
Keiauwee *see* Kayauwee
Keimanoeitoh *see* Kitlope
Kein [Subgens] *Omaha* (H)
Keinouche [MI] *Ottawa* (BE)
Keiscatch-ewan *see* Cree
Keiskatchewan *see* Cree
Kei-u-gue *see* Cayuga
Keiugue *see* Cayuga
Ke-jawn *see* Yuma
Kejawn *see* Yuma
Kek *see* Kake
Ke-ka-alns *see* Kikiallu
Kekaalns *see* Kikiallu
Kekapo *see* Kickapoo
Kekapou *see* Kickapoo
Kekaupoag *see* Kickapoo
Kekayeken [Can] *Songish* (BE)
Kekchi [Gua, Bel, MX] (LC)
Kekchian [Lang] *Mayan* (O)
Kekch-kon *see* Kake
Kekerannon-rounon *see* Nipiss-
   ing
Kekies *see* Kichai
Ke-kin *see* Kekin [Kansa]
Kekin [Clan] *Kansa* (H)
Kekin [Gens] *Osage* (H)
K-ek-k'enox *see* Kyekykyenok
Kekkenox *see* Kyekykyenok
Kekowhatan *see* Kecoughtan
Ke'k-pa *see* Hekpa
Kekpa *see* Hekpa
Kekuvskoe *see* Kake

Kelamouche *see* Comanche
Kelatl [BC] *Cowichan* (H)
Kelatl [Can] *Stalo* (BE)
Kele (H) *see also* Karankawa (LC)
Kele [Can] *Hopi* (H)
Ke-le-nyu-muh *see* Kele
Kelenyumuh *see* Kele
Ke-le win-wu *see* Kele
Kele winwu *see* Kele
Kelewinwu *see* Kele
Keliopoma [CA] *Pomo* (H)
Kelistenos *see* Cree
Kellamuck *see* Tillamook
Kellespem *see* Kalispel
Kel-seem-aht *see* Kelsemaht
Kelseemaht *see* Kelsemaht
Kel-sem-aht *see* Kelsemaht
Kelsemaht [Can] *Nootka* (BE)
Kelsey *see* Makhelchel
Kelta (Contri, v.3)
Keltakkaua [Clan] [BC] *Nuhalk* (H)
K-eltsma-ath *see* Kelsemaht
Keltsmaath *see* Kelsemaht
Kel-ut-sah *see* Kilutsai
Kelutsah *see* Kilutsai
Kemahwivi *see* Chemehuevi
Kemanks [BC] *Salish* (H)
Ke'na *see* Kainah
Kena *see* Kainah
Kenabe *see* Norridgewock
Kenabe *see* Kennebec
Kenabeca *see* Norridgewock
Ke-na-big *see* Kenabig
Kenabig [Clan] *Chippewa* (H)
Kenai *see* Knaiakhotana
Kenaian *see* Athapascan
Kenaies *see* Knaiakhotana
Kenai-tena *see* Knaiakhotana
Kenaitena *see* Knaiakhotana
Kenaitses *see* Knaiakhotana
Kenaitze *see* Knaiakhotana
Kenaiyer *see* Knaiakhotana
Kenaiyut *see* Knaiakhotana
Kenaize *see* Knaiakhotana
Kenaizen *see* Knaiakhotana
Kenaizer *see* Athapascan
Kenajer *see* Knaiakhotana
Kenake'n *see* Okinagan
Kenas *see* Knaiakhotana
Kenath tui ex *see* Kinuhtoiah
Kenathtuiex *see* Kinuhtoiah
Kenay *see* Knaiakhotana
Kenayern *see* Knaiakhotana
Kenayzi *see* Knaiakhotana
Kendawa [Clan] *Miami* (H)
Kenebecka *see* Kennebec
Kenebecke Indians *see* Norridgewock
Kenebeke *see* Norridgewock
Kenehawa *see* Conoy
Keneku'n *see* Kainah
Kenesti *see* Wailaki

Ken-es-ti [Self-designation] *see* Wailaki
Ke-ni'kaci-ka *see* Kenikashika
Kenikacika *see* Kenikashika
Kenikashika [Clan] *Quapaw* (H)
Ke nika-shing-ga *see* Kekin [Kansa]
Kenikashingga *see* Kekin [Kansa]
Kenim Lake [BC] *Shuswap* (H)
Ke-nip-sim *see* Kenipsim
Kenipsim [Can] *Cowichan* (BE)
Ke-nish-te-no-wuk *see* Cree
Kenishtenowuk *see* Cree
Kenisteno *see* Cree
Kenistenoag *see* Cree
Ke-nis-te-noag *see* Cree
Kenistenoo *see* Cree
Kenk *see* Southern Tehuelche
Kenka *see* Ken-ka
Ken-ka [CA] *Patwin* (Pub, v.29, no.4)
Kenkateye [Br] *Canella* (O)
Kennebec (LC) *see also* Norridgewock (LC)
Kennebec *Eastern Abnaki* (Hdbk15)
Kennebeki *see* Norridgewock
Kenneck Indians *see* Norridgewock
Kenondadie *see* Wyandot
Ke-noushay *see* Kenozhe
Kenoushay *see* Kenozhe
Kenowiki *see* Conoy
Ke-no-zha *see* Kenozhe
Kenozha *see* Kenozhe
Ke-no-zhe *see* Kenozhe
Kenozhe [Clan] *Chippewa* (H)
Ke-nunctioni *see* Iroquois
Kenunctioni *see* Iroquois
Keo Haade *see* Aokeawai
Keomee *see* Keyauwee
Keope-e-no *see* Koprino
Keotuc [KS] *Potawatomi* (H)
Keowewallah *see* Clowwewalla
Keoxa *see* Kiyuksa
Kepatawangachik [Q] (H)
Kepikeriwat *see* Kepikiriwat
Kepikiriwat [Br] (O)
Kepo *see* Quepo
Keq! *see* Kake
Kequoughtan *see* Kecoughtan
Kera *see* Keres
Keralite *see* Eskimos
Keran *see* Keres
Keras *see* Keres
Kerchi *see* Kichai
Kerechun [Subgens] *Winnebago* (H)
Kerem-eeos *see* Keremeus
Keremeeos *see* Keremeus
Keremen [TX] (H)
Keremeus *Similkameen* (H)
Keremya'uz *see* Keremeus

K'eres *see* Keres
Keres [Lang] (BE)
Keres [NM] (LC)
Keres Indians *see* Keres
Keretsa *see* Navajo
Kerimen *see* Keremen
Kern River (BE) *see also* Tubatulabal (LC)
Kern River [CA] *Shoshone* (H)
Kerokia *see* Cahokia
Keroopinough *see* Koprino
Kershaw *see* Catawba
Kertani *see* Lower Kutenai
Kesagami Lake [Can] *Sakawininiwug* (BE)
Kesale *see* Hueyhueyquetzal
Kescacon *see* Kishkakon
Keseruma [Lang] *Makusi* (UAz, v.28)
Keshase *see* Kitzeesh
Keshok [WI] *Menominee* (BE)
Keshwa *see* Quechua
Ke'so *see* Keshok
Keso *see* Keshok
Ke-spi-co-tha *see* Kispokotha
Kespicotha *see* Kispokotha
Kespoogwit [Can] *Micmac* (BE)
Kessler *see* Makhelchel
Kes-whaw-hay *see* Keres
Keswhawhay *see* Keres
Keswick [Lang] *Wintu* (CA-8)
Ketahn-hah-mwits [Lang] *Chumash* (JCB, v.4, no.2, pp.222–232)
Ketahto *Comanche* (BE)
Ket a Mat *see* Kitamat
Ketamat *see* Kitamat
Ket-an-dou *see* Kitunto
Ketandou *see* Kitunto
Ketawauga *see* Cherokee
Ketchegamins *see* Kitchigami
Ketchewaundaugenink [MI] *Chippewa* (H)
Ketcheyes *see* Kichai
Ketchies *see* Kichai
Ketchigamin *see* Kitchigami
Ketchigumiwisuwugi [Gens] *Sauk* (H)
Ke'tcifamiwisuwagi *see* Ketchitumiwisuwugi
Ketcifamiwisuwagi *see* Ketchigumiwisuwugi
Ke-tdoa *see* Ke
Ketdoa *see* Ke
Ketehigamins *see* Kitchigami
Keteta *see* Shanwappom
Ketetas *see* Kittitas
K'e'tgo hit tan *see* Ketgohittan
Ketgohittan [Subclan] *Nanyaayi* (H)
Ket-ka-kesh *see* Kitkehahki
Ketkakesh *see* Kitkehahki
Ketl'ahi *see* Pima

Ketlane *see* Kitlani
Ketlaynup [Can] *Salish* (H)
Ketlitk-Kutchin *see* Unakhotana
Ketnas-hadai [Sub-family] [AK]
　[*Yaku-lanas*] (H)
Ke-to-wa *see* Ke
Ketowa *see* Ke
Ketschetnaer *see* Ahtena
Ketschet-naer *see* Ahtena
Ke'tsi *see* Katsey
Ketsi *see* Katsey
Ketsilind [NM] *Jicarilla Apache*
　(BE)
Kettle Band *see* Oohenonpa
Kettle Falls *see* Colville
Kettle Indians *see* Colville
Ket-wilk-ci-pa *see* Kitwilksheba
Ketwilkcipa *see* Kitwilksheba
Ketyagoos *see* Kittizoo
Kevalingamiut [AK] *Eskimos* (BE)
Kevalinye Mutes *see* Ke-
　valingamiut
Kevalinyes *see* Kevalingamiut
Kevalinyes *see* Kivalinigmiut
Kevilkivashala [Can] *Salish* (H)
Kevil-kwa-sha-lah *see* Kevilki-
　vashala
Keviller'chini *see* Cathlamet
Kewatsana [TX] *Comanche* (BE)
Ke-waugh-tchen-emach *see* Ke-
　waughtohenemach
Kewaughtchenemach *see* Ke-
　waughtohenenmach
Ke-waught-chen-naugh *see* Ke-
　waughtohenemach
Kewaughtchenunaugh *see* Ke-
　waughtohenemach
Kewaughtohenemach [WA] *Oki-
　nagan* (H)
Kewawee *see* Kayauwee
Keweah *see* Kawia [Yokuts]
Kewevikopaya [AZ] *Yavapai* (BE)
Keweyipaya *see* Southeastern
　Yavapai
Keya [Clan] [NM] *Pueblo Indians*
　(H)
Keyauwee [Lang] *Eastern Siouan*
　(H)
Keyauwee [NC] (LC)
Keyawee *see* Keyauwee
Keycchies *see* Kichai
Keyche *see* Kichai
Keychies *see* Kichai
Keyes *see* Kichai
Keyeshees *see* Kichai
Keys *see* Kichai
Keyuse *see* Cayuse
Keze *Sisseton* (H)
Kfwetragottine [Can] *Kawchottine*
　(BE)
Kha-a *see* Cheghita
Kha-a *see* Khra
Khaa (PC) *see also* Cheghita (H)

Khaa (PC) *see also* Khra (H)
Khaa [Clan] *Oto* (H)
Khaamotene [CA] (H)
Khaap [BC] *Ntlakyapamuk* (H)
Khabenapo [CA] *Pomo* (H)
Khagan-taya-khun-khin (H) *see
　also* Aleuts (LC)
Khagan-taya-khun-khin [AK]
　[*Unung'un*] (Contri, v.1)
Khaguach *see* Agua Caliente
Khahitan *Pueblo Indians* (H)
Khahkhahton *see* Chippewa
K'haibhai *see* Santa Clara [NM]
Khaibhai *see* Santa Clara [NM]
Khai-ler-te-tang *see* Qailertetang
Khailertetang *see* Quailertetang
Khakhaton *see* Chippewa
Khakhatonwan *see* Chippewa
Khakupin *see* Agua Caliente
Khalam *see* Clallam
Khaltso [Clan] *Navajo* (H)
Khana [CA] (H)
Khanukh *see* Goch
K'ha-po-o *see* Santa Clara [NM]
K'hapoo *see* Santa Clara [NM]
Khapoo *see* Santa Clara [NM]
Kharatanumanke *see* Horatamu-
　make
Khashhlizhni [Clan] *Navajo* (H)
Khaskankhatso [Clan] *Navajo* (H)
Kha-t'a-ottine *see* Kawchottine
Khataottine *see* Kawchottine
Kha-tcho-gottine *see* Kaw-
　chogottine
Khatchogottine *see* Kawchogot-
　tine
Khecham *see* Luiseño
Khech-am *see* Luiseño
Khekhu *see* Kake
Khemnichan [MI] *Matantonwan*
　(H)
Khenipsim *see* Kenipsim
Kheyataotonwe [MI] *Mdewakan-
　ton* (H)
Kheyatawichasha (H) *see also*
　Upper Brule (BE)
Kheyatawichasha [NE] *Brule* (H)
Khidh [Clan] *Quapaw* (H)
Khidhenikashika [Gens] *Quapaw*
　(H)
Khionontatehronon *see* Tionon-
　tati
Khionontateron *see* Tionontati
Khionontateronon [Self-
　designation] *see* Wyandot
Khionontaterrhonon *see* Tionon-
　tati
Khitanumanke (H) *see also* Ki-
　tanemake (H)
Khitanumanke *Mandan* (H)
Khlel-ta *see* Kelta
Khoghanhlani [Clan] *Navajo* (H)
Khometwoli *see* Hometwoli

Khomtinin [CA] *Yokuts* (H)
Khonagani [Clan] *Navajo* (H)
Khoonkhwuttunne [CA] *Tolowa*
　(H)
Khootznahoo *see* Hutsnuwu
Khosatunne [CA] *Tolowa* (H)
Khosminin (H)
Khoso *see* Hopi
Khotachi [Clan] *Iowa* (H)
Khotana (LC) *see also* Koyukon
　(LC)
Khotana [AK] (H)
Khra [Subclan] *Iowa* (H)
Khrahune [Subclan] *Iowa* (H)
Khrahune [Subclan] *Iowa* (H)
Khrakreye [Subclan] *Iowa* (H)
Khrapathan [Subclan] *Iowa* (H)
Khu-a nika-shing-ga *see* Khra
Khuanikashingga *see* Khra
Khube [Subgens] *Omaha* (H)
Khudhapasan [Subgens] *Osage*
　(H)
Khuilchan *see* Kulchana
Khuilchana *see* Kulchana
Khulpini (H)
Khundjalan [Subgens] *Kansa* (H)
Khundtse [Subgens] *Osage* (H)
Khung [Clan] *Santa Clara* (H)
Khun-tdoa *see* Kun
Khuntdoa *see* Kun
Khustenete *see* Kwaishtunne
Khutsno *see* Hutsnuwu
Khuya [Clan] *Kansa* (H)
Khuyeguzhinga [Subgens] *Kansa*
　(H)
Khwaishtunnetunne *see* Wishte-
　natin
Khwakhamaiu [CA] *Pomo* (H)
Ki-a-a *see* Pueblo Alto
Kiaa *see* Pueblo Alto
Kiabaha [TX] (H)
Kiaboha *see* Kiabaha
Kiackennneck *see* Qairnirmiut
Kiaffess *see* Kuasse
Kiahl [Clan] *Pecos* (H)
Kiahoba *see* Kiabaha
Kiaini *see* Kinaani
Kiakatsmovi *see* Kyakotsmovi
Kiakichomovi *see* Kyakotsmovi
k'iakima *see* Kiakima
Kiakima *Zuni* (Hdbk9)
k'iakime *see* Kiakima
Kiaknukmiut *see* Kinipetu
Kiaknukmiut *see* Qairnirmiut
Kiakotsmovi *see* Kykotsmovi
Kialdagwuns [Subclan] *Haida* (H)
Kianamara *see* Gallinomero
Kia-na-wa *see* Kechipauan
Kianawa *see* Kechipauan
Ki-a-ni *see* Kegi
Kiani *see* Kegi
Kianosili *see* Kianusili
Kia'nusili *see* Kianusili

Kianusili [Clan] *Haida* (H)
Kiapaha *see* Quapaw
Kiaskusis [Clan] *Cree* (BE)
Kiasses *see* Kuasse
Kiasses-chancres *see* Kuasse
Kiatagmiut [AK] *Eskimos* (BE)
Kiatagmute *see* Kiatagmiut
Kiataro *see* Coyotero Apache
Kiataw *see* Coyotero Apache
Kiatenes *see* Kiatagmiut
Kiatenses *see* Knaiakhotana
Kiatero *see* Coyotero Apache
Kiawa (H) *see also* Kiowa (LC)
Ki-a-wa *see* Kiowa
Kiawa [SC] *Cusabo* (BE)
Kiawaw [SC] *Cusabo* (H)
Kiaway *see* Kiowa
Kiawetni *see* Ki-a-wet-ni
Ki-a-wet-ni *Yokuts* (Contri, v.3, p.370)
Kiawpino *see* Koprino
Kicapoo *see* Kickapoo
Kicapou *see* Kickapoo
Kicapoux *see* Kickapoo
Kicapu *see* Kickapoo
Kicara *see* Arikara
Kiccapoo *see* Kickapoo
Kicha *see* Luiseño
Kichae *see* Kichai
Kichai [TX, OK] (BE)
Kichamguchum *see* Diegueño
Kichamkochem *see* Kamia
Kichamkuchum *see* Kamia
Kichamkwangakh *see* Diegueño [Lang]
Kichaoneiak *see* Kishkakon
Kichaoueiak *see* Kishkakon
Kichapac *see* Kickapoo
Kiche *see* Kichai
Kiche *see* Quiche
Kichean *see* Quichean
Kichesipiiriniouek *see* Kichesipirini
Kichesipirini [Can] *Algonkin* (BE)
Kichesipiriniwek *see* Kichesipirini
Kichis *see* Kichai
Ki-chi-tcac *see* Kichai
Kichitcac *see* Kichai
Kichiyali (H)
Kichkagoneiak *see* Kishkakon
Kichkankoueiak *see* Kishkakon
Kicho *see* Quijo
Kichtages *see* Illinois
Kichtawan *see* Kitchawank
Kichtawanc *see* Kitchawank
Kichtawanck *see* Kitchawank
Kichtawanghs *see* Kitchawank
Kichtawons *see* Kitchawank
Kichtewangh *see* Kitchawank
Kichtowanghs *see* Kitchawank
Kichwa *see* Quechua
Ki-ci-ku-cuc *see* Wichita

Kicikucuc *see* Wichita
Ki-ci-tcac *see* Kichai
Kicitcac *see* Kichai
Kickakon *see* Kishkakon
Kickapo *see* Kickapoo
Kickapoo (H) *see also* Kispokotha (BE)
Kickapoo [OK, MX, WI] (LC)
Kickapoos of the Prairies *see* Prairie Kickapee
Kickapoos of the Vermilion *see* Vermilion
Kickapou *see* Kickapoo
Kickatanck *see* Accomac
Kickatanck *see* Kiquotank
Kicked-in-their-bellies *see* Erarapi'o
Kick in the Belly *Crow* (H)
Kickipoo *see* Kickapoo
Kickotank *see* Assateague
Kick-sa-tee *see* Kiksadi
Kicksatee *see* Kiksadi
Kicktages *see* Illinois
Kicktawanc *see* Kitchawank
Kickuallis *see* Kikiallu
Kicoagoves *see* Kickapoo
Kicoapou *see* Kickapoo
Kicopoux *see* Kickapoo
Kicquotank *see* Accomac
Kictawanc *see* Kitchawank
Kidelik *see* Kidnelik
kiditikadi *see* idutokado
kidji'sa *see* Chiricahua Apache
Kidnelik (H) *see also* Copper Eskimos (H)
Kidnelik [Can] *Central Eskimos* (H)
Kidutokado *Northern Paiute* (Hdbk11)
Kiechee *see* Kichai
Kienketons *see* Sisseton
Kieoux *see* Cayuse
Kiequotank *see* Kiquotank
Kietsash *see* Kichai
Ki-e-wah *see* Kiowa
Kiewah *see* Kiowa
Ki-gaktag'myut *see* Kigiktagmiut
Ki-gal-twa-la *see* Cascades
Kigaltwala *see* Cascades
Ki-gal-twal-la *see* Cascades
Ki-gal-twal-la *see* Watlala
Kigaltwalla *see* Cascades
Kigaltwalla *see* Watlala
Kigamies *see* Kaigani
Kigani *see* Kaigani
Kigarnee *see* Kaigani
Kigenes *see* Kaigani
Kighahnixons *see* Patuxent
Kighetawkigh Roanu *see* Illinois
Kighigufi *see* Atka
Kightages *see* Illinois
Kightewangh *see* Kitchawank
Kightowan *see* Kitchawank

Kigi *see* Cogui
Kigikh-khun *see* Atka
Kigikhkhun *see* Atka
Kigiktagmiut [Can] *Labrador Eskimos* (BE)
Kigiktagmyut *see* Kigiktagmiut
Kigirktarugmiut [Can, AK] *Mackenzie Eskimos* (BE)
Kiglacka *see* Kiglashka
Kiglashka *Hunkpapa* (H)
Kiglaska *see* Kiglashka
Kiglinirmuit [Can] *Central Eskimos* (BE)
Kiguel *see* Mishikhwutmetunne
Kigukhtagmyut *see* Kigiktagmiut
Ki-gu-ksa *see* Kiyuksa [Mdewakanton]
Kiguksa *see* Kiyusksa [Mdewakanton]
Kihigouns *see* Unalaska
Kihnatsa *see* Crow
Ki-hu *see* Kegi
Kihu *see* Kegi
Ki-hua *see* Santo Domingo
Kihua *see* Santo Domingo
Kiiataigmiuty *see* Kiatagmiut [Rus]
Kiiataigmiuty [Rus] *see* Kiatagmiut
Kiiatemfsy *see* Kiatagmiut
Kiiatenfsy [Rus] *see* Kiatagmiut
kiikaapoa *see* Kickapoo
Ki'imilit *see* Eskimos
Kiimilit *see* Eskimos
Kij *see* Gabrielino
Kijataigmjuten *see* Kiatagmiut
Kijataigmuten *see* Kiatagmiut
Kijaten *see* Kiatamiut
Kik [Clan] *Hopi* (H)
Kikabeux *see* Kickapoo
Kikabon *see* Kickapoo
Kikabou *see* Kickapoo
Kikaboua *see* Kickapoo
Kikabu *see* Kickapoo
Kikanona *see* Karanakawa
Kikapau *see* Kickapoo
ki-kapo *see* Kickapoo
kikapo *see* Kickapoo
Kikapoes *see* Kickapoo
Kikapoo *see* Kickapoo
Kikapou *see* Kickapoo
Kikapoux *see* Kickapoo
Kikapouz *see* Kickapoo
Kikapu *see* Kickapoo
Kikasta *see* Crow
Ki'kat'sik *see* Kikatsik
Kikatsik [CA] *Shasta* (H)
Kikealans *see* Kikiallu
Kikhtagmiut *see* Chugach
Kikhtagmiut *see* Koniag
Kikhtagyuk *see* Qikiqtagrungmiut
Kikhtog'amut (Contri, v.1, p.15)

Kikhtog'amut (H) *see also* Ei-whuelit (BE)
Kikialli *see* Kikiallu
Kikiallu [WA] *Skagit* (H)
Kik-i-allus *see* Kikiallu
Ki-kia-loos *see* Kikiallu
Kikialoos *see* Kikiallu
Kikialos *see* Kikia'los
Kikia'los [WA] *Swinomish* (BE)
Kikialtis *see* Kikiallu
Kikima *see* Halyikwamai
Kikitagmyut [Can] [*Inuit (Quebec)*] (Hdbk5)
Kikitamkar *see* Kitanemuk
Kikitanum *see* Kitanemuk
Kikkapoo *see* Kickapoo
Kikotanke *see* Kiquotank
Kikpouz *see* Kickapoo
Kiks-adi *see* Kiksadi
Kiksa-di *see* Kiksadi
Kiksadi [AK] *Tlingit* (H)
Kiksan *see* Kitksan
Kiktagamute *see* Qikiqtagrung-miut
Kikua [Moiety] *Miwok* (Pub, v.11, no.5, p.293)
Kik-wun-wu *see* Kik
Kikwunwu *see* Kik
Kilamook *see* Tillamook
Kil a mox *see* Tillamook
Kilamox *see* Tillamook
Kilamuke *see* Tillamook
Kilamute *see* Tillamook
Kilat *see* Tsimshian
Kilataks *see* Kilatika
Kilatica *see* Kilatika
Kilatika [IL] *Miami* (H)
Kilauwitawi'nmium *see* Kunmiut
Kilawalaks *see* Kitlakdamix
Kil-cah-ta *see* Kitkahta
Kilcahta *see* Kitkahta
Kilemoka [BO] (O)
Kilgat *see* Tsimshian
Kilgonwah *see* Kitwingach
Kilikunom [CA] *Witukomnom* (H)
Kilingmyut *see* Kilinigmiut
Kilinigmiut [Can] *Suhinimiut Eskimos* (H)
Ki lin'ig myut *see* Kilinigmiut
Kilisteno *see* Cree
Kilistinaux *see* Cree
Kilistino *see* Cree
Kilistinon *see* Cree
Kilistinon Alimibegouek *see* Alimibegouek
Kilistinons of the Nipisiriniens *Cree* (H)
Kilistinous *see* Cree
Kilitika *see* Kilatika
Kiliu *see* Trio
Kiliwa [BaC, MX] (LC)
Kiliwa [Lang] *California Yuman* (Hdbk10)

Kiliwatsal *see* Kalawatset
Kiliwatshat *see* Kalawatset
Kiliwee *see* Kiliwa
Kiliwi *see* Kiliwa
Kil-kat *see* Tsimshian
Kilkat *see* Tsimshian
Killacinga *see* Quillacinga
Killamook *see* Tillamook
Killamouck *see* Tillamook
Killamouk *see* Tillamook
Killamox *see* Tillamook
Killamuck *see* Tillamook
Killamuk *see* Tillamook
Killawat *see* Kalawatset
Killaxthocle *see* Killaxthokle
Killaxthokl *see* Killaxthokle
Killaxthokle [WA] *Chinookan* (H)
Kil-laxt-ho-kle's T *see* Killaxthokle
Killaythocle *see* Killaxthokle
Kill Close By *see* Nitotsiksisstaniks
Killemook *see* Tillamook
Killernoux *see* Tillamook
Killestinoes *see* Cree
Killewatsis *see* Kalawatset
Killikmiut [AK] *Interior North Alaska Eskimos* (Hdbk5)
Killimoucks *see* Tillamook
Killimous *see* Tillamook
Killimux *see* Tillamook
Killinek [Can] [*Inuit (Quebec)*] (Hdbk5)
Killinermiut [AK] *Eskimos* (BE)
Killini *see* Cree
Killiniq *see* Copper Eskimos
Killinirmiut *see* Copper Eskimos
Killinunmiut [Can] *Labrador Eskimos* (BE)
Killirmiut [AK] *North Alaska Coast Eskimos* (Hdbk5)
Killisnoo *Tlingit* (Ye)
Killisteneaux *see* Cree
Killistenoes *see* Cree
Killistinaux *see* Cree
Killistini *see* Cree
Killistinoer *see* Cree
Killistinoes *see* Cree
Killistinon *see* Cree
Killistinous *see* Cree
Killistins *see* Cree
Killiwashat *see* Kalawatset
Killiwatshat *see* Kalawatset
Kill-on-chan *see* Kilutsai
Killonchan *see* Kilutsai
Killoosa *see* Kilutsai
Killowitsa *see* Kilutsai
Killsmaht *see* Kelsemaht
Killumucks *see* Tillamook
Killutsar *see* Kilutsai
Kilootsa *see* Kilutsai
Kil-pan-hus *see* Kilpanlus
Kilpanhus *see* Kilpanlus

Kilpanlus [Can] *Cowichan* (BE)
Kilsamat *see* Kelsemaht
Kilshaidagai *see* Kils-haidagai
Kils-haidagai [BC] [*Kagialskegawai*] (H)
Kilstlai-djat-takinggalung [*Klgahetgu-lanas*] (H)
Kilusiktomiut [Can] *Central Eskimos* (BE)
Kil-utsai *see* Kilutsai
Kilutsai [BC] *Tsimshian* (H)
Kim [Clan] *Isleta* (H)
Kim [Clan] *Tigua* (H)
Kimmooenim *see* Kamiah
Kimnepatoo *see* Kinipetu
Ki-mni-can *see* Khemnichan
Kimnican *see* Khemnichan
Kimoenim *see* Kamiah
Ki-moo-e-nim *see* Kamiah
Kimooenim *see* Kamiah
Kimsquit [Can] *Bella Coola* (BE)
Kim-t'ainin *see* Kim
Kimtainin *see* Kim
Ki-na *see* Kainah
Kina *see* Kainah
Kinaa'ni *see* Kinaani
Kinaani [Clan] *Navajo* (H)
Kinabik *see* Kenabig
Kinaetzi *see* Knaiakhotana
Kinaghi *see* Kaniagmiut
K'inahi-piako *see* Tonkawa
Kinahipiako *see* Tonkawa
Kinai *see* Knaiakhotana
Kinaitsa *see* Knaiakhotana
Kinaitze *see* Knaiakhotana
Kinaitzi *see* Knaiakhotana
Kinaizi *see* Knaiakhotana
Kinajut *see* Knaiakhotana
Kinakanes [WA] *Okinagan* (H)
Kin-a-roa-lax *see* Kitlakdamix
Kinaroalax *see* Kitakdamix
Kinawa *see* Kiowa
Kin-a-wa-lax *see* Kitlakdamix
Kinawalax *see* Kitlakdamix
Kinbaskets (Hdbk12) *see also* Shuswap Band
Kinbaskets [BC] *Upper North Thompson* (Hdbk12)
Kinebikowininiwak *see* Northern Shoshone
Kinebikowininiwak *see* Shoshone
Kinegans *see* Kinugumiut
Kine-ne-ai-koon *see* Kainah
Kineneaikoon *see* Kainah
Kinep *see* Kingep
kine-piko-nini *see* Shoshone
kinepikonini *see* Shoshone
Kineuwidishianun *see* Kine'u wi'dishi'anun
Kine'u wi'dishi'anun [Phratry] *Menominee* (H)
Kingee'ga-mut (H) *see also* Kinugumiut (BE)

Kingee'ga-mut [Can] [*Kaviag-mut*] (Contri, v.1, p.16)
Kingep *Kiowa* (BE)
Kingigumute *Bering Strait Eskimos* (Hdbk5)
Kingikmiut *see* Kinugumiut
King Island *Bering Strait Eskimos* (Hdbk5)
Kingnaitmiut [Can] *Central Eskimos* (BE)
Kingnaitmiut [Can] *Okomiut Eskimos* (H)
King's River *see* King's River
Kings River [CA] (H)
Kings River [Lang] *Foothill Yokuts* (CA-8)
Kinguamiut (H)
K'inguamiut *see* Kinguamiut
Kinhlitshi [Clan] *Navajo* (H)
Kinibeki *see* Kennebec
Kinikinao (O) *see also* Tereno (O)
Kinikinao [Br] *Guana* (O)
Kinik Mute *see* Kinugumiut
Kinimia *see* Guayabero
Kinipetu (Hdbk5) *see also* Qairnirmiut (Hdbk5)
Kinipetu *Central Eskimos* (H)
Kinipissa *see* Acolapissa
Kinishtinak *see* Cree
Kinishtino *see* Cree
Kinisquit [BC] *Bella Coola* (H)
Kinisteneaux *see* Cree
Kinistinaux *see* Cree
Kinistineaux *see* Cree
Kinistinoes *see* Cree
Kinistinons *see* Cree
Kinistinuwok *see* Cree
Kiniwa *see* Kiowa
Kin-Kash *see* Kinkash
Kinkash [IN] *Potawatomi* (H)
Kin Klechini *see* San Juan [NM]
Kinklechini *see* San Juan [NM]
Kin Klekai Ni *see* Santo Domingo
Kinklekaini *see* Santo Domingo
Kin-krash *see* Kinkash
Kinkrash *see* Kinkash
Kinlitcini *see* Kinhlitshi
Kinlitsi (H) SE Kinhlitshi (H)
Kinlitsidine *see* Kinhlitshi
Kin Naazt'i *see* Shongopovi
Kinnaazti *see* Shongopovi
Kin-nas-ti *see* Shongopovi
Kinnasti *see* Shongopovi
Kinnat *see* Knaiakhotana
Kin-nato-iks *see* Kinuhtoiah
Kinnatoiks *see* Kinuhtoiah
Kinnats-Khotana *see* Knaiakhotana
Kinnatz-kokhtana *see* Knaiakhotana
Kinnebeck Indians *see* Norridgewock

Kinnepatoo *see* Qairnirmiut
Kinnepatu *see* Kinipetu
Kinnewoolun *see* Kitlakdamix
Kinngarmiut [Lang] *Eastern Canada* (Hdbk5)
Kinnipetu *see* Kinipetu
Kinnipiak *see* Quinnipiac
Kin Nodozi *see* Sandia
Kinnodozi *see* Sandia
Kinnstoucks *see* Kinuhstoiah
Ki-no *see* Kainah
Kino *see* Kainah
Kinoga [Clan] *Chippewa* (H)
Kinojan *see* Kenozhe
Kinonchepiirinik *see* Keinouche
Kinonchepirinik *see* Keinouche
Kinongeouilini *see* Nameuilini
Kinouche *see* Keinouche
Kinouchebiiriniouek *see* Keinouche
Kinounchepirini *see* Keinouche
Kinse *see* Cayuse
Kinstenaux *see* Cree
Kinstinaux *see* Cree
Kintlitci *see* Kinhlitshi
Kinugmut *see* Kinugumiut
Kinugumiut [AK] *Eskimos* (BE)
Kinugumiut *North Alaska Coast Eskimos* (Hdbk5)
Kinugumut *see* Kinugumiut
Kinuhtoiah [BC] *Tsimshian* (H)
kinya-inde *see* Jicarilla Apache
kinya-ini *see* Jicarilla Apache
Kio [Clan] *Jemez* (H)
Ki-o-a-me *see* Santo Domingo
Kioboba *see* Kiabaha
Kioch's Tribe [BC] *Salish* (H)
Kiocsies *see* Kiyuksa
Kiohican *see* Kiowa
Kiohuan *see* Kiowa
Kiohuhahan *see* Kiowa
Kioose *see* Cayuse
Kiotsaa *see* Kio
Kiouahaa *see* Kiowa
Kious *see* Dakota
Kiova *see* Kiowa
Kiowa [KS] (LC)
Kiowa Apache (LC)
Kiowah *see* Kiowa
Kiowan [Lang] (H)
Kiowan Indians *see* Kiowa
Kiowa-Tanoan (Hdbk10) *see also* Tanoan (LC)
Kiowa-Tanoan [Lang] (BE)
Kioway *see* Kiowa
Ki-o-wummi *see* Santo Domingo
ki-padikadi *see* Kupadokado
kipadikadi *see* Kupadokado
Kipawa [Can] *Algonkin* (BE)
Kipea [Br] (O)
Kipea [Lang] *Kariri* (O)
Kipikavvi *see* Pepikokia
Kipikawi *see* Pepikokia

Kipikuskvvi *see* Pepikokia
Kipisa'kia Wini'wiwuk [WI] *Menominee* (BE)
Ki-pomas *see* Kato
Kiqatsa *see* Crow
Kiquotank *Accomac* (Hdbk15)
Kiratika *see* Kilatika
Kirauash (H) *see also* Querecho (H)
Kirauash (Hdbk10) *see also* Apache (LC)
Kirauash [NM] (H)
Kirhawguagh Roanu *see* Karhagaghrooney
Kirikiri [OK] *Wichita* (BE)
Kirikirigoto [Br, Sur] *Tiriyo* (O)
Kirikuru *see* Wichita
Kiriri [Br] (LC)
Kiriri-Sapuya *see* Sapuya
Kirishana *see* Yanoama
Kirishkitsu *Wichita* (H)
Kiristinon *see* Cree
Kirokikhoche [Subgens] *Iowa* (H)
Ki-ro-ko-qo-tce *see* Kirokokche
Kironnona *see* Karankawa
Kironomes *see* Karankawa
Kironona *see* Karankawa
Kiruhikwak *see* Yurok
Kisalas *see* Kitzilas
Kisambaeri [Lang] [PE] *Harakmbet* (O)
Kisambaeri [PE] (O)
Kiscacon *see* Kishkakon
Kiscacones *see* Kishkakon
Kiscakon *see* Kishkakon
Kiscakou *see* Kishkakon
Kiscapocke *see* Kispokotha
Kischigamins *see* Kitchigami
Kisch-pach-la-ots *see* Kishpachlaots
Kischpachlaots *see* Kishpachlaots
Kiscopoke *see* Kispokotha
Kisgagas *see* Kitgargas
Kis-ga-gas *see* Kishgagass
Kisgagas *see* Kishgagass
Kisgegos *see* Kishgagass
Kis-go-gas *see* Kishgagass
Kisgogas *see* Kishgagass
Kishai *see* Kichai
Kishakevira *see* Hupa
Kishey *see* Kiski
Kish-ga-gass *see* Kishgagass
Kishgagass [BC] *Kitskan* (H)
Kishgahgehs *see* Kishgagass
Kishi [Clan] *Caddo Confederacy* (H)
Kishkako *see* Kishkakon
Kishkakon [MI] *Ottawa* (BE)
Kishkallen [WA] *Chehalis I* (H)
Kishkat [OK] *Wichita* (BE)
Kishkawbawee [MI] *Chippewa* (H)
Kishke-gas *see* Kishgagass

Kishkipquis [Society] *Sauk* (His/T, v.2, p.357)
Kishkoa [Gens] *Sauk* (His/T, v.2, p.147)
Kishpachlaots [BC] *Tsimshian* (H)
Kish-pi-yeoux *see* Kishpiyeoux
Kishpiyeoux [BC] *Kitksan* (H)
Kish-pi-youx *see* Kishpiyeoux
Kishpiyoux *see* Kishpiyeoux
Kishpochalots *see* Kishpachlaots
Kishpootwada [Society] *Niska* (H)
Kishqra [Clan] *Cochiti* (H)
Kishqra-hanuch *see* Kishqra
Kisinahi *see* Kiowa Apache
Kiskacoueiak *see* Kishkakon
Kiskagahs *see* Kishgagass
Kiskakon *see* Kishkakon
Kiskakonk *see* Kishkakon
Kiskakoumac *see* Kishkakon
Kiskakoun *see* Kishkakon
Kiskapocoke *see* Kispokotha
Kiskey *see* Kiski
Kiski [CA] *Maidu* (H)
Kiskiack *see* Chiskiac
Kiskiak *see* Chiskiac
Kiskieck *see* Chiskeac
Kis Kies *see* Kiski
Kiskies *see* Kiski
Kiskokan *see* Kishkakon
Kiskuskia *see* Kaskaskia
Kisky *see* Kiski
Kislistinons *see* Cree
Kis-pa-cha-laidy *see* Kishpach-laots
Kispachalaidy *see* Kishpachlaots
Kispachlohts *see* Kishpachlaots
Kispaioohs *see* Kishpiyeoux
Kispapoou *see* Kickapoo
Kispayaks *see* Kispoix
Kispiax *see* Kishpiyeoux
Kispiyox *see* Gitksan
Kispococoke *see* Kispokotha
Kispogogi *see* Kispokotha
Kispoix [Can] *Kitksan* (BE)
Ki-spo-ko-tha *see* Kispokotha
Kispokotha [TN] *Absentee Shawnee* (BE)
Kispyaths *see* Kishpiyeoux
Kispyox *see* Kishpiyeoux
Kissah *see* Coosa
Kissgarrase *see* Kishgagass
Kiss-ge-gaas *see* Kishgagass
Kissgegaas *see* Kishgagass
Kisteneaux *see* Cree
Kitaesches *see* Kichai
Kitaesechi *see* Kichai
Kitaheeta *see* Hitchiti
Kitalaska *see* Kitzilas
Kitamah *see* Kitamat
Kitamaht *see* Kitamat
Kitamat [Can] *Bellabella* (LC)
Kitamatt *see* Kitamat

Kitamet *see* Kitamat
Kitami *see* Kita'mi
Kita'mi [Clan] *Menominee* (H)
Kit-an-doh *see* Kitunto
Kitandoh *see* Kitunto
Ki-ta-ne-make *see* Khitanu-manke
Kitanemake *Mandan* (H)
Kitanemuk [CA] *Serrano* (CA)
Kitanemuk [Lang] *[Serrano-Gabrielino]* (Hdbk10)
Kit-an-maiksh *see* Kitanmaiksh
Kitanmaiksh [BC] *Kitksan* (BE)
Kitans *see* Gituns
Kitanweliks *see* Kitanwilksh
Kitanwilksh [Can] *Niska* (BE)
Kitash *see* Kichai
Ki-tatash *see* Kittitas
Kitatel *see* Kitkala
Kitaunlhu [Br] *Southern Nam-bicuara* (O)
Kitcathla *see* Kitkala
Ki'tcha *see* Kichai
Kitch-a-clalth *see* Kitsalthlal
Kitchaclalth *see* Kitsalthlal
Kitchatlah *see* Kitkala
Kitchawanc *see* Kitchawank
Kitchawank [NY] *Wappinger* (BE)
Kitchawonck *see* Kitchawank
Kitchawong (Hdbk15)
Kitche kla la *see* Kitsalthlal
Kitcheklala *see* Kitsalthlal
Kitchemkalem *see* Kitzimgaylum
Ki-tchesh *see* Kichai
Kitchies *see* Kichai
Kitchigami [WI] (H)
Kitchigamich *see* Kitchigami
Kitchigamick *see* Kitchigami
Kitchigamiwinniwak *see* Kitchigumiwininiwug
Kitchigumiwininiwug [MI, WI, MN] *Chippewa* (H)
Kitchimkale *see* Kitzimgaylum
Kitchisibi-wininiwak *see* Kitchis-ibiwininiwug
Kitchisibiwininiwug [MN] *Chippewa* (H)
Kitchtawanghs *see* Kitchawank
Kitchu lass *see* Kitzilas
Kitchulass *see* Kitzilas
Kitcigamiwininiwag *see* Kitchigumiwininiwug
Kitcoonsa *see* Kitwingach
Kite *see* Crow
Kitegarent [Can] *Eskimos* (H)
Kite Indians *see* Staitan
Kites *see* Staitan
Kitestues *see* Kittizoo
Kitgargas [Can] *Kitksan* (BE)
Kitgigenik [Can] *Niska* (BE)
Kitha-ata *see* Kitkahta
Kithaata *see* Kitkahta
Kithateen *see* Kitkahteen

Kithateh [Can] *Niska* (BE)
Kithatla *see* Kitkala
Kithigami *see* Kitchigami
Kithkatla *see* Kitkala
Kitiga'ru *see* Kitegareut
Kitigaru *see* Kitegareut
Kit-ih-shian *see* Kitksan
Kitihshian *see* Kitksan
Kitikitish *see* Wichita
Kitimat *see* Kitamat
Kitimat *see* Haisla
Kitinah *see* Kitanmaiksh
Kitistzoo *see* Kittizoo
Kitisu *Southern Coast Tsimshian* (Anthro, v.9, no.3, p.159)
Kititas [WA] (Ye)
Kit-ka *see* Kitkehahki
Kitka *see* Kitkehahki
Kitka-ata *see* Kitkahta
Kitkaata *see* Kitkahta
Kitkada *see* Kitkahta
Kitkadusshade *Haida* (H)
Kitkaet *see* Kitkahta
Kit-ka-gas *see* Kishgagass
Kitkagas *see* Kishgagass
Kitkaha'ki *see* Kitkehahki
Kitkahoets *see* Kitkehahki
Kitkaht *see* Kitkahta
Kit-kahta *see* Kitkahta
Kitkahta [BC] *Tsimshian* (H)
Kitkahteen *Can* [Niska] (BE)
Kitkahtla *Southern Coast Tsimshian* (Anthro, v.9, no.3, p.159)
Kitkala [BC] *Tsimshian* (H)
Kitkathla *see* Kitkala
Kitkatla *see* Kitkala
Kit-kats *see* Kithkahta
Kitkats *see* Kitkahta
Kitkehahki [Pawnee] (BE)
Kitkehahki ov [NE] *Republican Pawnee* (Oregon)
Kit-ke-hak-i *see* Kitkehahki
Kitkehaki *see* Kitkehahki
Kit-khall-ah *see* Kitkala
Kitkhallah *see* Kitkala
Kit-khatla *see* Kithala
Kitkhatla *see* Kithala
Kitksa'n *see* Kitksan
Kitksan [BC] (LC)
Kitksan [Lang] *Chimmesyan* (H)
Kit-ksum *see* Kitksan
Kitksum *see* Kitksan
Kit-ksun *see* Kitksan
Kitksun *see* Kitsan
Kitlacdamax *see* Kitlakdamix
Kitlach-damak *see* Kitlakdamix
Kitlach-damax *see* Kitlakdamix
Kit-lak-damix *see* Kitlakdamix
Kitlakdamix [BC] *Niska* (H)
Kitlan *see* Kitlani
Kitlani [BC] *Tsimshian* (H)
Kitlan Kilwilpeyot *see* Kitlani

Kitlatamox *see* Kitlakdamix
Kitlermiut *see* Killirmiut
Kitloop *see* Kitlope
Kitlop *see* Kitlope
Kit-lope *see* Kitlope
Kitlope [BC] *Kwakiutl* (H)
Kitlope [Lang] *Haisla* (BE)
Ki-tona-qa *see* Kutenai
Ki'tona'qa *see* Upper Kutenai
Kitona'qa [Lang] *Kitunahan* (H)
Kitoonitza *see* Kitkala
Kitqata *Southern Coast Tsimshian*
   (Anthro, v.9, no.3, p.159)
Kitrauaiiks [BC] *Tsimshian* (H)
Kits-ach-la-al'ch *see* Kitsalthlal
Kitsagas *see* Kishgagass
Kitsagatala *see* Kitsalthlal
Kitsahlaalch *see* Kitsalthlal
Kitsaiches *see* Kichai
Kitsalas *see* Kitzilas
Kitsalass *see* Kitzilas
Kitsallas *see* Kitzilas
Kitsalthlal [BC] *Tsimshian* (H)
Kitsanaka *Haidu* (H)
Kitsaoi *see* Kichai
Ki'tsash *see* Kichai
Kitsash [Self-description] *see*
   Kichai
Kitsash [Self-designation] *see*
   Kichai
Kitsasi *see* Kichai
Kits de Singes *see* Kichai
Kitseesh *see* Kitzeesh
Kitseguecla *see* Kitzegukla
Kitsegukla (BE) *see also*
   Kitzegukla (H)
Kitse-gukla *see* Kitzegukla
Kitsegukla [Can] *Kitksan* (BE)
Kitsei *see* Kichai
Kit-se-lai-so *see* Kitzilas
Kitselaiso *see* Kitzilas
Kitselassir *see* Kitzilas
Kitsellase *see* Kitzilas
Kitsenelah *see* Kitzegukla
Kitsequahla *see* Kitzegukla
Kit-se-quahla *see* Kitzegukla
Kit-se-quak-la *see* Kitzegukla
Kitsequakla *see* Kitzegukla
Kits-ge-goos *see* Kishgagass
Kitsgegoos *see* Kishgagass
Kits-go-gase *see* Kishgagass
Kitsgogase *see* Kishgagass
Kitsigeukle *see* Kitzegukla
Kitsiguchs *see* Kitzegukla
Kitsiguhli *see* Kitzegukla
Kits-iisch *see* Kitzeesh
Kitsiisch *see* Kitzeesh
Kitsis *see* Kitzeesh
Kitsoss *see* Kichai
Kitspayuchs *see* Kishpiyeoux
Kits-pious *see* Kishpiyeoux
Kits-piouse *see* Kishpiyeoux
Kitspiouse *see* Kishpiyeoux

Kitspioux *see* Kishpiyeoux
Kits-piox *see* Kishpiyeoux
Kitspiox *see* Kishpiyeoux
Kitspukaloats *see* Kishpachlaots
Kits-pyonks *see* Kishpiyeoux
Kitspyonks *see* Kishpiyeoux
Kits-se-quec-la *see* Kitzegukla
Kitssequecla *see* Kitzegukla
Ki'tsu *see* Kichai
Kitsumkalem *see* Kitzimgaylum
Kitswingachs *see* Kitwingach
Kitswinscolds *see* Kitwinskole
Kit ta maat *see* Kitamat
Kittamaat *see* Kitamat
Kittamark *see* Kitamat
Kit-ta-muat *see* Kitamat
Kittamuat *see* Kitamat
Kittando *see* Kitunto
Kitte-ga-re-ut *see* Kitegareut
Kittegareut *see* Kitegareut
Kitte-garroe-oot *see* Kitegareut
Kittegarroeoot *see* Kitegareut
Kit-te-ga-ru *see* Kitegareut
Kittegaru *see* Kitegareut
Kittegaryumiut [AK] *North Alaska*
   Coast Eskimos (Hdbk5)
Kittegaryumiut [Can] *Mackenzie*
   Eskimos (BE)
Kittimat *see* Kitamat
Kit-tist-zu *see* Kittizoo
Kittistzu *see* Kittizoo
Kittitas *see* Kitates
Kit-tizoo *see* Kittizoo
Kittizoo [BC] *Tsimshian* (H)
Kittlean *see* Kitlani
Kittlope *see* Kitlope
Kit-too-nuh-a *see* Kutenai
Kittoonuha *see* Kutenai
Kittralchla *see* Kitkala
Kittumark *see* Kitamat
Kittuwa *see* Cherokee
Kituanaha *see* Kutenai
Kituanahan *see* Kutenai
Kituhwagi *see* Cherokee
Kituitsach-hade [BC] *Haidu* (H)
Kitunaha (H) *see also* Kutenai
   (LC)
Kitunahan *see* Kutenai
Kitunahan [Lang] (H)
Kitunana *see* Kutenai
Kitunaxa *see* Kutenai
Kitunto [BC] *Tsimshsian* (H)
Kitwancole *see* Kitwinskole
Kit-wan-cool *see* Kitwinskole
Kitwancool (PC) *see also* Kitwin-
   skole (H)
Kitwancool [BC] *Kitksan* (LC)
Kitwanga [Can] *Kitksan* (BE)
Kit-wang-agh *see* Kitwingach
Kitwangagh *see* Kitwingach
Kitwanger *see* Kitwingach
Kitwilgioks [BC] *Tsimshian* (H)
Kitwilksheba [BC] *Tsimshian* (H)

Kit-will-coits *see* Kitwilgioks
Kitwillcoits *see* Kitwilgioks
Kitwillquoitz *see* Kitwilgioks
Kit-will-su-pat *see* Kitsilksheba
Kitwillsupat *see* Kitwilksheba
Kitwinga *see* Kitwingach
Kit-win-gach *see* Kitwingach
Kitwingach [BC] *Kitksan* (H)
Kitwinshilk [Can] *Niska* (B)
Kit-win-skole *see* Kitwinskole
Kitwinskole (LC) *see also* Kitwan-
   cool (LC)
Kitwinskole [BC] *Kitksan* (H)
Kit-wulg-jats *see* Kitwilgioks
Kitwulgjats *see* Kitwilgioks
Kitwulkesebe *see* Kitwilksheba
Kit-wulkse-be *see* Kitwilksheba
Kit-wun-kool *see* Kitwinskole
Kitwunkool *see* Kitwinskole
Kityagoo *see* Kittizoo
Kitzeesh [BC] *Tsimshian* (H)
Kitze-gukla *see* Kitzegukla
Kitzegukla [BC] *Kitksan* (H)
Kitzegulka (H) *see also* Kitsegulka
   (BE)
Kit zilas *see* Kitzilas
Kitzilas [BC] *Tsimshian* (H)
Kit-zilass *see* Kitzila
Kitzilass *see* Kitzilas
Kit-zim-gay-lum *see* Kitzimgay-
   lum
Kitzimgaylum [BC] *Tsimshian*
   (H)
Kiua [Self-designation] *see* Santo
   Domingo
Kiu-ahs-dee *see* Shongopovi
Kiuahsdee *see* Shongopovi
Kiuaten *see* Kiatagmiut
Kiukusweskitchimi-uk *see* Male-
   cite
Kiuses *see* Cayuse
Kivalhioqua *see* Kwalhioqua
Kivalinag-miut *see* Kevalingmiut
Kivalinagmiut *see* Kivalinigmiut
Kivalinigmiut [AK] *Kotzebue*
   Sound Eskimos (Hdbk5)
Kive-za-ku *see* Kivezaku
Kivezaku [AZ] *Yuman* (H)
Kivome *see* Santo Domingo
Kivualinagmyut *see* Kivalinig-
   miut
Kivuse *see* Cayuse
Ki-wa *see* Santo Domingo
Kiwaa *see* Kiowa
Kiwahka [*Mosquito-Sumo*] (BE)
Kiwaw *see* Cayuse
Kiwefapawa *see* Kickapoo
Kiwigapawa *see* Kickapoo
Ki-wo-mi [Self-designation] *see*
   Santo Domingo
Ki'xmi *see* Kinugumiut
Kiyahami [Clan] *Apache* (H)
Ki-ya-hanni *see* Kiyahani

Ki-ya-jani *see* Kiyahani
Kiyataigmeuten *see* Kiatagmiut
Kiyataygmyut *see* Kiatagmiut
Kiyatentsy *see* Kiatagmiut
Ki'yis *see* Kiyis
Kiyis [MN] *Piegan* (BE)
Ki-yu-ksa *see* Kiyuska [Mde-
    wakanton]
Kiyuksa [MN] (LC)
Kiyuksa [MN] *Brule* (H)
Kiyuksan *see* Kiyuska [Mde-
    wakanton]
Kiyuska *Mdewakanton* (H)
Kiyuska [SD] *Oglala* (H)
Kiyuska *Upper Yanktonai* (H)
Kizh *see* Gabrielino
Kjotsuni *see* Uru
K'kasawi *see* Kowasayee
Kkoest'ayle-kle *see* Athabasca
Kkra-lon-Gottine *see* Kraylon-
    gottine
K'kwa'kum *see* Kukwakum
Klaamen *see* Sliammon
Klaat-sop *see* Clatsop
Klaatsop *see* Clatsop
Klabalpom [CA] *Wintu* (BE)
Klachatah *see* Klikitat
Klackama *see* Clackamas
Klackamat *see* Clackamas
Klackamu *see* Clackamas
Klackamus *see* Clackamas
Klackamuss *see* Clackamas
Klackarpan *see* Thompson Indi-
    ans
Klackarpun *see* Ntlakyapamuk
Klackatack *see* Klickitat
Klackatat *see* Klikitat
Klackatuck *see* Klikitat
Kla'gulaq *see* Katlagulak
Klagulaq *see* Katlagulak
Klahars *see* Klahosaht
Klahinks *see* Yakutat
Klah-oh-quaht *see* Clayoquot
Klahohquaht *see* Clayoquot
Klahoose *see* Clahoose
Klahoquaht *see* Clayoquot
Klahosaht [Can] *Nootka* (BE)
Klahose *see* Clahoose
Klahous *see* Clahoose
Klah-wit-sis *see* Tlauitsis
Klahwitsis *see* Tlauitsis
Klaizart *see* Makah
Kla-iz-zar *see* Makah
Klaizzar *see* Makah
Klakalama *see* Thlakalama
Klakamat *see* Clackamas
Klakatack *see* Klikitat
Klaki'mass *see* Clackamas
Kla-kwul-lum *see* Cloquallam
Klakwullum *see* Cloquallam
Klalakamish [WA] *Lummi* (H)
Klallam *see* Clallam
Klamac *see* Klamath

Klamak *see* Klamath
Klamat *see* Klamath
Klamath (LC) *see also* Yurok (LC)
Klamath [OR] (LC)
Klamath Lake Indians *see* Kla-
    math
Klamath River [Lang] [CA] *Shasta*
    (CA-8)
Klamatk *see* Klamath
Klamet *see* Klamath
kla'met *see* Klamath
Klameth *see* Klamath
Kla'moix *see* Katlamoik
Klamoix *see* Katlamoik
Klanoh-klatklam *see* Kalispel
Klantlala *see* Kwatami
Klaokwat *see* Clayoquot
Kla-oo-qua-aht *see* Clayoquot
Klaooquaaht *see* Clayoquot
Kla-oo-quate *see* Clayoquot
Klaooquate *see* Clayoquot
Klarkino *see* Klaskino
Klashoose *see* Clahoose
Klas-kaino *see* Klaskino
Klaskaino *see* Klaskino
Klaskino [Can] *Koskimo* (BE)
Klasset *see* Makah
Klass-ki-no *see* Klaskino
Klasskino *see* Klaskino
Klatanar [BC] *Cowichan* (H)
Klatawar *see* Klatanar
Klat-ol-klin *see* Katshikotin
Klatolklin *see* Katshikotin
Klatolseaquilla *see* Tlatlasikoala
Klatrap *see* Clatsop
Klatsap *see* Clatsop
Klatscanai *see* Tlatskanai
Klatskanai *see* Tlatskanai
Klatskanai *see* Clatskanie
Klatskania *see* Tlatskanai
Klatskanie *see* Clatskanie
Klatskanie *see* Tlatskanai
Klats-kanuise *see* Tlatskanai
Klatskanuise *see* Tlatskanai
Klatsonis *see* Tlatskanai
Klatsop *see* Clatsop
Kla-wit-sis *see* Tlauitsis
Klawitsis *see* Tlauitsis
Kla-wi-tsush *see* Tlauitsis
Klawitsush *see* Tlauitsis
Klawmut *see* Klamath
Klaychala *see* Thlingchadinne
Klay-cha-la-tinneh *see*
    Thlingchadinne
Klay quoit *see* Clayoquot
Klayquoit *see* Clayoquot
Klay-tinneh *see* Thlingchadinne
Klaytinneh *see* Thlingchadinne
Klbalt [WA] *Puyallup* (BE)
Kleketat *see* Klikitat
Klemook *see* Tillamook
Kleyne Siconese *see* Little
    Siconese

Klicatat *see* Klikitat
Klickataat *see* Klikitat
Klick-a-tack *see* Klikitat
Klickatack *see* Klikitat
Klickatat *see* Klikitat
Klickatates *see* Klikitat
Klickitat *see* Klikitat
Klikalat *see* Klikitat
Klikatat *see* Klikitat
Kliketan *see* Klikitat
Kliketat *see* Klikitat
Klikitarik (Hdbk5) *see also* Qikiq-
    tagrungmiut (Hdbk5)
Klikitarik *Bering Strait Eskimos*
    (Hdbk5)
Klikitat [WA] (LC)
Klimmim [WA] *Chehalis* (H)
Klinget *see* Tlingit
Klinquit (H)
Klin-tchanpe *see* Lintchanre
Klintchanpe *see* Lintchanre
Klin-tchonpeh *see* Lintchanre
Klintchonpeh *see* Lintchanre
Kliquital *see* Klikitat
Klistinaux *see* Cree
Klistinon *see* Cree
Klistinos *see* Cree
Klo-a-tsul-tshik *see* Tutchone
Kloatsultshik *see* Tutchone
Klochwatone [Family] *Tlingit* (H)
Klodesseottine [Can] *Etchaottine*
    (BE)
Klogi [Clan] *Navajo* (H)
Klogicine *see* Klogi
Klogidine *see* Klogi
Klogni *see* Klogi
Klokadakaydn *Pinal Apache* (H)
Klokadakoydn *San Carlos Apache*
    (H)
Klokegottine [Can] *Nahane* (H)
Kl'o-ke-ottine *see* Klokegottine
Klokeottine *see* Klokegottine
Klo-kke-Gottine *see* Klokegot-
    tine
Klokkegottine *see* Klokegottine
Klo-kke-ottine *see* Klokegottine
Klokkeottine *see* Klokegottine
Kloven Koutcchin *see*
    Tukkuthkutchin
Klo-ven-Kouttchin *see*
    Tukkuthkutchin
Kloven Kuttchin *see*
    Tukkuthkutchin
Klo-ven-Kuttchin *see*
    Tukkuthkutchin
Klowanga *see* Bloods [Sarsi]
Klowitshis *see* Tlauitsis
Kltlassen [Can] *Songish* (BE)
Kluck-hait-kwee *see* Kluck-
    haitkwu
Kluckhaitkwee *see* Kluckhaitkwu
Kluckhaitkwu [WA] *Okinagan*
    (H)

Kluck-ulium *see* Kwaiailk
Kluckulium *see* Kwaiailk
Kluckwaton *see* Klochwatone
Kluckwatone *see* Klochwatone
Klugadacayn *see* Klokadakaydn
Klu'ka-tat *see* Klikitat
Klukatat *see* Klikitat
Kluk-ha-tat *see* Klikitat
Klukhatat *see* Klikitat
kluk-nachadi *see* Tluknahadi
kluknachadi *see* Tluknahadi
Klumaitumsh [WA] *Chehalis I*
(H)
kmike *see* Seri
Knacsitare *see* Gnacsitare
Knaiakhotana (BE) *see also* Aleuts
(LC)
Knaiakhotana (BE) *see also*
Tanaina (LC)
K'nai-a-kho-ta-na *see* Kna-
iakhotana
Knaiakhotana [AK] *Tinne* (H)
Knaiakhotans *see* Knaiakhotana
Knaina *see* Knaiakhotana
Knaiokhotana *see* Knaiakhotana
Knatsomita [Society] *Piegan* (H)
Kneestenoag *see* Cree
Knife Indians *see* Ntlakyapamuk
Knife Indians *see* Esbataottine
Knife Indians *see* Thompson In-
dians
Knife Lake [MI, WI] *Chippewa*
(H)
Knight's Landing [CA] (BE)
Knight's Landing [Lang] [CA]
River Patwin (BE)
Knik *Knaiakhotana* (H)
Knikamut *see* Knik
Kniktagemiut *Kaviagmiut* (H)
Kniktag'emut *see* Kniktagemiut
Knisteaux *see* Cree
Knistenaus *see* Cree
Knistenaux *see* Cree
Knisteneau *see* Cree
Knisteneaux *see* Cree
Knisteneux *see* Cree
Knisteno *see* Cree
Knistenoo *see* Cree
Knistinaux *see* Cree
Knistineaux *see* Cree
Knistino *see* Cree
Knives *see* Ntlakyapamuk
Knives *see* Thompson Indians
K'nou *see* Knou
Knou [Clan] *Potawatomi* (H)
Koa *see* Koi
Koa'aga'itoka (Hdbk11) *see also*
Yahandeka (Hdbk10)
Koaagaitoka *see* Koa'aga'itoka
Koa'aga'itoka *Northern Paiute*
(Hdbk11)
Koa'antel *see* Kwantlen
Koaantel *see* Kwantlen

Koahualla *see* Cahuilla
Koahualla *see* Kawia [Luiseño]
Koaia [Br] (O)
Koaikar *see* Cuaiquer
Koakia *see* Cahokia
Koakotsalgi [Clan] *Creek* (H)
Koakramint *see* Koksoagmiut
K'oa'la *see* Hoya
Koanalalis [Gens] *Nimkish* (H)
Koaratira *see* Amniape
Koas [AK] (H)
Koasaota *see* Koasati
Koasati [AL] *Potawatomi* (LC)
Koassati *see* Koasati
koatoava *see* Cochiti
Kobena *see* Cubeo
Kobeua *see* Cubeo
Kobewa *see* Cubeo
Kobuk (Hdbk5) *see also* Kuuvang-
miut (Hdbk5)
Kobuk [CA] (CA)
Kobukmiut [AK] *Eskimos* (Ye)
Kochayli *see* Ayticha
Koche *see* Camsa
Kocheche Wenenewak *see* Koje-
jewiniewug
Kocheyali (BE) *see also* Ayticha
(CA)
Kocheyali [CA] *Yokuts* (BE)
Kochi *see* Camsa
Kochimberi *Mashco* (O)
Ko-chi-mi *see* Cochimi
Kochimi *see* Cochimi
Kochinakwa *see* Havasupai
Kochinish [Clan] *Acoma* (H)
Kochinish-yaka [Clan] *Laguna*
(H)
Kochinish-yaka [Subclan] *Laguna*
(H)
Kochinish-yaka-hanoch *see* Ko-
chinish-yaka
Kochinishyaka-hanoqch *see* Ko-
chinish-yaka
Ko-chi-ti *see* Cochiti
Kochiti *see* Cochiti
Kochiyali *see* Kocheyali
Kochonino *see* Havasupai
kochutikwe *see* Cochiti
Ko-cke *see* Cochiti
Kocke *see* Cochiti
Koco *see* Hopi
K'odalpa-K'inago *see* Dakota
Kodenees *see* Kutenai
Kodhell-ven-Kouttchin *see*
Kwitchakutchin
Kodiak [Lang] *Koniag* (Hdbk5)
Kodjaksky *see* Kaniagmiut
Koeats [NV] *Ute* (H)
Koechies *see* Kichai
Koeetenays *see* Kutenai
Koekoaainok [Clan] *Kwakiutl* (H)
Koeksotenok [Can] *Kwakiutl*
(BE)

Koeracoenetanon *see* Coiracoen-
tanon
Koes *see* Cowasuck
K-oe'tas *see* Koetas
Koetas [Family] [AK] *Haida* (H)
Koetenais *see* Kutenai
Koetenay *see* Kutenai
Koetenok [Clan] *Bellabella* (H)
Koeton *see* Nassauaketon
koets *see* Koso
Kofan *see* Cofan
Kofane *see* Cofan
Kogaahl-lanas [Subfamily] [BC]
Haida (H)
K-og-a'ngas *see* Kogangas
Kogangas [Family] [BC] *Haida*
(H)
Koggaba *see* Kagaba
Kogholaghi *see* Unalaska
Kogi *see* Kagaba
Kogloktogmiut [Can] *Central Es-
kimos* (BE)
Kogohue *Green River Snakes* (Ye)
Ko'gui (H)
Ko'gui *see* Kogui
Kogui (LC) *see also* Kagaba (LC)
Kogui *Kiowa* (BE)
Kogui [SA] *see* Cogui
Kohadk [Lang] *Papago* (Hdbk10)
Ko'hai *see* Kuhaia
Kohai (PC) *see also* Kuhaia (H)
Kohai [Clan] *Keres* (H)
Kohaia [Clan] *Laguna* (H)
Kohaia-hanoch *see* Kuhaia
Kohai-hano *see* Kuhaia
Kohaio *see* Kuhaia
Kohani [TX] (BE)
Kohatk *see* Quahatika
Kohatsoath [Sept] *Toquart* (H)
Ko-ha-yo *see* Kuhai
Kohayo *see* Kuhaia
Kohenin *see* Yavapai
Kohkang *see* Kokyan
Kohkannanmu *see* Kokyan
Ko-hni-na *see* Havasupai
Kohnina *see* Havasupai
Koho (H) *see also* Tanaha (H)
Koho [Clan] *Caddo Confederacy*
(H)
Kohoaldje *see* Sihvwits
Kohoaldje *see* Southern Paiute
Koho'hlte *see* Taos
Kohohlte *see* Taos
Kohonino *see* Havasupai
Koht-ana *see* Knaiakhotana
Kohtana *see* Knaiakhotana
Kohuana (BE) *see also* Coano
(BE)
Kohuana (BE) *see also* Cowina
(BE)
Kohuana (BE) *see also* Kahwan
(Hdbk10)
Kohuana [AZ] (BE)

Kohuana [Lang] [CA] *Yuman* (He)

Kohun *see* Yuma

kohwailce *see* Southern Paiute

Koi [CA] *Southeastern Pomo* (Pub, v.36, no.6)

Koi [Phratry] *Chickasaw* (H)

koi-aw'we-ek *see* Northern Paiute

koiawweek *see* Northern Paiute

Koienkahe *see* Karankawa

Koikahtenok [Can] *Kwakiutl* (H)

Koikpagamute *see* Ikogmiut

Koiks *see* Laguna [NM]

Ko-in-chush *see* Koinchush

Koinchush [Clan] *Chickasaw* (H)

Ko-intchush *see* Koinchush

Kointchush *see* Koinchush

Koiotero *see* Coyotero Apache

Ko-i-yak *see* Coos

Koiyak *see* Coos

koi-yu-wak *see* Northern Paiute

koiyuwak *see* Northern Paiute

Ko-je-je-win-in-e-wug *see* Koje-jewininewug

Kojejewininewug [MN] *Chippewa* (BE)

Kokaitk [BC] *Bellabella* (H)

K'o'k-aitq *see* Kokaitk

Kokama *see* Cocama

ko'kee'eit *see* Flathead

kokeeeit *see* Flathead

Kokenu'k'ke *see* Okinagan

Kokesailah *see* Koksilah

Kok hit tan *see* Kokhittan

Kokhittan [Social group] *Tlingit* (H)

Kokh-lit-innuin *see* Yuit

Kokh'lit innuin *see* Okiogmiut

Kokhlitinnuin *see* Okiogmiut

Kokhlitinnuin *see* Yuit

Kokhuene *see* Cajuenche

Kokhwaiu *see* Luiseño

Kokmalect *see* Numukmiut

Koknas-hadai [AK] *Haida* (H)

Kokob (H) *see also* Kukuch (H)

Kokob [Clan] *Hopi* (H)

Ko-k'oc *see* Coos

Kokoc *see* Coos

Kokoheba (Pub, v.4, no.3, p.119) *see also* Holkoma (BE)

Kokoheba [CA] *Mono* (Pub, v.4, no.3, p.119)

Kokokiwak *see* Crow

Kokomcar [Lang] [CA] (Pub, v.8, no.1, p.1)

Kokomish *see* Skokomish

Kokonino *see* Havasupai

Kokop (H) *see also* Kokob (H)

Kokop [Phratry] *Hopi* (H)

Ko-ko-pa *see* Cocopa

Kokopa *see* Cocopa

Ko-kop nyu-mu *see* Kokop

Kokop nyumu *see* Kokop

Kokop winwu *see* Kokop

Ko-kop-wun-wu *see* Kokop

Kokop wunwu *see* Kokop

K'ok-o-ro-t'u-yu *see* Pecos

Kokorotuyu *see* Pecos

Kokoskeeg (H)

Kokraimoro [Br] *Cayapo* (O)

Kokraymoro *see* Kokraimoro

Koksilah [Can] *Cowichan* (BE)

Koksoagmiut [Can] *Sukinimiut Eskimos* (H)

Koksoagmyut *see* Koksoagmiut

Koksoak Innuit *see* Koksoagmiut

Koksoakmiut [Can] *Labrador Eskimos* (BE)

Koksoak River People *see* Koksoagmiut

Koksoak River People *see* Kokyan

Koktu *see* Coto

Kokvontan *see* Kagmantan

Kok-wai-y-toch *see* Kokaitk

Kokwaiytoch *see* Kokaitk

Kokwapa *see* Cocopa

Kokwiat [BC] *Bellabella* (Anthro, v.9, no.3, p.159)

Kokyan [Clan] *Hopi* (H)

Ko-kyan-a *see* Kokyan

Kokyana *see* Kokyan

Kokyan winwu *see* Kokyan

Ko-kyun-uh wunwu *see* Kokyan

Kokyunuh wunwu *see* Kokyan

Kolapissa *see* Acolapissa

Kolash *see* Tlingit

Kolatica *see* Kilatika

Kolchaina *see* Hankutchin

Kolchaina *see* Kutchakutchin

Kolchan *see* Kulchana

Kolchane *see* Kulchana

Kolchina *see* Kulchana

Kolimsi *see* Sabane

Kolina *see* Culina

Koliugi *see* Tlingit

Koljuches *see* Tlingit

Koljuschen *see* Tlingit

Koljush *see* Tlingit

Kolla *see* Colla

Kollahuaya *see* Callahuaya

Kollasuyo *see* Callahuaya

Kollina *see* Culina

Kolloshians *see* Tlingit

Kolnit *see* Skilloot

Koloches *see* Tlingit

Kolodai *see* Kolo'di

Kolo'di [Lang] *Papago* (Hdbk10)

Ko-lo-ma *see* Koloma

Koloma [CA] *Nishinam* (H)

Kolomi [AL, FL] *Muskogee* (BE)

Kolomisi [Self-designation] *see* Sabane

Koloshes *see* Tlingit

Koloshi *see* Tlingit

Koloshians *see* Tlingit

Kolouches *see* Tlingit

Kolshani *see* Kulchana

Kolshina *see* Ahtena

Kolshina *see* Hankutchin

Kolshina *see* Tinne

Kolsid (H) *see also* Colcene (H)

Kolsid [WA] *Twana* (BE)

Kolsin *see* Colcene

Kol-sin *see* Kolsid

Kolsin *see* Kolsid

Koltchane *see* Kulchana

Koltschane *see* Kulchana

Koltschaner *see* Kulchana

Koltshan *see* Kulchana

Koltshane *see* Kulchana

Koltshanen *see* Kulchana

Koltshani *see* Kulchana

Koltshany *see* Kulchana

Koltsiowotl [VanI] *Nanaimo* (H)

Koluschan (LC) *see also* Tlingit (LC)

Koluschan [Lang] (H)

Kolush *see* Tlingit

Kolwa *see* Koroa

Kolyuzhi *see* Tlingit

Ko-ma-cho *see* Komacho

Komacho [CA] *Pomo* (H)

Komantsu *see* Comanche

Komaplix [WA] *Okinagan* (BE)

Komats *see* Comanche

Kom-bo *see* Yana [CA]

Kom-bo *see* Yahi

Kombo *see* Yana [CA]

Kombo *see* Yahi

Komenok [BC] *Lekwiltok* (H)

K'o'm'enoq *see* Komenok

Komiu'tis *see* Komkyutis

Komiutis *see* Komkyutis

Komiuvedo *see* Witoto

komkak *see* Seri

Komkome *see* Tonkawa

Komkutis *see* Komkyutis

K'o'mkyutis *see* Komkyutis

Komkyutis [Sept] [[BC] *Kwakiutl* (H)

Ko'm-maidum *see* Achomawi

Kommaidum *see* Achomawi

Ko'moks *see* Comox

Komoks *see* Comox

Ko-mookhs *see* Comox

Komookhs *see* Comox

Ko-mo-yah *see* Kamia

Komoyah *see* Kamia

K'o-moyue *see* Komoyue [Gens]

Komoyue [Gens] [BC] *Kueha* (H)

Komoyue [Sept] *Kukwakum* (H)

Komoyue [VanI] *Kwakiutl* (H)

Ko'mpabi-anta *see* Kiowa

Kompabianta *see* Kiowa

Kompa'go *see* Kiowa

Kompago *see* Kiowa

Komparia *see* Campa

Komseka-Ki'nahyup *see* Arapaho
Komseka-Kinahyup *see* Arapaho
Komuk *see* Comox
Ko-mun-i-tup-i-o *see* Nez Perce
Komunitupio *see* Nez Perce
Komux *see* Comox
Komux *see* Comox
Konagen *see* Kaniagmiut
Konages *see* Kaniagmiut
Konagis *see* Kaniagmiut
Konakegawai *see* Kona-kegawai
Kona-kegawai [Family] *Haida* (H)
Konasgi *see* Kaniagmiut
Konatine *see* Kanohatino
Konaz *see* Kansa
Konce *see* Kansa
Konea *see* Arapaso
Ko-ne-a kun *see* Comiakin
Koneakun *see* Comiakin
Kone-Konep *see* Konekonep
Konekonep [WA] *Okinagan* (H)
Konekonl'p *see* Konekonep
Konekotay [NJ] *Delaware* (H)
Kongigamiut *see* Kangigmiut
Kongigamut *see* Kungugemiut
Kongigamute *see* Kungugemiut
Kong-lo *see* Konglo
Konglo [Clan] *Hano* (H)
Konglo [Clan] *Tewa* (H)
Kongtalyui *Kiowa* (BE)
Kongya [Clan] *Tesuque* (H)
Koni (Pub, v.6, no.1, p.353) *see also* Amador (Pub, v.6, no.1, p.353)
Koni [CA] *Miwok* (H)
Koniag [Lang] *Pacific Yupik* (Hdbk5)
Koniaga *see* Koniag
Koniagi *see* Kaniagmiut
Koniagi *see* Koniag
Koniagmute *see* Kaniagmiut
Konino *see* Havasupai
Konithlushuamiut [Can] *Labrador Eskimos* (BE)
Konjagen *see* Eskimauan
Konjagen *see* Koniagmiut
Konjagen *see* Koniag
konkaak [Self-designation] *see* Seri
Kon-kau *see* Konkow
Konkau *see* Konkow
Konkhandeenhronon *see* Conkhandeenrhonon
Konkone *see* Tonkawa
Konkonelp [WA] *Sinkaietk* (BE)
Konkow [CA] *Maidu* (BE)
Konkow [Lang] *Maiduan* (CA-8)
Ko-nlo *see* Konglo
Konlo *see* Konglo
Konoatinno *see* Kanohatino
Konomihu [CA] (LC)
Konomihu [Lang] [CA] *Shasta* (CA-8)

Konoshioni *see* Iroquois
Konossioni *see* Iroquois
Konowiki *see* Conoy
Konsa *see* Kansa
Kon-ses *see* Kansa
Konses *see* Kansa
Konta'lyui *see* Kongtalyui
Kontareahronon *Huron* (H)
Konungzi Oniga *see* Iroquois
Konya *see* Kongya
Konya-tdoa *see* Kongya
Konza *see* Kansa
Kon-za *see* Kanze [Omaha]
Konza *see* Kanze [Omaha]
Ko-o *see* Koo
Koo [Clan] *Tewa* (H)
Kooagamute *see* Kowagmiut
Kooagomute *see* Kunmiut
Koo a sah te *see* Koasati
Kooasahte *see* Koasati
Koo-cha-koo-chin *see* Utchakutchin
Koochakoochin *see* Kutchakutchin
Koo-chee-ta-kee *see* Kotsoteka
Koocheetakee *see* Kotsoteka
Koo-che-ta-ker *see* Kotsoteka
Koochetaker *see* Kotsoteka
Koochin *see* Kutchin
Koo-chi-ta-ker *see* Kotsoteka
Koochitaker *see* Kotsoteka
Koogmute *see* Kunmiut
Ko-oh-lok-ta-que *see* Kalokta
Koohloktaque *see* Kalokta
Kooji (H)
Kook-a-tee *see* Hokedi
Kookatee *see* Hokedi
Kook-koo-oose *see* Coos
Kookkoooose *see* Coos
Kookotlane [BC] *Bella Coola* (H)
Kookpovoros *see* Kukpaurung-miut
Kook-wai-wai-toh *see* Kokaitk
Koolsaticara *see* Kotsoteka
Koolsatik-ara *see* Kotsoteka
Koolsatikara *see* Kotsoteka
Koo-nah-mich *see* Koonahmich
Koonahmich [BC] *Salish* (H)
koonzi *see* ko'onzi
ko'onzi *Western Shoshone* (Hdbk11)
Koo-og-ameut *see* Kowagmiut
Kooogameut *see* Kowagmiut
Koopowro Mutes *see* Kukpau-rungmiut
Koopowromutes *see* Kukpau-rungmiut
Kooq Mute *see* Kunmiut
Kooqmute *see* Kunmiut
Kooqotla'ne *see* Kookotlane
Koosharem *Ute* (Hdbk11)
Kooskimo *see* Koskimo
Koos-koo *see* Kooskoo

Kooskoo [Clan] *Abnaki* (H)
Koossawin [Chippewa] (H)
Koot *see* Got
Koo-tames *see* Kutenai
Kootames *see* Kutenai
Kootamies *see* Kutenai
Kootanaes *see* Kutenai
Kootanay *see* Kutenai
Kootanie *see* Kutenai
Koo-tche-noo *see* Kutsnuwu
Kootchenoo *see* Hutsnuwu
Koo-tchin *see* Kutchin
Kootchin *see* Kutchin
Koo-tdoa *see* Koo
Kootdoa *see* Koo
Kootenai *see* Kutenai
Kootenaies *see* Kutenai
Kootenaise *see* Kutenai
Kootenay *see* Kutenai
Kootenia *see* Kutenai
Koote-nuha *see* Kutenai
Kootenuha *see* Kutenai
Kootones *see* Kutenai
Kootoonais *see* Kutenai
Kootsenoo *see* Hutsnuwu
Kootsnahoo *see* Hutsnuwu
Kootsnovskie *see* Hutsnuwu
Kootznoo *see* Hutsnuwu
Kootznov *see* Hutsnuwu
Kooukopai *see* Ko'o'u-kopai
Ko-o-u-kopai [AZ] *Walapai* (BE)
Koo-wa-ho-ke *see* Koowahoke
Koowahoke [Subclan] *Delaware* (H)
Kopa *see* Creek
Kopaalk [BC] *Salish* (H)
Kopagmiut (H) *see also* Mackenzie Delta Eskimos (Hdbk5)
Kopagmiut [Can] *Eskimos* (H)
Kopa'g-mut *see* Kopagmiut
Kopag-mut *see* Kopagmiut
Kopagmut *see* Kopagmiut
Kopan'g-meun *see* Kopagmiut
Kopang-meun *see* Kopagmiut
Kopangmeun *see* Kopagmiut
Kopano [TX] (BE)
Ko-paya *see* Tulkepaia
Kopaya *see* Tulkepaia
Ko-pe *see* Copeh
Kope *see* Copeh
Ko-pe-li *see* Kopeli
Kopeli [Clan] *Hano* (H)
Kopeli [Clan] *Tewa* (H)
Kopeli-towa *see* Kopeli
Kopin [Clan] *Tewa* (H)
Kopin-tdoa *see* Kuping
Koprino [BC] (BE)
Koprino [Lang] *Koskimo* (BE)
K'op-tagui *see* Jicarilla Apache
Koquieightuk *see* Kokaitk
Koquitan *see* Coquitlam
Koracocnitonon *see* Coiracoen-tanon

Korakoenitanon *see* Coiracoen-
tanon
Korebahu *see* Coreguaje
Korekaru *see* Baniwa
Korekin *see* Karkin
Korenkake *see* Karankawa
Koretau *see* Baniva
Koripako *see* Curripaco
Korkone *see* Tonkawa
Koroa [MS] (BE)
Koronk *see* Karankawa
Koru [CA] *Patwin* (Pub, v.29,
no.4)
Ko-ru-si *see* Korusi
Korusi [CA] (H)
Kosale'ktawi *see* Kosalektawi
Kosalektawi [CA] *Achomawi*
(Pub, v.23, no.5)
Ko-sa-te'han-ya *see* Koasati
Kosatehanya *see* Koasati
Koseallakte *see* Ko-se-al-lak-te
Ko-se-al-lak-te [CA] *Achomawi*
(BE)
Ko-se-a-ne-nyon *see* Cayuga
Koseanenyon *see* Cayuga
Kosetah [CA] (H)
Koshkiemo *see* Koskimo
Koshkogemut [AK] *Chnagmiut
Eskimos* (H)
Kosho *see* Apache
Kosho *see* Hopi
Kosho *see* Koso
Kosho *see* Shikaviyam
Kosh-sho-o *see* Gashowu
Kosh-sho-o *see* Kassovo
Koshshoo *see* Gashowu
Koshshoo *see* Kassovo
Kosimo *see* Koskimo
Ko-si-pa tu-wi-wa-gai-yu *see*
Kosipatuwiwagaiyu
Ko-si-pa tu-wi-wa-gai-yu *see*
Toedokado
Kosipatuwiwagaiyu (PC) *see also*
Toedokado (Hdbk11)
Kosipatuwiwagaiyu [NV] *Paviotso*
(H)
Kosk'e'di *see* Koskedi
Koskedi [Clan] *Tlingit* (H)
Koskedi [Social group] *Huna* (H)
Koskeemo *see* Koskimo
Kos-keemoe *see* Koskimo
Koskeemoe *see* Koskimo
K'osk-e'moq *see* Koskimo
Kos-ki-mo *see* Koskimo
Koskimo [Lang] [Can] *Kwakiutl*
(BE)
Kos-ki-mu *see* Koskimo
Koskimu *see* Koskimo
Koskoquim *see* Kuskwogmiut
Koskumo *see* Koskimo
K'o-s-o *see* Hopi
Koso (LC) *see also* Panamint (LC)
Koso [CA, NV] (CA)

ko-son *see* Hopi
koson *see* Hopi
K'o-so-o- *see* Hopi
Kosoo *see* Hopi
Ko-stete *see* Laguna [NM]
Kostete *see* Laguna
Kosumnes *see* Cosume
Kosunato (BE) *see also* Uintah
Ute (H)
Kosunato [UT] *Ute* (BE)
Kotaba *see* Catawba
Kotakoutouemi *see* Otaguot-
touemin
Kot-a-Kutchin *see*
Kutchakutchin
Kotakutchin *see* Kutchakutchin
Kotch-a Kutchin *see*
Kutchakutchin
Kotchakutchin *see*
Kutchakutckin
Kotchitchi-wininiwak *see* Koje-
jewininewug
Kotedia *see* Guanano
Kotemoka *see* Pakaanova
Ko-te-yi-mik *see* Kutaiimiks
Koteyimik *see* Kutaiimiks
Kotiria [Self-designation] *see*
Guanano
Kotite *see* Cochiti
Kotitia *see* Guanano
Kot-ji-ti *see* Cochiti
Kotjiti *see* Cochiti
Kotlenok [Gens] *Kwakiutl* (H)
Kotlschanen *see* Kulchana
Koto *see* Orejon
Ko-toh-spi-tup-i-o *see* Salish
Kotohspitupio *see* Salish
K'otsaa *see* Kio
Kotsaa [Clan] [NM] *Pecos* (H)
Kotsai [TX] *Comanche* (BE)
Kotsava (H) *see also* Kutsavi-
dokado (Hdbk11)
Kots-a'va *see* Kotsava
Kots-a'va *see* Kutsavidokado
Kotsava [CA] *Mono* (H)
Kotsento *see* Navajo
Kotsokhotana *see* Kungugemiut
Ko'tso-te-ka *see* Kotsoteka
Kotso-te'ka *see* Kotsoteka
Kotsoteka *Comanche* (BE)
Kot-ta *see* Kotta
Kotta [Clan] *Mohave* (H)
Kotuiti *see* Cochiti
Kotu-ti *see* Cochiti
Kotyit *see* Cochiti
ko-tyit *see* Cochiti
Ko-tyi-ti *see* Cochiti
Kotyiti *see* Cochiti
Kotze *see* Camsa
Kotzebue Sound Eskimos [AK]
(Hdbk5)
Kouan *see* Kohani
Kouas *see* Kawas

Ko-uavi *see* Tulkepaia
Kouavi *see* Tulkepaia
Kouayan *see* Kouyam
Kouayon *see* Kouyam
Kouchnas-hadai [Subfamily]
Haida (H)
Kouera *see* Koroa
Kouerakouitenoux *see* Coira-
coentanon
Kouivakouintanouas *see* Coira-
coentanon
Koukhontan *see* Kagwantan
Kouksoarmiut *see* Koksoagmiut
Ko-un *see* Tonto Apache
Koun *see* Tonto Apache
Ko'un *see* Tulkepaia
Koun *see* Tulkepaia
Kounaouons [MA, ME] (H)
Koungmiut (H) *see also* Kuung-
miut [Paallirmiut] (Hdbk5)
Koungmiut [Can] *Eskimos* (H)
Kourouas *see* Koroa
Kourova *see* Koroa
Kouse *see* Coos
Koushca Kouttchin *see*
Kutchakutchin
Koushcakouttchin *see*
Kutchakutchin
Koushnou *see* Hutsnuwu
Kouskokhantse *see* Kuskwogmiut
Koutaines *see* Kutenai
Koutani *see* Kutenai
Ko-utchan *see* Yuma
Koutchan *see* Yuma
Koutonais *see* Kutenai
Koutzenoo *see* Hutsnuwu
Koutznou *see* Hutsnuwu
Kouyam [TX] (H)
Kouyou *see* Kuiu
kowacdikni *see* kowa'cdikni
kowa'cdikni [OR] *Klamath* (BE)
Kowagmiut [AK] *Eskimos* (LC)
Kowag-mut *see* Kowagmiut
Kowagmut *see* Kowagmiut
Kowai *see* Salmon River
Kowailchew (H) *see also*
Cowichan (LC)
Kowailchew [Can] *Coast Salish*
(H)
Kow-ait-achen *see* Cowichan
Kowaitachen *see* Cowichan
Kowalitsks *see* Cowlitz
kowame *see* Santa Clara [NM]
Kowan'g-meun *see* Kowagmiut
Kowangmeun *see* Kowagmiut
Kow-a-sah *see* Kawaiisu
Kowasah *see* Kawaiisu
Kowasayee [OR] *Tenino* (BE)
Kowavi *see* Tulkepaia
Kowelits *see* Cowlitz
Kowelitsk *see* Cowlitz
Kowes *see* Coos
Kowes Bay *see* Coos

Kowitchan *see* Cowichan
Kowitsin *see* Cowichan
Kowlith *see* Wiyot
Kowlitz *see* Cowlitz
Kowmook *see* Comox
Kowrona *see* Koroa
Kowsis [CA] (H)
Kowwassayee *see* Kowasayee
Kowwassayes *see* Kowasayee
Ko-ya-ta *see* Koyeti
Koyata *see* Koyeti
Ko-ya-te *see* Koyeti
Koyate *see* Koyeti
Koyeti [CA] *Yokuts* (BE)
Ko-ye-to *see* Koyeti
Koyeto *see* Koyeti
Ko-yet-te *see* Koyeti
Koyette *see* Koyeti
Ko'yoang kaui *see* Konkow
Koyoangkaui *see* Konkow
koyo-iyemise *see* Northern
  Paiute
Ko-yo-konk-ha-ka *see* Cayuga
Koyokonkhaka *see* Cayuga
Koyona winwu *see* Koyonya
Ko-yo-no wun-wu *see* Koyonya
Koyono wunwu *see* Koyonya
Koyonya [Clan] *Hopi* (H)
Koyoukon *see* Koyukukhotana
Koyoukouk-kouttanae *see*
  Koyukukhotana
Koyu *see* Kuiu
Koyugmiut [AK] *Malemiut* (H)
Koyug'mut *see* Koyugmiut
Koyuhkhotana *Tinne* (H)
Ko-yu-hon *see* Atsakudoka tuvi-
  warai
koyuhon *see* Atsakudoka tuvi-
  warai
Ko-yu-how *see* Koyuhow
Ko-yu-how' *see* Atsakudoka tu-
  viwarai
Koyuhow (PC) *see also* Atsaku-
  doka tuviwarai (Hdbk11)
Koyuhow [NV] *Paviotso* (H)
Koyuk *Bering Strait Eskimos*
  (Hdbk5)
Koyukon [AK] (LC)
Koyukukh-otana *see* Tinne
Koyu-kukh-ota'na *see*
  Koyukukhotana
Koyukukhotana [AK] *Koyukon*
  (BE)
Koyukun *see* Koyukukhotana
Koyukuns *see* Koyukukhotana
Koyukunskoi *see* Koyukukhotana
Koyungmiut (H)
Ko-za'-bi-ti-kut'-eh *see* Kutsavi-
  dokado
Kozabitikuteh *see* Kutsavidokado
Ko-za-bi-ti-kut-teh *see* Kotsava
Kozabitikutteh *see* Kotsava
Kozarene [Br] *Paressi* (O)

Kozarini *see* Kozarene
kpuspat *see* Northern Paiute
K'qlo-qwec tunne *see* Siuslaw
K'qlo-qwec tunne *see* Coos
K'qlo-qwec'tunne *see* Kalawatset
Kqoptl'nik *see* Colville
Kraho *see* Craho
Kranhacarore *see* Kreen-Akarore
Krayiragottine [Can] *Etchaottine*
  (H)
Kraylongottine [Can] *Nahane* (H)
Krazlongottine (H)
Kre-akarore *see* Arara
Kreakarore *see* Arara
Kree *see* Cree
Kreek *see* Creek
Kreen-Akarore *see* Kreen-Akrore
Kreen-Akrore [Br] (LC)
Kreluits *see* Skilloot
Kremye *see* Krem-ye
Krem-ye [Br] *Timbira* (O)
Krenak [Br] *Botocudo* (O)
Krenje *see* Krem-ye
Krenkataje *see* Canella
Krenkateye [Br] (O)
Kren-ye *see* Krem-ye
Krenye *see* Krem-ye
Kre-tan *see* Kretan
Kretan [Subclan] *Missouri* (H)
Kreye *see* Krem-ye
Kricho *see* Creek
Krie *see* Cree
Krieq *see* Cree
Krihk *see* Creek
Krikati [Br] *Eastern Timbira* (O)
Krinkati *see* Krikati
Kriq *see* Cree
Kris *see* Cree
Krishana *see* Yawaperi
Kristenaux *see* Cree
Kristeneaux *see* Cree
Kristinaux *see* Cree
Kristino *see* Cree
Krixana *see* Yawaperi
Ksalokul [VanI] *Nanaimo* (H)
ksanka [Self-designation in MT]
  see Kutenai
Ksapsem [VanI] *Songish* (BE)
K'tata *see* Shanwappom
K'tatas-le'ma *see* Shanwappom
Ktlaeshatlkik [WA] *Cathlamet*
  (H)
ktunaxa [Self-designation] *see*
  Kutenai
Ku [Clan] *Tewa* (H)
Ku [NI] *Sumo* (BE)
Kua [Clan] *Taos* (H)
Ku-ag'mut *see* Kowagmiut
Kuagmut *see* Kowagmiut
Kua'hadi *see* Kwahari
Kuahadi *see* Kwahari
Kuaiath *Seshat* (H)
Kuaja *see* Kwahu

Kuakumchen [BC] *Squawmish*
  (H)
Kua'kumtcen *see* Kuakumchen
Kuakumtcen *see* Kuakumchen
Kuangmiut *see* Kowagmiut
Kuasse [TX] (H)
Kua-taiina *see* Kua
Kuataiina *see* Kua
K'uato *see* Kuato
Kuato *Kiowa* (H)
Kuaua *Tigua* (H)
Kubakhye *see* Kawaiisu
Ku-baratpat *see* Penateka
Kubaratpat *see* Penateka
Kubenbrankegn *see* Kuben-
  Kran-Kegn
Kubenbranken *see* Kuben-Kran-
  Kegn
Kuben-Kamrekti *see* Asurini I
Kubenkamrekti *see* Asurini I
Kubenkragmotire *see* Kuben
  Kragmotire
Kuben Kragmotire [Br] *Cayapo*
  (O)
Kubenkrankegn *see* Kuben Krag-
  motire
Kuben-Kran-Kegn [Br] *Cayapo*
  (O)
Kubeo *see* Cubeo
Kubeu *see* Cubeo
Kubewa *see* Cubeo
Kubewana *see* Cubeo
kucadikadi *see* Kutsavidokado
kuccuntikka *see* Lemhi
kuccuntikka [Self-designation]
  see Pohogwe
ku-che-sa *see* Chiricahua Apache
Kuchiana *see* Yuma
Ku-chi-bich-i-wa-nap Pal-up *see*
  Pahkanapils
Ku-chi-bich-i-wa-nap Pal-up *see*
  Tipatolapa
Ku-chi-bich-i-wa-nap Pal-up *see*
  Tubatulabal
Kuchibichiwanap Palup *see*
  Pahkanapils
Kuchibichiwanap Palup *see*
  Tipatolapa
Kuchibichiwanap Palup *see* Tu-
  batulabal
Kuchichiwininiwug *Kojejewinini-
  wug* (His/T, v.1, p.346)
Kuchin *see* Kutchin
Kuchnikwe *see* Havasupai
kudi-q *see* Eskimos
kudi-q *see* Eyak
kudiq *see* Eskimos
kudiq *see* Eyak
Kud-witcaca *see* Kutawichasha
Kudwitcaca *see* Kutawichasha
Kueh'a *see* Komoyue
Kueha (PC) *see also* Komoyue (H)
Kueha [BC] *Lekwiltok* (H)

Kuehe *see* Komoyue
Kuenyugu-haka *see* Cayuga
Kue'qa *see* Komoyue
Kue'qa *see* Kueha
Kueqa *see* Komoyue
Kueqa *see* Kueha
Kue'xa *see* Komoyue
Kuexa *see* Komoyue
Ku-ga *see* Kokop
Kuga *see* Kokop
Kugapakori *see* Cogapocori
Kugaramiut [AK] *Malemiut Eskimos* (H)
Kugmiut (H) *see also* Kunmiut (BE)
Kugmiut [AK] *North Alaska Coast Eskimos* (Hdbk5)
Kuhaia [Clan] *Keres* (H)
Kuhaia-hanuch *see* Kuhaia
Kuhinedi [AK] *Tlingit* (H)
Kuhinedi [Clan] *Henya* (H)
Kuhkweai *see* Laguna [NM]
Kuhlanapo [CA] *Eastern Pomo* (H)
Kuhn *see* Tulkepaia
Kuhnauwantheew *see* Conoy
Kuhni kwe *see* Havasupai
Ku'h-nis *see* Havasupai
Kuhnis *see* Havasupai
Kuhns *see* Tonto Apache
Kuh-pat-ti-kut-teh *see* Kuhpattikutteh
Kuh'-pat-ti-kut'-teh *see* Kupadokado
Kuhpattikutteh *see* Kupadokado
Kuhpattikutteh [NV] *Paviotso* (H)
Ku'htche-tecka *see* Kotsoteka
Kuhtchetecka *see* Kotsoteka
Kuiba *see* Cuiva
Kuicha *see* Komoyue
Kuigpagmiut [AK] *Eskimos* (Hdbk5)
Kuikni *see* Molala
Kuikuro *see* Kuikuru
Kuikuru [Lang] [Br] *[Bakairi-Nahukwa]* (LC)
Kuilchana *Tinne* (H)
Kuilka *see* Kaskaskia
Kuille-pate *see* Quileute
Kuillepate *see* Quileute
Kuin-ae-alt *see* Quinault
Kuinaealt *see* Quinault
Kuin-ruk *see* Kuinruk
Kuinruk [AK] *Knaiakhotana* (H)
Kuishkosh [Clan] *Acoma* (H)
Kuishkoshyaka [Clan] *Acoma* (H)
Ku'ishkoshyaka-hanoqch *see* Kuishkoshyaka
Kuishtiti *see* Kuishtitiyaka
Kuishtitiyaka [Clan] *Acoma* (H)
Ku'ishtitiyaka-hanoqch *see* Kuishtitiyaka

Kuitare-i *see* Pawnee
Kuitarei *see* Pawnee
Ku-itc *see* Kuitsh
Kuitc *see* Kuitsh
Kuitsh [OR] (LC)
Kuiu (PC) *see also* Ku'iu (Contri, v.1, p.38)
Kuiu [AK] *Tlingit* (BE)
Ku'iu *[Sitka-kwan]* (Contri, v.1, p.38)
Kuiva *see* Cuica
Kuivaduka *see* Smith Creek Valley
Kuiwanva [Clan] *Hopi* (H)
kúixpáymiut *see* Kuigpamiut
Kuiyaduka *see* Smith Creek Valley
Kuiyui'tikadu *see* Kuyuidokado
Kuiyuitikadu *see* Kuyuidokado
Kuiza'n *see* Yuma
Kuizan *see* Yuma
Kujeedi *see* Kuyedi
Kukalaya *[Mosquito-Sumo]* (BE)
Kukanish [Clan] *Acoma* (H)
Ku'kanis-hyaka-hanoqch *see* Kukinishyaka
Kukanishyakahanoqch *see* Kukinishyaka
Kukapa *see* Cocopa
Kukettan *see* Kokhittan
Kukhpagmiut *see* Kopamiut
Kukinishyaka [Clan] *Acoma* (H)
Kukinish-yaka [Sub-clan] *Laguna* (H)
Ku'kinishyaka-hanoch *see* Kukinishyaka
Kukittan *see* Kokhittan
Kukkuiks [Society] *Piegan* (H)
Kukoak [VanI] *Songish* (BE)
Kukparungmiut [AK] *Eskimos* (BE)
Kukra *see* Sumo
Kukuch [Clan] *Hopi* (H)
Kukulek [VanI] *Songish* (BE)
Kukunski *see* Koyukukhotana
Ku-ku-tci *see* Kukuch
Kukutci *see* Kukuch
Kukutc winwu *see* Kukuch
Kukuth-kutchin *see* Takkuthkutchin
Kukuthkutchin *see* Takkuthkutchin
Kukuts *see* Kukuch
Kukutsi *see* Kukuch
Kukuyana (O) *see also* Tiriyo (O)
Kukuyana *Pianokoto* (O)
Kukwa'kum *see* Kukwakum
Kukwakum [Gens] [VanI] *Kwakiutl* (H)
Kukwil *see* Mishikhwutmetunne
Ku-kwil tunne *see* Mishikhwutmetunne
Kukwiltunne *see* Mishikhwutmetunne

Ku-kwil-tun tunne *see* Mishikhwutmetunne
Kukwiltuntunne *see* Mishikhwutmetunne
Ku-la Kai Pomo *see* Keliopoma
Kulakai Pomo *see* Keliopoma
Kulanapan [Lang] [CA] (H)
Kulanapan (LC) *see also* Pomo (LC)
Kulanapo *see* Pomo
Kula'napo *see* Pomo
Kulanopo *see* Kuhlanapo
Kulchana [AK] *Ahtena* (BE)
Kuldo (H) *see also* Kauldaw (H)
Kuldo [Can] *Kitsan* (BE)
Kuldoe *see* Kauldaw
Kuldoe *see* Kuldo
Ku-lees *see* Kulleets
Kulees *see* Kulleets
Ku-leets *see* Kulleets
Kuleets *see* Kulleets
Kul-hul-atsi *see* Kadohadacho
Kulhulatsi *see* Kadohadacho
Kulias Palus *see* Kalispel
Kuliaspalus *see* Kalispel
Kulina *see* Culina
Kulino *see* Culina
Ku-lis-kitc hitc'lum *see* Taltushtuntude
Kuliskitchitclum *see* Taltushtuntude
Kulkuisala *see* Koksilah
Kulleets [VanI] *Cowichan* (BE)
Kullespelm *see* Kalispel
Kullespen *see* Kalispel
Kullyspell *see* Kalispel
Kulmeh *see* Kul-meh
Kul-meh [CA] *Maidu* (Contri, v.3, p.282)
Ku-lo-mum *see* Kulomum
Kulomum [CA] *Maidu* (H)
Ku-lon-to-wa *see* Konglo
Kulontowa *see* Konglo
K'ul-pa-ki-a-ko *see* Kretan
Kuls-wa *see* Kulswa
Kulswa [Clan] *Miami* (H)
Kulua *see* Koroa
Kulumi *see* Kolomi
Ku-lu-shut *see* Kulushut
Kulushut [AK] *Ahtena* (BE)
Kuma *see* Kunipalgi
Kumachisi [CA] *Yokuts* (CA)
Kumachisi [Lang] *Poso Creek* (CA-8)
Kumadamnainai [VE] *Wakuenai* (O)
Ku-mad-ha *see* Kumadha
Kumadha [Clan] *Mohave* (H)
Ku-man-i-a-kwe *see* Comanche
Kumaniakwe *see* Comanche
Kumaya ay *see* Kamia
Kumayaay *see* Kamia
Kumayena [Lang] *Trio* (UAz, v.28)

Kumbatkni *see* Kumbatuash
Kumbatuash [CA] (H)
Kumbatuashkni *see* Kumbatuash
Kumbatwash *see* Kumbatuash
Kum-cutes *see* Komkyutis
Kumcutes *see* Komkyutis
Kumeyaa *see* Kamia
Kumeyaay *see* Kamia
Kumkewtis *see* Komkyatis
Kumnom *see* Nuimok
kumo-its *see* Cedar
Ku-mu *see* Kunipalgi
Kumumbar *see* Cumumbah
Kun (BE) *see also* Yuma (LC)
Kun (H) *see also* Tulkepaia (H)
Kun [Clan] *Pueblo Indians* (H)
Kuna *see* Cuna
Kunaii-tdoa *see* Kungaii
Kunailanas *see* Kuna-lanas
K'unak-e-owai *see* Kona-kegawai
Ku'na lanas *see* Kuna-lanas
Kuna-lanas [Family] *Haida* (H)
Kunana *see* Nahane
Kunechin [BC] *Seechelt* (BE)
Kuneste [CA] (H)
Kuneyil *see* Kamia
Kunfetdi-tdoa *see* Kungfetdi
Kungaii [Clan] *San Ildefonso* (H)
Kungeeg-ameut *see* Kun-
　gugemiut
Kungfetdi [Clan] *Tewa* (H)
Kungmiut *see* Kuungmiut [Paal-
　lirmiut]
Kungpi [Clan] *Tewa* (H)
Kungtsa [Clan] *Tewa* (H)
Kungtsei [Clan] *Tewa* (H)
Kungtsoa [Clan] *Tewa* (H)
Kungugemiut [AK] *Malemiut* (H)
Kungugemut *see* Kungugemiut
Kungya [Clan] *Tewa* (H)
Kungye *see* Kungya
Kungyi [Clan] *Nambe* (H)
Kunhittan *Tlingit* (H)
Kunimia *see* Guayabero
Kuni-palgi *see* Kuniopalgi
Kunipalgi [Clan] *Creek* (H)
Kunis'tunne *see* Alsea
Ku-nis tunne *see* Alsea
Kunistunne *see* Alsea
Kunis'unne *see* Alsea
Kunisunne *see* Alsea
Kunivadeni *see* Dani
Kun la'nas *see* Kuna-lanas
Ku'nmium *see* Kunmiut
Kunmium *see* Kunmiut
Kunmiut [AK] *Eskimos* (BE)
Kunmu'd'lin *see* Kangmaligmiut
Kun-na-nar-wesh *see* Arapaho
Kunnanarwesh *see* Arapaho
Kunnas-hadai [Family] *Haida* (H)
Kunniwunneme [OR] (H)
Kunpi-tdoa *see* Kungpi
Kunqit *see* Gunghet-haidagai

Kunri-t'ainin *see* Kurni
Kunta-witcaca *see* Kutawichasha
Kun-tdoa *see* Kun
Kuntsa-tdoa *see* Kungtsa
Kuntsei-tdoa *see* Kungtsei
Kuntsoa-tdoa *see* Kungtsoa
Kunuana *see* Kunuhana
Kunuhana [VE] *Yecuana* (O)
Kunu-hayanu *see* Potawatomi
Kunuhayanu *see* Potawatomi
Kun-un-ah *see* Tahltan
Kununah *see* Tahltan
Kunwica'sa *see* Kutawichasha
Kunya [Clan] *Tewa* (H)
Kunya-tdoa *see* Kungya
Kunyil *see* Kamia
Kun-za *see* Kanze [Omaha]
Kunza *see* Kanze *Omaha*
Kuoolt-e *see* Kwantlen
Kupa *see* Cupeño
Kupadokado *Northern Paiute*
　(Hdbk11)
Kupi [Clan] *Santa Clara* (H)
Kupin *see* Kuping
Kuping [Clan] *Tewa* (H)
Kupin-tdoa *see* Kuping
Kupi-tdoa *see* Kuping
Kupkipcock *see* Caposepock
Kupondirideri *Mashco* (O)
Kupunmium *see* Kopagmiut
Kura *see* Bakairi
Kuraintu-kwakats *see* Kwaiantik-
　wokets
Kurina *see* Culina
Kuripako *see* Curripaco
Kurni [Clan] *Tigua* (H)
Kuroskiana *see* Yabarana
Kurrim [Self-designation] *see*
　Curripaco
Kurripako *see* Curripaco
Kurso *see* Moro
Kursu *see* Moro
Kurts [Clan] [NM] *Keres* (H)
Kur'ts-hanoqch *see* Kurts
Kurtshanoqch *see* Kurts
Kurtsi [Clan] *Laguna* (H)
Kur-tsi-hanoch *see* Kurts
Kurtsihanoch *see* Kurts
Kurtz *see* Kurts
Kuruaya [Br] (O)
Kurugmiut [Can] *Mackenzie Eski-
　mos* (BE)
Kurukuru *see* Paumari
Kuruparia *see* Campa
Kurvik *see* Kopagmiut
Kus *see* Miluk
Kus *see* Coos
Kus *see* Okuwa
Kusa *see* Abihka
Kusa *see* Coos
Kusa *see* Creek
Kusan (LC) *see also* Coos (LC)
Kusan [Lang] (BE)

Kuscarawaok *see* Cuscarawaoc
Kuscarawock *see* Cuscarawaoc
Kusch-ke-ti *see* Koskedi
Kuschketi *see* Koskedi
Kusch-kuk-chwak-mut *see*
　Kuskowogmiut
Kuschkukchwak-muten *see*
　Kuskwogiut
Kusesh [Clan] *Acoma* (H)
Kuseshyaka [Clan] *Acoma* (H)
Kuseshyaka-Hanoqch *see* Kuse-
　shyaka
Ku-shap Ok-la *see* Kushapokla
Kushapokla [Phratry] *Choctaw*
　(H)
Kushiksa [Clan] *Choctaw* (H)
Kush-Kish *see* Usal
Kushkish *see* Usal
Kushkukkhvakmiuty *see*
　Kusquqvagmiut
Kushokwagmut *see* Kuskwog-
　miut
Kushpelu *see* Kalispel
Kusikia [BO] (O)
Ku'si-pah *see* Kosipatuwiwagaiyu
Ku'si-pah *see* Toedokado
Kusipah *see* Kosipatuwiwagaiyu
Kusipah *see* Toedokado
kusitta *see* Gosiute
Kusi-Utahs *see* Gosiute
Kuskaranaocke *see* Cuscarawaoc
Kuskarawack *see* Cuscarawaoc
Kuskarawaokes *see* Nanticoke
Kusk-edi *see* Koskedi
Kuskedi *see* Koskedi
Kuskeiskee *see* Kaskaskia
Kus-ke-mu *see* Koskimo
Kuskemu *see* Koskimo
Kusko kuax tana *see* Kuskwog-
　miut
Kuskokuaxtana *see* Kuskwogmiut
Kuskokvigmiuty *see* Kusquq-
　vagmiut
Kuskokvigmyut *see* Kusquq-
　vagmiut
Kuskokvimtsy *see* Kusquq-
　vagmiut
Kuskokwagmut *see* Kuskwog-
　miut
Kuskokwigmjuten *see* Kuskwog-
　miut
Kuskokwig-mut *see* Kuskwog-
　miut
Kuskokwim (H) *see also* Kulchana
　(BE)
Kuskokwim *Yupik Eskimos* (LC)
Kuskokwimer *see* Kuskokwim
Kuskokwimjut *see* Kuskokwim
Kuskokwimtsi *see* Kuskwogmiut
Kuskoquimer *see* Kulchana
Kuskowagamiut *see* Kukquq-
　vagmiut
Kuskuske *see* Kaskaskia

Kuskutchewak *see* Kuskwogmiut
Kuskutshewak *see* Kuskwogmiut
Kuskwogmiut (Hdbk5) *see also*
  Kusquqvagmiut (Hdbk5)
Kuskwogmiut [AK] *Eskimos* (BE)
Kuskwog'mut *see* Kuskwogmiut
Kuskwogmut *see* Kuskwogmiut
Kus-me'tunne *see* Coos
Kusmetunne *see* Coos
Kuspelu *see* Kutenai
kúsquafáymiut *see* Kusquq-
  vagmiut
Kusquqvagmiut [AK] *Eskimos*
  (Hdbk5)
Kusso [SC] (LC)
Kussoe *see* Coosa
Kustenau *see* Kutenabu
Kustsheotin [Can] *Northern Car-
  rier* (BE)
Kuta [Clan] [NM] *Santo Domingo*
  (H)
Kut-ai-im-ik *see* Kutaiimiks
Kutaiimiks [MN] *Piegan* (BE)
Kut-ai-sot-si-man *see* Kutaisotsi-
  man
Kutaisotsiman [MN] *Piegan* (BE)
Kutaki *see* Chippewa
Ku-taki *see* Ottawa
Kutaki *see* Ottawa
Kutana *see* Kutenai
Kutani *see* Kutenai
Kutawichasha [Clan] *Brule* (H)
Kuta-witcaca *see* Kutawichasha
Kutawitcaca *see* Kutawichasha
Kutcan *see* Yavasupai
Kutchaa Kuttchin *see*
  Kutchakutchin
Kutcha'kut-chin *see* Tinne
Kutcha'kut-chin *see*
  Kutchakutchin
Kutch-a kutch'in *see*
  Kutchakutchin
Kutch a Kutchin *see*
  Kutchakutchin
Kutcha-kutchin *see*
  Kutchakutchin
Kutchakutchin [AK] (LC)
Kutchamakin *see* Kutshamakin
Kutchan *see* Yuma
Kutchia-Kuttchin *see*
  Kutchakutchin
Kutchiakuttchin *see*
  Kutchakutchin
Kutchi-kutchi *see* Kutchakutchin
Kutchikutchi *see* Kutchakutchin
Kutchin [AK] *Tinne* (LC)
Kutchin [Lang] *Athapascan* (BE)
Kutcitciwininiwag *see* Kojejew-
  ininewug
K'u-tdoa *see* Ku [Pueblo]
Kutenabu [Br] (O)
Kutenae *see* Kutenai
Kutenaekwan *see* Kutenai

Kutenai [MT, BC] (LC)
Kutenay *see* Kutenai
Kutia-Diapa *see* Catoquina
Kutia-Diapa *see* Katukina
  [Panoan]
Kutish (Oregon)
Kutja'am *see* Ashluslay
K'utja'am *see* Yitaa
Kutneha *see* Kutenai
Kutona *see* Kutenai
Kutonacha *see* Kutenai
Kutona'qa *see* Kutenai
Ku-towa *see* Ku [Tewa]
Kutowa *see* Ku [Tewa]
Kut'qakut'qin *see* Loucheux
Kutqakutqin *see* Loucheux
Ku-t'qin *see* Kutchin
Kutqin *see* Kutchin
Kuts [Clan] *Cochiti* (H)
Kutsavidokado *Northern Paiute*
  (Hdbk11)
Kutsha-Kutshi *see*
  Kutchakutchin
Kutshakutshi *see* Kutchakutchin
Kutshamakin [MA] *Massachuset*
  (BE)
Kutshamaquin *see* Kutshamakin
Ku'ts-hano *see* Kurts
Kutshano *see* Kurts
Kutshi *see* Kutchin
Kutshin *see* Kutchin
Kutshittan [Family] *Tlingit* (H)
Kutsh'undika *see* Kutsshundika
Kutshundika *see* Kutsshundika
Kutsnovskoe *see* Hutsnuwu
Kutssemhaath [Can] *Nootka* (H)
Kutsshundika [ID] *Bannock* (BE)
Kuttelspelm *see* Kalispel
Kuttoowauw *see* Cherokee
kutuaiua *see* Kutenai
Kutuhano [MX] (Hdbk10)
Kutzan *see* Yuma
Kuuanguala *see* Pecos
kuugaalimmiut [Can] [*Inuit
  (Quebec)*] (Hdbk5)
Kuungmiut [AK] *Eskimos* (Hdbk5)
Kuungmiut *Kotzebue Sound Eski-
  mos* (Hdbk5)
Ku-u'sha *see* Muskogee
Ku-u-sha *see* Creek
Kuusha *see* Creek
Kuusha *see* Muskogee
Kuuts [Clan] *Keres* (H)
Kuuts-hano *see* Kurts
Kuuvangmiut *Kotzebue Sound Es-
  kimos* (Hdbk5)
Kuuvanmiit *Eskimos* (LC)
Kuuvaum Kangianigmiut *Kotze-
  bue Sound Eskimos* (Hdbk5)
Ku-ux-aws *see* Kiyuksa [Yank-
  tonai]
Kuuxaws *see* Kiyuksa [Yank-
  tonai]

Kuvahaivima *see* Serrano
Kuvahaivima *see* Gitanemuk
kuvahya *see* Kawaiisu
Kuvakhye *see* Kawaiisu
Kuvugmiut *North Alaska Coast
  Eskimos* (Hdbk5)
Ku-wa-ku-che *see* Koakotsalgi
Kuwakuche *see* Koakotsalgi
Kuwaltisk *see* Cowlitz
Ku-we-ve-ka pai-ya *see* Yavapai
Kuwevekapaiya *see* Yavapai
Kuwhaia [Clan] *Acoma* (H)
Kuwhaia-hanoqch *see* Kuwhaia
Kuwichpackmuten *see* Ikogmiut
Kuwu'nmium *see* Kowagmiut
Kuwunmium *see* Kowagmiut
K'u'xinedi *see* Kuhinedi
Kuyakinchi *see* Koyukukhotana
Ku-yan-we *see* Kuyanwe
Kuyanwe [Clan] *Pueblo Indians*
  (H)
Kuyanwe-to-wa *see* Kuyanwe
Kuyawa *see* Kiowa
Kuyedi [Social group] [AK] *Kuiu*
  (H)
kuyeti *see* Koyeti
Kuyo [CA] *Southern Valley Yokuts*
  (BE)
kuyudikka *see* Kuyuidika
Ku-yu-i-di-ka *see* Kuyuidika
Ku yu-i-di ka *see* Kuyuidokado
Kuyuidika (PC) *see also*
  Kuyuidokado (Hdbk11)
Kuyuidika [NV] *Paviotso* (H)
kuyuidikado *see* Kuyuidokado
Kuyuidokado *Northern Paiute*
  (Hdbk11)
Kuyuitkuht [NV] *Northern Paiute*
  (NVAP)
Kuyui'tukede *see* Kuyuidokado
Kuyuitukede *see* Kuyuidokado
kuyui-yekade *see* Kuyuidokado
kuyuiyekade *see* Kuyuidokado
Kuyukantsi *see* Koyukukhotana
Kuyuku-haga *see* Cayuga
Kuyukuhaga *see* Cayuga
Kuyukuks *see* Koyukukhotana
Kuyukunski *see* Koyukukhotana
Kuyut-koe *see* Kuiu
Ku'-yu-wi-ti-kut'-teh *see*
  Kuyuidokado
Kuyuwitikutteh *see* uyuidokado
Kvikhlyuagmyut *see* Kayaligmiut
Kvikhpagmyut *see* Kuigpagmiut
Kvikliuagmiuty *see* Kayaligmiut
Kvikpagmute *see* Ikogmiut
Kwa *see* Kwahu
Kwaak-sat *see* Hoh
Kwaaymi (LC) *see also* Diegueño
  (LC)
Kwaaymi [CA] (MM, Sun. 1995,
  pp.8–9)
Kwaaymii *see* Kamia

kwaca'n [Self-designation] *see* Yuma

Kwachelanokumae [Gens] *Kwakiutl* (H)

Kwadsakbiuk *see* Kwa'dsakbiuk

Kwa'dsakbiuk [WA] *Swinomish* (BE)

Kwag'ul *see* Kwakiutl

Kwa-g'utl *see* Kwakiutl

Kwagutl *see* Kwakiutl

Kwahadi (BE) *see also* Kotsoteka (BE)

Kwa'hadi *see* Kwahari

Kwahadi (PC) *see also* Kwahari (BE)

Kwahadi *Comanche* (BE)

Kwahadk *see* Quahatika

Kwahare tetchaxane *see* Kwahari

Kwahari (BE) *see also* Kotsoteka (BE)

Kwa'hari *see* Kwahari

Kwahari [TX] *Comanche* (BE)

Kwahkewlth *see* Kwakiutl

Kwahlaonan [Subclan] *Tewa* (H)

Kwahnt-len *see* Kwantlen

Kwa-hu *see* Kwahu

Kwahu [Clan] *Hopi* (H)

Kwahu winwu *see* Kwahu

Kwa-hu wun-wu *see* Kwahu

Kwahu wunwu *see* Kwahu

Kwai-ailk *see* Kwaiailk

Kwaiailk [Lang] [WA] *Salishan* (BE)

Kwai-an-ti-kwok-ets *see* [NM]

Kwaiantikwokets (PC) *see also* San Juan [NM] (Hdbk11)

Kwaiantikwokets [AZ] *Paiute* (H)

Kwai-an-ti-twok-ets *see* Kwa-iantitwok-ets

Kwaiantitwokets *see* Kwaiantit-wok-ets

Kwaiantl *see* Quinault

Kwaiker *see* Cuaiquer

Kwaikmut *see* Kwaik-mut

Kwaik-mut *Kaviagmiut* (Contri, v.1, p.16)

Kwaishtunne [OR] *Tututni* (BE)

Kwaitlen *see* Kwantlen

Kwakina *Zuni* (Hdbk9)

Kwakiool *see* Kwakiutl

Kwa-kiutl *see* Kwakiutl

Kwakiutl [*BC*] (LC)

Kwakiutl [Lang] *Wakashan* (Anthro, v.9, no.3, pp.157–158)

Kwa'kok-ul *see* Kwakokutl

Kwakokul *see* Kwakokutl

Kwakokutl [Gens] *Kwakiutl* (H)

Kwakoom *see* Kukwakum

Kwakowenok [Gens] *Kwakiutl* (H)

Kwa'kowenox *see* Kwakowenok

Kwa-kuhl *see* Kwakiutl

Kwakuhl *see* Kwakiutl

Kwakukemalenok [Clan] *Koskimo* (H)

Kwakukemlaenok *see* Kwakukemlenok

Kwak'waka-wakw (NPeos, v.7, no.2, p.12)

Kwakwakawakw *see* Kwak'waka-wakw

Kwa-le-cum *see* Saamen

Kwalecum *see* Saamen

Kwalhiokwa *see* Kwalhioqua

Kwalhioqua [WA] (BE)

Kwalinsadndesu [Br] *Southern Nambicuara* (O)

Kwaliokwa *see* Kwalhioqua

Kwan [Clan] [Hopi] (H)

Kwan-le-cum *see* Saamen

Kwanlecum *see* Saamen

Kwa'ntlen *see* Kwantlen

Kwantlen [Can] *Stalo* (BE)

Kwantlin *see* Kwantlen

Kwantlum *see* Kwantlen

Kwantlun *see* Kwantlen

Kwan wiñwu *see* Kwan

Kwan wuñ-wu *see* Kwan

Kwapa *see* Quapaw

kwapa [Self-designation] *see* Co-copa

Kwapa Cegiha *see* Quapaw

Kwapa-Dhegiha *see* Quapaw

Kwapahag *Abnaki* (H)

kwasan *see* Yuma

kwasa-nt *see* Yuma

kwasant *see* Yuma

Kwashi *Comanche* (BE)

Kwashila *see* Goasila

Kwashilla *see* Goasila

Kwa-ta-me tunne *see* Kwatami

Kwatametunne *see* Kwatami

Kwatami (H) *see also* Quahtomah (H)

Kwa-ta-mi *see* Kwatami

Kwatami [OR] *Tututni* (BE)

Kwat-kewlth *see* Kwakiutl

Kwatkewlth *see* Kwakiutl

Kwatsei [Clan] *Tewa* (H)

Kwatsei-tdoa *see* Kwatsei

Kwat-se-no *see* Quatsino

Kwatseno *see* Quatsino

Kwats'enoq *see* Quatsino

Kwatsenoq *see* Quatsino

Kwatsino *see* Quatsino

K'watumati-tene *see* Kwatami

Kwat-zi-no *see* Quatsino

Kwatzino *see* Quatsino

Kwauaenoq *see* Guauaenok

Kwa-wa-ai-nuk *see* Guauaenok

Kwawaainuk *see* Guauaenok

Kwa'wa'a'nuk *see* Guauaenok

Kwawaanuk *see* Guauaenok

Kwaw-kelch *see* Kwakiutl

Kwawkelch *see* Kwakiutl

Kwawkewklth *see* Kwakiutl

Kwaw-kewlth *see* Kwakiutl

Kwaw-ma-chin *see* Quamichan

Kwawmachin *see* Quamichan

Kwawshela *see* Goasila

Kwaw-she-lah *see* Goasila

Kwawshelah *see* Goasila

Kwawt-se-no *see* Quatsino

Kwawtseno *see* Quatsino

Kwa-yo *see* Kwayo

Kwayo [Clan] *Hopi* (H)

Kwayo wiñwu *see* Kwayo

Kwa-yo wuñ-wu *see* Kwayo

Kwa-zackmash *see* Kwazackmash

Kwazackmash [WA] (H)

Kwe-ah-kah *see* Komogue

Kweahkah *see* Komogue

Kwe-ah-kah-Saich-kioie-tachs *see* Kueha

Kweahkahsaichkioietachs *see* Kueha

Kwe-dee-tut *see* Quileute

Kwedeetut *see* Quileute

Kweet *see* Quaitso

Kwehtl-ma-mish *see* Kwehtl-mamish

Kwehtlmamish [WA] *Salish* (H)

Kwehts-hu *see* Quaitso

Kwehtshu *see* Quaitso

K'we'k-sot'enoq *see* Koeksotenok

Kwelech *see* Mohawk

Kwenaiwitl *see* Quinault

Kwe-net-che-chat *see* Makah

Kwenetchechat *see* Makah

Kwe-net-sat'h *see* Makah

Kwenetsath *see* Makah

Kwenio'gwen *see* Cayuga

Kweniogwen *see* Cayuga

Kwent-le-ah-mish *see* Kwehtl-mamish

Kwentleahmish *see* Kwehtl-mamish

Kweres *see* Keres

Kwesh *Tonkawa* (H)

Kwetah *see* Holkoma

Kwe'tela *see* Tsimshian

Kwetela *see* Tsimshian

Kwetso *see* Quaitso

Kwevakapai *see* Kwe'va-kapai

Kwe'va-kapai [AZ] *Walapai* (BE)

Kwevkpaya *see* Kewevikopaya

Kwewu [Clan] *Hopi* (H)

Kwe-wu-uh wuñ-wu *see* Kwewu

Kwewuuh wunwu *see* Kwewu

Kwewu wunwu *see* Kwewu

Kwexa *Kwakiutl* (Anthro, v.9, no.3, p.158)

Kwi-ah-kah *see* Komogue

Kwiahkah *see* Komogue

kwica'n *see* Yuma

Kwichag-mut *see* Kwichagmut

Kwichagmut (H)

Kwichagmut (H) *see also* Kiatagiut (BE)

Kwichan *see* Yuman

Kwichana [Self-designation] *see*
Yuma

Kwichljuamjuten *see* Ikogmiut

Kwichpacker *see* Ikogmiut

Kwichpagmjuten *see* Ikogmiut

Kwichpak *see* Ikogmiut

Kwichyana [Self-designation] *see*
Yuma

kwiciti *see* Cochiti

Kwick-so-te-no *see* Koeksotenok

Kwi-en-go-mats *see* Las Vegas

Kwiengomats (PC) *see also* Las
Vegas (Hdbk11)

Kwiengomats [NV] *Paiute* (H)

Kwigunts [UT] *Paiute* (H)

Kwi-ha *see* Kueha

Kwiha *see* Kueha

Kwikapa *see* Cocopa

kwikapat *see* Cocopa

Kwikhluagemut *see* Kwikluagmiut

Kwikhpag'emut *see* Ekogmut

Kwikhpag'emut *see* Kwikpagmiut

Kwikhpagemut *see* Ekogmut

Kwikhpagemut *see* Kwikpagmiut

Kwikh-pag-mut *see* Ikogmiut

Kwikhpagmut *see* Ikogmiut

Kwikluagmiut [AK] *Ikogmiut* (H)

Kwikoaenok [Gens] *Kwakiutl* (H)

Kwi'koaenox *see* Kwikoaenok

Kwikoaenox *see* Kwikoaenok

Kwikotlem *see* Coquitlam

Kwikpagmiut (Hdbk5) *see also*
Kuigpagmiut (Hdbk5)

Kwikpagmiut [AK] *Ikogmiut* (H)

Kwikpagmiut *see* Kwikpagmiut

Kwiksot'enoq *see* Koeksotenok

Kwik-so-tino *see* Koeksotenok

Kwi'kwitlem *see* Coquitlam

Kwikwitlem *see* Coquitlam

Kwikwu'lit *see* Cascades

Kwikwu'lit *see* Hood River Indians

kwilegi'i *see* San Felipe

Kwille-hate *see* Quileute

Kwillehate *see* Quileute

Kwille-hiut *see* Quileute

Kwillehiut *see* Quileute

Kwilleut *see* Quileute

Kwilleyhut *see* Quileute

Kwilleyute *see* Quileute

Kwillu'chini *see* Cathlamet

Kwilsieton [OR] *Chasta* (H)

Kwimguchum *see* Cahuilla

Kwimkwangakh *see* Cahuilla
[Lang]

kwi'naduva *see* Atsakudoka tuviwarai

kwinaduva *see* Atsakudoka tuviwarai

kwi'naduvaa *see* Atsakudoka tuviwarai

kwinaduvaa *see* Atsakudoka tuviwarai

Kwinaith *see* Quinault

Kwinaitl *see* Quinault

Kwinaiult *see* Quinault

Kwinaiutl *see* Quinault

kwi-napa-ti *Owens Valley Paiute*
(Hdbk11)

kwinapati *see* kwi-napa-ti

Kwin-eek-cha *see* Kwineekcha

Kwineekcha [Subclan] *Delaware*
(H)

Kwingyap [Clan] *Hopi* (H)

Kwi-nobi *see* Kwingyap

Kwinobi *see* Kwingyap

kwi-nodiba *see* Atsakudoka tuviwarai

kwinodiba *see* Atsakudoka tuviwarai

kwi'nodub *see* Atsakudoka tuviwarai

kwinodub *see* Atsakudoka tuviwarai

kwin-yap wuñ-wu *see* Kwingyap

Kwinyap wunwu *see* Kwingyap

Kwinyil *see* Kamia

Kwis-aese-kees-to *see* Kwisaesekeesto

Kwisaesekeesto [Clan] *Delaware*
(H)

Kwitanemum *see* Cahuilla

Kwitara-a *see* Pawnee

Kwitchakutchin [Can] *Kutchin*
(H)

Kwitcha-Kuttchin *see*
Kwitchakutchin

Kwitchakuttchin *see*
Kwitchakutchin

Kwitchia-Kutchin *see*
Kwitchakutchin

Kwitchiakutchin *see*
Kwitchakutchin

Kwitchluag'emut *see* Kwikluagmiut

Kwitcyan *see* Yuma

Kwitcyana *see* Yuma

Kwithluag'emut *see* Ekogmut

Kwit'qakut'qin *see* Loucheux

Kwitqakutqin *see* Loucheux

Kwi-um-pus *see* Beaver

Kwiumpus (PC) *see also* Beaver
(Hdbk11)

Kwiumpus [UT] *Paiute* (H)

Kwohatk *see* Quahatika

Kwok-woos *see* Coos

Kwokwoos *see* Coos

Kwoneatshatka [VanI] *Nootka*
(BE)

Kwoshonipu *see* Chimariko

Kwo-to-a *see* Kwotoa

Kwotoa [CA] *Maidu* (H)

Kwowahtewug *see* Mandan

Kwtsaan *see* Yuma

Kwu'da *see* Kiowa

Kwuda *see* Kiowa

kwukwokwum [Clan] *Kwexa* (Anthro, v.9, no.3, p.158)

Kwulseet *see* Colcene

Kwun Lennas *see* Kuna-lanas

Kwusatthlkhuntunne *see* Cosuttheutun

Kwu-teh-ni *see* Kwaiailk

Kwutehni *see* Kwaiailk

Kwuts *see* Koso

Kxagantaiahouhin *see* Aleuts

Kyacks *see* Kake

Kyaishi-ateuna [Phratry] *Zuni*
(H)

Kyakiima *see* Kiakima

Kyakotsmovi *Hopi* (Hdbk9)

Kyakyali [Clan] *Zuni* (H)

K'ya'k'yali-kwe *see* Kyakyali

Kyalish *see* Kyiahl

K'yalishi-ateuna *see* Kyalishi-
ateuna

Kyana [Clan] *Zuni* (H)

K'yana-kwe *see* Kyana

Kyanamara *see* Gallinomero

K'ya-na-thlana-kwe *see* Laguna

K'ya'na'we *see* Kechipauan

Kya'nusla *see* Kianusili

Kyanusla *see* Kianusili

Kyaukev *see* Tillamook

Kyaukw *see* Tillamook

Kyaway *see* Kiowa

Kychtagmytt *see* Chugach

Kychtagmytt *see* Koniag

Kycu-cut *see* Kyoquot

Kycucut *see* Kyoquot

Kyekykyenok [Gens] *Kwakiutl*
(H)

Kyemuse *see* Cayuse

Kye-use *see* Cayuse

Kyeuse *see* Cayuse

Kyewaw *see* Kiawaw

Kygani *see* Kaigani

Kyganies *see* Kaigani

Kygany *see* Kaigani

Kygargey *see* Kaigani

Kygarney *see* Kaigani

Kyiahl [Clan] *Jemez* (H)

Kyia'hlash *see* Kyiahl

Kyiahlash *see* Kyiahl

Kyia'ltkoangas *see* Kialdagwuns

Kyialtkoangas *see* Kialdagwuns

Kyiataash *see* Kiahl

Kyia'taash *see* Kyiahl

Kyiks'ade *see* Kiksadi

Kyiksade *see* Kiksadi

Kyis *see* Kichai

Kyisapang *see* Sanapana

Kykhtagmiut *see* Chugach

Kykhtagmiut *see* Koniag

Kyktagagmiut *see* Qikiqtagrung-
miut

Kyoma *see* Angaite

Kyoose *see* Cayuse
Kyo-p'enoq *see* Koprino
Kyopenoq *see* Koprino
Kyoquot [Can] *Nootka* (BE)
Kyspyox *see* Kishpachlaots
Ky-u-kaht *see* Kyoquot
Ky-uk-aht *see* Kyoquot
Kyukaht *see* Kyoquot
Kyu-kutc'hitclum *see* Takelma
Kyukutchitclum *see* Takelma
Kyungan-tdoa *see* Kyunggang
Kyunggang [Clan] *Tewa* (H)
Kyunu [Clan] *Pueblo Indians* (H)
Kyunu'ash *see* Kyunu
Kyunuash *see* Kyunu
Kyunu'tsaah *see* Kyunu
Kyunutsaah *see* Kyunu
Kyu-nutsa-ash *see* Kyunu
Kyunutsaash *see* Kyunu
Ky-wk-aht *see* Kyoquot
Kywkaht *see* Kyoquot
Ky-yoh-quaht *see* Kyoquot
Kyyohquaht *see* Kyoquot

-L-

Laalaksentaio [Clan] *Guetela* (H)
Laa'laqsent'aio *see* Laalaksentaio
La'alaxsent'aio *see* Laalaksentaio
Laalaxsentaio *see* Laalaksentaio
Laa'luis *see* Tlaaluis
Laaluis *see* Tlaaluis
La-aptin *see* Nez Perce
Laaptin *see* Nez Perce
Labrador [Can] *Eskimos* (BE)
Labrador Eskimo [Lang] *Eastern Canada* (Hdbk5)
Labrador Inuttut [Lang] *see* Labrador Eskimo [Lang]
Labradormiut *see* Inuit [Labrador]
Labrodaor Inuit [Self-designation] *see* Inuit [Labrador]
Lacandon [Gua, MX] *Mayas* (LC)
Lac Court d'Oreille *see* Lac Court Oreilles
Lac Court Oreilles [WI] *Betonukeengainubejig* (H)
Lac Court Orville *see* Lac Court Oreilles
Lac Coutereille *see* Lac Court Oreilles
Lac des Quinze [Can] *Algonkin* (BE)
Lac du Flambeau *Chippewa* (Char, v.2, pt.1, p.23)
La-ches *see* Tachi
Laches *see* Tachi
Lack-Bows *see* Sans Arcs

Lack-que-libla *see* Lekwiltok
Lackquelibla *see* Lekwiltok
Lac la Hache (Hdbk12) *see also* Williams Lake Band (Hdbk12)
Lac la Hache [BC] *Lake Sushwap* (Hdbk12)
Lac la Pluie Indians *see* Kojejew-ininewug
La Concepcion de Quarac *see* Quarai
La Dalle *see* Dalles
Lacopseles *see* Tlascopsel
Lac qui Parle *see* Mdeiyedan
Lacquiparle *see* Mdeiyedan
Lac Traverse Band *see* Kahra
Laenukhuma [Gens] *Quatsino* (H)
La Feuille's band *see* Kiyuksa [Medewakanton]
Lagana *see* Laguna
Laghkeak [Social group] *Niska* (H)
Laghkepo [Social group] *Niska* (H)
Lagoons *see* Tolowa
Lagouna *see* Laguna
La Gran Quivira *see* Tabira
La Grue *see* Atchatchakangouen
Laguna [CA] *Pomo* (H)
Laguna [NM] (Hdbk11) *see also* Timpanogots (Hdbk11)
Laguna [NM] (Hdbk11) *see also* Timpanogots (Hdbk11)
Laguna [NM] (LC)
Laguna [NM] (LC) *see also* Tatagua (H)
Laguna [NM] (LC) *see also* Timpaiavats (H)
Lagune *see* Laguna
Lagunero [MX] (BE)
Lagunian *see* Laguna
La haguna *see* Laguna
Lahaguna *see* Laguna
Lahama *see* Lahanna
Lahanna (H)
La-hanna *see* Lahanna
Lahayikqoan *see* Yakutat
Lahayi'kqoan [Self-designation] *see* Yakutat
Lahtoh *see* Methow
Laich-kwil-tacks *see* Lekwiltok
Laidukatuwiwait [NV] *Paviotso* (H)
Lai-ku-ka-tu-wi-wait *see* Laidukatuwiwait
Laimon [BaC] (H)
Laitanes *see* Ietan
Lak *see* Clear Lake Indians
Lakamello *see* Clear Lake Indians
La Kar *see* Ietan
La Kar *see* Ietan
Lakar *see* Ietan
Lake [Can] *Upper Lillooet* (BE)
Lake Calhoun Band *see* Kheyataotonwe

Lake Camedu *Dakota* (BE)
Lake Division (Hdbk12) *see also* Shuswap Lake Division (Hdbk12)
Lake Division [BC] *Shuswap* (Hdbk12)
Lake Indians (BE) *see also* Senijextee (BE)
Lake Indians (H)
Lake Indians (H) *see also* Dwamish (LC)
Lake Indians (H) *see also* Lower Kutenai (BE)
Lake Indians (H) *see also* Timpaiavats (H)
La'k!elak *see* Clatsop
Lakelak *see* Clatsop
La'k!elaq *see* Clatsop
Lakelaq *see* Clatsop
Lake Lillooet [BC] *Upper Lillooet* (Hdbk12)
Lake Miwok [CA] *Miwok* (BE)
Lake Miwok [Lang] [CA] *Western Miwokan* (CA-8)
Lake Northern Pomo [Lang] [CA] (Pub, v.6, no.1, pp.155–159)
Lake Patwin [Lang] *Wintuan* (CA-8)
Lake People *see* Min-i-shi-nak-a-to
Lakes [BC, WA] (Hdbk12)
Lake Wappo *see* Lileek
Lake Winnipeg band *see* Nibow-isibiwininiwak
Lakhamute *see* Ugalakmiut
Lakisamni [CA] *Northern Valley Yokuts* (BE)
Lakloukst [BC] *Niska* (H)
Lakmiuk *see* Luckiamute
Lakmiut *see* Luckiamute
Lakonde [Br] *Northern Nambicuara* (O)
Lakota (BE) *see also* Sioux (LC)
Lakota (LC) *see also* Teton Indians (LC)
Lakota [Self-designation] (BE)
Laksamshu [Phratry] *Carrier Indians* (Bull133)
Lakseel [BC] *Niska* (H)
Laksilyu [Phratry] *Carrier Indians* (Bull133)
Lakskiyek [Clan] *Chimmesyan* (H)
Laktiaktl [BC] *Niska* (H)
Laktsemelik [BC] *Niska* (H)
Lakus [Hon, NI] *Sumo* (BE)
Lakweip [AK, BC] (BE)
Lakyebo [Clan] *Chimmesyan* (H)
La-la-ca *see* Modoc
lalaca *see* Modoc
Lalachsent'aio *see* Laalaksentaio
La'lasiqoala *see* Tlatlasikoala
Lalasiqoala *see* Tlatlasikoala
La'lasiqwala *see* Tlatlasikoala

Lalasiqwala *see* Tlatlasikoala
La'lauilela *see* Lalauitlela
Lalauilela *see* Lalauitlela
Lalauitlela [Gens] *Tlatlasikoala* (H)
Lalela'min *see* Tlatlelamin
Laleshiknom *see* Kato
La litanes *see* Ietan
Lalitanes *see* Ietan
Lalkutno'm [CA] *Yuki* (CA)
Lal Linches *see* Dalinchi
Lallinches *see* Dalinchi
'La'loalgi *see* Hlahloalgi
Laloalgi *see* Hlahloalgi
Lama [PE] (O)
La-malle *see* Chelamela
Lamalle *see* Chelamela
Lamancus [Lang] [CA] (Pub, v.8, no.1, p.6)
Lamano *see* Lama
La Mar *see* Omaha
Lamar Culture (LC)
Lamasconson [MD] *Patuxent* (H)
Lamasket *see* Namasket
Lamatan *see* Huron
Lameco *see* Chiaha
Lamika *see* Rancoca
Lamista *see* Lama
Lamisto *see* Lama
lamma-we *see* Goose Lake
　　Modoc
Lamoine *see* Laimon
Lamparack *see* Ditsakana
Lamtama [ID] *Nez Perce* (BE)
Lana *see* Tano
Lanachaadus *see* Lana-chaadus
Lana-chaadus [Family] [BC]
　　Haida (H)
Lanagukunhlin-hadai [Sub-
　　family] *Haida* (H)
Lanaguqantimxadai *see*
　　Lanagukunhlin-hadai
La'na gu qa'n-tin xa'da-i *see*
　　Lanagukunhlin-hadai
La'na tca-adas *see* Lana-chaadus
Lana tcaadas *see* Lana-chaadus
Lanatcaadas *see* Lana-chaadus
la Nation du Sault *see* Saulteaux
Lance *see* Shemaukan
Land Pitches *see* Sanpet
Lanecy *see* Lipan Apaches
Lanegado *see* Anegado
l'Anguille *see* Eel River
Lanos *see* Manso
Laousteque *see* Texas
La Paddo *see* Comanche
Lapaho *see* Arapaho
Lapahogi *see* Arapaho
Lapan *see* Lipan Apache
Lapana *see* Lipan Apache
Lapane *see* Lipan Apache
Lapanne *see* Lipan Apache
Lapiene's House Indians *see*
　　Takkuth-kutchin

Lapiene's House Indians *see*
　　Takuthkutchin
La Plais *see* Comanche
LaPlais *see* Comanche
La Play *see* Comanche
La Playes *see* Comanche
La Plurisima de Zuni *see* Zuni
La Pong *see* Ponca
La Porcelaine *see* Metoac
La Posta [CA] *Mission Indians*
　　(H)
Lapototot *see* Lopotatimini
Laptambif [OR] *Calapooya* (H)
La Purisima de Zuni *see* Zuni
Lapwewe [ID] *Nez Perce* (BE)
Laqkyebo *see* Lakyebo
Laqlo'ukst *see* Lakloukst
Laqloukst *see* Lakloukst
Laqse *see* Haailakyemal
Laqse'el *see* Lakseel
Laqseel *see* Lakseel
Laqski'yek *see* Lakskiyek
Laqt'ia'k tl *see* Laktiaktl
Laqtiaktl *see* Laktiaktl
Laq'uyi'p *see* Lakweip
Laquyip *see* Lakweip
Laramari *see* Tarahumare
Larapihu *see* Arapaho
Lari [Pan, CR] *Terraba* (BE)
La'ri'hta *see* Comanche
Larihta *see* Comanche
Lar-li-e-lo *see* Spokan
Larlielo *see* Spokan
Lartielo *see* Spokan
Lar-ti-e-to's Nation *see* Spokan
Lartieto's Nation *see* Spokan
Las Candelas [Col] *Yuko* (O)
L'a'sq'enox *see* Klaskino
Lasqenox *see* Klaskino
Las-sik *see* Lassik
Lassik [CA] [(CA)
Lassik [Lang] [CA] *Wailaki* (He)
Lastekas *see* Texas
Lastikas *see* Texas
Last-Lodge *see* Kanze [Kansa]
Las Vegas *Southern Paiute*
　　(Hdbk11)
La-ta-ca *see* Modoc
Lataca *see* Modoc
La-ta-da *see* Dhatada
Latada *see* Dhatada
Late-Comedu *Dakota* (H)
Lat'gaawa *see* Upper Takelma
Latgaawa *see* Upper Takelma
Latgawa [OR] (BE)
Latilentask *see* Adirondack
Lati-u *see* Molala
Latiu *see* Molala
La-tiwe *see* Molala
Latiwe *see* Molala
latiwi [Self-designation] *see*
　　Northern Molola
Latsop *see* Clatsop

Latunde [Br] *Northern Nam-
　　bicuara* (O)
Lau'itsis *see* Tlauitsis
Lawokla [Clan] *Choctaw* (H)
Lawrence, St. *see* Picuris
Lawrence Iroquois, Saint
　　(Hdbk15)
Lawrence Islanders, Saint *Asiatic
　　Eskimos* (Hdbk5)
Lawrence Island Yupik, Saint *see*
　　Yuit
La'xse *see* Haailakyemae
Laxse *see* Haailakyemae
Layamon *see* Laimon
Layano [Par, Br] (O)
Layma *see* Laguna
Laymi [Br] (O)
Laymon (H) *see also* Laimon (H)
Laymon [MX] *Cochimi* (BE)
Laymona *see* Laimon
Laymones *see* Laimon
Lazars *see* Illinois
La Zoto *see* Oto
Lcta'mectix *see* Seamysty
Lda'ldji tama-i *see* Tlduldjitamai
Leachers *see* Oto
Lean Bear *Sioux* (BE)
Leapers *see* Chippewa
Lecatuit (H) SE Likatuit (H)
Lecawgo *see* Secawgo
Lecha *see* Gachwechnagechga
Lecle'cuks *see* Spokan
Leclecuks *see* Spokan
Leco [Lang] [BO] (O)
L'Ecoree *see* Ecorce
Lee-Biches *see* Shivwits
Leebiches *see* Shivwits
Lee-ha-taus *see* Ietan
Leehataus *see* Ietan
Lee-kwin-a-i' *see* Leekwinai
Leekwinai [Subclan] *Delaware*
　　(H)
LEEL-wat *see* Lillooet
Lee Panis *see* Lipan Apache
Leepanis *see* Lipan Apaches
Lee Pawnees *see* Lipan Apache
Leepawnees *see* Lipan Apaches
Leequeeltoch *see* Lekwiltok
Left Hand *see* Assiniboin
Lehigh Indians *see* Gachwech-
　　nagechga
Lehu [Clan] *Hopi* (H)
Le-hu wun-wu *see* Lehu
Lehu wunwu *see* Lehu
leilliuit *see* Lillooet
Leja-ga-dat-cah *see* Lejagadatcah
Lejagadatcah *Miniconjou* (H)
Lekahtewutke *see* Marin-Bodega
Lek-a'mel *see* Nicomen
Lekamel *see* Nicomen
Lekulk *see* Sokulk
Lekwiltok [BC] *Kwakiutl* (BE)
Le'kwiltoq *see* Lekwiltok

Lekwiltoq see Lekwiltok
Le'lacha see Lelaka
Lelacha see Lelaka
Lelaka [Gens] *Nakomgilisala* (H)
Lelek [Can] *Songish* (BE)
Lelengtu [Clan] *Hopi* (H)
Lelentu winwu see Lelengtu
Lelewagyila [Gens] *Kwakiutl* (H)
Le-le-wa-you see Lelewayou
Lelewayou [Subclan] *Delaware* (H)
Leliotu *Hopi* (H)
Le-li-o-tu wun-wu see Leliotu
Leliotu wunwu see Leliotu
Le'lqet see Tletket
Lelqet see Tletket
Le'lqete see Tletket
Lelqete see Tletket
Lema'tlca see Lilmalche
Lemerlauans see Paouites
Lemhi *Northern Shoshone* (Hdbk11)
Lemitas [NM] (H)
LeMotte see Le Motte
Le Motte [WI] *Menominee* (BE)
Lemparack see Ditsakana
Lenahuon [CA] (H)
Lenais see Leni Lenape
Lenalenap see Leni Lenape
Lenalenape see Leni Lenape
Lenalinepies see Leni Lenape
Lenap see Leni Lenape
Lenape [Self-designation] see Leni Lenape
Lenape [Self-designation] see Leni Lenape
Lenapegi see Leni Lenape
Lenappe see Leni Lenape
Lenappy see Leni Lenape
Lenawpe see Leni Lenape
Le-nay-wosh see Tenawa
Lenaywosh see Tenawa
Lenbaki see Lelengtu
Lenca [ES, Hon] (LC)
Lencan [Lang] [ES, Hon] (Bull44)
L'ene'di see Tlenedi
Lenedi see Tlenedi
Lenekee see Seneca
Lenelenape see Leni Lenape
Lenelenoppe see Leni Lenape
Lenepee see Leni Lenape
Lengua [Par] (LC)
Lengua-Mascoi [Lang] [Par] (LC)
Lengua-Maskoy see Lengua-Mascoi
Lengya [Clan] *Hopi* (H)
Leni Lenape *Delaware* (BE)
Leni-Lenape [Self-designation] (H) see also Leni Lenape (BE)
Lenna-lenape see Leni Lenape
Lennape see Leni Lenape
Lennapewi see Leni Lenape

Lenni-lappe see Leni Lenape
Lennilappe see Leni Lenape
Lenni Lenape see Leni Lenape
Lennilenape see Leni Lenape
Lenni-Lennape see Leni Lenape
Lenno Lenapee see Leni Lenape
Lenno Lenapi see Leni Lenape
Lenno-Lennape see Leni Lenape
Lenopi see Leni Lenape
Lenoppea see Leni Lenape
Lentes *Tigua* (H)
Lenya see Lenguya
Leonopi see Leni Lenape
Leonopy see Leni Lenape
Leon's Creek see Lions Creek
Lepan see Lipan Apache
Le Panis see Lipan Apache
le Pe see Peoria
Lepeguanes see Tepehuan
Le Plays see Comanche
Le'q'em see Tlekem
Leqem see Tlekem
Les Caribou (H) see also Attikirin-iouetch (H)
Les Folles see Menominee
Les Fols see Menominee
les Moines see Moingwena
Les Noire Indians (H)
Les Paisans see Seneca
Les pancake see Kansa
les peuples de Mississagué see Mississauga
les Pez see Peoria
Lespoama [MX] (Hdbk10)
Les Pongs see Ponca
Les Radiqueurs see Shoshoko
Lesser Osage see Utsehta
Les Souliers see Amahami
Letaiyo [Clan] *Hopi* (H)
Letaiyo winwu see Letaiyo
Le-tai-yo wun-wu see Letaiyo
Letaiyo wunwu see Letaiyo
Let-e-nugh-shonee see Iroquois
Letenughshonee see Iroquois
Letniki-Takaiak see Takaiak
Letniki-Takaiak see Takaiak
Let-tegh-segh-nig-egh-tee see Onondaga
Letteghseghnigeghtee see Onondaga
Letuama see Yahuna
Letuama see Letuana
Letuana [Col] (O)
Lewis River Band see Klikitat
Leyva *Tigua* (H)
Lezar see Illinois
Lgalaiguhl-lana [BC] *Haida* (H)
Lhtaten see Nahane
Lhtaten see Sekani
Lia see Sia
Liahtan Band see Ietan
Liards see Etchieridiegottine
Liard Slaves see Etcheridiegottine

L'Iatan see Ietan
Liaywas (H)
Li-ay-was see Liaywas
Libby Band [MN] *Kutenai* (BE)
Licatiut [CA] *Gallinomero* (H)
Lichagotegodi [SA] *Caduveo* (O)
Lienkwiltak see Lekwiltok
Liew-kwil-tah see Lekwiltok
Li-hit see Ponca
Lihit see Ponca
Li-icks-sun see Tateke
Liickssun see Tateke
Li-kat-u-it see Likatuit
Likatuit [CA] *Olamentke* (H)
Like-Big-Fish see Ho'ke
lik-si-yu see Cayuse
liksiyu see Cayuse
li'kwa'ama'i see Halyikwamai
likwaamai see Halyikwamia
Li-kwil-tah see Lekwiltok
Likwiltah see Lekwiltok
Likwiltoh see Lekwiltok
Lileek see Lile'ek
Lile'ek [CA] *Wappo* (BE)
lillewaite see Lillooet
lilliwhit see Lillooet
Lillooet [BC] *Salish* (LC)
Lillooet [BC] *Upper Lillooet* (Hdbk12)
Lillooet River [Can] *Lower Lillooet* (BE)
Lilmalche [Can] *Cowichan* (BE)
Lilooet see Lillooet
lilooitt see Lillooet
Lilowat see Lillooet
Lilshiknom [CA] *Round Valley Yuki* (H)
Lilshimnom see Lilshi'mnom
Lilshi'mnom *Grindstone Creek Wintu* (Pub, v.29, no.4)
li'luet see Lillooet
liluet see Lillooet
lilwat see Lillooet
lilwat see Lower Lillooet
lilwat'ut [BC] *Lower Lillooet* (Hdbk12)
Lima [PE] (O)
Limanu see Alabama
Limitas see Lemitas
Limonies see Laimon
Linapi see Leni Lenape
Linapiwi see Leni Lenape
Lingua Geral Amazonica see Nheengatu
Liniouck see Illinois
Linkinse see Sinkiuse
Linnelinopies see Leni Lenape
Linneways see Illinois
Linni linapi see Leni Lenape
Linnilinopes see Leni Lenape
Linnope see Leni Lenape
Lin-ok-lu-sha see Linoklusha
Linoklusha [Clan] *Choctaw* (H)

Linpoilish *see* Sanpoil
Linslow *see* Siuslaw
Lintcanre *see* Lintchanre
Lint-canre *see* Thlingchadinne
Lintcanre *see* Thlingchadinne
L'in-tchanpe *see* Lintchanre
Lintchanpe *see* Lintchanre
Lin-tchanre *see* Lintchanre
Lintchanre [Can] *Thlingchadinne* (BE)
Linways *see* Illinois
Lion Eaters *see* Tanima
Lion's Creek *see* Lions Creek
Lions Creek [BC] *Salish* (H)
Lipajen-ne *see* Lipan Apache
Lipajenne *see* Lipan Apache
Lipallanes *see* Lipillanes
Lipan Apache [TX, NM] (LC)
Lipane *see* Lipan Apache
Lipanes *see* Lipan Apache
Lipanes Abajo [NM, TX] *Lipan Apache* (BE)
Lipanes de Abajo *see* Lipanes Abajo
Lipanes de Arriba [TX] *Lipan Apache* (BE)
Lipanes del Norte *see* Lipanes de Arriba
Lipanes del Sur *see* Lipanes Abajo
Lipanes Llaneros *see* Lipan Apache
Lipanis *see* Lipan Apache
Lipanjenne [TX] *Lipan Apache* (BE)
Lipanos *see* Lipan Apache
Lipau *see* Lipan Apache
Lipaw *see* Lipan Apache
Lipillanes *Llaneros* (H)
Lipiyan *see* Lipillanes
Lipiyanes *see* Lipillanes
Lippan *see* Lipan Apache
Lisguegue *see* Iliguigue
l'Isle de Sancte Marie *see* Ekaentoton
Litanes *see* Ietan
Litltle Shuswap Band [BC] *Shuswap Lake Division* (Hdbk12)
Little Bainoa [HA] *Guaccaiarima* (BE)
Little Diomede *Bering Strait Eskimos* (Hdbk5)
Little Dogs [Can] *Paskwawininiwug* (BE)
Little Falls Band *see* Inyancheyaka-atonwan
Little Foolish Dogs *see* Hosukhaunukarerihu
Little Forks [MI] *Chippewa* (H)
Little Girl Assiniboines *see* Itscheabine
Little Hats *see* Manso

Little Kitkehahki *Pawnee* (BE)
Little Klamath [OR, CA] *Modoc* (BE)
Little Klamath Lake [CA] *Modoc* (Oregon)
Little Lakes *see* Mitomkai
Little Mingo *see* Huron
Little Osage (H) *see also* Utsehta (H)
Little Osage [MO] *Osage* (BE)
Little Ossage *see* Utsehta
Little Prairie Indians *see* Macouten
Little Rapids *see* Inyancheyaka-atonwan
Little River Band of Ottawa [newly recognized Oct. 94] (IndT, Oct.1994, p.4)
Little Robes *see* Inuksiks
Little Rock Band (H)
Little Sand Dune people *see* Sua'makosa Tusi'niniu
Little Shushwap Lake [BC] *Shuswap* (H)
Little Siconese *Delaware* (Hdbk15)
Little Six *see* Taoapa
Little Spokan *see* Upper Spokan
Little Taensa *see* Avoyel
Little Talasse *see* Tali
Little Tioux *see* Tiou
Little Tohome *see* Naniaba
Lituya [AK] *Huna* (H)
Live Oak People *see* Kaichichekaiya
Liver Eater Band *see* Tanima
Liwahali *see* Hothliwahali
Li-woch-o-nies *see* Tawakoni
Liwochonies *see* Tawakoni
Lizarva *Achagua* (O)
Lku'men *see* Songish
Lkumen *see* Songish
L'kungen *see* Songish
L'kungen *see* Songish
Lku'ngen *see* Songish
Lkungen [Self-designation] *see* Songish
Llagua *see* Yagua
Llakwash [Self-designation] *see* Lama
Llamparica *see* Ditsakana
Llanero (H) *see also* Guhlkainde (H)
Llanero (H) *see also* Kwahari (BE)
Llanero *Apache* (H)
Llegeeno *see* Diegueño
Lleni-lenape *see* Leni Lenape
Lleta *see* Isleta
Llieta *see* Isleta
Lliguno *see* Diegueño
Ll'inkit *see* Tlingit
Llinkit *see* Tlingit
Ll-mache *see* Lilmalche

Llmache *see* Lilmalche
Ll-mal-che *see* Lilmalche
Llmalche *see* Lilmalche
Loaiza [PR] (BE)
Loasau [CA] *Buena Vista Yokuts* (BE)
Locaguiniguara [MX] (Hdbk10)
Lock-wearer *see* Tsishusindt-sakdhe
Lo-co *see* Tonto Apache
Loco *see* Tonto Apache
Locollomillo *see* Clear Lake Indians
Locomo *see* Locono
Locono [Ve, Guy, Sur, FrG] (LC)
Lodge-in-the-rear *see* Kanze [Kansa]
Lodges charged upon *see* Ahacik
Lodges without horses *Crow* (H)
Lodovic, San *see* Sevilleta
Lo-him *see* Lohim
Lohim *Northern Paiute* (Hdbk11)
Lohim [OR] (BE)
Loh-whilse *see* Quaitso
Lohwhilse *see* Quaitso
Loka [Clan] *Navajo* (H)
Loka-dine *see* Loka
Loko *Northern Paiute* (Hdbk11)
Loko [NV] *Paviotso* (H)
Lokono *see* Locono
Lo'-kuili'la *see* Komkyutis
Lokulk *see* Sokulk
Lolangkok Sinkyone [Lang] [CA] *Wailaki* (He)
Lold-la *see* Lolsel
Loldla *see* Lolsel
Lo-lon-kuk [CA] (Contri, v.3, p.113)
lolowakamux *see* Nicola
Lol-sel *see* Lolsel
Lolsel [CA] *Patwin* (H)
Lomotugua [MX] *Coahuiltecan* (Hdbk10)
Lone Eaters *see* Nitawyiks
Lo-ne-ka-she-ga *see* Lunikashinga
Lonekashega *see* Lunikashinga
Long Haired Indians *see* Crow
Long Island Indians *see* Metoac
Long-isle *see* Eel River
Long Lake [MI, WI, Ont] *Chippewa* (H)
Longo [EC] (O)
Long People *see* Western Choctaw
Longs Cheveux *see* Nipissing
Long Sioux [SD] *Dakota* (BE)
Long Swamp Indians *see* Mikasuki
Long Swamp Indians *see* Seminole
Long Tom *see* Chelamela
Long Tom Creek Indians *see* Chelamela

Long-tongue-buff *see* Laptambif

Long-ush-har-kar-to *see* Longushharkarto

Longushharkarto [Sub-clan] *Delaware* (H)

Long Valley Paiute [CA] *Paiute* (Pub, v.33, no.2)

Long-wha *see* Tonkawa

Longwha *see* Tonkawa

Loo-choos *see* Kutchin

Loochoos *see* Kutchin

Loo-coo-rekah *see* Tukuarika

Loocoorekah *see* Tukuarika

Looking-like-Ghosts *see* Tuwan'hudan

Loomnears *see* Tumna

Loo-nika-shing-ga *see* Lunikashinga

Loonikashingga *see* Lunikashinga

Loo's *see* Mahican

Loos *see* Skidi Pawnee

Lopas *see* Tolowa

Lopillamillo *see* Clear Lake Indians

Lopotalimne *see* Lopatatimni

Lopotatimne *see* Lopotatimni

Lopotatimni [CA] *Miwok* (H)

Lopstatimne *see* Lopotatimni

Loque *see* Zoque

Loquilt Indians *see* Lillooet

Lorenzan [Lang] [SA] *Arawakan* (LC)

Lorenzan Indians *see* Amuesha

Lorenzano *see* Moxo

Lorenzo *see* Amuesha

Lorenzo de los Picuris, San *see* Picuris

Lorenzo de Pecuries, San *see* Picuris

Lorenzo de Picuries, San *see* Picuris

Lorenzo de Tezuqui, San *see* Tesuque

Lorenzo Tezuqui, San *see* Tesuque

Loreto [BaC, MX] *Cochimi* (BE)

Loretronon *see* Huron of Lorette

Lorica *see* Yorica

Lorretto *see* Canelo

Los Angeles Mission Indians *see* Pecos

Los Coyotes (Pub, v.26) *see also* Mountain Cahuilla (BE)

Los Mechos *see* Comanche

Los Mecos *see* Comanche

Lost Lodges *see* Ashinadea

Lost River Valley [OR, CA] *Modoc* (BE)

Lotlemaga [Gens] *Nakomgilisala* (H)

Lo'tlemaq *see* Lotlemaga

Lototen *see* Tututni

Lou *see* Skidi Pawnee

Louches *see* Tukkuthkutchin

Louchetchouis *see* Uzutiuhi

Loucheux (BE) *see also* Nakotchokutchin (BE)

Loucheux (Contri, v.1, p.31) *see also* Vuntakutchin (LC)

Loucheux (Contri, v.1, pp.30–31) *see also* Natsitkutchin (LC)

Loucheux (LC) *see also* Kutchin (LC)

Loucheux [AK] (BE)

Loucheux [Lang] *Athapascan* (BE)

Loucheux-Batards *see* Batard Loucheux

Louchieux Proper *see* Takkuthkutchin

Louchioux *see* Kutchin

Louchioux Proper *see* Tukkuthkutchin

Louchoux *see* Kutchin

Loud Voices Band *see* Katepoisipi-wiinuuk

Louis Indians, San *see* Luiseño

Loup (BE) *see also* Leni Lenape (BE)

Loup (BE) *see also* Mahican (LC)

Loup (BE) *see also* Pawnee (LC)

Loup (H) *see also* Catskill (BE)

Loup [Lang] *Algonquian* (Hdbk15)

Loupelousa *see* Opelousa

Loupes *see* Skidi Pawnee

Loupitousa *see* Opelousa

Loup Pawnees *see* Skidi Pawnee

Loups *see* Mahican

Lowako (H)

lo-wa-ni *see* Miami

lowani *see* Miami

Lowaniwi *see* Lowako

Lowanuski *see* Lowako

Lower Brule (BE)

Lower Brule (H) *see also* Kutawichasha (H)

Lower Brusle *see* Kutawichasha

Lower Chehalis [WA] *Salish* (H)

Lower Chinook [WA] (H)

Lower Coquille *see* Miluk

Lower Coquille *see* Nasumi

Lower Creek (BE) *see also* Seminole (LC)

Lower Creek (H)

Lower Dhegiha (H)

Lower Gens de fou *see* Hankutchin

Lower Indians *see* Tatsakutchin

Lower Inlet [AK] *Tanaina* (BE)

Lower Kalispel [ID, BC] (BE)

Lower Karok [CA] (H)

Lower Kootanai *see* Lower Kutenai

Lower Kootanie *see* Lower Kutenai

Lower Kootenay *see* Lower Kutenai

Lower Kutenai (H) *see also* Aqkoqtl'atlqo (H)

Lower Kutenai [MN, ID, BC] (BE)

Lower Kvichpaks *see* Magemiut

Lower Lake Division [Lang] *Northern Moquelumnan* (Pub, v.6, no.1, pp.317–318)

Lower Lake Pomo *Southeastern Pomo* (Pub, v.29, no.4)

Lower Lillooet [BC] *Lillooet* (BE)

Lower Nez Perce (W)

Lower Okinagan (Ye)

Lower Oraibi *see* Kyakotsmovi

Lower Pend d'Oreille *see* Lower Kalispel

Lower Pima *see* Pima Bajo

Lower Piman [Lang] [MX] *Tepiman* (Hdbk10)

Lower Quarter Indians [NC] (H)

Lower Rogue River Indians *see* Tututni

Lower Sauratown *see* Cheraw

Lower Similkameen [BC, WA] (BE)

Lower Sioux *see* Santee

Lower Sisseton *see* Miakechakesa

Lower Spokan (H) *see also* Skaischiltnish (H)

Lower Spokan [WA] (BE)

Lower Thompson [BC] *Ntlakyapamuk* (BE)

Lower Umpqua [Lang] (Bull40)

Lower Umpqua Indians *see* Kuitsh

Lower Umpwua *see* Kuitsh

Lower Wahpeton *see* Inyancheyaka-atonwan

Lower Wakpeton *see* Inyancheyaka-atonwan

Lower Yakima *see* Shallattoo

Lower Yakima *see* Skaddal

Lower Yakima *see* Squannaroo

Lower Yancstons *see* Yankton

Lower Yanctonai *see* Hunkpatina

Lower Yanctonnai *see* Hunkpatina

Lower Yanktonai (H) *see also* Hunkpatina (H)

Lower Yanktonai [SD] (BE)

Lower Yanktonnai *see* Hunkpatina

Low-him *see* Lohim

Lowhim *see* Lohim

Lowland Brule *see* Kutawichasha

Lowland Cree *see* Mamikininiwug

Lowland Dogs *see* Thlingchadinne

Lowlanders *see* Kaiyuhkhotana

Low-landers *see* Kutchakutchin

Lowlanders *see* Kutchakutchin

Lowland Guarijio [Lang] *Guarijio* (Hdbk10)

Lowland Mayan *see* Mayoid
Lowland People *see* Kutchakutchin
Lowland People *see* Mamikinini-wug
Lowland Pima [Lang] (Hdbk9)
Lowland Takelma *see* Takelma
Lowushkis *see* Lowako
Ltaoten *see* Tautin
Ltautenne *see* Tautin
Ltavten *see* Tautin
Lthyhellun Kiiwe *see* Hleilung-keawai
Ltsxe'als *see* Nisqually
Ltuiskoe *see* Lituya
Lu *see* Lunikashinga
Lucayan [Bah] (LC)
Luccumi *see* Arawak
luch *see* Paloos
Lu-chih *see* Ruche
Luckamiut *see* Luckiamute
Luck-a-mi-ute *see* Luckiamute
Luckamiute *see* Luckiamute
Luckamuke *see* Luckiamute
Luckamute *see* Luckiamute
Luckiamut *see* Luckiamute
Luckiamute [OR] (BE)
Luckimiute *see* Luckiamute
Luckimute *see* Luckiamute
Luck-ton *see* Luckton
Luckton [OR] (H)
Lugare *see* Mataco
Lugh-se-la *see* Sanyakoan
Lughsela *see* Sanyakoan
Lugplapiagulam *Coahuiltecan* (Hdbk10)
Lugua-mish *see* Suquamish
Luguamish *see* Suquamish
Luisah *see* Cupan
Luis de Seuilleta, San *see* Sevilleta
Luisenian, San *see* Luiseño
Luiseño, San *see* Luiseño
Luiseño [CA] (LC)
Luiseño [Lang] *Cupan* (Hdbk10)
Luiseño [Lang] [*Luiseño-Cahuilla*] (Pub, v.4, no.3, p.145)
Luiseño [Lang] [*Luiseño-Kawia*] (H)
Luiseño-Cahuilla [Lang] *Southern California* (Pub, v.4, no.3, p.97)
Luiseño-Kawia [Lang] *Southern California* (H)
Luisieno, San *see* Luiseño
Luis Obispo, San [Lang] [CA] *Chumashan* (H)
Luis Obispo Sevilleta, S. *see* Secilleta
Luis Rey, San *see* Luiseño
Lukahs *see* Succaah
Luk-a-ta't *see* Klikitat
Lukatat *see* Klikitat
Luk-a-tatt *see* Klikitat

Lukatatt *see* Klikitat
Lukatimu'x *see* Ntlakyapamuk
Lukatimu'x *see* Thompson
Lukemayuk *see* Luckiamute
Lukhselee *see* Sanyakoan
Lukisamni (CA)
Lukton *see* Luckton
Lulak *see* Lulakiksa
Lu-lak Ik-sa *see* Lulakiksa
Lulakiksa [Clan] *Choctaw* (H)
Lule [Arg] (LC)
Lumano *see* Jumano
Lumbee [NC] (LC)
Lume *see* Hume [TX]
Lummas *see* Lummi
Lummi [BC, WA] (LC)
Lummi [Lang] *Coastal Salishan* (Oregon)
Lummie *see* Lummi
Lummi-neuk-sack *see* Lummi
Luna *see* Tuneboo
Lungs *see* Chagu
Luni *see* Zuni
Lunikacinga *see* Lunikashinga
Lunikashinga [Clan] *Kansa* (H)
Lupaca [PE] *Aymara* (O)
Lu-pa-yu-ma *see* Clear Lake Indians
Lupayuma *see* Clear Lake Indians
Lupies *see* Pawnee
Lupilomi *see* Clear Lake Indians
Lu-pi-yu-ma *see* Clear Lake Indians
Lupiyuma *see* Clear Lake Indians
Lurcee *see* Sarsi
Lushootseed [Lang] [WA] (Hdbk12)
Lusolas *see* Susolas
Lute-ja *see* Rukhcha
Luteja (PC) *see also* Rukhcha (H)
Luteja [Clan] *Oto* (H)
Lutmawi *see* Modoc
Lutnami *see* Lutuamian
Lutuam *see* Modoc
Lutuami *see* Modoc
Lutuami *see* Lutuamian
lutuami *see* Modoc
Lutuamian [Lang] [CA, OR] *Shapwailutan* (LC)
Lutuani *see* Lutuamian
Lutumani *see* Lutuamian
Luturim *see* Lutuamian
lutwa-mi [isc] *see* Tule River Modoc
lxale'xamux *see* Lillooet
Lyach-sun *see* Tateke
Lyachsun *see* Tateke
Lyacksum *see* Tateke
Lytton Band [BC] *Thompson Indians* (Hdbk12)
Lytton Band [BC] *Upper Thompson* (H)

-M-

Ma [Br] *Cinta Larga* (O)
Maak [Clan] *Potawatomi* (H)
Maa'koath *see* Maakoath
Maakoath [Sept] *Nootka* (H)
Ma-am *see* Maam
Maam [Social group] *Pima* (H)
Maa'mtag-ila *see* Maamtagyila
Maamtagila *see* Maamtagyila
Maamtagyila [BC] *Kwakiutl* (H)
Ma-an-greet *see* Maangreet
Maangreet [Subclan] *Delaware* (H)
Maapiguara [MX] (Hdbk10)
Maaqua *see* Mohawk
Maarmiut [AK] *Eskimos* (Hdbk5)
Maastoetsjkwe *see* Hopi
Maawi [Clan] [NM] *Zuni* (H)
Maawi-kwe *see* Maawi
Mabenaro [Lang] [BO] *Tacanan* (O)
Mabila *see* Mobile
Mabile *see* Mobile
Mabodamaca [PR] (BE)
Ma-buc-sho-roch-pan-ga *see* Northern Shoshone
Mabucshorochpanga *see* Northern Shoshone
Mabucshorochpanga *see* Shoshone
Ma-buc-sho-roch-pang-ga *see* Shoshone
Maca *see* Matsaki
Maca [Br] *Payagua* (O)
Maca [Par, Guy, Arg] (LC)
Macaca [CU] (BE)
Macachusetts *see* Massachuset
Macacuy [MX] *Coahuiltecan* (Hdbk10)
Macaguaje [Col, EC] [Angotero] (O)
Macaguane *see* Makaguane
Macahua *see* Mazahua
Macanabi *see* Mishongnovi
Macanas *see* Tawakoni
Macanas *see* Tonkawa
Macanipa *see* Omagua
Macapao *Coahuiltecan* (BE)
Macapaqui [MX] *Coahuiltecan* (Hdbk10)
Macapiras [FL] (BE)
Macaque *see* Matsaki
Macatiguin [MX] (Hdbk10)
Macatiguire *see* Macatiguin
Macatu [MX] *Coahuiltecan* (Hdbk10)
Macau *see* Makah
Ma-caw *see* Makah
Macaw *see* Makah
Maccaw *see* Makah
Maccazina [HA] *Bainoa* (BE)

Maccoa [SC] (H)
Maccou *see* Maccoa
Macetuchet *see* Massachuset
Macetusete *see* Massachuset
Machachac *see* Mequachake
Machachee *see* Shawnee
Machaculi *see* Masaculi
Machakandibi *see* Michacondibi
Machandibi *see* Michacondibi
Machantiby *see* Michacondibi
Machapunga [NC] (BE)
Machateege *see* Accomac
Machateego *see* Matchapunga
Mac-ha-ves *see* Mohave
Machaves *see* Mohave
Mac-ha-vis *see* Mohave
Machavis *see* Mohave
Machecous *see* Muskogee
Machegamea *see* Michigamea
Machemeton *see* Mechemeton
Machemni [CA] *Miwok* (H)
Machepungo (Hdbk15) *see also*
  Machapunga (BE)
Machepungo *Accomac* (Hdbk15)
Macheye *see* Mayeye
Macheyenga *see* Machiganga
Machias Tribe *see* Pas-
  samaquoddy
Machichac *see* Mequachake
Machicui *see* Lengua-Mascoi
Machicuy *see* Toba-Maskoy
Machies Tribe *see* Pas-
  samaquoddy
Machigama *see* Michigamea
Machigamea *see* Michigamea
Machiganga [PE] *Campa* (LC)
Machiguenga *see* Machiganga
Machingan *see* Mahican
Machkentiwomi *see* Mechken-
  towoon
Machkoutench *see* Mascouten
Machkoutenck *see* Mascouten
Machkouteng *see* Mascouten
Machkoutenk *see*
Machoatick *see* Matchotic
Machoeretini *see* Conestoga
Machui [BO] *Araona* (O)
Machuvi [BO] *Araona* (O)
Maciguara [MX] *Coahuiltecan*
  (Hdbk10)
Macilenya winwu *see* Masilengya
Macjave *see* Mohave
Mackacheck *see* Mequachake
Mackah *see* Makah
Mackanotin [OR] *Tututni* (H)
Mackasookos *see* Mikasuki
Mackensie Eskimos *see* Macken-
  zie Delta Esskimos
Mackenzie [Can] *Eskimos* (BE)
Mackenzie Delta Eskimos [AK]
  (Hdbk5)
Mackenzie Flats Kutchin *see*
  Nakotcho-kutchin

Mackenzie River Delta [Lang]
  [*Inuit-Inupiaq Eskimo*]
  (Hdbk5)
Mackenzie River Eskimo *see*
  Kopagmiut
Mackenzie's River Louchioux *see*
  Nakotcho-kutchin
mackoke *see* Muskogee
Mackuchi *see* Macusi
Macku'ke *see* Muskogee
Mackwaes *see* Mohawk
Mackwasii *see* Mohawk
Mackwes *see* Mohawk
Maclatzinca *see* Ocuiltec
Maco *see* Macoita
Maco *see* Piapoco
Macoa [Lang] *Motilon* (UAz,
  v.28)
Macoas *see* Macoita
Macocoma [Coahuiltecan] (BE)
Macoita [VE] *Yukpa* (O)
Macomala [MX] *Coahuiltecan*
  (Hdbk10)
Macomile *see* Menominee
Maconabi *see* Mishongnovi
Maconagua *see* Mayoruna
Maconi *see* Masacali
Macono *see* Nacono
Macoraena [MX] *Coahuiltecan*
  (Hdbk10)
Macorajora *see* Macuarera
Macorix [HA] *Caizcimu* (BE)
Macorixe [Cu] (BE)
Macoryzes [SanD, HA] *Hubabo*
  (BE)
Macos *see* Piaroa
Macoushi *see* Macusi
Macouten *see* Mascouten
Macoutin *see* Mascouten
Macoyahui [MX] (BE)
Macqs *see* Mohawk
Macquaas *see* Mohawk
Macquaaus *see* Mohawk
Macquaejeet *see* Beothuk
Macquas *see* Mohawk
Macquaus *see* Mohawk
Macques *see* Mohawk
Macquess *see* Mohawk
Ma-cqui *see* Matsqui
Macqui *see* Matsqui
Macquis *see* Mohawk
Macquiss *see* Mohawk
Macro-Chibchan [Lang] (O)
Macro-Otomangue [Lang] (BE)
Macro-Penutian (LC) *see also*
  Penutian (LC)
Macro-Penutian [Lang] (BE)
Mactcingeha *see* Ute
Mactciñgeha wain *see* Ute
Mactotata *see* Oto
Macu [Br, Col] (LC)
Macuarera [MX] *Coahuiltecan*
  (Hdbk10)

Macu-Bara [SA] *Macu* (O)
Macu-Bravos [SA] *Macu* (O)
Macuchy *see* Macusi
Macu de cubes *see* Cacua
Macu de desano *see* Cacua
Macu de guanano *see* Cacua
Macu de tucano *see* Jupda
Macueque *see* Hopi
Macuna [Br, Col] (LC)
Macuni *see* Masacali
Macurap *see* Makurap
Macusari [Self-designation] *see*
  Jivaro
Macushi *see* Macusi
Macusi [Br, Guy, VE] (LC)
Macusi [Lang] *Carib* (UAz, v.28)
Macusy *see* Macusi
Macuxi *see* Macusi
Madaha *see* Anadarko
Madan *see* Mandan
Madaouaskairini *see*
  Matawachkarini
Mad-a-wakantoan *see* Mde-
  wakanton
Madawakantoan *see* Mdewakan-
  ton
Madawakanton *see* Mdewakan-
  ton
Ma-da-weh-soos *see*
  Madawehsoos
Madawehsoos [Clan] *Abnaki* (H)
Maddy Band *see* Chemapho
Madehsi [CA] *Achomawi* (LC)
Madeqsi *see* Puisu
Made'si *see* Madehsi
Madesi *see* Madehsi
Madesiwi [Lang] *Achomawi* (CA-
  8)
Madhinka-gaghe *see* Mandhink-
  agaghe
Madiha *see* Culina
Madija [Self-designation] *see*
  Culina
Madnussky *see* Mednovskie
Madoc *see* Modoc
Madocteg *see* Medoctec
Madowesians *see* Dakota
Mad River Indians *see* Batawat
Maechachtinni *see* Seneca
Maechibaeys *see* Mohawk
Ma-etsi-daka *see* Mitcheroka
Maetsidaka *see* Mitcheroka
Mag-a-bo-das *see* Putetemini
Magabodas *see* Putetemini
Magagmiut *see* Maarmiut
Magagmjuten *see* Magemiut
Magag-mut *see* Magemiut
Magalibo *see* Maguhleloo
Magamute *see* Magemiut
Magatch *see* Maca
Magatch *see* Payagua
Magayuteshni (BE) *see also*
  Maghayuteshni (H)

Ma-ga-yu-tesh-ni *see* Maga-
yuteshni
Magayuteshni *Mdewakanton* (BE)
Maga-yute-sni *see* Magayuteshni
Magayutesni *see* Magayuteshni
Magemiut (Hdbk5) *see also*
Maarmiut (Hdbk5)
Magemiut [AK] *Eskimos* (BE)
Mag'emut *see* Magemiut
Magemut *see* Magemiut
Magemute *see* Magemiut
Magenesito *see* Yagenechito
Maghai *see* Mayeye
Maghayuteshni [MN] *Matanton-
wan* (H)
Magimut *see* Magemiut
Magimuten *see* Magemiut
Magirona *see* Mayoruna
Magmiut *see* Magemiut
Magmiut *see* Maarmiut
Magmjuten *see* Magemiut
Magmute *see* Magemiut
Magmuti *see* Magemiut
Mago *see* Mayo
Magrias *see* Tano
Maguana [HA] (BE)
Maguano [Cu] (BE)
Maguas *see* Tano
Maguck *see* Shawnee
Magueck *see* Mequachake
Ma-guh-le-loo *see* Maguhleloo
Maguhleloo [Clan] *Abnaki* (H)
Magui *see* Hopi
Maguiaqui [MX] *Varohio* (H)
Maguipamacopini *see* Maquispa-
macopini
Ma-gwa (H) *see also* Magwa (H)
Magwa (PC) *see also* Ma-gwa (H)
Ma-gwa [Clan] *Shawnee* (H)
Magwa [Clan] *Shawnee* (H)
Maha (BE) *see also* Omaha (LC)
Maha (PC) *see also* Ma-ha (H)
Ma-ha [Clan] *Mohave* (H)
Maha [Clan] *Mohave* (H)
Ma-ha-bit-tuh *see* Petenegowats
Mahabittuh *see* Petenegowats
Mahacks *see* Mohawk
Mahacqs *see* Mohawk
Mahacu *see* Macu
Mahaer *see* Omaha
mahaguaduka *Western Shoshone*
(Hdbk11)
Mahah *see* Omaha
Mahah *see* Skidi Pawnee
Mahaha *see* Amahami
Mahaitin [HA, WInd] *Cahibo*
(BE)
Mahak *see* Mohawk
Mahakan *see* Mahican
Mahakander *see* Mahican
Mahakas *see* Mohawk
Mahakes *see* Mohawk
Mahakinbaas *see* Mohawk

Mahakinbas *see* Mohawk
Mahakobaas *see* Mohawk
Mahakuaas *see* Mohawk
Mahakuase *see* Mohawk
Mahakuasse *see* Mohawk
Mahakwa *see* Mohawk
Mahamomowi *Guahibo* (O)
Mahan *see* Comanche
Mahan *see* Omaha
Mahana *see* Comanche
Mahane *see* Klikitat
Ma ha os *see* Mohave
Mahaos *see* Mohave
Mahar *see* Omaha
Maharha *see* Omaha
Maharim *see* Meherrin
Maharineck *see* Meherrin
Maharmar *see* Amahami
Ma-har-o-luk-ti *see* Maharolukti
Maharolukti [Subclan] *Delaware*
(H)
Mahas *see* Skidi Pawnee
Mahaton *see* Manhattan
Mahaukes *see* Mohawk
Mahauvies *see* Mohave
Mahaw *see* Omaha
Mahawha *see* Amahami
Maha-wi *see* Mohave
Mahawi *see* Mohave
Mahcander *see* Mahican
Mahegan (BE) *see also* Mohegan
(LC)
Mahegan (H) *see also* Mahican
(LC)
Mahegan [CN] (BE)
Maheigan *see* Mahican
Mahekander *see* Mahican
Maherin *see* Meherrin
Maherine *see* Meherrin
Mahering *see* Meherrin
Maherries *see* Meherrin
Maherrin *see* Meherrin
Maherring *see* Meherrin
Maherron *see* Meherrin
Maheye *see* Mayeye
Mahhekaneew *see* Mahican
Mahibarez *see* Nambicuare
Mahican [Lang] [NY] *Eastern Al-
gonquian* (Hdbk15)
Mahican [NY] (LC)
Mahican Confederacy (BE)
Mahicander *see* Mahican
Mahicanni *see* Mahican
Mahiccan *see* Mahican
Mahiccani *see* Mahican
Mahiccon *see* Mahican
Mahicon *see* Mahican
Mahigan *see* Catskill
Mahigan *see* Mahican
Mahiganathicoit *see* Mahican
Mahigan-Aticois *see* Mahican
Mahiganaticois *see* Mahican
Mahigane *see* Mahican

Mahiganiouetch *see* Mahican
Mahiggin *see* Mahican
Mahik *see* Mahican
Mahikan *see* Mahican
ma-hi-kan *see* Mahican
Mahikander *see* Mahican
ma-hi-kani-w *see* Mahican
mahikaniw *see* Mahican
Mahikaune [CA] *Pomo* (Pub,
v.40, no.2)
Mahikkander *see* Mahican
Mahillendras *see* Mahican
Mahinacu *see* Mehinacu
Mahingan *see* Mahican
Mahinganak *see* Mahican
Mahinganiois *see* Mahican
Mahingans *see* Mahican
Mahingaus *see* Mahican
Mah'le-Mat *see* Malemiut
Mahlemoot *see* Malemiut
Mahlemut *see* Malemiut
Mahlemute *see* Malemiut
Mah-ma-lil-le-kulla *see* Ma-
malelekala
Mahmalillekulla *see* Ma-
malelekala
Mah-ma-lil-le-kullah *see* Ma-
malelekala
Mahmalillekullah *see* Ma-
malelekala
Mahmatilleculaat *see* Ma-
malelekala
mah'-nah'-tse'-e *see* Washo
mahnahtsee *see* Washo
Mahna-Narra *see* Mandan
Mahnanarra *see* Mandan
Mahnewsheet *see* Malecite
Mahnomoneeg *see* Menominee
Mahnomonie *see* Menominee
Mahoc *see* Manahoac
Mahock *see* Manahoac
Mahogs *see* Mohawk
Mahohivas [Society] *Cheyenne*
(H)
Mahongwis *see* Iroquois
Mahora *see* Tamaroa
Ma-ho-yum *see* Mahoyum
Mahoyum [SD] *Cheyenne* (BE)
Mahpiyamaza *Mdewakanton* (H)
Mahpiyato *see* Arapaho
Mahpiyawichasta *Mdewakanton*
(H)
Mah sihk'ku ta *see* Masi'kota
Mahsihkkuta *see* Masi'kota
Mahsolamo [VanI] *Salish* (H)
Mahta [NJ] *Unalachtigo* (BE)
Mah-tah-ton *see* Matantonwan
Mahtahton *see* Matantonwan
Mah-tee-cetp *see* Matilpe
Mahteecetp *see* Matilpe
Mahtilpi *see* Matilpe
Mahtulth-pe *see* Matilpe
Mahuame *see* Siaguan

Mahuames [MX, TX] (H)
mahuopani *see* Apwurage
Mahwawa *see* Moah
Mahwukes *see* Mohawk
Mahycander *see* Mahican
Maiaguarite [HA] *Bainoa* (BE)
Maiaiu *see* Mai-ai-u
Mai-ai-u [CA] *Yokuts* (Contri, v.3, p.370)
Maicander *see* Mahican
Maico *see* Maitho
Maiconeras [MX] *Lagunero* (BE)
Mai-dec-kiz-ne *see* Jemez
Maideckizne *see* Jemez
Mai-deh *see* Maidu
Maideh *see* Maidu
Maideski'z *see* Maitheshkizh
Maideski'zni *see* Maitheshkizh
Maidnorskie *see* Ahtena
Mai-du *see* Maidu
Maidu [CA] (LC)
Maiduan [Lang] [CA] *Penutian* (CA-8)
Maiece *see* Mayeye
Maieye *see* Mayeye
Maii Deeshgaiizh *see* Jemez
Ma'ii Deeshgiizh *see* Jemez
Ma'ii Deeshgiizhnii *see* Jemez
Maii Deeshgiizhnii *see* Jemez
Maikan *see* Mahican
Maiken *see* Mahican
Mailam-ateuna [Phratry] *Zuni* (H)
Maima *see* Miami
Maina *see* Mayna
Maingan *see* Mahican
Maingcong *see* Yecuana
Mainland Cuna [Pan] *Cuna* (O)
Mainu [Self-designation] *see* Jivaro
Maiongcong *see* Yecuana
Maiongking *see* Yecuana
Maiongkong *see* Yecuana
Maiongong *see* Yecuana
Maipure [Lang] [SA] (O)
Maipurean [Lang] [SA] (O)
Maipuridjana *see* Okomoyana
Maises *see* Manso
Maisi [Cu] (BE)
Ma-i-sin-as *see* Sans Arcs
Maisinas *see* Sans Arcs
Maisqui *see* Matsqui
Maitheshkizh [Clan] *Navajo* (H)
Maitho [Clan] *Navajo* (H)
Maitiff *see* Mixed bloods
Maito *see* Maitho
Maito'dine *see* Maitho
Maitsi *see* Yecuana
Maiyakama *see* Wappo
Maiyakma *see* Makoma
Maiye [Cu] (BE)
Majabos *see* Mohave
Majanale [MX] *Coahuiltecan* (Hdbk10)

Majanani *see* Mishongnovi
Majave *see* Mohave
Majubim *see* Paranawat
Majur *see* Zoro
Majuruna *see* Mayoruna
Maka *see* Makah
Maka *see* Maca
Mak'a *see* Maca
Makache [Clan] *Oto* (H)
Ma kadawagami'tigweya-wininiwag *see* Mekadewagamitigweyawinini-wak
Makadawagamitigweyawininiwag *see* Medakewagamitigweyaw-ininiwak
Ma kadawagamitigweya-wininiwug *see* Mekadewagamitigweyawinini-wak
Makadewana-ssidok *see* Siksika
Makag'mut *see* Ekogmut
Makaguane [Col] (O)
Makah (H) *see also* Omaha (LC)
Makah [Lang] *Nootka* (LC)
Makah [Lang] *Wakashan* (Oregon)
Makah [WA] (LC)
Makaitserk *see* Klamath
makaitserk *see* Modoc
Makamitek *see* Makomitek
Makamotcemei [CA] *Southern Pomo* (Pub, v.40, no.2)
Makan (H) *see also* Makah (LC)
Makan [Clan] *Ponca* (H)
Makan [Clan] *Wazhazhe* (H)
Ma'kandwawininiwag *see* Pillagers
Makandwawininiwag *see* Pillagers
Makandwewininiwag *see* Pillagers
Makapu [ID] *Nez Perce* (BE)
Makatapi (H)
Ma'katawimeshikakaa *see* M'ke-tashshekakah
Makatawimeshikakaa *see* M'ke-tashshekakah
Ma-ka-tce *see* Makache
Makatce *see* Mackache
Makaw *see* Makah
Makha *see* Makah
Makha-v *see* Mohave
Makhe [Clan] *Quapaw* (H)
Makh-el-chel *see* Makhelchel
Makhelchel [CA] (H)
Makhenikashika (H) *see also* Wakantaenikashika
Makhenikashika [Gens] *Quapaw* (H)
Makhpiyamaza [MN] *Matanton-wan* (H)
Maki *see* Hopi

Makicander *see* Mahican
Makihander *see* Mahican
Makimane *see* Mahican
Makingan *see* Mahican
Makiritare *see* Yecuana
Makka *see* Maca
Mak-kah *see* Makah
Makkah *see* Makah
Maklak *see* Lutuamian
Maklaks *see* Klamath
ma'klaks *see* Klamath
Maklaks [Self-designation] *see* Modoc
Makoateeaukee *see* Kaskaskia
Makoma [CA] (H)
Makomitek [WI] *Algonquian* (H)
Makostrake *see* Mequachake
Makostrake *see* Shawnee
Ma-ko-ta *see* Dakota
Makota *see* Dakota
Ma-kotch *see* Makache
Ma-kotch *see* Mankoke
Makotch (PC) *see also* Makache (H)
Makotch (PC) *see also* Mankoke (H)
Makotch [Clan] *Oto* (H)
Makou *see* Makoua
Makoua [WI] (H)
Makoucoue *see* Makoukuwe
Makoueoue *see* Makoukuwe
Makoukuwe [WI] (H)
Makoumoue *see* Makoukuwe
Makouten *see* Mascouten
Makoutensak *see* Mascouten
Makquas *see* Mohawk
Maksav *see* Mohawk
Makskouteng *see* Mascouten
Ma'ktl'aiath *see* Maklaiath
Maktlaiath (PC) *see also* Maklaiath (H)
Maktlaiath [Sept] [Can] *Nootka* (H)
Maku *see* Macu
Maku-Bara *see* Macu-Bara
Maku-Bravos *see* Macu-Bravos
Makuhadokado *Northern Paiute* (Hdbk11)
Makuna *see* Macuna
Makunabodo *see* Macu
Makundwawininiwug *see* Pillagers
Ma'kundwawininiwug [Self-designation] *see* Pillagers
Makurap [Lang] [Br] *Tupi* (O)
Makushi *see* Macusi
Makusi *see* Macusi
Makuxi *see* Macusi
ma-kwa *see* Makwa
Ma'kwa *see* M'ko
Makwa (PC) *see also* M'ko (H)
Makwa [Clan] *Mahican* (H)
Makwaes *see* Mohawk
Ma-kwis-so-jik *see* Makwisuchigi

Makwissojik *see* Makwisuchigi
Makwisuchigi [Clan] *Fox* (H)
Ma-kwisutcig *see* Makwicuhigi
Makwisutcig *see* Makwisuchigi
Malacite *see* Malecite
Malaguita *Coahuiltecan* (Hdbk10)
Malaka [CA] *Patwin* (H)
Ma-lak-ka *see* Malaka
Malakka *see* Malaka
Malakut [Can] *Cowichan* (BE)
Ma'lakyilatl *see* Spukpukolemk
Malakyilatl *see* Spukpukolemk
Malamech *see* Marameg
Malana *see* Marameg
Malaque *see* Matsaki
Malataute *see* Oto
Malayo [Col] (LC)
Malayo [Lang] *see* Chibchan
Malbala *see* Mataco
Malecete *see* Malecite
Malechite *see* Malecite
Malecite [ME, Can] (LC)
Malegmjuti *see* Malemiut
Maleigmjuten *see* Malemiut
Maleimioute *see* Malemiut
Maleku [CR] (O)
Ma'leleqala *see* Mamalelekam
Maleleqala *see* Mamalelekam
Malemiut [AK] *Eskimos* (BE)
Malemuke *see* Malemiut
Malemut *see* Malemiut
Malemutes *see* Malemiut
Malesite *see* Malecite
Maleygmyut *see* Malemiut
Malhomin *see* Menominee
Malhoming *see* Menominee
Malhomini *see* Menominee
Malhominy *see* Menominee
Malhomme *see* Menominee
Malhommi *see* Menoiminee
Maliacones [TX] (H)
Malibu [Col] (O)
Malicans *see* Maliacones
Malicete *see* Malecite
Malicite *see* Malecite
Malicococa [MX] *Coahuiltecan*
   (Hdbk10)
Maliconas *see* Maliacones
Malicones *see* Maliacones
Maliegmut *see* Malemiut
Ma-li-ka (H) *see also* Malika (H)
Malika *see* ASLO Ma-li-ka
Ma-li-ka [Clan] *Mohave* (H)
Malika [Clan] *Mohave* (H)
Malimiut Indians *see* Malemiut
Malimiut Inupiaq [Lang] [AK]
   Inupiaq (Hdbk5)
Malimuten *see* Malemiut
Malimyut *see* Malemiut
Malinchenos [MX] *Tamaulipec*
   (BE)
Maliseet [Self-designation] *see*
   Malecite

Maliseet-Passamaquoddy [Lang]
   [NB] (Hdbk15)
Malisit *see* Malecite
Malleye *see* Mayeye
Mallopeme [TX] *Coahuiltecan*
   (BE)
Malmiut *see* Malemiut
Malnombre *see* Mal Nombre
Mal Nombre *Coahuiltecan*
   (Hdbk10)
Malockese [OH] (H)
Malomeni *see* Menominee
Malomimi *see* Menominee
Malomine *see* Menominee
Malominese *see* Menominee
Malomini *see* Menominee
Malouin *see* Menominee
Maloumine *see* Menominee
Malouminek *see* Menoiminee
Malowwack *see* Metoac
Mals-sum *see* Malssum
Malssum [Clan] *Abnaki* (H)
Maltshokamut [AK] *Kna-*
   iakhotana (H)
Mal-tsho-qa-mut *see* Maltshoka-
   mut
Maltshoqamut *see* Maltshokamut
Maluche *see* Araucanian
Malukander *see* Mahican
Malungeons *see* Melungeons
Mam [Hon] *Mosquito* (BE)
Mam [MX, Gua] (LC)
Mama *see* Omaha
Mamainde [Br] *Northern Nam-*
   bicuara (LC)
Mamaine *see* Mamainde
Mamaitum [Clan] *Serrano* (Pub,
   v.26)
Mamakans Apeches *see*
   Mescalero Apache
Mamakata'wana-si'ta'ak *see* Sik-
   sika
Mamakitce-wiinuuk [Can]
   Paskwawininiwug (BE)
Mamaleilakitish *see* Ma-
   malelekala
Mamaleilakulla *see* Mamalelekala
Ma'malelek-ala *see* Mamalelekala
Mamalelekala [BC] *Kwakiutl* (BE)
Ma'malelek-am *see* Ma-
   malelekam
Mamalelekam [Gens] *Ma-*
   malelekala (H)
Ma'maleleqala *see* Mamalelekala
Mama-lil-a-cula *see* Ma-
   malelekala
Mamalilacula *see* Mamalelekala
Ma-ma-lil-li-kulla *see* Ma-
   malelekala
Mamalillikulla *see* Mamalelekala
Mambare *see* Paressi
Mambe *see* Nambe
Mambo *see* Nambe

Mambyara *see* Nambicuara
Mambyuara *see* Nambicuara
Mamean [Lang] [MX, Gua]
   Mayan (O)
Mamekoting [NY] *Esopus* (BE)
Ma-me-li-li-a-ka *see* Ma-
   malelekala
Mameliliaka *see* Mamalelekala
Mamelute *see* Malemiut
Ma-me-o-ya *see* Mameoya
Mamikininiwug [Can] *Paskwaw-*
   ininiwug (BE)
Mamikiwininiwag *see*
   Mamikininiwug
Mamikiyiniwok *see* Mamikinini-
   wug
Mam-il-i-li-a-ka *see* Ma-
   malelekala
Mamililiaka *see* Mamalelekala
Mamite *Concho* (BE)
M'amiwis *see* Miami
Mamiwis *see* Miami
Mammapacun *see* Menapacunt
Ma-mo an-ya-di *see* Alabama
Mamoanyadi *see* Alabama
Ma-mo han-ya *see* Alabama
Mamohanya *see* Alabama
Ma-mo ha-yan-di *see* Alabama
Mamohayandi *see* Alabama
Mamskey *see* Matsqui
Mamtum [VanI] (H)
Mamun-gitunai [Sub-family]
   [BC] *Haida* (H)
Mamuqui *Coahuiltecan* (BE)
Man [Lang] [CA] (Pub, v.8, no.1,
   p.4)
Manabaho [HA] *Cahibo* (BE)
Manabaxao [HA] *Guaccaiarima*
   (BE)
Manabusho *see* Ma'nabu'sho
Ma'nabu'sho [WI] *Menominee*
   (BE)
Manacica [BO] (LC)
manacts *see* Washo
Managog *see* Manahoac
Managua *see* Cashibo
Manahoac [Lang] *Monacan* (H)
Manahoac [VA] (LC)
Manahoac Confederacy [VA] (H)
Manahoack *see* Manahoac
Manahoak *see* Manahoac
Manahock *see* Manahoac
Manahoke *see* Manahoac
Manairisu [Br] *Nambiguara* (O)
Manajo *see* Amanaye
Manam [TX] *Coahuiltecan* (BE)
Manamabobo *see* Sipibo
Manamabobo *see* Sipibo
Mananye *see* Amanaye
Manapacumter *see* Menapacunt
Manaries *see* Machiguenga
Manasica *see* Manacica
Manaskson *Assateague* (Hdbk15)

Manastara [Lang] *Motilon* (UAz, v.28)

Manatahqua [MA] *Massachuset* (BE)

Manathane *see* Manhattan

Manathanes *see* Manhattan

Manathen *see* Manhattan

Ma-na-to (H) *see also* Manato (H)

Ma-na-to [Clan] *Shawnee* (H)

Manato [Clan] *Shawnee* (H)

Manaure [Col] *Yuko* (O)

Manava *see* Sipibo

Manaxo *see* Amanaye

Manaye *see* Amanaye

Manazewa *see* Amanaye

Mancantequut *see* Maquantequat

Manche (LC) *see also* Mopan (LC)

Manche [Hon] (BE)

Manchester Pomo *Pomo* (J/Anthro, v.1, no.1, Winter 1974, pp.206–219)

Manchinere *see* Maxineri

Manchineri *see* Piro [Peru]

Manchokatous *see* Mdewakanton

Mancinka-gaxe *see* Mandhinkagaghe

Mandahuaca *see* Mandawaka

Mandals *see* Mandan

Mandam *see* Mandan

Mandan [Lang] *Siouan* (H)

Mandan [ND] (LC)

Mandane *see* Mandan

Mandani *see* Mandan

Mandanne *see* Mandan

Mandaus *see* Mandan

Mandawaka [VE, Br] (O)

Mandawakanton *see* Mdewakanton

Mande *see* Manta [NJ]

Manden *see* Mandan

Mandeouacanton *see* Mdewakanton

Mandhinkagaghe [Gens] *Omaha* (H)

Mandian *see* Mandan

Mandin *see* Mandan

Mandinga (O) *see also* San Blas (O)

Mandinga *Cuna* (BE)

Mandoages *see* Nottaway

Mandon *see* Mandan

Mandong *see* Nottaway

Maneater Indians *see* Tonkawan Tribes

Man eaters *see* Attacapa

Man-eaters *see* Tonkawa

Man-Eaters *see* Mohawk

Manessings *see* Minisink

Maneteneri *see* Maniteneri

Manetineri *see* Maniteneri

Manetore *see* Hidatsa

Maneus *see* Malecite

Manewquesend *see* Conoy

Mangakekias *see* Mengakonkia

Mangakekis *see* Mengakonkia

Mangakokis *see* Mengakonkia

Mangakonkia *see* Mengakonia

Mangeurs de cariboux *see* Etheneldeli

Mangoac *see* Nottaway

Mangoack *see* Nottaway

Mangoag *see* Nottaway

Mangoak *see* Nottaway

Mangoako *see* Nottaway

Mangoang *see* Nottaway

Mangon [Cu] (BE)

Mangue [CR, NI] (LC)

Mangus Colorado's Band *see* Mimbreno Apache

Manhanset *see* Manhasset

Manhasset [NY] *Metoac* (BE)

Manhassett *see* Manhasset

Manhate *see* Manhattan

Manhates *see* Munsee

Manhatesen *see* Manhattan

Manhattae *see* Manhattan

Manhattan (Hdbk15) *see also* Munsee (LC)

Manhattan [NY] *Wappinger Confederacy* (LC)

Manhattanese *see* Manhattan

Manhattes *see* Manhattan

Manhattons *see* Manhattan

Manhikan *see* Mahican

Manhikani *see* Mahican

Manhingan *see* Mahican

Maniabon [Cu] (BE)

Maniataries *see* Hidatsa

Maniba *see* Baniva

Manicheneri *see* Maniteneri

Manico [TX] *Coahuiltecan* (BE)

Manieneri *see* Maniteneri

Manikan *see* Mahican

Manilla *see* Mobile

Manimapacan *see* Inapanam

Manipo [BO] *Araona* (O)

manise *see* Ommunise

Manissing *see* Minisink

Manitaries *see* Hidatsa

Maniteneiri *see* Maniteneri

Maniteneri (LC) *see also* Piro [Peru] (LC)

Maniteneri [Br] (O)

Mani-ti *see* Maniti

Maniti *Sisseton* (H)

Manitineri *see* Maniteneri

Manitou Place people *see* Manitowuk Tusi-niniwug

Manitowuk tusininiwug *see* Mani'towuk Tusi'niniwug

Mani'towuk Tusi'niniwug [WI] *Menominee* (BE)

Manitsawa [Br] (O)

Maniuk *see* Choroti

Maniva *see* Baniva

Maniwaki [Can] *Algonkin* (BE)

Manjuy *Chorote* (O)

Mankato [MN] *Mdewakanton* (H)

Mankikani *see* Mahican

Man-ko-ke *see* Mankoke

Mankoke [Clan] *Iowa* (H)

Mankutquet [MA] *Wampanoag* (BE)

Mannahannock *see* Manahoac

Mannahoack *see* Manahoac

Mannahoag *see* Manahoac

Mannahoak *see* Manahoac

Mannahock *see* Manahoac

Mannahoke *see* Manahoac

Mannanokin *see* Pocomoke

Mannature *see* Hidatsa

Manna-wousut *see* Manosaht

Mannawousut *see* Manosaht

Mannissing *see* Minisink

Manoa (O) *see also* Panobo (O)

Manoa [Lang] *Maipurean* (O)

Man-oh-ah-saht *see* Manosaht

Manohahsaht *see* Manosaht

Manoita *see* Setebo

Manokin [MD] *Nanticoke* (BE)

Manomanee *see* Menominee

Mano-meh *see* Menominee

Manomeh *see* Menominee

Manomine *see* Menominee

Manominik *see* Menominee

mano-miniwa *see* Menominee

manominiwa *see* Menominee

Manomoy [MA] *Nauset* (BE)

Manoomina *see* Menominee

Manosaht [VanI] *Nootka* (LC)

Manos Coloradas *see* Manos Colorados

Manos Coloradas *Coahuiltecan* (BE)

Manos de Perros [TX] *Coahuiltecan* (BE)

Manosit *see* Manosaht

Manosprietas *see* Manos Prietas

Manos Prietas [MX, TX] *Coahuiltecan* (BE)

Manostamenton *see* Menostamenton

Manrhoat *see* Kiowa

Manrhout *see* Kiowa

Mansa *see* Manso

Manses *see* Manso

Manshkaenikashika [Clan] *Quapaw* (H)

Manso [NM, TX, MX] (BE)

Manta *see* Mantaes

Manta [EC] (LC)

Manta [NJ] *Delaware* (H)

Mantaa *see* Manta [NJ]

Mantachuset *see* Massachuset

Mantaes (H) *see also* Manta [NJ] (H)

Mantaes *Delaware* (Hdbk15)

Mantaesy *see* Manta [NJ]

Mantanes *see* Mandan
Mantantan *see* Matantonwan
Mantanton *see* Matantonwan
Mantanton Scioux *see* Matantonwan
Mantantous *see* Matantonwan
Mantaquak *see* Nanticoke
Mantautous *see* Matantonwan
Mantaw *see* Manta [NJ]
Mante *see* Manta [NJ]
Mantera *see* Cherokee
Manteran *see* Cherokee
Manteses *see* Manta [NJ]
Manteses *see* Mantaes
Mantinacock *see* Matinecock
Mantinecock [NY] *Montauk* (BE)
Manto *see* Manta [NJ]
Manton *see* Mandan
Manton *see* Mento
Mantonumanke *see* Matonumanke
Mantopanatos *see* Assiniboin
Mantotin *see* Santotin
mantoue *see* Mantoueck
Mantouek *Southeastern Ojibwa* (H)
Mantu [Clan] *Quapaw* (H)
Mantuenikashika [Clan] *Quapaw* (H)
Man-tu-we *see* Mento
Mantuwe *see* Mento
Manua [PE] *Campa* (O)
Manuk *Chorote* (O)
Man-um-aig *see* Marameg
Manumaig (PC) *see also* Marameg (H)
Manumaig [Clan] *Chippewa* (H)
Manunejo [MX] *Coahuiltecan* (Hdbk10)
Manuquiari [PE] *Toyeri* (O)
Manwarno *see* Galibi
Manworne *see* Galibi
Manxo *see* Manso
Manyateno *Coahuiltecan* (Hdbk10)
Many Beasts *see* Ahkotashiks
Many Horses *see* Tashunkeota
Many Horse's Band *see* Young Buffalo Robe
Manyika [Clan] *Kansa* (H)
Manyikakhthi [Subgens] *Iowa* (H)
Ma-nyi-ka-qci *see* Manyikakhthi
Manyikaqci *see* Manyikakhthi
Manyikazhinga [Subclan] *Kansas* (H)
Manyinka [Clan] *Kansa* (H)
Manyinkagaxe *see* Manyika
Manyinkainihkashina [Social group] *Osage* (H)
Manyinkainiukacina *see* Manyinkainihkashina
Manyin'ka i'niyk'acin'a *see* Mayinkainihkashina

Manyinkatanga [Subclan] *Kansa* (H)
Many Lodge Poles *see* Ahkwonistsists
Many Lodges *see* A c'araho
Manzana *see* Mishongnovi
Maon (H)
Maopidian *see* Maopityan
Maopidian *see* Mapidian
Maopityan (O) *see also* Mapidian (O)
Maopityan [Br] *Atorai* (O)
Maouila *see* Mobile
Mapanai [Lang] *Maipurean* (O)
Mapaniguara [MX] *Coahuiltecan* (Hdbk10)
Maparina *see* Aguano
Mape *see* Bari
Mapes *see* Motilon
Mapeshana *see* Wapisiana
Mapeya *see* Sandia
Mapicopa *see* Maricopa
Mapidian [Br] *Wapisiana* (O)
Mapili [MX] *Coahuiltecan* (Hdbk10)
Mapollo *see* Mapoyo
Maporcan *Coahuiltecan* (Hdbk10)
Mapoyo [Lang] *Carib* (UAz)
Mapoyo [VE] (O)
Mapuche [CH] *Araucanian* (O)
Mapudungu *see* Mapuche
Mapudungun *see* Mapuche
Mapulcan *Coahuiltecan* (Hdbk10)
Mapumary [BO] *Araona* (O)
Maqa *see* Mohawk
Maqaise *see* Mohawk
Maqe-nikaci-ka *see* Makhenikashika
Maqenikacika *see* Makhenikashika
Maqkuanani (PC) *see also* Ma'qkuana'ni (H)
Ma'qkuana'ni [Clan] *Menominee* (H)
Maqkuanani [Clan] *Menominee* (H)
maqlaqs [Self-designation] *see* Klamath
Maqpi'ato *see* Arapaho
Maq-pi'ato *see* Arapaho
Maqua *see* Mohawk
Maquaa *see* Mohawk
Maquache (Hdbk11) Moache (LC)
Maquache *see* Moache
Maquache Utes *see* Moache
Maquaes *see* Mohawk
Maquaese *see* Mohawk
Maquahache *see* Moache
Maquais *see* Mohawk
Maquaise *see* Mohawk
Maquamticough (H) *see also* Maquantequat (H)

Maquamticough *Choptank* (Hdbk15)
Maquasas *see* Mohawk
Maquase *see* Mohawk
Maquash *see* Mohawk
Maquass *see* Mohawk
Maquasse *see* Mohawk
Maquatequat [MD] (H)
Maqude *see* Iowa
Maque *see* Mohawk
Maquems *Coahuiltecan* (BE)
Maquez *see* Mohawk
Maqui *see* Hopi
Maquiapem *Coahuiltecan* (Hdbk10)
Maquichee *see* Mequachake
Maquinna *Mooachaht* (H, p.804)
Maquiritare [Lang] *Carib* (UAz, v.28)
Maquiritare Indians *see* Yecuana
Maquis *see* Mohawk
Maquispamacopini [MX] (Hdbk10)
Maquoas *see* Mohawk
Maquoche Utahs *see* Moache
Maquois *see* Mohawk
Maquot *see* Pequot
Maraca [Col] *Yuko* (O)
Maraca [Lang] *Motilon* (UAz, v.28)
Maracano (O) *see also* Cahuarano (O)
Maracano [PE] *Iquito* (O)
Maracasero *see* Malayo
Marachie *see* Malecite
Maracho *see* Pianokoto
Maracopa *see* Maricopa
Maragua *see* Maue
Marahtxo *see* Pianokoto
Marahua *see* Mayoruna
Maraka *see* Yuko
Marameg *Chippewa* (H)
Maramoskee *see* Machapunga
Marangakh *see* Serrano
Marangakh *see* Morongo
Marani [BO] *Araona* (O)
mar-an-sho-bish-ko *see* Dakota
maranshobishko *see* Dakota
Maraquites *Coahuiltecan* (BE)
Marashite *see* Malecite
Maraso *see* Pianokoto
Maraticund *see* Moratico
Maratin *Coahuiltecan* (Hdbk10)
Maratino *see* Maratin
Maraughquaick *Assateague* (Hdbk15)
Marawa [Lang] *Maipurean* (O)
Marayam *see* Serrano
Marayam *see* Morongo
Marayo *see* Bora
Marcpeeah Mahzah *see* Makhpiyamaza
Marechite *see* Malecite

Marechkawieck *see* Canarsee
Marecopa *see* Maricopa
Mareschite *see* Malecite
Marguerite, Ste. *see* Oumamiwek
Marho *see* Navajo
Maria, Santa [EC] *Secoya* (O)
Mariames (BE) *see also* Muruam (BE)
Mariames [TX] *Coahuiltecan* (H)
Marian (H) *see also* Mariames (H)
Marian *Huron* (H)
Mariana *see* Bora
Marianes *see* Mariames
Mariarves *see* Mariames
Mariate [Lang] *Maipurean* (O)
Maribichicoa-Guatajigiala [ES] (BE)
Maricheet *see* Malecite
Maricopa [AZ] (LC)
Marien [HA, DR] (BE)
Mariguan *see* Mariguanes
Mariguanes [MX] *Tamaulipec* (BE)
Marin [Lang] [CA] *Coast Miwok* (CA-8)
marina [Clan] *Serrano* (Pub, v.26, 1929)
Marinahua *see* Marinawa
Marinahua *see* Sharanahua
Marinawa (LC) *see also* Sharanahua (LC)
Marinawa [Br, PE] *Sharanahua* (O)
Marin-Bodega [Lang] [CA] *Miwok* (Pub, v.9, no.3, p.293)
Marineoueia *see* Piankashaw
Maringayam *see* Serrano
Maringayam *see* Morongo
Maringints *see* Serrano
Maringints *see* Morongo
Mariposa (LC) *see also* Yokuts (LC)
Mariposa [Lang] [CA] *Miwok* (Pub, v.6, no.3, p.353)
Mariposa-Chowchilla [Lang] *Southern Sierra Miwok* (BE)
Mariposan [Lang] *see* Mariposa
Mariposa Indians *see* Yokuts
Marisiz *see* Malecite
Marisizi *see* Malecite
Maritise *see* Manta
Mariusa [Guy] *Warrau* (O)
Markiritare *see* Yecuana
Marlain *see* Staitan
Marlin *see* Staitan
Mar-ma-li-la-cal-la *see* Mamalelekala
Marmalilacalla *see* Mamalelekala
Mar-ma-sece *see* Marmasece
Marmasece [WA] (H)
Marmusckits *see* Machapunga
Maroa *see* Tamaroa
Maroba *see* Maruba

Marobo [Lang] *Panoan* (O)
Marocasero *see* Malayo
Marohans *see* Tamaroa
Marona [CA] *Serrano* (Pub, v.26, 1929)
Maronge *see* Morongo
Maronge *see* Serrano
Maroni River Carib [Lang] *Galibi* (UAz, v.28)
Maropa *see* Maruba
Marospinc *see* Massapequa
Marossepinck *see* Massapequa
Marota *see* Tamaroa
Maroumine *see* Menominee
Marova *see* Maruba
Ma-rpi-wi-ca-xta *see* Kheyatao-tonwe
Marpiwicaxta *see* Kheyataotonwe
Ma-rpi-ya-ma-za *see* Makhpiya-maza
Marpiyamaza *see* Makhpiyamaza
Marracou [FL] (H)
Marraganeet *see* Narraganset
Marraugh tocum *see* Moratico
Marricoke *see* Merric
Marsapeag *see* Massapequa
Marsapeage *see* Massapequa
Marsapeague *see* Massapequa
Marsapege *see* Massapequa
Marsapequa *see* Massapequa
Marsepain *see* Massapequa
Marsepeack *see* Massapequa
Marsepeake *see* Massapequa
Marsepequa *see* Massapequa
Marsepin *see* Massapequa
Marsepinck *see* Massapequa
Marsepingh *see* Massapequa
Marsepyn *see* Massapequa
Marsey *see* Massapequa
Marshpang *see* Mashpee
Marshpee *see* Mashpee
Marsh Village Dakotas *see* Sisseton
Marsh Villagers *see* Sisseton
Martha's Vineyard Indians [MA] (H)
Mar-til-par *see* Matilpe
Martilpar *see* Matilpe
Martin *see* Maratin
Martinez [CA] (H)
Martinne houck *see* Matinecoc
Maru [BO] *Araona* (O)
Maruba [Br] (LC)
Marubo *see* Maruba
Marychkenwikingh *see* Canarsee
Mary River *see* Chepenafa
Marys River Indinas *see* Chepenafa
Marysville *see* Chepenafa
Masa *see* Matsaki
Masa *see* Macuna
Masacali [Br] (LC)
Masacara *see* Kamakan

Masacuajulam *Coahuiltecan* (Hdbk10)
Masagnebe *see* Mishongnovi
Masagneve *see* Mishongnovi
Masaka *see* Aikana
Masanais *see* Mishongnovi
Masanani *see* Mishongnovi
Masapequa *see* Massapequa
Masaqueve *see* Mishongnovi
Masathulet *see* Massachuset
Masatibu [BO] *Araona* (O)
Masawomekes *see* Iroquois
Mascalero *see* Mescalero Apache
Mascautins *see* Mascouten
Mascelero *see* Mescalero Apache
Maschongcong *see* Yecuana
Maschongkong *see* Yecuana
Masco *see* Mashco
Mascoaties *see* Mascouten
Mascoi *see* Lengua-Mascoi
Mascoi *see* Toba-Maskoy
Mascoian (LC) *see also* Lengua-Mascoi (LC)
Mascoian [Lang] [Par] (O)
Mascontan *see* Mascouten
Masconten *see* Mascouten
Mascontenec *see* Mascouten
Mascontin *see* Mascouten
Mascontire *see* Mascouten
Mascordin *see* Mascouten
Mascotain *see* Mascouten
Mascoten *see* Mascouten
Mascotin *see* Mascouten
Mascouetech *see* Mascouten
Mascoutech *see* Mascouten
Mascouteins Nadouessi *see* Teton
Mascouten (Hdbk15) *see also* Fox (LC)
Mascouten *Peoria* (BE)
Mascouten [WI] *Potawatomi* (LC)
Mascoutin *see* Mascouten
Mascoutons *see* Mascouten
Mascoy *see* Toba-Maskoy
Ma-seip-kih *see* Kadohadacho
Ma'-seip'-kih *see* Kadohadacho Confederacy
Maseipkih *see* Kadohadacho Confederacy
Ma'se'p *see* Kadohadacho
Masep *see* Kadohadacho
Masepeage *see* Massapequa
Ma-se-sau-gee *see* Missisauga
Masesaugee *see* Missisauga
Masetuset *see* Massachuset
masgalen *see* Mescalero Apache
Mashacali *see* Masacali
Mashantucket (LC)
Mashantucket (LC) *see also* Pequot (LC)
Mashapeag *see* Massapequa
Masha-Peage *see* Massapequa
Mashawatoc *Accomac* (Hdbk15)

Mashco [PE] (LC)
Mashcouqui *see* Muskogee
Ma-she-ma-tak *see* Mashematak
Mashematak [Gens] *Sauk and Fox* (H)
Mashgale *see* Mescalero Apache
Mashgalende *see* Mescalero Apache
Mashgalene *see* Mescalero Apache
Mashgali *see* Mescalero Apache
Mashikuhta *see* Masi'kota
Mashkegon *see* Maskegon
Mashkegonhyrinis *see* Maskegon
Mashkegous *see* Maskegon
Mashkotens *see* Potawatomi
Mashkoutens *see* Mascouten
Mashongcong *see* Yecuana
Mashongkong *see* Yecuana
Mashongnavi *see* Mishongnovi
Ma-shong-ni-vi *see* Mishongnovi
Mashongnivi *see* Mishongnovi
Mashoniniptuovi *see* Mishongnovi
Mashpeage *see* Massapequa
Mashpee [MA] (LC)
Mashpege *see* Mashpee
Mashukhara *see* Shasta
Masi [Clan] *Hopi* (H)
Masiassuck *see* Missisquoi
Masichewsett *see* Massachuset
Ma sih kuh ta *see* Masi'kota
Masi'kot *see* Masi'kota
Masikot *see* Masi'kota
Masikota *see* Masi'kota
Masi'kota [SD] *Cheyenne* (BE)
Masilengya [Clan] *Hopi* (H)
Ma-si-len-ya wun-wu *see* Masinlengya
Masilinya wunwu *see* Masinlengya
Masipa (PC) *see also* Ma-si-pa (H)
Ma-si-pa [Clan] *Mohave* (H)
Masipa [Gens] *Mohave* (H)
Masi winwu *see* Masi
Ma-si wunwu *see* Masi
Ma-si wun-wu *see* Masi
Masiwunwu *see* Masi
Mas-ka-gau *see* Maskegon
Maskagau *see* Maskegon
Maskasinik (H) *see also* Achiligouan (H)
Maskasinik [Can] *Ottawa* (H)
Maskco *see* Mashco
Maskego *see* Maskegon
Maskegon (LC) *see also* Cree (LC)
Maskegon [Cree] (BE)
Maskegonehirini *see* Maskegon
Maskegous *see* Maskegon
Maskegowuk *see* Maskegon
Maskigoes *see* Maskegon
Maskigonehirini *see* Maskegon
Maskoge *see* Muskogee

Masko'ge *see* Muskogee
Maskogi *see* Muskogee
Maskokalgi *see* Muskogee
Maskokal'gi *see* Muskogee
Maskoke *see* Muskogee
Maskoki *see* Creek
Maskoki *see* Mucsogee
Maskoki Hatchata *see* Lower Creek
Maskoki Harchapale *see* Upper Creek
Masko'ki Hatchapale *see* Upper Creek
Masko'ki Hatchata *see* Lower Creek
maskokulki *see* Muskogee
Maskoutech *see* Mascouten
Maskouteck *see* Mascouten
Maskoutein *see* Mascouten
Maskouten *see* Mascouten
Maskoutench *see* Mascouten
Maskoutenek *see* Mascouten
Maskoutens-Nadouessians *see* Teton
Maskoutin *see* Mascouten
Maskouting *see* Mascouten
Maskoy *see* Toba-Maskoy
Maskutick *see* Mascouten
Masnipiwiniuuk [Can] *Paskwawininiwug* (BE)
Masonah *see* Nasumi
Maspeth [NY] (H)
Masphi *see* Mashpee
Masquachki *see* Muskogee
Masquikoukiak *see* Maskegon
Masquikoukiouek *see* Maskegon
Masquitamis *see* Fox
Masrodawa *see* Masronhua
Masronhua *Jaminaua* (O)
Massa-adchu-es-et *see* Massachuset
Massaca *see* Huari
Massacara *see* Kamakan
Massachewset *see* Massachuset
Massachisan *see* Massachuset
Massachuselt *see* Massachuset
Massachuset [Lang] *Eastern Algonquian* (Hdbk15)
Massachuset [MA] (LC)
Massachusett *see* Massachuset
Massachuseuk *see* Massachuset
Massachusiack *see* Massachuset
Massachusuk *see* Massachuset
Massaco [CT, NY] *Wappinger* (BE)
Massacoe *see* Wappinger
Massadchueset *see* Massachuset
Massadzosek *see* Massachuset
Massajoset *see* Massachuset
Massakiga *see* Arosaguntacook
Mas-sang-na-vay *see* Mishongnovi
Massangnavay *see* Mishongnovi

Massapeag *see* Massapequa
Massapee *see* Mashpee
Massapege *see* Massaspequa
Massapequa *Delaware* (Hdbk15)
Massapequa [NY] *Metoac* (H)
Massapequa [NY] *Monatauk* (BE)
Massasagues *see* Missisauga
Massasauga *see* Missisauga
Massasoiga *see* Missisauga
Massasoit [MA] *Wampanoag* (BE)
Massassuk *see* Missiassik
Massathuset *see* Massachuset
Massatuchet *see* Massachuset
Massatusitt *see* Massachuset
Massauwu *see* Masi
Massauwuu *see* Masi
Massawamacs *see* Iroquois
Massawomacs *see* Iroquois
Massawomecks *see* Iroquois
Massawomees *see* Iroquois
Massawomeke *see* Iroquois
Massawomekes *see* Iroquois
Massawonacks *see* Iroquois
Massawonaes *see* Iroquois
Massechuset *see* Massachuset
Massepeake *see* Massapequa
Massesague *see* Missisauga
Massetuset *see* Massachuset
Mas-si kwa-yo *see* Massikwayo
Massikwayo [Clan] *Hopi* (H)
Massinacac [VA] *Monacan Confederacy* (H)
Massinacack *see* Massinacac
Massinague *see* Missisauga
Massinnacack *see* Massinacac
Massorite *see* Missouri
Massoritte *see* Missouri
Massourite *see* Misiouri
Massowomeks *see* Iroquois
Masstachusit *see* Massachuset
Mastanahua [PE] *Sharanahua* (O)
Mastanawa *see* Mastanahua
Ma-stoh-pa-ta-kiks *see* Mastohpatakiks
Mastohpatakiks [Society] *Siksika* (H)
Mastutc-kwe *see* Hopi
Mastutckwe *see* Hopi
Masut [CA] *Northern Pomo* (Pub, v.40, no.2)
Matabantowaher *see* Matantonwan
Matabesec *see* Mattabesec
Matabezeke *see* Mattabesec
Matachuses *see* Massachuset
Matachuset *see* Massachuset
Mataco [Arg, BO, Par] (LC)
Matacoan [Lang] [Par, Arg] (O)
Matagalpa [EC, NI, Hon, ES] *Sumo* (LC)
Matagalpan [Lang] *Misumalpan* (BE)
Matage *see* Kiowa Apache

Mataguaya *see* Mataco
Mataguayo *see* Mataco
Matahuinala *Coahuiltecan*
  (Hdbk10)
Mataitaikeok [Can] *Cree* (BE)
Mataki'la *see* Maamtagyila
Matakila *see* Maamtagyila
Matako *see* Mataco
Matakwarapa *see* Haka-whatapa
Matambu [CR] (O)
Matamusket *see* Machapunga
Matanakons [NJ] *Delaware* (H)
Matantonwan [MN] *Mdewakan-*
  ton (H)
Mataouachkarinien *see*
  Matawachkarini
Mataouakirinouek *see*
  Matawachkarini
Mataouchkairinik *see*
  Matawachkarini
Mataouchkairiniouek *see*
  Matawachkarini
Mataouchkairni *see*
  Matawachkarini
Mataouchkarini *see*
  Matawachkarini
Mataouiriou *see* Mattawan
Mataovan *see* Mattawan
Matapaman *see* Mattapanient
Matapan [MX] *Tehueco* (H)
Matapeake [MD] (H)
Matapi (LC) *see also* Yecuna (LC)
Matapi [Col] (O)
Matapoll *see* Mattapony
Matarango [CA] (H)
Matascuco [MX] *Coahuiltecan*
  (Hdbk10)
Matathusett *see* Massachuset
Matatiquiri [MX] *Coahuiltecan*
  (Hdbk10)
Matatoba *Dakota* (H)
Matauwake *see* Metoac
Matavakopai *see* Mata'va-kopai
Mata'va-kopai [AZ] *Walapai* (BE)
Mataveke-paya *see* Hualapai
Matawachkarini [Can] (H)
Matawachwarini *see*
  Matawachkarini
Matawang *see* Mattawan
Matawin *see* Mattawan
Matchagamia *see* Michigamea
Matchapango *see* Machapunga
Matchapongo *see* Machapunga
Matchapungo *see* Machapunga
Matchedach *see* Matchedash
Matchedash [Ont] *Missisauga* (H)
Matchemne *see* Machemni
Mat-che-naw-to-waig *see* Iro-
  quois
Matchenawtowaig *see* Iroquois
Matchepungo *see* Machapunga
Matchinadoaek *see* Iroquois
Matchitashk *see* Matchedash

Matchoatick *see* Matchotic
Matchopungo *see* Machapunga
Matchotic [VA] *Powhatan Con-*
  federacy (H)
Matcsuamako Tusininiu *see*
  Matc Sua'mako Tusi'niniu
Matc Sua'mako Tusi'niniu [WI]
  Menominee (BE)
Matebeseck *see* Mattabesec
Matechitache *see* Matchedash
Mateiros *see* Txakamekra
Matelpa *see* Matilpe
Matelthpah *see* Matilpe
Matetiguara *see* Matatiquiri
Mat-hat-e-vatch *see* Chemehuevi
Mathatevatch *see* Chemehuevi
Mathatuset *see* Massachuset
Mathatusitt *see* Massachuset
Mat-haupapaya (BE) *see also*
  Wikutepa (BE)
Mathaupapaya *see* Mat-
  haupapaya
Mat-haupapaya [AZ] *Yavepe* (BE)
Mathesusete *see* Massachuset
Mathiaca [FL] *Timuqua* (H)
Mathiaqua *see* Mathiaca
Mathkoutench *see* Mascouten
Mathomeni *see* Menominee
Mathomini *see* Menominee
Mathue [MD] (H)
M'ath-wa (H) *see also* Mathwa
  (H)
Mathwa (PC) *see also* M'-ath-wa
  (H)
M'-ath-wa [Clan] *Shawnee* (H)
Mathwa [Clan] *Shawnee* (H)
Maticones *see* Maliacones
Ma-tilhpi *see* Matilpe
Matilhpi *see* Matilpe
Ma-tilpe *see* Matilpe
Matilpe [Sept] [BC] *Kwakiutl* (H)
Ma'tilpis *see* Matilpe
Matilpis *see* Matilpe
Matinecoc (H) *see also* Manti-
  necock (BE)
Matinecoc [NY] (H)
Matinecoce *see* Matinecoc
Matinecocke *see* Matinecoc
Matinecogh *see* Matinecoc
Matineocock *see* Matinecoc
Matinicock *see* Matinecoc
Matiniconck *see* Matinecoc
Matinnekonck *see* Matinecoc
Matipu [Br] (O)
Matipuhy *see* Matipu
Matis *see* Matses
Ma-tis-ab-its *see* Panaca
Matisabits *see* Panaca
Mat-jus *see* Chemehuevi
Matjus *see* Chemehuevi
Matkawatapa [AZ] *Walkamepu*
  (BE)
Matkitwawipa [AZ] *Yavepe* (BE)

Matlaltzinca *see* Matlatzinca
Matlame [Lang] [MX] *Matlatz-*
  inca (BE)
Matlame [MX] (BE)
Matlazahua *see* Mazahua
Matninicongh *see* Matinecoc
Mato [CA] *Northern Pomo* (Pub,
  v.40, no.2)
Matokatagi *see* Oto
Matolagua *Coahuiltecan* (Hdbk10)
Matole *see* Mattole
Mato-Mihte *see* Matonumanke
Matomihte *see* Matonumanke
Matomkin *Accomac* (Hdbk15)
Matompkin *see* Matomkin
Ma-to-no-make *see* Matonu-
  manke
Matonomake *see* Matonumanke
Matontenta *see* Oto
Matonumake *see* Matonumanke
Mato-Numangkake *see* Matonu-
  manke
Matonumangkake *see* Matonu-
  manke
Ma-to nu-man-ke *see* Matonu-
  manke
Matonumanke *Manda* (H)
Ma-toosh-ats *see* Gunlock
Matooshats *see* Gunlock
Matora (H) *see also* Mento (H)
Matora [AR] (H)
Matotante *see* Oto
Matou-ouescarini *see*
  Matawachkarini
Matoua *see* Mento
Matoutenta *see* Oto
Matowack *see* Metoac
Matowepesack *see* Mattabesec
Matox *see* Matchotic
Matpanient *see* Mattapanient
Matses [PE, Br] (O)
Matshingenga *see* Machiganga
Matsiapungo *see* Machapunga
Matsigamea *see* Michigamea
Matsiganga *see* Machiganga
Matsigenga *see* Machiganga
Matsigenka *see* Machiganga
Matsiguenga [Self-designation]
  see Nomatsiguenga
Matsi'shkota *see* Masi'kota
Matsishkota *see* Masi'kota
Matsqui [BC] *Cowichan* (H)
Mattabeeset *see* Mattabesec
Mattabesec [CT] *Wappinger* (BE)
Mattabeseck *see* Mattabesec
Mattabesett *see* Mattabesec
Mattabesicke *see* Mattabesec
Mattacco *see* Mataco
Mattachucett *see* Massachuset
Mattachusett *see* Massachuset
Mattachussett *see* Massachuset
Mattacuset *see* Massachuset
Mattanawcook *see* Mattinacook

Mattapament *see* Mattapanient
Mattapament *see* Mattapony
Mattapanian *see* Mattapanient
Mattapanient [MD] *Conoy* (BE)
Mattapany *see* Mattapony
Mattapeaset *see* Mattabesec
Mattapomen *see* Mattapony
Mattapoment *see* Mattapony
Mattaponies *see* Mattapony
Mattapony [VA] *Powhatan Confederacy* (BE)
Mattasoon *see* Amahami
Mattassin *see* Mistassin
Mattathusett *see* Massachuset
Mattatusett *see* Massachuset
Mattaugwessawacks *see* Dakota
Mattawa *see* Mattawan
Mattawan [Ont] *Chippewa* (H)
Mattawoman *Conoy* (Hdbk15)
Mattebeseck *see* Mattabesec
Mattehatique *see* Matchotic
Matthiaqua *see* Mathiaca
Mattikongy *see* Naraticon
Mattinacock (H) *see also* Matinecoc (H)
Mattinacook [ME] *Penobscot* (H)
Mattinnekonck *see* Matinecoc
Mattinnicock *see* Matinecoc
Mattinnicock *see* Matinecoc
Mattinnicoek *see* Matinecoc
Mat-Toal *see* Mattole
Mattoal *see* Mattole
Mattole [CA] (CA)
Mattole [Lang] [CA] [Athabascan] (He)
Mattououescarini *see* Matawachkarini
Mattouwacky *see* Metoac
Mattowax *see* Metoac
Mattpament *see* Mattapanient
Matucapam *Coahuiltecan* (Hdbk10)
Matucar *Coahuiltecan* (BE)
Matu-es-wi skitchu-nu-uk *see* Micmac
Matueswi skitchunuuk *see* Micmac
Matuime *Coahuiltecan* (BE)
Matuimi *see* Matuime
Matuku [CA] *Pomo* (CA)
Mat-ul-pai *see* Matilpe
Matulpai *see* Matilpe
Matuwack *see* Metoac
Maubedan *Coahuiltecan* (BE)
Maubela *see* Mobile
Maubila *see* Mobile
Maubile *see* Mobile
Maubileans *see* Mobile
Maubilians *see* Mobile
Maucu *see* Macu
Maudaus *see* Mandan
Maudowessies *see* Dakota
Maue [Lang] [Br] *Tupi* (LC)

Mauguawog *see* Mohawk
Mauhauk *see* Mohawk
Mauhe *see* Maue
Mauilla *see* Mobile
Mauitzi *see* Yecuana
Maukquogges *see* Mohawk
Mauliapeno *see* Mayapem
Maulieni [Lang] [AZ] *Maipurean* (O)
Maume *see* Miami
Maumee *see* Miami
Maumie *see* Miami
Mau-os-aht *see* Manosaht
Mauosaht *see* Manosaht
Mauquaoys *see* Mohawk
Mauquas *see* Mohawk
Mauquauogs *see* Mohawk
Mauquaw *see* Mohawk
Mauquawog *see* Mohawk
Mauquawos *see* Mohawk
Mauques *see* Mohawk
Mauraigan *see* Mahican
Mauraygan *see* Mahican
Maure *see* Baure
Mausand *see* Mishongnovi
Mauscouten *see* Mascouten
Mauthaepi [Q] *Montagnais* (H)
Mauton *see* Mento
Mauvais Monde (H) *see also* Etchaottine (H)
Mauvais Monde *Nehaunee* (Contri, v.1, p.33)
Mauvais Monde des Pieds-Noirs *see* Sarsi
Mauvila *see* Mobile
Mauvilians *see* Mobile
Mauviliens *see* Mobile
Mauyga *Coahuiltecan* (BE)
maviatem [Clan] [CA] *Serrano* (Pub, v.26)
Mavila *see* Mobile
Mavilians *see* Mobile
Mavilla *see* Mobile
Ma-wahota *see* Mawakhota
Mawahota *see* Mawakhota
Mawakhota [*Two-Kettle*] (H)
Ma-waqota *see* Mawakhota
Mawaqota *see* Mawakhota
Ma-wa-ta-dan *see* Mandan
Mawatadan *see* Mandan
Mawatani *see* Mandan
Ma-wa-tanna *see* Mandan
Mawatanna *see* Mandan
Maw-dan *see* Mandan
Mawdan *see* Mandan
Mawe *see* Maue
Mawhakes *see* Mohawk
Mawhauog *see* Mohawk
Mawhaw *see* Omaha
Mawhawkes *see* Mohawk
Mawkey *see* Hopi
Mawmee *see* Miami
Mawooshen *see* Abnaki

Mawques *see* Mohawk
Maw-soo-tah *see* Mawsootah
Mawsootah [Subclan] *Delaware* (H)
Mawtawmauntowah *see* Mdewakanton
Maxa-bomdu *see* Putetemini
Maxabomdu *see* Putetemini
Maxacali *see* Masacali
Maxakali *see* Masacali
Maxaruna *see* Mayoruna
Maxa-yute-cni *see* Magayuteshni
Maxayutecni *see* Magayuteshni
Ma'xe *see* Kdhun
Maxe *see* Kdhun
Maxineri (O) *see also* Piro [Peru] (LC)
Maxineri [Br, PE] (O)
Maxirona *see* Mayoruna
Maxubi *see* Arikapu
Maxuki *see* Arikapu
Maxuruna *see* Mayoruna
Maya (H) *see also* Mayo (LC)
Maya [Br] (O)
Mayacma *see* Makoma
Mayaguex [PR] (BE)
Mayaguiguara *Coahuiltecan* (Hdbk10)
Mayaintalap *see* Serrano
Mayaintalap *see* Gitanemuk
Mayain-talap *see* Gitanemuk
Mayajuanguara [MX] *Coahuiltecan* (Hdbk10)
Maya-Mopan *see* Mopan
Mayan [Lang] [MX, Gua, ES, Bel] (LC)
Mayan Indians *see* Mayas
Mayapem *Coahuiltecan* (Hdbk10)
Mayas [MX, BrH] (LC)
Mayasquere *see* Cuaiquer
Mayawaug [MA] *Pocomtoc* (BE)
Maye *see* Mayeye
Mayece *see* Mayeye
Mayee *see* Mayeye
Mayeguara *Coahuiltecan* (Hdbk10)
Mayekander *see* Mahican
Mayeye [TX] *Tonkawan* (BE)
Mayganathicoise *see* Mahican
Mayimeuten *see* Magemiut
Mayintalap *see* Serrano
Mayiruna *see* Mayoruna
Maykander *see* Mahican
maykis oob *see* Highland Pima
maymiut *see* Maarmiut
Mayna (O) *see also* Maina (O)
Mayna [Lang] [EC, Pe] *Jivaro* (LC)
Mayna [Lang] [PE] *Quecha* (O)
Mayndeshkish [Clan] *San Carlos Apache* (H)
Mayne Island [Sept] [VanI] *Sanetch* (BE)

Maynoa [JA] (BE)

Mayo (O) *see also* Maya [SA] (O)

Mayo [Lang] [MX] *Cahita* (Hdbk10)

Mayo [MX] (LC)

Mayoahc *see* Kiowa

Mayoid [Lang] *Choloid* (BE)

Mayonggong *see* Mayongong

Mayongong [Br] (O)

Mayoruna [Br, PE] (LC)

Mayu *see* Maya [SA]

Mayu *see* Mayoruna

Mayuca [FL] *Seminole* (Ye)

Mayupi [BO] *Araona* (O)

Mayuzuna *see* Mayoruna

Mazahua (H) *see also* Omaha (LC)

Mazahua [MX] (LC)

Mazames *see* Mazapes

Mazapes [NM. TX] (BE)

Mazaque *see* Matsaki

Mazaqui *see* Matsaki

Ma-za-ro-ta *see* Magayuteshni

Mazarota *see* Magayuteshni

Mazatec [MX] (LC)

Mazateco *see* Mazatec

Mazatzal *Southern Tonto Apache* (BE)

mazipskoi *see* Missisquoi

mazipskoiak *see* Missisquoi

mazipskoik *see* Missisquoi

Mazpegnaka *Sans Arc* (H)

Mbaia *see* Mbya

Mbaya [Arg, Par] (LC)

Mbaye *see* Mbya

Mbia *see* Kaiwa

Mbia *see* Mbua

Mbia *see* Mbya

Mbia [Self-designation] *see* Sirono

Mbocobi *see* Mocobi

Mboyo *see* Mapoyo

Mbua [Br] (O)

Mbwiha *see* Mbya

Mbya [Br] *Guaycuru* (LC)

Mbya Guarani *see* Guarayo

McCloud River [Lang] [CA] *Wintu* (CA-8)

McGilvery [MS] *Chickasaw* (BE)

McGrath [AK] *Ingalik* (BE)

Mdawakonton *see* Mdewakanton

Mdawakontonwan *see* Mdewakanton

M'day-wah-kaun-twan Dakota *see* Mdewakanton

Mdaywahkauntwan Dakota *see* Mdewakanton

M'day-wah-kauntwaun *see* Mdewakanton

Mdaywahkauntwaun *see* Mdewakanton

M'daywakanton *see* Mdewakanton

Mdaywakanton *see* Mdewakanton

M'daywawkawntwawn *see* Mdewakanton

Mdaywawkawntwawn *see* Mdewakanton

Mdeiyedan (H) *see also* Mdewakanton (LC)

Mdeiyedan [MN] *Wahpeton* (H)

Mde-wahantonwan *see* Mdewakanton

Mdewahantonwan *see* Mdewakanton

M'dewakanton *see* Mdewakanton

Mdewakanton *see* Mdewakanton

Mdewakanton [Lang] [*Dakota-Assiniboin*] (H)

Mdewakanton [MN, WI, SD] (LC)

Mde-wa-kan-ton-wan *see* Mdewakanton

Mdewakantonwan *see* Mdewakanton

M'de-wakan-towwan *see* Mdewakanton

Mdewakantowwan *see* Mdewakanton

M'dewakant'wan *see* Mdewakanton

Mdewakantwan *see* Mdewakanton

Md-Wakan *see* Mdewakanton

Mdwakan *see* Mdewakanton

Mdwakantonwan *see* Mdewakanton

Meade and Ikpikpuk River Eskimos *Interior North Alaska Eskimos* (Hdbk5)

Meadow Indians *see* Mascouten

Meame *see* Miami

Me-a-me-a-me *see* Miami

Meameame *see* Miami

Meami *see* Miami

Meamskinisht [Can] *Kitksan* (BE)

Meamuyna *see* Bora

Meandan *see* Mandan

Meantaukett *see* Montauk

Meat-who *see* Methow

Meatwho *see* Methow

Mebengokre *see* Cayapo

Mecawa *see* Pesawa

Mech-cha-ooh *see* Tooksetuk

Mechchaooh *see* Tooksetuk

Mechecauki *see* Fox

Mechecouaki *see* Fox

Mechegame *see* Michigamea

Mechemeton [MN] *Sisseton* (H)

Mechemiton *see* Mechemeton

Mechkentiwoom *see* Mechkentowoon

Mechkentowoon [NY] *Mahican Confederacy* (BE)

Mechuouaki *see* Fox

Meco (LC) *see also* Chichimeca-Jonaz (LC)

Meco [Lang] [MX] (BE)

Mecontin *see* Mascouten

Mecosukee *see* Mikasuki

Mecoutin *see* Mascouten

Me-dama-rec *see* Bidamarek

Medamarec *see* Bidamarek

Medaquakantoan *see* Mdewakanton

Medawah-Kanton *see* Mdewakanton

Medawahkanton *see* Mdewakanton

Med-a-wakan-toan *see* Mdewakanton

Medawakantoan *see* Mdewakanton

Med-a-wa-kanton *see* Mdewakanton

Medawakanton *see* Mdewakanton

Medawakantwan *see* Mdewakanton

Me-da-we-con-tong *see* Mdewakanton

Medawecontong *see* Mdewakanton

Medaykantoan *see* Mdewakanton

Med-ay-wah-kawn-t'waron *see* Mdewakanton

Medaywahkawntwaron *see* Mdewakanton

Medaywakanstoan *see* Mdewakanton

Med-ay-wa-kan-toan *see* Mdewakanton

Medaywakantoan *see* Mdewakanton

Medaywokant'wan *see* Mdewakanton

Me-de-wah-kan-toan *see* Mdewakanton

Medewahkantoan *see* Mdewakanton

Medewakantoan *see* Mdewakanton

Medewakanton *see* Mdewakanton

Mede-wakan-t'wan *see* Mdewakanton

Medewakantwan *see* Mdewakanton

Medicine *see* Hanga

Mediwankton *see* Mdewakanton

Mednofski *see* Ahtena

Mednofski *see* Mednovskie

Mednoftski *see* Mednovskie

Mednovskie [Lang] *Eskimo* (BE)

Mednovtze *see* Mednovskie

Medocktack *see* Medoctec

Medockteck *see* Medoctec

Medoctec [NewB] *Abnaki* (H)

Medoctek *see* Medoctec

Medoctet *see* Medoctec

Medocthek *see* Medoctec
Medoktek *see* Medoctec
Medostec *see* Medoctec
Medsigamea *see* Michigamea
Medwakantonwan *see* Mdewakanton
Meeches *see* Michigamea
Me-em-ma *see* Chimariko
Meemma *see* Chimariko
Mee-ne-cow-e-gee *see* Miniconjou
Meenecowegee *see* Miniconjou
Meesee Contee *see* Amaseconti
Mee-see-qua-guilch *see* Miseekwigweelis
Meeseequaguilch *see* Miseekwigweelis
Mee-shom-o-neer *see* Mishongnovi
Meeshomoneer *see* Mishongnovi
Meesucontu *see* Amaseconti
Meethco-thinyoowuc *see* Kainah
Meewa *see* Miwok
Meewie *see* Miwok
Meewoc *see* Miwok
Megancockia *see* Mengakonkia
Megesiwisowa *see* Mikissioua
Megezi *see* Mgezawa
Me'gezi *see* Mgezewa
Meghay *see* Mayeye
Meghey *see* Mayeye
Meghty *see* Mayeye
Me-giz-ze *see* Omegeeze
Megizze *see* Omegeeze
Me-gizzee *see* Omegeeze
Meguak *see* Mohawk
Megual *see* Mohawk
Meguatchaiki *see* Shawnee
Megue *see* Mohawk
Meguenodon *see* Tututni
Megwe *see* Mohawk
Me-ha-shun-ga *see* Mehashunga
Mehashunga [Gens] *Kansa* (H)
Meherin *see* Meherrin
Meherine *see* Meherrin
Meheron *see* Meherrin
Meherries *see* Meherrin
Meherrin [VA, NC] (BE)
Meherring *see* Meherrin
Meherron *see* Meherrin
Mehethawa *see* Cree
Mehihammer *see* Mahican
Mehinacu [Br] (LC)
Mehinaku *see* Mehinacu
Mehinkaku *see* Mehinacu
Meh-ko-a *see* Mehkoa
Mehkoa [Clan] *Abnaki* (H)
Mehta *see* Carapana
Meidoo *see* Maidu
Meihite *see* Mayeye
Meinaco *see* Mehinacu
Meipontsky (H) *see also* Christianna Indians (H)

Meipontsky [VA] (H)
Meipoutsky *see* Meipontsky
Mejeraja [Clan] *Oto* (H)
Mejia *Piro* (H)
Mejia *Tigua* (H)
Mekadewagamitigweyawininiwak [MI, WI] *Chippewa* (H)
Mekasousky *see* Mikasuki
Mekem [Br] (O)
Mekka *see* Witoto
Mekoateeaukee *see* Kaskaskia
Mekrangnonti *see* Mekranoti
Mekranoti [Br] *Cayapo* (LC)
Mekrononty *see* Mekranoti
Mekronotire *see* Mekranoti
Mekusuky *see* Mikasuki
Melchora [NI] *Chibchan* (BE)
Melecite *see* Malecite
Melemisimok-ontilka *see* Coast Yuki
Meletecunk [NJ] *Unami* (BE)
Melhominy *see* Menominee
Melicete *see* Malecite
Melicite *see* Malecite
Meli-lema *see* Tenino
Melilema *see* Tenino
Meliquenes [PE] *Aguano* (O)
Melisceet *see* Malecite
Melomelinoia *see* Menominee
Melominee *see* Menominee
Melukutz [OR] *Kusan* (H)
Melungeons (LC)
Memaconjo *see* Miniconjou
Memankitonna [DE] *Unalachtigo* (BE)
Membrenos *see* Mimbreno Apache
Membres culture (LC) *see also* Mogollon Culture (LC)
Memeoya [MN, Can] *Kainah* (BE)
Memesoon *see* Comanche
Memi *see* Miami
Memilounioue *see* Miami
Me-mogg-ins *see* Memoggyins
Memoggyins [Clan] *Koeksotenok* (H)
Memonomier *see* Menominee
Memottins *see* Memoggyins
Memramcook [Can] *Sigunikt* (BE)
Memwaylaka [Lang] *River Nomlaki* (CA)
Menache *see* Moache
Menamenies *see* Menominee
Menanque *see* Menenquen
Menanquen *see* Menenquen
Menapacunt [VA] *Algonquian* (Hdbk15)
Menapacute *see* Menapacunt
Menaquen *see* Menenquen
Menatopa *see* Otaopabine
Mencami *see* Miami

Menchaerink *see* Menherrin
Menchokatonx *see* Mdewakanton
Menchokatouches *see* Mdewakanton
Menchon *see* Huron
Mencouacanton *see* Mdewakanton
Mendawahkanton *see* Mdewakanton
Men-da-wa-kan-ton *see* Mdewakanton
Mendawakanton *see* Mdewakanton
Mendeouacanton *see* Mdewakanton
Mendeouacantous *see* Mdewakanton
Menderink *see* Meherrin
Mendewacantong *see* Mdewakanton
Mende Wahkan toan *see* Mdewakanton
Mendewahkantoan *see* Mdewakanton
Mende-Wakan-Toann *see* Mdewakanton
Mendewakantoann *see* Mdewakanton
Mendica [TX] (H)
Mendoerink *see* Meherrin
Mendouca-ton *see* Mdewakanton
Menduwakanton *see* Mdewakanton
Mendwrink *see* Meherrin
Menearo [PE] *Campa* (O)
Meneca [Col, PE] *Witoto* (O)
Menekka *see* Witoto
Menekut'thegi *see* Mequachake
Menenquen [TX] *Coahuiltecan* (BE)
Me-ne-sharne *see* Itazipcho
Menesharne *see* Itazipcho
Menesikns *see* Minisink
Menesouhatoba *Dakota* (H)
Menessinghs *see* Minisink
Menetare *see* Hidatsa
Me-ne-ta-ree *see* Hidatsa
Menetaree *see* Hidatsa
Me ne tar re *see* Hidatsa
Mene tar re *see* Hidatsa
Menetarre *see* Hidatsa
Mengakonkia [IL] *Miami* (H)
Mengala [Gua] (O)
Mengua *see* Iroquois
Mengues *see* Iroquois
Menguy *see* Iroquois
Mengwe *see* Nottaway
Mengwe *see* Iroquois
Mengwee *see* Iroquois
Mengwi *see* Iroquois
Menherring *see* Meherrin
Menheyricks *see* Meherrin

Menian see Kamakan
Men-i-cou-zha see Miniconjou
Menicouzha see Miniconjou
Menien see Kamakan
Menisink see Minisink
Menissinck see Minisink
Menissing see Minisink
Menissinges see Minisink
Menissins see Minisink
Menitegow [MI] Chippewa (H)
Menkranotire see Mekranoti
Menkrononty see Mekranoti
Mennissinck see Minisink
Mennominee see Menominee
Men of the Wood see Nopeming
Menomene see Menominee
Me-no-me-ne-uk see Menominee
Menomeneuk see Menominee
Menomienies see Menominee
Menominee [MI, WI] (LC)
Menomini see Menominee
Menominny see Menominee
Menomoee see Menominee
Menomone see Menominee
Menomonee see Menominee
Menomonei see Menominee
Menomoni see Menominee
Menomonies see Menominee
Menomony see Menominee
Menonomee see Menominee
Menonomies see Menominee
Menoquet's Village [MI]
    Chippewa (H)
Menostamenton Dakota (BE)
Menowa Kautong see Mde-
    wakanton
Menowa Kontong see Mde-
    wakanton
Mententon see Matantonwan
Mento (H)
Menton see Mento
Mentonton see Matantonwan
Mentou see Mento
Mentuktire [Br] Cayapo (O)
Menunkatuck [NY, CT] Wap-
    pinger (BE)
Menunkatuk see Wappinger
Meosigamia see Michigamea
Mepayaya [TX] (H)
Mepene Abipone (LC)
Mepontsky (BE) see also Ont-
    ponea (BE)
Mepontsky [VA] (BE)
Mequa see Mohawk
Mequachake (H) see also Spitotha
    (H)
Mequachake [TN] Shawnee (BE)
Mequashake see Mequachake
Meracock see Merric
Meracouman [TX] (H)
Meraquaman see Meracouman
Merced [CA] (H)

Mercedes see Merced
Merced-Yosemite [Lang] Southern
    Sierra Miwok (CA-8)
Mereo see Emerillon
Mereyo see Emerillon
Merguan see Menenquen
Merhuan see Menenquen
Mericock see Merric
Mericoke see Merric
Merikoke see Merric
Merocomecook see Rocameca
Meroke see Merric
Merriack see Merric
Merric [NY] Montauk (BE)
Merricocke see Merric
Merrimac see Pennacook
Merrimack see Pennacook
Mersapege see Massapequa
Mertowack see Metoac
Mesasagah see Missisauga
Mescal see Mescales
Mescaler see Mescalero Apache
Mescalere see Mescalero Apache
Mescalero Apache [MX, NM,
    TX] (LC)
Mescales [MX] Coahuiltecan (BE)
Mescallaro see Mescalero Apache
Mescalo see Mescalero Apache
Mescaloro Apaches see Mescalero
    Apache
Mescalos see Mescalero Apache
Mescaluro see Mescalero Apache
Mescata see Mescales
Mescate see Mescales
Mescatera see Mescalero Apache
Mescato see Mescales
Mescolero see Mescalero Apache
Meshal (Hdbk12) see also Mishal-
    pam (Hdbk12)
Meshal [WA] Southern Coast Sal-
    ish (Hdbk12)
Me-she-ka see Mesheka
Mesheka [Clan] Chippewa (H)
Meshingomesia's band see Miami
Meshkemau Ottawa (H)
Meshkwaki see Fox
Meshkwakihug see Fox
Mesh-kwa-kihug [Self-
    designation] see Fox
Meshkwa kihugi see Fox
Meshkwakihugi see Fox
Meshkwakiwug see Fox
Meshon see Methow
Me-shong-a-na-we see Mishong-
    novi
Meshonganawe see Mishongnovi
Meshongnavi see Mishongnovi
Meshsunganawe see Mishong-
    novi
Me-shung-a-na-we see Mishong-
    novi
Me-shung-ne-vi see Mishong-
    novi

Meshungnevi see Mishongnovi
Mesigameas see Michigamea
Meskemau see Meshkemau
Meskigouk see Maskegon
me-ško-te-waki see Peoria
meskotewaki see Peoria
Me-skwa-da-re see Meskwadare
Meskwadare [Clan] Chippewa (H)
Meskwaki see Fox
Meskwa'ki'ag see Fox
Meskwakiag see Fox
Mesoamerican (LC)
Meso-American see Mesoameri-
    can
Mespacht see Maspeth
Mespadt see Maspeth
Mespaetches see Maspeth
Mespat see Maspeth
Mespath see Maspeth
Mespath's Kill see Maspeth
Mespat Kil see Maspeth
Mespatkil see Maspeth
Mespats-kil see Maspeth
Mesquabuck see Mesquawbuck
Mesquaki see Fox
Mesquakie see Fox
Mesquawbuck Potawatomi (H)
Mesquita see Mesquite
Mesquite [MX] Concho (BE)
Mesquittes see Mesquite
Messachusett see Massachuset
Messachusiack see Massachuset
Messagnes see Missisauga
Messague see Missisauga
Messasaga see Missisauga
Messasagies see Missisauga
Messasagoes see Missisauga
Messasagues see Missisauga
Messasaugues see Missisauga
Messassaga see Missisauga
Messathusett see Massachuset
Messawomes see Iroquois
Messcothin see Mascouten
Messenack see Fox
Messen-Apaches see Navajo
Messenecqz see Fox
Messesagas see Missisauga
Messesagnes see Missisauga
Messesago see Missisauga
Messesagues see Missisauga
Messessagues see Missisauga
Messiasics see Missiassik
Messinagues see Missisauga
Messisaga see Missisauga
Messisage see Missisauga
Messisague see Missisauga
Messisauga see Missisauga
Messisauger see Missisauga
Messissaga see Missisauga
Messissauga see Missisauga
Messissauger see Missisauga
Messorite see Missouri
Messthusett see Massachuset

Mestigo *see* Mestizo
Mestizo (H)
Metaharta *see* Hidatsa
Metapawnien *see* Mattapanient
Metchagamis *see* Michigamea
Metchigame *see* Michigamea
Metchigamea *see* Michigamea
Metchis *see* Mechigamea
Met-co-we *see* Methow
Metcowwe *see* Methow
Metcowwee *see* Methow
Me-te-ah-ke *see* Meteahke
Meteahke *Mandan* (H)
Metehigamis *see* Michigamea
Meteowwee *see* Methow
Meterries *see* Meherrin
Metesigamias *see* Michigamea
Methau *see* Methow
Methew *see* Methow
Methom *see* Methow
Met-how *see* Methow
Methow [WA] *Salish* (BE)
Metis (H)
Metis (H) *see also* Mixed bloods
  (LC)
Metkuyak-ontilka *see* Coast Yuki
Metoac [NY] (H)
Metoctire *see* Mentuktire
Me-too-ta-hak *see* Mandan
Metootahak *see* Mandan
Metotire *see* Mentuktire
Metotonta *see* Oto
Metouscepriniouek (H)
Metouwack *see* Metoac
Metowack *see* Metoac
Metsahamomowi *Guahibo* (O)
Metsepe *see* Maspeth
Metsigameas *see* Michigamea
Metsmetskop (H)
Metsto'asath *see* Metstoasath
Metstoasath [Sept] *Nootka* (H)
Metsupda [Lang] *Konkow* (CA-8)
Metuktire *see* Mentuktire
Metutahanke *see* Mandan
Meviras [MX] *Lagunero* (BE)
Mewah *see* Miwok
Mewan (LC) *see also* Miwok (LC)
Mewan [Lang] (CA-8)
Mewko *see* Plains Miwok
Mexica *see* Aztecs
Mexican Diegueño *see* Bajino
  Diegueño
Mexican Diegueño *see* Tipai
Mexicano *see* Nahuas
Meye *see* Mayeye
Meyemma *see* Chimariko
Meynomeney *see* Menominee
Meynomeny *see* Menominee
Meynominey *see* Menominee
Meyo [Clan] *Laguna* (H)
Meyo-hano *see* Meyo
Meyo-hanock *see* Meyo
Mezcal *see* Miscal

Mezcalero *see* Mescalero Apache
Mezquites *see* Mesquite
Meztitlanec [MX] (BE)
Meztitlaneca *see* Meztitlanec
Meztizo (H) *see also* Mixed bloods
  (LC)
M-ge-ze-wa *see* Mgezewa
Mgezewa [Clan] *Potawatomi* (H)
Mhikana *see* Mahican
Mi [Clan] *Quapaw* (H)
Miahao *see* Kreen-Akrore
Mi-ah-kee-jack-sah *see* Mi-
  akechakesa
Miahkeejacksah *see* Mi-
  akechakesa
Mi-ah-ta-nes *see* Mandan
Miahtanes *see* Mandan
Mi-ah-wah-pit-siks *see* Miah-
  wahpitsiks
Miahwahpitsiks [MN] *Piegan*
  (BE)
Mia Kechakesa *see* Miakechakesa
Miakechakesa [MN] *Sisseton* (H)
Mialat [Br] *Kawahib* (O)
Miame *see* Miami
Miamee *see* Miami
Miami [OK, IN] (LC)
Miamia *see* Miami
Miamiack *see* Miami
Miamiha *see* Miami
Miamik *see* Miami
Miamiouek *see* Miami
Miamis de la Grue *see* Atchatch-
  akangouen
Miamunaa [Self-designation] *see*
  Bora
Miankish *see* Piankashaw
Miarra [Br] (O)
Mi-aw-kin-ai-yiks *see* Miawki-
  naiyiks
Miawkinaiyiks *Piegan* (BE)
Miayuma *see* Mahoyum
Micacoupsiba [MN] *Dakota* (BE)
Mi ca cu op si ba *see* Mi-
  cacuopsiba
Micai *see* Mical
Mical [WA] *Pshwanwapam* (BE)
Micasukey *see* Mikasuki
Micasukies *see* Mikasuki
Micasukys *see* Mikasuki
Mi-caw *see* Makah
Micaw *see* Makah
Micawa *see* Misshawa
Miccasooky *see* Mikasuki
Miccosaukie *see* Mikasuki
Mic-co-sooc-e *see* Mikasuki
Miccosooce *see* Mikasuki
Miccosukee *see* Mikasuki
Miccosukee *see* Seminole
Miccosuki *see* Mikasuki
Michacondibi *Algonquian* (H)
Michael, St. *Bering Strait Eskimos*
  (Hdbk5)

Michaha *see* Michahai
Michahai [CA] *Kings River Yokuts*
  (BE)
Michahay *see* Michahai
Miche Michequipi *see* Metsmet-
  skop
Michemichequipi *see* Metsmet-
  skop
Miche-Miche-Quipy *see*
  Metsmetskop
Michemichequipy *see* Metsmet-
  skop
Mich-en-dick-er *see* Fox
Michendicker *see* Fox
Michesaking *see* Missisauga
Michiaba [MX] *Coahuiltecan*
  (Hdbk10)
Michiagamias *see* Michigamea
Michibousa (H)
Michif [Lang] *Cree* (LC)
Michigamas *see* Michigamea
Michigamea [AR] *Illinois Confed-*
  eracy (BE)
Michigamias *see* Michigamea
Michigamis *see* Michigamea
Michigania *see* Michigamea
Michiganians *see* Michigamea
Michigans *see* Michigamea
Michigourras *see* Michigamea
Michikamau [Can] [*Montagnais-*
  Naskapi] (BE)
Michilimackinac [MI, WI]
  Chippewa (H)
Michilimackinac People (BE) *see*
  also Menominee (LC)
Michilimackinac People (BE) *see*
  also Misi'nimak Kimiko
  Wini'niwuk (BE)
Michinipicpoets *see* Etheneldeli
Michipicoten [Ont] *Chippewa*
  (BE)
Michirache [Clan] *Iowa* (H)
Michisagnek *see* Missauga
Michisaguek *see* Mississauga
Michiskoui *see* Missiassik
Michiskoui *see* Missisquoi
Michoacana *see* Tarascan
Michonguave *see* Mishongnovi
Michopdo *see* Mich-op-do
Mich-op-do *Maidu* (Contri, v.3,
  p.282)
Michuacana *see* Tarascan
Mi-ci-kqwut-me'tunne *see*
  Mishikhwutmetunne
Micikqwutmetunne *see*
  Mishikhwutmetunne
Mi-ci-qwat *see* Mishikhwut-
  metunne
Miciqwat *see* Mishikhwut-
  metunne
Mickasauky *see* Mikasuki
Mickasukian *see* Mikasuki
Micka Sukle *see* Mikasuki

Mickasukle *see* Mikasuki
Mickmak *see* Micmac
Micksucksealton *Kalispel* (H)
Micksucksealton *Tushepaw* (H)
mickyashe *see* Shoshone
Mi-Clauq-tcu-wun-ti *see* Klikitat
Miclauqtcuwunti *see* Klikitat
Micmac [Can] *Central Algonquian*
(LC)
Micognivi *see* Mishongnovi
Mi-con-in-o-vi *see* Mishongnovi
Miconinovi *see* Mishongnovi
Miconovi *see* Mishongnovi
Mictawayang *see* Mishtawayaw-
ininiwak
Middle Assiniboin *see* Opposite
Assiniboin
Middle Blackfeet *Siksika* (H)
Middle Cherokee [Lang] [NC]
(H)
Middle Columbia River [WA]
Salish (Hdbk12)
Middle Columbia Salish (LC) *see
also* Sinkiuse-Columbia (LC)
Middle Columbia Salish [WA]
(UW)
Middle Creek (BE) *see also* Tal-
lapoosa (BE)
Middle Creek [AL] *Creek* (H)
Middle Indians *see* Tangeratsa
Middle Inlet [AL] *Tenaina* (BE)
Middle Mewuk *see* Tuolumne
Middle-Settlement Indians [GA,
NC] *Cherokee* (H)
Middle Spokan (LC) *see also*
South Spokan (BE)
Middle Spokan [WA] *Spokan*
(LC)
Middle Spokane *see* Middle
Spokan
Middle Spo-ko-mish *see* Sin-
tootoolish
Middle Spokomish *see* Sin-
tootoolish
Midewakanton *see* Mdewakan-
ton
Mide'wigan *see* Midewiwin
Midewigan *see* Midewiwin
Mide'wiwin *see* Midewiwin
Midewiwin [Society] *Ojibwa* (An-
nual, v.7, 1885/86)
Midinakwadshiwininiwak [ND]
Chippewa (BE)
Miditadi *see* Hidatsa
Midnookies *see* Mednovskie
Midnooski *see* Mednovskie
Midnoosky *see* Mednovskie
Midnovtsi *see* Mednovskie
Midnusky *see* Mednovskie
Midu *see* Maidu
Miduusky [AK] *Ahtena* (BE)
Miednoffskoi *see* Mednovskie
Miednofskie *see* Mednovskie

Miembre *see* Mimbreno Apache
Miembrenos *see* Mimbreno
Apache
Mie-mis-souks *see* Miemissouks
Miemissouks [WA, BC] (H)
Mi-em-ma *see* Chimariko
Miemma *see* Chimariko
Mienbre *see* Miembreno Apache
Mi e'nikaci'ka *see* MIenikashika
Mienikacika *see* Mienikashika
Mienikashika [Gens] *Quapaw* (H)
Migichihiliniou (H)
Migichihilinious *see* Migichi-
hiliniou
Mi-gisi *see* Omegeeze
Migisi *see* Omegeeze
Migisiwininiwug *see* Migichi-
hiliniou
Migiziwininiwug *see* Migichi-
hiliniou
Migmac *see* Micmac
Miguel, San [CA] *Salinan* (BE)
Migueleño [Lang] [CA] *Salinan*
(CA)
Migueliño *see* Migueleño
Miguel Taxique, San *see* Tajique
Miguel Ures, San *see* Ures
Miheconder *see* Mahican
Mihicander *see* Mahican
Mihtukmechakick [MA] (H)
Miitsr [Clan] *Keres* (H)
Miitsr-hano *see* Miitsr
Mije *see* Mixe
Mika-ati *see* Northern Shoshone
mika-ati *see* Shoshone
Mikaati *see* Northern Shoshone
mikaati *see* Shoshone
Mikadeshitchishi *see* Nez Perce
Mikakh [Clan] *Quapaw* (H)
Mikakhenikashika [Gens] *Qua-
paw* (H)
Mika nika-shing-ga *see* Mikau-
nikashinga
Mikanikashingga *see* Mikau-
nikashinga
Mika'q'e ni'kaci'ka *see*
Mikakhenikashika
Mikaqenikacika *see*
Mikakhenikashika
Mikaqlajinga *see* Mikau-
nikashinga
Mika qla junga *see* Mikau-
nikashinga
Mikasaukies *see* Mikasuki
Mikasi [Subgens] *Omaha* (H)
Mikasi-unikacinga *see* Mand-
hinkagaghe
Mikasuki [FL] (LC)
Mikasuky *see* Mikasuki
Mika unikachinga *see* Mikau-
nikashinga
Mikaunikachinga *see* Mikau-
nikashinga

Mikaunikashinga [Subgens] *Kansa*
(H)
Mikechuse [CA] (H)
Mikikiwoman *Conoy* (Hdbk15)
Mikikoues *see* Nikikouek
Mikikouet *see* Nikikouek
Mi'kina'k *see* Mikonoh
Mikinak *see* Mikonoh
Mi kina'kiwadshiwininiwag *see*
Mikinakwadshiwininiwak
Mikinakiwadshiwininiwag *see*
Mikinakwadshiwininiwak
Mi kina'kiwadshiwininiwug *see*
Mikinakwadshiwininiwak
Mikinakiwadshiwininiwug *see*
Mikinakwadshiwininiwak
Mikinakwadshi-wininiwak *see*
Mikinakwadshiwininiwak
Mikinakwadshiwininiwak [MN,
ND, SD] *Chippewa* (H)
Mikissioua [Gens] *Sauk and Fox*
(H)
Mikissoua *see* Mikissioua
Mikkesoeke *see* Mikasuki
Mikmakiques *see* Micmac
Mikonah [Clan] *Chippewa* (H)
Mik-o-noh *see* Mikonoh
Mikonoh [Gens] *Chippewa* (H)
Mikonotunne *see* Mackanotin
Mikonotunne *see* Mikono tunne
Mikono tunne [OR] *Tututni* (BE)
Mikouachakhi *see* Miskouaha
Mikouest *see* a Mikouest
Mikouest *see* Amikwa
Mi'kowa *see* Mehkoa
Mikowa *see* Mehkoa
Mikwak *see* Micmac
Mikwanak *see* Micmac
Mi'kyashe *see* Northern Shoshone
Mi'kyashe *see* Shoshone
Mikyashe *see* Northern Shoshone
Mikyashe *see* Shoshone
Mil-a-ket-kun *see* Milakitekwa
Milaketkun *see* Milakitekwa
Milakitekwa [WA] *Okinagan* (H)
Milakitewa *see* Similkameen
Milaug-tcu-wun-ti *see* Klikitat
Milbauks-chim-zi-an *see*
Tsimshian
milena *see* Navajo
Milicete *see* Malecite
Milicite *see* Malecite
Milijae *see* Milijaes
Milijaes [MX, TX] *Coahuiltecan*
(BE)
Milkemaxi'tuk *see* Similkameen
Millbank Indians *see* Bellabella
Millbank Sound Indians *see*
Bellabella
Mill Creek culture [IA] (LC)
Mill Creek Indians *see* Yana
Mille Lac Band *see* Misis-
agaikaniwininiwak

Milli-hhlama *see* Tenino
Milowack *see* Metoac
Miluk [OR] (BE)
Miluk Coos *see* Miluk
Mimbre *see* Mimbreno Apache
Mimbrenas *see* Mimbreno
   Apache
Mimbreno Apache [AZ] *Gileños*
   (LC)
Mimbrereños *see* Mimbreno
   Apache
Mimbres (H) *see also* Mimbreno
   Apache (LC)
Mimbres culture (LC)
Mimetari *see* Hidatsa
Mimiola *Coahuiltecan* (Hdbk10)
Mimvre *see* Mimbreno Apache
Mina [Clan] *Keres* (H)
Minacaguapo [MX] (Hdbk10)
Minaco *see* Mehinacu
Minacu *see* Mehinacu
Mina-hano *see* Mina
Minas [NS] *Micmac* (H)
Minatare *see* Hidatsa
Minataree *see* Hidatsa
Minatari *see* Hidatsa
Minatories *see* Hidatsa
Minchumina Lake [AK] *Tanana*
   (BE)
Minckquas *see* Iroquois
Minckus *see* Conestoga
Mincquaas *see* Iroquois
Min-da-war-car-ton *see* Mde-
   wakanton
Mindawarcarton *see* Mdewakan-
   ton
Mineamies *see* Menominee
Mineamies *see* Miami
Minecogue *see* Miniconjou
Minecosias *see* Miniconjou
Minecougan *see* Miniconjou
Mi-ne-kanj'zus *see* Miniconjou
Minekanjzus *see* Miniconjou
Mineoes *see* MIngo
Minesepere *see* Mine'sepere
Mine'sepere [MN] *Crow* (BE)
Mine-set-peri *see* Minesetperi
Minesetperi *Crow* (H)
Minesupe'rik *see* Minesetperi
Minetaire *see* Hidatsa
Minetare *see* Hidatsa
Minetaree *see* Hidatsa
Minetare of the Prairie *see* Atsina
Minetari *see* Hidatsa
Minetaries *see* Hidatsa
Minetarre *see* Hidatsa
Minetarries *see* Hidatsa
Mingaes *see* Iroquois
Mingan [Can] [*Montagnais-
   Naskapi*] (BE)
Minghakokia *see* Mengakonkia
Minghasanwetazhi [Subgens]
   Omaha (H)

Minghaska [Subgens] *Osage* (H)
Minghaskainihkashina [Subgens]
   Osage (H)
Ming-ko *see* Mingko
Mingko [Clan] *Chickasaw* (H)
Mingo (H) *see also* Mingko (H)
Mingo [PA] *Iroquois* (LC)
Mingwe *see* Iroquois
Mingwe *see* Mingo
Mingwee *see* Mingo
Miniamies *see* Menominee
Miniaterree (BE)
Mini-cala *see* Itazipcho
Minicala *see* Itazipch
Minicau *see* Piniquu
Minicau *see* Manico
Mini-con-gsha *see* Miniconjou
Minicongsha *see* Miniconjou
Mini-Conjou *see* Miniconjou
Miniconjou [Lang] *Teton* (H)
Miniconjou *Teton* (LC)
Minicoughas *see* Miniconjou
Minikaniwininiwuk *see*
   Minika'ni Wini'niwuk
Minika'ni Wini'niwuk [WI]
   Menominee (BE)
Mini-kan-jou *see* Miniconjou
Minikanjou *see* Miniconjou
Minikanjzu *see* Miniconjou
Minikan oju *see* Miniconjou
Minikanoju *see* Miniconjou
Minikanyes *see* Miniconjou
Minikanye wozupi *see* Minicon-
   jou
Minikiniad-za *see* Miniconjou
Minikomjoos *see* Miniconjou
Minikonga *see* Miniconjou
Minikongaha *see* Miniconjou
Mininihkashina [Subgens] *Osage*
   (H)
Min-in-kanj'zu *see* Miniconjou
Minipata *see* Minnepata
Mini-sala *see* Itazipcho
Minisala *see* Itazipacho
Min-i-sha *see* Itazipcho
Min-i-sha *see* Minisha
Minisha (PC) *see also* Itazipcho (H)
Minisha [SD] *Oglala* (BE)
Minishinakato *see* Min-i-shi-
   nak-a-to
Min-i-shi-nak-a-to [MN] *Assini-
   boin* (BE)
Minishupako *see* Dakota
Minishupsko *see* Dakota
Minisincks *see* Minisink
Minising *see* Minisink
Minisink [NY, NJ, PA] *Munsee*
   (LC)
Miniskuyakichun [Brule] (H)
Miniskuyakitchun *see*
   Miniskuyakichum
Miniskuya-kitc'un *see*
   Miniskuyakichum

Minissens *see* Minisink
Minissingh *see* Minisink
Minissinks *see* Minisink
Ministeneaux *see* Cree
Minisuk *see* Minisink
Minitare *see* Hidatsa
Minitaree *see* Hidatsa
Minitare of the Prairie *see* Atsina
Minitari *see* Miniaterree
Minitari *see* Hidatsa
Minitari *see* Hidatsa
Minkekhanye [Subgens] *Iowa* (H)
Minke'yin'e *see* Minkeyine
Minkeyine [Subgens] *Iowa* (H)
Min k'in *see* Minkin
Minkin [Gens] *Kansa* (H)
Minkin [Gens] *Osage* (H)
Minnake-nozzo *see* Min-
   nakineazzo
Minnakenozzo *see* Min-
   nakineazzo
Min-na-kine-az-so *see* Minicon-
   jou
Minnakineazzo (PC) *see also*
   Miniconjou (LC)
Minnakineazzo *Miniconjou* (H)
Minnecarguis *see* Miniconjou
Minnecausha *see* Miniconjou
Minnecogoux *see* Miniconjou
Minnecojou *see* Miniconjou
Minnecongew *see* Miniconjou
Minnecongou *see* Miniconjou
Minneconjon *see* Miniconjou
Minneconjos *see* Miniconjou
Minne Conjoux *see* Miniconjou
Minneconjoux *see* Miniconjou
Minnecoujos *see* Miniconjou
Minnecoujou *see* Miniconjou
Minne-cousha *see* Mininconjou
Minnecousha *see* Miniconjou
Minnecowzue *see* Miniconjou
Minneh-sup-pay-deh *see* Mine-
   setperi
Minnehsuppaydeh *see* Mineset-
   peri
Minnekonjo *see* Miniconjou
Min-ne-pa-ta *see* Minnepata
Minnepata *Hidatsa* (H)
Minnessinck *see* Minisink
Minnetahree *see* Hidatsa
Minnetahse *see* Hidatsa
Min-ne-ta-re *see* Hidatsa
Minnetare *see* Hidatsa
Minnetaree *see* Hidatsa
Minnetaree Metaharta *see* Hidatsa
Minnetaree of Fort de Prairie *see*
   Atsina
Minnetaree of Fort Prairie *see*
   Atsina
Minnetaree of Knife River *Hi-
   datsa* (H)
Minnetaree of the Plains *see*
   Atsina

Minnetaree of the Prairies *see* Atsina

Minnetaree of the Willows *see* Hidatsa

Minnetaroes *see* Hidatsa

Minnetarre *see* Hidatsa

Minneways *see* Illinois

Minnicongew *see* Miniconjou

Minnikan-jous *see* Miniconjou

Minnikanye Wozhipu *see* Miniconjou

Minnishupsko *see* Dakota

Minnisink *see* Minisink

Minnissincks *see* Minisink

Minnissingh *see* Minisink

Minnissinke *see* Minisink

Minnitaree *see* Miniaterree

Minnitaree *see* Hidatsa

Minnitaree Metaharta *see* Hidatsa

Minnitaree of the Willows *see* Hidatsa

Minntaree *see* Hidatsa

Minokantong *see* Mdewakanton

Minominee *see* Menominee

Minominies *see* Menominee

Minomonee *see* Menominee

Minoniones *see* Menominee

Minoomenee *see* Menominee

Minoosky *see* Mednovskie

Minowakanton *see* Mdewakanton

Minowa Kantong *see* Mdewakanton

Minowakantong *see* Mdewakanton

Minowas *see* Iowa

Minoway-Kantong *see* Mdewakanton

Minow Kantong *see* Mdewakanton

Minowkantong *see* Mdewakanton

Min-qe qan-ye *see* Minkekhanye

Minqeqanye *see* Minkekhanye

Minqua [Lang] *Iroquois* (BE)

Minquaa *see* Conestoga

Minquaas *see* Iroquois

Minquaes *see* Conestoga

Minqua Indians *see* Conestoga

Minquaos *see* Conestoga

Minquas *see* Iroquois

Minquase *see* Conestoga

Minquays *see* Conestoga

Minque *see* Conestoga

Minquino *see* Conestoga

Minquosy *see* Conestoga

Minsi *see* Munsee

Mintou *see* Mento

Minusing *see* Minisink

Minusky *see* Mednovskie

Minxa-san-wet'aji *see* Minghasanwetazhi

Minxasanwetaji *see* Mingasanwetazhi

Minxa'ska *see* Minghaska

Minxaska *see* Minghaska

Minxa'ska i'niyk'acin'a *see* Minghaskainihkashina

Minxaskainiykacina *see* Minghaskainihkashina

Miook *see* Miwok

Miopacoas [MX] *Laguenero* (BE)

Mipacma *see* Makoma

Mipegoes *see* Winnebago

Miqkano *see* Miqka'no

Miqka'no [Clan] *Menominee* (H)

Miqui *see* Hopi

Miquiaguin *see* Moquiaguin

Miquira [PE] (O)

Miracoa *see* Maricopa

Miragua *see* Miraña

Mirami *see* Miami

Miraña [Col] (O)

Miraña-Carapana-Tapuyo *see* Bora

Miranha *see* Miraña

Mirania *see* Miraña

Miraño *see* Miraña

Miranya *see* Miraña

Mirayo *see* Miraña

Miriti *see* Miriti-Tapuya

Miriti-Tapuya [Col] *Tucano* (O)

Mirocopa *see* Maricopa

Mirrachtauhacky *see* Montauk

Mirrica *see* Manico

Misalla-Magun [CA] *Gallinomero* (Contri, v.3, pp.183–186)

Miscal (Hdbk10) *see also* Mescales (BE)

Miscal [MX] (Hdbk10)

Miscalero *see* Mescalero Apache

Miscothins *see* Mascouten

Miscotins *see* Mascouten

Miscouaguis *see* Fox

Miscouaqui *see* Fox

Miseekwigweelis *Skagit* (H)

Mishalpam [WA] (Hdbk12)

Mi-shan-qu-na-vi *see* Mishongnovi

Mishanqunavi *see* Mishongnovi

Mishara *see* Yagua

Mishbul-ontilka *see* Coast Yuki

Mishigamaw *see* Michigamea

Mishikhwutmetunne [OR] (BE)

Mishisagaiganiwininiwag *see* Misisagaikaniwininiwak

Mishkei-ontilka *see* Coast Yuki

Mishkemau *see* Meshkemau

Mishkeun-ontilka *see* Coast Yuki

Mi-shong-i-niv *see* Moshongnovi

Mishonginiv *see* Mishongnovi

Mi-shong-i-ni-vi *see* Mishongnovi

Mishonginivi *see* Mishongnovi

Mi-shong-in-ovi *see* Mishongnovi

Mishonginovi *see* Mishongnovi

Mi-shong-no-vi *see* MIshongnovi

Mishongnovi *see* Mishongnovi

Mishongnovi *Pueblo Indians* (BE)

Mishongop-avi *see* Mishongnovi

Mi-shon-na-vi *see* Mishongnovi

Mishonnavi *see* Mishongnovi

Mishtawaya-wininiwak *see* Mishtawayawininiwak

Mishtawayawininiwak [Ont] *Chippewa* (H)

Mishumash [CA] *Chumash* (H)

Misiassins *see* Mistassin

Misiassuck *see* Missiassik

Misinimak Kimiko Wininiwuk *see* Misi'nimak Kimiko Wini'niwuk

Misi'nimak Kimiko Wini'niwuk [WI] [Menominee] (BE)

mi'sis *see* Omisis

Misis *see* Omisis

Misisagaikani-wininiwak *see* Misisagaikaniwininiwak

Misisagaikaniwininiwak [MN, ND, SD] *Chippewa* (BE)

Misisagakaniwininiwak [MN] *Kitchisibiwininiwug* (H)

Misisaga's *see* Missisauga

Misisagas *see* Missisauga

Misisagey *see* Missisauga

Misiskoui *see* Missiassik

Misiskuoi *see* Missisquoi

Misitague *see* Missisauga

Mis-kai-whu *see* Miseekwigweelis

Miskaiwhu *see* Miseekwigweelis

Mis-Keeges *see* Maskegon

Miskeegoes *see* Maskegon

Mis-ke-toi-i-tok *see* Hupa

Misketoiitok *see* Hupa

Miskigula *see* Pascagoula

Miskito [NI, Hon] (Bull106)

Miskito (O) *see also* Mosquito (LC)

Miskitu *see* Miskito

Miskogonhirini *see* Maskegon

Miskouaha [Q] *Nippising* (H)

Misku-Gami-Saga-igananishinabeg *see* Miskwagamiwigaigan

Miskugamisagaiganinishinabeg *see* Miskwagamiwigaigan

Mis-kut *see* Hupa

Miskut *see* Hupa

Miskwadasi *see* Meskwadare

Miskwa-gamiwi-saga-igan *see* Miskwagamiwisagaigan

Miskwagamiwisagai-i-gan *see* Miskwagamiwisagaigan

Miskwagnmiwisagaigan [MN] *Chippewa* (BE)

Miskwa-ka Mewe Sagagan Wene-
newak *see* Miskwagamiwis-
agaigan
Miskwakamewesagaganwenenewak
see Miskwagamiwisagaigan
Miskwikeeyuk *see* Fox
Misonk *see* Mietmissouks
Misouri *see* Missouri
Misquachki *see* Fox
Missada *see* Missisauga
Missage *see* Missisauga
Missasaga *see* Missisauga
Missasago *see* Missisauga
Missasague *see* Missisauga
Missasauga *see* Missisauga
Missassago *see* Missisauga
Missassuga *see* Missisauga
Missaugee *see* Missisauga
Missequek *see* Missisauga
Missesaga *see* Missisauga
Missesagoes *see* Missisauga
Missesague *see* Missisauga
Missesaque *see* Missisauga
Mis-sha-wa *see* Misshawa
Misshawa [Clan] *Potawatomi* (H)
Missiago *see* Missisauga
Missiassik [VT] *Abnaki* (BE)
Missinasague *see* Missisauga
Mission [BC] *Seaton Lake Lillooet*
(H)
Mission [BC] *Squamish* (H)
Mission [BC] *Upper Lillooet* (H)
Mission Indians [CA] (LC)
Mission Iroquois *see* Caugh-
nawaga
Mission Valley [BC] *Salish* (H)
Missiosagaes *see* Missisauga
Missiouri *see* Missiouri
Missiqueck *see* Missisauga
Missisaga *see* Missisauga
Missisagaes *see* Missisauga
Missisage *see* Missisauga
Missisagi *see* Missisauga
Missisago *see* Missisauga
Missisague *see* Missisauga
Missisaguez *see* Missisauga
Missisaguy *see* Missisauga
Missisak *see* Missisauga
Missisaki *see* Missisauga
Missisaque *see* Missisauga
Missisaquees *see* Missisauga
Missisauga [Ont] *Chippewa* (LC)
Missisauge *see* Missisauga
Missisco *see* Missisquoi
Missiscoui *see* Missiassik
Missiscoui *see* Missisquoi
Missisiga *see* Missisauga
Missiskouy *see* Missiassik
Missisque *see* Missisquoi
Missisquoi (IndL, nos.27–28) *see
also* Missiassik (BE)
Missisquoi [VT, Q] *Abnaki*
(Hdbk10)

Mississaga *see* Missisauga
Mississaget *see* Missisauga
Mississageyes *see* Missisauga
Mississagez *see* Missisauga
Mississagies *see* Missisauga
Mississagua *see* Missisauga
Mississague *see* Missisauga
Mississagura *see* Missisauga
Mississaki *see* Missisauga
Mississaque *see* Missisauga
Mississauge *see* Missisauga
Mississauger *see* Missisauga
Mississaugies *see* Missisauga
Mississaugue *see* Missisauga
Mississgua *see* Missisauga
Mississippian culture (LC)
Mississippi bands *see* Kitchisibi-
wininiwug
Missitague *see* Missisauga
Missogkonnog [MA] (H)
Missoori *see* Missouri
Missounta *see* Missouri
Missouri [Lang] *Chiwere* (LC)
Missouri [MO, IA, KS] (LC)
Missouri [OK] (W) *see also* Oto
(LC)
Missouria *see* Missouri
Missourian *see* Missouri
Missourien *see* Missouri
Missouries *see* Missouri
Missouri River Souk *see* Sauk
Missourita *see* Missouri
Missourite *see* Missouri
Missoury *see* Missouri
Misstassin *see* Mistassin
Missuri *see* Missouri
Missurier *see* Missouri
Missurys *see* Missouri
Mistapnis *see* Mistassin
Mistasiniouek *see* Mistassin
Mistasirenois *see* Mistassin
Mistasirinin *see* Mistassin
Mistassin [Q] *Algonquian* (LC)
Mistassini *see* Mistassin
Mistassinni *see* Mistassin
Mistassirinin *see* Mistassin
Mistissinnys *see* Mistassin
Misumalpan [Lang] [CAm] (BE)
Misuri *see* Missouri
Mitahawiye *see* Kitkehahki
Mitaoam Kai Pomo *see* Mito-
mkai
Mitaui *see* Methow
Mitawit *see* Mita'wit
Mita'wit [Society] (Annual, v.14,
pt.1)
Mitchagami *see* Michigamea
Mit-che-ro-ka *see* Mitcheroka
Mitcheroka [Clan] *Hidatsa* (H)
Mitchif *see* Michif
Mitchigamea *see* Michigamea
Mitchigamias *see* Michigamea
Mitchitamou *see* Mistassin

Mi-tcu-mac *see* Chumash
Mitcumac *see* Chumash
Mithouies *see* Methow
Mi-til-ti *see* Hupa
Mitilti *see* Hupa
Mitiuhana [Self-designation] *see*
Karine
Mi-toam Kai Po-mo *see* Mito-
mkai
Mitomkai [CA] *Pomo* (H)
Mitom Pomo [CA] *Northern
Pomo* (Pub, v.40, no.2)
Mitsita *see* Wichita
Mitua [Self-designation] *see*
Guayabero
Miuneconjou *see* Miniconjou
Miuxsen *see* Tonkawan
Mivera *see* Quivira
Mi-wa *see* Miwok
Miwa *see* Miwok
Mi-wi *see* Miwok
Miwi *see* Miwok
Mi-wok *see* Miwok
Miwok [CA] (LC)
Miwokan [Lang] *Utian* (CA-8)
Miwokan Indians *see* Miwok
Miwuk *see* Miwok
Mixe [Lang] [MX] *Zoquean* (LC)
Mixed bloods (LC)
Mixed bloods (LC) *see also* Mes-
tizo (H)
Mixed bloods (LC) *see also* Metis
(H)
Mixed Shoshones [*Bannock,
Tukuarika*] (H)
Mixtec [MX] (LC)
Mixteca Alta [MX] (BE)
Mixteca Baja [BaC, MX] (BE)
Mixtecan [Lang] *Mixtecan* (BE)
Mixteco *see* Mixtec
Miyami *see* Miami
Miyi *see* Mayeye
Mizocuavean (BE)
Miztecan [MX] (BE)
Mkatewetiteta *see* Siksika
M'ke-tash-she-ka-kah *see* M'ke-
tashshekakah
Mketashshekakah *see* M'ke-
tashshekakah
M'ketashshekakah [Gens] *Sauk
and Fox* (H)
Mko *see* M'ko
M'ko [Clan] *Potawatomi* (H)
Mkwa *see* M'-kwa
M'-kwa [Clan] *Shawnee* (H)
Mnakho-tana *see* Unakhotana
Moache [Col, NM] *Ute* (LC)
Moacks *see* Mohawk
moadika-a *see* Aga'ipani-
nadokado
Moadoc *see* Modoc
Mo-a-dok *see* Modoc
Moadok *see* Modoc

Moadokado *see* Aga'ipaninadokado

Moadokkni *see* Modoc

Moadok Maklak *see* Modoc

Mo-ah *see* Moah

Moah [Clan] *Potawatomi* (H)

Moahtockna *see* Modoc

Moak *see* Mohawk

Moan-au-zi *see* Northern Paiute

Moanauzi *see* Northern Paiute

Moanauzi *see* Mono

Moanunts [UT] *Ute* (Hdbk11)

Mo-apa *see* Moapa

Moapa *Southern Paiute* (Hdbk11)

Moapan *see* Mopan

Moapariat [NV] *Paiute* (H)

Mo-a-pa-ri-ats *see* Moapariats

Mo-a-pa-ri-ats *see* Moapa

Moa-pariats *see* Moapa

Moapariats (PC) *see also* Moapa
(Hdbk11)

Mo-a-pats *see* Moapa

Moapats *see* Moapa

Moasham *see* Abnaki

Moasson *see* Abnaki

Moassone *see* Abnaki

Moatakish *see* Modoc

Moatokgish *see* Modoc

Moatokni (H) *see also* Modoc
(LC)

Moatokni [CA] (BE)

Moavinunts *see* Moanunts

Mo-a-wa-ta-ve-wach *see* Tabeguache

Moawatavewach *see* Tabeguache

Moawk *see* Mohawk

Mobeluns *see* Mobile

Mobilas *see* Mobile

Mobile [AL] (LC)

Mobileans *see* Mobile

Mobilian (H) *see also* Creek (LC)

Mobilian [Lang] (LC)

Mobilian Indians *see* Mobile

Mobiliens *see* Mobile

Mobima *see* Movima

Moca *see* Hopi

Mocama [Lang] *Timucuan* (H)

Mocama Indians *see* Timucua

Moccasin-with-Holes *see* Bannock

Mochda [Tucanan] [Self-
designation] *see* Carapana

Moche *see* Mochica

Mochgonnekonck *see* Shinnecock

Mochgonnekouck *see* Shinnecock

Mochi *see* Hopi

Mochica (LC) *see also* Yunca (LC)

Mochica [PE] (LC)

Mochies *see* Hopi

Mocho [Lang] *Mayan* (LC)

Mochomes *see* Delaware

Mo-cko-ki *see* Muskogee

Mockoki *see* Muskogee

Mockway *see* Mohawk

Mocoa *see* Camsa

Mocobi [Arg] (LC)

Mococo [FL] (BE)

Mocorito [MX] (BE)

Mocovi *see* Mocobi

Mocquages *see* Mohawk

Mocquayes *see* Mohawk

Moctobi [MS, LA] (BE)

Moctoby *see* Moctobi

Modanks *see* Modoc

Modesse *see* Madehsi

Modoc [CA, OR] (LC)

Mo-docks *see* Modoc

Modocks *see* Modoc

Modoes *see* Modoc

Mo-dok *see* Modoc

Modok *see* Modoc

Mo-dokish *see* Modoc

Modokish *see* Modoc

Mo-dokni *see* Modoc

Modokni *see* Modoc

Modokni maklaks *see* Modoc

Mo-dok-us *see* Modoc

Modokus *see* Modoc

Modook *see* Modoc

Mo-e-ka-ne-ka-she-ga *see*
Manyika

Moekanekashega *see* Manyika

Mo-e-kwe-ah-ha *see* Chedunga

Moekweahha *see* Chedunga

Moencopi *see* Moenkopi

Moenkapi *see* Moenkopi

Moenkopi *Hopi* (Hdbk9)

Moennitarri *see* Hidatsa

Moeno *see* Mashco

Moeroahkongy *see* Meletecunk

Mo-e-twas *see* Palaihnihan

Moetwas *see* Palaihnihan

Mogall *see* Mogollon

Mogallones *see* Mogollon

Mogeri *see* Hopi

Mogin *see* Hopi

Mogogones *see* Mogollon

Mogoll *see* Mogollon

Mogollon *Gileños* (LC)

Mogollon culture (LC)

Mogollone *see* Mogollon

Mogollones *see* Mogollon

Mogosnae *see* Mocobi

Mogoyones *see* Mogollon

Moguache *see* Moache

Moguachi *see* Moache

Moguachis *see* Moache

Moguex [Col] (LC)

Moguex [Lang] (LC) *see also*
Chibchan (LC)

Moguez *see* Moguex

Mogui *see* Hopi

Moha *see* Moxo

Mohaakx *see* Mohawk

Mohace *see* Hopi

Mohack *see* Mohawk

Mohacqs *see* Mohawk

Mohacques *see* Mohawk

Mohacs *see* Mohawk

Mohaes *see* Mohawk

Mohag *see* Mohawk

Mohagg *see* Mohawk

Mohahue *see* Mohave

Mohak *see* Mohawk

Mohansick *see* Manhasset

Mohaokx *see* Mohawk

Mohaq *see* Mohawk

Mohaqe *see* Mohawk

Mohaques *see* Mohawk

Mo-har-a-la *see* Moharala

Moharala [Subclan] *Delaware* (H)

Mohauck *see* Mohawk

Mohaug *see* Mohawk

Mohaukes *see* Mohawk

Mohauks *see* Mohawk

Mohauog *see* Mohawk

Mohauvies *see* Mohave

Mohave [CA, AZ] (LC)

Mohave Apache *see* Yavapai

Mohavi *see* Mohave

Mohavies *see* Mohave

Mohawa *see* Mohave

Mohawa [Clan] *Miami* (H)

Mohawck *see* Mohawk

Mohawe *see* Mohave

Mohawk [NY, Can] *Iroquois* (LC)

Mohawk [OR] *Luckiamute* (H)

Mohawkes *see* Mohawk

Mohawques *see* Mohawk

Mohaws *see* Mohawk

Moheakanneew *see* Mahican

Moheakenunk *see* Mahican

Moheakounuck *see* Mahican

Moheakunnuk *see* Mahican

Mohecan *see* Mahican

Moheckon *see* Mahican

Moheconnock *see* Mahican

Mo-heegan *see* Mahican

Moheegan *see* Mahican

Moheg *see* Mohawk

Mohegan [CT, NY] (LC)

Mohekennuk *see* Mahican

Mohekin *see* Mahican

Mo-he-kun-e-uk *see* Mahican

Mohekuneuk *see* Mahican

Mohekunuh *see* Mahican

Mohemencho [Lang] *Monacan*
(H)

Mohetan (BE)

mohiatniyum [Clan] *Serrano*
(Pub, v.26)

Mohican *see* Mahican

Mohican *see* Mohegan

Mohicand *see* Mahican

Mohicander *see* Mahican

Mohiccon *see* Mahican

Mohickan *see* Mahican

Mohickander *see* Mahican
Mohicken *see* Mahican
Mohickon *see* Mahican
Mohigon *see* Mahican
Mohiguara *Coahuiltecan*
  (Hdbk10)
Mohikan *see* Mahican
Mohikander *see* Mahican
Mohikon *see* Mahican
Mohikonder *see* Mahican
Mohineyam (H) *see also* Serrano
  (LC)
Mohineyam [CA] (Pub, v.4, no.3,
  pp.139–140)
Mohingan *see* Mahican
Mohingaus *see* Mahican
Mohino *see* Ese Ejja
Mohinyam *see* Mohineyam
Mohkach [Clan] *Cochiti* (H)
Mohkuh [Clan] *Ponca* (H)
Mohoakk *see* Mohawk
Mohoc *see* Mohawk
Mohocander *see* Mahican
Mohoce *see* Hopi
Mohocks *see* Mohawk
Mohog *see* Mohawk
Mohogan *see* Mahican
Mohoges *see* Mohawk
Mohogg *see* Mohawk
Mohok *see* Mohawk
Mohokander *see* Mahican
Mohokes *see* Mohawk
Mohoqui *see* Hopi
Mohose *see* Hopi
Mohotlath [Sept] *Opitchesaht* (H)
Mohotze *see* Hopi]
Mohoukes *see* Mohawk
Mohowaugsuck *see* Mohawk
Mohowauuck *see* Mohawk
Mohowawog *see* Mohawk
Mohowk *see* Mohawk
Mohox *see* Mohawk
Moh-tau-hai-ta-ni-o *see* Ute
Mohtauhaitanio *see* Ute
Mohtawa *see* Kansa
Moh-ta-wa-ta-ta-ni-o *see* Sihas-
  apa
Mohtawatatanio *see* Sihasapa
Mohuache *see* Moache
Mohuache Utahs *see* Moahce
Mohuache Utes *see* Moache
Mohuccon *see* Mahican
Mohuccories *see* Mahican
Mohuck *see* Mohawk
Mohuhache *see* Moache
moieomini tan *see* Shoshone
Moi-ka nika-shing-ka *see*
  Manyika
Moika nikashingka *see* Manyika
Moingoena *see* Moingwena
Moingwena *Illinois* (Hdbk15)
Moins *see* Illinois
Moiseyu [SD] *Cheyenne* (BE)

Moja *see* Moxo
Mojaoes *see* Mohave
Mojaris *see* Mohave
Mojave (Hdbk10) *see also* Mohave
  (Hdbk10)
Mojave *Fort Mojave and Colorado
  River* (Hdbk10, p.69)
Moje *see* Hopi
Mojeno *see* Baure
Mojo *see* Moxo
Mojose *see* Hopi
M'okahoki *see* Okahoki
Mokahoki *see* Okahoki
Mokaich [Clan] *Keres* (H)
Mokalumne *see* Plains Miwok
Mokaus *see* Mohawk
Mokawkes *see* Mohawk
Moke *see* Hopi
Mokee *see* Hopi
Mokhaba *see* Mohave
Moki *see* Hopi
Mo-ki *see* Hopi
Mokoit [Self-designation] *see*
  Mocobi
Mokozumne *see* Plains Miwok
Mokumiks [MN] *Piegan* (BE)
Mokushi *see* Macusi
Mokwats [CA] *Chemehuevi* (BE)
Molafoka *see* Mola-foka
Mola-foka (Pub, v.29, no.4) *see
  also* Lower Lake Pomo (Pub,
  v.29, no.4)
Mola-foka [CA] (Pub, v.29, no.4)
Molala [OR] (LC)
Molale *see* Molala
mo-lalis *see* Molala
Molalis *see* Molala
Molalla *see* Molala
Mo-lal-la-la *see* Molala
Molallala *see* Molala
Mole [Lang] *see* Moré
Molel *see* Molala
Molia *see* Pomuluma
Molibal *see* Tubatulabal
Molina *Coahuiltecan* (Hdbk10)
Mollala *see* Molala
Mollalla *see* Molala
Molma [CA] *Maidu* (H)
Molsem *see* Malssum
Moluche [CH] *see* Araucanian
Moluche [EC] *see* Huao
Molxave *see* Mohave
Momi [Subclan] *Missouri* (H)
Momobi [Clan] *Hopi* (H)
Momon *Coahuiltecan* (Hdbk10)
mona *see* Mono
Monacan [Lang] *Eastern Siouan*
  (H)
Monacan [VA] (LC)
mo-na-che *see* Mono
monache *see* Mono
Monachi *see* Mono
Mona'ci *see* Northern Paiute

Monaci *see* Northern Paiute
Monadji *see* Mono
Monahassano *see* Nahyssan
Monahassanugh *see* Nahyssan
Monahegan *see* Mohegan
Monahiganeuck *see* Mohegan
mo-nahk *see* Northern Paiute
monahk *see* Northern Paiute
Monahoac *see* Manahoac
Monakin *see* Manokin
mo-na-mus-se *see* Northern
  Paiute
monamusse *see* Northern Paiute
Monan *Coahuiltecan* (Hdbk10)
mo'nasa *see* Waho
monasa *see* Washo
Monaton *see* Manhattan
Monatun *see* Manhattan
Monaxo *see* Masacali
mon-ay-a *see* Mono Lake North-
  ern Paiute
Moncoca [BO] (O)
Mondaque *see* Anadarko
Monde [Br] (O)
Mondorocu *see* Mundurucu
Monecoshe *see* Miniconjou
Mon-eka-goh-ha *see* Mandhink-
  agaghe
Monekagohha *see* Mandhinka-
  gaghe
Moneton [WV, VA] (BE)
Mong [Clan] *Chippewa* (H)
Mongwa [Clan] *Miami* (H)
Monhauset *see* Manhasset
Monhigg *see* Mohegan
Moni *see* Menominee
Monichi [Self-designation] *see*
  Muniche
Monkee Indians *see* Hopi
Monkoka *see* Moncoca
Mon-mish *see* Samamish
Monmish *see* Samamish
Monnato [Clan] *Miami* (H)
Monnesick *see* Minisink
Mono [CA] (CA)
Mono [Lang] *Western Numic*
  (Hdbk11)
mo-nok *see* Northern Paiute
monok *see* Northern Paiute
Mono Lake Northern Paiute
  (Hdbk11)
Monomeni *see* Menominee
Monomin *see* Menominee
Monomonee *see* Menominee
Monomoy *see* Manomoy
Monomunies *see* Menominee
mo-no-ni-o *see* Mandan
mononio *see* Mandan
Mono-Paviotso [Lang] (Hdbk11)
  see also Mono-Bannock
  (Hdbk11)
Mono-Paviotso [Lang] *Western
  Numic* (Hdbk11)

Monoponson *Choptank* (Hdbk15)
Monosho *see* Masacali
Monozi *see* Northern Paiute
Monqui [BaC, MX] *Waicuri* (BE)
Monquoi *see* Hopi
Mons [Clan] *Menominee* (H)
Monsee *see* Munsee
Monsey *see* Munsee
Monshoro *see* Zoro
Monsonabi *see* Mishongnovi
Monsonavi *see* Mishongnovi
Monsoni [Can] *Upeshipow* (H)
Mons widishianun *see* Mons wi'dishi'anun
Mons wi'dishi'anun [Phratry] *Menominee* (H)
Montagnais (H) *see also* Chipewyan (LC)
Montagnais (H) *see also* Nahane (LC)
Montagnais [Q] [*Montagnais-Naskapi*] (LC)
Montagnais-Naskapi [Can] (BE)
Montagnards *Tinne* (H)
Montagne *see* Onondaga
Montagnees *see* Chipewyan
Montagnes *see* Chipewyan
Montagnese *see* Mikinakwadshi-wininwak
Montagneurs *see* Onondaga
Montagnez *see* Chipewyan
Montagues *see* Onondaga
Montauk [Lang] *Eastern Algonquian* (Hdbk15)
Montauk [NY] (LC)
Monterey [CA] *Costanoan* (BE)
Montese *see* Caingua
Montochtana [Clan] *Knaiakhotana* (H)
Mon-to-to *see* Nutunutu
Montoto *see* Nutunutu
Montowese [CT] *Mattabesec* (H)
Mooachaht [Can] *Nootka* (BE)
moo-dus-sey *see* Navajo
moodussey *see* Navajo
Moohag *see* Mohawk
Mookwungwahoki [Subclan] *Delaware* (H)
Moo-lal-le *see* Molala
Moolalle *see* Molala
Moon-calves *see* Menominee
Mooncalves *see* Menominee
Mooncha (H) *see also* Tunanpin [Oto] (H)
Moon-cha *see* Tunanpin [Oto]
Mooncha [Clan] *Oto* (H)
Moonhartarne [Sublan] *Delaware* (H)
Moonpidenne *see* Maopityan
Moonsee *see* Munsee
Mooqui *see* Hopi
Moor *see* Nanticoke

Moose Factory Band [Can] *Sakawininiwug* (BE)
Moosehead Lake [ME] *Penobscot* (H)
Mooshahneh *see* Mishongnovi
Mooshkaooze [Clan] *Chippewa* (H)
Mooshongae nayvee *see* Mishongnovi
Mooshongeenayvee *see* Mishongnovi
Moo-song-na-ve *see* Mishongnavi
Moosongnave *see* Mishongnavi
Mo-o-tza *see* Hopi
Mootza *see* Hopi
Mopan [Gua, Bel, BrH] (LC)
Mopanero *see* Mopan
Moq *see* Hopi
Moqni *see* Hopi
Moqtavhaitan *see* Moqtavhaita'niu
Moqtavhaita'niu [SD] *Cheyenne* (BE)
Moqua *see* Hopi
Moquache *see* Moache
Moquaches *see* Moache
Moquaes *see* Mohawk
Moquakues *see* Mohawk
Moquas *see* Mohawk
Moquase *see* Mohawk
Moquat *Paiute* (H)
Mo-quats *see* Las Vegas
Moquats *see* Las Vegas
Moquauks *see* Mohawk
Moquawes *see* Mohawk
Moque *see* Hopi
Moquelemne *see* Moquelumnan
Moquelumnan [CA] (LC)
Moquelumnan [Lang] [CA] *Costanoan* (H)
Moqui *see* Hopi
Moqui *see* Mohawk
Moquiaguin [MX] *Coahuiltecan* (Hdbk10)
Moquian Pueblo *see* Hopi
Moquin *see* Hopi
Moquina *see* Hopi
Moquino *see* Hopi
Moquitch *see* Hopi
Moquois *see* Hopi
Moquy *see* Hopi
Moqwai'o [Clan] *Menominee* (H)
Moqwai'o wi'dishi'anun [Phratry] *Menominee* (H)
Morahicander *see* Mahican
Moraigane *see* Mahican
Moraigun *see* Mahican
Moraleños *Coahuiltecan* (Hdbk10)
Morales *Coahuiltecan* (Hdbk10)
Morargan *see* Mahican
Moratico [VA] (Hdbk15)
Moratik *see* Moratuc

Morato [Lang] *see* Candoshi
Moratok [NC] (BE)
Moratuc (Hdbk15) *see also* Moratok (BE)
Moratuc [NC] *Algonquian* (Hdbk15)
Moraughtacund [VA] *Powhatan* (BE)
Moravian Indians (LC)
Moravian Indians (LC) *see also* Christian Indians (LC)
Morbah [Clan] [NM] *Pecos* (H)
Morbanas *Coahuiltecan* (BE)
Moré [BO, Br] (O)
Moreno [Gua] (O)
Morerebi [Br] (O)
Morhicans *see* Mohegan
Moriwene [Lang] *Maipurean* (O)
Mormon Lake *Northern Tonto Apache* (BE)
Moro [BO, Par] (LC)
Moroba *see* Maruba
Morochoco *see* Morochucan
Morochucan [PE] (LC)
Morochuco *see* Morochucan
Morocosi [Lang] *see* Moxo
Morongo (Pub, v.4, no.3, p.133) *see also* Serrano (LC)
Morongo [CA] (CA)
Morotico *see* Moratuc
Morotoco *see* Moro
Morqui *see* Hopi
Moruba *see* Mayoruna
Morumsce *Pocomoke* (Hdbk15)
Morunahua [PE] (O)
mo'rzhumae *see* Navajo
morzhumae *see* Navajo
Mosanais *see* Mishongnovi
Mosanis *see* Mishongnovi
Mosasnabi *see* Mishongnovi
Mosasnave *see* Mishongnovi
Mosca *see* Chibcha
Moscalara *see* Mescalero Apache
Moscama *see* Mocama
Mosco *see* Miskito
Moses Band *see* Sinkiuse
Moses-Columbia [WA] [*Sinkiuse-Columbia*] (BE)
Mosetene *see* Mosetenos
Mosetene *see* Chimane
Mosetenos [BO] (LC)
Moshaich [Clan] *Acoma* (H)
Moshanganabi *see* Mishongnovi
Moshi *see* Moré
Moshkos *see* Fox
Moshkos *see* Mascoutens
Moshome *see* Navajo
Moshongnave *see* Mishongnovi
Mosi *see* Hopi
Mosicha *see* Hopi
Mosilian [NJ] (H)
Moskoky *see* Muskogee
Mosnala [CAm] *Concho* (BE)

Mosobiae *see* Mocobi
Mosopelea [OH] *Ofo* (BE)
Mosquagsett *see* Mohawk
Mosquies *see* Hopi
Mosquitans *see* Mascoutens
Mosquito [Hon, NI] (LC)
Mosquitoan [Lang] *Misumalpan* (BE)
Mosquitos (H) *see also* Mascouten (LC)
Mossa *see* Moxo
Mossanganabi *see* Mishongnovi
Mossi *see* Moré
Mossonganabi *see* Mishongnovi
Moszasnani *see* Mishongnovi
Motahtosiks *Piegan* (BE)
Motantee *see* Oto
Motarctin *see* Mascouten
Mo'tawa *see* Kansa
Motawa *see* Kansa
Moteawaughkin *Assateague* (Hdbk15)
Moterequoa *see* Pauserna
Mother People *see* Tukkuthkutchin
Motilon [Col, VE] (LC)
Motilon [Lang] (UAz, v.28)
Motilone *see* Motilon
Motilones Bravos *see* Bari
Motilon of the North *see* Yukpa
Motochintlec *see* Mocho
Motochintlec *see* Motozintlec
Motomkin *see* Matomkin
Mototzintlec *see* Mocho
Mototzintlec *see* Motozintlec
Motozintlec (LC) *see also* Mocho (LC)
Motozintlec [MX] (LC)
Motozintleca [Lang] (Bull44)
Motozintleca Indians *see* Motozintlec
Mo-ts *see* Hopi
Mots *see* Hopi
Motsai [TX] *Comanche* (BE)
motse-heone-tane *see* Apache
Mo-tsi *see* Hopi
Motsi *see* Hopi
Motsonitanio *see* Woksihitanio
Moturicu *see* Mundurucu
Motutatak *see* Oto
Motwainaiks [MN] *Piegan* (BE)
Mouache *see* Moache
Mouaches *see* Moache
Mougui *see* Hopi
Mouhak *see* Mohawk
Moukou *see* Mohkuh
Mouloubis *see* Moctobi
Mound-builders (LC)
Mountain Assinaboins *see* Tschantoga
Mountain Cahuilla [CA] (BE)
Mountain Cahuilla [Lang] (CA-8)

Mountain Comanche *see* Apache
Mountain Crow (H)
Mountain Diegueño [Lang] [CA] *Yuman* (He)
Mountainee *see* Montagnais
Mountaineer *see* Chipewyan
Mountaineer Indians *see* Montagnais
Mountaineers *see* Onondaga
Mountain Eskimos *Interior North Alaska Eskimos* (Hdbk5)
Mountain Indians *see* Tsethaottine
Mountain Indians *see* Tutchone
Mountain Indians *see* Chipewyan
Mountain Indians *see* Etagottine
Mountain Indians *see* Tenankutchin
Mountain Indians *Intermedidate Denes* (H)
Mountain Maidu *Northeastern Maidu* (Pub, v.29, no.4)
Mountain Men *see* Tenankutchin
Mountain People *see* Xe'bina
Mountain People *see* Xe'natonwan
Mountain People *see* Atai-Kutchin
Mountains *see* Chipewyan
Mountain-Sheep-Eaters *see* Tukuarika
Mountain Sheep Men *see* Abbatotine
Mountain Shoshone *see* Tukudeka
Mountain Snake *see* Shoshone
Mountain Stoneys *see* Tshantoga
Mountain Ute (JCB, v.11, no.1, 1989, pp.35–49)
Mount Currie Lillooet [Lang] *Interior Salish* (Hdbk12)
Mourigan *see* Mahican
Mouskouasoak *see* Malecite
Mousonee [Phratry] *Chippewa* (H)
Moustiquais *see* Miskito
Moustiques *see* Miskito
Mouuache Utes *see* Moache
Mouvill *see* Mobile
Mouvilla *see* Mobile
Mouville *see* Mobile
Movas [MX] *Pima Bajo* (Bull44)
Move (LC) *see also* Guaymi (LC)
Move [Pan] *Northern Guaymi* (BE)
Moviats [CA] *Chemehuevi* (BE)
Movila *see* Mobile
Movill *see* Mobile
Movima [BO] (LC)
Movina *see* Movima
Moving Lodges *Ahacik* (H)

Movwiat *Paiute* (H)
Mo-vwi-ats *see* Las Vegas
Movwiats (PC) *see also* Las Vegas (Hdbk11)
Mowa [AL] *Choctaw* (IT, v.24, no.4, p.19)
Mowack *see* Mohawk
Mowakes *see* Mohawk
Mowaks *see* Mohawk
Mowatak *see* Modoc
Mo-wata-k *see* Modoc
mowataviwatsiu *see* Uncompahgre
Mowatchi *see* Moache
Mowatodkni *see* Modoc
Mowatsi *see* Moache
Mowhak *see* Mohawk
Mowhakes *see* Mohawk
Mowhakues *see* Mohawk
Mowhaug *see* Mohawk
Mowhauk *see* Mohawk
Mowhawk *see* Mohawk
Mowhawkes *see* Mohawk
Mowhoake *see* Mohawk
Mowhok *see* Mohawk
Mowill *see* Mobile
Mowquakes *see* Mohawk
Mow-shai-i-na *see* Mishongnovi
Mowshaiina *see* Mishongnovi
Moxa *see* Moxo
Moxainabe *see* Mishongnovi
Moxainavi *see* Mishongnovi
Moxeño *see* Moxo
Moxi *see* Hopi
Moxionavi *see* Mishongnovi
Moxitae *see* Moxo
Moxo (LC) *see also* Ignaciano (LC)
Moxo [BO, Br, Par] (LC)
Moxonaui *see* Mishongnovi
Moxonavi *see* Mishongnovi
Moyana [BO] *Araona* (O)
Moyaoncer *see* Conoy
Moyave *see* Mohave
Moyawance [MD] *Conoy* (BE)
Moyma *see* Movima
Moyoack *see* Nottoway
Moyowance *see* Conoy
Mozan *see* Mishongnovi
Mpoyo *see* Mapoyo
Msepase *see* M'-se'-pa-se
M'-se'-pa-se [Clan] *Shawnee* (H)
M'shkudan'nik *see* Prairie Band of Potawatomi
Mshkudannik *see* Prairie Band of Potawatomi
Mtlakapmah *see* Thompson
Mtom-kai *see* Mitomkai
Muache *see* Moache
Muahuache *see* Moache
Mu-apots *see* Moapa
Muapots *see* Moapa
muappa *see* Moapa

muappacimi *see* Moapa
Muares *see* Moache
Mu'atokni *see* Modoc
Muatokni *see* Modoc
Muca *see* Hopi
Mu-ca-la-moes *see* Mescalero Apache
Mucalamoes *see* Mescalero Apache
Muchalat [Can] *Nootka* (BE)
Muchimo [PE] *Muniche* (O)
Much-quanh *see* Makwa
Muchquanh *see* Makwa
Much-quauh *see* Makwa
Muchquauh *see* Makwa
Mu-cin-t'a tunne *see* Coos
Mucintatunne *see* Coos
Muck-aluc *see* Klamath
Muckaluc *see* Klamath
Muckaluck *see* Klamath
Muckhekanies *see* Mahican
Muckleshoot [WA] (LC)
Mucoco *see* Mococo
Mucogulgee *see* Muskogee
Muddy Creek Paiute *see* Moapa
Muddy River Indians *see* Piegan
Mudjetire *see* Surui II
Muellama [Col] (O)
Muenane *see* Muinane
Mu-gua *see* Hopi
Mugua *see* Hopi
Mugulasha (BE) *see also* Quinipissa (BE)
Mugulasha [LA] (BE)
mugunuwu *see* Kawaiisu
Muhekannew *see* Mahican
Muhheakunneuw *see* Mahican
Muhheakunnuk *see* Mahican
Muhheconnew *see* Stockbridge
Muhheconnuk *see* Stockbridge
Muhheeckanew *see* Mahican
Muh-hee-kun-eew *see* Mahican
Muhheekuneew *see* Mahican
Muhhekaneew *see* Mahican
Muhhekaneok *see* Mahican
Muhhekanew *see* Stockbridge
Muhhekaniew *see* Mahican
Muhhekanneuk *see* Mahican
Muhhekanok *see* Mahican
Muhhekenow *see* Mahican
Muhhekunneau *see* Mahican
Muhhekunneyuk *see* Mahican
Muhhowekaken [Subclan] *Delaware* (H)
Muhkarmhukse [Subclan] *Delaware* (H)
Muhkrentharne [Subclan] *Delaware* (H)
Muhuache *see* Moache
Muhwa'o Se'peo Wini'niwuk [WI] *Menominee* (BE)
Muinane [Col] (LC)
Muinane [PE] *Witoto* (O)

Muinyan [Clan] *Hopi* (H)
Muisca *see* Chibcha
Muite [Pan] (BE)
Mujetire *see* Surui II
Muk (H)
mu-ka kyula *see* Navajo
mukakyula *see* Navajo
Muk-a-luk *see* Klamath
Mukaluk *see* Klamath
Mukanti (H) *see also* Molala (LC)
Mukanti [OR] *Molala* (BE)
Mu-ke *see* Hopi
Muke *see* Hopi
Mukickan *see* Mahican
Mukickkaneew *see* Mahican
Muk-im-dua-win-in-e-wug *see* Pillagers
Mukimduawininewug *see* Pillagers
Mukkekaneaw *see* Mahican
Mukkudda Ozitunnug *see* Siksika
Mukkundwas *see* Pillagers
Mukkwaw *see* Makwa
Muk-kwaw *see* Mawka
Muklasa [AL, FL] (BE)
Muklasalgi [Clan] *Creek* (H)
Muk-me-dua-win-in-e-wug *see* Pillagers
Mukmeduawininewug (PC) *see also* Pillagers (H)
Mukmeduawininewug [MN] *Chippewa* (BE)
Muk-ud-a-shib *see* Sheshebe
Mukudashib *see* Sheshebe
Mukundua *see* Pillagers
Muk-un-dua-win-in-e-wing *see* Pillagers
Mukunduawininewing *see* Pillagers
Muk-un-dua-win-in-e-wug *see* Pillagers
Mukunduawininewug *see* Pillagers
Mukundwa *see* Pillagers
Muk-wah *see* Makwa
Mukwah *see* Makwa
Mula [Clan] *Zuni* (H)
mulalis *see* Molala
Mulatos *Coahuiltecan* (BE)
mule-lis *see* Molala
Muleye *see* Mayeye
Mulian *see* Pomuluma
Mulknomans *see* Mutlnomah
Multnomah [OR] (LC)
Mum-i-o-yiks *see* Mameoya
Mumioyiks *see* Mameoya
Mummapacune [VA] *Powhatan* (BE)
Munangomo *see* Mayongong
Munangone *see* Mayongong
Mun-an-ne-qu'tunne *see* Klickitat

Munannequtunne *see* Klickitat
Munapume [MX] *Coahuiltecan* (Hdbk10)
Muncey [Ont] *Munsee* (BE)
Munchies *see* Hopi
Munchirache *see* Tunanpi
Muncie *see* Munsee
Muncu *see* Manico
Mundaywahkanton *see* Mdewakanton
Munday Wawkanton *see* Mdewakanton
Munde *see* Aikana
Mundruca *see* Mundurucu
Mundrucu *see* Mundurucu
Mun-dua *see* Mantouek
Mundua *see* Mantouek
Munduka [Br] *Southern Nambicuara* (O)
Mundurucu [Br] (LC)
Munduruku *see* Mudurucu
Mungwas *see* Iroquois
Muniche [PE] (O)
Munichi *see* Muniche
Munichino *see* Muniche
Munitsche *see* Muniche
Munku *see* Iranxe
Munnawtawkit *see* Montauk
Mun-noa'min-nee *see* Menominee
Munnoaminnee *see* Menominee
Munominikasheenhug [WI, MN] *Chippewa* (BE)
Munque concabe *see* Moenkopi
Munsee [NJ, NY] *Delaware* (LC)
Munsey *see* Munsee
Munsy *see* Munsee
Munxar *see* Zoro
Muoi [Pan] *Northern Guaymi* (BE)
Muqui *see* Hopi
Muqui concabe *see* Moenkopi
Mura [Br] (LC)
Mura [Lang] [Col] *Paezan* (LC)
Muracumane *see* Meracouman
Muradicos *see* Shoshoko
Murato (O) *see also* Candoshi (LC)
Murato [PE] (O)
Murire (LC) *see also* Guaymi (LC)
Murire [Pan] *Northern Guaymi* (BE)
Muro *see* Moro
Mur til par *see* Matilpe
Murtilpar *see* Matilpe
Muru *see* Moro
Muruam *see* Muruam
Muruam [TX] *Coahuiltecan* (BE)
Murui [Col] *Witoto* (LC)
Murzibusi [Clan] *Hopi* (H)
Mus [Clan] *Mohave* (H)
Musagulge *see* Muskogee
Musalero *see* Mescalero Apache

Mu-sal-la-kun *see* Missalla
   Magun
Musallakun *see* Misalla Magun
Muscagee *see* Muskogee
Muscagoes *see* Maskegon
Mus-ca-lar-oes *see* Mescalero
   Apache
Muscalaroes *see* Mescalero
   Apache
Muscalero *see* Mescalero Apache
Muscallaro *see* Mescalero Apache
Muscogee *see* Creek
Muscogee *see* Muskogee
Muscogeh *see* Muskogee
Muscogulge *see* Muskogee
Muscolgee *see* Muskogee
Musconoge *see* Maskegon
Musconogee *see* Maskegon
Muscoten *see* Mascouten
Muscoutan *see* Mascouten
Muscow *see* Muskogee
Musgogee *see* Muskogee
Mu-shai-e-now-a *see* Mishong-
   novi
Mushaienowa *see* Mishongnovi
Mu-shai-i-na *see* Mishongnovi
Mushaiina *see* Mishongnovi
Mushangene-vi *see* Mishongnovi
Mushangnevi *see* Mishongnovi
Mushangnevy *see* Mishongnovi
Mu-shang-newy *see* Mishong-
   novi
Mushangnewy *see* Mishongnovi
Musha-ni *see* Mishongnovi
Mushani *see* Mishongnovi
Mushauguewy *see* Mishongnovi
Mush-co-desh *see* Mascouten
Mushcodesh *see* Mascouten
Mushkeag *see* Maskegon
Mushkodain *see* Mascouten
Mush-ko-dain *see* Mascouten
Mush-ko-dains-ug *see* Mas-
   couten
Mushkodainsug *see* Mascouten
Mushongnovi *see* Mishongnovi
mushshailekwe *see* Mishongnovi
Musica *see* Chibcha
Muskagoes *see* Maskegon
Muskagowuk *see* Maskegon
Mus-ka-g-wuk *see* Makegon
Mus-ka-le-ra *see* Mescalero
   Apache
Muskalera *see* Mescalero Apache
Mus-ka-lero *see* Mescalero
   Apache
Muskalero *see* Mescalero Apache
Muskantin *see* Mascouten
Muskeegoo *see* Maskegon
Muskeg *see* Maskegon
Muskeggouck *see* Maskegon
Muskegoag *see* Maskegon
Muskegoag *see* Nopeming
Muskegoe *see* Maskegon

Muskegon *see* Maskegon
Muskegoo *see* Maskegan
Muskego Ojibway *see* Maskegan
Muskelera *see* Mescalero Apache
Muskelero *see* Mescalero Apache
Musketoons *see* Mascouten
Musketoous *see* Mascouten
Muskhogean [Lang] (LC)
Muskhogean Indians *see* Musko-
   gee
Muskigo *see* Maskegon
Muskigok *see* Maskegon
Musk-keeg-oe *see* Maskegon
Muskkeegoe *see* Maskegon
Muskoge *see* Muskogee
Muskogean *see* Muskhogean
Muskogee [AL, FL] (BE)
Muskoghe *see* Mascouten
Muskogolgee *see* Muskogee
Muskohge *see* Muskogee
Muskohgee *see* Muskogee
Muskoke *see* Muskogee
Musko'ke *see* Muskogee
Muskoki *see* Muskogee
Mus-koo-gee *see* Muskogee
Muskotanje *see* Mascouten
Mus-ko-ta-we-nuk *see*
   Paskwaniniwug
Muskotawenuk *see* Paskwanini-
   wug
Muskrat *see* Malecite
Muskrat Indians *see* Malecite
Muskulthe *see* Mascouten
Muskutawa *see* Mascouten
Mus-kwa-ka-uk *see* Fox
Muskwakauk *see* Fox
Muskwake *see* Fox
Muskwaki *see* Fox
Muskwakiwuk *see* Fox
Muskwoikakenut [Can] *Cree* (BE)
Muskwoikauepawit [Can] *Cree*
   (BE)
Musqua *see* Muskogee
Musquabuck *see* Mesquawbuck
Musquacki *see* Fox
Mus-quack-ki-uck *see* Fox
Musquackkiuck *see* Fox
Musquake *see* Fox
Musquakee *see* Fox
Musquakie *see* Fox
Musquakkink *see* Fox
Musquaro [Can] [*Montagnais-
   Naskapi*] (BE)
Musquattamies *see* Fox
Musquattamies *see* Mascouten
Musquawkee *see* Fox
Musqueam [Can] *Stalo* (BE)
Musqueten *see* Mascouten
Musqueton *see* Mascouten
Musquetoon *see* Mascouten
Musquiakis *see* Fox
Musquitan *see* Mascouten
Musquitoes *see* Mascouten

Musquiton *see* Mascouten
Musscovi *see* Missouri
Mussisakies *see* Missisauga
Mussundumnis [Clan] *Chippewa*
   (H)
Mustassin *see* Mistassin
Mustee *see* Mestizo
Mustegan *see* Maskegan
Musten *see* Mutsen
Musteses *see* Mixed bloods
Musu *see* Moxo
musumi *see* Navajo
Musutepes [CAm] *Suman* (BE)
Mutea *see* Carapana
mu-ti-ci *see* Moapa
mutici *see* Moapa
mu-ti-cimi *see* Moapa
muticimi *see* Moapa
Mutilones *see* Motilon
mu-ti-nukkinti *see* Moapa
mutinukkinti *see* Moapa
Mutsen [CA] (CA-8)
Mutsen [Lang] [CA] *Northern
   Costonoan* (CA-8)
Mutsiana-taniu *see* Kiowa
   Apache
Mutsianata'niuw *see* Apache
Muvinabore [TX] *Comanche* (BE)
Muwa *see* Miwok
Muwach *see* Moache
Muwekma [CA] (CA)
Muwekma Ohlone [CA] (News,
   Fall 1997, pp.8–9)
Muxtawatan *see* Ute
Muxtsuhintan *see* Apache
Muynku *see* Irantxe
Muysca *see* Chibcha
Muzo [Col] (LC)
Mwawa *see* M'-wa-wa
M'-wa-wa [Clan] *Shawnee* (H)
Myacma *see* Makoma
Myacomap *see* Makoma
Myami *see* Miami
Myamick *see* Miami
Myanamak *see* Manumaig
Myeengun [Clan] *Chippewa* (H)
Mynckussar *see* Conestoga
Myncqueser *see* Conestoga
Mynky *see* Irantxe
Mynomamies *see* Menominee
Mynomanies *see* Menominee
Mynonamies *see* Menominee

-N-

N.D. du Secour *see* Socorro
N.S. de la Assuncion de Zia *see*
   Sia
N.S. de los Dolores de Sandia *see*
   Sandia

N.S. *see also* Nuestra Señora (H)
N.S. *see* Nuestra Señora
N. Señora del Socorro *see* Socorro del Sur
Na. Señora del Socorro *see* Socorro del Sur
Na [Clan] *Tewa* (H)
Naa'ance *see* Nehane
Naaance *see* Nahaunee
Naa-anee *see* Nahane
Naaanee *see* Nahane
Naabeeho *see* Navajo
Na-ah-ma-o *see* Naahmao
Naahmao [Clan] *Mahican* (H)
Naa'i *see* Naai
Na-ai *see* Nahane
Naai (PC) *see also* Nahane (LC)
Naai [Clan] *Navajo* (H)
Naa-icine *see* Naai
Naaicine *see* Naai
Naa'idine *see* Naai
Naaidine *see* Naai
Naaketl'ahi *see* Pima
Naalem *see* Nehalem
Naalgus-hadai [Subclan] *Haida* (H)
Na-al-ye *see* Naalye
Naalye [OR] *Skoton* (H)
Naamhock *see* Amoskeag
Naamhok *see* Naumkeag
Naamkeek *see* Amoskeag
Naamkeke *see* Naumkeag
Na-ane *see* Nahane
Naane *see* Nahane
Na-ane-ottine *see* Nahane
Naaneottine *see* Nahane
Na'an-ne *see* Nahane
Na anne *see* Nahane
Naanne *see* Nahane
Naansi [TX] *Hasinai Confederacy* (BE)
Naantucke *see* Niantic
Naa-nu-aa-ghu *see* Nanyaayi
Naanuaaghu *see* Nanyaayi
naapeexwoh *see* Navajo
Naas *see* Chimmesyan
Naashashi *see* Santa Clara [NM]
Naashashi *see* Tewa
Naashgali *see* Mescalero Apache
Naasht'ezhi *see* Zuni
Naaskaak *see* Naasumetunne
Naas River Indians *see* Niska
Naass *see* Chimmesyan
Na-a-su me'tunne *see* Naasumetunne
Naasumetunne [OR] (H)
Naaticoke *see* Nanticoke
Naatoohi *see* Laguna
Naatooho *see* Isleta
Naatooho *see* Laguna
Naausi *see* Naasumetunne
Nabadache *see* Nabedache
Nabadachies *see* Nabedache

Nabadatsu *see* Nabedache
Nabaducho *see* Nabedache
Nabaduchoe *see* Nabedache
Nabaho *see* Navajo
Nabahoes *see* Navajo
Nabaho-no *see* Navajo
Nabahuna *see* Navajo
Nabahunae *see* Navajo
nabahunaema *see* Navajo
Nabahydache *see* Nabedache
Na-bai-da-che *see* Nabedache
Nabaidache *see* Nabedache
Nabaidatcho *see* Nabedache
Na-ba-i-da-tu *see* Nabedache
Nabaidatu *see* Nabedache
Nabajay *see* Navajo
Nabajo *see* Navajo
Nabajoa *see* Navajo
Nabajo Apaches *see* Navajo
Nabajoe *see* Navajo
Nabari *see* Nabiri
Nabato *see* Nabedache
Nabatutuei (H)
Nabaydacho *see* Nabedache
Nabbehoes *see* Navajo
Nabedache [TX, LA] *Hasinai Confederacy* (BE)
Nabedoche *see* Nabedache
Nabeho *see* Navajo
Nabeidacho *see* Nabedache
Nabeidatcho *see* Nabedache
Nabeidtacho *see* Nabedache
Nabejo *see* Navajo
nabe li *see* Navajo
Nabeli *see* Navajo
Nabesna [AK] (LC)
Nabesnatana (LC) *see also* Tanana (LC)
Nabesnatana [AK] *Tenankutchin* (H)
Nabeyeyxa [TX] *Hasinai Confederacy* (BE)
Nabeyxa *see* Nabeyeyxa
Nabidachos *see* Nabedache
Nabihos *see* Navajo
Nabil-tse *see* Hupa
Nabiltse *see* Hupa
Nabiri [TX, AR] (H)
Nabites *see* Nabiri
Nabiti *see* Namidish
Nabiti *see* Nabiri
Nabittse *see* Hupa
Nabobish [MI] *Chippewa* (H)
Nabochi *see* Napochi
Nabojas *see* Navajo
Nabojo *see* Navajo
Nabowu winwu *see* Nabowu
Nabowu [Clan] *Hopi* (H)
Na-bowu wun-wu *see* Nabown
Nabowu wunwu *see* Nabowu
Nabuggindegbaig *see* Choctaw
Nacacahoz *see* Natchitoches
Nacacha *see* Nacachau

Nacachao *see* Nacachau
Nacachau [TX] *Hasinai Confederacy* (BE)
Nacachez *see* Nacisi
Na-ca-ci-kin *see* Hano
Nacacikin *see* Hano
Nacado-cheeto *see* Nacogdoche
Nacane *see* Detsanayuka
Nacaniche [TX] *Nabedache* (H)
Nacanish [TX, LA] *Hasinai Confederacy* (BE)
Nacanne *see* Detsanayuka
Nacao [TX] *Nacanish* (BE)
Nacassa *see* Nacisi
Nacasse *see* Nacisi
Nacatches *see* Nacisi
Nacau *see* Nacao
Nacaxes *see* Nacao
Na-ce-doc *see* Natchitoches
Nacedoc *see* Natchitoches
Nacha *see* Natchez
Nachee *see* Natchez
Naches *see* Natchez
Naches *see* Neche
Nachetes *see* Natchitoches
Nachez *see* Natchez
Nachiche [Subclan] *Iowa* (H)
Nachillee *see* Netchilirmiut
Nachis *see* Natchez
Nachitock *see* Natchitoches
Nachitooches *see* Natchitoches
Nachitos *see* Natchitoches
Nachittoo *see* Natchitoches
Nachittos *see* Natchitoches
Nachizh-o-zhi'n *see* Dechizhozhin
Nachodoches *see* Nacogdoches
Nachtichoukas *see* Natchitoches
Nachvlke *see* Natchez
Nachy *see* Natchez
Nacisi [LA, TX] (H)
Nacitos *see* Natchitoches
Nac-nanuc *see* Tapuya
Nacnanuc *see* Tapuya
Naco *see* Chamelcon
Nacoches *see* Nacachau
Nacochtant *see* Nacotchtank
Nacocodochy *see* Nacogdoches
Nacocqdoxez *see* Nacogdoches
Nacodissy *see* Nacogdoches
Nacodocheets *see* Nacogdoches
Nacodoches *see* Nacogdoches
Nacodochitos *see* Nacogdoches
Nacogdoches [TX, LA] *Hasinai Confederacy* (BE)
Nacogdochet *see* Nacogdoches
Nacoho *see* Nacao
Nacomen *see* Nicomen
Nacomones *see* Nacono
Nacono [TX] *Hasinai Confederacy* (BE)
Naconome *see* Detsanayuka
Nacooks *see* Souhegan

Nacostines (H) *see also* Nacotch-
tank (BE)
Nacostines *Conoy* (Hdbk15)
Nacota *see* Assiniboin
Nacotah *see* Dakota
Na-co-tah O-see-gah *see*
Itscheabine
Nacotah Oseegah *see* Itscheabine
Nacotchtank [MD] *Conoy* (BE)
Nacotchtanke *Conoy* (Hdbk15)
Nactchitoches *see* Natchitoches
Nactocovit *see* Toba
Nactythos *see* Natchitoches
Nacuache *see* Pacuaches
Na-cu-mi tunne *see* Nasumi
Nacumitunne *see* Nasumi
Nacune *see* Detsanayuka
Nadaco *see* Anadarko
Nadacoe *see* Anadarko
Nadacogdoches *see* Nacogdoches
Nadacogs *see* Anadarko
Nadaho *see* Anadarko
Nada'ko *see* Anadarko
Nadako *see* Anadarko
Nadaku *see* Anadarko
Nadaku hayanu *see* Anadarko
Nadamin [TX] *Hasinai Confeder-
acy* (BE)
Nadatcho *see* Anadarko
Nadatcho *see* Nabedache
Nadawessi *see* Dakota
Na-da-wessy *see* Dakota
Nadches *see* Natchez
Nadchito *see* Natchitoches
Nadchitoches *see* Natchitoches
Nadchitoe *see* Natchitoches
Naddawessy *see* Dakota
Naddouwessioux *see* Dakota
Nadeb [SA] *Macu* (O)
Nadeche *see* Nabedache
Nadeches *see* Natchez
Nadeicha *see* Kiowa Apache
Nadeicha *see* Nabedache
Na-de-ne *see* Na-dene
Nadene *see* Na-dene
Na-dene [Lang] [NA] (LC)
Nadenhadai *see* Naden-hadai
Naden-hadai [Subclan] [AK]
Haida (H)
Nadesis *see* Dakota
Nadezes *see* Natchez
Nadiisha-dena [Self-designation]
see Kiowa Apache
Nadiousioux *see* Dakota
Nadishdena *see* Kiowa Apache
Nad'ish-dena [Self-designation]
see Kiowa-Apache
Nadissioux *see* Dakota
Nadococ *see* Anadarko
Nadocogs *see* Anadarko
Nadoeses *see* Dakota
Nadoessi *see* Dakota
Nadoessians *see* Dakota

Nadoessi Mscouteins *see* Iowa
Nadoessious *see* Dakota
Nadohotzosn (Hdbk10) *see also*
Coyotero Apache (H)
Nadohotzosn *Chiricahua Apache*
(H)
Nadonaisi *see* Dakota
Nadonaisioug *see* Dakota
Nadonechiouk *see* Dakota
Nadonessioux *see* Dakota
Nadonessis *see* Dakota
Nadooessis *see* Dakota
Nadooessis of the Plains *see*
Teton
Nadouags *see* Dakota
Nadouagssioux *see* Dakota
Nadouaissioux *see* Dakota
Nadouayssioux *see* Dakota
Nadoucious *see* Dakota
Nadouechiouec *see* Dakota
Nadouechiouek *see* Dakota
Nadouecis *see* Dakota
Nadouesciouz *see* Dakota
Nadouesiouack *see* Dakota
Nadouesiouek *see* Dakota
Nadouesioux *see* Dakota
Nadouesiouz *see* Dakota
Nadouessans *see* Dakota
Nadouesse *see* Dakota
Nadouessians *see* Dakota
Nadouessies *see* Dakota
Nadouessi-Maskoutens *see* Iowa
Nadouessions *see* Dakota
Nadouessiou *see* Dakota
Nadouessiouak *see* Dakota
Nadouessiouek *see* Dakota
Nadouessioux *see* Dakota
Nadouessioux des prairies *see*
Iowa
Nadouessioux Maskoutens *see*
Iowa
Nadouessis *see* Dakota
Nadouessons *see* Dakota
Nadouessoueronons *see* Dakota
Nadouissious *see* Dakota
Nadoussians *see* Dakota
Nadoussieux *see* Dakota
Nadoussioux *see* Dakota
Nadouwesis *see* Dakota
Nadovesaves *see* Dakota
Nadovessians *see* Dakota
Nadowa (BE) *see also* Iroquois
(LC)
Nadowa (BE) *see also* Wyandot
(BE)
Nadowa (H)
Nadowa (H) *see also* Huron (H)
Na-do-wage *see* Iroquois
Nadowage *see* Iroquois
Nadowaig *see* Iroquois
Na-do-wa-see-wug *see* Dakota
Nadowaseewug *see* Dakota
Nadowasis *see* Dakota

Nadowassis *see* Dakota
Nadowayaioux *see* Dakota
Nadowe *see* Iroquois
Nadowesee *see* Dakota
Nadowesi *see* Dakota
Nadowesioux *see* Dakota
Nadowessi *see* Dakota
Nadowessiern *see* Dakota
Nadowessies *see* Dakota
Nado-wes-siouex *see* Dakota
Nadowessiouex *see* Dakota
Nadowessioux *see* Dakota
Nadowestesus *see* Dakota
Nadsonites *see* Nasoni
Nadsoo *see* Nanatsoho
Nadsou *see* Nanatsoho
Naduessiouck *see* Dakota
Nadussians *see* Dakota
Naduwessi *see* Dakota
Nadvesiv *see* Dakota
Naehiaok *see* Cree
Nae kun k-eraua'i *see* Naikun-
kegawai
Naekunkerauai *see* Naikun-
kegawai
Naeku'n stastaai *see* Nekun-
stustai
Naelim *see* Nehalem
Na-e-lum *see* Nehalem
Naelum *see* Nehalem
Naembeck *see* Naumkeag
Naemkeck *see* Naumkeag
Naemkeek *see* Naumkeag
Naenshya [Gens] *Kwakiutl* (H)
Na-fhi-ap *see* Sandia
Nafhiap *see* Sandia
Nafiad *see* Sandia
Na-fi-ap *see* Sandia
Nafiap *see* Sandia
Nafiat *see* Sandia
Nafihuide *see* Sandia
Nafugua *see* Nafuqua
Nafukwa *see* Nafuqua
Nafuqua [Br] (O)
Nagail *see* Takulli
Nagailas *see* Takulli
Nagailer *see* Takulli
Nagalier *see* Takulli
Nagarotu [Br] *Northern Nam-
bicuara* (O)
Nagcodoches *see* Nacogdoches
Na-ge-uk-tor-me-ut *see*
Nageuktormiut
Nageuktormeut *see* Nageuk-
tormiut
Nageuktormiut [Can] *Eskimos*
(H)
Naggiuktop-meut *see* Naguek-
tormiut
Naggoe-ook-tor-moe-oot *see*
Naguektormiut
Nagodoches *see* Nacogdoches
Nagogdoches *see* Nacogdoches

Nagokaydn [AZ] *Pinal Apache*
(H)
Nagonabe [MI] *Chippewa* (H)
Nagosugn [AZ] *Pinal Apache* (H)
Nagrandan [NI] *Mangue* (BE)
Naguadaco *see* Natchitoches
Naguateeres *see* Natchitoches
Nagusi *see* Nacisi
Nagyuktogmiut [Can] *Central Es-
kimos* (BE)
Nagyuktogmiut *Copper Eskimos*
(Hdbk5)
Nahacassi *see* Nacisi
Na-hae-go *see* Nahaego
Nahaego [NV] (H)
Nahakhotane *Umpqua* (BE)
Nahamcok *see* Naumkeag
Nahanais *Intermediate Denes* (H)
Nah ane *see* Nahane
Nahane [BC] *Western Denes* (LC)
Nahanesten *see* Nahane
Nah-anes tene *see* Nahane
Nahani *see* Nahane
Nahanies *see* Nahane
Nahanies of the Upper Stikine *see*
Tahltan
Nahan-ne *see* Nahane
Nahanne *see* Nahane
Nahannie *see* Nahane
Nahantick *see* Niantic
Nahanticut *see* Niantic
Nahari *see* Nabiri
Nahat-dinne *see* Etagottine
Nahatdinne *see* Etagottine
Nahathaway *see* Cree
Nahaton [MA] *Massachuset* (BE)
Nahaunee *see* Tutchone
Nahauni *see* Nahane
Nahaunies *see* Nahane
Nahawas-hadai [Sub-family]
Haida (H)
Nahawni *see* Nahane
Nah-aw-ny *see* Nahane
Nahawny *see* Nahane
Nah-bah-too-too-ee *see*
Nabatutuei
Nahbahtootooee *see* Nabatutuei
Nahchee *see* Natchez
Nahcoktaws *see* Nakoaktok
Nahcotah *see* Dakota
Nah-dah-waig *see* Iroquois
Nahdahwaig *see* Iroquois
Nahdawessy *see* Dakota
Nahdooways *see* Iroquois
Nahdowasch *see* Dakota
Nahdoways *see* Iroquois
Na-he-ah-wuk *see* Sakawithini-
wuk
Naheahwuk *see* Sakawithiniwuk
Naheawak *see* Cree
Nahelem *see* Nehalem
Na-hel-ta *see* Nahelta
Nahelta [OR] *Chasta* (H)

Nahhahwuk [Self-designation]
see Cree
Nahiawah *see* Cree
Nahicans *see* Narraganset
Nahiganiouetch *see* Narraganset
Nahiganiouetch *see* Mahican
Nahiganset *see* Narraganset
Nahiganneucks *see* Narraganset
Nahiggonike *see* Narraganset
Nahiggonset *see* Narraganset
Nahiggonsick *see* Narraganset
Nahigonset *see* Narraganset
Nahigonsick *see* Narraganset
Nahigonsick *see* Narraganset
Nahigonsiks *see* Narraganset
Nahioak *see* Cree
Nahirir *see* Nabiri
Nahjo *see* Navajo
Nahkeeockto *see* Nakoaktok
Nah-keoock-to *see* Nakoaktok
Nah-keuck-to *see* Nakoaktok
Nahkeuckto *see* Nakoaktok
Nah-knock-to *see* Nakoaktok
Nahknockto *see* Nakoaktok
Nahkwoch-to *see* Nakoaktok
Nah-ma-bin *see* Namabin
Nahmabin *see* Namabin
Nahoas *see* Nahuas
Nahodiche *see* Nabedache
Nahopani *see* Nakhopani
Nahordikhe *see* Nabedache
Nahoudikhe *see* Nabedache
Nahpahpa *see* Nakhpakhpa
Nah-poo-itle *see* Cathlapotle
Nahpooitle *see* Cathlapotle
Nah-shah-shai *see* Hano
Nahshahshai *see* Hano
Nahtooessies *see* Dakota
Nahto-tin *see* Nataotin
Nahtotin *see* Nataotin
Nah-t'singh *see* Natesa
Nahtsingh *see* Natesa
Na-hu *see* Nahu
Nahu [Clan] *Hopi* (H)
Nahua *see* Nahuas
Nahuas [MX] (LC)
Nahuatl [MX] *Aztec* (BE)
Nahuatlan *see* Aztecoidan
Nahuatlato [NI] *Aztec* (BE)
Nahuatlecas *see* Nahuas
Nahudique *see* Nabedache
Nahukua [Br] (O)
Nahukwa *see* Nahukua
Nahum-keag *see* Naumkeag
Nahumkeag *see* Naumkeag
Nahuqua *see* Nahukua
Nahwahta *see* Nakoaktok
Nahwahtoh *see* Nakoaktok
Nahy *see* Natchez
Nahyssan (H) *see also* Tutelo (LC)
Nahyssan [VA, NC] (BE)
Naiatukq-ut *see* Niantic
Naicha *see* Neche
Naichoas *see* Natchez

Naiemkeck *see* Naumkeag
Naihantick *see* Niantic
Naikunkegawai *see* Naikun-
kegawai
Naikun-kegawai [Family] *Haida*
(H)
Na-iku'n qe'gawa-i *see* Naikun-
kegawai
Naikunqegawai *see* Naikun-
kegawai
Na-iku'n qe'gaw-i *see* Naikun-
kegawai
Naikunqegawi *see* Naikun-
kegawai
Na-im-bai *see* Nambe
Naimbai *see* Nambe
Na-im-be *see* Nambe
Na-imbe *see* Nambe
Naimbe *see* Nambe
Na-i-mbi *see* Nambe
Naimbi *see* Nambe
Na-i-shan-dina *see* Kiowa Apache
Naishandina *see* Kiowa Apache
Na-ishi Apache *see* Kiowa
Apache
Naishi Apache *see* Kiowa Apache
Naish-tiz-a *see* Zuni
Naishtiza *see* Zuni
Nai-te-zi *see* Zuni
Naitezi *see* Zuni
Na-izha'n *see* Lipan Apache
Naizhan [Self-designation] *see*
Lipan Apache
Naiz Percez *see* Amikwa
Najack *see* Canarsee
Nakai [Clan] *Navajo* (H)
Nakalas-hadai [Sub-family] [AK]
Haida (H)
Nakalnas-hadai *Haida* (H)
Na'ka'na'wan *see* Nakanawan
Nakanawan *Caddo* (H)
Nakasa (H) *see also* Nacisi (H)
Nakasa [LA] *Yatasi* (BE)
Nakase [LA] *Yatasi* (BE)
Na'kasine'na *see* Nakasinena
Nakasinena [CO, WY] *Northern
Arapaho* (H)
Nakasine'na [Self-designation] *see*
Nakasinena
Na-ka-si-nin *see* Nakasinena
Nakasinin *see* Nakasinena
Na-kas-le-tin *see* Nikozliautin
Nakasletin *see* Nikozliautin
Nakawawa *see* Cree
Nakawewuck *see* Cree
Nakawewuck *see* Cree
Naka-we-wuk *see* Cree
Nakaydi [Clan] *White Mountain
Apache* (H)
Nakazeteo-ten *see* Kikozliautin
Nakazeti *see* Kawahib
Na-ka-ztli-tenne *see* Nikozli-
autin

Nakaztlitenne see Nikozliautin
Nakchi'sh-hlama [WA] *Yakima*
(BE)
Naked Indians see Miami
Nakeduts-hadai [Sub-family]
Haida (H)
Nakeh see Eskimos
Naketoe's see Natchitoches
Naketosh see Natchitoches
Nakhopani [Clan] *Navajo* (H)
Nakhotodhanyadi [Clan] *Biloxi*
(H)
Nakhpakhpa *Brule* (H)
Nakitoches see Natchitoches
Nakkawinininiwak [Can] *Cree*
(H)
Nakkawinininiwak *Chippewa* (H)
Naknahula [Gens] *Kwakiutl* (H)
Nakoaktok [BC] *Kwakiutl* (BE)
Na'k-oartok see Nakoaktok
Nakoartok see Nakoaktok
Nakodotch see Nacogdoches
Nakodo'tche see Nacogdoches
Nakodotche see Nacogdoches
Nakohodotse see Nacogdoches
Na-ko-hodo-tsi see Nacogdoches
Nakohodotsi see Nacogdoches
Nakoktaw see Nakoaktok
Nakomgilasala [Can] *Nawiti* (BE)
Nak o'mguilisila see
Nakomgilasala
Nakomgyilisila see Nakomgilasala
Na-ko-nies see Detsanayuka
Nakonies see Detsanayuka
Nakonkirhirinous see Nameuilini
Nakonshadai see Nakons-hadai
Nakons-hadai [Sub-family] *Haida*
(H)
Nakoozetenne see Nikozliautin
Nakopozna [Clan] *Ponca* (H)
Nakota see Dakota
Nakotchokutchin see Nakotcho-
kutchin
Nakotcho-kutchin [Can] *Kutchin*
(BE)
Nakotcho-Kuttchin see
Nakotcho-kutchin
Nakotchokuttchin see Nakotcho-
kutchin
Nakotchpotschig Koutcchin see
Kutchakutchin
Na-Kotchpo-tschig-Kouttchin
see Kutchakutchin
Nakotco-ondjig-kut'qin *Loucheux*
(H)
Nakoulouhirinous see Nakkaw-
inininiwak
Na-kra-ztli-tenne see Nikozli-
autin
Nakraztlitenne see Nikozliautin
Nakrehe [Br] *Botocudo* (O)
Naksad see Mohave
Naks-at see Mohave

Naksat see Mohave
Naktche see Natchez
Nakudotche see Nacogdoches
Nakuhedotch see Nacogdoches
Na'kuimana [SD] *Cheyenne* (BE)
Nakuimana *Southern Cheyenne*
(H)
Nakum see Na-kum
Na-kum [CA] *Maidu* (Contri,
v.3, p.282)
Na-kutch-oo-un-jeek see
Nakotch-kutchin
Nakutchoounjeek see Nakotcho-
kutchin
Na-kutch-u-un-juk kutchin see
Nakotcho-kutchin
Nakutchuunjuk kutchin see
Nakotcho-kutchin
Nakwartoq see Nakoaktok
Na-kwok-to see Nakoaktok
Nakwokto see Naloaktok
Nalal se moch see Natalsemoch
Nalalsemoch see Natalsemoch
Na'lani see Comanche
Na'la'ni see Kiowa
Nalani see Comanche
Nalani see Kiowa
Nalatchwaniak see Norridgewock
Nalatsenoch see Natalsemoch
Nalekuitk [Clan] *Wikeno* (H)
Nalkitgoniash [NS] *Micmac* (H)
Nalo-tin see Nulaautin
Nal'tene tunne see Naltun-
netunne
Naltenetunne see Naltunnetunne
Nal-tun-ne tunne see Natlun-
netunne
Naltunnetunne [OR] (BE)
Nalvotogy see Norwootuc
Nalwetog see Norwootuc
Nam *Coahuiltecan* (Hdbk10)
Na-ma see Nama
Nama [Clan] *Chippewa* (H)
Namaaskeag see Naumkeag
Namabas see Naniaba
Nam-a-bin see Namabin
Namabin [Clan] *Chippewa* (H)
Namakaus see Navajo
Namananim see Kathlaminimin
Namanaxin see Kathlaminimin
Namanu see Nama'nu
Nama'nu [Clan] *Menominee* (H)
Namaoskeag see Amoskeag
Namao Wikito Tusiniu see Na-
ma'o Wikito Tusi'niu
Nama'o Wikito Tusi'niu [WI]
Menominee (BE)
Namascet see Namasket
Namaschaug see Amoskeag
Namaschet see Namasket
Namascheucks see Namasket
Namaske see Amoskeag
Namasket [MA] (H)

Namassachusett see Namasket
Namassakett see Namasket
Namassekett see Namasket
Na-ma-tha see Namatha
Namatha [Clan] *Shawnee* (H)
Na-ma-we-so-uk see Numaw-
isowugi
Namawesouk see Numawisowugi
Namawinini see Nameuilini
Namawisowagi see Numaw-
isowugi
Namba see Nambe
Nambe [Lang] *Northern Tewa*
(BE)
Nambehun see Nambe
Nambeke see Naumkeag
Nambi see Nambe
Nambicuara [Br] (LC)
Nambikuara see Nambicuara
Nambikwara see Nambicuara
Nambiquara see Nambicuara
Namburuap see Nambe
Name (H) see also Nama (H)
Name [VE] (O)
Nameanilieu see Nameuilini
Namekeake see Amoskeag
Nameuilini [Ont] *Chippewa* (BE)
Namewilini see Nameuilini
Namguack see Norridgewock
Namidish [TX] (BE)
Namikh-hua see Atka
Namikh-hun see Nikhu-khnin
Nami Te see Nambe
Namkeake see Amoskeag
Namkeake see Naumkeag
Namkeg see Naumkeag
nammo-lo-na see Nambe
nammolona see Nambe
Namollo see Siberian Eskimos
Namollos see Yuit
Namolly see Siberian Eskimos
Nampe see Nambe
Namset see Nauset
Namtainin see Num
Nan (H) see also Nang (H)
Nan (H) see also Nung (H)
Nan [Clan] *Tewa* (H)
Nana [Clan] *Nambe* (H)
Nanaa'ri see Nanyaayi
Nanaari see Nanyaayi
Nanabine'nan see Nakasinena
Nanaccejin see Nanashthezhin
Nanaganset see Narraganset
Nanaha see Navajo
Nanahaws see Navajo
Nanaigua see Tapiete
Nanaimo [Can] *Cowichan* (BE)
Nanaimuk [Clan] *Nanaimo* (H)
Nanainio [Clan] *Nanaimo* (H)
Na-na-ma-kew-uk see Nana-
makewuk
Nanamakewuk [Gens] [*Sauk, Fox*]
(H)

Nananawi [Clan] *Hopi* (H)
Nanankhuotana [OR] *Umpqua* (BE)
Nanashthezhin [Clan] *Navajo* (H)
Nanaste'zin *see* Nanashthezhin
Nanastezin *see* Nanashthezhin
Nana-tdoa *see* Nana
Nanatscho *see* Nanatsoho
Nanatsoho [LA] *Caddo Confederacy* (BE)
Nanawu [Clan] *Hopi* (H)
Na-na-wu wun-wu *see* Nanawu
Nanbikuara *see* Nambicuara
Nancaushy Tine *see* Nikozliautin
Nancemondies *see* Nansemond
Nanchagetan *see* Ankakehittan
Nancokoueten *see* Nassauaketon
Nancymond *see* Nansemond
Nandacaho *see* Anadarko
Nandako *see* Anadarko
Nandakoes *see* Anadarko
Nandaquees *see* Anadarko
Nandaquies *see* Anadarko
Nandawissees *see* Dakota
Nandesu [Br] *Southern Nambicuara* (O)
Nandeva *see* Avachiripa
Nandeva *see* Guarani
Nandeva *see* Nhandeva
Nandewy *see* Nandue
Nandoesi *see* Dakota
Nandoessies *see* Dakota
Nandoquies *see* Anadarko
Nandowese *see* Dakota
Nandowessies *see* Dakota
Nandsamund *see* Nansemond
Nandswesseis *see* Dakota
Nandtanghtacund *see* Nansatico
Nandtaughtacund *see* Nantaughtacund
Nandue *Accomac* (Hdbk15)
Nanduye *see* Nanticoke
Nanduye *see* Nandue
Nanemond *see* Nansemond
Nanenor *see* Naskapi
Nanenot *see* Naskapi
Nanepashemet [MA] *Massachuset* (BE)
Nanerna [PE] *Campa* (O)
Nang [Clan] *Pueblo Indians* (H)
Nangatu *see* Nheengatu
Nangatu *see* Tupi
Nan-gche-ari *see* Nanyaayi
Nangcheari *see* Nanyaayi
Nangemaick *see* Conoy
Nangemy *see* Conoy
Nanheygansett *see* Narraganset
Nanhiganset *see* Narraganset
Nanhigg *see* Narraganset
Nanhigganeuck *see* Narraganset
Nanhigganset *see* Narraganset
Nanhiggansick *see* Narraganset
Nanhiggon *see* Narraganset

Nanhiggonset *see* Narraganset
Nanhiggonsick *see* Narraganset
Nanhiggontick *see* Narraganset
Nanhigonset *see* Narraganset
Nanhigonsick *see* Narraganset
Nanhugansit *see* Narraganset
Nanhygansett *see* Narraganset
Naniaba [AL] *Tohome* (BE)
Naniba *see* Naniaba
Nanihiggonsick *see* Narraganset
Na'nita *see* Comanche
Nanita *see* Comanche
Nanitch *see* Sanetch
Nanjemy *see* Conoy
Nank'haanseine'nan *see* Nakasinena
Nankin-wahlum *see* Round Valley Yuki
Nanni (H) *see also* Nunni (H)
Nanni [Clan] *Chickasaw* (H)
Nannogan *see* Narraganset
Nannotansett *see* Narraganset
Nanohigganeuk *see* Narraganset
Nanohigganset *see* Narraganset
Nanohiggunset *see* Narraganset
Nanoniks-kare'niki *see* Cheyenne
Nanonikskareniki *see* Cheyenne
Nanoni'ks-kare'niku *see* Cheyenne
Nanonikskareniku *see* Cheyenne
Nanoos *see* Snonowa
Nanoose *see* Snonowas
Nanortalik *Greenland Eskimos* (BE)
Nanpanta (H) *see also* Panhkawashtake (H)
Nanpanta [Clan] *Osage* (H)
Nanpanta [Clan] *Quapaw* (H)
Nanpantaqtsi *see* Panhkawashtake
Nanrantsoak *see* Norridgewock
Nanrantsouak *see* Norridgewock
Nanrantswac *see* Norridgewock
Nanrantswak *see* Norridgewock
Nansamond *see* Nansemond
Nansamund *see* Nansemond
Nansatico [VA] *Algonquian* (Hdbk15)
Nanscud-dinneh *see* Naskotin
Nanseman *see* Nansemond
Nansemond [VA] *Powhatan* (BE)
Nansemun *see* Nansemond
Nansi *see* Naansi
Nansiatico *see* Nansatico
Nansimum *see* Nansemond
Nansoakouaton *see* Nassauaketon
Nansoua *see* Nassauaketon
Nansouaketon *see* Nassauaketon
Nantansouak *see* Norridgewock
Nantaquack *see* Nanticoke
Nantaquaes *see* Nanticoke
Nantaquak *see* Nanticoke

Nantaughs tacum *see* Nansatico
Nantaughtacund [VA] *Powhatan* (BE)
Nantautacund *see* Nantaughtacund
Nan-tdoa *see* Nang
Nantdoa *see* Nang
Nantecoke *see* Nanticoke
Nantégo *see* Nanticoke
Nantekokies *see* Nanticoke
Nanteqet *see* Niantic
Nantequit *see* Niantic
Nan-te-we-ki *see* Seneca
Nanteweki *see* Seneca
Nantiakokies *see* Nanticoke
Nantiatico *see* Nansatico
Nantico *see* Nanticoke
Nanticock *see* Nanticoke
Nanticoes *see* Nanticoke
Nanticoke [Lang] *Eastern Algonquian* (Hdbk15)
Nanticoke [MD, DE] (LC)
Nanticoke Confederacy (H)
Nanticoks *see* Nanticoke
Nanticook *see* Nanticoke
Nanticoque *see* Nanticoke
Nantigansick *see* Narraganset
Nantikoke *see* Nanticoke
Nantikokies *see* Nanticoke
Nantiock *see* Nanticoke
Nantioke *see* Nanticoke
Nantiquack *see* Nanticoke
Nantiquak *see* Nanticoke
Nantley Tine *see* Natliatin
Nantoüe *see* Mantouek
Nan-towa *see* Nang
Nantowa *see* Nang
Nantsattaqunt *see* Nansatico
Nantue *see* Nanticoke
Nantunagunk *see* Ontonagon
Nantuxet [PA, DE] *Unalachtigo* (BE)
Nantycoke *see* Nanticoke
Nantygansick *see* Narraganset
Nantyggansik *see* Narraganset
Nanualikmut [AK] *Knaiakhotana* (H)
Na-nua-li-q'mut *see* Nanualikmut
Nanualiqmut *see* Nanualikmut
Na-nu-a-luk *see* Nanualikmut
Nanualuk *see* Nanualikmut
Na-nus-sus-so-uk *see* Nanussussouk
Nanussussouk [Clan] [*Sauk, Fox*] (H)
Nanuya *see* Nonuya
Nanwacinaha'anan *see* Southern Arapaho
Nanwuine'nan *see* Nawunena
Nanya'ayi *see* Nanyaayi
Nanyaayi [AK] *Southern Tlingit* (H)

Nanyiee [Family] *Tahltan* (H)
Nanzaticoe *see* Nansatico
Naodiche *see* Nabedache
Na-o-geh *see* Naogeh
Naogeh [Clan] *Seneca* (H)
Naolingo *see* Totonec
Naonediche *see* Nabedache
Naotchtant *see* Nacotchtank
Naotetain *see* Nataotin
Naouadiche *see* Nabedache
Naoudiche *see* Nabedache
Naoudishes *see* Nabedache
Naouediches *see* Nabedache
Naouidiche *see* Nabedache
Naouydiche *see* Nabedache
Naovediche *see* Nabedache
Napa [CA] *Patwin* (Contri, v.3, p.218)
Napa [Lang] [CA] *Patwin* (CA-8)
Napaaqtugmiut *Kotzebue Sound Eskimos* (Hdbk5)
Napaches *see* Napochi
Napakato Mutes *see* Napaaqtug-miut
Napakato Mutes *see* Nuataag-miut
Napanam *see* Inapanam
Napao *see* Navajo
Napé [SA] (O)
Napeya *see* Sandia
Na'pfe'ta *see* Sandia
Napfeta *see* Sandia
Napgitache *see* Natchitoches
Napgitoches *see* Natchitoches
naphetho *see* Sandia
Naphiat *see* Sandia
Na-pi-ap *see* Sandia
Napiap *see* Sandia
Na-pi-hah *see* Sandia
Napihah *see* Sandia
napikerenu *see* Picuris
Napissa [MS] (BE)
Napo *see* Canelo
Napo *see* Quijo
Napobatin (H)
Napochi [AL] (BE)
Napochies *see* Napochi
Napoya [Clan] *Timucua* (H)
Nappa-arktok-towock *see* Nageuktormiut
Nappaarktoktowock *see* Nageuk-tormiut
Napuat *see* Carrizo [MX]
Naputsemack [WA] (Hdbk12)
Napyosa *see* Napissa
Napyssa *see* Napissa
Naqkyina *see* Lakweip
Na'q'oaqtoaq *see* Nakoaktok
Na'q'oaqtôq *see* Kanoaktok
Naqoaqtoq *see* Nakoaktok
Naqoartoq *see* Nakoaktok
Naqo'mg ilisala *see* Nakomgilisala

Naqomgilisala *see* Nakomgilisala
Naqomqilis *see* Nakomgilisala
Naqopani *see* Nakhopani
Naqpaqpa *see* Nakhpakhpa
Naquitoches *see* Natchitoches
Naquizcoza *see* Arkokisa
Naragancett *see* Narraganset
Naraganset *see* Narraganset
Naragansick *see* Narraganset
Naraghenses *see* Narraganset
Naragooe *see* Norridgewock
Naragooe *see* Kennebec
Narako *see* Anadarko
Naranchouak *see* Norridgewock
Naranchouek *see* Norridgewock
Naranckouak *see* Kennebec
Narangaqock *see* Kennebec
Narangawock *see* Norridgewock
Narangawook *see* Norridgewock
Narankamigdok epitsik arenan-back *see* Abnaki
Naransett *see* Narraganset
Narantsoak *see* Norridgewock
Narantsouak *see* Norridgewock
Narantsouan *see* Norridgewock
Narantswouak *see* Norridgewock
Nar-a-tah *see* Comanche
Naratah *see* Comanche
Naratekon *see* Naraticon
Naraticon [NJ] *Unalachtigo* (BE)
Naraticonck *Delaware* (Hdbk15)
Narautsouak *see* Norridgewock
Narautsouak *see* Kennebec
Narauwing *see* Norridgewock
Narauwing *see* Kennebec
Naravute (O) *see also* Naruvot (O)
Naravute [Lang] *Xingu* (UAz, v.28)
Narcotah *see* Dakota
Nardichia *see* Kiowa Apache
Narent Chouan *see* Norridge-wock
Nar-go-des-giz-zen *see* Akonye
Nargodesgizzen *see* Akonye
Narhiganset *see* Narraganset
Narhiggansett *see* Narraganset
Narhiggon *see* Narraganset
Naricanset *see* Narraganset
Narices [MX] *Coahuiltecan* (BE)
Naricon *see* Naraticon
Naridgewalk *see* Norridgewock
Naridgwalk *see* Norridgewock
Nariganset *see* Narraganset
Narigansette *see* Narraganset
Narigansset *see* Narraganset
Narigenset *see* Narraganset
Narigganset *see* Narraganset
Narihganset *see* Narraganset
Narises *see* Narices
Narizes *see* Narices
Nar-kock-tau *see* Nakoaktok
Narkocktau *see* Nakoaktok
Nar-ode-so-sin *see* Natootzuzn

Narodesosin *see* Natootzuzn
Narogansett *see* Narraganset
Narohiganset *see* Narraganset
Narrackomagog *see* Rocameca
Narragancett *see* Narraganset
Narragangsett *see* Narraganset
Narraganses *see* Narraganset
Narraganset [RI] (LC)
Narragansett *see* Narraganset
Narrahamegock *see* Rocameca
Narrakamegock *see* Rocameca
Narrangansett *see* Narraganset
Narraticong *see* Naraticon
Narraticonse *see* Naraticon
Narratikonck *see* Naraticon
Narreganset *see* Narraganset
Narrhagansitt *see* Narraganset
Nar-rit-i-cong *see* Naraticon
Narriticong *see* Naraticon
Narroganset *see* Narraganset
Narrohiganset *see* Narraganset
Narrohigganset *see* Narraganset
Narrohiggenset *see* Narraganset
Narrohiggin *see* Narraganset
Narrohiggonset *see* Narraganset
Narrowbiggonset *see* Narraganset
Narrowgancett *see* Narraganset
Narrowganneuch *see* Narraganset
Narrowganneuck *see* Narraganset
Narrow Ganset *see* Narraganset
Narrowganssit *see* Narraganset
Narrowganzet *see* Narraganset
Narrow-Higansett *see* Narraganset
Narrowhigansett *see* Narraganset
Narrow Higgansent *see* Narraganset
Narrowhiggansent *see* Narraganset
Narsh-tiz-a *see* Pima
Narsh-tiz-a *see* Zuni
Narshtiza *see* Pima
Narshtiza *see* Zuni
Naruvot [Br] (O)
Nar-wah-ro *see* Delaware
Narwahro *see* Delaware
Narwootuck *see* Norwootuc
Narygansett *see* Narraganset
Nasa [Self-designation] *see* Paez
Nasagas-haidagai [Subclan] *Haida* (H)
Na s'a'gas qa'edra *see* Nasagas-haidagai
Nasagasqaedra *see* Nasagas-haidagai
Nas-ah-mah *see* Nasumi
Nasahmah *see* Nasumi
Nasahossez *see* Nacogdoches
Nasal *see* Nisal
Nasamond *see* Nansemond
Nasas *see* Nazas
Na s'a'yas qa'etqa *see* Nasagas-haidagai

Nasayasqaetqa *see* Nasagas-
haidagai
Nascah *see* Niska
Nascapee *see* Naskapi
Nascapi *see* Naskapi
Nascar *see* Niska
Nascha *see* Neche
Nascopi *see* Naskapi
Nascopie *see* Naskopi
Nascotin *see* Naskotin
Nascud *see* Naskotin
Nascud Denee *see* Naskotin
Nascupi *see* Naskapi
Nashaue *see* Nashua
Nashaway *see* Nashua
Nashawog *see* Nashua
Nashawogg *see* Nashua
Nashedosh *see* Natchitoches
Nashitosh *see* Natchitoches
Nashi'tosh *see* Natchitoches
Confederacy
Nashkali dinne *see* Mescalero
Apache
Nashkoten *see* Naskotin
Nashlizhe *see* Zuni
Nashoba *see* Nashola
Na-sho-la *see* Nashola
Nashola [Clan] *Chickasaw* (H)
Nashoway *see* Nashua
Nashteise *see* Pima
Nashtezhe *see* Zuni
Nashua [NH, MA] *Pennacook*
(BE)
Nashuay *see* Nashua
Nashuway *see* Nashua
Nashuya *see* Nashua
Nasiampaa [MN] *Mdewakanton*
(H)
Na-si-ap *see* Sandia
Nasiap *see* Sandia
Nasitt *see* Nauset
Nasitti *see* Natchitoches
Naskapi [Q] (LC)
Naskapit *see* Naskapi
Naskoaten *see* Naskotin
Nas-koo-tain *see* Naskotin
Naskootain *see* Naskotin
Naskopi *see* Naskapi
Naskopie *see* Naskapi
Naskotin [Can] (BE)
Naskupi *see* Naskapi
Na-sku-tenna *see* Naskotin
Naskutenne *see* Naskotin
Nasohmah [OR] *Tututni* (H)
Nas-o-mah *see* Nasumi
Nasomah *see* Nasumi
Na-son *see* Nasumi
Nason *see* Nasumi
Nasone *see* Nasoni
Nasoni [TX] (BE)
Nasony *see* Nasoni
Nasori *see* Nasoni
Nasoui *see* Nasoni

Naspapee *see* Naskapi
Naspatl *see* Chaicclesaht
Naspatle *see* Chaicclesaht
Naspatte *see* Chaicclesaht
Nasqa *see* Niska
Nasqua *see* Niska
Nasqually *see* Nisqualli
Nasqually *see* Nisqually
Nasquapee *see* Naskapi
Nasquapick *see* Naskapi
Nasrad-Denee *see* Naskotin
Nass *see* Chimmesyan
Nass *see* Niska
Nassamond *see* Nansemond
Nassauaketon [MI, WI] *Ottawa*
(BE)
Nassauakuetuon *see* Nassauake-
ton
Nassawach *see* Nashua
Nassawaketon *see* Nassauaketon
Nasse *see* Chimmesyan
Nasshaway *see* Nashua
Nassitoches *see* Natchitoches
Nassomte *see* Nasoni
Nassoni *see* Nasoni
Nassonian *see* Nasoni
Nassonit *see* Nasoni
Nassonites *see* Nasoni
Nas-sou *see* Nasumi
Nassou *see* Nasumi
Nassoway *see* Nashua
Nass River Indians *see* Niska
Nasswatex *Pocomoke* (Hdbk15)
Nastanahua [Lang] *Panoan* (O)
Nas-tedi *see* Nastedi
Nastedi [Social group] [AK] *Tlin-
git* (H)
Nastedi [Social group] *Kuiu* (H)
Nasto-kegawai [Family] [BC]
Haida (H)
Nas-tu-kin-me'tunne *see* Nes-
tucca
Nastukinmetunne *see* Nestucca
Nasuia kwe *see* Ute
Nasumi (H) *see also* Nasohmah
(H)
Na-su-mi *see* Nasumi
Nasumi [OR] (H)
Nata [Pan] (BE)
Na'taa *see* Comanche
Nataa *see* Comanche
Natab'hu-tu-ei *see* Nabatutuei
Natache [LA] [Yatasi] (BE)
Natacook *see* Souhegan
Natadowa *see* Nottoway
Natafe *see* Kiowa Apache
Natagaima [Col] (LC)
Natage (H) *see also* Kiowa Apache
(LC)
Natage (Hdbk10) *see also*
Mescalero Apache (LC)
Natage *Apache* (Hdbk10)
Natagee *see* Kiowa Apache

Natagees *see* Natage
Natages *see* Natage
Natageses *see* Natage
Natahe *see* Mescalero Apache
natahe *see* Natage
Natahi'n *see* Mescalero Apache
Natahin *see* Mescalero Apache
Nata-hinde *see* Nataini
Natahinde *see* Nataini
Nataina *see* Natage
Nata-i'ni *see* Nataini
Nataini [NM] *Mescalero Apache*
(H)
Nataje *see* Kiowa Apache
Natajee *see* Kiowa Apache
Nata-Kebit *see* Toba
Natakebit *see* Toba
Natale *see* Kiowa Apache
Natal-se-moch *see* Natalsemoch
Natalsemoch [BC] (H)
Na-ta-ne *see* Mescalero Apache
Natane *see* Mescalero Apache
Natano *see* Hupa
Natao (H) *see also* Adai (BE)
Natao *Coahuiltecan* (BE)
Nataotin [Can] *Carrier* (BE)
Natashkwan [Can] [*Montagnais-
Naskapi*] (BE)
Natasi [LA] *Caddo* (BE)
Natatladiltin *Apache* (H)
Na-taw-tin *see* Nataotin
Natawtin *see* Nataotin
Natche *see* Natchez
Natchee *see* Natchez
Natche-kutchin *see* Nat-
sitkutchin
Natchekutchin *see* Natsitkutchin
Natches *see* Natchez
Natchesan [Lang] [MS, LA] (H)
Natchesan Indians *see* Natchez
Natchese *see* Natchez
Natchets *see* Natchez
Natchez [MS] (LC)
Natchidosh *see* Natchitoches
Natchiloches *see* Natchitoches
Natchites *see* Natchitoches
Natchitoches [TX, LA] *Caddo
Confederacy* (BE)
Natchitoches Confederacy [LA]
(BE)
Natchitochis *see* Natchitoches
Natchitotches *see* Natchitoches
Natchitto *see* Natchitoches
Natchon *see* Tulkepaia
Natchoo *see* Nanatsoho
Natchous *see* Tulkepaia
Na'tci-tce *see* Nachiche
Natcitce *see* Nachiche
Na-tcte tunne *see* Takelma
Natctetunne *see* Takelma
Na-tdoa *see* Nang
Natdoa *see* Nang
Natekebit *see* Toba

Natenehima *see* Dakota
Nat-e-ne-hin-a *see* Dakota
Natenehina *see* Dakota
Nate-ote-tain *see* Nataotin
Nateotetain *see* Nataotin
Natesa (H) *see also* Natsahi (H)
Nate-sa *see* Natesa
Natesa [Family] *Kutchakutchin*
    (H)
Nathannas *see* Nahane
Nathehwywintinyoowuc *see* Cree
Nathehwy-within-yoowuc *see*
    Cree
Nathe-wywithin-yu *see* Cree
Nathewywithinyu *see* Cree
Nathoso *see* Nanatsoho
Nathsoo *see* Nanatsoho
Na-tick *see* Niantic
Natick *see* Massachuset
Natick *see* Niantic
Natilantin *see* Natliatin
Natimolo *see* Totonac
Natinnoh-hoi *see* Hupa
Natio Euporum *see* Abnaki
Natio Luporum *see* Abnaki
Nation d'Atironta *see* Aren-
    dahronon
Nation de Bois *see* Missisauga
Nation de Chat *see* Erie
Nation de Feu *see* Mascouten
Nation de Fourche *see* Nas-
    sauaketon
Nation de Grand-Rat *see* Cree
Nation de la folle avoine *see*
    Menominee
Nation de la Grande Montagne
    see Seneca
Nation de la Grue *see* Miami
Nation de la Grue *see* Pepikokia
Nation de la Loutre *see* Nikik-
    ouek
Nation de la Montagne *see*
    Onondaga
Nation de la Pierre *see* Oneida
Nation de la Roche *see* Aren-
    dahronon
Nation de l'Isle *see* Kichesipirini
Nation de l'Ours *see* Attig-
    nawantan
Nation d'Entauaque *see* At-
    tigneenongnahac
Nation des Chats *see* Erie
Nation des Forts *see* Sisseton
Nation des Ours *see* Attignawan-
    tan
Nation des Porc epics *see* Kak-
    ouchaki
Nation des Sorciers *see* Nipissing
Nation detruite *see* Neutral Na-
    tion
Nation d'Iroquet *see* Onon-
    chataronon
Nation du boeuf *see* Santee

Nation du Castor *see* Amikwa
Nation du Chat *see* Erie
Nation du Chien *see* Cherokee
Nation du chien *see* Ofo
Nation du Feu *see* Potawatomi
Nation du petum *see* Tionontati
Nation du Petun *see* Tionontati
Nation du Porc-Epic *see* Piek-
    ouagami
Nation du Rocher *see* Aren-
    dahronon
Nation du Sault *see* Chippewa
Nation of Bread *see* Pascagoula
Nation of Fire *see* Potawatomi
Nation of Fire *see* Shawnee
Nation of the Beaver *see* Amikwa
Nation of the Dog *see* Ofo
Nation of the Great Water *see*
    Assiniboin
Nation of the Otter *see* Niki-
    houek
Nation of the Porcupine *see*
    Kakouchaki
Nation of the Snake *see*
    Shoshone
Nation of the Wild Oats *see*
    Menominee
Nation of the Willows *see* Hava-
    supai
Nation of Tobacco *see* Tionon-
    tati
Natio perticarum *see* Conestoga
Natleh-hwo'tenne *see* Natliatin
Natliantin *see* Natliatin
Natliatin [Can] (BE)
Natliatin [Clan] *Takulli* (H)
Natliautin *see* Natliatin
Natlo'tenne *see* Natliatin
Natlotenne *see* Natliatin
Natni *see* Dakota
Natnihina *see* Dakota
Na-to *see* Sa
Nato *see* Sa
Na-too-na-ta *see* Nutunutu
Natoonata *see* Nutunutu
Nato-o-tzuzn *see* Natootzuzn
Natootzuzn *Apache* (H)
Natotin Tine *see* Nataotin
Na-to-utenne *see* Nataotin
Natoutenne *see* Nataotin
Na'towewok *see* Nottoway
Natowewok *see* Nottoway
Na-to-wo-na (BE)
Natowona *see* Dakota
Natsagana *see* Abnaki
Nat-sah-i *see* Natesa
Natsahi (PC) *see also* Natesa (H)
Natsahi [Clan] *Kutchakutchin* (H)
Natschitos *see* Natchitoches
Na-tsik-ku-chin *see*
    Naisitkutchin
Natsikkuchin *see* Natsitkutchin
Natsik-kutchin *see* Natsitkutchin

Natsikkutchin *see* Natsitkutchin
Natsilik *see* Netchilirmiut
natsilik *see* Netsiik
Natsilingmiut [AK] *Netsilik*
    (Hdbk5)
Nat-singh *see* Natesa
Natsingh (PC) *see also* Natesa (H)
Natsingh [Caste] [AK] *Loucheux*
    (H)
Na-ts'it kutchi-in *see* Nat-
    sitkutchin
Natsit-kutchin *see* Natsitkutchin
Natsitkutchin [AK] *Kutchin* (LC)
Natsitoches *see* Natchitoches
Natsoho *see* Nanatsoho
Natsohock *see* Nanatsoho
Natsohok *see* Nanatsoho
Natsoo *see* Nanatsoho
Natsshostanno (H) *see also*
    Natchitoches (BE)
Natsshostanno [TX, LA] (BE)
Natsytos *see* Natchitoches
Nattamonge *see* Nansemond
Nattechez *see* Natchez
Nattlewitinne [BC] *Carrier Indi-
    ans* (Bull133)
Nattsae-Kouttchin *see*
    Tukkuthkutchin
Nattukkog *see* Souhegan
Natu [Br] (O)
Natuagi *see* Iroquois
Natuesse *see* Dakota
Natuessuag *see* Dakota
Nau-do-ques *see* Anadarko
Nauajo *see* Navajo
Nauajoa *see* Navajo
Nauchee *see* Natchez
Naudacho *see* Anadarko
Naudawissees *see* Dakota
Naudewessioux *see* Dakota
Naudoessi *see* Dakota
Naudoouessis *see* Dakota
Naudoques *see* Anadarko
Naudouescioux *see* Dakota
Naudouessi *see* Dakota
Naudouisioux *see* Dakota
Naudouisses *see* Dakota
Naudouwessies *see* Dakota
Naud-o-waig *see* Iroquois
Naudowaig *see* Iroquois
Naud-o-wa-se *see* Dakota
Naudowase *see* Dakota
Naud-o-wa-se-wug *see* Dakota
Naudowasewug *see* Dakota
Naudowasses *see* Dakota
Naudowesies *see* Dakota
Naudowesse *see* Dakota
Naudowesseeg *see* Dakota
Naudowessies *see* Dakota
Naudtaughtacund *see* Nantaugh-
    tacund
Naudussi *see* Dakota
Nauduwassies *see* Dakota

Naugatuck *see* Wappinger
Naugdoches *see* Nacogdoches
Naukanski *Siberian Yupik*
    (Hdbk5)
naukantsy *see* Naukanski
Naumkeag [MS] *Pennacook* (BE)
Naumkeak *see* Naumkeag
Naumkeck *see* Naumkeag
Naumkeek *see* Naumkeag
Naumkek *see* Naumkeag
Naumkuk *see* Naumkeag
Naune *see* Comanche
Na-u-ni *see* Comanche
Nauni *see* Comanche
Nauniem *Comanche* (BE)
Naupaktomiut *see* Napaaqtug-
    miut
Naurantsouak *see* Norridgewock
Naurantsouak *see* Kennebec
Naurautsoak *see* Norridgewock
Naurautsouak *see* Norridgewock
Nausamund *see* Nansemond
Nauscud Dennies *see* Naskotin
Nause [MD] *Nanticoke* (BE)
Nauset [MA] (LC)
Naushawag *see* Nashua
Nausit *see* Nauset
Nausites *see* Nauset
Na-ussins *see* Navasink
Naussins *see* Navasink
Nautaquake *see* Nanticoke
Nautaughtacund *see* Nantaugh-
    tacund
Nautaugue *see* Nottaway
Nauticoke *see* Nanticoke
Nau-tle-atin *see* Natliatin
Nautleatin *see* Natliatin
Nautowaig *see* Iroquois
Nautowas *see* Iroquois
Nautoway *see* Iroquois
Nauwanatat [NV] *Paiute* (H)
Nau-wan-atats *see* Moapa
Nauwanatats (PC) *see also* Moapa
    (Hdbk11)
Nauyarmiut *see* Aivilingmiut
Navadacho *see* Nabedache
Navago *see* Navajo
Navaho *see* Navajo
Na-va-ho *see* Navajo
Navahoe *see* Navajo
Navahoes *see* Navajo
Navahu *see* Navajo
Navahua *see* Navajo
Navajai *see* Navajo
Navajo [NM, AZ] [1969 officially
    adopted by Navojo Nation]
    (LC)
Navajoas *see* Navajo
Navajoes *see* Navajo
Navajoes *see* Navajo
Navajoos *see* Navajo
Navajosa *see* Navajo
Navajoses *see* Navajo

Navajoso *see* Navajo
Navajosos *see* Navajo
Navaosos *see* Navajo
Navasink *Delaware* (Hdbk15)
Navasink [NJ] *Unami* (BE)
navaxo *see* Navajo
Navaxu *see* Navajo
Navecinx *see* Navasink
Navedacho *see* Nabedachoe
Navejo *see* Navajo
Navenacho *see* Nabedache
Navesand *see* Navasink
Navesinck *see* Navasink
Navesink *see* Navasink
Navesu-pai *see* Havasupai
Navicarao [HA] *Guaccaiarima*
    (BE)
Navidacho *see* Nabedache
Navidad di Nuestra Señora *see*
    Chilili [Tigua]
Navidgwock *see* Norridgewock
Navijoes *see* Navajo
Navijos *see* Navajo
Navisink *see* Navasink
Navison *see* Navasink
Naviti *see* Nabiri
navo *see* Navajo
Navoasos *see* Navajo
Navohos *see* Navajo
Navone *see* Lipan Apache
Nawaas [CN] (H)
Nawadishe *see* Nabedache
na-waho *see* Navajo
nawaho *see* Navajo
Nawahona *see* Navajo
Nawahonae *see* Navajo
Nawas *see* Nawaas
Nawathi'neha (H) *see also*
    Nawunena
Nawathineha *see* Nawathi'neha
Nawathi'neha [OK] *Southern
    Arapaho* (W)
Nawazi-Montji *see* Chimane
Nawdowessie *see* Dakota
Nawdowissnees *see* Dakota
Naweho *see* Navajo
Nawes *see* Nawaas
Nawiti [Lang] *Kwakiutl* (BE)
Nawotsi [Clan] *Caddo* (H)
Nawsamond *see* Nansemond
Nawsel *see* Nauset
Nawset *see* Nauset
Nawsit *see* Nauset
Na-wunena *see* Nawunena
Nawunena [OK] *Southern Ara-
    paho* (H)
Na-wuth-i-ni-han *see* Nawunena
Nawuthinihan *see* Nawunena
Nayack *see* Canarsee
Nayaerita [Self-designation] *see*
    Cora
Nayantacott *see* Niantic
Nayantakick *see* Niantic

Nayantakoog *see* Niantic
Nayantaquist *see* Niantic
Nayantaquit *see* Niantic
Nayantiaquct *see* Niantic
Nayantick *see* Niantic
Nayantik *see* Niantic
Nayantuk *see* Niantic
Nayantuqiqt *see* Niantic
Nayantuquit *see* Niantic
Nayari *see* Cora
Nayarit *see* Cora
Nayarit *see* Cora
Nayarita *see* Cora
Nayariti *see* Cora
Nayariti *see* Cora
Nayerits *see* Cora
Nayhantick *see* Niantic
Nayhautick *see* Niantic
Nayhiggonsik *see* Narraganset
Nayohygunsic *see* Narraganset
Na yu-ans qa'edra *see* Nayuuns-
    haidagai
Nayuansqaedra *see* Nayuuns-
    haidagai
Na yu'ans qa'etqa *see* Nayuuns-
    haidagai
Nayuansqaetqa *see* Nayuuns-
    haidagai
Nayuuns-haidagai [BC] *Haida*
    (H)
Naywaunaukauraunah (H)
Nay-Waunaukauraunah *see* Nay-
    waunaukauraunah
Naywaunaukau-raunuh *see* Mis-
    sisauga
Nazacahoz *see* Natchitoches
Nazadachotzi *see* Nacogdoches
Nazaganset *see* Narraganset
Nazanne *see* Comanche
Nazas [MX] *Coahuiltecan* (BE)
Nazatica *see* Nansatico
Nazca culture [PE] (LC)
Nazkutenne *see* Naskotin
Nazone *see* Nasoni
Nazpercies *see* Nez Perce
Naz-te-zi *see* Zuni
Naztezi *see* Zuni
Naz-tuk-e-me tunne *see* Nestucca
Naztukemetunne *see* Nestucca
ndaabixunde *see* Navajo
Ndakotah *see* Dakota
Nda kun-dadehe *see* Karankawa
Ndakundadehe *see* Karankawa
Ndatahe *see* Mescalero Apache
Ndatonatendi *see* Potawatomi
N'day *see* Apache
Nday *see* Apache
Nde [Self-designation] *see*
    Apache
N'de [Self-designation] *see*
    Apache
nde [Self-designation] *see*
    Mescalero Apache

Nde Ndai *see* Chiricahua Apache
Ndu-tcho-ottine *see* Etcheri-
diegottine
Ndutchoottinne *see* Etcheri-
diegottine
Neagottine *see* Nigottine
Neagwaih [Clan] *Seneca* (H)
Neahawanak *see* Newichawanoc
Neamitch *see* Dwamish
Neantick *see* Niantic
Neanticot *see* Niantic
Neanticutt *see* Niantic
Neantucke *see* Niantic
Neaquiltough *see* Lekwiltok
Ne-ar-de-on-dar-go-war *see*
Oneida
Neardeondardgowar *see* Oneida
Ne-a-ya-og *see* Chippewa
Ne-a-ya-og *see* Cree
Neayaog *see* Chippewa
Neayaog *see* Cree
Nebagindibe *see* Salish
Nebagindibed *see* Salish
Nebajos *see* Navajo
Nebdache *see* Nabedache
Nebedache *see* Nabedache
Nebicerini *see* Nipissing
Nebome (H) *see also* Nevome
(LC)
Nebome [MX] *Pima Bajo* (BE)
Nebomes Baxos *see* Nevome
Necait *see* Niciat
Ne'c'asath *see* Neshasath
Necasath *see* Neshasath
Neccope *see* Skopamish
Necha *see* Neche
Nechacohee *see* Nechacokee
Nechacoke *see* Nechocoke
Nechacokee [OR] *Multnomah* (BE)
Ne-cha-co-lee *see* Nechasokee
Nechacolee *see* Nechacokee
Nechaui [TX] *Hasinai* (BE)
Neche [TX] (BE)
Nechecolee *see* Nechacokee
Nechegansett *see* Pennacook
Nechegansitt *see* Narraganset
Nechijilli *see* Netchilirmiut
Nechimuasath [Sept] *Nootka* (H)
Ne-ci-he-nen-a *see* Kiowa
Necihenena *see* Kiowa
Neckpercie *see* Nez Perce
Necochincos *Conoy* (Hdbk15)
Ne-com-ap-oe-lox *see* Spokan
Necomapoelox *see* Spokan
Neconbacistes *see* Nekoubaniste
Necootimeigh [OR] (H)
Necosts (H) *see also* Nacotchtank
(BE)
Necosts *Conoy* (Hdbk15)
Necpacha *Coahuiltecan* (BE)
Necta *see* Neshta
Ne-cul-ta *see* Lekwiltok
Neculta *see* Lekwiltok

Nedlungmiut [Can] *Central Eski-
mos* (BE)
nedna *see* Southern Chiricahua
Apache
Ned-ni (Hdbk10)
Nedni *see* Ned-ni
Nedouessaus *see* Dakota
Neds percés *see* Amikwa
Neds-percez *see* Amikwa
Ne-e-ar-gu-ya *see* Neagwaih
Neearguya *see* Neagwaih
Ne-e-ar-guy-ee *see* Montagnais-
Naskapi
Neearguyee *see* Neagwaih
Neecelowes *see* Neeslous
Neecelows *see* Neeslous
Neechaokee *see* Nechacokee
Nee-cow-ee-gee *see*
Neecoweegee
Neecoweegee *Miniconjou* (BE)
Needle Hearts *see* Skitswish
Neegatú *see* Nheengatu
Neenoa *see* Miriti-Tapuya
Neenoilno *see* Montagnais-
Naskapi
Neepemut *see* Nipmuc
Neepercil *see* Nez Perce
Neepmuck *see* Nipmuc
Neepnet *see* Nipmuc
Ne-er-che-ki-oo *see* Neer-
chokioon
Neerchekioo *see* Cascades
Neerchekioo *see* Neerchokioon
Neerchokioo *see* Neerchokioon
Neerchokioon [OR] *Chinookan*
(H)
Neerchokioon [OR] *Shahala* (H)
Neerchokioon [OR] *Watlala* (BE)
Nees-lous *see* Neeslous
Neeslous [BC] *Tsimshian* (H)
Neetlakapakuch *see* Thompson
Indians
Nee-wam-ish *see* Dwamish
Neewamish *see* Dwamish
Negaouich *see* Negaouichirin-
iouek
Negaouichiriniouek [WI] (H)
Negarote *see* Nagarotu
Ne-ga-tce *see* Chippewa
Negatce *see* Chippewa
Ne-gatc-hi-jan *see* Chippewa
Negatchijan *see* Chippewa
Negrito [Lang] [MX] (Hdbk10)
Neguadoch *see* Natchitoches
Neguecaga Temigii *see* Negue-
cactemic
Neguecatemiji *see* Niguecactemic
Neguecogatemegi *see* Nigue-
cactemic
Neguicactemi *see* Niguecactemic
Nehadi [AL] *Tlingit* (H)
Nehalem [OR] *Tillamook* (LC)
Nehalim *see* Nehalem

Nehalin *see* Nehalem
Nehalta *see* Nahelta
Nehaltmoken [BC] *Salish* (H)
Nehane *see* Nahane
Nehanien *see* Nahane
Nehanne *see* Nahane
Nehannee *see* Nahane
Nehannes *see* Ahtena
Nehanni *see* Nahane
Nehantic *see* Niantic
Nehantick *see* Niantic
Neharontoq *see* Oneida
Nehaunay *see* Nahane
Nehaunce *see* Nehane
Nehaunee *see* Ahtena
Nehaunee *see* Nahane
Nehaunee *see* Tutchone
Nehaunees of the Chilkaht River
see Takutine
Ne-haw-re-tah-go *see* Oneida
Nehawretahgo *see* Oneida
Ne-haw-re-tah-go-wah *see*
Oneida
Nehawretahgowah *see* Oneida
Ne-haw-teh-tah-go *see* Oneida
Nehawtehtahgo *see* Oneida
Ne-heth-a-wa *see* Cree
Nehethawa *see* Cree
Nehethe-wuk *see* Cree
Nehethewuk *see* Cree
Nehethowuck *see* Cree
Nehethwa *see* Cree
Nehiyaw *see* Cree
Nehiyawok *see* Cree
Ne-h-ja-o *see* Nehajao
Nehjao [Clan] *Mahican* (H)
Nehlchikyokaiya *Wailaki* (Pub,
v.20, no.6, p.100)
Nehogatawonah [MN, WI]
Lakota (BE)
Nehogatawonaher *see* Nehogata-
wonah
Neholohawee (H)
Nehum-kek *see* Naumkeag
Nehumkek *see* Naumkeag
Neibaimao [HA, WInd] *Bainoa*
(BE)
Neibaymao *see* Neibaimao
Neighbor People *see* Keliopoma
Neihahat [TX] *Hasinai Confeder-
ation* (BE)
Ne-i-lem *see* Nehalem
Neilem *see* Nehalem
Neine Katlene *see* Ahtena
Neinekatlene *see* Ahtena
Neiosioke *see* Neusiok
Neipnett *see* Nipmuc
Neita *see* Neche
Neitchille *see* Netchilirmiut
Neitchillee *see* Netchilirmiut
Neitschillik *see* Netchilirmiut
Neitshillit-Eskimos *see*
Netchilirmiut

Neitteelik *see* Netchilirmiut
Ne-kah *see* Nikah
Nekah (PC) *see also* Nikah (H)
Nekah [Clan] *Chippewa* (H)
Nek-a'men *see* Nicomen
Nekamen *see* Nicomen
Nekaslay *see* Nikozliautin
Nekaslayan *see*Nikozliautin
Nekasly *see* Nikozliautin
Nekekowannock *see*
  Newichawanoc
Neketmeuk [WA] *Salish* (BE)
Neklakapamuk *see* Ntlakyapa-
  muk
Neklakussamuk *see* Ntlakyapa-
  muk
Nekoubaniste [Q] (H)
Nekuaix *see* Cathlanaquick
Ne-kum-ke-lis-la *see*
  Nakomgilisala
Nekumkelisla *see* Nakomgilisala
Neku'n stasta-i *see* Nekun-
  stustai
Nekunstastai *see* Nekun-stustai
Nekun-stustai [Sub-family]
  Haidu (H)
Nekwichoujik-kutchin *Loucheux*
  (IndN, v.2, no.3, July 1925,
  pp.172-177)
Nekwun Kiiwe *see* Naikun-
  kegawai
Nekwunkiiwe *see* Naikun-
  kegawai
Nelcelchumnee [CA] (H)
Nellagottine [Can] *Kawchottine*
  (BE)
Neloubanistes *see* Nekoubaniste
Ne-lus-te *see* Neluste
Neluste [Clan] *Cherokee* (H)
Nemaha *Sauk* (Hdbk15)
Ne'malnomax *see* Multnomah
Nemalnomax *see* Multnomah
Nemalquinner (BE) *see also*
  Clowwewalla (BE)
Nemalquinner [OR] *Multnomah*
  (BE)
Ne-mal-quin-ners *see* Ne-
  malquinner
Nemascut *see* Namasket
Nemasket *see* Namasket
Nemausin *see* Comanche
Ne-me-ne *see* Comanche
Neme ne *see* Comanche
Nemene *see* Comanche
Nemerexka *see* Tonakawan
Nemeroke [MA] *Pocomtuc* (BE)
Nemiseau *see* Comanche
Nemonsin *see* Comanche
Nemosen *see* Comanche
Ne-mo-sin *see* Comanche
Nemosin *see* Comanche
Nemousin *see* Comanche
Ne-moy *see* Nemoy

Nemoy [MT] *Snake* (H)
Nemqic *see* Nimkish
Nemqisch *see* Nimkish
Nemshan *see* Nimsewi
Nemshaw *see* Nimsewi
Nemshoos *see* Nimsewi
Nemshous *see* Nimsewi
Nemsu [Lang] *Penutian* (CA-8)
Nenachtach *see* Tenaktak
Nenawehk *see* Cree
Nenawewehk *see* Cree
Nena Wewhok *see* Cree
Nenawewhok *see* Cree
Ne'nelk-enox *see* Nenelkyenok
Nenelkenox *see* Nenelkyenok
Nenelkyenok [Clan] *Kwakiutl* (H)
Ne'nelpae *see* Nenelpae
Nenelpae [Clan] *Kwakiutl* (H)
Neneme'kewagi *see* Nana-
  makewuk
Nenemekewagi *see* Nana-
  makewuk
Ne ne not *see* Nascapee
Nenenot *see* Nascapee
Nenitagmiut [Can] *Central Eski-
  mos* (BE)
Nennequi [CA] (H)
Ne-nooth-lect *see* Nenoothlect
Nenoothlect [OR] *Chinookan* (H)
Nenpersaas *see* Nez Perce
Nentegowi *see* Nanticoke
Nentico *see* Nanticoke
Nenuswisowagi *see* Nanussus-
  souk
Ne-o-ge-he *see* Missouri
Neogehe *see* Missouri
Neojehe *see* Missouri
Neomai-taneo *see* Neomaitaneo
Neomaitaneo [CO] *Cheyenne* (H)
Neosho-Senecas *see* Mingo
Ne-o-ta-cha *see* Missouri
Neotacha *see* Missouri
Nepajan [MX] *Coahuiltecan*
  (Hdbk10)
Nepeelium *see* Nespelim
Nepercy *see* Nez Perce
Neperink *see* Nipissing
Ne persa *see* Iowa
Nepersa *see* Iowa
Nepesang *see* Nipissing
Nepesink *see* Nipissing
Nepessin *see* Nipissing
Nepgitoches *see* Natchitoches
Nephite (LC)
Nepicerini *see* Nipissing
Nepicinquis *see* Nipissing
Nepicirenian *see* Nipissing
Nepicirinien *see* Nipissing
Nepiscenicen *see* Nipissing
Nepiserinien *see* Nipissing
Nepisin *see* Nipissing
Nepisinguis *see* Nipissing
Nepisirini *see* Nipissing

Nepissen *see* Nipissing
Nepisseninien *see* Nipissing
Nepisserinien *see* Nipissing
Nepissing *see* Nipissing
Nepissingue *see* Nipissing
Nepissinien *see* Nipissing
Nepissirien *see* Nipissing
Nepissirinien *see* Nippising
Nepmet *see* Nipmuc
Nep mock *see* Nipmuc
Nepmock *see* Nipmuc
Nepnet *see* Nipmuc
Nepoyo *see* Mapoyo
Neragonsitt *see* Narraganset
Nerankamigdok *see* Abnaki
Neridgewalk *see* Norridgewock
Neridgewok *see* Norridgewock
Neridgiwack *see* Norridgewock
Neridgwock *see* Norridgewock
Neridgwook *see* Norridgewock
Nerigwok *see* Norridgewock
Nerm [Self-designation] *see* Co-
  manche
Ner-mon-sin-nan-see *see*
  Nawunena
Nermonsinnansee *see* Nawunena
Ner Percee *see* Nez Perce
Nerridgawock *see* Norridgewock
Nerridgewock *see* Norridgewock
Nesadi [Society] *Kake* (H)
Nesahuaca [PE] *Campa* (O)
Nesaquake [NY] *Montauk* (BE)
Nescope *see* Skopamish
Neselitch *see* Siletz
Neshamani *see* Neshamini
Neshamina *see* Neshamini
Ne-sham-i-ne *see* Neshamini
Neshamine *see* Neshamini
Neshamini [PA, DE] *Unalachtigo*
  (BE)
Neshaminies *see* Neshamini
Neshasath [Sept] [Can] *Nootka*
  (H)
Neshta [Subgens] *Ponca* (H)
Nesilextci'n *see* Sanpoil
Nesioke *see* Neusiok
Neskainlith [BC] *Shuswap* (H)
Neskaupe *see* Naskapi
Neskonlith Band [BC] *Shuswap*
  (Hdbk12)
Nesonee *see* Asahani
Nespectum *see* Nespelim
Nes-pee-lum *see* Nespelim
Nespeelum *see* Nespelim
Nespelem *see* Nespelim
Nespelim [WA] *Sanspoil* (LC)
Nes Perces *see* Nez Perces
Nespilim *see* Nespelim
Nespods *see* Chaicclesaht
Nesqualli *see* Nisqualli
Nesqually *see* Nisqualli
Nestackee *see* Nestucca
Nestockies *see* Nestucca

Nestucalips *see* Nestucca
Nestucals *see* Nestucca
Nestucca [OR] *Tillamook* (BE)
Nestucka *see* Nestucca
Nestuckah *see* Nestucca
Nestuckers *see* Nestucca
Nestuckia *see* Nestucca
Ne-ta-ka-ski-tsi-pup-ik *see* Ni-takoskitsipupiks
Netakaskitsipupik *see* Ni-takoskitsipupiks
Netcetumiut [Can] *Labrador Eskimos* (BE)
Netches *see* Natchez
Netchilirmiut (H) *see also* Netsilik (Hdbk5)
Netchilirmiut [Can] *Central Eskimos* (H)
Netchilli *see* Netsilik
Netchillik *see* Netchilirmiut
Netchillirmiut *see* Netchilirmiut
Netcimu'asath *see* Nechimuasath
Netela *see* Juaneño
Netidli'wi *see* Netchilirmiut
Netion Neuht *see* Neutral Nation
Netschilluk Innuit *see* Netchilirmiut
Netsepoye *see* Siksika
Netsilik [AK] *Central Eskimos* (Hdbk5)
Netsilik [Lang] *[Inuit-Inupiaq]* (Hdbk5)
Netsilingmiut (BE) *see also* Netsilik (Hdbk5)
Netsilingmiut [Can] *Central Eskimos* (BE)
Netsilley *see* Ettchaottine
Net-tee-lek *see* Netchilirmiut
Netteelek *see* Netchilirmiut
Nettinat *see* Nitinat
Neu-chad-lits *see* Nuchatlitz
Neuchadlits *see* Nuchatlitz
Neuchalits *see* Nuchatlitz
Neuchallet *see* Nuchatlitz
Ne-u-cha-ta *see* Missouri
Neuchata *see* Missouri
Neuk-sach *see* Nootsack
Neuksack *see* Nooksack
Neuk-sak *see* Nooksack
Neuk-wers *see* Nuchwugh
Neukwers *see* Nuchwugh
Ne-u-lub-vig *see* Neutubvig
Neulubvig *see* Neutubvig
Neum *see* Comanche
Ne-uma *see* Comanche
Neuma *see* Comanche
Ne-ume *see* Comanche
Neume *see* Comanche
Neumkeage *see* Naumkeag
Neuse *see* Neusiok
Neuses *see* Neusiok
Neus Indians *see* Neusiok

Neusiok [NC] (BE)
Ne-u-tach *see* Missouri
Neutach *see* Missouri
Neu-ta-che *see* Missouri
Neu-tache *see* Missouri
Neutache *see* Missouri
Neuter Nation *see* Neutral Nation
Neutral Nation [NY] (LC)
Neutre Nation *see* Neutral Nation
Neutrios *see* Neutral Nation
Ne-u-tub-vig *see* Neutubvig
Neutubvig [WA] (H)
Neuusiooc *see* Neusiok
Neuwesink *see* Navasink
Nevacho *see* Nabedache
Nevada City [Lang] [CA] (CA-8)
Nevada Northern Paiute *Northern Paiute* (Hdbk11)
Nevadizo *see* Nabedache
Nevajoes *see* Navajo
Neversinck *see* Navasink
Neversingh *see* Navasink
Neversink *see* Navasink
Nevesin *see* Navasink
Neve-Sinck *see* Navasink
Nevesinck *see* Navasink
Nevesing *see* Navasink
Nevesink *see* Navasink
Nevichumnes *see* Newichumni
Nevisan *see* Navasink
Nevoma *see* Pima Bajo
Nevome [Lang] *Upper Piman* (LC)
Nevuqaq *see* Naukanski
Newashe *see* Nawaas
Newasiwac *see* Neusiok
Newasol pakawai *see* Pakawa
Newason *see* Navasink
Ne Was tar ton *see* Newastarton
Newastarton [MN] *Mdewakanton* (BE)
Newatchumne *see* Newichumni
Newcalenous *see* Wea
Newcastle Toronsite *see* Newcastle Townsite
Newcastle Townsite [BC] *Salish* (H)
Newchawanick *see* Newichawanoc
Newchemass [Can] (H)
New-chow-we *see* Nuchawayi
Newchowwe *see* Nuchawayi
New-dar-cha *see* Missouri
Newdarcha *see* Missouri
Newesingh *see* Navasink
Newesink *see* Navasink
Newgeawanacke *see* Newichawanoc
Newgewanacke *see* Newichawanoc
New Gummi Lurk *see* Nugumiut

Newichawanick *see* Newichawanoc
Newichawannicke *see* Newichawanoc
Newichawanoc [ME, NH] *Pennacook* (BE)
Newichawanock *see* Newichawanoc
Newichewannock *see* Newichawanoc
Newichumni [CA] *Miwok* (H)
Newichuwenoq *see* Newichawanoc
Newichwanicke *see* Newichawanoc
Newichwannock *see* Newichawanoc
Newickawanack *see* Newichawanac
Newithimomowi *Guahibo* (O)
New Netherland (AI)
Newoo'-ah *see* Kawaiisu
Newooah *see* Kawaiisu
New Oraibi *see* Kyakotsmovi
New River [Lang] *Shastan* (CA-8)
New River Indians (BE) *see also* Kamia (LC)
New River Indians (H) *see also* Comeya (H)
New River Indians [CA] *Shasta* (H)
New River Shasta Indians (H) *see also* Chimalakwe (H)
New River Shastan [Lang] [CA] *Shastan* (He)
New Sevilla *see* Sevilleta
Nexadi *see* Nehadi
Nextuca *see* Nestucca
Neyantick *see* Niantic
Neyetse-kutchi *see* Natsitkutchin
Neyetsekutchi *see* Natsitkutchin
Neyetse-Kutchin *see* Natsitkutchin
Neyetsekutchin *see* Natsitkutchin
Neyetse-Kutshi *see* Natsitkutchin
Neyetsekutshi *see* Natsitkutchin
Neyick *see* Canarsee
Ne-yu-ta-ca *see* Missouri
Neyutaca *see* Missouri
Ne-yutka *see* Oneida
Ne'yutkanonu'ndshunda *see* Oneida
Nezierce *see* Nez Perce
Nez Perce (H) *see also* Chinook (LC)
Nez Perce [OR, ID] (LC)
Nez Perce Flatheads *see* Nez Perce
Nez Perce Kayuse *see* Cayuse
Nez-Perces (H) *see also* Amikwa (LC)

Nez Perce's *see* Nez Perce
Nezperces *see* Nez Perce
Nez Percez (H) *see also* Amikwa (LC)
Nez Percez *see* Nez Perce
Nezpercies *see* Nez Perce
Nezperee *see* Nez Perce
Nez Perse *see* Nez Perce
Nez Pierces *see* Nez Perce
Nez-quale *see* Nisqualli
Nez qually *see* Nisqualli
Nezqually *see* Nisqually
Neztrucca *see* Nestucca
Nez Tucca *see* Nestucca
Neztucca *see* Nestucca
Ngobe *see* Guaymi
Ngoberre *see* Guaymi
Nhambicuara *see* Nambicuara
Nhandeva [Br] (O)
Nheengatu (O) *see also* Geral (O)
Nheengatu [Col, BR] (O)
Nhikana *see* Mahican
N-hla-kapm-uh *see* Ntlakyapamuk
Nhlakapmuh *see* Ntlakyapamuk
Niabaha *see* Kiabaha
Niacomala *see* Macomala
Niagagarega *see* Neutral Nation
Niantaquit *see* Niantic
Niantecutt *see* Niantic
Niantic [MA] (LC)
Niantick *see* Niantic
Nianticut *see* Niantic
Niantig *see* Niantic
Niantique *see* Niantic
Niantuck *see* Niantic
Niantucut *see* Niantic
Nia'rhari's-kurikiwa'ahuski *see* Arapaho
Niarhariskurikiwaahuski *see* Arapaho
Nia-rhari's-kurikiwa-shuski *see* Arapaho
Niarhariskurikiwashuski *see* Arapaho
Nibenet *see* Nipmuc
Nibissirinien *see* Nipissing
Nibowi-sibi-wininiwak *see* Nibowisibiwininiwak
Nibowisibiwininiwak [Ont] *Chippewa* (H)
Nicarao [MX, NI] (LC)
Nicassias [CA] *Moquelumnan* (H)
Nichigmut *see* Nuchig'mut
Ni-chihine'na *see* Kiowa
Nichihinena *see* Kiowa
Nichikun [Can] [*Montagnais-Naskapi*] (BE)
Nichora *see* Nifora
Nichoras *see* Nixora
Nichoras *see* Yavapai
Niciat [BC] *Upper Lillooet* (H)
Niciatl *see* Seechelt

Ni'ciatl *see* Seechelt
Ni'ckite hitclum *see* Dakubetede
Nickitehitclum *see* Dakubetede
Nickomin [WA] *Chehalis* (H)
Nicoamen *see* Nicomen
Nicohe *see* Doosedoowe
Nicola [BC] *Upper Ntlakyapamuk* (H)
Nicola [BC] *Upper Thompson* (H)
Nicola [Can] *Ntlakyapamuk* (BE)
Nicolas, San [Lang] [CA] (Hdbk10)
Nicolena [CA] (LC)
Nicoleño, San [CA] (Ye)
Nicomen [Can] *Stalo* (BE)
Nicondiche *see* Nacaniche
Nicoutameen *see* Ntlakyapamuk
Nicoutamuch *see* Ntlakyapamuk
Nicoya [CR] *Orotina* (BE)
Nicpapa *see* Hunkpapa
Nicudje *see* Missouri
Niculuite *see* Wishram
Nicute-much *see* Ntalakyapamuk
Nicutemuch *see* Ntalakyapamuk
Ni'ekeni *see* Bear River Indians
Niekeni *see* Bear River Indians
Nien'tken *see* Brotherton
Niere'rikwats-kuni'ki *see* Cheyenne
Nieskakh-itina *see* Unalaska
Nieusinck *see* Navasink
Nieuwesinck *see* Navasink
Nifora (H) *see also* Nixora (H)
Nifora (Hdbk10)
Nifora (Hdbk10) *see also* Yabipai (Hdbk10)
Niforas *see* Yavapai
Nifore *see* Nixora
Nifores *see* Yavapai
Nigco [TX] *Coahuiltecan* (BE)
Nige-tanka *see* Nighetanka
Nigetanka *see* Nighetanka
Nighetanka *Miniconjou* (H)
Night Cloud [SD] *Oglala* (H)
Night-hawks [MN] *Atsina* (BE)
Nigik *see* Nikikouek
Nigora *see* Nixora
Ni-gottine *see* Nigottine
Nigottine [Can] *Kawchottine* (BE)
Nigouaouichirinik *see* Neyauouichiriniouek
Niguecactemic [Br] *Tereno* (O)
Niguecactemic [Par] *Chana* (O)
Niguicactemia *see* Niguecactemic
Nihaloitih *see* Tlakliut
Nihaloitih *see* Wishram
Nihaloth [Lang] *Chinookan* (Bull15)
Nihamwo [Self-designation] *see* Yagua
Nihantick *see* Niantic
Nih-a-o-cih-a-is *see* Oahenonpa

Nihaocihais *see* Oahenonpa
Niharuntagoa *see* Oneida
Niharuntaquoa *see* Oneida
Nihatiloendagowa *see* Oneida
Ni-he-ta-te-tup-i-o *see* Kalispel
Nihetatetupio *see* Kalispel
Nih'ka wakan'taki *see* Kdhun
Nihkawakantaki *see* Kdhun
Nihorontagowa *see* Oneida
Nihouhin *see* Atka
Niigugis [AK] (Hdbk5)
Nijoas *see* Nacao
Nijor *see* Nixora
Nijor *see* Yavapai
Nijora *see* Nixora
Nijora *see* Nifora
Nijoras *see* Yavapai
Nijore *see* Nixora
Nijores *see* Yavapai
Nijote *see* Nifora
Nijotes *see* Yavapai
Ni'ka *see* Nekah
Nika *see* Nestucca
Nika *see* Nekah
Nikaa *see* Nestucca
Nika-da-ona *see* Nikapashna
Nikadaona *see* Nikapashna
Nikapashna (H) *see also* Nakapozna (H)
Nikapashna [Clan] *Ponca* (H)
Nikhu-khinin [CA] [*Unung'un*] (Contri, v.1, p.22)
Nikhu-khnin (H) *see also* Atka (BE)
Nikiata [Clan] *Quapaw* (H)
Nikic *see* Noquet
Nikicouek *see* Nikikouek
Nikikouek *Ojibwa* (H)
Nikikoues *see* Nikikouek
Nikikoüet *see* Nikouek
Nikoaliantin *see* Nikozliautin
Nikozliautin [Can] *Northern Carrier* (BE)
Nikozliautin [Clan] [BC] *Takulli* (H)
Ni kuta muk *see* Thompson Indians
Nikutamuk *see* Thompson Indians
Nikutemikh (Hdbk15) *see also* Thompson Indians (Hdbk15)
Nikutemukh [Lang] *Salishan* (Contri, v.1, p.248)
Nilsumack [BC] *Salish* (H)
Nim (H) *see also* North Fork Mono (Pub, v.11, no.5, p.293)
Nim [CA] [*Mono-Paviotso*] (H)
Nimaca [HA, WInd] *Guacca-iarima* (BE)
ni-maha-haki *see* Sauk
Nimapu *see* Nez Perce
Nimenim *see* Comanche
Nimeteka *see* Tonkawa

nimi [Self-designation] *see* Northern Paiute

nimi [Self-designation] *see* Owens Valley Paiute

nimi [Self-designation] *see* Shoshone

nimi [Self-designation] *see* Bannock

Ni-mi-ou-sin *see* Comanche

Nimiousin *see* Comanche

ni-mi-pu [Self-designation] *see* Nez Perce

Nimipu [Self-designation] *see* Nez Perce

Nim-keesh *see* Nimkish

Nimkeesh *see* Nimkish

Nimkis *see* Nimkish

Nim-kish *see* Nimkish

Nimkish [Can] *Kwakiutl* (BE)

Nimpkish *see* Nimkish

Nim Sewi *see* Nimsewi

Nimsewi [CA] *Maidu* (H)

Nim-shu *see* Nimsewi

Nimshu *see* Nimsewi

Nim-sirs *see* Nimsewi

Nimsirs *see* Nimsewi

Nimskew *see* Nimsewi

Nim-sus *see* Nimsewi

Nimsus *see* Nimsewi

Ninam *see* Yanoama

Ninatic *see* Niantic

Ninchopan [Clan] *Tonkawa* (H)

Nindahe (H) *see also* Tidendaye (H)

Nindahe *Central Chiricahua Apache* (Hdbk10)

Ninibatan [Subclan] *Omaha* (H)

Ninkannichkaiya *Wailaki* (Pub, v.20, no.6, pp.99–100)

Ninneway *see* Illinois

Ninnipaskulgee [AL] *Upper Creek* (H)

Ninniwa *see* Chippewa

Ninny-pask-ulgee *see* Ninnipaskulgee

Ninnypaskulgee *see* Ninnipaskulgee

ninsHye *Koskimo* (Anthro, v.9, no.3, p.158)

Ninstints People *see* Gunghethaidagai

Nintchopan *see* Ninchopan

Nintropan *see* Ninchopan

Nio [MX] (BE)

Niojara *see* Nixora

Niondago'a *see* Oneida

Niopwatuk [Can] *Paskwawininiwug* (BE)

nipakanticimi *see* Las Vegas

Nipan *see* Lipan Apache

Nipegon *see* Winnebago

Nipecerinien *see* Nipissing

Nipercinean *see* Nipissing

Nipicirinien *see* Nipissing

Nipisierinij *see* Nipissing

Nipising *see* Nipissing

Nipisingue *see* Nippissing

Nipisink *see* Nippising

Nipisirinien *see* Nipissing

Nipissa *see* Acolapissa

Nipissin *see* Nipissing

Nipissing [Ont] (LC)

Nipissingue *see* Nipissing

Nipissirinien *see* Nipissing

Nipissirinioek *see* Nipissing

Nipistingue *see* Nipissing

Nipmoog *see* Nipmuc

Nipmuc [MA] (LC)

Nipmuck *see* Nipmuc

Nipmug *see* Nipmuc

Nipmuk *see* Nipmuc

Nipnet *see* Nipmuc

Nipnett *see* Nipmuc

Nippsingue *see* Nipissing

Nipsang *see* Nipissing

Niquiranos *see* Nicarao

Niquiras *see* Nicarao

Niquisan *see* Nicarao

Ni-ris-hari's-ki'riki *see* Kadohadacho

Ni'ris-hari'ski'riki *see* Kadohadacho

Nirishariskiriki *see* Kadohadacho

Nisak (H)

Nisal [WA] *Chinook* (H)

Niscotin *see* Naskotin

Nisenan [CA] *Maidu* (LC)

Nishamines *see* Neshamini

Nishga *see* Niska

Nishgar *see* Niska

Nishidawa *see* Nishinahua

Nishinahua (O) *see also* Morunahua (O)

Nishinahua [SA] *Jaminaua* (O)

Nishinam (BE) *see also* Nisenan (LC)

Ni-Shi-Nam *see* Nishinam

Nishinam [CA] *Southern Maidu* (BE)

Nishka *see* Niska

Nishmumta *see* Tsimshian

Nishram *see* Tlakliut

Nishram *see* Wishram

Nisibourounik *Cree* (H)

Nisigas Haade *see* Nasagashaidagai

Nisione *see* Nasoni

Nisk-a *see* Niska

Niska [BC] (LC)

Niskah *see* Niska

Nis-kah *see* Niska

Nis-se-non *see* Nishinam

Niskap (H) *see also* Skopamish (BE)

Niskap [WA] (H)

Niskwali *see* Nisqualli

Niskwalli *see* Nisqualli

Nisquali *see* Nisqualli

Nisqualies *see* Nisqualli

Nisqualli [WA] (LC)

Nisqually *see* Nisqualli

Nissenon *see* Nishinam

Nissohone *see* Nasoni

Nisson *see* Nasoni

Nissone *see* Nasoni

Nistoki Ampafa amim *see* Newtucca

Nitahende *see* Ni't'ahende

Ni't'ahende *Mescalero Apache* (Hdbk10)

Nitajende *see* Ni't'ahende

Nitakoskitsipupiks [MN] *Piegan* (BE)

Nit-ak-so-kit-si-pup-ik *see* Nitakoskitsipupiks

Nitawalik [BC] *Chimmesyan* (H)

Ni-taw-yik *see* Nitawyiks

Nitawyiks [MN] *Piegan* (BE)

Nitchequon [Can] *Naskapi* (H)

Nitches *see* Natchez

Nitchihi *see* Kiowa

Nitchik *see* Nitchequon

Nitchik Irionetz *see* Nitchequon

Nitchik Ironionetch *see* Nitchequon

Niten aht *see* Nitinat

Nitenaht *see* Nitinat

Ni-the-wuk *see* Cree

Nithewuk *see* Cree

Nit-ik-skik *see* Nitikskiks

Nitikskiks [MN, Can] (BE)

Nitinaht *see* Nitinat

Nitinat [VanI] *Nootka* (BE)

Ni'tinath *see* Nitinat

Nitinath *see* Nitinat

Nitlakapamuk *see* Ntlakyapamuk

Ni-tot-si-ksis-stan-ik *see* Nitotsiksisstaniks

Nitotsiksisstaniks [NM] *Piegan* (BE)

Nittanet *see* Nitinat

Nittaweega *see* Nottaway

Nitten-aht *see* Nitinat

Nittenaht *see* Nitinat

Nittenat *see* Nitinat

Nittinaht *see* Nitinat

Nittinat *see* Nitinat

Nitutinni *see* Nataotin

nitxktayu *see* Cascades

Ni-uam *see* Comanche

Niuam *see* Comanche

Ni-ue-Uom O-kai *see* Niueuomokai

Niueuomokai [Clan] *Pima* (H)

Niukonska *see* Osage

Ni-U-Ko'n-Ska *see* Osage

Niuna *see* Comanche

Niunda-ko'wa *see* Oneida

Niutachi [Self-designation] *see* Missouri

Ni-u-t'a-tci *see* Missouri

Niutatci *see* Missouri

Ni-ut'ati *see* Missouri

Niutati *see* Missouri

Nivacle *see* Ashluslay

Nivakle *see* Ashluslay

Ni'wace *see* Tsishuwashtake

Niwace *see* Tsishuwashtake

Ni-wan-ci-ke *see* Niwanshike

Niwancike *see* Niwanshike

Niwanshike [Clan] *Iowa* (H)

niwi *see* Kawaiisu

niwi [Self-designation] *see* Shoshone

niwini *see* Shoshone

niwiwi *see* Kawaiisu

Nixamvo *see* Yagua

Nixe-tanka *see* Nighetanka

Nixetanka *see* Nighetanka

Nixinahua [Lang] *Panoan* (O)

Nixora (H)

Nixora (Hdbk10) *see also* Nifora (Hdbk10)

Nixoras *see* Yavapai

Nixotas *see* Yavapai

Niyalhosu [Br] *Southern Nambicuara* (O)

Nizorae *see* Nixora

Njith *see* Tukkuthkutchin

Nkamaplix [Can] *Okinagan* (H)

N-Kamip *see* Nkamip

Nkamip [Can] *Okinagan* (BE)

Nkamtci'nemux *see* Spences Bridge

Nkee'us [WA] [*Sinkiuse-Columbia*] (Oregon)

Nko'atamux *see* Ntlakyapamuk

Nkoatamux *see* Ntlakyapamuk

Nktusem *see* Dakota

Nku'kumamux *see* Upper Thompson

Nkukumamux *see* Upper Thompson

Nkuo-osai *see* Nkuoosai

Nkuoosai [Clan] [BC] *Squawmish* (H)

Nkuo-ukten *see* Nkuoukten

Nkuoukten [Gens] *Squawmish* (H)

N-ku-tam-euh *see* Ntlakyapamuk

Nkutameuh *see* Ntlakyapamuk

Nkutemixu *see* Ntlakyapamuk

Nlak-a'pamux *see* Ntlakyapamuk

Nlakapamux *see* Ntalkyapamuk

Nl'du'ne *see* Navajo

Nldune *see* Navajo

N-ma *see* Nma

Nma [Clan] *Potawatomi* (H)

N-ma-pe-na *see* Nmapena

Nmapena [Clan] *Potawatomi* (H)

Nnea-gottine *see* Nigottine

Nne-la-gottine *see* Nellagottine

Nnelagottine *see* Nellagottine

Nne-lla-Gottine *see* Nellagottine

Nnellagottine *see* Nellagottine

Nni-Gottine *see* Nigottine

Nnigottine *see* Nigottine

Nni-ottine *see* Nigottine

Nniottine *see* Nigottine

Noaches *see* Mariposa

Noachi *see* Nasoni

Noadiches *see* Nabedache

No-ah-ha *see* Towahhah

Noahha *see* Towahhah

Noahonirmiut [Can] *Central Eskimos* (BE)

Noalingo [MX] (BE)

Noam-kekhl *see* Yuki

Noamkekhl *see* Yuki

Noam-kult *see* Yuki

Noamkult *see* Yuki

Noamlaki *see* Nomlaki

Noanama [Lang] *see* Waunana

Noanama Indians *see* Choco

Noaname *see* Nonuya

Noanawa *see* Nonuya

Noan-kakhi *see* Saia

Noankakhi *see* Saia

Noapeeming *see* Nopeming

Noatagamute *see* Nunatogmiut

Noatagmiut (Hdbk5) *see also* Nuataagmiut (Hdbk5)

Noatagmiut *North Alaska Coast Eskimos* (BE)

Noatches *see* Natchez

Nobows *see* Sans Arcs

Noca *see* Notha

Nocacine *see* Notha

Nocaman [Lang] *Panoan* (O)

Nocantick *see* Niantic

Nocao *see* Nacao

Noces *see* Yana [CA]

Noche *see* Yokuts

Noche *see* Mariposa

Noches Colteches *see* Kawaiisu

Nochi *see* Mariposa

Noch-Peem *see* Nochpeem

Nochpeem *Delaware* (Hdbk15)

Nochpeem [NY] *Wappinger* (LC)

Nochways *see* Eskimos

Nocké *see* Noquet

Nocodoch *see* Nacogdoches

No-co-me *see* Detsanayuka

Nocome *see* Detsanayuka

Noconee *see* Detsanayuka

Noconi *see* Detsanayuka

No-coo-nee *see* Detsanayuka

Nocoonee *see* Detsanayuka

Nocotchtanke *see* Nachotchtank

Noctene *see* Mataco

Noddouwessces *see* Dakota

Nodehs *see* Navajo

Nod-o-waig *see* Iroquois

Nodowaig *see* Iroquois

Nodoways *see* Iroquois

Nod-o-way-se-wug *see* Dakota

Nodowaysewug *see* Dakota

Nodoweisa *see* Dakota

Nodowessies *see* Dakota

Nodswaig *see* Iroquois

Nodways *see* Eskimos

Noenama *see* Waunana

No-ga-ie *see* Nogaie

Nogaie [NV] *Paviotso* (H)

Noguet *see* Noquet

No-gwats *see* Nogwats

No-gwats *see* Las Vegas

Nogwats (PC) *see also* Las Vegas (Hdbk11)

Nogwats [NV] *Paiute* (H)

Nohannaies *see* Nahane

Nohanni *see* Nahane

Nohannies *see* Nahane

Nohar-taney *see* Mandan

Nohartaney *see* Mandan

Noh-ga *see* Makan

Nohga (PC) *see also* Makan (H)

Nohga [Clan] *Ponca* (H)

Noh'ha-i-e *see* Etagottine

Nohhaie *see* Etagottine

Nohhana *see* Nahane

Nohhannies *see* Nahane

Noh-tin-oah *see* Hupa

Nohtinoah *see* Hupa

Nohtooksaet [MA] *Wampanoag* (BE)

Nohuntsitk [Can] *Bellabella* (BE)

Nohuntsitk [Lang] *Wakashan* (H)

Noi Muck *see* Nuimok

Noimuck *see* Nuimok

Noire *see* Les Noire Indians

Noi-Sas *see* Yana [CA]

Noisas *see* Yana [CA]

Noisy Pawnee *see* Pitahauerat

Noi-Yucan *see* Noyuki

Noiyucan *see* Noyuki

Noka [Clan] *Chippewa* (H)

No-kaig *see* Noka

Nokaig *see* Noka

No'ke *see* Noka

Nok'e *see* Noka

Noke *see* Noquet

Noke *see* Noka

Noket *see* Noquet

Noketrota [CA] (H)

Nokoni *see* Detsanayuka

No-ko-ni *see* Detsanayuka

No'koni *see* Detsanayuka

Nokonmi *see* Pomo

Nokosalgi [Clan] *Creek* (H)

Nokumktesilla *see* Nakomgilisala

No-kuse *see* Nokosalgi

Nokuse *see* Nokosalgi

Nol-cha *see* Nolcha

Nolcha [Clan] *Mohave* (H)

Nolongewock *see* Norridgewock

Noltanana *see* Naltunnetunne
Noltnachnah *see* Naltunnetunne
Nolt-nat-nah *see* Naltunnetunne
Noltonatria *see* Naltunnetunne
Nomakokun sepeo tusininitug *see* Noma'kokun Se'peo Tusi'niniwug
Noma'kokun Se'peo Tusi'niniwug [WI] *Menominee* (BE)
Nomas (H)
Nomatsiguenga [PE] *Campa* (LC)
Nome'e *see* Nambe
Nomee Cults *see* Yuki
Nomee Lack *see* Nomlaki
Nome Lackee *see* Nomlaki
Nomelackee *see* Nomlaki
Nomenuches *see* Weeminuche
Nominies *see* Onawmanient
Nomlaka [Lang] [CA] *River Nomlaki* (CA-8)
Nomlaki [CA] (LC)
Nommuk *see* Nummuk
Nomoqois (H)
Nomsu's *see* Nomsus
Nomsus [CA] *Wintu* (BE)
Nomtipom (CA-8)
Nonama *see* Waunana
Nonapho [TX] *Coahuiltecan* (BE)
Nonatum *see* Massachuset
No-na-um *see* Nauniem
Nonaum *see* Nauniem
Noncottecoe *see* Nansatico
Nondacao *see* Anadarko
Nondaco *see* Anadarko
Nondage *see* Onondaga
Nondaque *see* Anadarko
Nongatl [CA] (CA)
Nongatl [Lang] [CA] *Wailaki* (He)
Nonharmin [Subclan] *Delaware* (H)
Non-hde-i-ta-zhi *see* Nonhdetazhi
Nonhdeitazhi [Subgens] *Omaha* (H)
Nonotuc [MA] *Pocomtuc* (BE)
Nonsowhaticond *see* Nansatico
Nontagues *see* Onondaga
Nontaguez *see* Onondaga
Nonto-wa-ka *see* Seneca
Nontowaka *see* Seneca
Nonuya [Col, PE] *Bora* (O)
Nooachhummilh [WA] *Chehalis I* (H)
Nooatok *see* Nunatogmiut
Nooatoka Mute *see* Nunatogmiut
Noobimuck *see* Normuk
Noochahlaht *see* Nuchatlitz
Nooch-aht-aht *see* Nuchatlitz
Noochahtaht *see* Nuchatlitz
Nooch-ahtl-aht *see* Nuchatlitz
Noochahtlaht *see* Nuchatlitz
Nooch-alh-laht *see* Nuchatlitz

Noochalhlaht *see* Nuchatlitz
Noochartl-aht *see* Nuchatlitz
Noochatl-aht *see* Nuchatlitz
No-ochi *see* Ute
No-o-chi *see* Ute
Noochi *see* Ute
No-o-chi-uh *see* Ute
Noochiuh *see* Ute
Nooda'i *see* Ute
Nooghe [Clan] *Ponca* (H)
Nooh-lum-mi *see* Lummi
Noohlummi *see* Lummi
Noohooultch [WA] *Chehalis* (H)
Nookachamos [WA] *Skagit* (Oregon)
Nookachamps [WA] *Skagit* (BE)
Nookalit [Can] *Yuit Eskimos* (BE)
Nookalthu [WA] *Chehalis I* (H)
Nook-choo *see* Nukchu
Nookchoo *see* Nukchu
Nooklulumic *see* Lummi
Nooklulumu *see* Lummi
Nooklummie *see* Lummi
Nooknachamish *see* Nukwatsamish
Nook-saak *see* Nooksack
Nooksaak *see* Nooksack
Nook-sac *see* Nooksack
Nooksac *see* Nooksack
Nooksach *see* Nooksack
Nooksack [WA] (LC)
Nook-sahk *see* Nooksack
Nooksahk *see* Nooksack
Nooksak *see* Nooksack
Nookuolamic *see* Lummi
Noolamarlarmo [Subclan] *Delaware* (H)
Nool-a-mar-mo *see* Noolamarlarmo
Nool-ke-o-tin *see* Nulaautin
Noolkeotin *see* Nulaautin
Noo-na-cham-ish *see* Nukwatsamish
Noonah *see* Kwahari
No-onch *see* Ute
Noonch *see* Ute
Noonitagmioot *see* Nunatogmiut
Nooscope *see* Niskap
Nooscope *see* Skopamish
Noosdalum *see* Clallam
Noo-seh-chatl *see* Nusehtsatl
Noosehchatl *see* Nusehtsatl
Nooselalum *see* Clallam
Noosiatsks [WA] *Chehalis I* (H)
Nooskoh [WA] *Chehalis I* (H)
Noo-ta *see* Noota
Noota *Crow* (H)
Noo-taa *see* Noota
Nootaa *see* Noota
Nootanana *see* Naltunnetunne
Nootapareescar *see* Noota
Noothlakamish [Can] *Bella Coola* (BE)

Noot-hum *see* Lummi
Noothum *see* Lummi
Noot-hum-mic *see* Lummi
Noothummic *see* Lummi
Nootka [BC, WA] (LC)
Nootka-Columbian *see* Nootka
Nootsaak *see* Nooksack
Nootsak *see* Nooksack
Noo-wha-ha *see* Towahhah
Noowoo Mute *see* Nuwukmiut
Noowoomute *see* Nuwukmiut
Noowootsoo *see* Seamysty
No Parfleche *see* Kutaisotsiman
Nopchinchi (CA-8) *see also* Nupchinche (BE)
Nopchinchi [Lang] [CA] *Yokutsan* (CA-8)
Nope *see* Martha's Vineyard
Nopemen d'Achirini *see* Nopeming
Nopemetus Aineeg *see* Nopeming
Nopeming [Ont] *Chippewa* (H)
Nopemin of Archirini *see* Nopeming
Nopemit Azhinneneeg *see* Nopeming
Nopiming daje inini *see* Nopeming
Nopimingdajeinini *see* Nopeming
No'pimingtashineniwag *see* Nopeming
Nopimingtashineniwag *see* Nopeming
Nopnat *see* Nipmuc
Nopochinches *see* Nopthrinthres
Nopthrinthres [CA] *Yokuts* (H)
Noptinte *see* Nupchinche
Noquai *see* Noquet
Noquet [WI, MI] *Southwestern Ojibwa* (BE)
No-qui-quahko *see* Noquiquahko
No-si *see* Yana [CA]
Noquiquahko [BC] *Salish* (H)
Norague *see* Nixora
Norbos *Copehan* (H)
Norboss *see* Norbos
Nordgawock *see* Norridgewock
Nord ouests *see* Dakota
Nordouests *see* Dakota
Norelmuk [CA] *Wintu* (CA)
Noreo [MX] *Coahuiltecan* (Hdbk10)
Nor-har-min *see* Nonharmin
Norharmin *see* Nonharmin
Noridgewalk *see* Norridgewock
Noridgewoc *see* Norridgewock
Noridgewock *see* Norridgewock
Noridgwoag *see* Norridgewock
Noridgwock *see* Norridgewock
Normoc *see* Normuk

Nor-mok *see* Normuk
Normok *see* Normuk
Normuk [CA] *Wintun* (H)
Norragansett *see* Narraganset
Norredgewock *see* Norridgewock
Nor-rel-mok *see* Normuk
Norrelmok *see* Normuk
Norridegwock *see* Norridgewock
Norridgawock *see* Norridgewock
Norridgewalk *see* Norridgewock
Norridgewock [ME] *Abnaki*
    (LC)
Norridgowock *see* Norridgewock
Norridgwak *see* Norridgewok
Norridgwalk *see* Norridgewock
Norridgwock *see* Norridgewock
Norridgwog *see* Norridgewock
Norridgwogg *see* Norridgewock
Norrigawake *see* Norridgewock
Norrigewack *see* Norridgewock
Norrigewock *see* Norridgewock
Norrigwock *see* Norridgewock
Norrijwok *see* Norridgewock
Norriwook *see* Norridgewock
Norrywok *see* Norridgewock
Norteño (O) *see also* Northern
    Guaymi (O)
Norteño [Pan, CR] *Terraba* (O)
Norteños (BE) *see also* Pira
    [Pueblo] (LC)
Nortenyo *see* Guaymi
North Alaska Coast Eskimos
    (Hdbk5)
North Blackfeet *Siksika* (H)
North Canyon Band [BC] *Canyon
    Shuswap* (Hdbk12)
North Carolina Algonquians
    (Hdbk15)
North Dale Indians *see* Klikitat
Northeastern Choctaw (His/T,
    v.1, p.71)
Northeastern Columbia-Venezuela
    Border [Lang] *Yukpa* (UAz,
    v.28)
Northeastern Maidu [CA] (BE)
Northeastern Pomo [Lang] [CA]
    (Pub, v.6, no.3, pp.237–245)
Northeastern Sierra *see* Amador
Northeastern Yavapai [AZ] *Yava-
    pai* (Pub, v.29, no.3)
Northeast Sahaptin [WA] *Sahap-
    tin* (Hdbk12)
Northern Apaches *see* Jicarillo
    Apache
Northern Arapaho (BE) *see also*
    Nakasinena (H)
Northern Arapaho [WY] (BE)
Northern Assiniboin (H)
Northern Athapaskan [Lang]
    [AK] (BE)
Northern Barasana *see* Bara
Northern Brazilian Outliers
    [Lang] *Txicao* (UAz, v.28)

Northern Brule *see* Khey-
    atawichasha
Northern Carib [Lang] (UAz,
    v.28)
Northern Carrier [Can] (BE)
Northern Cayapo (O)
Northern Cheyenne [Fort
    Laramie Treaty, Sep.17, 1851]
    (BE)
Northern Choco [Col] (O)
Northern Chorote [Arg] (O)
Northern Coast *see* Lake Miwok
    [Lang]
Northern Comanche (H)
Northern Costonoan [Lang]
    Penutian (CA-8)
Northern Cree *see* Sakawithini-
    wuk
Northern Death Valley *Western
    Shoshone* (Hdbk11)
Northern Denes *Tinne* (H)
Northern Diegueño [CA, MX]
    (BE)
Northern Diegueño [Lang]
    Yuman (He)
Northern Embera [Lang] *see*
    Catio [Lang]
Northern Epera [Lang] *see* Catio
    [Lang]
Northerners *see* Khwakhamaiu
Northerners *see* Tahagmiut
Northern Foothill Division [CA]
    Yokuts (BE)
Northern Guaymi [Pan] (O)
Northern Hills Yokuts *see*
    Chukchansi
Northern Indians *see* Etheneldeli
Northern Iroquois (Hdbk15)
Northern Kalapoian [Lang] (BE)
Northern Mewuk *see* Amador
Northern Miwok [CA] (BE)
Northern Molala [Lang] [OR]
    (Hdbk12)
Northern Moquelumnan [Lang]
    [CA] (Pub, v.6, no.1, pp.314–17)
Northern Nambicuara [Br] (O)
Northern Okinagan [BC, WA]
    (LC)
Northern Paiute (Hdbk10) *see also*
    Paviotso (CA)
Northern Paiute [CA, NV, OR]
    (BE)
Northern People *see* Wazi'a
    wintca'cta
Northern People *see* Northern
    Assiniboin
Northern Pomo [CA] (CA-8)
Northern Shoshone [ID, WY]
    (BE)
Northern Shoshone [Lang] *Cen-
    tral Numic* (Hdbk11)
Northern Sierra Miwok [Lang]
    Eastern Miwokan (CA-8)

Northern Tehuelche [Arg] (O)
Northern Tepehuan [Lang] [*Uto-
    Aztecan*] (Hdbk10)
Northern Tepehuan [MX]
    (Hdbk10)
Northern Tete de Boule [Can]
    Sakawininiwug Cree (BE)
Northern Tewa [NM] (BE)
Northern Tonto *Western Apache*
    (Hdbk10)
Northern Unami [Lang]
    (Hdbk15)
Northern Ute (Bull157)
Northern Uttawawa *see* Cree
Northern Valley Yokuts [Lang]
    (Anthro, v.11, no.3)
Northern Wappo [CA] (BE)
Northern West Greenlandic
    [Lang] *West Greenlandic*
    (Hdbk15)
Northern Wintu [Lang] [CA]
    Wintun (He)
Northern Yana [CA] *Yana* (BE)
Northern Yana [Lang] [CA]
    Hokan (CA-8)
North Fork [Lang] [CA] *Wailaki*
    (He)
Northfork Mono (BE) *see also*
    Northern Paiute (BE)
North Fork Mono [CA] (Pub,
    v.11, no.5, p.293)
Northfork Mono [NV] (BE)
North Greenlandic *see* Polar Es-
    kimos
North Slope Inupiaq [Lang] [AK]
    Unupiaq (Hdbk5)
North Susseeton *see* Kahra
North Thompson [BC, Can]
    Shuswap (BE)
North Thompson Band [BC]
    North Thompson Shuswap
    (Hdbk12)
North Thompson Division [BC]
    Shuswap (Hdbk12)
Northwest Coast *Western Province*
    (AI)
Northwestern Maidu [Lang] [CA]
    Maidu (CA)
Northwestern Sierra *see* Plains
    Miwok
Northwest Hill Maidu [CA]
    (Pub, v.33, no.2)
Northwest River [Can]
    [*Montagnais-Naskapi*] (BE)
Northwest Sahaptin (Hdbk12)
North Yanktons *see* Upper Yank-
    tonai
Norwalk [CN] (H)
Norwidgewalk *see* Norridgewock
Norwootuc [MA] *Algonquian* (H)
Norwootuck *see* Norwootuc
Norwottock *see* Norwootuc
Norwottuck *see* Norwootuc

Norwuthick *see* Norwootuc
Nosa *see* Yana [CA]
Noser *see* Yana [CA]
Nosi *see* Yana [CA]
Nossoni *see* Nasoni
Nostlalaim *see* Clallam
Nota *see* Notha
Nota-a *see* Ute
Notadine *see* Notha
Nota-osh *see* Comanche
No-taw *see* Comanche
Notaw *see* Comanche
Notch *see* Ute
Notchees *see* Natchez
Notches *see* Natchez
Notchitoches *see* Natchitoches
Notha [Clan] *Navajo* (H)
Notinnonchioni *see* Iroquois
Notkitz *see* Noquet
Notlnatnah *see* Naltunnetunne
Notoanaiti *see* Nutunutu
No-toan-ai-ti *see* Nutunutu
Notonato *see* Nutunutu
No-ton-no-to *see* Nutunutu
Notonnoto *see* Nutunutu
No-ton-too *see* Nutunutu
Notontoo *see* Nutunutu
Notoowtha *see* Nutunutu
Notototen *see* Nutunutu
Notowega *see* Nottaway
Notowegee *see* Nottaway
No-tow-too *see* Nutunutu
Notowtoo *see* Nutunutu
Notre Dame de Betsiamits *see* Bersiamite
Nottawagee *see* Seneca
Nottawagees *see* Iroquois
Nottaway [VA. SC] (LC)
Nottawayes *see* Nottoway
Nottawegas *see* Iroquois
Nottawessie *see* Dakota
Notteweges *see* Iroquois
Nottoway *see* Nottaway
Nottoweasses *see* Dakota
Nouadiche *see* Nabadache
Nouga *see* Kawchottine
Nouidiches *see* Nabedache
Nouista [TX] (H)
Noukek *see* Noquet
Noumpoli *see* Numpali
Nouquet *see* Noquet
Nousaghauset *see* Narraganset
Noutka *see* Nootka
Nova *see* Pakaanova
Novadiches *see* Nabedache
Novajos *see* Navajo
Novangok [Can] [*Inuit (Quebec)*] (Hdbk5)
no-vintc *see* Ute
Novisan *see* Navasink
Nov-seh-chatl *see* Nusehtsatl
Novsehchatl *see* Nusehtsatl
No-wah-ah *see* Towahhah

Nowahah *see* Towahhah
Nowamish *see* Dwamish
Nowhaha *see* Towahhah
Nowonthewog *see* Norwootuc
No'xunts'itx *see* Nohuntsitk
Noxuntsitx *see* Nohuntsitk
Noyatagameut *see* Nunatogmiut
Noykewel [Lang] [CA] (CA-8)
No-yu-ki *see* oyuki
Noyuki [CA] *Maidu* (H)
Noza *see* Yana [CA]
Noze *see* Yana [CA]
Nozhi *see* Yana [CA]
No-zi *see* Yana [CA]
Nozi *see* Yana [CA]
Nozone *see* Nasoni
N'pochele *see* Sanpoil
Npochele *see* Sanpoil
N'poch-le *see* Sanpoil
Npochle *see* Sanpoil
N'pockle *see* Sanpoil
Npockle *see* Sanpoil
N'qua'cha'mish *see* Nukwatsamish
Nquachamish *see* Nukwatsamish
N'Quentl-ma-mish *see* Kwehtlmamish
Nquentlmamish *see* Kwehtlmamish
N'Quentlmaymish *see* Kwehtlmamish
Nquentlmaymish *see* Kwehtlmamish
N'quutl-ma-mish *see* Kwehtlmamish
Nquutlmamish *see* Kwehtlmamish
Nra del Socorro *see* Socorro del Sur
Nra Sra del Socorro *see* Soccoro
Nsekau's *see* Clackamas
N'selixtci'n *see* Sanpoil
Nselixtcin *see* Sanpoil
Nsietshawas Indians *see* Tillamook
Nsietshawus (H) *see also* Tillamook (LC)
Nsietshawus [Lang] *Salishan* (BE)
Nsi'mpxemux *see* North Thompson Band
Nsimpxemux *see* North Thompson Band
Nsirtshaus *see* Tillamook
N'skwali *see* Nisqally
nspilm *see* Nespelim
Nsqualli *see* Nisqualli
Ns tiwat *see* Clackamas
Nstiwat *see* Clackamas
N'sualli *see* Nisqualli
Ntaauotin *see* Nataotin
N'tla-ka-pa-moh *see* Thompson Indians

Ntlakapamoh *see* Thompson Indians
N'tlaka-pamuq *see* Ntlakyapamuk
N'tlaka'pamuq *see* Thompson Indians
Ntlakapamuq *see* Ntlakyapamuk
Ntlakapamuq *see* Thompson Indians
N'tla-ka-pe-mooh *see* Thompson Indians
Ntlakapemooh *see* Thompson Indians
N-tla-ka-pe-mook *see* Ntalakyapamuk
Ntlakapemook *see* Ntlakyapamuk
N'tla-kap-moh *see* Thompson Indians
Ntlakapmoh *see* Thompson Indians
Ntlakyapamuk (Hdbk12) *see also* Thompson (Hdbk12)
Ntlakyapamuk (LC) *see also* Thompson Indians (Hdbk15)
Ntlakyapamuk [BC, WA] *Salish* (LC)
Ntlakyapamuk [Lang] [BC, WA] *Salishan* (LC)
Ntlakya'pamuq *see* Ntlakyapamuk
Ntlakyapamuq *see* Ntlakyapamuk
Ntocouit *see* Toba
Ntogapid *see* Itogapuk
Ntokowit *see* Toba
Ntshaautin [Can] *Southern Carrier* (BE)
Ntshaautin [Clan] *Takulli* (H)
Ntsietshaw *see* Tillamook
Ntsietshawus *see* Tillamook
Nu-a-gun-tits *see* Nuaguntits
Nu-a-gun-tits *see* Las Vegas
Nuaguntits (PC) *see also* Las Vegas (Hdbk11)
Nuaguntits [NV] *Paiute* (H)
Nua'ka'hn *see* Missisauga
Nuakahn *see* Missisauga
Nuataagmiut *Kotzebue Sound Eskimos* (Hdbk5)
Nubenaigooching *see* Nopiming
Nucekaʼyi *see* Nushekaayi
Nuchalkmx *see* Nuhalk
Nuchatlitz [VanI] *Nootka* (BE)
Nuch-a-wan-ack *see* Newichawanoc
Nuchawanack *see* Newichawanoc
Nuchawayi (H) *see also* Yawdanchi
Nuchawayi [CA] *Yokuts* (H)
Nuchig'mut [CA] (Contri, v.1, p.21)
Nuchimases *see* Newchemass

Nu-chow-we *see* Nuchawayi
Nuchowwe *see* Nuchawayi
Nuchschi [AK] (H)
Nuchu [CA] *Miwok* (H)
Nuchwugh [WA] *Salish* (H)
nuci *see* Ute
nu-ci [Self-designation] *see* Ute
nu-ciu *see* Ute
nuciu *see* Ute
Nuculaha [Subclan] *Timucua* (H)
Nuestra Señora de Guadalupe
  [BCa] *Mission Indians* (H)
Nuestra Señora de Guadalupe del
  Sur *see* Nuestra Señora de
  Guadalupe
Nuestra Señora de Guadalupe de
  Pojoaque *see* Pojoaque
Nuestra Señora de Guadalupe de
  Pojuaque *see* Pojoaque
Nuestra Señora de Guadalupe de
  Zuni *see* Zuni
Nuestra Señora de la Asumpcion
  de Zia *see* Sia
Nuestra Señora de la Purisma
  Concepcion *see* Sia
Nuestra Señora de la Soledad
  [CA] *Mission Indians* (H)
Nuestra Señora de los Angeles de
  Pecos *see* Pecos
Nuestra Señora de los Angeles de
  Porciuncula de Pecos *see* Pecos
Nuestra Señora de los Angeles de
  Porcuncula *see* Pecos
Nuestra Señora de los Angeles de
  Tecos *see* Pecos
Nuestra Señora de los Dolores del
  Norte [BCa] *Mission Indians*
  (H)
Nuestra Señora de los Dolores de
  Sandia *see* Sandia
Nuestra Señora de los Dolores y
  San Antonio de Sandia *see*
  Sandia
Nuestra Señora del Socorro *see*
  Socorro del Sur
Nuestra Señora de Pecos *see*
  Pecos
Nuestra Señora de Portiuncula de
  los Angeles de Pecos *see* Pecos
Nueva Sevilla *see* Sevilleta
Nuey-kech-emk *see* Ni-
  ueuomokai
Nueykechemk *see* Niueuomokai
Nugh-Kwetle-babish *see* Kwehtl-
  mamish
Nughkwetlebabish *see* Kwehtl-
  mamish
Nugh-lemmy *see* Lummi
Nughlemmy *see* Lummi
Nugh-sahk *see* Nooksack
Nughsahk *see* Nooksack
Nugsuak *Greenland Eskimos* (BE)
Nugumeute *see* Nugumiut

Nugumiut [Can] *Central Eskimos*
  (BE)
Nugumut *see* Nuwukmiiut
Nuhalk [BC] *Bella Coola* (H)
Nuhiyup *see* Tulalip
Nuh-lum-mi *see* Lummi
Nuhlummi *see* Lummi
Nu-i-mok *see* Nuimok
Nuimok [CA] *Wintun* (H)
Nuite *see* Northern Guaymi
Nukak [Col] (O)
Nukchu (H) *see also* Nuchu (H)
Nukchu [CA] (H)
Nukfalalgi *see* Timucua
Nukfila *see* Timucua
Nukhe [Clan] *Wazhazhe* (H)
Nukhe [Gens] *Ponca* (H)
Nukhlesh *see* Lummi
Nuk-hotsi *see* Timucua
Nukhotsi *see* Timucua
Nukh-tum-mi *see* Lummi
Nukhtummi *see* Lummi
Nukluktana [AK] *Tenankutchin*
  (H)
Nuk-mut (Contri, v.1, p.16)
Nukmut *see* Nuk-mut
Nuksahk *see* Nooksack
Nuk-sak *see* Nooksack
Nuksak *see* Nooksack
Nuksiwepu [ID] *Nez Perce* (BE)
Nuktusem *see* Dakota
Nukuini [Br] (O)
Nu-kwat-samish *see* Nukwat-
  samish
Nukwatsamish [WA] *Salish* (H)
Nu-kwints *see* Unkapanukuint
Nukwints *see* Unkapanukuint
Nuk wul tuh *see* Nakoaktok
Nukwultuh *see* Nakoaktok
Nulaantin *see* Nulaautin
Nulaautin [Sept] [BC] *Takulli*
  (H)
Nulatokhotan *see* Nula'to-kho-
  tan
Nula'to-kho-tan [*Kar-Yuh-Kho-
  Ta'Na*] (Contri, v.1, p.26)
Nulpe *see* Cuaiquer
Nult-nort-nas *see* Naltun-
  netunne
Nultnortnas *see* Naltunnetunne
Nul-to-nat-na *see* Naltun-
  netunne
Nultonatna *see* Naltunnetunne
Nulto-nat-tene *see* Naltun-
  netunne
Nultonattene *see* Naltunnetunne
Num [Clan] *Pueblo Indians* (H)
num [Self-designation] (Pub, v.4,
  no.3, p.105) *see also* Cheme-
  huevi (LC)
Numa *see* Comanche
Numa *see* Nama
Numa *see* Paiute

Numa *see* Northern Paiute
Numa *see* Numic
Numa-bin *see* Namabin
Numabin *see* Namabin
Numakaki *see* Mandan
Numakshi *see* Mandan
Numangkake *see* Mandan
Numawisowugi [Phratry] *Fox* (H)
Numawisowugi [Phratry] *Sauk*
  (H)
Numbiai [Br] (O)
Num-ee-muss *see* Hupa
Numeemuss *see* Hupa
Numepo *see* Nez Perce
Nu-me-poo *see* Nez Perce
Numepoo *see* Nez Perce
Numi *see* Nambe
Numic [Lang] (LC)
Numipo *see* Nez Perce
Numipu *see* Nez Perce
nu-mi-pu *see* Nez Perce
Num-kes *see* Nimkish
Numkes *see* Nimkish
Numleki *see* Nomlaki
Nummastaquyt *see* Namasket
Num-mok *see* Nummuk
Nummok *see* Nummuk
Nummuk [CA] *Wintun* (H)
Numpali [CA] *Olamentke* (H)
Num-t'ai'nin *see* Num
Numtainin *see* Num
Numu [Self-designation] *see*
  Northern Paiute
Numurano *see* Omurano
Nun (H) *see also* Nung (H)
Nun [Clan] *Koskimo* (H)
Nuna-mish *see* Dwamish
Nunamish *see* Dwamish
Nunamiut *Interior North Alaska
  Eskimos* (Hdbk5)
Nunataagmiut *Kotzebue Sound Es-
  kimos* (Hdbk5)
Nunatagmiut *North Alaska Coast
  Eskimos* (BE)
Nunatagmut *see* Nunatagmiut
Nuna-tangmeun *see* Nunatag-
  miut
Nunatangmeun *see* Nunatagmiut
Nunatañmiun *see* Nunatagmiut
Nuna-to'g-mut *see* Nunatagmiut
Nunato'g-mut *see* Nunatagmiut
Nunatogmut *see* Nunatagmiut
Nunatsiaqmiut [Self-designation]
  see Baffinland Eskimos
Nuna-tun'g-meun *see* Nunatag-
  miut
Nunatungmeun *see* Nunatag-
  miut
Nun-da-wa-o-no *see* Seneca
Nundawaono *see* Seneca
Nundawaronah *see* Seneca
Nun'dawe'gi *see* Seneca
Nundawegi *see* Seneca

Nundowaga *see* Seneca
Nunemasek-a'lis *see* Nune-
    masekalis
Nunemasekalis [Gens] *Tlauitsis*
    (H)
Nu'nemaseqalis *see* Nune-
    masekalis
Nunemaseqalis *see* Nune-
    masekalis
Nu'nemeasqalis *see* Nune-
    masekalis
Nunemeasqalis *see* Nune-
    masekalis
Nunenumiut [Can] *Labrador Es-
    kimos* (BE)
Nung [Clan] *Hano* (H)
Nung [Clan] *Tewa* (H)
Nunivaaq *see* Nunivagmiut
Nunivagmiut [AK] *Eskimos* (BE)
Nunivagmut *see* Nunivagmiut
Nunivagmute *see* Nunivagmiut
Nunivak Central Yupik [Lang]
    (Hdbk5)
Nunivak Eskimo [AK] (Hdbk5)
Nunivak people *see* Magemiut
Nunivak People *see* Nuni-
    vagmiut
nuni-va-q *see* Nunivagmiut
nunivaq *see* Nunivagmiut
nuni-va-ymiut *see* Nunivagmiut
nunivaymiut *see* Nunivagmiut
nuni-wax *see* Nunivagmiut
nuniwax *see* Nunivagmiut
nuni-wa-ymiut *see* Nunivagmiut
nuniwaymiut *see* Nunivagmiut
Nun-ni *see* Nunni
Nunni [Clan] *Chickasaw* (H)
Nuntaly *see* Nuntaneuck
Nuntaneuck *Siouan* (H)
Nupchinche (BE) *see also* Nopch-
    inchi (CA-8)
Nupchinche [CA] *Northern Valley
    Yokuts* (BE)
Nuqa-lkh *see* Nuhalk
Nuqalkh *see* Nuhalk
Nuqa'lkmh *see* Nuhalk
Nuqalkmh *see* Nuhalk
Nuqe *see* Nukhe
Nuqtu *see* Dakota
Nuquencaibo [Self-designation]
    see Capanahua
Nuqueno *see* Nootka
Nurhantsuak *see* Norridgewock
Nus-klai-yum *see* Clallam
Nusche-kaari *see* Nushekaayi
Nuschekaari *see* Nushekaayi
Nusdalum *see* Clallam
Nusehtsatl [WA] *Salish* (H)
Nushagagmiut (BE) *see also* Ki-
    atagmiut (Hdbk5)
Nushagagmiut [AK] *Eskimos* (BE)
Nushagag-mut *see* Nushagagmiut
Nushagagmut *see* Nushagagmiut

Nushaltkagakni [OR] *Modoc* (H)
Nushegagmut *see* Nushagagmiut
Nushekaayi [AK] *Tlingit* (H)
Nushemouck [Conoy] (Hdbk15)
Nushergagmute *see* Nushagagmiut
Nusiok *see* Neusiok
Nuskarawaok *see* Cuscarawaoc
Nusklaim *see* Clallam
Nu-sklaim *see* Clallam
Nusklaiyum *see* Clallam
Nu-so-lupsh *see* Kwaiailk
Nu-so-lupsh *see* Cowlitz
Nusolupsh *see* Cowlitz
Nusolupsh *see* Kwaiailk
Nuss-ka *see* Niska
Nusska *see* Niska
Nustoc *see* Neusiok
Nuswattax (Hdbk15) *see also*
    Nasswatex (Hdbk15)
Nuswattax *Pocomoke* (Hdbk15)
Nuswattock *Accomac* (LC)
Nuta *see* Yawdanchi
Nutaa *see* Northern Paiute
Nutaa *see* Yawdanchi
Nutaa *see* Mono
Nut'aa *see* Mono
Nutabe [Col] (O)
Nutantisha *see* Nutunutu
Nutcatenna *see* Ntshaautin
Nutca'tlath *see* Nuchatlitz
Nutcatlath *see* Nuchatlitz
Nut-chu *see* Nuchu
Nutchu *see* Nuchu
Nutha *see* Mono
Nut-ha [Self-designation] *see*
    Mono
Nutimiiniuuk *see* Nutimi-iniuuk
Nutimi-iniuuk [Can] *Paskwaw-
    ininiwug Cree* (BE)
Nutka *see* Nootka
Nutonetoo *see* Nutunutu
Nutqui [Society] *Cheyenne* (H)
Nutrecho [CA] (H)
Nuts *see* Ute
Nutschichgi [Clan] *Knaiakhotana*
    (H)
Nutseni *see* Nu'tseni
Nu'tseni [BC] *Carrier Indians*
    (Bull133)
Nutuntu *see* Nutunutu
Nutunutu [CA] *Southern Valley
    Yokuts* (BE)
nutuwic [[Moiety] [CA] *Yokuts*
    (Pub, v.11, no.5, p.293)
nutuwuts *see* Nutuwic
Nutzotin [AK] *Nabesna* (BE)
Nutzotin [AK] *Tenankutchin* (H)
Nuu-chah-nulth *see* Nootka
Nuuchahnulth *see* Nootka
Nuvorugmiut [Can] *Mackenzie
    Eskimos* (BE)
Nuvugmiut [Can] *Labrador Eski-
    mos* (BE)

Nuvungmiut *North Alaska Coast
    Eskimos* (Hdbk5)
nuvunnguq *see* Novangok
Nuweta *see* Mandan
Nuwichawanick *see*
    Newichawanoc
Nuwukmiut [AK] *Eskimos* (BE)
Nuwuk-mut *see* Nuwukmiut
Nuwukmut *see* Nuwukmiut
Nuwun'g-meun *see* Nuwukmiut
Nuwung-me-un *see* Nuwukmiut
Nuwungmeun *see* Nuwukmiut
Nuwu'nmiun *see* Nuwukmiut
Nuwunmiun *see* Nuwukmiut
Nuxa'lk *see* Nuhalk
Nuxalk *see* Bella Coola
Nuxalk *see* Nuhalk
Nuxe *see* Nukhe
Nuxsklai'yem *see* Clallam
Nwa-ka *see* Chippewa
Nwaka *see* Chippewa
N'Wamish *see* Dwamish
Nwamish *see* Dwamish
Nwasabe *see* Navajo
N'wh-ah-tk-hm *see* Lummi
Nwhahtkhm *see* Lummi
Nyack [NY] *Unami* (H)
Nyantecet *see* Niantic
Nyantecutt *see* Niantic
Nyanticke *see* Niantic
Nyavapai *see* Yavapai
Nyavi Pais *see* Yavapai
Nyavipais *see* Yavapai
Nyavkopai *see* Nyav-kopai
Nyav-kopai [AZ] [Walapai] (BE)
Nyengatu *see* Nheengatu
Nyhantick *see* Niantic
Nyhatta [LA] (H)
Nyonuxa *see* Nanuya
Nypissing *see* Nipissing
Nypsin *see* Nipissing

-O-

Oa *see* Pamoa
Oabano *see* Ouabano
Oaboponoma *see* Hoabonoma
Oadauwau *see* Ottawa
Oahpap *see* Maricopa
Oaiapi *see* Oyampi
Oaica *see* Waica
Oaimpik *see* Oyampi
Oajana *see* Oyana
Oajuenche *see* Cajuenche
Oakanagan *see* Okinagan
Oak Creek *Northern Tonto Apache*
    (BE)
Oak Creek Canyon *see* Wipukyi-
    pai
Oakfuskee *see* Okfuskee

Oakinacken see Okinagan
Oakinagan see Okinagan
Oaklafalaya see Oklafalaya
Oak-pa-pa see Hunkpapa
Oakpapa see Hunkpapa
Oaktashippas see Octashepas
Oalpe see Walpi
Oanancocke see Onancock
Oanoska see Ohanhanska
Oat [Clan] Caddo Confederacy
  (H)
Oate-lash-schute see Ootlashoot
Oatelashschute see Ootlashoot
Oathkaqua see Onathaqua
Oa-tish-tye see San Felipe
  [Keres]
Oatishtye see San Felipe [Keres]
Oat-la-shoot see Ootlashoot
Oatlashoot see Ootlashoot
Oat-lash-shoot see Ootlashoot
Oatlashshoot see Ootlashoot
Oat-lash-shute see Ootlashoot
Oatlashshute see Ootlashoot
Oatouat see Ottawa
Oatsees see Yazoo
o-badi see Opata
obadi see Opata
Obayo [Lang] [MX] Coahuiltecan
  (H)
Obekaws see Abishka
Obeloussa see Opelousa
O-benaki see Abnaki
Obenaki see Abnaki
Obidgewong [Ont] Chippewa (H)
Obika see Abihka
Obinack see Abnaki
Obispeño [Lang] [CA] Chumash
  (BE)
Objibway see Ojibwa
Obodeus [TX] (H)
Obone [MX] Concho (BE)
Obozi Coahuiltecan (BE)
Obstinate Indians see Ni-
  takoskitsipupiks
Obunego see Abnaki
Obwahnug see Dakota
O-bwah-nug see Dakota
Ocage see Osage
Ocaina [PE, Col] Witoto (LC)
Ocala see Olagale
Ocale (H) see also Olagale (H)
Ocale [FL] (BE)
Ocali see Olagala
Ocaly see Olagale
Ocam see Ocana
Ocama Waica [Br] Yanorama (O)
Ocameches see Occoneechee
Ocana [TX] Coahuiltecan (BE)
Ocanes see Lipan Apache
Ocanes see Ocana
Ocansa see Quapaw
Ocapa see Quapaw
Ocara see Maricopa

Ocatameneton Dakota (BE)
Occaanechy see Occoneechee
Occahannock Accomac (Hdbk15)
Occahanock (H) see also Acco-
  hanoc (BE)
Occaneches see Occoneechee
Occaneeches see Occoneechee
Occaneechi see Occoneechee
Occaneechi see Occoneechee
Occanichi see Occoneeche
Occanuchee see Occoneeche
Occoneachey see Occoneechee
Occoneechee [Lang] Siouan (LC)
Occoneechee [VA, NC] (LC)
Occouy see Oconee
"occupants of big igloos" see illu-
  alummiut
"occupants of igloos" see Igdlu-
  miut
"occupants of little igloos" see
  Iglurarsome
"occupants of the islands" see
  Kikiktagmyut
"occupants of the other side of
  the country" see Itivimiut
"occupants of the shady side" see
  Tahagmiut
"occupants of the sunny side" see
  Suhinimyut
Ocean People see Usal
Oceti sakowin see Dakota
Ocetisakowin see Dakota
Ocha see O-cha
O-cha [Clan] Mohave (H)
Ochahananke see Accohanoc
Ochahannauke see Quacko-
  hamaock
Ochan see Yaochane
Ochasteguin see Huron
Ochatagin see Huron
Ochataiguin see Huron
Ochategin see Huron
Ochateguin see Huron
Ochatequin see Huron
O-che see Odshisalgi
Oche see Odshisalgi
Ochecames see Yachikamni
Ochecamnes see Yachikamni
Ochechote [WA] Shahaptian (BE)
Ochecole see Ochechote
Ochee see Yuchi
Ochehak see Plains Miwok
Ochekhamni see Okechumne
Ocheneechee see Occoneechee
Ochente Shakoan see Dakota
Ochente Shakoan see Seven
  Council Fires
Ochente Shakona see Dakota
Ocheo's Band see Tuziyammos
O'chepe'wag see Ojibwa
Ochepewag see Ojibwa
Ochese Creek see Creek
Ochesee see Muskogee

Ochesees see Lower Creek
Ochesse see Yuchi
Ochessigiriniooek see Oukeses-
  tigouek
Ochessigiriniouek see Oukeses-
  tigouek
Ochestgooetch see Oukeses-
  tigouek
Ochestgouetch see Oukeses-
  tigouek
Ochestigoueck see Oukeses-
  tigouek
Ocheti shakowin see Dakota
Ocheti Shaowni see Dakota
Ocheti Shaowni see Seven Coun-
  cil Fires
Ochi see San Juan [NM]
Ochiakenen (H)
Ochiatagonga [IL] (H)
Ochiatenen see Wea
Ochie'tari-ronnon see Cherokee
Ochietarironnon see Cherokee
Ochinakein see Okinagan
Ochineeches see Occoneechee
Ochingita see O-ching-i-ta
O-ching-i-ta [CA] Yokuts (Con-
  tri, v.3, p.370)
Ochipawa see Ojibwa
Ochipawa see Chippewa
Ochipewa see Ojibwa
Ochipoy see Ojibwa
Ochippewais see Ojibwa
Ochiro see Chamacoco
Ochiro see Orio
Ochocumnes see Yachikamni
Ochoes [MX] Lagunero (BE)
Ochomazo see Uru
Ochozuma see Uru
O-chunga-raw see Winnebago
Ochungaraw see Winnebago
O-chunk-o-raw see Winnebago
Ochunkoraw see Winnebago
oci-pi-w see Ojibwa
ocipiwa see Ojibwa
očipwe'w see Ojibwa
Ocita [FL] (BE)
Ockinagee see Occoneechee
Ocki Pah-Utes see Agaihtikara
Ocki Pi-Utes see Agaihtikara
Ocki Pi-Utes see Aga'idokado
Ockiwere see Chiwere
Ockneharuse (H)
Oclawaha see Seminole
Ocole see Mataco
Ocona see Oconee
Ocone see Oconee
Oconee [GA] (BE)
Oconery's see Oconee
Oconi [FL] Timucua (BE)
Ocoroni [Lang] Taracahitian (BE)
Ocosaus see Arkokisa
Ocotegueguo Caduveo (O)
Octagros see Winnebago

Octashepas (H)
Octata *see* Oto
Octenai *see* Mataco
Octguanes *see* Yuma
Octguanes *see* Kahwan
Octi *see* Agaihtikara
Octoctatas *see* Oto
Octogymists *see* Ottawa
Octolacto *see* Oto
Octolata *see* Oto
Octonagon *see* Ontonagon
Octootata *see* Oto
Octota *see* Oto
Octotale *see* Oto
Octotata *see* Oto
Octotota *see* Oto
Ocuiltec [Lang] [MX] *Matlatz-inca* (LC)
Ocute (BE) *see also* Hitchiti (BE)
Ocute [GA] (BE)
Odagami *see* Fox
Odagumaig *see* Fox
Odahwah *see* Ottawa
O-dah-wah *see* Ottawa
Odahwah *see* Ottawa
Odahwaug *see* Ottawa
Odakeo *see* Odukeo's band
O'dam *see* Tepehuan
Odam *see* Tepehuan
Odame *see* Tepehuan
Odami [Self-designation] *see* Te-pehuan
Odamich *Coahuiltecan* (Hdbk10)
Odawa *see* Ottawa
Odchipewa *see* Ojibwa
O-de-eilah *see* Kikatsik
Odeeilah *see* Kikatsik
O-de-i-lah *see* Kikatsik
Odeilah *see* Kikatsik
Odgiboweke *see* Ojibwa
Odishk-wa-gami *see* Nipissing
Odishkwagami *see* Nipissing
Odishkwagamig *see* Nipissing
Odishkwa-Gamig *see* Nipissing
O-dish-quag-um-ee *see* Nipissing
Odishquagumee *see* Nipissing
Odishquáhgumme *see* Nipissing
O-dish-quaq-um-eeg *see* Nipissing
Odishquaqumeeg *see* Nipissing
Odistastagheks *see* Mascouten
Odjibewais *see* Ojibwa
Odjibwa *see* Ojibwa
Odjibwa *see* Ojibwa
Od-jib-wag *see* Ojibwa
Odjibwag *see* Ojibwa
Odjibwe *see* Ojibwa
Odjibwek *see* Ojibwa
Odlkat-no'm *see* Round Valley Yuki
Odoary [BO] *Araona* (O)
Odoesmades [TX] *Coahuiltecan* (BE)

Odshisalgi [Clan] *Creek* (H)
O-dug-am-eeg *see* Fox
Odugameeg *see* Fox
Odugamies *see* Fox
O-dug-augeeg (H) SE Fox (LC)
Odugaugeeg *see* Fox
O-duk-e-o's band *see* Odukeo's band
Odukeo's band [NV] *Paviotso* (H)
Odzibwe *see* Ojibwa
O'ealilx *see* Oealitk
Oealilx *see* Oealitk
Oealitk [Sept] [BC] (H)
O'ealitq *see* Oealitk
Oealitq *see* Oealitk
Oenne *see* Eskimos
Oenock *see* Eno [NC]
Oenronronnon *see* Wenro
Oepoeroei *see* Guayana
Oetsoenhwotenne *see* Natliatin
O-e-tun-i-o *see* Crow
Oetunio *see* Crow
Oewaku *see* Auaka
Ofagoula *see* Ofo
Ofaye [Br] (O)
Ofaye-Xavante *see* Ofaye
Ofegaula *see* Ofo
Offagoula *see* Ofo
Offegoula *see* Ofo
Offogoula *see* Ofo
Ofi okla *see* Mosopolea
Ofiokla *see* Mosopolea
Ofo [MS] (BE)
Ofogoula *see* Ofo
Ofugula *see* Ofo
Ogablalla *see* Oglala
O-ga-la-la *see* Oglala
Ogalala *see* Oglala
Ogalalab Yokpah *see* Oglala
Ogalala Dacota *see* Oglala
Ogalalla *see* Oglala
Ogalallah *see* Oglala
O'Galla *see* Oglala
Ogalla *see* Oglala
Ogallah *see* Oglala
O'Gallala *see* Oglala
Ogallala *see* Oglala
Ogallalla *see* Oglala
Ogallallah *see* Oglala
Ogallallee *see* Oglala
O-ga-pa *see* Quapaw
Ogapa *see* Quapaw
O-ge-chee *see* Ogeechee
Ogechee *see* Ogeechee
Ogechi *see* Ogeechee
Ogeeche *see* Ogeechee
Ogeechee [CA] *Yuchi* (H)
Ogeelala *see* Oglala
Ogehage *see* Conestoga
Ogellah *see* Oglala
Ogellala *see* Oglala
Ogellalah *see* Oglala
Oghiny-yawee *see* Ogeechee

Ogibois *see* Ojibwa
Ogillallah *see* Oglala
O-gla-la *see* Oglala
Og-la-la *see* Oglalaichichagha
Oglala (PC) *see also* Oglalaichichagha (H)
Oglala *Oglala* (LC)
Oglala hca *see* Oglala
Oglalaichichagha [Brule] (H)
Oglala-icicaga *see* Oglalaichichagha
Oglalaicicaga *see* Oglalaichichagha
Oglala-itc-itcaxa *see* Oglalaichichagha
Oglala proper *see* Oglala
Oglala-qtca *see* Iteshica
Oglalaqtca *see* Iteshica
Oglalatcitcaxa *see* Oglalaichichagha
Oglallah *see* Oglala
Oglemut *see* Aglemiut
Oglemute *see* Aglemiut
Ogoh pae *see* Quapaw
Ogohpae *see* Quapaw
Ogoize *see* Bannock
Ogolawla *see* Oglala
O-guah-pa *see* Quapaw
Oguahpa *see* Quapaw
O-guah-pah *see* Quapaw
Oguahpah *see* Quapaw
Oguapas *see* Quapaw
Oguecolomo *Coahuiltecan* (Hdbk10)
Ogue Loussa *see* Opelousa
Ogueloussa *see* Opelousa
O'Gullala *see* Oglala
Ogullala *see* Oglala
Og'ulmut *see* Aglemiut
O'gulmut *see* Aglemiut
Ogulmut *see* Aglemiut
Ohaguame (Hdbk10) *see also* Siaguan (BE)
Ohaguames [MX] *Coahuiltecan* (BE)
Ohah-hans-hah *see* Ohanhanska
Ohahhanshah *see* Ohanhanska
O-hah-kas-ka-toh-y-an-te *see* Ohanhanska
Ohahkaskatohyante *see* Ohanhanska
Ohamiel *see* Ohamil
O'Hamil *see* Ohamil
Ohamil [BC] *Stalo* (BE)
Ohamille *see* Ohamil
Ohanapa *see* Oahenonpa
Ohanhanska [MN] *Magayuteshni* (BE)
Ohantonwanna *see* Yanktonai
Ohdada *see* Oglala
Ohdihe *Sisseton* (H)
O-he-nom-pa *see* Ohenonpa
Ohenompa *see* Oohenonpa

Ohe-nonpa *see* Oohenonpa
Ohenonpa *see* Oohenonpa
Ohenonpa Dakotas *see*
  Oohenonpa
Oherokouaehronon [Can] (H)
Ohey-aht *see* Oiaht
oh-hon [VE] (O)
Ohiat *see* Oiaht
Ohke *see* San Juan [NM]
Ohk to unna *see* Oqtoguna
Ohktounna *see* Oqtoguna
Oh-la-qu-hoh *see* Hoh
Ohlaquhoh *see* Hoh
Ohlone [CA] *Costanoan* (CA)
Ohlwa *see* Ulva
Ohno-wal-a-gantle *see* Onoalag-
  ona
Ohnowalagantle *see* Onoalagona
Ohnowalagantles *see* Schenec-
  tady
Oho-homo *see* Dakota
Ohohomo *see* Dakota
Ohongeeoquena [Clan] [PA]
  Susquehanna (BE)
Oho-omo-yo *see* Dakota
Ohoomoyo *see* Dakota
Ohopesha *see* O'hope'sha
O'hope'sha [WI] *Menominee* (BE)
O-hot-du-sha *see* Ohotdusha
Ohotdusha *Crow* (H)
Ohotoma *see* Pima
Ohque *see* San Juan [NM]
Oh-sa-ra-ka *see* Saratoga
Ohsaraka *see* Saratoga
Ohshahch [Clan] *Laguna* (H)
Ohshahch-hanoch *see* Oshahch
Ohuaqui *see* Pojoaque
Ohuqui *see* Pojoaque
ohya *see* o'hya
o'hya *Panamint* (Hdbk11)
Ohyat *see* Oiaht
Oiaht [VanI] *Nootka* (BE)
Oiampi *see* Oyampi
Oiatenon *see* Wea
Oiatuch *see* Oiaht
Oico *see* Orinoco Waica
Ointemarhen [TX] (H)
Oiochronon *see* Cayuga
Oiogernon *see* Cayuga
Oiogoen *see* Cayuga
Oiogoenhronnon *see* Cayuga
Oiogouan *see* Cayuga
Oiogouanronnon *see* Cayuga
Oiogouen *see* Cayuga
Oiogouenronnon *see* Cayuga
Oiogouin *see* Cayuga
Oïogueronnon *see* Cayuga
Oiongoiconon *see* Cayuga
Oiougovene *see* Cayuga
O'irauash *see* Kirauash
Oi-ra-uash *see* Querecho
Oirauash *see* Kirauash
Oirauash *see* Querecho

Oiudachenaton *see* Oughetge-
  odatons
Oi'viman *see* Oi'vamana
Oiviman *see* Oi'vimana
O'ivima na *see* Oivimana
Oivimana *see* Oi'vimana
Oi'vimana [SD] *Cheyenne* (BE)
Oiyurpe *see* Oyukhpe
Ojadagochroehne *see* Catawba
Ojadagochroene *see* Cherokee
Ojana *see* Guyana
Ojana *see* Urukuyana
Ojarikoelle *see* Oyaricoulet
O-jebway *see* Ojibwa
Ojebway *see* Ojibwa
Ojeebois *see* Ojibwa
Ojeegwyahnug (H)
Ojeeg Wyahnug *see* Ojeegwyah-
  nug
O-jee-jok *see* Ojeejok
Ojeejok [Clan] *Chippewa* (H)
Ojibaway *see* Ojibwa
Ojibbewaig *see* Ojibwa
Ojibbeway *see* Ojibwa
Ojibeway *see* Ojibwa
Ojibois *see* Ojibwa
Ojibua *see* Ojibwa
Ojibwa (LC)
O-jib-wage *see* Ojibwa
Ojibwaig *see* Ojibwa
O-jib-wa-uk *see* Ojibwa
Ojibwauk *see* Ojibwa
Ojibway *see* Ojibwa
Ojibway-ug *see* Ojibwa
Ojibwayug *see* Ojibwa
Ojibwe *see* Ojibwa
Ojipas *Yuman* (H)
Ojitlan [Lang] [MX] *Chinantec*
  (BE)
Ojitlan [MX] (BE)
Oj-ke *see* San Juan [NM]
Ojke *see* San Juan [NM]
Ojo Caliente *see* Warm Springs
Ojogoüen *see* Cayuga
Ojongovere *see* Cayuga
Ojos de la Tierra *Coahuiltecan*
  (Hdbk10)
Oj-que *see* San Juan [NM]
Ojque *see* San Juan [NM]
Ojuaque *see* Pojoaque
Oka [Q] (LC)
Okadada *see* Oglala
Okaga-wicasa *see* Ok-
  aghawichasha
Okagawicasa *see* Ok-
  aghawichasha
Okaghawichasha *Brule* (H)
O-ka-ho-ki *see* Okahoki
Okahoki [PA] *Unalachtigo* (BE)
Okahoki [Subclan] *Delaware* (H)
Okaina *see* Ocaina
Okaktowininiwuk *see* Oka'to
  Wini'niwuk

Okames *see* Kansa
Okams *see* Kansa
Okanagam *see* Okinagan
Okanagan *see* Okinagan
Okanagan-Colville [Lang] *Interior
  Salish* (Hdbk12)
Okanagan Lake [BC] *Okinagan*
  (H)
Okana'gen *see* Okinagan
Okanagen *see* Okinagan
Okanagon *see* Okinagan
O-kan-a-kan *see* Okinagan
Okanakanes *see* Okinagan
Okanakans *see* Okinagan
Okanaken *see* Okinagan
Okanandan *see* Oglala
Okana'qen *see* Okinagan
Okanaqen *see* Okinagan
Okanaqe'nix *see* Okinagan
Okanaqenix *see* Okinagan
O-kan-dan-da *see* Oglala
Okandanda *see* Oglala
O'Kanies-kanies *see* Okinagan
O'kawa'siku *see* Okawasiku
Okanieskanies *see* Okinagan
Okanis *see* Kansa
Okanogan *see* Okinagan
Okanogon *see* Okinagan
Okatlituk *see* Oealitk
Oka'to Wini'niwuk [WI] *Menom-
  inee* (BE)
Okawasiku [Clan] *Menominee* (H)
Okaxa-witcaca *see* Okagh-
  wichasha
Okchai [AL] *Muskogee* (BE)
Okdada *see* Oglala
Oke-choy-atte *see* Alabama
Okechoyatte *see* Alabama
Okechumne [CA] (H)
Okee-og-mut *see* Okiogmiut
Okeeog-mut *see* Okiogmiut
Okeeogmut *see* Okiogmiut
Okeeogmute *see* Okiogmiut
Okehocking *Delaware* (Hdbk15)
Okelousa [LA, MS] (BE)
Okenaganes *see* Okinagan
Okenakanes *see* Okinagan
Okena quai'n *see* Okinagan
Okenaquain *see* Okinagan
Okenechee *see* Occoneechee
Okfuskee [AL] *Coosa* (BE)
Okhaganak *see* Okiogmiut
Okiakanes *see* Okinagan
O-ki-li-sa *see* Okilisa
Okilisa [Clan] *Creek* (H)
Okinagan [Lang] *Interior Salish*
  (LC)
Okinagan [WA, BC] (LC)
Okinaganes *see* Okinagan
Okinagenes *see* Okinagan
Okinahane *see* Okinagan
Okinakain *see* Okinagan
Okinakan *see* Okinagan

O'Kinakanes see Okinagan
Okinakanes see Okinagan
O'kina'k-en see Okinagan
Okina'k-en see Okinagan
Okinaken see Okinagan
Okina'qen see Okinagan
Okinaqen see Okinagan
Okin-e-Kanes see Okinagan
Okinekanes see Okinagan
O'kin-i-kaines see Okinagan
Okinikaines see Okinagan
Okinokan see Okinagan
Okiogmiut Eskimos (H)
O-ki-wah-kine see Okinagan
Okiwahkine see Okinagan
Okla falaya see Oklafalaya
Oklafalaya Choctaw (H)
Oklahaneli see Oklahannali
Okla hannali see Oklahannali
Oklahannali Choctaw (H)
Okla-humali-hosh see Oklahan-
    nali
Oklahumalihosh see Oklahannali
Okmulgee (BE)
Oknagan River see Okinagan
Oknaka see Oglala
Oknanagan see Okinagan
Okomiut Eskimos (H)
Okomoyana [Br, Sur] [Tiriyo]
    (O)
Okonagan see Okinagan
Okonagon see Okinagan
Okonegan see Okinagan
Okopeya Tizaptan (H)
Okoro see Arikara
Okoromomowi Guahibo (O)
O-kos see Okos
Okos Arikara (H)
Okshee see Klamath
Oktchunualgi [Clan] Creek (H)
Okuaho see Toryohne
Okuvagamute see Ukivogmiut
O-ku-wa see Okuwa
Okuwa [Clan] Pueblo Indians (H)
okuwaregeowinge see Sia
oku warege owing Sia (Hdbk9)
O-ku-wa-ri see Sia
Okuwari see Sia
Okuwa-tdoa see Okuwa
Okuwatdoa see Okuwa
O-ku-wun see Okuwa
Okuwun see Okuwa
Okwanuchee [Lang] Shastan (CA-
    8)
Ok-wa-nu-chu see Okwanuchu
Okwanuchu [CA] (CA)
Okwanuchu [Lang] [CA] Shastan
    (He)
Olagale [FL] (H)
Olahmenko see Olamentka
O-lah-ment-ko see Olamentka
Olalla see Oraibi
Olamentka [CA] (H)

Olamentko see Marin-Bodega
Olanche [CA] [Mono-Paviotso]
    (H)
Olanches see Yawdanchi
Olancho [Hon] Nahuatl (BE)
Olchipwe see Ojibwa
Olchones see Ohlon
Old Chilili see Chilili [Tigua]
Old Colony Indians see Mashpee
Old Cordilleran see Cascade
    Phase
Old Dogs [Society] Hidatsa (H)
Oldnass see Niska
Old Oraibi see Oraibi
Old Sarcee's Band see Uterus
Old Skin Necklace [SD] Oglala
    (H)
Oleachshoot see Ootlashoot
Oleepa see Ololopa
Ole-har-kar-me-kar-to see Ole-
    harkarmekarto
Oleharkarmekarto [Subclan]
    Delaware (H)
Olelachshook see Ootlashoot
Olelackshoot see Ootlashoot
Oleo Caduveo (O)
Ol-hones see Ohlon
Olhones see Ohlon
Olibahalies see Alabama
Olilefeleia see Oklafalaya
Olinack see Abnaki
O-lip-as see Ololopa
Olipas see Ololopa
O-lip-pas see Ololopa
Olippas see Ololopa
Olive [Lang] [MX] (Bull44)
Olive [MX] (BE)
Oljon see Ochon
Ol-la see Olla
Olla [CA] Maidu (Contri, v.3,
    p.282)
Olla-jocue see Aiyaho
Ollero see Saidinde
Ollo's see Oto
Olmeca see Olmecs
Olmecs [MX] (LC)
Olobayaguame [MX] Concho (BE)
Olojasme Concho (BE)
Ololopa [CA] (H)
Ololopai see Ololopa
Olomega see Nahuatlato
Olon-ko see Moquelumnan
Olonko see Moquelumnan
Olotule [Self-designation] see
    Cuna
Olowitok [CA] (H)
Ol-po-sel see Olposel
Olposel [CA] (H)
Olua see Ulva
Ol-u-la-to see Olulato
Olulato [CA] Patwin (H)
O-lum-a-ne see Olumane
Olumane [Subclan] Delaware (H)

Oluta [MX] Popoloca (BE)
Olwere see Chiwere
Oma-a see Omowuh
Omaa see Omowuh
Omage see Amuesha
Omagua (LC) see also Carijona
    (LC)
Omagua [Br] (O)
O-ma-ha see Omaha
Omaha [Lang] Siouan (H)
Omaha [NE] (LC)
Omaha hcaka see Omaha
Omahah see Omaha
Omahahcaka see Omaha
Omahanes see Okinagan
Omahaw see Omaha
Omahua see Omaha
Omail see Ohamil
Omalia see Omaha
Omameeg see Miami
oma-mi see Miami
omami see Miami
Omamiwininiwak [Q] (H)
Oman see Omaha
O-man-ee see Mdewakanton
Omanee see Mdewakanton
O-man-ha see Omaha
Omanha see Omaha
O-man-ha-hca see Omaha
Omanhahca see Omaha
Omanitsenok [Gens] Kwakiutl
    (H)
Omanominee see Menominee
Omanomineu [Self-designation]
    see Menominee
Omanomini see Menominee
omano-mini see Menominee
Omaonhaon see Omaha
Omashkekok see Maskegon
Omaskos see Oma'skos
Oma'skos [Clan] Menominee (H)
Omasuyo [BO] Aymara (O)
Omat see Houma
Omatchamne see Machemni
Omates see Onondaga
Omatl [Gens] Tlatlasikoala (H)
O-mau see Okuwa
O-mau see Omowuh
Omau see Okuwa
Omau see Omowuh
Omau-hau see Omaha
Omauhau see Omaha
O-maum-ee see Mdewakanton
Omaumee see Mdewakanton
O-maum-eeg see Miami
Omaumeeg see Miami
Omaumeg see Miami
Omauwu [Clan] Hopi (H)
Omawhaw see Omaha
Omawhawes see Omaha
Omawuu see Omowuh
Omeaoffe see Omenaosse
Omeaosse see Omenaosse

Omeaotes *see* Omenaosse

O-me-gee-ze *see* Omegeeze

Omegeeze [Clan] *Chippewa* (H)

Omenaosse [TX] (H)

O'mene *see* Nootka

Omene *see* Nootka

Omianick *see* Miami

Omie *see* Miami

Omikoues *see* Amikwa

O'mi'sis (H) *see also* Northern
Cheyenne (BE)

Omisis *see* O'mi'sis

Omisis (PC) *see also* Northern
Cheyenne (BE)

O'mi'sis [SD] *Cheyenne* (BE)

O'mi'sists *see* O'mi'sis

Omisists *see* O'mi'sis

O missis *see* O'mi'sis

Omissis *see* O'mi'sis

Omkwa *see* Umpqua

Omma *see* Houma

Ommunise [MI] *Chippewa* (H)

Omochumnies *see* Machemni

Omouhoa *see* Omaha

Omowhow *see* Omaha

Omowuh [Clan] *Hopi* (H)

O-mow-uh wun-wu *see*
Omowhu

Omowuh wunwu *see* Omowuh

Omuhaw *see* Omaha

O-mun-o-min-eeg *see* Menominee

Omunomineeg *see* Menominee

Omurano [PE] (O)

Omushkasug *Chippewa* (H)

Omush-ke-goag *see* Maskegon

Omushkegoag *see* Maskegon

Omushke-goes *see* Maskegon

Omushkegoes *see* Maskegon

Omutchamne *see* Machemni

Omutchumne *see* Machemni

Ona (O) *see also* Selk'nam (O)

Ona [Arg, CH] (LC)

Onace *see* Ouasourini

Onadago *see* Onondaga

Onadahkos *see* Anardarko

Onadaicas *see* Anadarko

Onagongue *see* Abnaki

Onagunga *see* Abnaki

Onagungee *see* Abnaki

Onalkeopa (BE) *see also* Walka-
mepa (BE)

Onalkeopa (BE) *see also* Wikedjasapa (BE)

Onalkeopa [AZ] (BE)

Onanadages *see* Onondaga

Onancock *Accomac* (Hdbk15)

Onancocke *see* Onancock

Onandaga *see* Onondaga

Onandager *see* Onondaga

Onandago *see* Onondaga

Onandoga *see* Onondaga

Onanikins *see* Ouanakina

Onantague *see* Onondaga

Onaouackecinatouek *see* Huron

Onapiem [TX] (H)

Onapien *see* Onapiem

Onapienes *see* Onapiem

Onathaqua [FL] (H)

Onathequa [FL] *Timucua* (BE)

Onaumanient *see* Onawmanient

Onawaraghhare *see* Oneida

Onawmanient [VA] *Powhatan*
(BE)

Onayaut *see* Oneida

Onayiut *see* Oneida

O-na-yote-ka-o-na *see* Oneida

Onayotekaona *see* Oneida

O-na-yote'-ka-o-no *see* Oneida

Onayotekaono *see* Oneida

Oncapapa *see* Hunkpapa

Onch-pa-pah *see* Hunkpapa

Onchpapah *see* Hunkpapa

Oncida *see* Oneida

Onconntehock *see* Abnaki

Onc-pah-pa *see* Hunkpapa

Oncpahpa *see* Hunkpapa

Oncpapa *see* Hunkpapa

Oncydes *see* Oneida

Ondadeonwas *see* Cherokee

Ondage *see* Onondaga

Ondataouaouat *see* Ottawa

Ondataouatouat *see* Illinois

Ondataouatouat *see* Ottawa

ondatauauat *see* Ottawa

Ondatawawat *see* Ottawa

Ondatouatandy *see* Oto

Ondatouatandy *see* Potawatomi

Ondawaga *see* Seneca

Ondiake *see* Abnaki

Ondieronu *see* Neutral Nation

Ondiondago *see* Onondaga

Ondironon *see* Aondironon

Ondoutaouaheronnon *see* Ondoutaouaka

Ondoutaouaheronnon *see* Ottawa

Ondoutaouaka [Q] (H)

Oneata (H) *see also* Oneida (LC)

O-nea-ya-ta-au-cau *see* Oneida

Oneayotaaucau *see* Oneida

One-ca-papa *see* Hunkpapa

Onecapapa *see* Hunkpapa

One-daugh-ga-haugh-ga *see*
Onondaga

Onedaughgahaughga *see*
Onondaga

Oneday *see* Oneida

Onedes *see* Oneida

Onedoes *see* Oneida

Oneiada *see* Oneida

Oneiadd *see* Oneida

Oneiades *see* Oneida

Oneida [NY] *Iroquois* (LC)

Oneidaes *see* Oneida

Oneidas of the Thames [Ont]
Oneida (H)

Oneides *see* Oneida

Oneidoes *see* Oneida

Oneids *see* Oneida

Oneijde *see* Oneida

Oneiochronon *see* Oneida

Oneiotchronon *see* Oneida

Oneiouks *see* Oneida

Oneiouronon *see* Oneida

Oneiout *see* Oneida

Oneioutchronnon *see* Oneida

Oneiyuta *see* Oneida

Onei-yu-ta-augh-a *see* Oneida

Oneiyutaaugha *see* Oneida

Onejage *see* Abnaki

Onejagese *see* Sokoki

Onejda *see* Oneida

Onejde *see* Oneida

Onejoust *see* Oneida

Onendagah *see* Onondaga

Oneniuteaka *see* Seneca

Oneniute'a'ka *see* Seneca

Oneniuteronnon *see* Seneca

Oneniute'ron'non *see* Seneca

O-nen-ta-ke *see* Onondaga

Onentake *see* Onondaga

Oneota *Lakota* (LC)

Oneout *see* Oneida

Oneoutchoueronon *see* Oneida

Onepowesepewenenewak [MN,
SD, ND] *Chippewa* (H)

Onepowe Sepe Wenenewok *see*
Onepowesepewenenewak

Onepowesepewenenewok *see*
Onepowesepewenenewak

Oneronon (H)

Oneronon (Hdbk15) *see also*
Wenro (Hdbk15)

Oneyades *see* Oneida

Oneyda *see* Oneida

Oneyder *see* Oneida

Oneydes *see* Oneida

Oneydese *see* Oneida

Oneydey *see* Oneida

Oneydoes *see* Oneida

Oneydos *see* Oneida

Oneyds *see* Oneida

Oneyede *see* Oneida

Oneyonts *see* Oneida

Oneyote *see* Oneida

Oneyoust *see* Oneida

Oneyut *see* Oneida

Onghetgechaton *see* Oughetgeodatons

Onghetgeodatons *see* Oughetgeodatons

Ongmarahronon *see* Neutral Nation

Ongniaahra [NY] *Neutrals* (BE)

Ongniarahronon [Lang] *Neutral
Nation* (H)

Onguiarahronon *see* Neutral Nation

Ongwa *see* Hoti

Ongwanonsionni *see* Iroquios
On-gwa-non'syon'n *see* Iroquois
Ongwanonsyonni *see* Iroquois
Oniada *see* Oneida
Oniades *see* Oneida
Oniansont-Keronon *see* Honniasontkeronon
Oniasontke *see* Honniasontkeronon
Oniasontkeronon *see* Honniasontkeronon
Onicoin [Self-designation] *see* Sharanahua
Onids *see* Oneida
Onieda *see* Oneida
Oniedes *see* Oneida
Onie-le-toch *see* Oealitk
Onieletoch *see* Oealitk
Onieoute *see* Oneida
Oni'ha *see* Omaha
Oniha *see* Omaha
O-ni-ha-o *see* Omaha
Onihao *see* Omaha
Onioenhronnon *see* Cayuga
Onioet *see* Oneida
Onionenhronnon *see* Cayuga
Oniouenhronon *see* Cayuga
Oniout *see* Oneida
Onioutcheronon *see* Oneida
Onipowisibiwininiwag *see* Onepowesepewenenewak
Onipowisibiwininiwug *see* Onepowesepewenenewak
Oniyouth *see* Oneida
O-ni-yu-ta *see* Oneida
Oniyuta *see* Oneida
Oniyutaaugha *see* Oneida
onjadikadi *Northern Paiute* (Hdbk11)
Onkapas *see* Oyukhpe
Onkdaka *see* Oglala
Onkilon *see* Siberian Eskimos
Onkinegan *see* Okinagan
Onkolukomno'm [CA] *Yuki* (BE)
Onkouagannha *see* Ontwaganha
Onkpahpah *see* Hunkpapa
Onkpapah *see* Hunkpapa
Onktokadan (H)
Onlogamies *see* Fox
Onnagonge *see* Abnaki
Onnagongue *see* Abnaki
Onnagongwe *see* Abnaki
Onnagonque *see* Abnaki
Onnandages *see* Onondaga
Onnatague *see* Onondaga
Onneiochronnon *see* Oneida
Onneious *see* Oneida
Onneioust *see* Oneida
Onneiout *see* Oneida
Onneioutchoueronon *see* Oneida
Onneioute *see* Oneida
Onneiouthronnon *see* Oneida

Onnejioust *see* Oneida
Onnejochronon *see* Oneida
Onnejohronnon *see* Oneida
Onnejoust *see* Oneida
Onnejout *see* Oneida
Onnetague *see* Onondaga
Onneyatte *see* Oneida
Onneyde *see* Oneida
Onneyotchronon *see* Oneida
Onneyout *see* Oneida
Onneyouth *see* Oneida
Onneyuttehaga *see* Oneida
Onnieotchronnon *see* Oneida
Onnogonges *see* Abnaki
Onnogongwae *see* Abnaki
Onnogontes *see* Oneida
Onnoncharonnon *see* Ononchataronon
Onnondaga *see* Onondaga
Onnondage *see* Onondaga
Onnondagoes *see* Onondaga
Onnondagues *see* Onondaga
Onnongonge *see* Abnaki
Onnoniote *see* Oneida
Onnonlage *see* Onondaga
Onnontae *see* Onondaga
Onnontaé *see* Onondaga
onnontaeeronnon *see* Onondaga
Onnontaehronnon *see* Onondaga
Onnontaeronnon *see* Onondaga
Onnontae'ronnon *see* Onondaga
Onnontaghe *see* Onondaga
Onnontagk *see* Onondaga
Onnontague *see* Onondaga
Onnontaguehronnon *see* Onondaga
Onnontagueronnon *see* Onondaga
Onnontaguese *see* Onondaga
Onnontaguez *see* Onondaga
Onnontaheronnon *see* Onondaga
Onnontatae *see* Onondaga
Onnontcharonnon *see* Ononchataronon
Onnontgué *see* Onondaga
Onnon-Tioga *see* Onnontioga
Onnontioga [NY] (H)
Onnontoeronnon *see* Onondaga
Onnotague *see* Onondaga
Onnoyotes *see* Oneida
Onnoyoute *see* Oneida
Onoalagona [NY] *Mohawk* (H)
O-no-a-la-gone-na *see* Onoalagona
O-no-a-la-gone-na *see* Schenectady
Onoalagonena *see* Onoalagona
Onoalagonena *see* Schenectady
Onoconcquehaga *see* Abnaki
Onocow *see* Konkow
Onodo *see* Oneida
Onogange *see* Abnaki
Onogongoes *see* Abnaki

Onogonguas *see* Abnaki
Onogungo *see* Abnaki
Onoiochrhonon *see* Oneida
Onojake *see* Oneida
Onokonquehaga *see* Abnaki
Ononchataronon [Can] *Algonkin* (BE)
Ononda-ago *see* Onondaga
Onondaago *see* Onondaga
Onondades *see* Onondaga
Onondaeronnon *see* Onondaga
Onondaga [NY] *Iroquois Confederacy* (LC)
Onondagaes *see* Onondaga
Onondagah *see* Onondaga
Onondage *see* Onondaga
Onondagez *see* Onondaga
Onondagha *see* Onondaga
Onondaghe *see* Onondaga
Onondagheronon *see* Onondaga
Onondago *see* Onondaga
Onondagoes *see* Onondaga
Onondague *see* Onondaga
Onondaja *see* Onondaga
Onondake *see* Onondaga
Onondawgaw *see* Onondaga
Onondega *see* Onondaga
O-non-e-ka-ga-ha *see* Mandhinkagaghe
Ononekagaha *see* Mandhinkagaghe
Onongongues *see* Abnaki
Ononiiote *see* Oneida
O-no-ni-o *see* Arikara
Ononio *see* Arikara
Ononiote *see* Oneida
Ononjete *see* Oneida
Ononjote *see* Oneida
Onontae *see* Onondaga
Onontaehronon *see* Onondaga
Onontaerhonon *see* Onondaga
Onontaeronon *see* Onondaga
Onontaerrhonon *see* Onondaga
Onontaez *see* Onondaga
Ononta'ge *see* Onondaga
Onontage *see* Onondaga
Onontager *see* Onondaga
Onontageronon *see* Onondaga
Onontages *see* Onondaga
Onontaghes *see* Onondaga
Onontaghronon *see* Onondaga
Onontago *see* Onondaga
Onontague *see* Onondaga
Onontaguehronnon *see* Onondaga
Onontagueronon *see* Onondaga
Onontaguese *see* Onondaga
Onontaguez *see* Onondaga
Onontaharonon *see* Onondaga
Onontahe *see* Onondaga
Onontakaes *see* Ottawa
Onontake *see* Onondaga
Onontatacet *see* Onondaga

Onontchataranon *see* Onon-
chataronon
Onontchateronon *see* Onon-
chataronon
Ononthaca *see* Onathaqua
Ononthague *see* Onondaga
Onontioga *see* Onnontioga
Onoontaugaes *see* Onondaga
Onossky *see* Ahtena
Onoto *see* Paraujano
Onoundage *see* Onondaga
Onoyat *see* Oneida
Onoyaut *see* Oneida
Onoyote *see* Oneida
Onoyout *see* Oneida
Onoyut *see* Oneida
Onquilouza *see* Opelousa
Ontaanak *see* Ottawa
Ontagamies *see* Fox
Ontague *see* Onondaga
Ontanaak *see* Ottawa
Ontaonatz *see* Ottawa
Ontarahronon (H)
Ontarahronon (Hdbk15) *see also*
Kickapoo (LC)
Ontarraronon *see* Ontarahronon
Ontastoes *see* Conestoga
Ontationoue *see* Noottoway
Ontdwawies *see* Ottawa
Ontehibouse *see* Ojibwa
Ontiayanadi [Clan] *Biloxi* (H)
Ontoagannha *see* Ontwaganha
Ontoagaunha *see* Ontwaganha
Ontonagon [MI, WI] *Chippewa*
(BE)
Ontoouaganha *see* Ontwaganha
Ontotonta *see* Oto
Ontouagannha *see* Ontwaganha
Ontouagennha *see* Ontwaganha
Ontponea [VA] *Manahoac* (BE)
Ontponies *see* Ontponea
Onttaouactz *see* Ottawa
Ontwagana *see* Shawnee
Ontwaganha (H)
Ontwaganha (H) *see also* Shawnee
(LC)
Ontwagannha *see* Ontwaganha
Onughkaurydaaug *see* Seneca
O-nun-da-ga-o-no *see*
Onondaga
Onundagaono *see* Onondaga
Onundagega *see* Onondaga
Onundagega-nonondshunda *see*
Onondaga
Onundawaga *see* Seneca
Onundawgoes *see* Onondaga
Onuntewakaa *see* Seneca
Onyades *see* Oneida
Onyapes *see* Quapaw
Onydan *see* Oneida
Onyedaun *see* Oneida
oob *see* Highland Pima
Oochepayyan *see* Chipewyan

Oo-chuk-ham *see* Oochukham
Oochukham [Subclan] *Delaware*
(H)
Oocooloo-Falaya *see* Oklafalaya
O-o-dam *see* Tepehuan
o'odam *see* Lowland Pima
oodam *see* Lowland Pima
Oodam *see* Tepehuan
O'odham *see* Upper Piman
Oodham *see* Upper Piman
Ooe-Asa *see* Tawasa
Ooeasa *see* Tawasa
Oofe-ogoola *see* Ofo
Oogahlensie *see* Ugalakmiut
Oogalenskie *see* Ugalakmiut
Oo-geoolik *see* Ugjulirmiut
Oogeoolik *see* Ugjulirmiut
Oogueesik Salik *see* Ukusiksalair-
miut
Ooguensik-salik-Innuits *see*
Ukusiksalirmiut
Oo-gwapes *see* Quapaw
Oogwapes *see* Quapaw
Oohe-nonpa *see* Oohenonpa
Oohenonpa [SD] *Oglala* (LC)
Oohenoupa *see* Oohenonpa
O-o-ho-mo-i-o *see* Dakota
Oohomoio *see* Dakota
Oohp *see* Hualapai
Oohp *see* Navajo
Ooikaxtenox *see* Koikahtenok
Oo-ka-na-kane *see* Okinagan
Ookanakane *see* Okinagan
Ookanawgan *see* Okinagan
Ook-joo-lik *see* Ugjulirmiut
Ookjoolik *see* Ugjulirmiut
Ookwolik (H) *see also* Ugjrlirmiut
(H)
Ookwolik *Eskimos* (H)
Oolukak *see* Ulukakhotana
Oo-ma-ha *see* Omaha
Oomaha *see* Omaha
Oominutqui *see* Oomi-nutqui
Oomi-nutqui [Society] *Cheyenne*
(H)
Oomi-nu-tquin *see* Himoiyoqis
Oominutquin *see* Himoiyoqis
Oomoojeks *see* Eiwhuelit
Oonaligmiut *Bering Strait Eskimos*
(Hdbk5)
Oonaligmute (H) *see also* Unalig-
miut (BE)
Oonangan *see* Aleuts
Ooncow *see* Konkow
Oonontaeronnon *see* Onondaga
Oop *see* Apache
Oop *see* Navajo
Oopa *see* Maricopa
Oopap *see* Maricopa
Ooqueesiksillik *see* Ukusiksalir-
miut
Oo-sa-bot-*see see* Oosabotsee
Oosabotsee *Crow*

O'o-sa tun'ne *see* Khosatunne
Oosatunne *see* Khosatunne
Oosemite *see* Awani
Oosoomite *see* Awani
Oostomas *see* Ustoma
Ootagamis *see* Fox
Ootam *see* Pima
O'otam (Hdbk9)
Ootam *see* O'otam
Oote-lash-shoot *see* Ootlashoot
Ootelashshoot *see* Ootlashoot
Oote-lash-shute *see* Ootlashoot
Ootelashshute *see* Ootlashoot
Ootkeaviemute *see* utkiavinmiut
Ootkeavies *see* Utkiavinmiut
Ootlashoot (Hdbk12) *see also* Flat-
head (Hdbk12)
Ootlashoot *Tushepaw Nation* (H)
Ootooka Mutes *see* Utukamiut
Ootookas *see* Utukamiut
Ootslashshoot *see* Ootlashoot
Ootyi-ti *see* Cochiti
Ootyti *see* Cochiti
Ooukia *see* Cahokia
Ooukkea *see* Cahokia
Oowekeeno [BC] (LC)
Oo-yapes *see* Quapaw
Ooyapes *see* Quapaw
Oo-za-tau *see* Otsehta
Oozatau *see* Utsehta
'Oozei *see* Hopi
'Oozei *see* Oraibi
Oozei Biyaazh *see* Moenkopi
Op *see* Apache
Opa *see* Maricopa
O'pa *see* Upan
Opa *see* Kavelchadom
Opa *see* Upan
Opaguiguara *see* Ipajuiguara
Opaia *see* Obayo
Opaina *see* Yahuana
Opa-la *see* Opata
Opalusa *see* Opelousa
Opanguaimas *see* Upanguayma
Opan Guamas *see* Upanguayma
Opata [Lang] [MX] *Opatan*
(Hdbk10)
Opata [MX] (LC)
Opataice *see* Opata
Opatan [Lang] [MX] *Taracahitan*
(Hdbk10)
Opatas Coguinachis *see* Cogu-
inachi
Opatas teguimas *see* Teguima
Opate *see* Opata
Opatoro [Hon] *Lenca* (BE)
Opaua *see* Opata
Opea *see* Peoria
Opechisaht *see* Opitchesaht
Opecluset *see* Opitchesaht
Ope-eis-aht *see* Opitchesaht
Opeeisaht *see* Opitchesaht
Opelousa (BE) *see also* Paloos (LC)

Opelousa [LA] (BE)
Opelouse see Opelousa
Opeluassa see Opelousa
Opemens d'Acheling see
  Nopeming
Openadyo see Abnaki
Openagi see Abnaki
Openago see Abnaki
Openango see Abnaki
Openoches see Pohonichi
Opet-ches-aht see Opitchesaht
Opetchesaht see Opitchesaht
Opichiken [BC] Salish (H)
Opii see Hopi
Opillako see Pilthlako
O'pimittish Ininiwac see
  Nopeming
Opimittishininiwac see Nopem-
  ing
O'pimmitish Ininiwuc see Cree
Opimmitishininiwuc see Cree
Opinadkom see Arara
Opine see Wappinger
Oping see Pompton
Oping see Wappinger
O-ping-ha-ki see Opinghaki
O-ping-ho-ki see Opinghaki
Opinghoki [Subclan] Delaware
  (H)
Opiscopank [VA] Algonquian
  (Hdbk15)
Opitches-aht see Opitchesaht
Opitchesaht [BC] Nootka (BE)
Opocoula see Ofo
O-po-nagh-ke see Abnaki
Oponaghke see Abnaki
Opone [Lang] Carib (O)
Oponoche [CA] (H)
O-po-que see San Ildefonso
Opoque see San Ildefonso
Oposian see Opossian
Oposime see Obone
Oposine see Obone
Oposme see Obone
Opossian [NC] Warrasqueoc (H)
Oppelousa see Opelousa
Oppenago see Abnaki
Opposite Assiniboin [MN] Atsina
  (BE)
O-puh-nar-ke see Abnaki
Opuhnarke see Abnaki
Opuhnarke see Delaware
O-puh-nark-ke see Delaware
O-puhn nika-shing-ga see Upan
Opuhnnikashingga see Upan
Oqomiut see Okomiut
Oqtogon see Oqtoguna
Oqtogona see Oqtaguna
Oqtoguna [SD] Cheyenne (BE)
O-qua-pa see Quapaw
Oquapa see Quapaw
Oquapaso see Quapaw
Oque-Loussa see Opelousa

Oqueloussa see Opelousa
Oquwa [Clan] Tewa (H)
Oquwa tdoa see Okuwa
Oquwa tdoa see Oquwa
Orage see Osage
Oraibi Hopi (BE)
Orapak [VA] Algonquian (Hdbk15)
Orapakes see Orapak
Orari [Br] Eastern Bororo (O)
Orarians (Contri, v.1)
Orarians (H) see also Eskimauan
  (BE)
Oraw-it see Warrau
Orawit see Warrau
Oraybi see Oraibi
Orchard Party Oneida (H)
Orcocoyana see Urukuyana
Orcoquisa see Arkokisa
Orcoquisac see Arkokisa
Orcoquiza see Arkokisa
Ore see Opata
Orebe see Ocaina
Orechon see Orejon
Oregon [Lang] Shasta (CA-8)
Oregon House [Lang] Nisenan
  (CA)
Oregon Indians [SA] see Orejon
Oregon jargon see Chinookan
  jargon
Oregon Northern Paiute (Hdbk5)
Oregon Trade Language [Lang]
  Chinookan jargon (BE)
Oreintales see Penateka
Orejon [PE] Witoto (O)
Orejones Faraon Apache (H)
Orejones [Pacific Northwest] (H)
Orejones [TX] Coahuiltecan (BE)
Orejon-Koto see Orejon
Orelha de Pau see Numbiai
Orendake see Adirondack
Orinoco Waica [Br] Yanoama (O)
Orio [BO, Par] Chamacoco (O)
Oriskayek see Warrasqueoc
Orista see Edisto
Oristan [JA] (BE)
Oristanum see Edisto
Orke see San Juan [NM]
Orkokoyana see Guayana
Orleans Indians see Karok
Ornofay [Cu] (BE)
Oro At [Br] Pakaanova (O)
Oro Eu [Br] Pakaanova (O)
Orohpikes see Orapak
Oro Mun [Br] Pakaanova (O)
Oro Nao [Br] Pakaanova (O)
Orondack see Adirondack
Orondock see Adirondack
Orondoes see Adirondack
Orongouen see Cayuga
Oron-nygh-wurrie-gughre see
  Onoalagone
Oronnyghwurriegughre see
  Onoalagone

Oroondok see Adirondack
Oroonduck see Adirondack
Orosi [CR] Orotina (BE)
Orotina [CR] Chorotega (BE)
Orotinan [Lang] [CR] (Bull44)
Orowari see Pakaanova
Oro Warm [Br] Pakaanova (O)
Oro Warmxijein [Br] Pakaanova
  (O)
Orp see Apache
Orphans Southern Brule (TW,
  v.39, no.6, June 1992)
Orquisaco see Arkokisa
Orriparacogi see Tocobaga
Orriparagi see Tocobaga
Orriygua see Tocobaga
Orundack see Adirondack
Orunge see Mahican
Oruro see Aymara
Osa [CR] Boruca (BE)
Osach [Clan] Acoma (H)
Osach-hano see Oshach
Osach-hanoqch see Oshach
Osage [MO, OK] (LC)
Osage des Chenes see Santsukhd-
  hin
Osages of the Oaks see
  Santsukhdhin
Osagi see Sauk
Osaij see Hopi
Osaki see Sauk
Osakik see Sauk
Osa'kiwug [Self-designation] see
  Sauk
Osakiwugi see Sauk
Osan-algi see Osanalgi
Osanalgi [Clan] Creek (H)
Osankies see Sauk
Osarge see Osage
Osasi'gi see Osage
Osasigi see Osage
Osass see O'sass
O'sass [Clan] Menominee (H)
Osatoves see Uzutiuhi
Osaugeeg see Sauk
Osaukies see Sauk
O-saw-kee see Sauk
Osawkee see Sauk
O-saw-se see Osage
Osawse see Osage
Osay see Hopi
Osaye see Osage
Oscameches see Occoneechee
Oschekkamega Wenenewak see
  Oschekkamegawenenewak
Oschekkamegawenenewak [MN,
  WI] Chippewa (BE)
Oscouarahronon (H)
Oseca see Maricopa
Osedshi maklak see Osage
Osedshmaklak see Osage
O-see-gah see Tschantoga
Oseegah Assiniboin (H)

O-se-elth *see* Ozette
Oseelth *see* Ozette
Osegah *see* Tschantoga
Osegah *see* Oseegah
O-se-ilth *see* Ozette
Oseilth *see* Ozette
Osera *see* Maricopa
Osgeegah *see* Itscheabine
Oshach [Clan] *Keres* (H)
O'shach-hano *see* Oshach
Oshachhano *see* Oshach
O'shach-hanuch *see* Oshach
Oshachhanuch *see* Oshach
Oshahak *see* Dakota
Osha'kamigawininiwag *see* Os-
chekkamegawenenewak
Oshakamigawininiwag *see* Os-
chekkamegawenenewak
Osha'kumi-gawininiwug *see* Os-
chekkamegawenenewak
Oshakumigawininiwug *see* Os-
chekkamegawenenewak
O-sharts *see* Oshach
Osharts *see* Oshach
Oshatsh *see* Oschach
Oshawanoog *see* Shawnee
Oshcush [Society] *Sauk* (His/T,
v.2, p.357)
Osheraca *see* Fox
O-sher-a-ca *see* Fox
Osheti Shakowin *see* Dakota
Oshetishakowin *see* Dakota
Oshibek *see* Ojibwa
Oshkasha [Gens] *Sauk* (His/T,
v.2, p.147)
Oshkosh *see* Osh'kosh
Osh'kosh [WI] *Menominee* (BE)
Osinies *see* Ozinies
Osinipoille *see* Assiniboin
Osipee *see* Ossipee
Oskemanettigon *see* Oukiski-
manitouk
Oskemanitigous *see* Oukiski-
manitouk
Os-ken-o-tah *see* Oskenotoh
Oskenotah *see* Oskenotoh
Oskenotoh [Clan] *Huron* (H)
Oskquisaquamai (H)
Osochi [AL] *Creek* (BE)
Osooyoo *see* Nkamip
Osotonoy *see* Uzutiuhi
Osottoeoez *see* Uzutiouhi
Osoyoos *see* Nkamip
Osquake [NY] *Mohawk* (H)
Osquisakamai *see* Oskquisaqua-
mai
Ossachile *see* Timucua
Ossage *see* Osage
Os'se *see* Osse
Osse [Gens] *Menominee* (H)
Ossegah (PC) *see also* Tshantoga
(H)
Ossegahs *see* Tschantoga

Ossepe *see* Ossipee
Ossikanna *see* Seneca
Ossikaunnehak *see* Seneca
Ossineboine *see* Assiniboin
Ossiniboine *see* Assiniboin
Ossipe *see* Mosopelea
Ossipee [ME] *Abnaki* (BE)
Ossnobian *see* Assiniboin
Ossoteoez *see* Uzutiuhi
Ossoteoue *see* Uzutiuhi
Ossotonoy *see* Uzutiuhi
Ossotoues *see* Uzutiuhi
Ossotteoez *see* Uzutiuhi
Ossoztoues *see* Uzutiuhi
Os-sweh-ga-da-ga-ah *see* Osswe-
hgadagaah
Osswehgadagaah [Clan] *Seneca*
(H)
Ostiagaghroone *see* Ojibwa
Ostiagaghroone *see* Saulteaux
Ostiagahoroones *see* Chippewa
Ostiagahroone *see* Ojibwa
Otagamies *see* Fox
Otaguottouemin [Can] *Algo-
nquian* (H)
Otaha *see* Ottawa
O-ta-har-ton *see* Otekhiatonwan
Otaharton *see* Otekhiatonwan
otaka-mi-k *see* Fox
otakamik *see* Fox
O-ta-ki *see* Otaki
Otaki [Lang] [CA] *Maiduan* (CA-
8)
Otama [Self-designation] *see*
Pima
Otanabe *see* Muniche
Otanave *see* Muniche
Otaoas *see* Ottawa
Otaopabine [Clan] *Assiniboin* (H)
Otaou *see* Ottawa
Otaouak *see* Ottawa
Ota's-ita'niuw *see* Kadohadacho
Otasitaniuw *see* Kadohadacho
Ota'tshia *see* Otatshia
Otatshia [Phratry] *Menominee*
(H)
Ota-tshia wi'dishi'anun *see* Otat-
shia
Otatshiawidishianun *see* Otatshia
Otatsightes *see* Oneida
Otaua *see* Ottawa
Otaulubis *see* Outurbi
Otavala *see* Otavalo
Otavalo [EC] (LC)
O-ta-wa *see* Ottawa
Ota'wa *see* Ottawa
Otawa *see* Ottawa
Otawau *see* Ottawa
Otawawa *see* Ottawa
Otayachgo *see* Nanticoke
Otcenake *see* Okinagan
Otcenaqai'n *see* Okinagan
Otchagra *see* Winnebago

Otchaqua *see* Onathaqua
Otchente Chakowie *see* Sioux
Otchenti-Chakoang *see* Dakota
Otchepose *see* Ojibwa
Otchipoeses *see* Chippewa
Otchipois *see* Ojibwa
Otchipoises *see* Ojibwa
Otchipwe *see* Ojibwe
Otchipwe *see* Chippewa
O-tchun-gu-rah *see* Winnebago
Otchungurah *see* Winnebago
Otcitca'konsag *see*
Outchichagami
Otehatonwan *see* Otekhiatonwan
Otehiatonwan *see* Otekhiaton-
wan
Otekhiatonwan *Wahpeton* (H)
Ot'el'nna *see* Eskimos
Otelnna *see* Eskimos
Otenmarhen *see* Ointemarhen
Otenmarkem *see* Ointemarhen
Otenta *see* Oto
Oteqi-atonwan *see* Otekhiaton-
wan
Ote-toe *see* Oto
Otetoe *see* Oto
Otheues *see* Oto
Otheuess *see* Oto
Otho *see* Oto
Othoe *see* Oto
Othonez *see* Oto
Othoues *see* Oto
Othouez *see* Oto
Othoves *see* Oto
Oticki-waga-mi *see* Nipissing
Otickiwagami *see* Nipissing
O-til-tin *see* Kutchakutchin
Otiltin *see* Kutchakutchin
Otinanchahe *see* Joassek
Otjibwek *see* Ojibwa
Otkialnaas-hadai *Haida* (H)
Otnaas-hadai *Haida* (H)
Otno-khotana *see* Ahtena
Otnokhotana *see* Ahtena
Otnox tana *see* Ahtena
Otnoxtana *see* Ahtena
Oto [NE] (LC)
Otocomanes (H)
Otoctata *see* Oto
Otoctota *see* Oto
Otoe *see* Oto
Otoetata *see* Oto
Otogamies *see* Fox
Otoge *see* Apinage
O-toh-son *see* Oglala
Otohson *see* Oglala
Oto-kog-ameut *see* Utukamiut
Otokogameut *see* Utukamiut
Otolptpuemi *see* Otaguot-
touemin
Otomaco [Achagua] (LC)
Otomanguean [Lang] [MX] (LC)
Otomaque *see* Otomaco

Otomi [MX] (LC)
Otomian [Lang] [MX] (LC)
Otomie *see* Omaha
Otonnnica *see* Tunica
Otontagan [Ont] *Ottawa* (H)
Otopachgnato [Clan] *Assiniboin* (H)
Otopplata *see* Oto
Otoptata *see* Oto
Ototanta *see* Oto
Ototata *see* Oto
Ototchassi *see* Uzutiuhi
Otoutanta *see* Oto
Otoutantas Paote *see* Oto
Otoway *see* Ottawa
Otsotchaue *see* Uzutiuhi
Otsotchoue *see* Uzutiuhi
Otsotchove *see* Uzutiuhi
Otsote *see* Uzutiiuhi
Ottagamies *see* Fox
Ottagaugami *see* Fox
Ottagaumies *see* Fox
Ottah-wah *see* Ottawa
Ottahwah *see* Ottawa
Ot-tah-way *see* Ottawa
Ottahway *see* Ottawa
Ottaouai *see* Ottawa
Ottaouet *see* Ottawa
Ottapoas *see* Ojibwa
Ottar-car-me *see* Fox
Ottarcarme *see* Fox
Ot-tar-gar-me *see* Fox
Ottargarme *see* Fox
Ottauwah *see* Ottawa
Ottavois *see* Ottawa
Ottawa [MI] (LC)
Ottawac *see* Ottawa
Ottawack *see* Ottawa
Ottawaes *see* Ottawa
Ottawaga *see* Ottawa
Ottawaies *see* Ottawa
Ottawak *see* Ottawa
Ottawa Lake Men (H) *see also* Lac Court Oreilles (H)
Ottawa Lake Men [WI] *Chippewa* (BE)
Ottawaw *see* Ottawa
Ottawawa *see* Ottawa
Ottawawaa *see* Ottawa
Ottawawe *see* Ottawa
Ottawawooes *see* Ottawa
Ottaway *see* Ottawa
Ottawwaw *see* Ottawa
Ottawwawwag *see* Ottawa
Ottawwawwug *see* Ottawa
Otteaus *see* Oto
Otter People *see* Atonthrataronon
Otter Tail [MI] *Pillager Chippewa* (H)
Ottewa *see* Ottawa
Ottigamie *see* Fox
Ottigaumies *see* Fox

Ottiquamies *see* Fox
Otto *see* Oto
Ottoas *see* Oto
Ottoawa *see* Ottawa
Ottoe *see* Oto
Ottogamis *see* Fox
Ottomacque *see* Otomaco
Ottomaku *see* Otomaco
Ottoo *see* Oto
Otto's *see* Oto
Ottos *see* Oto
Ottotatoc *see* Oto
Ottotatoes *see* Oto
Ottova *see* Ottawa
Ottowa *see* Oto
Ottowa *see* Ottawa
Ottowaes *see* Ottawa
Ottowais *see* Ottawa
Ottowata *see* Ottawa
Ottowaus *see* Ottawa
Ottowauway *see* Ottawa
Ottowaw *see* Ottawa
Ottowawa *see* Ottawa
Ottowawe *see* Ottawa
Ottoway *see* Ottawa
Ottowayer *see* Ottawa
Ottowose *see* Ottawa
Ottwasse *see* Ottawa
O'tu'gunu *see* Oqtoguna
Otugunu *see* Oqtoguna
Otuke *see* Otuquis
Otuki *see* Otuquis
O-tun-nee *see* Cree
Otunnee *see* Crow
Otuquis [BO] (LC)
Oturkagmiut [AK] *North Alaska Coast Eskimos* (Hdbk5)
Otusson [MI] *Chippewa* (H)
Otutache *see* Oto
Otzen-ne *see* Otzenne
Otzenne [BC] *Sekani* (H)
Oua *see* Wea
Ouabano (H)
Ouabans *see* Ouabano
Ouabe *see* Guale
Ouabenakiouek *see* Abnaki
Ouabenaqui *see* Abnaki
Ouabenaquis *see* Abnaki
Ouabnaquia *see* Abnaki
Ouace *see* Ouasourini
Ouacha *see* Washa
Ouachibes *see* Washita
Ouachipuanes *see* Chipewyan
Ouachita *see* Washita
Ouachites *see* Washita
Ouachtenon *see* Wea
Ouade *see* Guale
Ouadiche *see* Nabedache
Ouagoussac *see* Fox
Ouaitiadeho *Caduveo* (O)
Ouakich *see* Nootka
Oualeanicou [WI] (H)
Ouali *see* Ouasourini

Ou-a-luck *see* Oualuck's Band
Ou-aluck *see* Oualuck's Band
Oualuck's Band [OR] *Snake* (H)
Ouanahinan *see* Kannehouan
Ouanakina [AL] (H)
Ouaouiartanon *see* Wea
Ouaouiatanoukak *see* Wea
Ouapishana *see* Wapisiana
Ouapishane *see* Wapisiana
Ouapisiana *see* Wapisiana
Ouapon [MI] (H)
Ouaronon *see* Wenro
Ouasaouanik *see* Ouasourini
Ouasita *see* Washita
Ouasouarim *see* Ouasourini
Ouasouarini *see* Ouasourini
Ouasourini [Ont] *Chippewa* (H)
Ouasoy *see* Osage
Ouassi *see* Ouasourini
Ouassita *see* Washita
Ouatawais *see* Ottawa
Ouatchita *see* Washita
Ouatemaneton *see* Ocatameneton
Ouatoieronon *see* Sauk
Ouatouax *see* Ottawa
Ouavaous *see* Warrau
Ouayana *see* Oyana
Ouayeome *see* Waiwai
Ouayeoue *see* Waiwai
Oubenaki *see* Abnaki
Oubestamiouek *see* Bersiamite
Oucahipoues *see* Ojibwa
Ouchage *see* Osage
Ouchaouanag *see* Shawnee
Ouchawanag *see* Shawnee
Ouchee *see* Yuchi
Ouchessigiriniouek *see* Oukesestigouek
Ouchestigouek *see* Oukesestigouek
Ouchestigouet *see* Oukesestigouek
Ouchestigouetch (H) *see also* Oukesestigouek (H)
Ouchestigouetch [Can] [*Montagnais-Naskapi*] (BE)
Ouchibois *see* Ojibwa
Ouchipawah *see* Chippewa
Ouchipoe *see* Chippewa
Ouchipoves *see* Ojibwa
Ouchuchlisit *see* Uchucklesit
Ou-chuk-lis-aht *see* Uchucklesit
Ouchuklisaht *see* Uchuclesit
Oudataouatouat *see* Ottawa
Ouemessourit *see* Missouri
Ouendat *see* Huron
Ouenebegonhelini *see* Ouinebigonhelini
Ouentouoronon *see* Seneca
Oueschekgagamiouilimy [MN, Ont] *Chippewa* (BE)
Ouesperie *see* Mosopelea

Oues-peries *see* Uzutiuhi
Ouesperies *see* Uzutiuhi
Oufeagaoula *see* Ofo
Oufe Agoula *see* Ofo
Oufeogoula *see* Ofo
Oufe Ogula *see* Ofo
Oufeogula *see* Ofo
Oufe-ougla *see* Ofo
Oufeougla *see* Ofo
Oufe Oyoula *see* Ofo
Oufi-Ougula *see* Ofo
Oufiougula *see* Ofo
Oufotu *see* Uzutiuhi
Ougagliakmuzi-Kinaia *see* Kna-
iakhotana
Ougalachmioutsy *see* Ugalakmiut
Ougalentze *see* Ugalakmiut
Ougapa *see* Quapaw
Ougebowy *see* Ojibwa
Oughalakmute *see* Ugulakmiut
Oughalentze *see* Ugulakmiut
Oughetgeodatons *Dakota* (BE)
Oughtella *see* Awaitlala
Ouguapa *see* Quapaw
Ouh-papa *see* Hunkpapa
Ouhpapa *see* Hunkapapa
Ouiagies *see* Mahican
Ouias *see* Wea
Ouiatanon *see* Wea
Ouichaatcha *see* Osage
Ouichram *see* Tlakluit
Ouidachenaton *see* Oughetge-
odatons
Ouidaougeomaton *see* Oughet-
geodatons
Ouidaougeouaton *see* Oughetge-
odatons
Ouidaougeounaton *see* Oughet-
geodatons
Ouidaugeounaton *see* Oughetge-
odatons
Ouidiches *see* Nabedache
Ouikaliny *see* Onikaliny
Ouileute *see* Quileute
Ouillequegaw *see* Kwalhioqua
Ouimiamies *see* Miami
Ouinebigonhelini *Maskegon* (H)
Ouiochrhonon *see* Oneida
Ouioenrhonon *see* Cayuga
Ouionenronnon *see* Cayuga
Ouiouenronnon *see* Cayuga
Ouispe *see* Mosopelea
Ouispe *see* Ofo
Ouititchakouk *see* Kickapoo
Ouitoto *see* Witoto
Ouitoupa *see* Ibitoupa
Oujalespious *see* Oujatespouitons
Oujalespoitons *see* Oujate-
spouitons
Oujalespoitous *see* Oujate-
spouitons
Oujatespouetons *see* Oujate-
spouitons

Oujatespouitons *Dakota* (BE)
Oukesestigouek [Lab] *Montagnais*
(H)
Oukinegan *see* Okinagan
Oukiskimanitouk [Clan]
Chippewa (H)
Oukotoemi [Q] *Montagnais* (H)
Oukskenah *see* Klamath
Oulchioni *see* Doustioni
Oulchionis *see* Doustioni
Oulgampaya *see* Walapai
Ouloulatines *see* Olulato
Ouma *see* Houma
Oumalomini *see* Menominee
Oumaloumine *see* Menominee
Oumalouminek *see* Menominee
Oumalouminetz *see* Menominee
Oumamen *see* Miami
Oumami *see* Miami
Oumamik *see* Miami
Oumamiois *see* Bersiamite
Oumamiois *see* Oumamiwek
Oumamiouck *see* Bersiamite
Oumamiwek (H) *see also* Bersi-
amite (H)
Oumamiwek [Can] [*Montagnais-
Naskapi*] (BE)
Oumanies *see* Miami
Oumaniouet *see* Oumamiwek
Oumanois *see* Oumamiwek
Oumaominiec *see* Menominee
Oumatachi [Q] *Algonquian* (H)
Oumatachiiriouetz *see* Oumatchi
Oumeami *see* Miami
Oumiamies *see* Miami
Oumisagai *see* Missisauga
Ou-missouri *see* Missouri
Oumissouri *see* Missouri
Ounabonim *see* Menominee
Ounachkapiouek *see* Naskapi
Ounadcapi *see* Naskapi
Ounagountchagueliougiout *see*
Juglemute
Ounangan *see* Eskimauan
Ounasacoetois *see* Nassauaketon
Ounascapi *see* Naskapi
Ouneiout *see* Oneida
Ounejout *see* Oneida
Ouneyouths *see* Oneida
Ounhann-Kaouttanae *see* Un-
akhotana
Ounikanes *see* Amikwa
Ounneiout *see* Oneida
Ounontcharonnous *see* Onon-
chataronon
Ounountchatarounongak *see*
Ononchataronon
Ounspik *see* Ofo
Ountaussogoe (Coll, 1st, v.4)
Ountaussookoe (Coll, 1st, v.4)
Ountchatarounounga *see* Onon-
chataronon
Oupapa *see* Quapaw

Oupapinachiouek *see* Papina-
chois
Oupinagee *see* Apinage
Oupouteouatamik *see*
Potawatomi
Ourage *see* Mahican
Ouragies *see* Mahican
Ouramanichek *see* Oumamiwek
Ouraouakmikoug *see*
Outaouakamigouk
Our Lady of Sorrow and Saint
Anthony of Sandia *see* Sandia
Our Lady of Sorrows and Saint
Anthony of Sandia *see* Sandia
Ourous *see* Puquina
Ous *see* Osage
Ousaki *see* Sauk
Ousakiouek *see* Sauk
Ousason *see* Osage
Ousasoy *see* Osage
Ousatannock *see* Stockbridge
Ousatounnuck *see* Stockbridge
Ousetannuck *see* Stockbridge
Ousita *see* Wichita
Ousola *see* Uzutiuhi
Ousontiwi *see* Uzutiuhi
Ousoutiwy *see* Uzutiuhi
Ouspie *see* Ofo
Oussipe *see* Ofo
Oustestee *see* Ustisti
Oustonnoc *see* Stockbridge
Out *see* Oat
Outabitibek *see* Abitibi
Outabytibi *see* Abitibi
Outachepa *see* Ojibwa
Outagami *see* Fox
Outagamie-ock *see* Fox
Outagamieouek *see* Fox
Outagamy *see* Fox
Outagomies *see* Fox
Outakouamiouek *see* At-
tikamegue
Outakouamiwek *see* Attikamegue
Outantes *see* Oto
Outaois *see* Ottawa
Outaoise *see* Ottawa
Outaonaes *see* Ottawa
Outaoua *see* Ottawa
Outaouac *see* Ottawa
outaouaes *see* Ottawa
Outaouaga *see* Ottawa
Outaouagamis *see* Fox
Outaouaies *see* Ottawa
Outaouais *see* Ottawa
Outaouak *see* Ottawa
Outaouakamigouk [Can] *Ottawa*
(H)
Outaouak of the Sable *see* Sable
Outaouaks Sinagaux *see* Sinago
Outaouan *see* Ottawa
Outaouas *see* Ottawa
Outaouasinagouk *see* Sinago
Outaouasinagrouc *see* Sable

Outaouas of Talon *see* Otonta-
gan
Outaouats *see* Ottawa
Outaouaus *see* Ottawa
Outaouax *see* Ottawa
Outaouay *see* Ottawa
Outaouea Sinago *see* Sinago
Outaoues *see* Ottawa
Outaouis *see* Bouscoutton
Outaouisbouscottous *see* Bous-
coutton
Outaouois *see* Ottawa
Outaoutes *see* Ottawa
Outaovacs *see* Ottawa
Outaovas *see* Ottawa
Outaowaies *see* Ottawa
Outapa *see* Ibitoupa
Outarwas *see* Ottawa
Outatibes *see* Abitibi
Outauaes *see* Ottawa
Outauas *see* Ottawa
Outauies *see* Ottawa
Outauois *see* Ottawa
Outava *see* Ottawa
Outavis *see* Ottawa
Outavois *see* Ottawa
Outawa *see* Ottawa
Outawacs *see* Ottawa
Outawais *see* Ottawa
Outawase *see* Ottawa
Outawawa *see* Ottawa
Outaway *see* Ottawa
Outawies *see* Ottawa
Outawois *see* Ottawa
Outaype *see* Ibitoupa
Outchibouec *see* Ojibwa
Outchibous *see* Ojibwa
Outchichagami [Can] (H)
Outchichagamiouetz *see*
Outchichagami
Outchioung *see* Uchium
Outchiouns *see* Uchium
Outchipoue *see* Ojibwa
Outchipwais *see* Ojibwa
Outchougai [Q] (H)
Outchouguet *see* Outchougai
Outduaois *see* Ottawa
Outehipoues *see* Ojibwa
Outemiskamegs *see* Temiscaming
Outeonas *see* Ottawa
Outetontes *see* Oto
Outichacouk *see* Atchatchakan-
gouen
Outigamis *see* Fox
Outimac *see* Ottawa
Outimagami [Can] *Algonquian*
(H)
Outiskouagami *see* Nipissing
Outisquagami *see* Nipissing
Outitchakiiok *see* Kickapoo
Outitchakouk *see* Atchatchakan-
gouen
Outlaw *see* Pinutgu

Outoagamis *see* Fox
Outontagan *see* Ottawa
Outouacks *see* Ottawa
Outouacs *see* Ottawa
Outouagamis *see* Fox
Outouais *see* Ottawa
Outouaouas *see* Ottawa
Outougamis *see* Fox
Outouloubys *see* Outurbi
Outouvas *see* Ottawa
Outowacs *see* Ottawa
Outpanka *see* Ontponea
Outponies *see* Ontponea
Outsotin *see* Hwotsotenne
Outtagamies *see* Fox
Outtagaume *see* Fox
Outtagomies *see* Fox
Outtais *see* Ottawa
Outtamack *see* Ottawa
Outtaouacts *see* Ottawa
Outtaouatz *see* Ottawa
Outtaouis *see* Ottawa
Outtauois *see* Ottawa
Outtawa *see* Ottawa
Outtawaats *see* Ottawa
Outtoaets *see* Ottawa
Outtongamis *see* Fox
Outtouagamis *see* Fox
Outtouatz *see* Ottawa
Outtougamis *see* Fox
Outurbi [Ont] *Algonquian* (H)
Ouxeinacomigo *see* Sinago
O-uxtxitan *see* Osage
Ouxtxitan *see* Osage
Ou Yaku Ilnige *see* Aoyakulnagai
Ouyakuilnige *see* Aoyakulnagai
Ouyana *see* Guayana
Ouyana *see* Urukuyana
Ouyapes *see* Quapaw
Ouyapez *see* Quapaw
Ouyatespony *see* Oujate-
spouitons
Ova *see* Jova
Ovas *see* Iowa
Overhill Creek *see* Upper Creek
Owaha *see* Omaha
Owandaet *see* Wyandot
Owandoat *see* Huron
Owaragees *see* Pennacook
Owasse *see* Owa'sse
Owa'sse [Clan] *Menominee* (H)
Owasse widishianun *see* Owa'sse
wi'dishi'anun
Owa'sse wi'dishi'anun [Phratry]
Menominee (H)
Oway *see* Kiowa
Oweekano *see* Oowekeeno
O-wee-kay-no *see* Oowekeeno
Oweekayno *see* Oowekeeno
Oweekayo *see* Oowekeeno
Owenagunga *see* Abnaki
Owenagunge *see* Abnaki
Owenagungies *see* Abnaki

Owendaet *see* Huron
Owendat *see* Huron
Owendot *see* Huron
Owen's River Indians *see* Kot-
sava
Owens Valley [CA] *Paiute* (BE)
Owens Valley Paiute (H) *see also*
Petenegowats (H)
Owenunga *see* Abnaki
Owhat [Clan] *Tesuque* (H)
Owhat tdoa *see* Okuwa
Owhillapsh *see* Kwalhioqua
Owhu [Clan] *Nambe* (H)
Owhu tdoa *see* Okuwa
Owhyhee [Self-designation] [HI]
(H)
Owia-lei-toh *see* Oealitk
Owialeitoh *see* Oealitk
Owikeno *see* Oowekeeno
Owiklit [BC] *Bellabella* (Anthro,
v.9, no.3, p.159)
Owilapsh *see* Kwalhioqua
Owileitoh *see* Oealitk
Owit-lei-toh *see* Oealitk
Oxomiut *see* Okomiut
Oxquoquire *see* Arkokisa
Oyacoulet *see* Oyaricoulet
Oyadackuchraono *see* Cherokee
Oyadagahroene *see* Catawba
Oyadagahroene *see* Cherokee
Oyadage-ono *see* Cherokee
Oyadageono *see* Cherokee
O-ya-da-go-o-no *see* Cherokee
Oyalit [BC] *Bellabella* (Anthro,
v.9, no.3, p.159)
Oyambi *see* Oyampi
Oyampi (LC) *see also* Oyana (LC)
Oyampi [Br, FrG, Su] (LC)
Oyana [Br, Su, FrG] (LC)
Oyanders *see* Mohawk
Oyanpik *see* Oyampi
Oyapi *see* Oyampi
Oyaricoulet [Su] (LC)
Oyata'ge'ronon *see* Cherokee
Oyatageronon *see* Cherokee
Oyataysheeeka *see* Oyateshicha
O-ya-tay-shee-ka *see* Oy-
ateshicha
Oyate-citca *see* Oyateshicha
Oyatecitca *see* Oyateshicha
Oyateshicha [MN] *Mdewakanton*
(H)
Oyateshicha *Yankton* (H)
Oyate sica *see* Oyateshicha
Oyatesica *see* Oyateshicha
Oyaudah *see* Cherokee
Oydica *see* Oydican
Oydican (BE) *see also* Doaquioy-
dacam (Hdbk10)
Oydican [TX] (BE)
Oyelloightuk *see* Oealitk
Oyer-lal-lah *see* Oglala
Oyerlallah *see* Oglala

Oyike *Tesuque* (H)
Oyoa *see* Iowa
Oyogouin *see* Cayuga
Oy-pat-oo-coo-la *see* Oypatukla
Oypatoocoola *see* Oypatukla
Oypat oocooloo *see* Oypatukla
Oypatoocooloo *see* Oypatukla
Oypatukla [MS] *Choctaw* (H)
Oyty-aht *see* Oiaht
Oytyaht *see* Oiaht
Oyukhpe [SD] *Oglala* (H)
Oyulipe *see* Oyukhpe
Oyuqpe *see* Oyukhpe
Oza *see* Osage
Ozage *see* Osage
Ozaje *see* Osage
Ozanbogus (H)
Ozange *see* Osage
Ozara *see* Maricopa
Ozarar *see* Maricopa
Ozark [MO, AR] *Quapaw* (H)
Ozaukie *see* Sauk
ozavdiki *see* Pakwidokado
Ozembogus *see* Ozanbogus
Ozenies *see* Ozinies
Ozette [WA] *Makah* (BE)
Ozimies *see* Ozinies
Ozine *see* Wicomese
Ozinies [MD] *Nanticoke* (BE)
ozokwakiak *see* Sokoki
Ozotheoa *see* Uzutiuhi
Ozotoues *see* Uzutiuhi

-P-

Pa [Clan] *Pueblo* (H)
Pa-a-bi-a *see* Payaba
Paabia *see* Payaba
Paac [TX] *Coahuiltecan* (BE)
Paachiqui [TX, MX] (BE)
Paachiquis (H) *see also* Pacuaches (BE)
Paalat *see* Pajalat
Paallirmiut *Caribou Eskimos* (Hdbk5)
Paanamaka [CAm] *Sumo* (O)
pa-anepiccih *see* Northern Paiute
paanepiccih *see* Northern Paiute
Paanese *see* Saponi
pa-anetti *see* Northern Paiute
paanetti *see* Northern Paiute
Pa'ankotshonk *see* Northern Tehuelche
Paankotshonk *see* Northern Tehuelche
Pa'ankun'k *see* Northern Tehuelche
Paankunk *see* Northern Tehuelche
Pa-ash *see* Pa [Pecos]

Paash *see* Pa [Tewa]
Paatsiaja [PE] *Andoke* (O)
Pabaksa [MN, ND] *Upper Yanktonai* (H)
Pabanoton *see* Yecuana
Pa Bda-ska *see* Salish
Pabdaska *see* Salish
Pabierni'n *see* Keres
Pabor (Hdbk10) *see also* Bobol (Hdbk10)
Pabor [TX] *Terocodame* (BE)
Pa-ca *see* Patha
Paca *see* Patha
Pacaanova *see* Pakaanova
Pacaa-Novo *see* Pakaanova
Pacaca [CR] *Cabecar* (O)
Pacaca [MX] *Guetare* (BE)
Pacaguara *see* Sipibo
Pacaguara *see* Pacanuara
Pacaha *see* Quapaw
Pacahuara *see* Pacanuara
Pacahuche *see* Pacuaches
Pacahuches *see* Pakawa
Pacaje *see* Aymara
Pacajudeus [SA] *Caduveo* (O)
Pacama *see* Pakana
Pacamteho *see* Pocomtuc
Pacamtekock *see* Pocomtuc
Pacamtekookes *see* Pocomtuc
Pacana *see* Pakana
Pacanawkite *see* Pokanoket
Pacanua *see* Pakaanova
Pacanuara [BO] (O)
Pacaos (H) *see also* Pakawa (BE)
Pacaos [TX] *Coahuiltecan* (H)
Pacarabo *see* Cheyenne
Pacaruja [TX] *Coahuiltecan* (BE)
Pacasa [BO] *Aymara* (O)
Pacavara *see* Pacanuara
Paceo *see* Patzau
Pacer band of Apache .*see* Kiowa Apache
Pacgal *see* Pachal
Pacha *see* Patzau
Pachac *see* Patzau
Pachagues *see* Pacuaches
Pachagues *see* Pacuaches
Pachai *see* Patzau
Pachajuen *see* Patague
Pachal [TX] (BE)
Pachalaca *see* Pachalaque
Pachalaque *Coahuiltecan* (BE)
Pachalate *see* Pachalaque
Pachales *see* Pachal
Pachalgagu *see* Pachalaque
Pachaloco (Hdbk10) *see also* Pastaloca (BE)
Pachaloco [MX] *Pachal* (BE)
Pachalque *see* Pachalaque
Pachami *see* Nochpeem
Pachamin *see* Nochpeem
Pachamis *see* Tankiteke
Pachan *see* Pachal

Pachanova *see* Pakaanova
Pachany *see* Tankiteke
Pachao *see* Pakawa
Pacha-oglouas *see* Pascagoula
Pachaogloues *see* Pascagoula
Pacha-Ogoula *see* Pascagoula
Pachaogoula *see* Pascagoula
Pachaque *see* Parchaque
Pachaque *see* Pachaquen
Pachaquen *Coahuiltecan* (BE)
Pachaques *see* Pachuaches
Pachaques *see* Pacuaches
Pachat *see* Pachal
Pachaug *Coahuiltecan* (BE)
Pachaxa *see* Patzau
Pacheena *see* Pacheenaht
Pacheenaht [Can] *Nootka* (BE)
Pacheenett *see* Pacheenaht
Pachenah *see* Pacheenaht
Pachera [MX] *Tarahumare* (BE)
Paches *see* Apache
Pachima *Coahuiltecan* (Hdbk10)
Pachimis *see* Tankiteke
Pachizerco [MX] *Coahuiltecan* (Hdbk10)
Pacho *see* Patzau
Pachoches *see* Pachal
Pachoches *see* Pacuaches
Pachoches *see* Pacuaches
Pachoches *see* Pakawa
Pachuag (H) *see also* Patzau (BE)
Pachules *see* Pachal
Pacific Bribri [Pan] *Bribri* (O)
Pacific Yupik *Alaskan Yupik* (Hdbk5)
Paciguima [MX] *Coahuiltecan* (Hdbk10)
Pacin wasabe *see* Wichita
Packamins *see* Tankitchke
Packanocott *see* Pokanoket
Pacoas [TX] *Coahuiltecan* (H)
Pacoatal *see* Pacoas
Pa-co-ha-mo-a *see* Pacohamoa
Pacohamoa [Clan] *Sauk* (H)
Pacomtuck *see* Pocomtuc
Paconahua *see* Morunahua
Pacos *see* Pakawa
Pacpoles *see* Pacpul
Pacpul [MX] *Coahuiltecan* (BE)
pacu *see* Navajo
Pacuaches (H) *see also* Pakawa (BE)
Pacuaches [MX, TX] *Coahuiltecan* (BE)
Pacuachiam (Hdbk10) *see also* Pacuaches (BE)
Pacuachiam [TX] *Coahuiltecan* (BE)
Pacuas *see* Pakawa
Pacuasin *see* Pacuaches
Pacuchiani *see* Pacuachiam
Pacuq *see* Pacoas
Padacus *see* Comanche

Padahuri *see* Yanoama
Pa-dai-na *see* Pawnee
Padaina *see* Pawnee
Padana *see* Pawnee
Padani *see* Arikara
Pa-da-ni *see* Pawnee
Padani *see* Pawnee
Padani Masteta *see* Pawnee
Padanka *see* Comanche
Padaw *see* Comanche
Paddlers *see* Wato'pabin
paddlers *see* Kalispel
Padduca *see* Comanche
Padeuyami *see* Palewyami
Padlermiut *see* Paallirmiut
Padlimiut (BE) *see also* Paalirmiut
  (Hdbk5)
Padlimiut [Can] *Central Eskimos*
  (BE)
Padoka *see* Comanche
Padonee *see* Comanche
Padonka *see* Comanche
Padoo *see* Comanche
Padoosha *see* Balwisha
Padouca (H) *see also* Comanche
  (LC)
Padouca (Hdbk10)
Padoucah *see* Comanche
Padoucee *see* Comanche
Padoucha *see* Comanche
Padoucies *see* Comanche
Padowaga *see* Seneca
Paduca *see* Comanche
Paducah *see* Comanche
Paduka *see* Comanche
Paece *see* Paez
Paegan *see* Piegan
Paego *see* Pecos
Pa-e-gun *see* Piegan
Paegun *see* Piegan
Pa-eps *see* Kaibab
Paeps *see* Kaibab
Pae-qo *see* Pecos
Paeqo *see* Pecos
Pac-quina-la *see* Pecos
Paequinala *see* Pecos
Paequiu *see* Becos
Paequiuala *see* Pecos
Pa-erks *see* Eskimos
Paerks *see* Eskimos
Paex *see* Paez
Pae-yoq'ona *see* Pecos
Paeyoqona *see* Pecos
Paez [Col] (LC)
Paez [Lang] *see* Chibchan
Paezan [Lang] [Col] *Chibchan*
  (O)
Pafalto *see* Paxalto
Pagaiame *see* Bagname
Pagait [NV] *Paiute* (H)
Pa-ga-its *see* Las Vegas
Pagaits *see* Las Vegas
Pagampache *see* Pagampachi

Pagampache *see* Pahvant
Pagampache *Cobarde* (H)
Pagampachi (Hdbk11) *see also*
  Kaibab (BE)
Pagampachi *Southern Paiute*
  (Hbk11)
Pagan *see* Piegan
Paganavo *see* Cheyenne
Paganpachi *see* Kaibab
Paganpachi *see* Pagampachi
Pa-gan-tso *see* Pagantso
Pagantso [NV] (H)
Pagasett *see* Paugusset
Pa-gatsu *see* Pagatsu
Pagatsu [TX] *Comanche* (BE)
Pa-gaump-ats *see* Kaibab
Pagaumpats *see* Kaibab
Pagayuats [UT] *Gosiute* (H)
Pagnache *see* Pacuaches
Pago *see* Pecos
Pagogowatsnunts *see* Moanunts
Pa'gonotch *see* Southern Paiute
Pa'gonotch *see* Paiute
Pagonotch *see* Paiute
Pagonotch *see* Southern Paiute
pagönunts *see* Moanunts
pagonunts *see* Timpanogots
Pagouitik *see* Saulteaux
pagowadziu *see* Timpanogots
Pagowitch *see* Navajo
Pagowits *see* Navajo
Paguaches *see* Pacuaches
Paguachis *see* Pacuaches
Paguachis *see* Pakawa
Paguampe *see* Pahvant
Paguan *see* Paguanan
Paguanan [TX] *Coahuiltecan* (BE)
Paguit (PC) *see also* Panguitch
  (Hdbk11)
Paguit [UT] *Paiute* (H)
Pa-gu-its *see* Paguit
Pa-gu-its *see* Panguitch
Pagu-uits *see* Navajo
Paguuits *see* Navajo
Pa-gu-wets *see* Navajo
Pagu-wets *see* Navajo
Paguwets *see* Navajo
Pagwaki *see* Pequawket
pag-wa-nu-chi *see* Uinta
Pa-gwi-ho *see* Pagwiho
Pagwiho [CA] *Paviotso* (H)
Pa'-gwi-ho-tu *see* Pakwidokado
Pagwihotu *see* Pakwidokado
Pa'-gwi-ho-tuviwagaiyu *see* Pak-
  widokado
Pagwihotuviwagaiyu *see* Pak-
  widokado
Pa-ha-hi-a *see* Payaba
Pahahia *see* Payaba
Pa-ha-sa-be *see* Mescalero
  Apache
Pahasabe *see* Mescalero Apache
Pa-ha-sca *see* Pahatsi

Pahasca *see* Pahatsi
Pahatsi [Lang] *Osage* (H)
Pahaya *see* Paya
Pah Baxa *see* Pabaksa
Pahbaxa *see* Pabaksa
Pah-bax-ah *see* Pabaksa
Pahbaxah *see* Pabaksa
Pah-Edes *see* Paiute
Pah-Edes *see* Southern Paiute
Pahedes *see* Paiute
Pahedes *see* Southern Paiute
Pahenguichia *see* Piankashaw
Pahhuhhachis *see* Pohonichi
Pah-huh-hack-is *see* Pohonichi
pa-hi-ka *see* watatikka
pahika *see* watatikka
Pahi Mahas *see* Skidi Pawnee
Pahimahas *see* Skidi Pawnee
Pah-kah-nah-vo *see* Cheyenne
Pahkahnahvo *see* Cheyenne
Pahkanapil *see* Tubatulabal
Pahkanu [CA] (H)
Pah-kee *see* Siksika
Pahkee *see* Siksika
Pahkepunnasso [MA] *Wampanoag*
  (BE)
Pahlachocolo *see* Apalachicola
Pa hlai *see* Cochiti
Pahlai *see* Cochiti
Pah-lo-cho-ko-lo *see*
  Apalachicola
Pahlochokolo *see* Apalachicola
Pahmetes *see* Paiute
Pahneug *see* Pawnee
Pahn-kech-emk *see* Pan
Pahnkechemk *see* Pan
Pahnutes Utahs *see* Paiute
Pa-ho-cha *see* Iowa
Pahocha *see* Iowa
Pahodja *see* Iowa
Pa-ho-dje *see* Iowa
Pahodje *see* Iowa
Pa-ho-ja *see* Iowa
Pahoja *see* Iowa
pahongtha *see* Ponca
pa-hon-gthe *see* Ponca
Pahosalgi [Clan] *Creek* (H)
Pahoüiting dach *see* Saulteaux
Pahquetooai *Tigua* (H)
Pah Ranagat *see* Paranigut
Pahranagat (PC) *see also* Paranigut
  (H)
Pahranagat *Southern Paiute*
  (Hdbk11)
Pah-ran-ne *see* Paranigut
Pahranne *see* Paranigut
Pah-Reneg-Utes *see* Paranigut
Pahreneg Utes *see* Paranigut
Pah-ru-sa-pah *see* Southern
  Paiute
Pah-ru-sa-pah *see* Paiute
Pahrusapah *see* Paiute
Pahrusapah *see* Southern Paiute

Pah-to-cah *see* Comanche
Pahtocah *see* Comanche
Pah-Tout *see* Paiute
Pahtout *see* Paiute
Pahuanan *see* Paguanan
Pahucae *see* Iowa
Pa-hu-cha *see* Iowa
Pahucha *see* Iowa
pahumu witu *see* Pakwidokado
Pahusitah *see* Paiute
Pah Utah (Hdbk11) *see also* Paiute (LC)
Pahutah *see* Paiute
Pah Utah [UT] *Northern Paiute* (Hdbk11)
Pah Utes *see* Paiute
Pah-Utes *see* Southern Paiute
Pahutes *see* Paiute
Pah-Van *see* Pahvant
Pahvan *see* Pahvant
Pah-vant *see* Pahvant
Pahvant [UT] *Ute* (BE)
pahva-ntits *see* Pahvant
pahvantits *see* Pahvant
Pah Vaut *see* Pahvant
Pahvaut *see* Pahvant
Pah Vent *see* Pahvant
Pahvent *see* Pahvant
Pahvontee *see* Pahvant
pahwa'lita *see* San Ildefonso
p'ahwia'hliap *see* San Ildefonso
pahwiahliap *see* San Ildefonso
Pa-i *see* Pawnee
Pai *see* Pawnee
Pai [Self-designation] *see* Secoya
Paia *see* Payaya
Paiabun *see* Payuguan
Paiagua *see* Payagua
Paiaia *see* Payaya
Paialla *see* Payaya
Paiapan *see* Payuguan
Pai a'ti *see* Paiute
Paiati *see* Paiute
Paiaya *see* Payaya
Paicayua *see* Pai-Cayua
Pai-Cayua [Par] (O)
Paicone *see* Paunaca
Paiconeca [Lang] *Maripurean* (O)
Paifan amim *see* Alsea
Paifanamim *see* Alsea
Paignkenken *see* Northern Tehuelche
Paiguan *see* Payuguan
Paii [Br] *Kawahib* (O)
Pai-Ide *see* Paiute
Paiide *see* Paiute
Pai Indians *see* Walapai
Paik *see* Siksika
Paikananavo *see* Cheyenne
Paikandoo *see* Cheyenne
Paikawa (BE)
Paikawan *see* Paikawa
Paikise *see* Mundurucu

Paikyce *see* Mundurucu
Paillailles *see* Payaya
Pailsk *see* Copalis
Pail-uk-sun *see* Sailupsun
Pailuksun *see* Sailupsun
Paimeru [Br] *Tiriyo* (O)
Paine *see* Pawnee
Paingua *see* Caingua
Painima [ID] *Nez Perce* (BE)
painkwitikka *Western Shoshone* (Hdbk11)
painkwitikka *see also* Fish Eaters (Hdbk11)
Pain-pe-tse-menay *see* Dakota
Painpetsemenay *see* Dakota
Paint Creek town *see* Chillicothe
Painted Heart Indians *see* Skitswish
Painted Indians *see* Pintados
Painted People *see* Masnipiwini-uuk
Painya *see* Pima
Paipai *see* Akwa'ala
Paiquize *see* Mundurucu
Paisano *see* Pausanes
Paisau *see* Patzau
Pai-Taviyera *see* Pai-Cayua
Paiter *see* Surui I
Paiuches *see* Paiute
Paiuches *see* Southern Paiute
Paiugan *see* Payuguan
Paiulee *see* Paiute
Pai-Ute *see* Pa-Ute
Pai-Ute *see* Pi-Ute
Paiute (LC) *see also* Northern Paiute (Hdbk11)
Paiute (LC) *see also* Owens Valley Paiute (Hdbk11)
Paiute (LC) *see also* Southern Paiute (Hdbk11)
Paiute (PC) *see also* Pa-Ute (Hdbk11)
Paiute [CA, AZ] (LC)
Paiute [Lang] [*Ute-Chemehuevi*] (LC)
Paiute Snakes [OR] *Shoshone* (H)
Pai-u-ti *see* Paiute
Pai-uches *see* Paiute
Paiuti *see* Paiute
Pai-yu'chimu *see* Paiute
Paiyuchimu *see* Paiute
Pai-yudshi *see* Paiute
Paiyudshi *see* Paiute
Pai-yu-tsi *see* Paiute
Paiyutsi *see* Paiute
Paiztat *see* Patzau
Pajaca *see* Paac
Pajague *see* Pojoaque
Pajalache *see* Pachalaque
Pajalaches *see* Pajalat
Pajalames *see* Pajalat
Pajalaques *see* Pachalaque
Pajalaques *see* Pajalat

Pajalat [TX] *Coahuiltecan* (BE)
Pajalatames *see* Pajalat
Pajalates *see* Pajalat
Pajalet *see* Pajalet
Pajalve *see* Pasalves
Pajamara [MX] *Coahuiltecan* (Hdbk10)
Pajarito (H) *see also* Troomaxi-aquino (H)
Pajarito [TX] *Coahuiltecan* (BE)
Pajaro Pinto *see* Tshirege
Pajatiles *see* Pajalat
Pa'jeh *see* Patkoi
Pajeh *see* Patki
Pajoaque *see* Pojoaque
Pajonalino [PE] *Campa* (O)
Pajuagne *see* Pojoaque
Pajuaque *see* Pojoaque
Pajuguan *see* Payuguan
Pakaanawa *see* Pakaanova
Pakaa Nova *see* Pakaanova
Pakaanova [Br] (O)
Pakab [Phratry] *Hopi* (H)
Pakabaluyu *see* San Juan [NM]
Pa-kab nyu-mu *see* Pakab
Pakab nyumu *see* Pakab
Pakab wiñwû *see* Pakab
Pa-kab wuñwû *see* Pakab
Pakab wuñwû *see* Pakab
Pakamali [CA] *Maidu* (H)
Pa-ka-mal-li *see* Pakamali
Pakamalli *see* Pakamali
Pakana [TX] *Muskogee* (BE)
Pa ka na vo *see* Cheyenne
Pakanavo *see* Cheyenne
Pa-ka-na-wa *see* Cheyenne
Pakanawa *see* Pakaanova
Pakanawa *see* Cheyenne
Pa-kan-e-pul *see* Tubatulabal
Pakanepul *see* Tubatulabal
Pa-ka-ni *see* Pakani
Pakani [Gens] *Tonkawa* (H)
Pakanokick *see* Pokanoket
Pakarara [Br] (O)
Pa ka-san-tse *see* Nez Perce
Pakasantse *see* Nez Perce
Pakaud *see* Pequot
Pakawa [TX] *Coahuiltecan* (BE)
Pakawan [Lang] [MX] (Bull44)
Pakawara *see* Pacanuara
paka-wi-cci *see* Navajo
pakawicci *see* Navajo
Pakhpuinihkashina [Society] *Osage* (H)
Pakhtha [Clan] *Iowa* (H)
Pakidai (O) *see also* Yanoama (LC)
Pakidai [Br, VE] *Yanoama* (O)
pakiucimi *see* Panguitch
Pa'kiut'-le'ma *see* Yakima
Pakiutlema *see* Yakima
Pa'kiut'lema [Self-designation] *see* Yakima

Pak-ka-na *see* Pacana
Pakkana *see* Pacana
Pakoango *see* Unami
Pakota *see* Dakota
Pa-kua *see* Pakwa
Pakua *see* Pakwa
Pa-kuh-tha *see* Iowa
Pa-kuh-tha *see* Pakhtha
Pakuhtha *see* Iowa
pakupala *see* San Juan [NM]
Paku'parai *see* San Juan [NM]
pakuparai *see* San Juan [NM]
Pakuqhalai *see* San Juan [NM]
Pakutha *see* Pakhtha
Pakwa [Clan] *Hopi* (H)
Pa-kwa win-wu *see* Pakwa
Pakwa wiñwû *see* Pakwa
Pa-kwa wuñ-wû *see* Pakwa
Pakwa wuñwû *see* Pakwa
pakwidikadi *see* Pakwidokado
Pakwidokado *Northern Paiute*
  (Hdbk11)
pakwihu [Phratry] [CA] *Mono*
  (Pub, v.11, no.5, p.293)
pakwiti *see* San Ildefonso
Pa'l-ab *see* Cochiti
Palab *see* Cochiti
Palache *see* Apalachee
Palachicola *see* Apalachicola
Palachocala *see* Apalachicola
Palachoocla *see* Apalachicola
Pa-la-chooc-le *see* Apalachicola
Palachoocle *see* Apalachicola
Palachuckola *see* Apalachicola
Palachuola *see* Apalachicola
Palagewan (BE) *see also* Tubatula-
  bal (LC)
Palagewan [CA] (BE)
Palagueque *see* Palaquesson
Palaguesson *see* Palaquesson
Palaguin [MX] *Coahuiltecan*
  (Hdbk10)
Pa-lahuide *see* Cochiti
Palaihnih *see* Palaihnihan
Palaihnihan [Lang] *Hokan* (CA-8)
Palaik *see* Palaihnihan
Palakahu [OR] (BE)
Palalgueque *Coahuiltecan*
  (Hdbk10)
Palana wiñwû *see* Paluna
Palanches *see* Apalachee
Pa-la-ni *see* Pawnee
Palani *see* Pawnee
Palank *see* Palenque
Palanoa *see* Barasana
Palanshan *see* Tsulamsewi
Palanshawl *see* Tsulamswei
Palaquechaune *see* Palaquesson
Palaquechaure *see* Palaquesson
Palaquechone *see* Palaquesson
Palaquesones *see* Palaquesson
Palaquesson [TX] (H)
Palaquessous *see* Palaquesson

Palatcy *see* Apalachee
Palauiyang *see* Paraviyana
Pa-la-wa (H) *see also* Palewa (H)
Palawa *see* Pa-la-wa
Palawa *see* Palewa
Pa-la-wa [Clan] *Shawnee* (H)
Palawi *see* Coyotero Apache
Palaxy *see* Apalachee
Palenca *see* Palenque
Palenke *see* Palenque
Palenque [Lang] *Tamanco* (UAz,
  v.28)
Palenque [VE] (LC)
Paleo-Indians (LC)
Pal-e-um-mi *see* Palewyami
Paleummi *see* Palewyami
Paleuyami *see* Palewyami
Palewa [Clan] *Shawnee* (H)
Palewyami [Lang] *Poso Creek*
  (CA-8)
Paleyami *see* Palewyami
Palicur [Br, FrG] (LC)
Palikur *see* Palicur
Pa liren ab ponin *see* Chiricahua
  Apache
Palirenabponin *see* Chiricahua
  Apache
Palish *see* Copalis
Palish *see* Copalis
Pal-la-a-me *see* Palewyami
Pallaame *see* Palewyami
Pal-lace *see* Paloos
Pallace *see* Paloos
Pal-lah-weah-e-am *see*
  Palewyami
Pallahweaheam *see* Palewyami
Pallalat *see* Pajalat
Pallalt *see* Pilalt
Pallatapalla *see* Paloos
Pallegawonap (H) *see also* Tubat-
  ulabal (LC)
Pallegawonap [CA] (Pub, v.4,
  no.3, p.125)
Pallet to Pallas *see* Paloos
Pal-li-ga-wo-nap *see* Palliga-
  wonap
Palligawonap *see* Pallegawonap
Palloatpallah *see* Paloos
Palloats *see* Paloos
Pallotepaller *see* Paloos
Pallotepallor *see* Paloos
Pallotepellow *see* Paloos
Palmela [Br] (O)
Palmela [Lang] *Carib* *see* Palmela
Palmella (UAz, v.28)
Palmeños *Coahuiltecan* (Hdbk10)
Palmitos *Coahuiltecan* (Hdbk10)
Paloas *see* Paloos
Paloguessen *see* Palaquesson
Palomas (Hdbk10)
Palona *see* Palomas
Palonies [CA] *Chemehuevi* (H)
Palonnas *see* Palomas

Palooche *see* Paloos
Paloos [WA, ID] *Sahaptian* (LC)
Paloose *see* Paloos
Palooshis *see* Paloos
Palosse *see* Paloos
Palouches *see* Paloos
Palous *see* Paloos
Palouse *see* Paloos
Paloyama *see* Palewyami
Palquesson *see* Palaquesson
Pa'lu *see* Paviotso
Palu *see* Paviotso
Paluna [Phratry] *Pakab* (H)
Pa-lun-am wuñ-wu *see* Paluna
Palunam wuñwû *see* Paluna
Pa-lus *see* Paloos
Palus *see* Paloos
Palus [WA] *Paloos* (BE)
Paluses *see* Paloos
Paluunun *see* Palwunun
paluus *see* Paloos
paluuspam *see* Paloos
Palux [WA] *Chinook* (H)
Paluxies *see* Biloxi
Paluyam *see* Palewyami
Palvas *see* Paloos
Pal-wish-a *see* Badwisha
Palwisha *see* Balwisha
Pal-wu-nuh (H) *see also* Palwu-
  nun (H)
Palwunuh *see* Pal-wu-nuh
Palwunuh (Pub, v.4, no.3, p.125)
  see also Palwunun (H)
Pal-wu-nuh [CA] (Contri, v.3,
  p.393)
Palwunun [CA] (H)
Pamacacack *see* Pamacocack
Pamacas *see* Pamaque
Pamacocack *Conoy* (BE)
Pamakeroy *see* Pamunkey
Pamanes *see* Pausanes
Pamanuk *see* Pamunkey
Pamanuke *see* Pamunkey
Pamaomeck *see* Pamunkey
Pamaque [TX] *Coahuiltecan* (BE)
Pamareke *see* Pamunkey
Pamari *see* Paumari
Pamauke *see* Pamunkey
Pamaunck *see* Pamunkey
Pamaunk *see* Pamunkey
Pamaunke *see* Pamunkey
Pamaunkie *see* Pamunkey
Pamauri *see* Paumari
Pamauuaioc *see* Pomouic
Pamavukes *see* Pamunkey
Pamaya *Coahuiltecan* (BE)
Pambadeque *see* Cocamilla
Pambizimina *see* Dakota
Pame [Lang] [MX] (Bull44)
Pame [Lang] [MX] *Otomanguean*
  (Hdbk10)
Pame [MX] (LC)
Pames *see* Pausanes

Pamiagdluk *Greenland Eskimos*
(BE)
Pamisahagi *see* Pamissouk
Pa-mis-so-uk *see* Pamissouk
Pamissouk [Gens] *Sauk* (H)
Pamitoy [NV] *Paviotso* (H)
Pamiwa [Self-designation] *see*
Cubeo
Pamlico [NC] (BE)
Pamlicough *see* Pamlico
Pammahas *see* Skidi Pawnee
Pammari *see* Paumari
Pam-mi-toy (H) *see also* Pamitoy
(H)
Pammitoy *see* Pam'-mi-toy
Pam'-mi-toy *Northern Paiute*
(Hdbk11)
Pamnaouamske *see* Penobscot
Pamoa [Col] *Barasana* (LC)
Pa-moki-abs *see* Beaver
Pamokiabs *see* Beaver
Pamonke *see* Pamunkey
Pamonkies *see* Pamunkey
Pamoranos *Coahuiltecan* (BE)
Pamoranos [TX] *Tamaulipan* (H)
Pamozanes *see* Pamoranos
Pampa [Arg] (LC)
Pampapas *see* Pampopas
Pampean Indians *see* Pampa
Pampe Chyimina *see* Dakota
Pamphleco *see* Pamlico
Pampleco *see* Pamlico
Pamplicoes *see* Pamlico
Pampoas *see* Pampopas
Pampopas [TX] *Coahuiltecan*
(BE)
Pampos *see* Pampopas
Pamptaco *see* Pamlico
Pamptecough *see* Pamlico
Pamptego *see* Pamlico
Pamptichoe *see* Pamlico
Pampticoes *see* Pamlico
Pampticoke *see* Pamlico
Pampticough *see* Pamlico
Pamptucough *see* Pamlico
Pamtico *see* Pamlico
Pamticough *see* Pamlico
Pamuenkok *see* Pamunkey
Pamulian *see* Pomuluma
Pamunckye *see* Pamunkey
Pamuncoroy *see* Pamunkey
Pamunkey [VA] *Powhatan Con-
federacy* (LC)
Pamunkies *see* Pamunkey
Pamunkii *see* Pamunkey
Pamunky *see* Pamunky
Pan [Clan] *Pima* (H)
Pana *see* Ponca
Pana *see* Panobo
Pana *see* Pawnee
Panac *see* Papanaca
Panaca (H) *see also* Pacana (H)
Panaca *Southern Paiute* (Hdbk11)

Panack *see* Bannock
Panagamsde *see* Penobscot
Panagoto *see* Pianokoto
Panague *see* Pamaque
Panahamsequit *see* Penobscot
Panai Proper *see* Chavi
Panai'ti *see* Bannock
Panaiti [Self-designation] *see*
Bannock
Panaitu *see* Bannock
Panak *see* Bannock
Panakhil [Self-designation] *see*
Agua Caliente
pan-akwati *see* Northern Paiute
panakwati *see* Northern Paiute
Panaloga *see* Comanche
Panama *see* Pawnee
Panama *see* Pawnee
Panamaha *see* Pawnee
Panamaka [NI, Hon] *Sumo* (BE)
Panamint [CA] *Western Shoshone*
(LC)
Panamint [Lang] *Central Numic*
(Hdbk10)
Panamnuk *see* Panamint
Panampskewi *see* Penobscot
Panamske *see* Penobscot
Panamske [Lang] *Cariban*
(Hdbk15)
Panana *see* Kiowa
Pananaioc *see* Pomouic
Pananan *see* Pawnee
Pananarock *see* Pomouic
Pananke *see* Penobscot
Panannojock *see* Pomouic
Pananuaioc *see* Pomouic
Pana-ompskek *see* Penobscot
Panaompskek *see* Penobscot
Panaomske *see* Penobscot
Panaonke *see* Penobscot
Panaouameske *see* Penobscot
Panaouamke *see* Penobscot
Panaouamsde *see* Penobscot
Panaouamske *see* Penobscot
Panaouamsquee *see* Penobscot
Panaouanbskek *see* Penobscot
Panaouanke *see* Penobscot
Panaouankskek *see* Penobscot
Panaouaske *see* Penobscot
Panaoumski *see* Penobscot
Panaounke *see* Penobscot
Panaouske *see* Penobscot
Panaquakike *see* Quinnipiac
Panare [Lang] *Carib* (UAz, v.28)
Panare [Lang] *Cariban* (LC)
Panare [VE] (LC)
Panari *see* Panare
Pana's *see* Ponca
Panascan *see* Pasnacanes
Panasht *see* Bannock
panati *Owens Valley Paiute*
(Hdbk11)
Panauuaioc *see* Pamlico

Panawamske *see* Penobscot
Panawamske *see* Penobscot
Panawamskik *see* Penobscot
Panawaniske *see* Penobscot
Panawanscot *see* Penobscot
Panawanskik *see* Penobscot
Panawiock *see* Pamlico
Panawopskeyal *see* Penobscot
Panaxki *see* Abnaki
Panazelo [EC] (O)
Panazelo [Lang] *Chibchan* (O)
Panca *see* Ponca
Pancacola *see* Pensacola
Pancarara *see* Pancaruru
Pancararu [Br] (LC)
Pancare [Br] *Pancararu* (O)
Pancaru *see* Pancararu
Pancaw *see* Ponca
Pancho [ES] *Pipil* (O)
Pandabequeo *see* Cocamilla
Pandoga *see* Comanche
Pandouca *see* Comanche
Panea Republicans *see* Kitke-
hahki
Paneas *see* Pawnee
Paneassa *see* Wichita
Panee *see* Chaui
Panego *see* Pamaque
Panego *see* Panequo
Pa-nel-a-kut *see* Penelukut
Panelakut *see* Penelakut
Paneloga *see* Comanche
Panelogo *see* Comanche
Paneloza *see* Comanche
Panemaha *see* Skidi Pawnee
Panequo [TX] (H)
Paneroa [Col] (O)
Panetoca *see* Comanche
Panetonka *see* Comanche
Pang [Clan] *Pueblo* (H)
Pangayo *Conoy* (Hdbk15)
Pangeyen *see* Zoro
Pangkaw *see* Ponca
Pangoa (LC) *see also* Nomat-
siguenga (LC)
Pangoa [PE] *Campa* (O)
Panguay *Coahuiltecan* (Hdbk10)
Panguayes [MX] *Tamaulipec* (BE)
Panguitch *Southern Paiute*
(Hdbk11)
Pangwa [Clan] *Hopi* (H)
Pangwiduka *see* Cache Valley
Shoshone
Pangwiduka *see* Fish Eaters
Panhandle Culture [OK] (LC)
Panhka *see* Ponca
Panh'ka wacta'ke *see*
Panhkawashtake
Panhkawactake *see* Panhkawash-
take
Panhkawashtake [Clan] *Osage* (H)
Pani (BE) *see also* Arikara (LC)
Pani (H)

Pani (H) *see also* Dakota (LC)
Pani (LC) *see also* Pawnee (LC)
Pania *see* Pawnee
Pania *see* Ponca
Pania Loups *see* Skidi Pawnee
Pania Lousis *see* Skidi Pawnee
Pania Luup *see* Skidi Pawnee
Pania Proper *see* Chaui
Pania propre *see* Chaui
Pania Republican *see* Kitkehahki
Panias Loups *see* Skidi Pawnee
Panias republicians *see* Kitkehahki
Pani Blanc [Can] *Cree* (H)
Panies *see* Pawnee
Paniete *Itgua* (H)
Panimachas *see* Skidi Pawnee
Pani-Maha *see* Skidi Pawnee
Panimaha *see* Skidi Pawnee
Pani-Mahaws *see* Skidi Pawnee
Panimahaws *see* Skidi Pawnee
Pa-ni-mahu *see* Skidi Pawnee
Panimahu *see* Skidi Pawnee
Panimaka *see* Skidi Pawnee
Panimalia *see* Skidi Pawnee
Panimalis *see* Skidi Pawnee
Panimint *see* Panamint
Panimoas *see* Skidi Pawnee
Panimoha *see* Skidi Pawnee
Pan-in *see* Pawnee
Panin *see* Pawnee
Panini (H)
Panipique *see* Tawehash
Panipique *see* Skidi Pawnee
Pani Pique *see* Wichita
Panipiquet *see* Tawehash
Paniquiapem *see* Tenicapeme
Paniquita [Col] *Paez* (O)
Panis *see* Pawnee
Panis-Blancs *see* Pawnee
Panisciowa *see* Pineshow
Panislousa *see* Skidi Pawnee
Panismahans *see* Skidi Pawnee
Panis Mahas *see* Skidi Pawnee
Panis noirs *see* Wichita
Panis piques *see* Wichita
Panis Republican *see* Kitkehahki
Panis ricara *see* Arikara
Panivacha *see* Skidi Pawnee
Panka (H) *see also* Ponca (LC)
Pan-ka *see* Ponca
Panka [Clan] *Kansa* (H)
Pan'kan *see* Ponca
Pankan *see* Ponca
Pankara *see* Pancararu
Pankarara *see* Pancararu
Pankarare *see* Pancararu
Pankaravu *see* pancararu
Pankaravu *see* Pancararu
Pankaroru *see* Pancararu
Pankaru *see* Pancararu
Pankwi duka [ID] *Northern Shoshone* (Anthro, v.8, no.3, p.264)

Pannack *see* Bannock
Pannah *see* Bannock
pannaihti *see* Northern Paiute
pannaitti *see* Northern Paiute
Pannakee *see* Bannock
Pannamaha *see* Skidi Pawnee
Pannaoumske *see* Penobscot
Pannawanbskek *see* Penobscot
Panneh *see* Allakaweah
Pannimalia *see* Skidi Pawnee
Pano *see* Panobo
Pano *see* Setebo
Panoan Indians [Br, PE, BO] (LC)
Panobo (O) *see also* Setebo (O)
Panobo [PE] (O)
Panouamke *see* Penobscot
Panouamsde *see* Penobscot
Panouamske *see* Penobscot
Panouca *see* Comanche
Panoumsque *see* Penobscot
Panouske *see* Penobscot
Panpoc *see* Pampopas
Panquechin [VanI] *Sanetch* (H)
Panquechip [Can] *Sanetch* (BE)
Pansacola *see* Pensacola
Pans falaya *see* Choctaw
Pansfalaya *see* Choctaw
Pantasma (BE)
Pa'ntch pinunkansh *see* Chitimacha
Pantch pinunkansh *see* Chitimacha
Pan-tdoa *see* Pang
Pantdoa *see* Pang
Panther Gens *see* Tanghantanhkaenikashika
Pantico *see* Pamlico
Panticoes *see* Pamlico
Panticough *see* Pamlico
Pantiguara [MX] *Coahuiltecan* (Hdbk10)
Pantipora [MX] (Hdbk10)
Pants Mahas *see* Skidi Pawnee
Pantsmahas *see* Skidi Pawnee
Panukkog *see* Pennacook
Panulam *see* Pomuluma
Panumints *see* Serrano
Panumits *see* Serrano
panumunt *see* panamint
Pan-Utahs *see* Paiute
Pa'n-wa *see* Pangwa
Panwa *see* Pangwa
Panwapskik *see* Penobscot
Pan-wa win-wu *see* Pangwa
Pan-wa wüñwû *see* Pangwa
Panwa wüñwû *see* Pangwa
Panwu winwu *see* Pangwa
Pañwû wiñwû *see* Pangwa
Panyi *see* Pawnee
Panyi puca *see* Arikara
Panyipuca *see* Arikara
Panyi Wacewe *see* Wichita

Panyiwacewe *see* Wichita
Panys *see* Pawnee
Panza *see* Pawnee
Panzacola *see* Pensacola
Panzas *see* Pawnee
Paobdeca *see* Salish
Pa O-bde-ca *see* Salish
Paoduca *see* Comanche
Paogas [MX] *Lagunero* (BE)
Paola *see* Puaray
Paoneneheo *see* Pawnee
Paoninihieu *see* Pawnee
Paonis *see* Pawnee
Paote *see* Iowa
Paouichtigouin *see* Chippewa
Paouitagoung *see* Chippewa
Paouites [TX] (H)
Paouitigouieuhak *see* Chippewa
Paouitingouach-irini *see* Chippewa
Paoutagoung *see* Saulteaux
Paoutees *see* Iowa
Paoutes *see* Iowa
Paoutez *see* Iowa
Papabi-Ootam *see* Papago
Papabiootam *see* Papago
Papabi-Otawas *see* Papago
Papabiptawas *see* Papago
Papabo *see* Papago
Papabota *see* Papago
Papabuco [Lang] [MX] *Chatino* (LC)
Papaconck *see* Papagonk
Papaga *see* Papago
Papagi *see* Papago
Papago (LC) *see also* Tohon O'Odham (LC)
Papago [AZ, MX] (LC)
Papago [Lang] *Upper Piman* (Hdbk10)
Papago-cotam *see* Papago
Papagocotam *see* Papago
Pa-Pagoe *see* Papago
Papagoe *see* Papago
Papagoes *see* Papago
Papagonck *see* Papagonk
Papagonk [NJ, NY] (H)
Papagoose *see* Papago
Papah-a'atam *see* Papago
Papahaatam *see* Papago
Papahanna *see* Rappahannock
Papahi-Ootam *see* Papago
Papahiootam *see* Papago
Papah'o *see* Papago
Papahota *see* Papago
Papajo *see* Papago
Papalote *see* Papago
Papanac *see* Papanaca
Papanaca [TX, MX] (BE)
papani *see* Papago
Papani *see* Papanaca
Pa-panti *see* Pahvant
papanti *see* Pahvant

Papantla [Lang] *Totonac* (BE)
Papa-Otam *see* Papago
Papaotam *see* Papago
papapi numakaki *see* Flathead
Papap Ootam *see* Papago
Papapootam *see* Papago
Papapootans *see* Papago
Papap-Otam *see* Papago
Papapotam *see* Papago
Paparo (LC) *see also* Choco (LC)
Paparo [Pan, Col] *Embera* (BE)
Papavicotam *see* Papago
Papavo *see* Papago
Papawar *see* Papago
papawin *see* Papago
Papayeca [Hon] *Nahuatl* (BE)
Papayo *see* Papago
Papelotes *see* Papago
Papenachois *see* Papinachois
Papia Louisis *see* Skidi Pawnee
Papigo *see* Papago
Papikaha *see* Quapaw
Papinachaux *see* Papinachois
Papinaches *see* Papinachois
Papinachiois *see* Papinachois
Papinachois [Can] [*Montagnais-Naskapi*] (BE)
Papinakois *see* Papinachois
Papinanchois *see* Papinachois
pa-piocco *see* Paviotso
papiocco *see* Paviotso
Papipanachois *see* Papinachois
Papiragad'ek *see* Papinachois
Papitsinima *see* Dakota
Papivaches *see* Papinachois
Pa'pk'um *see* Popkum
Papkum *see* Popkum
Paponal *see* Papanaca
Paponeches *see* Papinachois
pappanaiht *see* Northern Paiute
Papshpun'lema *see* Kalispel
Papshpunlema *see* Kalispel
papsire numakaki *see* Flathead
Papspe'lu *see* Sinkiuse-Columbia
Papspelu *see* Sinkiuse-Columbia
Papudo [Lang] [MX] *Acaxee* (BE)
Papudo [MX] (BE)
Paqamali *see* Pakamali
Pa-qca *see* Pakhtha
Paqca *see* Pakhtha
Pa-qo-tce *see* Iowa
Paqotce *see* Iowa
Paquaanocke *see* Poquonock
Paquache *Coahuiltecan* (BE)
Paquakig *see* Pequawket
Paquanaug *see* Poquonock
Paquanick *see* Poquonock
Paquatanog *see* Pequot
Paquea *see* Piqua
P'a-qu-lah *see* Pecos
Paqulah *see* Pecos
Pa-qu-te *see* Iowa
Paqute *see* Iowa

Para *see* Puretuay
Parabuyeis *see* Jumano
Paracana *see* Parakana
Parachuctaus *see* Apalachicola
Parachukla *see* Apalachicola
Paraconosko [VA] *Algonquian* (Hdbk15)
Paracoxi *see* Tocobaga
Paracpoola *see* Apalachicola
Pa-ra-goons *see* Cedar
Pa-ra-goons *see* Panguitch
Paragoons *see* Cedar
Paragoons *see* Panguitch
Pa-ra-guns *see* Cedar
Pa-ra-guns *see* Panguitch
Paraguri *see* Yanoama
Parahuri *see* Parichuri
Parahuri *see* Yanoama

Parajota [MX] *Coahuiltecan* (Hdbk10)
Parakana [Br] (O)
Parakateye *see* Gavioes
Parakuto *see* Paricuto
Paramona *see* Patamona
Parampamatuju *Coahuiltecan* (Hdbk10)
Paramuni *see* Patamona
Parana [Lang] *Maipurean* (O)
Paranagats *see* Paraniguts
Paranagats *see* Pahranagat
Paranapura [PE] *Jebero* (O)
Paranawat [Br] *Kawahib* (O)
Paranigut (PC) *see also* Pahranagat (Hdbk11)
Paranigut [NV] *Paiute* (H)
Pa-ran-i-guts *see* Paranigut
Pa-ran-i-guts *see* Pahranagat
Parannhahua [Lang] *Panoan* (O)
Parano *see* Pahranagat
Parant *see* Pahvant
Parantones [TX] *Coahuiltecan* (BE)
Parant Utah *see* Pahvant
Paranukh *see* Shivwits
Paraogwan *see* Paraujano
Paraokan *see* Paraujano
Paraonez *see* Faraon
Paratapuio *see* Pira-Tapuyo
Parathees [TX] (H)
Parauana *see* Paraviyana
Parauano *see* Paraujano
Parauiana *see* Paraviyana
Parauillana *see* Paraviyana
Paraujano [VE] (LC)
Paravan Yuta *see* Pahvant
Paravilhana (O) *see also* Par-aviyana (O)
Paravilhana [Lang] *Makusi* (UAz, v.28)
Paraviyana (O) *see also* Wapisiana (LC)
Paraviyana [Br] (O)

Parawan *see* Paruguns
Parawat Yutas *see* Parguns
Parawgwan *see* Paraujano
Parawkan *see* Paraujano
Paray *see* Puaray
Parchaca *see* Parchaque
Parchaque (H) *see also* Pacuaches (BE)
Parchaque [TX] *Coahuiltecan* (BE)
Parche Corn Indians (H)
Parchinas [TX] *Coahuiltecan* (BE)
Pareche *see* Paressi
Pareci *see* Paressi
Pareescar (H) *see also* Pariscar (H)
Pa-rees-car *see* Pariscar
Pareescar *Crow* (H)
Parenisati *see* Capa del Alto Perene
Parentintin *see* Parintintim
Paresi *see* Paressi
Paressi [Br] (LC)
Paressi-Cabishi *see* Paressi
Pareti *see* Paressi
Parhowka *see* Paraujano
Pari *see* Mundurucu
Paria [Aymara] (O)
Pariana *see* Omagua
Paribitete *see* Pari-bi-tete
Pari-bi-tete [Br] *Apiaca* (O)
Parihuri [VE, Br] (O)
Pariki *see* Pawnee
Parikoto *see* Paricoto
Parintintim (LC)
Parintintin *see* Parintintim
Pariri (LC) *see also* Arara (LC)
Pariri [Lang] *Arara* (UAz, v.28)
Pariri [Lang] *Motilon* (UAz, v.28)
Pariri [VE] *Yukpa* (O)
Par-is-ca-oh-pan-ga *see* Crow
Pariscaohpanga *see* Crow
Pariscar *Crow* (H)
Paritiguara *see* Pantiguara
Paritin *see* Kawahib
Pariza [Pan] *Guaymi* (BE)
Parkateye *see* Gavioes
Par-keeh *see* Siksika
Parkeeh *see* Siksika
Parkeenaum (H) *see also* Pagatsu (BE)
Par-kee-na-um *see* Parkeenaum
Parkeenaum [TX] *Comanche* (BE)
Par-lar-nee *see* Pawnee
Parlarnee *see* Pawnee
Par-lar-we *see* Chiricahua Apache
Parlarwe *see* Chiricahua Apache
Parokonosko *see* Paraconosko
Parokoto *see* Paricoto
Pa-room-pai-ats *see* Moapa
Paroompaiats *see* Moapa
Pa-room-pats *see* Las Vegas
Paroompats *see* Las Vegas

Pa-roos-its *see* Saint George
Paroosits *see* Saint George
Parowan Paiutes *see* Cedar
Parquenahua [PE] (O)
Parrot [Clan] *Isleta* (H)
Parrot People *see* Pichikwe
Partamona *see* Patamona
Par-too-ku *see* Comanche
Partooku *see* Comanche
Parua *see* Kayabi
Parugun [UT] *Paiute* (H)
Pa-ru-guns *see* Paruguns
Parukoto *see* Puricoto
Parukoto-Charuma *see*
　Parukoto-Xarume
Parukoto-Pemon [VE] *Puricoto*
　(O)
Parukoto-Xaruma [Br] *Puricoto*
　(O)
Parukutu *see* Puricoto
Parumpaiat *Paiute* (H)
Parumpat *Paiute* (H)
Paru-pdeari *see* Yuruna
Pa-rup-its *see* Cedar
Pa-rup-its *see* Panguitch
Parupits *see* Cedar
Parupits *see* Panguitch
Parupodeari *see* Yuruna
Parusanuch (Hdbk11) *see also*
　White River Utes (W)
Parusanuch [CO] *Ute* (Hdbk11)
Parusi (H) *see also* Paiute (LC)
Parusi *Cobarde* (H)
Parussi *see* Saint George
Parvain *see* Pahvant
Parvan *see* Pahvant
Par Vans *see* Pahvant
Pasagoula *see* Pascagoula
Pasaju *see* Patzau
Pa-sa-kun-a-mon *see* Pasakuna-
　mon
Pasakunamon [Sub-clan]
　Delaware (H)
Pasalves [TX] *Coahuiltecan* (BE)
Pasamaquoda *see* Passamaquoddy
Pasatiko Wininiwuk *see*
　Pa'sa'tiko Wini'niwuk
Pa'sa'tiko Wini'niwuk [WI]
　Menominee (BE)
Pascaganlas *see* Pascagoula
Pascagolas *see* Pascagoula
Pascagoula [TX, LA] (LC)
Pasca Ogoula *see* Pascagoula
Pascaogoula *see* Pascagoula
Pasca Oocola *see* Pascagoula
Pasca-Oocoolo *see* Pascagoula
Pascaoocoolo *see* Pascagoula
Pascatacon *see* Piscataway
Pascataqua *see* Piscataqua
Pascatawaye *see* Conoy
Pascatawayes *see* Piscataqua
Pascatoe *see* Conoy
Pascatoway *see* Conoy

Pascatowies *see* Piscataway
Pascattawaye *see* Conoy
Paschal *see* Pachal
Paschales *see* Paschal
Paschtoligmeuten *see* Pastolig-
　miut
Paschtoligmjuten *see* Pastolig-
　miut
Paschtoligmuten *see* Pastoligmiut
Paschtuligmuten *see* Pastoligmiut
Pasco [PE] (O)
Pascoboula *see* Pascagoula
Pascogoula *see* Pascagoula
Pascoticon *see* Conoy
Pascual, San [CA] *Digueno* (H)
Pascual, San [NM] *Piro* (H)
Pasé [Lang] *Maipurean* (O)
Pa-sha-ga-sa-wis-so-uk *see*
　Pashagasawissouk
Pashagasawissouk [Clan] *Sauk*
　(H)
Pashcatoway *see* Piscataway
Pashilqua *see* Cayoosh Creek
Pashilquia *see* Cayoosh Creek
Pashir [Clan] *Pueblo Indians* (H)
P'ashir-t'anin *see* Pashir
Pashirtanin *see* Pashir
pashiukwa *see* Nambe
Pashohan *see* Iowa
Pashtolegmutis *see* Pastoligmiut
Pashtolits *see* Pastoligmiut
pasiatikka *Shoshone* (Hdbk11)
Pasitas [MX] *Coahuiltecan* (BE)
Paskagoula *see* Pascagoula
Paskaguna *see* Pascagoula
Paskattaway *see* Piscataway
Pas-ke-sa *see* Poskesa
Paskesa *see* Poskesa
Paskokopa-wiinuuk [Can]
　Paskwawininiwug (BE)
Paskwawiginiwok *see* Paskwaw-
　ininiwug
Paskwawininiwug [Can] *Cree*
　(BE)
Paskwawiyiniwok *see* Paskwaw-
　ininiwug
Pasnacan *see* Pasnacanes
Pasnacanes *Coahuiltecan* (BE)
Pa-so-ods *see* Nim
Pasos (H)
Paspagola *see* Pascagoula
Paspahe *see* Paspahegh
Paspahegas *see* Paspahegh
Paspahegh [VA] *Powahatan Con-
　federacy* (BE)
Paspaheghes *see* Paspahegh
Paspaheyan *see* Paspahegh
Paspatank *see* Pasquotank
Paspeiouk *see* Paspahegh
Paspihae *see* Paspahegh
Pa-spi-kai-vat *see* Paspikaivat
Paspikaivat (PC) *see also* Kaibab
　(BE)

Paspikaivat [UT] *Paiute* (H)
Pa-spi-kai-vats *see* Kaibab
Pa-spika-vats *see* Kaibab
Paspitank *see* Pasquotank
Pasqual, San *see* San Pascual
　[CA]
Pasqual *Coahuiltecan* (BE)
Pasquenan *see* Pacana
Pasquotank [NC] *Weapemeoc*
　(BE)
Passacola *see* Pensacola
Passaguaniguara [Lang] *Quinigua*
　(Hdbk10)
Passamacadie *see* Passamaquoddy
Passamaquoda *see* Pas-
　samaquoddy
Passamaquodda *see* Pas-
　samaquoddy
Passamaquoddy [ME, NewB] *Ab-
　naki Confederacy* (LC)
Passamaquodie *see* Pas-
　samaquoddy
Passamequado *see* Pas-
　samaquoddy
Pas-sam-ma-quod-dies *see* Pas-
　samaquoddy
Passammaquoddies *see* Pas-
　samaquoddy
Passayonk [PA, DE] *Unalachtigo*
　(BE)
Pass Cahuilla (BE) *see also* West-
　ern Cahuilla (BE)
Pass Cahuilla [CA] *Cahuilla* (CA-
　8)
Passemaquoddy *see* Pas-
　samaquoddy
Passimaquodies *see* Pas-
　samaquoddy
Passinchan *see* Iowa
Passing Hail's Band [MN] *Mde-
　wakanton* (H)
Passonagesit *see* Massachuset
Passtaquack *see* Piscataqua
Pastalac *see* Pastalaco
Pastaloca [TX] *Coahuiltecan* (BE)
Pastaloco *see* Pastaloca
Pastaluc *see* Pastaloca
Pastalve *see* Pasalves
Pastalve *see* Pastaloca
Pastancoyas [MX] *Coahuiltecan*
　(BE)
Pastannowna *see* Castahana
Pasta-now-na *see* Castahana
Pastanowna *see* Castahana
Pastanquia [MX] *Coahuiltecan*
　(Hdbk10)
Pasteal (Hdbk10) *see also* Pachal
　(BE)
Pasteal [MX, TX] *Coahuiltecan*
　(BE)
Pastia (H) *see also* Pasteal (BE)
Pastia *Coahuiltecan* (Hdbk10)
Pasto [Col, EC] (LC)

Pastoligmiut [AK] *Unaligmiut Eskimos* (H)
Pastolig'mut *see* Unaligmiut
Pastoligmut *see* Pastoligmiut
Pastolik *Bering Strait Eskimos* (Hdbk5)
Pastoloca *see* Pastaloca
Pastulac *see* Pastaloca
Pasuchis *see* Paiute
p'asuiap *see* Pojoaque
pasuiap *see* Pojoaque
Pasuque *see* Pojoaque
Pasxa *see* Patzau
Patacal *Coahuiltecan* (Hdbk10)
Patacales *see* Pastaloca
Patacales *see* Patacal
Patacho *see* Patasho
Patagahan *see* Patague
Patagahu *see* Patague
Patagon [Lang] [PE] *Cariban* (O)
Patagone *see* Tehuelche
Patagonians *see* Tehuelche
Patagu *see* Patague
Patagua *see* Patague
Pataguan *see* Patague
Pataguaque *see* Patague
Patague [TX, MX] *Coahuiltecan* (BE)
Pataguita *see* Patague
Pataguo *see* Patague
Pa-taiina *see* Paw
Pataiina *see* Paw
Pa-take-e-no-the *see* Patakeenothe
Patakeenothe [Clan] *Shawnee* (H)
Patalca *see* Pitalac
Pataloco *see* Pastaloca
Patamack *see* Potomac
Patamona [Guy, VE] *Acawai* (LC)
Patamona [Lang] *Pemong* (UAz, v.28)
Patamuno *see* Patamona
Patan [Coahuiltecan] (BE)
Patanium *Coahuiltecan* (BE)
Patao *see* Patague
Pataomecke *see* Potomac
Pataquakes *see* Patague
Pataque *see* Patague
Pataquilla [TX] *Coahuiltecan* (BE)
Patarabueye (H) *see also* Jumano (LC)
Patarabueye [MX, TX] (LC)
Patarabye *see* Jumano
Patarabye *see* Patarabueye
Pataromerke *see* Potomac
Patashoo [Br] (LC)
Patas-negras *see* Siksika
Pataunck [VA] *Powhatan Confederacy* (BE)
Patavo *see* Patague
Pat-a-Wat *see* Patawat
Pat-a-wat *see* Batawat

Patawat (Pub, v.9, no.3, p.384)
Patawat (Pub, v.9, no.3, p.384) *see also* Batawat (BE)
Patawatimes *see* Potawatomi
Patawattamies *see* Potawatomi
Patawattomies *see* Potawatomi
Pat-a-we *see* Wintu
Patawe *see* Wintu
Patawoenicke *see* Potomack
Patawomeck *see* Potomac
Patawomeck *see* Potomac
Patawomeke *see* Potomac
Pataxo *see* Patasho
Patayan (AI, p.30)
Patchal *see* Pachal
Patch-a-we *see* Wintu
Patchawe *see* Patwin
Patcheena *see* Pacheenaht
Patchisagi *see* Apache
Patchoag [NY] *Metoac* (H)
Patchogue [NY] *Montauk* (BE)
Patchuh *see* Apache
Patcina'ath *see* Pacheenaht
Patcinaath *see* Pacheenaht
Pa-tco-ka *see* Comanche
Patcoka *see* Comanche
Pa-tco ka-ja *see* Comanche
Patcokaja *see* Comanche
Pa-tdoa *see* Pa [Tewa]
Pa-tdoa *see* Pang
Patdoa *see* Pa [Tewa]
Patdoa *see* Pang
Patehal *see* Pachal
Patesick *see* Karok
Patha [Clan] *Oto* (H)
Patica *Chibchan* (BE)
Patih-rik *see* Karok
Patihrik *see* Karok
Patipora *see* Pantipora
Patiquilid [CA] (H)
Patiri [TX] (BE)
Patki [Phratry] *Hopi* (H)
Pat-ki-nyu-mu *see* Patki
Patkinyumu *see* Patki
Pat-ki win-wu *see* Patki
Patki wiñwû *see* Patki
Pat-ki wüñ-wû *see* Patki
Patki wüñwû *see* Patki
Patlapigua *see* Potlapigua
Pa-toas *see* Paloos
Patoas *see* Paloos
Patomac *see* Potomac
Patomeck *see* Potomac
Patonca *see* Comanche
Patoo [MX] *Coahuiltecan* (Hdbk10)
Patou (Hdbk10) *see also* Patague (BE)
Patou *Coahuiltecan* (BE)
Patowamack *see* Potomac
Patowmeck *see* Potomac
Patowomack *see* Potomac
Patowomeek *see* Potomac

Patowomek *see* Potomac
Patrantecooke *see* Pocomtuc
Patshenin (BE) *see also* Oconeechee (LC)
Patshenin [Ont] (H)
Patsjoe *see* Navajo
Patsuiket *see* Sokoki
Pattawatamies *see* Potawatomi
Pattawatima *see* Potawatomi
Pattawatimee *see* Potawatomi
Pattawatimy *see* Potawatomi
Pattawatomie *see* Potawatomi
Pattawattamee *see* Potawatomi
Pattawattomi *see* Potawatomi
Pattawattomies *see* Potawatomi
Pattawomeke *see* Potomac
Patti Corbeau's band *see* Kapozha
Pattiwatima *see* Potawatomi
Pattsau *see* Patzau
Pattuxunt *see* Patuxent
P'atu'ak *see* San Felipe [Keres]
Patuak *see* San Felipe [Keres]
Pa-tu-atami *see* Potawatomi
Patuatami *see* Potawatomi
Pa-tuh-ku *see* Comanche
Patuhku *see* Comanche
Pa-tu-ka *see* Comanche
Patuka *see* Comanche
patukunancimi *see* Cedar
Patumaco *Coahuiltecan* (Hdbk10)
Patuñ *see* Patung
Patung [Clan] *Hopi* (H)
Patung [Phratry] *Hopi* (H)
Patunke *see* Comanche
Patun wiñwû *see* Patung
Pa-tun-wuñ-wu *see* Patung
Patunwunwu *see* Patung
Patun wuñwu *see* Patung
Patuxant *see* Patuxent
Patuxent [MD] *Conoy* (BE)
Patuxon *see* Patuxent
Patwae *see* Patwin
Patween *see* Patwin
Pat-win *see* Patwin
Patwin [Lang] [CA] *Wintuan* (LC)
Pat-wish-a *see* Badwisha
Patwisha *see* Badwisha
P'a-tyu-la *see* Pecos
p'atyula *see* Pecos
Patyula *see* Pecos
Patzar *see* Patzau
Patzau *Coahuiltecan* (BE)
Pauana *see* Pawnee
Pau Cerna *see* Pauserna
Paucerna *see* Pauserna
Pa-uches *see* Paiute
Pauches *see* Tabeguache
Pauches *see* Paiute
Paucomtuck *see* Pocomtuc
Paucomtuckqut *see* Pocomtuc
Pa-u-da *see* Paiute

Pauda *see* Paiute
Pauda tuviwarai *see*
  Makuhadokado
Paugassett *see* Paugusset
Paugusset [CN, NY] *Wappinger*
  (LC)
Paugussett *see* Paugusset
Pauhoochees *see* Iowa
Pauide tuviwarai *see*
  Makuhadokado
Pauishana [Br] (LC)
Paukwechin *see* Panquechin
Pa-Ulche *see* Southern Paiute
Paulche *see* Paiute
Pa-ulche [Self-designation] *see*
  Paiute
Paulches *see* Southern Paiute
Paumari (LC) *see also* Purupuru
  (LC)
Paumari [Br] *Purupuru* (O)
Paumary *see* Paumari
Paumtonnauweew *see* Wyandot
Paumuca *see* Chiquitano
Pauna *see* Paunaca
Paunaca [Lang] [BO] *Maipurean*
  (O)
Paunaka *see* Paunaca
Paunaque *see* Bannock
Paunch Indians *see* Allakaweah
Paunee *see* Pawnee
Paunee Republics *see* Kitkehahki
Paüoitigoüeieuhak *see* Saulteaux
Pauray *see* Puaray
Paus *see* Paloos
Pausanas *see* Pausanes
Pausane *see* Pausanes
Pausane *see* Pausanes
Pausanes [TX] *Coahuiltecan* (BE)
Pausaqui *Coahuiltecan* (BE)
Pausay *Coahuiltecan* (BE)
Pauserna [BO] (LC)
Pau-shuk *see* Paushuk
Paushuk *Arikara* (H)
Pautawatimi *see* Potawatomi
Pautawattamies *see* Potawatomi
Pa-Utche *see* Southern Paiute
Pautches *see* Southern Paiute
Pa-ute (H) *see also* Paiute (LC)
Paute *see* Paiute
Paute *see* Pa-Ute
Pa-Ute *Paiute* (Hdbk11)
Pauteaumi *see* Potawatomi
Pa-utes *see* Southern Paiute
Pautes *see* Southern Paiute
Pautuxuntes *see* Patuxent
Pauvans *see* Pahvant
Pauvante *see* Pahvant
pauwuii *see* pauwu'ii
pauwu'ji *Western Shoshone*
  (Hdbk11)
pauwu'jiji *see* pauwu'ji
Pauxi [Lang] *Chikena* (UAz, v.28)
Pauxiana [Lang] *Carib* (UAz, v.28)

Pauzanes *see* Pausanes
pavandüts *see* Pahvant
Pavant *see* Pahvant
Pavant Utahs *see* Pahvant
Pavant Yuta *see* Pahvant
Pavatiya [Clan] *Hopi* (H)
Pavatiya wiñwû *see* Pavatiya
Pa-va-ti-ya wuñ-wû *see* Pavatiya
Pavatiya wuñwû *see* Pavatiya
Pavilion (Hdbk12) *see also* Paloos
  (LC)
Pavilion [BC] *Shushwap* (H)
Pavilion [BC] *Upper Lillooet*
  (Hdbk12)
Pavillon (Hdbk12) *see also* Paloos
  (LC)
Paviotso (CA) *see also* Paiute (LC)
Pa-vi-o-tso *see* Paviotso
Paviotso [CA, NV] (CA)
Paviotso [Lang] [*Mono-Paviotso*]
  (H)
Paviotso [Lang] *Western Numic*
  (Hdbk10)
Pa-vi-o-tsoes [Self-designation]
  see Paviotso
pavi-wats *see* Moanunts
paviwats *see* Moanunts
pavogowunsin (Hdbk11) *see also*
  Moanunts (Hdbk11)
Pavogowunsin [UT] (BE)
Pa-vu-wi-wu-yu-ai *see* Pavuwi-
  wuyuai
Pavuwiwuyuai [UT] *Paviotso* (H)
Paw [Clan] *Taos* (H)
Pawalu *see* Pa'walu
Pa'walu [NV] (BE)
Pawana *see* Yecuana
Pawate *see* Paranawat
Pawating [MI, WI] *Chippewa* (H)
Pawaustic-eythin-yoowuc *see*
  Atsina
Pawcompt *see* Pocomtuc
Pa-Weapits *see* Pawipits
Pa-weap-its *see* Moapa
Paweapits *see* Moapa
Paweapits *see* Pawipits
Pawgassett *see* Paugusset
Pawgasuck *see* Paugusset
Pawghksuck *see* Paugusset
Pawha'hlita *see* San Ildefonso
Pawhahlita *see* San Ildefonso
Pawikya [Clan] *Hopi* (H)
Pawikya wiñwû *see* Pawikya
Pa-wi-kya wuñ-wû *see* Pawikya
Pawikya wuñwû *see* Pawikya
Pawilkna *see* Coyotero Apache
Pawipit [NV] *Paiute* (H)
Pawishana [Lang] [Br] *Cariban*
  (O)
Paw-is-tick I-e-ne-wuch *see*
  Atsina
Pawistick Ienewuch *see* Atsina
Pawistucienemuk *see* Atsina

Pawistuck-Ienewuck *see* Atsina
Pawkees *see* Siksika
Pawkunnawkutt *see* Pokanoket
Pawluch *see* Paloos
Pawnaka *see* Paunaca
Pawnawnee *see* Pawnee
Pawne *see* Pawnee
Pawnee (H) *see also* Lipan Apache
  (LC)
Pawnee [OK, NB, KN, WY] (LC)
Pawnee Loup *see* Skidi Pawnee
Pawnee Loupes *see* Skidi Pawnee
Pawnee Mahas *see* Skidi Pawnee
Pawnee Mahaw *see* Skidi Pawnee
Pawnee Markar *see* Skidi Pawnee
Pawnee Mohaw *see* Skidi Pawnee
Pawnee O'Mahaws *see* Skidi
  Pawnee
Pawneeomawhaws *see* Skidi
  Pawnee
Pawnee O'Mohaws *see* Skidi
  Pawnee
Pawneer *see* Pawnee
Pawnee Republic *see* Kitkehahki
Pawnee-Rikasree *see* Arikara
Pawnee Tappage *see* Pitahauerat
Pawnee Tappah *see* Pitahauerat
Pawnee Tappaye *see* Pitahauerat
Pawnemahas *see* Skidi Pawnee
Pawni *see* Pawnee
Pawnye *see* Pawnee
Pawokti [FL, AL] *Creek Confeder-
  acy* (BE)
Pawtucket *see* Wamesit
Pawtuckett *see* Wamesit
Pawtuxunt *see* Patuxent
Pawyer *see* Paya
Paxac *see* Paac
Paxalto *Coahuiltecan* (Hdbk10)
paxiniwis *see* Flathead
Paxuado ameti *see* Hualapai
Paya [Hon] (LC)
Payaba [SD] *Oglala* (H)
Payabyeya *see* Payaba
Payagua (H) *see also* Payaya (LC)
Payagua [Par] (LC)
Payaguanes *see* Pajuguan
Payagui *see* Orejon
Payahan *see* Payuguan
Payai *see* Payaya
Payaia *see* Payaya
Payairkets *see* Eskimos
Payalla *see* Payaya
Payan [MX] (BE)
Payangitchaki *see* Piankashaw
Payankatank *see* Piankatank
Payankatonk *see* Pinakatank
payapadika'a *Northern Paiute*
  (Hdbk11)
Payaque *see* Pojoaque
Payavan *see* Payuguan
Payay *see* Payaya
Payaya [TX] *Coahuiltecan* (BE)

Payayasa *see* Payaya
Payaye *see* Payaya
Paygan *see* Piegan
Payi *see* Pawnee
Payi *see* Pawnee
pa-yice *see* Southern Paiute
payice *see* Southern Paiute
Payin *see* Pawnee
Payin-manhan *see* Skidi Pawnee
Payinmanhan *see* Skidi Pawnee
Payin'qtci *see* Chaui
Payinqtci *see* Chaui
Payinqtsi *see* Chaui
payipki *see* Sandia
Payma *see* Pima
Payne Inuit (Hdbk5)
Payni-Ken *see* Northern
  Tehuelche
Payniken *see* Northern
  Tehuelche
Paynute *see* Paiute
Payoan *see* Payuguan
Payoche *see* Paiute
payoci *see* Southern Paiute
Pa-yo-go-na *see* Pecos
Payogona *see* Pecos
payopi *see* Sandia
Payoqona *see* Pecos
Payories *see* Peoria
payowci *see* Southern Paiute
Paysan *see* Pausanes
Payseyas *see* Payaya
Payucha *see* Paiute
Payuchas *see* Southern Paiute
Payuches *see* Paiute
Payuches *see* Southern Paiute
Payuchi *see* Southern Paiute
payuci *see* Southern Paiute
payucimi *see* Southern Paiute
payu-cimi *see* Southern Paiute
payuc *see* Southern Paiute
payu-di *see* Paiute
payudi *see* Paiute
Payugan *see* Payuguan
Payuguan [MX] *Coahuiltecan*
  (BE)
Payuhan *see* Payuguan
Payuhuan *see* Payuguan
Payukue *see* Paiute
payunggish'ah *see* Piankashaw
Payupki (H) *see also* Sandia (BE)
Payupki [NM] (BE)
Payuta *see* Paiute
Payutas *see* Southern Paiute
Payute *see* Paviotso
Payute *see* Pa-Ute
payutih *see* Paiute
Payutsin dinne *see* Paiute
Payutsindinne *see* Paiute
Paza *see* Patzau
Pazac *see* Patzau
Pazajo *see* Patzau
Pazaju *see* Patzau

Pazatican *Conoy* (Hdbk15)
Pazaug *see* Patzau
Pazhajo *see* Patzau
Pazoods *see* Nim
Pazo-ods *see* Nim
Pazuchis *see* Paiute
Pe [Clan] [*Pueblo Indians*] (H)
Peacemaker *see* Chizhuwashtage
Peacott *see* Pequot
Pea Creek Band [FL] *Seminole*
  (H)
Peadea *see* Pedee
Peagan *see* Piegan
Peagin *see* Piegan
Peaginou *see* Piegan
Pe-a-go *see* Pecos
Peago *see* Pecos
Pe-ah-cun-nay *see* Piegan
Peahcunnay *see* Piegan
Peahko *see* Pecos
Peahs *see* Grand River Ute
Pe-ah's band of Utes *see* Grand
  River Ute
Peahushaw *see* Pinkashaw
Pe-a-ko *see* Pecos
Peako *see* Pecos
P'e-a-ku *see* Pecos
p'eaku *see* Pecos
Pe-a-ku *see* Pecos
Peaku *see* Pecos
Peakuni *see* Pecos
Pe-a-ku-ni *see* Pecos
Peana *Coahuiltecan* (BE)
Peanghichia *see* Piankashaw
peangišia [Self-designation] *see*
  Piankashaw
Peanguichea *see* Piankashaw
Peanguichia *see* Piankasahw
Peanguischia *see* Piankashaw
Peanguisein *see* Piankashaw
Peankshaws *see* Piankashaw
Peanquicha *see* Piankashaw
Peantias (H)
Peanzichia Miami *see* Pi-
  ankashaw
Peaouaria *see* Peoria
Peaquitt *see* Pequot
Peaquod *see* Pequot
Peaquot *see* Pequot
Pe'ash *see* Pe
Peash *see* Pe
Peau de Lievre *see* Kawchottine
Peauguichea *see* Piankashaw
Peaux *see* Kalispel
Peaux-de-Lievres *see* Kawchottine
Peba *see* Yagua
Pebo *see* Cogui
Pecaneaux *see* Piegan
Pecankeeshaw *see* Piankashaw
Pecan Point *see* Nanatsoho
Pecari *see* Picuris
Pecas *see* Pecos
Pecawa *see* Piqua

Peccos *see* Pecos
Pecegesiwag *see* Pashagawissouk
Pech *see* Paya
Pechange *see* Pachanga
Pechir *see* Piechar
Peckawee *see* Shawnee
Peckwalket *see* Pequawkat
Pe-cla *see* Peshla
Pecla *see* Peshla
Pe-cla-ptcetcela *see* Pesh-
  laptechela
Peclaptcetcela *see* Peshlaptechela
Peco *see* Pecos
Pecoat *see* Pequot
Pecoates *see* Pequot
Pecod *see* Pequot
Pecoit *see* Pequot
Pecoites *see* Pequot
Pecompticks *see* Pocomtuc
Pecomptuk *see* Pocomtuc
Pecora *see* Picuris
Pecos [Lang] *Jemez* (BE)
Pecos [NM] (BE)
Pecott *see* Pequot
Pecowick *see* Shawnee
Pecucio *see* Picuris
Pecucis *see* Picuris
Pecuri *see* Picuris
Pecuria *see* Peoria
Pecuries *see* Picuris
Pecuris *see* Picuris
Pecuwesi *see* Piqua
Pedadumies *see* Potawatomi
Pe-dahl-lu *see* Petdelu
Pedahllu *see* Petdelu
Pedani *see* Pawnee
Pedea *see* Embera
Pedee [Lang] *Eastern Siouan* (H)
Pedee [SC] (BE)
Pedgan *see* Piegan
Pedilonians (H)
Pedraza *see* Tunebo
Pedro, San *see* Acoma
Pedro y Sant Pablo, Sant *see* Sia
Peduca *see* Comanche
Pee-allipaw-mich *see* Puyallup
Peeallipawmich *see* Puyallup
Pee Dee *see* Pedee
Peedee *see* Pedee
Peegan *see* Peagan
Pe-e-ki-ce *see* Peekishe
Peekice *see* Peekishe
Peekishe [MO] (H)
pe'ekit *see* Naukanski
Peelig *see* Pilingmiut
Peel River Kutchin *see* Tatlit-
  kutchin
Peel River Kutchin *see* Tellet-
  kutchin
Peel's River Indians *see* Tatl-
  itkutchin
Peel's River Loucheux *see* Tatl-
  itkutchin

Peenecook *see* Pennacook
Peequot *see* Pequot
Pegan *see* Piegan
Peganes *see* Piegan
Pe-gan-o *see* Piegan
Pegano *see* Piegan
Peganoe-koon *see* Piegan
Peganoekoon *see* Piegan
Peganoo-eythinyoowuc *see* Piegan
Pe ga-zan-de *see* Nez Perce
Pegazande *see* Nez Perce
Pegoa *see* Pecos
Pegod *see* Pequot
Pegouakky *see* Pequawkat
Pegoucoquia *see* Pepikokia
Peguampaxte [MX] *Coahuiltecan* (Hdbk10)
Peguenche *see* Pehuenche
Pegwacket *see* Pequawket
Pegwackit *see* Pequawket
Pegwackuk *see* Pequawket
Pegwaggett *see* Pequawket
Pegwaket *see* Pequawket
Pe-hi-pte-ci-la *see* Peshlaptechela
Pehiptecila *see* Peshlaptechela
Pehqwoket *see* Pequawket
Peh-tsik *see* Karok
Pehtsik *see* Karok
Pehuenche [Arg, CH] (LC)
Peici *see* Pecos
Peicis *see* Pecos
Peicj *see* Pecos
Peigan *see* Piegan
Peiki *see* Siksika
Peikuagamiu *see* Piekouagami
Pe-iltzun *see* Peiltzun
Peiltzun *San Carlos* (H)
Peimtegouet *see* Penobscot
Peioria *see* Peoria
Peisacho *see* Peissaquo
Pe-i-si-e-kan *see* Peisiekan
Peisiekan [Can] *Cree* (BE)
Peissaque [TX] (H)
Peixoloe (H)
Pe-ji-wo-ke-ya-o-ti *see* Shoshone
Pejiwokeyaoti *see* Shoshone
Pejodque *see* Pojoaque
Pe-kan-ne *see* Piegan
Pekanne *see* Piegan
Pekanne-koon *see* Piegan
Pekannekoon *see* Piegan
Pekansantse *see* Nez Perce
Pe ka-san-tse *see* Nez Perce
Pekash *see* Pequot
Peki'neni *see* Potawatomi
Pekineni *see* Potawatomi
Pekineni'hak *see* Potawatomi
Pe-ko *see* Pecos
Peko *see* Pecos
Pekoath *see* Pequot

Pekoct *see* Pequot
Pekot *see* Pequot
Pekoweu *see* Piqua
pekowi *see* Shawnee
Peku *see* Pecos
Pekuegi *see* Piqua
Pekush *see* Pecos
Pe-kush [Self-designation] *see* Pecos
pe-kwile *see* Picuris
pekwile *see* Picuris
pekwileta *see* Picuris
Pe'kwilita *see* Picuris
Pekwilita *see* Picuris
Pelado *see* Penobo
Pelagisia *see* Piankashaw
Pela'tlq *see* Pilalt
Pelatlq *see* Pilalt
Peleuche *see* Apalachee
Peleuyi *see* Palewyami
Pe-le-wa *see* Palewa
Pelewa *see* Palewa
Pelheli [BC] (H)
Pelicaguaro *see* Pericaguera
Pel-late-pa-ler *see* Paloos
Pellatepaler *see* Paloos
Pelloat pallah *see* Paloos
Pelloatpallah *see* Paloos
Pel-lote-paller *see* Paloos
Pellotepaller *see* Paloos
Peloose *see* Paloos
Pelouchs *see* Paloos
Pelouse *see* Paloos
Pelouze *see* Paloos
Pe'lqeli *see* Pelheli
Pelqeli *see* Pelheli
Pelu-cpu *see* Paloos
Pelus *see* Paloos
Pelusbpa *see* Paloos
Peluse *see* Paloos
Pelushes *see* Paloos
Pema *see* Pima
Pemberton [BC] *Lower Lillooet* (BE)
Pemberton Meadows [BC] *Lower Lillooet* (H)
Pembina Band *see* Anibiminanis-ibiwininiwak
Pemblicos *see* Pamlico
Pemedenick *see* Huron
Pemetegoit *see* Penobscot
Pemlico *see* Pamlico
Pemlicoe *see* Pamlico
Pemo *see* Pima
Pemon [VE] (LC)
Pemong (O) *see also* Arecuna (LC)
Pemong (O) *see also* Arekuna (LC)
Pemong [Lang] *Carib* (UAz, v.28)

Pemplico *see* Pamlico
Pemptagoiett *see* Penobscot
Pemptico *see* Pamlico
Pemtegoit *see* Penobscot
Pemveans (H)
Penacook *see* Pennacook
Pe-na-doj-ka *see* Penateka
Penadojka *see* Penateka
Penagooge *see* Pennacook
Pe-nai-na *see* Pawnee
Penaina *see* Pawnee
Penakook *see* Pennacook
Penal Apaches *see* Pinalino Apache
Penalenos *see* Pinalino Apache
Pena'leqat *see* Penelakut
Penaleqat *see* Penelakut
Penalhut *see* Penelakut
Penalikutson *see* Penelakut
Penande *see* Penateka
Penard *see* Fox
Penaske *see* Penobscot
Pen-a-tacker *see* Penateka
Penatacker *see* Penateka
Penataka *see* Penateka
Pe'nate'ka *see* Pi'nutgu
Penateka (PC) *see also* Pi'nutgu (BE)
Penateka *Comanche* (BE)
Penaubsket *see* Penobscot
Penboscot *see* Penobscot
Penboscut *see* Penobscot
Pençacola *see* Pensacola
Pencoana (H)
Pençocolo *see* Pensacola
Penday *see* Canelo
Pend d'Oreille (H) *see also* Kalispel (LC)
Pend d'Oreille [MT] (Hdbk12)
Pend d'Oreilles of the Lower Lake *see* Kalispelm
Pend d'Oreilles of the Upper Lake *see* Slka-tkml-schi
Pends Oreilles *see* Kalispel
Penduhut *see* Penelakut
Penechon *see* Pineshow
Penecooke *see* Pennacook
Penelaka *see* Penateka
Penelakut [Can] *Cowichan* (BE)
Penelethka *see* Penateka
Penetakee *see* Penateka
Penetaker *see* Penateka
Peneteghka *see* Penateka
Pene-teh-ca *see* Penateka
Peneteka *see* Penateka
Pe-neteka-Comanches *see* Penateka
Peneteka Comanches *see* Penateka
Penetethca *see* Penateka
Penetethka *see* Penateka
Penetoghko *see* Penateka
Pen-ha-teth-ka *see* Penateka

Penhatethka *see* Penateka
Pen-ha-teth-kah *see* Penateka
Penhatethkah *see* Penateka
Penichon *see* Pineshow
Penicoock *see* Pennacook
Penicook *see* Pennacook
Penikikonau (H) *see also* Pe'niki'konau (H)
Pe'niki'konau [Clan] *Menominee* (H)
Penikikonau [Clan] *Menominee* (H)
Pen'ikis *see* Abnaki
Penikis *see* Abnaki
Penikook *see* Pennacook
Penition *see* Pineshow
Penjeacu (H)
penkwitikka *see* Fish Eaters
Pen loca *see* Comanche
Penloca *see* Comanche
Penna [Clan] *Potawatomi* (H)
Pennacoke *see* Pennacook
Pennacook [NH] *Pennacook Confederacy* (LC)
Pennacook Confederacy *Algonquian* (H)
Pennacooke *see* Pennacook
Pennagog *see* Pennacook
Pennakook *see* Pennacook
Pennecooke *see* Pennacook
Pennekokes *see* Pennacook
Pennekook *see* Pennacook
Pennekooke *see* Pennacook
Pennelaka *see* Penateka
Penne-taha *see* Penateka
Pennetaha *see* Penateka
Penneteka *see* Penateka
Pennicook *see* Pennacook
Pennikook *see* Pennacook
Pennobscot *see* Penobscot
Pennokook *see* Pennacook
Pennoukady *see* Passamaquoddy
Penny Cook *see* Pennacook
Penny-Cooke *see* Pennacook
Pennykoke *see* Pennacook
Penobesutt *see* Penobscot
Penobscot [Lang] *Eastern Algonquian* (Hdbk15)
Penobscot [ME] *Abnaki Confederacy* (LC)
Penobscotes *see* Penobscot
Penobscott *see* Penobscot
Penobscut *see* Penobscot
Penobskeag *see* Penobscot
Penobsot *see* Penobscot
Penointik-ara *see* Penointikara
Penointikara [ID] *Bannock* (BE)
Penoki *see* Penoqui
Peñol *see* Acoma
Peñoles *see* Acoma
Penomeno [Pan] (BE)
Penoqui [BO] (O)
Penoy (H)

Pensacola [FL, MS] (BE)
Pensicola *see* Pensacola
Pentagoet *see* Penobscot
Pentagoiett *see* Penobscot
Pentagonett *see* Penobscot
Pentagouet *see* Penobscot
Pentagouetch *see* Penobscot
Pentagovett *see* Penobscot
Pentegoet *see* Penobscot
Pentepec [MX] (BE)
Penticton [WA] *Okanagon* (BE)
P-e'ntlatc *see* Puntlatsh
Pentlatc *see* Puntlatsh
Penttakers *see* Penateka
Pentucket [MA] *Pennacook* (BE)
Peñunde [MX] (H)
Penutian [Lang] [CA] (LC)
Penxayes *Plains Apache* (Hdbk10)
Penzocolo *see* Pensacola
Peoaria *see* Peoria
Peoira *see* Utagami
Peola *see* Utagami
peolia *see* Peoria
Peona *see* Utagami
Peonies *see* Peoria
People in a Circle *see* Detsanayuka
people of Bellot Strait *see* Arviqtuurmiut
people of Pelly Bay *see* Arviligyuarmiut
people of the Canyon *see* Akonye
People of the Desert *see* Kwahari
People of the Earth *see* Tongva
People-of-the-flat-roof-houses *see* Querecho
People of the Fork *see* Nassauaketon
people of the head of the big river *see* Kuuvaum Kangianigmiut
people of the intervening country *see* Akudnirmiut
people of the Killilk River *see* Killikmiut
people of the Kuskokwim *see* Kusquqvagmiut
People of the Lake *see* Mdewakanton
people of the leggings *see* Akiyenik
People of the Lowlands *see* Maskegan
people of the marshy or muddy lowlands *see* Maarmiut
people of the Nushagak River *see* Nushagagmiut
People of the Outlet *see* Sauk
People of the Pheasants *see* Sipushkanumanke
People of the Place of the Fire *see* Mascouten
People-of-the-Place-of-the Flying-Head *see* Tobacco Plains

people of the place with bones *see* Hauniqtuurmiut
People of the Plains *see* Paskwawininiwug
People of the Prairie *see* Paskwawininiwug
people of the ridgepole *see* Aglurmiut
people of the river *see* Kuungmiut
people of the sea *see* Tagiutmiut
People of the Submerged Pin Tree *see* Ka-te-nu'a'ka
people of the Togiak River *see* Tuyuryarmiut
people of the upper lakes *see* Akiskenukinik
People of the Upper Reaches [BC] *North Thompson Shuswap* (Hdbk12)
people of the whirlpools *see* Harvaqtuurmiut
People of the Willows *see* Havsupai
People of the Woods *see* Tcan'xe wintca'cta
People of the Woods *see* Sakawininiwug
People of the Woods *see* Sakawithiniwuk
People of the Yellow Earth *see* Sauk
people of the Yukon River *see* Kuigpagmiut
people of Tulugak Lake *see* Tulugakmiut
People That Don't Laugh *see* Kutaiimiks
People who hold aloof [Can] *Sarsi* (BE)
Peoreana *see* Peoria
Peores *see* Peoria
Peoria [IL, OK, IA] *Illinois Confederacy* (LC)
Peorian *see* Peoria
Peoualen *see* Peoria
Peouanguichia *see* Piankashaw
Peouanguihia *see* Piankashaw
Peouarea *see* Peoria
Peouareona *see* Peoria
Peouarewi *see* Peoria
Peouaria *see* Peoria
Peouarius *see* Peoria
Peouaroua *see* Peoria
Peoucaria *see* Peoria
Peoueria *see* Peoria
Peouria *see* Peoria
Peourya *see* Peoria
Peoutewatamie *see* Potawatomi
Pepatlenok [Clan] *Tenaktak* (H)
Pepawitlenok [Clan] *Klaskino* (H)
Pepegewizzains [Clan] *Chippewa* (H)

Pepegewizzains [Clan] *Ottawa*
(H)
Pepepicokia *see* Pepicokia
Pepepoake *see* Pepicokia
Pepicokia *Miami* (H)
Pepicoqui *see* Pepicokia
Pepicoquia *see* Pepicokia
Pepikoki *see* Pepicokia
Pepikokia *see* Pepicokia
Pepikoukia *see* Pepicokia
Pepuahapitski Sawanogi *see* Absentee Shawnee
Peqouaki *see* Pequawhet
Pequaket *see* Pequawket
Pequaket *see* Pequawhket
Pequant *see* Pequot
Pequanucke *see* Poquonock
Pequanucke *see* Poquonock
Pequaquaukes *see* Pequawket
Pequat *see* Pequot
Pequatit *see* Pequot
Pequatoa *see* Pequot
Pequatt *see* Pequot
Pequauket *see* Pequawket
Pequawett *see* Pequawket
Pequawket [ME, NH] *Abnaki*
(LC)
Pequea *see* Shawnee
Pequeat *see* Pequot
Pequent *see* Pequot
Pequente *see* Pequot
Pequet *see* Pequot
Pequetan *see* Pequot
Pequett *see* Pequot
Pequid *see* Pequot
Pequim *see* Pequot
Pequin *see* Pequot
Pequiot *see* Pequod
Pequite *see* Pequot
Pequitoog *see* Pequot
Pequitt *see* Pequot
Pequoadt *see* Pequot
Pequod *see* Pequot
Pequoid *see* Pequot
Pequoit *see* Pequot
Pequoite *see* Pequot
Pequooyt *see* Pequot
Pequot [RI, CN] *Algonquian* (LC)
Pequote *see* Pequot
Pequot Nayantaquit *see* Niantic
Pequotoh *see* Pequot
Pequottoog *see* Pequot
Pequt *see* Pequot
Pequt Nayantaquit *see* Niantic
Pequtt *see* Pequot
Pequut *see* Pequot
Pequuttoog *see* Pequot
Peqvat *see* Pequot
Peqwit *see* Pequot
Pera *Plains Indians* (H)
Perces *see* Nez Perce
Pericaguera *Coahuiltecan*
(Hdbk10)

Perico *see* Pericaguera
Pericú [Lang] [BaC] (J/Anthro,
v.2, no.2, pp.180–182)
Pericu [MX, BaC] (BE)
Perocodame *see* Terocodame
Perouacca *see* Peoria
Perouasca *see* Peoria
Peroueria *see* Peoria
Perpacug *Coahuiltecan* (Hdbk10)
Perpapug *see* Perpepug
Perpepug *Coahuiltecan* (Hdbk10)
Perquiman [NC] *Weapemeoc* (BE)
Peruka [Clan] *Keres* (H)
Pe'ruka-hano *see* Peruka
Perukahano *see* Peruka
Perun *see* Tionontati
Peruu *see* Tionontati
Pe-sa-wa (H) *see also* Pesawa (H)
Pe-sa-wa [Clan] *Shawnee* (H)
Pesawa [Clan] *Shawnee* (H)
Pescado *Coahuiltecan* (BE)
Pescagola *see* Pascagoula
Peshegesiwug *see* Pashagasawissouk
Peshla [SD] *Oglala* (H)
Peshlaptechela *Oglala* (BE)
Peshtigo River people *see*
Pa'sa'tiko Wini'niwuk
Peshtiko *see* Pesh'tiko
Pesh'tiko [WI] *Menominee* (BE)
Peskadaneeoukkanti *see* Passamaquoddy
Peskamaquonty *see* Passamaquoddy
Peskedemakadi *see* Passamaquoddy
Peskodamukotik *see* Passamaquoddy
Pe-sla *see* Peshla
Pesla *see* Peshla
Pe-sla-ptecela *see* Peshlaptechela
Peslaptecela *see* Peshlaptechela
Pesmaquady *see* Passamaquoddy
Pesmocady *see* Passamaquoddy
Pesmokanti *see* Passamaquoddy
Pesquis (H)
Pes-ta-moka'tiuk *see* Passamaquoddy
Pestamokatiuk *see* Passamaquoddy
Pestumagatick *see* Passamaquoddy
Petaakwe *see* Aiyaho
Pe-ta-ha-ne-rat *see* Pitahaurat
Petahanerat *see* Pitahauerat
Pe-tane'nikaci'ka *see* Petangenikashika
Petanenikacika *see* Petangenikashika
Petang [Clan] *Quapaw* (H)
Petangenikashika [Clan] *Quapaw*
(H)
Petao [TX] (H)

Petaro *see* Petao
Petawomeek *see* Potomac
Petaz *see* Petao
Petcares *see* Petas
petceq'cicen *see* Sugarcane Band
petceq'cicen *see* Williams Lake
Band
petceqcicen *see* Williams Lake
Band
petceqcicien *see* Sugarcane Band
petceq'musemx *see* Green Timber Band
petceqmusemx *see* Green Timber
Band
Pe-tchale-ruh-pa-ka *see*
Petchaleruhpaka
Petchaleruhpaka [Clan] *Crow* (H)
Petchisagi *see* Apache
Petdelu [Clan] *Pecos* (H)
P'etdelu ash *see* Petdelu
Petdeluash *see* Petdelu
Pe-tdoa *see* Pe
Petdoa *see* Pe
Petenegowat Pau-Ute *see* Petenegowats
Petenegowats *see* Owens Valley
Paiute
Petenegowats [NA, CA] *Mono*
(H)
Pethahanerat *see* Pitahauerat
Pethowerat *see* Pitahauerat
Peticado [TX] *Caddoan* (H)
Petikokia *see* Pepicokia
Petikokia *see* Pepicokia
Petisikapau [Can] [*Montagnais-Naskapi*] (BE)
Petitisick *see* Karok
Petit Osage *see* Utsehta
Petits Acansas *Quapaw* (H)
Petitscotia *see* Pepicokia
Petitscotia *see* Pepicokia
Petits Eskimaux *see* Montagnais
Petit-sick *see* Karok
Petit Zo *see* Utsehta
Petkhaninikashina [Social group]
Osage (H)
Petodseka [NV] *Paviotso* (H)
Pe-tod-si-ka *see* Petodseka
Petonaquat *see* Petenegowats
Petonoquats *see* Owens Valley
Paiute
Pe-tou-we-ra *see* Pitahauerat
Petouwera *see* Pitaheauerat
Petqan *see* Petkhaninikashina
Pe'tqan i'nihk'acin'a *see*
Petkhaninikashina
Pe-tsaa *see* Pe
Petsaa *see* Pe
Petsare *see* Petao
Pe'tse i'nihk'acin'a *see* Kansa
Petseinihkacina *see* Kansa
Petsika *see* Karok
Petsikła *see* Karok

Pet-tan-i-gwut *see* Petenegowats
Pettanigwut *see* Petenegowats
Pettikokia *see* Pepicokia
Petun *see* Tionontati
Petuneur *see* Cayuga
Petuneux *see* Tionontati
Petzare *see* Petao
Peumepuem *see* Peupuetam
Peuple de Faisans *see* Sipuskanu-manke
Peupuetam *Coahuiltecan* (Hdbk10)
pe-wa-le *see* Peoria
pewale *see* Peoria
pewalia *see* Peoria
Pewaria *see* Peoria
Pewin *see* Winnebago
Pex-ge *see* Jicarilla Apache
Pexge *see* Jicarilla Apache
Peyakwagami *see* Piegouagami
Peyaya *see* Payaya
Pey metes Utahs *see* Paiute
Peymetes Utahs *see* Paiute
peyokhona *see* Pecos
Peytre *Pueblo* (H)
Pey-ute *see* Paiute
Pey-ute *see* Paviotso
Pey-ute *see* Southern Paiute
Peyute *see* Paiute
Peyute *see* Paviotso
Peyute *see* Southern Paiute
Pe-zhew *see* Besheu
Pezhew (PC) *see also* Besheu (H)
Pezhew [Clan] *Chippewa* (H)
Pezhi'wokeyotila *see* Northern Shoshone
Pezhi-wokeyotila *see* Shoshone
Pezo *see* Pissuh
Pezpacuz *see* Perpacug
Pfia [Clan] *Taos* (H)
Pfialola [Clan] *Taos* (H)
Pfialola-taiina *see* Pfialola
Pfia-taiina *see* Pfia
Pfiataiina *see* Pfia
Pfiataikwa'hlaonan *see* Pfiataik-wahlaonan
Pfiataikwahlaonan [Clan] *Taos* (H)
P'hallatillie *see* Tubatulabal
Phallatillie *see* Tubatulabal
Phampleco *see* Pamlico
Pharaona *see* Faraon
Pharaones *see* Faraon
Pheasant Rump Nakota (IA, Fall 1997, pp.50–53)
Pheasants *see* Shiyotanka
Phelipe, S. *see* San Felipe [Keres]
Phelipe, San *see* San Felipe [Keres]
Phelipe, Sant *see* San Felipe [Keres]
Phelipe, Sn. *see* San Felipe [Keres]

Phelippe, San *see* San Felipe [Keres]
Philepe, Sant *see* San Felipe [Keres]
Philip, Saint *see* San Felipe [Keres]
Philip, St. *see* San Felipe [Keres]
Philip de queres , Sn. *see* San Feleipe [Keres]
Philippe, San *see* San Felipe [Keres]
Philippe, St. *see* San Felipe [Keres]
Philips, St. *see* San Felipe [Keres]
Philip's Indians *see* Wampanoag
Phillipe, St. *see* San Felipe [Keres]
Phillippe, San *see* San Felipe [Keres]
Phillippe, St. *see* San Felipe [Keres]
P'ho *see* Po [Clan]
Pho *see* Po [Clan]
P'ho doa *see* Po [Clan]
Phodoa *see* Po [Clan]
P'Ho'juo-ge *see* San Ildefonso
Phojuoge *see* San Ildefonso
Phonecha *see* Pohonichi
P'ho-se *see* Poseuingge
Phose *see* Pseuingge
P'Ho-zuang-ge *see* Pojoaque
Phozuangge *see* Pojoaque
Phurhembe *see* Tarascan
Pia *see* Sia
Piaarhaus *see* Piraha
Piagouagami *see* Piekouagami
Piah Band *see* Grand River Ute
Piakouakamy *see* Piekouagami
Piakuakamits *see* Piekouagami
Piakwagami *see* Pickouagami
Pialpies *see* Cuaiquer
Pianakoto *see* Pianokoto
Pianbotinu [Clan] *Taos* (H)
Pianbotinu-taiina *see* Pianbotinu
Piancashaw *see* Piankashaw
Piangeshaw *see* Piankashaw
Pianguicha *see* Piankashaw
Pianguisha *see* Piankashaw
Piankashaw [OK] *Miami* (LC)
Piankaskouas *see* Piankashaw
Piankatank [VA] *Powhatan Confederacy* (BE)
Piankeshas *see* Piankashaw
Piankeshaw *see* Piankashaw
Piankichas *see* Piankashaw
Piankishas *see* Piankashaw
Piankishaw *see* Piankashaw
Piankshaw *see* Piankashaw
Piannacotou *see* Pianokoto
Piannocotou *see* Pianokoto
Pianocoto *see* Pianokoto
Pianoghotto *see* Pianokoto
Pianogoto *see* Pianokoto

Pianoi *Aramagoto* (O)
Pianokoto [Br] (O)
Pianquicha *see* Piankashaw
Pianquiches *see* Piankashaw
Pianquishaw *see* Piankashaw
Pianria *see* Peoria
Piant *see* Piowant
Piantia *see* Peoria
Piapoco [Col, VE] (LC)
Piapot's Band [Can] *Paskwaw-ininiwug Cree* (BE)
Piaroa [VE] (LC)
Piato [MX] (BE)
Piatos (Hdbk10) *see also* Pimas Altos (Hdbk10)
Piattuiabbe [NV] *Paviotso* (H)
Pi-auk-e-shaw *see* Piankashaw
Piaukeshaw *see* Piankashaw
Piawkashaw *see* Piankashaw
Pi'ba *see* Piba
Pi-ba *see* Sa
Piba [Clan] *Hopi* (H)
Pi-ba nyûwû *see* Piba
Piba nyûwû *see* Piba
Piba wiñwû *see* Piba
Piba wûnwû *see* Piba
Piba-Yagua *see* Yagua
Pib-wuñi-wu *see* Piba
Pibwuñiwu *see* Piba
Pi-ca *see* Piska
Pica *see* Piska
Picacheños *Coahuiltecan* (Hdbk10)
Picaneaux *see* Piegan
Picanipalish *see* Puyallup
Picaris *see* Picuris
Piccakches *see* Pitkachi
Piccuries *see* Picuris
Pichanga *see* Pachanga
Pichango *see* Pachenga
Pichar *see* Piechar
Pichares *see* Piechar
Picheno *see* Pischenoas
Pichi [Clan] *Zuni* (H)
Pichikwe [Clan] *Zuni* (H)
Pichons *see* Pisquows
Pichouagamis *see* Piekouagami
Pi-ci-kse-bi-tupii-o *see* Northern Shoshone
Piciksebitupiio *see* Northern Shoshone
Pi-ci-kse-ni-tup-i-o *see* Shoshone
Piciksenitupio *see* Shoshone
Pickan *see* Piegan
Pickar *see* Piechar
Pickawa *see* Piqua
Pickaway *see* Piqua
Pickaway *see* Shawnee
Pickawee *see* Piqua
Pickawes *see* Piqua
Pickerel Gens *see* Keinouche
Pickovagam *see* Piekouagami

Pickpocket *see* Pequawket
Pickpockett *see* Pequawket
Picks *see* Wichita
Pickwacket *see* Pequawket
Pickwocket *see* Pequawket
Picone *see* Picunche
Picoris *see* Picuris
Picos *see* Piro [Pueblo]
Picoweu *see* Piqua
Picque *see* Piqua
Picquemyan [Can] *Algonquian*
  (H)
Picqwaket *see* Pequawket
Pic River [Can] *Chippewa* (H)
Pictoris *see* Picuris
Pictou [Can] *Sigunikt* (BE)
Pictured People *see* Masnipiwini-
  uuk
Picunche *Araucanian* (O)
Picuni *see* Picuris
Picuri *see* Picuris
Picuria *see* Picuris
Picuries *see* Picuris
Picuris (BE)
Picux *see* Picuris
Picwocket *see* Pequawket
Pida-Diapa [Lang] *Catuquina* (O)
Pidee *see* Pedee
Pidian *see* Maopityan
Pidian *see* Mapidian
Pieb *see* Piba
Piechar [TX] (H)
Piecis *see* Pecos
Pi-Edes *see* Paiute
Piedes *see* Paiute
Pi-Edes *see* Southern Paiute
Piedes *see* Southern Paiute
Piedgan *see* Piegan
Piedras Blancas [TX] *Coahuiltecan*
  (BE)
Piedras Blancos *see* Piedras Blan-
  cas
Piedras Chicas *see* Piedras Chiq-
  uitas
Piedras Chiquitas *Coahuiltecan*
  (Hdbk10)
Pieds-noirs *see* Siksika
Pi-eed *see* Paiute
Pieed *see* Paiute
Pie Edes *see* Paiute
Piegan [MN] *Siksika* (LC)
Piekane *see* Piegan
Piekann *see* Piegan
Piekouagami [Can] (H)
Piekouagamiens *see* Piekouagami
Piekovagamiens *see* Piekouagami
Pierced Nose Indians *see* Nez
  Perce
Pierced Noses *see* Iowa
Pierced Noses *see* Nez Perce
Pierced Noses *see* Amikwa
Pierce Noses *see* Nez Perce
Pi-er-ru-i-ats *see* Pierruiats

Pierruiats [UT, NV] *Gosiute* (H)
Pieuse *see* Paloos
Pie-Utaws *see* Southern Paiute
Pieutaws *see* Southern Paiute
Pieutes *see* Paiute
Pieutes *see* Southern Paiute
Pigan *see* Piegan
Piggwacket *see* Pequawket
Pigocket *see* Pequawket
Piguachet *see* Pequawket
Piguicane *see* Piguique
Piguique [TX] (H)
Pigwachet *see* Pequawket
Pigwachitt *see* Pequawket
Pigwacket *see* Pequawket
Pigwocket *see* Pequawket
Pigwoket *see* Pequawket
Pigwolket *see* Pequawket
Pihcha [Clan] *Hopi* (H)
Pihkash [Clan] *Hopi* (H)
Pihnique *see* Piquique
Pi'h-tca *see* Pihcha
Pihtca *see* Pihcha
Pihugati [Br] *Eastern Timbira* (O)
Pihuique (H) *see also* Piguique
  (H)
Pihuique [TX] *Coahuiltecan* (H)
Pijao [Col] (LC)
Pijiao [Lang] *Cariban* (O)
Pijiu *see* Pissuh
Pijmo *see* Pima
Pi-ka-kwa-na-rat *see* Pikakwa-
  narat
Pikakwanarats [UT] (BE)
Pikani *see* Piegan
Pik-cak-ches *see* Pitkachi
Pike *see* Siksika
Pi-ke-e-wai-i-ne *see* Jicarilla
  Apache
Pikeewaiine *see* Jicarilla Apache
Pike Place people *see* Oka'to
  Wini'niwuk
Pikmiktaligmiut [AK] *Unaligmiut
  Eskimos* (H)
Pikmikta'lig-mut *see* Unalig-
  miut
Pikmikta'lig-mut *see* Pikmiktal-
  igmiut
Pikogami *see* Piekouagami
Pikoweu *see* Piqua
pi-ksi-ksinaitapi-wa *see*
  Shoshone
piksiksinaitapiwa *see* Shoshone
pikuli *see* Picuris
Pikun-i *see* Piegan
Pikuni *see* Piegan
pikuri *see* Picuris
Pikuri'a *see* Picuris
pikuria *see* Picuris
Pilabo *see* Socorro
Pilaca *see* Pilaga
Pilaga [Arg] (LC)
Pilaho *see* Socorro

Pilalt [BC] *Stalo* (BE)
Pila-tlq *see* Pilalt
Pilatlq *see* Pilalt
Pi-la-wa *see* Pilawa
Pilawa [Clan] *Miami* (H)
Pilcosumi [PE] *Campa* (O)
Pilgan *see* Piegan
Piling *see* Pilingmiut
Pilingmiut [AK] *Iglulingmiut*
  (Hdbk5)
Pilingmiut [Can] *Eskimos* (H)
Pillagers (BE) *see also* Mukmedu-
  awininewug (BE)
Pillagers [MN] *Chippewa* (H)
Pilleurs *see* Pillagers
Pilliers *see* Pillagers
Pilopue *see* Socorro
Pilthlako [AL] (BE)
Pim [Clan] *Isleta* (H)
Pima [AZ, MX] (LC)
Pima [Lang] *Upper Piman*
  (Hdbk10)
Pima Aytos *see* Pima
Pima Bajo [MX] (LC)
Pima Gileños *see* Gileños
Pimahaitu *see* Pima
Pimahito *see* Pima
Pimal *see* Pinalino Apache
Piman [Lang] [MX] *Nahuatl* (H)
Pima of the Gila River *see*
  Gileños
Pima-Papabota *see* Papago
Pimas Altos [Lang] (Bull44)
Pimas de el Sur *see* Nevome
Pimases *see* Pima
Pimas frijoleros *see* Papago
Pimas Gileños *see* Pima
Pimas Ileños *see* Pima
Pime *see* Pima
Pimenteira [Lang] *Carib* (UAz,
  v.28)
Pimera *see* Pima
Pimes *see* Pima
Pimese *see* Pima
Pimez *see* Pima
Pimi *see* Pima
Pimica *see* Pima
Pimo *see* Pima
Pimo Galenos *see* Pima
Pimole *see* Pima
Pimos Illños *see* Pima
Pim-t'ainin *see* Pimtainin
Pimtainin [Clan] *Tigua* (H)
Pinage *see* Apinage
Pinal Apache (H) *see also* Pinalino
  Apache (H)
Pinal Apache *San Carlos* (BE)
Pinal Apachen *see* Pinalino
  Apache
Pinal Coyotero *see* Pinal Apache
Pinaleños *see* Pinalino Apache
Pinalino Apache (H)
Pinal Leñas *see* Pinalino Apache

Pinal Leño *see* Pinalino Apache
Pinal Llanos *see* Pinalino Apache
Pinals Apaches *see* Pinalino
  Apache
Pinanaca [TX] (BE)
Pinao *see* Pijao
Pinare *see* Apinage
Pinashiu *see* Pinash'iu
Pinash'iu [Clan] *Menominee* (H)
Pinbico *see* Pinbitho
Pinbicocine *see* Pinbitho
Pinbitho [Clan] *Navajo* (H)
Pin bito *see* Pinbitho
Pinbito *see* Pinbitho
Pin bito'dine *see* Pinbitho
Pinbitodine *see* Pinbitho
Pinche *see* Taushiro
Pinchi *see* Taushiro
Pinchon *see* Pineshow
Pinchow *see* Pineshow
Pincos *see* Pima
Pinechon *see* Pineshow
Pineifu *see* Chepenafa
Pine Indians *see* Natchez
Pinelores *see* Pinalino Apache
Pine Nut Eaters *Western Shoshone*
  (Hdbk11)
Pinery *see* Pinal Apache
Pineshow [MN] *Wahpeton* (BE)
Pineshow's band *see* Pineshow
Pinewewewixpu [ID] *Nez Perce*
  (BE)
Pingangnaktogmiut [Can] *Central*
  Eskimos (BE)
Ping-gwi *see* Picuris
Pinggwi *see* Picuris
Ping-ul-tha *see* Picuris
Pingultha *see* Picuris
Pinichon *see* Pineshow
Pininos *see* Pima
Piniquu [MX] *Coahuiltecan* (BE)
Pinisca *see* Acolapissa
Pinkeshaw *see* Piankashaw
Pinnanca *see* Pinanaca
Pinnekook *see* Pennacook
Pinneshaw *see* Pineshow
Pinnokas (H)
Pinol *see* Pinalino Apache
Piñoleno *see* Pinalino Apache
Pinolero *see* Pinalino Apache
Pinoles *see* Pinalino Apache
Piñol-Indianer *see* Pinalino
  Apache
Piñon Lano *see* Pinalino Apache
Piñon Llano Apache *see* Pinalino
  Apache
Pintadi *see* Pintados
Pintados [MX] (H)
Pintagone *see* Penobscot
Pin-ti-ats *see* Pintiats
Pin-ti-ats *see* Moapa
Pintiats (PC) *see also* Moapa
  (Hdbk11)

Pintiats [NV] *Paiute* (H)
Pintos (H) *see also* Pakawa (BE)
Pintos [MX] *Tamaulipec* (BE)
Pintos [TX] *Coahuiltecan* (BE)
Pinuelta *see* Picuris
Pinutgu *see* Pi'nutau
Pi'nutqu [SD] *Cheyenne* (BE)
Pinyaha *see* Piraha
Pioche *see* Sioni
Pioche *see* Encabellado
Piocobges *see* Gavioes
Piograpapaguarco [MX] *Coahuil-*
  tecan (Hdbk10)
Pioje *see* Sioni
Pionicuagura [MX] *Coahuiltecan*
  (Hdbk10)
Pioria *see* Peoria
Piouanguichia *see* Piankashaw
Piouaroua *see* Peoria
Piowant [MA] *Wampanoag* (BE)
Pip *see* Piba
Pipas *see* Maricopa
Pi-pa-s [Self-designation] *see*
  Maricopa
Pipatsje [Self-designation] *see*
  Maricopa
Pipeli *see* Pipil
Pipil [ES, MX, Gu, Hon] *Nahutl*
  (LC)
Pipil [Lang] *General Aztec*
  (Hdbk10)
Pipili *see* Pipil
Pipos-altos *see* Pima
Pipu'inimou [ID] *Nez Perce* (BE)
Pipuinimu *see* Pipu'inimu
Piqo'sha *see* Piqosha
Piqosha [Clan] *Hopi* (H)
Piqua (H) *see also* Bicowetha (H)
Piqua [TN] *Shawnee* (BE)
Piquachet *see* Pequawket
Piquaw *see* Shawnee .
Piquique *Coahuiltecan* (BE)\
Pir *see* Piro [Pueblo]
Pira *see* Piro [Pueblo]
Pira *see* Piro [Peru]
Piraha [Br] *Mura* (O)
Piraheus *see* Piraha
Piratapuio *see* Pira-Tapuya
Piratapuyo *see* Pira-Tapuyo
Pira-Tapuyo [Br] (O)
Piri *see* Piro [Peublo]
Piriaha *see* Piraha
Piriahai *see* Piraha
Pirianaus *see* Piraha
Piriatapuya *see* Pira-Tapuyo
Pirinda [Lang] [MX] (Bull44)
Pirinda [MX] *Matlatzinca* (BE)
Pirio *see* Piro [Peru]
Pirj *see* Piro [Pueblo]
Pirna *see* Pima
Piro [Lang] *Tanoan* (H)
Piro [Peru] (LC)
Piro [Pueblo] [NM] (LC)

Pirro *see* Piro [Peru]
Piruas *see* Piro [Pueblo]
Pisa [Clan] *Hopi* (H)
Pisabo [PE, Br] (O)
Pisagua *see* Pisabo
Pisahua *see* Pisabo
pi save *see* Western Apache
pisave *see* Western Apache
Piscahoose *see* Pisquows
Piscaous *see* Pisquows
Piscataqua [ME, NH] *Pennacook*
  Confederacy (H)
Piscataquaukes *see* Piscataqua
Piscataway (BE) *see also* Conoy
  (LC)
Piscataway *Conoy* (BE)
Piscatawese *see* Conoy
Piscatawese *see* Piscataway
Piscatchecs *see* Pitkachi
Piscatoway *see* Conoy
Piscatoway *see* Piscataway
Piscatowayes *see* Conoy
Piscatowayes *see* Piscataway
Piscattawayes *see* Conoy
Piscattawayes *see* Piscataway
Piscatua *see* Conoy
Piscatua *see* Piscataway
Pischenoas [MS] (H)
Pischoule *see* Pisquows
Pischous *see* Pisquows
Pisch quit pas *see* Pishquitpah
Pischquitpas *see* Pishquitpah
Piscous *see* Pisquows
Pisha [Clan] *Hopi* (H)
Pishakulk *see* Dakota
Pishekethe *see* Psakethe
Pishenoa [FL] (BE)
Pishiu *see* Besheu
Pi-shla ateuna *see* Pishla-ateuna
Pishlaateuna *see* Phisla-ateuna
Pishla-ateuna [Phratry] *Zuni* (H)
Pishquibo [PE] (O)
Pishquitpah [WA] *Shahaptian* (H)
Pishquitpaw *see* Pishquitpah
Pishquitpow *see* Pishquitpah
Pishwanwapum (H) *see also*
  Yakima (LC)
Pishwanwapum [WA] (Hdbk12)
Pisiatari [PE] *Campa* (O)
Pisierinii *see* Nipissing
Pisierinij *see* Nipissing
Pisinahua *see* Sharanahua
Pisiqsarfik *Greenland Eskimos*
  (BE)
Pisirinin *see* Nipissing
Pisisumi *see* Campa
Piskakauakis [Can] [Cree] (BE)
Piskatang *see* Piskitang
Piskitang [Can] *Algonquian* (H)
Pisko [WA] *Yakima* (BE)
Piskwas *see* Pisquows
Piskwaus *see* Pisquows
Pisone [Lang] [MX] (Bull44)

Pisone [MX] (BE)
Pispis [NI, Hon] *Sumo* (BE)
Pispiza-wicasa *see* Pispizawichasha
Pispquitpah *see* Pishquitpah
Pisquibo *see* Pishquibo
Pisquibo *see* Sipibo
Pisquitpak *see* Pishquitpah
Pisquous *see* Pisquows
Pisquouse *see* Pisquows
Pisquow (BE) *see also* Wenatchi (LC)
Pisquow [WA] *Salish* (H)
Pissasec [VA] *Powhatan Confederacy* (BE)
Pissaseck *see* Pissasec
Pissassack *see* Pissasec
Pissassees *see* Pissasec
Pisscattaway *see* Conoy
Pisscattaway *see* Piscataway
Piss-cows *see* Pisquows
Pisscows *see* Pisquows
Pis-suh *see* Pissuh
Pissuh [Clan] *Abnaki* (H)
Pistol River Indians *see* Chetleschantunne
Pita [MX] *Tamaulipec* (BE)
Pita [TX] *Coahuiltecan* (BE)
Pi-ta-da *see* Pawnee
Pitagmiut *Kotzebue Sound Eskimos* (Hdbk5)
Pitagoriciens *see* Pythagoreans
Pitagoricos *see* Pythagoreans
Pit-a-hau-e-rat *see* Pitahauerat
Pitahauerat [NE] *Pawnee Confederacy* (BE)
Pitahawirata *see* Pitahauerat
Pitahay [TX] (BE)
Pitalac *Coahuiltecan* (Hdbk10)
Pitaleae *see* Pilaga
pitanapati *see* pitan-apa-ti
pitan-apa-ti *Owens Valley Paiute* (Hdbk11)
Pitanay *see* Pitahay
Pitanisha *see* Tubatulabal
Pitannisuh *see* Pi-tan-ni-suh
Pi-tan-ni-suh (H) *see also* Tubatulabal (LC)
Pitannisuh *see* Tubatulabal
Pi-tan-ni-suh [CA] *Kern River Indians* (Contri, v.3, p.393)
Pitanta *see* Serrano
Pitanta *see* Mohineyam
Pitavirate Noisy Pawnee *see* Pitahauerat
Pitayo [Col] *Paez* (O)
Pit-cach-es *see* Pitkachi
Pitcaches *see* Pitkachi
Pit-cat-chee *see* Pitkachi
Pitcatchee *see* Pitkachi
Pitcatches *see* Pitkachi
Pitchakies *see* Pitkachi
Pitchiboucouni *see* Pitchibourenik

Pitchiboueouni *see* Pitchibourenik
Pitchibourenik [Can] (H)
Pitchiboutounibuek *see* Pitchibourenik
Pitchinavo *see* Wichita
Pitch Indians *see* Wailaki
Pitch Wailaki [Lang] [CA] *Wailaki* (He)
Pit-cuch-es *see* Pitkachi
Pitcuches *see* Pitkachi
Pitelaha *see* Pilaga
Pithlako *Creek* (BE)
Pitiaches *see* Pitkachi
Piticado *see* Peticado
Pitilaga *see* Pilaga
Pitisfiafuil *Coahuiltecan* (Hdbk10)
Pit-ka-chi *see* Pitkachi
Pitkachi [CA] *Yokuts* (CA)
Pitkachi [Lang] [CA] *Mariposan* (H)
Pit-kah-che *see* Pitkachi
Pitkahche *see* Pitkachi
Pit-kah-te *see* Pitkachi
Pitkahte *see* Pitkachi
Pitkati *see* Pitkachi
Pitonakingkainapitcig *see* Betonukeengainubejig
Pi'tona'kingkain-upichig *see* Betonukeengainubejig
Pitonakingkainupichig *see* Betonukeengainubejig
Pi'tona'kinkgainapitcig *see* Betonukeengainubejig
Pit River Indians *see* Madehsi
Pit River Indians *see* Achomawi
Pit River Indians *see* Atsugewi
Pit River Nation [CA] (CA)
Pittal *see* Pita [TX]
Pitt River Indians *see* Palaihnihan
Pituiaro [Br] *Northern Cayapo* (O)
Pitukmiut *see* Pitagmiut
Pi-u-cha *see* Paiute
Piucha *see* Paiute
Pi-u-chas *see* Southern Paiute
Piuchas *see* Southern Paiute
Piutaay *see* Pitahay
Pi-utah *see* Paviotso
Pi-utah *see* Paiute
Piutah *see* Paiute
Piutah *see* Paviotso
Pi-ute *see* Paiute
Piute *see* Southern Paiute
Piute *see* Paiute
Piute Snakes *see* Paiute Snakes
Piuwani *see* Pivwani
Piva *see* Piba
Pi-vwa-ni *see* Pivwani
Pivwani [Clan] *Hopi* (H)
Piwa'qtinet [WI] *Menominee* (BE)
Piyakkwagami *see* Piekouagami
Pizpiza-witcaca *see* Pispizawichasha

Pkiwi-leni *see* Miami
Pkiwileni *see* Miami
Pkiwi-lenigi *see* Miami
Pkiwilenigi *see* Miami
Placerville [Lang] *Nisenan* (CA)
Plaikni (BE) *see also* Klamath (LC)
Plaikni (H) *see also* Modoc (LC)
Plai'kni (H) *see also* Paviotso (CA)
Plaikni (PC) *see also* Paviotso (CA)
Plaikni [OR] (H)
Plain Assineboin *see* Assiniboin of the Plains
Plainfield Indians *see* Quinebaug
Plains Cree *see* Paskwawininiwug
Plains Miwok [CA] *Miwok* (BE)
Plains Miwok [Lang] *Eastern Miwokan* (CA-8)
Plains Salish (Hdbk12) *see also* Pend d'Oreille (Hdbk12)
Plains Salish [MT] (Hdbk12)
Planidore *see* Coaque
Plankishaw *see* Piankashaw
Plano Culture (AI, pp.21–22)
Plascotez de Chiens *see* Thlingchadinne
Plat cote de Chien *see* Thlingchadinne
Plateau Indians *Western Province* (AI)
Plateau Shoshonean (LC) *see also* Numic (LC)
Plateau Shoshonean [Lang] [*Ute-Chemehuevi*] (Pub, v.4, no.3)
Plats cotee de Chiens *see* Thlingchadinne
Plats-Cotes-de-Chien *see* Thlingchadinne
Plats-cotes de Chien *see* Thlingchadinne
Plats-côtes-de-chien du fort Raë *see* Lintchanre
Plats cotez de Chiens *see* Thlingchadinne
Playano [CA] *Salinan* (CA)
Playero [Col, VE] (O)
Playsanos *see* Gabrielino
Pleureurs *see* Coaque
Ploluse *see* Paloos
Plumes *see* Frozen Indians
Plutuo [MX] *Coahuiltecan* (Hdbk10)
P'o *see* Po [Clan]
Po [Clan] *Pueblo Indians* (H)
Poackyaks *see* Potchayick
Poala *see* Puaray
Poam Pomo *see* Ballokai
P'oanin *see* Apache
Poanin *see* Apache
Poatsituhtikuteh [NV] *Paviotso* (H)
Poat-sit-uh-ti-kut-teh *see* Poatsituhtikuteh

Poat'-sit-uh-ti-kut'-teh *see* poz'idadikadi

Poatsituhtikutteh (PC) *see also* poz'idadikadi (Hdbk11)

Pobawotche Utah *see* Tabeguache

Pocan *see* Ponca

Pocanahua *see* Morunahua

Pocatello *Shoshone* (NatPeos, p.297-98)

Pochaick *see* Potchayick

Pochutec [Lang] *Aztecan* (Hdbk10)

Pochutla [MX] (BE)

Pociwu winwu *see* Poshiwu

Pociwuwinwu *see* Poshiwu

Pockaguma *see* Piekouagami

Pocoman *see* Pocoman

Pocoman [Gu, ES] (O)

Pocoman [Lang] [Gu, ES] *Eastern Mayan* (O)

Pocomchi *see* Pokonchi

Pocomoke (Hdbk15)

Pocompheake *see* Pocomtuc

Pocomptuck *see* Pocomtuc

Pocomtakukes *see* Pocomtuc

Pocomtock *see* Pocomtuc

Pocomtuc [MA] (BE)

Pocomtuck *see* Pocomtuc

Poconchi *see* Pokonchi

Pocora [MX] (BE)

Pocosi [CR] *Bribri* (BE)

Pocoughtaonack *see* Bocootawwonauke

Pocoughtronack *see* Bobootawwonauke

Pocra [PE] (LC)

Pocumptuck *see* Pocomtuc

Pocumtuc *see* Pocomtuc

Po-da-wand-um-ee *see* Potawatomi

Podawandumee *see* Potawatomi

Po-da-waud-um-eeg *see* Potawatomi

Podawaudumeeg *see* Potawatomi

Podunck *see* Podunk

Podunk [CN] *Wappinger* (BE)

Po-e-lo *see* Poelo

Poelo [CA] (Pub, v.4, no.3, p.125)

Poenese *see* Pawnee

Poeomtuck *see* Pocomtuc

Poes *see* Potawatomi

Poetan *see* Powhatan

Poetan *see* Werowocomoco

Pofuaque *see* Pojoaque

Po-ge-hdo-ke *see* Nez Perce

Pogehdoke *see* Nez Perce

Pogesas *see* Posisiga

Pogodque *see* Pojoaque

Poha *see* Bannock

Po-ha-ha-chi *see* Pohonichi

Pohahachi *see* Pohonichi

Pohalin tinliu *see* Pohallintinleh

Pohalintinliu *see* Pohallintinleh

Po-hal-lin-Tin'leh *see* Pohallintinleh

Pohallintinleh [CA] (H)

Pohbantes *see* Pahvant

Pohena *see* Callahuaya

Poh-he-gan *see* Mahican

Pohhegan *see* Mahican

Pohic *see* Potchayick

Pohliklah *see* Yurok

Pohogue *see* Pohogwe

Pohogwe (Hdbk11)

Po-hoi *see* Pohoi

Pohoi [TX] *Comanche* (BE)

pohokwi *see* Pohogwe

Pohomoosh [NS] *Micmac* (H)

Poho-neche *see* Pohonichi

Pohoneche *see* Pohonichi

Po-ho-ne-chee *see* Pohonichi

Pohonechee *see* Pohonichi

Pohoneechee *see* Pohinichi

Po-ho-neech-es *see* Pohonichi

Pohoneeches *see* Pohonichi

Po-ho-neich-es *see* Pohonichi

Pohoneiches *see* Pohonichi

Pohonichi [CA] *Miwok* (Pub, v.4, no.4, p.202)

Pohonichi [CA] *Moquelumnan* (H)

Pohoy [FL] (BE)

Po-hua-gai *see* San Ildefonso

Pohuagai *see* San Ildefonso

Pohuaque *see* Pojoaque

Po-hu-lo *see* Pohulo

Pohulo [Clan] *Pueblo Indians* (H)

Pohuniche *see* Pohonichi

pohwake *see* Pojoaque

Po-hwa-ki *see* Pojoaque

Pohwaki *see* Pojoaque

Poil leué *see* Ottawa

Poils leue *see* Missisauga

Pointed Hearts *see* Skitwish

poisi nimi *see* Yohandika

Poissons blancs *see* Attikamegue

Pojake *see* Pojoaque

Pojanque *see* Pojoaque

Pojanquiti *see* Pojoaque

Pojaugue *see* Pojoaque

Pojiniguara [MX] *Coahuiltecan* (Hdbk10)

Po-jo *see* Pohoi

Pojo (PC) SE Pohoi (BE)

Pojoague *see* Pojoaque

Pojoaque (BE)

Pojoaque (JSW, v.32, no.3, 1990, pp.268-277) *see also* Nambe (BE)

Pojodque *see* Pojoaque

Pojoi *see* Pohoy

Pojouque *see* Pojoaque

Pojuague *see* Pojoaque

Po-juo-ge *see* San Ildefonso

Pojuoge *see* San Ildefonso

Po-juo-que *see* San Ildefonso

Pojuoque *see* San Ildefonso

Pokagon band of Potawatomi (IndT, Oct. 1994)

Pokanga (O) *see also* Bara (O)

Pokanga *Tucano* (O)

Pokanga-Tapuya *see* Bara

Pokanoket (LC) *see also* Wampanoag (LC)

Pokanoket [RI] (Hdbk15)

Pokanokit *see* Pokanoket

Pokcra *see* Pocra

Po-ke-as *see* Poskesa

Pokeas *see* Poskesa

Pokegama [MI, ND, SD] *Chippewa* (H)

Poke-koo-un-go *see* Pokekooungo

Poke-koo-un-go *see* Unami

Pokekooungo [Clan] [DE] (H)

Po-ken-well *see* Bokinwad

Pokenwell *see* Bokinwad

Po-ken-welle *see* Bokinwad

Pokenwelle *see* Bokinwad

Pokkenvolk *see* Hopi

Pokomam [Gu, ES] (LC)

Pokomchi *see* Pokonchi

Pokomoke *see* Pocomoke

Pokomtakuke *see* Pocomtuc

Pokomtock *see* Pocomtuc

Po-ko-na-ti *see* Pohonichi

Pokonchi [Gu] (LC)

Pokonino *see* Bokninuwad

Pokosi *see* Pocosi

Pokwadi *see* Pojoaque

pokwadi *see* San Ildefonso

Po'k-woide *see* Pojoaque

Pokwoide *see* Pojoaque

Polachucola *see* Apalachicola

Polacme *Concho* (BE)

Po-la-ga-mis *see* Tubatulabal

Polagamis *see* Tubatulabal

Polanches *see* Paloos

Polar *see* Polar Eskimos

Polar Eskimos *Greenland Eskimos* (Hdbk5)

Polar Inuit *see* Polar Eskimos

Pole-cat band *see* Hokarutcha

Polecat band *see* Hokarutcha

Politos *Coahuiltecan* (Hdbk10)

Pollaca [Pueblo] (Hdbk9)

Pollotepallor *see* Paloos

Polokawynahs *see* Tubatulabal

Polonatri *see* Pohonichi

Polonches *see* Paloos

Polooca [Pueblo] (H)

Polu'ksalgi *see* Biloxi

Poluksalgi *see* Biloxi

Pololuma *see* Pomuluma

Pol-we-sha *see* Badwisha

Polwesha *see* Badwisha

Poma *see* Ballokai

Pomaliqui [MX] *Coahuiltecan*
(Hdbk10)
Pome *see* Ballokai
Po-mo *see* Pomo
Pomo [CA] (LC)
Pomoan [Lang] *Hokan* (CA-8)
Pom-o Jo-ua *see* Pomojoua
Pomojoua [NM] *Pueblo* (H)
Pomonick *see* Pomouic
Pomonkeye *see* Pamunkey
Pomonky *see* Pamunkey
Pomouic [NC] *Algonquian* (H)
Pomouik *see* Pamlico
Pomouik *see* Pomouic
Pompeton *see* Pompton
Pom-Pomo *see* Ballokai
Pompton (Hdbk15) *see also* Wap-
pinger (LC)
Pompton [NJ] *Munsee* (BE)
Pompton [NJ] *Unami* (BE)
Pomucke *see* Pamunkey
Pomulum *see* Pomuluma
Pomuluma [MX] *Coahuiltecan*
(BE)
Pomunkey *see* Pamunkey
Pona *see* Puna
Ponack *see* Bannock
Ponacock *see* Pennacook
Ponacok *see* Pennacook
Ponak [Clan] *Hopi* (H)
Ponakñyamu Pona *see* Ponak
Ponar *see* Ponca
Ponarak *see* Dakota
Ponashita *see* Bannock
Ponashta *see* Bannock
Ponca [Lang] [NE] *Dheiga* (LC)
Ponca [NE] (LC)
Poncah *see* Ponca
Poncan *see* Ponca
Pon'car *see* Ponca
Poncar *see* Ponca
Poncar *see* Ponca
Poncarar *see* Ponca
Poncare *see* Ponca
Poncarer *see* Ponca
Poncaries *see* Ponca
Poncaw *see* Ponca
Ponch *see* Allakaweah
Poncha *see* Ponca
Poncrar *see* Ponca
Poncye *see* Ponca
Pond d'Oreilles *see* Kalispel
Pond d'Oreilles *see* Pend d'Or-
eille
Pondecas *see* Kalispel
Pondera *see* Kalispel
Ponderas *see* Kalispel
Ponderay *see* Kalispel
Pond Orrilles *see* Kalispel
Pond Orrilles *see* Pend d'Oreille
Ponduras *see* Kalispel
Pone *see* Ballokai
Pongkaw *see* Ponca

Poni *see* Pawnee
Poniar *see* Ponca
P'onin *see* Apache
Ponin *see* Apache
Ponishta Bonack *see* Bannock
Ponka *see* Ponca
Ponkah *see* Ponca
Ponkeontami *see* Potawatomi
Ponobscot *see* Penobscot
Ponobscut *see* Penobscot
Ponoetaneo (H)
Po-no-i-ta-ni-o *see* Ponoetaneo
Po-no-i-ta-ni-o *see* Southern
Cheyenne
Ponoitanio *see* Ponoetaneo
Ponoitanio *see* Southern
Cheyenne
Po-no-kix *see* Ponokix
Ponokix *Kainah* (H)
Ponouike *see* Pamlico
Pons *see* Ponca
Ponsar *see* Ponca
Ponteatamies *see* Potawatomi
Ponteotamies *see* Potawatomi
Pontewatami *see* Potawatomi
Ponton *see* Pompton
Pontowattimies *see* Potawatomi
Po-nyi Numbu *see* Ponyinumba
Ponyinumbu [NM] *Tewa* (H)
P'o-nyi Pa-kuen *see* Ponyi-
pakuen
Ponyipakuen [NM] *Tewa* (H)
Poodawahduhme *see* Potawatomi
Pooemocs *see* Puimuk
Pooesoo *see* Puisu
Poo-joge *see* San Ildefonso
Poojoge *see* San Ildefonso
Poollachuchlaw *see* Apalachicola
Po-o-mas *see* Siksika
Poomas *see* Siksika
Poong-car *see* Ponca
Poongcar *see* Ponca
Poor *see* Honowa
Poo-reh-tu-ai *see* Puretuay
Poorehtuai *see* Puretuay
Poor-ones [MN] *Atsina* (BE)
Poosepatuck (H) *see also* Patchoag
(H)
Poosepatuck [NY] (H)
Poosoona *see* Pusune
Poospatuck *see* Poosepatuck
Pootatuck [CN] (Eagle, v.9, no.3,
p.4)
Pooy *see* Pohoy
Popaghtunk *see* Papagonk
Popan *see* Papanaca
Popcum *see* Popkum
Popinoshees *see* Papinachois
Popkum [Can] *Stalo* (BE)
Poplar People *see* Nutimi-iniuuk
Popocatoque [MX] *Coahuiltecan*
(Hdbk10)
Popolo Bruciato *see* Tzenatay

Popoloca [Gu] *Xincan* (BE)
Popoloca [Puebla, MX] (LC)
Popoluca [Lang] (BE)
Popoluca [Veracruz, MX] *Mixe*
(LC)
Popya *see* Paya
Poquan'noc *see* Poquonock
Poquannoc *see* Poquonock
Poquannock *see* Poquonock
Poquonnoc *see* Poquonock
Poquonock [CN] *Wappinger* (BE)
Porcupine People *see* Piek-
ouagami
Porcupine River Indians *see*
Takkuth-kutchin
Porcupine River Indians *see*
Tukkuthkutchin
Porcupine Tribe *see* Kakouchaki
Porocoto *see* Puricoto
Porokoto *see* Puricoto
Portaback *see* Potopaco
Portage Band [WI] *Winnebago*
(H)
Portage de Prairie [Can]
Chippewa (H)
Portage people *see* Kaka'nikone
Tsu'niniwug
Port Clarence *Bering Strait Eski-
mos* (Hdbk5)
Porteurs *see* Takulli
Port Madison *see* Suquamish
Portobaccoes *see* Potopaco
Portoback *see* Potopaco
Port Orchard *see* Dwamish
Port Orchard *see* Suquamish
Port Orford Indians *see* Kalt-
sergheatunne
Port Orford Indians *see* Kwatami
Port Stuart Indians (H) Ahealt
(H)
Port-Tabago *see* Potopaco
Port Townsend Indians *see* Chi-
makum
Posalme *Concho* (BE)
Posch *see* Paya
Poseuingge [Pueblo] *Tewa* (H)
Posgisa [NV] (BE)
Poshgisha *see* Posgisa
Poshiwu [Clan] *Hopi* (H)
Po-si-o *see* Poshiwu
Posio *see* Poshiwu
Posiwu *see* Poshiwu
Posiwuu *see* Poshiwu
Po-si-wuwuñ-wu *see* Poshiwu
Posiwuwunwu *see* Poshiwu
Pos-ke-as *see* Poskesa
Poskeas *see* Poskesa
Pos-ke-sa *see* Poskesa
Poskesa [CA] *Mono* (H)
Posnama *see* Pusuama
Poso Creek [CA] *Yokuts* (CA)
Poso Creek [Lang] *Foothill* (CA-
8)

Posonwu *see* San Ildefonso
Posowe *see* San Ildefonso
Posoy *see* Pohoy
Posoye *see* Pohoy
Po-suan-gai *see* Pojoaque
Posuangai *see* Pojoaque
Pota-aches *see* Potoyanti
Potaaches *see* Potoyanti
Potameos Indians *see* Tututni
Potano [FL] *Timucua* (BE)
Potanou *see* Potano
Potapaco [MD] *Conoy* (BE)
Potato-eating people *see* Northeastern Choctaw
Potaucac *see* Potaunk
Potaunk (Hdbk15)
Potavalamia *see* Potawatomi
Potavncak *see* Potaunk
Potavou *see* Potano
Potawackati [CA] *Moquelumnan* (H)
Potawackaties *see* Potawackati
Potawahduhmee *see* Potawatomi
Potawatama *see* Potawatomi
Potawatami *see* Potawatomi
Potawatamies *see* Potawatomi
Potawatamie tribe of Indians of the Prairie *see* Prairie Band of Potawatomi
Potawatimie *see* Potawatomi
Po-ta-w'a-to-me *see* Potawatomi
Potawatomi [MI] (LC)
potawatomink *see* Potawatomi
Potawatomi of Huron [MI] (H)
Potawatomi of the Wabash [IN] (H)
Potawatomi of the Woods [KS] (BE)
Potawattamies *see* Potawatomi
Potawattimie *see* Potawatomi
Potawattomies *see* Potawatomi
Potawatumies *see* Potawatomi
Po-ta-waw-to-me *see* Potawatomi
Potawawtome *see* Potawatomi
Po-ta-wot-me *see* Potawatomi
Potawotme *see* Potawatomi
Potawtumies *see* Potawatomi
Potawunkack *see* Potaunk
Potchayick (Hdbk15)
Potchiack *see* Potchayick
Po-tdoa *see* Po
Potdoa *see* Po
P'o-tdoa *see* Po [Clan]
Poteotami *see* Potawatomi
Poteouatami *see* Potawatomi
Poteskeet [NC] *Weapemeoc* (BE)
Poteskeit *see* Poteskeet
po-te-wa-tami *see* Potawatomi
Potewatamies *see* Potawatomi
Potewatamik *see* Potawatomi
potewatmi *see* Potawatomi
Poticara *see* Potiguara

Potiguar *see* Potiguara
Potiguara [Br] (LC)
Potiwattimeeg *see* Potawatomi
Potiwattomies *see* Potawatomi
Potlapigua [MX] *Pima Alta* (H)
Potlapiqua *see* Potlapigua
Po'tlas *see* Potlas
Potlas [BC] *Nuhalk* (H)
Potoachos *see* Potoyanti
Potoancies *see* Potoyanti
Potoashees [WA] *Salish* (H)
Potoashs *see* Potoashees
Potoencies *see* Potoyanti
po-to iwe *see* Laguna
potoiwe *see* Laguna
Potomac [VA] *Powhatan Confederacy* (BE)
Potomack *see* Potomac
Potomana *see* Patamona
Potopaco (Hdbk15)
Potorera *see* Poturero
Po-tosh *see* Potawatomi
Potosh *see* Potawatomi
Potosino [MX] (BE)
Potoskite *see* Poteskeet
Potowatameh *see* Potawatomi
Potowatamies *see* Potawatomi
Potowatomies *see* Potawatomi
Potowmack *see* Potomac
Potowotamies *see* Potawatomi
Potoyantes *see* Potoyanti
Po-to-yan-ti *see* Potoyanti
Potoyanti [CA] *Moquelumnan* (H)
Po-to-yan-to *see* Potoyanti
Potoyanto *see* Potoyanti
Poto-yau-te *see* Potoyanti
Potoyaute *see* Potoyanti
Po-toy-en-tre *see* Potoyanti
Potoyentre *see* Potoyanti
Potre [NM] *Pueblo* (H)
Po-tsid'a-tu *see* poz'idadikadi
Potsidatu *see* poz'idadikadi
Po-tsid'a-tuviwagaiyu *see* poz'idadikadi
Potsidatuviwagaiyu *see* poz'idadikadi
Pottawatameh *see* Potawatomi
Pottawataney *see* Potawatomi
Pottawatimies *see* Potawatomi
Pottawatomi *see* Potawatomi
Pottawatomies *see* Potawatomi
Pottawattamie *see* Potawatomi
Pottawattamies *see* Potawatomi
Pottawatumie *see* Potawatomi
Potta-wat-um-ies *see* Potawatomi
Pottawaudumies *see* Potawatomi
Pottawotamies *see* Potawatomi
Pottawottomies *see* Potawatomi
Pottewatemies *see* Potawatomi
Pottiwattamies *see* Potawatomi
Pottowatamies *see* Potawatomi

Pottowatomie *see* Potawatomi
Pottowatomy *see* Potawatomi
Pottowattomies *see* Potawatomi
Pottowautomie *see* Potawatomi
Pottowotomee *see* Potawatomi
Poturero [BO] (O)
Potzua-ge *see* Pojoaque
Potzuage *see* Pojoaque
Po-tzu-ye *see* Potzuye
Potzuye [Pueblo] (H)
Poualac *see* Dakota
Poualak *see* Dakota
Poualake *see* Dakota
Pouanak *see* Dakota
Pouankikia *see* Piankashaw
Pouans *see* Winnebago
Poueatami *see* Potawatomi
Poues *see* Potawatomi
Pouhatamies *see* Potawatomi
Pouhatan *see* Powhatan Confederacy
Poujuaque *see* Pojoaque
Pouka *see* Ponca
Poulteattemi *see* Potawatomi
Poulx *see* Potawatomi
Poulx teattemis *see* Potawatomi
Pous *see* Potawatomi
Poutauatemi *see* Potawatomi
Poutawatamies *see* Potawatomi
Poutawottamies *see* Potawatomi
Pouteami *see* Potawatomi
Pouteaouatami *see* Potawatomi
Pouteatami *see* Potawatomi
Pouteatimies *see* Potawatomi
Pouteauatami *see* Potawatomi
Pouteotami *see* Potawatomi
Pouteouatami *see* Potawatomi
Pouteouatami *see* Potawatomi
Pouteouatamiouec *see* Potawatomi
Pouteouatimi *see* Potawatomi
Pouteouetamites *see* Potawatomi
Pouteouitami *see* Potawatomi
Pouteouotami *see* Potawatomi
Poutewatamies *see* Potawatomi
Poutoualami *see* Potawatomi
Poutouami *see* Potawatomi
Poutouatami *see* Potawatomi
Poutouatamittes *see* Potawatomi
Poutoucsis *see* Biloxi
Poutouotami *see* Potawatomi
Poutouwatami *see* Potawatomi
Poutowatomies *see* Potawatomi
Poutuatami *see* Potawatomi
Poutwatami *see* Potawatomi
Pouutouatami *see* Potawatomi
Poux *see* Potawatomi
Pouz *see* Potawatomi
Povantes *see* Pahvant
Poverty Point culture (LC)
Povoli *see* Buli
Powahekune Tusininiwug *see* Powahe'kune Tusi'niniwug

Powahe'kune Tusi'niniwug [WI] *Menominee* (BE)
Powáhtan *see* Powhatan
Powaith *see* Powhatan
Powchay-icks *see* Potchayick
Powcomputck *see* Pocomtuc
Powhatan [Lang] *Eastern Algonquian* (Hdbk15)
Powhatan [VA] *Powhatan Confederacy* (LC)
Powhatan Confederacy [VA] *Algonquian* (H)
Powhatanic Confederacy *see* Powhatan Confederacy
Powhattan *see* Powhatan Confederacy
Powhawneches *see* Pohonichi
Powhites *see* Powhatan
Powhoge *see* San Ildefonso
Powite *see* Powhatan
Powmunkey *see* Pamunkey
Powquaniock *see* Poquonock
Powtawatami *see* Potawatomi
Powtewatami *see* Potawatomi
Powtewattimies *see* Potawatomi
Powtowottomies *see* Potawatomi
Poxen [NM] *Tigua* (H)
Poxuaki *see* Pojoaque
Poya *see* Paya
Poyai *see* Paya
Poyanahua *see* Poyanawa
Poyanawa [Br] (O)
Poye-kwe *see* Poyi
Poyekwe *see* Poyi
Poyenisati [Self-designation] *see* Caquinte
Poyer *see* Paya
Poyi [Clan] *Zuni* (H)
Poyi-kwe *see* Poyi
Poyikwe *see* Poyi
Poza *see* Macuna
Poze *see* Potre
pozidadikaki *see* poz'idadikaki
poz'idadikaki [Northern Paiute] (Hdbk11)
Po-zuan-ge *see* Pojoaque
Pozuange *see* Pojoaque
P'o-zuang-ge *see* Pojoaque
Pozuang-ge *see* Pojoaque
Pozuangge *see* Pojoaque
Pozuanque *see* Pojoaque
Prairie Apache *see* Kiowa Apache
Prairie Band of Potawatomi [WI, IL, IN] *Potawatomi* (H)
Prairie Chicken *see* Seechkaberuhpaka
Prairie Chicken *see* Sipushkanumanke
Prairie Dog *see* Achepabecha
Prairie Grosscentres *see* Atsina
Prairie Hen *see* Seechkaberuhpaka
Prairie-hen People *see* Sipushkanumanke

Prairie hens *see* Sipushkanumanke
Prairie Indians *see* Teton
Prairie Kickapoo [IL] *Kickapoo* (H)
Prairie Potawatomi [KS] *Potawatomi* (BE)
Prairie Wolf *see* Shomakoosa
Prairie-wolf people *see* Mandhinkagaghe
Praying Indians (H)
Precolumbian (LC)
Pre-Columbian *see* Precolmbian
Preguey [NM] *Pueblo* (H)
Premorska *see* Chnagmiut
Premorski *see* Chnagmiut
Presumpscot [ME] (H)
Presumscott *see* Presumscot
Pribilof *Aleuts* (TT, v.15, no.25, June 21, 1978, pp.1, 7, 9)
Prickled Panis *see* Wichita
Priest's Rapids *see* Sokulk
Prietos *Coahuiltecan* (BE)
Prietos [TX] *Aranama* (H)
Primahaitu *see* Pima
Primoske *see* Chnagmiut
Prince Edward Island [Can] *Micmac* (BE)
Prince William Sound *Tlingit* (Ye)
Prinoski *see* Chnagmiut
Prinsu *Sumo* (O)
Printed Hearts *see* Skitswish
Prinzo [NI] *Ulua* (BE)
Progoto *see* Puricoto
Projoaque *see* Pojoaque
Prominent Jaws *see* Oqtoguna
Promontory Point Shoshone (Bull120)
Pronaria *see* Peoria
Pronesea *see* Peoria
Pronevoa *see* Peoria
Proto-Tzeltal-Tzotzil [Lang] *Mayan* (LC)
Prouaria *see* Peoria
Prouyana [Br, Su] *Tiriyo* (O)
Proven *Greenland Eskimos* (BE)
Proyana *see* Prouyana
Pruara *see* Puaray
Psake-the *see* Psakethe
Psakethe [Clan] *Shawnee* (H)
Psarsavina *see* Sobaipuri
Psaupsau (H) *see also* Patzau (BE)
Psaupsau [TX] *Coahuiltecan* (BE)
Pschwan-wapp-am (H) *see also* Shanwappom (BE)
Pschwanwappam (PC) *see also* Shanwappom (BE)
Pshwa'napum *see* Shanwappom
Pshwanapum *see* Shanwappom
Pshwanwapam [WA] (BE)
Pshwanwapam [WA] (BE)
Pshwanwappam (H) *see also* Yakima (LC)

Pshwanwappam (Hdbk12) *see also* Piswanwapum (Hdbk12)
Psinchaton [MN] *Dakota* (BE)
Psinontanhinhintons *see* Psinoutanhinhintons
Psinoumanitons [WI] *Santee* (BE)
Psinoutanhhintons *see* Psinoutanhinhintons
Psinoutanhinhintons *see* Psinoutanhinhintons
Psinoutanhinhintons [MN] (BE)
Pswanwapam *see* Pshwanwapam
Pte-yute-eni *see* Pteyuteshni
Pteyuteeni *see* Pteyuteshni
Pteyuteshni *Hunkpatina* (H)
Pte-yute-sni *see* Pteyuteshni
Pteyutesni *see* Pteyuteshni
Ptolme [CA] (H)
Puab *see* Winnebago
Puaguampe *see* Pahvant
Puala *see* Puaray
Puallip *see* Puyallup
Puallipamish *see* Puyallup
Pualli-paw-mish *see* Puyallup
Puallipawmish *see* Puyallup
Pualliss *see* Puyallup
Puan *see* Winnebago
Puanipuatama *see* Peripatama
Puant *see* Metsmetskop
Puant *see* Winnebago
Puara *see* Puaray
Puarai *see* Puaray
Puaray [NM] *Tigua* (H)
Puary *see* Puaray
Pucapacuri *see* Cogapocori
Pucapacuri *see* Machiganga
Pucapacuri *see* Toyeri
Pucara *see* Arikara
Puca-Uma *see* Iquito
Pucauma *see* Iquito
Pucha *see* Patzau
Puchkohn [Can] *Hopi* (H)
Puckanokick *see* Pokanoket
Pudding River Indians *see* Ahantchuyuk
Pueblo [Lang] *Shoshonean* (Pub, v.4, no.3)
Pueblo Alto [Pueblo] [NM] (H)
Pueblo Blanco [Pueblo] (H)
Pueblo Bonito [Pueblo] [NM] (H)
Pueblo Caja del Rio [Pueblo] [NM] (H)
Pueblo Colorado (H) *see also* Tzemantuo (H)
Pueblo Colorado [Pueblo] [NM] (H)
Pueblo del Alto [Pueblo] (H)
Pueblo de la Parida [Pueblo] (H)
Pueblo de Tunque *see* Tungge
Pueblo Indians (LC)
Pueblo of the Bird *see* Tshirege
Puelche [CH, Arg] (LC)
Puelchu *see* Puelche
Pueripatama [MX] (Hdbk10)

Pugallipamish *see* Puyallup
Pugallup *see* Puyallup
Puguahiam *see* Pacuaches
Puh-ksi-nah-mah-yiks *see*
  Puhksinahmahyiks
Puhksinahmahyiks [MN] *Siksika*
  (BE)
Puiale *see* Puyallup
Puimem [CA] *Wintum* (H)
Pu-i-mim *see* Piumem
Puimim *see* Puimem
Pu-i-mok *see* Puimuk
Puimok *see* Puimuk
Puimuk [CA] *Wintun* (H)
Puinabe *see* Puinave
Puinabi *see* Puinave
Puinabo *see* Puinave
Puinahau *see* Poyanawa
Puinahua *see* Puinave
Puinahua *see* Setebo
Puinave [Col, VE] (O)
Puisascamin (H)
Puisortok *Greenland Eskimos* (BE)
Pu-i-su *see* Puisu
Puisu [CA] (H)
Puivlirmiut [Can] *Central Eskimos*
  (BE)
pujjunarmiut [Can] [*Inuit (Que-
  bec)*] (Hdbk5)
Pujuaque *see* Pojoaque
Pujunan (LC) *see also* Maidu (LC)
Pujunan [Lang] [CA] (H)
Pujuni *see* Pusune
Pukina *see* Puquina
Pukirieri [PE] *Toyeri* (O)
Pukobke [Br] *Eastern Timbira*
  (O)
Pukobye [Br] *Gavioes* (LC)
Pukopye *see* Pukobye
Puk-tis *see* Omaha
Puktis *see* Omaha
Puku-Diapa [Lang] *Catuquina*
  (O)
Pulacman *see* Pulacuam
Pulacuam *Coahuiltecan* (BE)
Pulga [Lang] *Konkow* (CA-8)
Pullaeu *see* Unalachtigo
Pul-la-ook *see* Pullaook
Pul-la-ook *see* Unalachtigo
Pullaook [Clan] [DE] (H)
Pulpene *see* Bolbone
Pulpone *see* Bolbone
Puma *see* Pima
Pume [Self-designation] *see*
  Yaruro
Pumpoa *see* Pampopa
Pumpton *see* Pompton
Puna [Clan] *Hopi* (H)
Punames *see* Sia
Pu-nañ nyu-mu *see* Puna
Punan nyumu *see* Puna
Punaryou [Sub-clan] [DE] (H)
Punashly *see* Bannock

Pu-na'wuñ-wu *see* Puna
Puna wunwu *see* Puna
Punca *see* Ponca
Puncah *see* Ponca
Puncataguo *see* Juanca
Puncaw *see* Ponca
Puncha *see* Ponca
Punchaw *see* Ponca
Puncuri *see* Pukirieri
Pu'n-e *see* Puna
Pune *see* Puna
Pungelika *see* Erie
Pungotege *Accomac* (Hdbk15)
Pungoteque *see* Pungotege
Punjuni *see* Pusune
Punka *see* Ponca
Pun-nak *see* Bannock
Punnak *see* Bannock
Puntale *see* Cuaiquer
Puntlatsh [VanI] (BE)
Punt-ledge *see* Puntlatsh
Puntledge *see* Puntlatsh
Pun-ush *see* Bannock
Punush *see* Bannock
Puotwatemi *see* Potawatomi
Puqina [BO] (LC)
Puquiri [PE] *Mashco* (O)
Pura *see* Puretuay
Puray *see* Puaray
Purepecha *see* Tarascan
Pur-e Tu-ay *see* Puretuay
Puretuay [Pueblo] [NM] (H)
Purhe *see* Tarasco
Purhepecha *see* Tarasco
Puri [Br] (LC)
Puricoto [Guy, VE] (LC)
Purigotos *see* Ipurucoto
Purigotos *see* Puricoto
Purisimeno [CA] *Chumash* (CA)
Purisimeño [Lang] [CA] (He)
Purisma *see* Purisimeno
Puro [Br] *Northern Cayapo* (O)
Puruai *see* Puaray
Puruay *see* Puaray
Purubora [Br] (O)
Purucoto *see* Paricoto
Purucutu *see* Paricoto
Puruha [EC, PE] (LC)
Purukoto *see* Paricoto
Purupuru [Br] (LC)
Puscattaway *see* Piscattaway
Pusciti *see* Akwe-Shavante
Pushune *see* Pusune
Pu-shush *see* Puisu
Pushush *see* Puisu
Pusto *see* Pasto
Pusuama *Coahuiltecan* (Hdbk10)
Pusuaque *see* Pojoaque
Pu-su-na *see* Pusune
Pusuna *see* Pusune
Pu-su-ne *see* Pusune
Pusune [CA] *Nishinam* (H)
Putaay [TX] (BE)

Putah Creek [Lang] [CA] *Mo-
  quelumnan* (Pub, v.6, no.1,
  pp.316–17)
Putai *see* Pitahay
Putavatimes *see* Potawatomi
Putawatame *see* Potawatomi
Putawatimi *see* Potawatomi
Putawatimies *see* Potawatomi
Putawatomie *see* Potawatomi
Putawawtawmaw *see* Potawatomi
Putc-ko-hu *see* Puchkohu
Putckohu *see* Puchkohu
Putetemini [SD] *Hunkpatina* (H)
Pu-te-wa-ta *see* Potawatomi
Putewata *see* Potawatomi
Pu-te-wa-ta-dan *see* Potawatomi
Putewatadan *see* Potawatomi
Putewatimes *see* Potawatomi
Puthlavamiut *Labrador Eskimos*
  (BE)
Putos (H) *see also* Copeh (H)
Putos [CA] *Patwin* (Contri, v.3,
  p.219)
Putowatomey's *see* Potawatomi
Puttawattimies *see* Potawatomi
Puttcotung *see* Potawatomi
Puttewatimies *see* Potawatomi
Puttowatomies *see* Potawatomi
Puttwatimee *see* Potawatomi
Puukong [Clan] *Hopi* (H)
Puukoñ wiñwu *see* Puukong
Puxiti *see* Akwe-Shavante
Puyallop *see* Puyallup
Puyallup [WA] *Nisqualli* (LC)
Puyallupahmish *see* Puyallup
Pu-yallup-a-mish *see* Puyallup
Puyallupamish *see* Puyallup
Puyalup *see* Puyallup
Puyatye *see* Tano
Puye Mesa [Pueblo] [NM] (H)
Puymok [Lang] [CA] *River Nom-
  laki* (CA-8)
Puyon *see* Winnebago
puzaots [Clan] [CA] *North Folk
  Mono* (Pub, v.11, no.5, p.293)
Puzhune *see* Pusune
Puzlumne *see* Pusune
Pwiya'lap *see* Puyallup
Pwiyalap *see* Puyallup
Pxanai *see* Modoc
Pyankashee *see* Piankashaw
Pyankeesha *see* Piankashaw
Pyankeha *see* Piankashaw
Pyankeshaw *see* Piankashaw
Pyankishaw *see* Piankashaw
Pyedes *see* Pa-Ute
Py-eed *see* Paiute
Pyeed *see* Paiute
Py-eeds *see* Southern Paiute
Pyeeds *see* Southern Paiute
Pyentes *see* Paiute
Pyquag *see* Pyquauq
Pyquauq [CN] *Mattabesec* (H)

Pyramid Lake *Paiute* (Char, v.11)
Pyros *see* Piro [Pueblo]
Pythagoreans (H)
Py-ute *see* Paviotso
Py-ute *see* Paiute
Pyute *see* Paiute
Pyute *see* Paviotso

-Q-

Q!a'ad na'as Xada-i *see* Kaad-
naas-hadai
Qaadnaas Xadai *see* Kaadnaas-
hadai
Qa-a-mo' te-ne *see* Khaamotene
Qaamotene *see* Khaamotene
Qa'aqe *see* Kaake
Qaaqe *see* Kaake
Qackanqatso *see* Khashkankhatso
Qaclij *see* Khashhlizhni
Qaclijni *see* Khashhlizhni
Q!a'dasgo qe'gawa-i *see*
Kadusgo-kegawai
Qadasgo qegawai *see* Kadusgo-
kegawai
Qaernermiut *see* Qairnirmiut
Qaernermiut [Can] *Central Eski-
mos* (BE)
Qagaan Tayagungin [Lang] [AK]
Eastern Aleut (Hdbk5)
Qa'gials qe'gawa-i *see* Kagials-
kegawai
Qagils qegawai *see* Kagials-
kegawai
Qagutl *see* Kwakiutl
Qagyuhl [Self-designation] *see*
Kwakiutl
Qahatika *see* Quahatika
Qa-iat la'nas *see* Kaiahl-lanas
Qaiat lanas *see* Kaiahl-lanas
Qaibabitc *see* Kaibab
Qai'dju qe'gawa-i *see* Kaidju-
kegawai
Qaidju qegawai *see* Kaidju-
kegawai
Qailertetang (H)
Qairnirmiut *Caribou Eskimos*
(Hdbk5)
Qaisla *see* Kitamat
Q'a'ketan *see* Ankakehittan
Qaketan *see* Ankakehittan
Qala'ltq *see* Hellelt
Qalda'ngasal *see* Huldanggat
Qaldangasal *see* Huldanggat
Qaldo *see* Kuldo
Q'ale'ts *see* Kulleets
Qalto *see* Khaltso
Qaltsodine *see* Khaltso
Qamil'lema *see* Camiltpaw
Qamillema *see* Camiltpaw

Qanab *see* Kaibab
Qa'ngual la'nas *see* Kangguatl-
lanas
Qangual lanas *see* Kangguatl-
lanas
Qanikilak (H)
Q'anikilaq *see* Qaanikilak
Qanikilaq *see* Qanikilak
Qapnish-lema *see* Topinish
Qa-qamatses *see* Hahamatse
Qaqa!o's hit tan *see* Kakos-hit-
tan
Qa'qaqatilik-a *see* Kakawatilikya
Qa-qa-ton-wan *see* Chippewa
Qaqatonwan *see* Chippewa
Qaqawatilika *see* Kakawatilikya
Qaqlets *see* Kulleets
Qaqoshittan *see* Kakos-hit-tan
Qa-ra-ta nu-man-ke *see* Horata-
mumake
Qarata numanke *see* Horatamu-
make
Q'ash-tre-tye *see* San Felipe
[Keres]
Qashtretye *see* San Felipe [Keres]
Q!as la'nas *see* Kas-lanas
Qaslanas *see* Kas-lanas
Qa-sta qe-gawa-i *see* Daiyuahl-
lanas
Qastaqegawai *see* Daiyuahl-lanas
Qa'tcadi *see* Katchadi
Qatcadi *see* Katchadi
Q!a'tgu hit tan *see* Ketgohittan
Qatguhittan *see* Ketgohittan
Qatgui-tga'xet gitina-i *see*
Kahlguihlgahet-gitinai
Qa'tiguaxa-idaga-i *see* Kahligua-
gitinai
Qatiguaxaidagai *see* Kahligua-
gitinai
Q!a'tkaayi *see* Katkaayi
Qatlaayi *see* Katkaayi
Qauitcin *see* Cowichan
Qaumauangmiut [Can] *Central
Eskimos* (BE)
Qaupaw *see* Quapaw
Qaviaragmiut *see* Kaviagmiut
Qawalangin [Lang] [AK] *Eastern
Aleut* (Hdbk5)
Qawasqar [CH, TDF] (O)
Qawiaraq Inupiq [Lang] *Inupiaq*
(Hdbk5)
Qawpaw *see* Quapaw
Qaxun (Hdbk5)
qeme-spelu *see* Kalispel
qemespelu *see* Kalispel
Qe-mini-tcan *see* Khemnichan
Qeminitcan *see* Khemnichan
Qemnitca *see* Khamnichan
qemuynu *see* Nez Perce
Qen [Clan] *Nambe* (H)
Qe'nipsen *see* Kenipsim
Qenipsen *see* Kenipsim

Qen-tdoa (H) *see also* Kang (H)
Qentdoa (PC) *see also* Kang (H)
Qentdoa *see* Qen
Qe'qaes *see* China Hat
Qeqaes *see* China Hat
Qeqertarmiut *see* Qiqiqtarmiut
Qetlk-oan *see* Hehlkoan
Qetlkoan *see* Hehlkoan
Qeyata-otonwe *see* Kheyatao-
tonwe
Qeyataotonwe *see* Kheyatao-
tonwe
Qeyata-tonwan *see* Khayatao-
tonwe
Qeyatatonwan *see* Kheyatao-
tonwe
Qeyata-witcaca *see* Khey-
atawichasha
Qeyatawitcaca *see* Khey-
atawichasha
Qhechwa *see* Quechua
Qichun *see* Yuma
Qidneliq *see* Kidnelik
Qigiigun [Lang] *Eastern Aleut*
(Hdbk5)
Qiimiut [Lang] *Central Alaskan
Yupik* (Hdbk5)
qikextaymiut *see* Chugatchigmut
Qikiqtagrungmiut *Kotzebue Sound
Eskimos* (Hdbk5)
qikirmiut *see* Kikiktagmyut
qikirtamiut [Can] [*Inuit
(Quebec)*] (Hdbk5)
Qinaboag *see* Quinebang
Qinguamiut (H) *see also*
Kinguamiut (H)
Qinguamiut [Can] *Central Eski-
mos* (BE)
Qinnepioka *see* Quinnipiac
Qinnipiac *see* Quinnipiac
Qiqiqtarmiut [AK] *Eskimos*
(Hdbk5)
Q'i-ra-vash *see* Querecho
Qiravash *see* Querecho
Qi-ta nu-man-ke *see* Khitanu-
manke
Qitanumanke *see* Khitanumanke
qlispel *see* Kalispel
qlspilx *see* Kalispel
Q'ma'shpal *see* Skitwish
Qmashpal *see* Skitswish
Qnicaapou *see* Kickapoo
Qoasi'la *see* Goasila
Qoasila *see* Goasila
Qoe'qoaainox *see* Koekoaainok
Qoeqoaainox *see* Koekoaainok
Qoe'qomatlxo *see* Homalko
Qoeqomatlxo *see* Homalk
Q!oe'tas *see* Koetas
Qoetas *see* Koetas
Q'oe'tenox *see* Koetenok
Qoetenox *see* Koetenok
Qoe'xsot/enox *see* Koeksotenok

Qoexsotenox *see* Koeksotenok
Qoga'nas *see* Kogangas
Qoganas *see* Kogangas
Qo-ganlani *see* Khoghanhlani
Qoganlani *see* Khoghanhlani
Qo-gat la'nas *see* Kogahl-lanas
Qogatlanas *see* Kogahl-lanas
Qoi'k-axtenox *see* Koikahtenok
Qoke'de *see* Hokedi
Qokede *see* Hokedi
Q'o'lenox *see* Kotlenok
Qolenox *see* Kotlenok
Qolla *see* Colla
Qollahuaya *see* Callahuaya
Q'o'm'enox *see* Komenok
Qomenox *see* Komenok
Q'o'mk-utis *see* Komkyutis
Qomkutis (PC) *see also* Komlyutis
  (H)
Qomkutis *Kwakiutl* (Anthro, v.9,
  no.3, p.158)
Q'o'moyue *see* Komogue
Qomoyue *see* Komogue
Qonaga'ni *see* Khonagani
Qonagani *see* Khonagani
Q!o'no qe'gawa-i *see* Kone-
  kegawai
Qonoqegawai *see* Kone-kegawai
Qo-on-gwut-tun'ne *see*
  Khoonkhwuttunne
Qoonqwuttunne *see*
  Khoonkhwuttunne
Q'o'qa-itx *see* Kokaitx
Qoqaitx *see* Kokaitx
Qosalektawi [Lang] *Achomawi*
  (CA-8)
Qospimo *see* Koskimo
Qo'sqemox *see* Koskimo
Qosqemox *see* Koskimo
Qo-ta-tci *see* Khotachi
Qotatci *see* Khotachi
Qouarra *see* Quarai
Qq'ueres *see* Keres
Qra *see* Khra
Qra-qtci *see* Nachiche
Qraqtci *see* Nachiche
Qsa'loqul *see* Ksalokul
Qsaloqul *see* Ksalokul
Qsa'psem *see* Ksapem
Qsapsem *see* Ksapsem
Qset-so-kit-pee-tsee-lee *see*
  Shipaulovi
Qsetsokitpeetseelee *see*
  Shipaulovi
Qsisilla *see* Goasila
Qtla'sen *see* Kltlasen
Qtlasen *see* Kltlasen
Qtlumi *see* Lummi
Quaahda *see* Kwahari
Quaasada *see* Koasati
Quaauenoq *see* Guauaenok
Quabaag *see* Quabaug
Quabaconk *see* Quabaug

Quabage *see* Quabaug
Quabagud *see* Quabaug
Quabajai *see* Serrano
Quabajay *see* Serrano
Quabakuft *see* Quabaug
Quabaog *see* Quabaug
Quabaquick *see* Quabaug
Quabaug [MA] (H)
Quabauk *see* Quabaug
Quaboag *see* Quabaug
Quaboagh *see* Quabaug
Quabog *see* Quabaug
Quaboug *see* Quabaug
Quachita *see* Washita
Quach-snah-mish *see* Squaxon
Quachsnahmish *see* Squaxon
Quack-ena-mish *see* Squaxon
Quackenamish *see* Squaxon
Quackeweth *see* Kwakiutl
Quackewlth *see* Kwakiutl
Quackohamaock [VA] (Hdbk15)
Quackohowaon *see* Quacko-
  hamaock
Quackolls *see* Kwakiutl
Quacksis *see* Fox
Quacohamaock *see* Quacko-
  hamaock
Qua-colth *see* Kwakiutl
Quacolth *see* Kwakiutl
Quacos *see* Kwakiutl
Quaddies *see* Passamaquoddy
Quaddy Indians *see* Pas-
  samaquoddy
Quadodaquees *see* Kadohadacho
Quadodaquious *see* Kadohada-
  cho
Qua'dos *see* Huados
Quados *see* Huados
Quagheuil *see* Kwakiutl
Quagyuhl *see* Kwakiutl
Quahada Comanche *see* Kwahari
Quahade-Comanche *see* Kwahari
Quaha-dede-chatz-Kenna *see*
  Kwahari
Quahadedechatzkenna *see* Kwa-
  hari
Qua-ha-de-dechutz-Kenna *see*
  Kwahari
Quahadedechutzkenna *see* Kwa-
  hari
Quahades *see* Kwahari
Quahatika [AZ] *Piman* (BE)
Quahkeulth *see* Kwakiutl
Qua-ho-dah *see* Kwahari
Quahodah *see* Kwahari
Quah-tah-mah *see* Kwatami
Quahtahmah *see* Kwatami
Quah-to-mah *see* Kwatami
Quahtomah (PC) *see also*
  Kwatami (BE)
Quahtomah [OR] *Tututni* (H)
Quahuila *see* Coahuileño
Quaiantl *see* Quinault

Quainacona *see* Kinikinao
Quainacona *see* Tereno
Qua-i-nu *see* Guauaenok
Quainu *see* Guauaenok
Quaitlin *see* Kwantlen
Quaitso (BE) *see also* Queets (BE)
Quai'tso *see* Quaitso
Quaitso [WA] *Salish* (H)
Quajote *see* Kohadk
Qua-kar *see* Komogue
Quakar *see* Komogue
Quakers *see* Oto
Quakoumwah *see* Kwatami
Quakouwah *see* Kwatami
Quak-s'n-a-mish *see* Squaxon
Quaksnamish *see* Squaxon
Qualacu [Pueblo] *Piro* (H)
Qualhioqua *see* Kwalhioqua
Qualicum *see* Saamen
Qualiogua *see* Kwalhioqua
Qualliamish *see* Nisqualli
Quallyamish *see* Nisqualli
Qualquilth *see* Kwakiutl
Qualquioqua *see* Kwalhioqua
Quamichan [VanI] *Cowichan*
  (BE)
Quamitchan *see* Quamichan
Quanataguo [TX] *Coahuiltecan*
  (BE)
Quandanquian *Pocomoke*
  (Hdbk15)
Quane [VanI] (H)
Quannepague *see* Quinebaug
Quanoatinno *see* Kanohatino
Quanoatino *see* Kanohatino
Quanoouatino *see* Kanohatino
Quanouatin *see* Kanohatino
Quanquiz (H)
Quans *see* Kansa
Quant-lum *see* Kwantlen
Quantlum *see* Kwantlen
Quapa *see* Quapaw
Quapau *see* Quapaw
Quapaw [AR] (LC)
Quapaw [Lang] *Dhegiha* (H)
Quapaws-Arkansas *see* Quapaw
Quapois *see* Quapaw
Quappas *see* Quapaw
Quappaw *see* Quapaw
Qu'Appelle *see* Katepoisipi-
  wiinuuk
Quappelle *see* Katepoisipi-
  Wiinuuk
Quaqua [VE] (O)
Quaquima *see* Kiakima
Quaquina *see* Wakina
Quaquiolts *see* Kwakiutl
Quara *see* Quarai
Quarac *see* Quarai
Quarai [Pueblo] [NM] (H)
Quarlpi *see* Colville
Quarra *see* Quarai
Quarrelers *see* Kutchin

Quarrelers *see* Tukkuthkutchin
Quarrellers *see* Vuntakutchin
Quarrellers *see* Tukkuthkutchin
Quarro *see* Quarai
Quarrydechocos *see* Kwahari
Qua-saw-da *see* Koasati
Quasawda *see* Koasati
Quash-sua-mish *see* Squaxon
Quashsuamish *see* Squaxon
Quasmigdo [Self-designation] *see* Bidai
Quasquen (H)
Quasquen (H) *see also* Kaskaskia (LC)
Quassarte *see* Koasati
Quata [MX] (BE)
Quatanon *see* Wea
Quataquois *see* Kiowa Apache
Quataquon *see* Kiowa Apache
Quathlahpohtle *see* Cathlapotle
Quathlahpothle *see* Cathlapotle
Quathlahpotle *see* Cathlapotle
Quathl-met-ha *see* Comeya
Quathlmetha (PC) *see also* Comeya
Quathlmetha [CA] *Comeya* (H)
Qua'tl *see* Kwantlen
Quatl *see* Kwantlen
Quatoge *see* Huron
Quatoge *see* Wyandot
Quatoghee *see* Huron
Quatoghies *see* Huron
Quatoghies of Loretto *see* Huron
Quatokeronon *see* Sauk
Quatomah *see* Kwatami
Qua-tou-wah *see* Kwatami
Quatouwah *see* Kwatami
Quatseno *see* Quatsino
Quatsinas *see* Goasila
Quatsino [Can] *Koskimo* (BE)
Quat-si-nu *see* Quatsino
Quatsinu *see* Quatsino
Quattamya *see* Kwatami
Quaumauangmiut *see* Kaumauangmiut
Quaupaw *see* Quapaw
Quawbaug *see* Quabaug
Quawbawg *see* Quabaug
Quawguults *see* Kwakiutl
Quawlicum *see* Saamen
Quawpa *see* Quapaw
Quawpaug *see* Quabaug
Quawpaw *see* Quapaw
Quaw-she-lah *see* Goasila
Quawshelah *see* Goasila
Quayneos *see* Kannehouan
Quayoughcohanek *see* Quiouco-hanock
Quazula *see* Ute
Queackar *see* Komogue
Quebaug *see* Quabaug
Quebec of the Southwest *see* Acoma

Quebira *see* Quivira
Quecha (LC) *see also* Yuma (LC)
Quecha *Andes Region* (LC)
Quechal [Lang] *see* Quechan
Quechal *see* Hueyhueyquetzal
Quechan [Lang] *Yuma* (Hdbk10)
Quechua *see* Quecha
Quedejeño [Coahuiltecan] (Hdbk10)
Queeakah *see* Kueha
Quee-ha-ni-cul-ta *see* Kueha
Queehaniculta *see* Kueha
Quee ha Qna coll *see* Komogue
Queehaqnacoll *see* Komogue
Quee-ha-qua-coll *see* Komogue
Queehaquacoll *see* Komogue
Queelquelu (H)
Queenapaug *see* Quinebaug
Queenapiok *see* Quinnipiac
Queenapoick *see* Quinnipiac
Queenhithe *see* Quinault
Queen Hythe *see* Quinault
Queenhythe *see* Quinault
Queenioolt *see* Quinault
Queercho *see* Querecho
Queets (H) *see also* Quaitso (H)
Queets [WA] (BE)
Queet-see *see* Quaitso
Queetsee *see* Quaitso
Quehts *see* Quaitso
Quejanaquia [MX] *Coahuiltecan* (Hdbk10)
quejatsa *see* Hidatsa
Quejuen *see* Tulkepaia
Quekchi *see* Kekchi
Que-lai-ult *see* Quileute
Quelaiult *see* Quileute
Quelamoueches *see* Karankawa
Quelancouchis *see* Karankawa
Quelanhubeches *see* Karankawa
Quelene *see* Tzotzil
Quellehute *see* Quileute
Queloktrey [NM] *Jumano* (H)
Quelotetreny *see* Quelotetrey
Quelotretrey *see* Quelotetrey
Quelshose [BC] *Salish* (H)
Quemaya *see* Kamia
Quemaya *see* Comeya
Quems [MX] *Coahuiltecan* (BE)
Quemult *see* Quinault
Quenait chechat *see* Makah
Quenaitchechat *see* Makah
Que-nait-sath *see* Makah
Quenaitsath *see* Makah
Quenebage *see* Quinebaug
Quenebaug *see* Quinebaug
Quenebec Indians *see* Norridge-wock
Quenepiage *see* Quinnipiac
Quenepiake *see* Quinnipiac
Queniauitl *see* Quinault
Quenibaug *see* Quinebaug
Quenipisa *see* Acolapissa

Quenistinos *see* Cree
Que-ni-ult *see* Quinault
Queniult *see* Quinault
Quenoil *see* Quinault
Quenoith *see* Quinault
Quenongebin *see* Keinouche
Quenopiage *see* Quinnipiac
Quentuse *see* Maca
Queoues coupees *see* Kishkakon
Queouescoupees *see* Kishkakon
Quepanos *Coahuiltecan* (BE)
Quepas *see* Quapaw
Quepo [CR] (BE)
Queppa *see* Quapaw
Quequashkecasquick *Assateague* (Hdbk15)
Quequesal *see* Hueyhueyquetzal
Quequexque [Pan, CR] *Terraba* (O)
Quera *see* Keres
Querandi [Arg] (LC)
Querca *see* Quarai
Quercho *see* Querecho
Querechaos *see* Querecho
Quereches *see* Querecho
Querecho (Hdbk10) *see also* Navajo (LC)
Querecho [NM, TX] *Apache* (H)
Querechos *see* Apache
Quereho *see* Querecho
Querejeño *see* Quedejeño
Queremeteco *Coahuiltecan* (Hdbk10)
Querendi *see* Querandi
Querene *see* Tzotzil
Querepee *see* Quinnipiac
Queres *see* Keres
Quereses *see* Keres
Queres Gibraltar *see* Acoma
Querez *see* Keres
Queris *see* Keres
Queristinos *see* Cree
Quernermiut (Hdbk5) *see also* Qairnirmiut (Hdbk5)
Queroma *see* Caurame
Queros *see* Keres
Querphas *see* Quapaw
Querra *see* Quarai
Quesada *see* Koasati
Quesal (Hdbk10) *see also* Gueiquesales (H)
Quesal (Hdbk10) *see also* Hueyhueyquetzal (Hdbk10)
Quesal [MX] *Coahuiltecan* (BE)
Queseda *see* Koasati
Quetahtore *see* Carrizo [MX]
Quetapon [MX] *Coahuiltecan* (Hdbk10)
Queues coupees *see* Kishkakon
Quevene *see* Kohani
que Vira *see* Quivira
quevira *see* Quivira
Quevoil *see* Quinault

Queyches *see* Kichai
Queyugwe *see* Cayuga
Queyugwehaughga *see* Cayuga
Quezedan *see* Koasati
Quhlicum *see* Saamen
Quialpo [NM] (H)
Quiana [Pueblo] [AZ] [Hopi] (H)
Quianna *see* Quiana
Quiapo [NM] (H)
Quiarlpi *see* Colville
Quiatolte [MX] *Coahuiltecan* (Hdbk10)
Quiauaane *see* Quiguasguama
Quibira *see* Quivira
Quibobima [MX] *Coahuiltecan* (Hdbk10)
Quibonoa *Coahuiltecan* (Hdbk10)
Quiborique *Coahuiltecan* (BE)
Quicama *see* Halyikwamai
Quicama *see* Quigyuma
Quicamopa *see* Quigyuma
Quicana *see* Halyikwamai
Quicapause *see* Kickapoo
Quicapons *see* Kickapoo
Quicapou *see* Kickapoo
Quichaais *see* Kichai
Quichais *see* Kichai
Quichan *see* Kiowa
Quiche [Lang] *Highland* (LC)
Quichean [Lang] *Eastern Mayan* (LC)
Quicheigno *see* Kichai
Quiches *see* Kichai
Quichoid *see* Quichean
Quichua (LC) *see also* Quechua (LC)
Quichua [EC] (O)
Quichuan *see* Kiowa
Quicima *see* Quigyuma
Quick-sul-i-nut *see* Kocksotenok
Quicksulinut *see* Koeksotenok
Quicoma *see* Quigyuma
Quicoma *see* Halyikwamai
Quicunontateronons *see* Tionontati
Quidaho *see* Kichai
Qui-dai-elt *see* Quinault
Quidaielt *see* Quinault
Quide [TX] *Coahuiltecan* (BE)
Quidehaio *see* Kichai
Quidehais *see* Kichai
Quieetso *see* Quaitso
Quieha Ne cub ta *see* Kueha
Quiehanecubta *see* Kueha
Quiemltutz *see* Tionontati
Quien *Coahuiltecan* (Hdbk10)
Quiennontateronon *see* Nipissing
Quiennontateronon *see* Tionontati
Quietaroes *see* Coyotero Apache
Quieunontateronon *see* Nipissing

Quieunontateronon *see* Tionontati
Quieunontati *see* Tionontati
Quiguantiguara [MX] *Coahuiltecan* (Hdbk10)
Quiguasguama [MX] *Coahuiltecan* (Hdbk10)
Quigui *see* Santo Domingo
Quigyama *see* Quigyuma
Quigyuma (BE) *see also* Halyikwamai (BE)
Quigyuma [AZ] *Yuman* (H)
Quihuima *see* Quigyuma
Quijo [EC] (LC)
Quilaco *see* Quillaca
Quilahute *see* Quileute
Quilaielt *see* Quinault
Quil-cene *see* Kolsid
Quilcene *see* Kolsid
Quilehute *see* Quileute
Quileute [WA] (LC)
Quiliapiack *see* Quinnipiac
Quilipiacke *see* Quinnipiac
Quil-i-ute *see* Quileute
Quiliute *see* Quileute
Quillaca [BO] *Aymara* (O)
Quillacinga [EC, Col] (LC)
Quillagua *see* Quillaca
Quillalyute *see* Quileute
Quillasinga *see* Quillacinga
Quillayute *see* Quileute
Quil-leh-ute *see* Quileute
Quillehute *see* Quileute
Quilleouoqua *see* Kwalhioqua
Quillequaqua *see* Kwalhioqua
Quillequeogna *see* Kwalhioqua
Quillequeoqua *see* Kwalhioqua
Quilleute *see* Quileute
Quilleyute *see* Quileute
Quillihute *see* Quileute
Quillipeage *see* Quinnipiac
Quillipeage *see* Quiripi
Quillipiacke *see* Quinnipiac
Quillipieck *see* Quinnipiac
Quillipiog *see* Quinnipiac
Quillipiuk *see* Quinnipiac
Quillipyake *see* Quinnipiac
Quilliute *see* Quileute
Quilloyath *see* Quileute
Quillypieck *see* Quinnipiac
Quillypieck *see* Quiripi
Quilmur [AZ] (H)
Quilomene [WA] *Sinkiuse* (Hdbk12)
Quil-si-eton *see* Kwilsieton
Quilsieton *see* Kwilsieton
Quimac *see* Quigyuma
Quimbaya [Col] (LC)
Qui-me *see* Cochiti
Quime *see* Cochiti
Quimicoa *Coahuiltecan* (Hdbk10)
Quiminipao *see* Cuiminipaco
Quimipeiock *see* Quinnipiac

Quimis *see* Quems
Quims *see* Quems
Qui-nai-elt *see* Quinault
Quinaielt *see* Quinault
Quin-aik *see* Quinault
Quinaik *see* Quinault
Quinailee *see* Quinault
Quinaimo *see* Guinaima
Quinaiult *see* Quinault
Quinapeag *see* Quinnipiac
Quinapeake *see* Quinnipiac
Quinaqui *see* Ese Ejja
Quinaquois *see* Kickapoo
Quinault [WA] (LC)
Quinayat *see* Quinault
Quincapou *see* Kickapoo
Quinebaug [CN] (H)
Quinechart *see* Makah
Quinegaayo [MX] *Coahuiltecan* (Hdbk10)
Quinemeguete [MX] *Coahuiltecan* (Hdbk10)
Quineres *see* Karankawa
Quinet (H) *see also* Karankawa (LC)
Quinet [TX] (H)
Quingas *see* Keres
Quingoes *see* Cayuga
Quingoi *see* Kwingyap
Quini *see* Zuni
Quiniacapem *Coahuiltecan* (Hdbk10)
Quiniapin *Coahuiltecan* (Hdbk9)
Quinibauge *see* Quinebaug
Quinicuan *see* Quinicuanes
Quinicuanes [MX] *Tamaulipec* (BE)
Quinielt *see* Quinault
Quinigual [MX] *Coahuiltecan* (Hdbk10)
Quiniguio [MX] *Coahuiltecan* (Hdbk10)
Quiniilt *see* Quinault
Quinilt *see* Quinault
Quiniltz *see* Quinault
Quinimicheco [MX] *Coahuiltecan* (Hdbk10)
Quinipiac *see* Quinnipiac
Quinipieck *see* Quinnipiac
Quinipisa *see* Acolapissa
Quinipisa *see* Quinipissa
Quinipissa (H) *see also* Acolapissa (BE)
Quinipissa [LA] (BE)
Quinipiuck *see* Quinnipiac
Quiniquijo *see* Quiniguo
Quiniquissa *see* Acolapissa
Quiniquissa *see* Quinipissa
Quinira *see* Quivira
Quiniult *see* Quinault
Quiniutles *see* Quinault
Quinnabaug *see* Quinebaug
Quin-na-chart *see* Makah

Quinnachart see Makah
Quinnechant see Makah
Quinnechart see Makah
Quinnepa see Quinnipiac
Quinnepaeg see Quinnipiac
Quinnepauge see Quinnipiac
Quinnepiack see Quinnipiac
Quinne-pyooghq see Quinnipiac
Quinnepyooghq see Quinnipiac
Quinnipauge see Quinnipiac
Quinnipiac (Hdbk15) see also
  Quiripi (Hdbk9)
Quinnipiac [CN] Wappinger (LC)
Quinnipiak see Quinnipiac
Quinnipieuck see Quinnipiac
Quinnipieuck see Quiripi
Quinnipieuck see Keres
Quinnipieuk see Quinnipiac
Quinnipiog see Quinnipiac
Quinnipioke see Quinnipiac
Quinnipissa see Acolapissa
Quinnipissa see Quinipissa
Quinnipiug see Quinnipiac
Quinnippiuck see Quinnipiac
Quinnopiage see Quinnipiac
Quinnuboag see Quinebaug
Quinnypiag see Quinnipiac
Quinnypiock see Quinnipiac
Quinnypiock see Quiripi
Quinnypiog see Quinnipiac
Quinopiocke see Quinnipiac
Quinopiocke see Quiripi
Quinquima see Quigyuma
Quinticook see Connecticut
Quintimiri [PE] Campa (O)
Quinult see Quinault
Quinypiock see Quinnipiac
Quioborique [TX] (H)
Quiocohanoes see Quiouco-
  hanock
Quiocohanses see Quiocohanock
Quiocqahannock see Quiouco-
  hanock
Quiohohouan see Kiowa
Quiomaqui [NM] (H)
Quiotanck see Kiquotank
Quiotank see Accomac
Quiotraco [NM] (H)
Quiouaha see Kiowa
Quiouahan see Kiowa
Quioucohanock [VA] Powhatan
  Confederacy (H)
Quipana see Pawnee
Quipano see Pawnee
Quipea see Kariri
Quipu [PE] (BE)
Quiquima see Quigyuma
Quiquima see Halyukwamai
Quiquimo see Quigyuma
Quiquiona see Quigyuma
Quiquoga see Cayuga
Quirasquiris see Wichita
Quirepeys see Quinnipiac

Quirequire [Lang] Tamanaco
  (UAz, v.28)
Quires see Keres
Quirex see Keres
Quiria see Keres
Quiriba see Quivira
Quiripeys see Quinnipiac
Quiripeys see Quiripi
Quiripi (Hdbk9) see also Quin-
  nipiac (LC)
Quiripi [Lang] Eastern Alquon-
  quian (Hdbk9)
Quiriquitiniguera [MX] Coahuil-
  tecan (Hdbk10)
Quirireches see Querecho
Quirix see Keres
Quiros see Keres
Quirruba see Quirrubu
Quirrubu Achagua (O)
Quisabas Coahuiltecan (BE)
Quisal see Quesal
Quisqueyano (LC)
Quitacas [TX] Coahuiltecan (BE)
Quitaguriaguilo [MX] Coahuilte-
  can (Hdbk10)
Quitemo (O)
Quitirrisi [CR] (O)
Quito see Iquito
Quitoks see Quitoles
Quitoles [TX] Coastal Coahuilte-
  can (H)
Quitres see Kichai
Quitrey see Kichai
Quits see Quaitso
Quitsei see Kichai
Quitseigus see Kichai
Quitseings see Kichai
Quituchiis see Kichai
Quiturran see Iquito
Quitway see Miami
Quitxix see Kichai
Quitzaene see Kichai
Quiubaco [NM] (H)
Quiuira see Quivira
Quiuirien see Quivira
Qui-ump-uts see Beaver
Quiumputs see Beaver
Quiuquuh see Cayuga
Quiutcanuaha [TX] Tonkawan
  (BE)
Quiva see Cuiva
Quivera see Quivira
Quivi [TX] Coahuiltecan (BE)
Quivica see Quivira
Quivina see Quivira
Quivira Wichita (H)
Quivirae see Quivira
Quivirans see Quivira
Quivirenses see Quivira
Quivix see Keres
Quixo see Quijo
Quiyougcohanock see Quiouco-
  hanock

Quiyoughcohanock see
  Quioucohanock
Quiyoughqnohanock see
  Quioucohanock
Quize see Kichai
Qujane see Kohani
Qumault see Quinault
Qumie'qen see Comiakin
Qumieqen see Comiakin
qumiutarmiut [Can] [Inuit (Que-
  bec)] (Hdbk5)
Qundj-alan see Khundjalan
Qundjalan see Khundjalan
Qune'tcin see Kunechin
Qunetcin see Kunechin
Qunkmamish see Kwehtlmamish
Qunnipiuck see Quinnipiac
Qunnubbagge see Quinebaug
Quntse see Khundtse
Quoan see Kohani
Quoboag see Quabaug
Quoboge see Quabaug
Quodadiquio see Kadohadacho
Quoddies see Passamaquoddy
Quoddy see Passamaquoddy
Quoddy see Passamaquoddy
Quoisilla see Goasila
Quoitesos see Quaitso
Quokim see Cawina
Quokim see Kohuana
Quo-kim see Cawina
Quonantino see Kanohatino
Quondiats see Ute
Quon-di-ats see Ute
Quonoatinno see Kanohatino
Quoqui see Coaque
Quoquoulth see Kwakiutl
Quoratean [Lang] [CA] (H)
Quor-ra-da-chor-koes see Kwa-
  hari
Quorradachorkoes see Kwahari
Quotoa see Kwotoa
Quouarra see Quarai
Quowaughkutt Choptank
  (Hdbk15)
Quppas see Quapaw
Quqoa'q see Kukoak
Quqoaq see Kukoak
Ququ'lek see Kukulek
Qusutas see Ute
Quts hit tan see Kutshittan
Qutshittan see Kutshittan
Quunnipieuck see Quinnipiac
Qu-wun-kqwut see
  Khoonkhwuttunne
Quwunkqwut see Khoonkhwut-
  tunne
Quya see Khuya
Quyegu jinga see Khuyeguzhinga
Quyegujinga see Khuyeguzhinga
Quyunikacinga see Husada
Qvinipiak see Quinnipiac
Qvivira see Quivira

Qwan-s'a-a-tun *see* Khosatunne
Qwansaatun *see* Khosatunne
Qwapas *see* Quapaw
Qweenylt *see* Quinault
Qwe'qu sot!e'noxu *see* Koek-
sotenok
Qwequ sotenoxu *see* Koek-
sotenok
Qwikties *see* Miami
Qwuc-tcu-micl-tun tunn'e *see*
Kaltsergheatunne
Qwuctcumicltuntunne *see* Kalt-
sergheatunne
Qwu'lh-hwai-pum *see* Klikitat
Qwulhhwaipum *see* Klikitat

-R-

Rabbit Assiniboin [Can] (H)
Rabbit Lake [MN] *Chippewa* (BE)
Rabbit Lake [MN] *Kitchisibi-
wininiwug* (H)
Rabbit Skins *see* Wabuswaianuk
Rabbitskins *see* Kawchottine
Rabbit Skins (PC) *see also* Rabbit-
skins (PC)
Rabbitskins (PC) *see also* Rabbit
Skins (PC)
Rabinal [Gua] *Achi* (O)
Raccoon *see* Mikaunikashinga
Raccoon Nation *see* Erie
Rackeaway *see* Rockaway
Racre *see* Arikara
Rafael, San (H) *see also* Jukiusme
(H)
Rafael, San [CA] (Contri, v.3,
p.195)
Ragged People *see*
Kutchakutchin
Ragu *see* Prouyana
Ragupuis *see* Bagiopa
Rahowacah *see* Monacan
Rainbow-house people *see* Taol-
naas-hadai
Rain Pueblo *see* Chettrokettle
Rainy Lake *see* Tecamamiouen
Rainy-Lake Indians *see* Kojejew-
ininewug
Rakouagega *see* Neutral Nation
Ralamari [Self-designation] *see*
Tarahumare
Ral-la-wat-set *see* Kalawatset
Rallawatset *see* Kalawatset
Rama [NI] *Voto* (BE)
Rama-Corobici *Chibchan* (BE)
Ramarama [Br] *Kawahib* (O)
Ramarama [Lang] [Br] (O)
Ramaya *see* Santa Ana [NM]
Ramaytush [Lang] [CA] *Northern
Costonoan* (CA-8)

Ramcocameca *see*
Ramkokamekra
Ramcock *see* Remkoke
Ramkokamekra [Br] *Canella* (O)
Ramkokes *see* Rancoca
Ramock *see* Rancoca
Rampart Indians *see* Trot-
sikkutchin
Rampart People *see* Tatsakutchin
Ranatshganha *see* Mahican
Rancheria Grande [TX] (H)
Rancheria of Alonso *Apache*
(Hdbk10)
Rancheria of Capitan Vigotes
Apaches (Hdbk10)
Rancheria of El Ligero *Apache*
(Hdbk10)
Rancheria of Pasqual *Apache*
(Hdbk10)
Ranchos [Pueblo] [NM] (H)
Rancoca [NJ, DE] (H)
Rancocus *see* Ancocus
Rancoka *see* Rancoca
Ranger-Piki *see* Prouyana
Rankoka *see* Rancoca
Rankokamekra *see*
Ramkokamekra
Ranquel *see* Ranqueles
Ranquelches *see* Ranqueles
Ranqueles [BO, CH] (LC)
Rapahanna *see* Rappahannock
Rapahanock *see* Rappahannock
Rapaho *see* Arapaho
Raparpuas *see* Tapouaro
Rapid Indians *see* Atsina
Rappahannock [VA] *Powhatan*
(LC)
Rappahannocke *see* Rappahan-
nock
Rappahanoc *see* Rappahannock
Rappaho *see* Arapaho
Raramuri *see* Tarahumara
Ra-ra-to-oan *see* Chippewa
Raratooan *see* Chippewa
Ra-ra-t'wan *see* Chippewa
Raratwan *see* Chippewa
Raretangh *see* Raritan
Raritan DO NOT *see* Raritanoo
Raritan [NJ] *Unami* (BE)
Raritang *see* Raritan
Raritanoo (Hdbk15)
Raritanus *see* Raritan
Rarondak *see* Adirondack
Rasaoua koueton *see* Nassauake-
ton
Rasaouakoueton *see* Nassauake-
ton
Rascal Indians *see* Tututni
Rasoughteick *Choptank* (Hdbk15)
Rathroche [Subgens] *Pakhtha* (H)
Rat Indians *see* Takkuth-kutchin
Rat Indians *see* Tukkuthkutchin
Rat Indians *see* Vuntakutchin

Ratiruntak *see* Adirondack
Rat People *see* Vuntakutchin
Rat River Indians *see* Takkuth-
kutchin
Rat River Indians *see*
Tukkuthkutchin
Rattling Moccasin Band [MN]
Mdewakanton (BE)
Rat Tribe *see* Kake
Raudauqua-quank *see* Bear River
Raudauquaquank *see* Bear River
Ravin Indians *see* Crow
Rawekhangye [Subgens] *Iowa* (H)
Raweyine [Subgens] *Iowa* (H)
Rawrenoc *see* Roanoak
Rayado *see* Jumano
Raymneecha *see* Khemnichan
Rayouse *see* Cayuse
Rchaketan [Clan] [AK] *Tlingit*
(H)
Rchauutass-hade [BC] *Haida* (H)
Rchuch-e'di *see* Hokedi
Rchuchedi *see* Hokedi
Real Ponka [Subclan] *Ponca* (H)
Rea Ratacks *see* Klikitat
Rearatakcs *see* Klikitat
Reatkin *see* Yadkin
Reaum's Village [MI] *Chippewa*
(H)
Recar *see* Arikara
Rechahecrian *see* Cherokee
Rechehecrian *see* Cherokee
Rechgawawanc *see* Manhattan
Rechgawawanc *see* Reck-
gawawanc
Rechgawawanck *see* Reck-
gawawanc
Rechgawawanck *see* Manhattan
Rechgawawank *see* Reck-
gawawanc
Rechgawawank *see* Reck-
gawawanc
Rechkawick *see* Manhattan
Rechkawick *see* Reckgawawanc
Rechkawyck *see* Manhattan
Rechkawyck *see* Rockaway
Rechkewick *see* Rockaway
Rechkewick *see* Manhattan
Rechkewick *see* Reckgawawanc
Rechouwhacky *see* Rockaway
Rechowacky *see* Rockaway
Rechqua Akie *see* Rockaway
Rechquaakie *see* Rockaway
Reckawanck *see* Manhattan
Reckawanck *see* Manhattan
Reckawawanc *see* Manhattan
Reckawawanc *see* Reckgawawanc
Reckewacke *see* Manhattan
Reckewacke *see* Reckgawawanc
Reckgawawanc (BE) *see also* Man-
hattan (LC)
Reckgawawanc [NY] *Unami* (BE)
Reckkeweck *see* Rockaway

Reckkouwhacky *see* Rockaway
Reckomacki *see* Rockaway
Reckonhacky *see* Rockaway
Reckowacky *see* Rockaway
Recuyeene *see* Rucuyen
Recuyenne *see* Urukuyana
Redais *see* Bidai
Red Ants *see* Vultures
Red-Butt *see* Hu'deca'bin
Red butte dwellers *see* Atsaku-doka tuviwarai
Red Cedar Lake [WI, MI] *Chippewa* (H)
Red Cliff [MI, WI, ND, SD] *Chippewa* (H)
Red Crayfish *see* Chakchiuma
Red Eagle *see* Tsishuwashtake
Red Earth People *see* Fox
red-eye people *see* Churan
Red Indians *see* Beothuk
Red Indians of Newfoundland *see* Beothuk
Red Iron Band [MN] *Sisseton* (H)
Red-Knife Indians *see* Tatsanottine
Red Knives *see* Tatsanottine
Red Leg's Band [MN] *Wahpekute* (BE)
Red-lips *see* Ihasha
Red Lobsters *see* Chakchiuma
Red Lodge [SD] *Oglala* (H)
Red Mouths *Crow* (H)
Red Paint People *see* Eastern Chiricahua
Red Paint People *see* Warm Springs Apache
Red People *see* Suwuki Ohimal
Red Peoples *see* Vultures
Red River Assiniboin (H)
Red River Chippewa [MN] (H)
Red Shield *see* Mahohivas
Red Shield *see* Kichai
Red Sticks *see* Mikasuki
Red Sticks *Creek* (H)
Red Sticks *Seminole* (H)
red-stream people *see* Cedar
Red Tipi *see* Mahoyum
Red water band *see* Itazipcho
Red Water Band *see* Minisha
Red-willow Indians *see* Taos
Red-willow place *see* Taos
Red Wing's *see* Khemnichan
Redwood (BE) *see also* Huchnom (CA)
Redwood *Dakota* (BE)
Redwood Indians (BE) *see also* Whilkut (CA)
Redwoods (H) *see also* Huchnom (CA)
Ree (LC) *see also* Arikara (LC)
Ree [SD] *Northern Cheyenne* (BE)
Reese River Indians *see* Nahaego
Regis, St. [Q, NY] *Mohawk* (LC)

Re-Ho *see* Reho
Reho [CA] *Patwin* (Contri, p.218)
Reiners *see* Fox
Re-ka-ra *see* Arikara
Rekara *see* Arikara
Re-ke-rah *see* Arikara
Rekerah *see* Arikara
Remahenoc *see* Haverstraw
Reminica Band *see* Khemnichan
Remkoke (H) *see also* Rancoca (H)
Remkoke *Delaware* (Hdbk15)
Remnichah *see* Khemnichan
Remo [Br, PE] (O)
Renapi *see* Delaware
Renapoak [NC] (H)
Renards *see* Fox
Renarhonon *see* Arendahronon
Renars *see* Fox
Renarz *see* Fox
Rencour *see* Fox
Renecuey *see* Senecu
Re-nis-te-nos *see* Cree
Renistenos *see* Cree
Renni Renape *see* Delaware
Renni Renape *see* Leni Lenape
Republic *see* Kitkehahki
Republican Pawnee *see* Kitke-hahki
Republick *see* Kitkehahki
Republiques *see* Kitkehahki
Resigaro *see* Resigero
Resigero [Col, PE] (LC)
Resiggaro *see* Resigero
Resiguaro *see* Resigero
Ressigaro *see* Resigero
Restigouche [Can] *Sigunikt Mic-mac* (BE)
Rewechnongh *see* Haverstraw
Reweghnome *see* Haverstraw
Reweghnonck *see* Manhattan
Reweghnongh *see* Haverstraw
Reyata Band *Santee* (H)
Reyataotonwe *see* Kheyatao-tonwe
Reyesano [Bo] (O)
Reynards *see* Fox
Reyre [HA, WInd] *Caizcimu* (BE)
Rhaap [BC] *Ntlakyapamuk* (H)
Rhaap [BC] *Upper Thompsons* (H)
Rhagenratka *see* Neutral Nation
Rhea *see* Arikara
Rheno *see* Remo
Rhett Lake *see* Tule Lake
Rhiierrhonon *see* Erie
Rhoanoke *see* Roanoak
Ri *see* Arikara
Riana *see* Kiowa
Ricapou *see* Kickapoo
Ricar *see* Arikara
Ric-ara *see* Arikara
Ricara *see* Arikara
Ricaree *see* Arikara

Ricari *see* Arikara
Ricarie *see* Arikara
Riccaree *see* Arikara
Riccarree *see* Arikara
Rice-gathering-place people *see* Powahe'kune
Rice Indians *see* Menominee
Rice Lake [WI, MI] *Chippewa* (BE)
Richara *see* Arikara
Rich Prairie Dog Indians *see* Achepabecha
Rickapoo *see* Kickapoo
Rickara *see* Arikara
Rickaree *see* Arikara
Rickeree *see* Arikara
Rickohockan *see* Yuchi
Rickohockans *see* Cherokee
Rickree *see* Arikara
Ricora *see* Arikara
Ri-ga-ta-a-ta-wa *see* Kheyatao-tonwe
Rigataatawa *see* Kheytaotonwe
Rigneronnon *see* Erie
Rigué *see* Erie
Rigueronnon *see* Erie
Rihit *see* Ponca
Rikara *see* Arikara
Rikbaktsa [Lang] [Br] (LC)
Rikkara *see* Arikara
Rikpakca *see* Aripaktsa
Rikpaktsa *see* Rikbaktsa
Rimachu *see* Mayna
Rionegrino [VE] *Yukpa* (O)
Riparian Peoples (AI)
Riquehronnon *see* Erie
Rising Sun Men *see* Etheneldeli
Riske Creek Band [BC] *Canyon Shuswap* (Hdbk12)
Rito [Pueblo] [NM] *Laguna* (H)
Ritwan [CA] (BE)
River Campa *see* Ashinanca
River Cree *see* Sipiwininiwug
River Crow (H)
River Crow (H) *see also* Mineset-peri (H)
River Desert (BE) *see also* Mani-waki (BE)
River Desert *Algonquian* (H)
River du Lievre [Q] *Algonquian* (IndN, v.6, no.3, July 1929, pp.225+)
River Indians (BE) *see also* Mahi-can (LC)
River Indians (BE) *see also* Mohe-gan (BE)
River Indians (H)
River Mouth people *see* Kip-isa'kia Wini'wiwuk
River Nisinan *Riverine* (JCB, v.1, pp.8–9)
River Nomlaki [Lang] [CA] (CA-8)

River Patwin [Lang] [CA] (BE)
River People *see* Cipi-winiuuk
River People *see* Sipiwininiwug
river people *see* Kuungmiut
River Pomo [Lang] (Pub, v.6, no.1, pp.235-239)
River that Flies *Miniconjou* (H)
River Wintun *Riverine* (JCBf, v.1, pp.8-9)
River Yuman [Lang] (Hdbk10)
Rivière aux Feuilles [Can] [*Inuit (Labrador)*] (Hdbk5)
Road Indians *see* Ninnipaskulgee
Roakaway *see* Rockaway
Roamaina *see* Omurano
Roanoak [NC, VA] (H)
Roanoke *see* Roanoak
Roasters *see* Dakota
Robber Indians *see* Bannock
Robbers *see* Pillagers
Robeson County Indians (BE)
Robes with Hair on the outside *see* Isisokasimiks
Rocameca [ME] *Abnaki* (BE)
Roccamecco *see* Rocameca
Ro'c'hilit *see* Eskimos
Rochilit *see* Eskimos
Rockamagug *see* Rocameca
Rockamecook *see* Rocameca
Rockaway [NY] *Montauk* (BE)
Rock Creek [OR] (Ye)
Rockeway *see* Rockaway
Rock Indians *see* Kumbatuash
Rock Mountain Indian *see* Nahane
Rock People *see* In'yanton'wanbin
Rock People *see* Arendahronon
Rock-people *see* Hanahawinena
Rocks *see* Jatonabine
Rockway *see* Rockaway
Rocky Mountain Indians *see* Sekani
Rocky Mountain People *see* Etagottine
Rocomeco *see* Rocameca
Rocouyenne *see* Oyani
Rodela [Br] (O)
Rodinunchsiouni *see* Iroquois
Roeamasa [Col] *Macuna* (O)
Roger's River *see* Tututni
Rogue Indians *see* Tututni
Rogue River *see* Takelma
Rogue River (H) *see also* Shasta (CA)
Rogue River (H) *see also* Tututni (LC)
Rogue River [Lang] [CA] *Oregon* (He)
Rogues *see* Pillagers
Rogue's River *see* Tututni
Roil-roil-pam *see* Klikitat
Roilroilpam *see* Klikitat

Roinsac *see* Kaskaskia
Rokorona *see* Poakaanova
Romaine *see* Musquaro
Romanan *see* Romonan
Ro-mo-nan *see* Romonan
Romonan [CA] *Costanoan* (H)
Ronaninhohonti *see* Seneca
Ronaok *see* Roanoak
Ronatewisichroone [GL] (H)
Rondax *see* Adirondack
Rondaxe *see* Adirondack
Ronhugati [Br] *Eastern Timbira* (O)
Ronoke *see* Roanoak
Root Diggers *see* Ditsakana
Root-Diggers *see* Shoshone
Root Eaters *see* Ditsakana
Root Eaters *see* Shoshoko
Root-Eaters *see* Yambadika
Roquai *see* Noquet
Rosa de Santa Maria, Santa *see* Pachera
Rosa Indians, Santa *see* Chumash
Rosa Island, Santa [Lang] [CA] *Chumashan* (H)
Rosalia di Mulege, S. *see* Santa Rosalia Mulege
Rosalia Mulege, Santa (H)
Rosebud Sioux (Char, v.1)
Rosino, Santa *see* Canelo
Rosino, Santa *see* Quijo
Roskeemo *see* Koskimo
Rouameuo *see* Rocameca
Roucouyene [Lang] *Eastern Carib* (UAz, v.28)
Roucouyenne (LC) *see also* Oyana (LC)
Roucouyenne (LC) *see also* Rucuyen (O)
Roucouyenne (O) *see also* Guayana (LC)
Roucouyenne (O) *see also* Urukuyana (O)
Rouinsac *see* Kaskaskia
Round Heads *see* Tetes de Boule
Round Town People *see* Yuchi
Roving Dakotas *see* Gens du Large
Rowanan *see* Romonan
Rowanoke *see* Roanoak
Rsarsavina *see* Sobaipuri
Rua *see* Tigua
Rucana *see* Rucuyen
Rucana *see* Urukuyana
Rucana *see* Guyana
Ruche [Clan] *Iowa* (H)
Rucouyenne *see* Oyana
Rucuyen (O) *see also* Guayana (LC)
Rucuyen (O) *see also* Urukuyana (O)
Rucuyen [FrG] (O)
Rukhcha [Clan] *Oto* (H)

Rukuyenne *see* Oyana
Rukuyenne *see* Rucuyen
Ruma [EC] *Secoya* (O)
Rumachenanck *see* Haverstraw
Rumo *see* Ruma
Rumsen [CA] (H)
Rumsen [Lang] [CA] *Northern Costonoan* (CA-8)
Rumsenes *see* Rumsen
Rumsien *see* Rumsen
Runaways *see* Seminole
Runcienes *see* Rumsen
Runica *see* Tunica
Runsenes *see* Rumsen
Runsienes *see* Rumsen
Rupert House [Can] [*Montagnais-Naskapi*] (BE)
Ruslen *see* Rumsen
Russian Mission (Hdbk5)
Russian River [CA] *Pomo* (Pub, v.6, no.1, pp.213-24)
Ru-tce *see* Ruche
Rutce *see* Ruche
Ru-ya-pa *see* Tintaotonwe
Ruyapa *see* Tintaotonwe
Ryawa *see* Kiowa
Ryuwa *see* Kiowa

-S-

S. *see* Saint
Sa [Clan] [NM] *Pueblo Indians* (H)
Saa-Kaalituck *see* Saukaulutuchs
Saakaalituck *see* Saukaulutuchs
Saakiees *see* Sauk
Sa-akl *see* Yaquina
Saakl *see* Yaquina
Saalis *see* Salish
Saaman *see* Saame
Saamen [Can] *Puntlatsh* (BE)
Saanitch *see* Sanetch
Sa aptin *see* Nez Perce
Saaptin *see* Nez Perce
Sa arcez *see* Sarsi
Saarcez *see* Sarsi
Sa-arcix *see* Sarsi
Saarcix *see* Sarsi
Saaskies *see* Sauk
Saasskies *see* Sauk
Sababiruna *see* Sanavirona
Sababish *see* Samamish
Sabaguana *see* Akanaquint
Sabaibo *Acapee* (BE)
Sabane [Br] *Nambicuara* (O)
Sabaneque [Cu] (BE)
Sabanero *see* Guaymi
Sabanoes *see* Shawnee
Sabassa [BC] (H)
Sabatini [BO] *Araona* (O)

sa-be *see* Apache
sa-be *see* Navajo
sabe *see* Apache
sabe *see* Navajo
Sabela [Lang] (LC)
Sabenaki *see* Abnaki
Sable [MI] *Ottawa* (BE)
Sablez *see* Sable
Sabone *see* Sabane
Sabril *see* Japreria
Sabrile *see* Japreria
Sabuagana *see* Akanaquint
Sabuagana Gutas *see* Akanaquint
Sac *see* Sauk
Sacahaye [LA] (H)
Sacalanes *see* Saclan
Sacapultec *see* Sacapulteco
Sacapulteco [Gua] (O)
Sacayo *Conoy* (Hdbk15)
Saccha *see* Colorado [SA]
Sacha,wan,ooes *see* Shawnee
Sachal [WA] (H)
Sachap *see* Satsop
Sachdagugh-roonaw *see*
   Powhatan
Sachdagughs *see* Powhatan
Sa-cher-i-ton *see* Sacheriton
Sacheriton [OR] *Skoton* (H)
Sachet *see* Skagit
Sachi *see* Sauk
Sachia *Conoy* (Hdbk15)
Sachimers *see* Sakumehu
Sa-chin-ko *see* Tait
Sackanoir *see* Luckiamute
Sackaweethinyoowuc *see* Sakaw-
   ithiniwuk
Sacket *see* Skagit
Sacks *see* Sauk
Sacky *see* Sauk
Saclan [CA] (LC)
Saclan [Lang] *Eastern Miwokan*
   (CA-8)
Sac-me-ugh *see* Sakumehu
Sacmeugh *see* Sakumehu
Saconet *see* Sakonnet
Saconnet *see* Sakonnet
Sacramanteno *see* Mescalero
   Apache
Sacramento Apaches *see*
   Mescalero Apache
Sacramento Valley [CA] *Pomo*
   (Pub, v.6, no.1, p.124)
Sacred Head *see* Ponca
Sacs *see* Sauk
Sacuache *Coahuiltecan* (Hdbk10)
Saczo *see* Cenizo
Sadalsomte-k'iago *see* Kiowa
   Apache
Sadalsomtekiago *see* Kiowa
   Apache
Sadammo *Apache* (H)
Sadamon *see* Sadammo
Saddal *see* Skaddal

Sadedndesu *see* Nambicuara
Sadi *see* Seri
Sadjugahl-lanas [BC] *Gituns* (H)
Sadjugahl-lanas [Subclan] *Haida*
   (H)
Sadujames *see* Sadammo
Saeamo *see* Itonama
Saelis *see* Chehalis
Sae-lis *see* Salish
Saelis *see* Salish
Saelo *see* Tepehuan
Sa-essau-dinneh *see* Etheneldeli
Saessaudinneh *see* Etheneldeli
Saesse *Coahuiltecan* (Hdbk10)
Sagahiganirini *see* Sagaiguninini
Sagaiganinini *see* Sagaiguninini
Sagaiguninini [Ont] *Algonkin*
   (BE)
Sag-a-na-ga *see* Delaware
Saganaga *see* Delaware
Sagangusili [Subclan] [BC] *Haida*
   (H)
Sagasey *see* Sauk
Sagayayumnes *see* Sakaikumne
Sagdlirmiut [Can] *Central
   Eskimos* (BE)
Sage-nom-nas *see* Sagenomnas
Sagenomnas [CA] (H)
Sage-nom-nis *see* Sagenomnas
Sagenomnis *see* Sagenomnas
Sagetaen-ne *see* Chiricahua
   Apache
Sagetaenne *see* Chiricahua
   Apache
Sage Wenenewak *see* Sagewene-
   newak
Sagewenenewak *Man* (H)
Sagi [Clan] *Yuchi* (H)
Saginaw [MI] *Chippewa* (H)
Sagi taha *see* Sagi
Sagitaha *see* Sagi
Sagitawawininiwag *see*
   Sagewenenewak
Sagiwa *see* Sauk
Sagkonate *see* Saconnet
Sagnitaouigama [Ont] *Algonkin*
   (H)
Sagosanagechteron *see* Onondaga
Sagua [Cu] (BE)
Saguaguana *see* Akanaquint
Sa'gua la'nas *see* Sagua-lanas
Sagualanas *see* Sagua-lanas
Sagua-lanas [Subclan] *Haida* (H)
Saguanos *see* Shawnee
Saguenay [Q] *Naskapi* (H)
Sagui gitana-i *see* Sagui-gituanai
Saguigitanai *see* Sagui-gitunai
Sagui-gitunai [Subclan] *Haida*
   (H)
Saguikun-lnagai [Subclan] *Haida*
   (H)
Saguimaniguara [MX] (Hdbk10)
Saguna *see* Laguna

Sahagi *see* Dakota
Sahagungusili *see* Sagangusili
Sahaidagai *see* Sa-haidagai
Sa-haidagai *Kunalanas* (H)
Sahajugwan alth Lennas *see*
   Sadjugahl-lanas
Saha'ntla *see* Siksika
Sahantla *see* Siksika
Sahapotin *see* Nez Perce
Sahaptain *see* Nez Perce
Sahaptan *see* Nez Perce
Sahaptanian *see* Nez Perce
Sahaptin *see* Nez Perce
Sahaptin *see* Shahaptian
Sahaptini *see* Nez Perce
Sahatpu [ID] *Nez Perce* (BE)
Sahawahmish *see* Sahehwamish
sa-he *see* Cree
sahe *see* Cree
Sa-heh-wamish *see* Sahehwamish
Sahehwamish [WA] *Nisqually* (BE)
Sahe'wabsch *see* Sahehwamish
Sahewabsch *see* Shehwamish
Sahe'wabsh *see* Sahehwamish
Sahewabsh *see* Sahehwamish
Sah-halah *see* Shahala
Sahhalah *see* Shahala
Sah haptinnay *see* Nez Perce
Sahhaptinnay *see* Nez Perce
Sahhihwish *see* Sahehwamish
Sa-hi-ye-na *see* Cheyenne
Sahiyena *see* Cheyenne
Sah-ku-mehu *see* Sakumehu
Sahkumehu *see* Sakumehu
Sahmamish *see* Samamish
Sahohes *see* Saone
Sa-hone *see* Saone
Sah-o-ne *see* Saone
Sahone *see* Saone
Sah-o-ne-hont-a-par-par *see*
   Saone [Hunkpapa]
Sahonehontaparpar *see* Saone
   [Hunkpapa]
Sahonies *see* Saone
Sah-own *see* Sangona
Sahown *see* Sangona
Sah-se-sah tinney *see* Etheneldeli
Sahsesahtinney *see* Etheneldeli
Saht-lil-kwu *see* Sahtlilkwu
Sahuaripa *see* Jova
Sah-wah-mish *see* Sawamish
Sahwahmish *see* Sawamish
Sah-wau-noo *see* Shawnee
Sahwaunoo *see* Shawnee
Saia (BE) *see also* Nongatl (CA)
Saia [CA] *Hupa* (H)
Sai-a-kwa *see* Sia
Saiakwa *see* Sia
Sai-az (H) *see also* Saia (H)
Saiaz *see* Saia
Saiaz *see* Sai-az
Sai-az [CA] (Contri, v.3, pp.122–
   24)

Saich-kioie-tach see Lekwiltok
Saichkioietach see Lekwiltok
Saich-kwil-tach see Lekwiltok
Saichkwiltach see Lekwiltok
Saidinde *Jicarilla Apache*
 (Hdbk10)
Saidoka see Modoc
Saidokado see Saiduka
Saiduka (H) *see also* Nez Perce
 (LC)
Saiduka (Hdbk11)
Saiduka'a see Modoc
Saidukadu see Saiduka
Saie'kuun see Cree
Saiekuun see Cree
saikihne see Maricopa
saikihne see Pima
Saikine see Maricopa
Saikine see Pima
Saikinne see Papago
Saiksaikinpu [ID] *Nez Perce* (BE)
Sai-letc see Siletz
Sailetc see Siletz
Sai-letc-ic-me-tunne see Siletz
Sailetcicmetunne see Siletz
Sailksun see Sailupsun
Sail-up-sun see Sailupsun
Sailupsun [BC] *Salish* (H)
Sainct Iean see Etarita
Sainipame [MX] *Coahualtecan*
 (Hdbk10)
Sainoscos see Sarnosas
Sainoscos [MX] *Tamaulipec* (BE)
Sainstkla see Siuslaw
Sainstskla see Yakonan
Saintctiean see Etarita
Saintiean see Etarita
Sai-o-kwa see Sia
Saiokwa see Sia
Saiopines see Tiopanes
Sa-i-sa-'dtinne see Etheneldeli
Saisadtinne see Etheneldeli
Saitinda [NM] *Jicarilla Apache*
 (BE)
Sait-inde see Saitinde
Saituka (H) *see also* Shahaptian
 (LC)
Saituka [OR, ID] (H)
Saiustkla see Siuslaw
Saiustla see Siuslaw
Sai-wash see Shasta
Saiwash see Shasta
Sai-yiks see Saiyiks
Saiyiks [MN] *Siksika* (BE)
Sai-yu-sla-me tunne see Siuslaw
Saiyuslametunne see Siuslaw
Sai-yus-t'cu-me tunne see Sius-
 law
Saiyustcumetunne see Siuslaw
Sa-jiu Uing-ge see Sajiuwingge
Sajiuuingge see Sajiuwingge
Sajiuwingge [Pueblo] [NM] (H)
Saka *Patwin* (Pub, v.29, no.4)

Sakacawone see Secacawoni
Sakahiganiriouek see Sagai-
 guninini
Sakahl [BC] *Cowichan* (H)
Sakaikumne [CA] *Miwok* (H)
Sakanma [ID] *Nez Perce* (BE)
Sakawininiwug [Can] *Cree* (BE)
Sakawinouuk see Saka-winouuk
Saka-winouuk [Can] *Paskwaw-
 ininiwug* (BE)
Sakawis see Sauk
Sakawithiniwuk *Cree* (H)
Sakawiyiniwok see Sakawithini-
 wuk
Sakbwatsuk [Can] *Paskwawinini-
 wug* (BE)
Sakes see Sauk
Saketupiks see Siksika
S'a-ke-w'e see Sauk
Sakewes see Sauk
Sakewi see Sauk
Sa-ke-yu see Sakeyu
Sakeyu [Pueblo] [NM] (H)
Sak'hutka see Abihka
Sakhutka see Abihka
Saki see Sauk
Sakikegawai see Saki-kegawai
Saki-kegawai [Subclan] *Haida*
 (H)
Sa-ki-na-nk see Sauk
Sa'ki qe'gawa-i see Saki-kegawai
Sakiqegawai see Saki-kegawai
Sakittawawininiwug [Can]
 Sakawininiwuk (BE)
Sakittawawithiniwuk *Sakawithini-
 wuk* (H)
Sa-ki-waki see Sauk
Sa-kiyá see Sauk
Sá-ki-ya see Sauk
Sá-kiyah see Sauk
Sa-ki-yu see Sauk
Sakiyu see Sauk
Saklan see Saclan
Sakonnet [RI] *Wampanoag* (LC)
Sak o'ta see Cheyenne
Saks see Sauk
Sak-si-nah-mah-yiks see Saksi-
 nahmahyiks
Saksinahmahyiks [MN, Can]
 Kainah (BE)
Saktabsh [WA] *Suquamish* (BE)
Saktci homma see Houma
Saktcihomma see Houma
Sakuma [AZ, CA] (H)
Sa-ku-me-hu see Sakumehu
Sakumehu [WA] *Salish* (H)
Sakutenedi *Kake* (H)
Sakutenedi [Subclan] [AK] *Tlingit*
 (H)
Sakuya see Remo
Sakwiabsh see Sakwi'absh
Sakwi'absh [WA] *Nisqualli* (Ore-
 gon)

Saky see Sauk
Sa-la-bi see Salabi
Salabi [Clan] *Hopi* (H)
Salab wiñwu see Salabi
Sa-lab wuñ-wu see Salabi
sa'ladebc see Sinkiuse-Columbia
saladebc see Sinkiuse-Columbia
Salamai see Monde
Salan [CA] *Mono* (H)
Salapaque [TX] *Coahuiltecan*
 (BE)
Salaphueme see Saulapaguem
Salasca [EC] (O)
Salem Indians see Manta [NJ]
Salendas [Subclan] *Haida* (H)
S'ale'ndas sa-t see Northern
 Paiute
Saliba see Saliva
Salic see Ntlakyapamuk
Sa-lic see Ntlakyapamuk
Sa'lic see Thompson Indians
Salinan [CA] (LC)
Salinan [Lang] [CA] (H)
Salinas [TX] (BE)
Saline Apaches see Mescalero
 Apache
Salineros [MX] *Seri* (BE)
Salineta *Piro* (H)
Salineta *Tigua* (H)
Salish [ID, MN] (LC)
Salishan [Lang] (LC)
Salishan Indians see Salish
Salish Coastal see Coast Salish
Saliua see Saliva
Saliutla see Siuslaw
Saliva [VE, Col] (LC)
Sallenche see Dalinchi
Sallirmiut [AK] *Central Eskimos*
 (Hdbk5)
Sallirmiut [AK] *Iglulingmiut*
 (Hdbk5)
Sallumiut (Ye) *see also* Baffin Is-
 land (Ye)
sallumiut [Can] [*Inuit (Quebec)*]
 (Hdbk5)
Salmeros see Salineros
Salmon River Indians [OR]
 Tillamook (BE)
Salmon River Snakes see
 Tukuarika
Salonde see Saluma
Salsen see Salsona
Salses see Salsona
Salsona [CA] (H)
Salsxuyilp see Colville
Salt Chuck (H)
Salteaux see Saulteaux
Salteaux see Chippewa
Salteur see Chippewa
Salt Lake Diggers see Hohandika
Salt People see Oktchunualgi
Salt Pomo [CA] *Pomo* (BE)
Salt River Pima (Char, v.4)

Salt-water band *see* Lower
  Chehalis
Saltwater band *see* Lower
  Chehalis
Saluda [SC] (BE)
Saluma [Br] (LC)
Saluma [Lang] *Chikena* (UAz,
  v.28)
Salvador, San [ES] *Pokomam* (BE)
Salwepu [ID] *Nez Perce* (BE)
Salzon *see* Salsona
Sam-ab-mish *see* Samamish
Samabmish *see* Samamish
Samackman *see* Samahquam
Samacoalapem [Coahuiltecan]
  (Hdbk10)
Sam-ahmish *see* Samamish
Samahmish *see* Samamish
Samahquam [BC] *Douglas Tribe*
  (Hdbk12)
Samahquam [BC] *Salish* (H)
Samamhoo *see* Semiahmoo
Samampac *Coahuiltecan* (BE)
Samena *see* Thompson Indians
Sa-milk-a-niugh *see* Nicola
Sa-milk-a-nuigh *see* Similka-
  meen
Samilkanuigh *see* Similkameen
Samipoa *see* Sanipao
Samish [WA] (LC)
Sam-na'i *see* Picuris
Samnai *see* Picuris
samnan *see* Picuris
Samococis *see* Moro
Samoupavi *see* Shonogpovi
Sampanal [TX] *Coahuiltecan* (BE)
Samparicka *see* Ditsakana
Sampeetches *see* Sanpits
Sampiche *see* Sanpits
Sampichya *see* Sanpits
Sampit *see* Sanpits
Sampits [UT] (BE)
sampi-viwants *see* Sanpits
Sampuches *see* Sanpits
Samtsh *see* Sanetch
Samucan *see* Zamucoan Indians
Samuco *see* Zamucoan Indians
Samuku *see* Zamuco
Sana [TX] (BE)
Sanakhanskoe *see* Sanyakoan
Sanakiwa *see* Choctaw
Sa'nak-oan *see* Sanyakoan
Sanakoan *see* Sanyakoan
Sanamaika *see* Monde
Sanamiguara *see* Coyoquipiguara
Sanapana [Par] (O)
Sanaque *Coahuiltecan* (Hdbk10)
Sanaviron *see* Sanavirona
Sanavirona [Arg] (LC)
Sancican *see* Sankhikan
San-da-to-ton *see* Sandatoton
Sandatoton [AZ] *Chiricahua
  Apache* (H)

Sandea *see* Sandia
Sandedotan *see* Sandatoton
Sand-hill people *see* Neomaita-
  neo
Sandia [NM] *Tigua* (BE)
San-Diaz *see* Sandia
Sandiaz *see* Sandia
Sandilla *see* Sandia
Sand Papago (Hdbk10) *see also*
  Hiac'ed O'odham adai
  (Hdbk10)
Sand Papago [CA] (H)
Sand People *see* Saitinde
Sand People *see* Saidinde
Sandpipers *see* Kialdagwuns
Sandusky Senecas *see* Mingo
Sandy Hill [Ont] (H)
Saneca *see* Senecu del Sur
Sanema *see* Sanuma
Sanema-Yanoama *see* Yanoama
Sanetch [VanI] *Salish* (BE)
Sangican *see* Sankhikan
Sangiesta *see* Saugiesta
Sangireni [PE] *Campa* (O)
Sangona [SD] *Hunkpatina* (H)
Sanha *see* Sanka
Sanha [Lang] *see* Damana [Lang]
Sanhican *see* Sankhikan
Sanich *see* Sanetch
Sanima *see* Sanuma
Sa-ni-pa-o *see* Sanipao
Sanipao [TX] *Coahuiltecan* (BE)
Sanish *see* Arikara
Sa-nish *see* Arikara
Sani'ti'ka *see* Arapaho
Sanitika *see* Arapaho
Sanja *see* Malayo
Sanja [Lang] *see* Damana [Lang]
Sanka (BE) *see also* Comanche
  (LC)
San'ka *see* Kutenai
Sanka *see* Kutenai
Sanka [Col] (O)
Sanka [Lang] *see* Damana [Lang]
Sankaskitons *see* Sisseton
Sankawee *see* Tsankawi
Sankewi *see* Sauk
Sankhicani *see* Mohawk
Sankhikan *Delaware* (Hdbk15)
Sankikan *see* Sankhikan
Sankikani *see* Sankhikan
Sanko *see* Comanche
Sanks *see* Sauk
Sannager *see* Seneca
Sanoma *see* Sanuma
San-ona *see* Sangona
Sanona *see* Sangona
Sanonawantowane *see* Cayuga
Sanoni-Hunkpapa *see* Saone
  [Hunkpapa]
Sanoniwicasa *see* Saone
Sanpanal *see* Sampanal
Sanpanale *see* Sampanal

Sanpet (BE) *see also* Sampits (BE)
Sanpet [UT] *Ute* (H)
San-Petes *see* Sanpits
Sanpetes *see* Sanpits
Sanpiche Utah *see* Sanpits
Sanpit *see* Sanpits
Sanpitc *see* Sanpits
San Pitch *see* Sanpits
Sanpitch *see* Sanpits
San Pitches *see* Sanpits
Sanpitches *see* Sanpits
San Poel *see* Sanpoil
Sanpoel *see* Sanpoil
Sanpoil [Lang] [WA] (Oregon)
Sanpoil [WA] (LC)
Sanpoil [WA] (LC)
Sansarcs *see* Sans Arcs
Sans Arcs [SD] *Teton* (LC)
Sansarcs Dakota *see* Sans Arcs
San *see* Saint
Sanshkia-a-runu *see* Miami
Sanspoële *see* Sanpoil
Sans Puelles *see* Sanpoil
Sanspuelles *see* Sanpoil
Santacrucino (O)
Santacrucino (O) *see also* Aguano
  (O)
Santaim *see* Santiam
Santainas *see* Santiam
Santana *see* Santa Ana [NM]
Santana *see* Shawnee
Santas *see* Santee
Santa *see* Saint
Santeaux *see* Chippewa
Santee [Lang] *Catawba* (H)
Santee [SC] *Dakota* (LC)
Santena *see* Chippewa
Santeurs *see* Chippewa
Santiago (H) *see also* Pecos (BE)
Santiago del Espero *see* Quechua
Santiagueños *Bocas Prietas*
  (Hdbk10)
Santiam [OR] (BE)
Santian *see* Santiam
Santie *see* Santee
Santo *see* Tonto Apache
Santo *see also* Saint
San-to-tin *see* Santotin
Santotin [AK] *Nabesna* (BE)
Sant *see* Saint
Santse'pasu *see* Santsukhdhin
Santsepasu *see* Santsukhdhin
Santsukhdhi [MO] *Osage* (H)
Sanukh [Clan] *Tonkawa* (H)
Sanuma [VE, Br] (O)
Sanux *see* Sanukh
San-wap-pum *see* Shanwappon
Sanya [AK] *Tlingit* (BE)
S!a'nya koan *see* Sanyakoan
Sanyakoan [AK] *Tlingit* (H)
Sanyakwan *see* Sanyakoan
Sanyaqwon *see* Sanyakoan
Sanze-Ougrin *see* Santsukhdhin

Saone (H) *see also* Sangona (H)
Saone *Hunkpapa* (H)
Saone *Teton* (H)
Saopi *see* Farmers Band
Saoustla *see* Siuslaw
Saoux *see* Dakota
Saoyn *see* Cheyenne
Saoynes *see* Saone
Sa-pani *see* Atsina
Sapani *see* Atsina
Sapara [Lang] *Makusi* (UAz, v.28)
Sapa wicasa *see* Ute
Sapawicasa *see* Ute
Sapa wichasha *see* Ute
Sapawichasha *see* Ute
Sape *see* Kalina
Sapenys *see* Saponi
Sapes *see* Esopus
Sapetan *see* Nez Perce
Sapeten *see* Nez Perce
Sapiboca [Lang] [BO] *Tacanan*
  (O)
Sapiny *see* Saponi
Sapiteri *see* Sirineiri
Sapon *see* Saponi
Sapon *see* Tisepan
Sapona *see* Saponi
Saponees *see* Saponi
Sapones *see* Saponi
Saponeys *see* Saponi
Saponi [Lang] *Tutelo Confederacy*
  (H)
Saponi [VA] (BE)
Saponie *see* Saponi
Saponys *see* Saponi
Sapoonies *see* Saponi
Sapotan *see* Nez Perce
Sapototot *see* Lopotatimni
Sappona *see* Saponi
Sapponces *see* Saponi
Sapponees *see* Saponi
Sapponey *see* Saponi
Sapponi *see* Saponi
Sapponie *see* Saponi
Sappony *see* Saponi
Sapriria *see* Japreria
Saps *see* Saponi
Sap Suckers *see* Minesetperi
Sapsuckers *see* Minesetperi
Saptan *see* Nez Perce
Sap'tin *see* Nez Perce
Saptin *see* Nez Perce
Sapuquis [Par] *Sanapana* (O)
Sapuya [Br] (LC)
Sapwell *see* Sanpoil
Saqeootina *see* Sazeutina
Saqgui'gyit'inai *see* Sagui-gitunai
Saqguigyitinai *see* Sagui-gitunai
Saquaacha *see* Kwatami
Saquan *see* Seguan
Saquechuma *see* Chakchuima
Saquenets *see* Saguenay
Saques *see* Sauk

Saquis *see* Sauk
Saqute'nedi *see* Sakutenedi
Sara (H) *see also* Cheraw (LC)
Sara [BO] *Aroana* (O)
Saracuam [TX] *Coahuiltecan* (BE)
sarade *see* Zuni
Saraguro [EC] (O)
Sarai *see* Zuni
Sarame *see* Xarame
Saramo *see* Itonama
Saran *see* Zuni
Saranai *see* Sichomovi
Saranna *see* Shawnee
Sarannahs *see* Shawnee
Sarapinagh [MD] (H)
Sarapjon *Pamaque* (Hdbk10)
Sarare [Br] *Nambicuara* (O)
Sararpatin *see* Wanapam
Saratiguara [MX] (Hdbk10)
Saratoga [NY] *Mohawk* (H)
Sarau *see* Cheraw
Saraveca [BO, Br] (O)
Saraveka *see* Saraveca
Saraw *see* Cheraw
Sarawa *see* Cheraw
Saray *see* Zuni
Sarcee *see* Sarsi
Sarcess *see* Sarsi
Sarcix *see* Sarsi
Saretika *see* Arapaho
Saringue [Br] *Paiagua* (O)
Sariramiut [AK] *Tununirmiut*
  (Hdbk5)
Saritch-ka-e *see* Arapaho
Saritchkae *see* Arapaho
Sa-ritc-ka-e *see* Arapaho
Saritckae *see* Arapaho
Sa-ri-te-ka *see* Arapaho
Sariteka *see* Arapaho
Sar-lit-hu *see* Kalispel
Sarlithu *see* Kalispel
Sarnosas *Coahuiltecan* (Hdbk10)
Sarpa-wee-cha-cha *see* Ute
Sarpaweechacha *see* Ute
Sarraw *see* Cheraw
Sarritehca *see* Arapaho
Sarsee *see* Sarsi
Sarsewi *see* Sarsi
Sarsi [BC] *Dane* (LC)
Saruma *see* Saluma
Sarxi *see* Sarsi
Sasa *see* Cheraw
Sasabaithi [WY] *Arapaho* (BE)
Saschutkenne [BC] *Sekani* (H)
Sas-chu-tqene *see* Saschutkenne
Saschutqene *see* Saschutkenne
Sas-chut-qenne *see* Saschutkenne
Saschutqenne *see* Saschutkenne
Sa-Sis-e-ta *see* Cheyenne
Sasiseta *see* Cheyenne
Sasitka *see* Siksika
Saskatchewan Assiniboin [Sas]
  (H)

Saskinan (Hdbk5)
Saskwihanang *see* Conestoga
Sasquahana *see* Conestoga
Sasquahannah *see* Conestoga
Sasquehannock *see* Conestoga
Sasquesahanock *see* Conestoga
Sasquesahanoug *see* Conestoga
Sasquisahanoughes *see* Conestoga
Sassasouacotton *see* Nassauake-
  ton
Sassasouakoueton *see* Nassauake-
  ton
Sassassaoua Cotton *see* Nas-
  sauaketon
Sassassaouacotton *see* Nassauake-
  ton
Sassee *see* Sarsi
Sassi *see* Sarsi
Sassory *see* Nasoni
Sassquahana *see* Conestoga
Sastaghretsy *see* Huron
Saste *see* Sastean
Saste *see* Shasta
Saste *see* Shastan
Sastean *see* Shastan
Sastean [Lang] [CA] *Shasta* (H)
Sastharhetsi *see* Huron
Sastise *see* Shasta
Sastotene *see* Sekani
Sasuchan [Can] *Sekani* (BE)
Sasuten *see* Sasuchan
Sa-t *see* Northern Paiute
Sat *see* Northern Paiute
Satana *see* Shawnee
Satans *see* Shawnee
Satare *see* Maue
Satawomeck *see* Pomotac
Satawomeke *see* Potomac
Satcap *see* Satsop
Satchap *see* Clatsop
Satchap *see* Satsop
Satchin [AZ] *San Carlos Apache*
  (H)
Sa-tcho-gottine *see* Satchotugot-
  tine
Satchogottine *see* Satchotugot-
  tine
Satcho t'u gottine *see* Satchotu-
  gottine
Satchotugottine [Can] *Kawchot-
  tine* (BE)
Sa-tdoa *see* Sa
Satdoa *see* Sa
Sat-e-loo-ne *see* Saschutkenne
Sateloone *see* Saschutkenne
Satere [Lang] *see* Maue
Satipo [PE] *Campa* (O)
Satiroua *see* Saturiwa
Satoeronnon *see* Sauk
Satoeronnon *see* Houat-
  toehronon
Satoriva *see* Saturiwa
Satos *see* Uzutiuhi

Sa-to-tin *see* Tatlit-kutchin
Satotin *see* Tatlit-kutchin
Satouriona *see* Saturiwa
Satourioua *see* Saturiwa
Satrahe *see* Arikara
Sat-sa-pich *see* Satsop
Sats-a-pish *see* Satsop
Satsapish *see* Satsop
Sa-tshi-o-tin *see* Clatchotin
Satshiotin *see* Clatchotin
Sat-siaqua *see* Siksika
Satsiaqua *see* Siksika
Satsikaa *see* Siksika
Satsop [WA] *Chehalis I* (BE)
Sattana *see* Shawnee
Satudene *see* Bear Lake
Satunra Island [Can] *Sanetch* (BE)
Saturiba *see* Saturiwa
Saturiora *see* Saturiwa
Saturiwa [FL] (BE)
Satzi *see* Sauk
Sauckeys *see* Sauk
Saucs *see* Sauk
Saudia *see* Sandia
Saugies *see* Sauk
Saugiesta (H)
Saugkonnet *see* Saconnet
Sau-hto *see* Comanche
Sauhto *see* Comanche
Sauk [WA] *Skagit* (LC)
Saukaulutuchs [VanI] (H)
Sau-kau-lutuck *see* Saukaulu-
tuchs
Saukaulutuck *see* Saukaulutuchs
Saukeas *see* Sauk
Saukee *see* Sauk
Saukey *see* Sauk
Saukies *see* Sauk
sauk'i-ni *see* Navajo
saukini *see* Navajo
Saulapaguem *Coahuiltecan*
(Hdbk10)
Saulapaguet *Coahuiltecan*
(Hdbk10)
Saulier *see* Amahami
Saulteaux [MN] *Chippewa* (BE)
Saulteur *see* Saulteaux
Saulteur *see* Chippewa
Saulteuse *see* Chippewa
Saulteux *see* Chippewa
Sault Indians *see* Chippewa
Saumingmiut [Can] *Central Eski-
mos* (BE)
Sauniktumiut (Hdbk5) *see also*
Hauniqtuurmiut (Hdbk5)
Sauniktumiut [Can] *Eskimos* (H)
Sau'nto *see* Comanche
Saunto *see* Comanche
Sauouans *see* Shawnee
Sauounon *see* Shawnee
Saura *see* Cheraw
Sauro *see* Cheraw
Saussetons *see* Sisseton

Sautain *see* Santiam
Sauteaux *see* Chippewa
Sauters *see* Chippewea
Sauteurs *see* Chippewa
Sauteus *see* Chippewa
Sauteux *see* Chippewa
Sauteux *see* Saulteaux
Sauthouis *see* Uzutiuhi
Sautor *see* Chippewa
Sautor *see* Saulteaux
Sautous *see* Chippewa
Sautoux *see* Chippewa
Sautoux *see* Saulteaux
Sau-tux *see* Comanche
Sautux *see* Comanche
Sa'u'u *see* Zuni
Sauu *see* Zuni
Sauvages de l'Isle *see* Kich-
esipirini
Sau-va-no-gee *see* Shawnee
Sauvanogee *see* Shawnee
Sauwanew *see* Shawnee
Sauwanew *see* Savanoo
Sau-wa-no-gee *see* Shawnee
Sauwanogee *see* Shawnee
Sauwanous *see* Shawnee
Sauwontiat [NV] *Paiute* (H)
Saux *see* Dakota
Saux of the Wood *see* Santee
Sauxpa *see* Sissipahaw
Savages of the Lake *see* Senijextee
Savana *see* Shawnee
Savanah *see* Shawnee
Savanau *see* Shawnee
Savanna *see* Maskegon
Savanna *see* Shawnee
Savanna *see* Yuchi
Savannah *see* Shawnee
Savannecher *see* Shawnee
Savanneher *see* Shawnee
Savannuca *see* Shawnee
Savano *see* Shawnee
Savanoes *see* Shawnee
Savanois *see* Maskegon
Savanoo *Delaware* (Hdbk15)
Savanore *see* Shawnee
Savansa *see* Quapaw
Savanuca *see* Yuchi
save *see* Navajo
Savinards *see* Savinnars
Savinars *see* Savinnars
Savinnars [VanI] (H)
Savints *see* Shivwits
Savvanormiout *see* Harevaqtuur-
miut
sawagatidi *see* Sawawaktodo tu-
viwari
Sa-wa'-ga-ti-ra *see* Sawawaktodo
tuviwari
Sawagativa (Hdbk11) *see also*
Sawawaktodo tuviwari
(Hdbk11)
Sawagativa [NV] *Paviotso* (H)

sawagudakwa *see* Sawawaktodo
tuviwari
sawa-kate *see* Sawawaktodo tuvi-
wari
Sawakhtu *see* Sa-wakh-tu
Sa-wakh-tu *Yokuts* (Contri, v.3,
p.370)
Sawakola *see* Shawnee
Sawakudokwa tuviwari *see*
Sawawaktodo tuviwari
Sawala *see* Shawala
Sawala *see* Shawnee
Sa-wa-mish *see* Sawamish
Sawamish [WA] *Salish* (H)
Sawana *see* Shawnee
Sawanee *see* Shawnee
Sawani [CA] *Cholovone* (H)
Sawano *see* Shawnee
Sawanogi *see* Shawnee
Sawanoo *see* Shawnee
Sa-wa-no-o-no *see* Shawnee
Sawanoono *see* Shawnee
Sawanuh *see* Shawnee
Sawa'nu-haka *see* Shawnee
Sawanuháka *see* Shawnee
Sa-wa-nu-ka *see* Shawnee
Sawanúka *see* Shawnee
Sawanwa *see* Shawnee
Sa-wan-wa [Self-designation] *see*
Shawnee
Sa-wan-wa-kee *see* Shawnee
Sawanwakee *see* Shawnee
Sawara *see* Cheraw
Sawassaw-tinney *see* Etheneldeli
Sawassawtinney *see* Etheneldeli
Sawawaktodo tuviwari (Hdbk11)
see also Kupadokado (Hdbk11)
Sawawaktodo tuviwari *Northern
Paiute* (Hdbk11)
Saw-cesaw-dinnah *see*
Etheneldeli
Saw-cesaw-dinneh *see*
Etheneldeli
Sawcesawdinneh *see* Etheneldeli
Sawcessawdinnah *see* Etheneldeli
Sawedndesu [Br] *Southern Nam-
bicuara* (O)
Saw-eessaw-dinneh *see*
Etheneldeli
Saweessawdinneh *see* Etheneldeli
Sawekela *Shawnee* (His/T, v.1,
p.39)
Sawessaw tinney *see* Etheneldeli
Sawessawtinney *see* Etheneldeli
Sawkee *see* Sauk
Sawketakix *see* Siksika
Sawkey *see* Sauk
Sawkies *see* Sauk
Sawkis *see* Sauk
Saw-meena *see* Ntlakyapamuk
Saw-meena *see* Siamannas
Saw-meena *see* Thompson Indi-
ans

Sawmeena *see* Ntlakyapamuk
Sawmeena *see* Siamannas
Sawmeena *see* Thompson Indians
Sawokli [AL] *Creek* (BE)
Sawonoca *see* Shawnee
Sawons *see* Saone
Sawra *see* Cheraw
Sawraw *see* Cheraw
Sawro *see* Cheraw
Sa-wu-no-ki *see* Shawnee
Sawunoki *see* Shawnee
Sawwanew *see* Shawnee
Sawwannoo *see* Shawnee
Sawwanoo *see* Shawnee
Sa xa-idaga-i *see* Sa-haidagai
Saxaidagai *see* Sa-haidagai
Saxapahaw *see* Sissipahaw
Saxes *see* Sauk
saxlat *see* Wasco
Saxlatks *see* Wasco
Saxsano [ID] *Nez Perce* (BE)
Saxtila *see* Colorado [SA]
Sayaco *see* Amahuaca
Sayaqua-kwa *see* Sia
Sayaquakwa *see* Sia
Sayaque *see* Tesuque
Say-do-carah *see* Paviotso
Saydocarah *see* Paviotso
Sayenagi *see* Cheyenne
Say-hah-ma-mish *see* Sahe-
wamish
Sayhahmamish *see* Sahewamish
Say-hay *see* Samamish
Sayhay *see* Samamish
Say-hay-ma-mish *see* Sahe-
wamish
Sayhaymamish *see* Sahewamish
Sayhaynamish *see* Sahewamish
Sayhaywamish *see* Sahewamish
Sayi *see* Klamath
Sayonstla *see* Siuslaw
Sayopina *see* Tiopane
Sayopines *see* Tiopine
Sayousla *see* Siuslaw
Sayouslaw *see* Siuslaw
Sayula [MX] *Popoluca* (BE)
Sayulime [MX] *Coahuiltecan*
(Hdbk10)
Sayultec [MX] (BE)
Sayupane *see* Tiopane
Sayuskla *see* Siuslaw
Sayuskla *see* Yakonan
Sayustkla *see* Siuslaw
Saywamines *see* Sawami
Sa-ze-oo-ti-na *see* Sazeutina
Sazeutina [BC] *Nahane* (H)
Sbaleuk *see* Sba'leuk
Sba'leuk [WA] *Skagit* (BE)
Scabby band *see* Oivimana
Scad-dal *see* Skaddal
Scaddal *see* Skaddal
Scad-jat *see* Skagit
Scadjat *see* Skagit

scaelamxex *see* Chelan
Sca-goines *see* Shregegon
Scagoines *see* Shregegon
S'calam *see* Clallam
Scalam *see* Clallam
Scam-namnack [WA] (Hdbk12)
Scanehaderadeyghroones *see*
Nanticoke
Scaniadaradighroona *see* Nanti-
coke
Scanihaderadighroones *see* Nan-
ticoke
Scarci *see* Sarsi
Scarred-Arms *see* Cheyenne
Scatchae *see* Skagit
Scatchat *see* Skagit
Scaticook [CN, NY] (LC)
Scatoneck *see* Saconnet
scelamx *see* Chelan
Sceouex *see* Dakota
Sceoux *see* Dakota
Sceth-tessessay-tinneh *see*
Etcheridiegottine
Scethtessessaytinneh *see* Etcheri-
diegottine
Schaghticoke *see* Scaticook
Schaha *see* Arapaho
Schahi *see* Cree
Schahswintowaher *see* Sisseton
Schanadarighroenes *see* Nanti-
coke
Schaniadaradighroona *see* Nanti-
coke
Schanihadeiadyaghroonees *see*
Nanticoke
Schani-ha-dei-adygh-roon-ees *see*
Nanticoke
Schaouanos *see* Shawnee
Schaunactadas *see* Schenectady
Schavanna *see* Shawnee
Schaveno *see* Shawnee
Schawanese *see* Shawnee
Schawanno *see* Shawnee
Schawanoah *see* Shawnee
Schawanooes *see* Shawnee
Schawenoes *see* Shawnee
Schawenon *see* Shawnee
Schee-et-st-ish *see* Schuelstish
Scheetstish *see* Schuelstish
Schenectady [NY] *Mohawk* (H)
Schengo-kedi *see* Shunkukedi
Schengokedi *see* Skunkukedi
Schetibo *see* Setebo
Scheyenne *see* Cheyenne
Schian *see* Cheyenne
Schianese *see* Cheyenne
Schiannesse *see* Cheyenne
Schiarame *see* Xarame
Schilra [Clan] [*San Felipe (Keres)*]
(H)
Schilra-Hano *see* Schira
Schimilacameachs *see* Similka-
meen

schimilicameachs *see* Nicola
Schimilicameachs *see* Similka-
meen
S-chinkit *see* Tlingit
Schinkit *see* Tlingit
Schinouk *see* Chinook
Schipibo *see* Sipibo
Schipuwe *see* Chippewa
Schira [Clan] [NM] *Sia* (H)
Schischlachtana [Clan] [AK] *Kna-
iakhotana* (H)
Schissatuch *see* Seshart
S-chitcha-chon *see* Sitka
Schitchachon *see* Sitka
Schit-hu-a-ut *see* Okinagan
Schithuaut *see* Okinagan
Schit-hu-a-ut-uh *see* Okinagan
Schithuautuh *see* Okinagan
Schitka *see* Sitka
Schitka-kon *see* Sitka
Schitkakon *see* Sitka
Schitkhakhoan *see* Sitka
Schizuumsh *see* Coeur d'Alene
S'chkoe *see* Siksika
Schkoe *see* Siksika
S'chkoeishin *see* Siksika
Schloss [BC] *Upper Lillooet* (H)
Schoccories *see* Shakori
Schockoores *see* Shakori
Schoeishin *see* Siksika
Scholkleng *see* Shokleng
Schoneschioronon [Clan] *Iroquois*
(H)
Schoomadits [VanI] (H)
Schoomads *see* Schoomadits
Schouchouaps *see* Shuswap
Schre-gon *see* Shregegon
Schregon *see* Shregegon
Schroo-yel-pi *see* Colville
Schrooyelpi *see* Colville
Schu-el-stish *see* Schuelstish
Schuelstish [WA] *Salish* (H)
Schugatschi *see* Chugatchigmut
Schuylkill *Delaware* (Hdbk15)
Schwarzfussige *see* Siksika
Schwo-gel-pi *see* Colville
Schwogelpi *see* Colville
Schwoyelpi *see* Colville
Schyarame *see* Xarame
Sciaguan *see* Siaguan
Sciatoga *see* Shahaptian
Scibole *see* Zuni
Scidi *see* Skidi Pawnee
Scietoga *see* Shahaptian
Scietoga *see* Saiduka
Scieux *see* Dakota
Sci'li *see* Skidi Pawnee
Scili *see* Skidi Pawnee
Scinslaw *see* Siuslaw
Scione Sioux *see* Saone
Sciou *see* Dakota
Scious of the Prairies *see* Teton
Scioux *see* Dakota

Scioux de la Chasse *see* Hictoba
Scioux des Lacs *see* Menesouha-
toba
Scioux of the East *see* Santee
Scioux of the Prairies *see* Teton
Scioux of the West *see* Teton
Scioux of the Woods *see* Santee
Scipxame *see* Sijame
Scitico [MA] *Pocomtoc* (BE)
Sciuslau *see* Siuslaw
Sclallum *see* Clallam
Scloavthamuk *see* Lillooet
Scocomish *see* Skokomish
Scoffies *see* Naskapi
Sconta *see* Skoton
Scootle-mam-ish *see* Shotle-
mamish
Scootlemamish *see* Shotlemamish
Scootuks *see* Passamaquoddy
Scoresbysund Eskimos *see* itto-
qqortoormeermiit
Scoresbysundimiut *see* ittoqqor-
toormeermiit
Scorpions *see* Alacrane
Scoton *see* Skoton
Scott's Valley Indians *see* Iruaitsu
Scott Valley [Lang] [CA] *Shasta*
(CA-8)
Scott Valley People *see* Iruaitsu
Scotuks *see* Passamaquoddy
Scowlits [BC] *Stalo* (BE)
Scowlitz *see* Scowlits
scqescitni *see* Lower Spokan
Scungsicks *see* Sauk
Scyatoga *see* Saiduka
SDiaz *see* Sandia
SDies *see* Sandia
Sdoh-kwhlb-bhuh *see* Sno-
qualmie
Sdok-al-biwh *see* Snoqualmie
Sdokalbiwh *see* Snoqualmie
Sdo'kwalbiuq *see* Snoqualmie
Sdokwalbiuq *see* Snoqualmie
Sdug-wadskabsh *see* Sdugwadsk-
absh
Sdugwadskabsh [WA] *Snohomish*
(BE)
Se [Clan] [NM] (H)
Se [Clan] *San Ildefonso* (H)
Seaconet *see* Saconnet
Seaconnet *see* Sakonnet
Seacos *see* Shiegho
Seacotauk *see* Secatogue
Sead-ler-me-oo *see* Sagdlirmiut
Seadlermeoo *see* Sagdlirmiut
Seaketaulke *see* Secatogue
Seakonnet *see* Saconnet
Sealy [MS] *Chickasaw* (BE)
Seamysty [WA, OR] *Silloot* (BE)
Seaneca *see* Seneca
Seantre [CA] (H)
Seapcat *see* Siapkat
Seapkat *see* Siapkat

Seaquatalke *see* Setauket
Seaquetalke *see* Setauket
Searcies *see* Sarsi
Se-a-sa-pa *see* Sihasapa
Seasapa *see* Sihasapa
Seashelth *see* Seechelt
Se-ash-ha-pa *see* Sihasapa
Seashhapa *see* Sihasapa
Seaside People *see* Mohegan
Seatakot *see* Setauket
Seatalcott *see* Setauket
Seatalcutt *see* Setauket
Seatalkot *see* Setauket
Sea-Talkott *see* Setauket
Seatalkott *see* Setauket
Seataucok *see* Setauket
Seaton Lake *see* Seton Lake
Seauex *see* Dakota
Seaux *see* Dakota
Seawee *see* Sewee
Sebassa *see* Sabassa
Sebollita *see* Sevilleta
Sebondoy *see* Camsa
Se-ca-ca-co-nies *see* Secacawoni
Secacaconies *see* Secacawoni
Secacaonies *see* Secacawoni
Secacawoni [VA] *Powhatan* (BE)
Secakoonies *see* Secacawoni
Secanais *see* Sekani
Se-cang'cos *see* Brule
Secangcos *see* Brule
Secatague *see* Secatogue
Secataug *see* Secatogue
Secatoag *see* Secatogue
Secatogue [NY] *Montauk* (BE)
Secatoket *see* Secatogue
Secatong *see* Secatogue
Secawgo (H)
Seccherpoga [FL] (H)
Sechel *see* Seechelt
Sechels *see* Seechelt
Sechokiyahang *Wailaki* (Pub,
v.20, no.6, p.97)
Se-cho-ma-we *see* Sichomovi
Sechomawe *see* Sichomovi
Sechs Nationem *see* Iroquois
Sechumevay *see* Sichomovi
Se-chum-e-way *see* Sichomovi
Sechumeway *see* Sichomovi
Sechura *see* Tallan
Seckoneses *see* Siconessi
Secmoco [TX] *Coahuiltecan* (BE)
Seco [MX, Hon] *Paya* (BE)
Secoffee *see* Naskapi
Seconet *see* Sakonnet
Seconett *see* Sakonnet
Seconnett *see* Sakonnet
Seconondihago [Clan] [PA]
Susquehanna (BE)
Secotan (BE) *see also* Machapunga
(BE)
Secotan [NC] (BE)
Secoton *see* Secotan

Secoutagh *see* Secatogue
Secowocomoco [MD] *Conoy* (BE)
Secoya (LC) *see also* Encabellado
(O)
Secoya [EC, PE, Col] (LC)
Seculusepa [PE] *Aguano* (O)
Secunnie *see* Sekani
Secwepemc [Self-designation] *see*
Shuswap
Sedentary Nadouesserons *see*
Santee
See [Clan] [NM] (H)
See ash *see* Seh
Seeash *see* Seh
Seechelt [Lang] [BC] *Salishan*
(LC)
Seech-ka-be-rah-pa-ka *see*
Seechkaberuhpaka
Seechkaberuhpaka *Hidatsa* (H)
See-cho-mah-wee *see* Sichomovi
Seechomahwee *see* Sichomovi
Seed People *see* Ataakwe
See-har-ong-o-to *see* Seeharon-
goto [Wolf Clan]
Seeharongoto [Clan] *Delaware*
(H)
See-issaw-dinni *see* Etheneldeli
Seeissawdinni *see* Etheneldeli
Seelawik Mutes *see* Selawigmiut
Seelawikmutes *see* Selagwigmiut
See-oo-nay *see* Saone
Seeoonay *see* Saone
Seepans *see* Lipan Apache
See-pohs-ka-mi-mah-ka-kee *see*
Sipushkanumanke
Seepohskamimahkakee *see* Si-
pushkanumanke
See-poosh-ka *see* Sipushkanu-
manke
Seepooshka (PC) *see also* Si-
pushkanumanke (H)
Seepooshka *Mandan* (H)
Se-ere *see* Seri
Seere *see* Seri
Seeseetoan *see* Sisseton
See-see-ton *see* Sisseton
Seeseeton *see* Sisseton
Seeseetwaun *see* Sisseton
See-see-wan *see* Sisseton
Seeseewan *see* Sisseton
Seesetoan *see* Sisseton
See-se-ton *see* Sisseton
Seeseton *see* Sisseton
Seetauke *see* Setauket
Seethenskie *see* Sitka
Seewa *see* Sewee
Seganiateratickrohne *see* Nanti-
coke
Segatajenne *see* Chiricahua
Apache
Segatajen-ne *see* Chiricagui
Segatajen-ne *see* Chiricahua
Apache

Segilande *see* Chiricagui
Segilande *see* Chiricahua Apache
Segujulapem *Coahuiltecan*
 (Hdbk10)
Seguna *see* Laguna
Segutmapacam *Coahuiltecan*
 (Hdbk10)
Segwallitsu *Nisqualli* (H)
Seh [Clan] [NM] (H)
Sehalatak *see* Clackamas
Se-hehwa-mish *see* Sahewamish
Sehehwamish *see* Sahewamish
Sehlchikyokaiya *Wailaki* (Pub,
 v.20, no.6, pp.100–01)
Sehtsaash *see* Seh
Se-huapm-uh *see* Shuswap
Sehuapmuh *see* Shuswap
Sei Bee Hooghan *see* San Felipe
 [Keres]
Seibeehooghan *see* San Felipe
 [Keres]
sei'leqamuq *see* Nicola
seileqamuq *see* Nicola
Seinslaw Eneas *see* Siuslaw
Seinslaweneas *see* Siuslaw
Seipa *see* Seyupa
Sejen-ne *see* Mescalero Apache
Sejenne *see* Mescalero Apache
Sekacawone *see* Secacawoni
Sekacowone *see* Secacawoni
Se-ka-mish *see* Sekamish
Sekamish [WA] *Muckleshoot* (BE)
Sekanai *see* Sekani
Sekanais *see* Sekani
Sekanais toene *see* Sekani
Sekan-es *see* Sekani
Sekanes *see* Sekani
Sekani [BC] *Dane* (BE)
Sekhushtuntunne [OR]
 Mishikhwutmetunne (H)
Sek-mo-ko *see* Secmoco
Sekmoko *see* Secmoco
Sekonett *see* Sakonnet
Sekoselar *see* Sikosuilarmiut
Sekoselar Innuit *see* iko-
 suilarmiut
Sekoya *see* Secoya
Seksekai *see* Siksika
Sekunnet *see* Sakonnet
Selakampom *see* Comanche
Selawigamute *see* Selawigmiut
Selawigamute *see* Siilvingmiut
Selawigmiut (Hdbk5) *see also* Si-
 ilvingmiut (Hdbk5)
Selawigmiut [AK] *Eskimos* (BE)
Selawig'mut *see* Selawigmiut
Selawigmut *see* Selawigmiut
Selawikmiut *see* Selawigmiut
Selcaisanende *see* Faraon
Seldom Lonesome *see* Miahwah-
 pitsiks
Selelot [BC] *Squawmish* (H)
Selis *see* Thompson Indians

Selish *see* Salishan
Selknam *see* Ona
Selk'nam (O) *see also* Ona (LC)
Selknam *see* Selk'nam
Selk'nam [Arg] (O)
Selloat-pallah *see* Paloos
Selloatpallah *see* Paloos
Sels [Subclan] *Haida* (H)
Selugrue *see* Wea
Semaccom *see* Samahquam
Sema'mila *see* Ntlakyapamuk
Sema'mila *see* Siamannas
Sema'mila *see* Thompson Indians
Semamila *see* Ntlakyapamuk
Semamila *see* Siamannas
Semamila *see* Thompson Indians
Semanole *see* Seminole
Semat *Kiowa Apache* (BE)
Sematuse (Oregon) *see also*
 Spokan (LC)
Sematuse [MN] [*Pend d'Oreille*]
 (BE)
Semena [Lang] [WA] *Salishan*
 (Oregon)
Semiahmoo [WA, BC] (BE)
Semiahoo *see* Semiahmoo
Semia-mo *see* Semiahmoo
Semiamo *see* Semiahmoo
Semigae *see* Shimigae
Semillete *see* Sevilleta
Seminola *see* Seminole
Seminole [FL, OK] (LC)
Seminoleans *see* Seminole
Seminolie *see* Seminole
Seminolulki *see* Seminole
Seminu'niak *see* Seminole
Seminuniak *see* Seminole
Sem-mi-an-mas *see* Semiahmoo
Semmianmas *see* Semiahmoo
Semonan [TX] *Coahuiltecan* (BE)
Sempiche Utah *see* Sanpits
Sem-po-a-pi *see* Sempoapi
Sempoapi [NM] (H)
Sempoil *see* Sanpoil
Semte'use *see* Sematuse
Semteuse *see* Sematuse
Senaca *see* Seneca
Senacaes *see* Seneca
Senacar *see* Seneca
Senacu *see* Seneca
Senahuow *see* Lenahuon
Senakee *see* Seneca
Senan [Clan] *Yuchi* (H)
Sena'ntaha *see* Senan
Senantaha *see* Senan
Senatuch [VanI] *Nootka* (H)
Sencase *see* Secmoco
Sende *see* Mescalero Apache
Sendia *see* Sandia
Sene *see* Senecu
Seneca [NY] *Iroquois Confederacy*
 (LC)
Senecaes *see* Seneca

Senecashága *see* Seneca
Senecas of Ohio *see* Mingo
Senecas of Sandusky *see* Mingo
Senecas of Sandusky and Stony
 Creek *see* Mingo
Senecas of the Glaize *see* Mingo
Senecca *see* Seneca
Seneckes *see* Seneca
Seneco *see* Senecu del Sur
Senecque *see* Seneca
Senecu [NM] (BE)
Senecu del Sur (BE)
Senedo [VA] (H)
Senegar *see* Seneca
Seneka *see* Seneca
Senekaa *see* Seneca
Senekaes *see* Seneca
Senekee *see* Seneca
Seneker *see* Seneca
Senekes *see* Senenca
Senekies *see* Seneca
Senekoes *see* Seneca
Senequaes *see* Seneca
Senequas *see* Seneca
Seneques *see* Seneca
Senequois *see* Seneca
Senestun [OR] *Chastacosta* (H)
Seni *see* Caddo
Senicaes *see* Seneca
Seniczo *see* Sinicu
Seniczo *see* Cinizo
Sen-i-jex-tee *see* Senijextee
Sen-i-jex-tee (Hdbk12) *see also*
 Lakes (Hdbk12)
Senijextee (Hdbk12) *see also* Lakes
 (Hdbk12)
Senijextee [WA] (BE)
Seniker *see* Seneca
Senisos [MX] *Coahuiltecan* (BE)
Sennagar *see* Seneca
Sennaka *see* Seneca
Sennaker *see* Seneca
Senneca *see* Seneca
Sennecca *see* Seneca
Senneches *see* Seneca
Senneckes *see* Seneca
Sennecks *see* Seneca
Sennekaes *see* Seneca
Sennekas *see* Seneca
Sennekee *see* Seneca
Sennekies *see* Seneca
Senneks *see* Seneca
Sennekus *see* Seneca
Sennenes [CA] *Costnoan* (H)
Sennequan *see* Seneca
Senneque *see* Seneca
Sennequen *see* Seneca
Sennickes *see* Seneca
Sennicks *see* Seneca
Senontouant *see* Seneca
Senottoway *see* Seneca
Senoxami'naex *see* Spokan
Senoxma'n *see* Spokan

Sensi *see* Setebo
Senslaw Eneas *see* Siuslaw
Senslaweneas *see* Siuslaw
Sentutu *see* Spokan
Senxome *see* Upper Spokan
Sepascoot [NY] *Munsee* (H)
Se-pa-ua *see* Sepawi
Sepaua *see* Sepawi
Se-pa-ue *see* Sepawi
Sepaue *see* Sepawi
Sepawi [NM] (H)
Se-peh *see* Seh
Sepeh *see* Seh
Sepin [Clan] [NM] (H)
Sepinpacam *Coahuiltecan* (Hdbk10)
Sepin-tdoa *see* Sepin
Sepintdoa *see* Sepin
Sepoous *see* Tunxis
Sepos *see* Tunxis
Septem ciuitatum *see* Zuni
Sepuanabo [PE] *Campa* (O)
Sepunco *see* Secmoco
Sepus *see* Esopus
Sepus *see* Tunxis
Sequalchin *see* Kwatami
Sequan [CA] *Diegueño* (H)
Sequa'pmuq *see* Shuswap
Sequapmuq *see* Shuswap
Sequarchin *see* Kwatami
Sequatake *see* Secatogue
Sequatogue *see* Secatogue
Sequawaughteick *Choptank* (Hdbk15)
Sequeen *see* Mattabesec
Se-queh-cha *see* Kwatami
Sequehcha *see* Kwatami
Sequetauke *see* Secatogue
Sequin *see* Mattabesec
Sequotan *see* Secotan
Seqvin *see* Mattabesec
Se-qwut tunne *see* Na-hankhuotane
Seqwuttunne *see* Nahankhuotane
Sera *see* Seri
Ser-a-goines *see* Shregegon
Seragoines *see* Shregegon
Ser-a-goins *see* Shregegon
Seragoins *see* Shregegon
Seranna *see* Shawnee
Serates *see* Santee
Seratic *see* Arapaho
Seratickk *see* Arapaho
Serente *see* Sherente
Seretee *see* Santee
Seri [MX] (LC)
Seromet *Coahuiltecan* (Hdbk10)
Serpents *see* Shoshone
Serragoin *see* Shregegon
Serran [Lang] [*Serrano-Gabrieliño*] (Hdbk10)
Serrano (H) *see also* Comeya (H)
Serrano [CA] (LC)

Serrano [Lang] *Serran* (Hdbk10)
Serrano [Lang] [*Southern California Shoshonean*] (H)
Serrano [MX] *Seri* (BE)
Serrano-Gabrieliño [Lang] *Takic* (Hdbk10)
Servushamne [CA] (H)
Se-seetoan *see* Sisseton
Seseetoan *see* Sisseton
Se-see-t'wawn *see* Sisseton
Seseetwawn *see* Sisseton
Sesepaulaba *see* Shipaulovi
Seseton *see* Sisseton
Ses'h-aht *see* Seshart
Seshaht *see* Seshart
Seshal *see* Seechelt
Seshart [VanI] *Nootka* (BE)
Sesiton *see* Sisseton
Sessatone *see* Sisseton
Sessatons *see* Sisseton
Sesseton *see* Sisseton
Seta *see* Heta
Se-ta-a-ye *see* Setaaye
Setaaye [OR] *Chastacosta* (H)
Setakaiya *Wailaki* (Pub, v.20, no.6, pp.105–106)
Setaket *see* Setauket
Seta Koxniname *see* Hualapai
Setakoxniname *see* Hualapai
Setalcket *see* Setauket
Setaltcitcokaiya *see* Set'altcit-cokaiya
Set'altcitcokaiya [CA] (Pub, v.20, no.6)
Setandongkiyahang *Wailaki* (Pub, v.20, no.6)
Setaslema (PC) *see also* Se'tas-lema (BE)
Se'tas-lema [WA] *Yakima* (BE)
Setaslema [WA] *Yakima* (H)
Setauck *see* Setauket
Setauket [NY] *Montauk* (BE)
Se-t'ca-tun *see* Setthatun
Setcatun *see* Setthatun
Se-tco-mo-we *see* Sichomovi
Setcomowe *see* Sichomovi
Se-tdoa *see* Se
Setdoa *see* Se
Setebo [PE] (O)
Setlemuk [Can] *Shuswap* (BE)
Setlomuk *see* Setlemuk
Setocende *see* Gila Apache
Setocende *see* Gileños
Setokett *see* Setauket
Seton Lake [BC] *Upper Lillooet* (H)
Setorokamiut *see* Sidarumiut
Setshomave *see* Sichomovi
Setshomove *see* Sichomovi
Settebo *see* Setebo
Setthatun [OR] *Chetco* (H)
Setuket *see* Setauket
Seu-a-rits *see* Seuvarits

Seuarits *see* Seuvarits
Seueni *see* Witoto
Seuh-nau-ka-ta *see* Onondage
Seuhnaukata *see* Onondaga
Seuh-no-keh'te *see* Onondaga
Seuhnokehte *see* Onondaga
Seuh-now-ka-ta *see* Onondaga
Seuhnowkata *see* Onondaga
Seuilleta *see* Sevilleta
Seuvarits (BE) *see also* Uinta (LC)
Seuv-a-rits *see* Seuvarits
Seuvarits [UT] (BE)
Seven Castles *see* Seven Nations of Canada
Seven Cities of Cibola *see* Zuni
Seven Cities of gold *see* Zuni
Seven Council Fires *Lakota* (H)
Seven Fires *see* Seven Council Fires
Seven Nations of Canada (H)
Seven Nations of Lower Canada Indians *see* Seven Nations of Canada
Seven Tribes on the River St.Lawrence *see* Seven Nations of Canada
Severnovskia *see* Khwakhamaiu
Severnovze *see* Khwakhamaiu
Severnovzer *see* Khwakhamaiu
Severnovzi *see* Khwakhamai
Seviches *see* Shivwits
Sevilleta [NM] *Piro* (H)
Sevillete *see* Sevilleta
Sevilletta *see* Sevilleta
Sevinta *see* Shivwits
Se-wa-acl-tcu-tun *see* Se-waathlchutun
Sewaacltcutun *see* Se-waathlchutun
Sewaathlchutun [OR] *Takelma* (H)
Sewa'cen *see* Sewathen
Sewacen *see* Sewathen
Sewan-akies *see* Metoac
Sewanakies *see* Metoac
Sewanne *see* Shawnee
Sewapois *Delaware* (Hdbk15)
Sewapoo [NJ, DE] *Delaware* (H)
Sewathen [BC] [Stalo] (BE)
Se wat palla *see* Paloos
Sewatpalla *see* Paloos
Sewee [Lang] *Catawba* (H)
Sewee [SC] (LC)
Sewernowskije *see* Aglemiut
Sewickley *see* Shawnee
Sewoe *see* Sewee
Sewonkeeg *see* Siwanoy
sexqeltkemx *see* Eastern Shush-wap Band
seyadankaiya *see* Slakaiya
Se-ya Pae-la *see* Seyupa
Seyapaela *see* Seyupa
Seymos *see* Eskimos

Se-yu-pa *see* Seyupa
Seyupa [NM] *Pecos* (H)
Se-yu-pa-lo *see* Seyupa
Seyupalo *see* Seyupa
Seywamines *see* Sawani
Sezaro Mutes *see* Sidarumiut
Sg-adze'guatl la'nas *see*
    Sadjugahl-lanas
Sgadzeguatllanas *see* Sadjugahl-
    lanas
Sg-aga-ngsilai *see* Sagangusili
Sgagangsilai *see* Sagangusili
Sg-anag-wa *see* Skanuka
Sganagwa *see* Skanuka
Sganiateratieh-rohne *see* Nanti-
    coke
Sgoielpi *see* Colville
Sha [Clan] *Yuchi* (H)
Sha-ap-tin *see* Nez Perce
Shaaptin *see* Nez Perce
sha-bi *see* Navajo
shabi *see* Navajo
Shabor *see* Shakori
Shabwasing [MI] *Chippewa* (BE)
Shacco *see* Shakori
Shacioes *see* Shakori
Shackaconia [VA] *Manahoac* (BE)
Shackakonies *see* Shackaconia
Shackamaxon [PA] *Unalachtigo*
    (BE)
Shack-a-po *see* Kickapoo
Shackapo *see* Kickapoo
Shackory *see* Shakori
Shacktau *see* Choctaw
Shacriaba *see* Xakriaba
Sha-de-ka-ron-ges *see* Seneca
Shadekaronges *see* Seneca
Shadjwane [Clan] *Yuchi* (H)
Sha-en *see* Cheyenne
Shaen *see* Cheyenne
Shagelook *see* Jugelnute
Shageluk *see* Jugelnute
Shagen *see* Cheyenne
Shaglook *see* Jugelnute
Shagsowanoghroona [Can] (H)
Shagwau Lennas *see* Sagua-lanas
Shagwikitone *see* Sagui-gitunai
Shahala (BE) *see also* Watlala (BE)
Shahala (Hdbk12) *see also* Cas-
    cades (Hdbk12)
Shahala [OR] (H)
Shahalah *see* Shahala
Shahan *see* Dakota
Shahana *see* Dakota
Shahana *see* Shahala
Shahaptain *see* Nez Perce
Shahaptan *see* Nez Perce
Shahaptanian *see* Nez Perce
Shahaptemish *see* Nez Perce
Shahaptian [Lang] [ID, WA, OR]
    (LC)
Shahapts *see* Nez Perce
Shahe *see* Cree

Shah-ha-la *see* Shahala
Shahhala *see* Shahala
Shahindahua *see* Shahindawa
Shahindawa [PE] *Yaminawa* (O)
Sha-hi'yena *see* Cheyenne
Shahi'yena *see* Cheyenne
Shahiyena *see* Cheyenne
Shahlee *see* Ootlashoot
Sha-ho *see* Cheyenne
Shaho *see* Cheyenne
Shahsweentowah *see* Sisseton
Shaiande *see* Sha'i'ande
Sha'i'ande [Chiricahua Apache]
    (Hdbk10)
Sha-i-a-pi *see* Cheyenne
Shaiapi *see* Cheyenne
Shai-ela *see* Cheyenne
Shaiela *see* Cheyenne
Sha-i-e-na *see* Cheyenne
Shai-ena *see* Cheyenne
Shaiena *see* Cheyenne
Shaircula *see* Shawnee
sha-i-ye *see* Cree
shaiye *see* Cree
Shakahamai *see* Mentuktire
Shakahonea *see* Shackaconia
Sha-ka-pee's band *see* Taopa
Shakapee's band *see* Taopa
Shakchukla [Clan] *Choctaw* (H)
Shake-kah-quah *see* Kickapoo
Shakekahquah *see* Kickapoo
Shakian [Clan] *Yuchi* (H)
Shakian taha *see* Shakian
Shakies *see* Sauk
Shakirs *see* Sauk
Shakitok *see* Sha'kitok
Sha-kitok [WI] *Menominee* (BE)
Shakkeen [BC] *Salish* (H)
Shakopee *see* Taopa
Shakor *see* Shakori
Shakori [NC] (BE)
Shakpa *see* Taopa
Shakpay *see* Taopa
Shakriaba *see* Xakriaba
Shakshakeu *see* Shakshak'eu
Shakshak'eu [Clan] *Menominee*
    (H)
S'hak-tabsh *see* Shaktabsh
Shak-tabsh *see* Shaktabsh
Shaktabsh [WA] *Salish* (H)
Shaktci homma *see* Chakchiuma
Shaktcihomma *see* Chakchiuma
Shaktoligmiut [AK] *Malemiut* (H)
Shakto'ligmut *see* Shaktoligmiut
Shaktoligmut *see* Shaktoligmiut
Shaktoolik *Bering Strait Eskimos*
    (Hdbk5)
Shakwalengya [Clan] *Hopi* (H)
Sha-la-la *see* Shelala
Shalala *see* She-la-la
Shalee *see* Ootlashoot
Shallate *see* Shallattoo
Shallatolo *see* Shallattoo

Shal-lat-ta *see* Shallattoo
Shallatta *see* Shallattoo
Shal-lat-to *see* Shallattoo
Shallattoo [WA] *Pisquows* (H)
Shallee *see* Ootlashoot
Shallna-rooners *see* Shawnee
Shalsa'ulk *see* Kutenai
Shalsaulk *see* Kutenai
Shamanese *see* Shawnee
Shamapa [VA] *Powhatan Confed-
    eracy* (H)
Shamapent *see* Shamapa
Shamatari [Br] *Yanoama* (O)
Shambioe *see* Caraja
Shamboia *see* Xamboia
Shaminahua [Lang] *Panoan* (O)
Shana [Clan] *Yuchi* (H)
Shanaki *see* Cherokee
Shanana *see* Dakota
Shanaw *see* Shawnee
Shanel-kaya *see* Shnalkeya
Shanelkaya *see* Shnalkeya
Shangke [Clan] *Quapaw* (H)
Shaniadaradighroona *see* Nanti-
    coke
Shanihadaradighroones *see* Nan-
    ticoke
Shan-ke-t'wans *see* Yankton
Shanketwans *see* Yankton
Shank't'wannons *see* Yankton
Shanktwannons *see* Yankton
Shank-t'wans *see* Yankton
Shanktwans *see* Yankton
Shannack *see* Cherokee
Shannaki *see* Cherokee
Shannakiak *see* Cherokee
Shannoah *see* Shawnee
Shanoa *see* Shawnee
Shanwans *see* Shawnee
Shanwappom (H) *see also* Yakima
    (LC)
Shanwappom [WA] *Pisquows*
    (BE)
Shanwappones *see* Yakima
Shanwappum *see* Shanwappom
Shaodawa *see* Juminaua
Shaodawa *see* Shaonahua
Shaonahua *Jaminaua* (O)
Shaonois *see* Shawnee
Shaononon *see* Shawnee
Shapalawee *see* Shipaulovi
Sha-pan-la-vi *see* Shipaulovi
Shapanlavi *see* Shipaulovi
Shapanlobi *see* Shipaulovi
Shaparru [Lang] *Motilon* (UAz,
    v.28)
Shaparru [VE] *Yukpa* (O)
Shaparu *see* Shaparru
Shapata (PC) *see also* Sha-pa-ta
    (H)
Sha-pa-ta [Clan] *Shawnee* (H)
Shapata [Clan] *Shawnee* (H)
Sha-pau-lah-wee *see* Shipaulovi

Shapaulahwee *see* Shipaulovi
Shapeinihkashina [Society] *Osage* (H)
Shapera *see* Shapra
Shapra (LC) *see also* Candoshi (LC)
Shapra [PE] (LC)
Shara *see* Cheyenne
Sharanahua [Br, PE] (LC)
Sharetikeh *see* Arapaho
Shar'ha *see* Cheyenne
Sharha *see* Cheyenne
Sharp-eyed Indians *see* Kutchin
Sharsha *see* Cheyenne
Shashones *see* Shoshone
Shask [Clan] *Acoma* (H)
Shasta [CA, OR] (CA)
Shasta [Lang] *Shasta* (CA-8)
Shasta-Achomawi *see* Shastan
Shastacosta *see* Chastacosta
Shasta County [Lang] [CA] *Wintu* (CA-8)
Shastan [Lang] *Hokan* (CA-8)
Shastasla *see* Shahaptian
Shasta Valley [Lang] *Shasta* (CA-8)
Shasteeca *see* Shasta
Shas-te-koos-tee *see* Chastacosta
Shastekoostee *see* Chastacosta
Shas-ti-ka *see* Shasta
Shastika *see* Shasta
Shasty *see* Shasta
Sha taha *see* Shana
Shataha *see* Shana
Shatchet *see* Skagit
Shatckad *see* Sha'tckad
Sha'tckad [WA] *Puyallup* (BE)
Shatera *see* Tutelo
Shateras *see* Tutelo
Shathiane [Clan] *Yuchi* (H)
Shat'hiane taha *see* Shathiane
Shati *see* Koasati
Shatnauilak *see* Kawaiisu
Shatnau ilak *see* Kawaiisu
Shauano *see* Shawnee
Sha-u-ee *see* Shawni
Shauee (PC) *see also* Shawi (H)
Shauee [Clan] *Chickasaw* (H)
Shaugwaumikong [MI, WI] *Chippewa* (H)
Shaukimmo [MA] (H)
Shaumeer *see* Saumingmiut
Shauna *see* Shawnee
Shavano *see* Shawnee
Shavante *see* Akwe-Shavante
Shavante *see* Xavante
Shavante-Akwe *see* Akwe-Shavante
Shaved heads *see* Pawnee
Shaw *see* Shawnee
Shawahah *see* Shawnee
Shawahlook *see* Skwawalooks
Shawala (BE) *see also* Shawnee (LC)

Shawala *Brule* (H)
Shawan *see* Chowanoc
Shawana *see* Shawnee
Shawanah *see* Shawnee
Shawanahaac *see* Shawnee
Shawanapi *see* Shawnee
Shawanaw *see* Shawnee
Shawanawa *see* Sharanahua
Shawane *see* Shawnee
Shawanee *see* Shawnee
Shawaneise *see* Shawnee
Shawaneles *see* Shawnee
Shawanese *see* Shawnee
Shawanesse *see* Shawnee
Shawaneu *see* Shawnee
Shawanies *see* Shawnee
Shawanna *see* Shawnee
Shawannoh *see* Shawnee
Shawannos *see* Shawnee
Shawano-Algonkin *see* Shawnee
Shawanoe *see* Shawnee
Shawanoes *see* Shawnee
Shawanoese *see* Shawnee
Shawanoh *see* Shawnee
Shawanois *see* Shawnee
Shawanon *see* Shawnee
Shawano's *see* Shawnee
Shawanos *see* Shawnee
Shawanose *see* Shawnee
Shawanous *see* Shawnee
Shawanowi *see* Shawnee
Shawans *see* Shawnee
Shawash *see* Achomawi
Shawatharott *see* Beothuk
Shawati [Clan] *Acoma* (H)
Shawaunoes *see* Shawnee
Shaway *see* Cheyenne
Shawdtharut *see* Beothuk
Shawendadies *see* Tionontati
Shawenoes *see* Shawnee
Shaweygira *see* Shawnee
Shaw-ha-ap-ten *see* Nez Perce
Shawhaapten *see* Nez Perce
Shaw Haptens *see* Nez Perce
Shawhaptens *see* Nez Perce
Shawhay *see* Cheyenne
Shawhena *see* Shawnee
Shawi (H) *see also* Shauee (H)
Shawi [Clan] *Chickasaw* (H)
Sha-wi-ti *see* Shawiti
Shawiti [Clan] [NM] (H)
Shawiti-hano *see* Shawiti
Shawiti-hanoch *see* Shawiti
Shawiti-hanoq *see* Shawiti
Shawiti-hanoqch *see* Shawiti
Shawnee [TN] (LC)
Shawneese *see* Shawnee
Shawnese *see* Shawnee
Shawnesse *see* Shawnee
Shawney *see* Shawnee
Shawno *see* Shawnee
Shawnoah *see* Shawnee
Shawnoes *see* Shawnee

Shawonese *see* Shawnee
Shawoniki *see* Shawnee
Shawonoes *see* Shawnee
Shawpatin *see* Sokulk
Shawpatin *see* Wanapam
Shawun *see* Shawnee
Shaw-un-oag *see* Shawnee
Shawunoag *see* Shawnee
Shawunogi *see* Shawnee
Shaxshurunu *see* Fox
Shaya (H) *see also* Caya (H)
Shaya [Clan] *Yuchi* (H)
Shayabit *see* Chayahuita
Shayage *see* Cherokee
Shayen *see* Cheyenne
Shayenna *see* Cheyenne
Sh-chee-tso-ee *see* Skitswish
Shcheetsoee *see* Sksitswish
Sheastuckles *see* Siuslaw
Sheastukles *see* Siuslaw
Sheavwits *see* Shivwits
She-bal-ne Poma *see* Kelispoma
Shebalnepoma *see* Kelispoma
She-banlavi *see* Shipaulovi
Shebanlavi *see* Shipaulovi
She-ba-retches *see* Seuvarits
Shebaretches *see* Seuvarits
Shebaula-vi *see* Shipaulovi
Shebaulavi *see* Shipaulovi
Shebayo (O)
Sheberetch *see* Seuvarits
Sheberetches *see* Seuvarits
Sheberiches *see* Seuvarits
She-be-riches *see* Seuvarits
She-be-Ucher *see* Seuvarits
Shebeucher *see* Seuvarits
She-bo-pav-wee *see* Shipaulovi
Shebopavwee *see* Shipaulovi
Shechart *see* Seshart
Shee-ah-whib-bahk *see* Isleta
Sheeahwhibbahk *see* Isleta
Shee-ah-whib-bak *see* Isleta
Sheeahwhibbak *see* Isleta
Shee-e-huib-bac *see* Isleta
Sheeehuibbac *see* Isleta
Shee-eh-whib-bak *see* Isleta
Sheeehwhibbak *see* Isleta
Sheeourkee *see* Sichomovi
Sheepeater Indians *see* Tukudeka
Sheep-Eaters *see* Tukuarika
Sheep-Eaters *see* Tukudeka
Sheepeaters *see* Tukuarika
Sheepeaters *see* Tukudeka
Sheep Indians *see* Abbatotine
Sheeponarleeve *see* Shipaulovi
Sheepowarleeve *see* Shipaulovi
Sheep People *see* Abbatotine
Sheethltunne [OR] (H)
Shehees *Calapooya* (H)
She-kom *see* Shigom
Shekom *see* Shigom
Shekri *see* Xikrin
Shelknam *see* Ona

Shelk'nam *see* Selk'nam

Shelknam *see* Selk'nam

Shell Earring Band *see* Inyanhaoin

Shelter Bay [Can] [*Montagnai-Naskapi*] (BE)

She-mau-kau *see* Shimaukan

Shemaukau *see* Shimaukan

Shemigae *see* Shimigae

Sheminawa *see* Cashinawa

She-mo-pa-ve *see* Shongopovi

Shennoquankin *see* Shennosquankin

Shennoskuankin *see* Shennosquankin

Shennosquankin [BC] *Similkameen* (H)

She-noma *see* Hopi

Shenoma *see* Hopi

She-nos-quan-kin *see* Shennosquankin

Shenosquankin *see* Shennosquankin

Sheo *Oglala* (H)

Shepalave *see* Shipaulovi

Shepalawa *see* Shipaulovi

She-pa-la-wee *see* Shipaulovi

Shepalawee *see* Shipaulovi

She-pau-la-ve *see* Shipaulovi

Shepaulave *see* Shipaulovi

Shepauliva *see* Shipaulovi

Shepawee *see* Chippewa

Shepewa *see* Chippewa

Shepeweyan *see* Chipewyan

Shepolavi *see* Shipaulovi

She-powl-a-we *see* Shipaulovi

Shepowlawe *see* Shipaulovi

Shepuway *see* Chippewa

Sherente [Br] (LC)

Sherry-dika *Shoshone* (Ye)

Sherwits *see* Shivwits

She-sha-aht *see* Seshart

Sheshaaht *see* Seshart

She-shebe *see* Sheshebe

Sheshebe [Clan] *Chippewa* (H)

Sheshebug *see* Sheshebe

She-she-gwah *see* Kenabig

Sheshegwah *see* Kenabig

She-she-gwun *see* Kenabig

Sheshegwun *see* Kenabig

Sheshel *see* Seechelt

She-shell *see* Seechelt

Sheshell *see* Seechelt

Sheta [Br] (O)

Shetebo *see* Setebo

Shetimasha *see* Chitimacha

Shevanor *see* Shewanee

Shewena *see* Zuni

Shewhap *see* Shuswap

Shewhapmuch *see* Shuswap

Shewhapmuh *see* Shuswap

Shewhapmukh *see* Shuswap

She-whaps *see* Shuswap

Shewhaps *see* Shuswap

She-wo-na *see* Zuni

Shewona *see* Zuni

Sheyen *see* Cheyenne

Sheyenne *see* Cheyenne

Shgali Dine'e *see* Athapascan

Shian *see* Cheyenne

Shia'navo *see* Cheyenne

Shianavo *see* Cheyenne

Shi-an-hti *see* Shiankya

Shianhti *see* Shiankya

Shiank'ya *see* Shiankya

Shiankya [Clan] *Pecos* (H)

Shiannes *see* Cheyenne

Shi-ap-a-gi *see* Santa Clara [NM]

Shiapagi *see* Santa Clara [NM]

Shiarish *see* Cheyenne

Shiaska [Clan] *Laguna* (H)

Shiastuckles *see* Siuslaw

Shibalna Pomo *see* Keliopoma

Shi-bal-ni Po-mo *see* Keliopoma

Shibalni Pomo *see* Keliopoma

Shibalta *see* Nestucca

Shicha'am *see* Chishamne'e

Shichaam *see* Chiushamne'e

Shi-choam-a-vi *see* Sichomovi

Shichoamavi *see* Sichomovi

Shi-e-a-la *see* Cree

Shieala *see* Cree

Shie'da *see* Cheyenne

Shieda *see* Cheyenne

Shiegho [CA] *Pomo* (H)

Shiene *see* Cheyenne

Shiennes *see* Cheyenne

Shiens *see* Cheyenne

Shiewhibak *see* Isleta

Shi-e-ya *see* Cree

Shieya *see* Cree

Shi-fu-ni'n *see* Shifunin

Shifunin [NM] *Isleta* (H)

Shigapo *see* Kickapoo

Shigom [CA] *Pomo* (H)

Shihwapmukh [Lang] *Salish* (Contri, v.1, p.247)

Shi'ini *see* Lipan Apache

Shiini *see* Lipan Apache

Shikaich *see* Koso

Shikana *see* Hoti

Shikapo *see* Kickapoo

Shikapu *see* Kickapoo

Shikaviyam (Hdbk11) *see also* Koso (BE)

Shikaviyam [CA] *Mono* (Pub, v.4, no.3, pp.68–69)

Shi-ke *see* Shike

Shike [Clan] *Sia* (H)

Shike-hano *see* Shsike

Shikiana [Br] (O)

Shikshichela (H)

Shikshichena *Upper Yanktonai* (H)

Shil-an-ottine *see* Thilanottine

Shilanottine *see* Thilanottine

Shiliveri [PE] *Harakmbet* (O)

Shillicoffy *see* Chillicothe

Shi-ma-co-vi *see* Shongopovi

Shimacovi *see* Shongopovi

Shimacu *see* Urarina

Shimagan *see* Shemaukan

Shimaku *see* Urarina

Shimiahmoo *see* Semiahmoo

Shimigae [PE] (O)

Shimizya *see* Chimila

Shimopavi *see* Shongopovi

Shimopova *see* Shongopovi

Shimopovy *see* Shongopovi

Shimps-hon *see* Shimpshon

Shimpshon [BC] *Salish* (H)

Shimshyan *see* Tsimshian

Shinabu *see* Sinabu

Shinacock *see* Shinnecock

Shinalutaoin *Sans Arc* (H)

Shinana [NM] *Tigua* (H)

Shinecock *see* Shinnecock

Shineshean *see* Tsimshian

Shinicok *see* Shinnecock

Shinicook *see* Shinnecock

Shinikes *see* Seneca

Shinikook *see* Shinnecock

Shinnacock *see* Shinnecock

Shinnecock [NY] *Montauk* (LC)

Shinome *see* Hopi

Shi-nu-mo *see* Hopi

Shinumo *see* Hopi

Shiohinowutz-hita'neo *see* Comanche

Shi-oui *see* Zuni

Shioui *see* Zuni

Shipanahua *see* Xipinawa

Shipanawa *see* Xipinawa

Shi-pau-a-luv-i *see* Shipaulovi

Shipaualuvi *see* Shipaulovi

Shi-pau-i-luv-i *see* Shipaulovi

Shipauiluvi *see* Shipaulovi

Shi-pau-la-vi *see* Shipaulovi

Shipaulavi *see* Shipaulovi

Shipaulovi [AZ] *Hopi* (BE)

Shi-pav-i-luv-i *see* Shipaulovi

Shipaviluvi *see* Shipaulovi

Shipaya *see* Chipaya

Shipi *see* Kuta

Shipibo (O)

Shipibo (O) *see also* Sipibo (LC)

Shipipo *see* Sipibo

Shipolovi *see* Shipaulovi

Shi-powl-ovi *see* Shipaulovi

Shipowlovi *see* Shipaulovi

Shippailemma *see* Shipaulovi

Shiptatse *see* Shiptetze

Shiptetsa *see* Shiptetza

Ship-tet-sa *see* Shiptetza

Ship-tet-za *see* Shiptetza

Shiptetza *Crow* (H)

Shira-hano *see* Schira

Shiriana (LC) *see also* Yanoama (LC)

Shiriana [Br] (O)
Shirianan *see* Shiriana
Shirianan *see* Yanoama
Shirianna *see* Shiriana
Shirineri *see* Sirineiri
Shiripuno *see* Sabela
Shirishana *see* Shiriana
Shirishana *see* Yanoama
Shirixana *see* Shiriana
Shirixana *see* Yanorama
Shirrydikas *see* Shoshone
Shishiniwotsitan *see* Comanche
Shi'shinowutz-hita'neo *see* Comanche
Shishinowutzhitaneo *see* Comanche
Shish-i-nu-wut-tsit-a-ni-o *see* Kiowa
Shishinuwuttsitanio *see* Kiowa
Shiship *see* Shesheba
Shishmaref *Bering Strait Eskimos* (Hdbk5)
Shis-Inday *see* Apache
Shisinday *see* Apache
Shistakoostee [OR] *Tututni* (H)
Shista-kwusta *see* Chastacosta
Shistakwusta *see* Chastacosta
Shiu [Clan] *Isleta* (H)
Shi-ua-na *see* Zuni
Shiuana *see* Zuni
Shiuano *see* Zuni
Shi-uo-na *see* Zuni
Shiuona *see* Zuni
Shiu-t-ainin *see* Shiu
Shiutainin *see* Shiu
Shiuwimi-hano *see* Shuwimi
Shivakuadeni [Br] *Dani* (O)
Shivawach [CA] *Chemehuevi* (BE)
Shivawats *see* Shivawach
Shiveytown *see* Sisseton
Shi-vo-la *see* Zuni
Shivola *see* Zuni
Shivwit *see* Shivwits
Shi-vwits *see* Shivwits
Shivwits [AZ, UT] *Paiute* (H)
Shivwitz *see* Shivwits
Shiwahpi *see* Siwapi
Shi-wa-na *see* Zuni
Shiwana *see* Zuni
Shi'wanish *see* Nez Perce
Shiwanish *see* Nez Perce
Shiwanu [Clan] *Hopi* (H)
Shiwi *see* Zuni
Shi'wi [Self-designation] *see* Zuni
Shiwian *see* Aridian
Shiwian *see* Zuni
Shiwila *see* Jebero
Shi-wi-na *see* Zuni
Shiwina *see* Zuni
Shi-wi-na-kwin *see* Zuni
Shiwinakwin *see* Zuni
Shi-win-e-wa *see* Sichomovi

Shiwinewa *see* Sichomovi
Shi-win-na *see* Sichomovi
Shiwinna *see* Sichomovi
Shi-wo-kug-mut *see* Eiwhuelit
Shiwokugmut *see* Eiwhuelit
Shiwona *see* Zuni
Shiwora *see* Jivaro
Shix River *see* Kwatami
Shi-ya *see* Cheyenne
Shiyan *see* Cheyenne
Shiyosubula *Brule* (H)
Shiyotanka *Brule* (H)
Shkanatulu [Clan] [*NM*] [Sia] (H)
Shkanatulu-hano *see* Shkanatulu
Shkashtun [OR] *Takelma* (H)
Shkopa *see* Tapishlecha
Shlakatat *see* Klikitat
Shltuja *see* Lituya
Shmel-a-ko-mikh *see* Similkameen
Shnalkeya [CA] *Kulanapan* (H)
Shoalwater Bay Indians *see* Atsmitl
shoaufoka *see* shoa'u-foka
shoa'u-foka [CA] *Patwin* (Pub, v.29, no.4)
Sho-bar-boo-be-er *see* Shobarboobeer
Shobarboobeer [OR] *Shoshone* (H)
Shoccories *see* Shakori
Shockays *see* Sauk
Shocktau *see* Choctaw
Shoco [Br] (LC)
Shocu *see* Shoco
Shodakhai [CA] *Pomo* (H)
Sho-do Kai Po-mo *see* Shodakhai
Shodokai Pomo *see* Shodakhai
Shoe Indians *see* Amahami
Shohi *see* Sewee
Shohoaigadika [ID] *Shoshone* (H)
Shohoita [Clan] [NM] *Zuni* (H)
Shohoita-kwe *see* Shohoita
Shohu [Clan] *Hopi* (H)
Shokhowa [CA] *Pomo* (H)
Shokleng [Br] (LC)
Shoko *see* Shoco
S'Homahmish *see* Shomamish
Shomahmish *see* Shomamish
Sho-ma-koo-sa *see* Shomakoosa
Shomakoosa [Clan] *Kansa* (H)
S'Homamish *see* Shomamish
Sho-mam-ish *see* Shomamish
Shomamish [WA] *Salish* (H)
Shomonpavi *see* Shongopovi
Shomoparvee *see* Shongopavi
Shomo Takali *see* Chonakera
Shomotakali *see* Chonakera
Shonack *see* Micmac
Shoneanawetowah *see* Cayuga
Shongapave *see* Shongopovi

Shong-a-pa-vi *see* Shongopovi
Shongapavi *see* Shongopovi
Shongoba-vi *see* Shongopovi
Shongobavi *see* Shongopovi
Shongopovi [AZ] (BE)
Shonivikidika *Shoshone* (H)
Shonk-chun-ga-da *see* Shungikikarachada
Shonkchungada *see* Shungikikarachada
Shononowendo *see* Cayuga
Shook-any *see* Shookany
Shookany *Calapooya* (H)
Shoo-schawp *see* Shuswap
Shooschawp *see* Shuswap
Shooshaps *see* Shuswap
Shooswaap *see* Shushwap
Shooswwabs *see* Shuswap
Shooter *see* Khemnichan
Shoo-wha-pa-mooh *see* Shuswap
Shoowhapamooh *see* Shuswap
Sho-o-yo-ko *see* Shooyoko
Shooyoko [Clan] *Hopi* (H)
Shopumish *see* Nez Perce
Shorihtefoka *see* Shorihte-foka
Shorihte-foka [CA] *Patwin* (Pub, v.29, no.4)
Shoro *see* Zoro
Short-Ears *see* Ottawa
Short Hair *see* Peshla
Short Hair *see* Shorthair
Shorthair [SD] *Oglala* (H)
Short hair band *see* Peshlaptechela
Sho-sho-co *see* Shoshoko
Shoshoco *see* Shoshone
Shoshoco *see* Shoshoko
Sho-sho-coes *see* Shoshoko
Shoshocoes *see* Shoshoko
Shoshoki *see* Shoshone
Shoshoko (H)
Shoshokoes *see* Shoshoko
Sho-sho-kos *see* Shoshoko
Shoshon *see* Shoshone
Sho-Sho-nay *see* Shoshone
Shoshonay *see* Shoshone
Sho-sho-ne *see* Shoshone
Shoshone [Self-designation] [WY] (Hdbk11)
Shoshonean [Lang] [*Mono-Paviotso*] (LC)
Shoshonean [Lang] [*Uto-Aztecan*] (BE)
Shoshone-Comanche [Lang] *Shoshonean* (H)
Shoshonee *see* Shoshone
Shoshonee Diggers *see* Shoshone
Shoshone-Goship *see* Gosiute
Sho-shones *see* Shoshone
Shoshoni *see* Shoshone
Shoshoni-Comanche *see* Shoshone-Comanche
Shoshoni-Goship *see* Gosiute

Shos-shone *see* Shoshone
Shosshone *see* Shoshone
Shossoonies *see* Shoshone
Shot-at-some-white-object *see* Hunkpatine
Shothones *see* Shoshone
S'ho-ti-non-na-wan-to-na *see* Cayuga
Shotinonnawantona *see* Cayuga
S'Hotle-ma-mish *see* Shotlemamish
Shotlemamish [WA] *Salish* (H)
S'Hotlmahmish *see* Shotlemamish
Shotlmahmish *see* Shotlemamish
S'hotlmamish *see* Shotlemamish
Shotlmamish *see* Shotlemamish
Shoto [OR] *Multnomah* (LC)
Shotoes *see* Shoto
Shoudamunk *see* Montagnais-Naskapi
Shoudamunk *see* Naskapi
Shoughey *see* Sauk
Shounaus *see* Shawnee
Shoushwap *see* Shuswap
Shouwapemoh *see* Shuswap
Shouwapemot *see* Shuswap
Showammers *see* Shawnee
Showanhoes *see* Shawnee
Showannee *see* Shawnee
Showannoes *see* Shawnee
Showanoes *see* Shawnee
Showati [Clan] [*San Felipe (Keres)*] (H)
Sho'wati-hano *see* Shawati
Showatihano *see* Shawiti
Showay *see* Cheyenne
Showita [Clan] *Pueblo Indians* (H)
Sho'wi-ti-hano *see* Shawiti
Showitihano *see* Shawiti
Show-mowth-pa *see* Shongopovi
Showmowthpa *see* Shongopovi
Showonese *see* Shawnee
Showonoes *see* Shawnee
Shquwi [Clan] *Acoma* (H)
Shquwi-hanoq *see* Shquwi
Shquwi-hanoq *see* Shruhwi
Shquwi-hanoqch *see* Shquwi
Shquwi-hanoqch *see* Shruhwi
Shrotsona [Clan] [*San Felipe (Keres)*] (H)
Shrotsona-hano *see* Shrotsona
Shruhwi [Clan] [NM] (H)
Shruhwi-hanuch *see* Shruhwi
Shrutsuna [Clan] [NM] (H)
Shrutsuna-hanuch *see* Shrutsuna
Shu [Clan] *Yuchi* (H)
Shuar *see* Jivaro
Shuara *see* Jivaro
Shubenacadie [NS] *Kespoogwit Micmac* (BE)
Shu-chum-a-vay *see* Sichomovi

Shuchumavay *see* Sichomovi
Shuckers *see* Shoshoko
Shuck-stan-a-jumps *see* Sktahlejum
Shuckstanajumps *see* Sktahlejum
Shugarski *see* Chugatchigmut
Shuhlanan [Clan] *Yuchi* (H)
Shukahamae *see* Mentuktire
Shukhtutakhlit [AK] *Ahtena* (BE)
Shukshansi *see* Chukchansi
Shu'lanan taha *see* Shuhlanan
Shulanantaha *see* Shuhlanan
Shul-ya *see* Shulya
Shulya [Clan] *Mohave* (H)
Shuman *see* Jumano
Shumeia *see* Yuki
Shumhami-hanuch *see* Shuwimi
Shumi *see* Hopi
Shummahpawa *see* Shongopovi
Shum-nac *see* Shumnac
Shumnac [NM] *Tigua* (H)
Shu-mo-pa-vay *see* Shongopovi
Shumopavay *see* Shongopovi
Shumopavi *see* Shongopovi
Shu-muth-pa *see* Shongopovi
Shumuthpa *see* Shongopovi
Shu-muth-pai-o-wa *see* Shongopovi
Shumuthpaiowa *see* Shongopovi
Shumuyu [Clan] *Isleta* (H)
Shung-a-pa-vi *see* Shongopovi
Shungapavi *see* Shongopovi
Shungapovi *see* Shongopovi
Shungikcheka [SD] *Hunkpatina* (H)
Shungikcheka *Yanktonai* (H)
Shungikikarachada [Gens] *Winnebago* (H)
Shungkahanapin *Brule* (H)
Shungkoyuteshni *Miniconjou* (H)
Shung-o-pah-wee *see* Shongopovi
Shungopahwee *see* Shongopovi
Shungopavi *see* Shongopovi
Shung-o-pa-we *see* Shongopovi
Shungopawe *see* Shongopovi
Shungopawee *see* Shongopovi
Shung-op-ovi *see* Shongopovi
Shungopovi *see* Shongopovi
Shung-opovi *see* Shongopovi
Shu'nien *see* Shu'nu ni'u
Shunien *see* Shu'nu Shungkayuteshni
Shunkasapa *see* Ohanhanska
Shunkukedi [AK] *Tlingit* (H)
Shunopovi *see* Shongopovi
Shunshun-wichasha *see* Shoshone
Shununiu *see* Shu-nu ni'u
Shu'nu ni'u [WI] *Menominee* (BE)
Shu-par-la-vay *see* Shipaulovi
Shuparlavay *see* Shipaulovi

Shupaulavi *see* Shipaulovi
Shupaulovi *see* Shipaulovi
Shupowla *see* Shipaulovi
Shupowlewy *see* Shipaulovi
Shu-qtu-ta-qlit *see* Shukhtutakhlit
Shuqtutaqlit *see* Shukhtutakhlit
Shuren *see* Churan
Shurmuyu [Clan] *Pueblo Indians* (H)
Shurmuyu-t'ainin *see* Shurmuyu
Shurshka [Clan] *Laguna* (H)
Shu'rshka-hano *see* Skurshka
Shurshkahano *see* Skurshka
Shu'rshka-hanock *see* Skurshka
Shurshkahanock *see* Skurshka
Shurts-un-na *see* Shrutsuna
Shurtsunna *see* Shrutsuna
Shu-sho-no-vi *see* Sichomovi
Shushonovi *see* Sichomovi
Shushwap *see* Shuswap
Shushwapumsh *see* Shuswap
Shuswap [BC] (LC)
Shuswap Band [BC] (Hdbk12)
Shuswap Lake [Can] *Shuswap* (BE)
Shuswap-much *see* Shuswap
Shu'ta *see* Shuta
Shuta [Clan] [NM] *Sia* (H)
Shu-taha *see* Shu
Shutaha *see* Shu
Shuta-hano *see* Shuta
Shutson [Clan] [*Santa Ana (NM)*] (H)
Shutson-hano *see* Shrutsuna
Shutsun-hano *see* Shrutsuna
Shutzuna *see* Shrutsuna
Shuwhami [Clan] *Cochiti* (H)
Shuwimi [Clan] *Keres* (H)
Shu'wimi-hano *see* Shuwimi
Shuwimi-hano *see* Shuwimi
Shuwimihanoch *see* Shuwimi
Shu'w-imi-hanock *see* Shuwimi
Shuyelpee *see* Colville
Shuyelphi *see* Colville
Shuyelpi *see* Colville
Shwalz *see* Nisqualli
Shwanoes *see* Shawnee
Shwoi-el-pi *see* Colville
Shwoielpi *see* Colville
Shwoyelpi [Lang] *Salishan* (Contri, v.1, p.248)
Shyamo *see* Shuwimi
Shyatagoes *see* Shahaptian
Shyatogo *see* Saiduka
Shy Clan *see* Tutoimana
Shyennes *see* Cheyenne
Shye-ui-beg *see* Isleta
Shyeuibeg *see* Isleta
Shyick *see* Shyik
Shyik [WA] (H)
Shyoutemacha *see* Chitimacha
Shy-to-ga *see* Shahaptian

Shytoga *see* Shahaptian
Sia [Pueblo] (LC)
Siaban *see* Siaguan
Siaexe *see* Saesse
Siaexer *see* Haesar
Siaguan [TX] *Coahuiltecan* (BE)
Siaguane *see* Siaguan
siahs *see* Saia
Si-a-ko *see* Shiegho
Siako *see* Shiegho
Siakua *see* Maca
Siakumne [CA] *Northern Valley Yokuts* (BE)
Siamannas (H)
Sia-man-nas *see* Siamannas
Siamomo [MX] *Coahuiltecan* (Hdbk10)
Sianabone *see* Cheyenne
Si-a-na-vo *see* Cheyenne
Sianavo *see* Cheyenne
Sianekee *see* Seneca
Sians *see* Saia
Siansi (Hdbk10) *see also* Saesse (Hdbk10)
Siansi [MX] *Coahuiltecan* (BE)
Siapane *see* Lipan Apache
Si'apkat *see* Siapkat
Siapkat [WA] *Wenatchi* (BE)
Siasconsit [MA] (H)
Siatlhelaak [BC] *Nuhalk* (H)
Siatlqela'aq *see* Siatlhelaak
Siausi *see* Saesse
Siaws *see* Saia
Siay *see* Sia
Siaywas *see* Liaywas
Sibanga [Lang] [CA] (Pub, v.8, no.1, p.11)
Sibapa *see* Kitkala
Sibayones [MX] *Tamaulipec* (BE)
Sibelleta *see* Sevilleta
Siberian Eskimos [Sib] (Hdbk5)
Siberian Eskimos [Sib] *Eskimos* (Hdbk5)
Siberian Yupik (LC) *see also* Yuit (BE)
Siberian Yupik [Lang] [Sib] (Hdbk5)
Sibillela *see* Sevilleta
Sibola *see* Zuni
Sibolla *see* Zuni
Siboney *see* Ciboney
Sibubapa [MX] *Nevome* (H)
Sibundoy [Self-designation] *see* Camsa
Sica'be *see* Siksika
Sicabe *see* Siksika
Sicaca *see* Chickasaw
Sicacha *see* Chickasaw
Sicajayapaguet *see* Sicujulampaguet
Sicanees *see* Etagottine
Sicangu *see* Brule

Sicangu *see* Kheyatawichasha
Sicannes *see* Sazeutina
Sicannis *see* Sekani
Sicanny *see* Sekani
Sicaog [CN] *Wappinger* (BE)
Sicasica *Aymara* (O)
Si'catl *see* Seechelt
Sicatl *see* Seechelt
Si-ca-tugs *see* Secatogue
Sicatugs *see* Secatogue
Sicauger *see* Brule
Sicaunies *see* Sekani
Si-ca-wi-pi *see* Tinazipeshicha
Sicawipi *see* Tinazipeshicha
Siccameen [VanI] *Cowichan* (BE)
Siccane *see* Sekani
Siccanies *see* Sekani
Siccannies *see* Sekani
Siccony *see* Sekani
Sichanetl [VanI] *Songish* (BE)
Sichangu [Self-designation] *see* Brule
Si-chan-koo *see* Brule
Sichankoo *see* Brule
Sichimovi *see* Sichomovi
Si-choan-avi *see* Sichomovi
Sichoanavi *see* Sichomovi
Sichomavi *see* Sichomovi
Sichomivi *see* Sichomovi
Sichomovi *Hopi* (BE)
Si-chum-a-vi *see* Sichomovi
Sichumavi *see* Sichomovi
Sichumnavi *see* Sichomovi
Sichumniva *see* Sichomovi
Sichumovi *see* Sichomovi
Siciatl *see* Seechelt
Si'ciatl [Self-designation] *see* Seechelt
Sickameen *see* Siccameen
Sick-a-mun *see* Siccameen
Sickamun *see* Siccameen
Sickanies *see* Sekani
Sickannies *see* Sekani
Sickenames *see* Pequot
Sicketauykacky *see* Secatogue
Sicketawach *see* Secatogue
Sicketawagh *see* Secatogue
Sicketeuwacky *see* Secatogue
Sicketweackey *see* Secatogue
Sickmunari *see* Sichomavi
Sick-naa-hulty *see* Siknahadi
Sicknaahulty *see* Siccameen
Sickoneysinck *see* Big Siconese
Sickoneysincks *see* Siconesse
Sicomout *see* Sichomovi
Siconescinque *see* Siconesse
Siconesse [NJ] *Unalachtigo* (BE)
Siconi *see* Sekani
Siconysy *see* Siconesse
Sicosuilarmiut *see* Sikosuilarmiut
Sicouex *see* Dakota
Sicuane [VE, Col] (LC)
Sicuani *see* Sicuane

Sicujulampaguet *Coahuiltecan* (Hdbk10)
Sicxacames *see* Ssijames
Sidaru *see* Sidarumiut
Sidarumiut [AK] *Eskimos* (BE)
Sida'runmiun *see* Sidarumiut
Sidarunmiun *see* Sidarumiut
Sid-is-kine *see* Tzetseskadn
Sidiskine *see* Tzetseskadn
Sidocaw (H) *see also* Paviotso (CA)
Sidowaw (Hdbk11)
Siehwib-ag *see* isleta
Siemas [Pueblo] [NM] (H)
Sierra Blanca Apache (Hdbk10)
Sierra Miwok [Lang] *Eastern Miwokan* (CA-8)
Siete Arroyos *see* Tenabo
Siete Cibdades *see* Zuni
Siete-Ciudades de Cibola *see* Zuni
Sigaitsi *Western Shoshone* (Hdbk11)
si-gawiyam *see* Koso
sigawiyam *see* Koso
Sig-gwal-it-chie *see* Nisqualli
Siggwalitchie *see* Nisqualli
Sigilande *see* Rancheria of Capitan Vigotes
Sigua [Pan] (BE)
Sigunikt [Can] *Micmac* (BE)
Siguniktawak [NS] *Micmac* (H)
Sigwa'letcabsh [WA] *Nisqualli* (BE)
Si-ha-sa-pa *see* Sihasapa
Si-ha-sa-pa *see* Siksika
Sihasapa *Teton* (LC)
Sihasapakhcha *Sihasapa* (H)
Siha-sapa-qtca *see* Sihasapakhcha
Sihasapaqtca *see* Sihasapakhcha
Sihasapa-rca *see* Sihasapakhcha
Sihasaparca *see* Sihasapakhcha
Si-him-e-na *see* Siamannas
Sihimena *see* Siamannas
Sihlama *see* Si-hlama
Si-hlama [WA] *Yakima* (BE)
Sihu [Clan] *Hopi* (H)
Sihu winwu *see* Sihu
Si-hu wuñ-wu *see* Sihu
Sihuwunwu *see* Sihu
Si-i *see* Sii
Sii [Clan] *Acoma* (H)
Sii -hano *see* Sii
Sii-hanoq *see* Sii
Sii-hanoqch *see* Sii
sii'lexamux *see* Nicola
Siilvingmiut *Kotzebue Sound Eskimos* (Hdbk5)
Sijame [TX] *Coahuiltecan* (BE)
Sikacha *see* Chickasaw
Si-kah-ta-ya *see* Sikyataiyo
Sikahtaya *see* Sikyataiyo
Sikahtayo *see* Sikyataiyo

Sikaium *see* Koso
Sikanis *see* Sekani
Sikanni *see* Sekani
Sikannies *see* Sekani
Sik-a-pu *see* Kickapoo
Sikapu *see* Kickapoo
Si-ka-tsi-po-maks *see* Sikutsipumaiks
Sikatsipomaks *see* Sikutsipumaiks
Sikauyam *see* Koso
Sikauyam *see* Shikaviyam
Sikcitano *see* Siksika
Si-ke-na *see* Maricopa
Si-ke-na *see* Papago
Si-ke-na *see* Pima
Sikena *see* Maricopa
Sikena *see* Papago
Sikena *see* Pima
Sikennies *see* Sekani
Siketeuhacky *see* Secatogue
Sikiana [Br] (O)
Siknahadi [Clan] [AK] *Tlingit* (H)
Siknaq'a'de *see* Siknahadi
Siknaqade *see* Siknahadi
S!iknaxa'di *see* Siknahadi
Siknaxadi *see* Siknahadi
Sikne *see* Seneca
Si-koh-i-tsim *see* Sikokitsimiks
Sikohitsim *see* Sikokitsimiks
Sik-o-kit-sim-iks *see* Sikokitsimiks
Sikokitsimiks [MN] *Piegan* (BE)
Sikonesses *see* Siconesse
Sik-o-pok-si-maiks *see* Sikopoksimaiks
Sikopoksimaiks [MN] *Piegan* (BE)
Sikosuilarmiut [Can] *Central Eskimos* (BE)
Sikoua *see* Pecos
Siks-ah-pun-iks *see* Siksahpuniks
Siksahpuniks [MN, Can] *Kainah* (BE)
Siksekai *see* Siksika
Sik'ses-tene *see* Kwatami
Siksestene *see* Kwatami
Siksicela *see* Shikshichela
Siksicena *see* Sikshichena
Sik-si-ka *see* Siksika
Siksika [Can, MN] (LC)
Siksikai *see* Siksika
Sik-si-no-kai-iks *see* Siksinokaks
Siksinokaiiks *see* Siksinokaks
Siks-in-o-kaks *see* Siksinokaks
Siksinokaks [MN] *Kainah* (BE)
Sikskekuanak *see* Siksika
Sikuani *see* Sicuane
Sik-ut-si-pum-aiks *see* Sikutsipumaiks
Sikutsipumaiks [MN] *Piegan* (BE)
Sikuye *see* Pecos
Sikwigwi'lts [WA] *Skagit* (BE)

Sikyachi [Clan] *Hopi* (H)
Sikyataiyo [Clan] *Hopi* (H)
Sikyataiyo wiñwu *see* Sikyataiyo
Si-kya-tai-yo wuñ-wu *see* Sikyataiyo
Sikyatchi wiñwu *see* Sikyachi
Si-kya-tci *see* Sikyachi
Sikyatci *see* Sikyachi
Si-kya-tci wuñ-wu *see* Sikyachi
Silahlama *see* Si'la-hlama
Si'la-hlama [WA] *Yakima* (BE)
Silam [NI, Hon] *Sumo* (BE)
Silan [CAm] *Sumo* (O)
Silawi'nmiun *see* Selawigmiut
Silawinmiun *see* Selawigmiut
Silela *Kuitsh* (Oregon)
Siletz [OR] (LC)
Silez *see* Thompson Indians
Silka *see* Coyotero Apache
Silkhkemechetatun [OR] *Choastacosta* (H)
Silla *see* Sia
Sillanguagyas [MX] *Coahuiltecan* (BE)
Sille *see* Sia
Silqkemetcetatun (H)
Sil-qke-me-tce-ta-tun *see* Silkhkemechetatun
Siltaden *see* Tsiltaden
Siltcoos [OR] *Kuitsch* (Oregon)
Silveno *see* Gambiano
Silvia *see* Moguex
Sima *see* Pima
Simacu *see* Urarina
Simamamish *see* Samamish
Sim-a-mish *see* Samamish
Simano'lalgi *see* Seminole
Simanolalgi *see* Seminole
Simano'la'li *see* Seminole
Simanolali *see* Seminole
Sim-a-no-le (H) SES Seminole (LC)
Simanole *see* Seminole
Simaomo [TX] *Coahuiltecan* (BE)
Simariguan *Coahuiltecan* (Hdbk10)
Simbalakee *see* Tamuleko
Sim-e-lo-le *see* Seminole
Simelole *see* Seminole
Sim-e-no-le *see* Seminole
Simenole *see* Seminole
Simenolies *see* Seminole
Simiahmoo *see* Semiahmoo
Simiamo *see* Semiahmoo
Si-mi-lacamich *see* Smilkameen
Similacamich *see* Smimlkameen
Similaton [Hon] (BE)
Similikameen *see* Similkameen
Similkameen [WA, BC] *Okinagan* (BE)
Similoculgee *see* Seminole
Siminekempu [ID] *Nez Perce* (BE)

Siminole *see* Seminole
Simiranch *see* Piro [Peru]
Simiranche *see* Piro [Peru]
Simirenche *see* Piro [Peru]
Simirenchi *see* Chuntaquiro
Simirinche *see* Piro [Peru]
Simiza *see* Chimila
Simizya *see* Chimila
Simkoehlama *see* Si'mkoe'hlama
Si'mkoe-hlama [WA] *Yakima* (BE)
Simmagons *see* Seneca
Simojueve *see* Chemehuevi
Simomo *see* Simaoma
Simonde *see* Seminole
Simonolay *see* Seminole
Simpsian *see* Tsimshian
Simsean *see* Tsimshian
Sim-u-no-li *see* Simenole
Simunoli *see* Seminole
Simupapa *see* Sibubapa
Simza *see* Chimila
Sinabo *see* Sinabu
Sinabu [BO] *Pacanuara* (O)
Sinacanai *Coahuiltecan* (Hdbk10)
Sinacantan [Gua] *Xinca* (BE)
Sinachicks *see* Lakes
Sinacks *see* Seneca
Sinacsop *see* Smackshop
Sinagar *see* Seneca
Sinago [MI] *Ottawa* (BE)
Sinagoux *see* Sinago
Sinaitskstx *see* Lakes
Sinakaiausish *see* Sinkiuse
Sinakee *see* Seneca
Sinaker *see* Seneca
Sinako *see* Sinago
Sinaloa [MX] *Cahita* (BE)
Sina-luta-oin *see* Shinalutaion
Sinalutaoin *see* Shinalutaion
Sinamaica *see* Paraujano
Sinamiut *see* Sinimiut
Sinapans *see* Lipan Apache
Sinapoil *see* Sanpoil
Sinapoiluch *see* Sanpoil
Sinarghutlitun [OR] *Chastacosta* (H)
Si-na-rxut-li-tun *see* Sinarghutlitun
Sinarxutlitun *see* Sinarghutlitun
Sinatchegg (H) Senijextee (BE)
Sinca *see* Xinca
Sincayuse *see* Sinkiuse-Columbia
Sincoalne *Coahuiltecan* (Hdbk10)
Sindagua *see* Cuaiquer
Sindeagdhe [Subclan] *Ponca* (H)
Sindiyui *see* Kongtalui
Sineca *see* Seneca
Sineckes *see* Seneca
Sinecu *see* Senecu del Sur
Sine-gain-see *see* Sinegainsee
Sinegainsee [Clan] *Huron* (H)
Sinek *see* Seneca

Sineka *see* Seneca
Sinekee *see* Seneca
Sinekes *see* Seneca
Sinekies *see* Seneca
Sineque *see* Seneca
Singacuchusca *see* Urarina
Singo *see* Sinago
Singsing *see* Sintsink
Sing-sings *see* Sintsink
Singsink *see* Sintsink
Sinhomene *see* Lower Spokan
Sinhomenish *see* Middle Spokan
Sinialkumuk *see* Sinia'lkumuk
Sinia'lkumuk [WA] *Wenatchi* (BE)
Sinica *see* Seneca
Sinicaes *see* Seneca
Sinicker *see* Seneca
Sinicu (H) *see also* Senecu (BE)
Sinicu (Hdbk10) *see also* Cenizo
  (Hdbk10)
Sinicu [TX] *Coahuiltecan* (BE)
Siniker *see* Seneca
Sinimiut [Can] *Central Eskimos*
  (BE)
Sinipoual *see* Sanpoil
Sinique *see* Seneca
Siñis *see* Zuni
sinitciskatariwis *see* Nez Perce
Si ni-te-li *see* Tillamook
Si ni-te-li *see* Nestucca
Siniteli *see* Nestucca
Siniteli *see* Tillamook
Si ni-te-li tunne *see* Alsea
Sinitelitunne *see* Alsea
Sinixzo *see* Cenizo
Sinkaielk *see* Sinkaietk
Sinkaietk (Hdbk12) *see also*
  Southern Okinagan (Hdbk12)
Sinkaietk [WA] (BE)
Sinkakaius [WA] *Salishan* (BE)
Sinkayus *see* Sinkiuse
Sinkayuse *see* Sinkiuse
Sinkine *see* Sinkyone
Sin-ki-use *see* Sinkiuse
Sinkiuse (LC) *see also* Sinkiuse-
  Columbia (LC)
Sinkiuse [WA] *Salish* (H)
Sinkiuse-Columbia [WA] (LC)
Sinkolkoluminuh (Oregon)
Sinkowarsin (Oregon)
Sinkquaius [WA] (Ye)
Sinkuaili *see* Okinagan
Sinkumchi'muk [WA] *Wenatchi*
  (BE)
Sinkumkunatkuh (Oregon)
Sinkyone [CA] (LC)
Sinnacock *see* Shinnecock
Sinnager *see* Seneca
Sinnakee *see* Seneca
Sinnaker *see* Seneca
Sinnakes *see* Seneca
Sinnaques *see* Seneca
Sinneca *see* Seneca

Sinneche *see* Seneca
Sinneck *see* Seneca
Sinneckes *see* Seneca
Sinneco *see* Seneca
Sinnecus *see* Seneca
Sinnedowane *see* Seneca
Sinnek *see* Seneca
Sinneka *see* Seneca
Sinnekaes *see* Seneca
Sinneke *see* Seneca
Sinnekee *see* Seneca
Sinneken *see* Seneca
Sinneken *see* Oneida
Sinnekies *see* Seneca
Sinnekis *see* Seneca
Sinnekus *see* Seneca
Sinneqars *see* Seneca
Sinnequaas *see* Seneca
Sinnequen *see* Seneca
Sinnequois *see* Seneca
Sinnica *see* Seneca
Sinnicar *see* Seneca
Sinnichee *see* Seneca
Sinnick *see* Seneca
Sinnickes *see* Seneca
Sinnickin *see* Seneca
Sinnicus *see* Seneca
Sinnikaes *see* Seneca
Sinnikes *see* Seneca
Sinniques *see* Seneca
Sinnodowanne *see* Seneca
Sinnodwannes *see* Seneca
Sinnokes *see* Seneca
Sinnondewannes *see* Seneca
Sinodouwas *see* Seneca
Sinodowannes *see* Seneca
Sinojo *see* Sinago
Sinoloa *see* Sinaloa
Sinondowan *see* Seneca
Sin-o-pah *see* Sinopah
Sinopah [Society] *Piegan* (H)
Sinoquipe [MX] *Opata* (H)
Sinpaivelish *see* Sanpoil
Sinpauelish *see* Sanpoil
Sin-poh-ell-ech-ach *see* Sanpoil
Sinpohellechach *see* Sanpoil
Sinpoil *see* Sanpoil
Sin-poil-er-hu *see* Sanpoil
Sinpoilerhu *see* Sanpoil
Sin-poil-schne (H) *see also* San-
  poil (LC)
Sinpoilschne *see* Sin-poil-schne
Sin-poil-schne *Salish* (H)
Sinpulame *see* Xupulame
Sinpusko'isok [WA] *Wenatchi*
  (BE)
Sinselan *see* Siuslaw
Sinselano *see* Siuslaw
Sinselau *see* Siuslaw
Sinselaw *see* Siuslaw
Sinsheelish *see* Sin-shee-lish
Sin-shee-lish *Salish* (H)
Sinsinck *see* Sintsink

Sinsincq *see* Sintsink
Sinsing *see* Sintsink
Sinsink *see* Sintsink
Sinsitwans *see* Sisseton
Sin-slih-hoo-ish *see* Sins-
  likhooish
Sinslihhooish *see* Sinslikhooish
Sin-slik-hoo-ish *see* Sins-
  likhooish
Sinslikhooish [ID] *Salish* (H)
Sin-spee-lish *see* Nespelim
Sinspeelish *see* Nespelim
Sin-te-hda wi-ca-sa *see* Northern
  Shoshone
Sin-te-hda wi-ca-sa *see* Shoshone
Sintehda wicasa *see* Northern
  Shoshone
Sintehda wicasa *see* Shoshone
Sintiatkumuk *see* Sintia'tkumuk
Sintia'tkumuk [WA] *Wenatchi*
  (BE)
Sin-too-too *see* Sintootoolish
Sintootoo *see* Sintootoolish
Sintootoolish [ID] *Salish* (H)
sintotoluh *see* Upper Spokan
Sintou-tou-oulish *see* Sin-
  tootoolish
Sintoutououlish *see* Sintootoolish
Sintsinck *see* Sintsink
Sint-sings *see* Sintsink
Sintsings *see* Sintsink
Sintsink [NY] *Wappinger* (BE)
Sint-Sinks *see* Sintsink
Sintsnicks *see* Sintsink
Sintutuuli *see* Upper Spokan
sinua'ikstuk *see* Lakes
Sinuitskistuk *see* Lakes
Sinuitskistux *see* Senijextee
Sin-who-yelp-pe-took *see*
  Colville
Sinwhoyelppetook *see* Colville
Sioane *see* Saone
Sioki *see* Zuni
Si-o-ki-bi *see* Zuni
Siokibi *see* Zuni
Si-o-me *see* Zuni
Siome *see* Zuni
Siona *see* Sioni
Siones *see* Saone
Sioni [Col] (LC)
Sionimone *see* Sichomovi
Sionne *see* Saone
Siooz *see* Dakota
Sios *see* Dakota
Siou *see* Dakota
Siouan [Lang] (H)
Sioune *see* Saone
Siouones *see* Saone
Siouse *see* Dakota
Sioushwap *see* Shuswap
Siouslaw *see* Siuslaw
Sious Medeouacanton *see* Mde-
  wakanton

Sioust *see* Dakota

Sioux (BE) *see also* Lakota, Dakota (LC)

Sioux (H) *see also* Tiou (BE)

Sioux de L'Est *see* Santee

Sioux des prairies *see* Teton

Siouxes *see* Dakota

Sioux Mindawarcarton *see* Mdewakanton

Sioux nomades *see* Teton

Sioux occidentaux *see* Teton

Sioux of the Lakes *see* Mdewakanton

Sioux of the Meadows *see* Teton

Sioux of the Plains *see* Teton

Sioux of the Prairies *see* Matatobe

Sioux of the River *see* Mdewakanton

Sioux of the River *see* Santee

Sioux of the Rocks *see* Assiniboin

Sioux of the Savannahs *see* Teton

Sioux of the Woods *see* Santee

Sioux orentaux *see* Santee

Siouxs *see* Dakota

Sioux sedentaires *see* Santee

Siouxs of the River St. Peter's *see* Santee

Sioux-Tentons *see* Teton

Sioux Teton *see* Teton

Siowes *see* Saone

Sioxes *see* Dakota

Sipacapense [Gua] (O)

Sipan *see* Lipan Apache

Sipapo *see* Piaroa

sipawlivt *see* Shipaulovi

Sipibo [PE] (LC)

Sipiwininiwug [Can] *Paskwawininiwug* (BE)

Sipiwithiniwuk *Sakawithiniwuk* (H)

Siposka-numakaki *see* Sipushkanumanke

Sippahaw *see* Sissipahaw

Sipposkanumakaki *see* Sippushkanumanke

Si-pu-cka nu-man-ke *see* Sipushkanumanke

Sipuckanumanke *see* Sipushkanumanke

Sipushkanumanke *Mandan* (H)

Sipushkenumanke (H) *see also* Seepooshka (H)

Sipuske-Numangkake *see* Sipushkanumanke

Sipuskenumangkake *see* Sipushkanumanke

ši-p-uwe *see* Ojibwa

šipuwe *see* Ojibwa

Siqinirmiut (Hdbk5) *see also* Inuit [Labrador] (Hdbk5)

siqinirmiut (Hdbk5) *see also* Suhinimyut (Hdbk5)

Siqinirmiut [Can] [*Inuit (Quebec)*] (Hdbk5)

Siquipil *Coahuiltecan* (Hdbk10)

Siquitchib *see* Kwatami

Sira-grins *see* Shregegon

Siragrins *see* Shregegon

Sircie *see* Sarsi

Sireneire *see* Sirineiri

Sirenikski [Lang] *Siberian Eskimos* (Hdbk5)

sireniktsy *see* Sirenikski

sirenkovtsy *see* Sirenikski

Siriana *see* Xiriana I

Siriano (LC) *see also* Shiriana (O)

Siriano (LC) *see also* Yanoama (LC)

Siriano [Col] (O)

Sirineiri [PE] (O)

Sirineri *see* Sirineiri

Sirineyri *see* Sirineiri

Sirinueses *see* Shawnee

Sirione *see* Siriano

Siriono [BO] (LC)

Sirixana *see* Shiriana

Sirixana *see* Yanoama

Siros *see* Piro [Pueblo]

Siroux *see* Dakota

Sirunes [NM] (H)

Sisaghroana *see* Missisauga

Sisapapa *see* Sihasapa

Sisatoon *see* Sisseton

Sisatoone *see* Sisseton

Siseton *see* Sisseton

Sisetwan *see* Sisseton

Sishat *see* Seshart

Sishiatl *see* Seechelt

Sishiatl *see* Sliammon

Sisibotari [MX] *Nevome* (H)

Sisika [Clan] [NM] (H)

Sisika-hano *see* Sisika

Si'sin lae *see* Sisintlae

Sisinlae *see* Sisintlae

Sisintlae [Clan] *Goasila* (H)

Sisintlae [Clan] *Kwakiutl* (H)

Sisintlae [Clan] *Nakoaktok* (H)

Sisintlae [Clan] *Nimkish* (H)

Sisintlae [Clan] *Tlauitsis* (H)

Sisin-towanyan *see* Sisseton

Sisintowanyan *see* Sisseton

Sisi toan *see* Sisseton

Sisitoan *see* Sisseton

Sisiton *see* Sisseton

Si-si-ton-wan *see* Sisseton

Sisitonwan *see* Sisseton

Si-si-t'wans *see* Sisseton

Sisitwans *see* Sisseton

si-si-ye-nin *see* Shoshone

sisiyenin *see* Shoshone

Sisizhanin *see* Northern Shoshone

Sisizhanin *see* Shoshone

Sis-qun-me'tunne *see* Yaquina

Sisqunmetunne *see* Yaquina

Sissaton *see* Sisseton

Sissatones *see* Sisseton

Sisseeton *see* Sisseton

Sissetoan *see* Sisseton

Sisseton [SD] *Santee* (LC)

Sisseton Dakota [Official name after 1993] (ICT, v.13, no.18, Oct.27, 1993, pp.B1, B2)

Sissetong *see* Sisseton

Sissetonwan *see* Sisseton

Sissipahau *see* Sissipahaw

Sissipahaw [NC] (BE)

Sissisaguez *see* Missisauga

Sissispahaw *see* Sissipahaw

Sissitoan *see* Sisseton

Sissiton *see* Sisseton

Sissitong *see* Sisseton

Sissit'wan *see* Sisseton

Sissitwan *see* Sisseton

Sis-stsi-me *see* Sitsime

Sisstsime *see* Sitsime

Sistasoona *see* Sisseton

Sistasoone *see* Sisseton

sistavana-tewa *see* San Ildefonso

Siston *see* Sisseton

Si-stsi-me *see* Sitsime

Sistsime *see* Sitsime

Si-tanga *see* Chedunga

Sitanga *see* Chedunga

Sitca *see* Sitka

Sitca'netl *see* Sichanetl

Sitcanetl *see* Sichanetl

Sitcan-xu *see* Brule

Sitcanxu *see* Brule

Sitcha *see* Sitka

Sitchom-ovi *see* Sichomovi

Sitchomovi *see* Sichomovi

Sitcomovi *see* Sichomovi

Sitconski *see* Sitcon-ski

Sitcon-ski [MN] *Assiniboin* (BE)

Si-tcum-o-vi *see* Sichomovi

Sitibo *see* Setebo

Sitka [AK] *Tlingit* (BE)

Sitka-kwan *see* Sitka

Sitka-qwan *see* Sitka

Sitkhinskoe *see* Sitka

Sitkias *see* Siksika

Sitkoedi [AK] *Tlingit* (H)

Siton *see* Teton

S!itqoe'di *see* Sitkoedi

Sitqoedi *see* Sitkoedi

Sits [Clan] *Laguna* (H)

Sits-hanoch *see* Tsits

Sitsime [Pueblo] [NM] (H)

Sitskabinohpaka *see* Seechkaberuhpaka

Sitteoui *see* Uzutiuhi

Si'twans *see* Sisseton

Sitwans *see* Sisseton

Siuola *see* Zuni

Siupam [TX] *Coahuiltecan* (BE)

Siur Poil *see* Sanpoil

Siusclau *see* Siuslaw

Siuselaw *see* Siuslaw
Siuslaw [OR] (LC)
Siuslawan *see* Siuslaw
Siusy-Tapuya (O) *see also* Baniwa (O)
Siusy-Tapuya [Col] *Wakuenai* (O)
Sivilleta *see* Sevilleta
Sivinte *see* Shivwits
Sivits *see* Shivwits
Sivokakhmeit *see* Saint Lawrence Islanders
Sivokakmeit *see* Yuit
Sivola *see* Zuni
Sivolo *see* Zuni
Sivulo *see* Zuni
Sivuqaq *see* Saint Lawrence Islanders
Sivux *see* Dakota
Si-vwa-pi *see* Siwapi
Sivwapi *see* Siwapi
Sivwapi wiñwu *see* Siwapi
Siwahoo *see* Siwanoy
Siwaihsu [Br] *Southern Nambicuara* (O)
Siwanoy *Delaware* (Hdbk15)
Siwanoy [NY] *Wappinger* (LC)
Siwapi [Clan] *Hopi* (H)
Siwaro *see* Jivaro
Siwash *see* Salishan
Siwer *see* Dakota
Siwhipa *see* Isleta
siwi *see* Zuni
Siwinna *see* Sichomovi
Six *see* Kwatami
Sixacama *see* Sijame
Six Allied Nations *see* Iroquois
Sixame *see* Sijame
Sixes *see* Kwatami
Sixes River Indians *see* Kwatami
Sixhehiekoon *see* Siksika
Six-he-kie-koon *see* Siksika
Sixikau'a *see* Siksika
Six Nations (BE)
Six Nations (H) *see also* Iroquois (LC)
Six Nations Living at Sandusky *see* Mingo
Six Towns Indians *see* Oklahannali
Siya *see* Sia
Siyanguayas *see* Sillanguagyas
siya-va *see* Sia
siyava *see* Sia
Siyelpa *see* Colville
Siyi'ta *see* Siyita
Siyita [Can] *Stalo* (BE)
Siyo-subula *see* Shiyosubula
Siyo-tanka *see* Siyotanka
Skaap *see* Khaap
Skacewanilom *see* Abnaki
Skaddal [WA] *Wenatchi* (BE)
Skad-dat *see* Skaddal

Skaddat *see* Skaddal
Skadjat *see* Skagit
Skadjet *see* Skagit
Skaemena *see* Sokulk
Skaget *see* Skagit
Skaghnanes *see* Nipissing
Skaghquanoghrono *see* Nipissing
Skagit [WA] *Swinomish* (LC)
Ska-hak-bush *see* Skahakmehu
Skahakbush *see* Skahakmehu
Ska-hak-mehu *see* Skahakmehu
Skahakmehu [WA] *Salish* (H)
Skahene-hadai [AK] [*Chaahllanes*] (H)
Skaiakos [Can] *Seechelt* (BE)
Skai-na-mish *see* Skihwamish
Skainamish *see* Skihwamish
Skai-schil-t'nish *see* Skaischiltnish
Skaischiltnish [WA] *Salish* (H)
Skaisi *see* Kutenai
Skaiwhamish *see* Skihwamish
Skai-who-mish *see* Skihwamish
Sk'a-jub *see* Skagit
Skajub *see* Skagit
Ska-ka-bish *see* Skokomish
Skakabish *see* Skokomish
Skakalapiak [WA] *Colville* (BE)
Ska-ka-mish *see* Skokomish
Skakamish *see* Skokomish
Skakies *see* Sauk
Skakobish *see* Skokomish
Skala'li *see* Tuscarora
Skalali *see* Tuscarora
Skal-lum *see* Clallam
Skallum *see* Clallam
Skalza *see* Kutenai
Skalzi *see* Kutenai
Ska-moy-num-achs *see* Skamoynumachs
Skamoynumachs *Okinagan* (H)
Ska-moy-num-acks *see* Wanapam
Skamoynumacks *see* Wanapam
Skanatiarationo *see* Nanticoke
Skaniadaradighroona *see* Nanticoke
Skaniatarati-haka *see* Nanticoke
Skaniatarationo *see* Nanticoke
Skanigadaradighroona *see* Nanticoke
Skaniodaraghroona *see* Nanticoke
Ska-no-wecl tunne *see* Skanowethltunne
Skanowecltunne *see* Skanowethltunne
Skanowethltunne [OR] *Takelma* (H)
Skanuka (H)
Ska-ru-ren *see* Tuscarora
Skaruren *see* Skaru'ren
Skaruren *see* Tuscarora

Skaru'ren [NC] *Tuscarora* (H)
Ska-sah-ah *see* Skasahah
Skasahah [VanI] *Cowichan* (H)
Skasquamish *see* Skokomish
Sk'au'elitsk *see* Scowlits
Skauelitsk *see* Scowlits
Skaukisagi *see* Fox
Skaun-ya-ta-ha-ti-hawk *see* Nanticoke
Skaunyatahatihawk *see* Nanticoke
Ska'utal *see* Skaddal
Skautal *see* Skaddal
Skawah-look *see* Skwawalooks
Skawahlook *see* Skwawalooks
Skawhahmish *see* Skihwamish
Ska-whamish *see* Skihwamaish
Skawhamish *see* Skihwamish
Skawuahmish *see* Skokomish
Skaxshurunu *see* Fox
Skea-wa-mish *see* Skihwamish
Skecaneronon *see* Nipissing
Skec-e-ree *see* Skidi Pawnee
Skeceree *see* Skidi Pawnee
Ske-chei-a-mouse *see* Skeckeramouse
Skecheiamouse *see* Shackeramouse
Skecheramouse [WA] *Salish* (H)
Skedans *Southern Haidu* (Anthro, v.9, no.3, pp.160–61)
Skedee *see* Skidi Pawnee
Skee-cha-way *see* Sitswish
Skeechaway *see* Skitswish
Skee-de *see* Skidi Pawnee
Skeede *see* Skidi Pawnee
Skeedee *see* Skidi Pawnee
Skee-e-ree *see* Skidi Pawnee
Skeeeree *see* Skidi Pawnee
Skeelsomish *see* Skitswish
Skeen *see* Skinpah
Skeena *see* Tsimshian
Skeeree *see* Skidi Pawnee
Skeetchestn (Hdbk12) *see also* Deadman's Creek Band (Hdbk12)
Skeetchestn (Hdbk12) *see also* skemqunemx (Hdbk12)
Skeetchestn [BC] *Shuswap* (Hdbk12)
Skeetshoo *see* Coeur d'Alene
Skeetshues *see* Coeur d'Alene
Skeetsomish *see* Skitswish
Skeetsonish *see* Coeur d'Alene
Skein-tla-ma [OR] (Forg)
Skekaneronon *see* Nipissing
Skekwanenhronon *see* Nipissing
Skelsa-ulk *see* Kutenai
Skelsaulk *see* Kutenai
Ske-luh *see* Okinagan
Skeluh *see* Okinagan
skemqinemx [BC] *Shuswap* (Hdbk12)

Skenchiohronon *see* Fox
Skequaneronon *see* Nipissing
Skere *see* Skidi Pawnee
Skerreh *see* Skidi Pawnee
Sketch Hue *see* Coeur d'Alene
Sketch Hughe *see* Coeur d'Alene
Sketsomish *see* Coeur d'Alene
Sketsoomish *see* Skitswish
Sketsui *see* Coeur d'Alene
Sketsui *see* Skitswish
Skeuyelpi *see* Colville
Skeysehamish *see* Shihwamish
Ske-yuh *see* Ntlakyapamuk
Skeyuh *see* Ntlakyapamuk
Skey-wah-mish *see* Skihwamish
Skeywahmish *see* Skihwamish
Skeywhamish *see* Skihwamish
S'khinkit *see* Tlingit
Skhinkit *see* Tlingit
Skida-i la'nas *see* Skidai-lanas
Skidailanas *see* Skidai-lanas
Skidai-lanas [Family] *Haida* (H)
Ski'di *see* Skidi Pawnee
Skidi Pawnee [NE] *Pawnee Confederacy* (BE)
Skidirahru [NE] *Skidi Pawnee* (H)
Skidi rah'ru *see* Skidirahru
Skien *see* Skinpah
Skighquan *see* Nipissing
Skihikintnub *see* Sinkiuse-Columbia
Skihwamish (IndL, no.32) *see also* Skykomish (BE)
Skihwamish [WA] *Salish* (H)
Skijistin *see* Skeetchestn
Skillool *see* Skilloot
Skilloot [WA] (BE)
Skillute *see* Skilloot
Skillutt *see* Skilloot
Skilumaak [WA] *Colville* (BE)
Skim-i-ah-moo *see* Semiahmoo
Skimiahmoo *see* Semiahmoo
Skin (H) *see also* Skinpah (BE)
Sk-inge'nes *see* Skingenes
Skingenes [VanI] *Songish* (BE)
Skin Indians [WA] (BE)
Skinnacock *see* Shinnecock
Ski'npa *see* Skinpah
Skinpa *see* Skinpah
Skin-pah *see* Skinpah
Skinpah [WA, OR] *Tenino* (BE)
Skinpaw *see* Skinpah
Skin pricks *see* Tawehash
Skiquamish *see* Skokomish
Skiri Pawnee *see* Skidi Pawnee
Ski-shis-tin *see* Skeetchestn
Skishistin *see* Skeetchestn
Skislainaixadai *see* Skistlainai-hadai
Sk!i'sla-i na-i xasa-i *see* Skist-lainai-hadai
Skistlainai-hadai [Subclan] *Haida* (H)

Skitawish *see* Coeur d'Alene
Skit-mish *see* Skitmish
Skitsaih *see* Skitswish
Skitsaish *see* Skitswish
Skitsamuq *see* Skitswish
Skitsui *see* Skitswish
Skitsuish *see* Skitswish
Skitswish [ID] [*Coeur d'Alene*] (LC)
Skittagetan [Lang] *Haida* (LC)
Skiuse *see* Cayuse
Skiwhamish *see* Skihwamish
Sk-Khabish *see* Sekamish
Skkhabish *see* Sekamish
S'Klallam *see* Clallam
Sklallam *see* Clallam
S'Klallan *see* Clallam
Sklallan *see* Clallam
Sklarkum *see* Sanpoil
Skoahchnuh *see* Sinkiuse-Columbia
Skoa'tl'adas *see* Skwahladas
Skoffie *see* Naskapi
Skog *see* Skooke
Skoiel-poi *see* Colville
Skokamish *see* Skokomish
Sko-ki han-ya *see* Muskogee
Sko-ki han-ya *see* Creek
Skoki hanya *see* Creek
Skoki hanya *see* Muskogee
Sko-kobc *see* Skokomish
Skokobc *see* Skokomish
Skokomish [WA] *Twana* (LC)
Sko-ko-nish *see* Skokomish
Skokonish *see* Skokomish
Skolsa *see* Kutenai
S'komook *see* Comox
Skomook *see* Comox
Skooke [Clan] *Abnaki* (H)
Skookum Chuck [BC] *Salish* (H)
Sko-pabsh *see* Skopamish
Skopabsh *see* Skopamish
Skopahmish *see* Skopamish
Skopamish [WA] *Muckleshoot* (BE)
Skope-ahmish *see* Skopamish
Skopeahmish *see* Skopamish
Skope-a-mish *see* Skopamish
Skopeamish *see* Skopamish
Sko-sko-mish *see* Skokomish
Skoskomish *see* Skokomish
S'Kosle-ma-mish *see* Shotle-mamish
Skoslemamish *see* Shotlemamish
Skotlbabsh *see* Sko'tlbabsh
Sko'tlbabsh [WA] *Puyallup* (BE)
Skoton (BE) *see also* Chastacosta (BE)
Skoton [OR] *Umpqua* (H)
Skowall *see* Skwawalooks
skowa'xlsenex *see* Sinkiuse-Columbia
skowaxlsenex *see* Sinkius-Columbia

Skowliti *see* Scowlits
Skowtous [BC] *Upper Thompson* (H)
Skoyelpi *see* Colville
Skoylpeli [Lang] *Salishan* (Contri, v.1, p.248)
Skraeligjar *see* Eskimos
Skraelingar *see* Eskimos
Skraelingr *see* Eskimos
Skraelings *see* Eskimos
Skraellingar *see* Eskimos
S Kraellings *see* Eskimos
Skraellings *see* Eskimos
Skrellings *see* Eskimos
Skroelingues *see* Eskimos
Skstellnemuk [Can] *Shuswap* (BE)
Sk-tah-le-gum *see* Sktahlejum
Sktahlegum *see* Sktahlejum
Sk-tah-le-jum *see* Sktahlejum
Sktahlejum [WA] *Salish* (H)
Sk-tahl-mish *see* Sktehlmish
Sk-tehlmish *see* Sktehlmish
Sktehlmish [WA] *Salish* (H)
Skuaisheni *see* Siksika
Skuakisagi *see* Fox
Skuck-stan-a-jumps *see* Sktahlejum
Skuingkung [BC] *Songish* (BE)
Skukem Chuck *see* Skookum Chuck
Skukulat'kuh *see* Sinkiuse-Columbia
Skull Valley *Gosiute* (Hdbk11)
Skultaqchi'mh *see* Sinkiuse-Columbia
Skulteen [BC] *Salish* (H)
Skunnemoke *see* Attacapa
Skurghut [OR] *Chastacosta* (H)
Skurshka [Clan] [NM] *Laguna* (H)
Sku-rxut *see* Skurghut
Skurxut *see* Skurghut
Sku'tani *see* Atsina
Skutani *see* Atsina
Skuyelpi *see* Colville
Skwadabsh *see* Skwada'bsh
Skwada'bsh [WA] *Swinomish* (BE)
Skwahladas [BC] *Haida* (H)
Skwak-sin *see* Squaxon
Skwaksin *see* Squaxon
Skwale *see* Nisqualli
Skwale'absh *see* Nisqualli
Sk'wa-le-ube *see* Nisqualli
Skwaleube *see* Nisqualli
Skwali *see* Nisqualli
Skwalliahmish *see* Nisqualli
Skwallyamish [Lang] *Salishan* (BE)
Skwapabsh *see* Skwapa'bsh
Skwapa'bsh [WA] *Puyallup* (BE)
Skwawahlook *see* Skwawalooks
Skwawalooks [Can] *Stalo* (BE)

Skwayaithlhabsh [WA] *Sahe-
hwamish* (BE)
Skwilsidiabsh *see* Skwilsi'dia-bsh
Skwilsi'dia-bsh [WA] *Snohomish*
(BE)
Skwlotsid *see* Skwlo'tsid
Skwlo'tsid [WA] *Puyallup* (BE)
Skykomish [WA] *Snoqualmie*
(BE)
Sky-Man *see* Kheyataotonwe
Skynse *see* Cayuse
Skyuse *see* Cayuse
Sky-wa-mish *see* Skihwamish
Skywamish *see* Skihwamish
Slakaiya *Wailaki* (Pub, v.20, no.6,
pp.103–105)
Sla-na-pa *see* Tzlanapah
Slanapa *see* Tzlanapah
Slave (H) *see also* Kawchottine
(LC)
Slave (H) *see also* Thlingchadinne
(LC)
Slave Indians (H) *see also* Etchaot-
tine (H)
Slave Indians (H) *see also*
Etchareottine (H)
Slave Indians [BC] (LC)
Slave Indians of Ft. Liard (H) *see
also* Etcheridiegottine (BE)
Slaves (H) *see also* Etchareottine
(H)
Slaves of Lower Hay River *see*
Klodesseottine
Slaves of Upper Hay River *see*
Klodesseottine
Slaves proper *see* Etchaottine
Slavey *see* Etchareottine
Slaxa'yux *see* Upper Fraser
Slaxayux *see* Upper Fraser
Sledge Island *Bering Strait Eski-
mos* (Hdbk5)
Sleepy Eyes Band *see* Chans-
dachikana
Sleepy Kettle Band *see* Cheokhba
Slender Bows *see* Kutenai
Sliammon [BC] *Comox* (BE)
slide people *see* Baskaiya
Slka-tkml-schi *Kalispee* (H)
Slosh *see* Schloss
Slub-e-a-ma *see* Slubeama
Slubeama [Can] *Salish* (H)
Slumach [BC] *Katsey* (H)
Slumagh *see* Slumach
Smackshop [WA] *Chilluckitte-
quaw* (BE)
Smacshop *see* Smackshop
Smacsop *see* Smackshop
S'Mag'emut *see* Magemiut
Smagemut *see* Magemiut
Sma-hoo-men-a-ish (H) *see also*
Spokan (LC)
Smahoomenaish *see* Sma-hoo-
men-a-ish

Sma-hoo-men-a-ish *Salish* (H)
Smakshop *see* Smackshop
Sma-leh-hu *see* Smalihu
Smalehhu *see* Smalihu
Smalh *see* Simulkamish
Smalh-kahmish *see* Smulkamish
Smalhkahmish *see* Smulkamish
Sma-lih-hu *see* Smalihu
Smalihhu *see* Smalihu
Smali-hu *see* Smalihu
Smalihu [WA] *Salish* (H)
Small Robes *see* Inuksiks
Smascop *see* Smackshop
smela'kamux *see* Nicola
smelekamux *see* Nicola
Smelekamux *see* Similkameen
smelekemux *see* Nicla
smele'qemux *see* Nicola
smeleqemux *see* Nicola
Smelkameen *see* Similkameen
Smel-ka-mish *see* Smulkamish
Smelkamish *see* Smulkamish
smelkamix *see* Nicola
Smichunulauk [WA] *Colville* (BE)
Smile-kamuq *see* Nicola
Smilekamuq *see* Nicola
Smile-qamux *see* Similkameen
Smileqamux *see* Similkameen
Smilkameen *see* Similkameen
Smilkamin *see* Similkameen
Smilkemix *see* Similkameen
Smith Creek Valley *Western
Shoshone* (Hdbk11)
Smith River Indians *see*
Khaamotene
Smith Sound Eskimos *see* Ita
Smith Sound Eskimos *see* Polar
Eskimos
smlkamix *see* Nicola
smlqamix *see* Similkameen
Smockshop *see* Smackshop
Smo'en *see* Smoen
Smoen [BC] *Bellacoola* (H)
Smokshop *see* Smackshop
Smopoy *see* Shongopovi
Smulcoe *see* Smulkamish
Smul-ka-mish *see* Smulkamish
Smulkamish [WA] *Muckleshoot*
(BE)
Smuttuns [WA] *Salish* (H)
Sn. *see* Saint
S-na-a-chikst *see* Senijextee
Snaachikst *see* Senijextee
Snahaim *see* Snakaim
snaichksti *see* Lakes
Snai'tcekst *see* Lakes
Snaitcekst *see* Lakes
Snai'tcekstek *see* Lakes
Snaitcekstek *see* Lakes
snai'tckstka *see* Lakes
snaitckstka *see* Lakes
Snakaim [BC] *Upper Thompsons*
(H)

Snake (BE) *see also* Comanche
(LC)
Snake (BE) *see also* Walpapi (LC)
Snake (H) *see also* Comanche
(LC)
Snake (H) *see also* Togwingani
(H)
Snake (Hdbk11) *see also* Eastern
Shoshone [on the Plains]
(Hdbk11)
Snake (Hdbk11) *see also* Shoshone
(LC)
Snake (Hdbk11) *see also* Yahuskin
(LC)
Snake [OR] *Northern Paiute*
(Hdbk11)
Snake Diggers *see* Southern
Paiute
Snake Diggers *see* Paiute
Snake Diggers *see* Shoshone
Snake Indians (BE) *see also* Wal-
papi (LC)
Snake River [MN] *Chippewa* (H)
Snake Root Diggers *see*
Shoshoko
Snakes *see* Walpapi
Snake Valley *Western Shoshone*
(Hdbk11)
Snalatine *see* Atfalati
Snanaimooh [Clan] *Nanaimo* (H)
Snanaimuk [Lang] *Salishan* (BE)
Snanaimuq [Clan] *Nanaimo* (H)
Snanaimux *see* Snanaimuk
Snchalik [WA] *Colville* (BE)
Snchumutast [WA] *Colville* (BE)
Snegs *see* Shoshone
Snekwa?etkwemx [BC] *Bonaparte
Division* (Hdbk12)
Sniekos *see* Seneca
Snilaminak [WA] *Colville* (BE)
snke'iwsx *see* Sinkiuse
Snkuasik [WA] *Colville* (BE)
Snoa *see* Northern Shoshone
Snoa *see* Shoshone
Sno-dom-ish *see* Snohomish
Snodomish *see* Snohomish
Sno-ho-mish *see* Snohomish
Snohomish [WA] *Salish* (LC)
Sno-kwal-mi-yukh *see* Sno-
qualmie
Snokwalmiyukh *see* Snoqualmie
Snokwalmu *see* Snoqualmie
Snonkwe'ametl *see*
Snonkweametl
Snonkweametll [Can] *Stalo* (BE)
Snonoos *see* Snonowas
Snonowas (BE) *see also* Nanaimo
(BE)
Snonowas [VanI] *Salish* (H)
Sno-no-wus *see* Snonowas
Snonowus *see* Snonowas
Sno-qual-a-mick *see* Snoqualmie
Snoqualamick *see* Snoqualmie

Sno-qual-a-muhe *see* Sno-
qualmie
Snoqualamuhe *see* Snoqualmie
Sno-qual-a-muke *see* Sno-
qualmie
Snoqualamuke *see* Snoqualmie
Snoqualimich *see* Snoqualmie
Sno-qualimick *see* Snoqualmie
Snoqualimick *see* Snoqualmie
Snoqualmi *see* Snoqualmie
Sno-qual-mie *see* Snoqualmie
Snoqualmie [WA] *Nisqualli* (BE)
Snoqualmoo *see* Snoqualmie
Sno-qual-mook *see* Snoqualmie
Snoqualmook *see* Snoqualmie
Snoqualmu [WA] *Snoqualmie* (H)
snpesqwawsexw *see* Wenatchi
Snpuelish *see* Sanpoil
snqa'aws *see* Sinkiuse
Snrai'tcskstex *see* Lakes
Sntutu'u *see* Middle Spokan
Soacatino [TX, LA] *Caddo* (BE)
Soariapode *see* Pira-Tapuya
Soatlkobsh [WA] *Twana* (BE)
Soayalpi *see* Colville
Soba [MX] *Papago* (H)
Sobahipuri *see* Sobaipuri
Sobaibo [MX] *Acaxee* (BE)
Sobaihipure *see* Sobaipuri
Sobaipori *see* Sobaipuri
Sobaipoti *see* Sobaipuri
Sobaipure *see* Sobaipuri
Sobaipuri [AZ] (LC)
Sobaipuris Pimas *see* Sobaipuri
Sobal-ruck *see* Smulkamish
Sobalruck *see* Smulkamish
Sobaypure *see* Sobaipuri
Sobaypuri *see* Sobaipuri
Soccoki *see* Sokoki
Soccoqui *see* Sokoki
Soccoro *see* Socorro del Sur
Soccorro *see* Socorro del Sur
Soccouky *see* Sokoki
Sockacheenum *see* Shuswap
Sock-a-muke *see* Sakumehu
Sockamuke *see* Sakumehu
Sockegones *see* Sokoki
Sockeyes *see* Sauk
Sockhigones *see* Sokoki
Sock Indians *see* Sooke
Soclan *see* Saclan
Socoas *see* Shokhowa
Socoisuka [CA] *Thamien* (H)
Socoki *see* Sokoki
Socollomillo *see* Lear Lake Indi-
ans
Socoqui *see* Sokoki
Socoquio *see* Sokoki
Socoquioi *see* Sokoki
Socora *see* Socorro
Socoro *see* Socorro
Socorra *see* Socorro
Socorre *see* Socorro

Socorro [NM] *Piro* (H)
Socorro del Sur [NM] *Piro* (H)
Socouky *see* Sokoki
Soda Creek [BC] *Fraser River
Shuswap* (H)
Sogkonate *see* Sakonnet
Sogup *Ute* (H)
Sohhweihlp *see* Colville
Sohl [Clan] [NM] (*Pueblo*) (H)
Sohol [Clan] [NM] *Pecos* (H)
Sohonut [CA] (H)
Soieenos *see* Somenos
Soi-il-enu *see* Tsawatenok
Soiilenu *see* Tsawatenok
Soi it inu *see* Tsawatenok
Soiitinu *see* Tsawatenok
Sok *see* Sooke
Soke *see* Zoque
sok'ein *see* Navajo
sokein *see* Navajo
sok'e'ina *see* Navajo
sokeina *see* Navajo
Sokes *see* Sooke
Sokkie *see* Sauk
Soko *see* Shoco
So-ko-a *see* Shokhowa
Sokoa *see* Shokhowa
Sokoki [ME] *Abnaki* (LC)
Sokokiois *see* Sokoki
Sokomba [Col] *Yuko* (O)
Sokoqui *see* Sokoki
Sokoquiois *see* Sokoki
Sokoquis *see* Sokoki
Sokoueki *see* Sokoki
Sokulk (Hdbk12) *see also* Wana-
pam (Hdbk12)
Sokulk [WA] *Paloos* (BE)
Solameco *see* Chiaha
Solano [Lang] [*TX*] (Hdbk10)
Soledad [CA] *Chalon* (BE)
Soloagua [MX] (Hdbk10)
Sologuegue [MX] (Hdbk10)
Solomec [CAm] *Mamean* (O)
Soloti [SA] *Chorote* (O)
Soltec [Lang] *Chatino* (BE)
Solumnee *see* Tuolumne
Somass *see* Tsomosath
Somehulitk [Can] *Heiltsuk* (BE)
Somena *see* Ntlakyapamuk
Some-na *see* Siamannas
Somena *see* Siamannas
So-me-nau *see* Somenos
Somenau *see* Somenos
Somenos [VanI] *Cowichan* (BE)
So'mexulitx *see* Somehulitk
Somexulitx *see* Somehulitk
Somi *see* Zuni
Son [Clan] *Jemez* (H)
Sonaque [TX] *Coahuiltecan* (BE)
Sonayam *see* Sonayan
Sonayan [TX] *Coahuiltecan* (BE)
Soneme (LC) *see also* Soneñes (O)
Soneñes [PE] *Ese Ejje* (O)

Songars *see* Songish
Songasketon *see* Sisseton
Songaskicons *see* Sisseton
Songasquiton *see* Sisseton
Songastikon *see* Sisseton
Songat *see* Sisseton
Songatskiton *see* Sisseton
Songees *see* Songish
Songeskiton *see* Sisseton
Songeskitoux *see* Sisseton
Songestikon *see* Sisston Sioux
Songhies *see* Songish
Songish [VanI] (BE)
Songoapt *see* Shongopovi
Sonik'ni *see* Wichita
Sonikni *see* Wichita
Sonkaskiton *see* Sisseton
Sonkawas *see* Tonkawa
Sonnonteronnon *see* Seneca
Sonnonthouan *see* Seneca
Sonnontoehronnon *see* Seneca
Sonnontouaheronnon *see* Seneca
Sonnontoüan *see* Seneca
Sonnontoueronnon *see* Seneca
Sonnontovan *see* Seneca
Sonontoen *see* Seneca
Sonontoerrhonon *see* Seneca
Sonontouan *see* Seneca
Sonontouanhrronon *see* Seneca
Sonontouehronon *see* Seneca
Sonontouon *see* Seneca
Sonontrerrhonon *see* Seneca
Sonora *see* Opata
Sonoran [Lang] [*Southern Uto-
Aztecan*] (Hdbk10)
Sonsa [Clan] [NM] *Jemez* (H)
Sonsaash *see* Sonsa
Sontaouan *see* Ottawa
Sontouaheronnon *see* Seneca
Sontouhoironon *see* Seneca
Sontouhouethonon *see* Seneca
So-nus-ho-gwa-to-war *see*
Cayuga
Sonushogwatowar *see* Cayuga
Soo *see* Sioux
Sooke [VanI] *Songish* (BE)
Soones *see* Zuni
Soon-noo-daugh-we-no-wenda
see Cayuga
Soonnoodaughwenowenda *see*
Cayuga
Soopis *see* Esopus
Soopus *see* Esopus
Soo-wan-a-mooh *see* Okinagan
Soowanamooh *see* Okinagan
Sopaktalgi [Clan] *Creek* (H)
So-pak-tu *see* Sopaktalgi
Sopaktu *see* Sopaktalgi
Sopes *see* Esopus
Sopez *see* Esopus
Sopus *see* Esopus
Soqenaqai'mex *see* Okinagan
Soquachjck *see* Sokoki

Soquackick *see* Sokoki
Soquagkeeke *see* Squawkeag
Soquatuck *see* Sokoki
Soque *see* Zoque
Soquenaqai'mex *see* Okinagan
Soquoki *see* Sokoki
Soquoqui *see* Sokoki
Soquoquisii *see* Sokoki
Soraphanigh *see* Sarapinagh
Sorcerers *see* Nipissing
Sore Backs *see* Chankaokhan
Sorora Teguime *see* Opata
Sorsi *see* Sarsi
Sosemiteiz *see* Awani
Sosemity *see* Awani
Soshawnee *see* Shoshone
Soshka [Clan] *Pueblo* (H)
Sosh'ka-hano *see* Soshka
Soshone *see* Shoshone
So-so-ba *see* Shobarboobeer
Sosoba *see* Shobarboobeer
So-so-bu-bar *see* Shobarboobeer
Sosobubar *see* Shobarboobeer
So-so-i-ha-ni *see* Shoshone
Sosoihani *see* Shoshone
Sosokos *see* Shoshoko
So-so-na *see* Shoshone
Sosona *see* Shoshone
Sosone *see* Shoshone
Sosonee *see* Shoshone
Sosones *see* Shoshone
So-so-ni *see* Shoshone
Sosoni *see* Shoshone
Sosuties *see* Chippewa
Sotegaraik *see* Ashluslay
Sotenna *see* Sarsi
Soteomellos *see* Wappo
Sothoues *see* Uzutiuhi
Sothouis *see* Uzutiuhi
Sothuze *see* Chippewa
Sotiagai *see* Ashluslay
Sotiagay *see* Ashluslay
Soto *see* Chippewa
Soto *see* Saulteaux
Soto [Lang] *Algonquian* (Bull13)
Sotoes *see* Chippewa
Sotolvekopai *see* Soto'lve-kopai
Soto'lve-kopai [AZ] *Walapai* (BE)
Sotomieyos *see* Wappo
Sotonis *see* Uzutiuhi
Sotoos *see* Chippewa
Sotoriva *see* Saturiwa
Sotos *see* Uzutiuhi
Sotouis *see* Uzutiuhi
Sotto *see* Chippewa
Soturiba *see* Satuirwa
Souanetto [LA] (H)
Souchitioni *see* Doustioni
Souchitionij *see* Doustioni
Souchitiony *see* Doustioni
Souchitiony *see* Uzutiuhi
Soudaye *see* Kadohadacho
Soues *see* Dakota

Souex *see* Dakota
Sougaskicon *see* Sisseton
Souhegan [NH] *Pennacook Confederacy* (BE)
Souis *see* Dakota
Soulier Noir *see* Amahami
Soulteaux *see* Chippewa
Sounes *see* Zuni
Sounikaeronon (H)
Souon *see* Saone
Souon-Teton *see* Saone
Souriquois [Lang] *Algonquian* (BE)
Souriquois Indians *see* Micmac
Sous *see* Sioux
Soushwap *see* Shuswap
Sousitoon *see* Sisseton
Souteus *see* Chippewa
Southampton Indians *see* Shinnecock
South Andrian *Shuswap* (H)
South Bands *see* Pawnee
South Bay *see* Nusehlsatl
South Blackfeet *Siksika* (H)
South Canyon Band [BC] *Canyon Shuswap* (Hdbk12)
Southeast Baffin Inuktitut *Eastern Canada* (Hdbk5)
Southeastern Colombia Carib [Lang] *Carijona* (UAz, v.28)
Southeastern Ojibwa (Hdbk15)
Southeastern Pomo [CA] (BE)
Southeastern Yavapai (Hdbk10) *see also* Kewevkapaya (BE)
Southeastern Yavapai [AZ] (Pub, v.29, no.3, p.177)
Southeast Greenlanders *Greenland Eskimos* (Hdbk5)
Southerly Wintun [Lang] [CA] (Pub, v.6, no.1, pp.290–300)
Southern *see* Nootka
Southern Apache *see* Faraon
Southern Apache *see* Gila Apache
Southern Arapaho (H) *see also* Nawunena (H)
Southern Arapaho [WY] (BE)
Southern Band *see* Nawunena
Southern Brule (TW, p.39, no.6, Je 1992)
Southern California [Lang] *Shoshonean* (H)
Southern Carib [Lang] (UAz, no.28)
Southern Carrier [Can] (BE)
Southern Cayapo [Br] (O)
Southern Cheyenne (H)
Southern Chiricahua (H) *see also* Chiricahua Apache (LC)
Southern Chiricahua [MX] (Hdbk10)
Southern Choco [Col] (O)
Southern Chorote [Arg] (O)
Southern Coast *see* Marin-Bodega

Southern Comanche *see* Penateka
Southern Costonoan [Lang] *Utian* (CA-8)
Southern Diegueño [BaC, MX] (BE)
Southern Diegueño [Lang] *see* Kamia
Southern Embera [Lang] (LC)
Southern Eskimos *see* Kaniagmiut
Southern Guaymi [Pan, CR] (O)
Southern Guiana Carib [Lang] *Southern Carib* (UAz, v.28)
Southern Hunters (BE)
Southern Indians *see* Cree
Southern Indians *see* Mashpee
Southern Killamuk *see* Yakonan
Southern Killamuk *see* Yaquina
Southern Maidu (Pub, v.20, no.3)
Southern Mewuk *see* Mariposa
Southern Minquas *see* Conestoga
Southern Miwok [CA] *Miwok* (BE)
Southern Molala [Lang] [OR] *Molala* (Hdbk12)
Southern Moquelumnan [Lang] [CA] (Pub, v.6, no.1, pp.305–14)
Southern Motilones *see* Bari
Southern Nambicuara [Br] (O)
Southern Nisenan [Lang] [CA] *Maidu* (He)
Southern Numic [Lang] [*Uto-Aztecan*] (Hdbk11)
Southern Okinagan [WA] *Middle Columbia River Salish* (Hdbk12)
Southern Paiute [NV] (BE)
Southern Pimas *see* Nevome
Southern Pomo [CA] (BE)
Southern Sierra *see* Mariposa
Southern Sierra Miwok [Lang] (CA-8)
Southern Tarahumara [Lang] (Hdbk10)
Southern Tehuelche [Arg] (O)
Southern Tepehuan [Lang] *Tepiman* (Hdbk10)
Southern Tete de Boule [Can] *Sakawininiwug* (BE)
Southern Tewa *see* Tano
Southern Tiwa [Pueblo] (Hdbk9)
Southern Tonto *Western Apache* (Hdbk10)
Southern Tsimshian *Coast Tsimshian* (Anthro, v.9, no.3, p.139)
Southern Unami [Lang] (Hdbk15)
Southern Ute [CO, UT, NM] (H)
Southern Uto-Aztecan [Lang] (Hdbk10)
Southern Valley [Lang] *Yokutsan* (CA-8)

Southern Wappo [CA] (BE)
Southern Wappo [Lang] *Yuki* (Pub, v.6, no.1, p.266)
Southern West Greenlandic [Lang] *West Greenlandic* (Hdbk5)
Southern Yana [CA] (BE)
South Fork *Western Shoshone* (Hdbk15)
Southois *see* Uzutiuhi
Southon *see* Shinnecock
Southouis *see* Uzutiuhi
South Sea Indians *see* Mashpee
South Spokan [WA] *Spokan* (BE)
South Susseton *see* Miakechakesa
Southward Indians (H)
Southwestern Pomo (BE) *see also* Gualala (H)
Southwestern Pomo [CA] (BE)
Southwestern Pomo [Lang] [CA] (He)
South Wind People *see* Kansa
South Wind People *see* Quapaw
Southwood Indians *see* Southward Indians
South Yanktons *see* Yankton
Souties *see* Saulteaux
Soutouis *see* Uzutiuhi
Soux *see* Sioux
Sowa *see* Ashluslay
Sowahegan *see* Souhegan
Sowanakas *see* Shawnee
So-wania *see* Southern Cheyenne
Sowania *see* Southern Cheyenne
Sowanokas *see* Shawnee
Sowanokee *see* Shawnee
Sowans *see* Saone
Sow-a-to *see* Comanche
Sowato *see* Comanche
So-wi *see* Sowi
Sowi [Clan] *Hopi* (H)
Sowiinwa [Clan] *Hopi* (H)
So-wi-in-wa wun-wu *see* Sowi-inwa
Sowinu winwu *see* Sowiinwa
So-win-wa *see* Sowiinwa
Sowinwa *see* Sowiinwa
Sowi wiñwu *see* Sowi
Sowocatuck *see* Sokoki
Sowocotuck *see* Sokoki
Sowonia *see* Southern Cheyenne
Sow-on-no *see* Shawnee
Sowonno *see* Shawnee
Sowquackick *see* Sokoki
Sowuash *see* Ashluslay
Soyennom *see* Soyennow
So-yen-now *see* Soyennow
Soyennow [ID] *Chopunnish* (H)
Soyopas *see* Mohave
Soyote [Sib] (LC)
Spalacin *see* Spallumcheen
Spallamcheen *see* Spallumcheen
Spallum-acheen *see* Spallumcheen

Spallumacheen *see* Spallumcheen
Spallumcheednspalu'sox *see* Paloos
Spallumcheen [BC] *Shuswap* (H)
spalu'sox *see* Paloose
Spanish Yutes *see* Ute
Spatsatlt [Clan] [BC] *Taliomh* (H)
Speakers of Cree *see* Cahi'a 'ye'skabin
Spearmaro *see* Squannarro
Speckled Pawnee *see* Wichita
Spelemcheen *see* Spallumcheen
Spellamcheen *see* Spallumcheen
Spellammachum *see* Spallumcheen
spemoc [sic[*see* Santo Domingo
Spences Bridge [BC] *Ntlakyapamauk* (BE)
Spia [Clan] [NM] *Sia* (H)
Spia-hano *see* Spia
Spicheats *see* Spichehat
Spicheet *see* Spichehat
Spichehat [TX] (H)
Spitotha *Shawnee* (H)
Split Livers *see* Tapishlecha
Spo.qe'in *see* Spokan
Spogan *see* Spokan
Spokain *see* Spokan
Spokan [WA] (LC)
Spokane *see* Spokan
Spo-kehmish *see* Spokan
Spokehmish *see* Spokan
Spokehnish *see* Spokan
Spokein *see* Spokan
Spoke'n *see* Spokan
Spoken *see* Spokan
Spokenish *see* Sma-hoo-men-a-ish
Spo-kih-nish *see* Spokan
Spokihnish *see* Spokan
Spokineish *see* Spokan
Spokines *see* Spokan
Spokomish *see* Spokan
Spoqein *see* Spokan
Spring Creek *see* Bidai
Spring-people *see* Nushaltkagakni
Spring Valley *Western Shoshone* (Hdbk11)
"spruce tree people" *see* Napaaqtugmiut
Spuka'n *see* Spokan
Spukpukolemk [Clan] [BC] *Nuhalk* (H)
Spuqpuqo'lemq *see* Spukpukolemk
Spwiya'laphabsh [WA] *Puyallup* (BE)
Sqahe'ne xa'da-i *see* Skahenehadai
Sqai'aqos *see* Skaiakois
Sqnamishes *see* Squawmish

Sqoa'ladas *see* Skwahladas
Sqowi [Clan] *Laguna* (H)
Sqowi-hano *see* Shruhwi
Sqowi-hanoch *see* Shruhwi
Sqsa'nitc *see* Sanetch
Squa-aitl *see* Squiatl
Squabage *see* Quabaug
Squabang *see* Quabaug
Squabaug *see* Quabaug
Squabauge *see* Quabaug
Squaboag *see* Quabaug
Squabog *see* Quabaug
Squacum [BC] *Salish* (H)
Squaghkie *see* Fox
Squ-agh-kie *see* Squawkihow
Squaghkie *see* Squawkihow
Squahalitch *see* Chilliwack
Squaheag *see* Squawkeag
Squahksen *see* Squaxon
Squah-sin-aw-mish *see* Squaxon
Squahsinawmish *see* Squaxon
Squai-aitl *see* Squiatl
Squaiaitl *see* Squiatl
Squakeage *see* Squawkeag
Squakeay *see* Squawkeag
Squakeg *see* Sokoki
Squakheag *see* Squawkeag
Squakheig *see* Squawkeag
Squakies *see* Squawkihow
Squakkeag *see* Squawkeag
Squakshin *see* Squaxon
Squakskin *see* Squaxon
Squaks'na-mish *see* Squaxon
Squaksnamish *see* Squaxon
Squakson *see* Squaxon
Squalees *see* Nisqualli
Squalli-ah-mish *see* Nisqualli
Squalliahmish *see* Nisqualli
Squalli-a-mish *see* Nisqualli
Squalliamish *see* Nisqualli
Squally-ah-mish *see* Nisqualli
Squallyahmish *see* Nisqualli
Squallyamish *see* Nisqualli
Squam [MA] (H)
Squam-a-cross *see* Squannaroo
Squamacross *see* Squannaroo
Squam-a-ross *see* Squannaroo
Squamaross *see* Squammaroo
Squamish [BC] *Squawmish* (H)
Squamscot [NH] *Pennacook Confederacy* (H)
Squan-nan-os *see* Squannaroo
Squannanos *see* Squannaroo
Squannaroo [WA] *Pisquows* (H)
Squannor-oss *see* Squannaroo
Squannoross *see* Squannaroo
Squan-nun-os *see* Squannaroo
Squannunoss *see* Squannaroo
Squa'pamuq *see* Shuswap
Squapamuq *see* Shuswap
Squapaukc *see* Quabaug
Squa-sua-mish *see* Squaxon
Squasuamish *see* Squaxon

Squatchega *see* Squawkihow
Squatchegas *see* Fox
Squatehokus *see* Squawkihow
Squatets *see* Squawtits
Squatils *see* Squawtits
Squatits *see* Squawtits
Squaw-a-tosh *see* Colville
Squawatosh *see* Colville
Squawkeag [MA] *Pocomtuc* (BE)
Squawkeague *see* Squawkeag
Squawkey *see* Squawkihow
Squawkheag *see* Squawkeag
Squawkiehah *see* Fox
Squawkihow [NY] *Fox* (H)
Squawmish [BC] (LC)
squawmisht *see* Squawmish
Squawskin *see* Squaxon
Squawtas *see* Squawtits
Squawtits [BC] *Stalo* (BE)
Squaxin *see* Squaxon
Squaxon [WA] *Nisqualli* (BE)
Squeer-yer-pe *see* Colville
Squeeryerpee *see* Colville
Squeit-letch *see* Squiatl
Squeitletch *see* Squiatl
Squekaneronon *see* Nipissing
Squ-hano *see* Shruhwi
Squhano *see* Shruhwi
Squiaelp *see* Colville
Squi-aitl *see* Squiatl
Squiath *see* Nisqualli
Squiatl [WA] *Salish* (H)
Squierhonon (H)
S'quies-tshi *see* Arikara
Squiestshi *see* Arikara
Squi'nqun *see* Skiungkung
Squinqun *see* Skuingkung
Squinters *see* Tukkuthkutchin
Squint Eyes *see* Kutchin
Squint-Eyes *see* Tukkuthkutchin
Squohamish *see* Squawmish
Squorin *see* Squaxson
Squoxsin *see* Squaxon
Sratt-kemer *see* Srattkemer
Srattkemer [BC] *Salish* (H)
Sri-gon *see* Shregegon
Srigon *see* Shregogon
Sroo-tle-mam-ish *see* Shotle-
  mamish
Srootlemamish *see* Shotlemamish
Ssabela *see* Sabela
Ssangha-kon *see*
ssanyakoan (H)
Ssetebo *see* Setebo
Ssik-nachadi *see* Siknahadi
Ssiknachadi [isc] *see* Siknahadi
Ssikossuilar-miut *see* Siko-
  suilarmiut
Ssimaku *see* Huambisa
Ssimaku *see* Urarina
Ssipipo *see* Shipibo
S'slo-ma-mish *see* Shomamish
Sslomamish *see* Shomamish

St. *see* Saint
Stabbernowles *see* Shawnee
Stactan *see* Staitan
Sta-e-tan *see* Staitan
Staetan *see* Staitan
Staeton *see* Staitan
Staga'ush [Self-designation] *see*
  Nestucca
Sta'gi la'nas *see* Stagilanas
Stagilanas [Clan] *Haida* (H)
Stahabsh *see* Sta'habsh
Sta'habsh [WA] *Nisqualli* (BE)
Sta-he-tah *see* Staitan
Stahetah *see* Staitan
Stahlouk [BC] *Salish* (H)
Stailan *see* Staitan
Stairing haires *see* Ottawa
Staitan (H)
Staitan (Ye) *see also* Crow (LC)
Staked Plain Indians *see* Kwahari
Staked Plains Omaions *see* Kwa-
  hari
Staked Plains Onawas *see* Kwahari
Stakhin-kwan *Tlingit* (Contri, v.1,
  pp.38–39)
Staktabsh [WA] *Salish* (H)
Staktaledjabsh *see* Stakta'ledjabsh
Stakta-ledjabsh [WA] *Snoqualmie*
  (BE)
Stak-ta-le-jabsh *see* Sktahlejum
Staktalejabsh *see* Sktahlejum
Stak-ta-mish *see* Skaiailk
Staktamish *see* Kwaiailk
Staktomish *see* Kwaiailk
Stalame [SC] (H)
Stallo *see* Stalo
Stalo [BC] (LC)
Stalo [Lang] *Salishan* (LC)
Standing Stone People *see*
  Oneida
Stankekan *see* Sankhiken
Staq-tubc *see* Chehalis
Staq-tube *see* Chehalis
Staqtube *see* Chehalis
Star Band *Mdewakanton* (BE)
Star Gens *see* Mikakhenikashika
Starrahe *see* Arikara
Star-rah-he *see* Arikara
Starrahhe *see* Arikara
Stasaos-kegawai [Family] *Haida*
  (H)
Stasa'os la'nas *see* Stasaos-lanas
Stasaoslanas *see* Stasaos-lanas
Stasaos-lanas [BC] *Haida* (H)
Stasa'os qe'gawa-i (H) Stasaos-
  lanas (H)
Stasaosqegawai *see* Stasaos-lanas
Stasausk'e'owai *see* Stasaos-
  kegawai
Stastas *see* Stustas
Stataketux *see* Stata'ketux
Stata'ketux [WA] *Sinkiuse Colum-
  bia* (BE)

Statca'sabsh [WA] *Sahehwamish*
  (BE)
Staten Island Indians [NY]
  Delaware (Hdbk15)
Stationary Minetare *see* Hidatsa
Statlamchu *see* Lillooet
Stat-lam-shu *see* Lillooet
Sta-tlum-ooh *see* Lillooet
Statlumooh *see* Lillooet
Stauacen *see* Sewathen
Stawas-haidagai [Clan] *Haida* (H)
Sta-wih-amuh *see* Nicola
Stawihamuh *see* Nicola
stawi'xemux *see* Nicola
stawixemux *see* Nicola
Stawtubc *see* Chehalis
Stchitsui *see* Skitswish
Stcuwa'cel *see* Sewathen
Ste. *see* Sainte
Steamtshi *see* Crow
Stebbins *Bering Strait Eskimos*
  (Hdbk5)
Steelar *see* Skidi Pawnee
Stegara *see* Stegaraki
Stegarakes *see* Stegaraki
Stegaraki [VA] *Manahoac Confed-
  eracy* (BE)
Stegarakies *see* Stegaraki
Stegerakies *see* Stegaraki
Stegora *see* Stegaraki
Steh-cha-sa-mish *see* Steht-
  sasamish
Stehchasamish *see* Stehtsasamish
Stehchass *see* Stehtsasamish
Stehchop *see* Stehtsasamish
Stehtsasamish [WA] *Salish* (H)
Steilacoom (H) *see also* Steila-
  coomamish (H)
Steilacoom [WA] *Puyallup* (BE)
Steilacoomamish [WA] *Salish* (H)
Steilakimahmish *see* Steila-
  coomamish
Steilaquamish *see* Stillaquamish
Steil-la-qua-mish *see* Stil-
  laquamish
Steillaquamish *see* Stillaquamish
Stekchar *see* Stehtsasamish
Stekini *see* Stikine
Stela-coom-a-mish *see* Steila-
  coomamish
Stelatin [Can] *Southern Carrier*
  (BE)
Stell-cha-sa-mish *see* Steht-
  sasamish
Stellchasamish *see* Stentsasamish
Stemchi *see* Crow
Stemtchi *see* Crow
Stenkenocks *see* Stegaraki
Steptoe Valley *Western Shoshone*
  (Hdbk11)
Stetch-as *see* Stehtsasamish
Stetchas *see* Stehtsasamish
Stetlum *see* Lillooet

Stewart's Lake Indians see Nikozliautin

Ste'wi'x see Nicola

Stewix see Nicola

ste'wi'xaemux see Nicola

stewixaemux see Nicola

ste'wi'xemux see Nicola

stewi-xemux see Nicola

stewixemux see Nicola

stewixtci'n see Nicola

Stiaggeghroano see Chippewa

Stiagigroone see Chippewa

Stickens see Stikine

Stickienes see Stikine

Stick Indians (H)

Stickine see Stikine

Sticks see Nuchwugh

Stiel Shoi see Skitswish

Stietamuk [Can] Shuswap (BE)

Stietshoi see Skitswish

Stikin see Stikine

Stikine [AK] Tlingit (BE)

Stili see Skidi Pawnee

Stillaguamish see Stillaquamish

Stillaquamish [WA] (LC)

Stillo-qua-mish see Stillaquamish

Stilloquamish see Stillaquamish

Stillwater [Lang] Wintu (CA-8)

Stimk see Crow

Stincards (H)

Stincards (H) see also Metsmetskop (H)

Stinkards see Stincards

Stinkards see Winnebago

Stinks see Winnebago

Stitchafsamish see Stehtsasamish

Stitcha-saw-mich see Stehtsasamish

Stitchasawmich see Stehtsasamish

Stitcheo-saw-mish see Stehtsasamish

Stitcheosawmish see Stehtsasamish

St-ka-bish see Sekamish

Stkabish see Sekamish

St-kah-mish see Sekamish

Stkahmish see Sekamish

St'kamish see Sekamish

Stkamish see Sekamish

Stkamlu'lep see Kamloop

Stkamlulepsemuk [Can] Shuswap
(BE)

stkemlups see Shuswap

S'tlaht-tohtlt-hu see Comox

Stlahttohtlthu see Comox

Stla-Sli-muk see Lillooet

STLA-tlei-mu-wh see Lillooet

stla'tlimQ see Lillooet

Stlat-limuh see Lillooet

Stlatlimuh see Lillooet

stl'atl'imx see Lillooet

Stla-tlium see Liliooet

Stlatlium see Lillooet

Stla'tliumh see Lillooet

Stlemhulehamuk [Can] Shuswap
(BE)

Stlenga-lanas [Family] [BC]
Haida (H)

Stl'enge la'nas see Stlenga-lanas

Stlenge lanas see Stlenga-lanas

Stling Lennas see Stlenga-lanas

Sto. see Santo

Stoam Ohimal see Coyotes

Sto'am O'himal see Stoamohimal

Stoam Ohimal see Stoamohimal

Stoamohimal [Phratry] Pima (H)

Stobshaddat see Yakima

Stockbridge [NY] Mohican Confederacy (LC)

Stogaras see Stegaraki

Stohenskie see Stikine

Sto-lo-qua-baish see Stillaquamish

Stoloquabaish see Stillaquamish

Sto-luch-wamish see Stil-
laquamish

Stoluch-wa-mish see Stil-
laquamish

Stoluchwamish see Stillaquamish

Sto-luck-qua-mish see Stillaquamish

Stoluckquamish see Stil-
laquamish

Stoluck-wha-mish see Stillaquamish

Stoluckwhamish see Stil-
laquamish

Stolutswhamish see Stillaquamish

Stone Chilcotin [Can] (BE)

Stone Earring Band see Inyanhaoin

Stone Indians see Assiniboin

Stone Indians see Jatonabine

Stone Kettle Esquimaux see
Ukusiksalirmiut

Stone People see Asinskau-
winiuuk

Stone Roasters see Assiniboin

Stone Sioux see Assiniboin

Stone Sukiniiut see Siqinirmiut

Stone Tsilkotin [BC] Tsilkotin
(H)

Stoney see Assiniboin

Stoney Indians see Assiniboin

Stonies see Assiniboin

Stonies see Chilcotin

Stonies see Tschantoga

Stono [SC] Cusabo (BE)

Stonoes see Stone

Stony Creek Band see Nulaautin

Stony Creek Indians see Asuun-
pink

Stony Indians see Assiniboin

Strangers see Tidendaye

Stratten [BC] Salish (H)

Street Natives see Tlingit

Strong bow see Etcheridiegottine

Strong Bows People see Ditche-
ta-ut-tinne

Strong People see Loucheux

Strong Wood Assiniboines see
Tschantoga

Strongwood Assinniboines see
Tschantoga

Strongwood Cree see Sakawithiniwuk

Stsababsh [WA] Salish (H)

Stsa'nges see Songish

Stsa'nges see Stsanges

Stsanges (PC) see also Songish
(BE)

Stsanges [VanI] Songish (BE)

Stsketamihu see Stske'tamihu

Stske'tamihu [WA] Wenatchi
(BE)

Stskitcestn see Skeetchestn

Stuckre [WA] Salish (H)

Stuichamukh [BC] Athapascan
(H)

Stulnaas-hadai [Subfamily] [AK,
Can] [Chaahl-lanas] (H)

Stu-miks see Stumiks

Stumiks [Society] Piegan (H)

Sturgeon Bay People see Nama'o
Wikilo Tusi'niniu

Sturgeon Indians see Nameuilini

Stustas [Family] Haida (H)

Stuweixmux see Nicola

Stuwi'h see Nicola

Stuwih see Nicola

Stuwihamuk [Can] (BE)

Stuwihamuk [Can] (BE)

Stuwi'hamuq see Stuichamukh

Stuwihamuq see Stuichamukh

Stuwi'x see Nicola

Stuwix see Nicola

stuwi'xamux see Nicola

stuwixamux see Nicola

stuwixemux see Nicola

Stwixmxw see Nicola

Stxuaixn see Siksika

Su see Dakota

sua-ciq see Chugatchigmiut

suaciq see Chugatchigmiut

sua-cit see Chugatchigmiut

suacit see Chugatchigmiut

Suahuaches [TX] Coahuiltecan
(BE)

Sualatine see Atfalati

Suali see Cheraw

Sualy see Cheraw

Suamakosa Tusininiu see Sua'-
makosa Tusi'niniu

Sua'makosa Tusi'niniu [WI]
Menominee (BE)

Suanaimuchs [Clan] Nanaimo
(H)

Su-a-na-muh see Okinagan

Suanamuh see Okinagan

Suanas *see* Suanes
Suanes [TX] *Coahuiltecan* (BE)
Suaque *see* Zuaque
Suaqui *see* Zuaque
Suatae *see* Cuatache
Subaipure *see* Sobaipuri
Subaipuri *see* Sobaipuri
Subartic Denes *Tinne* (H)
Subinha [MX] (BE)
Subtiaba [NI] (BE)
Subtiaban [Lang] [CAm]
  (Bull44)
Sucayi [CAm] *Concho* (BE)
Suc-ca-ah *see* Succaah
Succaah [CA] (H)
Suc-co-ah *see* Succaah
Succoah *see* Succaah
Suchamnier *see* Luckiamute
Sucheen *see* Stikine
Suchongnewy *see* Sichomovi
Suck-a-mier *see* Luckiamute
Suckamier *see* Luckiamute
Suckemos *see* Eskimos
Suckiaug *see* Sukiaug
Suckieag *see* Sukiaug
Suckquakege *see* Sokoki
Sucltaqotca *see* Sushttakhot-
  thatune
Sucl-ta-qo-t'ca tunne *see* Susht-
  takhotthatune
Suco *see* Acoma
Suco *see* Pecos
Suc-qua-cha-to-ny *see* Kwatami
Sucquachatony *see* Swatami
Sucuriuy-Tapuya [Col] *Wakunai*
  (O)
Sucuyama *Coahuiltecan* (Hdbk10)
Su-dce *see* Kadohadacho
Sudce *see* Kadohadacho
Sud Killamuk *see* Yakonan
Sue *see* Dakota
Suerra [CR] (BE)
Suerro [NI] (O)
Sugarcane Band [BC] *Fraser River
  Shuswap* (Hdbk12)
Sugar Eater band *see* Penateka
Sugar-Eaters *see* Penointikara
Sugaus *see* Sugeree
Sugcestun *see* Pacific Yupik
Sugeree [Lang] *Catawba* (BE)
Sugeree Indians [SC] (BE)
Sugpiaq *see* Eskimos
Sugpiaq *see* Pacific Yupik
Sug-wau-dug-ah-win-in-e-wug
  see Sugwaundugahwininewug
Sugwaudugahwininewug *see*
  Sugwaundugahwininewug
Sug-waun-dug-ah-win-ine-wug
  see Sugwaundugahwininewug
Sugwaundugahwininewug [MI,
  WI] *Chippewa* (BE)
Sugwundugahwininewig *see* Sug-
  waundugahwininewug

Sug-wun-dug-ah-win-in-e-wug
  see Sugwaundugahwininewug
Suhin *see* Ashluslay
Suhinikyut (H) *see also* Suhinim-
  iut (H)
Suhinimiut *Labrador Eskimos* (H)
Suhinimyut (H) *see also* Suhinim-
  iut (H)
Suhinimyut [*Inuit (Quebec)*]
  (Hdbk5)
Suh'tai *see* Sutaio
Suhtai *see* Sutaio
Suhub *see* Suhubi
Suhubi [Clan] *Hopi* (H)
Su-hub wuñ-wu *see* Suhubi
Suhub wuñwu *see* Suhubi
Suh-ut-it *see* Sukhutit
Suhutit *see* Sukhutit
Sui *see* Sowi
Suia *see* Suya
Suiattle [WA] *Skagit* (BE)
Suil *see* Dakota
Suipam *see* Siupam
Suisan [Lang] *Patwin* (CA-8)
Suisi [Lang] *Maipurean* (O)
Su-i-sun *see* Suisun
Suisun [CA] *Patwin* (H)
Suivirits *see* Seuvarits
Suj-el-pa *see* Colville
sujo *see* Zuni
suk/suk *see* Pacific Yupik
Sukaauguning [MI, WI]
  Chippewa (H)
Sukanom [CA] *Yuki* (H)
Sukechunetunne [OR]
  Chastacosta (H)
Su-ke-tcu-ne tunne *see*
  Sukechunetunne
Suketcunnetunne *see* Sukechune-
  tunne
Suketi'kenuk *see* Nisqualli
Suketikenuk *see* Nisqualli
Sukhinimyut *see* Suhinimiut
Sukhutit *Arikara* (H)
Sukiang *see* Sukiaug
Sukiaug [CN] *Algonquian* (H)
Sukiaugk *see* Sukiaug
Sukkertoppen *Greenland Eskimos*
  (BE)
Suk-kwe-tce *see* Kwatami
Sukkwetce *see* Kwatami
Suko [Clan] *Caddo* (H)
Sukoti'kenuk *see* Nisqualli
Sukotikenuk *see* Nisqulli
Suksanchi *see* Chukchansi
Sukshaltatano'm [CA] *Yuki* (BE)
Sukshudltatum-no'm *see* Round
  Valley Yokuts
Sukshultaatanom *see* Sukshal-
  tatano'm
Suk-wa-bish *see* Squamish
Sukwabish *see* Squamish
Sukwames *see* Suquamish

Sukwamish *see* Suquamish
Sulajame *see* Sulujame
Sulatelak [Self-designation] [CA]
  Wiyot (Pub, v.9, no.3, pp.384)
Sulawig-meut *see* Selawigmiut
Sulluggoes *see* Cherokee
Sulolumne *see* Tuolumne
Sulujam *see* Sulujame
Sulujame [TX] *Coahuiltecan* (BE)
Suma (BE) *see also* Jumano (LC)
Suma [MX, TX] (BE)
Sumagualapem *see* Sama-
  coalapem
Suman [MX] (BE)
Sumana *see* Jumano
Sumass [BC] *Stalo* (BE)
Su-mat-se *see* Sumass
Sumdum [AK] *Tlingit* (BE)
Sume *see* Suma
Sumi *see* Zuni
Summit Lake [NV] *Pauite* (Char,
  v.11)
Sumo [NI, Hon] (LC)
Sumonpavi *see* Shongopovi
Sumo-porvy *see* Shongopovi
Sumoporvy *see* Shongopovi
Sumopowy *see* Shongopovi
Sumosirpe *see* Sumo-Sirpe
Sumo-Sirpe [CAm] [*Misquito-
  Sumo*] (BE)
Sumu *see* Sumo
Sumy *see* Zuni
Suna *see* Suma
Suna *see* Tatuyo
Sunahumes *see* Snohomish
Sunananahogwa [NV] *Paviotso*
  (H)
Sundia *see* Sandia
Sundowns *see* Sumdum
Su-ne-na'na-ho'gwa *see*
  Sunananahogwa
Sun-Flower-Seed-Eaters *see*
  Shonivikidika
Sun Gens *see* Mienikashika
Sungki [Clan] [NM] *Jemez* (H)
Sungkitsaa [Clan] [NM] *Jemez*
  (H)
Sungti [Clan] [NM] *Pecos* (H)
Sun-hunters *see* Tabeguache
Suñi *see* Zuni
Sun ikceka *see* Shungikcheka
  [Yanktonai]
Sunikceka *see* Shungikcheka
  [Yanktonai]
Sunkaha napin *see* Shungka-
  hanapin
Sunkahanapin *see* Shungka-
  hanapin
Sunka ute-sni *see*
  Shungkayuteshni
Sunkayuteshni *Miniconjou* (H)
Sunkayutesni
  Shungkayuteshni

Sunkitsaa *see* Sungkitsaa
Sunne *see* Zuni
Sunnekes *see* Seneca
Sun-nun-at *see* Dakota
Sunnunat *see* Dakota
Sunset Indians *see* Natchez
Sunsunnestunne [OR]
 Mishikhwutmetunne (H)
Sun-tea-coot-a-coot *see* Suntea-
 chooacoot
Sunteacootacoot [BC] (H)
Sunti-ash *see* Sungkitsaa
Suntiash *see* Sungkitsaa
Suny *see* Zuni
Sunyitsa *see* Zuni
Sunyitsi *see* Zuni
Su'nyuitsa *see* Zuni
Suouex *see* Dakota
Supai *see* Havasupai
Supanecan [Lang] [CAm] (BE)
Supi *see* Havasupai
Supie *see* Havasupai
Suponolevy *see* Shipaulovi
Supowolewy *see* Shipaulovi
Suppai *see* Havasupai
Suquahmish *see* Suquamish
Suquamish (LC) *see also*
 Squawmish (LC)
Suquamish [WA] *Nisqualli* (LC)
Su'quapmuq *see* Shuswap
Suquapmuq *see* Shuswap
Suraminis *see* Sawani
Surara *see* Pakidai
Surcee *see* Sarsi
Surci *see* Sarsi
Surcie *see* Saesi
Surini [Self-designation] *see*
 Asurini II
Surira *see* Siriano
Suroamasa [Col] *Macuna* (O)
Surrech *see* Surruque
Surrillo *see* Castake
Surruque [FL] (BE)
Sursi *see* Sarsi
Surui I [Br] *Rondonia* (LC)
Surui II [Br] *Para* (LC)
Susa [Col] *Yuko* (O)
Susanville [Lang] *Maidu* (CA-8)
Suscahannaes *see* Conestoga
Suscohannes *see* Conestoga
Sushaidagai *see* Sus-haidagai
Sus-haidagai [Subfamily] [BC]
 Haida (H)
Sushetno *see* Sus-haidagai
Sushltakhotthatune [OR]
 Mishikhwutmetunne (H)
Sushwap *see* Shuswap
Susitna (H) *see also* Sus-haidagai
 (H)
Susitna [AK] *Tanaina* (BE)
Suski [Clan] [NM] *Keres* (H)
Suski-kwe *see* Suski
Sus-kso-yiks *see* Susksoyiks

Susksoyiks [MN] *Piegan* (BE)
Susolas [TX] *Coahuiltecan* (H)
Susoles *see* Susolas
Susquahanna *see* Susquehanna
Susquahannock *see* Susquehanna
Susquamish *see* Suquamish
Susquehana *see* Susquehanna
Susquehanna [PN] *Conestoga*
 (LC)
Susquehannagh *see* Susquehanna
Susquehannah Minquays *see*
 Conestoga
Susquehannock *see* Conestoga
Susquehannock *see* Susquehanna
Susquehannoes *see* Susquehanna
Susquehanons *see* Susquehanna
Susquehanock *see* Susquehanna
Susquehanoes *see* Susquehanna
Susquhannok *see* Susquehanna
Susquihanough *see* Susquehanna
Sussec *see* Sarsi
Susseeton *see* Sisseton
Sussekoon *see* Sarsi
Susseton *see* Sisseton
Sussetong *see* Sisseton
Sussetonwah *see* Sisseton
Sussez *see* Sarsi
Sussi *see* Sarsi
Sussitong *see* Sisseton
Sussitongs of Roche Blanche *see*
 Kahra
Su-su-ne *see* Shoshone
Susune *see* Shoshone
susuni *see* Shoshone
Sus xa-idaga-i *see* Sus-haidagai
Susxaidagai *see* Sus-haidagai
Su'tai *see* Sutaio
Sutai *see* Sutaio
Sutaio [SD] (BE)
Su-tasi'na *see* Sutaio
Sutasina *see* Sutaio
Suta'ya *see* Sutaio
Sutayo *see* Sutaio
Suthsetts *see* Seshart
Su'ti *see* Sutaio
Suti *see* Sutaio
Sutsets *see* Seshart
Sutuami *see* Lutuamian
Suturee *see* Sugeree
Suwa'dabc *see* Sinkiuse-
 Columbia
Suwal [WA] *Kwalhioque* (BE)
Suwanoes *see* Shawnee
Suwapamuck *see* Shuswap
Suweri [PE] *Harakmbet* (O)
Suwu'ki O'himal *see* Suwuki
 Ohimal
Suwuki Ohimal (H) *see also* Vul-
 tures (H)
Suwuki Ohimal [Phratry] *Pima*
 (H)
suxpiaq *see* Eskimos
Suxwa'pmux *see* Shuswap

Suya [Br] *Cayapo* (LC)
Suysum *see* Suisun
Svernofftsi *see* Aglemiut
Swa'dab.c *see* Sinkiuse-Columbia
Swadabc *see* Sinkiuse-Columbia
Swalarh *see* Swalash
Swalash (BE) *see also* Swallah (BE)
Swa-lash *see* Swalash
Swalash [WA] *Salish* (H)
Swali *see* Cheraw
Swallah (BE) *see also* Swallah (BE)
Swallah [WA] (BE)
Swamp Cree *see* Western Woods
 Cree
Swamp Cree Swamp Indians *see*
 Maskegon
Swampee *see* Maskegon
Swampies *see* Maskegon
Swampy Cree *see* Maskegon
Swampy Creek Indians *see*
 Maskegon
Swampy Ground *Assiniboin* (H)
Swampy Kree *see* Maskegon
Swampys *see* Maskegon
Swa'namc *see* Sinkiuse-Columbia
Swanamc *see* Sinkiuse-Columbia
Swan Creek [KS] *Chippewa* (BE)
Swasti'djanadji *see* Itsatawi
Sweat-lips *see* Putetemini
Swees *see* Sarsi
Sweielpa *see* Colville
Sweke-aka *see* Grand River Indi-
 ans
Swekeaka *see* Grand River Indi-
 ans
Swi-el-pree *see* Colville
Swielpree *see* Colville
Swinomish [WA] (LC)
Swo-Kwabish *see* Suquamish
Swokwabish *see* Suquamish
Sxoe'lpix *see* Colville
Sxoie'lpu *see* Colville
Sxqomic *see* Squamish
sxstelenemx *see* Eastern Shuswap
 Band
sxste'llnemux *see* Eastern
 Shuswap Band
Sxuie'ylpix *see* Colville
Sxwei'lpex *see* Colville
S'yars *see* Saia
Syars *see* Saia
Sycuan *see* Sequan
Syilalkoabsh *Salish* (H)
Syneck *see* Seneca
Synek *see* Seneca
Synekees *see* Seneca
Synekes *see* Seneca
Synicks *see* Seneca
Synnekes *see* Seneca
Synneks *see* Seneca
Syouslaw *see* Siuslaw
Sypanes *see* Lipan Apache
Sypouria (H)

Syquan *see* Sequan
Sywanois *see* Siwnoy

-T-

T. Son-non-ta-tex *see* Tionon-
tati
T. Son-non-thu-ans *see* Seneca
T. Sonnontouans *see* Seneca
Ta [Clan] *Pueblo Indians* (H)
Taa [Clan] *Zuni* (H)
Taa Ashiwani *see* Zuni
Taadine *see* Navajo
T'aa diné *see* Navajo
Taahl-lanas [Family] [BC] *Haida*
(H)
Ta'a-kwe *see* Taa
Taakwe *see* Taa
T!a'al *see* Taahl-lanas
Taal *see* Taahl-lanas
Taaovaiazes *see* Tawehash
Taaovayases *see* Tawehash
Taasey *see* Toosey
Ta-ashi *see* Apache
Taashi *see* Apache
Taas nei *see* Knaiakhotana
Taasnei *see* Knaiakhotana
Taatem'hlanah-kwe *see* Taa
Tab *see* Tabo
Tabaguache *see* Uncompahgre
Tabahtea [CA] *Pomo* (H)
Tabahuache *see* Tabeguache
Tabaino [Col] (O)
Tabaquache *see* Uncompahgre
Tabaroa *see* Tamaroa
Tabasco [MX] *Mazatec* (BE)
Tabayase *see* Tawehash
Tabbywatts *see* Uncompahgre
Tabea *see* Tapa [Yuchi]
Tabechya *see* Tabeguache
Tabeguache [CO] (LC)
Tabeguachi *see* Tabeguache
Tabegwaches *see* Tabeguache
Tabehuaches *see* Uncompahgre
Tabehuachi *see* Tabeguache
Tabe-nache *see* Tabeguache
Tabenache *see* Tabeguache
Tabensa *see* Taensa
Tabequache *see* Tabeguache
Tabequache *see* Uncompahgre
Tabewache *see* Tabeguache
Tabiachi *see* Tabeguache
Tabin [CA] (H)
Ta-bi-ra *see* Tabira
Tabira [NM] *Piro* (H)
Tabitibi *see* Abitibi
Tabittibi *see* Abitibi
Tabittiki *see* Abitibi
Tabkepaya *see* Hualapai
Table Bluff Band [CA] *Wiyot*

(News, v.10, no.1, Fall 1976,
pp.4–7)
Tab nyû-mû *see* Tabo
Tabnyumu *see* Tabo
Ta-bo *see* Tabo
Tabo [Phratry] *Hopi* (H)
Taboayas *see* Tawehash
Tabogimkik [NS] (H)
Tabo-Pita [Phratry] *Hopi* (H)
Tabotirojejeamasa [Col] *Macuna*
(O)
Tabo wiñwû *see* Tabo
Tabracki *see* Tabeguache
Tabuache *see* Tabeguache
Tab wuñ-wû *see* Tabo
Tabwunwu *see* Tabo
Ta-cab-ci-nyu-muh *see* Navajo
Tacabcinyumuh *see* Navajo
Tacabuy *see* Navajo
Tacabuy *see* Yavapai
Tacaguista *Coahuiltecan* (Hdbk10)
Tacamane *see* Tacame
Tacame [TX] *Coahuiltecan* (BE)
Tacana [BO] (LC)
Tacanan [Lang] [BO] (LC)
Tacaneco [Gua] (O)
Ta-can-rpi-sa-pa *see* Tacanhpis-
apa
Tacanrpisapa *see* Tacanhpisapa
Tacasnanes *see* Pasnacanes
Tacatacuru [FL] (BE)
Tacci *see* Dogi
Tache *see* Tachi
Tachekarorein *see* Tuscarora
Taches *see* Texas
Ta-chi *see* Tachi
Tachi [CA] *Southern Valley Yokuts*
(CA)
Tachies *see* Texas
Tachigmyut *see* Unaligmiut
Tackankanie *see* Tawakoni
Tack-chan-de-see-char *see*
Tackchandeseechar
Tackchandeseechar *Saone* (H)
Tack-chan-de-su-char *see*
Tackchandeseechar
Tackchandesuchar *see* Tackchan-
deseechar
Tackies *see* Texas
Tacllan *see* Tallan
Taco *see* Huchnom
Taco *see* Taku
Tacokoquipesceni *see* Pineshow
Tacone *see* Tacame
Tacoon *see* Yaquina
Tacopate [MX] *Coahuiltecan*
(Hdbk10)
Tacoposca *see* Taposa
Tacos *see* Taos
Tacos *see* Tewa
Tacoullie *see* Takulli
Tacuanama [MX] *Coahuiltecan*
(Hdbk10)

Tacueyo [Col] *Paez* (O)
Taculli *see* Takulli
Ta-cullies *see* Takulli
Tacullies *see* Takulli
Tacunyape [Br] (O)
Tade [BO] *Araona* (O)
Taderighrone *see* Tutelo
Tadirighrone *see* Catawba
Tadirighrone *see* Catawba
Tadiva [TX] *Hasinai Confederacy*
(BE)
Tadjedjayi *see* Tachi
Tadjezhinga [Subclan] *Kanze* (H)
Tadjii *see* Tachi
Ta'dji la'nas *see* Tadji-lanas
Tadjilanas *see* Tadji-lanas
Tadji-lanas [Family] *Raven* (H)
Tado [Col] (O)
Tadousac [Q] [*Montagnais-
Naskapi*] (BE)
Ta-ee-tee-tan *see* Tihittan
Taeeteetan *see* Tihittan
Taenca *see* Taensa
Taensa *see* Taensa
Taensa [LA] (LC)
Taenza *see* Taensa
Taesapaoa *see* Tangipahoa
Tafique *see* Tajique
Tagahosh *see* Nestucca
Tageque *see* Tajique
Tagiacana *see* Tawakoni
Tagique *see* Tajique
Tagish [BC] *Nahane* (BE)
tagitika'a *see* Tagotoka
Tagiugmiut [AK] *Coastal Eskimos*
(Hdbk5)
Tagna *see* Tewa
Tagnani *see* Tawande
Tagno *see* Tano
Tagotoka *Northern Paiute*
(Hdbk11)
Tagua *see* Catawba
Taguaca *see* Jicaque
Taguaca *see* Twahka
Taguacanes *see* Tawakoni
Taguache *see* Pacuaches
Taguaguan *Pamaque* (Hdbk10)
Tagualillo *Coahuiltecan* (Hdbk10)
Tagualilos [MX] *Tamaulipec* (BE)
Tagualito *see* Tagualillo
Ta'gugala *see* Kiowa Apache
Tagugala *see* Kiowa Apache
Tagui *see* Kiowa Apache
Tagui *see* Apache
Tagukeresh *see* Apache
Tagukeresh *see* Jicarillo Apache
Tagukerish *see* Kiowa Apache
Taguna *see* Laguna
Tahagmiut [*Inuit (Quebec)*]
(Hdbk5)
Tahagmiut *Labrador Eskimos* (H)
Ta hag myut *see* Tahagmiut
Tahagmyut *see* Tahagmiut

Ta'hana *see* Ute
Tahana *see* Tano
Tahana *see* Ute
Tahano *see* Tano
Tahawrehogeh *see* Mohawk
Ta'hba *see* Maricopa
Tah'ba *see* Papago
Ta'hba *see* Papago
Tahba *see* Maricopa
Tahba *see* Papago
Tahca-pa *see* Takhchapa
Tahcapa *see* Takhchapa
Tah-che *see* Tachi
Tahche *see* Tachi
Tah-chunk wash taa *see* Oy-ateshicha
Tahchunkwashtaa *see* Oy-ateshicha
Tahco *see* Taku
Tahculi *see* Takulli
Tah-cully *see* Takulli
Tahcully *see* Takulli
Tah-cul-tu *see* Lekwiltok
Tahcultu *see* Lekwiltok
Tah-do *see* Huchnom
Tahdo *see* Huchnom
Tahelie *see* Takulli
Tahensa *see* Taensa
Tahiannihouq (H) *see also* Kan-nehouan (H)
Tahiannihouq [LA] (H)
Ta-hi-cha-pa-han-na (H) *see also* Kawaiisu (LC)
Tahichapahanna (PC) *see also* Kawaiisu (LC)
Tahichapahanna *see* Ta-hi-cha-pa-han-na [CA]
Tahichapahanna *see* Kawaiisu
Ta-hi-cha-pa-han-na [CA] (Contri, v.3, p.393)
Ta-hichp *see* Ta-hi-cha-pa-han-na
Ta-hichp *see* Kawaiisu
Tahichp *see* Ta-hi-cha-pa-han-na
Tahichp *see* Kawaiisu
Tahickpi-u *see* Kawaiisu
Tahitan [AK, BC] (Ye)
Tahiuharmiut [AK] *Paarlirmiut* (Hdbk5)
Tahka-li *see* Takulli
Tahkali *see* Takulli
Tahkallies *see* Takulli
Tahk-heesh *see* Tagish
Tahkheesh *see* Tagish
Tah-khl *see* Takulli
Tahkhl *see* Takulli
Tahkoli *see* Takulli
Tahko-tinneh *see* Tah-ko-tin'neh
Tah'ko-tin'neh (H) *see also* Taku-tine (BE)
Tahkotinneh *see* Tah-ko-tin'neh

Tah-ko-tin'neh *Nehaunee* (Contri, v.1, p.33)
Tah-le-wah *see* Tolowa
Tahlewah *see* Tolowa
Ta'hli'mnin *see* Navajo
Tahlimnin *see* Navajo
Tahlkoedi [AK] *Stikine* (H)
Tahl-tan *see* Tahltan
Tahltan [AK. BC] *Nahane* (LC)
Tahluptsi [Clan] [NM] *Zuni* (H)
Ta'hluptsi-kwe *see* Tahluptsi
Tahluptsikwe *see* Tahluptsi
Tahogale (H) *see also* Yuchi (LC)
Tahogale [TN, AL] (H)
Tahogalewi *see* Yuchi
Tahohyahtaydootah *see* Kapozha
Tahokia *see* Cahokia
Tahontaenrat *Huron* (H)
Tahookatuke *see* Tohookatokie
Tahos *see* Taos
Tah sau gaa *see* Tasagi's band
Tahsaugaa *see* Tasagi's band
Tah-se-pah *see* Tushepaw
Tahsepah *see* Tushepaw
Tahtoo *see* Huchnom
Tahuacana *see* Tawakoni
Tahuacane *see* Tawakoni
Tahuacano *see* Tawakoni
Tahuacany *see* Tawakoni
Tahuacaro *see* Tawakoni
Tahuaconi *see* Tawakoni
Tahue [Lang] [MX] *Taracahitian* (BE)
Tahuha-yuta *see* Takhuhayuta [Yanktonia]
Ta-hu-ka-ni *see* Tawakoni
Tahukani *see* Tawakoni
Ta'hu-un-de *see* Tahuunde
Tahuunde [TX, NM] *Mescalero Apache* (H)
Tahwaccaro *see* Tawakoni
Tah-wac-car-roes *see* Tawakoni
Tahwaccarroes *see* Tawakoni
Tahwaccona *see* Tawakoni
Tah-wae-carras *see* Tawakoni
Tahwaecarras *see* Tawakoni
Tah-wah-ca-roo *see* Tawakoni
Tahwahcaroo *see* Tawakoni
Tah-wah-carro *see* Tawakoni
Tahwahcarro *see* Tawakoni
Tahwaklero *see* Tawakoni
Taia *see* Paya
Taiahounhins *see* Aleuts
Tai-aq *see* Tyigh
Taiaq *see* Tyigh
Taiate [Br] *Northern Nambicuara* (O)
Taibano *see* Tabaino
Taichida *Maidu* (Contri, v.3, p.282)
Taidnapam [WA] (BE)
Taidnapum *see* Taidnapam
Taigas *see* Texas

Tai-ga-tah *see* Taos
Taigatah *see* Taos
Taighs *see* Tyigh
Ta-ih *see* Tyigh
Taih *see* Tyigh
Taiina *see* Taos
Taiinamu *see* Taos
Taijas *see* Texas
Tai-kie-a-pain *see* Taitinapam
Taikieapain *see* Taitinapam
Tai-lin-che *see* Dalinchi
Tailinche *see* Dalinche
Taimamares (H) *see also* Tuma-mar (BE)
Taimamares [TX] (BE)
Taina [Self-designation] *see* Taos
Ta-i-na-ma *see* Taos
Tainama *see* Taos
Tain-gees-ah-tsah *see* Tangeratsa
Taingeesahtsah *see* Tangeratsa
Tainkoyo *see* Nishinam
Taino [WInd, PR, Cu] (LC)
Tai'otl la'nas *see* Daiyuahl-lanas
Taiotl lanas *see* Daiyuahl-lanas
Taioux *see* Texas
Tairona [Col] (LC)
Tairtla *see* Tyigh
Tait [BC] *Cowichan* (H)
Tai-tim-pan *see* Taitinapam
Taitimpan *see* Taitinapam
Tai-tin-a-pam *see* Taitinapam
Taitinapam [WA] *Shahaptian* (BE)
Tait-inapum *see* Taitinapam
Taitinapum *see* Taitinapam
Taitinipan *see* Taitinapam
Taitnapam *see* Taitinapam
Taitsick-Kutchin *see* Tangeratsa
Taitzoga *see* Tesuque
Tai-tzo-gai *see* Tesuque
Taiwano *see* Tabaino
Taiyanyanokhotana [AK] *Kaiyuhkhotana* (H)
Tai-yayan-o-khotan'a *see* Taiyanyanokhotana
Tai-ya-yan-o-khotan-a *see* Taiyanyanokhotana
Ta-ji-que *see* Tajique
Tajique [Pueblo] *Tigua* (H)
Ta-jua *see* Tawa
Tajua *see* Tawa
Taka *see* Taku
Takadhe *see* Takkuth-kutchin
Takadhe *see* Tukkuthkutchin
Takahagane *see* Ontwaganha
Takahli *see* Takulli
Takaiak [AK] *Kaiyuhkhotana* (H)
Takaiaksa *see* Takaiak
Takai-yakho-tan'a (Contri, v.1, p.26)
Takai-yakho-tan'a (H) *see also* Jugelnute (H)

Takaiyakhotana *see* Takai-
yakho-tan'a
Takajaksen *see* Takaiak
Takali *see* Takulli
Takalli *see* Takulli
Takama *see* Yakima
Takamiut *see* Baffin Island
Takana *see* Tacana
Takapo ishak *see* Attacapa
Takapoishak *see* Attacapa
Takapsin-tonwanna *see*
Takapsintonwanna
Takapsintonwanna *Wahpeton* (H)
takastina *see* Takestina
Takawaro *see* Tawakoni
Takaz *see* Tukkuthkutchin
Takdentan [AK] *Tlingit* (H)
Takelly *see* Takulli
Ta-kel-ma *see* Takelma
Takelma [OR] (LC)
Takelman [Lang] [OR] (LC)
Takensa *see* Taensa
Takestina [AK] *Tlingit* (H)
Takfwelottine [Can] *Thlingchadi-
ine* (BE)
Takhayuna *see* Aleuts
Takhchapa *Miniconjou* (H)
Takhe *see* Taos
Takhtam *see* Serrano
Takhuhayuta [SD] *Hunkpatina*
(H)
Takhuhayuta *Yanktonai* (H)
Takic [Lang] [*Uto-Aztecan*]
(Hdbk10)
Takilma *see* Takelma
Takini *Upper Yanktonai* (BE)
Ta-kit kutchin *see* Tatlitkutchin
Takitkutchin *see* Tatlithutchin
Takkuth-kutchin [Can] (BE)
T'akkwel-ottine *see* Takfwelot-
tine
Takkwelottine *see* Takfwelottine
Takla-uedi *see* Daktlawedi
Taklauedi *see* Daktlawedi
Takla-vedi *see* Daktlawedi
Tako *see* Taku
Takon (H) *see also* Taku (BE)
Takon [AK, Can] *Han* (BE)
Takongoto [Subclan] *Delaware*
(H)
Takoo *see* Taku
Ta-ko-ong'-o-to *see* Takoongoto
Ta-koos-oo-ti-na *see* Takutine
Takoosootina *see* Takutina
Takopepeshane *see* Pineshow
Takoulguehronnon (H)
Takoulguehronnon (H) *see also*
Conestoga (LC)
Taksehepu [ID] *Nez Perce* (BE)
Takshik *see* Toba
Taksik [Arg] *Toba* (O)
Takten-tan *see* Takdentan
Taktentan *see* Takdentan

Taktum [Moiety] [CA] *Cahuilla*
(Pub, v.16, no.6, p.349)
Taku (H) *see also* Takutine (BE)
Taku [AK] *Tlingit* (BE)
Takuatep [Br] *Kawahib* (O)
Takudh *see* Takkuthkutchin
Taku-kon *see* Taku
Takukon *see* Taku
Ta-kuli *see* Takulli
Takuli *see* Takulli
Takulli (LC) *see also* Carrier (LC)
Takulli [BC] [Tinne] (H)
Takunape *see* Tucunyape
Taku-qwan *see* Taku
Takuqwan *see* Taku
Ta-ku-rth *see* Takkuthkutchin
Takurth *see* Takkuthkutchin
Takusalgi [Clan] *Creek* (H)
Ta-Kutchi *see* Eskimos
Takutchi *see* Eskimos
Ta-kuth Kutchin *see*
Tukkuthkutchin
Takutine [BC] *Nahane* (BE)
Takutsskoe *see* Taku
Takwanedi [AK] *Tlingit* (H)
Takya [Clan] [NM] *Zuni* (H)
Tak'yaiuna-kwe *see* Takya
Takyaiunakwe *see* Takya
Tak'ya-kwe *see* Takya
Takyakwe *see* Takya
Tala [Clan] *Yuchi* (H)
Talagan *see* Cherokee
Talamanca [CR] *Bribri* (LC)
Talamanca [Lang] *Chibchan* (LC)
Talamancan *see* Talamanca
[Lang]
Talamatan *see* Huron
Talamatun *see* Huron
Talamoh *see* Tillamook
Talangamanae *see* Khemnichan
Ta-laottine *see* Chintagottine
Talaottine *see* Chintagottine
Talapaguem *see* Saulapaguem
Talapoosa *Creek* (H)
Talarenos *see* Tularenos
Talarkoteen [Family] *Tahltan* (H)
Ta'la taha *see* Tala
Talataha *see* Tala
Talatui [CA] *Miwok* (H)
Talawa *see* Tolowa
Talawipiki [Clan] *Hopi* (H)
Talawipikiwiñwu *see* Talawipiki
Ta-la-wi-pi-ki wuñ-wu *see* Ta-
lawipiki
Tal-che *see* Tachi
Talche *see* Tachi
Talchedon *see* Alchedoma
Talchedum *see* Alchedoma
Talch-kuedi *see* Tahlkoedi
Talchkuedi *see* Tahlkoedi
Talcotin *see* Tautin
Talegan *see* Cherokee

Talegawe *see* Cherokee
Talemaya *see* Tututni
Talepuse *see* Middle Creek
Tali [TN] (BE)
Taliaseri *see* Tariana
Talicomish *see* Taliomh
Talinche *see* Dalinchi
Talinchi *see* Dalinchi
Talio *see* Bella Coola
Ta'lio *see* Taliomh
Talio *see* Taliomh
Taliomh (BE)
Talio'mh *see* Taliomh
Talipuce *see* Middle Creek
Talirpingmiut [Can] *Central Eski-
mos* (BE)
Talirpingmiut *Okomiut Eskimos*
(H)
Talkoaten *see* Tautin
Talkotin *see* Tautin
Tallagewy *see* Cherokee
Tallahaski *see* Seminole
Tallan [EC] (LC)
Tallapoosa [TN] *Shawnee* (BE)
Tallawa Thlucco *see* Apalachicola
Tallegewi *see* Talligewi
Tallegwi *see* Tallegwi
Tallegwi *see* Cherokee
Tallenche *see* Dalinchi
Talligeu *see* Cherokee
Talligewi (BE)
Talligewi (H) *see also* Cherokee
(LC)
Tallignamay *see* Quigyuma
Talliguamais *see* Quigyuma
Talliguamay *see* Quigyuma
Talliguamay *see* Halyikwamai
Talliguamayoue *see* Quigyuma
Tal-lin-che *see* Dalinchi
Tall-in-chee *see* Dalinchi
Tallinchee *see* Dalinchi
Tallion *see* Taliomh
Tallion Nation *see* Bella Coola
Tallium *see* Taliomh
Tall Man's band *see* Odukeo's
band
Tal-lo-wau thlucco *see*
Apalachicola
Tallowauthlucco *see* Apalachicola
Talluche *see* Dalinchi
Talmamiche [OR] *Takelma* (H)
Tal-ma-mi-tce *see* Talmamiche
Talohlafia [Clan] [NM] *Taos* (H)
Talo'lafia tai'na *see* Talohlafia
Talolafia taina *see* Talohlafia
Talomey *see* Taliomh
Talon [MI] *Ottawa* (H)
Ta-lo-na-pi *see* Talonapin
Talonapi *see* Talonapin
Talo-na p'in *see* Talonapin
Talonapin *Hunkpapa* (BE)
Ta-lo tunne *see* Talotunne
Talotunne [OR] *Takelma* (H)

Talqoe'di *see* Tahlkoedi
Tal-qua-tee *see* Tahlkoedi
Taltactunne *see* Taltushtundtude
Tal-tac tunne *see* Taltushtuntude
Talta'l-cane *see* Hakia tce-pai
Talta'l-kuwa *see* Hakia Tce-pai
Taltalkuwa *see* Hakia tce-pai
Taltotin *see* Tautin
T'altsan Ottine *see* Tatsanottine
Taltsanottine *see* Tatsanottine
Tal't-uc-tun tu-de *see* Taltush-
  tuntude
Taltuctuntude *see* Taltushtun-
  tude
Taltushtuntude (BE) *see also*
  Takelma (LC)
Taltushtuntude [OR] (BE)
Talua lako *see* Apalachicola
Talualako *see* Apalachicola
Taluit *see* Taliomh
Ta-lum-ne *see* Telamni
Talumne *see* Telamni
Talusa *see* Taensa
Talu-wa *see* Tolowa
Taluwa *see* Tolowa
Talwa lako *see* Apalachicola
Talwalako *see* Apalachicola
Talyan *see* Tahltan
Tam [Clan] [NM] *Pueblo Indians*
  (H)
Tama [Col] (O)
Tama [FL] (BE)
Tama [FL] (BE) *see also* Altamaha
  (BE)
Tamahita (BE)
Tamaicas *see* Timucua
Tamainde *see* Mamainde
Tamaiya *see* Santa Ana [NM]
Tamajab *see* Mohave
Tamakurideni *see* Dani
Tamakwa [Clan] *Abnaki* (H)
Tamakwapi [Clan] *Delaware* (H)
Tamal [CA] (H)
Tamalenos *see* Tamal
Tamales *see* Tamal
Tamalgi *see* Itamalgi
Tamali (BE)
Tamallos *see* Tamal
Tamanac [VE] (LC)
Tamanaco [Lang] *Carib* (UAz,
  v.28)
Tamanahua [Br] (O)
Tamanawa *see* Tamanahua
Tamankamyam *see* Serrano
Tamanmu [ID] *Nez Perce* (BE)
Tamarais *see* Tamaroa
Tamarca *see* Tamaroa
Tamare *see* Nambicuara
Tamaroa *Illinois Confederacy* (H)
Tamaroha *see* Tamaroa
Tamaroid *see* Tamaroa
Tamarois *see* Tamaroa
Tamaroja *see* Tamaroa

Tamarona *see* Tamaroa
Tamarono *see* Tamaroa
Tamarora *see* Tamaroa
Tamaroua *see* Tamaroa
Tamarouha *see* Tamaroa
Tamarous *see* Tamaroa
Tamaro'wa *see* Tamaroa
Tamarowa *see* Tamaroa
Tamasab *see* Mohave
Tamasabes *see* Mohave
tamat *see* Klamath
Tamathli [GA] *Tamali* (BE)
Tamaulipec [MX] (BE)
Tamaulipeco [MX] *Tamaulipec*
  (BE)
Tamawa *see* Tamaroa
Ta-ma-ya *see* Santa Ana [NM]
Tamaya *see* Santa Ana [NM]
ta-maya *see* Santa Ana [NM]
Tamazulteca [MX] (BE)
Tambeopa *see* Kaiwa
Tambiope *see* Kaiwa
Tambopata *see* Ese Ejja
Tambopata-Guarayo *see* Ese Ejja
Tamcan *Coahuiltecan* (BE)
Tamceca [NC, SC] (H)
Tame *see* Tunebo
Tame Motilon *see* Yukpa
Tames *see* Jemez
Tamescamengs *see* Tamiscaming
Tami *see* Tano
tamianutcem [Clan] [CA] *Serrano*
  (Pub, v.26, 1929)
Tamikurideni [Br] *Dani* (O)
Taminaua *see* Tamanahua
Tamique *Coahuiltecan* (BE)
Tamiquis *see* Tamique
Tamkan [CA] *Costanoan* (H)
Tamlocklock *see* Tamuleko
Tammalanos *see* Tamal
Tammasees *see* Yamasee
Tammoleka *see* Tamuleko
Tammoleka *see* Tamuleko
Tammukan [CA] *Cholovone* (H)
Tamoleca *see* Tamuleko
Ta-mo-le-ka *see* Tamuleko
Tamoria *see* Tamaroa
Tamorois *see* Tamaroa
Tamos *see* Pecos
Tampa *see* Campa
Tampacua *Coahuiltecan*
  (Hdbk10)
Tampacuases *see* Karankawa
Tamp-Pah Utes *see* Yampa
Tamppah Utes *see* Yampa
T'am-t'ainin *see* Tam
Tamtainin *see* Tam
Tamuleko [CA] (H)
Ta-mul-kee *see* Itamalgi
Tamulkee *see* Itamalgi
Tamy [Self-designation] *see*
  Santa Ana [NM]
Tamya *see* Santa Ana [NM]

Tamyen [Lang] *Northern*
  Costonoan (CA-8)
Tan (H) *see also* Tang (H)
Tan' *see* Tung
Tan [Clan] *Tewa* (H)
Ta'naha *see* Tanaha
Tanaha [Clan] *Caddo Confederacy*
  (H)
Tanahtenk *see* Tenaktak
Ta-nah-wee *see* Tenawa
Tanahwee *see* Tenawa
Tanai *see* Tainaina
Tanaina [AK] (LC)
Tanaka [Clan] *Hopi* (H)
Tanaka wiñwu *see* Tangyaka
Ta-na-ka wunwu *see* Tangyaka
Tanakawuñwu *see* Tangyaka
Tanak-tench *see* Tenaktak
Tanaktench *see* Tenaktak
Tanakteuch *see* Tenaktak
Tanakteuk *see* Tenaktak
Tana-kut'qin *see* Loucheux
Tanakutqin *see* Loucheux
Tanana [AK] (LC)
Tanan-Kuttchin *see* Ten-
  ankutchin
Tanaquiapem *see* Tenicapeme
Ta-na-tin-ne *see* Kawchottine
Tanatinne *see* Kawchottine
Ta-na-tsu-ka *see* Tanetsukanu-
  manke
Tanatsuka (PC) *see also* Tanet-
  sukanumanke (H)
Tanatsuka *Mandan* (H)
Ta-na-wun-da *see* Tonawanda
Tanawunda *see* Tonawanda
Tan-a-ya *see* Santa Ana [NM]
Tanaya *see* Santa Ana [NM]
Tancacoama [MX] *Coahuiltecan*
  (Hdbk10)
Tancaguas *see* Tonkawa
Tancagueis *see* Tonkawa
Tancagues *see* Tonkawa
Tancaguez *see* Tonkawa
Tancaguies *see* Tonkawa
Tancahuas *see* Tonkawa
Tancahues *see* Tonkawa
Tancahuos *see* Tonkawa
Tancamas *see* Tonkawa
Tancanes *see* Tonkawa
Tancaouay *see* Tonkawa
Tancaoves *see* Tonkawa
Tancaoye *see* Tonkawa
Tancards *see* Tonkawa
Tancaro *see* Tawakoni
Tancases *see* Tonkawa
Tancaveys *see* Tonkawa
Tanchipahoe *see* Tangipahoa
Tancl-tac tunne *see* Taltushtun-
  tude
Tancltactunne *see* Taltushtun-
  tude
Tancoways *see* Tonkawa

Ta'ne *see* Dyani
Tane *see* Tanyi
Tane *see* Dyani
Tane'di *see* Tanedi
Tanedi [AK] *Tligit* (H)
Ta'neeszahni (IndT, v.21, no.10, Oct. 1990, pp.19, 22)
Taneeszahni *see* Ta'neeszahni
Taneho [LA] (H)
Taneks anyadi *see* Biloxi
Taneksanyadi *see* Biloxi
Taneksayna *see* Biloxi
Taneks ayna [Self-designation] *see* Biloxi
Taneks hanyadi *see* Biloxi
Tanekshanyadi *see* Biloxi
Tanekshaya *see* Biloxi
Taneks haya [Self-designation] *see* Biloxi
Ta-nek-teuch *see* Tenaktak
Tanena *see* Tanana
Tanessee *see* Tawesa
Tanetsukanumanke (H) *see also* Tanatsuka (H)
Ta-ne-tsu-ka nu-man-ke *see* Tanetsukanumanke
Tanetsukanumanke *Mandan* (H)
Tanewa *see* Tenawa
Tanewah *see* Tanawa
Tang [Clan] *Hano* (H)
Tanga'c *see* Tongass
Tangac *see* Tongass
Tanga'sh *see* Tongass
Tangash *see* Tongass
Tangasskoe *see* Tongass
Tangdhangtanka [Clan] *Quapaw* (H)
Tangdhantangkaenikashika [Gens] *Quapaw* (H)
Tangeboa *see* Tangipahoa
Tangeesatsah [AK] *Loucheux* (H)
Tangeratsa *Kutchakutchin* (H)
Tanges-at-sa *see* Tangeratsa
Tangesatsa *see* Tangeratsa
Tangibac *see* Tangipahoa
Tangibao *see* Tangipahoa
Tangibaoa *see* Tangipahoa
Tan'gipaha *see* Tangipahoa
Tangipaho *see* Tangipahoa
Tangipahoa [LA] (BE)
Tangipao *see* Tangipahoa
Tangle Clan *see* Ta'neexzahni
Tanguay *see* Panguay
Tangyaka [Clan] *Hopi* (H)
Tani'banen *see* Kadohadacho
Tanibanen *see* Kadohadacho
Tani'banenina *see* Kadohadacho
Tanibanenina *see* Kadohadacho
Tani'batha *see* Kadohadacho
Tanibatha *see* Kadohadacho
Tanico (H) *see also* Tunica (LC)
Tanico [AR] (H)
Ta nika-shing-ga *see* Hangatanga

Tanikashingga *see* Hangatanga
Tanikwa *see* Tunica
Tani'ma *see* Tanima
Tanima *Comanche* (BE)
Tanimboka *see* Yahuna
Tanimboka *see* Tanimuko
Tanimuca *see* Yahuna
Tanimuca *see* Tanimuko
Tanimuco *see* Tanimuko
Tanimuka *see* Yahuna
Tanimuka *see* Tanimuko
Tanimuko [Col] (O)
Tanintabin *see* Tanin'ta'ben
Tanin'ta'bin [MN] *Assiniboin* (BE)
Tanintauci [Clan] *Assiniboin* (H)
Taniquo *see* Tanico
Tanish *see* Arikara
Ta-nish *see* Arikara
Taniyumh'h *see* Paviotso
Tanjibao *see* Tangipahoa
Tan-ka-wa *see* Tonkawa
Tankawa *see* Tonkawa
Tankaway *see* Tonkawa
Tank-heesh *see* Tagish
Tankheesh *see* Tagish
Tankiteke [NY, CN] *Wappinger Confederacy* (BE)
Tanko *see* Nishinam
Tanko *see* Tonkawa
Tanks *see* Tonkawa
Tankum *see* Nishinam
Tanna-kutchi *see* Tenankutchin
Tan-nah-shis-en *see* Jicarilla Apache
Tannahshisen *see* Jicarilla Apache
Tannakutchi *see* Tenankutchin
Tannock *see* Bannock
Tannocke *see* Bannock
Tan-no'm *see* Round Valley Yokuts
Tannontatez *see* Tionontati
Tano (H) *see also* Hano (BE)
Tano [Pueblo] (BE)
Tanoan [Lang] *Southern Tewa* (LC)
Ta-noch-tench *see* Tenaklak
Tanochtench *see* Tenaklak
Ta-nock-teuch *see* Tenaktak
Tanockteuch *see* Tenaktak
Tanoi *see* Hano
Tanom (PC) *see also* Ta'no'm (BE)
Ta'no'm [CA] *Yuki* (BE)
Tanom [CA] *Yuki* (H)
Ta-non Kutchin *see* Tenankutchin
Tanonkutchin *see* Tenankutchin
Tanoquevi *see* Hano
Tanoquibi *see* Hano
Tanos *see* Pecos
Tanotenne (H) *see also* Tsatsuotin (H)

Ta-no-tenne *see* Tanotenne
Tanotenne [Can] *Southern Carrier* (BE)
Tanpacuaze (Hdbk10) *see also* Tapacua (Hdbk10)
Tanpacuazes [TX] *Coahuiltecan* (H)
Tanquaay *see* Tonkawa
Tanquinno *see* Tanico
Tansipaho *see* Tangipahoa
Ta'nta hade *see* Tongass
Tantahade *see* Tongass
Ta'n-ta'wat *see* Chemehuevi
Tantawat *see* Chemehuevi
Tantawit *see* Chemehuevi
Tan-tdoa *see* Tan
Tantdoa *see* Tan
Tantin *see* Tautin
Tantos *see* Tonto Apache
Tan-uh-tuh *see* Tenaktak
Tanuhtuh *see* Tenaktak
Ta-nun kutch-in *see* Tenankutchin
Tanunkutchin *see* Tenankutchin
Tanus *see* Hano
Tanxnitania [VA] *Manahoac* (BE)
Tanx Powhatans *see* Powhatan
Tanxsnitania *see* Tanxnitania
Tanxsnitanian *see* Tanxnitania
Tanygua *see* Avachiripa
Tanyi [Clan] *Keres* (H)
Tanyi-hano *see* Tanyi
Tanyi-hanoq *see* Tanyi
Tanyi-hanoqch *see* Tanyi
Tanyi-hanuch *see* Tanyi
Tanyi hanutsh *see* Tanyi
Tao (H) *see also* Taos (LC)
Tao [Clan] *Caddo Confederacy* (H)
Taoapa [MN] *Mdewakanton* (H)
Taogaria *see* Ontwaganha
Taogria *see* Ontwaganha
Taol-naas-hadai *Haida* (H)
Taol na'as xa'da-i *see* Taol-naas-hadai
Taopi's Band *see* Farmers Band
Taoros *see* Taos
Taos (H) *see also* Moache (LC)
Taos [Pueblo] [NM] (LC)
Taosans *see* Taos
Taoses *see* Taos
Taosij *see* Taos
Taosis *see* Taos
Taosites *see* Taos
Taos Utes *see* Moache
Taosy *see* Taos
Taos Yutas *see* Moache
Taotin *see* Tautin
Taouacacana *see* Tawakoni
Taouacha *see* Tawasa
Taoucanes *see* Tawakoni
Taovayas *see* Wichita
Taowa *see* Tewa

Ta-o-ya-te-du-ta see Kapozha
Taoyateduta see Kapozha
Tao Yutas see Moache
Taoyutas see Moache
Tap see Tabo
Tapa [Clan] *Yuchi* (H)
Tapa [Gens] *Omaha* (H)
Tapa [Subgens] *Omaha* (H)
Tapaadji see Klamath
Tapaan see Tappan
Tapaanes see Tappan
Tapachula see Tapachultec
Tapachultec [MX, Gua] (BE)
Tapachulteca see Tapachutec
Tapacua see Akwe-Shavante
Tapage see Pitahauerat
Tapahanna see Quioucohanock
Tapahowerat see Pitahauerat
Tapaje see Pitahauerat
Tapajo [Br] (LC)
Tapakara see Kawahib
Tapana'sh see Tapanash
Tapanash [OR] *Tenino* (BE)
Tapanash [WA] (BE) *see also* Skin
   (BE)
Tapanash [WA] *Shahaptian* (H)
Tapanhuna see Beico do Pau
Tapanses see Tappan
Tapanyuna see Beico do Pau
Taparita *Achagua* (LC)
T'apa taha see Tapa [Yuchi]
Tapataha see Tapa [Yuchi]
Ta-pa-taj-je see Tapa [Omaha]
Tapatajje see Tapa [Omaha]
Tapatwa [Clan] *Yuchi* (H)
Tapatwa taha see Tapatwa
Tapatwataha see Tapatwa
Tapayotoque *Coahuiltecan*
   (Hdbk10)
Tapayuna [Br] *Kawahib* (O)
Tapeeksin [WA] (H)
Tapgucha see Taposa
Tapi [Clan] *Yuchi* (H)
Tapicletca see Tapishlecha
Tapiete [Par, BO] (O)
Tapii see Tapiete
Tapiksdabsh see Tapi'kdabsh
Tapi'ksdabsh [WA] *Sahehwamish*
   (BE)
Tapioca see Waiwai
Tapirape [Br] (LC)
Tapishlecha [SD] *Oglala* (H)
Tapisleca see Tapishlecha
Tapi taha see Tapi
Tapitaha see Tapi
Ta-pit-si-a-ma see Tapitsiama
Tapitsiama [Pueblo] *Acoma* (H)
Tapixulapan [CAm] *Zoque* (BE)
Tapkachmiut [AK] *Malemiut Es-
   kimos* (H)
Tapkhakgmut see Tapkachmiut
Tapoctough see Tenaktak
Tapohanock see Rappahannock

Tapoosa see Taposa
Taposa [MS] (BE)
Tapouaro *Illinois Confederacy* (H)
Tapoucha see Taposa
Tapouero see Tapouaro
Tapoura see Tapouaro
Tapousoa see Taposa
Tapoussa see Taposa
Tapowsa see Taposa
Tappa see Pitahauerat
Tappaen see Tappan
Tappage see Pitahauerat
Tappage Pawnee see Pitahauerat
Tappahanocke see Quiouco-
   hanock
Tappan [NY] *Unami* (BE)
Tapparies Comanches see Dit-
   sakana
Tappaye Pawnee see Pitahauerat
Tappen see Tappan
Tappensees see Tappan
Tappents see Tappan
Tapteal see Yakima
Tapteel see Yakima
Tapteet see Yakima
Tapteil see Yakima
Tap-teil-min see Yakima
Tapteilmin see Yakima
Tapuya [Br] (LC)
T!a'qdentan see Takdentan
Taqdentan see Takdentan
Taqsi't see Takestina
Taqsit see Takestina
Ta-qta see Choctaw
Taqta see Choctaw
Taquason *Choptank* (Hdbk15)
Taquenazabo [HA, WInd]
   Guaccaiarima (BE)
Taquha-yuta see Takhuhayuta
Taquhayuta see Takhuhayuta
Ta-qui-quc-ce see Tututni
Taquiqucce see Tututni
Ta-qu-quc-ce see Tututni
Taququece see Tututni
Ta-qu'-quo-ce see Tututni
Taququoce see Tututni
Taracahitan see Tarachaitan
Taracahitan see Cahita
Taracahitian [Lang] [*Uto-Aztecan*]
   (BE)
Taracone (H) *see also* Faraon (BE)
Taracone [TX] (H)
Taracton see Catskill
Taractou see Catskill
Taracuay see Characuay
Taraha [TX] (H)
Tarahumara see Tarahumare
Tarahumaran [Lang] [*Uto-
   Aztecan*] (Hdbk10)
Tarahumare [MX] (LC)
Tarahumari see Tarahumare
Tarakton see Catskill
Taramembe see Teremembe

taramil o'odham [Lang] *Highland
   Pima* (Hdbk10)
Tarancacuases see Karankawa
Taranteen see Abnaki
Taranu [BO] *Araona* (O)
Taraones see Farara
Tarapita see Taparita
Tarapototo [EC] (O)
Tararrais see Tamaroa
Tarascan [Lang] [MX] (LC)
Tarascan Indians see Tarasco
Tarasco [MX] (LC)
Tarateen see Abnaki
Taraumar see Tarahumare
Taraumares see Tarahumare
Tar-co-eh-parch see Takhchapa
Tarcoehparch see Takhchapa
Tar-coeh-parh see Takhchapa
Tarcoehparh see Takhchapa
Tarcoehparh *Miniconjou* (H)
Tareguano (H) *see also* Tarequano
   (H)
Tareguano *Coahuiltecan* (Hdbk10)
Tarena see Tereno
Tarenteen see Abnaki
Tarenteen see Tarrateen
Tarentin see Abnaki
Tarentine see Abnaki
Tareormeut see Kopagmiut
Tarepang see Taulipang
Tarequano [MX] *Coahuiltecan*
   (BE)
Tareumiut see Tagiugmiut
Taria see Tariana
Tariaca [CR] *Cabecar* (BE)
Tariaka see Tariaca
Tariana [Br] *Tucano* (LC)
Tariano see Tariana
Tarimari see Tarahumare
Tariumiut see Tagiugmiut
Tarken see Taku
Tarkoo see Taku
Taro see Yavapai
Taromari see Tarahumare
Taronas-hadai [AK] [*Yaku-lanas*]
   (H)
T'a'ro nas ihad'a'i see Taronas-
   hadai
Taronsihadai see Taronas-hadai
Tarracones see Faraon
Tarra-Iumane see Jumano
Tarraiumane see Jumano
Tarrakton see Catskill
tarramiut (Hdbk5) *see also* Tahag-
   miut (Hdbk5)
Tarramiut [Can] [*Inuit (Quebec)*]
   (Hdbk5)
Tarranteeri see Abnaki
Tarranteeri see Tarrateen
Tarranten see Abnaki
Tarranten see Tarrateen
Tarrantine see Abnaki
Tarrantine see Tarrateen

Tarrateen (LC)
Tarrateen *Abnaki* (LC)
Tarratin *see* Abnaki
Tarratin *see* Tarrateen
Tarrenteen *see* Abnaki
Tarrenteen *see* Tarrateen
Tarrenteene *see* Abnaki
Tarrenteene *see* Tarrateen
Tarrenten *see* Abnaki
Tarrenten *see* Tarrateen
Tarrentine *see* Abnaki
Tarrentine *see* Tarrateen
Tarreor-meut *see* Kopagmiut
Tarreormeut *see* Kopamiut
Tarthem [BC] *Salish* (H)
Taruarara *see* Tarahumare
Taruma [Guy] (O)
Tarwarsa *see* Tawasa
Tarwassaw *see* Tawasa
Tasabuess *see* Yavapai
Tasagi's Band *Wahpekute* (H)
Tasame *see* Navajo
Tasaning (H)
Ta-sa-un *see* Hopi
Tasaun *see* Hopi
tasavi *see* Navajo
tasavimi *see* Navajo
Tasawiks [WA] *Palouse* (BE)
Tascorins *see* Tuscarora
Tascororin *see* Tuscarora
Tascuache [MX] *Coahuiltecan* (Hdbk10)
Tascuroreus *see* Tuscarora
Tasha [Clan] *Caddo Confederacy* (H)
Tashash *see* Kadohadacho
Ta-sha-va-ma *see* Navajo
Tashavama *see* Navajo
Tash-e-pa *see* Tushepaw
Tashepa *see* Tushepaw
Tash-gatze *see* Tashkatze
Tashgatze *see* Tashkatze
Tashi *see* Mescalero Apache
tashihi *see* Apache
tashihin [sci] *see* Apache
Tashi'ine *see* Jicarilla Apache
Tashiine *see* Jicarilla Apache
Tashin *see* Apache
Tash-ka-tze *see* Tashkatze
Tashkatze [Pueblo] [NM] (H)
Tashnahecha [SD] *Oglala* (H)
Tashtye (H) *see also* Tawshtye (H)
Tashtye [Clan] [NM] *Pecos* (H)
Tashunkee-o-ta *see* Tashunkeota
Tashunkeeota *see* Tashunkeota
Tashunkeota *Sihasapa* (BE)
Tash-Yuta *see* Moache
Tashyuta *see* Moache
Tasiget tuviwarai *Northern Paiute* (Hdbk11)
tasigwaiti *see* Tasiget tuviwarai
Ta-sin-da *see* Tesinde
Tasinda *see* Tesinde

Ta sindje qaga *see* Hangatanga
Tasindjeqaga *see* Hangatanga
Tasio [PE] *Campa* (O)
tasiujaq *see* Tessiugak
Tasiusak *Greenland Eskimos* (BE)
Tasiuyarmiut [AK] *Tanunirmiut* (Hdbk5)
Taska'ho *see* Tuscarora
Taskaho *see* Tuscarora
T'as-ka-lo-len *see* Tuscarora
Taskalolen *see* Tuscarora
taskalónu *see* Tuscarora
Taskalo-nugi *see* Tuscarora
Taskalonugi *see* Tuscarora
Taskaroren *see* Tuscarora
Taskarosin *see* Tuscarora
Taskigi *see* Tuskegee
Taskirora *see* Tuscarora
Taskororin *see* Tuscarora
Tasks *see* Tuscarora
Tas la'nas *see* Tadji-lanas
Taslanas *see* Tadji-lanas
Tas Lennas *see* Tadji-lanas
Taslennas *see* Tadji-lanas
Tasmamares *see* Tumamar
Tasne *see* Knaiakhotana
Tassabuess *see* Navajo
Tassabuess *see* Yavapai
Tassautessus *see* Chickahominy
Tassenocogoula *see* Avoyel
Tassey *see* Toosey
Tastasagonia *see* Taztasagonies
Tastioteños [MX] *Seri* (Hdbk10)
Tatagua [CA] (H)
tatala *see* Cascades
Tatamaste [CAm] *Concho* (BE)
Tatankachesli *Sans Arc* (H)
Tatanka-tcelsi *see* Tatankachesli
Tatankatcelsi *see* Tatankachesli
Tataten *see* Ta-ta-ten
Ta-ta-ten *Tolowa* (Contri, v.3)
Tataviam *see* Alliklik
Tatchatotenne [BC] *Carrier* (Bull133)
Tatche *see* Tachi
Tatche band *see* Tatshiautin
Tatchee *see* Tachi
Tatchila *see* Colorado [SA]
Ta'tcqe *see* Tateke
Ta-tdoa *see* Ta [Tewa]
Tatdoa *see* Ta [Tewa]
Tate *see* Tait
Tateibombu's Band *Dakota* (BE)
Tateke [Can] *Cowichan* (BE)
T'a't'entsait *see* Ialostimot
Tatentsait *see* Ialostimot
Ta-te-poin *see* Kiyuksa [Mde-wakanton]
Tatepsin *see* Kiyuksa [Mde-wakanton]
T'a'teqe *see* Tateke
Tateqe *see* Tateke
Tatimolo [MX] *Totonac* (BE)

Tatiquilhati [Lang] [CAm] *Totonac* (BE)
Tatishokaiya *Wailaki* (Pub, v.20, no.6, pp.101–102)
Tatkannai *see* Takini
Tatla *see* Tatlatan
Tatla-Shequilla *see* Tlatlasikoala
Tatlatan [AK] *Ahtena* (H)
Tatlazan [AK] *Ahtena* (BE)
Tatliakhtana *see* Chugachigmut
Tat-li-em-a-nun *see* Navajo
Tatliemanun *see* Navajo
Ta-tlit-Kutchin *see* Tatlitkutchin
Tatlit-kutchin [BC] *Kutchin* (BE)
Tatlitkutchin *Tinne* (H)
Tatoama [MX] *Coahuiltecan* (Hdbk10)
Tatocuene [MX] *Coahuiltecan* (Hdbk10)
Tatouche *see* Makeh
Ta-towa *see* Ta [Tewa]
Tatowa *see* Ta [Tewa]
T'atpo'os *see* Tatpoos
Tatpoos [VanI] *Salish* (BE)
Tatqu'nma *see* Soyennow
Tatsah-Kutchin *see* Tatsakutchin
Ta-tsa Kutchin *see* Tatsakutchin
Tatsakutchin [BC] *Kutchin* (H)
Tatsanottine [Can] *Chipewyan* (BE)
Ta-tseh kutch-in *see* Tatsakutchin
Tatsehkutchin *see* Tatsakutchin
Tatshiantin *see* Tatshiautin
Tatshiautin [BC] *Northern Carrier* (BE)
Ta-tshi-ko-tin *see* Tatshiautin
Ta-tshik-o-tin *see* Tatshiautin
Tatshikotin *see* Tatshiautin
T'a-ts'un-ye *see* Tatsunye
Tatsunye [OR] *Chastacosta* (H)
Ta-tsur-ma *see* Tesuque
Ta-tu *see* Huchnom
Tatu *see* Huchnom
Tatutapuyo *see* Pamoa
Tatutapuyo *see* Tatuyo
Tatu-Tapuyo *see* Tatuyo
Tatuyo (LC) *see also* Pamoa (LC)
Tatuyo [Col] (O)
Tauarde *see* Nambicuara
Tauarde *see* Tawande
Taucos *see* Hano
Tau-hur-lin-dagh-go-waugh *see* Oneida
Tauhurlindaghgowaugh *see* Oneida
Ta-ui *see* Taos
Taukies *see* Sauk
Taulipang (O) *see also* Arekuna (LC)
Taulipang [Gua, VE] (O)
Taunde *see* Tawande
Taupane *see* Jicaque

Taurepa *see* Taulipang
Taurepane [*Parukoto-Pemon*] (O)
Taurepang *see* Arekena
Taurepang *see* Taulipang
Tauri *see* Atorai
Taushiro [PE] (O)
Tausitania [Lang] *Manahoac Confederacy* (H)
Ta-uth *see* Taos
Tautin [BC] *Southern Carrier* (BE)
Tautsa-wot-dinni *see* Tatsanottine
Taux *see* Nanticoke
Tauxania *see* Tanxnitania
Tauxenent [VA] *Powhatan Confederacy* (BE)
Tauxent *see* Tauxenent
Tauxinentes *see* Tauxenent
Tauxitania [Lang] *Manahoac Confederacy* (H)
Tauxsintania *see* Tauxnitania
Tauxuntania *see* Tauxnitatnia
Tauytera *see* Caingua
Tavakavas *see* Tawakoni
Tavaroas *see* Tamaroa
Tavashay [Arg, Par] *Ashluslay* (O)
Ta-ve *see* Tave
Tave [Clan] *Hopi* (H)
Tavewachi *see* Tabeguache
Taviachi *see* Tabeguache
Tavira *see* Tabira
Taviwach [Self-designation] *see* Uncompahgre
taviwatsiu *see* Parusanuch
Tavo *see* Tabo [Clan]
Tavossi *see* Tawasa
Tawa (BE) *see also* Ottawa (LC)
Tawa *see* Tewa
Tawa *see* Ottawa
Tawa [Clan] *Hopi* (H)
Tawaa *see* Ottawa
Ta-wac *see* Tawash
Tawacairoe *see* Tawakoni
Tawacamis *see* Tawakoni
Tawacanie *see* Tawakoni
Ta-wa-ca-ro *see* Tawakoni
Tawacaro *see* Tawakoni
Tawacarro *see* Tawakoni
Tawaccaras *see* Tawakoni
Tawaccomo *see* Tawakoni
Tawaccoroe *see* Tawakoni
Tawachguans *see* Nanticoke
Tawackanie *see* Tawakoni
Tawackguano *see* Nanticoke
Tawaconie *see* Tawakoni
Tawahka [Hon, NI] *Sumo* (BE)
Tawai *see* Catoquina
Tawai *see* Paku-Diapa
Tawakal *see* Tawakoni
Tawakanaks *see* Tawakoni
Tawakanas *see* Tawakoni

Tawakanay *see* Tawakoni
Tawakany *see* Tawakoni
Ta-wa-ka-ro *see* Tawakoni
Tawakaro *see* Tawakoni
Tawakenoe *see* Tawakoni
Tawakones *see* Tawakoni
Ta-wa-ko-ni *see* Tawakoni
Tawakoni [OK, TX] (LC)
Tawaktenk *see* Tenaktak
Tawakudi *see* Tawakoni
Tawalemne *see* Tuolumne
Tawalimnu [CA] *Northern Valley Yokuts* (BE)
Tawamana [Clan] *Hopi* (H)
Tawamana wiñwu *see* Tawamana
Ta-wa-ma-na wuñwu *see* Tawamana
Tawa-namu *see* Tawa
Tawanamu *see* Tawa
Tawande [Br] *Northern Nambicuara* (O)
Tawareka *see* Tawakoni
Tawas *see* Ottawa
Tawas *see* Tewa
Tawasa [FL] *Alabama* (BE)
Tawash [Clan] [NM] (H)
Tawasha *see* Tawasa
Tawash-hano *see* Tawash
Tawassa *see* Tawasa
Tawatawas *see* Miami
Tawatawee *see* Miami
Tawaw *see* Ottawa
Tawawinu *see* Tawa
Tawa wiñwu *see* Tawa
Tawa wuñ-wu *see* Tawa
Tawawunwu *see* Tawa
Taway *see* Ottawa
Taway *see* Tawa
Tawcullies *see* Takulli
Ta-we-hash *see* Tawehash
Tawe'hash (W) *see also* Wichita (LC)
Tawehash [OK] *Wichita Confederacy* (BE)
Ta-we-ka-she-ga *see* Ta [Kansa]
Tawekashega *see* Ta [Kansa]
Tawende *see* Tawande
Ta-wi-gi *see* Santo Domingo
Tawigi *see* Santo Domingo
Ta-wii *see* Taos
Tawii *see* Taos
Tawira [NI] *Mosquito* (BE)
Ta-wis-ta-wis *see* Doosedoowe
Tawistawis *see* Doosedoowe
Tawistwi *see* Miami
Tawitskash *see* Kadohadache
Tawixtawes *see* Miami
Ta Wolh *see* Taos
Tawolh *see* Taos
Tawshtye [Clan] [NM] *Pueblo Indians* (H)
Tawwarsa *see* Tawasa
Taw warse *see* Tautin

Tawwassa *see* Tawasa
Taw-wa-tin *see* Tautin
Tawwatin *see* Tautin
Taxe *see* Taos
Taxeju-na *see* Aleuts
Taxemna *see* Aleuts
Taxenent *see* Tauxenent
Taxique *see* Tajique
Taxkahe *see* Apache
Taxpa *see* Maricopa
Tayachquan *see* Nanticoke
Tayas *see* Texas
Tayberon *see* Taos
Tayopan [MX] *Guetare* (BE)
Tayos *see* Tohos
Tayude *see* Isleta
Tay-wah *see* Tewa
Taywah *see* Tewa
Tay-waugh *see* Tewa
Taywaugh *see* Tewa
Taza'aigadi'ka *see* Tazaaigadika
Tazaaigadika [ID] *Shoshone* (H)
Taze-char *see* Sans Arc
Tazechar *see* Sans Arcs
Taze-par-war-nee-cha *see* Sans Arcs
Tazeparwarneecha *see* Sans Arcs
Taztasagonies [TX] (H)
Tcacaatq *see* Nootka
Tca'i-ka-ka-ra-tca-da *see* Chaikikarachada
Tcaikikaratcada *see* Chaikikarachada
Tcaizra winwu *see* Chaizra
Tcai-zri-sa wun-wu *see* Chaizra
Tcaizrisa wunwu *see* Chaizra
Tcak *see* Chak
Tca-ka'ne *see* Delaware
Tcakane *see* Delaware
Tca-ka'nen *see* Delaware
Tcakanen *see* Delaware
Tca-ka-nha *see* Delaware
Tca-kwai-na *see* Chakwaina
Tcakwaina *see* Chakwaina
Tca-kwai-na nyu-mu *see* Asa
Tcakwaina nyumu *see* Asa
Tca-kwai-na-wun-wu *see* Chakwaina
Tcakwaina wunwu *see* Chakwaina
Tcalke *see* Cherokee
Tcami *see* Chaui
Tcanha *see* Delaware
Tcanka-oqan *see* Chankaokhan
Tcan-kaxa-otina *see* Chankaghaotine
Tcankaxaotine *see* Chankaghaotine
Tcan-kute *see* Chankute
Tcankute *see* Chankute
Tcan-ona *see* Chanona
Tcanona *see* Chanona
Tcanxe wintcacta *see* Tcan'xe wintca'cta

Tcan'xe wintca'cta [MN] *Assisini-boin* (BE)

Tcanxta'daa Unska'ha [MN] *Assiniboin* (BE)

Tcapokele *see* Chapokele

Tca-qta an-ya-di *see* Choctaw

Tcaqta anyadi *see* Choctaw

Tcaqtaanyadi *see* Choctaw

Tca-qta han-ha *see* Choctaw

Tcaqtahanha *see* Choctaw

Tcaqta hanya *see* Choctaw

Tcashtalalgi *see* Potawatomi

Tca-ta *see* Choctaw

Tcata *see* Choctaw

Tcawaxamux *see* Nicola

Tcawa'xamux *see* Nicola

Tcawi *see* Chaui

Tcaxu *see* Chagi

Tc'-eca'atq *see* Nootka

Tcedunga *see* Chedunga

Tceewadigi *see* Tsawarii

Tceewage *see* Tsawarii

Tcegnake-okusela *see* Cheg-nakeokisela

Tcei-ki-ka-ra-tca-da *see* Cheikikarachada

Tceindoqotdin *see* Cheindekhot-ding

Tcekiwere *see* Chiwere

Tceli *see* Cheli

Tce'metun *see* Tututni

Tcemetun *see* Tututni

Tc'e'natc'aath *see* Chenachaath

Tcenatcaath *see* Chenachaath

Tce-oqba *see* Cheokhba

Tceoqba *see* Cheokhba

Tcepocke *see* Cheposhkeyine

Tce p'o-cke yin-e *see* Chep-oshkeyine

Tceq-huha-ton *see* Chekhuhaton

Tcerokieco *see* Cherokee

Tcet-les-tcan tun'ne *see* Chetleschantunne

Tcewadi *see* Tsawarii

Tce-xi-ta *see* Cheghita

Tcexita *see* Chegita

Tce yin-ye *see* Cheyinye

Tceyinye *see* Cheyinye

Tchachagoulas [LA] (H)

Tchacta *see* Choctaw

Tcha gi'nduefte-I *see* Chagin-duftei

Tchagindueftei *see* Chagindueftei

Tcha helim *see* Chakelim

Tchahelim *see* Chahelim

Tchaihiksi-tcahiks *see* Pawnee

Tchakankni *see* Chakankni

Tch'akeipi *see* Chakeipi

Tchakenikai *see* Chankankni

Tchakh-toligmiouth *see* Shak-toligmiut

Tchaktchan *see* Chickasaw

Tcha kutpaliu *see* Chakutpaliu

Tchakutpaliu *see* Chakutpaliu

Tchalabone *see* Cholovone

Tcha lal *see* Chalal

Tchalal *see* Chalal

Tcha lawai *see* Chalawai

Tchalawai *see* Chalawai

Tcha mampit *see* Chamampit

Tchamampit *see* Chamampit

Tcha mifu amim *see* Chamifu

Tchamifuamim *see* Chamifu

Tch'ammifu *see* Chamifu

Tchammifu *see* Chamifu

Tch'ammiwi *see* Chamiwi

Tchammiwi *see* Chamiwi

Tch'ampikle amim *see* Champikle

Tchampikleamim *see* Champikle

Tchandjoeri-Kuttchin *see* Tangeratsa

Tchanhic [LA] (H)

Tchankaya *see* Tonkawa

Tchantchampenau amim *see* Chanchampeneau

Tchan-tchantu amim *see* Chan-chantu

Tchantchantuamim *see* Chan-Chantu

Tchan tkaip *see* Chantkaip

Tchantkaip *see* Chantkaip

Tchaouacha *see* Chaouache

Tchaouma *see* Chakchiuma

Tcha panaxtin *see* Chapanaghtin

Tchapanaxtin *see* Chapanaghtin

Tcha pungathpi *see* Chapun-gathpi

Tchapungathpi *see* Chapun-gathpi

tchaska *see* Apache

Tcha tagshish *see* Chatagshish

Tchatagshish *see* Chatagshish

Tchatake *see* Cherokee

Tchatake *see* Choctaw

Tch atakuin *see* Catakuin

Tchatakuin *see* Chatakuin

Tcha tamnei *see* Chatamnei

Tchatamnei *see* Chatamnei

Tchatchagoula *see* Tchachagoulas

Tchatchakigoa *see* Atchatchakan-gouen

Tchatchakigoa *see* Miami

Tchatchakigouas *see* Kaskaskia

Tchatchaking *see* Atchatchakan-gouen

Tcha tchambit mantchal *see* Chachambitmanchal

Tchatchamitmantchal *see* Chachambitmanchal

Tcha tchannim *see* Chachanim

Tchatchannim *see* Chachanim

Tcha-tchemewa *see* Chachimewa

Tchatchemewa *see* Chachemewa

Tch'atchif *see* Chachif

Tchatchif *see* Chachif

Tcha tchimmahiyuk *see* Chachimahiuk

Tchatchimmahiyuk *see* Chachimahhiyuk

Tchatchiun [Clan] *Yuchi* (H)

Tchatchiuntaha *see* Tchatchiun

Tcha tchmewa *see* Chachimewa

Tchatchmewa *see* Chachimewa

Tcha tchokuit *see* Chachokwith

Tchatchokuith *see* Chackokwith

Tchatc'huin taha *see* Tchatchiun

Tchatilkuei *see* Chatilkuei

Tcha-tilkuie *see* Chatilkuei

Tcha waye'd *see* Chawayed

Tcha-we *see* Chaui

Tchawe *see* Chaui

Tchaweyed *see* Chawayed

Tchaxsukush *see* Nez Perce

Tcha yakon amim *see* Yaquina

Tcha yakon amim *see* Yaquina

Tchayakonamim *see* Yaquina

Tcha-yamel-amim *see* Yamel

Tchayamelamim *see* Yamel

Tch'Ayanke'ld *see* Chayankeld

Tchayankeld *see* Chayankeld

Tchayankeld *see* Yoncalla

Tch'Ayanke'ld [Self-designation] *see* Yoncalla

Tcha yaxo amin *see* Alsea

Tchayaxoamin *see* Alsea

Tche-a-nook *see* Cheerno

Tcheanook *see* Cheerno

Tchefuncte [LA] [*Mound-builders*] (LC)

Tchelouit *see* Tlakluit

Tchenook *see* Chinook \

Tcheouelche *see* Tehuelche

Tcheshtalalgi *see* Potawatomi

Tche-wassan *see* Sewathen

Tchewassan *see* Sewathen

Tchiacta *see* Choctaw

Tchiaxsokush *see* Ponca

Tchicacha *see* Chicasaw

Tchidüajoüingoües *see* Miami

Tchiduakouingoues *see* Atchatchakangouen

Tchiduakouongue *see* Atchatch-akangouen

Tchiechrone *see* Eskimos

Tchiglit [Lang] *see* Mackenzie River Delta

Tchiglit Indians *see* Kopagmiut

Tchiguebo *Caduveo* (O)

Tchi-ha-hui-pah *see* Isleta

Tchihahuipah *see* Isleta

Tchihoga *see* Maricopa

Tchihogasat *see* Maricopa

Tchikao *see* Txicaos

Tchikasa *see* Chickasaw

Tchikemaha *see* Chitimacha

Tchikeylis *see* Chehalis

Tchi-kun *see* Pinalino Apache

Tchikun *see* Pinalino Apache

Tchilcat *see* Chilkat
Tchilkoten *see* Chilocotin
Tchilouit *see* Tlakluit
Tchinook *see* Chinook
Tchinouk *see* Chinook
Tchin-t'a-gottine *see* Chintagottine
Tchintagottine *see* Chintagottine
Tch'intchal *see* Chinchal
Tchintchal *see* Chinchal
Tchipan-Tchick-Tchick *see* Chippanchickchick
Tchipwayanawok *see* Chipeqyan
Tchishi dinne *see* Chiricahua Apache
Tchishidinne *see* Chiricahua Apache
Tchit-che-ah *see* Chitsa
Tchitcheah (PC) *see also* Chitsa (H)
Tchitcheah [Clan] *Kutchakutchin* (H)
Tchitimacha *see* Chitimacha
Tcho-la-lah *see* Chilula
Tchololah *see* Chilula
Tcholoone *see* Cholovone
Tcholovone *see* Cholovone
Tchonek *see* Tehuelche
Tchouchouma *see* Chakchium
Tchoueragak *see* Sqawkihow
Tchouktchi americani *see* Aglemiut
Tchouktchi Asiatiques (Contri, v.1, 1877, pp.13–15) *see* Yuit (BE)
Tchoutymacha *see* Citimacha
Tchoyopan *see* Choyapin
Tchrega *see* Tshirege
Tch tagithl *see* Chatagithl
Tchtagithl *see* Chatagithl
Tchu'hla *see* Chuhhla
Tchuhla *see* Chuhhla
Tchukarramei *see* Txukahamae
Tchukotalgi *see* Chukotalgi
Tchula *see* Chula
Tchula *see* Tchefuncte
Tchutpelit *see* Nez Perce
Tc'ib-io *see* Chubio
Tcibio *see* Chubio
Tci-ce-kwe *see* Tonto Apache
Tcicekwe *see* Tonto Apache
Tcicihi [Self-designation] *see* Lipan Apache
Tcieck-rune *see* Eskimos
Tcieck-runen *see* Eskimos
Tciglit *see* Kopagmiut
Tci hacin *see* Kanze
Tcihacin *see* Kanze
Tciju Wactage *see* Chizhuwashtage
Tci-ka-sa *see* Chickasaw
Tcikasa *see* Chickasaw
Tcik-au-atc *see* Chikauach

Tcikauatc *see* Chikauach
Tc'ileque'uk *see* Chilliwack
Tcil-qe-uk *see* Chilliwack
Tci'nat-li tunne *see* Tthinatlitunne
Tcinatlitunne *see* Tthinatlitunne
Tcingawuptuh *see* Ute
Tcinju *see* Chizhu
Tcin-tat tene *see* Chintagottine
Tcintattene *see* Chintagottine
Tcinuk *see* Chinook
Tci-nuña wuñ-wu *see* Chinunga
Tcinuña wuñwu *see* Chinunga
Tcipiya *see* Tsipiakwe
Tcipouaian-winiuuk [Can] *Paskwawininiwug Cree* (BE)
Tcipu *see* Chippewa
Tciruen-haka *see* Nottoway
Tci-sro wuñiwu *see* Chisro
Tcisro wuñiwu *see* Chisro
Tcits-hets *see* Chehalis
Tcitshets *see* Chehalis
Tcitxua'ut *see* Okinagan
Tciwere *see* Chiwere
Tcjamagmut *see* Kaviagmiut
Tckippewyan *see* Chipewyan
Tck'unge'n *see* Chkungen
Tckungen *see* Chkungen
Tclul-tci-qwut-me tunne *see* Thlulchikhwutmetunne
Tclultciqwutmetunne *see* Thlulchikhwutmetunne
Tcoka-kowela *see* Chokatowela
Tco'ko *see* Sarsi
Tcoko *see* Sarsi
Tcon-o *see* Chongyo
Tcono *see* Chongyo
Tcon wun-wu *see* Chongyo
Tconwunwu *see* Chongyo
Tco-ro wun'wu *see* Chosoro
Tcoro wunwu *see* Chosro
Tcorso winwu *see* Chosro
Tco-wa-tce *see* Tthowache
Tcowatche *see* Tthowache
Tco-zir *see* Chosro
Tcozir *see* Chosro
Tcqe-k'qu *see* Nestucca
Tcu *see* Chua
Tcua *see* Chua
Tcu-a nyu-mu *see* Chua
Tcuanyumu *see* Chua
Tcua'qamuq *see* Nicola
Tcuaqamuq *see* Nicola
Tcua winwu *see* Chua
Tcu-a-wun-wu *see* Chua
Tcubaa'bish [WA] *Skagit* (BE)
Tcubio wiñwu *see* Chubio
Tcub-i-yo wuñ-wu *see* Chubio
Tcubiyo wuñwu *see* Chubio
Tcuin nyumu *see* Chua
Tcu-kai *see* Chukai
Tcu-kai *see* Nung
Tcukai *see* Chukai

Tcukai *see* Nung
Tcu-Kutchi *see* Tsitoklinotin
Tcukutchi *see* Tsitoklinotin
Tcunoiyana *see* Atsugewi]
Tcu nyumu *see* Chua
Tcut-les-tcun tene *see* Chetleschantunne
Tc'ut-les-tcun-tun *see* Chetleshantunne
Tcutlestcuntun *see* Chetleschuantunne
Tcutzwa'ut *see* Okinagan
Tda'bo *see* Tabo
Tdabo *see* Tabo
Tda-wa *see* Tawa
Tdawa *see* Tawa
Tda-wu *see* Tung
Tdawu *see* Tung
Tdha-kke-Kuttchin *see* Tukkuthkutchin
Tdhakkekuttchin *see* Tukkuthkutchin
Tdha-Kouttchin *see* Tukkuthkutchin
Tdhakouttchin *see* Tukkuthkutchin
Tdha-kuttchin *see* Vuntakutchin
Tdha-kuttchin *see* Tukkuthkutchin
Tdhakuttchin *see* Tukkuthkutchin
Tdhakuttchin *see* Vuntakutchin
Tdjeunikashinga [Subclan] *Kanze* (H)
Tdu-wa *see* Tuwa
Tduwa *see* Tuwa
Te [Clan] *Pueblo Indians* (H)
Te [Clan] *Quapaw* (H)
Teachatz-kenna *see* Ditsakana
Teacuacitzica *see* Teacuacueitzisti
Teacuacitzisti *see* Teacuacueitzisti
Teacuacueitzisti [Lang] [MX] *Cora* (H)
Teagan *see* Piegan
Te-a-hin'kutch'in *see* Teachinkutchin
Teahinkutchin [AK] *Kutchin* (H)
Teakawreahogeh *see* Mohawk
Teakuaeitzizti *see* Teacuacueitzisti
Teana [TX] *Coahuiltecan* (BE)
Teao *see* Tohaha
Tearemetes *see* Tehauremet
Teatatunne *see* Kwatami
Teates *see* Tait
Teat Saws *see* Utsehta
Teatsaws *see* Utsehta
Teaxtkni *see* Tyigh
Teaxtkni maklaks *see* Tyigh
Teba *see* Tigua
Tebaca [MX] *Acaxee* (BE)

Tebas *see* Tiwa
Tebe *see* Tiwa
Tebe *see* Tigua
Te-bi *see* Tebi
Tebi [Clan] *Hopi* (H)
Te-bot-e-lob-e-lay *see* Tubatula-
  bal
Tebotelobelay *see* Tubatulabal
Tebti [Lang] (*Patwin*) (CA-8)
Tecahanqualahamo *Pueblo Indi-
  ans* (H)
Tecahuistes [TX] *Coahuiltecan*
  (BE)
Tecamamiouen [MN] *Chippewa*
  (H)
Tecamene *see* Tecame
Tecamenez *see* Tecame
Tecamoamiouen [CT] *Chippewa*
  (H)
Tecamones *see* Tecame
Tecargoni [MX] *Varohio* (H)
Tecas *see* Texas
Tecaya [CAm] *Acaxee* (BE)
Techachapi (Pub, v.4, no.3, p.110)
  see also Kawaiisu (LC)
Techbi *see* Terraba
Techbi *see* Teshbi
Techi *see* Teshbi
Techicha *see* Chicksaw
Techloel *see* Natchez
Techpa *see* Pima
Techpamais *see* Papago
Teckat Kenna *see* Ditsakana
Tec-li *see* Chelil
Teco (LC) *see also* Cuitlateco
  (LC)
Teco [MX, Gua] (LC)
Teco [Tupi] *see* Emerillon
Tecoripa [Pueblo] [MX] (Bull44)
Teco-Tecoxquin [MX] (BE)
Tecpanecas *see* Tepanecas
Tectileco *see* Teco
Tecua *see* Tewa
Tecual [MX] *Cora* (BE)
Tecualme *see* Tecual
Tecuexe [MX] (LC)
tecuge *see* Tesuque
Tecuiche *see* Cahuilla
Tecuiche *see* Kawia [Luiseño]
Tedamni *see* Telamni
Tedarighroones *see* Tutelo
Tedarrighroones *see* Tutelo
Ted-Chath-Kenna *see* Ditsakana
Tedchathkenna *see* Ditsakana
Tedchat-Kenna *see* Ditsakana
Tedderighroones *see* Tutelo
Tede *see* Athapascan
Tedexenos (H) *see also* Tejones
  (BE)
Tedexeños (Hdbk10) *see also*
  Quedejeños (Hdbk10)
Tedexeños [MX] *Tamaulipec* (BE)
Tedighroonas *see* Tutelo

Teek-a-nog-gan *see* Okinagan
Teekanoggan *see* Okinagan
Teelalup *see* Tulalip
Te e'nikaci'ka *see* Teenikashika
Teenikacika *see* Teenikashika
Teenikashika [Gens] *Quapaw* (H)
Teennenhighhunt *see* Seneca
Te-en-nen-hogh-hunt *see* Seneca
Teesgitunai *see* Tees-gitunai
Tees-gitunai [BC] (H)
Teeskun-Inagai [Subfamily] [BC]
  Haida (H)
Teet *see* Tait
Teeton *see* Teton
Teetonwan *see* Teton
Teetwan *see* Teton
Teetwaun *see* Teton
Tee-twawn *see* Teton
Teetwawn *see* Tigua
Teeuinge [Pueblo] [NM] (H)
Te-e-uing-ge *see* Teeuinge
Teeuningge *see* Teeuinge
Tee-wahn *see* Tigua
Te-e-wun-na *see* Hano
Teewunna *see* Hano
Teeytraan [Pueblo] [NM] (H)
Tega *see* Tewa
Teganatics *see* Tegninateo
Te-gat-ha *see* Taos
Tegatha *see* Taos
Tegesta (H) *see also* Tekesta (BE)
Tegesta [FL] *Seminole* (Ye)
Tegique *see* Tajique
Tegninateo [VA] *Manahoac Con-
  federacy* (BE)
Tegninaties *see* Tegninateo
Tegoneas *see* Tegnenateo
Tegotsugn *Pinal Apache* (H)
Tegua *see* Tewa
Teguampaxte *see* Peguampaxte
Teguas *see* Yavapai
Teguayos (H) *see also* Tawehash
  (BE)
Tegueco *see* Tehueco
Teguelche *see* Tehuelche
Tegui [MX] *Opata* (H)
Teguima [MX] *Opata* (H)
Tegwa *see* Tewa
Tehaas *see* Texas
Tehachapi [CA] (LC)
Tehacoacha *see* Chaouacha
Te-ha-hin Kutchin *see*
  Teachinkutchin
Tehahin Kutchin *see*
  Teachinkutchin
Tehama *see* Nomlaki
Tehanin-Kutchin (H) *see also*
  Knaiakhotana (H)
Tehanin-Kutchin *Tinne* (Contri,
  v.1, pp.35–36)
Tehas *see* Texas
Tehatchapi *see* Tehachapi
Tehauremet (H)

Tehawut [WA] *Salish* (H)
Tehawutun *see* Tehawut
Tehayesatlu *see* Alsea
Teheaman *see* Tacame
Teheili *see* Takulli
Tehoanoughroonaw (H)
Tehoel *see* Natchez
Tehon *see* Tejon
Tehotirigh *see* Tutelo
Tehoua *see* Puaray
Te-how-nea-nyo-hunt *see*
  Seneca
Tehowneanyohunt *see* Seneca
Tehua *see* Tejua
Tehua *see* Tewa
Tehua *see* Yavapai
Tehuacana *see* Tawakoni
Tehuantepec [MX] (BE)
Tehuaremet [TX] (H)
Tehueco [MX] *Cahita* (BE)
Tehuelche (LC) *see also* Tzoneca
  (LC)
Tehuelche [Arg] (LC)
Tehuelci *see* Tehuelche
Tehueleto *see* Tehuelche
Tehuelhet *see* Tehuelche
Tehuesh *see* Teuesh
Tehueshen *see* Teuesh
Tehueshenk *see* Teuesh
Tehuexe *see* Tecuexe
Tehuima *see* Teguima
Tehuiso *see* Tehuizo
Tehuizo [MX] *Nevome* (H)
Tehutili *see* Tutelo
Teh-wa *see* Hano
Tehwa *see* Hano
Teiakhochoe [OR] *Nevome* (H)
Te-iaq'otcoe *see* Teiakhochoe
Teiaqotcoe *see* Teiakhochoe
Teias *see* Texas
Teipana *see* Teypana
Teisa *see* Texas
Te'it (H) *see also* Tait (H)
Teit *see* Tait
Teit *see* Te'it
Te'it *Stalo* (BE)
Teixa *see* Texas
Tejano *see* Coahuiltecan
Tejano *see* Texas
Tejas *see* Taos
Tejas *see* Texas
Te-je Uing-ge O-ui-ping *see*
  Tejeuingge Ouiping
Tejeuingge Ouiping [Pueblo]
  [NM] (H)
Tejon [CA] (H)
Tejones (H) *see also* Tejon (H)
Tejones [MX] *Coahuiltecan* (BE)
Tejon Indians *see* Gitanemuk
Tejos *see* Taos
Tejua (H) *see also* Tewa (LC)
Tejua (Hdbk10) *see also* Yavapai
  (LC)

Tejua [AZ] *Apache* (H)
Tejuca *see* Tuyuca
Tejugne *see* Tesuque
Tejuneses *see* Tejon
Tekapu *see* Kickapoo
Te-kapwai *see* Penateka
Tekapwai *see* Penateka
Tekau-terigtego-nes *see* Mohawk
Tekesta [FL] (BE)
Tekin *see* Skinpah
Tekkekalt [Can] *Shuswap* (BE)
Tekkekaltemuk *see* Tekkakalt
Tekoedi [Phratry] [AK] *Tlingit*
    (H)
Tekopa *see* Tsankupi
tekuedi *see* Tekoedi
Tekuna *see* Tucuna
Te-kunr-a-tum *see* Tekunratum
Tekunratum [WA] *Okinagan* (H)
Telam *see* Telamni
Telamateno *see* Wyandot
Telamatenon *see* Wyandot
Telame *see* Telamni
Telamene [TX] (H)
Telamni [CA] *Southern Valley
    Yokuts* (CA)
Telamoteris *see* Telamni
Telategmiut [AK] *Chnagmiut*
    (H)\
Telateg'mut *see* Ekogmut
Telematino *see* Huron
Telembi [Col] (O)
Tel-emnies *see* Telamni
Telemnies *see* Telamni
Teletagmiut [AK] *Chnagmiut* (H)
Telhuemit *see* Tlakluit
Telhuemit *see* Wishram
Te'liemnim *see* Navajo
Teliemnim *see* Navajo
Telknikni *see* Tyigh
Tellet-kutchin *Loucheux* (IndN,
    v.2, no.3, July 1925,
    pp.172–177)
Tellilrpingmiut *see* Talirping-
    miut
Te-lu-a A-te-u-na *see* Telua-
    ateuna
Telua-ateuna [Clan] *Zuni* (H)
Te-lum-ni *see* Telamni
Telumni *see* Telamni
Teluski [CAm] *Chibchan* (BE)
Tema *see* Keres
Temagami (AIR, v.7, no.9, Sep-
    tember 1991, p.2)
Tembe [Br] *Guajajara* (O)
Tembekua *see* Kaivoa
Tembe-Tenetehara [Br] *Tenete-
    hara* (O)
Tembkua *see* Kaiwa
Temez *see* Jemez
Teminaguico [MX] *Coahuiltecan*
    (Hdbk10)
Temiscaming (H)

Temiscaming (H) *see also*
    Timiskaming (LC)
Temiscamis *see* Temiscaming
Temiskaming *see* Temiscaming
Temiskamink *see* Temiscaming
Temiskamnite *see* Temiscaming
Temoksee [NV] *Shoshonean* (H)
Temomoyami [Self-designation]
    see Winao
Temorais *see* Tamoroa
Temori [MX] (BE)
Temorias *see* Tamaroa
Tem-pan-ah-go *see* Timpaiavats
Tempanahgo *see* Timpanogots
Tempanahgo *see* Timpaiavats
Temque *see* Tesuque
Temtltemtleles [Gens] *Ma-
    matelekala* (H)
Temtltemtleles [Gens] *Nakoaktok*
    (H)
Ten'a (LC) *see also* Ingalik (LC)
Ten'a [AK] (Chapman)
Tena [AK] *see* Ten'a
Tena [EC] (O)
Ten-a-bo *see* Tenabo
Tenabo [Pueblo] [NM] *Tompiro*
    (H)
Tenahna *see* Kaniakhotana
Tenah'tah *see* Tenaktak
Tenahtah *see* Tenaktak
Tenahwit *see* Tenawa
Te-nahwit *see* Tenawa
Tenahwit *see* Tenawa
Tenaina *see* Knaikhotana
Tenaktak [BC] *Kwakiutl* (BE)
Tenak-tench *see* Tenaktak
Tenaktench *see* Tenaktak
Tenakteuk *see* Tenaktak
Tenama *see* Tenawa
Tenan-kut-chin *see* Ten-
    ankutchin
Tenankutchin (LC) *see also*
    Tanana (LC)
Tenankutchin [AK] *Tinne* (H)
Tenankuttchin *see* Tenankutchin
Tena'qtaq *see* Tenaktak
Tenaqtaq *see* Tenaktak
Tenaquel [NM] *Piro* (H)
Tenawa (BE) *see also* Tanima (BE)
Tena'wa *see* Tenawa
Tenawa *Comanche* (H)
T'ena'xtax *see* Tenaktak
Tena'xtax *see* Tenaktak
Tenaxtax *see* Tenaktak
Tendons [MN] *Atsina* (BE)
Tene *see* Athapascan
tene *see* Navajo
Te'nedi *see* Tenedi
Tenedi [AK] *Tihittan* (H)
Teneinamar [TX] (BE)
Tenetahara [Br] (LC)
Teneumama *see* Teneinamar
Tenewa *see* Tenawa

Tenez *see* Chinantec
Tengeratsekutchin *Dindjie* (H)
Tengeratsekutchin *Tinne* (H)
Tenge-rat-sey *see* Tangeratsa
Tengeratsey *see* Tangeratsa
Teng-rat-si *see* Tangeratsa
Tengratsi *see* Tangeratsa
Tenharem *see* Tenharim
Tenharim [Br] *Kawahib* (O)
Tenhua *see* Tenewa
Tenicapem *see* Tenicapeme
Tenicapeme [MX] *Coahuiltecan*
    (BE)
Tenino [CA] (Forg)
Tenino [OR] (BE)
Teniqueche *see* Serrano
Tenisaw *see* Taensa
Tenkahuas *see* Tonkawa
Tenkana *see* Tonkawa
Tennai *see* Athapascan
Ten-nai *see* Navajo
Tennai *see* Navajo
Tennankutchin *see* Ten-
    ankutchin
Tennan-tnu-kokh-tana *see* Ten-
    anjkutchin
Tennantnukokhtana *see* Ten-
    ankutchin
Tennawa *see* Tenawa
Tennis *see* Zuni
Tennuth-Kut-Chin *see* Ten-
    nuth-kutchin
Tennuth-kutchin [AK] *Tinne*
    (BE)
Tenoacha *see* Aztecs
Tenpenny Utahs *see* Timpaiavats
Tenpenny Utahs *see* Tim-
    panogots
Tensa *see* Taensa
Tensagini *see* Taensa
Tensau *see* Taensa
Tensaw *see* Taensa
Tentilves *see* Tutelo
Tenton *see* Teton
Ten-ton-ha *see* Teton
Tenton-ha *see* Teton
Tentouha *see* Teton
Tentpoles Worn Smooth *see* Op-
    posite Assiniboin
Tents Cut Down *see* Broad Grass
Tenu [TX] *Tonkawan* (BE)
Tenuai *see* Navajo
Tenucktau *see* Tenaktak
Te-nuckt-tau *see* Tenaktak
Tenuha *see* Tenawa
Te-nuh-tuh *see* Tanktak
Tenuhtuh *see* Tanktak
Tenuth *see* Tennuth-kutchin
Ten-uth Kutchin *see* Tennuth-
    kutchin
Tenuthkutchin *see* Tennuth-
    kutchin
Tenye *see* Navajo

Ten-yo *see* Tenyo
Tenyo [Clan] [AZ] *Pueblo Indians* (H)
Tenza *see* Taensa
Teoas *see* Tewa
Teoas *see* Tigua
Teoas *see* Tiwa
Teodocodamos *see* Terocodame
Teodoran *see* Terocodame
Teoux *see* Tiou
Tepachuaches [TX] (BE)
Tepagui *see* Tepahue
Tepaguy *see* Tepehue
Tepahue [MX] (BE)
Tepahui *see* Tepahue
Tepanecas [MX] (LC)
Tepave *see* Tepahue
Tepavi *see* Tepahue
Te-pda *see* Kiowa
Tepda *see* Kiowa
Tepecan [Lang] *Tepiman* (Hdbk10)
Tepecano [MX] *Tepehuan* (BE)
Tepeco *see* Tepocas
Tepegua *see* Tepehuan
Tepeguana *see* Tepehuan
Tepeguane *see* Tepehuan
Tepehua [MX] (LC)
Tepehuan [MX] *Tepecano* (LC)
Tepehuan *Pima* (LC)
Tepehuana *see* Tepehuan
Tepehuane *see* Tepehuan
Tepehuano *see* Tepehuan
Tepemaca [MX, TX] *Coahuiltecan* (BE)
Tepeoanes *see* Tepehuan
Tepeohuane *see* Tepehuan
Tepicon *see* Pepikokia
Tepiman [Lang] *Sonoran* (Hdbk10)
Tepk'i'nago *see* Kiowa
Tepocas [MX] *Seri* (BE)
Tepua *see* Tewa
Te-qoedi *see* Tekoedi
Teqoedi *see* Tekoedi
Te-qua *see* Tewa
Tequa *see* Tewa
Tequa *see* Tigua
Tequassimo [MD] *Choptank* (H)
Teque [VE] (LC)
Tequenica *see* Yahgan
Tequesta *see* Tekesta
Tequeste *see* Tekesta
Tequima *see* Opata
Tequiraca [Self-designation] *see* Awishiri
Tequistlatec [MX] (BE)
Tequistlateca [Lang] *see* Chontal [Lang]
Tequistlatecan *see* Chontal [Lang]
Terachitian [Lang] [MX] (BE)
Teremembaiz *see* Teremembe

Teremembe [Br] (LC)
Terena *see* Tereno
Tereno [Br] (LC)
Terenoa *see* Tereno
Terentine *see* Abnaki
Terentyne *see* Abnaki
Teriaca *see* Tariaca
Teriaka *see* Tariaca
Teriba *see* Teribe
Teriba *see* Terraba
Teribe [Pan] (O)
Terkodams *see* Terocodame
Terocadame [TX] *Coahuiltecan* (BE)
Terococodames *see* Terocadame
Terraba [Lang] *see* Chibchan
Terrebe *see* Terraba
Terre-Rouge *see* Fox
Terrerouge *see* Fox
Terrino *see* Tenino
Tersuque *see* Tesuque
Ter taitana *see* Tertaitatana
Tertaitana *see* Tertaitatana
Tertaitatana [NM] *Taos* (H)
Tesayan *see* Hopi
Tescarorin *see* Tuscarora
Teseque *see* Tesuque
Teshbi [CR, Pan] *Terraba* (BE)
Tesinde [Clan] *Omaha* (H)
T'es kunilnagai *see* Teeskun-Inagai
Teskunilnagai *see* Teeskun-Inagai
Tesonachas [LA] (H)
Tess-cho tin-neh *see* Desnede-yarelottine
Tesschotinneh *see* Desnede-yarelottine
Tessiugak [Can] [*Inuit (Quebec)*] (Hdbk5)
Testes de boeufs *see* Tetes de Boule
Tesuke *see* Tesuque
Tesuki *see* Tesuque
Tesuque *Northern Tewa* (BE)
Tesuqui *see* Tesuque
Tes-wan *see* Chilula
Teswan *see* Chilula
Tet [TX] *Coahuiltecan* (BE)
Tetamene *see* Telamene
Tetan *see* Teton
Tetanauoica [TX] *Coahuiltecan* (BE)
T'e't'anelenox *see* Tetanetlenok
Tetanetlenok [Clan] *Kwakutl* (H)
Tetankatane *see* Tintaotonwe
Tetans Saone *see* Saone
Tetarighroones *see* Tutelo
Tetarton *see* Tintaotonwe
T'e-ta tunne *see* Kwatami
Tetau *see* Ietan
Tetau *see* Teton
Te-tdoa *see* Te

Tetdoa *see* Te
Tetecores [MX] *Coahuiltecan* (BE)
Tete Coup *see* Pabaksa
Tete-Coupees *see* Pabaksa
Tetelcongo [Lang] *Aztec* (Hdbk10)
tetemide *see* Navajo
te temide [sic[*see* Navajo
te temnin *see* Navajo
tetemnin *see* Navajo
Tete Pelee *see* Comanche
Tete Plat *see* Thlingchadinne
Tetes Coupes *see* Pabaksa
Tetes de Boule [Q] *Sakawinini-wug Cree* (LC)
Tetes Pelees *see* Comache
Tetes Plates *see* Choctaw
Tetes Plates *see* Salish
Tetes-Plates *see* Chinook
Tetete [EC] (O)
Tetiquilhati [MX] (BE)
T'etliet-Kuttchin *see* Titl-itkutchin
Tetlietkuttchin *see* Tatlitkutchin
T'etllet-Kuttchin *see* Tatlitk-itchin
Tetlletkuttchin *see* Tatlitkutchin
Tetoan *see* Teton
Teton [ND, SD] *Sioux* (LC)
Tetones *see* Teton
Tetongue *see* Teton
Teton-Menna-Kanozo *see* Mini-conjou
Tetonmennakanozo *see* Mini-conjou
Te-ton-min-na-kine-az-so *see* Miniconjou
Teton minna kineazzo *see* Mini-conjou
Te-ton o-kan-da-das *see* Oglala
Tetonokandandas *see* Oglaga
Teton Okandandes *see* Oglala
Te-ton-sâh-o-ne *see* Saone
Tetonsahone *see* Saone
Teton sâhone *see* Saone
Teton Saone *see* Saone
Tetonsarans *see* Teton
Tetons errans *see* Teton
Tetons Mennakonozzo *see* Mini-conjou
Tetons Minnakenozzo *see* Mini-conjou
Tetons Minnekincazzo *see* Mini-conjou
Tetons of the Burnt Woods *see* Brule
Tetons Okandadas *see* Oglala
Tetons Sahone *see* Saone
Tetsogi *see* Tesuque
Tet-su-ge *see* Tesuque
Tetsuge *see* Tesuque
Tettchi-dhidie *see* Unakhotana

T'ettchie-Dhidie *see* Unakhotana
Tetuckough *see* Choptank
Tetzino [TX] *Coahuiltecan* (BE)
Te-tzo-ge *see* Tesuque
Tetzoge *see* Tesuque
Te-uat-ha *see* Taos
Teuatha *see* Taos
Teuesh [Lang] [Arg] (O)
Teuesson *see* Teuesh
Teui *see* Kaiova
Teul *see* Teule
Teule [Lang] [MX] *Piman* (BE)
Teuontowano *see* Seneca
Teutecas *see* Chinantec
Teuteloe *see* Tutelo
Teu-ton-ha *see* Teton
Teutonha *see* Teton
Teva *see* Tewa
Tewa [NM] (LC)
Tewanticut [MA] *Wampanoag*
  (BE)
Tewe *see* Hano
Tewelche *see* Tehuelche
Tewepu [ID] *Nez Perce* (BE)
Tewetken [VanI, BC] *Nanaimo*
  (H)
tewiai *see* Santo Domingo
Tewicktowes *see* Miami
tewige *see* Santo Domingo
Te-wi-gi *see* Santo Domingo
Tewigi *see* Santo Domingo
tewixtci'n *see* Nicola
Tewohomomy *see* Tuscarora
Texa [NM] *Piro* (H)
Texas *Hasinai* (H)
Texbi (O) *see also* Boruca (LC)
Texbi [CR] (O)
Texcocan *see* Tezcucan
Texia *see* Texas
Texixtepec [MX] *Popoloca* (BE)
Texon *see* Tejon
Texones *see* Tejones
Texpamais *see* Papago
Tex-pas *see* Pima
Texpas *see* Pima
Teya (BE)
Teyans *see* Texas
Teyaxa [NM] *Piro* (H)
Teyens *see* Texas
Teynas *see* Texas
Teyos *see* Texas
Teypama *see* Teypana
Teypana [NM] *Piro* (H)
Teystsekutshi *see* Teahinkutchin
Teytse-kutchi *see* Tatsakutchin
Te-yuwit *see* Penateka
Teyuwit *see* Penateka
Tezcucan [MX] (LC)
Tezuque *see* Tesuque
Tezuqui *see* Tesuque
Tgarihoge *see* Mohawk
Tgua *see* Tigua
Thacame *see* Tacame

Thah-a-i-nin *see* Apache
Thahainin *see* Apache
Tha'ka-hine-na *see* Kiowa
  Apache
Tha'kahine'na *see* Apache
Thakahinena *see* Apache
Thakahinena *see* Kiowa Apache
Tha'kaitan *see* Kiowa Apache
Thakaitan *see* Kiowa Apache
Thakhu *see* Taku
Thaltan *see* Tahltan
Thamien [CA] *Mission Indians*
  (H)
Thampa *see* Campa
Thanacahues *see* Tonkawas
Tha'neza *see* Thkhaneza
Thaneza *see* Thkhaneza
Tha'neza'ni *see* Thkhaneza
Thanezani *see* Thkhaneza
Thano *see* Tano
T'han-u-ge *see* Tano
Thaos *see* Taos
Tha'paha *see* Thkhapaha
Thapaha *see* Thkhapaha
Tha'pahadi'ne *see* Thkhapaha
Thapahadine *see* Thkhapaha
Tharahumara *see* Tarahumare
Tharhkarorin *see* Tuscarora
Thastchetci *see* Wyandot
Tha'to'dar'ho *see* Onondaga
Thatodarho *see* Onondaga
Thatsan-o'tinne *see* Tatsanottine
Thatsanotinne *see* Tatsanottine
Tha'tsini *see* Thkhatshini
Thatsini *see* Thkhatshini
Thco *see* Toho
Thearemets *see* Tehauremet
Theauremet *see* Tehauremet
Thecamene *see* Tacame
Thecamon *see* Tacame
Thecoel *see* Natchez
Thedirighroonas *see* Tutelo
Thegua *see* Tewa
Theguel-che *see* Tehuelche
Thehuelche *see* Tehuelche
The-ke-ne *see* Sekani
Thekene *see* Sekani
The-ken-neh *see* Sekani
Thekenneh *see* Sekani
The-ke-ottine *see* Sekani
Thekeottine *see* Sekani
The-kha-ne *see* Thekkane
Thekhane *see* Thekkane
The-khene *see* Sekani
Thekhene *see* Sekani
The-kka-ne *see* Sazeutina
The-kk'a-ne *see* Sekani
The-kka-ne *see* Sekani
Thekkane (PC) *see also* Sazeutina
  (H)
Thekkane *see* Sekani
Thekkane [BC] *Sekani* (H)
The-kke-Ottine *see* Sekani

Thekkeottine *see* Sekani
Theloel *see* Natchez
Theloelles *see* Natchez
Themiscamings *see* Temiscaming
Themiskamingues *see* Temis-
  caming
Themistamens *see* Temiscaming
The Nation *see* Upper Creek
Theonontateronon *see* Tionon-
  tati
The-Ottine *see* Etheneldeli
Theoux *see* Tiou
Therocodame *see* Terocodame
Theshtshini [Clan] *Navajo* (H)
Theskaroriens *see* Tuscarora
Thet'let-kut-qin *see* Loucheux
Thetletkutqin *see* Loucheux
Thetliantin *see* Thetliotin
Thetliotin [Clan] [BC] *Takulli*
  (H)
The-ushene *see* Teuesh
Theushene *see* Teuesh
The-ye Ottine *see* Etheneldeli
Theyeottine *see* Etheneldeli
Thezuque *see* Tesuque
Thickcannies *see* Sekani
Thickwood *see* Assiniboin
Thick Wood Cree *see* Sakawith-
  iniwuk
Thick-wood Indians *see* Stick
  Indians
Thick Woodsmen *see* Sug-
  waudugahwininewug
Thikanies *see* Sazeutina
Thikanies *see* Sekani
Thi-lan-ottine *see* Thilanottine
Thilanottine [Can] *Chipewyan*
  (BE)
Thildzhe [Clan] *Navajo* (H)
Thimagoa *see* Timucua
Thimagona *see* Timucua
Thimagoua *see* Timucua
Thimogoa *see* Timucua
Thingahadtinne *see*
  Thlingchadinne
Thing-e-ha-dtinne *see*
  Tlingchadinne
Thinthonha *see* Teton
Thinthonka *see* Teton
Thinthonna *see* Teton
Thintohas *see* Teton
Thionontati *see* Tionontati
Thionontatoronon *see* Tionon-
  tati
Thioux *see* Tiou
Thkhaneza [Clan] *Navajo* (H)
Thkhapaha [Clan] *Navajo* (H)
Thkhatshini [Clan] *Navajo* (H)
Thlakalama [WA] *Skilloot* (BE)
Thlakalamah *see* Thlakalama
Thlakalamah *see* Thlakalama
Thlakeimas *see* Clackamas
Thlala'h *see* Chinook

Thlalah see Chinook
Thlamalh see Klamath
Thlar-haryeek-gwan see Yakutat
Thlarharyeekgwan see Yakutat
Thleweechodezeth see Ukusik-
   salirmiut
Thlingcha see Thlingchadinne
Thlingcha see Thlingchadinne
Thlingchaddine see Dog-rib
Thlingchaddine see
   Thlingchadinne
Thlingchadinne [Can, OR] Tinne
   (LC)
Thlingcha-dinneh see
   Thlingchadinne
Thlingcha-dinneh see
   Thlingchadinne
Thlingchadinneh see
   Thlingchadinne
Thlingchadinneh see
   Thlingchadinne
Thlingcha tinneh see
   Thlingchadinne
Thlingcha-tinneh see
   Thlingchadinne
Thlingchatinneh see
   Thlingchadinne
Thlingchatinneh see
   Thlingchadinne
Thlingeha-dinneh see
   Thlingchadinne
Thlingehadinneh see
   Thlingchadinne
Thlingeha-dinni see
   Thlingchadinne
Thlingehadinni see
   Thlingchadinne
Thlinket see Tlingit
Thlinkiten see Tlingit
Thlinkithen see Tlingit
Thliwahali see Hothliwahali
Thljegonchotana see Tle-
   gonkhotana
Thlkwantiyatunne [OR]
   Mishikhwutmetunne (H)
Thlocochasses see Klokegottine
Thlo-co-chassies see Klokegot-
   tine
Thlowiwalla see Clowwewalla
Thltsusmetunne [OR]
   Mishikhwutmetunne (H)
Thlulchikhwutmetunne [OR]
   Mishikhwutmettune (H)
Thnaina see Athapascan
Thnaina see Knaiakhotana
Thobazhnaazhi [Clan] Navajo
   (H)
Thochalsithaya [Clan] Navajo (H)
Thoderighroonas see Tutelo
Thodhokongzhi [Clan] Navajo
   (H)
Thoditshini [Clan] Navajo (H)
Thoig'a-rik-kah see Nez Perce

Thokhani [Clan] Navajo (H)
Thomas, S. see Tome
Thome see Tohome
Thomez see Tohome
Thompson Indians (LC) see also
   Ntlakyapamuk (LC)
Thompson Indians Salish
   (Hdbk15)
Thompson River Indians see
   Shuswap
Thompsons see Ntlakyapamuk
Thongeith see Songish
Thops see Tups
Thornton party see Eel River In-
   dians
Thorntown party see Eel River
   Indians
Those That Carry Hunkpapa (H)
Thosethateatcrows see
   Kangkiyuha
Those That Eat No Dogs (H) see
   also Shungkayuteshni (H)
Those That Eat No Dogs (H) see
   also Sunkayuteshni (H)
Those That Eat No Dogs Mini-
   conjou (H)
Those Who Camp Next to the
   Last Hunkpapa (H)
Those Who Carry Hunkpapa (H)
"Those-who-do-not-give-away"
   see Tendons
"Those-who-water-their-horses-
   once-a-day" see Frozen Indi-
   ans
Those Who Have Water for
   Themselves Only Northern
   Assiniboin (H)
Those Who Keep Together see
   Young Buffalo Robe
Those Who Lodge Close To-
   gether Crow (H)
Those-who-stay-alone see Ic-
   na'umbisa
Thotsoni [Clan] Navajo (H)
Thottine see Etheneldeli
Thoucoue see Tiou
thoxtlawiama see San Felipe
   [Keres]
Thoyetlini [Clan] Navajo (H)
Three Affiliated Tribes (Booklist,
   June 1, 1992, p.1760)
Three Canes see Tawakoni
Three Cones see Tawakoni
Three Cranes see Tawakoni
Three Elder Brothers [Phratry]
   Mohawk (H)
Three Elder Brothers [Phratry]
   Onondaga (H)
Three Elder Brothers [Phratry]
   Seneca (H)
Three Fires (H)
Three Kettles see Oohnonpa
Threse [CA] (H)

Thuelchu see Tehuelche
Thule Culture [AK] (Hdbk5)
Thule-eskimoer see Polar Eski-
   mos
Thunder see Inshtansanda
Thunder Bay [MI] (H)
Thunder-bird see Cheghita
Thunder People see Hisada
Thunder People see Kdhun
Thuntotas see Teton
T'hur (H) see also Thur (H)
Thur (PC) see also T'hur (H)
T'hur [Clan] [Isleta] (H)
Thur [Clan] [NM] Pueblo Indians
   (H)
T'hur-t'ainin see Thur
Thurtainin see Thur
Thwle-lup see Tulalip
Thwspa-lûb see Clallam
Thy see Tyigh
Thycothe see Tukkuthkutchin
Thy-eye-to-ga see Shahaptian
Thyeyetoga see Shahaptian
Thynne see Tinne
Thysia see Tiou
Tiach see Tyigh
Ti-a-mi see Dyami
Tiami see Dyami
Tiaoux see Tiou
Tiapaneco see Tlapanec
Tiaquesco [MX] Coahuiltecan
   (Hdbk10)
Tiascons see Tirans
Tiatinagua see Ese Ejja
Ti'attluxa see Sinkiuse-Columbia
Tiattluxa see Sinkiuse-Columbia
Tiawco see Nanticoke
Tibex see Tigua
Tibilo see Tivilo
Tibitibi see Warrau
Tiburon [MX] Seri (BE)
tib-us-idikadi see Tovusidokado
Tice [MX] (BE)
Tichbi see Teshbi
Tichenos see Pischenoas
Tichuico see Pecos
Tickarneen see Siccameen
Ticmamar see Tumamar
Ticmanares see Tumamar
Ticori see Picuris
Ticorilla see Jicarilla Apache
Ticuic see Pecos
Ticuique see Pecos
Ticuna see Tucuna
Tiddoes see Caddo
Tideing Indians see Kiowa
Tideland Gatherers (Beals, p.5)
Tidendaye Central Chiricahua
   Apache
Tiedami see Telamni
Tiederighroenes see Tutelo
Tiederighroonas see Tutelo
Tiederighroones see Tutelo

Tiederigroenes *see* Tutelo
Tienique *see* Pecos
Tienonadies *see* Tionontati
Tienondaideaga *see* Tionontati
Ti-en-Ti-en *see* Tientien
Tientien [CA] *Wintun* (H)
Tierradentro [Col] *Paez* (O)
Tieton *see* Teton
Tigh *see* Tyigh
Tigikpuk [AK] *Knaiakhotana* (H)
Ti-gi-qpuk *see* Tigikpuk
Tigiqpuk *see* Tigikpuk
Tigitan *see* Tihittan
Ti-glabu *see* Tiglabu
Tiglabu *Brule* (H)
Tignes *see* Tigua
Tignex *see* Tigua
Tigninateos *see* Tegninateo
Tigoeux *see* Tigua
Tigouex *see* Puaray
Tigouex-on-the-rock *see* Puaray
Tigua (Hdbk9) *see also* Tiwa (BE)
Tigua [NM] (LC)
Ti-guan *see* Tigua
Tiguan *see* Tigua
Tiguasi *see* Tigua
Tigue *see* Tigua
Tiguean *see* Tigua
Tiguero *see* Tigua
Tigues *see* Tigua
Tigues *see* Tiwa
Tiguesh *see* Tigua
Ti'guesh [Self-designation, plural]
    see Tigua
Tiguet *see* Tigua
Tiguex *see* Tiwa
Tiguex *see* Puaray
Tiguex *see* Tigua
Tiguexa *see* Tigua
Tiguez *see* Tigua
Tiguez *see* Tiwa
Tiguns *see* Tigua
Ti-hil-ya *see* Tihilya
Tihilya [Clan] *Mohave* (H)
Tihiou *see* Tiou
Ti hit tan *see* Tihittan
Tihittan [AK] *Tlingit* (H)
Tihokahana *see* Pima
Tihua *see* Santo Domingo
Tihua *see* Tigua
Tihuas *see* Tiwa
Tihueq *see* Tigua
Tihues *see* Tiwa
Tihuex *see* Tigua
Tihuez *see* Tiwa
Tihuix *see* Tigua
Ti'ju *see* Tizhu
Tiju *see* Tizhu
Ti-ka-ja *see* Chickasaw
Tikaja *see* Chickasaw
Tikeramiut [AK] *Eskimos* (BE)
Tikuna *see* Tucuna
Ti'kwa *see* Seneca

Tikwa *see* Seneca
Tilamookhs *see* Tillamook
Tilamuk *see* Tillamook
Tilapani [LA] (H)
Ti'lawehuide *see* Acoma
Tilawehuide *see* Acoma
Ti'lawei *see* Acoma
Tilawei *see* Acoma
Tilhalluvit *see* Tlakluit
Tilhalumma *see* Kwalhioqua
Tilhanne *see* Tilkuni
Tilhiellewit *see* Tlakluit
Tilhilooit *see* Tlakluit
Tilhualwits *see* Tlakluit
Tilhulhwit *see* Tlakluit
Tilijae *see* Tilijaes
Tilijaes [TX] *Coahuiltecan* (BE)
Tilijais *see* Tilijaes
Tilijaya *see* Tilijaes
Tilijayas *see* Tilijaes
Tilijayos [TX] *Coahuiltecan* (H)
Tilkuni [OR] *Tenino* (BE)
Tillamook [OR] (LC)
Tillemookhs *see* Tillamook
Tillie *see* Tubatulabal
T'il-muk'tunne *see* Tillamuk
Tilmuktunne *see* Tillamuk
Tilofayas *see* Tilijaes
Tiloja *see* Tilijaes
Tilpacopal *Coahuiltecan* (Hdbk10)
Tilpales *see* Kilpanlus
Tilpayai *see* Tilijaes
Ti'lquni *see* Tilkuni
Tilquni *see* Tilkuni
Tiltiqui *Coahuiltecan* (Hdbk10)
Tiluex *see* Tigua
Tilyayas *see* Tilijaes
Timagoa *see* Timucua
Timbabachis *see* Timpaiavats
Timbachis *see* Timpaiavats
Timbalakee *see* Tamuleko
Timbira [Br] (LC)
Ti-mecl' tunne *see* Timethltunne
Timecltunne *see* Timethltunne
Timethltunne [OR] *Mishikhwut-
    metunne* (H)
Timigaming *see* Temiscaming
Timinaba *see* Tomraxo
Timinava *see* Tomraxo
Timiniha *see* Tomarxa
Timiscamiouetz *see* Temiscam-
    ing
Timiscimi *see* Temiscaming
Timiskaming (LC) *see also* Temis-
    caming (H)
Timiskaming [Can] *Algonkin* (LC)
timmiarmiit *see* Southeast
    Greenlanders
Timmiscamiens *see* Temiscaming
Timmiscamiens *see* Timiskaming
Timooka *see* Timucua
Timoqua *see* Timucua
Timpachis *see* Timpaiavats

Timpagtsis *see* Timpaiavats
Tim-pai-a-vats *see* Timpaiavats
Timpaiavats (Hdbk11) *see also*
    Timpanogots (Hdbk11)
Timpaiavats [UT] *Ute* (H)
timpa-nanunc *see* Timpanogots
timpananunc *see* Timpanogots
Timpana Yuta *see* Timpaiavats
Timpancouitzis *see* Timpaiavats
Timpangotzis *see* Timpaiavats
Timpanocutzis *see* Timpaiavats
Timpanocutzis *see* Timpanogots
Timpanoge *see* Timpaiavats
Timpanogo *see* Timpaiavats
Timpanogo *see* Timpanogots
Timpanogots (Hdbk11) *see also*
    Timpanogots (BE)
Timpanogots [UT] *Ute* (Hdbk11)
Timpanogotzes *see* Timpaiavats
Timpanogotzi *see* Timpanogots
Timpano-gotzis *see* Timpaiavats
Timpanogs *see* Timpaaiavats
Timpanois *see* Timpanogots
Timpanotzis *see* Timpaiavats
Timpashauwagotsit (BE) *see also*
    Tumpisagavatsits (BE)
Timpashauwagotsit [CA] *Paiute*
    (H)
Tim-pa-shau-wa-got-sits *see*
    Timpashauwagotsits
Timpenaguchya *see* Timpaiavats
Timpenaguchya *see* Timpanogots
Timpuaca *see* Timucua
Timuacana *see* Timucua
Timuca *see* Timucua
Timucua (LC) *see also* Utina (BE)
Timucua [FL] (LC)
Timucua [Lang] [SA] *Paezan* (O)
Timucuan [Lang] [FL]
    Muskhogean (LC)
Timuqan *see* Timucuan
Timuqua *see* Timucua
Timuquan *see* Timucuan
Timuquana *see* Timucua
Timuquanan *see* Timucua
Timusquana *see* Timucua
Tina *see* Tenu
Tinai *see* Athapascan
Tinaina *see* Knaiakhotana
Tinainu *see* Tenino
Tinalenos *see* Pinalino Apache
Tinapihuayas [MX, TX] *Pamaque*
    (BE)
Tina-zipe-citca *see*
    Tinazipeshicha
Tinazipecitca *see* Tinazipeshicha
Tinazipeshicha *Hunkpapa* (H)
Tinazipe-sica *see* Tinazipeshicha
Tinazipesica *see* Tinazipeshicha
Tindan *see* Quivera
Tindaw *see* Teton
Tinde [Self-designation] *see* Ji-
    carilla Apache

Tindi suxtana *see* Aglemiut
Tindisuxtana *see* Aglemiut
Tineyizhane *see* Tonkawa
Tingamirmiut *Greenland Eskimos* (BE)
Ting-ta-to-ah *see* Tintaotonwe
Tingtatoah *see* Tintaotonwe
Tini'ema *see* Tanima
tinihu-wi-ti *Owens Valley Paiute* (Hdbk11)
Tinina *see* Knaiakhotana
Tinja *see* Taensa
Tinjah *see* Taensa
Tinlinneh *see* Tejon
Tinlinneh *see* Tin-lin-neh
Tin-lin-neh *Yokuts* (Contri, v.3, p.370)
Tin'liu *see* Tejon
Tinliu *see* Tejon
Tin'llin-neh *see* Tejon
Tinna-ash *see* Apache
Tinnaash *see* Apache
Tinnats *see* Knaiakhotana
Tinnats-Khotana *see* Knaiakhotana
Tinnatte *see* Athapascan
Tinnatz-Kokhtana *see* Knaiakhotana
Tinne *Northern Athapascan* (LC)
Tinneh *see* Athapascan
Tinneh *see* Eskimauan
Tinneh *see* Tinne
Tinney *see* Athapascan
Tinnsal *see* Taensa
Tinontate *see* Tionontati
Tinpaynagoots *see* Timpaiavats
Tinpay nagoots *see* Timpanogots
Tinpaynagoots *see* Timpanogots
Tinqua *see* Timucua
Tinsa *see* Taensa
Tinssa *see* Taensa
Tin-tah-toh *see* Tintaotonwe
Tintahton *see* Tintaotonwe
Tintangaonthaton *see* Teton
Tintangaoughiaton *see* Teton
Tinta-otonwe *see* Tintaotonwe
Tintaotonwe [MN] *Mdewakanton* (H)
Tinta-tonwan *see* Teton
Tintatonwan *see* Teton
Tintatonwan *see* Tintaotonwe
Tinta tonwe *see* Tintaotonwe
Tintatonwe *see* Tintaotonwe
Tinthenha *see* Teton
Tinthona *see* Teton
Tinthonha *see* Teton
Tinthow *see* Teton
Tintinapain *see* Taitinapam
Tintinhos *see* Teton
Tinto *see* Tonto Apache
Tintoner *see* Teton
Tintones *see* Teton
Tintonhas *see* Teton

Tintons *see* Teton
Tintonwas *see* Teton
tinyitityame *see* Santa Clara [NM]
Tin'zit Kutch-in *see* Trotsikkutchin
Tinzitkutchin *see* Trotsikkutchin
Tioas *see* Tigua
Tioas *see* Tiwa
Tiohontates *see* Tionontati
Tiokeang *see* Kato
Tionionhagarawe *see* Seneca
Tionnontantes Hurons *see* Tionontati
Tionnontatehronnon *see* Tionontati
Tionnontatez *see* Tionontati
Tionnontatz *see* Tionontati
Tionnonthatez *see* Tionontati
Tionnotante *see* Tionontati
Tionondade *see* Tionontati
Tionontalies *see* Tionontati
Tionontates *see* Tionontati
Tionontati [Ont, WI] *Wyandot* (LC)
Tiopane [TX] *Coahuiltecan* (BE)
Tiopines [TX] *Coahuiltecan* (H)
tiotsokoma *see* Tesuque
Tiou [MS, LA] (BE)
Tioux *see* Tiou
Tipai (BE) *see also* Kamia (LC)
Tipai [CA] (CA-8)
Tipa'les *see* Kilpanlus
Tipanigos Yutas *see* Timpaiavats
tipatikka *see* Pine Nut Eaters
Tipatolapa *see* Tubatulabal
Ti-pa-to-la-pa (H) *see also* Tubatulabal (LC)
Tipatolapa *see* Ti-pa-to-la-pa
Ti-pa-to-la-pa *Paiute* (Contri, v.3, p.393)
Tiposies [CA] (H)
Tipoti [Pueblo] [NM] (H)
Tiputini *see* Sabela
Tique *see* Tigua
Tiquex *see* Tigua
Tiquexa *see* Tigua
Tiqui-Llapais *see* Hualapai
Tirangapui (H) *see also* Timpaiavats (H)
Tirangapui *Southern Paiute* (Hdbk11)
Tirangapuy (H) *see also* Timpaiavats (H)
Tirangapuy *see* Tirangapui
Tirans [NJ] *Unalachtigo* (BE)
Tiransgapuis *see* Timpaiavats
Tirapihu *see* Arapaho
Ti-re-wi *see* Chiwere
Tirewi *see* Chiwere
Tir hit tan *see* Tihittan
Tirhittan *see* Tihittan
Tiriyo (O) *see also* Trio (LC)

Tiriyo [Br, Sur] (O)
Tiriyometesem [Br, Sur] *Tiriyo* (O)
Tiroacarees *see* Tawakoni
Tirribi *see* Terraba
Tirub *see* Terraba
Tisagechroann *see* Mississauga
Tisagechroanu *see* Mississauga
Tisaiqdji *see* Yana [CA]
Tisaiqdjii *see* Yana [CA]
Tis-e-chu *see* Tisechu
Tisechu *Yokuts* (Contri, b.3, p.370)
Tisepan [AZ] *Chiricahua Apache* (H)
Tishechu *see* Tisechu
Tishim [TX] *Coahuiltecan* (BE)
Tishin [TX] *Tonkawan* (BE)
Tishomingo *Chickasaw* (BE)
Tishravarahi *see* Shasta
Tish-tan-a-tan *see* Hupa
Tishtanatan *see* Hupa
Tishum *see* Ti-shum
Ti-shum *Maidu* (Contri, v.3)
Tispaquin [MA] *Wampanoag* (BE)
Tistontaraetonga (H)
Tist'shinoie'ka *see* Detsanayuka
Tistshinoie'ka *see* Detsanayuka
Titamook *see* Tillamook
Titijay *see* Tilijaes
Ti-tji Han-at Ka-ma Tze-shu-ma *see* Pueblo Caja del Rio
Titji Hanat Kama Tzeshuma *see* Pueblo Caja del Rio
Titkainenom *see* Nomlaki
Ti toan *see* Teton
Titoan *see* Teton
Titoba *see* Teton
Titon *see* Teton
Titones *see* Teton
Titongs *see* Teton
Titonwan *see* Teton
Titsakanai *see* Ditsakana
Tit-sessinaye *see* Tizsessinaye
Titsessinaye (PC) *see also* Tizsessinaye (H)
Titsessinaye *Pinal Apache* (H)
Ti-tsho-ti-na *see* Titshotina
Titshotina [BC] *Nahane* (BE)
Titskanwatichatak [Clan] *Tonkawa* (H)
Titskanwatit *see* Tonkawa
Titskanwatitch *see* Tonkawa
Titskan watitch [Self-designation] *see* Tonkawa
Titskan wa'titch a'tak *see* Titskanwatichatak
Titwa *see* Miami
Ti-twan *see* Teton
Tit'wan *see* Teton
Titwan *see* Teton
Ti-t'wawn *see* Teton
Titwawn *see* Teton

Tiucara *see* Tucara

Tiuhex *see* Tigua

Tiutei *see* Tutelo

Tiuterih *see* Tutelo

Tiu'utlama'eka *see* Assiniboin

Tiuutlamaeka *see* Assiniboin

Tivacuno *see* Sabela

Ti'vati'ka *see* Paviotso

Tivatika *see* Paviotso

Tiverigoto [Lang] *Tamanaco* (UAz, v.28)

Tivitiva *see* Warrau

Tivitivi *see* Warrau

Tivolo [PE] *Aguano* (O)

Ti'wa *see* Tewa

Tiwa (LC) *see also* Tigua (LC)

Tiwa (PC) *see also* Tewa (LC)

Tiwa [NM, TX, MX] (BE)

Tiwan *see* Tigua

Ti'wan [Self-designation] *see* Tigua

tiwelqe *see* Northern Paiute

Tiwesh *see* Tiwa

Ti'wi *see* Santo Domingo

Tiwi *see* Santo Domingo

Ti-yakh'unin *see* Aleuts

Tiyakhunin *see* Aleuts

Tiyakh'unin *see* Aleuts

Tiyocesli *see* Tiyochesli

Tiyochesli [SD] *Oglala* (H)

Tiyopa-ocannunpa *see* Tiyopaoshanunpa

Tiyopaocannunpa *see* Tiyopaoshanunpa

Tiyopaoshanunpa *Sans Arc* (H)

Tiyopa-otcannunpa *see* Tiyopaoshanunpa

Tiyopaotcannunpa *see* Tiyopaoshanunpa

Tiyotcesli *see* Tiyochesli

Ti-zaptan *see* Tizaptan

Tizaptan *Sisseton* (H)

Tizaptanna *see* Tizaptan

Tizhu [Clan] *Quapaw* (H)

Tizsessinaye [AZ] *Apache* (H)

Tizua *see* Tigua

Tjon-a-ai *see* Tung

Tjonaai *see* Tung

Tjuiccu-hen-ne *see* Gila Apache

Tjuic-cujen-ne *see* Gila Apache

Tjuiccujen-ne *see* Gileños

Tjuiccujenne *see* Gila Apache

Tjusccujen-ne *see* Gila Apache

Tjusceu-jen-ne *see* Gila Apache

Tjuwanxa-ikc *see* Klikitat

T'ka *see* Kammatwa

Tka *see* Kammatwa

Tkai'waichash-hlama [WA] *Yakima* (BE)

Tk!ala'ma *see* Thlakalama

Tkalama *see* Thlakalama

Tkanoneoha *see* Oneida

Tkanonwaru'ha'r *see* Oneida

T'Kawkwamish *see* Tkwakwamish

Tkawkwamish *see* Tkwakwamish

tkemlupsemx [BC] *Kamloop* (Hdbk12)

Tketlcotins *see* Thetliotin

Tkhlunkhastunne [OR] *Mishikhwutmetunne* (H)

T'kitske *see* Trotsikkutchin

Tkitske *see* Trotsikkutchin

Tkulhiyogoa'ikc *see* Kwalhioqua

Tkulxiyogoa'ikc *see* Kwalhioqua

Tkwakwamish [WA] *Salish* (H)

T'Kwuratum *see* Tkwuratum

Tkwuratum [WA] *Okinagan* (H)

Tlaaluis [Sept] *Lekwiltok* [BC] (H)

Tlaamen *see* Sliammon

Tla'asath *see* Makah

Tlaasath *see* Makah

Tlachtana [Clan] [AK] *Knaiakhotana* (H)

Tlacopan [MX] *Nahuatl* (BE)

Tlacotepehua-Tepuzteca [MX] (BE)

Tlagga-silla *see* Trotsikkutchin

Tlaggasilla *see* Trotsikkutchin

Tlaglii *see* Haglli

Tlahoos *see* Clahoose

Tlahosath *see* Klahosaht

Tlahuica [MX] (LC)

Tlahu's *see* Clahoose

Tlaida *see* Haida

Tlaiyu Haade *see* Hlgaiu-lana

Tlakai'tat *see* Klikitat

Tlakaitat *see* Klikitat

Tlakalama [WA] *Skilloot* (BE)

Tlakatat *see* Klikitat

Tlakatlala [WA] *Skilloot* (BE)

Tlakaumoot [BC] *Bella Coola* (H)

Tlakimish *see* Clackamas

Tlakimish-pum *see* Clackamas

Tlakluit [WA] *Wishram* (LC)

Tlalam *see* Clallam

Tla'lem *see* Clallam

Tlalem *see* Clallam

Tlalliguamayas *see* Halyikwamai

Tlalliguamayas *see* Quigyuma

Tlalliquamalla *see* Quigyuma

Tlalum *see* Clallam

Tlamath *see* Klamath

Tlamatl *see* Klamath

Tlamatl *see* Lutuamian

Tlameth *see* Klamath

Tlanapanam *see* Clanapan

Tlanchuguin *see* Clancluiguyguen

Tlao kwiath (H) EE Clayoquot (LC)

Tlaoquatch *see* Clayoquot

Tlaoquatsh *see* Clayoquot

Tlapan *see* Apalachee

Tlapanec [MX] (LC)

Tlapaneco-Yopi *see* Tlapanec

Tlappanec *see* Tlapanec

Tlaqluit *see* Tlakluit

Tlascala *see* Sia

Tlascala *see* Tlaxcalan

Tlascalan *see* Tlaxcalan

Tlascaltec *see* Tlascalteca

Tlascalteca (LC)

Tlascan [Lang] [MX] (Bull44)

Tlascani *see* Tlatskanai

Tlascopsel [TX] (H)

Tlasenuesath (H) *see also* Tlasenuesath (H)

Tla'senuesath *see* Tlasenuesath

Tlasenuesath [Sept] *Seshart* (H)

Tlashgenemaki [WA] (H)

Tlaskanai *see* Tlatskanai

Tla'sk'enoq *see* Klaskino

Tlaskenoq *see* Klaskino

Tlastcini *see* Tlatshini

Tlastshini [Clan] *Navajo* (H)

Tlastsini *see* Tlatshini

T'la-then-koh-tin *see* Tlathenkotin

Tlathenkohtin *see* Tlathenkotin

Tlathenkotin [BC] *Chilcotin* (BE)

Tlatlashekwillo *see* Tlatlasikoala

Tlatlashequilla *see* Tlatlasikoala

Tlatlasik'oa'la *see* Tlatlasikoala

Tlatlasikoala [VanI] *Kwakiutl* (BE)

Tlatlasiqoala *see* Tlatlasikoala

Tlatlelamin [Gens] *Nimkish* (H)

Tlatlisikwila *see* Tlatlasikoala

Tla-tli-si-swila *see* Tlatlasikoala

Tlatsap *see* Clatsop

Tlatscanai *see* Tlatskanai

Tlats'e'noq *see* Klaskino

Tlatsenoq *see* Klaskino

Tlatskanai [WA, OR] (BE)

Tlatskanie *see* Tlatskanai

Tlat-skanie *see* Clatskinie

Tlatskanie *see* Clatskanie

Tlau'itsis *see* Tlauitsis

Tlauitsis [BC] (BE)

Tla-we-wul-lo *see* Clowwewalla

Tlawewullo *see* Clowwewalla

Tlaxcalan (H) *see also* Sia (LC)

Tlaxcalan [MX] *Nahuatl* (LC)

Tlaz'tenne *see* Tatshiautin

Tlaztenne *see* Tatshiautin

Tlduldjitamai [Clan] *Haida* (H)

Tlegon Khotana *see* Tlegonkhotana

Tlegonkhotana [AK] *Kaiyuhkhotana* (H)

Tlekem [Gens] *Walas Kwakiutl* (H)

Tlemtle'me-let *see* Clemlemalats

Tlenedi [Social group] [AK] *Auk* (H)

Tleqeti *see* Tletket

Tles-koh-tin *see* Tleskotin

Tleskohtin *see* Tleskotin
Tleskotin [BC] *Chilcotin* (BE)
Tletket [Gens] *Tlauitsis* (H)
Tletket [Gens] *Walas Kwakiutl*
(H)
Tlg-aio la'na *see* Hlgaiu-lana
Tlgaiolana *see* Hlgaiu-lana
Tlgaitguyitinai *see* Hlgahet-
gitinai
Tlg-a'it guyit'inau *see* Hlgahet-
gitinai
Tlickitack *see* Klikitat
T'likatat *see* Klikitat
Tlikatat *see* Klikitat
Tl'i'kutath *see* Tlikutath
Tlikutath [Sept] *Nootka* (H)
Tlingit [AK, Can] (LC)
Tlinket *see* Tlingit
Tlinkit *see* Tlingit
Tlinkit-antu-kwan *see* Tlingit
Tlip-pah-lis *see* Kilpanlus
Tlippahlis *see* Kilpanlus
Tlip-pat-lis *see* Kilpanlus
Tlippatlis *see* Kilpanlus
Tli'qalis *see* Tliaqalis
Tli'qalis *see* Tliqalis
Tliqalis [Gens] *Quatsino* (H)
Tlitk-atewu'mtlat *see* Shuswap
Tlitkatewumtlat *see* Shuswap
Tl'i'tlalas *see* Tlitlalas
Tlitlalas [Gens] *Quatsino* (H)
Tlizihlani [Clan] *Navajo* (H)
Tlizilani *see* Tlizihlani
Tlk-i-notl la'nas *see* Kagials-
kegawai
Tlkinotllanas *see* Kagials-kegawa
Tlogi *see* Sia
Tlokeang *see* Kato
Tlotoene *see* Klokegottine
Tlo-ton-na *see* Klokegottine
Tlotonna *see* Klokegottine
Tlqaiu la'na *see* Hlgaui-lana
Tlqaiulana *see* Hlgauilana
Tlsus-me tunne *see* Thltsusme-
tunne
Tlsusmetunne *see* Thltsusme-
tunne
Tluknahadi [AK] *Tlingit* (H)
Tlukoedi *Tlingit* (H)
Tlu'tlama'eka *see* Assiniboin
Tlutlamaeka *see* Assiniboin
Tmarois *see* Tamoroa
Tnac *see* Knaiakhotana
Tnai *see* Knaiakhotana
Tnaina *see* Knaiakhotana
Tnaina Ttynai *see* Knaiakhotana
To [Clan] *Yuchi* (H)
Toa *see* Tamathli
Toa *see* Paraujano
Toaa *see* Tohaha
Toagenha *see* Ontwaganha
Toagenha *see* Shawnee
Toags *see* Nanticoke

Toaguenha *see* Ontwaganha
Toah-waw-lay-neuch *see* Tsawa-
tenok
Toahwawlayneuch *see* Tsawa-
tenok
Toajgua *see* Tojagua
Toalaghreghroonees *see* Tutelo
Toalaghreghsoonees *see* Tutelo
Toalli *see* Tamathli
Toamar *Coahuiltecan* (Hdbk10)
Toamche *see* Toam-che
Toam-che *Maidu* (Contri, v.3)
Toanda *see* Twana
Toando *see* Twana
Toanho *see* Twana
To-an-hooch *see* Twana
Toanhooch *see* Twana
toanhoock *see* Twana
To-an-hu *see* Twana
Toanhu *see* Twana
Toan-huch *see* Twana
Toanhuch *see* Twana
To-an-kooch *see* Twana
Toankooch *see* Twana
Toao *see* Tohaha
Toarma *see* Toamar
Toas *see* Taos
Toas *see* Tewa
Toas *see* Tigua
Toasi *see* Tawasa
Toataghreghroones *see* Tutelo
Toaux *see* Tiou
Toa-waw-ti-e-neuh *see* Tsawa-
tenok
Toawawtieneuh *see* Tsawatenok
Toayas *see* Tawehash
Toba (H) *see also* Soba (H)
Toba [Arg, BO] (LC)
Tobacco Indians *see* Tionontati
Tobacco Nation *see* Tionontati
Tobacco People *see* Tionontati
Tobacco Plains [MN] *Kutenai*
(BE)
Tobacco Plains Kootanie (H) *see
also* Akanekunik (H)
Tobacco Plains Kootenay (H) *see
also* Akanekunik (H)
Tobamaskoy *see* Toba-Maskoy
Toba-Maskoy [Par] *Toba* (O)
Tobamiri *see* Toba-Miri
Toba-Miri [Par] *Toba* (O)
Tobawache *see* Uncompahgre
To'baznaaz *see* Thobazhnaoshi
Tobaznaaz *see* Thobazhnaozhi
To'baznaa-zi *see* Thobazhnaazhi
Tobaznaazi *see* Thobazhnaazhi
Tobc-a-dud *see* Yakima
Tobic *see* Tobique
Tobikhar *see* Gabrielino
Tobikhar [Lang] *see* Shoshonean
Tobique [NewB] *Malecite* (H)
Toboco *see* Toboso
Tobocore *Coahuiltecan* (Hdbk10)

Toboso [MX] (BE)
Tobosso *see* Toboso
tobowahamati *Owens Valley
Paiute* (Hdbk11)
Tocabago *see* Tocobaga
Tocamomon *Coahuiltecan*
(Hdbk10)
Tocaninambiches *see* Arapaho
Tocas [MX, TX] *Coahuiltecan* (BE)
To-che-wah-coo *see* Fox
Tochewahcoo *see* Fox
Tocholimafia [Clan] [NM] *Taos*
(H)
Tocholimafia tai'na *see* To-
cholimafia
Tochoquin [MX] *Coahuiltecan*
(Hdbk10)
Tocia [CA] *Chumashan* (H)
Tociniguara [MX] *Coahuiltecan*
(Hdbk10)
Tockwagh *see* Tocwogh
Tockwhogh *see* Tocwogh
Tockwock *see* Tocwogh
Tockwogh *see* Tocwogh
Tockwoghes *see* Tocwogh
Tockwoughes *see* Tocwogh
Tocobaga [FL] (BE)
Tocobaja *see* Tocobaga
Toco-baja-chile *see* Tocobaga
Tocobajachile *see* Tocobaga
Tocobajo *see* Tocobaga
Tocobaya *see* Tocobaga
Tocoboga *see* Tocobaga
Toco'it *see* Toba
Tocoit *see* Toba
Tocokiru [Br] *Northern Nam-
bicuara* (O)
Tocone [MX] *Concho* (BE)
Tocopata *see* Tocobaga
Tocovaga *see* Tocobaga
Tocovajachile *see* Tocobaga
Tocoytus *see* Toba
Toctata *see* Oto
Tocwogh [MD] *Nanticoke* (BE)
Tocwoy *see* Tocwogh
Toderechrones *see* Tutelo
Toderichronne *see* Tutelo
Toderichroone *see* Catawba
Todericks *see* Tutelo
Todetabi *see* Yodetabi
Todevighrono *see* Tutelo
Todichini *see* Thoditshini
Todirichrones *see* Tutelo
Todirichroones *see* Christanna
Indians
Todirichroones *see* Tutelo
To'ditsini *see* Thoditshini
Toditsini *see* Thoditshini
To'dokonzi *see* Thodhokongzhi
Todokonzi *see* Thodhokongzhi
Toebehe *see* Kawahib
Toedökado *Northern Paiute*
(Hdbk11)

To'e'k-tlisath *see* Chaicclesaht
Toektlisath *see* Chaicclesaht
Toelche *see* Tehuelche
Toelchi *see* Tehuelche
Toelchu *see* Tehuelche
Toene *see* Athapascan
Toeneche *see* Dalinchi
To-e-ne-che *see* Dalinchi
Toe-nen-hogh-hunt *see* Seneca
Toenenhoghhunt *see* Seneca
Toeni *see* Athapascan
Toepehe *see* Kawahib
Togabaja *see* Tocobaga
To Gad *see* Cochiti
Togad *see* Cochiti
To Gah *see* Cochiti
Togah *see* Cochiti
To Gahnii *see* Cochiti
Togahnii *see* Cochiti
Toghwock *see* Tocwogh
Togiagamiut *see* Togiagmiut
Togiagamiut *see* Tuyuryarmiut
Togiagamut *see* Togiagmiut
Togiagamute *see* Tuyuryarmiut
Togiagmiut [AK] *Eskimos* (BE)
Toguit-inai *see* Do-gitunai
To-gwing-a-ni *see* Togwingani
Togwingani [OR] *Paviotso* (H)
Tohacele *see* San Felipe [Keres]
To Hachele *see* San Felipe [Keres]
Tohaha [TX] (BE)
Tohahe *see* Tohaha
To'Hajiiloh *see* Santo Domingo
Tohajiiloh *see* Santo Domingo
To'Hajiilohnii *see* Santo Domingo
Tohajiilohnii *see* Santo Domingo
Tohaka *see* Tohaha
To-hak-ti-vi *see* Toahktivi
Tohaktivi [CA] *Paviotso* (H)
Tohaktivi *Owens Valley Paiute* (Hdbk11)
Tohan *see* Toho
To'hani *see* Thokhani
Tohani *see* Thokhani
Tohanni *see* Thokhani
Tohau *see* Toho
Tohlkagitunai *see* Tohlka-gitunai
Tohlka-gitunai [Clan] *Haida* (H)
Toho [TX] (BE)
Tohogaleas *see* Yuchi
Tohohai *see* Tuhohi
Tohohai *see* Chuxoxi
Tohohayi *see* Chuxoxi
Tohol [NM] *Piro* (H)
Toholo *see* Chawchila
Tohome [AL] *Choctaw* (BE)
Tohono O'Odham (LC) *see also* Papago (LC)
Tohono O'Odham [Self-designation] [MX, AZ] (LC)
Tohontaenras *see* Tohontaenrat

Tohontaenrat (Hdbk15) *see also* Tahontaenrat (H)
Tohontaenrat [Ont] *Huron* (H)
Tohookatokie [TX] (H)
Tohotaenrat *see* Tohontaenrat
Tohou [Clan] *Hopi* (H)
Tohouh [Clan] *Hopi* (H)
To-ho-uh wuñi-wu *see* Tohou
Tohou-wiñwu *see* Tohou
Tohouwuñwu *see* Tohou
Toihiche [CA] *Kings River Yokuts* (BE)
Toikhichi *see* Toihiche
Toiknimapu [ID] *Nez Perce* (BE)
Toinetche *see* Holkoma
To-i-nin-a *see* Atsina
Toinina *see* Atsina
To-i-wait *see* Toiwait
Toiwait [NV] *Paviotso* (H)
Tojar [Pan, CR] *Terraba* (BE)
Tojobaco *see* Tocobaga
Tojolabal (LC) *see also* Chanabal (LC)
Tojolabal [Lang] [CAm] *Western Mayan* (O)
Tojuma *see* Toamar
to-k'aelae *see* Jicarilla Apache
tokaelae *see* Jicarilla Apache
to-k'aelaecos *see* Jicarilla Apache
tokaelaecos *see* Jicarilla Apache
Tokala [Society] *Sioux* (SR, v.93, no.1, J/F 1993, p.4)
Tokalatoinu [ID] *Nez Perce* (BE)
Tokali *see* Takulli
Tokane *see* Yscani
Tokau *see* Toho
Tok'ele *see* Picuris
tokele *see* Picuris
To-ke-ma-che *see* Tuhukmache
Tokemache *see* Tuhukmache
Tok'oa'ath *see* Tokoaath
Tok'oa-ath *see* Toquart
Tokoaath (PC) *see also* Toquart (BE)
Tokoaath [Sept] *Nootka* (H)
Tok-oa'is *see* Tokoais
Tokoais [BC] *Nuhalk* (H)
Tokoanu [Clan] *Hopi* (H)
Tokoanu wiñwu *see* Tokoanu
To-ko-a-nu wun-wu *see* Tokoanu
To-ko-a-nu wuñi-wu *see* Tokoanu
Tokochi [Clan] *Hopi* (H)
Tokonabi [UT] *Hopi* (H)
Tokoonavi *see* Tokonabi
Tokotci wiñwu *see* Tokochi
To-ko-tci wuñi-wu *see* Tokochi
Tokotciwuñwu *see* Tokochi
Tokume *see* Apache
To-kum-pi *see* Northern Assini-boin
To-kum-pi *see* Tschantoga

Tokumpi *see* Northern Assini-boin
Tokumpi *see* Tschantoga
Tokuna *see* Tucuna
Tokwaht *see* Toquart
Tol *see* Jicaque
Tolameco *see* Chiaha
Tolana *see* Tolowa
Tolawa *see* Tolowa
Tolekopaya *see* Tulkepaia
Tolenos *see* Yolo
Tolera *see* Tutelo
Tolere *see* Tutelo
Toleri *see* Tutelo
To-le-wah *see* Tolowa
Tolewah *see* Tolowa
Tolgopeya *see* Tulkepaia
Tolimeca [MX] (BE)
Tolkapaya *see* Tolkepaya
Tolkepaya (H) *see also* Tulkepaia (H)
Tolkepaya [AZ] *Western Yavapai* (BE)
Tolkotin *see* Tautin
Tolkpaya *see* Tolkapaya
Tollinche *see* Dalinchi
Toloim *see* Bankalanchi
tolomma *see* Northern Paiute
Tol-o-wa *see* Tolowa
Tolowa [CA, OR] (LC)
Tolowarch *see* Apalachicola
Tolowar thlocco *see* Apalachicola
Tolowarthlocco *see* Apalachicola
Tolpan *see* Jicaque
Toltecs [MX] (LC)
Toltichi [CA] (CA)
Toltu [Clan] [NM] *Taos* (H)
Toltu tai'na *see* Toltu
Toltutaina *see* Toltu
Tolujaa *see* Tilijaes
To-lum-ne *see* Telamni
Tolumne *see* Telamni
Tolupan *see* Jicaque
Tolwatin [AK] *Tenankutchin* (H)
Tomacha *see* Tawehash
Tomachee *see* Timucua
Tomahitans *see* Yuchi
Tomales *see* Tamal
Tomaroa *see* Tamaroa
Tomarxa *see* Tomraxo
Tomasa *see* Tamasa
Tomaseños, San [BaC] (H)
Tome [Pueblo] [NM] (H)
Tomeas *see* Tohome
Tome Dominguez *see* Tome
Tomes *see* Tohome
Tomez *see* Tohome
Tomgass *see* Tongass
To-Mia *see* Santa Ana [NM]
Tomiscamings *see* Temiscaming
Tom-i-ya *see* Santa Ana [NM]
Tomiya *see* Santa Ana [NM]
Tomki *see* Mitomkai

Tommakee *see* Timucua
Tommakees *see* Tohome
Tomoco *see* Timucua
Tomoka *see* Timucua
Tomo'la *see* Tubatulabal
Tomola *see* To-mo-la
Tomola *see* Tubatulabal
To-mo-la [CA] (Contri, v.3, p.393)
Tompacua *see* Pakawa
Tompacuas *see* Tocobaga
tompanowotsnunts *see* Timpanogots
Tompira *see* Tompiro
Tompires *see* Tompiro
Tompiro [NM] *Piro* (H)
Tomraxo [Par, BO] *Chamacoco* (O)
Tom Tyler Indians [MA] *Wampanoag* (BE)
Ton [Clan] [NM] *Pueblo Indians* (H)
Tona [Clan] [NM] *Zuni* (H)
Tonaca *see* Totonac
Tona-kwa *see* Tona
Tonakwa *see* Tona
Tonasket [WA] *Sinkaietk* (BE)
Tonawanda [NY] *Seneca* (H)
Tonawando *see* Tonawanda
Tonawanta *see* Tonawanda
To-na-wits-o-wa *see* Tonawitsowa
Tonawitsowa [NV] *Shoshone* (H)
Toncahiras *see* Tonkawa
Toncahuas *see* Tonkawa
Toncas *see* Kutawichasha
Toncawes *see* Tonkawa
Ton-ch-un *see* Tonchuun
Tonchuun (H) *see also* Pecos (BE)
Tonchuun [Pueblo] [NM] (H)
Tondamans *see* Seneca
Tondo *see* Tonto Apache
Tone-ba-o *see* Tonebao
Tonebao [Phratry] *Mahican* (H)
Tong [Clan] [NM] *Pueblo Indians* (H)
Tongaria *see* Ontwaganha
Tongarois *see* Ontwaganha
Tongas *see* Tongass
Tongass [AK] *Tlingit* (LC)
Tong-o-na-o-to *see* Tongonaoto
Tongonaoto [Subclan] *Delaware* (H)
Tongues *see* Tonkawa
Tongva [CA] (CA)
Tonic *see* Tehelche
Tonica *see* Tunica
Tonicaus *see* Tunica
Tonicote *see* Tonocote
Tonika *see* Tunica
Tonikan [Lang] (LC)
Toniqua *see* Tanico
Tonkahans *see* Tonkawa

Tonkahaws *see* Tonkawa
Tonkahiras *see* Tonkawa
Tonkahuas *see* Tonkawa
Ton-ka-hues *see* Tonkawa
Tonkahues *see* Tonkawa
Ton-kah-ways *see* Tonkawa
Tonkahways *see* Tonkawa
Tonkawa [Lang] [TX, OK] (BE)
Tonkawa [TX, OK] (LC)
Tonkaway *see* Tonkawa
Tonkawe *see* Tonkawa
Tonkaweya *see* Tonkawa
Tonkeway *see* Tonkawa
Tonkhua *see* Tonkawa
Tonkonko *see* Siksika
Tonkowa *see* Tonkawa
Tonks *see* Tonkawa
Tonnewanta *see* Tonawanda
Tonnontoins *see* Seneca
Tonnoraunto *see* Tonawanda
To-noc-o-nies *see* Tawakoni
Tonocote [Arg] (LC)
Tonokote *see* Tonocote
Tono-Oohtam *see* Papago
Tono-Oohtam *see* Tohono O'Odham
Tonore *see* Txicaos
To-no-yiet *see* Tonoyiet's band
Tonoyiet *see* Tonoyiet's Band
Tonoyiet's Band [NV] *Paviotso* (H)
Tonoziet *see* Tonoyiet's Band
Ton-que-was *see* Tonkawa
Tonquewas *see* Tonkawa
Tonqueway *see* Tonkawa
Tonquoway *see* Tonkawa
Tonqus *see* Tonkawa
Tons *see* Taos
Ton tai'na *see* Ton
Tont-a-quans *see* Tongass
Tontaquans *see* Tongass
Ton-tdoa *see* Tong
Tonteac *see* Hopi
Tonteaca *see* Hopi
Tontears *see* Tonto Apache
Tontewait *see* Chemehuevi
Tonthratarhonon *see* Totontaratonhronon
Tonto (LC) *see also* Yavapai (LC)
Tonto Apache [AZ] (BE)
Tonto Cosnino *see* Havasupai
Tontoes *see* Tonto Apache
Tontonteac *see* Hopi
Tonto-Tinne *see* Tonto Apache
Tontthrataronon *see* Totontaratonhronon
Tontu *see* Tonto Apache
Tonwaina *see* Ton
Tonzaumacagua [TX] *Coahuiltecan* (BE)
Too *see* Toho
Tooahk [WA] *Salish* (H)
Too-an-hooch *see* Twana

Tooanhooch *see* Twana
Too-au-hooch *see* Twana
Tooauhooch *see* Twana
Too-au-hoosh *see* Twana
Tooauhoosh *see* Twana
Toocoo recah *see* Tukuarika
Toocoorecah *see* Tukuarika
Too-el-icans *see* Tooelicans
Tooelicans [OR] (H)
Toohtoowee [MA] *Wampanoag* (BE)
Took-a-rik-kah *see* Tukuarika
Tookarikkah *see* Tukuarika
Took-seat *see* Tookseat
Tookseat [Phratry] *Delaware* (H)
Took-se-tuk *see* Tooksetuk
Tooksetuk [Phratry] *Mahican* (H)
Tooleerayos *see* Tularenos
Toomedoc *see* Tumidok
Toomes *see* Tohome
Toom-na *see* Tumna
Toomna *see* Tumna
Toonoonee-roochiuh *see* Tununerusirmiut
Toonoonek *see* Tununirmiut
Toon-pa-ooh *see* Tonebao
Toonpaooh *see* Tonebao
Too-num-pe *see* Tunanpin
Toonumpe *see* Tunanpin
Too-qu-aht *see* Toquart
Tooquaht *see* Toquart
Toosey [BC] *Chilcotin* (BE)
Tooshkipakwisi [Subclan] *Delaware* (H)
Toosh-ki-pa-kwis-si *see* Tooshkipakwisi
Tooshkipakwissi *see* Tooshkipakwisi
Tooshwarkama [Subclan] *Delaware* (H)
Toothle *see* Maca
Too-too-ten *see* Tututni
Tootooten *see* Tututni
Too-too-te-ny *see* Tututni
Tootooteny *see* Tututni
Too-toot-nie *see* Tututni
Tootootnie *see* Tututni
Too-too-ton *see* Tututni
Tootooton *see* Tututni
Tootootone *see* Tututni
Too-war-sar *see* Tawehash
Toowarsar *see* Tawehash
Tooweehtoowee *see* Miami
Too-wos-sau (H) Tawasa (BE)
Toowossau *see* Tawasa
Topa-an *see* Thkhapaha
Topaan *see* Thkhapaha
Topacolme *Concho* (BE)
To-pai-di-sel *see* Topaidisel
Topaidisel [CA] *Patwin* (H)
Topehe *see* Kawahib
Topia *see* Cahita
Topinish [WA] *Yakima* (BE)

Topin-keua *see* Hopi
Topinkeua *see* Hopi
Top-in-te-ua *see* Hopi
Topinteua *see* Hopi
Topires *see* Tompiro
Topiro *see* Tompiro
Topnish *see* Topinish
Topocapa *see* Tocobaga
Topoliana-kuin *see* Taos
Topoqui *see* Tepocas
Toppahanock *see* Rappahannock
Toppaun *see* Tappan
Tops [TX] (H)
Toquaht *see* Toquart
Toquart [VanI] (*Nootka*) (BE)
Toquatux *see* Toquart
Toquegua [Hon] (BE)
To-quh-aht *see* Toquart
Toquhaht *see* Toquart
Toquimas [NV] *Mono* (H)
Tora [Br] (O)
Torape *see* Torepe's band
Toreon *see* Torreon
To-Repe's band *see* Torepe's
band
Torepe's band [NV] *Paviotso* (H)
Toreuna *see* Torreon
Toribio [Col] *Paez* (O)
Torica *see* Yorica
Torim *see* Telamni
Toriuash *see* Tawehash
Torn-trousers [Clan] [MN]
Atsina (BE)
Toromona [BO] (O)
To-ro-un to-go-ats *see* Toroun-
togoats
Torountogoats [UT, NV] *Gosiute*
(H)
Torreon [Pueblo] [NM] (H)
Torrupan *see* Jicaque
Tortero *see* Tutelo
Tortugas [TX] *Coahuiltecan* (H)
Tor-yoh-ne *see* Toryohne
Toryohne [Clan] *Iroquois* (H)
To-sarke *see* Tosarke's Band
Tosarke's Band [NV] *Paviotso* (H)
To'sa wee *see* Tussawehe
Tosawee *see* Tussawehe
Tosawitches *see* Tussawehe
Toscorora *see* Tuscarora
Tosepon *see* Tisepan
Tos-hit-tan *see* Toshittan
Toshittan [Social group] [AK]
Nanyaagi (H)
Tosikoyo *see* To-si-ko-yo
To-si-ko-yo [CA] *Maidu* (Contri,
v.3, p.282)
To-si-witches *see* Tussawehe
Tosiwitches *see* Tussawehe
To-si-withes *see* Tussawehe
Tosiwithes *see* Tussawehe
Toskiroro *see* Tuscarora
To-so-ee *see* Tussawehe

Tosoee *see* Tussawehe
To-so-wates *see* Tussawehe
Tosowates *see* Tussawehe
Tosowes *see* Tussawehe
To-so-witches *see* Tussawehe
Tosowwitches *see* Tussawehe
Tostl Engilnagai *see* Dostlan-
Inagai
Tosugui *see* Tesuque
To taha *see* To
Totaha *see* To
To'tak-amayaath *see* Totaka-
mayaath
Totakamayaath [Sept] *Toquart*
(H)
Totaly *see* Tutelo
Totaro *see* Tutelo
Totas Chee *see* Moratico
Totatkenne [BC] *Sekani* (H)
Toteloes *see* Tutelo
Totera *see* Tutelo
Toteri *see* Tutelo
Toteroes *see* Tutelo
Toteros *see* Tutelo
Totierono *see* Tutelo
Totiri *see* Catawba
Totiri *see* Tutelo
Totlgya guit'inai *see* Tohlka-
gitunai
Totlgyaguitinai *see* Tohlka-
gitunai
Toto *see* To-to
To-to *Maidu* (Contri, v.3, p.282)
Totoguan [Lang] *Papago*
(Hdbk10)
Totoimana [SD] *Cheyenne* (BE)
Totolaca *see* Totonac
Totonac [MX] (LC)
Totonaca *see* Totonac
Totonacan [Lang] [MX] (BE)
Totonaco *see* Totonac
Totonacos *see* Totonac
Totones *see* Tututni
Totonicapan *see* Totonac
Totonic tribes *see* Tututni
Totonoco *see* Totonac
Totontaratonhronon (H) *see also*
Atonthrataronon (H)
Totontaratonhronon [Can] *Algo-
nquian* (H)
Totonteac *see* Hopi
Totonteal *see* Hopi
Totontoac *see* Hopi
Totora *see* Tutelo
Totorame [MX] (BE)
Totoro [Col] *Paez* (O)
Totoson [MA] *Wampanoag* (BE)
Tototan *see* Tututni
To-to-taws *see* Tututni
Tototaws *see* Tututni
Tototeac *see* Hopi
Tototin [OR] *Tututni* (H)
To-to-tut-na *see* Tututni

Tototutna *see* Tututni
To'tsalsitaya *see* Thochalsithaya
Totsalsitaya *see* Thochalsithaya
totsema *see* Tesuque
To-tshik-o-tin *see* Trot-
sikkutchin
Totshikotin *see* Trotsikkutchin
To'tsoni *see* Thatsoni
Totsoni *see* Thotsoni
Tottero *see* Tutelo
Totteroy *see* Tutelo
Totuskey [VA] *Powhatan Confed-
eracy* (H)
Totutime *see* Tututni
Totutune *see* Tututni
Tou *see* Toho
Touacara *see* Tawakoni
Touacaro *see* Tawakoni
Touacha *see* Tawasa
Touagannha *see* Ontwaganha
To-ua-qua *see* Towakwa
Touaqua *see* Towakwa
Touashes *see* Tawehash
Touchon-ta-Kutchin *see*
Tutchone
Touchontakutchin *see* Tutchone
Touchon-tay Kutchin *see*
Tutchone
Touchontaykutchin *see*
Tutchone
Touchouaesintons *see* Tou-
chouasintons
Touchouasintons *Western Dakota*
(BE)
Toudamans *see* Seneca
Touguenha *see* Ontwaganha
Toukaways *see* Tonkawa
Touloucs *see* Ottawa
Toumacha *see* Tunica
Toumika *see* Tunica
Toungletat *see* Lekwiltok
Tounica *see* Tunica
Tounika *see* Tunica
Touquaht *see* Toquart
Touraxouslins [IL] (H)
Tourika *see* Tunica
Tous *see* Taos
Touscaroro *see* Tuscarora
Touse *see* Taos
Touserlemnies *see* Tuolumne
Toustchipas *see* Tushepqw
Tovare *see* Tubar
Tovok [Arg, Par] *Ashluslay* (O)
Tovoso *see* Toboso
Tovosso *see* Toboso
To'vu *see* Tovu
Tovu [Clan] *Hopi* (H)
Tovusidokado *Northern Paiute*
(Hdbk11)
Towa *Jemez* (Hdbk10)
Towaahach *see* Tawehash
Towacanies *see* Tawakoni
Towacanno *see* Tawakoni

Towacano *see* Tawakoni
Towacarro *see* Tawakoni
Towaccanie *see* Tawakoni
Towaccara *see* Tawakoni
Towachanies *see* Tawakoni
Towaches *see* Tawehash
To-wac-ko-nies *see* Tawakoni
Towackonies *see* Tawakoni
To-wac-o-nies *see* Tawakoni
Towaconies *see* Tawakoni
Towacoro *see* Tawakoni
Towaganha *see* Ontwaganha
Towahach *see* Tawehash
Tow-ah-ha *see* Towahhah
Towahha *see* Towahhah
Towahhah [WA] *Salish* (H)
Towahhans *see* Tawehash
Towahnahiooks (H) *see also* Kat-
   laminim (H)
Towahnahiooks [OR] *Shoshone*
   (H)
To-wa-ka *see* Seneca
Towaka *see* Seneca
Towa'kani *see* Tawakani
Towakarehu *see* Tawakoni
Towakarro *see* Tawakoni
Towakenos *see* Tawakoni
Towako *see* Ottawa
Towakon *see* Ottawa
Towakoni *see* Tawakoni
To-wa-kwa *see* Towakwa
Towakwa [Pueblo] [NM] *Jemez*
   (H)
To-wal-um-ne *see* Tuolumne
Towalumne *see* Tuolumne
Towanahioohs *see* Towah-
   nahiooks
Towanda *see* Twana
Towapummuk *see* Shuswap
To-wa-que *see* Taa
Towaque *see* Taa
Towarsa *see* Tawasa
Towas *see* Hano
Towas *see* Tewo
Tow-ash *see* Tawehash
Towash *see* Tawehash
Towash *see* Tawehash
Towcash *see* Tawehash
Tow-ce-ahge *see* Tawehash
Towceahge *see* Tawehash
Toweache *see* Tawehash
Toweash *see* Tawehash
Toweca *see* Tawakoni
Towecenego *see* Sinago
Toweeahge *see* Tawehash
Tow-eeash *see* Tawehash
Toweeash *see* Tawehash
Towha [Clan] [NM] *Taos* (H)
Towha tai-na *see* Towha
Towhataina *see* Towha
Towhayu [Clan] [NM] *Taos* (H)
Towhayu tai'na *see* Towhayu
Towhayutaina *see* Towhayu

Towiache *see* Tawehash
Towiache-Tawakenoes *see* Tawe-
   hash
Towiachs *see* Tawakoni
Towiash *see* Tawehash
Towih *see* Taos
To-win-che-ba *see* Holkoma
Towincheba *see* Holkoma
Towirnin *see* Taos
Towish *see* Tawehash
Town-Bend Indians *Dakota* (H)
Town of the Broken Promise *see*
   Tome
Towoash *see* Tawehash
Towoashe *see* Tawehash
Towoccaro *see* Tawakoni
Towoccaroes *see* Tawakoni
Towocconie *see* Tawakoni
Towockonie *see* Tawakoni
To-woc-o-roy Thycoes *see*
   Tawakoni
Towocoroy Thycoes *see* Tawakoni
Towoekonie *see* Tawakoni
Towrache *see* Tawehash
Towzash *see* Tawehash
toxelyuwic [Moiety] *Yokuts* (Pub,
   v.11, no.5)
Toxo *see* Toho
Toxocodame *see* Terocodame
Toyagua *see* Tojagua
Toyal *see* Tohaha
Toyash *see* Tawehash
Toyeri [PE] *Mashco* (O)
To'yetlini *see* Thoyetlini
Toyetlini *see* Thoyetlini
Toyhicha [Lang] [CA] *Kings River*
   (CA-8)
Toyn-aht *see* Toquart
Toynaht *see* Toquart
Toy Pah-Utes *see* Toiwait
Toypahutes *see* Toiwait
Toypehe *see* Kawahib
Toy Pi-Utes *see* Toiwait
Toypiutes *see* Toiwait
Toy-yu-wi-ti-kut-teh *see* Toi-
   wait
Toyyuwitikutteh *see* Toiwait
To-zan-ne *see* Laguna
Tozanne *see* Laguna
Tozjanna *see* Laguna
T'Peeksin *see* Tapeeksin
Tpeeksin *see* Tapeeksin
Tpelois *see* Natchez
Tpe-tliet-Kouttchin *see* Tatlit-
   kutchin
Tpetliet Kouttchin *see* Tatlit-
   kutchin
Tpe-ttchie-dhidie-Kouttchin *see*
   Natsitkutchin
Tpettchiedihidie Kouttchin *see*
   Natsitkutchin
Tqlun-qas tunne *see*
   Tkhlunkhastunne

Tqlunqastunne *see* Tkhlunkhas-
   tunne
T'Qua-quamish *see* Tkwak-
   wamish
Tquaquamish *see* Tkwakwamish
Traders *see* Ottawa
Traht *see* Tyigh
Trakouaehronnon *see* Conestoga
Tramaambe *see* Teremembe
Tran-jik-koo-chin *see* Trot-
   sikkutchin
Tranjikkutchin *see* Tranjik-
   kutchin
Tranjik-kutchin [AK] *Kutchin*
   (BE)
Transquakine *see* Trasquakin
Trantsaotthine *see* Tatsanottine
Tran-tsa ottine *see* Tatsanottine
Trappers *see* Nanticoke
Traskokin *see* Trasquakin
Trasquakin *Choptank II* (Hdbk15)
Tratse-kutshi *see* Trotsikkutchin
Tratsekutshi *see* Trotsikkutchin
Traverse Bay *Ottawa* (IndT, Oct.
   1994)
Traverse de Sioux [MN] *Sisseton*
   (BE)
Treaber Utes *see* Cumumbah
Treacherous Lodges *see* Ash-
   bochia
Treaty Party *Cherokee* (H)
Trelagu *Pueblo Indians* (H)
Trelaquepu *Pueblo Indians* (H)
Tremblers [AZ] *Apache* (H)
Tremembe *see* Teremembe
Trementinas *see* Tremblers
Trenaquel [Pueblo] [NM] *Piro*
   (H)
Tres-qui-ta *see* Pohoi
Tresquita *see* Pohoi
Treyey [NM] *Pueblo Indians* (H)
Treypual [NM] *Pueblo Indians*
   (H)
Tria *see* Sia
Tria *see* Sia
Triape *see* Triapi
Triapi [Pueblo] [NM] *Tewa* (H)
Triaque [Pueblo] [NM] *Tewa* (H)
Triati [Pueblo] [NM] (H)
Trickster Indians *see* Sitcon-ski
Trike *see* Trique
Triki *see* Trique
Trile Kalet *see* Klikitat
Trimati [Pueblo] [NM] (H)
Trinitario *see* Moxo
Trinity County [Lang] [CA]
   Wintu (CA-8)
Trinity Indians *see* Hupa
Trio (O) *see also* Tiriyo (O)
Trio [Lang] *Carib* (UAz, v.28)
Trio Indians [Sur, Br] (LC)
Triometesan [Lang] *Trio* (UAz,
   v.28)

Triometesem *see* Akurio

Trios *see* Sia

Tripanick [NC] *Algonquian* (H)

Tripanieks *see* Tripanick

Tripas Blancas [MX] *Coahuiltecan* (BE)

Trique [MX] (LC)

Triquean [Lang] [CAm] (BE)

Troc *see* Zoque

Troes *see* Zoe

Troiscanne *see* Tawakoni

Trokesen *see* Iroquois

Tronotes *see* Tionontati

Troo-maxia-qui-no *see* Troomaxiaquino

Troquois *see* Iroquois

Trotsikkutchin [AK] *Kutchin* (H)

Trot-tsik kutch-in *see* Trotsikkutchin

Trout Creek *Western Shoshone* (Hdbk11)

Trout Lake [MI, WI] *Chippewa* (H)

Trovmaxiaquino *see* Troomaxiaquino

Trudamans *see* Seneca

True Chiricahua *see* Central Chiricahua Apache

Trueños *Coahuiltecan* (Hdbk10)

True Thnaina *see* Tehanin-Kutchin

True Thnaina *see* Knaiakhotana

Truhohayi (CA) *see also* Chuxoxi (CA)

Truhohayi [CA] *Yokuts* (H)

Truhohi (CA) *see also* Chuxoxi (CA)

Truhohi *Yokuts* (Pub, v.4, no.4, p.209)

Truka [Br] (O)

Trula [NM] *Pueblo Indians* (H)

Trumai [Br] (LC)

Truni *see* Quni

Trypanik *see* Tripanick

Tsaagwi'gyit'inai *see* Djahuigitinai

Tsaagwigyitinai *see* Djahuigitinai

Tsaagwisguatl'adegai *see* Djahuiskwahladagai

Tsa-bah-bish *see* Dwamish

Tsabahbish *see* Dwamish

Tsaba'kosh *see* Dakota

Tsabakosh *see* Dakota

Tsacela *see* Colorado [SA]

Tsachila *see* Colorado [SA]

Tsaeqalalis [Gens] *Koskimo* (H)

Tsafiqui *see* Colorado [SA]

Tsaguedi [AK] *Tlingit* (H)

Tsahbahbish *see* Dwamish

Tsah-tu *see* Choctaw

Tsahtu *see* Choctaw

Tsah-tyuh *see* Tsattine

Tsahtyuh *see* Tsattine

Tsah-wau-tay-neuch *see* Tsawatenok

Tsahwautayneuch *see* Tsawatenok

Tsah-waw-ti-neuch *see* Tsawatenok

Tsahwawtineuch *see* Tsawatenok

Tsah-wit-ook *see* Tsahwitook

Tsahwitook [BC] *Salish* (H)

tsaiduka *Western Shoshone* (Hdbk11)

Tsaisuma *see* Washo

Tsakaitsetlins *see* Spokan

Tsakaitsitllin *see* Spokan

Tsa-ka-nha-o-nan *see* Delaware

Tsakanhaonan *see* Delaware

T'sakbahbish *see* Dwamish

Tsakbahbish *see* Dwamish

Tsaktono [CA] *Maidu* (H)

Tsa'k-tsak-oath *see* Tsaktsakoath

Tsaktsakoath [Sept] *Nootka* (H)

Ts'akua'm *see* Tsakuam

Tsakuam [BC] *Stalo* (BE)

Tsakwe'kwabsh [WA] *Nisqulli* (BE)

Tsalagi [Self-designation] *see* Cherokee

Tsalakies *see* Cherokee

Tsalakmiut [OR] *Luckiamute* (BE)

Tsa-lo-kee *see* Cherokee

Tsalokee *see* Cherokee

Tsamak [CA] *Maidu* (H)

Tsamiak [OR] *Luckiamute* (BE)

Tsampiak [OR] *Lakmiut* (H)

Tsa mpi'nefa ami'm *see* Chepenafa

Tsampinefaamim *see* Chepenafa

Tsan-alokual-amim *see* Calapooya

Tsanalokualamim *see* Calapooya

Tsan Ampkua amim *see* Umpqua

Tsanampkuaamim *see* Umpqua

Tsana-uta am'im *see* Siuslaw

Tsanautaamim *see* Siuslaw

Tsanchifin [OR] *Calapooya* (BE)

Tsanh-alokual amim *see* Calapooya

Tsan halpam amim *see* Santiam

Tsanhalpamamim *see* Santiam

Tsa-nish *see* Arikara

Tsanish *see* Arikara

Tsanklightemifa [OR] *Calapooya* (BE)

Tsankupi [OR] *Calapooya* (BE)

Tsanout *see* Tsawout

Tsantatawa [OR] *Luckiamute* (BE)

Tsan tcha-ishna amim *see* Salmon River

Tsantchaishnaamim *see* Salmon River

Tsan tchiffin ami'm *see* Tsanchifin

Tsantchiffinamim *see* Tsanchifin

Tsan-t'ie-ottine *see* Tsantieottine

Tsantieottine [Can] *Thlingchaddine* (BE)

Tsan tkupi ami'm *see* Tsankupi

Tsantkupiamim *see* Tsankupi

Tsan-tokayu *see* Tsantokayu

Tsantokayu *see* *see also* Chayankeld

Tsantokayu [OR] *Yoncalla* (BE)

Tsantuisha [OR] *Luckiamute* (BE)

Tsantuisha ami'm *see* Tsantuisha

Tsa-ottine *see* Tsattine

Tsaottine *see* Tsattine

Tsa-pa-kah *see* Tsapakah

Tsapakah [NV] *Paviotso* (H)

Tsaqtono *see* Tsaktono

Tsa-re-ar-to-ny *see* Kaltsergheatunne

Tsareartony *see* Kaltsergheatunne

Tsarout *see* Tsawout

Tsarragi *see* Cherokee

Tsarrua *see* Charrua

Tsartlip [VanI] *Sanetch* (BE)

Tsasadshamim *see* Siletz

Tsa Sadsh amin *see* Siletz

Tsashtla *see* Siuslaw

tsata-henit *see* Tsatenyedi

tsatahenit *see* Tsatenyedi

Tsatarghekhetunne [OR] *Mishikhwutmetunne* (H)

Tsatchela [EC] (IndNM, no.51)

Tsatchela [Self-designation] (LC) *see also* Colorado [SA] (LC)

Tsatchila *see* Colorado [SA]

Tsaten *see* Tsattine

Tsa-tenne *see* Tsattine

Tsatenne *see* Tsattine

Tsatenyedi [AK] *Tlingit* (H)

Tsa-tinneh *see* Tsattine

Tsatinneh *see* Tsattine

Tsatkenne [BC] *Sekani* (H)

Ts'atl la'na *see* Chaahl-lana

Tsatllana *see* Chaahl-lana

Tsa-tqenne *see* Tsattine

Tsatqenne *see* Tsattine

Tsatsaquits *see* Tlatlasikoala

Tsatsnotin *see* Tanotenne

Tsatsuotin (H) *see also* Tanotenne (BE)

Tsatsuotin [Clan] *Takulli* (H)

Tsattine (H) *see also* Tsatkenne (H)

Tsa-ttine *see* Tsattine

Tsattine [Can] (LC)

Tsa-ttinne *see* Tsattine

Tsattinne *see* Tsattine

Tsauat'enoq *see* Tsawatenok

Tsa-u-i *see* Chaui

Tsaui *see* Chaui

Tsaumas *see* Songish

Tsaumass *see* Songish
Tsauwarits *see* Tsuwaraits
Tsawadainoh *see* Tsawatenok
Tsawahtee *see* Tsawatenok
Tsawakot *see* Tsawokot
Tsawalinough *see* Tsawatenok
Tsawa'nemux *see* Okinagan
Tsawanemux *see* Okinagan
Tsawantiano *see* Tsawatenok
Tsa-wan-ti-e-neuh *see* Tsawatenok
Tsawantieneuh *see* Tsawatenok
Tsawantieneuk *see* Tsawatenok
Tsa-wa-ri-i *see* Tsawarii
Tsawarii [Pueblo] [NM] *Tewa* (H)
Tsawataineuk *see* Tsawatenok
Tsa'wateenoq *see* Tsawatenok
Tsawateenoq *see* Tsawatenok
Ts'a'wa-teenox *see* Tsawatenok
Tsawateenox *see* Tsawatenok
Tsawatenok [BC] *Kwakiutl* (BE)
Tsawat'enoq *see* Tsawatenok
Tsawatenoq *see* Tsawatenok
Tsawatli *see* Tsawatenok
Tsa-waw-ti-e-neuk *see* Tsawatenok
Tsawawtieneuk *see* Tsawatenok
Tsawi *see* Chaui
Tsawokot [OR] *Calapooya* (BE)
Tsa wo-okot amim *see* Tsawokot
Tsawookotamim *see* Tsawokot
Tsawout [VanI] *Sanetch* (BE)
Tsa-wut-ai-nuk *see* Tsawatenok
Tsawutainuk *see* Tsawatenok
Tsa-wutti-e-nuh *see* Tsawatenok
Tsawuttienuh *see* Tsawatenok
Tsawwassen *see* Sewathen
Tsaxta *see* Choctaw
Tsayiskithni [Clan] *Navajo* (H)
Tsayu (Bull133)
Tschaktaer *see* Choctaw
Tschantoga [Clan] *Assiniboin* (H)
Tschicgi [Clan] [AK] *Knaiakhotana* (H)
Tschicgi *see* Tschicgi
Tschihri *see* Pawnee
Tschilkat *see* Chilkat
Tschilkat-kon *see* Chilkat
Tschinjagmiut *see* Chingigmiut
Tschinkaten *see* Tenankutchin
Tschinuk *see* Chinook
Tschipeway *see* Chippewa
Tschippiweer *see* Chippewa
Tschirokesen *see* Cherokee
Tschischlkhathkhoan *see* Chilkat
Tschishlkhath *see* Chilkat
Tschishlkhathkhoan *see* Chilkat
Tschlahtsoptsch *see* Clatsop
Tschnagmeuten *see* Chnagmiut
Tschnagmjuten *see* Chnagmiut
Tschnag'mut *see* Unaligmiut
Tschnagmut *see* Unaligmiut

Tschnagmuten *see* Chnagmiut
Tscholban [CA] (H)
Tschuagmuti *see* Malemiut
Tschugatschi *see* Chugachigmut
Tschugazze *see* Chugachigmut
Tschugazzi *see* Chugachigmut
Tschukane'di *see* Chukanedi
Tschunguscetoner *see* Tschantoga
Tsclallum *see* Clallam
Ts'-co *see* Cheli
Tsco *see* Cheli
Tse [Clan] *Pueblo Indians* (H)
Tse-a *see* Sia
Tsea *see* Sia
Ts'eac'ath *see* Tseshaath
Tse-ah *see* Sia
Tseah *see* Sia
Tse Aminema *see* Tyigh
Tseaminema *see* Tyigh
Ts'eca'ath *see* Seshart
Tsecaath *see* Seshart
Tsecaath *see* Tseshaath
Tse'cqani *see* Tsethkhani
Tsecqani *see* Tsethkhani
Tsedahkin *see* San Felipe [Keres]
Tsedtuka [Gens] *Osage* (H)
Tsedtukaindtse [Gens] *Osage* (H)
Tse'dzinki'ni *see* Tsezhinkini
Tsedzinkini *see* Tsezhinkini
Tseghat'ahende *Chiricahua Apache* (Hdbk10)
Tsegoatl la'na *see* Djiguaahl-lana
Tsehalish *see* Chehalis
Tsehalish *see* Chehalis
Tsehum *see* Tsehump
Tsehump [VanI] *Sanetch* (BE)
Tse-itso-kit *see* Mishongnovi
Tseitsokit *see* Mishongnovi
Tse-itso-kit-bit-si-li *see* Shipaulovi
Tseitsokitbitsili *see* Shipaulovi
Tse'jinkini *see* Tsezhinkini
Tsejinkini *see* Tsezhinkini
Tsekani *see* Sekani
Tsekani [Can] *Sekani* (BE)
Tse-keh-na *see* Tsekehneaz
Tsekehna *see* Tsekehneaz
Tse'kehne *see* Sekani
Tsekehne *see* Sekani
Tse-keh-ne-az *see* Tsekehneaz
Tsekehneaz [BC] *Sekani* (H)
Tsekenne *see* Sekani
Tsekizthohi *see* Acoma
Tseklten [BC] *Squamish* (H)
Tsekum *see* Tsehump
Tse-kun *see* Tsehump
Tsekun *see* Tsehump
Tse la'kayat amim *see* Klikitat
Tselakayatamim *see* Klikitat
Tse-loh-ne *see* Tseloni
Tselohne *see* Tseloni
Tselone *see* Tseloni

Tseloni [BC] *Sekani* (BE)
Tsemakum *see* Chimakum
Tse-mo-e *see* Sitsime
Tsemoe *see* Sitsime
Ts'emsia'n *see* Tsimshian
Tsemsian *see* Tsimshian
Tsenacommacoh *Powhatan Confederacy* (H)
Tsenahapihlni [Clan] *Navajo* (H)
Tse'nahapilni *see* Tsenahapihlni
Tsenahapilni *see* Tsenahapihlni
Tsenes [Can] *Stalo* (BE)
Tsenkam [Subgens] (H)
Ts'e'nq'am *see* Tsenkam
Tsenqam *see* Tsenkam
Tsentsenkaio [Clan] [Can] *Walaskwakiutl* (H)
Tseokuimik [Clan] *Kwakiutl* (H)
Tseottine [Can] *Thlingchadinne* (BE)
Tsepcoen *see* Semonan
Tsepechoen frercuteas *see* Semonan
Tsepehoen *see* Semonan
Tsepehouen *see* Semonan
Ts'e-rxi-a tunne *see* Kaltsergheatunne
Tserxiatunne *see* Kaltsergheatunne
Tse-sa do hpa ka *see* Pawnee
Tsesadohpaka *see* Pawnee
Tsesaht *see* Seshart
Tsesaht *see* Seshart
Tse sa no hpa ka *see* Pawnee
Tsesanohpaka *see* Pawnee
Tsese [Self-designation] *see* Piapoco
Tseshaath [Sept] *Nootka* (H)
Tsesh-aht *see* Seshart
Tseshualliamim *see* Nisqualli
Tseskadin *Apache* (H)
Tse Skua'lli ami'm *see* Nisqualli
Tse Skualli amim *see* Nisqualli
Tse-ta-hwo-tgenne *see* Tsetautkenne
Tsetahwotqenne *see* Tsetautkenne
Tseta'kin *see* San Ildefonso
Tsetakin *see* San Ildefonso
Tsetautkenne [BC] *Sekani* (H)
Tse-taut-qenne *see* Tsetautkenne
Tsetautqenne *see* Tsetautkenne
Tse-tdoa *see* Tse
Tsetdoa *see* Tsa
Tse'thani *see* Tsethkhani
Tsethani (PC) Tsetkhani (H)
Tsethaottine [Can] *Nahane* (BE)
Tsetheshkizhni [Clan] *Navajo* (H)
Tsethkhani [Clan] *Navajo* (H)
Tsetistas *see* Cheyenne
Tse-tis-tas [Self-designation] *see* Cheyenne
Tse'tlani *see* Tsetlani

Tsetlani [Clan] *Navajo* (H)
Tse'tsaa *see* Tsetsaa
Tsetsaa [Gens] *Koskimo* (H)
Tsetsa'kin *see* San Felipe [Keres]
Tsetsakin *see* San Felipe [Keres]
T'set'sa'ut *see* Sekani
Ts'ets'a'ut *see* Tsetsaut
Tsetsaut *see* Sekani
Tsetsaut [AK, AL] *Western Na-hane* (LC)
Tsetsehet *see* Chechehet
Tsetseloa'laqEmae *see* Tsetset-loalakemae
Tsetsetloalakemae [Gens] *Kwaki-utl* (H)
Tsetseu *see* Tsetsaut
Tsetsohk'id *see* Mishongnovi
Tset-so-kit *see* Mishongnovi
Tsetsokit *see* Mishongnovi
Tse Tu Kinne *see* San Ildefonso
Tsetukinne *see* San Ildefonso
Ts'e'uitx *see* Tseokuimik
Tseuitx *see* Tseokuimik
Tsexiatene *see* Kaltsergheatunne
Tse'yanaco'ni *see* Tseyenathoni
Tseyanaconi *see* Tseyenathoni
Tse'yanato'ni *see* Tseyenathoni
Tseyanatoni *see* Tseyenathoni
Tseyenathoni [Clan] *Navajo* (H)
Tse'yikehe *see* Tseyikehe
Tseyikehe [Clan] *Navajo* (H)
Tse'yike-hedine *see* Tseyikehe
Tseyikehedine *see* Tseyikehe
Tsezhinkini [Clan] *Navajo* (H)
Tsezhinthiai [Clan] *Navajo* (H)
Tse-zi-a-tene *see* Kaltserghea-tunne
Tse'zindiai *see* Tsezhinthiai
Tsezindiai *see* Tsezhinthiai
Tshaahui *see* Chayahuita
Tsheheilis *see* Chehalis
Tshe-tsi-uetin-euerno *see* Mon-tagnais-Naskapi
Tshetsiuetineuerno *see* Montag-nais-Naskapi
Tshi-a-uip-a *see* Isleta
Tshiauipa *see* Isleta
Tshikchamen *see* Chickahominy
Tshilkotin *see* Chilocotin
Tshingit *see* Tlingit
Tshinkitani *see* Tlingit
Tshinuk *see* Chinook
Tshi-quit-e *see* Pecos
tshiquite *see* Pecos
Tshirege [Peublo] [NM] *Tewa* (H)
Tshishe *see* Apache
Tshithwyook *see* Chilliwack
Tshotinondowaga *see* Seneca
Ts-hot-ti-non-do-wa-ga *see* Seneca
Tshugazzi *see* Chugachigmut
Tshu-Kutshi *see* Tsitoklinotin

Tshukutshi *see* Tsitoklinotin
Tshya-ui-pa *see* Isleta
Tshyauipa *see* Isleta
Tsia *see* Sia
tsiaakwe *see* Sia
ts'i'a'kwe *see* Sia
Tsiama [Pueblo] [NM] (H)
Tsieu Wanun *see* Tsishusindt-sakdhe
tsiguhu matu *Owens Valley Paiute* (Hdbk11)
Tsihacin *see* Kdhun
Tsihaili-Selish *see* Chehalis
Tsihailish *see* Chehalis
Tsihalis *see* Chehalis
Tsi-hano *see* Tsina
Tsihano *see* Tsina
Tsi-he-lis *see* Chehalis
Tsihelis *see* Chehalis
Tsi-ka-ce *see* Chickasaw
Tsikace *see* Chickasaw
Tsikama'gi *see* Chickamauga
Tsikanni *see* Sekani
Tsi-klum *see* Tsehump
Tsiklum *see* Tsehump
tsikri *see* Skidi Pawnee
Tsi-ksu *see* Chickasaw
Tsiksu *see* Chickasaw
Tsik-u-su *see* Chickasaw
Tsikusu *see* Chickasaw
Tsilgopaya *see* Tolkopaya
Tsilgopeya *see* Tulkepaia
Tsilhtaden *see* Tsiltaden
Tsi-l-ina-inde *see* Tsihlinainde
Tsilinainde *see* Tsihlinainde
Tsilinainde [NM] *Mescalero Apache* (H)
Tsilkotin *see* Chilcotin
T'silkotinneh *see* Chilocotin
Tsilkotinneh *see* Chilcotin
Tsill-ane *see* Tsillane
Tsillane *Okinagan* (H)
Tsilla-ta-ut'tine *see* Etcheri-diegottine
Tsillatauttine *see* Etcheridiegot-tine
Tsilla-ta-ut-tinne *see* Etcheri-diegottine
Tsillatauttinne *see* Etcheridiegot-tine
Tsillawadoot *see* Etcheridiegottine
Tsillawawdoot *see* Etcheridiegot-tine
Tsillaw-awdut-dinne *see* Etcheri-diegottine
Tsillawawdutdinne *see* Etcheri-diegottine
Tsillawdawhoot-dinneh *see* Etcheridiegottine
Tsillawdawhoot Tinneh *see* Etcheridiegottine
Tsiltaden [AZ] *Chirichaua Apache* (H)

Tsiltarden *see* Tsiltaden
Tsimane *see* Chimane
Tsimchian *see* Tsimshian
T'simpheean *see* Tsimshian
Tsimpheean *see* Tsimshian
Tsimpsean *see* Tsimshian
T'simpshean *see* Tsimshian
Tsimpshean *see* Tsimshian
Tsimpsi-an *see* Tsimshian
Tsimpsian *see* Tsimshian
Tsimsean *see* Tsimshian
Tsimseyan *see* Tshimshian
Tsimsheean *see* Tsimshian
Tsimshian [Can, AK] (LC)
T'sim-si-an *see* Tsimshian
Tsimsian *see* Tsimshian
Tsin [Clan] *Cochiti* (H)
Tsina [Clan] *Acoma* (H)
Tsinadzi'ni *see* Tsinazhini
Tsina-hano *see* Tsina
Tsinahano *see* Tsina
Tsi'na-hanoch *see* Tsina
Tsinahanoch *see* Tsina
Tsina-hanoqch *see* Tsina
Tsinahanoqch *see* Tsina
Tsinajini *see* Tsinazhini
Tsinazhini [Clan] *Navajo* (H)
Tsineuhiu [CA] (BE)
Tsinha [Clan] [NM] *Santa Ana* (H)
Tsinha-hano *see* Tsina
Tsinhahano *see* Tsina
Tsi'n-hano *see* Tsina
Tsinhano *see* Tsina
Tsin-ik-sis-tso-yiks *see* Tsinksistsoyiks
Tsiniktsistsoyiks [MN] (BE)
Tsinsakathni [Clan] *Navajo* (H)
T'sinuk *see* Chinook
Tsinuk [Self-designation] *see* Chinook
Tsipiakwe (H)
Tsipu *see* Chippewa
Tsiqua'gis stastaai *see* Chawagis-stustae
tsirakawa *see* Chiricahua Apache
Tsi-se *see* Mescalero Apache
Tsise *see* Mescalero Apache
Tsishaat (Contri, v.9, no.3, pp.157–58)
Tsishu [Subgens] *Osage* (H)
Tsishusindtsakdhe [Gens] *Osage* (H)
Tsishuutsepedhungpa *Osage* (H)
Tsishuwashtake [Clan] *Osage* (H)
Tsi-stiks *see* Tsistiks
Tsistiks [Society] *Siksika* (H)
Tsistlatho band *see* Nakotin
Tsitka-ni *see* Sekani
Tsitkani *see* Sekani
Tsit-o-kliln-otin *see* Tsitoklinotin
Tsitoklinotin [BC, AK] *Han-kutchin* (H)

Tsits [Clan] [*San Felipe (Keres)*] (H)
Tsi'ts-hano *see* Tsits
Tsits-hano *see* Tsits
Tsitshano *see* Tsits
Tsits-hanoqch *see* Tsits
Tsitshanoqch *see* Tsits
Tsits-hanuch *see* Tsits
Tsitshanuch *see* Tsits
Tsitsimelekala [Gens] *Kwakiutl* (H)
Tsitsime'lEqala *see* Tsitsimelekala
Tsi-tska do hpa-ka *see* Seechkaberuhpaka
Tsitskadohpaka *see* Seechkaberuhpaka
Tsitsumevi *see* Sichomovi
Tsi-tsumo-vi *see* Sichomovi
Tsitsumovi *see* Sichomovi
Tsitumovi *see* Sichomovi
tsi-yame *see* Sia
tsiyame *see* Sia
Tsji'shekwe *see* Tonto Apache
Tskaisfshihlni *see* Middle Spokan
Tskaus *see* Sakahl
Tskiri rah'ru *see* Skidirahru
Tskirirahru *see* Skidirahru
tskowa'xtsenux (BE) *see also* Sinkiuse-Columbia (LC)
Tskowa'xtsenux [WA] (Oregon)
Tsnagmyut *see* Chnagmiut
Tsniuk *see* Chinook
Tsoes-tsieg-Kuttchin *see* Trotsikkutchin
Tsoestsiegkuttchin *see* Trotsikkutchin
tsogwiyuyugi *Western Shoshone* (Hdbk11)
Tsohaya *see* Yuchi
Tsohke *see* Sooke
Tsoi-gah *see* Nez Perce
Tsokolaikiinma [ID] *Nez Perce* (BE)
Tso'kwob *see* Wenatchi
Tsokwob *see* Wenatchi
Tsokwobe *see* Wenatchi
Tso'kwot *see* Wenatchi
Tsokwot *see* Wenatchi
Tsola *see* Paneroa
Tsoloa *see* Paneroa
Tsoloti *Chorote* (O)
Tsomass *see* Tsomosath
Tsomontatez *see* Tionontati
Tso'mos'ath *see* Tsomosath
Tsomosath [Sept] *Nootka* (H)
Tso'nai *see* Tsonai
Tsonai [BC] (BE)
Tsonantonon *see* Seneca
Tsonassan *see* Sewathen
Tsoneca *see* Tzoneca
Tsong *see* Songish
Tsonik *see* Tehuelche

Tson-krone *see* Thekkane
Tsonkrone *see* Thekkane
Tsonnontatex *see* Tiontati
Tsonnonthuans *see* Seneca
Tsonnontouans *see* Seneca
Tsonnontouen *see* Seneca
Tsonnontouens *see* Seneca
Tsononthouan *see* Seneca
Tsonontooas *see* Seneca
Tsonontouan *see* Seneca
Tsonontowan *see* Seneca
Tsonothouan *see* Seneca
Tsoo-ah-gah-rah *see* Nez Perce
Tsooahgahrah *see* Nez Perce
Tsooeawatah *see* Holkoma
Tsootine *see* Sarsi
Tso-Ottine *see* Sarsi
Tsösö ödö tuviwarai *Northern Paiute* (Hdbk11)
Tso-ta *see* Tesuque
Tsota *see* Tesuque
Tso-ta'ee *see* Tsotaee
Tsotaee [Clan] (H)
Ts'o'ts'ena *see* Tsotsena
Tsotsena [Gens] *Kwakiutl* (H)
Ts'otsqe'n *see* Tsimshian
Tsotsqen *see* Tsimshian
Tsouonthousaa *see* Seneca
Tsou-wa-ra-its *see* Tsuwarait
Tsouwaraits *see* Tsuwarait
Tsowassan *see* Sewathen
Tsoyaha *see* Yuchi
Tsoya'ha [Self-designation] *see* Yuchi
Tssetduka [Clan] *Osage* (H)
Tsugwa'lethal [WA] *Puyallup* (BE)
Tsuharukats *see* Nez Perce
Tsulakki *see* Cherokee
Tsulalgi [Clan] *Creek* (H)
Tsulam Sewi *see* Tsulamsewi
Tsulamsewi [CA] *Maidu* (H)
Tsu-lu-la *see* Chilula
Tsulu-la *see* Chilula
Tsulula *see* Chilula
Tsu'qos *see* Sarsi
Tsuqos *see* Sarsi
Ts'u-qus-li-qwut-me'tunne *see* Dakubetede
Tsuqusliqwutmetunne *see* Dakubetede
Tsushki (PC) *see also* Tsu'shki (H)
Tsushki [Clan] *Laguna* (H)
Tsu'shki [Clan] [NM] *Keres* (H)
Tsushki-hano *see* Shrutsuna
Tsushki-hanoch *see* Shrutsuna
Tsussie *see* Yekolaos
Tsutpeli [Self-designation] *see* Nez Perce
Tsuva *see* Suya
Tsuva *see* Aipatse
Tsuwa'diabsh [WA] *Nisqualli* (BE)

Tsuwarit [NV] *Paiute* (H)
Tsyenundady *see* Wyandot
Tte *see* Tovok
Tthinatlitunne [OR] *Mishikhwutmetunne* (H)
Tthowache [OR] *Takelma* (H)
T'tran-jik-kutch-in *see* Tangeratsa
Ttranjikkutchin *see* Tangeratsa
Ttse-ottine *see* Tseottine
Ttseottine *see* Tseottine
Ttynai *see* Athapascan
Ttynai-chotana *see* Athapascan
Ttynaichotana *see* Athapascan
Ttynnai *see* Athapascan
Tu [Clan] [NM] *Taos* (H)
Tuacana *see* Tawakoni
Tu-a'd-hu *see* Twana
Tu-ad-hu *see* Twana
Tuadhu *see* Twana
Tuak [*Inuit (Quebec)*] (Hdbk5)
Tuakay [Clan] [AZ] *Apache* (H)
Tualati *see* Atfalati
Tualatim *see* Atfalati
Tualatin *see* Atfalati
Tuality *see* Atfalati
Tuama [BO] *Araona* (O)
Tuamca *see* Juanca
Tuancas [MX, TX] *Coahuiltecan* (BE)
Tu-an-hu *see* Twana
Tuanhu *see* Twana
Tu-a-nooch *see* Twana
Tuanooch *see* Twana
Tu-a-noock *see* Twana
Tuanoock *see* Twana
Tuas *see* Taos
Tuata *see* Taos
Tu-a-wi-hol *see* Santo Domingo
Tuawihol *see* Santo Domingo
Tubaduka *see* Tuba Duka
Tuba Duka [UT] (Anthro, v.8, no.3)
tubahinagatu [Clan] [CA] (Pub, v.11, no.4, p.293)
Tu'-ba-na *see* Tewa
Tubana *see* Tewa
Tubar [Lang] *Sonoran* (Hdbk10)
Tubar [MX] (BE)
Tubarao *see* Aikana
Tubare *see* Tubar
Tu-ba-re *see* Tubar
Tubaris *see* Tubar
Tubatalabul *see* Tubatulabal
Tubatulabal [CA] (LC)
Tubbies *see* Choctaw
Tubessias *see* Yavapai
Tubian *see* Tano
Tubian *see* Tano
Tu-bi-an-wa-pu *see* Tubianwapu
Tubianwapu [NV] *Paviotso* (H)
Tubic wiñwu *see* Tubish
Tu-bic wuñ-wu *see* Tubish

Tubic wuñwu see Tubish
Tubiran see Tano
Tubish [Clan] *Hopi* (H)
Tucan see Hopi
Tucane see Tucara
Tucano see Hopi
Tucanoh see Twana
Tucano Maku see Jupda
Tucara [TX] (H)
Tucarica see Tukuarika
Tucayan see Hopi
Tuchano see Hopi
Tuchapae see Tushepaw
Tuchapak see Tushepaw
Tucheaap see Tesuque
Tuchiamas [Pueblo] (H)
Tuckankanie see Tawakoni
Tuckapa see Attacapa
Tuckapack see Tushepaq
Tuckapaus see Attacapa
Tuckclarwayde [Family] *Tahltan* (H)
Tuckis'a'th see Tushkisath
Tucknapax see Tushepaw
Tucumano see Cacan
Tucuna [Br, PE, Col] (LC)
Tucundiapa see Tukun-Diapa
Tucurrique [CR] *Cabecar* (BE)
Tucurriqui see Tucurrique
Tudamanes see Iroquois
Tudamanes see Seneca
Tude see Athapascan
Tudisishu [AZ] *Apache* (H)
Tudnunirmiut see Tununirmiut
Tudnunirossirmiut see Tununerusirmiut
Tu-ei see Isleta
Tuei see Isleta
Tuelche see Tehuelche
Tuelchu see Tehuelche
Tuerto [Pueblo] [NM] *Tano* (H)
Tue'tini'ni see Tuetinini
Tuetinini [TX] *Mescalero Apache* (H)
Tugumlepem *Coahuiltecan* (Hdbk10)
Tuha see Piaroa
Tuhakwilh see Tsimshian
Tu-hi'ts-pi-yet see Tuhitspiyet
Tuhitspiyet *Skidi Pawnee* (H)
Tuhk-pah-huks-taht see Tuhkpahhukstaht
Tuhkpahhukstaht *Skidi Pawnee* (H)
Tu'hlawai see Acoma
Tuhlawai see Acoma
Tu'hlawe see Acoma
Tuhlawe see Acoma
Tuhoa see Jemez
Tuhohi (CA) *see also* Chuxoxi (CA)
Tuhohi [CA] *Buena Vista Yokuts* (BE)

Tu-huc-mach see Tuhukmache
Tuhucmach see Tuhukmache
Tu-hue-ma-ches see Tuhukmache
Tuhukmache [CA] *Yokuts* (H)
Tu-huk-nahs see Tuhukmache
Tuhuknahs see Tuhukmache
Tuhuktukis see Tawakoni
Tuhuktukis see Tohookatokie
Tuhulaka see Tuhu'la-ka
Tuhu'la-ka [CA] *Patwin* (Pub, v.29, no.4)
Tu'hu tane see Clackamas
Tuhutane see Clackamas
Tuhuvtiaomokat see Siksika
Tuhu'vti-omokat see Siksika
Tuhwalati see Atfalati
Tuh-yit-yay see Tajique
Tuhyityay see Tajique
Tuh-yityay [Self-designation] *see* Tajique
Tu-iai see Santo Domingo
Tuiai see Santo Domingo
Tuiban [CA] (H)
Tuihtuihronoon see Miami
Tuim [Clan] [NM] *Tigua* (H)
Tuimama see Tumamar
Tuim-t'ainin see Tuim
Tuinondadecks see Tionontati
Tuinontatek see Tionontati
Tuis-kis-tiks see Tuiskistiks
Tuiskistiks [Society] *Siksika* (H)
Tuiunuk (H) *see also* Tyonok (BE)
Tuiunuk [AK] *Kaniakhotana* (H)
Tujutge see Toba-Maskoy
Tukabahchee [AL] *Muskogee* (BE)
Tukachoha see Piankasaw
Tukadka *Shoshone* (Ye)
Tuka Duka see Tukuduka
Tukaduka see Tukudeka
Tukahun (BE) *see also* Piro [Pueblo] (LC)
Tukahun (H)
Tu-ka-le see Tawakoni
Tukale see Tawakoni
Tukano Maku see Jupda
Tu-ka-nyi see Tawakoni
Tukanyi see Tawakoni
Tuka-rika see Tukuarika
Tukarika see Tukuarika
Tuke'liklikespu [ID] *Nez Perce* (BE)
Tukhe [Clan] *Quapaw* (H)
Tukhenikashika [Gens] *Quapaw* (H)
Tukinobi [Pueblo] [AZ] *Hopi* (H)
Tuk-ko see Takusalgi
Tukko see Takusalgi
Tukkola see Takulli
Tuk-kuth see Tukkuthkutchin
Tukkuth see Tukkuthkutchin
Tukkuth-kutchin see Tukkuthkutchin

Tukkuthkutchin [AK] *Kutchin* (LC)
tukkutikka see Tukudeka
Tukoratum [WA] *Sinkaieth* (BE)
Tuk-pa-han-ya-di see Attacapa
Tukpahanyadi see Attacapa
Tukpame [ID] *Nez Perce* (BE)
Tuk-spu'sh see John Day Indians
Tukspush (PC) *see also* John Day Indians (H)
Tukspush [OR] *Tenino* (BE)
Tukspu'sh-lema see John Day Indians
Tukspushlema see John Day Indians
Tukuaduka see Tukuarika
Tukuaduka see Tukuarika
Tu'kuari'ka see Tukuarika
Tukuarika (Hdbk11) *see also* Tukudeka (Hdbk11)
Tukuarika [ID, WY] *Western Shoshone* (LC)
Tukudeka [ID, MT, WY] *Northern Shoshone* (Hdbk11)
Tukudh see Tukkuthkutchin
Tukudh-kutchin see Tukkuthkutchin
Tukuku see Irapa
Tukumafed see Tukunafed
Tukum-Diapa see Tukun-Diapa
Tukuna see Tucuna
Tukunafed [Br] *Kawahib* (O)
Tukun-Diapa [Lang] *Catuquina* (O)
Tukuth-Kutchin see Tukkuthkutchin
Tukwet-babsh [WA] *Snohomish* (Oregon)
Tukwetlbabsh [WA] *Snohomish* (BE)
Tu'kwil-ma-k'i see Kuitsch
Tukwilmaki see Kuitsh
Tula see Tulareños
Tulalip [WA] (LC)
Tulalmina see Tulamni
Tulamni [CA] *Yokuts* (CA)
Tulara see Tulareños
Tulare Lake Indians see Tulareños
Tulareños [CA] (H)
Tulare River Indians see Tulareños
Tulares [CA] *Olamentke* (H)
Tularesin see Tulareños
Tulawei see Acoma
Tul'bush see Mattole
Tulbush see Mattole
Tule (O) *see also* San Blas [Cuna] (LC)
Tule [Pan] *Cuna* (BE)
Tuleamme see Lake Miwok
Tule-Kaweah [CA] *Yokuts* (BE)
Tule-Kaweah [Lang] [CA] *Foothill Yokutsan* (CA-8)

Tule Lake [OR, CA] *Modoc* (BE)
Tulelakle *see* Tule'lakle
Tule'lakle [WA] *Puyallup* (BE)
Tule River Indians *see* Tulareños
Tulkepa *see* Yavapai
Tulkepaia (H) *see also* Tolkepaya (BE)
Tulkepaia [AZ] *Yuman* (H)
Tulkepaia venuna tchehwale *see* Tulkepaia
T'ul-li-muks-me tunne *see* Tillamook
Tullimuksmetunne *see* Tillamook
Tu-lo-mos *see* Tulomos
Tulomos [CA] *Costanoan* (H)
Tulpkweyu [Gens] *Tonkawa* (H)
Tulsa [OK] *Coosa* (BE)
Tulse'tcakl (BE) *see also* Sahehwamish (BE)
Tulse'tcakl [WA] (BE)
Tultschina [AK] *Kaniakhotana* (H)
Tulugakmiut [AK] *Interior North Alaska Eskimos* (Hdbk5)
Tulumonos *see* Tulomos
Tuluraios *see* Tularenos
Tulwutmetunne [OR] *Mishikhwutmetunne* (H)
Tulykapaya *see* Tulkepaia
Tumaka *see* Yuki
Tu'ma-ka *see* Yuki
Tu-ma-leh-nia *see* Tumalenia
Tumalehnia *see* Tumalenia
Tumalenia [CA] *Moquelumnan* (H)
Tumamar [TX] *Coahuiltecan* (BE)
Tumangamalum *see* Gabrielino
Tumangamal-um *see* Gabrielino
Tumangangakh [Lang] *see* Gabrielino
Tumapacam *Coahuiltecan* (Hdbk10)
Tumayas *see* Yuma
tumbica *see* tu'mbica
tu'mbica *Panamint* (Hdbk11)
Tumecha *see* Tunicha
Tumeh *see* Athapascan
Tumewand *see* Mahican
Tumica *see* Timucua
Tumicha *see* Tunicha
Tu-mi-dok *see* Tumidok
Tumidok [CA] *Miwok* (H)
Tumkoaakya [BC] *Bella Coola* (H)
Tum-meli *see* Tummeli
Tummeli [CA] *Maidu* (H)
Tummewata *see* Clowwewalla
Tumna (H) *see also* Dumna (CA)
Tumna [CA] *Yokuts* (H)
Tumpanogots (BE) *see also* Timpaiavats (H)
tumpa'nogots *see* Tumpanogots

Tumpanogots [UT] (BE)
Tumpanuwach *see* Tumpanogots
Tumpataguo [TX] (H)
Tumpiros *see* Tompiro
Tumpisa *see* Panamint
Tumpisagavatsits [CA] *Chemehuevi* (BE)
Tumpzi [TX] *Coahuiltecan* (BE)
Tumrah *see* Tomraxo
Tumwater *see* Clowwewalla
Tunahe [MN] *Kutenai* (BE)
Tu'na-ji-i *see* Santa Ana [NM]
Tunajii *see* Santa Ana [NM]
Tunanpi [Clan] *Oto* (H)
Tu-nan-p'in *see* Tunanpin
Tunanpin [Clan] *Iowa* (H)
Tunanpin [Gens] *Missouri* (H)
Tunanpin [Gens] *Oto* (H)
Tunavwa *see* Sia
Tunawak *see* Tsia
Tunaxa [MN] *Kutenai* (BE)
Tuna'xe *see* Tunaxa
Tunaxe *see* Tunaxa
Tunca *see* Tunica
Tuncksis *see* Tunxis
Tundastusa [Pueblo] [AZ] (H)
Tunebo [Col, VE] (LC)
Tunebo [Lang] *see* Chibchan
Tunehepu [ID] *Nez Perce* (BE)
Tunevo *see* Tunebo
Tung [Clan] [AZ] *Tewa* (H)
Tungass *see* Tongass
Tungass-kon *see* Tongass
Tung-ge *see* Tungge
Tungge [Pueblo] [NM] *Tano* (H)
Tung-ke *see* Tungge
Tungke *see* Tungge
Tungla [NI, Hon] [*Mosquito-Sumo*] (BE)
Tungrass *see* Tongass
Tung-ul-ung-si *see* Tungulungsi
Tungulungsi [Subclan] *Delaware* (H)
Tungyaa [Pueblo] [NM] *Tewa* (H)
Tunica [MS, AK, LA] (LC)
Tunican [Lang] [LA] (BE)
Tunicha [NM] *Navajo* (H)
Tu-ni-cka an-ya-di *see* Tunica
Tunicka anyadi *see* Tunica
Tu-ni-cka han-ya *see* Tunica
Tunicka hanya *see* Tunica
Tunis *see* Zuni
Tunki [NI] *Panamaka* (BE)
Tunlepem *see* Tugumlepem
Tunne *see* Athapascan
Tunni [Clan] *Chickasaw* (H)
Tuno [BO] *Araona* (O)
Tunque *see* Tungge
tun save *see* Jicarilla Apache
tunsave *see* Jicarilla Apache
Tunsca *see* Tunica
Tuntu suxtana *see* Aglemiut

tunuamiut *see* East Greenlanders
Tunuka [Moiety] [CA] *Miwok* (Pub, v.11, no.5, p.292)
Tunuli *see* Txicaos
tunumiut *see* East Greenlanders
Tununerusirmiut [Can] *Central Eskimos* (BE)
Tununirmiut [AK] *Iglulik* (Hdbk5)
Tununirmiut [Can] *Central Eskimos* (BE)
Tununirusiriut (H) *see also* Tununerusirmiut (BE)
Tununirusirmiut [AK] *Tununirmiut* (Hdbk5)
Tunxis [CN] *Wappinger* (LC)
Tuohayi *see* Tuhohi
Tu-ol-um-ne *see* Tuolumne
Tuolumne [CA] *Miwok* (H)
Tuopa *see* Taos
Tupanagos *see* Timpaiavats
Tu-paranovits *see* Moanunts
tuparanovits *see* Moanunts
Tupari [Br] (LC)
Tupe *see* Ditsakana
Tupi [Br, Par] (LC)
Tupi-Kawahib *see* Kawahib
Tupi Moderno *see* Nheengatu
Tupinaki [Br] (O)
Tupinamba [Br] (LC)
Tup-kug-ameuts *see* Tapkachmiut
Tupkugameuts *see* Tapkachmiut
Tups [TX] (BE)
tupusiwitu *see* tupu-si witu
tu-pu-si wi-tu [CA] *Owens Valley Paiute* (Hdbk11)
Tu-pus-ti-kut-teh *see* Tupustikutteh
Tupustikutteh [NV] *Paviotso* (H)
Tupy *see* Tupi
Tuqteumi *see* Atuami
T'u-qwe-t'a'tunne *see* Tututni
Tuqwetatunne *see* Tutuni
Turatu [Clan] [NM] *Taos* (H)
Tura'tu tai'na *see* Turatu
Turatutaina *see* Turatu
Turcarora *see* Tuscarora
Turealemne *see* Tuolumne
Turimnainai [VE] *Wakuenai* (O)
Turiwa *see* Amanaye
Turiwara [Br] (O)
Turlitan *see* Atfalati
Turn Water *see* Stehtsasamish
Turriarba [CR] *Guatare* (BE)
Turrin [CAm] (BE)
Turtle Mountain [Man] (H)
Turtle Mountain Chippewa *see* Mikinakwadshiwininiwak
Turtle Portage [MI, WI] *Chippewa* (H)
Turtle Tribe *see* Unami

Turucaca (BE) *see also* Boruca
(LC)
Turucaca [Pan, CR] (BE)
Turwillana [Clan] [NM] *Taos* (H)
Turwil'lana tai'na *see* Turwillana
Turwillana taina *see* Turwillana
Tu-sa-be *see* Jicarilla Apache
Tusabe *see* Jicarilla Apache
Tu-sahn *see* Tzlanapah
Tusahn *see* Tzlanapah
Tusan *see* Hopi
Tusanes [MX, TX] *Coahuiltecan*
(BE)
Tusayan *see* Hopi
Tusayan *see* Tzlanapah
Tusayan Moqui *see* Hopi
tuscarara *see* Tuscarora
Tuscararo *see* Tuscarora
Tuscarera *see* Tuscarora
Tuscarooroes *see* Tuscarora
Tuscarora [NY, NC] *Six Nations*
(LC)
tusCarorase *see* Tuscarora
Tuscaroraw *see* Tuscarora
Tuscarore haga *see* Tuscarora
Tuscarorehaga *see* Tuscarora
Tuscaroren *see* Tuscarora
Tuscarories *see* Tuscarora
Tuscaroroes *see* Tuscarora
Tuscarow *see* Tuscarora
Tuscarura *see* Tuscarora
Tuscaruro *see* Tuscarora
Tus-che-pa *see* Tushepaw
Tuschepa *see* Tushepaw
Tuscorara *see* Tuscarora
Tuscorora *see* Tuscarora
Tuscororoes *see* Tuscarora
Tuscoroura *see* Tuscarora
Tuscorure *see* Tuscarora
Tuscouroro *see* Tuscarora
Tu-se-an *see* Hopi
Tusean *see* Hopi
Tusha *see* Rodela
Tushapaw *see* Tushepaw
Tus-he-pah *see* Tushepaw
Tushepaha *see* Tushepaw
Tushepau *see* Tushepaw
Tushepaw (H)
Tushepaw Flatheads *see*
Tushepaw
Tushinahua [Br] (O)
Tushinawa *see* Tushinahua
Tushipa *see* Tushepaw
Tushkisath [Sept] *Nootka* (H)
Tushshepah *see* Tushepaw
Tushtun [AZ] *San Carlos Apache*
(H)
Tushyityay *see* Tajique
Tush-yit-yay [Self-designation]
see Tajique
Tusk *see* Tuscarora
T'us-kai-y'en *see* Tuscarora
Tuskaiyen *see* Tuscarora

T'us-ka-o-wa *see* Tuscarora
Tuskaowa *see* Tuscarora
T'us-ka-o-wan *see* Tuscarora
Tuskaowan *see* Tuscarora
Tuskararo *see* Tuscarora
Tuskaroes *see* Tuscarora
Tuskarooroe *see* Tuscarora
tuskarora *see* Tuscarora
Tuskarorah *see* Tuscarora
Tuskarore *see* Tuscarora
Tuskarorers *see* Tuscarora
Tuskarorin *see* Tuscarora
Tuskaroro *see* Tuscarora
Tuskawres *see* Tuscarora
Tuskegee [OK, AL] *Creek* (BE)
T'us-ke-o-wa *see* Tuscarora
Tuskeowa *see* Tuscarora
T'us-ke-o-wan *see* Tuscarora
Tuskeowan *see* Tuscarora
Tuskeroode *see* Tuscarora
Tuskeruda *see* Tuscarora
Tuskeruro *see* Tuscarora
Tuski *see* Yuit
Tuskierore *see* Tuscarora
Tuskogee *see* Tuskegee
Tuskoraries *see* Tuscarora
Tuskorore *see* Tuscarora
Tuskroroes *see* Tuscarora
Tuskurora *see* Tuscarora
Tuskwawgomeeg *see* Nipissing
Tu-sla *see* Tzlanapah
Tusla *see* Tzlanapah
Tu-sla-na-pa *see* Tzlanapah
Tuslanapa *see* Tzlanapah
Tu-slan-go *see* Tzlanapah
Tuslango *see* Tzlanapah
Tusolivi [TX] (BE)
Tusonid [TX] *Coahuiltecan* (BE)
Tuspaquin *see* Tispaquin
Tusquarores *see* Tuscarora
Tusqueroro *see* Tuscarora
Tussapa *see* Tushepaw
Tussa-wehe *see* Tussawehe
Tussawehe *Shoshone* (H)
Tustans *see* Tustur
Tustatunkhuushi [OR]
Mishikhwutmetunne (H)
Tus-ta-tun qu-u-ci *see* Tus-
tatunkhuushi
Tustatunquuci *see* Tustatunkhu-
ushi
Tustur (H)
Tusuque *see* Tesuque
Tus-wa *see* Fusualgi
Tuswa *see* Fusualgi
Tusyan *see* Hopi
Tutahaco *Pueblo Indians* (H)
Tutahuco *see* Tutahaco
Tu-taiina *see* Tu
Tutaiina *see* Tu
Tutaliaco *see* Tutahaco
Tutaloes *see* Tutelo
Tutapi *see* Orejon

Tutatamy *see* Tututni
Tutchaco *see* Tutahaco
Tutchenoyika *see* Detsanayuka
Tut-chohn-kut-chin *see*
Tutchone
Tutchohnkutchin *see* Tutchone
Tutchone [AK, BC] (BE)
Tutchone-Kutchin *see* Tutchone
Tut-chone-kutchin *see*
Tutchone
Tutchonekutchin *see* Tutchone
Tutchone-kut'qin *see* Tutchone
Tutchonekutqin *see* Tutchone
Tutchon Kutchin *see* Tutchone
Tutch-un-tah' kutchin *see*
Tutchone
Tutchuntahkutchin *see*
Tutchone
Tutcone-kut'qin *see* Tutchone
Tutconekutqin *see* Tutchone
Tutecoes *see* Tutelo
Tuteeves *see* Tutelo
Tutelas *see* Tutelo
Tutele *see* Tutelo
Tutelo [VA] (LC)
Tutelo Confederacy [Lang]
Monacan (H)
Tuteloes *see* Tutelo
Tuteneiboica [TX] (BE)
Tuthea-uay *see* Acoma
Tutheauay *see* Acoma
Tuthla-huay *see* Acoma
Tuthlahuay *see* Acoma
Tuth-Lanay *see* Acoma
Tuthlanay *see* Acoma
Tuthlauay *Acoma* (H)
Tutie *see* Tutelo
Tutiloes *see* Tutelo
Tutloe *see* Tutelo
Tutoi band *see* Nahaego
Tutoimana *see* Totoimana
Tutoimanah *see* Totoimana
Tutonashikisd [Clan] [AZ] *San
Carlos Apache* (H)
Tutoten *see* Tututni
Tu-tsan-nde *see* Lipan Apache
Tutsannde *see* Lipan Apache
Tut-see-wa *see* Tushepaw
Tutseewa *see* Tushepaw
Tutsetcakl *see* Tutse'tcakl
Tutse'tcakl [WA] *Sahehwamish*
(BE)
Tutsoni *see* Thotsoni
Tutsoshin *Pinal Apache* (H)
Tutsuiba *see* Tesuque
tuts'uiba *see* Tesuque
Tuttelars *see* Tutelo
Tuttelee *see* Tutelo
Tutuhaco *see* Tutahaco
Tutulor *see* Tutelo
Tutunah *see* Tututni
Tututamys *see* Tututni
Tu-tuten *see* Tututni

Tututen *see* Tututni
Tututni [OR] (LC)
Tututunne *see* Tututni
Tututunne *see* Tototin
Tutzone (H) *see also* Thotsoni (H)
Tutzone (H) *see also* Tutzose (H)
Tutzone [AZ] *San Carlos Apache*
  (H)
Tutzose *Pinal Apache* (H)
Tuu *see* Toho
tuvaaluk *see* Tuak
Tuvachi [Clan] *Hopi* (H)
Tuvalim *see* Tubar
tuvaq *see* Tuak
Tuvatci wiñwu *see* Tuvachi
Tu'ven *see* Tewa
Tuven *see* Tano
Tuven *see* Tewa
Tuvinians *see* Soyote
Tuvou [Clan] *Hopi* (H)
Tuvou winwu *see* Tuvou
Tu-vo-u wuñ-wu *see* Tuvou
Tuvou wuñwu *see* Tuvou
Tuvuchi [Clan] *Hopi* (H)
Tu-vu-tci wuñ-wu *see* Tuvachi
Tuvutci wuñwu *see* Tuvachi
Tu-wa *see* Jemez
Tuwa (PC) *see also* Jemez (LC)
Tuwa [Clan] *Hopi* (H)
Tu-wa-hok-a-sha *see* Tuwa-
  hokasha
Tuwahokasha *Skidi Pawnee* (H)
Tuwakariwa *see* Tawakoni
Tuwa-Kukuch [Phratry] *Hopi* (H)
Tuwa-Kukutc *see* Tuwa-Kukuch
Tuwanek [Can] *Seechelt* (BE)
Tuwanhudan *see* Tu-wan'hudan
Tu-wan'hudan [MN] *Assiniboin*
  (BE)
T'uwanxa-ikc *see* Klikitat
Tuwanxaikc *see* Klikitat
Tu-wa nyu-mu *see* Tuwa
Tuwa nyumu *see* Tuwa
Tuwa wiñwu *see* Tuwa
Tu-wa wun-wu *see* Tuwa
Tu-wa wuñwu *see* Tuwa
Tuwa wuñwu *see* Tuwa
tuwéhtuwe *see* Miami
Tuwhakhabsh *see* Tuwhakhabsh
Tuwha'khabsh [WA] *Nisqualli*
  (BE)
Tuwi-ai *see* Santo Domingo
Tuwii *see* Santo Domingo
Tuwirat *see* Taos
tuwita *see* Santo Domingo
tu-wit-ha *see* Santo Domingo
tuwitha *see* Santo Domingo
Tu-wur-ints *see* Tuwurints
Tuwurints [UT, NV] *Gosiute* (H)
Tuxa [BR] (O)
Tuxaxa *see* Tohaha
Tuxinawa *see* Tushinahua
Tuxoxi *see* Chuxoxi

Tuxquet *see* Wichita
Tuyetchiske *see* Dakota
Tuyoneri *see* Toyeri
Tuyuca [Col] (LC)
Tuyuco *see* Tuyuca
Tuyuka *see* Tuyuca
Tuyuneri *see* Toyeri
Tuyuryarmiut [AK] *Eskimos*
  (Hdbk5)
tuyuyaymiut *see* Tuyuryarmiut
Tuzahe *Pueblo Indians* (H)
Tuzan *see* Hopi
Tuzantec *see* Mocho
Tuzhlani *see* Laguna
Tuzhune *see* Pusune
Tu-zi yam-mos *see* Tuziyammos
tu-zi'-yam-mos *see* Kidutokado
tuziyammos (PC) *see also* Kidu-
  tokado (Hdbk11)
Tuziyammos [OR] *Paviotso* (H)
Twaatwāā *see* Miami
Twadebshab *see* Twa'debshab
Twa'debshab [WA] *Puyallup* (BE)
Twa'ga'ha *see* Ontwaganha
Twagaha *see* Ontwaganha
Twahka [Hon] *Sumo* (O)
Twa'ka *see* Twahka
Twaka *see* Twahka
Twa-ka-nha *see* Chippewa
Twakanha *see* Chippewa
Twakanhahors *see* Missisauga
Twalaties *see* Atfalati
Twalaty *see* Atfalati
Twalites *see* Atfalati
Twallalty *see* Atfalati
Twaltatine *see* Atfalati
Twana [WA] (LC)
Twanhtwanh *see* Miami
Twanh twanh [Self-designation]
  see Miami
Twanoh *see* Twana
Twanug *see* Twana
T'wa-ru-na *see* Oneida
Twaruna *see* Oneida
Twautwāū *see* Miami
Twaxha *see* Twahka
Twechtwey *see* Miami
Tweeghtwee *see* Miami
Twe'tini'nde *see* Tuetinini
Twetininde *see* Tuetinini
Twghtwee *see* Miami
Twichtwee [Lang] *Algonquian*
  (Bull13)
Twichtwich *see* Miami
Twichtwick *see* Miami
Twichtwigh *see* Miami
Twichwiches *see* Miami
Twicktwick *see* Miami
Twicktwig *see* Miami
Twictwee *see* Miami
Twictwict *see* Miami
Twight *see* Miami
Twightee *see* Miami

Twighteey *see* Miami
Twighties *see* Miami
Twightwee *Miami* (BE)
Twightwicks *see* Miami
Twightwies *see* Miami
Twightwighs *see* Miami
Twightwis Roanu *see* Miami
Twigtees *see* Miami
Twigthwees *see* Miami
Twig-Twee *see* Miami
Twigtwee *see* Miami
Twigtwicks *see* Miami
Twigtwies *see* Miami
Twigtwig *see* Miami
Twiktwies *see* Miami
Twiswicks *see* Miami
Twitchwees *see* Miami
Twithuays *see* Miami
Twitwihenon *see* Miami
Twiwi *see* Santo Domingo
Two Cauldrons *see* Oohenonpa
Two Kettle *see* Oohenonpa
Two Kettles [Lang] *Teton* (H)
Two Kettle Sioux *see*
  Oohenonpa
Two Rille Band *see* Oohenonpa
Twowakanie *see* Tawakoni
T'wo'wo *see* Santo Domingo
Twowokana *see* Tawakoni
Twowokauaes *see* Tawakoni
Txakamekra [Br] (O)
Txapakura [Br, BO] (O)
Txicaos [Br] (LC)
Txijkao *see* Txicaos
Txikao *see* Txicaos
Txiripa *see* Avachiripa
txpa *see* Pima
txpa-may *see* Papago
Txukahamae (O)
Txukahamae (O) *see also* Mentuk-
  tire (O)
Txukahami *see* Txukahamae
Txukahami *see* Txukahamae
Txukahemei *see* Txukahamae
Txukarramae *see* Txukahamae
Txukarramai *see* Txukahamae
Txunhua-Djaba (O) *see also*
  Tukun-Diapa (O)
Txunhua-Djaba [Br] (O)
Tyaia [Clan] [NM] *Sia* (H)
Tya-juin-den-a *see* Tyajuindena
Tyajuindena [Pueblo] [NM]
  Jemez (H)
Tya-me *see* Dyami
Tyame *see* Dyami
Tyame hanutsh *see* Dyami
Tyami [Clan] *Pueblo Indians* (H)
Tyami-hano *see* Dyami
Tyamihano *see* Dyami
T'yami-hanoq *see* Dyami
Tyamihanoq *see* Dyami
Tyashk *see* Tyasks
Tyasks [MA] *Wampanoag* (BE)

Tyasoliwa [Pueblo] [NM] *Jemez* (H)
Tye *see* T'ye
T'ye [Clan] *Tesuque* (H)
Tye of Deshute *see* Tyigh
Tygh (H) *see also* Tyigh (BE)
Tygh [CA] *Tenino* (Forg, p.19)
Tyh *see* Tyigh
Ty-ich *see* Tyigh
Tyich *see* Tyigh
Tyick *see* Tyigh
Tyigh [OR] (BE)
Tykothee *see* Tukkuthkutchin
Tykothee-dinneh *see* Takkuth-kutchin
Tykothee-dinneh *see* Tukkuthkutchin
Tykotheedinneh *see* Takkuth-kutchin
Tykotheedinneh *see* Tukkuthkutchin
Tymangoua *see* Timucua
Tyndysiukhtana *see* Aglemiut
Tynondady *see* Wyandot
Tynyro *see* Moro
Tyo'na-wen-de't *see* Tonawanda
Tyonawendet *see* Tonawanda
Tyonek [AK] *Tanaina* (BE)
Tyo-non-ta-te-ka *see* Tionontati
Tyonontateka *see* Tionontati
tyucuko *see* Tesuque
Tyuga [CA] *Pomo* (H)
Tyupi [Clan] [NM] *Sia* (H)
Tyupi-hano *see* Tyupi
Tyu-tso-ku *see* Tesuque
Tyutsoku *see* Tesuque
Tza-e-delkay *see* Tzadelkay
Tzaedelkay [Clan] [AZ] *Apache* (H)
Tzah-dinneh *see* Tsattine
Tzahdinneh *see* Tsattine
Tze-binaste *see* Tzebinaste
Tzebinaste [Clan] [AZ] *San Carlos Apache* (H)
Tze-ches-chinne *see* Tzecheschinne
Tzecheschinne [AZ] *Black Rock Apache* (H)
Tzedoa *see* Tse
Tzej-gla *see* Coyotero Apache
Tzejgla *see* Coyotero Apache
Tzej-in-ne *see* Tzecheschinne
Tzejinne *see* Tzecheschinne
Tzekinne (H)
Tzekinne (H) *see also* Pima (LC)
Tze-kinne *see* Tzekinne
Tzekupama [CA, AZ] (H)
Tzeldal *see* Tzeltal
Tzel-tal *see* Tseltal
Tzeltal [MX] (LC)
Tzeltaloid *Mayan* (BE)
Tze-man Tu-o *see* Tzemantuo
Tzemantuo [Pueblo] (H)

Tzenatay [Pueblo] [NM] *Tano* (H)
Tzendal *see* Tzeltal
Tzental *see* Tzeltal
Tze-ojua *see* Tse
Tzeojua *see* Tse
Tzetseskadn [AZ] *San Carlos Apache* (H)
Tze-tzes-kadn *see* Tzetseskadn
Tzetzeskadn *see* Tzetseskadn
Tzi-a *see* Sia
Tzia *see* Sia
Tziame *see* Sijame
Tzibola *see* Zuni
Tziltadin [AZ] *Pinal Apache* (H)
Tzinachini *see* Tsinazhini
Tzina hanutsh *see* Tsina
Tzinahanutsh *see* Tsina
Tzi-na-ma-a *see* Mohave
Tzinamaa *see* Mohave
Tzintzilchutzikadn [AZ] *San Carlos Apache* (H)
Tzip-ia Kue *see* Tsipiakwe
Tzipiakue *see* Tsipiakwe
Tziquis *see* Tiwa
Tzi-quit-e *see* Pecos
Tziquite *see* Pecos
Tzi-re-ge *see* Tshirege
Tzirege *see* Tshirege
Tziseketzillan [AZ] *San Carlos Apache* (H)
Tzis-eque-tzillan *see* Tziseketzillan
Tzisequetzillan *see* Tziseketzillan
Tzitz hanutch *see* Tsits
Tziwiltzha-e *see* Osage
Tzlanapah [AZ] *San Carlos Apache* (H)
Tzoc *see* Zoque
Tzoes *see* Zoe
Tzolgan [AZ] *San Carlos Apache* (H)
Tzoneca (LC) *see also* Tehuelche (LC)
Tzoneca [SA] (LC)
Tzotzil [MX] (LC)
Tzuluki *see* Cherokee
Tzuni *see* Zuni
Tzuntuhil [Gu] (LC)
Tzuntuhile *see* Tzuntuhil
Tzutujil *see* Tzutuhil

-U-

Uabohy *see* Uaboi
Uaboi [Br] (LC)
Uacambabelte *see* Vilela
U-aha *see* Omaha
Uaha *see* Omaha
Ua-ha-tza-e *see* Uahatzae

Uahatzae [Pueblo] [NM] *Jemez* (H)
Uaica (LC) *see also* Waica (LC)
Uaica (O) *see also* Yanoama (LC)
Uaica [Lang] *Pemong* (UAz, v.28)
Uaicama *see* Pira-Tapuyo
Uaico *see* Orinoco Waica
Uaieue *see* Waiwai
Uaikena *see* Pira-Tapyuo
Uaimare *see* Waimare
Uaimiri *see* Waimari
U-ai Nu-int *see* Uainuit
U-ai-Nu-int *see* Saint George
Uainuint (PC) *see also* Saint George (Hdbk11)
Uainuint [UT] *Paiute* (H)
Uaiquire *see* Wokiare
Uaiuai [Lang] *Cariban* (LC)
Uajana *see* Urukuyana
Uajapi *see* Oyampi
Ualana *see* Picuris
Uala-to-hua *see* Jemez
Ualatohua *see* Jemez
Ualinarmiut *see* Pilingmiut
Ual-to-hua *see* Jemez
Ualtohua *see* Jemez
Uamana *see* Guanano
Uames [LA] (H)
Uamiri *see* Yawaperi
Uamue *see* Atikum
Uanana *see* Guanano
Uanano *see* Guanano
U-an-nu-ince *see* Saint George
Uannuince *see* Saint George
U-ano-intz *see* Saint George
Uanointz *see* Saint George
Uap-i-ge *see* Uapige
Uapige [Pueblo] [NM] *Tano* (H)
Uaradu-ne-e *see* Pauserna
Uaradunee *see* Pauserne
Uarakena *see* Arekena
Uarakena *see* Urukuyana
Uaranno *see* Warrau
Uarao *see* Warrau
Uarau *see* Warrau
Uaraw *see* Warrau
Uarequena *see* Arekena
Uariquena *see* Arekena
Uarow *see* Warrau
Uatadeo [SA] *Caduveo* (O)
Uateoteuo *see* Ua-teo-te-uo
Ua-teo-te-uo [CAm] *Caduveo* (O)
Uaui [BO] *Araona* (O)
Uaura *see* Waura
Uayana *see* Oyana
Uayemas *see* Guayma
Ubakhea [CA] *Pomo* (H)
Ubate *see* Tano
Ubde *see* Jupda
Ubina [PE] *Aymara* (O)
Uca *see* Yuki
Ucachile *see* Timucua

Ucalta *see* Lekwiltok
Ucataquerri *Achagua* (O)
Ucayale (LC) *see also* Cocama (LC)
Ucayale (LC) *see also* Ucayali (O)
Ucayali (O) *see also* Cocama (LC)
Ucayali [PE] (O)
Ucayalino [PE, Br] *Campa* (O)
Uche *see* Yuchi
Uchean [Lang] [CA] *Yuchi* (LC)
Uchean Indians *see* Yuchi
Uchee *see* Yuchi
Uchepowuch *see* Objiwa
Uches *see* Yuchi
Uchesee *see* Lower Creek
Uchi *see* Yuchi
Uchichak *see* Ojeejok
Uchichol *see* Ochechote
Uchi-chol *see* Ochechote
Uchies *see* Yuchi
Uchipwey *see* Chippewa
Uchita [BaC, MX] *Waicuri* (BE)
Uchium [CA] *Olamentke* (H)
Uchucklesit [BC] *Nootka* (BE)
Uchulta *see* Lekwiltok
Uchumi *see* Uru
Ucita *see* Ocita
Ucita *see* Pohoy
Uclenu [VanI, BC] (H)
U-cle-ta *see* Lewiltok
Ucleta *see* Lewiltok
Ucle-tah *see* Ucluelet
Ucletah *see* Ucluelet
Uclete *see* Lekwiltok
Ucluelet [VanI, BC] *Nootka* (BE)
Uclu-let *see* Ucluelet
Uctetah *see* Lekwiltok
Uculta *see* Lekwiltok
Ucu wiñwu *see* Ushu
Ucuwinwu *see* Ushu
U-cu wuñ-wu *see* Ushu
Ucuwuñwu *see* Ushu
Udawak *see* Ottawa
Uda-wak *see* Ottawa
Ude-kumaig *see* Udekumaig
Udekumaig [Clan] *Chippewa* (H)
Udi-kwininiwug *see* Attikirin-iouetch
Udikwininiwug *see* Attikiriniou-etch
Uech-e-neeti *see* Kuhinedi
Uecheneeti *see* Kuhinedi
Ueena-caw *see* Huna
Ueenacaw *see* Huna
U-en-u-wunts *see* Saint George
Uenuwunts *see* Saint George
Uerequema *see* Arekuna
Ufaina *see* Yakuna
Ufaina [Self-designation] *see* Tanimuko
Ugagogmiut [AK] *Aglemiut* (H)
Ugagog-mut *see* Ugagogmiut
Ugagogmut *see* Ugagogmiut

Ugakhpa *see* Quapaw
Ugakpa *see* Quapaw
Ugalachmiuti *see* Ugalakmiut
Ugalachmjuti *see* Ugalakmiut
Ugalachmut *see* Eyak
Ugalachmut *see* Ugalakmiut
Ugalah'mut *Southeastern Innuit* (Contri, v.1, pp.20–21)
Ugalakmiut [AK] *Eskimos* (BE)
Ugalak'mut *see* Ugalakmiut
Ugalakmut *see* Ugalakmiut
Ugalakmute *see* Ugalakmiut
Ugalakmutsi *see* Ugalakmiut
Ugalenschen *see* Ugalakmiut
Ugalense *see* Ugalakmiut
Ugalense *see* Eyak
Ugalenskoi *see* Ugalakmiut
Ugalents *see* Ugalakmiut
Ugalentses *see* Ugalakmiut
Ugalentsi *see* Ugalakmiut
Ugalentzes *see* Ugalakmiut
Ugalenz *see* Ugalakmiut
Ugalenzes *see* Ugalakmiut
Ugalenzi *see* Ugalakmiut
Ugaljachmjuten *see* Ugalakmiut
Ugaljachmutzi *see* Eskimauen
Ugaljachmutzi *see* Ugalakmiut
Ugaljakhmutsi *see* Ugalakmiut
Ugalukmute *see* Ugalakmiut
Ugalyachmutsi *see* Ugalakmiut
Ugalyachmutzi *see* Ugalakmiut
Ugalyackhmutsi *see* Ugalakmiut
Ugaqpa *see* Quapaw
U-ga-qpa-qti *see* Quapaw
Ugaqpaqti *see* Quapaw
Ugaranos *see* Moro
Ugashigmiut [AK] *Aglemiut* (H)
Ugas-hig-mut *see* Ugashigmiut
Ugashigmut *see* Ugashigmiut
Ugaxpa *see* Quapaw
Ugax-paxti *see* Quapaw
Ugaxpaxti *see* Quapaw
Ugjulirmiut [Can] *Eskimos* (H)
Ugluxlatuch *see* Ucluelet
"Ugly-Ones" *see* Opposite Assiniboin
Uguano *see* Aguano
Ugyulingmiut [AK] *Eskimos* (Hdbk5)
Uhitische *see* Apinage
Uiapii [Br] (O)
Uinkaret [AZ] *Paiute* (H)
U-in-ka-rets *see* Uinkaret
Uinta [UT] *Ute* (LC)
Uintah *see* Uinta
Uintahnints *see* Uinta
Uintahnunts *see* Moanunts
uintahnunts *see* Timpanogots
Uintah Valley Indians *see* Uinta
U-in-tats *see* Uinta
Uintats *see* Uinta
Uinta Yuta *see* Uinta
Uint-karit *see* Uinkaret

Uintkarit *see* Uinkaret
Uioto *see* Witoto
Uiquiare *see* Wokiare
Uiquire *see* Wokiare
Uirauasu-Tapuyo *see* Bora
Ujange wakixe *see* Manyika
Ujangewakixe *see* Manyika
Uj-e-jauk *see* Ojeejok
Ujejauk *see* Ojeejok
ujiji *see* pauwu'ii
Ujuiap [TX] (BE)
Ujuiapa *see* Ujuiap
Ukagemiut [AK] *Chnagmiut Eski-mos* (H)
Ukag'emut *see* Ukagemiut
Ukagemut *see* Ukagemiut
U-kah-pu *see* Quapaw
Ukahpu *see* Quapaw
Ukanakane *see* Okinagan
U-ka-na-nakane *see* Okinagan
Ukasa *see* Kansa
Ukasak *see* Kansa
Ukase *see* Kansa
U-ka-she *see* Mandan
Ukashe *see* Mandan
Ukdschulik *see* Ugjulirmiut
Ukdshulik *see* Ugjulirmiut
Uk-hoat-nom (Contri, v.3) *see also* Coast Yuki (BE)
Uk-hoat-nom (H) *see also* Uko-htontilka (H)
Ukhoatnom *see* Uk-hoat-nom
Uk-hoat-nom [CA] (Contri, v.3)
Ukhotno'm *see* Coast Yuki
Ukhotno'm *see* Uk-hoat-nom
Uk'hotnom *see* Ukohtontilka
Ukhotnom *see* Coast Yuki
Ukhotnom *see* Ukohtontilka
Ukivogmiut *Kaviagmiut Eskimos* (H)
Ukivog-mut *see* Ukivogmiut
Ukivok *see* Ukivogmiut
Ukivokgmut *see* Ukivogmiut
Ukkusiksaligmiut [Can] *Central Eskimos* (BE)
Ukla falaya *see* Oklafalaya
Uklafalaya *see* Oklafalaya
uknaqinx *see* Southern Okinagan
Ukohtontilka [CA] *Coast Yuki* (H)
Ukomnom *see* Ukomno'm
Ukomno'm [CA] *Yuki* (BE)
Ukua'yata *see* Ottawa
Ukuayata *see* Ottawa
Uk-um-nom *see* Ukomno'm
Ukumnom *see* Ukomno'm
Ukumnom *see* Yuki
Uk-um-nom [Self-designation] *see* Yuki
Ukusiksaliermiut [Can] *Central Eskimos* (H)
Ukusiksalik *see* Ukusiksalirmiut
Ukusiksalingmiut *see* Ukusik-salirmiut

Ukusiksillik *see* Ukusiksalirmiut
ukwnaqin *see* Okinagan
Ulastekwi *see* Malecite
Ullulata *see* Olulato
Ulmeca *see* Olmeco
Ulna [NI] (O)
Ulnobah *see* Beothuk
Ulno mequaegit *see* Beothuk
Ulnomequaegit *see* Beothuk
Ulseah *see* Alsa
Ultschna *see* Kulchana
Ultsehaga *see* Eskimos
Ultsehna *see* Eskimos
Ultzchna *see* Kulchana
Ulua (LC) *see also* Ulva (LC)
Ulua [NI] (BE)
Uluan [Lang] [NI] (BE)
Uluan Indians *see* Ulua
Uluca *see* Guilitoy
Ulukagmut *see* Ulukakhotana
Ulu'kakhotan'a *see*
  Ulukakhotana
Ulu-kakho-tan-a *see*
  Ulukakhotana
Ulukakhotana [AK]
  Kaiyuhkhotana (H)
Ulukuk *see* Ulukakhotana
Ululato *see* Olulato
Ulva [NI, Hon] *Sumo* (LC)
Ulwa *see* Ulva
Umah *see* Quecha
U-ma-ha *see* Omaha
Umaha *see* Omaha
Umalayapem *Coahuiltecan*
  (Hdbk10)
Umanak *Greenland Eskimos* (BE)
U-man-han *see* Omaha
Umanhan *see* Omaha
Umano *see* Jumano
Umashgohak *see* Creek
Umatalla *see* Umatilla
Umatallow *see* Umatilla
Umatila *see* Umatilla
Umatilla [OR] (LC)
Umaua (O) *see also* Omagua (O)
Umaua [Lang] *Carijona* (UAz,
  v.28)
Umawa *see* Carijona
Umbaqua *see* Umpqua
Umbiqua *see* Umpqua
Umbra *see* Anserma
Umcompahagre *see* Uncompaah-
  gre
Umeas *see* Quechan
Umgua *see* Umpqua
Umi'k *see* Ahmik
Umik *see* Ahmik
Umkwa *see* Umpqua
Umotima *see* Umotina
Umotina [BO, Br] *Bororo* (LC)
Umpkwa *see* Umpqua
Umpqua (H) *see also* Kuitsh (LC)
Umpqua [OR] (LC)

Umpquah *see* Umpqua
Umpqua Irins *see* Umpqua
Umpwua *see* Kuitsh
Umqua *see* Umpqua
Umque *see* Umpqua
Um-too-leaux *see* Humptulips
Umtooleaux *see* Humptulips
Umuamasa [Col] *Macuna* (O)
U'muchich-no'm *see* Round
  Valley Yokuts
Umuchichnom *see* Round Valley
  Yuki
Umudjek *see* Eiwhuelit
Umurano *see* Omurano
Umutina *see* Umotina
Unagounga *see* Abnaki
Unakatana *see* Unakhotana
Unakatana Yunakakhotana *see*
  Unakhotana
Un'a-kho-tana *see* Unakhotana
Un'akhotana *see* Unakhotana
Unakho-tana *see* Unakhotana
Unakhotana [AK] *Tinne* (H)
Unalachtgo *see* Unalachtigo
Unalachtigo [NJ] *Delaware* (BE)
Unalachtin *see* Unalachtigo
Unalakleet *Bering Strait Eskimos*
  (Hdbk5)
Unalakligemiut [AK] *Unaligmiut
  Eskimos* (H)
Unalaklig'emut *see* Unalaklige-
  mut
Unalaschkaer *see* Unalaska
Unalashkan *see* Unalaska
Unalaska [Lang] [AK] *Aleuts* (BE)
Unaleet *see* Unaligmiut
Unaligmiut [AK] *Eskimos* (BE)
Unalig'mut *see* Unaligmiut
Unaligmut *see* Unaligmiut
Unaligmutes *see* Unaligmiut
Unaliq [Lang] *Central Alaskan
  Yupik* (Hdbk5)
Unaliq Indians [AK] (Hdbk5)
Unaliskan *see* Unalaska
Unaluk *see* Unaliq
Unami *Delaware* (BE)
Unamines *see* Unami
Unamini *see* Unami
Unangan *see* Aleuts
Unangan *see* Eskimauan
Unatagua *see* Anadarko
Unataguous *see* Anadarko
Unataquas *see* Anadarko
Unavamiut *Labrador Eskimos*
  (BE)
Uncachogue *see* Poosepatuck
Uncas Indians *see* Mohegan
Uncaway *see* Uncowa
Unchagogs *see* Passamaquoddy
Unchechauge *see* Passamaquoddy
Unchechauge *see* Poosepatuck
Unchechauke *see* Passmaquoddy
Unckachohok *see* Poosepatuck

Unckeway *see* Uncowa
Uncoes *see* Wasco
Uncompahgre (H) *see also* Tabe-
  guache (LC)
Uncompahgre [CO] *Ute* (Hdbk11)
Uncompahgre Ute *see* Uncom-
  pahgre
Unconino [PE] *Campa* (O)
Uncowa [CN] (H)
Uncoway *see* Uncowa
Unc-pah-te *see* Hunkpatina
Uncpahte *see* Hunkpatina
Unc Papa *see* Hunkpapa
Uncpapa *see* Hunkpapa
Uncpappa *see* Hunkpapa
Uncpatina *see* Hunkpapa
Undatomatendi *see* Potawatomi
Undlskadjinsgitunai *see* Undl-
  skadjins-gitunai
Undl-skadjins-gitunai [BC] *Gi-
  tuns* (H)
Unechtgo *see* Nanticoke
Unedagoes *see* Onondago
Unegkurmiut *Pacific Eskimos*
  (Hdbk5)
ungava [Can] *Inuit Quebec*
  (Hdbk5)
Ungava [Can] [*Montagnais-
  Naskapi*] (BE)
Ungava Indians (H) *see also*
  Naskapi (LC)
Ungavamiut (H) *see also* Tahag-
  miut (H)
ungavamiut [Can] *Inuit Quebec*
  (Hdbk5)
Ungiayo-rono *see* Seminole
Ungiayorono *see* Seminole
Uniades *see* Oneida
Unikwa *see* Umpqua
Unimibigog *see* Alimigegouek
United Bands (H)
Uniutaka *see* Oneida
Univerrenay *Achagua* (O)
Un-ka-gar-its *see* Unkagarits
Unkagarits [UT, NV] *Gosiute* (H)
Unka-kanig-its *see* Kaibab
Unkakanigits *see* Kaibab
Unkakanigut *Paiute* (H)
Un-ka-ka-ni-guts *see* Un-
  kakaniguts
Un-ka-ka-ni-guts *see* Kaibab
Un-ka-pa *see* Unkapanukuint
Unkapa *see* Unkapanukuint
Unkapanukuint [UT] *Paiute* (H)
Unka'pa-Nu-kuints *see* Unka-
  panukuint
Un-ka-pa-Nu-kuints *see* Cedar
Unkar kauagato-Ta-Nouts *see*
  Unkakanigut
Unkarkauagatstanouts *see* Un-
  kakanigut
Unka-toma *see* Unkapanukuint
Unkatoma *see* Unkapanukuint

Unkce-yuta *see* Unkcheyuta
Unkcheyuta *Miniconjou* (H)
Unkechage *see* Poosepatuck
Unkepatine *see* Hunkpatina
Unkoah *see* Uncowa
Unkowa *see* Uncowa
Unkpapa *see* Hunkpapa
Unkpapa Dakota *see* Hunkpapa
Unktce-yuta *see* Unkcheyeuta
Unktceyuta *see* Unkcheyuta
Unktoka [WI] (H)
Unkwa *see* Uncowa
Unojita [TX] *Coahuiltecan* (BE)
Unpeghakhanye [Subclan] *Iowa* (H)
Unpeghathrecheyine [Subclan] *Iowa* (H)
Unpeghayine [Subclan] *Iowa* (H)
Unpuncliegut *Coahuiltecan* (Hdbk10)
Unquachack *see* Poosepatuck
Unquachog (Hdbk15) *see also* Poosepatuck (Hdbk15)
Unquachog [Lang] *Eastern Algonquian* (Hdbk15)
Unquechauge *see* Passamaquoddy
Unquehiett [PA] *Susquehanna* (BE)
Unshagogo *see* Passamaquoddy
Unugun *see* Eskimauan
U-nung'un *see* Aleuts
Unung'un [Self-designation] *see* Aleuts
Un-wu-si *see* Angwusi
Unwusi *see* Angwusi
Unxus *see* Tunxis
Uomo *see* Pakaanova
Upahuiguara *see* Ipajuiguara
Upan [Clan] *Kansa* (H)
Upanavadeni [Br] *Dani* (O)
Upanguayma [MX] *Seri* (BE)
Upaseppta [MX] *Coahuiltecan* (Hdbk10)
Upatsesatuch *see* Opitchesaht
Upernavik *West Greenlandic* (Hdbk5)
Upernivik *Greenland Eskimos* (BE)
Upe-shi-pow *see* Upeshipow
Upeshipow [Can] (H)
Upkhan [Clan] *Osage* (H)
Uplanders *see* Plaikni
Upland Guarijio [Lang] [MX] *Guarijio* (Hdbk10)
Upland Indians *see* Mohegan
Upland Yuman [Lang] *Yuman* (Hdbk10)
Up-pa *see* Hupa
Uppa *see* Hupa
Upper Brule (H) *see also* Kheyatawichasha (H)
Upper Brule *Brule* (BE)

Upper Chehalis *see* Kwaiailk
Upper Cheyenne *see* Northern Cheyenne
Upper Chihalis *see* Kwaiailk
Upper Chinook [OR] *Chinook* (H)
Upper Coquille *see* Mishikhwutmetunne
Upper Cowlitz [WA] *Cowlitz* (H)
Upper Cree *see* Sakawithiniwuk
Upper Creek [AL] *Creek* (H)
Upper Dakotas *see* Santee
Upper De Chutes *see* Tyigh
Upper Dhegiha [Lang] *Siouan* (H)
Upper Fraser [BC] *Ntlakyapamuk* (BE)
Upper Gens du fou *see* Trotsikkutchin
Upper Inlet [AL] *Tanaina* (BE)
Upper Iroquois *see* Iroquois Superieurs
Upper Kalispel [ID, MN] *Kalispel* (BE)
Upper Karok [CA] *Karok* (LC)
Upper Killamutes *see* Tillamook
Upper Klamath *see* Karok
Upper Kootanie *see* Upper Kutenai
Upper Kootenai *see* Upper Kutenai
Upper Kootenay *see* Upper Kutenai
Upper Kootenuha *see* Upper Kutenai
Upper Kutenai (H) *see also* Kitona'qa (H)
Upper Kutenai [MN, BC] *Kutenai* (BE)
Upper Lake Division [Lang] *Eastern Pomo* (Pub, v.6, no.1, pp.185–191)
Upper Lillooet [BC] *Lillooet* (BE)
Upper Matchotix *see* Matchotic II
Upper Mattapony [VA] *Powhatan* (BE)
Upper Mdewakanton [MN] *Mdewakanton* (H)
Upper Me-de-wakan-t'wan *see* Upper Mdewakanton
Upper Nasoni [TX] *Kadohadacho Confederacy* (BE)
Upper Natchitoches [TX] *Kadohadacho Confederacy* (BE)
Upper Pend d'Oreilles *Upper Kalispel* (H)
Upper Piman (Bull44) *see also* Pimo Alto (Bull44)
Upper Piman [Lang] [MX] *Tepiman* (Hdbk10)
Upper Platte Indians *see* Kheyatawichasha

Upper Porcupine River Kutchin *see* Takkuth-kutchin
Upper Puyallup *see* Tooahk
Upper Rogue River Indians *see* Takelma
Upper Sacramento [Lang] *Wintu* (CA-8)
Upper Saint Croix Lake *Munominikasheenhug* (H)
Upper Santiam *Molala* (Hdbk12)
Upper Sauratown *see* Cheraw
Upper Seesetoans *see* Kahra
Upper Similkameem [WA, BC] *Similkameem* (BE)
Upper Sioux *Sisseton* (H)
Upper Sioux *Wahpeton* (H)
Upper Spokan [WA] *Spokan* (BE)
Upper Takelma [OR] *Takelma* (H)
Upper Thompson [BC] *Ntlakyapamuk* (BE)
Upper Tsihalis *see* Kwaiailk
Upper Umpqua *see* Umpqua
Upper Verde Valley People *see* Matkitwawipa
Upper Wahpaton *see* Mdeiyedan
Upper Yakima *see* Pshwanwapam
Upper Yanctonais *see* Upper Yanktonai
Upper Yankotnai [SD] *Yanktonai* (BE)
Upper Yatasi [LA, TX] *Kadohadacho Confederacy* (BE)
Up-pup-pay *see* Nez Perce
Uppuppay *see* Nez Perce
Upputupet [WA] (H)
U'pqan *see* Upkhan
Upqan *see* Upkhan
Upsarauka *see* Crow
Upsaroca *see* Crow
Up-sa-ro-ka [Self-designation] *see* Crow
Up-shar-look-kar *see* Crow
Upsharlookkar *see* Crow
Upsook *see* Crow
Up-sor-ah-kay *see* Crow
Upsorahkay *see* Crow
Upsoroka *see* Crow
Upuri *see* Guarano
Upurui (LC) *see also* Oyana (LC)
Upurui [Br] (O)
Ura *see* Uva
Uraba *see* Taos
Uracha [TX] *Coahuiltecan* (BE)
Uragee *see* Mahican
Urai-Nuints *see* Uainuint
Urainuints *see* Uainuint
Uranico [BO] *Araona* (O)
Urarina [PE] (LC)
Urawi *see* Unami
Urayoan [PR] (BE)
Uren [MX] (BE)
Uren [Pan, CR] *Terraba* (O)

Ures [Lang] *Lowland Pima* (Hdbk10)

Ures [MX] *Pima Bajo* (BE)

Ures *Opata* (H)

Urhlaina [Clan] [NM] *Taos* (H)

Urihesahe [Clan] *Choctaw* (H)

Uriname [MX] *Bribri* (BE)

Urini *see* Asurini II

Uro *see* Uru

Urocalla *see* Uru

Urocolla *see* Uru

Uroquilla *see* Uru

Urraca [Pan] (BE)

Urribaracuxi *see* Tocobaga

Urripacoxit *see* Tocobaga

Urriparacoxi *see* Tocobaga

Ur'thlaina tai'na *see* Urhlaina

Urthlainataina *see* Urhlaina

Uru (LC) *see also* Puquina (LC)

Uru [BO] (LC)

Uruak *see* Auake

Urubu [Br] (LC)

Urubu-Diapa [Lang] *Catuquina* (O)

Urubu-Kaapor *see* Urubu

Urubu-Tapuya [Clan] *Karutana* (O)

Urucuiana *see* Oyana

Urueuwauwau *see* Urueu-Wau-Wau

Urueu-Wau-Wau [Br] (O)

Uruku [Br] (O)

Urukuena *see* Urukuyana

Urukuiana *see* Urukuyana

Urukuyana (O) *see also* Guyano (LC)

Urukuyana [FrG, Su, Br] (O)

Urumi [Br] (O)

Urupa [Br] (O)

Urutani *see* Auake

Usal [CA] *Sinkyone* (H)

Usapam *see* Uscapem

Usaya *see* Hopi

Usaya-kue *see* Hopi

Usayakue *see* Hopi

Usayan *see* Hopi

Uscamacu (H)

Uscapem *Coahuiltecan* (Hdbk10)

U-se *see* Ushu

Use *see* Ushu

Usheree *see* Catawba

Usherie *see* Catawba

Ushery *see* Catawba

Usherys *see* Catawba

Ush-ke-we-ah *see* Bannock

Ushkeweah *see* Bannock

Ushkimani'tigog *see* Oukiski-manitouk

Ushpee *see* Mosopelea

Ushpi *see* Ofo

Ushu [Clan] *Hopi* (H)

Usietshawus *see* Tillamook

Uskee *see* Eskimos

Uskee-mes *see* Eskimos

Uskeemes *see* Eskimos

Uskemau's *see* Eskimos

Uskemaw's *see* Eskimos

Uskimay *see* Eskimos

Usleta *see* Isleta

Uspantec *see* Upanteca

Uspanteca [MX, Gu] (LC)

Usquemows *see* Eskimos

Usququhaga [PA] *Susquehanna* (BE)

Ussagene'wi *see* Montagnais-Nakapi

Ussaghenick *see* Montagnais-Naskapi

Ussinebwoinug *see* Assiniboin

Ussinnewudj Eninnewug *see* Sari

Us-suc-car-shay *see* Mandan

Ussuccarshay *see* Mandan

Ustana *see* Timucua

Ustisti [Clan] *Cherokee* (H)

Us-to-ma *see* Ustoma

Ustoma [CA] *Maidu* (H)

Ustu *see* Ustoma

Uta *see* Ute

Utaca [TX] (BE)

Utagami *Peoria* (H)

Utagamig *see* Fox

Utahn *see* Ute

Utahs *see* Ute

U-tai-si-ta *see* Kadohadacho

Utaisita *see* Kadohadacho

Utalah *see* Umatilla

Utalla *see* Umatilla

Utalle *see* Umatilla

Utamis *see* Miami

Utamqt *see* Lower Thompson

Uta'mqt [Self-designation] *see* Lower Thompson

Uta'mqtamux *see* Lower Thompson

Utamqtamux *see* Lower Thompson

Utaobaes *see* Ottawa

Utas *see* Ute

Uta-seta *see* Kadohadacho

Utaseta *see* Kadohadacho

Utavois *see* Ottawa

Utaw *see* Ute

Utawas *see* Ottawa

Utawawa *see* Ottawa

Utaws *see* Ute

Utce-ci-nyu-muh *see* Apache

Utcecinyumuh *see* Apache

Utcena'qai'n *see* Okinagan

Utchi *see* Apache

Utcitcak *see* Ojeejok

Utciti *see* Uchita

Ute [Lang] *Southern Numic* (Hdbk11)

Ute [Lang] [*Ute-Chemehuevi*] (H)

Ute [UT, CO, NE] (LC)

Ute-Chemehuevi [Lang] *Plateau Shoshonean* (Pub, v.4, no.3, p.97)

Ute Diggers *see* Southern Paiute

Utella *see* Umatilla

Ute Mountain Ute Indians *see* Wiminuche

Uterus [Can] *Sarsi* (BE)

Utian [Lang] *Penutian* (CA-8)

Utilla *see* Umatilla

Utina (LC) *see also* Timucua (LC)

Utina [FL] (BE)

Utinom *see* Usal

Utinomanoc [CA] *Mission Indians* (H)

Utinosche *see* Apinage

Utitno'm [CA] *Yuki* (BE)

Utkiavigmiut [AK] *North Alaska Coast Eskimos* (Hdbk5)

Utkiavinmiut [AK] *Eskimos* (BE)

Utkiavwiñimiun *see* Utkiavinmiut

Utku-hikalik *see* Ukusiksalirmiut

Utkuhikalik *see* Ukusiksalirmiut

Ut-ku-hikaling-meut *see* Ukusiksalirmiut

Utkuhikalingmeut *see* Ukusiksalirmiut

Utkuhikhalingmiut [AK] *Eskimos* (Hdbk5)

Utkuhikjalingmiut *see* Utkuhikhalingmiut

Ut-ku-sik-kaling-me-ut *see* Ukusiksalirmiut

Utkusikkalingmeut *see* Ukusiksalirmiut

Utkusiksalik *see* Ukusiksalirmiut

Utkutciki-alin-meut *see* Ukusiksalirmiut

Utkutcikialinmeut *see* Ukusiksalirmiut

Utlateca *see* Quiche

Utlz-chna *see* Kulchana

Uto-Aztecan [MX] (LC)

Utovautes *see* Ottawa

Utsaamu *see* Apache

Utschim *see* Uchium

Utschium *see* Uchium

Utschiun *see* Uchium

Utschta [Lang] *Osage* (H)

Utsia *see* Ute

Utsushuat *see* Quapaw

Uttawa *see* Ottawa

Uttawaw *see* Ottawa

Utuado [PR] (BE)

Utugamig *see* Fox

Utukakgmut *see* Utukamiut

Utukamiut [AK] *Eskimos* (BE)

Utukokmiut *see* Utokok River Eskimos

Utukok River Eskimos [AK] *Interior North Alaska Eskimos* (Hdbk5)

Utumpaiat (PC) *see also* Moapa (Hdbk11)

Utumpaiat [NV] *Paiute* (H)
U-tum-pai-ats *see* Utumpaiat
U-tum-pai-ats *see* Moapa
Utunxtana *see* Ahtena
Utu Utu Gwaiti *Owens Valley Paiute* (Hdbk11)
Uulgo [MX] (H)
Uva [CA] *Chumashan* (H)
Uvaliarlit [AK] *Eskimos* (Hdbk5)
Uvkusigsalik *see* Ukusiksalirmiut
Uwaha *see* Omaha
Uwatayo-rono *see* Cherokee
Uwinty-Utahs *see* Uinta
Uxul *see* Lipan Apache
Uyada *see* Cherokee
Uyame *see* Kamiaxpu
Uzaje *see* Osage
Uzutiuhe *see* Uzutiuhi
U-zu-ti-u-hi *see* Uzutiuhi
Uzutiuhi *Quapaw* (H)
U-zu-ti-u-we *see* Uzutiuhi
Uzutiuwe *see* Uzutiuhi

-V-

Va-af *see* Vaaf
Vaaf [Clan] *Pima* (H)
Vacacoha *see* Awishiri
Vacoregue [MX] (BE)
Vacus *see* Acoma
Vaguero *see* Querecho
Va-had-ha *see* Vahadha
Vahadha [Clan] *Mohawk* (H)
Vajaribo *see* Guaharibo
Valachi *see* Apalachee
Vale do Cariri *see* Kariri
Valencia *see* Tome
Valiente (LC) *see also* Guaymi (LC)
Valiente [CAm] *Bribri* (O)
Valladolid *see* Taos
Vallatoa *see* Jemez
Valley [Lang] [CA] *Central Pomo* (Pub, v.6, no.1, pp.166–182)
Valley [Lang] [CA] *Nisenan* (CA-8)
Valley [Lang] [CA] *Northern Pomo* (CA-8)
Valley [Lang] [CA] *Southern Moquelumnan* (Pub, v.6, no.1, pp.309–313)
Valley Maidu [CA] *Northwestern Maidu* (Pub, c.29, no.4)
Valley Nomlaki [Lang] [CA] *Wintun* (CA-8)
Valley Yokuts (BE)
Valverde *see* Sempoapi
Vampe *see* Nambe
Vanae-ta-Kouttchin *see* Vuntakutchin

Vanaetakouttchin *see* Vuntakutchin
Vanagaoungo *see* Abnaki
Vanca [TX] (H)
Vancouvers *see* Klikitat
Van-tah-koo-chin *see* Vuntakutchin
Vantahkoochin *see* Vuntakutchin
Vanta-Kutchi *see* Vuntakutchin
Vantakutchi *see* Vuntakutchin
Vanta-Kutchin *see* Vuntakutchin
Vanta kutshi *see* Vuntakutchin
Vantakutshi *see* Vuntakutchin
Vanyume (H) *see also* Serrano (LC)
Vanyume [CA] *Serrano* (CA)
Vapidiana *see* Wapisiana
Vaquabo [JA, WInd] (BE)
Vaquero *see* Jicarillo Apache
Vaquero *see* Querecho
Varaa *see* Warrau
Varashedeni [Br] *Dani* (O)
Vareato [Pueblo] (H)
Variquena *see* Arekena
Varogio *see* Varohio
Varohio [MX] (BE)
Varojio *see* Varohio
Varojio *see* Guarijio
Varra *see* Warrau
Vassapalles [MX] *Lagunero* (BE)
Vassconia *see* Papago
Vayena *see* Guayano
Veado *see* Asurini II
Vedos *see* Asurini II
Vegas *see* Las Vegas
Vejareanos *Coahuiltecan* (Hdbk10)
Vejos *see* Mataco
Vejoz (LC)
Veliche *see* Huilliche
Venaambakaia [CA] *Pomo* (H)
Venados [TX] (BE)
Vende Flechas [TX] *Coahuiltecan* (BE)
Ven-ta-Kuttchin *see* Vuntakutchin
Ventakuttchin *see* Vuntakutchin
Venteguebo [SA] *Caduveo* (O)
Ventureno [CA] *Chumash* (LC)
Ventureño [Lang] [CA] *Chumash* (He)
Veracruzano [MX] (BE)
Vermilion [IN] *Kickapoo* (H)
Veshanack *see* Vesnak
Vesnack *see* Vesnak
Vesnak [CA] *Nishinam* (H)
Vespiric Indians (H)
Veyana *see* Guyana
Viakshi *see* Viaksi
Viaksi [VE] *Yukpa* (O)
Viandot *see* Huron
Viayam [TX] *Coahuiltecan* (BE)
Viayan *see* Viayam
Viceita [MX] *Bribri* (BE)

Vicente Diegueño, San [CA] (IndN, v.4, no.4, April 1927, p.154)
Vicieta *see* Viceita
Vicuris *see* Picuris
Vidae *see* Bidai
Vidai *see* Bidai
Viday *see* Bidai
Viddaquimamar [TX] (BE)
Vidshi itikapa *see* Papago
Vidshiitikapa *see* Papago
Vieux de la Mer *see* Nellagottine
Vigitega [MX] (BE)
Vikhit [AK] *Ahtena* (BE)
Vikhut *see* Vikhit
Vilela [Arg] (LC)
Vilimuluche *see* Araucanian
Village of Prairie *see* Tintaotonwe
Village of Sixes *see* Taoapa
Village of the Basket *see* Tungge
Village of the Insect *see* Puaray
Village of the Worm *see* Puaray
Village people *see* Minika'mi Wini'niwuk
Villegas *Coahuiltecan* (Hdbk10)
Vimaga *see* Vi-ma-ga
Vi-ma-ga *Mohave* (H)
Vineyard Indians *see* Martha's Vineyard
Viniettinen-ne *see* Tonto Apache
Vinni ettinenne *see* Tonto Apache
Vinni ettinen-ne *see* Tonto Apache
Vintukua *see* Arhuaco
Vi-qit *see* Vikhit
Viqit *see* Vikhit
Vi-ra-ri-ka *see* Huichol
Virarika *see* Huichol
Virginia Algonquians *Conoy* (Hdbk15)
Virgin River Paiute *see* Shivwits
Virgin River Paiute *see* Southern Paiute
Vishalika *see* Huichol
Vi-tapatu'i *see* Kiowa
Vitapatui *see* Kiowa
Vivais *see* Bidai
Vivit *see* Bibit
Vncheckaug *see* Passamaquoddy
Vnquechauke *see* Passamaquoddy
Voen Kuttchin *see* Vuntakutchin
Voenkuttchin *see* Vuntakutchin
Volvon *see* Bolbone
Vondt-way-Kutchin *see* Vuntakutchin
Vondtwaykutchin *see* Vuntakutchin
Voqueares [Guy, VE] (O)
Voragio *see* Varohio
Voto [CR, NI] (BE)

Vovol *see* Bobol
Vsacus *see* Acoma
Vttasantasough *see* Chicka-
hominy
Vuato *see* Guato
Vule Puga *see* Calapooya
Vulture *Pima* (H)
Vulture People (H) *see also*
Suwuki Ohimal (H)
Vumahein *Peublo Indians* (H)
Vun-tah ku-tch-in *see* Vun-
takutchin
Vunta-Kutchin *see* Vuntakutchin
Vuntakutchin [AK] (LC)
Vun-tta-kwi-chin *see* Vun-
takutchin
Vunttakwichin *see* Vuntakutchin

-W-

Waaih [TX] *Comanche* (BE)
Waapanahkiiha *see* Delaware
wa'atcem [Clan] *Serrano* (Pub,
v.26, 1929)
Waatenihts *see* Ute
Wabaage *see* Quabaug
Wabanackies *see* Abnaki
Wabanakee *see* Abnaki
Wabanaki *see* Abnaki
wabanakiiak *see* Abnaki
Wabanika *see* Abnaki
Wabanike *see* Abnaki
wabaniki *see* Delaware
Wabanoak *see* Abnaki
Wabanocky *see* Abnaki
Wabaquasset [CN] (IndL, nos.
27–28)
Wabasca *see* Athapascan
Wabasemowenenewak [MN, ND,
SD] *Chippewa* (H)
Wabasha's band *see* Kiyuksa
[Mdewakanton]
Wabashaw band *see* Kiyuksa
[Mdewakanton]
Wabashaw's sub-band of Mede-
wakan-t'wans *see* Kiyuksa
[Mdewakanton]
Wabashiu *see* Waba'shiu
Waba'shiu [Clan] *Menominee* (H)
Wabenakies *see* Abnaki
Wabenaki senobe *see* Abnaki
Wabenauki *see* Abnaki
Wabezhaze [Clan] *Chippewa* (H)
Wabinizhupye [Subgens] *Kansa*
(H)
Wablenicha [SD] *Oglala* (H)
Wab-na-ki *see* Abnaki
Wabnaki *see* Abnaki
Wabozo [Clan] *Potawatomi* (H)
Wabui [Lang] *Waiwai* (UAz)

Wabunaki *see* Abnaki
Wabushaw *see* Kiyuksa [Mde-
wakanton]
Wabuswaianuk *Paskwawininiwug
Cree* (BE)
Wacabe *see* Dtesanhadtadhishan
Wacalamus *see* Thlakalama
Wacamuc *see* Cathlacumup
Wacata *see* Guacata
Wacawai *Acawai* (O)
Waccamaw [Lang] *Eastern Siouan*
(H)
Waccamaw [SC, NC] (LC)
Wachape [SD] *Oglala* (H)
Wacheonpa [SD] *Oglala* (H)
Wachetak *Assateague* (Hdbk15)
Wachipaeri [PE] *Mashco* (O)
Wachipuanes *see* Chipewyan
Wachuset [NH, MA] (LC)
Waciazihyabin *see* Waci'azi
hyabin
Waci'azi hyabin [MN] *Assiniboin*
(BE)
Waco [TX, OK] (LC)
Wacoes *see* Wasco
Wa-come-app *see* Cathlacumup
Wacomeapp *see* Cathlacumup
Waculi *see* Tepecano
Wacutada *see* Oto
Wacuxca *see* Missouri
wadadika'a *see* Wadatoka
wadadikadi *see* Wadadokado
Wadadokado *Northern Paiute*
(Hdbk11)
Wadatickadu *see* Wadadokado
Wada'tikadu *see* Wadadokado
Wadatkuht *see* Wadadokado
Wadatkuht *see* Honey Lake
Paiute
Wadatoka *Northern Paiute*
(Hdbk11)
Wada'tukede *see* Wadadokado
Wadatukede *see* Wadadokado
Wad-doke-tah-tah *see* Oto
Waddoketahtah *see* Oto
Wadhigizhe [Subgens] *Omaha*
(H)
Wadiuparanin [Lang] *Catuquina*
(O)
Wadjuta tanga *see* Chedunga
Wa-dook-to-da *see* Oto
Wadooktoda *see* Oto
Wa-do-tan *see* Oto
Wadotan *see* Oto
Wadotada *see* Oto
Wadouissian *see* Dakota
waen-save *see* Navajo
Waerinnewangh *see* Warran-
gawankong
Waewae [Clan] *Chippewa* (H)
Waga *see* Wahga
Waganhaer *see* Ontwaganha
Waganhaer *see* Ottawa

Waganhaes *see* Ontwaganha
Waganhaes *see* Ottawa
Waganha's *see* Ottawa
Waganis *see* Ottawa
Wagannes *see* Ontwaganha
Wagannes *see* Ottawa
Wagenhanes *see* Ottawa
Wagenhanes *see* Shawnee
Wagh-toch-tat-ta *see* Oto
Waghtochtatta *see* Oto
Waglezaoin [Miniconjou] (H)
Waglukhe [SD] *Oglala* (H)
Wagosh *see* Fox
Wagrani *see* Huao
Wagunha *see* Ottawa
Wa'gushag *see* Fox
Wagushag *see* Fox
Waha [Clan] [NM] *Pueblo Indi-
ans* (H)
Wahaha [Clan] [NM] *Pecos* (H)
Wahai *see* Kawahib
Wahaikan [Lang] *Chinookan*
(Bull15)
Wahanna *see* Ontwaganha
Wahannas *see* Ottawa
Waharibo *see* Guahibo
Wahasha *see* Osage
Wa-ha-shaw *see* Kiyuksa
Wahashaw *see* Kiyuksa
Wa-ha-shaw's tribe *see* Kiyuksa
[Mdewakanton]
Wahclellah (Hdbk12) *see also* Cas-
cades (Hdbk12)
Wahclellah (Hdbk12) *see also*
Watlala (BE)
Wahclellah [Can, OR] *Shahala* (H)
Wahcoota Band *see* Khemnichan
Wahe *see* Cascades
Wahga [Clan] *Ponca* (H)
Wah-ho-na-hah *see* Potawatomi
Wahhonahah *see* Potawatomi
Wahibo *see* Guahibo
Wahiucaqa *see* Potawatomi
Wahiucaxa *see* Potawatomi
Wahiuyaha *see* Potawatomi
Wah-kah-towah *see* Chippewa
Wahkiakum [WA] *Chinook* (Ye)
Wahkiruxkanumanke *see*
Shoshone
Wah-koo-tay *see* Khemnichan
Wahkootay *see* Khemnichan
Wahkuti Band *see* Khemnichan
Wahlakalgi [Clan] *Creek* (H)
Wah-lal-la *see* Watlala
Wahlalla *see* Watlala
Wah-lik-nas-se *see* Tubatulabal
Wahliknasse *see* Tubatulabal
Wahl'lala *see* Watlala
Wahllala *see* Watlala
Wah ma dee Tunkah band *see*
Ohanhanska
Wahmadee Tunkah band *see*
Ohanhanska

Wahmi [MX] (BE)
Wah muk a-hah-ve *see* Mohave
Wahmukahahve *see* Mohave
Wahnachee *see* Wenatchi
Wahnookt *see* Klikitat
wahn-quints *see* Cedar
Wahnquints *see* Cedar
Wa-h'o-na-ha *see* Potawatomi
Wahonaha *see* Potawatomi
Wahopum [OR] *Tenino* (BE)
Wahpacoota *see* Wakpekute
Wahpekute [NE] *Santee* (LC)
Wahpeton [MN] *Santee* (LC)
Wah-ral-lah *see* Watlala
Wahrallah *see* Watlala
Wahsash *see* Osage
Wahshashe *see* Osage
Wah-Sha-She *see* Osage
Wah-shoes *see* Washo
Wahshoes *see* Washo
Wahshoo *see* Washo
Wahsuahgunewininewug [WI] *Chippewa* (BE)
Wahtani *see* Mandan
wah-tat-kin *see* Wadatoka
Wahtatkin *see* Wadatoka
Wah-teh-ta-na *see* Oto
Wahtehtana *see* Oto
Wahtohtanes *see* Oto
Wahtohtata *see* Oto
Wah-tok-ta-ta *see* Oto
Wahtoktata *see* Oto
Wah-tooh tah-tah *see* Oto
Wahtoohtahtah *see* Oto
Wahute Band *see* Khemnichan
Wah-we-ah-tung-ong *see* Wea
Wahweahtungong *see* Wea
Wah-ze-ah we-chas-ta *see* Northern Assiniboin
Wah-ze-ah we-chas-ta *see* Tschantoga
Wahzeah wechasta *see* Northern Assiniboin
Wahzeah wechasta *see* Tschantoga
Wahzhingka [Clan] *Quapaw* (H)
Wah-zi-ah *see* Northern Assiniboin
Wah-zi-ah *see* Tschantoga
Wahziah *see* Northern Assiniboin
Wahziah *see* Tschantoga
Waiam (BE) *see also* Wyam (LC)
Waiam [OR] *Tenino* (BE)
Waiana *see* Oyana
Waiapi *see* Oyampi
Waiatanwa *see* Wea
Waiboi [Br] (O)
Waica [Br, VE] *Akawoio* (LC)
Waicuri [BaC, MX] (BE)
Waicurian [Lang] *Hokan* (BE)
Waicuru *see* Guaycuru
Waiilatpu *see* Cayuse

Waiilatpuan [Lang] *see* Shapwailutan
Waika *see* Waica
Waikana *see* Pira-Tapuyo
Waikatdesu [Br] *Southern Nambicuara* (O)
Waikemi *see* Dau-pom
Waikena [Self-designation] *see* Pira-Tapuyo
Waiki lako *see* Okmulgee
Waikilako *see* Okmulgee
Waikino *see* Pira-Tapuyo
Waikosel *see* Wai-ko-sel
Wai-ko-sel [CA] *Patwin* (Contri, v.3, p.219)
Wailaki [CA] (LC)
Wailakki *see* Wailaki
Wai-lak-ki *see* Wailaki
Wailatpu *see* Cayuse
Wai'let-ma *see* Cayuse
Wailetma *see* Cayuse
Wailetpu *see* Cayuse
Waillatpu *see* Cayuse
Waimaha *see* Barasana
Waimaha *see* Waimaja
Waimaha [Self-designation] *see* Bara
Waimaja [Br, Col] *Barasana* (O)
Waimare [Br] *Paressi* (O)
Waimiri [Br, Guy] (LC)
Waimiry *see* Waimari
Waimuk (BE) *see also* Wintu (LC)
Waimuk [CA] (BE)
Wainoake *see* Weanock
Wainuma [Lang] [SA] *Maipurean* (O)
Waiomgomo *see* Mayongong
Wai-ri-ka *see* Shasta
Wairika *see* Shasta
waitikka *see* watatikka
Wait-lat-pu *see* Cayuse
Waitlatpu *see* Cayuse
Waiushr [Clan] [*San Felipe (Keres)*] (H)
Waiwai [Br, Guy] (LC)
Waiwe *see* Waiwai
Wai-yam (Forg)
Waiyam *see* Wai-yam
Waiyan *see* Guayano
Waiyana *see* Guayana
Wajaje *see* Osage
Wajaje *see* Ta
Wajapi *see* Oyampi
Wa-jibi *see* Guahibo
Wajibi *see* Guahibo
Wa-ju-xdca *see* Missouri
Wajuxdca *see* Missoui
Waka [Clan] *Oto* (H)
Wakada *see* Pira-Tapuyo
Wakalitdesu [Br] *Southern Nambicuara* (O)
Wakamass *see* Cathlacumup
Wakamuck *see* Cathlacumup

Wakan (H) *see also* Waka (H)
Wakan [Clan] *Iowa* (H)
Wakan [Clan] *Oto* (H)
Wakan *Hunkpapa* (H)
Wakan [SD] *Oglala* (H)
Wakanta [Clan] *Missouri* (H)
Wakanta [Clan] *Quapaw* (H)
Wakash *see* Nootka
Wakashan [Lang] [BC, WA] (LC)
Wakataneri *see* Amarakaeri
Wakazoo *see* Mekadewagamitigweyawininiwak
Wakeshi [Clan] *Potawatomi* (H)
Waki *see* Shipaulovi
Wakichi [CA] *Northern Valley Yokuts* (CA)
Wakidohka-numak *see* Northern Shoshone
Wakidohka-numak *see* Shoshone
Wakina *see* Arikara
Wakitaneri *Amarakaeri* (O)
Wakokai [AL] (BE)
Wakona [Br] (O)
Wakootay's Band *see* Khemnichan
Wakouiechiwek *see* Chisedec
Wa-kpa-aton-we-dan *see* Oyateshichan
Wakpaatonwedan *see* Oyateshichan
Wakpokinyan *Miniconjou* (H)
wakruxha ruwakaki *see* Shoshone
Waksachi [CA, NV] *Mono* (BE)
Waktonila *Dakota* (BE)
Wakuenai [VE, Col, Br] (O)
Wakusheg *see* Fox
Wakuta Band *see* Khemnichan
Wa-ku-te *see* Khemnichan
Wakute *see* Khemnicahn
Wakute's Band *see* Kheminchan
Wakynukaine *see* Wa-ky-nu-kaine
Wa-ky-nu-kaine [Lang] *Salishan* (Contri, v.1, p.248)
Walaiki *see* Wailaki
Walaikki *see* Wailaki
Walamskni *see* Chastacosta
Walamswash *see* Chastacosta
Wa-la-nah *see* Jemez
Walanah *see* Jemez
Walapai (LC) *see also* Hualapai (LC)
Walapai [AZ] (BE)
Walapai [Lang] *Upland Yuman* (Hdbk10)
Walapi *see* Walapai
Walas [Gens] *Kwakiutl* (H)
Walaskwakiutl [Sept] *Kwakiutl* (H)
Walatoa *see* Jemez
Walatowa *see* Jemez
Wa-la-tu-wa *see* Jemez
Walatuwa *see* Jemez

walawala *see* Walla Walla
walawalapam *see* Walla Walla
Wales *Bering Strait Eskimos* (Hdbk5)
Walhalla *see* Gualala
Walhomini *see* Menominee
Walhominies *see* Menominee
Wali *see* Guale
Waliperi-Dakenai [Lang] [SA] *Maipurean* (O)
Walitsum (H) *see also* Hahamatse (H)
Wa-lit-sum *see* Hahamatse
Walitsum *Kwakiutl* (H)
Walkamepa [AZ] *Yavapai* (BE)
Walker River *see* Aga'idokado
Walker River Paiute (Char, v.11)
Walker River Pi-Utes (H) *see also* Agaihtikara (H)
Walkers *see* Shoshoko
Walkers *see* Shoshone
Walker's Basin *see* Yutp
Walker's Basin *see* Yitpe
Walkey-anyahyepa [AZ] *Yavapai* (BE)
Wallamette *see* Clowwewalla
Wallamute *see* Ugalakmiut
Wallawalla *see* Walla Walla
Walla Walla [OR, WA] (LC)
Walli *see* Wal-li
Wal-li *Miwok* (Contri, v.3, p.349)
Wallirmiut [Can] *Central Eskimos* (BE)
Wallow Wallow *see* Walla Walla
Walpapi [OR] (LC)
Walpi *Pueblo Indians* (BE)
Walpiye *see* Walpi
Walpole Island [Ont] *Chippewa* (H)
Waltoykewel [Lang] [CA] *Hill Nomlaki* (CA-8)
Walua [WA] (Ye)
Waluga [OR] (Oregon)
Walula *see* Walla Walla
Walumskni *see* Latgawa
waluula *see* Walla Walla
waluulapam *see* Walla Walla
Walwama [ID] *Nez Perce* (BE)
Wal-wa-re-na *see* Barbareno
Walwarenna *see* Barbareno
Walyapai *see* Walapai
Wama [Br, Su] *Tiriyo* (O)
Wamaka'v *see* Mohave
Wamakava *see* Yuma
Wamaka'va *see* Mohave
Wamani [PE] (LC)
Wamanuche *see* Weeminuche
Wamari'i [CA] (BE)
Wambisa *see* Huambisa
Wamenuches *see* Weeminuches
Wamesit [MA, Q] *Pennacook* (LC)

Wamiitazhi [Subclan] *Ponco* (H)
Wa-mo-ka-ba *see* Mohave
Wamokaba *see* Mohave
Wamonae *see* Cuiva
Wampamag [MA] *Wampanoag* (BE)
Wampanoag [MA, RI] (LC)
Wampum-makers *see* Abnaki
Wamutanara [Col] *Barasana* (O)
wan *see* Jemez
Wanaco [Col] *Barasana* (O)
Wanaghe [Clan] *Kansa* (H)
Wanai [Self-designation] *see* Mapayo
Wanak *see* Dakota
Wanam [Br] (O)
Wanamakewajenenik [MN, ND, SD] *Chippewa* (H)
Wanami *see* Unami
Wanana (LC) *see also* Guanano (LC)
Wanana [Col, Br] (O)
Wanano *see* Guanano
Wanapam [WA] (BE)
Wa'napum *see* Sokulk
Wanapum (PC) *see also* Sokulk (BE)
Wanapum [OR, WA] (LC)
Wanat *see* Huron
Wanbanaghi *see* Abnaki
Wanbanaki *see* Abnaki
Wanbanakkie *see* Abnaki
Wanb-naghi *see* Abnaki
Wanbnaghi *see* Abnaki
Wandat *see* Huron
Wanderers *see* Detsanayuku
Wanderers *see* Missiassik
Wando [SC] *Cusabo* (BE)
Wandot *see* Huron
Wandot *see* Wyandot
wange owinge *see* Jemez
Wang-kat *see* Howungkut
Wangkat *see* Howungkut
Wangunk [CN] *Wappinger* (BE)
Waninahua *see* Catoquina
Waninawa *see* Catoquina
Wanjoak *see* Nottoway
Wanka *see* Huanca
Wanki [MX] *Mosquito* (BE)
Wannaton *see* Pabaksa
Wannawega *see* Cazazhita
Wannawegha (H) *see also* Wanneewackataonelar (H)
Wannawegha *Miniconjou* (H)
Wannewackataonelar *Miniconjou* (H)
Wantat *see* Huron
Wa-nuk-e-ye-na *see* Hidatsa
Wanukeyena *see* Hidatsa
Wanxue'ici [OK] *Arapaho* (BE)
Wanyam *Txapakura* (O)
Wao *see* Huao
Waodadi *see* Huao

Waoranec [NY] *Unami* (BE)
Waoraneck *see* Waoranec
Waorani [EC] (O)
Wa-otc *see* Iowa
Waotc *see* Iowa
Wa'pametant *see* Yakima
Wapametant *see* Yakima
Wapanachk *see* Abnaki
Wapanachki *see* Abnaki
Wapanachki *see* Delaware
Wapa'naki *see* Abnaki
Wapanaki *see* Abnaki
Wapanaki ha-akon *see* Abnaki
Wapanakihaakon *see* Abnaki
Wapanakihak *see* Abnaki
Wapanend *see* Abnaki
Wapanoos *see* Wampanoag
Wapasha's band *see* Kiyuksa [Mdewakanton]
Wapashaw's village *see* Kiyuksa [Mdewakanton]
Wa-pa-shee *see* Kiyuksa [Mdewakanton]
Wapashee *see* Kiyuksa [Mdewakanton]
Wapatha *see* Kiyuksa [Mdewakanton]
Wapato Lake *see* Atfalati
Wapatu *see* Atfalati
Wapatu Lake *see* Atfalati
Wapenacki *see* Abnaki
Wapenocks *see* Wampanoag
Wapeto *see* Atfalati
Wapiana *see* Wapisiana
Wapichana *see* Wapisiana
Wapichiyana *see* Wapisiana
Wapidian *see* Wapisiana
Wap-i-ge *see* Uapige
Wapige *see* Uapige
Waping *see* Pompton
Waping *see* Wappinger
Wapinger *see* Wappinger
Wapishana *see* Wapisiana
Wapisiana [Br, Guy] (LC)
Wapisiwisibiwininiwak [MI] *Chippewa* (BE)
Wapitxana *see* Wapisiana
Wapoos *see* Potawatomi
Wapoto Lake *see* Atfalati
Wappato *see* Multnomah
Wappato *see* Atfalati
Wappatoo *see* Atfalati
Wappatoo Lake Indians *see* Atfalati
Wappenackie *see* Abnaki
Wappeno *see* Abnaki
Wappinck *see* Wappinger
Wapping *see* Pompton
Wappinger [NY, CN] *Delaware* (LC)
Wappingo *see* Wappinger
Wappingoes *see* Wappinger
Wappings *see* Wappinger

Wappo [CA] (LC)
Waptai'lmin *see* Waptailmin
Wap-tail-min *see* Waptailmin
Waptailmin [WA] *Yakima* (BE)
Wapto *see* Atfalati
wa-puksa rupa-ka *see* Kiowa
wa-puksa rupa-ka *see* Shoshone
wapuksa rupaka *see* Kiowa
wapuksa rupaka *see* Shoshone
Wapumne [CA] *Nishinam* (H)
Wa-pum-ni *see* Wapumne
Wapumni *see* Wapumne
Wapumni *see* Wapumne
Wa-pu-nah-ki *see* Abnaki
Wapunahki *see* Abnaki
Wa-qotc *see* Iowa
Waqotc *see* Iowa
Waquithi [WY] *Arapaho* (BE)
Waraicu [Lang] [SA] *Mairupean*
(O)
Waranakarana *see* Naywau-
naukauraunah
Waranawonkong [NY] *Munsee*
(BE)
Warao [VE] (O)
War-are-ree-kas *see* Tazaaigadika
Wararereelas *see* Tazaaigadika
Wara-tikaru *see* Wadadokado
Waratikaru *see* Wadadokado
Warau *see* Warrau
Waraueti *see* Warrau
Waraweete *see* Warrau
Waraye *see* Osage
War Eagle People *see* Hangkau-
tadhantsi
Warekena *see* Arekena
Warenecker *see* Waoranec
Warequena *see* Arekena
Waresquokes *see* Warrasqueock
Wari *see* Huari
Wari [Self-designation] *see*
Pakaanova
Wariapana [Self-designation] *see*
Panobo
Wariapano *see* Panobo
Warihio *see* Guarijio
Warikena *see* Arekena
Warikyana *see* Arekena
Wariperidakena [VE] *Wakunai*
(O)
Waripi *see* Okomoyana
Wariscoyans *see* Warrasqueoc
Wariwa-Tapuya *see* Guariba
Warm Springs (H) *see also* Tenino
(BE)
Warm Springs Apache *Gilenos
Apache* (BE)
Warm Springs Indians (H) *see also*
Tenino (BE)
Warm Springs Indians (H) *see also*
Tilkuni (BE)
Warm Springs Indians [OR]
(Hdbk12)

Warm Springs Sahaptin *see*
Tenino
Warner's Ranch Indians *see* Cu-
peno
Warner's Ranch Indians *see* Agua
Caliente
Waronawanka *see* War-
ranawankong
Waroskoyack *see* Warrasqueoc
Warouwen *see* Warrau
Warow *see* Warrau
Warowocomo *see* Werowoco-
moco
Warpeshana *see* Wapisiana
Warraghtinook *see* Wea
Warran *see* Warrau
Warranawankong *Delware*
(Hdbk15)
Warraskoyack *see* Warrasqueoc
Warrasqueoc [VA] *Powhatan* (BE)
Warrau [Guy, Su, VE] (LC)
Warraw *see* Warrau
Warrawannankonck *see* War-
ranawankong
Warray *see* Warrau
Warrennuncock [Lang] *Catawba*
(H)
Warrow *see* Warrau
Waruwaru *see* Hoti
Warynawonck *see* War-
ranawankong
Wasa [Clan] *Quapaw* (H)
Wasaazj *see* Osage
Wasabane [NI, Hon] *Sumo* (BE)
Wasabe [Clan] *Kansa* (H)
Wasabe [Gens] *Ponca* (H)
Wasabehitazhi [Clan] *Chizhu* (H)
Wasage *see* Osage
Wasama [VE] *Yukpa* (O)
Wasape *Hanginihkashina* (H)
Wasapetun [Clan] *Osage* (H)
Wa-sa-sa-o-no *see* Dakota
Wasasaono *see* Dakota
Wa-sa-seh-o-no *see* Dakota
Wasasehono *see* Dakota
Wasashe *see* Osage
Wa'sassa *see* Osage
Wasassa *see* Osage
Wasawanik *see* Ouasourini
Wasawsee *see* Osage
Wasbasha *see* Osage
Wasco [OR, WA] (LC)
Was-co-pam *see* Wasco
Wascopam *see* Wasco
Wascoparn *see* Wasco
Wascopaw *see* Wasco
Wascopen *see* Wasco
Wascopum *see* Wasco
Wasco-Wishram [Lang] [OR,
WA] *Upper Chinook* (Hdbk12)
Washa (H) *see also* Osage (LC)
Washa [LA] (BE)
Washaba [Clan] *Ponca* (H)

Washabe [Clan] *Wazhazhe* (H)
Washaki [WI] *Shoshone* (H)
Washakie *see* Washaki
Wa-sha-she *see* Osage
Washashe *see* Osage
Washashewanun [Clan] *Osage*
(H)
Wash-a-tung *see* Inshtasanda
Washatung *see* Inshtasanda
Washaw *see* Washo
Washbashaw *see* Osage
Washee *see* Washo
Washew *see* Washo
Washinedi *see* Was-hinedi
Was-hinedi [Social group] *Kake*
(H)
Washita [LA] *Caddo* (BE)
Washiu *see* Washo
Washkie *see* Washaki
Wa-sho *see* Washo
Washo [CA, NV] (LC)
Washoe *see* Washo
Washoo *see* Washo
Washougal [OR, WA] *Watlala*
(BE)
Washo'xla *see* Oto
Washoxla *see* Oto
Washpa [Clan] *Cochiti* (H)
Washran *see* Washo
Washrotsi *see* Sandia
Wash-sashe *see* Osage
Washsashe *see* Osage
Wa'shutse *see* Sandia
Washutse *see* Sandia
Washu'tsi *see* Sandia
Washutsi *see* Sandia
wasisiw *see* Washo
wa-siu *see* Washo
wasiu *see* Washo
wasiw *see* Washo
wa-siw [Self-designation] *see*
Washo
wasiwi *see* Washoe
Wasko *see* Wasco
Waskopam *see* Wasco
Waskosin *see* Wasco
wasoinhiyeihits *see* Shoshone
wasqu *see* Wasco
wasqupam *see* Wasco
Wassam *see* Wishram
Wassash *see* Osage
Wassashsha *see* Osage
Was-saw *see* Washo
Wassaw *see* Washo
Wassawomees *see* Iroquois
Wasses *see* Ouasourini
Wasuhsu [Br] *Southern Nam-
bicuara* (O)
Waswagaming [Self-designation]
see Lac du Fambeau
Waswanipi [Can] [*Montagnais-
Naskapi*] (BE)
Watahpahata *see* Kiowa

Watakihulata [Phratry] *Choctaw* (H)

Watala *see* Cascades

Watanzizhidedhatazhi [Subgens] *Omaha* (H)

Watasoon *see* Amahami

watatikka *Western Shoshone* (Hdbk11)

Watawawininiwok *see* Ottawa

Wateknasi *see* Tubatulabal

Wateni'hte *see* Siksika

Watenihte *see* Siksika

Wate-pana-toes *see* Kiowa

Watepanatoes *see* Kiowa

Watepaneto *see* Kiowa

Water *see* Minnepata

Wateree [Lang] *Catawba* (H)

Wateree [SC, NC] (BE)

Watido [CA] *Shasta* (Shasta)

watikka *see* watatikka

Watiru (Shasta) *see also* Watido (Shasta)

Watiru [CA] *Shasta* (CA-8)

Watlala [OR, WA] (BE)

Watlalla *see* Watlala

Watohtata *see* Oto

Watopabin *see* Wato'pbin

Wato'pabin [MN] *Assiniboin* (BE)

Watopachnato (H) *see also* Big Devils (H)

Watopachnato [Clan] *Assiniboin* (H)

Watopaxnaonwan *see* Wato'paxna-on wan

Wato'paxna-on wan [MN] *Assiniboin* (BE)

Wato'paxnatun *see* Wato-paxna-on wan

Watopaxnatun *see* Wato'paxna-on wan

Wat'ota *see* Oto

Watota *see* Oto

Watoto *see* Oto

Wattasoon *see* Amahami

Watutata *see* Oto

Watuyu *Tesuque* (H)

Wau-ba-na-kee *see* Abnaki

Waubanakee *see* Abnaki

Waub-ose *see* Maskegon

Waub-ose *see* Sugwaundugah-wininewug

Waubose *see* Maskegon

Waubose *see* Sugwaundugah-wininewug

Waub-un-uk-eeg *see* Abnaki

Waubunukeeg *see* Abnaki

Waukouta Band *see* Khemnichan

Waulapta *see* Cayuse

Waulatpa *see* Cayuse

Waulatpu *see* Cayuse

Wau-lit-sah-mosk *see* Hahamatse

Waulitsahmosk *see* Hahamatse

Waunana (O) *see also* Choco (LC)

Waunana [Col] *Southern Choco* (O)

Waura [Br] (O)

Wauru *see* Waura

Wausashe *see* Osage

Waushee *see* Washo

Wauswagiming [MI, WI] *Chippewa* (H)

Wauyukma [WA] (BE)

Wavikopaipa *see* Southeastern Yavapai

Wawah *see* Maidu

Wawah *see* Wintu

Wa-wah *see* Maidu

Wawarsink [NY] *Munsee* (BE)

Wawawipu [ID] *Nez Perce* (BE)

Wawbunukkeeg *see* Abnaki

Wawenoc *see* Wawenock

Wawenock [ME] *Abnaki* (LC)

Wawenok *see* Wawenock

Wa-wha *see* Osage

Wawha *see* Osage

Waw-lit-sum *see* Hahamatse

Wawlitsum *see* Hahamatse

Wawping *see* Wappinger

Wawrigweck *see* Norridgewock

Wawrigwick *see* Norridgewock

Waw-sash *see* Osage

Wawsash *see* Osage

Waw-sash-e *see* Osage

Wawsashe *see* Osage

Wawyachtonoc [NY, CN] *Mahican* (BE)

Waxhaw [Lang] *Catawba* (H)

Waxhaw [SC, NC] (BE)

Wayacule *see* Wayarikure

Wayai *see* Paumari

Wayam (Forg) *see also* Chutes (H)

Wayam [CA] *Tenino* (Forg)

Wayampi *see* Oyampi

Wayana (LC) *see also* Oyana (LC)

Wayana (O) *see also* Guayano (LC)

Wayana [Lang] *Eastern Carib* (UAz, v.28)

Wayanaze *see* Kaingangue

Wayandott *see* Huron

Wayandott *see* Wyandot

Wayapi *see* Oyampi

Wayarikule *see* Wayankure

Wayarikure [Su, Br] *Tiriyo* (O)

Wa-ya-ta-no-ke *see* Miami

Wayatanoke *see* Miami

wayaxix *see* Cascades

Wayka *see* Akawaio

Waykewel [Lang] [CA] *Hill Nomlaki* (CA-8)

waylatpam *see* Cayuse

Waylette *see* Cayuse

Waynu *see* Huayno

Wayondot *see* Huron

Wayondott *see* Huron

Wayoro [Br] (O)

Wayu *see* Goajira

Wayumara [Lang] *Makusi* (UAz, v.28)

Wayundatt *see* Huron

Wayundatt *see* Wyandot

Wayundott *see* Huron

Wayundott *see* Wyandot

Wayuu [Self-designation] *see* Goajiro

Wazaizara *see* Guaja

Wazaza *see* Osage

Wazazies [SD] *Oglala* (H)

Wa-zhahez *see* Osage

Wazhahez *see* Osage

Wazhazha [Clan] *Ponca* (H)

Wazhazhe *see* Osage

Wazhazhe *Ponca* (H)

Wazhazhe [Self-designation] (BE) *see also* Osage (LC)

Wa-zha'zhe [Self-designation] *see* Osage

Wazhush [Clan] *Chippewa* (H)

Waziawintcacta *see* Wazi'a wintca'cta

Wazi'a wintca'cta [MN] *Assiniboin* (BE)

Wazi-kute *see* Chanona

Wazikute (PC) *see also* Chanona (H)

Wazikute *Yanktonai* (BE)

Wa-zi-ya-ta Pa-da-nin *see* Arikara

Waziyata Padanin *see* Arikara

Waziya wicasta *see* Tschantoga

Waziya wicasta *see* Wazi'a wintca'cta

Waz-za-ar-tar *see* Zaartaar

Wazzaartar *see* Zaartaar

Wazzaza *see* Waz-za-za

Waz-za-za *Brule* (TW, v.39, no.6, June 1992, p.49)

W'Banankee *see* Abnaki

Wchip-pow-waw *see* Ojibwa

Wdowo *see* Ottawa

Wea [OK] *Miami* (LC)

Weakaote *see* Khemnichan

Weandot *see* Huron

Weanock [VA] (Hdbk15)

Weapemeoc [NC] (BE)

Weasel-skin headdress Indians [Clan] [MN] *Atsina* (BE)

Weashkimek *see* Eskimos

Webbing *see* Winnebago

Weber *see* Cumumbah

Weber River Yutahs *see* Cumumbach

Weber-Utes *see* Cumumbah

Webing *see* Winnebago

We-che-ap-pe-nah *see* Itscheabine

Wecheappenah *see* Itscheabine

Wechihit [CA] *Southern Yokuts* (CA)
Wechikhit *see* Wechihit
Weciare *see* Wokiare
Wecquaesgeek [NY, CN] *Wappinger* (BE)
Wee hee skeu *see* Heviqs-ni'pakis
Weeheeskey *see* Heviqs-ni'pakis
Wee-ka-nah *see* Taos
Weekanah *see* Taos
Wee-kee-mack *see* Oowekeeno
Weekeemock *see* Oowekeeno
Weekenoch *see* Oowekeeno
Weeko (NAmI, v.19, 1978)
Weeminuche (LC) *see also* Wiminuch (LC)
Weeminuche [CO] *Ute* (Hdbk11)
Weepers *see* Assiniboin
Weepers *see* Coaque
Weesock *see* Waxhaw
Weesowhetko [Subclan] *Delaware* (H)
Weetamoe [MA] *Wampanoag* (BE)
Weetle-toch *see* Oealitk
Weetletoch *see* Oealitk
Weeyarkeek *see* Cascades
Weeyot *see* Wiyot
Weha [Clan] *Jemez* (H)
We hee skeu chien *see* Heviqs-ni'pahis
Wehee skeuchien *see* Heviqs-ni'pahis
Wehetara *see* Pira-Tapuya
Wehiko *see* Waco
wehka *see* Santo Domingo
Weianoack *see* Weanock
Weidyenye [Self-designation] *see* Mundurucu
Weitchpec [Yurok] (CA)
Weithspeh *see* Yurok
Weithspek *see* Yurok
Weitle toch *see* Oealitk
Weitletoch *see* Oealitk
Weits-pek *see* Yurok
Weiyot *see* Wiyot
Wejwo *see* Mataco
Wekanaqa'n *see* Okinagan
Welapakoteli *see* Wela'pakote'li
Wela'pakote'li [WA] *Kwalhioqua* (BE)
We-la-tah *see* Picuris
Welatah *see* Picuris
We'lmelti (BE) *see also* Washo (LC)
Welmelti *see* We'lmelti
We'lmelti [NV] (BE)
Welsh Indians (H) *see also* Hopi (LC)
Welsh Indians [NC] (LC)
Welunungsi [Subclan] *Delaware* (H)
Wemen *see* Siberian Eskimos

Wemenuche *see* Weeminuche
Wemessouret *see* Missouri
Wemiamik *see* Miami
wemintheew *see* Munsee
We-mi-nu-che *see* Weeminuche
Weminuche *see* Weeminuche
Wenachee *see* Wenatchi
Wename *see* Unami
Wenatcha *see* Wenatchi
Wenatchee *see* Wenatchi
Wenatchi [WA] (LC)
Wenaumeeu *see* Unami
Wenaumeew *see* Unami
Wendat *see* Huron
Wendat *see* Wyandot
wenepeko-w *see* Winnebago
Wenro *see* Wenrohronon
Wenrohronon [NY, PA] (LC)
Wentshepan *see* Wenatchi
Wenuhtokowuk *see* Nanticoke
We-ock-sock Willacum *see* Smackshop
Weocksockwillacum *see* Smackshop
Weocksock Willacum *see* Smackshop
Weopomiock *see* Weapemeoc
Wepawaug *see* Paugusset
weplapatsa *see* San Felipe
Wequadong [WI, MI] *Chippewa* (H)
Weramocomoco *see* Werowocomoco
Weraskoyks *see* Warrasqueoc
werckena *see* Arekena
Weroscoick *see* Warrasqueoc
Werowocomoco [VA] *Powhatan* (BE)
Wesa [Clan] *Quapaw* (H)
Wes'anikacinga *see* Northern Shoshone
Wes'anikacinga *see* Shoshone
Wesanikacinga *see* Northern Shoshone
Wesanikacinga *see* Shoshone
Weshacum [MA] *Pennacook* (BE)
Wesh-ham *see* Tlakliut
Wesh-ham *see* Wishram
Weshham *see* Tlakliut
Weshham *see* Wishram
Weskarini [Can] *Algonkin* (BE)
Wesorts [MD] *Mixed Bloods* (LC)
West Alaskan *Eskimos* (Ye)
West Central Sierra Miwok [Lang] [CA] (CA-8)
Westchester Indians *see* Wiechquaeskeck
Westenhuck [MA] *Mahican* (BE)
Western Abnaki (Hdbk15)
Western Aleut [Lang] [*Eskimo-Aleut*] (Hdbk5)
Western Apache (Hdbk10) *see also* San Carlos Apache (BE)

Western Apache [AZ, NM] (Hdbk10)
Western Bakairi [Br] (O)
Western Bororo [BO, Br] (O)
Western Cahuilla [CA] (BE)
Western Canada [*Inuit-Inupiaq*] (Hdbk5)
Western Carib [Lang] (UAz, v.28)
Western Coast *see* Marin-Bodega
Western Denes *Tinne* (H)
Western Diegueño *see* Northern Diegueño
Western Dog-ribbed Indians *see* Tsantieottine
Western Guiana Carib [Lang] *Panare* (UAz, v.28)
Western Indians *see* Creek
Western Keres [Lang] (H)
Western Mackenzie Innuit *see* Kangmaligmiut
Western Mackenzie Innuit *see* Kopagmiut
Western Mayan [Lang] [CAm] (O)
Western Miwokan [Lang] (CA-8)
Western Mono (JCB, v.12, no.2, 1990, pp.215–230) *see* Mono (CA)
Western Moquelumnan [Lang] [CA] (Pub, v.6, no.1, pp.303–305)
Western Niantic [RI, CN] (BE)
Western Numic [Lang] (Hdbk10)
Western Payutes *see* Owens Valley Paiute
Western Province (AI)
Western Pueblos (Ye)
Western Riparian (AI)
Western Shoshone (H) *see also* Shoshoko (H)
Western Shoshone [ID, UT] (BE)
Western Shuswap [Lang] *Interior Salish* (Hdbk12)
Western Sioux *see* Teton
Western Suya *see* Beico do Pau
Western Tarahumara [Lang] [MX] (Hdbk10)
Western Timbira *see* Apinage
Western Timbira *see* Toba
Western Toba [BO] (O)
Western Tukanoan (O)
Western Wappo [CA] (BE)
Western Wappo [Lang] [CA] *Yuki* (Pub, v.6, no.1, p.266)
Western White Mountain Apache *San Carlos Apache* (BE)
Western Woods *Cree* (BE)
Western Yavapai (Hdbk10) *see also* Toklapaya (BE)
Western Yavapai (Pub, v.29, no.4, p.177)

West Greenlanders *Greenland Es-*
kimos (H)
West Greenlandic *Greenland Eski-*
mos (Hdbk5)
Westo *Yuchi* (BE)
West Schious *see* Teton
We-suala-kuin *see* Sandia
Wesualakuin *see* Sandia
Weta-hato *see* Kiowa
Wetahato *see* Kiowa
Wetch-pec *see* Yurok
Wetch-peck *see* Yurok
Wetc-naqei'n *see* Okinagan
Wetcnaqein *see* Okinagan
We-te-pa-ha-to *see* Kiowa
Wetepahato *see* Kiowa
Wetersoon *see* Amahami
We-thlu-ella-kwin *see* San Felipe
[Keres]
Wethluellakwin *see* San Felipe
[Keres]
Wetitsaan *see* Hidatsa
Wetopahata *see* Kiowa
Wetshipweyanah *see* Chipewyan
Wettaphato *see* Kiowa
Wewamashkem [Gens] *Ma-*
malelekala (H)
Wewasee *see* We-wa-see
We-wa-see [Clan] *Shawnee* (H)
Weweenock *see* Wawenock
Wewenoc *see* Wawenock
We-wi-ca-sa *see* Kainah
Wewicasa *see* Kainah
Wewime *see* Wewi'me
Wewi'me [ID] *Nez Perce* (BE)
Weyandott *see* Huron
Weyarnihkato [Subclan] *Delaware*
(H)
Wey-eh-hoo *see* Yehuh
Wey-eh-hoo *see* Cascades
Weyehhoo *see* Cascades
Weyehhoo *see* Cascades
Weyehhoo *see* Yehuh
Weyet *see* Wiyot
Weyi-letpu *see* Cayuse
Weyonaques *see* Weanock
Weyondott *see* Huron
Weyondott *see* Wyandot
Wezhinshte [Subgens] *Omaha*
(H)
Whala [Clan] [NM] *Pecos* (H)
Whapi [Clan] *San Ildefonso* (H)
Whe-el-po *see* Colville
Wheelpo *see* Colville
Whe-el-poo *see* Colville
Wheelpoo *see* Colville
Whil-kut *see* Whilkut
Whilkut [CA] (CA)
Whilkut [Lang] [CA] *Hupa* (H)
Whinega *see* Huna
Whippanap *see* Abnaki
Whiskah [WA] *Chehalis* (H)
Whisklaleitch *see* Kittizoo

Whispering Pines Band (Hdbk12)
see also Clinton Band (Hdbk12)
Whispering Pines Band [BC]
Fraser River Shuswap (Hdbk12)
White Ants *see* Coyotes
White Bird Nez Perce *see* Lam-
tama
White Breasts *see*
Ahkaiyikokakiniks
White Cap [Can] *Dakota* (BE)
White Eagle (H) *see also* Khuya
(H)
White Eagle *Dakota* (BE)
White-Eared People *see* Tohon-
taenrat
White Earth Band *see* Gawababi-
ganikak
White Fish Indians *see* At-
tikamegue
White-Goose Eskimos *see* Kan-
gormiut
White Indians *see* Monominee
White Indians *see* Hopi
White Knife *see* White Knives
White Knives (H) *see also* Tus-
sawehe (H)
White Knives *Western Shoshone*
(Hdbk11)
White Minqua *see* Susquehanna
White Mountain Apache *Western*
Apache (Hdbk10)
White Mountain People *see* Pi-
anbotinu
White pani *see* Pawnee
White Pania *see* Pawnee
White People *see* Coyotes
White People *see* Stoamohimal
White Pueblo *see* Nabatatuei
White River [CO] *Ute* (Hdbk11)
White River *Western Shoshone*
(Hdbk11)
White River Indians (BE) *see also*
Kaviawach (BE)
White River Indians (H) *see also*
Klikitat (LC)
White River Indians (H) *see also*
Niskap (H)
White River Indians (H) *see also*
Skopamish (BE)
White River Indians (H) *see also*
Smulkamish (BE)
White Salmon [OR, WA]
(Hdbk12)
White Village *see* Nabatutei
White Whale River (BE) [Can]
[*Montagnais-Naskapi*] (BE)
Whiwunai *see* Hopi
Whonkentia [VA] *Monahoac* (BE)
Whull-e-mooch *see* Salish
Whullemooch *see* Salish
Whulwhaipum *see* Klikitat
Whulwhypum *see* Klikitat
wiachitoh *see* Wichita

wia chitoh *see* Wichita
Wi'alet-pum *see* Cayuse
Wialetpum *see* Cayuse
Wiam *see* Wyam
Wiananno *see* Iyanough
Wiandot *see* Huron
Wiandott *see* Huron
Wiapes *see* Quapaw
Wiaquahheckegumeeng [MI, WI]
Chippewa (H)
Wiaunyen *see* Mundurucu
Wibu-ka pa *see* Mohave
Wibukapa *see* Mohave
Wiccacomoco *see* Wicocomoco
Wiccimisses *see* Wicomese
Wiccocomico *see* Wicocomoco
Wiccomeese *see* Wicomese
Wichamni [CA] *Yokuts* (LC)
Wichamni [Lang] [*Tule-Kaweah*]
(CA-8)
Wi'chi'kik *see* Wechihit
Wichikik *see* Wechihit
Wichita [TX, OK] (LC)
Wichiyela *see* Yankton
Wichocomoco *see* Wicocomoco
Wiciyela *see* Yankton
Wickacomio *see* Wicocomoco
Wickerscreek Indyans *see*
Wiechquaeskeck
Wickicomoco *see* Wicocomoco
Wicocomico *see* Wicocomoco
Wicocomoco [VA] *Powhatan*
(BE)
Wicomese [MD] *Nanticoke* (BE)
Wicomesse *see* Wicomese
Wicomico *see* Wicocomoco
Wicomiss *see* Wicomese
Wicomocon (H) *see also* Sec-
owocomoco (BE)
Wicomocon *Conoy* (Hdbk15)
Wi'cxam *see* Tlakluit
Wicxam *see* Wishram
Wicxam *see* Tlakluit
Widge-e-te-ca-par *see* Maricopa
Widgeetecapar *see* Maricopa
Widshi itikapa *see* Maricopa
Widshi iti'kapa *see* Pima
Widshi itikapa *see* Papago
Widshiitikapa *see* Maricopa
Widshiitikapa *see* Papago
Widshiitikapa *see* Pima
Widyu *see* Ditsakana
Wi'dyu *see* Ditsakana
Wiechquaeskeck *Delaware*
(Hdbk15)
Wiekagjoc [NY] *Mahican* (BE)
Wiequaskeck *see*
Wiechquaeskeck
Wighcocomoco *see* Pocomoke
Wighcocomoco *see* Wicocomoco
wihinaitti [Self-designation] *see*
Northern Shoshone
wihinakwati *see* Shoshone

Wihinasht [OR, ID] (H)
Wi-ic-ap-i-nah *see* Itscheabine
Wiicapinah *see* Itscheabine
Wikainoh *see* Oowekeeno
Wikanee *see* Oowekeeno
Wikchamni [CA] *Yokuts* (LC)
Wikchamni [Lang] [*Tule-Kaweah*] (CA-8)
Wikchomni *see* Wikchamni
Wik-chum-ni *see* Wikchamni
Wikchumni *see* Wikchamni
Wikedjasapa [AZ] *Southeastern Yavapai* (BE)
Wikenichepa (BE) *see also* Mathaupapaya (BE)
Wikenichepa [AZ] *Northeastern Yavapai* (BE)
Wikeno (LC) *see also* Oowekeeno (LC)
Wik'eno *see* Ooweekeeno
Wikeno [Can] *Heiltsuk* (BE)
wikenox *see* Wikeno
Wiki [CA] *Wiyot* (BE)
Wiki-daredalil [CA] *Wiyot* (Pub, v.9, no.3, p.384)
Wikoktenok [Clan] *Bellabella* (H)
Wiksachi *see* Wik-sach-i
Wik-sach-i *Yokuts* (Contri, v.3, p.370)
Wikutepa [AZ] (BE)
Wikyuwamkamusenaikata [Can] *Cree* (BE)
wilac'u-kwe *see* Western Apache
Wilaksel *see* Wi'lak-sel
Wi'lak-sel [CA] *Patwin* (Contri, v.3, p.219)
Wilana *see* Picuris
wilatho *see* Picuris
Wilatsu'kwe *see* Coyotero Apache
Wild Coyotes *see* Navajo
Wild Creeks *see* Seminole
Wild Gentlemen *see* Polar Eskimos
Wild Motilones *see* Bari
Wild Nation *see* Etchaottine
Wild Rice *see* Menominee
Wild Rice Eaters *see* Menominee
Wild Rice Men *see* Menominee
Wi'lfa Ampa'fa am'im *see* Twana
Wilfa Ampafa amim *see* Twana
Wilfaampafaamim *see* Twana
Wi-li-gi *see* San Felipe [Keres]
Wiligi *see* San Felipe [Keres]
Wi-li-gi-i *see* San Felipe [Keres]
Wiligii *see* San Felipe [Keres]
Wili idahapa *see* Mohave
Wiliidahapa *see* Mohave
Willamette *see* Cathlacumup
Willamette Falls Indians *see* Clowwewalla
Willamette Indians *see* Clowwewalla

Willamette Tum-water band *see* Clowwewalla
Willammette Indians *see* Clowwewalla
Willapa *see* Kwalhioqua
Willa Walla *see* Walla Walla
Willetpo *see* Cayuse
Willhamett *see* Clowwewalla
Willi [CA] *Maidu* (H)
Williams Lake [BC] *Shuswap* (H)
Willinis *see* Illinois
Willow Creek Indians *see* Lohim
Willow People *see* Paskokopawiinuuk
Wiltaikapeya [AZ] *Western Yavapai* (Pub, v.29, no.4)
Wima *see* Wi-ma
Wi-ma *Maidu* (Contri, v.3, np.282)
Wimbee [SC] *Cusabo* (BE)
Wimilchi [CA] *Southern Valley Yokuts* (H)
Wiminuch *see* Weeminuche
Wiminuche (LC) *see also* Weeminuche (Hdbk11)
Wiminuche [CO] *Ute* (LC)
Wimonuch *see* Wiminuche
wimonuntci *see* Wiminuche
Wimonuntsi *see* Wiminuche
Wimosas *see* Yamassee
Wina *see* Desana
Winanghatal *see* Waksachi
Wi-nan-gik *see* Waksachi
Winangik *see* Waksachi
Winao [Lang] *Arawaka* (O)
Wina't ca *see* Wenatchi
Winatca *see* Wenatchi
winatsapam *see* Wenatchi
Winatshipum (LC) WEE Wenatchi (LC)
Winauk *see* Weanock
Winavi *see* Puinave
Windermere [BC] *Kutenai* (BE)
Win-de-wer-rean-toon *see* Mdewakanton
Windewerreantoon *see* Mdewakanton
Wind Family *see* Hutalgalgi
Wind People *see* Kiyuksa [Mdewakanton]
Wind People *see* Kansa
Wind River Shoshone [WY] (Anthro, v.5, no.5)
Windsor Indians *see* Podunk
Winebago *see* Winnebago
Winetaries *see* Hidatsa
Winibago *see* Winnebago
Winimen [CA] *Wintu* (BE)
winipeeaakoakee *see* Winnebago
wi-nipe-ko *see* Winnebago
winipeko *see* Winnebago
wi-nipi-ko *see* Winnebago
winipiko *see* Winnebago

winipikwa *see* Winnebago
winipyekohaki *see* Winnebago
Winiun *see* Wintu
Winnabago *see* Winnebago
Winnakenozzo *see* Miniconjou
Winnebago [WI, SD] (LC)
winnebagoag *see* Winnebago
Winnebegoshishiwininewak [MN] *Chippewa* (BE)
Winnebegoshishiwininiwak *see* Winnebegoshishiwininewak
Winnecowet [NH] *Pennacook* (IndL, nos.27–28)
Winnemem (CA) *see also* Winimem (BE)
Winnemem [CA] (CA)
Winnepeg *see* Winnebago
Winnepeskowuk [Can] *Upeshipow* (H)
Winnibago *see* Winnebago
Win-ni-mim *see* Winimen
Winnimim *see* Winimem
Winnipisauki [NH] *Pennacook* (IndL, nos.27–28)
Winpyeko *see* Winnebago
Winpyekok *see* Winnebago
Winta *see* Wintu
Wintaperi *Amarakaeri* (O)
Wintoon *see* Wintu
Wintu [Lang] [CA] *Penutian* (CA-8)
Wintuan *see* Wintu
Win-tun *see* Wintu
Wintun *see* Wintu
Winyaw [SC] (BE)
wipayutta *see* Skull Valley [Gosiute]
Wippanap *see* Abnaki
Wipukpaya [AZ] *Yavapai* (BE)
Wipukyipai [AZ] *Northeastern Yavapai* (Pub, v.29, no.4, p.177)
Wiquaeskeck *see* Wiechquaeskeck
Wira [Self-designation] *see* Desana
Wirafed [Br] *Kawahib* (O)
Wirina [Lang] [SA] *Maipurean* (O)
Wiruhikwairuk'a *see* Kammatwa
Wiruwhitsu *see* Katiru
Wisacky *see* Waxhaw
Wisagechroanu *see* Missisauga
Wischosk *see* Wiyot
Wisconsin River people *see* Wi'skos Se'peo Wini'niwuk
Wisham *see* Wishram
Wishham *see* Tlakluit
Wishham *see* Wishram
Wishoko [Clan] *Hopi* (H)
Wishosk *see* Wiyot
Wish-pooke *see* Yurok
Wishpooke *see* Yurok

Wish-ram *see* Tlakluit
Wishram *see* Wasco
Wish-ram *see* Wishram
Wishram (PC) *see also* Tlakluit (LC)
Wishram [WA] (BE)
Wishran *see* Tlakluit
Wishran *see* Wishram
Wishtenatin [OR] *Tututni* (H)
Wi'skos Se'peo Wini'niwuk [WI] *Menominee* (BE)
Wiskos Sepep Wininiwuk *see* Wi'skos Se'peo Wini'niwuk
Wissakodewinini *see* Mixed Bloods
Wissam *see* Tlakluit
Wiss-co-pam *see* Wasco
Wisscopam *see* Wasco
Wis-so-man-chuh *see* Hupa
Wissomanchuh *see* Hupa
Wisswham *see* Tlakluit
Wisswham *see* Wishram
Witahwicata *see* Pitahauerat
Witamky [FL] *Seminole* (His/T, v.2, p.372)
Witanghatal *see* Serrano
Witanghatal *see* Gitanemuk
Wi-ta-pa-ha *see* Kiowa
Witapaha *see* Kiowa
Witapa'hat *see* Kiowa
Witapahat *see* Kiowa
Wi'tapahatu *see* Kiowa
Wi'tapaha'tu *see* Kiowa
Witapahatu *see* Kiowa
Witap'atu *see* Kiowa
Witapa'tu *see* Kiowa
Witapatu *see* Kiowa
Witci-abin [MN] *Assiniboin* (BE)
Witcinyanpina *see* Itscheabine
Wi-tets-han *see* Hidatsa
Witetshan *see* Hidatsa
Without Bows *see* Sans Arcs
Witishaxtanu *see* Illinois
Witishaxtanu *see* Miami
witishaxtánu *see* Illinois
Witkispu [ID] *Nez Perce* (BE)
Witooilthaht *see* Ucluelet
Witoto [Col, PE] (LC)
Witoupo *see* Ibitoupa
Witowpa *see* Ibitoupa
Witowpo *see* Ibitoupa
Witsch-piks *see* Yurok
Witschpiks *see* Yurok
Witskamin *see* Wikchamni
Witsta *see* Bellabella
Witukomno'm [CA] *Yuki* (BE)
Witune *see* Kadohadacho Confederacy
Wi-tup-a-tu *see* Kiowa
Witupatu *see* Kiowa
Wiuini'em *see* Ditsakana
Wiwash *see* Nanticoke
Wiweakam [Gens] *Kueha* (H)

Wiwekae [Sept] [BC] *Lekwiltok* (H)
Wiwi [Self-designation] *see* Malayo
wiwi-nipye-ko-haki *see* Winnebago
Wiwohka [AL] *Muskogee* (BE)
Wiyandott *see* Huron
Wiyat *see* Wiyot
wiyitaka'a (Hdbk11)
Wiyok *see* Wiyot
Wiyot [CA] (LC)
W-ltoo-ilth-aht *see* Ucluelet
W'nalachtko *see* Unalachtigo
Wnalachtko *see* Unalachtigo
W'namiu *see* Unami
Wnamiu *see* Unami
Wo-a-pa-nach-ki *see* Abenaki
Woapanachki *see* Delaware
Woapanachki *see* Abnaki
Wobanaki *see* Abnaki
Wobonuch [CA, NV] *Mono* (BE)
Woccon [Lang] *Catawba* (H)
Woccon [NC] (BE)
Wociare *see* Wokiare
Wo-he-nom-pa *see* Oohenonpa
Wohenompa *see* Oohenonpa
Wohesh *see* Pawnee
Wohkpotsit *see* Woopotsi't
Wohuamis [Clan] *Koskimo* (H)
Wokiare [Guy, VE] (O)
Wokopee Indians *see* Owens Valley Paiute
Woksihitanio [Society] *Cheyenne* (H)
Wo'ladji *see* Wo'lasi
Woladji *see* Wo'lasi
Wo-la-si *see* Wo'lasi
Wolasi *see* Wo'lasi
Wo-lasi [CA] *Southern Valley Yokuts* (BE)
Wolf *see* Horatamumake
Wolf-Eaters *see* Coyotero Apache
Wolf Pawnee *see* Skidi Pawnee
Wolf People *see* Mandhinkagaghe
Wolf River people *see* Muhwa'o Se'peo Wini
Woll-pah-pe *see* Walpapi
Wollpahpe *see* Walpapi
Woll-pa-pe *see* Walpapi
Wollpape *see* Walpapi
Wols *see* Klamath
Wolutayuta *Sans Arc* (H)
Wolves *see* Skidi Pawnee
Womenunche *see* Weeminuche
Wonalatoko *see* Unalachtigo
Wonami *see* Unami
Wondats *see* Wyandot
Wong-ge *see* Jemez
Wongge *see* Jemez
Wongunk [CN] *Wappinger* (H)

Wo-ni-to-na-hi *see* Brule
Wonitonahi *see* Brule
wonsa-be *see* Navajo
wonsabe *see* Navajo
Wood Assiniboines *see* Tschantoga
Wood Cree *see* Sakawithiniwuk
Wooden-lips *see* Tlingit
Woodhouse people *see* Basawunena
Wood Indians *see* Tutchone
Wood Indians *see* Nopeming
Wood Indians *see* Nuchwugh
Woodland Cree *see* Sakawininiwug
Woodland Indians [Can] (LC)
Wood Lodge Men *see* Basawunena
Wood People *see* Hankutchin
Woods Bloods *see* Istsikainah
Wood Stoneys *see* Tshcantoga
Woolwa *see* Ulva
Woopotsi't [SD] *Cheyenne* (BE)
Wooselalim *see* Clallam
Woponuch *see* Wobonuch
Wopowage *see* Paugusset
Woraqa *see* Potawatomi
Wo-ra-qe *see* Potawatomi
Woraqe *see* Potawatomi
Woraxa *see* Potawatomi
Woraxe *see* Potawatomi
Workalgi [Clan] *Creek* (H)
Worm People *see* Esksinaitupiks
worowocomoco *see* Werowocomoco
Woscopom *see* Wasco
Wos-sosh-e *see* Osage
Wossoshe *see* Osage
Wotkalgi [Clan] *Creek* (H)
Wotuha [Self-designation] *see* Piaroa
Wouachita *see* Washita
Wounana *see* Waunana
Wowol (PC) *see also* Wo'lasi (BE)
Wowol [CA] *Southern Valley Yakuts* (CA)
Wowolasi [CA] *Yokuts* (H)
Wo-wul *see* Wo'lasi
Wowulasi *see* Wo'lasi
Woyamana *see* Waiwai
Wrinkled-Ankles *see* Sitcon-ski
wsaki *see* Sauk
W'sha'natu *see* Shallattoo
Wshanatu *see* Shallattoo
Wtanshekaunhtukko *see* Arsigantegoh
W'tassone *see* Oneida
Wtassone *see* Oneida
W'tawas *see* Ottawa
Wtawas *see* Ottawa
Wuchamni *see* Wikchamni
Wu'cxam *see* Wishram
Wucxam *see* Wishram

Wuhana see Macuna
Wukachmina see Wikchamni
Wukoanu [Clan] Hopi (H)
Wuksache see Waksachi
Wuksatche see Waksachi
Wula'stegwiak see Malecite
Wulastegwiak see Malecite
Wu'lastuk-wiuk see Malecite
Wulastukwiuk see Malecite
Wulwa see Ulva
Wulx see Shasta
Wulx see Upper Takelma
Wunalachtico see Unalachtigo
Wunalachtigo see Unalachtigo
Wunamuca's [the Second] band
    see Kuyuidika
Wun-a-muc-a's band [the Sec-
    ond] see Kuyuidika
Wunaumeeh see Unami
Wundat see Wyandot
Wunnashowatuckoog [MA] Nip-
    muc (IndL, nos.27–28)
Wu-sa-si see Osage
Wusasi see Osage
Wushketan [Social group] [AK]
    Hutsnuwu (H)
Wush-quma-pum see Tlakluit
Wushqumapum see Tlakluit
Wushuum see Wishram
Wusita see Wichita
Wusquowhananawkit [MA] Nip-
    muc (IndL, no.s27–28)
Wu'tap see Wu'tapiu
Wutap see Wu'tapiu
Wutapiu see Wu'tapiu
Wu'tapiu [SD] [Hevhaita'nio]
    (BE)
Wuteelit [AK] Yuit Eskimos (BE)
Wutshik see Wu'tshik
Wu'tshik [Clan] Menominee (H)
Wutsta see Bellabella
Wyam [OR] (LC)
Wyandot (LC) see also Huron
    (LC)
Wyandot [OH, OK after 1867]
    (BE)
Wyandote see Wyandot
Wyandott see Wyandot
Wyandotte see Wyandot
Wyanoke see Weanock
Wyapes see Quapaw
Wyatanon see Wea
Wy-eilat see Cayuse
Wyeilat see Cayuse
Wyendott see Wyandot
Wykenas see Oowekeeno
Wynaugh see Weanock
Wynoochee (LC) see also We-
    natchi (LC)
Wynoochee [WA] Chehalis I (BE)
Wyoming [WY] Susquehanna
    (BE)
Wyondat see Wyandot

Wyondatt see Wyandot
Wyondott see Wyandot
Wysox [NY] Susquehanna (BE)

-X-

Xabotaj see Hano
Xabotaos see Hano
Xacaje see Jacao
Xacatin see Soacatino
Xacupa'nya see Maricopa
Xaesar see Saesse
Xaeser see Haesar
Xaexaes see China Hat
Xa'exaes [Self-designation] see
    China Hat
Xagi-la'na see Hagi-lana
Xagilana see Hagi-lana
Xagua [HA, WInd] Caizcimu
    (BE)
Xagua'tc see Agua Caliente
Xaguetco see Caduveo
Xaguimaniguara see
    Saguimaniguara
Xa-he-ta-no see Apache
Xahetano see Apache
Xaida see Haida
Xa'ida [Self-designation] see
    Haida
Xaihais see China Hat
Xaimame see Cotonam
Xa-isla see Haisla
Xa-isla see Kitamat
Xaisla see Haisla
Xaisla see Kitamat
Xaixais Kwakiutl (Anthro, v.14,
    no.5, pp.341–347)
Xakleng see Shokleng
Xa-kpe-dan see Taoapa
Xakpedan see Taoapa
Xakriaba [Br] (O)
Xalan see Xarame
Xalay see Zuni
Xalda'ngats see Huldanggat
Xaldangats see Huldanggat
Xalpan [MX] Pueblo Indians (BE)
xalsiyum see Halchidhoma
Xamakxa'p see Mohave
Xamakxap see Mohave
Xamakxav see Mohave
xamakxa'va see Mohave
xamakxava see Mohave
Xamana [SanD, WInd, HA]
    Hubabo (BE)
Xamanao see Hamano
Xamanao see Hawmanao
Xamatari see Shamatari
Xambioa [Br] Caraja (O)
Xamunambe [SC] (H)
Xamunanuc see Xamunambe

Xanaksiala see Kitlope
Xana-ks'iala [Self-designation] see
    Kitlope
Xangopany see Shongopovi
Xantigui Coahuiltecan (Hdbk10)
Xapes see Hapes
Xapida [SC] (H)
Xapies see Hapes
Xapira see Xapida
xa-po see Santa Clara [NM]
xapo see Santa Clara [NM]
Xaqueuria see Quivira
Xaragua [HA, WInd] Bainao (BE)
Xaram see Xarame
Xarame [TX] Coahuiltecan (BE)
Xaramene see Aranama
Xarames see Harames
Xaraname see Aranama
Xaratenumanke see Pawnee
Xaray see Zuni
Xaruma [Br] (O)
Xatoe Piro (H)
Xatol see Xatoe
xatpa see Pima
Xatukwiwa see Wintu
Xavante [Br] (O)
Xavante Acuan see Akwe-
    Shavante
Xavante-Acuen see Akwe-
    Shavante
xavasu-k apay see Savasupai
Xa'xamatses see Hahamatse
Xaxamatses see Hahamatse
Xax'eqt see Kakekt
Xaxeqt see Kakekt
Xaxka-a see Crow
Xebero see Jebero
Xebina see Xe'bina
Xe'bina [MN] Assiniboin (BE)
Xegueteo [SA] Caduveo (O)
Xelkoan see Hehlkoan
xelyi'kuma'i see Halyikwamai
Xemes see Jemez
Xemez see Jemez
Xenatonwan see Xe'natonwan
Xe'natonwan [MN] Assiniboin
    (BE)
Xerente see Sherente
Xeres see Keres
Xeripam [TX] (H)
Xeta see Heta
Xevero see Jebero
Xevero-Munichi see Paranapura
Xharame see Xarame
Xhiahuam see Siaguan
Xhiahuan see Siaguan
Xiabu (H) see also Hiabu (BE)
Xiabu Coahuiltecan (BE)
Xiamela Pueblo Indians (H)
Xiancocodam Coahuiltecan
    (Hdbk10)
Xibitaono [PE] Cocama (O)
Xicaque see Jicaque

Xicarilla *see* Jicarilla Apache
Xicocoje *see* Gicocoge
Xicocossi *see* Gicocoge
Xicrin *see* Xikrin
Xiguan *see* Siaguan
Xijame *see* Sijame
Xijames *see* Hihames
Xikri *see* Xikrin
Xikriabi *see* Xakriaba
Xikrin [Br] *Northern Cayapo* (LC)
Xila *see* Gila Apache
Xilenos *see* Gila Apache
Xilotlatzinca [MX] (BE)
Ximiapa *see* Jimiopa
Xinca [Gu] (LC)
Xincan [Lang] [*Macro-Penutian*] (BE)
Xingu [Lang] *Carib* (UAz, v.28)
Xipaia *see* Chipaya
Xipaolabi *see* Shipaulovi
Xipianawa *see* Xipinawa
Xipinaw *see* Xipinawa
Xipinawa [Br] (O)
Xiriana I [Br, VE: Rio Branco] (O)
Xiriana II [Br, VE: Amazonas] (O)
Xirishana *see* Shiriana
Xirishana *see* Yanoama
Xitibo *see* Setebo
Xivari *see* Jivaro
Xivaro *see* Jivaro
xiwana *see* Apache
Xixame *see* Sijame
Xixime [MX] (BE)
Xiximole [MX] *Concho* (BE)
Xoco *see* Shoco
Xocomes *see* Jocomes
Xogleng *see* Shokleng
Xoi *see* Koi
Xokleng *see* Shokleng
Xokleng *see* Shokleng
Xoko (LC) *see also* Shoco (LC)
Xoko (O) *see also* Xukuru-Kariri (O)
Xoko [Br] (O)
Xokre *see* Shokleng
Xokreng *see* Shokleng
Xolata *see* Chorti
Xometwoli *see* Hometwoli
Xomi *see* Hume
Xommapavi *see* Shongopovi
Xomoks *see* Comox
Xonalus *see* Yonalus
Xongopabi *see* Shongopovi
Xongopani *see* Shongopovi
Xongopaui *see* Shongopovi
Xongopavi *see* Shongopovi
Xoq!e'di *see* Hokedi
Xoquinoe *see* Lacandon
Xorrhue [MX] *Chibchan* (BE)
Xorshio *see* Orio
Xougopavi *see* Shongopovi
Xoumane *see* Jumano

Xowalek [CA] *Eastern Pomo* (Pub, v.40, no.2)
Xowunkut *see* Howungkut
Xoxi *see* Sewee
Xo'yala *see* Hoyala
Xoyala *see* Hoyala
Xoya'les *see* Hoyala
Xoyales *see* Hoyala
Xptianos Manssos *see* Manso
Xuacaya [SC] (H)
Xu'adja-nao *see* Hutsnuwu
Xuadjinao *see* Hutsnuwu
Xuado's *see* Huados
Xuala *see* Cheraw
Xualla *see* Cheraw
Xuamitsan *see* Quamichan
Xuanes *see* Huanes
Xuarogio *see* Varohio
Xuikina-wo *Northern Chorote* (O)
Xuikua'yaxen *see* Huikuyaken
Xukru *see* Xikrin
Xukuru (O) *see also* Xukuru-Kariri (O)
Xukuru [Br] (O)
Xukuru-Kariri [Br] (O)
Xuma *see* Jumano
Xumana *see* Jumano
Xumane *see* Jumano
Xumaria *see* Jumano
Xumase *see* Jumano
Xumatcam *see* Tepecano
Xume'xen *see* Comiakin
Xumexen *see* Comiakin
Xumskhumesilis [Clan] *Quatsino* (H)
Xumsxumesilis *see* Xumskhumesilis
Xumunaumbe *see* Xamunambe
Xumupami *see* Shongopovi
Xumupani *see* Shongopovi
Xupulame *Coahuiltecan* (Hdbk10)
Xura *see* Witoto
Xurru [NI] (BE)
Xuts!hit tan *see* Kutshittan
Xuts!nuwu [Self-designation] *see* Hutsnuwu

-Y-

Ya [Clan] *Pecos* (H)
Yaagala *see* Ympqua
Yaai'Hak-emac *see* Yaaihakemae
Yaaihakemac *see* Yaaihakemae
Yaaihakemae [VanI] (H)
Yaai'x-aqemae *see* Yaaihakemae
Yaaixaqemae *see* Yaaihakemae
Yaaixyakami *see* ya'aixyakAmi
ya'aixyakAmi [Clan] *Kwexa* (Pub, v.9, no.3, p.158)
Yaa'kima *see* Yakima

Yaakima *see* Yakima
Ya'ash *see* Yangtsaa
Yaash *see* Yangtsaa
Ya-a-si-tun *see* Yaasitun
Yaasitun [OR] *Takelma* (H)
Yabaana *see* Yabarana
Yabapais *see* Yavapai
Yabarana [Br, VE] (LC)
Yabijoias *see* Yavapai
Yabipaees *see* Yavapai
Yabipai *see* Yavapai
Yabipai *see* Apache
Yabipai Cajuala *see* Southern Paiute
Yabipai Cajuala *see* Paiute
Yabipai Jabesua *see* Havasupai
Yabipai Lipan *see* Lipan Apache
Yabipais *see* Navajo
Yabipais Cuercomaches *see* Cuercomache
Yabipais Gileños *see* Gila Apache
Yabipais Jabesua *see* Havasupai
Yabipais Lipan *see* Lipan Apache
Yabipais Nabajay *see* Navajo
Yabipais Natage *see* Kiowa Apache
Yabipais Natage *see* Natage
Yabipais Tejua *see* Tejua
Yabipaiye *see* Yavapai
Yabipay *see* Yavapai
Yabipias *see* Yavapai
Yabuti *see* Jabuti
Yacaaw *see* Yakima
Yacamaw *see* Yakima
Yacana *see* Yecan
Yacavanes *see* Yojuane
Yacaw *see* Makah
Yacchicaua [MX] *Concho* (BE)
Yacco *see* Acoma
Yacdossa [TX] *Coahuiltecan* (BE)
Yachachumnes *see* Yachikamni
Yachakeenee *see* Ditsakana
Yachchumnes *see* Yachikamni
Yachies *see* Texas
Yachikamni [CA] *Cholovone* (H)
Yachimese (H) *see also* Yachikamni (H)
Yachimese [CA] *Cholovone* (H)
Yachimicha *see* Chitimacha
Ya-chin *see* Yachin
Yachin [AZ] *San Carlos Apache* (H)
Yacho *see* Acoma
Yachou *see* Yazoo
Yachoux *see* Yazoo
Yachyamelamim *see* Yamel
Yackaman *see* Yakima
Yackamaw *see* Yakima
Yackaw *see* Yakima
Yackima *see* Yakima
Yacoman *see* Yakima
Yacomanshaghking [NJ] *Unalachtigo* (BE)

Yacon see Yaquina
Yacona see Yaquina
Yacone see Yaquina
Yactaches see Yatasi
Yacuana see Yecuana
Yaculsari [MX] Concho (BE)
Yacum [CA] Diegueño (H)
Ya'das see Yadus
Yadas see Yadus
Yadkin [NC] (BE)
Yadus [Subclan] Stustas (H)
Yagala see Umpqua
Yagano see Yahgan
Ya-gats see Yagats
Ya-gats see Las Vegas
Yagats (PC) see also Las Vegas
  (Hdbk11)
Yagats [CA] Paiute (BE)
Yagenechito [LA] Choctaw (H)
Yaghan see Yahgan
Yagnetsito see Yagenechito
Yagochsanogechti see Onondaga
Yagoyecayn Pinal Apache (H)
Yagua [PE] (LC)
Yaguana [HA, WInd] Bainao
  (BE)
Yagueca [PR] (BE)
Yaguenechitons see Yagenechito
Yagueneschito see Yagenechito
Yaguma [Br] (O)
Yagunkun-lnagai [Subclan] Haida
  (H)
Ya'gun-kun'lnagi see Yagunkun-
  lnagai
Yagunstlan-lnagai [Subclan]
  Haida (H)
Ya-ha see Yahalgi
Yaha see Yahalgi
Yahalgi [Clan] Creek (H)
Yahandeka [Hdbk11] Northern
  Shoshone (H)
Yahandika see Yahandeka
Ya'handi'ka see Yahandika
Yahauranha see Yecuana
Yah-bay-paiesh see Yavapai
Yahbaypaiesh see Yavapai
Yahgan [CH, TDF] (LC)
Yahi [CA] (CA)
Yahkutat see Yakuta
Ya'hlahaimub'ahutulba see Taos
Yahlahaimubahutulba see Taos
Yahmayo see Yuma
Yahmayo see Quechan
Yahooshkin see Yahuskin
Yahooskin see Yahuskin
Yahooskin Snakes see Yahuskin
Yahowa see Iowa
Yah-quo-nah see Yaquina
Yahquonah see Yaquina
Yahshute [OR] Tututni (H)
Yahthe see Fulnio
Yahua see Yagua
Yahuna [Col] (LC)

Yahunahua [Lang] [Panoan] (O)
Yahup see Yohop
Yahuskin [OR, NV] Northern
  Paiute (LC)
Yah-wil-chin-ne see Yawilchine
Yahwilchinne see Yawilchine
yaia-hano see Tyaia
Ya-ide'sta see Molala
Yaidesta see Molala
Yainoma [Br] Yanoama (O)
Yais see Eyeish
Yak [Clan] [NM] Pueblo Indians
  (H)
Ya-ka see Yaka
Yaka [Clan] Pueblo Indians (H)
Yakahano see Yaka-hano
Yaka-hano [Clan] Keres (H)
Yakahanoch see Yaka-hanoch
Yaka-hanoch [Clan] Pueblo Indi-
  ans (H)
Yakahanoqch see Yaka-hanoqch
Yakahanuch see Yak'a-hanuch
Yak'a-hanuch [Clan] Cochiti (H)
Yakalamarure [Col] (LC)
Yaket-ahno-klatak-makanay see
  Akanekunik
Ya'k'et aqkinuqtle'et aqkts'-
  ma'kinik see Akanekunik
Yaket aqkinuqtleet aqktsmakinik
  see Akanekunik
Yakhano see Yak'hano
Yak'hano [Clan] [NM] Pueblo In-
  dians (H)
Yaki [Lang] [CA] Yana (He)
Ya-ki-as see Yokaia
Yakias see Yokaia
Ya-ki-ma see Yakima
Yakima [after 1994] see Yakama
Yakima [WA] (LC)
Yakimaw see Yakima
Yakka see Yaka
Yak'la'nas see Yaku-lanas
Yaklanas see Yaku-lanas
Yakna-Chitto [LA] (BE)
Yakoken kapai see Karankawa
Yakokenkapai see Karankawa
Yakokon kapai see Karankawa
Yakokonkapai see Karankawa
yakokxon-ecewin see Mescalero
  Apache
yakokxon-kapay [TX] (Hdbk10)
Yakon see Yaquina
Yakon see Yakonan
Yakona see Yaquina
Yakona see Yakonan
Yakonah see Yaquina
Yakonan [OR] (LC)

Yakone see Yaquina
Yakones see Yakonan
Yakoutat see Yakutat
Yakto'inu [ID] Nez Perce (BE)
Ya'ku gitina-I see Yaku-gitinai
Yakugitinai see Yaku-gitinai
Yaku-gitinai [Subclan] Haida (H)
Ya'ku la'nas see Yaku-lanas
Yakulanas see Yaku-lanas
Yaku-lanas [Clan] Haida (H)
Ya-kun-ni-me tunne see Yaquina
Yakunnime tunne see Yaquina
Yak'utat see Yakutat
Yakutat [AK] Tlingit (BE)
Yakutatskoe see Yakutat
Yakutatskoi see Yakutat
Yakwal [TX] (H)
Yakwina see Yakonan
Yakwu Lennas see Yaku-lanas
Yakwulennas see Yaku-lanas
Yalaas see Yazoo
Yalchedunes see Alchedoma
Yalipay see Yavapai
Yallashee see Yatasi
Yaltasse see Yatasi
Yaludnde [Br] Northern Nam-
  bicuara (O)
Yama see Yuma
Yama see Arara
Yamacan Coahuiltecan (Hdbk10)
Yamaces see Yamassee
Yamacraw see Yamassee
Yamaga see Mohave
Yamaica [Lang] [SA] Panoan (O)
Yamajab see Mohave
Yamamadi [Br] (O)
Yaman see Yahgan
Yamana see Yahgan
Yamas see Yamassee
Yamasecs see Yamassee
Yamasee see Yamassee
Yamases see Yamassee
Yamassalgi see Yamassee
Yamassee [FL, GA] (LC)
Yamassi see Yamassee
Yamaya see Mohave
Yam'badika see Yambadika
Yambadika Bannock (H)
Yamel [OR] (BE)
Yameo [PE] (O)
Yamesee see Yamassee
Yamhareek see Ditsakana
Yamhelas see Yamel
Yam Hill see Yamel
Yaminahua see Jaminaua
Yaminawa see Jaminaua
Yaminawa see Chandinahua
Yamiscaron see Yamassee
Yamkallie see Yoncalla
Yamkally see Yoncalla
Yamlocklock see Tamuleko
Yammassee see Yamassee
Yammonsee see yamassee

Yammosee *see* Yamassee
Yam-mos tu-wi-wa-gai-ya *see* Yammostuwiwagaiya
Yammostuwiwagaiya [NV] *Mono* (H)
Yam-mu's *see* Yammostuwiwagaiya
Yam-mus *see* Yamosopo tuviwarai
Yammus *see* Yammostuwiwagaiya
Yammus *see* Yamosopo tuviwarai
Yamoisee *see* Yamassee
Yamorai [PE] (O)
Yamosopo tuviwarai *Northern Paiute* (Hdbk11)
Yamossee *see* Yamassee
Yam-os-ukwaiti *see* Yamosopo tuviwarai
Yamosukwaiti *see* Yamosopo tuviwarai
Yampa (H) *see also* Yavapai (LC)
Yampa (Hdbk10) *see also* Havasupai (LC)
Yampa (Hdbk11) *see also* White River Utes (Hdbk11)
Yampa [UT, CO] *Ute* (LC)
Yampah *see* Comanche
Yampah *see* Yampa
Yampah Utahs *see* Yampa
Yam Pah-Utes *see* Yampa
Yampah Utes *see* Yampa
Yampai *see* Yavapai
Ya'mpaini *see* Comanche
Yampaini *see* Comanche
Yampai-o *see* Yavapai
Yampairi'kani *see* Comanche
Yampais *see* Yavapai
Yampais *see* Havasupai
Yampao *see* Yavapai
Yamparack *see* Ditsakana
Yamparaka *see* Ditsakana
Yampareck *see* Ditsakana
Yampareeka *see* Ditsakana
Yamparica *see* Ditsakana
Yamparika *see* Ditsakana
Yam'pari'ka *see* Ditsakana
Yamparika *see* Ditsakana
Yamparka *see* Yampa
Yamparkau *see* Yampa
Yam-pa-se-ca *see* Ditsakana
Yampaseca *see* Ditsakana
Yampateka *see* Ditsakana
Yampatick-ara *see* Yampa
Yampaxica *see* Ditsakana
Yampay *see* Yavapai
Yampequaw *see* Umpqua
Yamperack *see* Ditsakana
Yamperethka *see* Ditsakana
Yamper-rikeu *see* Ditsakana
Yamperrikeu *see* Ditsakana
Yam-pe-uc-coes *see* Ditsakana
Yampeuccoes *see* Ditsakana

Yampi *see* Yavapai
Yampias *see* Yavapai
Yampio *see* Yavapai
Yam-pi-ric-coes *see* Ditsakana
Yampiriccoes *see* Ditsakana
Yampi-Utes *see* Yampa
Yampoas *see* Yavapai
Yamp-Pah-Utahs *see* Yampa
Yamstills *see* Yamel
Yan [Clan] [NM] *Pueblo Indians* (H)
Yana [Lang] [CA] *Hokan* (CA-8)
Yana [Par] *see* Tapiete
Yanabopos [MX] *Lagunero* (BE)
Yanaconos [Andes] (LC)
Yanaigua *see* Tapiete
Yanakunas *see* Yanaconos
Yanam *see* Yanoama
Yanamaya [Br] *Yanoama* (O)
Yanapero [EC] (O)
Yanaygua *see* Tapiete
Yanche *see* Tonkawa
Yanckton *see* Yankton
Yancomo [NM] *Piro* (H)
Yanctannas *see* Yanktonai
Yancton *see* Yankton
Yanctonais *see* Yanktonai
Yanctonas *see* Yankton
Yanctonees *see* Yanktonai
Yanctongs *see* Yankton
Yanctonie *see* Yanktonai
Yanctonnais *see* Yanktonai
Yanctonnais Cutheads *see* Pabaksa
Yanctonwas *see* Yankton
Yanctorinans *see* Yankton
Yanctowah *see* Yankton
Yanesha *see* Amuesha
Yaneton *see* Yankton
Yanetong *see* Yankton
Yang [Clan] [NM] *Jemez* (H)
Yangala *see* Umpqua
Yangetongs *see* Yankton
Yangti [Clan] *Yuchi* (H)
Yangtons Ahnah *see* Yanktonai
Yangtsaa [Clan] [NM] *Jemez* (H)
Yanieyerono *see* Mohawk
Yanioseaves *see* Yamassee
Yankamas *see* Yakima
Yanka-taus *see* Yankton
Yankataus *see* Yankton
Yanktau-Sioux *see* Yankton
Yank toan *see* Yankton
Yanktoan *see* Yankton
Yanktoanan *see* Yanktonai
Yanktoanon *see* Yanktonai
Yankton [SD] *Lakota* (H)
Yanktona *see* Yanktonai
Yankton Ahna *see* Yanktonai
Yanktonahna *see* Yanktonai
Yankton ahnah *see* Yanktonai
Yanktonahnah *see* Yanktonai
Yanktonai [ND, SD] *Dakota* (H)

Yanktonaia *see* Yanktonai
Yanktonan *see* Yanktonai
Yank-ton-ees *see* Yanktonai
Yanktonees *see* Yanktonai
Yanktonians *see* Yanktonai
Yanktonias-Sioux *see* Yanktonai
Yanktonies *see* Yanktonai
Yanktonnan *see* Yanktonai
Yanktonnas *see* Yanktonai
Yankton of the North *see* Upper Yanktonai
Yankton of the plains *see* Yanktonai
Yanktons Ahna *see* Yanktonai
Yanktonsahna *see* Yanktonai
Yanktons Ahnah *see* Yanktonai
Yanktonsahnah *see* Yanktonai
Yank-ton-us *see* Yanktonai
Yanktonus *see* Yanktonai
Yanktoons *see* Yankton
Yanktown *see* Yankton
Yankwa-nan-syan-ni *see* Iroquois
Yankwanansyanni *see* Iroquois
Yannacook *see* Yannococ
Yannococ [NY] (H)
Yannocock *see* Yannococ
Yano *see* Jano
Yanoama [VE, Br] (LC)
Yanohami *see* Yanoama
Yanomam *see* Yainoma
Yanomama *see* Yanoama
Yanomami *see* Yanoama
Yanomamo *see* Yanoama
Yanoman *see* Yainoma
Yanomani *see* Yanoama
Yanomano *see* Yanoama
Yanomara *see* Yanoama
Yanomaya *see* Yanoama
Yanonami *see* Yanoama
Yan-pa-pa Utahs *see* Yampa
Yanpapa Utahs *see* Yampa
yantarii *see* Antarianunts
Ya'n-tdoa *see* Yan
Yantons *see* Yankton
Yantsaa *see* Yangtsaa
Yao [Lang] *Carib* (UAz, v.28)
Yaochane [MX] *Concho* (BE)
Yaocomico *see* Secowocomoco
Yaocomoco *see* Secowocomoco
Yaomacoes *see* Secowocomoco
Yaos *see* Taos
Yapa *see* Ditsakana
Yapaches *see* Apache
Yapaine *see* Ditsakana
Ya-pa-pi *see* Yavapai
Yapapi *see* Yavapai
Yaparehca *see* Ditsakana
Ya-pa-res-ka *see* Ditsakana
Yapareska *see* Ditsakana
Yapiam [CA] *Pomo* (H)
Yapitalga *see* Pilaga
Yapoco *see* Piapoco
Yapoo *see* Yahgan

Yapparichoes *see* Ditsakana
Yappariko *see* Ditsakana
Yapua *see* Desana
Yaqatlenlisch *see* Yaqatlenlish
Yaqatlenlish [Clan] *Kwakiutl* (H)
Yaqui [MX, AZ] *Cahita* (LC)
Yaquima *see* Yaqui
Yaquimi *see* Yaqui
Yaquimis *see* Yaqui
Yaquina [OR] (BE)
Yaquinigua [MX] *Cadereyta* (Hdbk10)
Ya-ra-hats-see *see* Yarahatssee
Yarahatssee [Clan] *Huron* (H)
Yari [Col] (O)
Yaru-Huanuco [Lang] [SA] *Quecha* (O)
Yaruma [Br] (O)
Yaruma [Lang] *Xingu* (UAz, v.28)
Yaruro [VE] *Achagua* (LC)
Yarurua *see* Yaruro
Yascha [Clan] *Pueblo Indians* (H)
Yascha-hano *see* Yascha
Yaschahano *see* Yascha
Ya-seem-ne *see* Awani
Yaseemne *see* Awani
Yasika [NI, Hon] *Sumo* (BE)
Yaskai *see* Yokaia
Yasones *see* Yazoo
Yasons *see* Yazoo
Yasoos *see* Yazoo
Yasou *see* Yazoo
Yasoux *see* Yazoo
Yasoves *see* Yazoo
Yassa *see* Yazoo
Yassaues *see* Yazoo
Yassouees *see* Yazoo
Yasus *see* Yazoo
Yatace *see* Yatasi
Yatacez *see* Yatasi
Yatache *see* Yatasi
Yatachez *see* Yatasi
Yatase *see* Yatasi
Yatasee *see* Yatasi
Yatasi [LA] *Caddo Confederacy* (BE)
Yatasi [LA] *Naitchitoches Confederacy* (BE)
Yatasie *see* Yatasi
Yatasse *see* Yatasi
Yatassee *see* Yatasi
Yatassez *see* Yatasi
Yatassi *see* Yatasi
Yatay *see* Yatasi
Yatcheethinyoowuc (BE) *see also* Chipewyan (LC)
Yatcheethinyoowuc (H)
Yatcheethinyoowuc (H) *see also* Siksika (LC)
Yat-chee-thin-yoowuc *see* Yatcheethinyoowuc
Yatchies *see* Texas
Yatchikamnes *see* Yachikamni

Yatchitcohes *see* Natchitoches
Yate *see* Fulnio
Yat-e-lat-lar-we *see* Navajo
Yatelatlarwe *see* Navajo
Yatilatlavi *see* Navajo
Yatl nas: had'a'i *see* Yehlnaas-hadai
Yatlnashadai *see* Yehlnaas-hadai
Yatoinu [ID] *Nez Perce* (BE)
Ya'tok'ya-kwe *see* Yatokya
Yatokyakwe *see* Yatokya
Yattapo *see* Yatasi
Yattasaee *see* Yatasi
Yattasces *see* Yatasi
Yattasees *see* Yatasi
Yattasie *see* Yatasi
Yattassee *see* Yatasi
Yauapery *see* Yawaperi
Yauapiti *see* Iaualapiti
Yauarana [VE] (O)
Yaucaniga *Abipone* (LC)
Yauco [PR] (BE)
Yaudanchi *see* Yawdanchi
Yauelmani *see* Yawelmani
Yaughtawnoon *see* Youghtanund
Ya-u-ko *see* Yauco
Yauko *see* Yauco
Yauktong *see* Yankton
Yauktons *see* Yankton
Yaulamni *see* Yawelmani
Yaulanchi *see* Yawdanchi
Yauna *see* Macuna
Yaunktwaun *see* Yankton
Yaun-ñi *see* Yaunyi
Yaunni *see* Yaunyi
Yaunyi (H)
Yaunyi-hano *see* Yaunyi
Yausapin *see* Weapemeoc
Yauyos [SA] (O)
Yava *see* Yagua
Yavai Suppai *see* Havasupai
Yavapai [AZ] (LC)
Yavapai Apache *see* Yavapai
Yavapaias *see* Yavapai
Yava-pais *see* Yavapai
Yavapaiso *see* Yavapai
Ya'vapay *see* Yavapai
Yavapay *see* Yavapai
Yavape (LC) *see also* Yavapai (LC)
Yavape [AZ] *Yavapai* (BE)
Yavape Kutcan *see* Yavapai
Yavapekutcan *see* Tulkepaia
Yavapekutcan *see* Yavapai
Ya-ve-pe-Ku-tcan *see* Tulkepaia
Yavepe-Kutchan *see* Yuma
Yavipai *see* Yavapai
Yavipai cajuala *see* Paiute
Yavipai Cuercomache *see* Cuercomache
Yavipai Javesua *see* Havasupai
Yavipai-Lipanes *see* Lipan Apache
Yavipai-Navajai *see* Navajo

Yavipai-navajoi *see* Navajo
Yavipais-caprala *see* Paiute
Yavipais-Nataje *see* Kiowa Apache
Yavipaistejua *see* Tejua
Yavipay *see* Yavapai
yav'i-pay *see* Yavapai
Yavitero [Lang] *Maipurean* (O)
Yavpay *see* Yavapai
Yavpe *see* Yavepe
Yawalapiti *see* Iaualapiti
Yawanawa *see* Yahunahua
Yawaperi [Br] (O)
Yawarana *see* Yecuna
Yawareta-Tapiiya *see* Kawahib
Yawareta-Tapiiya *see* Yawarete-Tapuya
Yawarete-Tapuya [Clan] *Karutana* (O)
Yawdanchi [CA] *Yokuts* (CA)
Yaweden'tshi *see* Yawdanchi
Yawedmo'ni *see* Yawdanchi
Yawelmani [CA] *Southern Yokuts* (CA)
Yawepe *see* Yavapai
Yawi *see* Tiriyo
Ya-wil-chine *see* Yawilchine
Yawilchine [CA] *Yokuts* (H)
Ya-wil-chuie *see* Yawilchine
Yawilchuie *see* Yawilchine
Yawitshenni *see* Yawilchine
Yawlamni *see* Yawelmani
Yawpim *see* Weapemeoc
Yawtanoone *see* Youghtanund
Yax-ka-a *see* Crow
Yaxkaa *see* Crow
yayantci [Phratry] [CA] *North Fork Mono* (Pub, v.11, no.5, p.293)
Yayaponchatu [AZ] (H)
Yayecha *see* Eyeish
Yazoo [MS] (BE)
Yazous *see* Yazoo
Yazoux *see* Yazoo
Ybaha *see* Guale
Ybdacax [TX] *Coahuiltecan* (BE)
Ybitoopa *see* Ibitoupa
Ybitoupa *see* Ibitoupa
Ycahuate [EC] *Secoya* (O)
Ycha-yamel-amim *see* Yamel
Ye [Clan] *Tewa* (H)
Yeannecock *see* Yannococ
Yeba-Masa *see* Yebamasa
Yebamasa [Br, Col] *Macuna* (O)
Yecan *Coahuiltecan* (Hdbk10)
Ye'ceqen *see* Yesheken
Yeceqen *see* Yesheken
Yechimicual [MX] *Coahuiltecan* (Hdbk10)
Yecora [MX] *Pima Bajo* (BE)
Yecuana (LC) *see also* Mayongong (O)
Ye'cuana *see* Yecuana

Yecuana [VE, Br] (LC)

Yecujen-ne *see* Mimbreno Apache

Yegaha [Self-designation] *see* Kansa

Yegua *see* Yagua

Yeguaces *see* Yguases

Yeguases *see* Yguases

Yeguaz *see* Yguases

Yeguazes *see* Yguases

Yeguecat [MX] *Concho* (BE)

Yehah *see* Yehuh

Yehah *see* Cascades

Yehhuh *see* Yehuh

Yehhuh *see* Cascades

Yehl (H) *see also* Hoya (H)

Yehl [AK] *Tlingit* (H)

Yehlnaas-hadai [Subfamily] *Haida* (H)

Yehuh (Hdbk12) *see also* Cascades (Hdbk12)

Yehuh [OR, Can] *Shahala* (BE)

Yeka *see* Kikatsik

Yekolaos [BC] *Cowichan* (BE)

Yekuana *see* Yecuana

Yekuhana *see* Yecuana

Yek'u-na-me-tunne *see* Yaquina

Yekunametunne *see* Yacone

Yekwana *see* Yecuana

Ye'kwana *see* Yecuna

Ye-let-po *see* Cayuse

Yeletpo *see* Cayuse

Yellowknife Indians *see* Ahtena

Yellow Knife Indians *see* Tatsanottine

Yellowknife Indians *see* Tatsanottine

Yellow Knives *see* Tatsanottine

Yellow Lake [MI, WI] *Chippewa* (H)

Yellow Liver *Sioux* (H)

Yellow Medicine's Band *see* Inyangmani

Yellow Wolf Band [SD] *Cheyenne* (BE)

Ye'l na'as xa'da-i *see* Yehlnaashadai

Yelnaasxadai *see* Yehlnaas-hadai

Yelyuchopa [AZ] (BE)

Yemasee *see* Yamassee

Yemassee *see* Yamassee

Yemasses *see* Yamassee

Yeme *Coahuiltecan* (BE)

Yemez *see* Jemez

Yemmassaw *see* Yamassee

Yendat *see* Huron

Yendot *see* Huron

Yenye'di *see* Yenyendi

Yenyendi [AK] *Tlingit* (H)

Yenyohol *see* Winyaw

Yeomansee *see* Yamassee

Yeopim *see* Weapemeoc

Yepa-Maksa *see* Yebamasa

Yepamaksa *see* Yebamasa

Yepa-Matso *see* Yebamasa

Yepamatso *see* Yebamasa

Yep-pe *see* Yampa

Yeppe *see* Yampla

Yeqolaos *see* Yekolaos

Yerbipiame *see* Ervipiame

Yerguiba *Coahuiltecan* (Hdbk10)

Yerington *Paiute* (Char, v.11)

Yeripiame *see* Ervipiame

Yesa *see* Nahyssan

Yesah *see* Tutelo

Yesan *see* Nahyssan

Ye-san *see* Tutelo

Yesan *see* Tutelo

Yesang *see* Tutelo

Yesheken [BC, VanI] *Nanaimo* (H)

Yetans *see* Ietan

Yeta-Ottina *see* Athabasca

Yetaottina *see* Athabasca

Yeta-Ottine *see* Etagottine

Yetaottine *see* Etagottine

Ye-tdoa *see* Ye

Yetdoa *see* Ye

Yete *see* Omagua

Yevepaya *see* Yavapai

Yguaces *see* Yguases

Yguaja *see* Guale

Yguases [TX] (H)

Yguaya *see* Guale

Yguazes *see* Yguases

Yhuata *see* Omagua

Yi'ata'tehenko *see* Carrizo [MX]

Yikirga-ulit *see* Eskimos

Yikirga-ulit *see* Imaklimiut

Yikirga'ulit *see* Inguklimiut

Yimaba [CA] *Northern Pomo* (Pub, v.40, no.2)

Yine *see* Piro [Peru]

Yingoteague *Pomoke* (Hdbk15)

yipinkatiti *see* Uinkaret

yipinkatiticimi *see* Uinkaret

Yisha'ktcabsh [WA] *Nisqualli* (BE)

Yita *see* Ute

Yitaa [Arg, Par] *Ashluslay* (O)

Yiuhta *see* Ute

Yiwinanghal [CA] *Monache* (Pub, v.4, no.3, p.122)

Yjar [Pueblo] [NM] *Jemez* (H)

Yldefonso, Sant *see* San Ildefonso

Yldefonzo, San *see* San Ildefonso

Ylefonso, Sant *see* San Ildefonso

Yman [TX] *Coahuiltecan* (BE)

Ymasaquajulam *see* Masacuajulam

Ymic [TX] *Coahuiltecan* (BE)

Y-Mitches *see* Imiche

Ymitches *see* Imiche

Yncagende *see* Alonso

Yncanabacte *see* Toba

Yncaopi [Pueblo] [NM] (H)

Yneci *see* Nabedache

Ynez, Santa [CA] *Chumash* (BE)

Ynezeño [Lang] [CA] *Chumash* (He)

Ynqueyunque *see* Yugeuinegge

Yntajen-ne *see* Faraon

Yoaka-yam [CA] (Pub, v.8, no.2)

Yoamaco *see* Secowocomoco

Yoamacoes *see* Secowocomoco

Yoamity *see* Awani

Yobotui [CA] *Eastern Pomo* (Pub, v.36, no.6, 1939)

Yocanis *see* Caddo

Yocolles *see* Yokol

Yocovanes *see* Yojuane

Yocut *see* Yokuts

Yo-det-a-bi *see* Yodetabi

Yodetabi [CA] *Patwin* (H)

Yodetabies *see* Yodetabi

Yodoi [CA] *Patwin* (Pub, v.29, no.4)

Yodunsu [Br] *Southern Nambicuara* (O)

Yoednani *see* Yawdanchi

Yoelchane *see* Yawilchine

Yoem *see* Yuma

Yoeme *see* Yaqui

Yoemem *see* Yaqui

Yoetaha *see* Navajo

Yofuaha *Choroti* (O)

Yoghtanunt *see* Youghtanund

Yogoyekaydn [AZ] *San Carlos Apache* (H)

Yohamite *see* Awani

Yohios *see* Yokaia

Yohop [SA] *Macu* (O)

Yohuane *see* Yojuane

Yoit *see* Yuit

Yojuane [TX] *Tonkawan* (BE)

Yo-kai-a *see* Yokaia

Yokaia (LC) *see also* Yokayo (LC)

Yokaia [CA] *Pomo* (H)

Yo-kai-a-mah *see* Yokaia

Yokaiamah *see* Yokaia

Yokayo [CA] (LC)

Yo-Kei *see* Yokaia

Yokei *see* Yokaia

Yo-ki *see* Patki

Yo-ki *see* Yoki

Yoki *see* Patki

Yoko *see* Yokol

Yokod (H) *see also* Yokol (H)

Yokod [CA] *Yokuts* (LC)

Yokod [Lang] [CA] [*Tule-Kaweah*] (CA-8)

Yokol (Pub, v.4, no.3, pp.124–125) *see also* Yawdanchi (CA)

Yokol [CA] *Yokuts* (H)

Yo-kols *see* Yokol

Yokon Flats Kutchin *see* Kutchakutchin

Yokpa [Self-designation] *see* Japreria

Yokpah *see* Oyukhpe
Yo-kul *see* Yokol
Yokul *see* Yokol
Yok'utat *see* Yakutat
Yokutat *see* Yakutat
Yo-kuts *see* Yokuts
Yokuts [CA] (LC)
Yokutsan [Lang] [CA] *Penutian* (CA-8)
Yokwa'lsshabsh [WA] *Nisqualli* (BE)
Yolanchas *see* Yawdanchi
Yolays *see* Yolo
Yoletta *see* Isleta
Yolhios *see* Yokaia
Yolo [CA] *Patwin* (H)
Yolox [MX] (BE)
Yoloy *see* Yolo
Yoloytoy *see* Yolo
Yo-lum-ne *see* Tuolumne
Yolumne *see* Tuolumne
Yomba *Shoshone* (Char, v.11)
Yomkallie *see* Yoncalla
Yom-pa-pa Utahs *see* Yampa
Yompapa Utahs *see* Yampa
Yonalins *see* Yonalus
Yonalus *Pueblo Indians* (H)
Yoncalla [OR] (LC)
Yoncolla *see* Yoncalla
Yongletats *see* Ucluelet
Yonh [Clan] *Yuchi* (H)
Yonh taha *see* Yonh
Yonkalla *see* Yoncalla
Yonkiousme *see* Jukiusme
Yonktins *see* Yankton
Yonktons *see* Yankton
Yonktons Ahnah *see* Yanktonai
Yon-sal-poma *see* Usal
Yonsalpomo *see* Usal
Yontuh [Clan] *Yuchi* (H)
Yontu'h taha *see* Yontuh
Yoo [Clan] *Navajo* (H)
Yoochee *see* Yuchi
Yookilta *see* Lekwiltok
Yookoomans *see* Yakima
Yoov'ta [Self-designation] *see* Uinta
Yoovte *see* Uinta
Yoqueechae *see* Yukichetunne
Yoquichachs *see* Yukichetunne
Yorbipianos *see* Ervipiame
Yoreme *see* Yaqui
Yorica [TX] *Coahuiltecan* (BE)
Yoron *see* Tunica
Yorotees [TX] (H)
Yosahmitti *see* Awani
Yosco [NI] (BE)
Yo-sem-a-te *see* Awani
Yosemate *see* Awani
Yosemeto *see* Awani
Yo-sem-ety *see* Awani
Yosemite *see* Awani
Yosemite Indians *see* Miwok

Yoshol *see* Usal
Yosimite *see* Awani
Yo-sol Poma *see* Usal
Yosol Poma *see* Usal
Yosoomite *see* Awami
Yostjeeme *see* Apache
Yota *see* Ute
yotam *see* Ute
Yotche-eme *see* Apache
Yotiya [CA] *Southern Pomo* (Pub, v.40, no.2)
Youay *see* Hainai
Youcan *see* Yukonikhotana
Youchee *see* Yuchi
Youchehtaht *see* Ucluelet
You-clul-aht *see* Ucluelet
Youclulaht *see* Ucluelet
Youcomako *Conoy* (Hdbk15)
Youcon *see* Yukonikhotana
Youcoolumnies *see* Yukolumni
Youghtamong *see* Youghtanund
Youghtamund *see* Youghtanund
Youghtanund [VA] *Powhatan* (BE)
Youghtanundo *see* Youghtanund
Youicomes *see* Yaquina
Youicone *see* Yaquina
Youikcones *see* Yaquina
Youikeones *see* Yaquina
Youikkone *see* Yaquina
Youkone *see* Yaquina
Youkon Louchioux Indians *see* Kutchakutchin
Youlolla *see* Yoncalla
Youmalolam *see* Umatilla
You-ma-talla *see* Umatilla
Youmatalla *see* Umatilla
You-matella *see* Umatilla
Youmatella *see* Umatilla
Young Buffalo Robe Band [Can] *Sarsi* (BE)
Young Dogs *see* Hachepiriiu
Younondadys *see* Tionontati
You-pel-lay *see* Santo Domingo
Youpellay *see* Santo Domingo
You-quee-chae *see* Yukichetunne
Youqueechae *see* Yukichetunne
Youruk *see* Yurok
Yout *see* Ute
Youta *see* Ute
Youtah *see* Ute
Yowa [Col] *Yuko* (O)
yowac *see* Owens Valley Paiute
Yowana *see* Hoti
Yoway *see* Iowa
Yowechani *see* Yawdanchi
Yow-el-man-ne *see* Yawelmani
Yowelmanne *see* Yawelmani
Yowkies *see* Yokol
Yowlumne *see* Yawelmani
Yo-woc-o-nee *see* Tawakoni
Yowoconee *see* Tawakoni
Yowuxua *Northern Chorote* (O)

Yoxica *see* Yorica
Yoxwaha [Self-designation] [Arg] *Southern Chorote* (O)
Ypolilos *see* Politos
Yrbipias *see* Ervipiame
Yrbipimas *see* Ervipiame
Yrekas *see* Kikatsik
Yrocois *see* Iroquois
Yrokoise *see* Iroquois
Yroquet *see* Ononchataronon
Yroquois *see* Iroquois
Ys *see* Ais
Ysa [Self-designation] *see* Catawba
Ysbupue [TX] *Coahuiltecan* (BE)
Yscan *see* Yscani
Yscanes *see* Caddo
Yscanes *see* Yscani
Yscani [OK] *Wichita* (BE)
Ysconis *see* Yscani
Ysleta *see* Isleta
Ysleta del Sur *see* Isleta
Yslete *see* Isleta
Ysleteños *see* Isleta
Ystete *see* Isleta
Ytimpabiches (H) *see also* Intimbich (H)
Ytimpabichi (Hdbk11) *see also* Southern Paiute (Hdbk11)
Ytimpabichi *Cobarde* (H)
Ytriza {Pueblo} [NM] (H)
Ytucali *see* Urarina
Yuahe *see* Iowa
Yuakayam *see* Chemehuvi
Yualapiti *see* Iaualapiti
Yuana *see* Hoti
Yuanes *see* Cocopa
Yuanes *see* Iguanes
Yu-ba *see* Yuba River
Yuba River (Pub, v.33, no.2, 1932/34, pp.139–232)
Yubipias *see* Yavapai
Yubissias *see* Yavapai
Yubuincarini *see* Yubuincariri
Yubuincariri (Hdbk11) *see also* Uinkaret (Hdbk11)
Yubuincariri [UT] *Cobarde* (H)
yucaipaiem [Clan] *Serrano* (Pub, v.26, 1929)
Yucal *see* Yokol
Yucaopi *see* Yncaopi
Yuca's *see* Palaihnihan
Yuca's *see* Yuki
Yucas *see* Yuki
Yucatat *see* Yakutat
Yucatec *see* Yucatecan
Yucatecan [Lang] [CAm] *Mayan* (LC)
Yucateco [MX, Bel] (O)
Yuchi [GA] (LC)
Yuchian [Lang] *see* Uchean [Lang]
Yuchian Indians *see* Yuchi

Yuchiha see Yuchi
Yuco see Yupa
Yuco see Yuko
Yucpa see Yukpa
Yucuna [Col] (LC)
Yudaha see Navajo
Yue Coahuiltecan (BE)
Yufala see Eufaula
Yufera (BE) see also Eufaula (BE)
Yufera [GA, FL] (BE)
Yugelnut see Juglenute
Yugeuinegge [Pueblo] [NM]
  Tewa (H)
Yuge-uing-ge see Yugeuinegge
Yugura see Leco
Yuguru [Self-designation] see Leco
yuhavetum [Clan] Serrano (Pub,
  v.36, 1929)
Yuhiktom see Cahuilla
Yu'hta see Ute
Yuhta see Ute
Yuhuana see Mapoyo
Yuhup see Maca
Yui [FL] (BE)
Yuit (Hdbk5) see also Siberian Es-
  kimos (Hdbk5)
Yuit [AK] Eskimos (BE)
Yuit [Lang] (Hdbk5) see also
  Siberian Yupik (Hdbk5)
Yuit [Lang] Siberian (BE)
Yu-i-ta see Navajo
Yu-ita see Navajo
Yuita see Navajo
Yu-Ite see Yuit
Yuite see Yuit
Yuittcemo see Apache
Yujuanes see Yojuane
yuk see Nunivak Central Yupik
yu-k see Yupik
Yuk see Yuit
Yuka see Yuki
Yukae see Yokaia
Yukai see Yokaia
Yukai see Yuki
Yukal see Yokol
Yukaliwa see Kiliwi
Yuke see Yuki
Yukeh see Yuki
Yukhakhonpom see Cahuilla
Yukhe [Subclan] Kansa (H)
Yukhitiishak see Attacapa
Yuk'hiti ishak [Self-designation]
  see Attacapa
Yu-ki see Yuki
Yu-ki see Yukichetunne
Yuki (PC) see also Yukichetunne
  (BE)
Yuki [CA] (LC)
Yuki [SA] see Yuqui
Yukian [Lang] [CA] (He)
Yukian Indians see Yuki
Yukichetunne (H) see also Eu-
  quachee (H)

Yukichetunne [OR] Tututni (BE)
Yu-ki-tce tunne see Yu-
  kichetunne
Yukitchetunne see Yukichetunne
Yukleta see Lekwiltok
Yuko [Col] (LC)
Yu-kol see Yokol
Yukol see Yokol
Yukolumni [CA] Cholovone (H)
Yukon-ikhotana see Unakhotana
Yukon-ikhotana see
  Yukonikhotana
Yukonikhotana [AK] Koyukon
  (BE)
Yukpa [Lang] Northern Carib
  (UAz, v.28)
Yukpa [VE] (O)
Yukuna see Yucuna
Yukuth see Tukkuthkutchin
Yukuth Kutchin see Takkuth-
  Kutchin
Yukuth Kutchin see
  Tukkuthkutchin
Yu-kwa-chi see Yukichetunne
Yukwachi see Yukichetunne
Yu-kwin-a see Yaquina
Yukwina see Yaquina
Yu-kwin-me tunne see Yaquina
Yukwinmetunne see Yaquina
Yu-kwi-tce tunne see Yu-
  kichetunne
Yukwitcetunne see Yukichetunne
Yula see Ute
Yulata see Taos
Yule see Cuna
Yulé see San Blas
Yullitt see Ahtena
Yulonee see Yuloni
Yu-lo-ni see Yuloni
Yuloni [CA] Miwok (H)
Yulugpiaq Yupik Eskimos (LC)
Yum see Kamia
Yum see Comeya
Yum see Yuma
Yuma (H) see also Suma (BE)
Yuma [AZ] (LC)
Yuma [SA] see Arara
Yuma [SA] see Cuna
Yuma-Apache see Yavapai
Yumagatok [CA] Maidu (H)
Yuman [Lang] (LC)
Yumana [SA] (O)
Yumanahua [Lang] Panoan (O)
Yuman Indians see Yuma
Yumano see Jumano
Yumatilla see Umatilla
Yumaya see Yuma
Yumba see Colorado [SA]
Yumbo [EC] (O)
Yumi see Huma
Yumi see Yuma
Yuminawa see Jaminaua
Yump see Yuma

yumpaka tewa see San Juan
  [NM]
Yumpatickara see Yambadika
Yum-pis see Yavapai
Yumpis see Yavapai
Yumpis see Yavapai
Yumsa see Yuma
Yu'mu see Yuma
Yumu see Yuma
Yumyum see Ute
Yuna-kho-tenne Tinne (H)
Yunca [PE] (LC)
Yunga (LC) see also Yunca (LC)
Yunga [BO] (O)
Yungya [Clan] Hopi (H)
Yunnakakhotana see
  Koyukukhotana
Yunque see Yugeuinegge
Yunssaka see Dakota
Yuntara-ye-ru'nu see Kickapoo
Yunu [CA] Maidu (H)
Yunu-kho-tenne see Yuna-kho-
  tenne
Yunukhotenne see Yuna-kho-
  tenne
Yuñu wiñwu see Yungyu
Yu-nu wuñ-wu see Yungyu
Yunu wuñiwu see Yungyu
Yunwiyah see Cherokee
Yun-wi-yah [Self-designation]
  see Cherokee
Yu'n-ya see Yungyu
Yunya see Yungu
Yupa (O) see also Yukpa (O)
Yupa [Col] (LC)
Yupaka see Guale
Yupapais see Yavapai
Yupe [Lang] Motilon (UAz, v.28)
Yupiak see Yupik
Yupiaq see Yupik
Yupiat see Yupik
Yu-pi'it see Yuit
Yupiit see Yuit
Yupik (LC) see also Yuit (BE)
Yup'ik see Yupik
Yupik [AK] Eskimos (LC)
yupis oob see Highland Pima
Yuquache see Yukichetunne
Yuques see Yuki
Yuqueyunk see Yugeuinegge
Yuqueyunque see Yugeuinegge
Yuqui [BO] (LC)
Yuqui Yanqui see Yugeuinegge
yuq-ye see Apache
yuqye see Apache
Yura [BO] (O)
Yuraba see Taos
Yuracare [BO] (LC)
Yuracarean see Yurucarean
Yurapari-Tapuya Karutana (O)
Yurapeis see Yavapai
Yurguimes [TX] Coahuiltecan
  (BE)

Yurmarjar *see* Yuma
Yuro *see* Yuracare
Yu-rok *see* Yurok
Yurok [CA] (LC)
Yurok Tsulu-la *see* Chilula
Yurpan-Tapuya *see* Karutana
Yurucarean [Lang] [SA] (LC)
Yurucari *see* Yuracare
Yurucaritia *see* Yurukarika
Yurujure *see* Yuracare
yu-ruk *see* Yurok
yuruk *see* Yurok
Yurukare *see* Yurucarean
Yurukarika [BO] (O)
Yurukarika [BO] (O)
Yuruna [Br] (LC)
Yuruna [Br] (LC)
Yurupari-Tapuya *see* Yurapari-
  Tapuya
Yuruti [Col] (O)
Yuruti [Col] *Eastern Tukanoan*
  (O)
Yuruxare *see* Yurucarean
Yusal Pomo *see* Usal
Yu-sal Poms *see* Usal
Yusan *see* Yussoih
Yusku [CAm] *Sumo* (O)
Yussoih [Clan] *Yuchi* (H)
Yusso-i'h taha *see* Yussoih
Yustaga [FL] (BE)
Yuta (LC) *see also* Ute (LC)
Yuta [TX] (H)
Yutacjen-ne *see* Navajo
Yutaha *see* Navajo
yutahani *see* Navajo
Yu-tah-kah *see* Navajo
Yutahkah *see* Navajo
Yutaje-ne *see* Navajo
Yuta-jenne *see* Faraon
Yutajen-ne *see* Navajo
Yutama *see* Ute
Yutamo *see* Ute
Yu-tar-har *see* Navajo
Yutarhar *see* Navajo
Yuta sabuagana *see* Akanaquint
Yutas Ancapagari *see* Tabeguache
Yutas Cobardes *see* Southern
  Paiute
Yutas Mogoachis *see* Moache
Yutas Payuchis *see* Southern
  Paiute
Yutas Sabuaganas *see* Uncom-
  pahgre
Yutas Talarenos *see* Tularenos
Yuta Tabehuachi *see* Tabeguache
Yutawat *see* Ute
Yutawats *see* Ietan
yutawits *see* Ute
Yutawotenne *see* Yuta'wotene
Yuta'wotenne [BC] *Carrier Indi-
  ans* (Bull133)
Yutcam *see* Yuma
Yutcana *see* Yuma

Yutchi *see* Yuchi
Yutci *see* Yuchi
Yu-tci *see* Yuchi
Yute *see* Ute
Yute-shay *see* Apache
Yuteshay *see* Apache
Yutila pa *see* Navajo
Yutilapa *see* Navajo
Yutilatlawi *see* Navajo
Yutlu-lath *see* Ucluelet
Yutlulath *see* Ucluelet
Yu'tsi *see* Yuchi
Yutsi *see* Yuchi
Yutsutkenne [BC] *Sekani* (H)
Yu-tsu-tqaze *see* Yutsutkenne
Yutsutqaze *see* Yutsutkenne
Yutta *see* Ute
yuttahi *see* Navajo
yu-tuk *see* Yurok
yutuk *see* Yurok
Yutuwichan [Can] *Sekani* (BE)
yuudaha *see* Navajo
Yuva-Supai *see* Havasupai

-Z-

Zaartaar *Upper Yanktonai* (H)
Za-ar-tar *see* Zaartaar
Zacapoaxtla [Lang] *Aztec*
  (Hdbk10)
Zacateca [MX] (LC)
Zacateco *see* Zacateca
Zacatil *Coahuiltecan* (Hdbk10)
Zacopines *see* Tiopines
Zage *see* Osage
Za-gí *see* Sauk
Zagí *see* Sauk
Zagoreni [PE] *Campa* (O)
Zaguaganas *see* Uncompahgre
Zaguagua *see* Abanaquint
Zaivovois *see* Iowa
Za-ke *see* Sauk
Zake *see* Sauk
Zakiah *Conoy* (Hdbk15)
Zaklohpakap *see* Mam
Zaktcinemuk [Can] [Shuswap]
  (BE)
Zalai *see* Zalaia
Zalaia *Coahuiltecan* (Hdbk10)
Zaltana [Clan] [AK] *Kna-
  iakhotana* (H)
Zamuco [Lang] [BO] (O)
Zamucoan Indians [BO, Par]
  (LC)
Zana *see* Sana
Zanana *see* Tenankutchin
Zancagues *see* Tonkawa
Zandia *see* Sandia
Zani *see* Zuni
Zanker-Indianer *see* Kutchin

Zantee *see* Santee
Zapa *see* Shapra
Zapara [Br] (O)
Zaparo [PE, EC] (O)
Zaparoan [Lang] [EC] (O)
Zaparoan Indains *see* Zaparo
Zapitalaga *see* Pilaga
Zapiteri [PE] *Mashco* (O)
Zapotec [MX] (LC)
Zapotecan [Lang] [MX] (BE)
Zapotecan Indians *see* Zapotec
Zapoteco *see* Zapotec
Zapoteros *Coahuiltecan* (Hdbk10)
Zarame *see* Xarame
Zatchila *see* Colorado [SA]
Zatienos *see* Moro
Zatoe *see* Xatoe
Zautoouys *see* Uzutiuhi
Zautooys *see* Uzutiuhi
Zavana [HA, WInd] (BE)
Zaxtci-nemux *see* Bonaparte Di-
  vision
Zayahueco [MX] *Cora* (BE)
Ze *see* Ge
Zea *see* Sia
Ze-gar-kin-a *see* Zuni
Ze-gar-kin-a *see* Pima
Zegarkina *see* Pima
Zegarkina *see* Zuni
Zegua [MX] (BE)
Ze-ka-ka *see* Kitkehahki
Zekaka *see* Kitkehahki
Zeka-thaka *see* Tangeratsa
Zekathaka *see* Tangeratsa
Zemas *see* Jemez
Zemboger *see* Ozanbogus
Zendal *see* Tzeltal
Zen-ecu *see* Senecu
Zenecu *see* Senecu
Zennecu *see* Senecu
Zesuqua *see* Tesuque
Zetocende *see* Gila Apache
Zetocende *see* Natage
Zeton *see* Teton
Zetonsende *see* Mescalero
  Apache
Zeven steden van Cibola *see*
  Zuni
Zhawe [Clan] *Quapaw* (H)
Zhawenikashika [Clan] *Quapaw*
  (H)
Zhiguan *see* Siaguan
Zhorquin [MX] (BE)
Zia *see* Sia
Ziaban *see* Siaguan
Ziaguan *see* Siaguan
Zian *see* Sia
Zibaro *see* Jivaro
Zibola *see* Zuni
Zibola *see* Matsaki
Zi-i *see* Sii
Zii *see* Sii
Zijame *see* Sijame

Zika hakisin *see* Kitkehahki
Zillgaw [AZ] *Apache* (H)
Zill-tar-den *see* Tsiltaden
Zilltarden *see* Tsiltaden
Zill-tar-din *see* Tsiltaden
Zilltardin *see* Tsiltaden
Zimitagui *Coahuiltecan* (Hdbk10)
Zimshian *see* Tsimshian
Zimshian-Indianer *see*
  Tsimshian
Zinantec *see* Chinantec
Zingomenes *see* Spokan
Zinogaba [CA] (H)
Ziñogova *see* Zinogaba
Zipias *see* Tsipiakwe
Zippia-Kue *see* Tsipiakwe
Zisagechroann *see* Missisauga
Zisagechrohne *see* Missisauga
Zi-unka-kutchi *see* Taugeratsa
Ziunkakutchi *see* Tangeratsa
Ziunka-kutshi *see* Tangeratsa
Ziunkakutshi *see* Tangeratsa
Zivaro *see* Jivaro
Zivola *see* Zuni
Zizika-akisi *see* Kitkehahki
Zizikaakisi *see* Kitkehahki
Zjen Kuttchin *see* Vuntakutchin
Zjenkuttchin *see* Vuntakutchin
Zjen-ta-Kouttchin *see* Vun-
  takutchin
Zjentakouttchin *see* Vun-
  takutchin
Zoc *see* Zoque
Zoe [MX] (BE)
Zoenji *see* Zuni
Zoke *see* Zoque
Zolahan *see* Sulujame

Zolajan *see* Sulujame
Zolata *see* Chorti
Zo-lat-e-se-djii *see* Zo-
  latungzezhii
Zolatesedjii *see* Zolatungzezhii
Zolatungzezhii [Pueblo] [NM]
  Jemez (H)
Zo-la-tun-ze-zhi-i *see* Zo-
  latungzezhii
Zolatunzezhii *see* Zolatungzezhii
Zolojan *see* Sulujame
Zolota *Chorti* (O)
Zolucan *see* Cherokee
Zooquagese *see* Sokoki
Zopex *see* Soba
Zopus *see* Esopus
Zoque [MX] (LC)
Zoquean [Lang] [MX] *Mi-*
  zocuavean (BE)
Zoquean Indians *see* Zoque
Zoro [Br] (LC)
Zorquan [TX] *Coahuiltecan* (BE)
Zotzil *see* Tzotzil
Zouni *see* Zuni
Zrohona [Clan] *Hopi* (H)
Zro-ho-na wuñwu *see* Zrohono
Zrohona wuñwu *see* Zrohono
Zrohono [Clan] *Hopi* (H)
Zrohono wiñwu *see* Zrohono
Ztolam *see* Sulujame
Zuanquiz *see* Quanquiz
Zuaque (H) *see also* Tehueco (BE)
Zuaque [MX] *Cahita* (BE)
Zue *see* Dakota
Zuelotetrey *see* Quelotetrey
Zugnis *see* Zuni
Zuidelijke Ute *see* Southern Ute

Zulaja *see* Sulujame
Zulajan *see* Sulujame
Zulocan *see* Cherokee
Zuma *see* Suma
Zumana *see* Jumano
Zumana *see* Suma
Zumaque [NM] *Pueblo Indians*
  (H)
Zumis *see* Zuni
Zun *see* Zuni
Zuña *see* Zuni
Zune *see* Zuni
Zuni [NM] (LC)
Zunia *see* Zuni
Zunian [Lang] [NM] (H)
Zunian Indians *see* Zuni
Zunias *see* Zuni
Zuni-Cibola *see* Zuni
Zunie *see* Zuni
Zunni *see* Zuni
Zunu *see* Zuni
Zuny *see* Zuni
Zunyits *see* Zuni
Zura *see* Zuni
Zures *see* Keres
Zutugil [Gu] (IndN, v.5, no.4,
  July 1928)
Zutuhil *see* Tzutuhil
Zuyi *see* Zuni
Zuzeca wi-Casa *see* Shoshone
zuzeca wichasa *see* Northern
  Shoshone
Zuzteca-kiyaksa *see* Kiyuksa
Zwan-hi-ooks *see* Towah-
  nahiooks
Zwanhiooks *see* Towahnahiooks

Bibliography

"Abenakis See Recognition." *Talking Leaf*, v. 42, no. 4 (April 1977), p. 5.

Agonito, Rosemary, and Joseph Agonito. "Resurrecting History's Forgotten Women: A Case Study from the Cheyenne Indians" in *Native American Women*, ed. by Women's Studies Program. Boulder: University of Colorado, 1981.

Alaska Geographic, v. 23, no. 2 (1996), entire issue.

Alphonse, Ephraim S. *Bulletin of American Ethnology Bulletin no. 16: Guaymi Grammar and Dictionary*. Washington, D.C.: U.S. Government Printing Office, Smithsonian Institution, 1956.

American Ethnological Society. *Monographs of the American Ethnological Society*. Locust Valley, NJ: J.J. Augustin, 1940–present.

_____. *Publications of the American Ethnological Society*. Leyden, Holland: E.J. Brill: Publications of the American Ethnological Society, vol.1–20, 1908–1936.

_____. *Transactions*. New York: Bartlett & Welford, 1845–1853.

Amsden, Charles. *Ancient Basketmakers: Southwest Museum Leaflets no. 1*. Los Angeles, CA: Southwest Museum, 1939.

Anderson, J.A. *Crying for a Vision: a Rosebud Sioux Trilogy, 1886–1976*. Dobbs Ferry, NY: Marogan, 1976.

Andrews, Ralph Warren. *Curtis' Western Indians*. Seattle: Superior, 1962.

"The Apache and Navajo." *El Palacio*, v. 27, nos. 1–7 (July 6/August 17, 1929), pp. 37–38.

Axelrod, Alan. *Chronicle of the Indian Wars: From Colonial Times to Wounded Knee*, New York: Prentice-Hall, 1993.

Bancroft-Hunt, Norman. *People of the Totem: Indians of the Pacific Northwest*. NY: Putnam, 1979.

Barker, Leo R., and Julia Costello (eds.) *Archaeology of Alta California*. New York: Garland, 1991.

Barrett, S.A. *Publications of the American Ethnological Society, v. 5, no. 4: The Material Culture of the Klamath Lake and Modoc Indians of Northeastern California and Southern Oregon*. Berkeley: University of California Press, 1910.

_____. *Publications of the American Ethnological Society, v. 6, no. 1: The Ethno-Geography of the Pomo and Neighboring Indians*. Berkeley: University of California Press, 1908.

_____. *Publications of the American Ethnological Society, v. 6, no. 2: Geography and Dialects of the Miwok Indians*. Berkeley: University of California Press, 1908.

Basgall, Mark E. "Archaeology and Linguistics: Pomoan Prehistory as Viewed from Northern Sonoma County, California." *Journal of California and Great Basin Anthropology*, v. 4, no. 2 (Summer 1982), pp. 3–22.

Basso, Ellen B. (ed.) *Carib-Speaking Indians: Culture, Society and Language; University of Arizona Anthropological Paper no. 28*. Tucson: University of Arizona, 1977.

Basso, Keith H., and Morris E. Opler (eds.) *Apachean Culture History and Ethnology; University of Arizona Anthropological Paper no. 21*. Tucson: University of Arizona, 1971.

Baumhoff, Martin A. *Anthropological Records, v. 16, no. 5: California Athabascan Group*. Berkeley: University of California Press, 1958.

Beals, Ralph L., and Joseph A. Hester, Jr. *California Indians I*. New York: Garland, 1974.

_____, *The Contemporary Culture of the Cahita Indians; Bureau of American Ethnology Bulletin no. 142*. Washington, D.C.: U.S. Government Printing Office, Smithsonian Institution, 1945.

_____. *Publications in American Archaeology and Ethnology, v. 31, no. 6: Ethnology of the Nisenan*. Berkeley: University of California Press, 1933.

Bechwith, Frank. "A Day in Acoma." *El Palacio*, v. 35, nos. 23–24 (Dec. 6–13, 1933), pp. 201–210.

Blackburn, Thomas C. *Flowers of the Wind*. Socorro, NM: Ballena, 1977.

Boas, Franz. Central Eskimo: Sixth Annual Report of the Bureau of Ethnology, 1884/85. Washington, D.C.: U.S. Government Printing Office, Smithsonian Institution, 1884/1885.

_____. *Chinook Texts; Bureau of American Anthology Bulletin no. 20*. Washington, D.C.: U.S. Government Printing Office, Smithsonian Institution, 1894.

_____. *Ethnology of the Kwakiutl: Thirty-Fifth Annual Report of the Bureau of American Ethnology, Pt. 1, 1913/14*. Washington, D.C.: U.S. Government Printing Office, Smithsonian Institution, 1921.

_____. *Ethnology of the Kwakiutl, Pt. 2: Thirty-Fifth Annual Report of the Bureau of American Ethnology, Pt. 2, 1913/14*. Washington, D.C.: U.S. Government Printing Office, Smithsonian Institution, 1921.

_____. *Publications in American Archaeology and Ethnology, v. 20, no. 1: Notes on the Tillamook*. Berkeley: University of California Press, 1923. 1820

_____. *Tsimshian Texts: Bureau of American Ethnology*

Bulletin no. 27. Washington, D.C.: U.S. Government Printing Office. Smithsonian Institution, 1902.

Boas, Franz (ed.) *Handbook of American Indian Languages: Bureau of American Ethnology Bulletin no. 40, Pt. 1.* Washington, D.C.: U.S. Government Printing Office, Smithsonian Institution, 1917.

_____. *Handbook of American Indian Languages: Bureau of American Ethnology Bulletin no. 40, Pt. 2.* Washington, D.C.: U.S. Government Printing Office, Smithsonian Institution, 1922.

Brinton, Daniel Garrison. *The American Race: A Linguistic Classification and Ethnographic Description of the Native Tribes of North and South America.* New York: Hodges, 1891.

Brinton, Daniel Garrison (ed.) *Library of Aboriginal American Literature, 8 v.* Philadelphia, PA: Brinton, 1882–1890.

Burch, Ernest S., Jr. *Eskimo Kinsmen: Changing Family Relationships in Northwest Alaska: Monographs of the American Ethnological Society no. 59.* St. Paul, MN: West, 1975.

Bureau of American Ethnology. *Anthropological Papers nos. 1–6, Bulletin no. 119.* Washington, D.C.: U.S. Government Printing Office, Smithsonian Institution, 1938.

_____. *Anthropological Papers nos. 7–12, Bulletin no. 123.* Washington, D.C.: U.S. Government Printing Office, Smithsonian Institution, 1939.

_____. *Anthropological Papers nos. 13–18, Bulletin no. 128.* Washington, D.C.: U.S. Government Printing Office, Smithsonian Institution, 1941.

_____. *Anthropological Papers nos. 19–26, Bulletin no. 133.* Washington, D.C.: U.S. Government Printing Office, Smithsonian Institution, 1944.

_____. *Anthropological Papers nos. 27–32, Bulletin no. 136.* Washington, D.C.: U.S. Government Printing Office, Smithsonian Institution, 1944.

_____. *Anthropological Papers nos. 33–44, Bulletin no. 151.* Washington, D.C.: U.S. Government Printing Office, Smithsonian Institution, 1953.

_____. *Anthropological Papers nos. 43–48, Bulletin no. 157.* Washington, D.C.: U.S. Government Printing Office, Smithsonian Institution, 1955. 1821

_____. *Anthropological Papers no. 49–56, Bulletin no. 164.* Washington, D.C.: U.S. Government Printing Office; Smithsonian Institution, 1957.

_____. *Anthropological Papers nos. 57–62, Bulletin no. 173.* Washington, D.C.: U.S. Government Printing Office; Smithsonian Institution, 1963.

_____. *Anthropological Papers nos. 63–67, Bulletin no. 186.* Washington, D.C.: U.S. Government Printing Office; Smithsonian Institution, 1963.

_____. *Anthropological Papers nos. 68–74, Bulletin no. 9173.* Washington, D.C.: U.S. Government Printing Office; Smithsonian Institution, 1964.

_____. *Anthropological Papers nos. 75–80, Bulletin no. 196.* Washington, D.C.: U.S. Government Printing Office; Smithsonian Institution, 1963.

_____. *Bulletin 1–200.* Washington, D.C.: U.S. Government Printing Office; Smithsonian Institution, 1887–1971.

Burrows, Don. *Indian Names, bicentennial ed.* Robinson, IL: Keller, 1976.

Burton, Art. *Black, Red and Deadly: Black and Indian Gunfighters of the Indian Territory, 1870–1907.* Austin, TX: Eakin, 1991.

Bush, Alfred L., and Lee Clark Mitchell. *The Photograph and the American Indian.* Princeton, NJ: Princeton University Press, 1994.

Bushnell, David I., Jr. *The Choctaw of Bayou Lacomb, St. Tammany Parish, Louisiana: Bureau of American Ethnology Bulletin no. 48.* Washington, D.C.: U.S. Government Printing Office; Smithsonian Institution, 1909.

_____. *Native Villages and Village Sites East of the Mississippi: Bureau of American Ethnology Bulletin no. 69.* Washington, D.C.: U.S. Government Printing Office; Smithsonian Institution, 1919.

_____. *Villages of the Algonquian, Siouan, and Caddoan Tribes West of the Mississippi: Bureau of American Ethnology Bulletin no. 77.* Washington, D.C.: U.S. Government Printing Office; Smithsonian Institution, 1922.

Byington, Cyrus. *A Dictionary of the Choctaw Language: Bureau of American Ethnology Bulletin no. 46.* Washington, D.C.: U.S. Government Printing Office; Smithsonian Institution, 1915.

California Historical Society. *Quarterly of the California Historical Society,* v. 1 – (1922 –).

California Indians I: Indian Land Use and Occupancy in California. American Indian Ethnohistory. California Basin-Plateau Indians. New York: Garland, 1974.

Canadian Association in Support of the Native Peoples. *Bulletin,* v. 17, no. 1 (March 1976), pp. 24–26.

Cardozo, Christopher (ed.) *Native Nations: First Americans as Seen by Edward S. Curtis.* Boston: Little Brown, 1993.

Champagne, Duane (ed.) *Native America: Portrait of the Peoples.* Detroit, MI: Visible Ink, 1994.

_____. *Native North American Almanac: A Reference Work on Native North Americans in the United States and Canada.* Detroit, MI: Gale Research, 1994.

Clark, Patricia A., et al. *Native American Index.* Los Angeles, CA: Los Angeles Public Library (www.lapl.org), 1989 to present.

Coe, Joffre L. "Cherokee Archaeology," *Symposium on Cherokee and Iroquois Culture no. 7: Bureau of American Ethnology Bulletin no. 180.* Washington, D.C.: U.S. Government Printing Office; Smithsonian Institution, 1961.

Coe, Michael D., et al. *Atlas of Ancient America.* New York: Facts on File, 1986.

Collins, June M. *Valley of the Spirits: the Upper Skagit Indians. Monographs of the American Ethnological Society no. 56.* Seattle: University of Washington Press, 1974.

Contributions from the Heye Museum, no. 1–9. New York: The Museum, 1913–1915.

Contributions from the Museum of the American Indian, Heye Foundation. New York: The Museum, no. 10-, 1916-.

Conzemius, Eduard. *Ethnographical Survey of the Miskito and Sumu Indians of Honduras and Nicaragua: Bureau of American Ethnology Bulletin no. 108.* Washington, D.C.: U.S. Government Printing Office; Smithsonian Institution, 1932.

Cook, S.F. *Anthropological Records, v. 16, no. 2: Aboriginal Population of the San Joaquin Valley, California.* Berkeley: University of California Press, 1955.

_____. *Anthropological Records, v. 16, no. 3: Aboriginal Population of the North Coast of California.* Berkeley: University of California Press, 1956.

_____. *Anthropological Records, v. 16, no. 4: Aboriginal Population of Alamadea and Contra Costa Counties, California.* Berkeley: University of California Press, 1957.

Cooper, John M. *Analytical and Critical Bibliography of the Tribes of Tierra del Fuego and Adjacent Territory: Bureau of American Ethnology Bulletin no. 63.* Washington, D.C.: U.S. Government Printing Office; Smithsonian Institution, 1917.

"Coquille Restoration Act (1989)." *Eagle*, v. 9, no. 2 (March/April 1991), pp. 20–21.

"Creeks Facing Tough Battle for Federal Recognition." *Indian Trader*, v. 21, no. 8 (August 1990), p. 26.

Curtis, Edward S. *Native Nations: First Americans as Seen by Edward S. Curtis.* Boston: Little Brown, 1993.

_____. *North American Indian, v. 1–20.* New York: Johnson Reprint, 1978.

Cushing, Frank Hamilton. *Zuni Fetiches [sic]: Second Annual Report of the Bureau of Ethnology, 1880/81.* Washington, D.C.: U.S. Government Printing Office; Smithsonian Institution, 1880/1881.

D'Azevedo, Warren L. (ed.) *Great Basin: v. 11: Handbook of North American Indians*, ed. William C. Sturtevant. Washington, D.C.: Smithsonian Institution, 1986.

Dall, W.H. *Remarks on the Origin of the Innui [sic]t: Contributions to North American Ethnology v. 1.* Washington, D.C.: U.S. Government Printing Office; Smithsonian Institution, 1877.

_____. *Terms of Relationship Used by the Innuit [sic]: Contributions to North American Ethnology v. 1.* Washington, D.C.: U.S. Government Printing Office; Smithsonian Institution, 1877.

_____. *Tribes of the Extreme Northwest: Contributions to North American Ethnology v. 1.* Washington, D.C.: U.S. Government Printing Office; Smithsonian Institution, 1877.

Damas, David (ed.) *Arctic: v. 5: Handbook of North American Indians, ed. William C. Sturtevant.* Washington, D.C.: Smithsonian Institution, 1984.

DeBoer, Warren R., and John H. Blitz. "Ceremonial Centers of the Chachi," *Expedition*, v. 33, no. 1 (1991), pp. 53–62.

"Delayed Justice for California Tribes?" *Eagle*, v. 9, no. 2 (March/April 1991), p. 16.

Denig, Edwin Thompson. *Indian Tribes of the Upper Missouri: Forty-Sixth Annual Report of the Bureau of American Ethnology, 1928–1929.* Washington, D.C.: U.S. Government Printing Office; Smithsonian Institution, 1930.

_____. *Of the Crow Nation: Bureau of American Ethnology Anthropological Paper no. 33, Bulletin no. 151.* Washington, D.C.: U.S. Government Printing Office; Smithsonian Institution, 1953.

Densmore, Francis. *The Belief of the Indian in a Connection between Song and the Supernatural: Bureau of American Ethnology Anthropological Paper no. 37, Bulletin no. 151.* Washington, D.C.: U.S. Government Printing Office; Smithsonian Institution, 1953.

_____. *Chippewa Customs: Bureau of American Ethnology Bulletin no. 86.* Washington, D.C.: U.S. Government Printing Office; Smithsonian Institution, 1929.

_____. *Mandan and Hidatsa Music: Bureau of American Ethnology Bulletin no. 80.* Washington, D.C.: U.S. Government Printing Office; Smithsonian Institution, 1923.

_____. *Music of Acoma, Isleta, Cochiti, and Zuñi Pueblos: Bureau of American Ethnology Bulletin no. 165.* Washington, D.C.: U.S. Government Printing Office; Smithsonian Institution, 1957.

_____. *Music of the Indians of British Columbia: Bureau of American Ethnology Anthropological Paper no. 27, Bulletin no. 136.* Washington, D.C.: U.S. Government Printing Office; Smithsonian Institution, 1944.

_____. *Nootka and Quileute Music: Bureau of American Ethnology Bulletin no. 124.* Washington, D.C.: U.S. Government Printing Office; Smithsonian Institution, 1939.

_____. *A Search for Songs among the Chitimacha Indians in Louisiana: Bureau of American Ethnology Anthropological Paper no. 19, Bulletin no. 133.* Washington, D.C.: U.S. Government Printing Office; Smithsonian Institution, 1943.

_____. *Technique in the Music of the American Indian: Bureau of American Ethnology Anthropolgical Paper no. 36, Bulletin no. 151.* Washington, D.C.: U.S. Government Printing Office; Smithsonian Institution, 1953.

_____. *Teton Sioux Music: Bureau of American Ethnology Bulletin no. 61.* Washington, D.C.: U.S. Government Printing Office; Smithsonian Institution, 1918.

_____. *Yuman and Yaqui Music: Bureau of American Ethnology Bulletin no. 110.* Washington, D.C.: U.S. Government Printing Office; Smithsonian Institution, 1932.

Denver Art Museum. Dept. of Indian Art. *Havasupai Indians: Indian Leaflet Series no. 33.* Denver: Denver Art Museum, 1931.

_____. *Hopi Indians: Indian Leaflet Series no. 13.* Denver, CO: Denver Art Museum, 1932.

_____. *Indian Linguistic Stocks or Families: Indian Leaflet Series nos. 51–52.* Denver, CO: Denver Art Museum, 1933.

_____. *Klamath Indians: Indian Leaflet Series no. 48.* Denver, CO: Denver Art Museum, 1932.

_____. *Long Island Indian Culture; Indian Leaflet Series no. 50.* Denver, CO: Denver Art Museum, 1932.

_____. *Long Island Indian Tribes; Indian Leaflet Series no. 49.* Denver, CO: Denver Art Museum, 1932.

_____. *Menomini Indians; Indian Leaflet Series no. 25.* Denver, CO: Denver Art Museum, 1932.

_____. *Northwest Coast Tribe; Indian Leaflet Series no. 72.* Denver, CO: Denver Art Museum, 1936.

_____. *Peyote Cult; Indian Leaflet Series no. 105.* Denver, CO: Denver Art Museum, 1950.

_____. *Tribes of the Great Lakes Regions; Indian Leaflet Series no. 81.* Denver, CO: Denver Art Museum, 1937.

_____. *Tribes of the Southwest; Indian Leaflet Series no. 55.* Denver, CO: Denver Art Museum, 1935.

_____. *The Wichita Indians and Allied Tribes: Waco, Towakoni, and Kichai; Indian Leaflet Series no. 40.* Denver, CO: Denver Art Museum, 1932.

Department of the Interior. U.S. Geographical and Geological Survey of the Rocky Mountain Region. *Contributions to North American Ethnology, v. 1–7, 9 (8 not published).* Washington, D.C.: U.S. Government Printing Office; Smithsonian Institution, 1877–1893.

Devereax, George. *Mohave Etiquette: Southwest Museum Leaflet no. 22.* Los Angeles, CA: Southwest Museum, 1948.

Dixon, R.B. *Publications in American Archaeology and Ethnology, v. 5, no. 5: The Chamariko Indians and Language.* Berkeley: University of California Press, 1910.

_____ and A.L. Kroeber. *Publications in American Archaeology and Ethnology, v. 16, no. 3: Linguistic Families of California.* Berkeley: University of California Press, 1919.

Doll, Don. *Vision Quest: Men, Women, and Sacred Sites of the Sioux Nation.* New York: Crown, 1994.

Dorsey, James Owen. *The Cecigha Language: Contributions to North American Ethnology v. 6.* Washington, D.C.: U.S. Government Printing Office; Smithsonian Institution, 1890.

_____. *Omaha and Ponka Letters: Bureau of American Ethnology Bulletin no. 11.* Washington, D.C.: U.S. Government Printing Office; Smithsonian Institution, 1889.

_____. *Omaha Sociology: Third Annual Report of the Bureau of Ethnology, 1881/82.* Washington, D.C.: U.S. Government Printing Office; Smithsonian Institution, 1881/1882.

_____. *Osage Traditions: Sixth Annual Report of the Bureau of Ethnology, 1884/1885.* Washington, D.C.: U.S. Government Printing Office; Smithsonian Institution, 1884/1885.

_____. *A Prehistoric Island Culture Area of America: Thirty-Fourth Annual Report of the Bureau of American Ethnology, 1912/13.* Washington, D.C.: U.S. Government Printing Office; Smithsonian Institution, 1922.

_____. *Siouan Sociology: A Posthumous Paper: Fifteenth Annual Report of the Bureau of Ethnology, 1897.* Washington, D.C.: U.S. Government Printing Office; Smithsonian Institution, 1897.

_____. *A Study of Siouan Cults: Eleventh Annual Report of the Bureau of Ethnology, 1894.* Washington, D.C.: U.S. Government Printing Office; Smithsonian Institution, 1894.

Downs, Ralph. "The Times They are a-Changing," *News from Native California,* v. 5, no. 1 (November/January 1990/1991), p. 17.

Dozier, Edward P. *Publications in American Archaeology and Ethnology, v. 44, no. 3: The Hopi-Tewa of Arizona.* Berkeley: University of California Press, 1954.

Drucker, Philip. *Anthropological Records, v. 2, no. 6: Kwakiutl Dancing Societies.* Berkeley: University of California Press, 1942.

_____. *Anthropological Records, v. 9, no. 3: Cultural Element Distributions: 26: Northwest Coast.* Berkeley: University of California Press, 1950.

_____. *The Native Brotherhoods: Modern Intertribal Organizations on the Northwest Coast; Bureau of American Ethnology Bulletin no. 168.* Washington, D.C.: U.S. Government Printing Office; Smithsonian Institution, 1958.

_____. *The Northern and Central Nootkan Tribes: Bureau of American Ethnology Bulletin no. 145.* Washington, D.C.: U.S. Government Printing Office; Smithsonian Institution, 1951.

_____. *Publications in American Archaeology and Ethnology, v. 35, no. 7: Contributions to Alsea Ethnography.* Berkeley: University of California Press, 1934.

_____. *Publications in American Archaeology and Ethnology, v. 36, no. 4: Tolowa and Their Southwest Oregon Kin.* Berkeley: University of California Press, 1934.

DuBois, Cora. *Anthropological Records, v. 3, no. 1: 1870 Ghost Dance.* Berkeley: University of California Press, 1939.

_____. *Publications in American Archaeology and Ethnology, v. 8, no. 3: Religion of the Luiseño Indians of Southern California.* Berkeley: University of California Press, 1908.

_____. *Publications in American Archaeology and Ethnology, v. 36, no. 1: Wintu Ethnography.* Berkeley: University of California Press, 1939.

Durlach, Theresa May. *Relationship Systems of the Tlingit, Haida, and Tsimshian: Publications of the American Ethnological Society v. 15.* New York: American Ethnological Society, 1928.

Eargle, Dolan H., Jr. *Earth is Our Mother: A Guide to the Indians of California, Their Locales and Historic Sites, 2nd ed.* San Francisco, CA: Trees, 1989.

Edmonson, Munro S. *Status Terminology and the Social Structure of North American Indians. Monographs of the American Ethnological Society no. 33.* Seattle: University of Washington Press, 1958.

Emerson, Nathaniel B. *Unwritten Literature of Hawaii: Sacred Songs of the Hula; Bureau of American Ethnology Bulletin 38.* Washington, D.C.: U.S. Government Printing Office; Smithsonian Institution, 1909.

Ewers, John C. *The Horse in Blackfoot Indian Culture, with Comparative Material from Other Western Tribes: Bureau of American Ethnology Bulletin no. 159.* Washington, D.C.: U.S. Government Printing Office; Smithsonian Institution, 1955.

Fay, George Emory (ed.) *Charters, Constitutions, and By-laws of the Indian Tribes of North America, v. 1–14.* Greeley, CO: Museum of Anthropology, Colorado State College, 1967–1981.

Faye, L. *Publications in American Archaeology and Ethnology, v. 20, no. 3: Notes on the Southern Maidu.* Berkeley: University of California Press, 1923.

Fewkes, Jesse Walter. *The Aborigines of Porto [sic] Rico and Neighboring Islands: Twenty-Fifth Annual Report of the Bureau of American Ethnology, 1903/04.* Washington, D.C.: U.S. Government Printing Office; Smithsonian Institution, 1907.

_____. *A Prehistoric Island Culture Area of America: Thirty-Fourth Annual Report of the Bureau of American Ethnology, 1912/13.* Washington, D.C.: U.S. Government Printing Office; Smithsonian Institution, 1922.

Finger, John R. "Termination and the Eastern Band of Cherokees," *American Indian Quarterly*, v. 15, no. 2 (Spring 1991), pp. 153–170.

Fleming, Paula Richardson, and Judith Lynn Luskey. *Grand Endeavors of American Indian Photography.* Washington, D.C.: Smithsonian Institution, 1993.

_____. *Indians of North America in Early Photos.* New York: Harper and Row, 1986.

Fletcher, Alice C., and Francis La Flesche. *The Omaha Tribe: Twenty-Seventh Annual Report of the Bureau of American Ethnology, 1905/06.* Washington, D.C.: U.S. Government Printing Office; Smithsonian Institution, 1911.

Forde, C. D. *Publications in American Archaeology and Ethnology, v. 28, no. 4: Ethnography of the Yuma Indians.* Berkeley: University of California Press, 1931.

Fortune, R.F. *Arapesh: Publications of the American Ethnological Society v. 19.* New York: J.J. Augustin, 1942.

"Forty Indian Groups Petition for Federal Recognition." *Wassaja* (January/February 1979), p. 16.

Foster, G.M. *Anthropological Records, v. 5, no. 3: A Summary of Yuki Culture.* Berkeley: University of California Press, 1944.

Frede, C. Daryll. *Publications in American Archaeology and Ethnology, v. 28, no. 4: Ethnography of the Yuma Indians.* Berkeley: University of California Press, 1931.

Freed, Stanley A. *Anthropological Records, v. 14, no. 6: Changing Washo Kinship.* Berkeley: University of California Press, 1960.

Gann, Thomas. *The Maya Indians of Southern Yucatan and Northern British Honduras: Bureau of American Ethnology Bulletin no. 64.* Washington, D.C.: U.S. Government Printing Office; Smithsonian Institution, 1918.

Garth, Thomas R. *Anthropological Records, v. 14, no. 2: Atsugewi Ethnography.* Berkeley: University of California Press, 1953.

Gatschet, Albert S., and John R. Swanton. *A Dictionary of the Atakapa Language: Bureau of American Ethnology Bulletin no. 108.* Washington, D.C.: U.S. Government Printing Office; Smithsonian Institution, 1932.

_____. *The Klamath Indians of Southwestern Oregon: Contributions to North American Ethnology v. 2.* Washington, D.C.: U.S. Government Printing Office; Smithsonian Institution, 1891.

Gattuso, John (ed.) *Circle of Nations: Voices and Visions of American Indians.* Hillsbor, OR: Beyond Word , 1993.

"Gay Head Wampanoags Receive Federal Assistance for Tribal Housing and Offices." *Eagle*, v. 9, no. 1 (January/February 1991), p. 4.

Gayton, A.H. *Anthropological Records, v. 10, no. 1: Yokuts and Western Mono Ethnography.* Berkeley: University of California Press, 1948.

_____. *Anthropological Records, v. 10, no. 2: Yokuts and Western Mono Ethnography: 2: Northern Foothill Yokuts and Western Mono.* Berkeley: University of California Press, 1948.

_____. *Publications in American Archaeology and Ethnology, v. 28, no. 3: The Ghost Dance of 1870 in South-Central California.* Berkeley: University of California Press, 1930.

Gendar, Jeannine. "Tribal Status," *News from Native California*, v. 7, no. 4 (Winter 1992/1993), pp. 33–35.

Gentry, Howard Scott. *The Wariho Indians of Sonora-Chihuahua: An Ethnographic Survey: Bureau of American Ethnology Anthropological Paper no. 65, Bulletin no. 186.* Washington, D.C.: U.S. Government Printing Office; Smithsonian Institution, 1963.

Gibbs, George. *Tribes of Western Washington and Northwestern Oregon: Contributions to North American Ethnology v. 1.* Washington, D.C.: U.S. Government Printing Office; Smithsonian Institution, 1877.

Gibbs, George, and W. H. Dall. *Comparative Vocabularies: Contributions to North American Ethnology v. 1.* Washington, D.C.: U.S. Government Printing Office; Smithsonian Institution, 1877.

Gibson, Arrell Morgan. *American Indians: Prehistory to the Present.* Lexington, VA: D.C. Heath, 1980.

Gifford, Edward Winslow. *Anthropological Records, v. 25: Ethnographic Notes on the Southwestern Pomo.* Berkeley: University of California Press, 1967.

_____. *The Kamia of Imperial Valley: Bureau of American Ethnology Bulletin no. 97.* Washington, D.C.: U.S. Government Printing Office; Smithsonian Institution, 1931.

_____. *Publications in American Archaeology and Ethnology, v. 11, no. 5: Dichotomous Social Organization in South Central California.* Berkeley: University of California Press, 1916.

_____. *Publications in American Archaeology and Ethnology, v. 12, no. 4: Miwok Moieties.* Berkeley: University of California Press, 1916.

_____. *Publications in American Archaeology and Ethnology, v. 12, no. 6: Tubatulabal and Kawaiisu Kinship Terms.* Berkeley: University of California Press, 1917.

_____. *Publications in American Archaeology and Ethnology, v. 14, no. 2: Clans and Moities in Southern California.* Berkeley: University of California Press, 1918.

_____. *Publications in American Archaeology and Ethnology, v. 18, no. 1: California Kinship Terminologies.* Berkeley: University of California Press, 1922.

_____. *Publications in American Archaeology and Ethnology, v. 18, no. 2: Clear Lake Pomo Society.* Berkeley: University of California Press, 1926.

_____. *Publications in American Archaeology and Ethnology, v. 18, no. 3: Miwok Cults.* Berkeley: University of California Press, 1926.

_____. *Publications in American Archaeology and Ethnology, v. 20, no. 5: Pomo Lands on Clear Lake.* Berkeley: University of California Press, 1923.

_____. *Publications in American Archaeology and Ethnology, v. 29, no. 3: The Southeastern Yavapai.* Berkeley: University of California Press, 1932.

_____. *Publications in American Archaeology and Ethnology, v. 31, no. 2: The Northfork Mono.* Berkeley: University of California Press, 1932.

_____. *Publications in American Archaeology and Ethnology, v. 31, no. 5: The Cocopa.* Berkeley: University of California Press, 1933.

_____. *Publications in American Archaeology and Ethnology, v. 34, no. 4: Northeastern and Western Yavapai.* Berkeley: University of California Press, 1936.

_____ and R.H. Lowie. *Publications in American Archaeology and Ethnology, v. 23, no. 7: Notes on the Akwa'ala Indians of Lower California.* Berkeley: University of California Press, 1928.

Gilbert, William Harlen, Jr. *The Eastern Cherokees: Bureau of American Ethnology Anthropological Paper no. 23, Bulletin no. 133.* Washington, D.C.: U.S. Government Printing Office; Smithsonian Institution, 1944.

Giles, Vesta. "Dorothy Grant," *Indian Art* (Fall 1997), pp. 38–41.

Gillin, John. *The Quichua-Speaking Indians of the Province of Imbabura (Ecuador) and Their Anthropometric Relations with the Living Populations of the Andean Area: Bureau of American Ethnology Archaeological Paper no. 16, Bulletin no. 128.* Washington, D.C.: U.S. Government Printing Office; Smithsonian Institution, 1941.

Goddard, Ives (ed.) *Languages: v. 17: Handbook of North American Indians,* ed. William C. Sturtevant. Washington, D.C.: Smithsonian Institution, 1996.

Goddard, Pliny Earle. *Publications in American Archaeology and Ethnology, v. 10, no. 6: Notes on the Chilula Indians of Northwestern California.* Berkeley: University of California Press, 1914.

_____. *Publications in American Archaeology and Ethnology, v. 17, no. 4: Habitat of the Pitch Indians, A Wailaki Division.* Berkeley: University of California Press, 1924.

_____. *Publications in American Archaeology and Ethnology, v. 20, no. 6: Habitat of the Wailaki.* Berkeley: University of California Press, 1903.

_____. *Publications in American Archaeology and Ethnology, v. 24, no. 5: The Bear River Dialect of Athapascan.* Berkeley: University of California Press, 1929.

Good, Diane L. "Sacred Bundles: History Wrapped up in Culture," *History News,* v. 45, no. 4 (July/August 1990), pp. 13–14, 27.

Granberry, Michael. "A Tribe's Battle for its Identity," *Los Angeles Times* (Sunday, March 13, 1994), pp. A1, A22-A23.

Haines, Elijah Middlebrook. *American Indian (Uh-nish-in-na-ba).* Chicago, IL: Mas-sin-na'-gan, 1888.

Hale, Horatio. "Iroquois Book of Rites," in *Library of Aboriginal American Literature v. 2,* ed. Daniel Garrison Brinton. Philadelphia, PA: Brinton, 1883.

Hall, Edwin S., Jr. "Kutchin Athapascan/Nunamiut Eskimo Conflict," *Alaska History and Arts of the North—Quarterly Journal,* v. 5, no. 4 (Autumn 1975), pp. 248–252.

Hall, Len. "A Mission Fulfilled," *Los Angeles Times* (December 1, 1993), pp. A3, A18.

Hanks, Lucien M., and Jane Richardson. *Observations on Northern Blackfoot Kinship: Monographs of the American Ethnology Society no. 9.* New York: J. J. Augustin, 1945.

Harrington, John Peabody. *The Ethnogeography of the Tewa Indians: Twenty-Ninth Annual Report of the Bureau of American Ethnology, 1907–1908.* Washington, D.C.: U.S. Government Printing Office; Smithsonian Institution, 1916.

_____. *The Original Strachey Vocabulary of the Virginia Indian Language: Bureau of American Ethnology Anthropological Paper no. 46, Bulletin no. 157.* Washington, D.C.: U.S. Government Printing Office; Smithsonian Institution, 1955.

_____. *Vocabulary of the Kiowa Language: Bureau of American Ethnology Bulletin no. 84.* Washington, D.C.: U.S. Government Printing Office; Smithsonian Institution, 1928.

Harrington, M.R. *Ancient Life among the Southern California Indians: Southwest Museum Leaflets no. 26.* Los Angeles, CA: Southwest Museum, 1955.

Healy, Donald T. "Flags of the Native Peoples of the United States," *RAVEN,* v. 3/4 (1996–1997), entire issue.

Heizer, Robert F. *The Indians of Los Angeles County: Hugo Reid's Letters 1852: Southwest Museum Papers, No. 21.* Los Angeles, CA: Southwest Museum, 1968.

_____. *Languages, Territories and Names of California Indian Tribes.* Berkeley: University of California Press, 1966.

Heizer, Robert F. (ed.) *California: v. 8: Handbook of North American Indians,* ed. William C. Sturtevant. Washington, D.C.: Smithsonian Institution, 1978.

Heizer, R.F., and M.A. Whipple. *California Indians, 2nd ed.* Berkeley: University of California Press, 1971.

Henry, Jeannette. "BIA to Samish Tribe: You Do Not Exist," *Wassaja,* v. 9. no. 3 (January/February 1983), pp. 1, 30.

Henshaw, H. W. *Anthropological Records, v. 15, no. 2: California Indian Linguistic Records: the Mission Indian Vocabularies of H.W. Henshaw.* Berkeley: University of California Press, 1955.

Hewitt, J.N.B. *Comparative Lexicology: Seventeenth Annual Report of the Bureau of Ethnology, Pt. 1, 1900.* Washington, D.C.: U.S. Government Printing Office; Smithsonian Institution, 1900.

_____. *Notes on the Creek Indians: Bureau of American Ethnology Anthropological Paper no. 10, Bulletin no. 123.* Washington, D.C.: U.S. Government Printing Office; Smithsonian Institution, 1939.

Heye Foundation. *Leaflets.* New York: Museum of the American Indian, 1919–1940.

Hiesinger, Ulrich W. *Indian Lives: A Photographic Record from the Civil War to Wounded Knee.* New York: te Neues, 1994.

Hines, Donald M. *Forgotten Tribes: Oral Tales of the*

Teninos and Adjacent Mid-Columbia River Indian Nations. Issaquah, WA: Great Eagle, 1991.

Hodge, Frederick Webb (ed.) *Handbook of American Indians North of Mexico: Bureau of American Ethnology Bulletin no. 30*, 2 v. Washington, D.C.: U.S. Government Printing Office; Smithsonian Institution, 1907.

_____. *Handbook of Indians of Canada, facsimile edition.* Toronto: C.H. Parmelee, 1974.

Hoffman, Bernard G. *Observations on Certain Ancient Tribes of the Northern Appalachian Province: Bureau of American Ethnology Anthropological Paper no. 70, Bulletin no. 191.* Washington, D.C.: U.S. Government Printing Office; Smithsonian Institution, 1964.

Hoffman, Walter James. *The Menomini Indians: Fourteenth Annual Report of the Bureau of Ethnology, Pt.1, 1896.* Washington, D.C.: U.S. Government Printing Office; Smithsonian Institution, 1897.

_____. *The Midi'wiwin or 'Grand Medicine Society' of the Ojibwa: Seventh Annual Report of the Bureau of Ethnology, 1885/86.* Washington, D.C.: U.S. Government Printing Office; Smithsonian Institution, 1885/1886.

Holden, Edward S. *Studies in Central American Picture–Writing: First Annual Report of the Bureau of Ethnology.* Washington, D.C.: U.S. Government Printing Office; Smithsonian Institution, 1879/1880.

Holmes, William H. *The Use of Gold and Other Metals among the Ancient Inhabitants of Chiriqui, Isthmus of Darien: Bureau of American Ethnology Bulletin no. 3.* Washington, D.C.: U.S. Government Printing Office; Smithsonian Institution, 1887.

Holt, Catherine. *Anthropological Records, v. 3, no. 4: Shasta Ethnography.* Berkeley: University of California Press, 1946.

Hook, Jason. *Geronimo: Last Renegade of the Apache.* Poole, Dorset, UK: Firebird, 1989.

Hooper, L. *Publications in American Archaeology and Ethnology, v. 16, no. 6: The Cahuilla Indians.* Berkeley: University of California, 1920.

Hoover, Herbert T. "Yankton Sioux Tribal Claims against the United States, 1917–1975," *Western Historical Quarterly*, v. 7, no. 2 (April 1976), pp. 125–142.

"Houma Denied Recognition." *Indian Country Today* (December 22, 1994), pp. A1, A2.

Howard, James H. *Dakota Winter Counts as a Source of Plains History: Bureau of American Ethnology Anthropological Paper no. 61, Bulletin 173.* Washington, D.C.: U.S. Government Printing Office; Smithsonian Institution, 1960.

_____. *The Ponca Tribe: Bureau of American Ethnology Bulletin no. 195.* Washington, D.C.: U.S. Government Printing Office; Smithsonian Institution, 1965.

Hrdliăka, Ales. *Anthropological Survey in Alaska: Forty-Six Annual Report of the Bureau of American Ethnology, 1928/29.* Washington, D.C.: U.S. Government Printing Office; Smithsonian Institution, 1930.

_____. *Early Man in South America: Bureau of American Ethnology Bulletin no. 52.* Washington, D.C.: U.S. Government Printing Office; Smithsonian Institution, 1912.

_____. *Physiological and Medical Observations Among the Indians of Southwestern United States and Northern Mexico: Bureau of American Ethnology Bulletin no. 34.* Washington, D.C.: U.S. Government Printing Office; Smithsonian Institution, 1908.

Hudson, Trevis. "Alliklik-Tataviam Problem," *Journal of California and Great Basin Anthropology*, v. 4, no. 2 (Winter 1982), pp. 222–232.

"Ihanktuwan Dacotah Oyate," *Indian Country Today*, v. 12, issue 44 (April 28, 1993), p. A4.

"Immokalee Seminole Receive Trust Status," *Eagle*, v. 8, no. 1 (January/February 1990), p. 8.

Indian Notes and Monographs no. 1–39. New York: Museum of the American Indian, Heye Foundation, 1919–1960.

Indian Place Names of New England. New York: The Museum (Museum of the American Indian, Heye Foundation), 1962.

Indiana Historical Society. *Prehistory Research Series, v. 1–7.* Indianapolis, IN: Indiana Historical Society, 1937–90.

Indians (Time/Life). Alexandria, VA: Time-Life, 1973.

"Indians Want Access to Sacred Land." *Eagle*, v. 9, no. 3 (May-June 1991), p. 4

Isbell, William H. "Honcompampa: Monumental Ruins in Peru's North Highlands." *Expedition*, v. 33, no. 3 (1991), pp. 27–36.

Jablow, Joseph. *Cheyenne in Plains Indian Trade Relations, 1795–1840: Monographs of the American Ethnological Society no. 19.* New York: J. J. Augustin, 1951.

Jacobs, Melville. "Texts in Chinook Jargon." *University of Washington Publications in Anthropology*, v. 7, no. 1 (1968), pp. 1–27.

Jelm, June (ed.) *Subarctic: v. 6: Handbook of North American Indians*, ed. William C. Sturtevant. Washington, D.C.: Smithsonian Institution, 1981.

Jenness, Diamond. *The Carrier Indians of the Bulkley River: Their Social and Religious Life: Bureau of American Ethnology Anthropological Paper no. 25, Bulletin no. 133.* Washington, D.C.: U.S. Government Printing Office; Smithsonian Institution, 1944.

Johnson, LeRoy. "Reconstructed Crow Terminology of the Titskanwatits, or Tonkawas, with Inferred Social Correlates." *Plains Anthropologist*, v. 39, no. 150 (November 94), pp. 377–413.

Jones, J.A. *The Sun Dance of the Northern Ute: Bureau of American Ethnology Anthropological Paper no. 47, Bulletin no. 157.* Washington, D.C.: U.S. Government Printing Office; Smithsonian Institution, 1955.

Jones, William. *Ethnography of the Fox Indians: Bureau of American Ethnology Bulletin no. 125.* Washington, D.C.: U.S. Government Printing Office; Smithsonian Institution, 1939.

_____. *Fox Texts: Publications of the American Ethnological Society, v. 1.* Leyden, Holland: E.J. Brill, 1912.

Kaliss, Tony. "Soviet Northern Native Peoples Become Organized," *Lakota Times*, v. 10, no. 41 (April 10, 1991), p. 1

Kearse, David. "Chief John A. James." *Palm Springs Life*, v. 39, no. 2 (October 1966), pp. 58–62.

Kluckhorn, Clyde. *The Ramah Navajo: Bureau of American Ethnology Anthropological Papers no. 79, Bulletin no. 196*. Washington, D.C.: U.S. Government Printing Office; Smithsonian Institution, 1966.

Krause, Aurel. *Tlingit Indians: Results of a Trip to the Northwest Coast of America and the Bering Straits*, trans. Erna Gunther. *Monographs of the American Ethnological Society no. 26*. Seattle: University of Washington Press, 1956.

Kroeber, A.L. *Anthropological Records, v. 11, no. 3: Yokuts Dialects Survey*. Berkeley: University of California Press, 1963.

_____. *Handbook of the Indians of California: Bureau of American Ethnology Bulletin no. 78*. Washington, D.C.: U.S. Government Printing Office; Smithsonian Institution, 1925.

_____. *Publications in American Archaeology and Ethnology, v. 2, no. 2: The Languages of the Coast of California South of San Francisco*. Berkeley: University of California, 1911.

_____. *Publications in American Archaeology and Ethnology, v. 2, no. 5: The Yokuts Language of South Central California*. Berkeley: University of California Press, 1907.

_____. *Publications in American Archaeology and Ethnology, v. 4, no. 3: Shoshonean Dialects of California*. Berkeley: University of California Press, 1907.

_____. *Publications in American Archaeology and Ethnology, v. 4, no. 5: The Washo Language of East Central California and Nevada*. Berkeley: University of California, 1907.

_____. *Publications in American Archaeology and Ethnology, v. 4, no. 6: The Religion of the Indians of California*. Berkeley: University of California, 1907.

_____. *Publications of the American Ethnological Society, v. 6, no. 3: On the Evidence of the Occupation of Certain Regions by the Miwok Indians*. Berkeley: University of California, 1908.

_____. *Publications in American Archaeology and Ethnology, v. 8, no. 1: A Mission Record of the California Indians*. Berkeley: University of California, 1908.

_____. *Publications in American Archaeology and Ethnology, v. 8, no. 2: Ethnography of the Cahuilla Indians*. Berkeley: University of California Press, 1908.

_____. *Publications in American Archaeology and Ethnology, v. 9, no. 2: Chumash and Coastanoan Indians*. Berkeley: University of California Press, 1910.

_____. *Publications in American Archaeology and Ethnology, v. 9, no. 3: "Languages of the Coast of California North of San Francisco*. Berkeley: University of California, 1911.

_____. *Publications in American Archaeology and Ethnology, v. 10, no. 1: Phonetic Constituents of the Native Languages of California*. Berkeley: University of California Press, 1911.

_____. *Publications in American Archaeology and Ethnology, v. 10, no. 3: Phonetic Elements of the Mohave Language*. Berkeley: University of California Press, 1911.

_____. *Publications in American Archaeology and Ethnology, v. 11, no. 4: Serian, Tequistlatecan and Hokan*. Berkeley: University of California Press, 1915.

_____. *Publications in American Archaeology and Ethnology, v. 12, no. 3: Arapaho Dialects*. Berkeley: University of California Press, 1916.

_____. *Publications in American Archaeology and Ethnology, v. 12, no. 9: California Kinship Systems*. Berkeley: University of California Press, 1917.

_____. *Publications in American Archaeology and Ethnology, v. 16, no. 8: Yuman Tribes of the Lower Colorado*. Berkeley: University of California Press, 1920.

_____. *Publications in American Archaeology and Ethnology, v. 20, no. 8: The History of Native Culture in California*. Berkeley: University of California Press, 1923.

_____. *Publications in American Archaeology and Ethnology, v. 22, no. 2: Types of Indian Culture in California*. Berkeley: University of California Press, 1904.

_____. *Publications in American Archaeology and Ethnology, v. 2, no. 9: Native Culture of the Southwest*. Berkeley: University of California Press, 1928.

_____. *Publications in American Archaeology and Ethnology, v. 24, no. 4: Valley Nisenan*. Berkeley: University of California Press, 1929.

_____. *Publications in American Archaeology and Ethnology, v. 29, no. 4: The Patwin and Their Neighbors*. Berkeley: University of California Press, 1932.

_____. *Publications in American Archaeology and Ethnology, v. 35, no. 2: Yurok and Neighboring Kin Term Systems*. Berkeley: University of California Press, 1934.

_____. *Publications in American Archaeology and Ethnology, v. 38, no. 12: Cultural and Natural Areas of Native North America*. Berkeley: University of California Press, 1939.

_____. *Southwest Museum Papers no. 6: The Seri*. Los Angeles, CA: Southwest Museum, 1931.

_____ and J. P. Harrington. *Publications in American Archaeology and Ethnology, v. 11, no. 2: Phonetic Elements of the Diegueño Language*. Berkeley: University of California Press, 1914.

Kyle, Robert. "400 Years Later: The Nanticoke Tribe." *Native Peoples*, v. 6, no. 3 (Spring 1993), pp. 72–75.

La Flesche, Francis. *A Dictionary of the Osage Language: Bureau of American Ethnology Bulletin no. 109*. Washington, D.C.: U.S. Government Printing Office; Smithsonian Institution, 1932.

_____. *The Osage Tribe: The Rite of Vigil: Thirty-Ninth Annual Report of the Bureau of American Ethnology, 1917/18*. Washington, D.C.: U.S. Government Printing Office; Smithsonian Institution, 1925.

Laboratory of Anthropology, Museum of New Mexico. *I am Here: Two Thousand Years of Southwest Indian Arts and Culture*. Santa Fe, NM: Museum of New Mexico Press, 1989.

Landberg, Leif C.W. *Chumash Indians of Southern California: Southwest Museum Papers no. 19*. Los Angeles, CA: Southwest Museum, 1965,

Lantis, Margaret. *Alaskan Eskimo Ceremonialism. Monographs of the American Ethnological Society no. 1.* New York: J. J. Augustin, 1947.

_____. *Eskimo Childhood and Interpersonal Relationships. Monographs of the American Ethnological Society no. 33.* Seattle: University of Washington Press, 1960.

La Vere, David. "Friendly Persuasions: Gifts and Reciprocity in Comanche-Euroamerican Relations." *Chronicles of Oklahoma*, v. 71, no. 3 (Fall 1993), pp. 322–337.

Lawler, Elizabeth. "Early Consultations with the Chemehuevis." *Malki Matters* (Summer 1995), pp. 5–7.

Lewis, Monte. "The Chickasaw on the Texas Frontier." *West Texas Historical Association Year Book, v. 58.* Abilene, TX: West Texas Historical Association, 1982.

Lewis, Oscar. *The Effects of White Contact upon Blackfoot Cult. Monographs of the American Ethnological Society no. 6.* New York: J. J. Augustin, 1942.

Library of Congress Subject Headings, 14th ed. Washington, D.C.: Cataloging Distribution Service, Library of Congress, 1991.

Lippard, Lucy R. (ed.) *Partial Recall.* New York: New Press, 1992.

Lounsbury, Floyd G. *Iroquois-Cherokee Linguistic Relations: Symposium on Cherokee and Iroquois Culture no. 2, Bureau of American Ethnology Bulletin no. 180.* Washington, D.C.: U.S. Government Printing Office; Smithsonian Institution, 1961.

Lowie, Robert H. *Publications in American Archaeology and Ethnology, v. 20, no. 9: The Cultural Connection of California and Plateau Shoshonean Tribes.* Berkeley: University of California Press, 1923.

_____. *Publications in American Archaeology and Ethnology, v. 36, no. 52: Ethnographic Notes on the Washo.* Berkeley: University of California Press, 1939.

_____. *Publications in American Archaeology and Ethnology, v. 39, no. 1: The Crow Language.* Berkeley: University of California Press, 1941

Luchetti, Cathy Lee. *Women of the West.* Berkeley: Antelope Island, 1982.

MacCauley, Clay. *Seminole Indians of Florida: Fifth Annual Report of the Bureau of Ethnology, 1883/84.* Washington, D.C.: U.S. Government Printing Office; Smithsonian Institution, 1883/1884.

McGee, W.J. *The Seri Indians: Seventeenth Annual Report of the Bureau of Ethnology, Pt. 1, 1900.* Washington, D.C.: U.S. Government Printing Office; Smithsonian Institution, 1900.

_____. *The Siouan Indians: A Preliminary Sketch: Fifteenth Annual Report of the Bureau of Ethnology, 1897.* Washington, D.C.: U.S. Government Printing Office; Smithsonian Institution, 1897.

McGinnis, Dale K., and Floyd W. Sharrock. *Crow People.* Phoenix, AZ: Indian Tribal Series, 1972.

McKenney, Thomas Loraine, and James Hall. *History of the Tribes of North America, 3v.* Edinburgh, Scotland: J.Grant, 1933–1934.

Magnaghi, Russell M. "Plains Indians in New Mexico: the Genizaro Experience." *Great Plains Quarterly*, v. 10, no. 2 (Spring 1990), pp. 86–95.

Maine Historical Society. *Collections of the Maine Historical Society, 1st–3rd Series.* Portland, ME: The Society, 1831–1887.

Marsden, W.L. *Publications in American Archaeology and Ethnology, v. 20, no. 11: The Northern Paiute Language of Oregon.* Berkeley: University of California Press, 1923.

Mason, John Alden. *Publications in American Archaeology and Ethnology, v. 10, no. 4: Ethnology of the Salinan Indians.* Berkeley: University of California Press, 1912.

_____. *Publications in American Archaeology and Ethnology, v. 11, no. 7: The Mutsun Dialect of Costanoan Based on the Vocabulary of De la Cuesta.* Berkeley: University of California Press, 1916.

_____. *Publications in American Archaeology and Ethnology, v. 14, no. 1: The Language of the Salinan Indians.* Berkeley: University of California Press, 1918.

_____. *Publications in American Archaeology and Ethnology, v. 20, no. 12: Preliminary Sketch of the Yaqui Indians.* Berkeley: University of California Press, 1923.

Mathes, W. Michael. "Some New Observations Relative to the Indigenous Inhabitants of La Paz." *Journal of California Anthropology*, v. 2, no. 2 (Winter 1975), pp. 180–182.

Mayfield, Thomas Jefferson. "Snaring Pigeons." *News from Native California*, v. 7, no. 4 (Fall/Winter 1994), pp. 10–11.

"Members of Kickapoo Indian Tribe in Texas to begin Taking Oath for U.S. Citizenship." *Los Angeles Times*, Pt.1 (November 21, 1985), p. 2.

Métraux, Alfred. *The Native Tribes of Eastern Bolivia and Western Matto Grosso: Bureau of American Ethnology Bulletin no. 134.* Washington, D.C.: U.S. Government Printing Office; Smithsonian Institution, 1942.

"Miami Indians Vow to Sue, if Necessary, to Regain Tribal Status." *Indian Trader*, v. 21, no. 8 (August 1990), p. 11.

Michelson, Truman. *Contributions to Fox Ethnology: Bureau of American Ethnology Bulletin no. 85.* Washington, D.C.: U.S. Government Printing Office; Smithsonian Institution, 1927.

_____. *Contributions to Fox Ethnology II: Bureau of American Ethnology Bulletin no. 95.* Washington, D.C.: U.S. Government Printing Office; Smithsonian Institution, 1930.

_____. *Fox Miscellany: Bureau of American Ethnology Bulletin no. 114.* Washington, D.C.: U.S. Government Printing Office; Smithsonian Institution, 1937.

_____. *Linguistic Classification of Cree and Montagnais-Naskapi Dialects: Bureau of American Ethnology Anthropological Paper no. 8, Bulletin no. 123.* Washington, D.C.: U.S. Government Printing Office; Smithsonian Institution, 1939.

_____. *Notes on the Fox WâpAnÿwiweni: Bureau of American Ethnology Bulletin no. 105.* Washington, D.C.: U.S. Government Printing Office; Smithsonian Institution, 1932.

_____. *Preliminary Report on the Linguistic Classification of Algonquian Tribes: Twenty-Eighth*

Annual Report of the Bureau of American Ethnology, 1906/07. Washington, D.C.: U.S. Government Printing Office; Smithsonian Institution, 1912.

Miller, Carl F. *Revaluation of the Eastern Siouan Problem, with Particular Emphasis on the Virginia Branches—the Occaneechi, the Saponi, and the Tutelo: Bureau of American Ethnology Anthropological Paper no. 52, Bulletin no. 164.* Washington, D.C.: U.S. Government Printing Office; Smithsonian Institution, 1957.

Miller, Jay. "Changing Moons: A History of Caddo Religion." *Plains Anthropologist,* v. 41, no. 157 (1966), pp. 243–259.

Mindeleff, Cosmos. *Localization of Tusayan Clans: Nineteenth Annual Report of the Bureau of Ethnology, Pt. 2, 1900.* Washington, D.C.: U.S. Government Printing Office; Smithsonian Institution, 1900.

Mishkin, Bernard. *Rank and Warfare among the Plains Indians. Monographs of the American Ethnological Society no. 3.* New York: J. J. Augustin, 1940.

"Montana Band Seeks Canadian Indian Status, Claims Reserve." *American Indian Report,* v. 7, no. 4 (April 1991), p. 2.

Mooney, James. *The Ghost-Dance Religion and the Sioux Outbreak of 1890: Fourteenth Annual Report of the Bureau of Ethnology, Pt. 2, 1896.* Washington, D.C.: U.S. Government Printing Office; Smithsonian Institution, 1897.

_____. *The Siouan Tribes of the East: Bureau of American Ethnology Bulletin no. 22.* Washington, D.C.: U.S. Government Printing Office; Smithsonian Institution, 1895.

Morley, Sulvanus Griswold. *An Introduction to the Study of the Maya Hieroglyphs: Bureau of American Ethnology Bulletin no. 57.* Washington, D.C.: U.S. Government Printing Office; Smithsonian Institution, 1915.

"Mowa Choctaws Continue Their Battle for Federal Recognition." *Indian Trader,* v. 24, no. 19 (April 1993), p. 19.

Murphy, Robert Francis, and Buell Quain. *Trumai Indians of Central Brazil. Monographs of the American Ethnological Society no. 24.* Locust Valley, N.J.: J. J. Augustin, 1955.

Myer, William Edward. *Indian Trails of the Southeast: Forty-Second Annual Report of the Bureau of American Ethnology, 1924/25.* Washington, D.C.: U.S. Government Printing Office; Smithsonian Institution, 1928.

"Narragansett Tribe Receives Formal Recognition." *Talking Leaf,* v. 49, no. 2 (February 1984), p. 5.

"Native American Affairs." *Akwesasne Notes,* v. 23, no. 2 (Summer 1991), p. 26.

Nelson, Edward William. *The Eskimo about Bering Strait: Eighteenth Annual Report of the Bureau of Ethnology, Pt. 1, 1901.* Washington, D.C.: U.S. Government Printing Office; Smithsonian Institution, 1901.

Nevada State Museum. *Anthropological Papers, no. 1-present.* Carson City, NV: Nevada State Museum, 1959-present.

"New Mexico State Fair award goes to artist Alice Yazzie." *Indian Trader,* v. 21, no. 10 (Oct.1990), pp. 19, 22.

Newman, Stanley. *Zuni Grammar: University of New Mexico Publications in Anthropology no. 14.* Albuquerque, NM: University of New Mexico Press, 1964.

Nichols, Frances Sellman Gaither (comp.) *Index to Schoolcraft's 'Indian Tribes of the United States, 4 vols.: Bureau of American Ethnology Bulletin no. 157.* Washington, D.C.: U.S. Government Printing Office; Smithsonian Institution, 1954.

Nichols, Roger L. (ed.) *American Indian: Past and Present, 3rd ed.* New York: Knopf, 1986.

Nightingale, Lewis. "Nelda Schrupp." *Indian Art* (Fall 1997), pp. 50–53.

Nomland, Gladys Ayer. *Anthropological Records, v. 2, no. 2: Bear River Ethnography.* Berkeley: University of California Press, 1938.

_____. *Publications in American Archaeology and Ethnology, v. 36, no. 2: Sinkyone Notes.* Berkeley: University of California Press, 1935.

Noriyuki, Duane. "Nation of One." *Los Angeles Times* (November 14, 1994), pp. E1, E4.

O'Brien, Sharon. *American Indian Tribal Governments.* Norman: University of Oklahoma Press, 1990.

Olson, James S. *The Indians of Central and South America: An Ethnohistorical Dictionary.* New York: Greenwood, 1991.

Olson, Ronald L. *Anthropological Records, v. 2, no. 5: Social Organization of the Haisla of British Columbia.* Berkeley: University of California Press, 1940.

_____. *Anthropological Records, v. 14, no. 5: Notes on the Bella Bella Kwakiutl.* Berkeley: University of California Press, 1955.

_____. *Anthropological Records, v. 14, no. 3: Social Life of the Owikeno Kwakiutl.* Berkeley: University of California Press, 1954.

_____. *Publications in American Archaeology and Ethnology, v. 33, no. 4: Clan and Moiety in Native America.* Berkeley: University of California Press, 1933.

Ortiz, Alfonso (ed.) *Southwest: v. 9: Handbook of North American Indians,* ed. William C. Sturtevant. Washington, D.C.: Smithsonian Institution, 1979.

_____. *Southwest: v. 10: Handbook of North American Indians,* ed. William C. Sturtevant. Washington, D.C.: Smithsonian Institution, 1983.

Petrullo, Vincenzo. *The Yururos of the Capanaparo River, Venezuela: Bureau of American Ethnology Anthropological Paper no. 11, Bulletin no. 123.* Washington, D.C.: U.S. Government Printing Office; Smithsonian Institution, 1939.

Pettitt, George A. *Anthropological Record v. 14, no. 1: Quileute of La Push.* Berkeley: University of California Press, 1953.

Pilling, James Constantine. *Bibliography of the Athapascan Languages: Bureau of American Ethnology Bulletin no. 14.* Washington, D.C.: U.S. Government Printing Office; Smithsonian Institution, 1892.

_____. *Bibliography of the Chinookan Languages (Including the Chinook Jargon): Bureau of American Ethnology Bulletin no. 15.* Washington, D.C.: U.S. Government Printing Office; Smithsonian Institution, 1893.

_____. *Bibliography of the Eskimo Languages: Bureau of American Ethnology Bulletin no. 1.* Washington, D.C.: U.S. Government Printing Office; Smithsonian Institution, 1887.

_____. *Bibliography of the Iroquoian Languages: Bureau of American Ethnology Bulletin no. 6.* Washington, D.C.: U.S. Government Printing Office; Smithsonian Institution, 1889.

_____. *Bibliography of the Muskhogean Languages: Bureau of American Ethnology Bulletin no. 9.* Washington, D.C.: U.S. Government Printing Office; Smithsonian Institution, 1889.

_____. *Bibliography of the Salishan Languages: Bureau of American Ethnology Bulletin no. 16.* Washington, D.C.: U.S. Government Printing Office; Smithsonian Institution, 1893.

_____. *Bibliography of the Siouan Languages: Bureau of American Ethnology Bulletin no. 5.* Washington, D.C.: U.S. Government Printing Office; Smithsonian Institution, 1887.

_____. *Bibliography of the Wakashan Languages: Bureau of American Ethnology Bulletin 19.* Washington, D.C.: U.S. Government Printing Office; Smithsonian Institution, 1894.

Pinart, Alphonse. *Anthropological Records, v. 15, no. 1: California Indian Linguistic Records: the Mission Indian Vocabularies of Alphonse Pinart.* Berkeley: University of California Press, 1952.

Pollard, John Garland. *Additional Studies of the Arts, Crafts, and Customs of the Guiana Indians, with Special Reference to those of Southern British Guiana: Bureau of American Ethnology Bulletin no. 91.* Washington, D.C.: U.S. Government Printing Office; Smithsonian Institution, 1929.

_____. *The Pamunkey Indians of Virginia: Bureau of American Ethnology Bulletin no. 17.* Washington, D.C.: U.S. Government Printing Office; Smithsonian Institution, 1894.

Porter, Frank W., III. "In Search of Recognition: Federal Indian Policy and the Landless Tribes of Western Washington." *American Indian Quarterly,* v. 14, no. 2 (Spring 1990), pp. 113–132.

"Potawatomi win Federal Recognition." *American Indian Report,* v. 10, no. 10 (October 1994), p. 3.

Powell, J.W. *Indian Linguistic Families of America North of Mexico: Seventh Annual Report of the Bureau of Ethnology, 1885/86.* Washington, D.C.: U.S. Government Printing Office; Smithsonian Institution, 1885/1886.

_____. *Wyandot Government: A Short Study of Tribal Society: First Annual Report of the Bureau of Ethnology, 1879/80.* Washington, D.C.: U.S. Government Printing Office; Smithsonian Institution, 1879/1880.

_____. (ed.) *Annual Report of the Bureau of Ethnology, 1892/93–1965.* Washington, D.C.: U.S. Government Printing Office; Smithsonian Institution (1896/1897–1965).

Powers, Stephen. *Tribes of California: Contributions to North American Ethnology v. 3.* Washington, D.C.: U.S. Government Printing Office; Smithsonian Institution, 1877.

"Pribilof Aleuts win Claims." *Tundra Times,* v. 15, no. 25 (June 21, 1978), pp. 1, 7, 9, 12.

"Project Clarifies Nipmuc Status." *Eagle,* v. 8, no. 5 (September/October 1990), p. 18.

Prucha, Francis Paul (ed.) *Documents of United States Indian Policy,* 2nd ed. Lincoln: University of Nebraska Press, 1990.

"Purported Indian Tribe Seeks Apology from Feds." *Indian Trader,* v. 22, no. 5 (May 1991), p. 34.

Rachlis, Eugene. *Indians of the Plains.* New York: American Heritage, 1960.

Radin, Paul. *Publications in American Archaeology and Ethnology, v. 14, no. 5: The Genetic Relationship of the North American Languages.* Berkeley: University of California Press, 1919.

_____. *Publications in American Archaeology and Ethnology, v. 27: A Grammar of the Wappo Language.* Berkeley: University of California Press, 1929.

_____. *The Winnebago Tribe: Thirty-Seventh Annual Report of the Bureau of American Ethnology, 1915/16.* Washington, D.C.: U.S. Government Printing Office; Smithsonian Institution, 1923.

Ray, Verne Frederick. "Lower Chinook Ethnographic Notes." *University of Washington Publications in Anthropology,* v. 7, no. 2 (May 1938), pp. 29–165.

_____. *Primitive Pragmatists; The Modoc Indians of Northern California. Monographs of the American Ethnological Society no. 38.* Seattle: University of Washington Press, 1963.

_____. "Sanpoil and Nespelem: Salishan Peoples of Northeastern Washington." *University of Washington Publications in Anthropology,* v. 5, no. 1, (Dec. 1932), pp. 1–235.

Reff, Daniel T. "The 'Predicament of Culture' and Spanish Missionary Accounts of the Tepehuan and Pueblo Revolts." *Ethnohistory,* v. 42, no. 1 (Winter 1995), pp. 63–90.

Reichard, Gladys Amanda. *Navaho Grammar: Publications of the American Ethnological Society v. 21.* New York: J.J. Augustin, 1951.

_____. *Publications in American Archaeology and Ethnology, v. 22, no. : Wiyot Grammar and Text.* Berkeley: University of California Press, 1925.

Renfro, Elizabeth. *The Shasta Indians of California and Their Neighbors.* Happy Camp, CA: Naturegraph, 1992.

Richardson, Jane. *Law and Status among the Kiowa Indians. Monographs of the American Ethnological Society no. 1.* New York: J.J. Augustin, 1940.

Riddell, Frances A. "Honey Lake Paiute Ethnography." *Anthropological Paper (Nevada State Museum),* no. 4 (1960), p. 3.

Riggs, James Owen. *Dakota Grammar, Texts, and Ethnography: Contributions to North American Ethnology v. 9.* Washington, D.C.: U.S. Government Printing Office; Smithsonian Institution, 1893.

Rose, Mark. "The Enduring Maya." *Archaeology,* v. 46, no. 3 (May/June 1993), pp. 56–58.

Roth, Walter Edward. "An Introductory Study of the Arts, Crafts, and Customs of the Guiana Indians." *Thirty-Eighth Annual Report of the Bureau of American Ethnology, 1916/17.* Washington, D.C.: U.S. Government Printing Office; Smithsonian Institution, 1924.

Royce, Charles C. *Cherokee Nation of Indians: Fifth*

Annual Report of the Bureau of Ethnology, 1883/84. Washington, D.C.: U.S. Government Printing Office; Smithsonian Institution, 1883/1884.

Ruby, Robert H., and John A. Brown. *Indians of the Pacific Northwest: A History.* Norman: University of Oklahoma Press, 1981.

Russell, Frank. *The Pima Indians: Twenty-Sixth Annual Report of the Bureau of American Ethnology, 1904/05.* Washington, D.C.: U.S. Government Printing Office; Smithsonian Institution, 1908.

Sapir, Edward. *Publications in American Archaeology and Ethnology, v. 13, no. 1: The Position of Yana in the Hokan Stock.* Berkeley: University of California Press, 1917.

_____. *Publications in American Archaeology and Ethnology, v. 13, no. 4: Yana Terms of Relationship.* Berkeley: University of California Press, 1918.

_____. *Publications in American Archaeology and Ethnology, v. 13, no. 6: The Fundamental Elementsof Northern Yana.* Berkeley: University of California Press, 1922.

Sapir, Edward, and Leslie Sapir. *Anthropological Records, v. 3, no. 3: Notes on the Culture of the Yana.* Berkeley: University of California Press, 1943.

Schenck, S.M., and W. E. Gifford. *Anthropological Records, v. 13, no. 6: Karok Ethnobotany.* Berkeley: University of California Press, 1952.

Schenck, W. E. *Publications in American Archaeology and Ethnology, v. 23, no. 2: Historical Aboriginal Groups of the California Delta Region.* Berkeley: University of California Press, 1926.

Scherer, Joanna Cohan. *Indians: The Great Photographs that Reveal North American Indian Life, 1847–1929.* New York: Crown, 1973.

Schuller, Rudolf. *Vanished Language of a Vanishing Indian People.* New York: Museum of the American Indian, Heye Foundation, 1930.

Secoy, Frank Raymond. *Changing Military Patterns on the Great Plains (17th Century through early 19th Century): Monographs of the American Ethnological Society no. 21.* New York: J. J. Augustin, 1953.

Sherrow, Victoria. *Political Leaders and Peacemakers.* New York: Facts on File, 1994.

Shimkin, D.B. *Anthropological Records, v. 5, no. 4: Wind River Shoshone Ethnography.* Berkeley: University of California Press, 1947.

_____. *The Wind River Shoshone Sun Dance: Bureau of American Ethnology Anthropological Paper no. 41, Bulletin 151.* Washington, D.C.: U.S. Government Printing Office, 1953.

Shipek, Florence C. "Mission Indians and Indians of California Land Claims." *American Indian Quarterly,* v. 13, no. 4 (Fall 1989), pp. 409–420.

Simmons, William S. "Indian Peoples of California." *California History,* v. 76, nos.1/2 (1997), pp. 48–78.

"Sioux Tribes Challenged to Develop Unified Front." *Lakota Times,* v. 10, no. 35 (February 26, 1991), pp. 1–2.

Skinner, Alanson. *Material Culture of the Menominee.* New York: Museum of the American Indian, Heye Foundation, 1921.

Slagle, Allogan. "Unfinished Justice: Completing the Restoration and Acknowledgment of California In-dians." *American Indian Quarterly,* v. 13, no. 4 (Fall 1989), pp. 325–345.

Smith, F. Todd. "The Kadohadacho Indians and the Louisiana-Texas Frontier, 1803–1815." *Southwestern Historical Quarterly,* v. 95, no. 2 (October 1991), pp. 177–204.

Smithsonian Institution. Bureau of American Ethnology. *Bulletin.* Washington, D.C.: U.S. Government Printing Office, 1887–1971.

_____. *Circular of Information Regarding Indian Popular Names, v. 1.* Washington, D.C.: U.S. Government Printing Office, 1959.

"South American Languages." *Athena Review,* v. 1, no. 3 (1997), pp. 31–24, 52–53.

Sparkman, P. S. *Publications in American Archaeology and Ethnology, v. 8, no. 4: The Culture of the Luiseño Indians.* Berkeley: University of California Press, 1908.

Speck, Frank G. *Beothuk and Micmic.* New York: Museum of the American Indian, Heye Foundation, 1922.

_____. *Boundaries and Hunting Groups of the River Desert Algonquin.* New York: Museum of the American Indian, Heye Foundation, 1929.

_____. *Chapters on the Ethnology of the Powhatan Tribes of Virginia.* New York: Museum of the American Indian, Heye Foundation, 1928.

_____. *Native Tribes and Dialects of Connecticut: A Mohegan-Pequot Diary: Forty-Third Annual Report of the Bureau of American Ethnology, 1925/26.* Washington, D.C.: U.S. Government Printing Office; Smithsonian Institution, 1928.

_____. *Rappahannock Indians of Virginia.* New York: Museum of the American Indian, Heye Foundation, 1925.

_____. *River Desert Indians of Quebec.* New York: Museum of the American Indian, Heye Foundation, 1927.

_____. *Territorial Subdivisions and Boundaries of the Wampanoag, Massachusett, and Nauset Indians.* New York: Museum of the American Indian, Heye Foundation, 1928.

Spencer, Robert F. *The North Alaskan Eskimo: A Study in Ecology and Society: Bureau of American Ethnology Bulletin no. 171.* Washington, D.C.: U.S. Government Printing Office; Smithsonian Institution, 1969.

Spier, Leslie. *Publications in American Archaeology and Ethnology, v. 30: Klamath Ethnography.* Berkeley: University of California Press, 1934.

Stanley, Sam (ed.) *American Indian Economic Development.* The Hague: Aldine, 1978.

Stern, Theodore. *The Klamath Tribe: A People and Their Reservation. Monographs of the American Ethnological Society no. 41.* Seattle: University of Washington Press, 1966.

Stevenson, Matilda Coxe. *The Sia: Eleventh Annual Report of the Bureau of Ethnology, 1894.* Washington, D.C.: U.S. Government Printing Office; Smithsonian Institution, 1894.

_____. *The Zuni Indians: Their Myth, Esoteric Fraternities, and Ceremonies: Twenty-third Annual Report of the Bureau of Ethnology, 1901/02.* Washington,

D.C.: U.S. Government Printing Office; Smithsonian Institution, 1904/1905.

Steward, Julian H. *Anthropological Records, v. 8, no. 3: Cultural Element Distributions: 23: Northern and Gosiute Shoshoni.* Berkeley: University of California Press, 1943.

_____. *Archaeological Reconnaissance of Southern Utah: Bureau of American Ethnology Archaeological Paper no. 18, Bulletin no. 128.* Washington, D.C.: U.S. Government Printing Office; Smithsonian Institution, 1941.

_____. *Basin-Plateau Aboriginal Sociopolitical Groups: Bureau of American Ethnology Archaeological Bulletin 120.* Washington, D.C.: U.S. Government Printing Office; Smithsonian Institution, 1938.

_____. *Panatübiji', an Owens Valley Paiute: Bureau of American Ethnology Anthropological Paper no. 6, Bulletin no. 119.* Washington, D.C.: U.S. Government Printing Office; Smithsonian Institution, 1938.

_____. *Publications in American Archaeology and Ethnology, v. 24, no. 2: Petroglyphs of California and Adjoining States.* Berkeley: University of California Press, 1929.

_____. *Publications in American Archaeology and Ethnology, v. 33, no. 3: Ethnography of the Owens Valley Paiute.* Berkeley: University of California Press, 1933.

_____. *Publications in American Archaeology and Ethnology, v. 33, no. 5: Two Paiute Autobiographies.* Berkeley: University of California Press, 1934.

_____. *Some Western Shoshoni Myths: Bureau of American Ethnology Anthropological Paper no. 31, Bulletin no. 136.* Washington, D.C.: U.S. Government Printing Office; Smithsonian Institution, 1944.

Steward, Julian H. (ed.) *Handbook of South American Indians, 8 v. : Bureau of American Ethnology Bulletin 143.* Washington, D.C.: U.S. Government Printing Office; Smithsonian Institution, 1946–1959.

Stewart, Omer C. *Anthropological Records, v. 2, no. 3: The Northern Paiute Bands.* Berkeley: University of California Press, 1938.

_____. *Publications in American Archaeology and Ethnology, v. 40, no. 3: Washo-Northern Paiute Peyotism: A Study in Acculturation.* Berkeley: University of California Press, 1944.

Stirling, Matthew W. *An Archaeological Reconnaissance in Southeastern Mexico: Bureau of American Ethnology Anthropological Paper no. 53, Bulletin no. 164.* Washington, D.C.: U.S. Government Printing Office; Smithsonian Institution, 1957.

_____. *Historical and Ethnographical Material on the Jivaro Indians: Bureau of American Ethnology Bulletin no. 117.* Washington, D.C.: U.S. Government Printing Office; Smithsonian Institution, 1938.

_____. *Stone Monuments of the Rio Chiquito, Veracruz, Mexico: Bureau of American Ethnology Anthropological Paper no. 43, Bulletin no. 157.* Washington, D.C.: U.S. Government Printing Office; Smithsonian Institution, 1966.

Stockel, H. Henrietta. *Survival of the Spirit: Chiricahua Apaches in Captivity.* Reno, NV: University of Nevada Press, 1993.

_____. *Women of the Apache Nation.* Reno, NV: University of Nevada Press, 1991.

Strong, W. D. *Publications in American Archaeology and Ethnology, v. 26: Aboriginal Society in Southern California.* Berkeley: University of California Press, 1929.

Sturtevant, William C. (ed.) *Handbook of North American Indians, v. 1-.* Washington, D.C.: Smithsonian Institution, 1978-present.

Suttles, Wayne (ed.) *Northwest Coast: v. 7: Handbook of North American Indians,* ed. William C. Sturtevant. Washington, D.C.: Smithsonian Institution, 1990.

Swanton, John R. *Aboriginal Culture of the Southeast: Forty-Second Annual Report of the Bureau of American Ethnology, 1924/25.* Washington, D.C.: U.S. Government Printing Office; Smithsonian Institution, 1928.

_____. *Early History of the Creek Indians and Their Neighbors: Bureau of American Ethnology Bulletin no. 73.* Washington, D.C.: U.S. Government Printing Office; Smithsonian Institution, 1922.

_____. *Haida Songs: Publications of the American Ethnological Society v. 3.* Leyden, Holland: E.J. Brill, 1912.

_____. *The Indian Tribes of North America: Bulletin of American Ethnology, Bulletin 145.* Washington, D.C.: U.S. Government Printing Office, Smithsonian Institution, 1945.

_____. *Indian Tribes of the Lower Mississippi Valley and Adjacent Coast of the Gulf of Mexico: Bureau of American Ethnology Bulletin no. 43.* Washington, D.C.: U.S. Government Printing Office; Smithsonian Institution, 1911.

_____. *The Indians of the Southeastern United States: Bureau of American Ethnology Bulletin 137.* Washington, D.C.: U.S. Government Printing Office; Smithsonian Institution, 1946.

_____. *Linguistic Material from the Tribes of Southern Texas and Northeastern Mexico: Bureau of American Ethnology Bulletin no. 127.* Washington, D.C.: U.S. Government Printing Office; Smithsonian Institution, 1940.

_____. *The Quipu and Peruvian Civilization: Bureau of American Ethnology Anthropological Paper no. 26, Bulletin no. 133.* Washington, D.C.: U.S. Government Printing Office; Smithsonian Institution, 1944.

_____. *Social and Religious Beliefs and Usages of the Chickasaw Indians: Forty-Fourth Annual Report of the Bureau of American Ethnology, 1926/27.* Washington, D.C.: U.S. Government Printing Office; Smithsonian Institution, 1928.

_____. *Social Conditions, Beliefs, and Linguistic Relationships of the Tlingit Indians: Twenty-Sixth Annual Report of the Bureau of American Ethnology, 1904/05.* Washington, D.C.: U.S. Government Printing Office; Smithsonian Institution, 1908.

_____. *Social Organization and Social Usages of the Indians of the Creek Confederacy: Forty-Second Annual Report of the Bureau of American Ethnology, 1924/25.* Washington, D.C.: U.S. Government Printing Office; Smithsonian Institution, 1928.

_____. *Source Material for the Social and Ceremonial Life of the Choctaw Indians: Bureau of American Eth-*

nology Bulletin no. 103. Washington, D.C.: U.S. Government Printing Office; Smithsonian Institution, 1931.

_____. *Source Material on the History and Ethnology of the Caddo Indians: Bureau of American Ethnology no. 132.* Washington, D.C.: U.S. Government Printing Office; Smithsonian Institution, 1942.

_____. *A Structural and Lexical Comparison of the Tunica, Chitimacha, and Atakapa Languages: Bureau of American Ethnology Bulletin no. 68.* Washington, D.C.: U.S. Government Printing Office; Smithsonian Institution, 1918.

_____ and James Owen Dorsey. *A Dictionary of the Biloxi and Ofo Languages: Bureau of American Ethnology Bulletin no. 47.* Washington, D.C.: U.S. Government Printing Office; Smithsonian Institution, 1912.

Swezey, Sean L., and Robert F. Heizer. "Ritual Management of Salmonid Fish Resources in California," *Journal of California Anthropology,* v. 4, no. 1 (Summer 1977), pp. 6–29.

Tanner, Helen Hornbeck (ed.) *Atlas of Great Lakes Indian History.* Norman, OK: University of Oklahoma Press, 1986.

Tantaquidgeon, Gladys. *Notes on the Gay Head Indians of Massachusetts.* New York: Museum of the American Indian, Heye Foundation, 1927.

Taylor, Douglas. *The Caribs of Dominica: Bureau of American Ethnology Anthropological Paper no. 3, Bulletin no. 119.* Washington, D.C.: U.S. Government Printing Office; Smithsonian Institution, 1938.

Teit, James H. *Salishan Tribes of the Western Plateaus: Forty-Fifth Annual Report of the Bureau of American Ethnology, 1927/28.* Washington, D.C.: U.S. Government Printing Office; Smithsonian Institution, 1930.

Temple, Thomas Workman, III. *Founding of San Gabriel Mission: Southwest Museum Leaflets no. 36.* Los Angeles, CA: Southwest Museum, 1971.

Theodoratus, Dorothea J. "Cultural and Social Change Among the Coast Central Pomo," *Journal of California Anthropology,* v. 1, no. 1 (Winter 1974), pp. 206–219.

Thomas, Cyrus. *Indian Languages of Mexico and Central America: Bureau of American Ethnology Bulletin no. 44.* Washington, D.C.: U.S. Government Printing Office; Smithsonian Institution, 1911.

Tooker, Elisabeth. *An Ethnology of the Huron Indians, 1615–1649: Bureau of American Ethnology Bulletin no. 190.* Washington, D.C.: U.S. Government Printing Office; Smithsonian Institution, 1964.

Treganza, A.E., and A. Bierman. *Anthropological Records, v. 20, no. 2: The Topanga Culture: Final Report of Excavations, 1948.* Berkeley: University of California Press, 1958.

Trigger, Bruce G. (ed.) *Northeast: v. 15: Handbook of North American Indians,* ed. William C. Sturtevant. Washington, D.C.: Smithsonian Institution, 1978.

Trimble, Stephen. *The People: Indians of the American Southwest.* Santa Fe, NM: School of American Research Press, 1993.

Trumbull, James Hammond. *Natick Dictionary: Bureau of American Ethnology Bulletin no. 25.* Wash-ington, D.C.: U.S. Government Printing Office; Smithsonian Institution, 1903.

"Tunica-Biloxi Recognized." *Indian Truth,* no. 241 (September 10, 1981), p. 1.

Turner, Allen C., and Robert C. Euler. "Brief History of the San Juan Paiute Indians of Northern Arizona," *Journal of California and Great Basin Anthropology,* v. 5, nos.1/2 (Summer/Winter 1983), pp. 199–207.

Turner, Lucien M. *Ethnology of the Ungava District, Hudson Bay Territory: Eleventh Annual Report of the Bureau of Ethnology, 1894.* Washington, D.C.: U.S. Government Printing Office; Smithsonian Institution, 1894.

Underhill, Ruth Murr. *Ceremonial Patterns in the Greater Southwest. Monographs of the American Ethnological Society no. 13.* NY: J. J. Augustin, 1948.

University of Arizona Anthropological Papers. Tucson: University of Arizona, 1959- .

University of California. *Anthropological Records, v. 1–28.* Berkeley: University of California Press, 1939–1973.

University of California, Archaeological Research Facility. *Contributions of the University of California Archaeological Research Facility.* Berkeley: University of California Press, 1965-present.

University of California. *Publications in American Archaeology and Ethnology.* Berkeley: University of California Press, 1908–1964.

University of New Mexico Publications in Anthropology no. 1–14. Albuquerque, NM: University of New Mexico Press, 1945–1965.

University of Washington Publications in Anthropology, v. 1-current. Seattle: University of Washington Press, 1920-present.

Vanderwerth, W.C. (ed.) *Indian Oratory: Famous Speeches by Noted Indian Chieftains.* Norman: University of Oklahoma Press, 1971.

Viola, Herman J. *After Columbus: The Smithsonian Chronicle of the North American Indians.* Washington, D.C.: Smithsonian, 1990.

Voegelin, C.F. *Map of North American Indian Languages: Publications of the American Ethnology Society v. 20.* New York: J.J. Augustin, 1944.

_____. *Publications in American Archaeology and Ethnology, v. 34, no. 2: Tubatulabal Grammar.* Berkeley: University of California Press, 1935.

Vogelin, Erminie W. *Anthropological Records, v. 2, no. 1: Tubatulabal Ethnography.* Berkeley: University of California Press, 1938.

Waldman, Carl. *Atlas of the North American Indian.* New York: Facts on File, 1985.

_____. *Encyclopedia of Native American Tribes.* New York: Facts on File, 1988.

_____. *Who was Who in Native American History: Indians and Non-Indians from Early Contacts through 1900.* New York: Facts on File, 1990.

Walker, Deward E., Jr. (ed.) *Plateau: v. 12: Handbook of North American Indians,* ed. William C. Sturtevant. Washington, D.C.: Smithsonian Institution, 1998.

Walker, Edwin F. *Indians of Southern California: Southwest Museum Leaflets no. 10.* Los Angeles, CA: Southwest Museum, 1937.

Walker, Paul Robert. *Spiritual Leaders*. New York: Facts on File, 1994.

Wall, Steve. *Wisdom's Daughter: Conversations with Women Elders of Native America*. New York: HarperCollins, 1993.

Wallace, Glenda. "Roadways to Native America: Homelands of the Confederated Salish and Kootenai Tribes," *Native Peoples*, v. 5, no. 1 (Fall 1997), pp. 52–56.

Ward, Duran J.H. "'Meshwakia' and 'Mesqwaki' People of Today," *Hawkeye Heritage*, v. 30, no. 3 (Autumn 1995), pp. 127–164.

Washburn, Wilcomb E. (ed.) *History of Indian-White Relations: v. 4: Handbook of North American Indians*, ed. William C. Sturtevan. Washington, D.C.: Smithsonian Institution, 1988.

Waterman, T. T. *Notes on the Ethnology of the Indians of Puget Sound*. New York: Museum of the American Indian, Heye Foundation, 1973.

_____. *Publications in American Archaeology and Ethnology, v. 10, no. 2: Phonetic Elements of the Northern Paiute Language*. Berkeley: University of California Press, 1911.

_____. *Publications in American Archaeology and Ethnology, v. 13, no. 2: The Yana Indians*. Berkeley: University of California Press, 1918.

Watkins, Frances E. *Navajo: Southwest Museum Leaflets no. 16*. Los Angeles, CA: Southwest Museum, 1943.

Way We Lived: California Indian Reminiscences, Stories, and Songs. Berkeley: Heydey, 1981.

Webber, Bert. *Indians along the Oregon Trail: The Tribes of Nebraska, Wyoming, Idaho, Oregon, and Washington Identified*. Medford, OR: Webb Research, 1989.

Wedel, Waldo Rudolph. *An Introduction to Pawnee Archaeology: Bureau of American Ethnology Bulletin no. 112*. Washington, D.C.: U. S. Government Printing Office; Smithsonian Institution, 1936.

Weibel-Orlando, Joan. *Indian Country, L.A.* Urbana: University of Illinois Press, 1991.

White, Leslie A. *The Acoma Indians: Forty-Seventh Annual Report of the Bureau of American Ethnology, 1929/30*. Washington, D.C.: U.S. Government Printing Office; Smithsonian Institution, 1932.

_____. *Publications in American Archaeology and Ethnology, v. 48, no. 2: Luiseño Social Organization*. Berkeley: University of California Press, 1963.

_____. *Publications in American Archaeology and Ethnology, v. 8, no. 3: Religion of the Luiseño Indians of Southern California*. Berkeley: University of California Press, 1908.

_____. *Some New Material from Acoma: Bureau of American Ethnology Anthropological Paper no. 32, Bulletin no. 136*. Washington, D.C.: U.S. Government Printing Office; Smithsonian Institution, 1944.

"With Respect. *News from Native California* (Fall 1997), pp. 8–9.Women's Studies Program (eds.) *Native American Women*. Boulder: University of Colorado, 1981. (also published as: *Frontiers, a Journal of Women Studies*, v. 6, no. 3, Fall 1981)

Wright, Muriel H. *A Guide to the Indian Tribes of Oklahoma*. Norman: University of Oklahoma Press, 1986.

Yenne, Bill. *Encyclopedia of North American Indian Tribes*. New York: Arch Cape, 1986.